HAWAII

KEVIN WHITTON
WITH KYLE ELLISON & BREE KESSLER

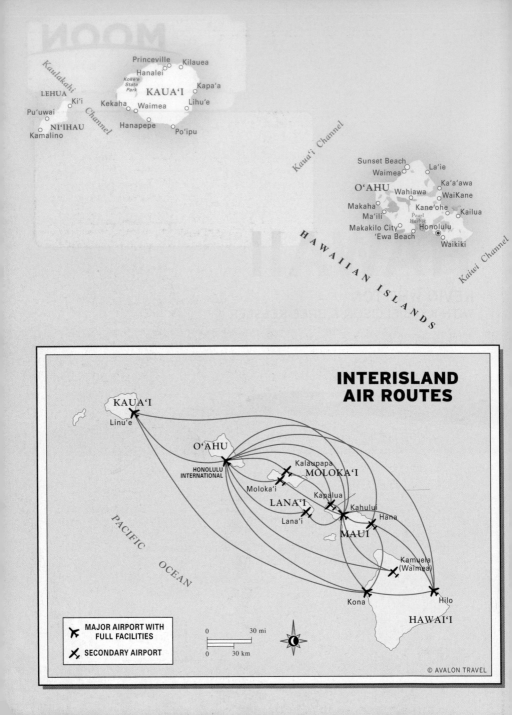

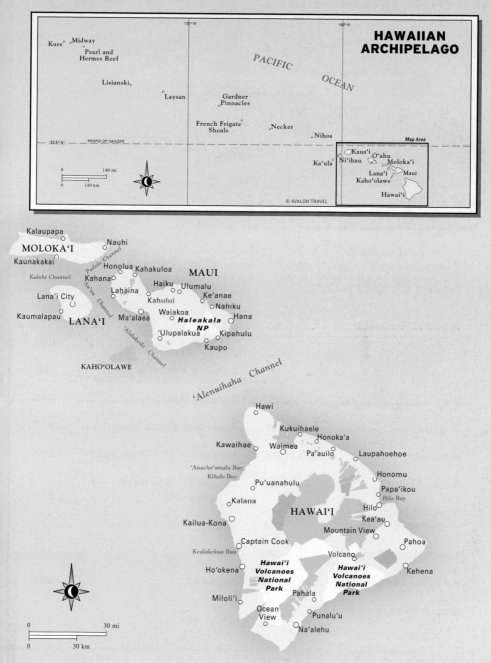

HAWAIIAN ARCHIPELAGO

Kure° °Midway
Pearl and
Hermes Reef

PACIFIC

OCEAN

Lisianski°

Laysan°

Gardner
Pinnacles°

French Frigate°
Shoals   °Necker

°Nihoa

Map Area

23.5° N   TROPIC OF CANCER

°Kaua'i O'ahu
Ni'ihau° °Moloka'i
Ka'ula° Lana'i °Maui
Kaho'olawe
Hawai'i

© AVALON TRAVEL

0   140 mi
0   140 km

Kalaupapa
°

Nauhi
°

MOLOKA'I

Kaunakakai

Pailolo Channel

Kalohi Channel

Honolua Kahakuloa

Kahana°

Au'au Channel

MAUI

Haiku Ulumalu

Lahaina°

Kahului°

Ke'anae

Waiakoa

°Nahiku

Lana'i City

Ma'alaea   °Hana

Kaumalapau

LANA'I

Haleakala
NP

°Ulupalakua Kipahulu

Kaupo°

KAHO'OLAWE

'Alenuihaha Channel

Hawi°

Kukuihaele
°

Kawaihae   Waimea   Honoka'a

Pa'auilo°   Laupahoehoe°

'Anaeho'omalu Bay
Kiholo Bay

Pu'uanahulu°

Honomu°

Papa'ikou°

Kalaoa°

HAWAI'I

Hilo Bay

°Hilo

Kailua-Kona

Kea'au°

Captain Cook°

Mountain View°   °Pahoa

Kealakekua Bay

Volcano°

Ho'okena°

Hawai'i
Volcanoes
National
Park

Hawai'i
Volcanoes
National
Park

°Kehena

Miloli'i°

Pahala°

Ocean
View°   Punalu'u°

Na'alehu°

0   30 mi
0   30 km

© AVALON TRAVEL

Contents

DISCOVER

Hawaii

Escape the world you know in Hawaii. Wander beautiful stretches of white sand. Swim in warm, crystal-clear water. Explore colorful reefs teeming with marine life. Lose yourself under a canopy of tropical rainforest. Cool off in passing rain showers and enjoy the rainbows that follow them.

One source of Hawaii's appeal is the diversity of the islands. As the most isolated archipelago on the planet, Hawaii is a place of geologic and biological extremes and a living experiment in evolution. Active volcanoes and erosion continually redefine a land populated by myriad endemic and native plant species found nowhere else on earth. The islands are also a true cultural melting pot. Their rich agricultural promise has attracted immigrants from all over the globe, contributing to Hawaii's eclectic cultural heritage, cuisine, and lifestyle.

At the heart of Hawaii's ambiance is aloha, a gift of hospitality from native Hawaiian tradition that resonates among all who live and travel here. Aloha brings with it a deeply ingrained reverence for nature: a respect for the land, the ocean, family, and friends. Read on to discover the treasures of all of the islands for yourself.

Clockwise from top left: Wailua Falls on Kaua'i; Hanauma Bay; Haiku Stairs hiking trail on O'ahu; snorkeler at Tunnels on Kaua'i; plumeria bloom; Hawaiian green sea turtle, or "Honu".

10 TOP
EXPERIENCES

1 **Diving and snorkeling:** Hawaii's reefs teem with marine life and are perfect for underwater exploration. No matter which island you visit, you can marvel at life under the sea. Try **Three Tables,** O'ahu (page 104), **Honolua Bay,** Maui (page 205), **Pawai Bay,** the Big Island (page 432), or **Ke'e Beach,** Kaua'i (page 595).

2 **Sunrise or Sunset at Haleakala:** Views from the top of Maui's dormant volcano will leave you in awe (page 307).

3 **Volcanoes National Park:** Learn all about the volcanoes that formed the Hawaiian Islands and see the lava glow (page 470).

> > >

4 **Surfing:** Whether you're a first-timer or a lifer, you can find the perfect wave on any island. Surf **Banzai Pipeline,** Oʻahu (page 102), **Kalapaki Beach,** Kauaʻi (page 560), **The Cove,** Maui (page 291).

5 **Pearl Harbor:** Hawaii holds a special place in World War II history (page 69).

>>>

6 **Hiking:** Some verdant treasures can only be seen by foot: **Diamond Head Summit Trail** (page 46), **Waipo'o Falls** and the **Canyon Trail** (page 651), **Pipiwai Trail** (page 354), and **Kilauea Iki Trail** (page 480).

<<<

7 **Whale-Watching:** see humpback whales off the coast of Maui (page 222) when they make their annual winter migration.

>>>

8 **Driving the Road to Hana:** This famous scenic drive offers unforgettable views and adventures (page 335).

<<<

9 **Waikiki Nightlife:** Iconic Waikiki is best explored after dark (page 48).

>>>

10 **Hawaiian culture:** To truly experience Hawaii, you need to understand its people. Visit the **Polynesian Cultural Center** (page 155), **'Iolani Palace,** (page 61), or even check out a **lu'au.**

<<<

Planning Your Trip

Where to Go

O'AHU

Home to world-famous **Waikiki** as well as 70 percent of the state's population, O'ahu is the marriage of big city and tropical paradise. Enjoy all the comforts of city life, including **diverse culture** and **nightlife**, alongside verdant mountains and crystal-clear water. State capital **Honolulu** is home to historical sites like 'Iolani Palace, the only royal residence in the United States, and World War II pilgrimage site **Pearl Harbor. Legendary surf** pounds the coast for much of the winter, while the summer offers magnificent diving. You can spend the morning sightseeing in downtown Honolulu, surrounded by crowds of people, but be on a secluded beach by noon, surrounded only by crashing waves.

MAUI, LANA'I, AND MOLOKA'I

The second largest island, Maui is lined with **endless, accessible sandy beaches,** especially along the south and west shores. With ample accommodations, Maui offers the **complete resort experience,** but much more spread out than the cluster of hotels in Waikiki. Maui is also the best island for **whale watching** and the windiest island—making it a mecca for **windsurfers.** The **Road to Hana** is Maui's most popular attraction: a **winding drive** to a sleepy town in a lush setting. A quick ferry ride or plane flight away, the islands of Moloka'i and Lana'i offer **secluded getaways**—and glimpses of the Hawaii of yesteryear.

BIG ISLAND OF HAWAI'I

Hawai'i, better known as the Big Island, is a raw and powerful place, the youngest island in geologic time. It's the site of **Hawai'i Volcanoes National Park,** with its barren lava fields and emerging native forests. Snow-capped Mauna Kea is one of the best spots on earth for **star gazing,** while Mauna Loa remains active and Kilauea has been continuously erupting since 1983. Agriculture still permeates the lives of island

Waikiki Beach in Honolulu

the red dirt of Waimea Canyon

residents. Hawaiian **cowboys** and **coffee plantations** mix with the **spacious resorts** that line the dry western coastline,

KAUA'I

Kaua'i is known as the Garden Isle for good reason. Its Mount Wai'ale'ale is one of the wettest spots on earth, where **waterfalls** pour down its vertical walls almost daily. **Botanical gardens** abound, as does **hiking,** both along the famous **Na Pali Coast** and in **Waimea Canyon**. Accommodations are split between the green north and the sunny south, where resorts, vacation rentals, and **golf courses** are abundant. Expect **romance, freedom,** and a **slower pace.**

High and Low Seasons

Hawaii is beautiful all year long, with a comfortable **tropical climate** that sees ocean and air temperature dip by only a few degrees between summer and winter. While winter and spring are known for more **rain,** showers and squalls are possible at any time, in any season. Thank the frequent passing showers for the **rainbows** they leave behind. The predominant **trade winds** keep the islands fresh and cool. The biggest seasonal difference is the **surf.** North shores see higher waves in **winter** (October-March), which produce **world-class surf breaks.** During this period, the south shore waters are flat, with better conditions for **snorkeling** and **diving.** The opposite is true during the **summer** (May-September), when south shore surf rises, although it's still gentler for beginners.

Hawaii experiences a defined high and low tourist season, with several spikes throughout the year. The state experiences an influx of visitors from Memorial Day to Labor Day weekends, or the end of May to the end of August. Room rates are higher and many hotels are operating at full capacity. There is a spike in visitors from the last two weeks of March to the end of April, thanks to North America's spring break holidays. Surprisingly, the busiest time to visit the islands is around Christmas and New Year. If you're planning to be here at that time, make hotel and airline reservations well in advance and plan on making reservations for most of your meals.

The Two-Week All-Island Trip

You can be forgiven for thinking that the islands are all the same. They're so close to each other and so isolated in the middle of the Pacific, how much could they differ? In fact, each island has its own unique personality, its own geography, plant and bird life, culture, activities, historical sites—and opportunities for new experiences. It's possible to see the best of all the islands in two weeks. If you have more time, follow the suggestions below to extend your stay to three weeks for full immersion in island living.

O'ahu, Maui, the Big Island, and Kaua'i all have airports servicing international, national, and interisland carriers. So with proper planning, you can begin a multi-week itinerary from any island. However, most national and international flights traffic through Honolulu International Airport, so O'ahu makes a great starting point. Whichever islands you're visiting, it's easy to spend an extra day or two on O'ahu at the beginning or end of your trip.

Getting between the islands is a quick flight: 30 minutes at most. Flight time across the entire state, tip to tip from the Big Island to Kaua'i, is about 90 minutes, although many flights stop for a quick layover on O'ahu. Car rental companies are located at all major airports and each island has ample accommodations. You'll have to pack up camp and get re-situated with each island hop, but it's a small price for enjoying the diversity of the islands.

O'ahu

DAY 1

After arriving on O'ahu, you'll most likely head straight to **Waikiki,** where most of the island's accommodations are located. Acclimate by swimming and relaxing on the beach. If you're ready for something more active, take **surf lessons,** go for an **outrigger canoe ride,** or hike the Diamond Head crater. Treat yourself to a delicious meal at **Duke's Waikiki** or **Sansei Seafood Restaurant and Sushi Bar** and get a good night's rest to adjust for any time difference.

Waikiki, Honolulu

sunset at Hale'iwa on the North Shore of O'ahu

DAY 2

Venture out and explore. Head to the **Pearl Harbor** historic sites, getting there early to beat the crowd. Heading back into **Downtown Honolulu,** visit the **Historic and Capitol District,** where museums and historic buildings abound. End the afternoon with some relaxing beach time. That evening, walk to **Chinatown,** just a few blocks away, and take in the burgeoning art and food scene. Restaurants, bars, clubs, markets, shops, and art galleries line the streets. Sample the culinary diversity with pizza and beer at **J.J. Dolan's,** or Chinese at **Little Village Noodle House.**

DAY 3

After breakfast, hop on the freeway and over to the windward side for one of the prettiest drives on the island. Take the coast highway up the windward side to the **North Shore.** If it's winter, relax at the beach and check out the waves. If it's summer, get in the water and snorkel. **Sharks Cove, Three Tables,** and **Waimea Bay** have the most marine life, but will also be the most crowded. Head back through historic **Hale'iwa** town where you can shop, eat, and drink. **Hale'iwa Joe's** is one of the best restaurants on the North Shore. And don't miss the legendary **Matsumoto Shave Ice.**

EXTEND YOUR STAY

If you have a few more days to spend on O'ahu, pack your bags and relocate to the **North Shore.** Consider a stay at **Turtle Bay Resort** or a **vacation rental** along the North Shore beaches, where you can really immerse yourself in the beauty of the area. Or stay put in your Waikiki hotel, using it as a base to visit the southeast corner of the island, from **Hawai'i Kai** to **Kailua.** Water activities abound in **Maunalua Bay,** with surf schools, fishing and dive charters, and recreational boating. **Koko Crater** is home to a dryland botanical garden, and there are hikes from Makapu'u to Kailua. **Yokohama Bay,** at the end of the road on the leeward side, is one of the most pristine and uncrowded spots on the island. It's also the starting point of a hike to **Ka'ena Point,** where a natural preserve is home to monk seals and seabirds.

Big Island of Hawai'i

DAY 4

You're Big Island bound! If ocean recreation is your priority, fly into **Kailua Kona** and set up

a telescope at Mauna Kea on the Big Island

a home base on the leeward side. If the volcanoes are your focus, base yourself in **Hilo.** Long driving distances separate the coasts, so you'll need to relocate your accommodations from one side to the other and plan your time wisely to see the whole island. Get an early start by exploring the beautiful waters and town of Kailua-Kona. No trip to the area is complete without a visit to the **Captain Cook Monument** and **Kealakekua Bay State Historical Park,** which can also serve as a starting point for a **kayaking** adventure. In the afternoon, explore the coffee plantations and tasting rooms around Kona. Or relax near your hotel, taking advantage of the sunshine.

DAY 5

Drive north to the Kohala Coast, stopping to enjoy the white sands of **Hapuna Beach** or the **Puako tide pools,** one of the best **snorkeling** spots on the island. In the afternoon, head inland to the upcountry paniolo town of **Waimea.** Head back to the coast to Kawaihae for dinner and dancing at **Blue Dragon Restaurant.** Another option is a prearranged guided tour to the top of **Mauna Kea** for sunset and stargazing. Stay the night on the Kohala Coast.

DAY 6

Take a scenic drive to beautiful **Waipi'o Valley.** Arrange for a scenic tour of the valley or hike down if you're adventurous. Drive along the **Hamakua Coast,** stopping at **Onomea Bay,** where a short trail leads down to a beautiful cove. Then drive into **Hilo** for the farmers market followed by dinner. Try delicious and popular **Café Pesto.** Stay the night in Hilo.

DAY 7

Today is all about **Hawai'i Volcanoes National Park.** After about an hour drive from Hilo, you'll enter the park, where you can explore the **visitors center, lava fields,** drive around and view and active volcano, and hike through **lava tubes** and **native Hawaiian forests.** After a full day in the park, enjoy food and art in **Volcano Village** before heading back to your hotel in Hilo.

EXTEND YOUR STAY

It's easy to extend a stay on the Big Island. Just hang tight for more in-depth exploration in the region of your choice. Add a day trip over the **Saddle Road** between **Mauna Kea** and **Mauna Loa.** Or spend more time in **Hawai'i Volcanoes National Park,** staying overnight

If you're interested in…

- **beaches:** Maui
- **nature:** Kaua'i and the Big Island
- **sailing:** O'ahu
- **surfing:** O'ahu and Maui
- **whale-watching:** Maui
- **snorkeling or scuba:** O'ahu, Maui, and Kaua'i
- **hiking:** O'ahu and Kaua'i
- **beachside bars:** O'ahu
- **views:** Kaua'i
- **a family vacation:** Maui
- **romance:** Kaua'i
- **authentic island culture:** the Big Island
- **history:** O'ahu and the Big Island
- **getting away from it all:** Moloka'i and Lana'i

view from the Kalalau Trail, O'ahu

at quaint lodgings in **Volcano Village** for a full two or more days of exploration.

Maui, Lana'i, and Moloka'i
DAY 8
A change of scenery is in store on Maui, where long stretches of beautiful sandy beaches are the main draw. Stay along in **Kihei** on the south side or around **Ka'anapali** on the west side. Greet Maui by soaking up the sun at **D. T. Fleming Beach Park** or **Keawakapu Beach.** Enjoy the refreshing water and take a long sunset stroll.

DAY 9
Head upcountry and visit **Haleakala,** a dormant volcano that dominates all of the views on the island. Drive to the top and hike around, or take a **biking tour** of the area. Guides can take you to the top to witness **sunrise above the clouds,** then cycle with you along the windy road down the mountain and through green pastures. Break up your ride with a stop in the upcountry town of **Kula.** Afterwards, check out **Pa'ia,** enjoying food and drink at **Charley's** or **Mama's Fish House.** Or head to the old whaling town of **Lahaina** to explore island history and enjoy dinner at **Kimo's.**

DAY 10
Take a **snorkeling, scuba diving, fishing,** or **whale-watching** tour. Tour operators leave from Lahaina, Ma'alaea Harbor, and Ka'anapali. You can select snorkeling and diving tours to Molokini, Lana'i, Moloka'i, and up and down Maui's coast. **Molokini** is a must see, but make sure to get the early boat to avoid the crowds. If a secluded beach day is more to your liking, head to **Moloka'i** or **Lana'i** for the day.

encountering dolphins off the coast of Lanaʻi

DAY 11

Today is the day: **Road to Hana.** Start off as early as possible. The drive takes at least three hours (from the beginning, just past **Hoʻokipa**), and you'll want to make lots of stops along the way. Take your time. **Hike to waterfalls,** eat at a **roadside fruit stand,** and take lots of pictures. Visit a *heiau* and botanical gardens in Hana, grab lunch from the **general store,** and find a nook on **Paʻiloa Beach** to relax and take it all in.

EXTEND YOUR STAY

If you extend your stay on Maui, take the time to enjoy the island at a slower pace. Spend the night in **Hana** to break up the drive over two days. Or plan on longer side trips to **Molokaʻi** and **Lanaʻi,** which are easiest to do from Maui. Or enjoy more **beach time** at your resort or vacation rental.

Kauaʻi

DAY 12

On Kauaʻi, choose either the North Shore or South Shore as a home base. The **South Shore** is much **sunnier,** while the **North Shore** is **lush** due to frequent showers. Begin with a beach day at **Poʻipu.** The **National Tropical Botanical Garden** and **Spouting Horn** blowhole nearby are available for exploration. The quaint town of **Koloa** is a perfect place to grab lunch. After lunch, head into Lihue for a stop at the **Kauaʻi Museum** and dinner at **Duke's** on Kalapaki Beach or **Gaylord's** at the Kilohana Plantation.

DAY 13

Wake early and drive to **Waimea Canyon,** where amazing photo-ops await at the lookout. If you're the adventurous type, take a hike in forested **Kokeʻe State Park.** On the way back to your hotel, stop in historic **Waimea town** and **Hanapepe,** full of art galleries and curious shops and eateries.

DAY 14

Time to explore the North Shore, one of the most beautiful places in all the state. Take your beach gear. Stop at the lighthouse in **Kilauea** and see the wildlife refuge, where seabirds nest in the cliffs. Continue on to **Hanalei Bay,** filled with shops and eateries. The perfect half-moon beach is great for **surfing** or stand-up **paddling.** After lunch in Hanalei, head north to the end of the road at **Keʻe Beach.** Swim, relax, and head to must-see **Limahuli Botanical Garden** when you need a break from the sun.

EXTEND YOUR STAY

Plan on splitting your time with a few days on both the North and South Shores to fully experience each region to its fullest. Spend an extra day taking a **helicopter tour** of **Waimea Canyon** and the inaccessible Na Pali Coast or a **boat tour** of the **Na Pali Coast.**

Oʻahu

Aptly named the Gathering Place, Oʻahu is the heartbeat of the Hawaiian Islands. The island is home to one million residents, about 72 percent of the state's total population, and is, by far, the most culturally and socially diverse of the eight main Hawaiian Islands.

It is a unique destination, where you can experience the comforts and convenience of city life and the natural beauty Hawaiʻi is famous for.

Oʻahu is home to Honolulu, the state's capital, main marine port and its economic and political center. By Hawaiʻi standards, Oʻahu is a big city. You might be surprised to encounter rush-hour traffic, skyscrapers, and suburban sprawl on a small island in the middle of the Pacific. Pull back the curtain of Oʻahu's urban landscape and there is a natural backdrop that informs the ebb and flow of island style and tropical living.

Thanks to 112 miles of coastline, beaches and ocean activities are the cornerstone of daily life here: there are myriad beaches and locales that are just right for the day's activity and weather conditions; the powerful waves of the North Shore draw the world's best surfers; the ledges off the leeward coast attract big game fish; Waikiki's calm water is the ultimate playground for the outrigger canoe; Kailua's fine, white sand rivals the most beautiful beaches in the world; and with two mountain ranges that span the island from north to south, valleys, ridges, and cliffs offer ample hiking and lush open space.

From the Polynesian roots of its first settlers, the gift of surfing and the spirit of aloha to Oʻahu's strategic role for the United States during World War II and its importance as an international agricultural hub, the breadth of the island's history and evolution is tangible from the leeward to the windward side. With no ethnic majority, Oʻahu best exemplifies the state's east-meets-west, melting-pot culture through its exceptional regional cuisine. In Honolulu, historic buildings and art museums pepper the city's historic district, while Kakaʻako and Chinatown are the epicenter of Oʻahu's local urban and fine art scene.

For every budget and every taste, for every tourist, visitor, backpacker, traveler, and globe-trotter seeking adventure or leisure, town or country, fine dining or food truck, mountains or beaches—Oʻahu has it all.

WHERE TO GO
Waikiki

The quintessential Oʻahu destination, Waikiki has beaches with **gentle surf** and **warm water,** great weather year-round, ocean activities, shopping, and dining, and is home to the majority of the hotels on the island. Waikiki's 2.5-mile strip of coastline is the stuff of legends. Not too far away is iconic landmark **Diamond Head.** The **Honolulu Zoo** and the **Waikiki Aquarium** exhibit local flora and fauna, while **Kapiʻolani Park** is a beautiful green space in the city. Waikiki's bars and restaurants offer cuisine from around the world and a **lively bar scene** once the sun sets.

Honolulu

The **economic and political center** of the state, Honolulu is also the capital of Hawai'i. Best known for its **historic district** and Chinatown, Honolulu stretches from Honolulu International Airport to the ridges and valleys of the Ko'olau Mountains. Here you'll find **stately government buildings** like the **Hawaii State Capitol** and historic sites such as **Washington Place** and **'Iolani Palace.** For museum enthusiasts, there's the **Hawai'i State Art Museum** and the **Honolulu Museum of Art.** Chinatown offers both **fine art galleries** and **Pacific Rim cuisine. Just west of Honolulu,** the **Pearl Harbor Historic Sites** are a must-see to grasp the history of Hawai'i and O'ahu and their role during World War II.

North Shore

O'ahu's rural North Shore is all about **beautiful beaches, diving, surfing,** and **snorkeling.** The coastline is natural and unspoiled, and the beaches are the hallmark of **tropical bliss.** During winter, the North Shore attracts surfers from around the world to ride the **powerful, barreling waves** that break all along the coast. During summer, the ocean surface remains calm and flat, the perfect conditions for diving and snorkeling at **Three Tables** and **Sharks Cove.** Relax at **Waimea Bay,** take a walk through a botanical garden and historic cultural site at **Waimea Valley,** or drive up to Pupukea to visit the **Pu'u O Mahuka Heiau,** an ancient Hawaiian temple site.

Southeast and Windward

The southeast shore spans affluent Kahala to Makapu'u. **Maunalua Bay** offers a variety of **water activities,** from Jet Skiing and wakeboarding to surfing and diving. **Sandy Beach** is the best bodysurfing beach on the island and **Hanauma Bay,** a protected marine preserve, offers the **best snorkeling** on the south shore.

From Makapu'u north to La'ie is the windward coast, hugging the spectacular **verdant cliffs** of the Ko'olau Mountains. The windward side is known for its numerous **white-sand beaches. Kailua** has a beautiful crescent beach with fine sand and calm water, and the town is full of boutiques and restaurants. Hike up to **Maunawili Falls** or along the **Kawainui Marsh** to see **native Hawaiian waterfowl.** Take the leisurely drive up the coast to the quiet town of La'ie, home of the **Polynesian Cultural Center.**

Leeward

The arid leeward side runs from the **Ko Olina Resort** to **Yokohama Bay** and **Ka'ena Point.** Ko Olina has fine dining, a golf course, and four artificial **seaside lagoons.** The predominantly calm conditions of the leeward beaches mean there is **great visibility** for snorkeling and diving. Hike out to **Ka'ena Point State Park,** the westernmost tip of the island, and look for **Hawaiian monk seals, spinner dolphins,** and **seabirds** nesting in the **sand dunes.**

O'AHU

Kuilima Point
Kahuku Point
Turtle Bay
TURTLE BAY RESORT

Sunset Beach

'Ehukai Beach
BONZAI PIPELINE

Kaua'i Channel

Waimea Bay Waimea
Waimea Beach

Pupukea-Paumalu Forest Reserve

WAIMEA VALLEY AUDUBON CENTER

Hale'iwa Beach County Park

83

Pu'u Ka'inapua'a 2,360ft

Mokule'ia Beach County Park

Ka'ena Point

Pu'u Pueo ▲ 768ft
DILLINGHAM AIRFIELD

930

Hale'iwa

Waialua

99

FARRINGTON HWY

803

KAMEHAMEHA

Ka'ena Point State Park

Kuaokala Forest Reserve

Yokohama Bay

KAUKONAHUA HWY

Whitmore Village

Wai'anae Range

93

Makua Keaau Forest Reserve

Mokuleia Forest Reserve

Mt Ka'ala 4,020ft ▲

KUKANILOKO BIRTHING STONES ★

Wahiawa
★ **WAHIAWA BOTANICAL GARDEN**

Kea'au Beach County Park

▲ Puu Kalena 3,504ft

Schofield Barracks

KANE'AKI HEIAU ★

Waianae Kai Forest Reserve

WHEELER AIR FORCE BASE

Makaha Beach

Makaha

750

Mililani

Wai'anae Harbor

Wai'anae

LUALUALEI

H2

99

Poka'i Bay Beach County Park

NAVAL

RESERVATION

KUNIA RD

Ma'ili

Lualualei

▲ Palikea 3,098ft

Patsy T. Mink Central Oahu Regional Park

Pearl City

PACIFIC

93

Nanakuli Forest Reserve

Waipahu

Nanakuli

Nanakuli Beach County Park

Kahe Point Beach County Park

OCEAN

Makakilo

H1

Pearl Harbor

FORT WEAVER RD

★ **USS MISSOURI**

KO'OLINA RESORT

FARRINGTON HWY

Kapolei

'Ewa

US NAVAL RESERVATION

'Ewa Beach

BARBERS POINT NAVAL AIR STATION

Barbers Point

Mamala Bay

0   5 mi

0   5 km

© AVALON TRAVEL

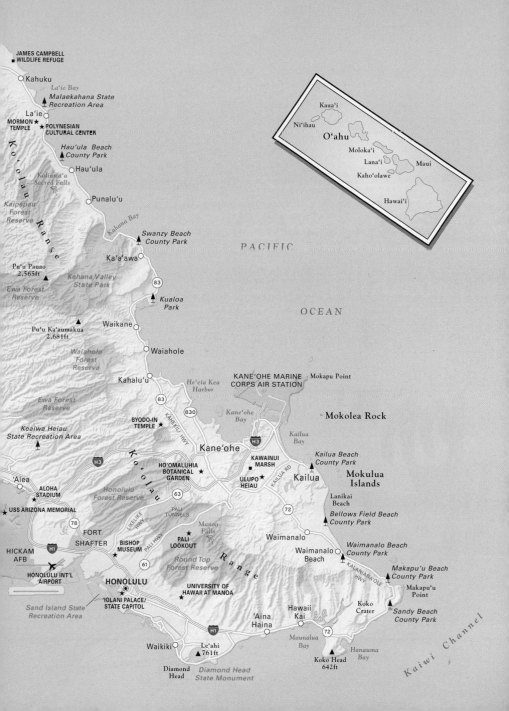

JAMES CAMPBELL
WILDLIFE REFUGE

○ Kahuku

La'ie Bay

▲ Malaekahana State
Recreation Area

La'ie
MORMON ★
TEMPLE ● POLYNESIAN
CULTURAL CENTER

Hau'ula Beach
▲ County Park

○ Hau'ula

Ko'olau Range

Kaliuwa'a
Sacred Falls

○ Punalu'u

Kaipapau
Forest
Reserve

Kahana Bay

Swanzy Beach
▲ County Park

Pu'u Pauao
2,565ft

○ Ka'a'awa

Kahana Valley
State Park

Ewa Forest
Reserve

83

▲ Kualoa
Park

Pu'u Ka'aumakua ▲
2,681ft

○ Waikane

Waiahole
Forest
Reserve

○ Waiahole

Ewa Forest
Reserve

○ Kahalu'u

He'eia Kea
Harbor

KANE'OHE MARINE
CORPS AIR STATION

Mokapu Point

Keaiwa Heiau
State Recreation Area

83

830

Kane'ohe
Bay

• Mokolea Rock

BYODO-IN ★
TEMPLE

Kailua
Bay

H3

Kane'ohe

Kailua Beach
▲ County Park

'Aiea

HO'OMALUHIA
BOTANICAL ★
GARDEN

KAWAINUI
MARSH

ALOHA
STADIUM

Honolulu
Forest Reserve

63

ULUPO
HEIAU

Kailua

Mokulua
Islands

● USS ARIZONA MEMORIAL

78

H3

Ko'olau

PALI
TUNNELS

Lanikai
Beach

Bellows Field Beach
▲ County Park

FORT
SHAFTER

LIKELIKE HWY

Manoa
Falls

KANEKILI HWY

PALI HWY

KAILUA RD

72

HICKAM
AFB

H1

BISHOP
MUSEUM

PALI ★
LOOKOUT

Waimanalo

Waimanalo Beach
▲ County Park

61

Round Top
Forest Reserve

Range

Waimanalo
Beach

KALANIANA'OLE HWY

Makapu'u Beach
▲ County Park

HONOLULU INT'L
AIRPORT

HONOLULU

UNIVERSITY OF
HAWAII AT MANOA

Makapu'u
Point

'IOLANI PALACE/
STATE CAPITOL

Hawaii
Kai

Koko
Crater

▲ Sandy Beach
County Park

Sand Island State
Recreation Area

H1

'Aina
Haina

Waikiki

Le'ahi
▲ 761ft

72

Maunalua
Bay

Koko Head
642ft

Hanauma
Bay

Kaiwi Channel

Diamond
Head

Diamond Head
State Monument

PACIFIC

OCEAN

Kaua'i

Ni'ihau

O'ahu

Moloka'i

Lana'i   Maui

Kaho'olawe

Hawai'i

Waikiki

White-sand beaches, swaying palm trees, surfers, stand-up paddle surfers, and outrigger canoes share the lineup at the famous Canoes and Queen's surfing breaks.

Swimmers and sunbathers grace the shoreline for a refreshing dip—with an average daytime high temperature in the low 80s and water temperatures in the mid-70s. It's no wonder Waikiki has long been a coveted destination for world travelers seeking the enchantment of a tropical oasis. But make no mistake, while the surf and sun rarely disappoint, you'll be hard pressed to find peace, solitude, or tranquility on Waikiki's narrow beaches, busy avenues, or in its packed restaurants.

A scant 2.5 miles of shoreline on the South Shore between Diamond Head and the Ala Wai Small Boat Harbor, Waikiki pulses year-round, with the footsteps of visitors from all over the world marching up and down Kalakaua and Kuhio Avenues and sinking their toes in the sand. Lined with high-rise hotels, condominiums, and apartment buildings, Waikiki is a complete destination, a beachside hamlet with all the amenities of city life within its mesmerizing embrace: shopping, dining, nightlife, health, fitness, spas, and, of course, ocean sports and activities. The Honolulu Zoo and the Waikiki Aquarium are a must for families. Kapiʻolani Park is a runner's delight, and tai chi and yoga are commonplace under the park's flowering canopy trees.

As cliché as it might sound, make sure to take a surf lesson or go on a canoe ride with a beachboy to become a part of a Waikiki tradition that harks back a century to the father of modern-day surfing and the original ambassador of aloha, Duke Kahanamoku. Across Waikiki, *pau hana* (happy hour) is celebrated every day with food and drink specials, and live music, to welcome the sunset. Once the sun goes down, Waikiki takes on a whole new tempo. The sidewalks of Kalakaua Avenue teem with street performers and swell with curious onlookers, and the clubs and bars welcome patrons till four in the morning.

Previous: It's always a beach day in Waikiki; Waikiki is the playground of the Pacific. **Above:** original ambassador of aloha Duke Kahanamoku.

Highlights

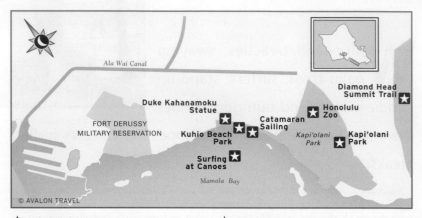

© AVALON TRAVEL

★ **Honolulu Zoo:** The Honolulu Zoo show-cases the African savannah, the Asian and American tropical forests, and the Pacific Islands in a great family outing (page 29).

★ **Kapi'olani Park:** It's Waikiki's outdoor gym. Play tennis, go for a run, stretch out with beachside yoga, or just throw down a blanket and enjoy lunch under flowering canopy trees (page 35).

★ **Duke Kahanamoku Statue:** Pay homage to the original ambassador of aloha, the man who grew up in Waikiki and brought the sport of surfing to the world (page 36).

★ **Kuhio Beach Park:** Relax under a palm tree, lay out on the beach, rent a surfboard, or take a canoe or catamaran ride (page 38).

★ **Surfing at Canoes:** No stay in Waikiki is complete without surfing, whether it's your first time getting your feet on the wax or you've been surfing your entire life. Become a part of the legacy (page 41).

★ **Catamaran Sailing:** Take a break from the crowds on the beach and get out on the open water. The sunset sails on the bigger boats offer a particularly good time (page 45).

★ **Diamond Head Summit Trail:** Combine O'ahu's unique volcanic geography, military history, and a short hike that will get your heart pumping. It's also home to the best views in Waikiki (page 46).

Waikiki is not without its blemishes, and the town can get rough and rowdy in the cool hours of early morning. Prostitution is illegal, but tolerated on Kuhio Avenue; homelessness is ever present; theft and muggings occur; and bar fights spill out onto the sidewalks after hours. But if you keep your eyes focused on the surf and sun, it's easy to find the paradise Waikiki is famous for.

PLANNING YOUR TIME

For first-time O'ahu travelers and many returning visitors, Waikiki is the perfect home base. The majority of the hotel and resort accommodations are found here and it's easy to take a day trip anywhere around the island and make it back in time for dinner. With high-end shopping, myriad restaurants, and plenty of sights and activities, you could spend your entire vacation in Waikiki and leave satisfied. It's the ideal locale to relax at the water's edge in very close proximity to your accommodations. To experience the gamut of Waikiki's sights and activities, set aside a day to spend in the Diamond Head area in addition to the time you plan for beach activities and shopping in Waikiki proper.

ORIENTATION

Waikiki is framed by the Ala Wai Canal to the north and west, Diamond Head to the east, and the beautiful Pacific Ocean to the south. Most streets in Waikiki are one-way thoroughfares: **Kalakaua Avenue,** the main drag, runs east to Diamond Head, **Ala Wai Boulevard** runs west, and in between them, **Kuhio Avenue** has two-way traffic east and west. Residents generally define directionality in relation to towns or major landmarks.

Sights

★ HONOLULU ZOO

Only a mere 2,392 miles from the nearest zoo, the **Honolulu Zoo** (151 Kapahulu Ave., 808/971-7171, www.honoluluzoo.org, 9am-4:30pm daily, $14 adults, $8 military adults, $6 children 3-12 with an adult, $4 military children with an adult, children 2 and under free) is a must-see in Waikiki. The plant and animal collections emphasize Pacific tropical ecosystems and are organized into three ecological zones: the African savannah, the Asian and American tropical forests, and the Pacific Islands. Mammals and birds are the spotlight here, with just a few reptiles on display, including a handful of Galapagos tortoises, a Komodo dragon, and dangerous-looking gharials. There's an expanded Indian elephant enclosure, opened in 2012, for the two playful inhabitants; the orangutans, Rusti and Violet, sleep mostly during the day; and the zebras, giraffes, hippos, and rhinoceroses on the savannah are a major draw. The baboons are quite interactive as well. The kids will love the massive jungle gym by the snack bar and the Sumatran tiger area. Right next door is the Keiki Zoo, with a crawl-through circular koi fish tank, lizards, farm animals, and a goat-petting area.

There are several after-hours events at the zoo, as well. Twilight Tours are held Friday and Saturday evenings. The guided, two-hour walk is a great chance to see who wakes up after everyone has left, and the Dinner Safari is a buffet and a two-hour guided night tour. Every Wednesday during the summer, the Wildest Show Summer Concert Series is a fun family event featuring local musicians. Check the website for the schedule. If you plan on returning to the zoo more than once during your stay or visit O'ahu several times a year, consider an annual pass. There are several levels of membership, but the average family can take advantage of the Chimpanzee Family membership: unlimited entrance and benefits for one year for two adults and up to four children under 18 ($55). There is a pay parking lot

Waikiki Northwest

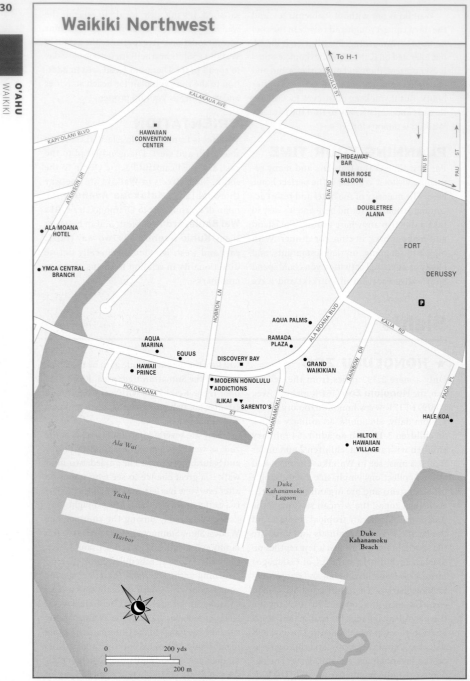

To H-1

MCCULLY ST

KALAKAUA AVE

KAPI'OLANI BLVD

ATKINSON DR

HAWAIIAN
CONVENTION
CENTER

HIDEAWAY
BAR

IRISH ROSE
SALOON

ENA RD

NIU ST

PAU ST

DOUBLETREE
ALANA

FORT

DERUSSY

ALA MOANA
HOTEL

YMCA CENTRAL
BRANCH

P

HOBRON LN

AQUA PALMS

ALA MOANA BLVD

KALIA RD

AQUA
MARINA

EQUUS

HAWAII
PRINCE

DISCOVERY BAY

RAMADA
PLAZA

GRAND
WAIKIKIAN

RAINBOW DR

PAOA PL

HOLOMOANA

MODERN HONOLULU
ADDICTIONS

ILIKAI

SARENTO'S

KAHANAMOKU ST

HALE KOA

Ala Wai

HILTON
HAWAIIAN
VILLAGE

Yacht

Duke
Kahanamoku
Lagoon

Harbor

Duke
Kahanamoku
Beach

0   200 yds

0   200 m

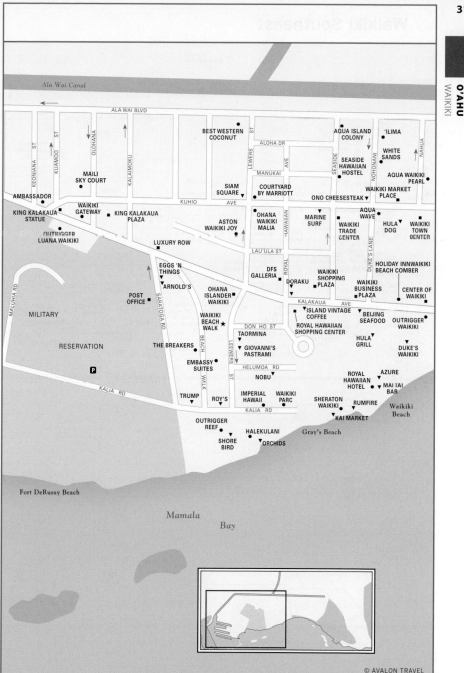

Ala Wai Canal

ALA WAI BLVD

MAILI SKY COURT

AMBASSADOR

KING KALAKAUA STATUE

WAIKIKI GATEWAY

KING KALAKAUA PLAZA

OUTRIGGER LUANA WAIKIKI

LUXURY ROW

BEST WESTERN COCONUT

ALOHA DR

MANUKAI

SIAM SQUARE

COURTYARD BY MARRIOTT

KUHIO AVE

ASTON WAIKIKI JOY

OHANA WAIKIKI MALIA

LAU'ULA ST

EGGS 'N THINGS

ARNOLD'S

OHANA ISLANDER WAIKIKI

POST OFFICE

MILITARY

RESERVATION

THE BREAKERS

WAIKIKI BEACH WALK

EMBASSY SUITES

TRUMP

ROY'S

DFS GALLERIA

DORAKU

DON HO ST

TAORMINA

GIOVANNI'S PASTRAMI

HELUMOA RD

NOBU

IMPERIAL HAWAII

WAIKIKI PARC

KALIA RD

OUTRIGGER REEF

SHORE BIRD

HALEKULANI

ORCHIDS

Gray's Beach

AQUA ISLAND COLONY

'ILIMA

WHITE SANDS

SEASIDE HAWAIIAN HOSTEL

AQUA WAIKIKI PEARL

WAIKIKI MARKET PLACE

ONO CHEESESTEAK

AQUA WAVE

MARINE SURF

WAIKIKI TRADE CENTER

HULA DOG

WAIKIKI TOWN CENTER

HOLIDAY INN WAIKIKI BEACH COMBER

WAIKIKI SHOPPING PLAZA

WAIKIKI BUSINESS PLAZA

CENTER OF WAIKIKI

KALAKAUA AVE

ISLAND VINTAGE COFFEE

BEIJING SEAFOOD

OUTRIGGER WAIKIKI

ROYAL HAWAIIAN SHOPPING CENTER

HULA GRILL

DUKE'S WAIKIKI

ROYAL HAWAIIAN HOTEL

AZURE

MAI TAI BAR

SHERATON WAIKIKI

RUMFIRE

KAI MARKET

Waikiki Beach

Fort DeRussy Beach

Mamala Bay

MALUHIA RD

KALIA RD

SARATOGA RD

BEACH WALK

LEEWERS ST

KEONIANA ST

KUAMOO ST

OLOHANA

KALAIMOKU

LEWERS ST

AVE

SEASIDE

NOHONANI

NAHUA

HAWAIIAN

ROYAL

DUKE'S LANE

© AVALON TRAVEL

Waikiki Southeast

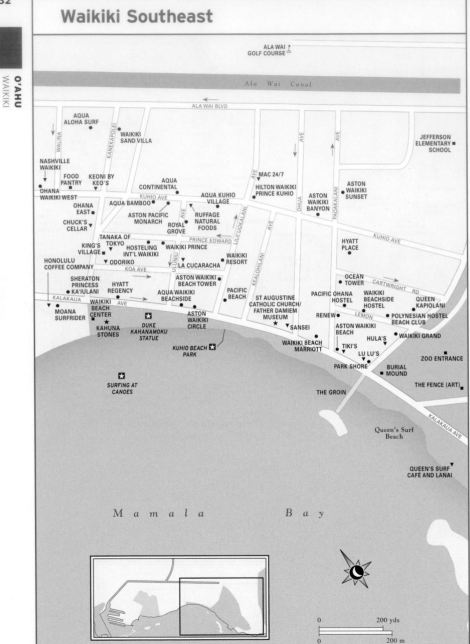

ALA WAI
GOLF COURSE

Ala Wai Canal

ALA WAI BLVD

AQUA
ALOHA SURF

WALINA

KANEKAPOLEI

WAIKIKI
SAND VILLA

AVE

AVE

JEFFERSON
ELEMENTARY
SCHOOL

NASHVILLE
WAIKIKI

FOOD   KEONI BY
PANTRY   KEO'S

MAC 24/7

AVE

ASTON
WAIKIKI
SUNSET

OHANA
WAIKIKI WEST

KUHIO AVE

AQUA
CONTINENTAL

HILTON WAIKIKI
PRINCE KUHIO

OHUA

PAOAKALANI

OHANA
EAST

AQUA BAMBOO

AQUA KUHIO
VILLAGE

ASTON
WAIKIKI
BANYON

KUHIO AVE

CHUCK'S
CELLAR

ASTON PACIFIC
MONARCH

ROYAL
GROVE

RUFFAGE
NATURAL
FOODS

AVE

TANAKA OF
TOKYO

PRINCE EDWARD

HYATT
PLACE

KING'S
VILLAGE

HONOLULU
COFFEE COMPANY

HOSTELING
INT'L WAIKIKI

ODORIKO

WAIKIKI PRINCE

LILIUOKALANI

WAIKIKI
RESORT

ULUNIU

KOA AVE

LA CUCARACHA

KEALOHILANI

OCEAN
TOWER

CARTWRIGHT RD

SHERATON
PRINCESS
KA'IULANI

HYATT
REGENCY

KALAKAUA

WAIKIKI
BEACH
CENTER

AVE

ASTON WAIKIKI
BEACH TOWER

AQUA WAIKIKI
BEACHSIDE

PACIFIC
BEACH

ST AUGUSTINE
CATHOLIC CHURCH/
FATHER DAMIEM
MUSEUM

PACIFIC
OHANA
HOSTEL

WAIKIKI
BEACHSIDE
HOSTEL

QUEEN
KAPIOLANI

MOANA
SURFRIDER

KAHUNA
STONES

DUKE
KAHANAMOKU
STATUE

ASTON
WAIKIKI
CIRCLE

SANSEI

RENEW

LEMON

ASTON WAIKIKI
BEACH

POLYNESIAN HOSTEL
BEACH CLUB

WAIKIKI GRAND

KUHIO BEACH
PARK

WAIKIKI BEACH
MARRIOTT

TIKI'S

HULA'S

LU LU'S

PARK SHORE

BURIAL
MOUND

ZOO ENTRANCE

SURFING AT
CANOES

THE GROIN

THE FENCE (ART)

Queen's Surf
Beach

KALAKAUA AVE

QUEEN'S SURF
CAFE AND LANAI

M a m a l a   B a y

0   200 yds

0   200 m

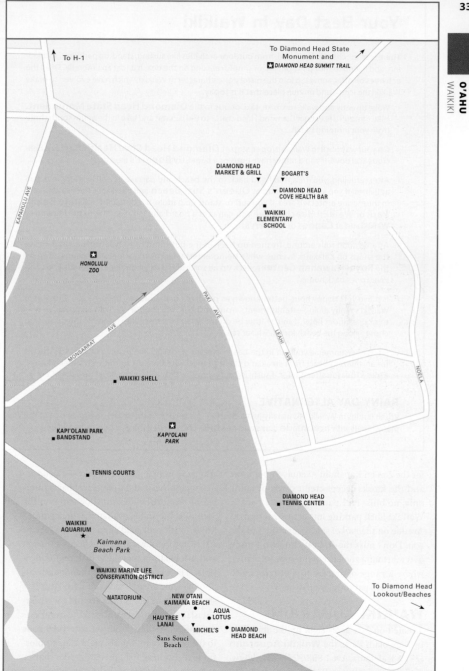

To H-1

To Diamond Head State
Monument and
★ DIAMOND HEAD SUMMIT TRAIL

KAPAHULU AVE

DIAMOND HEAD
MARKET & GRILL
▼

BOGART'S
▼

DIAMOND HEAD
COVE HEALTH BAR
▼

WAIKIKI
ELEMENTARY
SCHOOL

★
HONOLULU
ZOO

PAKI AVE

LEAHI AVE

NOELA

MONSARRAT AVE

WAIKIKI SHELL

KAPI'OLANI PARK
BANDSTAND

★
KAPI'OLANI
PARK

TENNIS COURTS

DIAMOND HEAD
TENNIS CENTER

WAIKIKI
AQUARIUM
★

Kaimana
Beach Park

WAIKIKI MARINE LIFE
CONSERVATION DISTRICT

To Diamond Head
Lookout/Beaches

NATATORIUM

NEW OTANI
KAIMANA BEACH

AQUA
LOTUS

HAU TREE
LANAI
▼

MICHEL'S
▼

DIAMOND
HEAD BEACH

Sans Souci
Beach

Your Best Day in Waikiki

There is so much to do in Waikiki, from outdoor activities like surfing, stand-up paddling, snorkeling, and hiking to shopping, dining, or simply relaxing on the beach under an umbrella. Of all the activities on offer, some tap into the history and character of Waikiki, which have evolved to make Waikiki the iconic and unique place that it is today.

- Wake up early and walk, run, bike, taxi, or bus to the **Diamond Head State Monument.** Hike through the extinct Diamond Head crater to the summit and take in the entire south shore from your morning perch.

- On your way back to Waikiki proper, stop at **Diamond Head Cove Health Bar** for a delicious acai bowl. If you'd rather have eggs or a bagel, try **Bogart's** next door.

- After refueling, you'll want to head back to the beach and partake in Waikiki's ample ocean activities. If you snorkel, post up at **Queen's Surf Beach** and check out the fish and reef in the marine protected area. If you surf or stand-up paddle, head straight to **Kuhio Beach Park** or **Waikiki Beach,** where you can rent a board and paddle out into the legendary Waikiki surf at **Canoes** or **Queen's.**

- As afternoon rolls around, freshen up back at the hotel and head back outside and cruise the shops on Kalakaua Avenue while being entertained by the street performers. Stop by the **Royal Hawaiian Center** to pick up all sorts of Hawaiian goodies for your friends and loved ones back home.

- Is it five yet? Happy hour, better known as *pau hana* in the islands, beckons you into one of Waikiki's many dining establishments. Your best bet is to choose one with an ocean view—think oceanfront hotel. If you'd rather be on the water for sunset, hop on one of the catamaran cruises along the beach for a 1.5-hour sail.

- For dinner, immerse yourself in the beach culture of Waikiki and head to **Duke's Waikiki** for an amazing beachfront steak and seafood meal with the best sunset views. Make sure to order a Hula Pie after dinner. If sushi is your game, try **Doraku** in the Royal Hawaiian Center.

RAINY-DAY ALTERNATIVE
When it rains in Waikiki, it's usually just a passing shower. If it persists, seek shelter in one of the many hotels with **oceanside bars** and **restaurants.** Have a drink or two, relax and enjoy.

for the zoo on Kapahulu Avenue, $1 per hour and the kiosks accept credit cards or coins only, no bills. Free parking is located at the Waikiki Shell parking lots across Monsarrat Avenue on the *makai* side (ocean side) of the zoo. Don't miss the **Art on the Zoo Fence** (www.artonthezoofence, 9am-4pm Sat.-Sun.), where a range of art, from photography to postcards to painting, is on display.

WAIKIKI AQUARIUM
Situated on 2.35 acres right on the shoreline in Kapi'olani Park, the **Waikiki Aquarium** (2777 Kalakaua Ave., 808/923-9741, www. waikikiaquarium.org, 9am-4:30pm daily, $12

adults, $8 military, $5 junior ages 4-12 and seniors, children 3 and under free) has a number of beautiful collections focusing on the South Pacific and Hawaiian marine communities. With your paid admission you receive a free audio tour wand, which gives insight and information on all the different collections. The aquarium has both indoor and outdoor viewing areas. Inside you'll find displays showcasing the marine life around the different islands and the creatures living in various marine ecosystems, from the intertidal zone to the open ocean. Corals, giant clams, colorful reef-dwelling fish, predators like sharks, trevally, and groupers, jellyfish, chambered nautilus, and even a gold American lobster (only one in 30 million American lobsters show this genetic disposition) are some of the curious residents at the aquarium. Outside you'll find the monk seal, a tidal pool with fish that reflect the marine life around Waikiki, an interactive area where people can hold hermit crabs and other little creatures, and a serene grassy open space under palm trees right next to the ocean for the kids to run around on and burn some energy or to sit and enjoy a snack.

The Waikiki Aquarium also has a signature summer concert series on the lawn that draws a more mature crowd than the zoo's summer concert series. Ke Kani O Ke Kai: The Sound of the Ocean runs June-August. Check the website for the latest schedule and information. Parking at the aquarium is limited. Park along Kalakaua Avenue, the ocean side is free and the mountain side is metered parking, $0.25 per half hour.

★ KAPI'OLANI PARK

Kapi'olani Park (intersection of Kapahulu and Kalakaua Avenues, www.kapiolanipark. net) is the oldest public park in Hawai'i, established in 1877 by King David Kalakaua, monarch of Hawai'i. What was once marshland and lagoons is now a 300-acre expanse of grass, sports fields, canopy trees, and a running trail. The park attracts all types of sports, from rugby and cricket to soccer and softball and has four lit tennis courts. It's a hub for picnics, birthdays, large family gatherings, and barbecues. The park also draws runners and walkers, who circle it on the three-mile running path. The park is the best spot for **bird-watching** on the South Shore, and birders set up binoculars and cameras to spy on the avian park goers in the mature shower trees, mesquite, and banyans.

The Waikiki Shell, an outdoor concert venue, and the Victorian-style **Kapi'olani Bandstand,** built in the late 1890s, are in close proximity, just across from the zoo. The park hosts festivals all year long to celebrate culture, food, and community, such as the Korean Festival and the Ukulele Festival. The park extends across Kalakaua Avenue, all the way to the beach. There is free parking along Monsarrat Avenue by the Waikiki Shell and the bandstand, along Paki Avenue, and on the ocean side of Kalakaua Avenue. There are parking meters (10am-6pm daily, $0.25/30 min., 4-hour limit) on the mountain side of Kalakaua Avenue.

Kapi'olani Park stretches all the way to the slopes of Diamond Head.

The Legacy of Duke

Born Duke Paoa Kahinu Mokoe Hulikohola Kahanamoku on August 24, 1890, **Duke** grew up in Waikiki near what is now the Hilton Hawaiian Village. In the course of his childhood on the beach, Duke quickly became a skilled waterman, mastering surfing, outrigger canoe paddling, and swimming. As one of the original Waikiki beachboys, Duke shared his passions with wealthy, upper-class tourists from the U.S. mainland, and by doing so saved the sport of surfing from near extinction. A champion swimmer, Duke won his first gold medal at the 1912 Olympics in Stockholm, Sweden. That same year he also traveled to Southern California to give swimming and surfing exhibitions, introducing surfing to America. In 1914, he traveled to Sydney, Australia, for more exhibitions and turned the Aussies on to surfing as well. In the 1920 Olympics in Antwerp, Belgium, he won two more gold medals in swimming. Duke's success and early relationships as a beachboy opened doors for him in the Hollywood film industry, where he played in nearly 20 films from 1925 until 1967. He also served as the sheriff of Honolulu from 1932 to 1961. Known as the original ambassador of aloha, Duke is immortalized in Hawai'i for sharing the sport of surfing with the world and embodying the aloha spirit throughout his life.

DIAMOND HEAD LOOKOUT

Where Kalakaua Avenue and Paki Avenue meet at the east end of Kapi'olani Park, Diamond Head Road begins its easy climb to the **Diamond Head Lookout.** At the apex, there are two designated areas to pull off the road and park right at the edge of the cliff for spectacular views up and down the coast. Keep in mind that the Waikiki Trolley and tour buses of all sizes also stop at the lookouts, so sometimes they are tranquil and uncrowded, while at other times they are infiltrated by mobs of visitors, taking pictures shoulder to shoulder. The tour buses will block any parked cars from leaving, but on the bright side, they usually don't stay long. From the lookout you can see the waves crashing on shallow reefs to the west, the surfers at Diamond Head's popular surf spots, and **Black Point** to the east, its rugged coastline fringed by palm trees and mansions.

Just before the first parking area on the ocean side of Diamond Head Road, coming from Waikiki, is the **Diamond Head Lighthouse** (3399 Diamond Head Rd.). First constructed in 1899, then rebuilt in 1917, the lighthouse still uses its original Fresnel lens, and its beacon can be seen more than 18 miles

out to sea. The lighthouse keeper's dwelling, where the lighthouse is situated, is a private residence, the quarters of the commander of the Fourteenth Coast Guard district. A gate restricts access to the lighthouse, but its close proximity to the gate, approximately 30 feet, still makes for a Kodak moment.

★ DUKE KAHANAMOKU STATUE

"The Father of Modern Surfing," **Duke Paoa Kahanamoku**, is immortalized in a larger-than-life bronze statue on the sidewalk fronting Kuhio Beach. Hang lei from his outstretched arms, pose with a loved one in front of Duke, and have someone snap a picture—a stop at the **Duke statue** is a must in Waikiki. Duke is the embodiment of Waikiki, of ocean recreation, and of aloha. Visit in the morning to avoid crowds and to catch the sunlight illuminating the statue. Duke grew up near the Hilton Hawaiian Village and was an accomplished surfer, canoe paddler, and Olympic gold-medalist swimmer. As Hawaii's first ambassador of aloha, Duke spread the sport of surfing around the world, traveling to the U.S. mainland and Australia for surfing exhibitions. Later in life he became a Hollywood star and held elected office in Honolulu for 29 years.

U.S. ARMY MUSEUM OF HAWAI'I

Located on Fort DeRussy Beach, the **U.S. Army Museum of Hawai'i** (808/955-9552, http://hiarmymuseumsoc.org, 9am-4:15pm Tues.-Sat., free) highlights O'ahu's military history. The museum is actually inside Battery Randolph, a massive concrete coastal defense structure with reinforced walls up to 12 feet thick. The battery was constructed in 1911 to house two 14-inch guns, part of a system set up to protect Honolulu Harbor from invasion. The battery was rendered obsolete by the rise of the aircraft carrier in World War II. Audio tours are available for $5. The museum validates parking tickets for the Fort DeRussy Parking Facility directly across the street.

Beaches

Waikiki's narrow beaches are generally packed shoulder to shoulder with people, or umbrella to umbrella, for most of the day. In the heart of Waikiki, the towering hotels have been built right to the water's edge, leaving anywhere from 20 to 50 feet of beach for public use. If a leisurely walk along the beach is your fancy, the feat is best accomplished during the first few hours after sunrise or after 6pm, when most people have made their way back to their hotels to prepare for dinner. It's not uncommon for the moon to rise over Diamond Head while the sun is still setting in the west. To get away from the crowds altogether, find a patch of sand along Diamond Head's seaside cliffs and revel in the fact that a short, steep walk down a gravelly path will deter most visitors.

DUKE KAHANAMOKU BEACH

At the west end, or 'Ewa (EH-va) side of Waikiki, is **Duke Kahanamoku Beach,** one of the wider beaches in Waikiki. Fronting the Hilton Hawaiian Village Waikiki Beach Resort, it stretches from the Ala Wai Small Boat Harbor to Hilton's catamaran pier. A shallow outer reef with great waves keeps the inner waters calm and very kid friendly. There's even an artificial ocean-fed lagoon between the beach and the hotel, the perfect spot to try out stand-up paddle surfing without having to worry about ocean chop or currents. The lagoon does have a synthetic feel to it, though, especially apparent in its coarse compacted shoreline that makes sand play an all out construction job.

There is a beach path that runs the length of Waikiki, but if you're coming from Kalakaua Avenue, you'll have to trek down Lewers Street, Beach Walk, or Saratoga Road to reach the sand. There is public beach access on the west side of the Outrigger Reef. Once you hit the beach path, keep walking west till you pass the catamaran pier. If you're coming by car, there is free parking in the Ala Wai Small Boat Harbor.

FORT DERUSSY BEACH

Just east of the catamaran pier, **Fort DeRussy Beach** runs all the way to the Outrigger Reef. Now a clean and tidy public beach and manicured park shaded by canopy trees, this military reservation was one of several shore batteries on O'ahu during World War II and served as an R&R locale for soldiers during the Vietnam War. The beach fronts the Hale Koa hotel, which caters strictly to armed forces personnel and their families, and the U.S. Army Museum, and has a distinct military presence and vibe. It's also known for its calm inner waters perfect for swimming or snorkeling and volleyball courts. An open-air parking lot across from Fort DeRussy Beach Park on Kalia Road is a relatively safe place to park for access to the beach. The rates are average for Waikiki standards at $3 per half hour, and it offers military discounts.

GRAY'S BEACH

Continuing east, the beach ends, and a raised cement walking path on top of the armored shoreline provides transport to **Gray's Beach,** a nook of coarse imported sand in between the Halekulani and Sheraton Waikiki Hotel. There is also beach access from Kalia Road between the two hotels.

WAIKIKI BEACH

Widened in the spring of 2012, **Waikiki Beach** is half of the heart of Waikiki. Stretching from the Royal Hawaiian to the Moana Surfrider, the first two hotels in Waikiki, this is prime real estate for visitors and the sand fills up quickly with beachgoers. This strip is lined with beach service providers and beachside bars and dining. Because of the sand bottom off Waikiki Beach, the water is a translucent aqua-green and perfect for swimming, stand-up paddling, or just floating on a fluorescent blow-up mat. There is a sandbar just offshore from the Royal Hawaiian that people wade or float out to in order to play in the knee-deep water and small surf. For snorkeling, there's not much to see in the way of marine life, save for the occasional green sea turtle. The famous surf spot Canoes breaks quite a way offshore, and while this part of the beach does have a small shore break—quite exciting for the kids—the inner waters are calm and sheltered from the prevailing trade winds.

The easiest way to get to Waikiki Beach is to walk down the shore from Kuhio Beach to the east. Otherwise, make your way through one of the big hotels on the beach to access the world-famous sand, sparkling waters, and iconic view of Diamond Head. Parking in Waikiki is very expensive whether you valet or self-park at one of the hotel parking garages. Your best bet is to park in the Waikiki Shell parking lot, which is free, and walk down Kalakaua Avenue. There is also free parking on the *makai* side of Kalakaua Avenue from Kapahulu Avenue all the way down to Diamond Head. Since landing one of the coveted free parking spots is hard to do, there is also metered parking on the *mauka* side (mountain side) of Kalakaua Avenue along Kapi'olani Park for a reasonable $0.25 per half hour.

★ KUHIO BEACH PARK

Stretching from the east side of the Moana Surfrider to the concrete pier where Kapahulu Avenue intersects Kalakaua Avenue, **Kuhio Beach Park** is the other half to the thumping

Waikiki Beach in the early morning

heart of Waikiki. It has a snack bar, restrooms, and showers at the west end, two lagoons for sheltered swimming, grassy knolls for relaxing in the shade under a palm tree, ample beach services, and one of the best waves in Waikiki—Queen's. Just as on Waikiki Beach, you'll want to arrive early to stake a claim in the sand with a beach towel or chair.

Kuhio Beach Park is the hub of surfing in Waikiki, with the forgiving waves of Queen's and Canoes breaking fairly close to shore by Hawaii standards. You'll find a host of beachboys in red shorts stoked to rent surfboards, stand-up paddleboards, bodyboards, and floating mats. They also offer surf lessons and outrigger canoe rides. Along the beach park you'll also find the iconic lei-adorned statue of Duke Kahanamoku and the statue of Prince Kuhio, as well. Once again, it's best to find parking around Kapi'olani Park and walk to Kuhio Beach Park. The beach park is closed 2am-5am.

QUEEN'S SURF BEACH

On the east side of the concrete pier, **Queen's Surf Beach** offers two things you won't find anywhere else in Waikiki: a "No Surfboard" zone and the **Waikiki Marine Life Conservation District**. Demarcated by buoys on the east side of the concrete pier, just off the shoreline, the No Surfboard zone sees small waves roll across the shallow waters and up the beach. While action of the water would be great for bodyboarding, the ocean floor is sharp, flat reef with the odd coral head, so swimming and bodysurfing are not good ideas.

On the east side of the jetty, the Waikiki Marine Life Conservation District stretches to the Waikiki War Memorial Natatorium's crumbling western wall. With fishing forbidden in this 76-acre marine conservation area and calm, shallow inner waters, this healthy reef ecosystem offers the best snorkeling in Waikiki.

Kapi'olani Park, with its wide-stretching banyan trees, runs the length of the beach. There are restrooms, showers, and a hip shoreline café open for breakfast, lunch, and dinner. The Waikiki Aquarium is at the Diamond Head end of the park. Publics is the main surfing wave along the beach, a dangerous left that breaks along a shallow reef of odd-shaped coral heads that rise above sea level on an extremely low tide. The beach and park area at Publics, where the beach ends, is a favorite for LGBT visitors. The park is also home to many of Waikiki's homeless population. Parking is

Kuhio Beach Park, the heart of Waikiki

available along Kalakaua Avenue and around Kapi'olani Park.

SANS SOUCI BEACH PARK

A small patch of sand between the eroding Waikiki War Memorial Natatorium and the New Otani Kaimana Beach Hotel, **Sans Souci Beach Park,** also known as **Kaimana Beach,** is a favorite spot for residents seeking easy access to a family-friendly beach and park without the hassle of getting in and out of Waikiki. There's limited free parking, restrooms, an outdoor shower at the beach, and indoor showers at the natatorium. In front of the natatorium is a great spot for snorkeling, and swimmers take advantage of a wide, deep channel through the reef and out to a wind sock fixed on its outer corner. Four laps from the beach to the wind sock is roughly a mile. The water is very calm, making it the perfect locale for children of all ages.

DIAMOND HEAD BEACH PARK

At the base of Diamond Head's seaside cliffs are some of the best beaches on the South Shore for escaping the crowds and enjoying the island's natural scenery. There's parking on both sides of Diamond Head Road and a paved footpath that cuts down the cliff. At the bottom of the path, **Diamond Head Beach Park** stretches out in both directions. The shoreline is lined with shells and sea glass, and there are tidepools on the west end of the beach. There are several surf breaks along the reef, but the pervasive trade winds, strong ocean currents, wind chop, and extremely shallow patches of reef make snorkeling and swimming dangerous. The beach below Diamond Head is a great spot for a romantic winter-season stroll as the sun sets straight off Waikiki. Diamond Head Beach Park is closed 10pm-5am.

Water Sports

SURFING

Surfing is synonymous with Waikiki. Not only did Hawaiians invent the sport of surfing, but the legendary Duke Kahanamoku—original beachboy, Olympic gold-medal swimmer, and the father of modern-day surfing, who hailed from Waikiki—introduced the fluid sport to the world. The surf breaks that Duke made famous riding on heavy wooden boards are the same spots that surfers seek out today. While the waves are biggest, best, and most consistent during summer, June-September, Waikiki has the potential to see surf at any time during the year. Whether you are a longboarder, a shortboarder, experienced, a novice, or a first-timer, Waikiki has a number of breaks that suit all abilities. Just remember that proper surfing etiquette applies at all breaks, and with so many people in the water, safety and respect for others are of the utmost importance. When in doubt, don't go out.

Fours to Populars

Straight out from the U.S. Army Museum, on the east side of a deep channel, is **Fours,** a wave that only comes alive when the surf gets big. Just to the east of Fours, way out over the outer reef, is **Threes,** a perfect right that breaks best on a low tide and holds its shape at all sizes. Threes is a favorite with local surfers and gets very crowded. To the east of Threes is **Paradise,** a surf zone with big, rolling, shifty peaks. It's a favorite for longboarders and stand-up paddle surfers. Continuing east, the next break is a favorite for all board riders—**Populars.** Locally referred to as Pops, this long right breaks over a sand-covered reef and can handle big surf. When the trade winds are stiff, Pops does get choppy.

★ Canoes

Canoes is straight out from the west end of Kuhio Beach Park. It breaks both right and left and has several takeoff zones. A slow, rolling longboard wave, Canoes is perfect for beginners. Start off slowly on the inside, catching the whitewater till you learn to stand up and balance on the board. Once you're more confident and comfortable, sit out the back with a mix of locals, beachboys, and people from all around the world sharing in this Hawaiian tradition. Canoes is very crowded with all types of watercraft, from 12-foot longboards to canoes and catamarans. Stay aware and, by all means, if something large is coming your way, don't be a deer in the headlights; paddle out of the way.

Queen's

Queen's, also called **Queen's Surf,** is one of the best waves in Waikiki. Straight off the beach from the east end of Kuhio Beach Park, before the lagoon, it's best for longboarding. Professional and amateur contests are often held here. The perfect turquoise rights draw a host of the best longboarders in Hawai'i, who hang ten down the line with style and ease. Queen's is usually very crowded, and if there's any swell in the water, Queen's is breaking.

Because of the tight takeoff zone and thick crowd, beginners should stick to Canoes.

Diamond Head

On the west end of **Diamond Head,** off Makalei Beach Park, is **Suicides,** a left for experts only. It's windy, quite a ways offshore, and subject to strong currents. Below the Diamond Head Lookout parking lots are several good breaks, the two most popular being **Lighthouse** and **Cliffs.** At the bottom of the trail down the cliff is a deep channel through the reef. From the beach, to the right of the channel is Lighthouse, a fast and powerful right for experts only. On the left of the channel is Cliffs, several peaks along the reef that break both right and left and are suited for all types of board riders. Diamond Head can get very windy as the trade winds blow right across the break, and is a favorite for kiteboarders and sailboarders during the extreme conditions.

Outfitters

Koa Board Sports (2420 Koa Ave., 808/923-0189, www.koaboardsports.com, 10am-6pm daily) has a huge selection of longboards and shortboards available for rent. Rates range from $15 for 1.5 hours to $60 for one day

Canoe surfing is definitely a team sport.

Waikiki Beachboys

If there's something about Waikiki that sets it apart from other tropical sea destinations, it's the **Waikiki beachboys.** Hailing back a century, the beachboy culture has evolved with the changing face of tourism in Hawai'i, but the gentlemen in the red shorts still practice the same core values of sharing the sports of surfing, outrigger canoeing, and aloha with visitors.

After Calvinist missionaries decimated the Hawaiian culture in the 19th century, the sport of surfing, a purely Hawaiian endeavor, was nearly extinguished. It was seen as sinful because of how much skin was shown while surfing. Only a few surfers remained at the end of the century, namely legendary waterman and three-time Olympic gold medalist Duke Kahanamoku and a few of his friends. As the first wave of wealthy American tourists arrived on steamers in the early decades of the 20th century, these few surfers took it upon themselves to entertain the visitors, teaching them to surf, ride canoes, and relax and have a good time in general. In essence, they created a way to earn a living surfing year-round on the beach at Waikiki. These first visitors came to Hawai'i for extended stays and were able to develop relationships with the beachboys, who became their tour guides and a bridge to the Hawaiian culture and a different lifestyle. After giving surfing lessons during the day, the beachboys entertained their guests with ukulele, song, and libations at night, a hedonistic lifestyle by all accounts.

The fun was curtailed by World War II, and as travel and tourism have changed since then, so too have the beachboys. With the ease and affordability of flying across the Pacific, a vacation to Waikiki is accessible for so many more people, not just the wealthy elite. Today, with thousands of visitors flocking to the beach daily, the beachboys focus on surfing and outrigger canoe surfing and have shifted roles from entertainers and tour guides to beach services. While only a few of Waikiki's beachboys can still trace their ties back to the original beachboys, any beachboy can still show you how to have the time of your life in Waikiki's gentle surf.

(24 hours), to $50 for two days. You can also switch the board anytime the shop is open. **Hans Hedemann Surf Adventures** (2586 Kalakaua Ave., 808/924-7778, www.hhsurf. com, 8am-5pm daily) is located in the Park Shore Hotel, between Starbucks and the hotel lobby. The surf school specializes in surf lessons out at Publics. You will have to carry a soft-top longboard from the retail outlet to the break, about a 10-minute walk. It also offers stand-up paddle lessons, guided surf adventures, and surfboard rentals.

If you prefer to rent your board right on the beach, or take a lesson with one of Waikiki's famous beachboys, then you'll want to check out some of Waikiki's vetted beach services. **Faith Surf School** (www.faithsurfschool. com), operated by the legendary Moniz family, offers its expertise at several beach locations: the Outrigger Reef (2169 Kalia Rd., 808/924-6084), the Outrigger Waikiki (2335 Kalakaua Ave., 808/926-9889), and the Sheraton (2255 Kalakaua Ave., 808/922-4422). Faith rents

longboards starting at $20 per hour and offers 1.5-hour group lessons for $60 and private lessons for $125.

Aloha Beach Services (808/922-3111, http://alohabeachservices.com, 8am-4pm daily), serving guests since 1932, has a small palapa but a lot of boards, in between the Outrigger Waikiki and the Moana Surfrider. It rents longboards for $20 and offers one-hour group lessons for $50 and private lessons for $90. A photo package is included with the group lesson. Aloha rents beach umbrellas, chairs, air mats, and rings and accepts cash only.

SNORKELING

The **snorkeling** in Waikiki is decent at best any time of year. Overuse and overfishing for decades have led to the decline in the number of species and fish in the nearshore waters, and all that fine white sand over the reef, which gives the water its clear, light-blue color, leaves little shelter for reef dwellers.

Patience, and the luck of being in the right place at the right time, can yield some great underwater exploring.

Duke Kahanamoku Beach and Fort DeRussy Beach

Since the nearshore waters off **Duke Kahanamoku Beach** and **Fort DeRussy Beach** are not heavily used, the potential to encounter marine life is definitely heightened. The water is shallow, waist to chest deep, all the way out to the waves breaking at Threes and Fours, and the bottom is a mix of reef and sand. As an added bonus, you won't have to keep your eye out for surfers, swimmers, canoes, or catamarans, so you can stay focused on what fish you can find.

Waikiki Marine Life Conservation District

The **Waikiki Marine Life Conservation District,** located along Queen's Surf Beach from the jetty to the Waikiki War Memorial Natatorium's western wall, is hands down the best snorkeling in Waikiki. The 76-acre marine conservation area is a regulated and patrolled no-take zone, where fishing or removing of any sea creature is illegal. The protection has allowed a plethora of reef-dwelling vertebrates and invertebrates to thrive. The shallow inner waters are generally calm, but heavy trade winds can texture the surface. Look for bonefish, funny face fish, wrasse, puffer fish, eel, and yellow tang. Chances are you'll even catch a glimpse of the sleek *humuhumunukunukuapua'a.*

Diamond Head

The nearshore waters off the beaches of **Diamond Head** are great for snorkeling but more suited for experienced snorkelers and swimmers. The reefs at Diamond Head attract all sorts of marine life, including sharks and the endangered Hawaiian monk seal. Shallow water and lots of nooks and crannies in the sharp reef make for great habitat, but beware of extremely shallow areas of reef, strong currents, and wind chop. Snorkeling

is best in winter, when the waves are small to nonexistent.

Outfitters

Whether you purchase your own snorkel gear or rent equipment is for you to decide. Renting allows you to travel without lugging around cumbersome snorkel gear, while owning gives you the luxury of a custom fit only your mouth knows. **Aqua Zone Scuba Diving & Snorkeling** (2552 Kalakaua Ave., 866/923-3483, www.aquazonescuba.com, 8am-5pm daily), in the Waikiki Beach Marriott, rents and sells gear and is a short walk from the Waikiki Marine Life Conservation District. It rents complete snorkel sets starting at $12 for 24 hours, $24 for three days, and $36 for five days.

Snorkel Bob's (702 Kapahulu Ave., 808/735-7944, www.snorkelbob.com, 8am-5pm daily), just outside of Waikiki, sells equipment and rents complete snorkeling sets, individual snorkels, fins, flotation devices, and wetsuits. The most basic equipment starts at $2.50 per day and $9 per week.

Nearly all the beach services at the beachfront hotels rent and sell snorkel gear, and most **ABC Stores** sell complete sets as well.

SCUBA DIVING

Once you get offshore from Waikiki, the seafloor slowly sinks away and the water becomes a rich, deep blue. At these greater depths are a few great dive sites, from reefs to shipwrecks. Offshore, the water teems with life, and turtles, eels, triggerfish, octopus, and a host of other reef fish abound. Diving off Waikiki is a year-round pursuit, weather and wave permitting.

In the heart of Waikiki you'll find two Professional Association of Diving Instructors (PADI) centers. **Waikiki Diving Center** (424 Nahua St., 808/922-2121, www.waikikidiving. com) dives two wrecks and 10 different sites right off Waikiki. With 32 years of experience, the center offers dives for every type of diver, rents and sells equipment, and offers PADI certification. Two-tank beginner dives start at $109, wreck dives start at $125, night dives start at $135, and PADI certification courses start at $250. **Aqua Zone Scuba Diving & Snorkeling** (2552 Kalakaua Ave., 866/923-3483, www.aquazonescuba.com) is in the Waikiki Beach Marriott. It includes free in-pool lessons for beginners and rusty divers and daily boat dives for all levels. It offers two levels of PADI certification and provides daily snorkel tours and equipment rental and sales. Two-tank boat dives with rental equipment start at $129. Both Waikiki Diving Center and Aqua Zone dive numerous locations outside of Waikiki as well.

STAND-UP PADDLING

Long before **stand-up paddling** became a full-fledged sport, a few of the Waikiki beach-boys were known to cruise around the line-ups kneeling or standing up on longboards and paddling with their canoe paddles. Now the equipment has been refined and stand-up paddling is popular both for surfing and flat-water paddling (also known as stand-up paddleboarding), both of which are full-body workouts. **Paradise, Populars,** and **Canoes** are the go-to surf breaks for stand-up paddle surfing in Waikiki. If you prefer to just paddle and check out the water from a different per-spective, get away from the crowds by pad-dling out beyond Canoes and **Queen's** and explore. Make your way to **Publics** and pad-dle in with the wind at your back. You'll be amazed that even at 10-15 feet deep, you'll still be able to see the bottom.

Faith Surf School (www.faithsurfschool.com) rents stand-up paddleboards from the Outrigger Reef (2169 Kalia Rd., 808/924-6084), Outrigger Waikiki (2335 Kalakaua Ave., 808/926-9889), and Sheraton (2255 Kalakaua Ave., 808/922-4422) starting at $25 for one hour and going up to $70 for all day. The school also offers stand-up paddle lessons starting at $65 up to $125 for a 1.5-hour pri-vate lesson.

Aloha Beach Services (808/922-3111, http://alohabeachservices.com, 8am-4pm daily), between the Outrigger Waikiki and the Moana Surfrider, rents stand-up paddle-boards for $30 for the first hour and $10 each additional hour. Lessons start at $60 and go to $80 for a private one-hour session. In Kuhio Beach Park, **Star Beachboys** (808/699-3750, www.starbeachboys.com, 6am-6pm daily) rent boards for $20 for the first hour and $10 for the second. Nearby, **Hawaiian Oceans Waikiki** (808/721-5443, 6am-6pm daily) rents stand-up paddleboards for $25 for the first hour and $10 for each additional hour.

BODYBOARDING

While you can bodyboard any of the waves around Waikiki, there are two areas where bodyboarders tend to congregate. Just off the cement pier at the east end of Kuhio Beach Park is a break called **Walls,** where war-bly waves break over very shallow reef and wash over the lagoon wall. To the east of the pier, along Queen's Surf Beach, is a specially marked No Surfboard zone. The waves here break over some shallow coral heads along the fringe reef and roll all the way to the shore.

Aloha Beach Services (808/922-3111, http://alohabeachservices.com, 8am-4pm daily), **Star Beachboys** (Kuhio Beach Park, 808/699-3750, www.starbeachboys.com, 6am-6pm daily), and **Hawaiian Oceans Waikiki** (Kuhio Beach Park, 808/721-5443, 6am-6pm daily) rents bodyboards for $5 per hour or $20 per day.

OUTRIGGER CANOEING

The outrigger canoe is one of the defining facets of Hawaiian culture. After all, it is how early Polynesian voyagers first arrived in these islands. Before surfboards came along, native Hawaiian fishers would stand up and "surf" their canoes back to shore. Outrigger canoe paddling and surfing have remained popular in Hawai'i to this day, and Waikiki offers the only place on O'ahu you'll be able to hop into a real six-person outrigger canoe with a profes-sional rudder operator to guide you through the surf.

Faith Surf School (www.faithsurfschool.com) runs six-person canoes at $25 each for three waves, with locations at the Outrigger Reef (2169 Kalia Rd., 808/924-6084, 8am-5:30pm daily), the Outrigger Waikiki (2335 Kalakaua Ave., 808/926-9889, 8am-5:30pm daily), and the Sheraton (2255 Kalakaua Ave., 808/922-4422, 8am-5:30pm daily). Note that the last surfboard rental is at 4:30pm. **Aloha Beach Services** (808/922-3111, http://alohabeachservices.com, 8am-4pm daily) runs eight-person canoes for $15 each for two waves. In Kuhio Beach Park **Star Beachboys** (808/699-3750, www.starbeachboys.com, 6am-6pm daily) canoe rides are $15 per person for three waves, and **Hawaiian Oceans Waikiki** (808/721-5443, 6am-6pm daily) runs a four-person canoe at $15 each for two waves.

★ CATAMARAN SAILING

There are seven catamaran cruises that launch from the beach and sail the waters off Waikiki almost every day, weather dependent, from Ala Moana to Diamond Head. The boats are different sizes and cater to different interests (some of the catamaran tours are known locally as the "booze cruise"), but the tours all offer a beautiful perspective of Waikiki, the city skyline, and the Ko'olau Mountains from out at sea. *Holokai* **Catamaran** (808/922-2210, https://sailholokai.com, 8am-7pm daily) is Waikiki's first new catamaran in almost two decades and launches from the beach fronting the Outrigger Reef. The company offers a tradewind sail for $35, a sunset sail for $55, a fireworks sail for $50 and a snorkeling sail for $60. Book online or at the beach.

On Waikiki Beach you'll find three catamaran operators. In front of the Royal Hawaiian is the *Kepoikai II* (808/224-9775, www.kepoikai.com), a 42-foot cat operating in Waikiki for more than 35 years. Its one-hour sail begins at 10:30am daily for $20 per person. Last sail is at 6pm during the summer. On board are sold $1 mai tais, $2 beer, juice, soda, and water. You'll need to make reservations or bookings from the beach.

The *Manu Kai* (808/792-1572, https://manukaicatamaran.com) beaches in front of the Outrigger Waikiki and offers one-hour trips ($25 pp with alcoholic beverages, $20 pp without). The 43-foot catamaran's last sail ($30 pp) is at 5:30pm and is a 1.5-hour trip. Right next to the Manu Kai you'll find the famous yellow and red *Na Hoku II* (808/554-5990, www.nahokuii.com, $30 pp with alcoholic beverages, $25 pp without). It offers 1.5-hour trips, and the first leaves the beach at 11:30am. A sunset sail departs at 5:30pm. Both of these boats have a 49-person maximum capacity and fill up quickly. If you're planning a weekend sunset sail, it's best to make a reservation at least a few days in advance.

At Kuhio Beach Park you'll find the *Mana Kai* (844/626-2524, http://waikikisailing.com, $20 pp), which holds up to 27 passengers, but will sail with just 6. The crew does not serve any beverages, but you are welcome to bring your own. The first one-hour sail departs at 9:30am, and the last sail is around 6pm, depending on the season.

PARASAILING

Parasailing offers the thrill of hang gliding while affixed by a prescribed length of line to a boat motoring across the warm Pacific Ocean. The parachute can soar up to 1,000 feet above the ocean, and as you can imagine, it really is a bird's-eye view. **Hawaiian Parasail** (1651 Ala Moana Blvd., slip 600B, 808/591-8884, http://hawaiianparasail.com, 8am-6pm daily) is located in the Ala Wai Small Boat Harbor. The slip is in between the two main free-parking areas and visible from the street. Rates start at $50 for 300 feet of line and three minutes in the air. Observers ride for $30. **Hawaii Active** (808/871-8884 or 866/766-6284, www.hawaiiactive.com) is an easy way to book a parasailing trip. There are four options for line length and time in the air, starting with the 300-foot line for 5-7 minutes for $44 per person, up to a 1,000-foot line for 10-12 minutes for $77.

Hiking and Biking

HIKING

You won't need a pair of hiking boots during your stay in Waikiki, even if you do plan on trekking the two "trails" on offer: the Diamond Head Summit Trail or the Waikiki Historic Trail that encircles the region.

TOP EXPERIENCE

★ Diamond Head Summit Trail

The **Diamond Head Summit Trail** is inside the Diamond Head crater, an extinct tuff cone volcano that erupted about 300,000 years ago, and is part of the **Diamond Head State Monument** (www.hawaiistateparks. org, 6am-6pm daily, $5 per vehicle, $1 walk-in visitor). The historic trail, built in 1908, climbs 560 feet from the crater floor to the summit in just 0.8 miles. The steep trail up the inner southwestern rim of the crater is a combination of concrete walkway, switchbacks, stairs, uneven natural terrain, and lighted tunnels. Inside the semiarid crater it's hot and rather dry, so bring plenty of water and sun protection. Along the hike you'll see remnants of O'ahu's natural and military history, punctuated by the breathtaking views of the entire South Shore from the observation station at the summit. Plan on 1.5-2 hours round-trip. The entrance to the Diamond Head State Monument is off Diamond Head Road between Makapu'u Avenue and 18th Avenue. The last entrance to hike the trail is 4:30pm. Visitors must exit the park by 6pm. To get there by bus, use routes 22, 23, or 24.

Waikiki Historic Trail

The self-guided **Waikiki Historic Trail** (www.waikikihistorictrail.com) takes you throughout Waikiki, covering fascinating historical, geological, and cultural sights with tidbits about Waikiki past and present. Informative surfboard markers at viewing areas correspond to a prescribed map and program available online. Print out a copy of the map and guide to take with you or use a personal electronic device while on the go. You can follow the order of sights in the program or just visit those areas you prefer. The trail begins at Queen's Surf Beach, hugs the coast to the west (the most scenic section of the trail), rounds up to the Ala Wai Canal and follows Kalakaua Avenue back into the heart of Waikiki. At a normal walking pace, the trail takes about two hours to complete.

BIKING

Since bicycles are prohibited on Waikiki sidewalks and the busy avenues of Waikiki, sans bike lanes, are not exactly bike friendly for those wishing to get around on two wheels, **biking** is best suited to near and around **Diamond Head,** where traffic is

Look for these surfboard markers along the Waikiki Historic Trail.

lighter and moves a bit slower. Biking to the Diamond Head lookout and beaches will also alleviate the task of finding parking and allow more time for exploring and enjoying your surroundings. You can circumnavigate Diamond Head easily by traveling from Diamond Head Road to Monsarrat Avenue (a great place to stop for a beverage and a bite to eat) to Paki Avenue and then back to Diamond Head Road.

Hawaiian Style Rentals (2556 Lemon Rd., 808/946-6733, www.hawaiianstylerentals.

com, 8:30am-5:30pm daily) rents bicycles with helmet, lock, map, front pouch, and rear rack starting at $15 for four hours, $20 per day, and $15 per day for three days or more. You'll also find bicycle rentals at **Adventure Rentals** (159 Kaiulani Ave., 808/924-2700, 8am-5:30pm daily) and **Big Kahuna Motorcycle Tours and Rentals** (407 Seaside Ave., 808/924-2736 or 888/451-5544, www.bigkahunarentals.com, 8am-5pm daily), which rents mountain bikes for $10 for four hours, $15 for 10 hours, and $100 weekly.

Shopping

ROYAL HAWAIIAN CENTER

The **Royal Hawaiian Center** (2201 Kalakaua Ave., 808/922-2299, www.royalhawaiiancenter.com, 10am-10pm daily), in the heart of Waikiki on Kalakaua Avenue, stretches from Lewers Street to the Outrigger Waikiki hotel. Here you'll find a mix of high-end retailers—clothing, accessories, and jewelry—surf shops and aloha wear, boutiques, beauty products, and food and drink from coffee to cocktails. If you're looking for a few comfortable T-shirts with some personality, check out **Crazy Shirts** (808/971-6024) on the second floor of building B. For women's swimwear, **Allure Swimwear** (808/926-1174) is located on the first level of building C. For those visiting Waikiki for romance, visit **Princesse Tam-Tam Lingerie** (808/922-3330) on the third level of building A for fine to moderate French lingerie. For all things leather, find **Pipeline Leather** (808/926-2288) on the first level of building C. The center has more than 110 shops and restaurants, including an **Apple Store** (808/931-2480) for your tech needs. Big-name stores front Kalakaua Avenue, but there is a parallel walkway through the mall with a host of other stores, a great way to get out of the sun. A small outdoor performance area with hewn stone seats under a banyan tree leads to a beautifully landscaped Hawaiian botanical garden and into the Royal Hawaiian hotel courtyard.

T GALLERIA

Just to the west of the Royal Hawaiian Center on Kalakaua Avenue, on the mountain side of the street, is **T Galleria by DFS** (330 Kalakaua Ave., 808/931-2700, www.dfs.com, 9:30am-11pm daily). The mall features the world's luxury brands and highly personalized service. International travelers can show their passport and purchase goods duty free, or with no tax added to the retail price. A word of caution, the mall is designed so that once you enter, it's hard to find the exit in order to keep you shopping.

LUXURY ROW

A few blocks west of T Galleria on Kalakaua Avenue, on the same side of the street, is **Luxury Row** (2100 Kalakaua Ave., 808/541-5136, www.luxuryrow.com, 9:30am-11pm daily). The name says it all. At Luxury Row you'll find high-end international brands like **Coach** (808/924-1677), **Chanel** (808/971-9011), **Tiffany & Co.** (808/926-2600), **Yves Saint Laurent** (808/924-6900), **Bottega Veneta** (808/923-0800), and **Gucci** (808/921-1000).

ART GALLERIES

Art abounds in Waikiki, with Hawaiian, ocean, and nature themes being the most prevalent. **Wyland Galleries Waikiki** (270 Lewers St., 808/924-1322, www.wyland.com, 10am-10pm daily) features Wyland's signature ocean art and is the most comprehensive Wyland source in Hawai'i. Also on Lewers Street in the Waikiki Beach Walk shops is the

Peter Lik Gallery (226 Lewers St., 808/926-5656, www.lik.com/galleries/waikiki.html, 10am-11pm daily), featuring bold prints from landscape photographer Peter Lik. Inside the **Sheraton Princess Kaiulani Hotel** (2352 Kalakaua Ave.) you'll find **Tabora Gallery** (808/922-5400, https://taboragallery.com, 9am-10:30pm daily), with originals from seascape painter Roy Tabora.

Entertainment and Events

TOP EXPERIENCE

NIGHTLIFE

LuLu's (2270 Kalakaua Ave., 808/979-7590, www.luluswaikiki.com, 7am-2am daily) serves breakfast, lunch, and dinner, but is more widely known as a place to hang out, have a beer, and enjoy its second-story view. Right on the corner of Kalakaua and Kapahulu Avenues, it's the spot for people-watching.

Sky Waikiki (2330 Kalakaua Ave., 808/921-9978, www.skywaikiki.com, 5pm-midnight Sun.-Thurs., 5pm-close Fri.-Sat.) is an upscale club, which offers amazing views, tapas, signature cocktails, and all the things nightclubs are known for. Expect a line to get in after 9pm and a cover charge at the door. You must get bottle service and a table if you'd like to order food.

Arnold's Beach Bar & Grill (339 Saratoga Rd., 808/924-6887, 10am-2am daily) is a kitschy throwback to the 1950s. It's warm and cozy, the service is friendly, and the drinks are priced just right.

One of the only true nightclubs in Waikiki, **Addiction Nightclub** (1775 Ala Moana Blvd., 808/943-5800, http://addictionnightclub.com, 10:30pm-3am Thurs.-Sat.) is in the chic Modern Honolulu hotel. DJs, dancing, bottle service—check the website for who's spinning while you're in town.

On the second floor of the Waikiki Grand hotel, **Hula's Bar & Lei Stand** (134 Kapahulu Ave., 808/923-0669, www.hulas.com, 10am-2am daily) is Waikiki's premier gay and lesbian bar. Famous for its open-air lanai and beautiful views from the rail, Hula's has DJs and dancing, daily drink specials, and a limited menu of entrées and appetizers. Check its website for a complete monthly events calendar.

LU'AU AND REVUES

There are two traditional lu'au in Waikiki. The **Waikiki Starlight Lu'au** at the **Hilton Hawaiian Village** (2005 Kalia Rd., 808/949-4321, www.hiltonhawaiianvillage.com) is an outdoor event featuring traditional Hawaiian, Tahitian, and Samoan live music and dance, as well as traditional lu'au fare, with accompanying dishes for the less adventurous like huli huli chicken and Hawaiian fried rice. Held Sunday-Thursday (weather permitting) on the rooftop of the Mid-Pacific Conference Center, the two-hour show begins at 5:30pm, with general seating at $99 for adults, $49.50 for children 4-11, and premier seating at $125 for adults, $62.50 for children 4-11. Children under 3 are free. The premier seating includes a fresh orchid lei greeting, preferred table seating closest to the stage, and first dibs at the buffet. All prices include two complimentary beverages.

The **Royal Hawaiian** (2259 Kalakaua Ave., 808/923-7311, www.royal-hawaiian.com) has a plated lu'au dinner and show held on the Ocean Lawn called **'Aha'aina,** a cultural journey through time. The special dinner is served Monday evenings 5:30pm-9pm for $175 for adults, $97 for children 5-12. There is a nominal charge for children under 5.

If you're in the mood for an evening with Elvis, check out **Burn'n Love Waikiki** (2300 Kalakaua Ave., 808/971-4321, www.burnnlove.com) at the Magic of Polynesia Theatre. The show relives Elvis's time in Hawaii and the influence it had on his life, his movies, and his music, including *Blue Hawaii* and the Aloha from Hawaii live concert broadcast.

LIVE MUSIC

A good portion of the restaurants and bars in Waikiki, especially the oceanfront establishments, have live music during *pau hana* and at night, usually a solo guitarist and singer or duo playing a mix of island-style classic rock peppered with a few island lounge classics. By far, the most popular free concert in Waikiki is **Duke's on Sunday.** From 4pm-6pm every Sunday at **Duke's Waikiki** (2335 Kalakaua Ave., 808/922-2268, www.dukeswaikiki.com) in the Outrigger Waikiki hotel, Hawaiian rock legend Henry Kapono plays a lively 2-hour rock-and-roll set of his own hits and classic rock covers done in his own style. Known as the "Wild Hawaiian," he draws residents and visitors alike to Duke's lower lanai, right on the sand, to catch the show, dance, and enjoy a few beverages in the afternoon sun. Kapono plays every Sunday unless he's on tour, in which case there are several other noteworthy bands in the lineup that put on a great show.

FESTIVALS AND EVENTS

There is no shortage of cultural events, festivals, and parades throughout the year that close down Kalakaua Avenue to vehicular traffic and bring out the live music and food vendors to invoke a celebratory atmosphere.

Spring

The **Waikiki Spam Jam** (www.spamjamhawaii.com) goes off at the end of April, with two stages on Kalakaua Avenue and featuring live music, food vendors, and a party till 10pm celebrating local Hawaiian culture. On May 1 **Lei Day** is celebrated with a colorful parade of flowers.

Summer

June is packed full of festivals: the **Honolulu Pride Parade and Celebration** (http://honoluluprideparade.blogspot.com) is in early June, the **Pan-Pacific Festival** (www.pan-pacific-festival.com) is a three-day event celebrating Pacific Rim culture with performances, food, events, and a parade, and the **Kamehameha Day Floral Parade** should not be missed if you're in Waikiki on June 11. In late July, the **Ukulele Festival** (www.ukulelefestivalhawaii.org) is a local favorite, when local and international ukulele talents entertain at the Kapi'olani Bandstand. **Duke's Oceanfest** (http://dukesoceanfest.com) is a weeklong series of ocean events in late August celebrating ocean sports and the legacy of Duke Kahanamoku. Competitions in longboarding, paddleboarding, swimming, tandem surfing, surf polo, beach volleyball, and other events go down from sunrise to sunset along Kuhio Beach Park.

Food

COFFEE

Honolulu Coffee Company (2365 Kalakaua Ave., 808/533-1500, ext. 4, www.honolulucoffee.com, 6am-10pm daily) can be found at the Moana Surfrider, but right on the sidewalk of Kalakaua Avenue, so you don't need to enter the hotel to find it. It has a wide variety of bagels, breads and pastries, and several tables, even sidewalk window seats.

QUICK BITES AND CAFÉS

Giovanni Pastrami (227 Lewers St., 808/923-2100, www.giovannipastrami.

com, 7am-midnight daily, $9-23) is a great New York-style deli and sports bar. With choice ingredients to nosh, 17 TVs, breakfast served till midnight, and a weekday happy hour 3pm-6pm, it's a great place to watch the game and have a sandwich and beer in style.

Bogart's Café (3045 Monsarrat Ave., 808/739-0999, http://bogartscafe.webs.com, 6am-6:30pm Mon.-Fri., 6am-6pm Sat.-Sun., $6-21) is a great little breakfast spot for escaping the bustle of Waikiki proper. The eggs, bagels, pancakes, waffles, and coffee are the perfect breakfast options after a walk or run across Kapiʻolani Park.

From homemade cakes, salads, and dips to cold sandwiches, local food, and burgers right off the grill, **Diamond Head Market & Grill** (3158 Monsarrat Ave., 808/732-0077, www.diamondheadmarket.com, 6:30am-9pm daily, $5-17) has a little bit of everything on offer. The grill has a walk-up window on the exterior of the building. Be prepared for a bit of a wait at lunch, as the food is popular with locals and visitors alike. And check out all the bakery delights inside. The scones—if there are any left—are beyond delicious.

BREAKFAST

Eggs 'n Things (343 Saratoga Rd., 808/923-3447, www.eggsnthings.com, 6am-2pm, 4pm-10pm daily, $8-17) is an extremely popular breakfast joint serving American-style breakfast with a few local variations. Meat, eggs, pancakes, waffles, and even crepes are the crux of the menu. Dinner is served as well. There is also a location on Kalakaua Avenue, called the **Waikiki Beach Eggspress** (2464 Kalakaua Ave., 808/926-3447, 6am-2pm, 4pm-10pm daily, $8-17), which has an interesting seating method. First you wait in line to order, then you wait in line to get seated, and then sometimes you have to wait a little longer for your food to arrive. With an average wait of 30-40 minutes from the moment it opens, it's apparent Eggs 'n Things has developed quite a following.

STEAK AND SEAFOOD

Azure (2259 Kalakaua Ave., 808/923-7311, www.azurewaikiki.com, 5:30pm-9pm daily, $26-52) is the pinnacle of fine seafood dining. Set inside the Royal Hawaiian, it serves the freshest seafood there is, hand selected from the Honolulu fish auction every morning. The focus is on high-heat, aromatic, herb-roasted

Eggs 'n Things is the "in" breakfast joint, so be prepared to wait at least 30 minutes for a stack of pancakes.

Hawai'i regional preparations with bright tropical flavors. Sommeliers can assist in selecting the perfect wine for your dinner. Azure has beachfront dining cabanas in addition to the dining room and a traditional six-course degustation menu, with samplings of the chef's signature dishes and wine pairings.

Roy's (226 Lewers St., 808/923-7697, http://royshawaii.com, 11am-9:30pm Mon.-Thurs., 11am-10pm Fri.-Sun., $15-45) has Hawaiian fusion wired, and the quality of ingredients, consistency, and service are exceptional. It is open for appetizer service 11am-5pm and offers a prix fixe menu with a sampling of favorites, a well-balanced offering of meat and fish entrées, and sushi.

Orchids (2199 Kalia Rd., 808/923-2311, www.halekulani.com/living/dining/orchids, 7:30am-10pm daily, $28-60) is located inside the Halekulani hotel. As the name suggests, colorful orchids abound, and the restaurant opens out to a breathtaking view of the Pacific Ocean unencumbered by beach umbrellas or sunbathers. The Sunday brunch is punctuated by a three-meat carving station, something you won't find at most Waikiki breakfast buffets, and the signature dinner entrée is a light *onaga* (snapper) Orchids style, with sesame oil, shoyu, and ginger. It also offers a lunch menu.

★ **Kai Market** (2255 Kalakaua Ave., 808/921-4600, www.sheraton-waikiki.com/dining/kai, 6am-11am, 5:30pm-9:30pm daily, breakfast $22-29, dinner $55-58) prides itself on locally sourcing all its products and ingredients, from the baked goods to the meat and produce. Kai Market is inside the Sheraton Waikiki, and both breakfast and dinner are buffet style. Kids 5 and under eat free anytime, and children 6-12 eat for half price.

Top of Waikiki (2270 Kalakaua Ave., 808/923-3877, http://topofwaikiki.com, 5pm-9:30pm daily, starting at $37) is truly a unique dining experience. On the top floor of the Waikiki Business Plaza, the three-tiered round restaurant slowly revolves 360 degrees per hour, offering guests a complete view of O'ahu's glowing South Shore. An open sit-down bar provides an additional level for viewing the sights. Great Pacific Rim cuisine and nightly happy hour specials—5pm-7pm and 9pm-11pm—complete the experience. Dinner is served until 9:30pm.

★ **Duke's Waikiki** (2335 Kalakaua Ave., 808/922-2268, www.dukeswaikiki.com, 7am-midnight daily, $15-33) is a must, whether it's for the breakfast buffet, lunch, dinner, or just cruising in the **Barefoot Bar** and watching the surfers out at Canoes and Queen's. Decorated with historic and recent pictures of the Waikiki beachboys and surf nostalgia, the relaxed, beachside atmosphere complements the excellent food and service Duke's has live music Monday-Thursday in the bar 4pm-6pm, and Friday-Sunday the show moves out to the lower lanai under the sun, the highlight being Duke's on Sunday, featuring Henry Kapono (unless he's on tour). For dinner, make reservations or be prepared to wait up to an hour during busy times, which isn't that bad if you retire to the bar and relax till your table is ready.

Hula Grill (2335 Kalakaua Ave., 808/923-4852, www.hulagrillwaikiki.com, 6:30am-11:30am and 3pm-10pm Mon.-Thurs.10pm, 6:30am-10pm Fri.-Sun., $20-34), in the Outrigger Waikiki and just upstairs from Duke's, is a great steak and seafood option if you don't have the time to wait for a table downstairs. With comfortable, Hawaiian home decor and live music nightly, 7pm-9pm, Hula Grill provides a comfortable ambience in which to savor several fish specialties, including the popular Macadamia Nut Crusted as well as the succulent Filet Steak Kiana, a take on the steak Diane. Hula Grill has a great Aloha Hour 4pm-6pm with half-off selected menu and drink items.

Michel's (2895 Kalakaua Ave., 808/923-6552, http://michelshawaii.com, 5:30pm-9pm Sun.-Thurs., 5:30pm-9:30pm Fri.-Sat., $40-75) is the pinnacle of French haute cuisine in Waikiki and has been recognized as the "Best Restaurant for Romance" by *Honolulu Magazine* since 1985. Overlooking a beautiful stretch of reef and ocean closer to Diamond Head and away from the Waikiki crowds, the stunning setting, live music, and delectable menu are worth the price for a truly special occasion. Michel's also offers a chef's choice six-course tasting menu.

MEXICAN

Buho Cocina Y Cantina (2250 Kalakaua Ave., 808/922-2846, http://buhocantina.com, 11am-1am Sun.-Thurs., 11am-2am Fri.-Sat., $10-29) is a great change of pace for your palate. The rooftop restaurant has mostly outdoor seating and a warm, festive atmosphere. Start with the guacamole appetizer and then dive into the many delicious entrées. You can't go wrong with the smoked brisket tacos and a signature margarita. From the sidewalk on Kalakaua, take the elevator from the street level directly to the restaurant.

ITALIAN

Perched at the top of the Ilikai hotel, **Sarento's** (1777 Ala Moana Blvd., 808/955-5559, www.sarentoswaikiki.com, dinner 5:30pm-9pm Sun.-Thurs., 5:30pm-9:30 Fri.-Sat., $24-42) has magnificent views of Waikiki and Honolulu's skyline. Fine Italian dining is accompanied with live piano music and great service.

JAPANESE

No detail has been left unexplored at **Nobu** (2233 Helumoa Rd., 808/237-6999, www. noburestaurants.com, dinner 5:30pm-10pm Sun.-Thurs., 5:30pm-10:30pm Fri.-Sat., bar lounge 5:30pm-close daily $3-48), where the architecture and interior help create an intimate and elegant setting, and the innovative and award-winning "New Style" Japanese cuisine is unmatched. Located in the Waikiki Parc Hotel, the sophisticated seafood-centric menu covers a range of hot and cold dishes, sushi and sashimi, complete dinners, and kushiyaki and tempura. The happy hour (5:30pm-7pm daily) has drink and food

specials that could suffice for a meal by themselves, though it's only available in the bar and lounge area.

Serving contemporary, inventive sushi and Asian-influenced dishes, ★ **Sansei Seafood Restaurant and Sushi Bar** (2552 Kalakaua Ave., 808/931-6286, www.sanseihawaii.com, 5:30pm-10pm Sun.-Thurs., 5:30pm-1am Fri.-Sat., starting at $8) is one of the most popular sushi restaurants in Waikiki. With its handful of award-winning sushi creations, the à la carte menu is perfect for sampling the gamut. Sansei has a popular early bird special 5:30pm-6pm Sunday and Monday, with half off most of the menu (people line up early at the door) and half-off drink specials 10pm-1am Friday and Saturday.

Doraku Sushi (2233 Kalakaua Ave., 808/922-3323, http://dorakusushi.com, noon-10pm Sun.-Thurs., noon-11pm Fri.-Sat., $4-44) features *izakaya* dining, where dishes are brought to the table throughout the meal to share. On the menu, you'll find hot and cold dishes as well as a beautiful assortment of specialty sushi rolls, sashimi, and soups and salads. A relaxing and enjoyable experience.

HEALTH FOOD

★ **Diamond Head Cove Health Bar** (3045 Monsarrat Ave., 808/732-8744, www. diamondheadcove.com, 9am-8pm Fri.-Mon., 9am-11pm Tues.-Thurs., $5-13) is a small juice and kava bar that also serves fresh omelets, hummus, salads, and is famous for its hearty and healthy *aiai* bowls. The staff is friendly, the food is fresh and delicious, and surf art, posters, and decorations fill every space on the walls and ceiling, creating a cool hangout to beat the midday heat. The Cove, as it's known by local patrons, stays open late for Kava Nights, Tuesday through Thursday, when it turns the lights low and lets the live musicians set the mood.

Honolulu

Look for ★ to find recommended sights, activities, dining, and lodging.

Highlights

★ **'Iolani Palace:** The only royal residence in the United States, this grand and stately palace sits on 11 grassy acres with beautiful shade trees (page 61).

★ **Historic Chinatown:** Chinatown is a hub for international dining, art, nightlife—and for Chinese food and goods, of course (page 64).

★ **Honolulu Museum of Art:** Hawaii's most prestigious art museum, with over 50,000 pieces spanning 5,000 years, was established in 1927. The museum's holdings include Asian, European, American, and African works of art (page 65).

★ **Foster Botanical Garden:** Century-old trees, palms, orchids, and cycads—curious leafy plants that date back to prehistoric times—can all be found in this majestic spot (page 66).

★ **Nu'uanu Pali State Wayside:** The Pali Lookout is a beautiful spot to take in the grandeur of the Ko'olau Mountains and the tropical splendor of Kane'ohe Bay (page 66).

★ **Tantalus-Round Top Drive:** This leisurely scenic drive winds up the Tantalus Crater to beautiful Pu'u 'Ualaka'a Park at the top of the volcano's cinder cone. The view scans Diamond Head, Punchbowl Crater, and greater Honolulu (page 67).

★ **Bishop Museum:** The premier museum in the Pacific explores Hawaiian culture and history, the other Polynesian and Pacific cultures, and the natural history of the islands. It also features a planetarium and interactive Science Adventure Center (page 68).

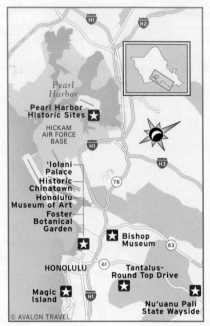

© AVALON TRAVEL

★ **Pearl Harbor Historic Sites:** Pay homage to the lives lost during the Pearl Harbor attack on December 7, 1941 (page 69).

★ **Magic Island:** Paths wind beneath the branches of beautiful trees. There's a protected beach and lagoon where *keiki* can safely play. Beautiful views along the coast make it perfect for a seaside picnic (page 72).

The capital of the Hawaiian Islands since 1845, Honolulu means "sheltered bay" in the Hawaiian language.

Honolulu is the political, cultural, and economic center of Oʻahu and the state of Hawaii, thanks largely to Honolulu Harbor's commercial port and the Honolulu International Airport. Its more than 400 high-rises create a skyline in stark contrast to the verdant backdrop of forested ridges and valleys. Honolulu combines the hustle, convenience, and abundance of a major city and an ethnically diverse population of 350,000 people with a history made unique by its architecture and thriving neighborhoods.

Just east of Pearl Harbor, Honolulu is defined by its city center, the economic heart of the county and state. Containing the Hawaii state capitol building that neighbors ʻIolani Palace, the only royal residence in the United States, the historic district is beset by towering skyscrapers. It gives way to Chinatown, a relic of Oʻahu's whaling, migrant worker, and war-torn past. Today, Chinatown is chock-full of art galleries, nightclubs, bars, and some of Oʻahu's best restaurants.

Honolulu's neighborhoods spread out in all directions and are as dynamic as the rainbows that hang over the mountains. Manoa Valley is home to the University of Hawaiʻi and Lyon Arboretum at the back of the valley. Kaimuki is known for its shopping and restaurants. Kakaʻako's industrial spaces have become the bastion for a burgeoning urban art scene, and Ala Moana Beach Park affords expansive grassy space, great waves, and a calm swimming area on the inside of the reef.

PLANNING YOUR TIME

Many of the activities in Honolulu, whether sightseeing in the historic district or hiking in the Koʻolau Mountains, require at least a half day's time. Mix in a meal or two and you have a packed schedule.

When heading downtown to see the historic district, leave early to beat the hot midday sun, since the best option is walking to the different buildings and museums. Downtown metered street parking has a two-hour time limit, so when it's time to get back to the car, head over to Chinatown, park in one of the municipal lots, and explore the small, historic city blocks. Plan on saving your appetite for eating in Chinatown, as the diversity of cuisine here will make your head spin.

Previous: downtown Honolulu; ʻIolani Palace. **Above:** the Pearl Harbor Historic Sites.

Greater Honolulu

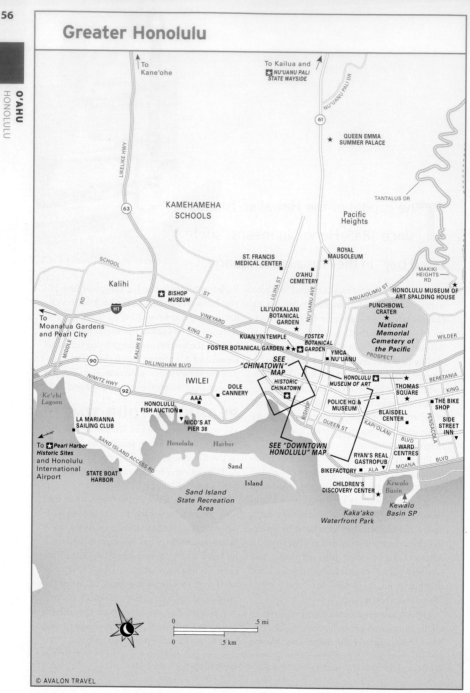

To
Kane'ohe

To Kailua and
✚ NU'UANU PALI
STATE WAYSIDE

61

QUEEN EMMA
SUMMER PALACE

TANTALUS DR

KAMEHAMEHA
SCHOOLS

Pacific
Heights

63

LIKELIKE HWY

ROYAL
MAUSOLEUM

ST. FRANCIS
MEDICAL CENTER

SCHOOL

MAKIKI
HEIGHTS
RD

O'AHU
CEMETERY

ULIHA ST

NU'UANU AVE

'ANUAIOLIMU ST

HONOLULU MUSEUM OF
ART SPALDING HOUSE

Kalihi

ST

✚ BISHOP
MUSEUM

PUNCHBOWL
CRATER

To
Moanalua Gardens
and Pearl City

VINEYARD

LILI'UOKALANI
BOTANICAL
GARDEN

National
Memorial
Cemetery of
the Pacific

H1

RD

KING   ST

WILDER

KALIHI ST

MIDDLE

90

KUAN YIN TEMPLE

FOSTER
BOTANICAL
GARDEN

FOSTER BOTANICAL GARDEN ★★✚

PROSPECT

YMCA
NU'UANU

DILLINGHAM BLVD

SEE
"CHINATOWN"
MAP

HONOLULU ✚
MUSEUM OF ART

BERETANIA

NIMITZ HWY

IWILEI

HISTORIC
CHINATOWN

THOMAS
SQUARE

KING

92

DOLE
CANNERY

Ke'ehi
Lagoon

AAA

BISHOP

POLICE HQ &
MUSEUM

■ THE BIKE
SHOP

PENSACOLA

HONOLULU
FISH AUCTION ■

BLAISDELL
CENTER

SIDE
STREET
INN

LA MARIANNA
SAILING CLUB

NICO'S AT
PIER 38

QUEEN ST

KAPI'OLANI

To ✚ Pearl Harbor
Historic Sites
and Honolulu
International
Airport

SAND ISLAND ACCESS RD

Honolulu   Harbor

SEE "DOWNTOWN
HONOLULU" MAP

BLVD

WARD
CENTRES

STATE BOAT
HARBOR

Sand

RYAN'S REAL
GASTROPUB

MOANA

BLVD

BIKEFACTORY ■   ALA ▼

Island

Sand Island
State Recreation
Area

CHILDREN'S
DISCOVERY CENTER ★

Kewalo
Basin

Kewalo
Basin SP

Kaka'ako
Waterfront Park

0   .5 mi

0   .5 km

© AVALON TRAVEL

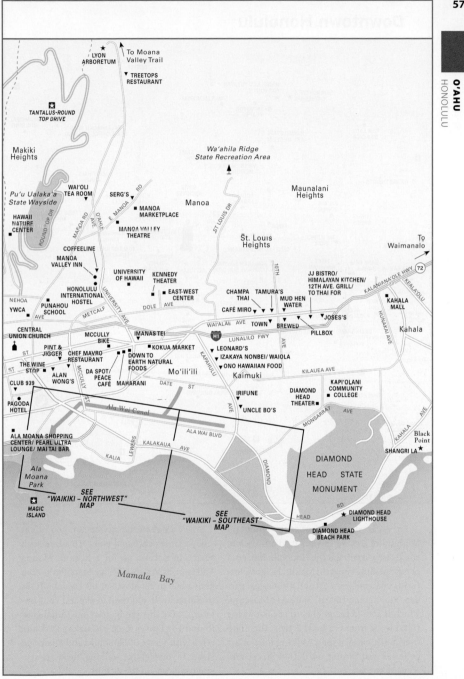

★ LYON ARBORETUM

To Moana Valley Trail

▼ TREETOPS RESTAURANT

✚ TANTALUS-ROUND TOP DRIVE

Makiki Heights

Wa'ahila Ridge State Recreation Area

Pu'u Ualaka'a State Wayside

WAI'OLI TEA ROOM

SERG'S ■

Manoa

Maunalani Heights

■ MANOA MARKETPLACE

HAWAII NATURE CENTER ■

■ MANOA VALLEY THEATRE

St. Louis Heights

To Waimanalo

COFFEELINE ■

MANOA VALLEY INN

UNIVERSITY OF HAWAII ■

KENNEDY THEATER

JJ BISTRO/ HIMALAYAN KITCHEN/ 12TH AVE. GRILL/ TO THAI FOR

HONOLULU INTERNATIONAL HOSTEL

NEHOA

■ EAST-WEST CENTER

CHAMPA THAI   TAMURA'S

MUD HEN WATER

KAHALA MALL

YWCA

PUNAHOU SCHOOL

DOLE   AVE

CAFÉ MIRO ▼

WAI'ALAE   AVE   TOWN   BREWED

JOSES'S ■

Kahala

CENTRAL UNION CHURCH

METCALF

METCALF

IMANAS TEI ■

LUNALILO FWY

PILLBOX

PINT & JIGGER

MCCULLY BIKE

■ KOKUA MARKET

LEONARD'S ■

THE WINE STOP ■

CHEF MAVRO RESTAURANT

DOWN TO EARTH NATURAL FOODS

IZAKAYA NONBEI/ WAIOLA

■ ONO HAWAIIAN FOOD

KILAUEA AVE

CLUB 939 ■

ALAN WONG'S ■

DA SPOT/ PEACE CAFÉ

MAHARANI

DATE   ST

Mo'ili'ili

Kaimuki

KAPI'OLANI COMMUNITY ■ COLLEGE

PAGODA HOTEL ■

IRIFUNE ■

DIAMOND HEAD THEATER ■

Ala Wai Canal

▼ UNCLE BO'S

ALA MOANA SHOPPING CENTER/ PEARL ULTRA LOUNGE/ MAI TAI BAR

KALAKAUA   AVE

ALA WAI BLVD

MONSARRAT   AVE

Black Point

SHANGRI LA ★

Ala Moana Park

SEE "WAIKIKI – NORTHWEST" MAP

DIAMOND

HEAD   STATE

MONUMENT

MAGIC ISLAND

SEE "WAIKIKI – SOUTHEAST" MAP

HEAD   RD

★ DIAMOND HEAD LIGHTHOUSE

■ DIAMOND HEAD BEACH PARK

Mamala   Bay

Downtown Honolulu

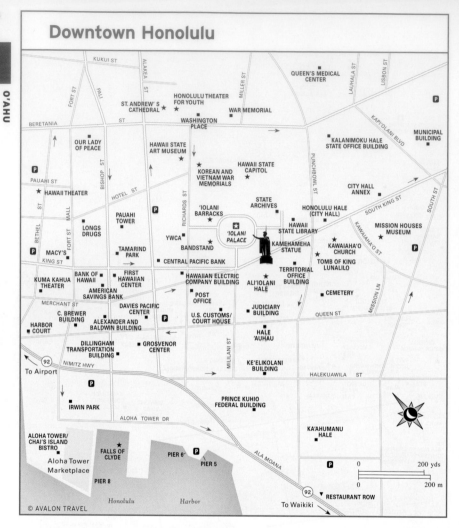

For an art day, start out at the Honolulu Museum of Art. With your paid admission, you'll also get entry at the Honolulu Museum of Art Spalding House in Makiki Heights, featuring contemporary art and a botanical garden. Stop by the Hawaii State Art Museum, which is free to the public, to check out the finest work from top local artists, then hop over to Chinatown for a walking tour of art galleries and dinner on Bethel Street and Nuuanu Avenue.

After a day in the city center, you might enjoy a little peace and quiet. To attain such solace in nature, go for a hike in Manoa Valley or at Wa'ahila Ridge State Park, then grab a bite to eat at one of the casual BYOBs in Kaimuki. If you need to expand your horizons, take the windy drive up Tantalus or Round Top Drives to Pu'u 'Ualaka'a Park and relax with views of Honolulu and Diamond Head. If you feel like walking, there are several trailheads in the vicinity.

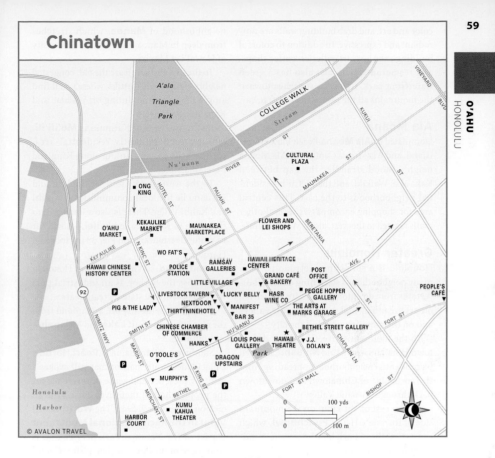

Chinatown

Honolulu might be urban, but it still has beaches. Spend the morning swimming, surfing, or stand-up paddling at Ala Moana Beach Park, then head across the street to Ala Moana Center for shopping and dining.

ORIENTATION
Downtown

Downtown is the epicenter of Honolulu and the financial and political center of the island and the state. Within downtown are the historic district, comprised of the state capitol, 'Iolani Palace, government buildings and offices, as well as other historical and cultural buildings. To the immediate west of the historic district is the financial district, where high-rise office buildings perch along one-way streets.

Chinatown

Just west of the financial district is the historic **Chinatown** neighborhood, which stretches from Vineyard Boulevard to the north to Aloha Tower along the harbor, with the Nu'uanu Stream as its western border. Chinatown is home to a curious mix of bars, hip ethnic restaurants, Chinese and Pacific Rim cuisine, Chinese grocery stores, small local eateries, art galleries, and chic coffee shops.

Kaka'ako

At the forefront of the urban art scene, much of **Kaka'ako** is industrial, especially the streets southeast of downtown. Young artists have transformed the area into an explosion of color and art, and drab building walls are now radiant and expressive. In addition to colorful building exteriors, art galleries, coffee shops, and restaurants, Kaka'ako also has a green waterfront park. Kaka'ako stretches toward the mountains all the way to the H-1 freeway.

Ala Moana

Dominated by **Ala Moana** Beach Park, Magic Island, and Ala Moana Center, the Ala Moana neighborhood straddles the gap between Kaka'ako, Waikiki, and the McCully residential neighborhoods to the east. This central area for shopping encompasses several other malls located to the west, along Ward Avenue.

Greater Honolulu

Honolulu is a sprawling metropolis, with many neighborhoods stretching out in all directions from downtown. Some are industrial, others are urban, and some are in the valleys and on the mountains behind the city.

In the mountains directly behind downtown Honolulu, you'll find **Nu'uanu,** defined by residential neighborhoods spreading from the north side of Chinatown and downtown back through Nu'uanu Valley.

To the east of Nu'uanu, on the mountain side of Interstate H-1, is **Punchbowl,** which consists of the old neighborhoods surrounding Punchbowl Crater.

Northeast of Punchbowl is the **Makiki** neighborhood, which snakes up the mountains.

Heading east takes you to the upscale neighborhood of **Manoa,** which stretches from deep in Manoa Valley to the University of Hawai'i at Manoa.

To the east and south are the old, congested neighborhoods of **Kaimuki,** where you'll find ample shopping and dining on Waialae and Kapahulu Avenues.

Just to the west of Kaimuki is **Mo'ili'ili,** another predominantly residential area, with some shops and dining along King and Beretania Streets.

To the west of downtown Honolulu and Nu'uanu lie the local communities of **Kalihi** and Kalihi Valley. There is also a small area to the south of Kalihi called **Iwilei,** known for its seafood restaurants on Pier 38 in Honolulu Harbor.

Sand Island, south of downtown Honolulu and across the harbor, is an industrial port with an oceanfront state recreation area.

To the west is the airport, and inland from the airport are the **Salt Lake** and **Moanalua** communities.

Southwest of Moanalua is **Pearl Harbor,** a placid, deepwater harbor that still evokes a military presence and sense of reverence for the people who lost their lives during the attack on December 7, 1941. The **World War II Valor in the Pacific National Monument** is part of the National Park Service and is comprised of the Pearl Harbor Visitor Center and four historic sites. It is the most heavily visited sight on O'ahu. The communities of Waipahu, Pearl City, 'Aiea, and Halawa border the harbor from west to east.

Your Best Day in Honolulu

While there are many neighborhoods that comprise Greater Honolulu, most of what appeals to visitors is centrally located in the downtown vicinity. For most visitors based out of Waikiki, plan your Honolulu visit around avoiding the daily rush-hour traffic to maximize your time.

- Instead of rushing immediately into the historic district in the morning and getting caught in traffic, head to **Lyon Arboretum** in Manoa Valley and explore the extensive trail system, bird-watch, and learn about native Hawaiian plants. If you'd like to be closer to downtown, try **Foster Botanical Garden,** just outside of Chinatown.

- Next, visit the historic district and take in the **Hawaii State Capitol** and **'Iolani Palace,** the only royal residence in the United States.

- For lunch, head to the **Ala Moana Center,** where you can grab lunch in the comfortable, open-air **Mai Tai Bar** on the upper lanai of the mall. Or, head into Kaka'ako, where you can find hip and unique shops and restaurants.

- A visit to the **Honolulu Museum of Art** is a must in the afternoon. If you have your own transportation, take advantage of the free same-day admission to the Spalding House in Makiki Heights, a museum of contemporary art.

- For dinner, head back into Chinatown and peruse the many restaurants and bars. Whether you're after Chinese food from **Little Village Noodle House** or pizza from Irish pub **J.J. Dolan's,** Chinatown has you covered.

- For those visiting **Pearl Harbor,** strike out as early as possible to avoid long lines and hours-long waits. Plan for at least a half day at the national monument.

RAINY-DAY ALTERNATIVE

A rainy day is a museum day. Purchasing admission to the **Honolulu Museum of Art** also allows you to visit the **Spalding House,** a contemporary art museum, for free. Take advantage of the two-for-one special.

Sights

DOWNTOWN

★ 'Iolani Palace

Set on a grassy 11 acres, shaded by canopy trees in the heart of the Capitol District, **'Iolani Palace** (364 S. King St., 808/522-0822, www.iolanipalace.org, 9am-5pm Mon.-Sat.) is the second royal palace to grace the grounds. The building, with its glass and ironwork imported from San Francisco and its Corinthian columns, is the only true royal palace in America. 'Iolani Palace, begun in late 1879 under orders of King Kalakaua, was completed in December 1882 at a cost of $350,000. It was the first electrified building in Honolulu, having electricity and telephones even before the White House in Washington DC. The palace served as the official residence of the monarch of Hawai'i until the overthrow of the Hawaiian kingdom in 1893. It then became the main executive building for the provisional government, with the House of Representatives meeting in the throne room and the Senate in the dining room, until 1968. It has since been elevated to a state monument and National Historic Landmark.

Through the first floor of this palace runs a broad hallway with a grand stairway that leads to the second story. On the east side of the building is the large and opulent Throne Room, the scene of formal meetings and major royal functions. On the west side are the smaller Blue Room, an informal reception area, and the dining room. The upstairs level was the private residence of the king and his family. It also has a wide hallway, and on each side are bedrooms, sitting rooms, a music room, and office. The basement held servants' quarters, the kitchen, and offices of certain government officials. On the palace grounds, you'll find the Coronation Pavilion, which originally stood directly in front of the palace, but was later moved to where it stands today as a bandstand for the Royal Hawaiian Band, and a raised earthen platform, the original site of the royal mausoleum, which was later moved out along the Pali Highway.

'Iolani Palace has docent-guided tours and self-guided tours of the first and second floors, both with self-guided exploration of the basement gallery. One-hour tours enter the palace every 15 minutes. Reservations are required for the **guided tour** (808/522-0832, palace-tickets@iolanipalace.org, 9am-10am Tues. and Thurs., 9am-11:15am Wed., Fri.-Sat., $21.75 adults, $6 children ages 5-12), but not for the **self-guided audio tour** (9am-4pm Mon., 10:30am-4pm Tues. and Thurs., noon-4pm Wed. and Fri.-Sat., $14.75 adults, $5 children ages 5-12, $1 fee for the audio recording). The **Basement Gallery exhibits** (9:30am-5pm Mon.-Sat., $7 adults, $3 children) are another option for touring. Tickets are also sold at the 'Iolani Barracks (9am-4pm Tues.-Sat.), behind the palace. Also in the barracks is the palace gift shop and bookstore (8:30am-4pm Mon.-Sat.).

There is limited metered parking on the palace grounds. From South King Street, turn left onto Likelike Street, a one-way drive, just before the major Punchbowl Street intersection. Turn left through the decorated gate onto the palace grounds.

Hawaii State Capitol

Directly behind 'Iolani Palace sits the unique **Hawaii State Capitol** (415 S. Beretania St., 808/587-0478, www.capitol.hawaii.gov), built in 1969. The structure is a metaphor for Hawaii: the pillars surrounding it are palms, the reflecting pool is the sea, and the cone-shaped rooms of the Legislature represent the volcanoes of Hawai'i. The walls are lined with rich *koa* wood from the Big Island and further graced with woven hangings, murals, and two gigantic, four-ton replicas of the State Seal

the only royal residence in the United States, 'Iolani Palace

the King Kamehameha I Statue

The Greek revival mansion was both Queen Lili'uokalani's home and also her prison beginning in 1893, when the Hawaiian kingdom was overthrown. She resided at Washington Place till her death in 1917. In 1918, the home became the official residence of the state governors of Hawaii. The mansion was converted into a museum in 2001, and a new governor's mansion was built behind it. Washington Place is still used for state dinners and official functions and remains the official residence of the governor. The mansion is on the mountain side of Beretania Street, directly across from the Hawaii State Capitol.

St. Andrew's Cathedral

Just to the west of Washington Place is **St. Andrew's Cathedral** (229 Queen Emma Sq., 808/524-2822, www.thecathedralofstandrew.org). Construction started in 1867 as an Anglican church, but it wasn't really finished until 1958. Many of its stones and ornaments were shipped from England, and its stained-glass windows, especially the large contemporary-style window on the narthex end, the bell tower, and its pipe organ, touted as the largest pipe organ in the Pacific, are of particular interest. Hawai'i's monarchs worshipped here, and the church is still active. There is a free guided tour following the 10:30am Sunday Episcopal service. After the service, simply wait below the pulpit for a docent. There is limited public parking on church grounds during the week.

Hawaii State Art Museum

The **Hawaii State Art Museum** (250 S. Hotel St., #2, 808/586-0900, http://hawaii.gov/sfca/HiSAM.html, 10am-4pm Tues.-Sat.) is on the second floor of the No. 1 Capitol District Building and has four galleries: the Diamond Head Gallery, the Ewa Gallery, the Sculpture Lobby, and the Sculpture Garden. The exhibitions highlight the finest collection of work by Hawai'i artists and the gallery displays rotate regularly. The museum gift shop is on the first floor.

hanging at both entrances. The inner courtyard has a 600,000-tile mosaic and standing at the *mauka* entrance to the building is a poignant sculpture of Saint Damien of Molokai, while the statue *The Spirit of Lili'uokalani* fronts the building on the ocean side. The State Legislature is in session for 60 working days, starting on the third Wednesday in January. The legislative session opens with dancing, music, and festivities, and the public is invited. Peek inside, then take the elevator to the fifth floor for outstanding views of the city. There is also a Korean-Vietnam War Memorial, paying tribute to those who died in the two wars.

Washington Place

Begun in 1841 by Captain John Dominis, **Washington Place** (320 S. Beretania St., 808/536-8040, www.washingtonplacefoundation.org) is best known as the home of Queen Lili'uokalani and her husband, John Owen Dominis, son of Captain Dominis.

King Kamehameha I Statue

The **King Kamehameha I Statue** is centered in a roundabout near the junction of King and Mililani Streets. Running off at an angle is Merchant Street, the oldest thoroughfare in Honolulu. This statue is much more symbolic of Kamehameha's strength as a ruler and unifier of the Hawaiian Islands than as a replica of the man himself. It is one of three. The original, lost at sea near the Falkland Islands en route from Paris, where it was bronzed, was later recovered, but not before the insurance money was used to cast this second one. The original now stands in the tiny town of Kapa'au, in the Kohala District of the Big Island, not far from where Kamehameha was born. The Honolulu statue was dedicated in 1883, as part of King David Kalakaua's coronation ceremony. Its black and gold colors are striking, but it is most magnificent on June 11, King Kamehameha Day, when 18-foot lei are draped around the neck and the outstretched arms. The third stands in Washington DC, dedicated when Hawai'i became a state.

Kawaiaha'o Church

The **Kawaiaha'o Church** (957 Punchbowl St., 808/522-1333, www.kawaiahao.org) was built between 1836 and 1842. The first Christian church in Hawaii, its New England-style architecture was crafted from 14,000 coral slabs, quarried by hand from local reefs. King Liholiho and his wife Queen Emma, who bore the last child born to a Hawaiian monarch, wed at the church, and on June 19, 1856, Lunalilo, the first king elected to the throne, took his oath of office in the church. Lunalilo is buried in a tomb at the front of the church, along with his father, Charles Kana'ina, and nearby lies the grave of his mother, Miriam Kekauluohi. In the graveyard at the rear of the church rest many members of the Parker, Green, Brown, and Cooke families, early missionaries to the islands. Most are recognizable as important and influential people in 19th-century Hawaiian history. Hidden away in a corner of the grounds is an unobtrusive

adobe building, the remains of a schoolhouse built in 1835 to educate Hawaiian children. Kawaiaha'o holds beautiful Christmas services with a strong Polynesian and Hawaiian flavor, and Hawaiian-language services are given here every Sunday, along with English-language services.

Mission Houses Museum

The days when tall ships with tattered sails bore in God-fearing missionary families dedicated to Christianizing the savage islands are alive in the halls and buildings of the **Mission Houses Museum** (553 S. King St., 808/447-3910, www.missionhouses. org, 10am-4pm Tues.-Sat.), now a registered National Historic Landmark. Set behind **Kawaiaha'o Church**, the complex includes two main houses, a printing house annex, a research library, and a gift shop. The printing office was the first in the islands just as the Frame House is the oldest wooden structure in Hawaii. One-hour guided tours are offered every hour 11am-3pm; admission is $10 adults, $6 students.

CHINATOWN
★ Historic Chinatown

Chinese immigrants came to Hawaii in the 1800s as the first contract laborers for the burgeoning sugar industry. They established a vibrant community with herb shops, restaurants, temples, and retail outlets in what is now **historic Chinatown.** Today, Chinatown is a vibrant mix of art galleries, coffeehouses, upscale restaurants, bars and clubs, outdoor markets, and quick and delicious ethnic food restaurants. It also has a seedy side of homeless sleeping in doorways, prostitution, and fights spilling out of dive bars onto the sidewalk, which gives the historic neighborhood depth and character.

The best way to see Chinatown is to park the car and explore the streets on foot. Chinatown is relatively small, and the square grid of streets makes it easy to get around quickly. There are six municipal parking lots across Chinatown, which have the best rates. There is one on River

Street, one on Maunakea Street, two on Smith Street, and two on Bethel Street.

On the east side of Chinatown, **Fort Street Mall** is a pedestrian area dominated by take-out restaurants and mingling students from Hawai'i Pacific University as they wait for classes. The art galleries are generally on the east end of Chinatown, on Smith Street, Nu'uanu Avenue, and Bethel Street. The cuisine on offer in Chinatown is truly international, from Irish and Cuban to French and Mediterranean, much of which is found on Bethel Street. But the main draw, traditional Chinese fare, is also readily available. The wealth of Chinese establishments is on Smith and Maunakea Streets. Noodle shops and Chinese restaurants merely complement the variety of Asian food found in the **Maunakea Marketplace Food Court,** on the corner of Maunakea and Hotel Streets. Chinese, Thai, Korean, Vietnamese, and Filipino plates are served from small market stalls with family-style seating available for enjoying the myriad flavors. Just across Beretania Street, on the outskirts of Chinatown, is the **Chinatown Cultural Plaza Center,** a small indoor mall with gift and herb shops, as well as a host of small eateries. There is paid parking at the plaza, as well.

Chinatown has an abundance of historical buildings dating back to the early 20th century, like the **Hawaii Theatre** on Bethel Street, which opened in 1922. The upper-story facades of the buildings along Hotel Street, between Bethel and Maunakea Streets, still retain vestiges from the World War II era. There is also the **Hawaii Kuan Yin Temple** on the mountain side of Vineyard Boulevard, at the entrance to Foster Botanical Garden. The temple is dedicated to the Chinese deity of compassion.

KAKA'AKO
★ Honolulu Museum of Art
With a rich history dating back to its opening in 1927, the **Honolulu Museum of Art** (900 S. Beretania St., 808/532-8700, http://honolulumuseum.org, 10am-4:30pm Tues.-Sat.,

1pm-5pm Sun.) has a collection of 50,000 pieces spanning 5,000 years of Asian art and textiles, American and European paintings and decorative art, works on paper, and traditional works from Africa, Oceania, and the Americas. Within its earthy, revival mission-style architecture, the museum also houses a library, an education wing, a contemporary gallery, a café, and a 280-seat theater. Admission is $10 adult, children 17 and under free. The fee also covers the Honolulu Museum of Art Spalding House for same-day entry.

Parking can be a bit tricky. There is metered street parking on the blocks around the museum, but make sure to check for time restrictions. The museum maintains two parking lots: the Honolulu Museum of Art School lot behind the Honolulu Museum of Art School, with entrances on Beretania Street and Young Street ($3 with validation for four hours), and the Kinau Street Lot (1035 Kinau St., 4:30pm-11pm Mon.-Fri., 10am-11pm Sat.-Sun., free). There are five spaces at the museum for visitors with disabilities.

Kaka'ako Waterfront Park and Kewalo Basin Park
Kaka'ako Waterfront Park is a 35-acre expanse of grassy rolling hills that runs to the water's edge on the west side of Kewalo Basin. There are restrooms, picnic tables, and a paved jogging path, but no sandy beach. If you want to jump in the water, there are cement steps that scale down the rocky jetty wall.

On the eastern flank of Kewalo Basin is **Kewalo Basin Park,** a small, coastal refuge with shade trees, restrooms, picnic tables, great views of the ocean, and a couple of popular surf breaks. If you've chartered a boat out of Kewalo Basin for diving or fishing, the park is the perfect place to kill some time before or after your tour. There are two small parking lots, which often fill up on the weekends.

Children's Discovery Center
The **Children's Discovery Center** (111 Ohe St., 808/524-5437, www.discoverycenterhawaii.org, 9am-1pm Tues.-Fri., 10am-3pm

Sat.-Sun.), at Kaka'ako Waterfront Park, is an interactive, hands-on children's museum and activity center focused on learning and discovering through play. The center has six exhibits, one for visitors five years and younger and five for older children. They can learn about their bodies, role play to discover how a community functions, find out about Hawaiian history and culture as well as cultures beyond Hawaiian shores, and explore and understand the importance of rainforests. Admission is $10 general, $6 senior citizen, children under one year are free.

NU'UANU
★ Foster Botanical Garden

Wedged between the H-1 freeway and downtown's skyscrapers **Foster Botanical Garden** (50 N. Vineyard Blvd., 808/522-7066, www1.honolulu.gov/parks/hbg/fbg. htm, 9am-4pm daily) finds itself in an unlikely area for abundant greenery. But once you set foot in the garden, you'll be mesmerized by the lush foliage and incredibly tall trees, and all things urban will melt away. Since some of the trees in the collection were planted back in 1853, when the grounds were the residence of German physician and botanist William Hillebrand, the enormity of the trees on the main lawn are a wonder of nature. There are 26 "Exceptional Trees" on the 13.5-acre property, and the garden boasts indoor and outdoor orchid sections, a palm section, as well as a cycad garden. Cycads are curious leafy plants that date back 200 million years, to the Jurassic period. Admission is $5 general, 13 and older, $1 children 6-12, and children 5 and under are free. The garden has ample parking.

Queen Emma Summer Palace

Hanaiakamalama, today known as the **Queen Emma Summer Palace** (2913 Pali Hwy., 808/595-3167, http://daughtersofhawaii. org, 9am-4pm daily), was King Kamehameha IV and Queen Emma's summer retreat from 1857 to 1885. Today the historic landmark is a museum set on beautifully landscaped grounds. Admission is $10 per adult and $1 per child. It also offers docent-led tours of the 19th-century home. To get to the palace, take the Pali Highway exit from the H-1 freeway. The palace is on the east side of the highway.

★ Nu'uanu Pali State Wayside

Better known as the Pali Lookout, the **Nu'uanu Pali State Wayside** is on the Honolulu side of the tunnels on the Pali Highway. The lookout has amazing views of Kane'ohe Bay, Kailua, and the Ko'olau Range. The lookout is often windy. If you're feeling adventurous, take the ramp that leads down to the Old Pali Road, which you can walk along till it is literally swallowed up by vegetation and decay.

PUNCHBOWL
National Memorial Cemetery of the Pacific

The **National Memorial Cemetery of the Pacific** (2177 Puowaina Dr., 808/532-3720, 8am-6:30pm daily Mar.-Sept., 8am-5:30pm daily Oct.-Feb.) is inside Punchbowl Crater. Established in 1949, the cemetery is a memorial to those who served in the U.S. Armed Forces and is listed on the National Register of Historic Places. Spreading across 112 acres, the beautiful, solemn grounds are a quiet place good for reflection. There is a small office and restrooms located at the entrance open 8am-4:30pm Mon.-Fri., and at the back of the cemetery, behind the main memorial, are restrooms and a pathway that leads to a magnificent viewing area on the crater rim overlooking Honolulu.

There are several ways to reach the cemetery and many signs around the crater indicating the way. From the H-1 freeway eastbound, take the Pali Highway exit, turn right on Iolani Avenue immediately after crossing the bridge, then take the next left onto Lusitana Street. Bear right onto Puowaina Drive and follow the signs. One-lane roads curve through the cemetery.

MAKIKI
★ Tantalus-Round Top Drive

One of only two roadways in Hawaii listed on the National Register of Historic Places, **Tantalus Drive** and **Round Top Drive** meet at the **Pu'u 'Ualaka'a State Wayside** on top of a cinder cone, with amazing views of Honolulu, from Diamond Head to Pearl Harbor, including Manoa Valley. Tantalus Drive approaches the wayside park from the west, while Round Top Drive comes in from the east. A round-trip on the winding roads is about 20 miles. The leisurely drive passes hillside homes, is thick with vegetation, and often quite narrow. If you're easily carsick, this is a drive you'll probably want to avoid. Reach Tantalus Drive from Auwaiolimu Street via Nehoa Street. Reach Round Top Drive from Makiki Street via Nehoa Street. You can also take Makiki Street, to Makiki Heights Drive, to Tantalus Drive. The wayside park is also the trailhead for several forest hiking trails and known for auto thefts, so be sure not to leave any valuables in your vehicle, even if you're just stopping for a few minutes to take in the view.

Honolulu Museum of Art Spalding House

Formerly the Contemporary Museum, the

Honolulu Museum of Art Spalding House (2411 Makiki Heights Dr., 808/526-0232, http://honolulumuseum.org, 10am-4pm Tues.-Sat., noon-4pm Sun., $10 adults, children 17 and under free) was gifted the entire contemporary art collection, covering from the 1940s to present, in 2011. The museum is set on 3.5 acres of terraced, sculpture, and botanical gardens. Admission also covers entry to the Honolulu Museum of Art for same-day entry. There is a one-hour docent-led walking tour at 1:30pm Tuesday-Sunday, and the museum is free to the public the first Wednesday of each month. Parking is also free. From Nehoa Street, turn onto Makiki Street, then take Makiki Heights Drive at the fork.

MANOA
University of Hawai'i at Manoa

On University Avenue, just off the H-1 freeway, the **University of Hawai'i at Manoa** (**UH Manoa**) is a beautiful, compact campus with mature landscaping and fascinating architecture spanning decades. Founded in 1907, University of Hawai'i at Manoa holds the distinction of being a land-, sea-, and space-grant research institution, with nine colleges rounding out its academic programs.

National Memorial Cemetery of the Pacific

Of particular interest on campus are the trees planted across its 320 acres. Stop by the botany department and pick up the **Campus Plants** pamphlet. It includes a map of the campus and identifies the myriad unique and unusual plants, making for a lovely walk. Also noteworthy is the art department's two free art galleries. The **University of Hawai'i Art Gallery,** off the main foyer, features local and international artists and thematic exhibitions in many different media. The **Commons Gallery,** upstairs, rotates exhibitions on a weekly basis and allows students to experiment with exhibition design and display. And don't miss the giant baobab tree on the west side of the art building—a natural work of art.

To get to UH Manoa, take the University Avenue exit from the H-1 freeway from either direction. There is free parking in the neighborhoods surrounding campus, requiring a bit of a walk, or there is paid meter parking on campus. You can access on-campus parking lots from East West Road, from Dole Street, or on Maile Way from University Avenue. A great time to visit is mid-May to mid-July, when the summer session is in, but the campus is rather empty.

Bishop Museum

Lyon Arboretum

Nestled in the back of lush and often misty Manoa Valley, **Lyon Arboretum** (3860 Manoa Rd., 808/988-0456, www.hawaii.edu/lyonarboretum, 8am-4pm Mon.-Fri., 9am-3pm Sat.) is a 194-acre botanical garden in a tropical rainforest setting. With over 5,000 tropical plants and a vast network of trails, you'll have the opportunity to see heliconias, gingers, aroids, native Hawaiian plants, and one of the largest collections of palms in Hawaii. Initially established as a watershed restoration project in 1918, the garden is shaded with a variety of far-reaching canopy trees, their trunks laden with bromeliads, moss, and ferns. With the arboretum receiving an average of 165 inches of precipitation annually, you should be prepared for long periods of rain, mud, and mosquitoes. Bring binoculars for **bird-watching.** Pick up a trail map at the visitors center and take the time to explore the smaller trails off the main artery that winds back up the valley.

To get to Lyon Arboretum, follow Manoa Road all the way back into the valley, past Paradise Park, and turn left onto the arboretum's private drive before the end of the road. There's a parking lot after a couple switchbacks. The visitors center also has a very nice bookstore focusing on conservation, biology, and botany.

KALIHI
★ Bishop Museum

The premier natural and cultural history institution in the Pacific and the largest museum in the state, **Bishop Museum** (1525 Bernice St., 808/847-3511, www.bishopmuseum.org, 9am-5pm daily), the Hawaii State Museum of Culture and Natural History, was founded in 1889 by Charles Reed Bishop in honor of his late wife, Princess Bernice Pauahi Bishop. It was erected as a bastion for her extensive collection of Hawaiian artifacts and royal family heirlooms as the last descendant of the royal Kamehameha family. The museum also has an extensive library and archives for research purposes.

Bishop Museum has both rotating and mainstay exhibits. Hawaiian Hall utilizes its three floors to explore the different realms of Hawaiian culture, from the gods and legends to the customs of daily life. Polynesian Hall, which opened in 2013, represents the peoples of Pacific cultures across Polynesia, Micronesia, and Melanesia. And the Abigail Kinoiki Kekaulike Kahili Room honors the kings of the Hawaiian monarchy and displays their *kahili* (feather standards) and other heirlooms. The Science Adventure Center has interactive exhibits focusing on Hawaii's volcanic origins and environment. It's a great installation to let the kids get hands-on and explore every nook and cranny. From the amazing collection of Pacific seashells to the planetarium, Bishop Museum explores Hawaii's culture through many different disciplines.

Admission is $22.95 adult, $19.95 senior, and $14.95 military and children age 4-12, under 4 are free. To get there from the H-1 freeway, take the Likelike Highway and turn right on Bernice Street.

MOANALUA
Moanalua Gardens

A large grassy park shaded by the famous Hitachi Tree and two other monkeypod trees with canopies creating beautiful, cooling shade, **Moanalua Gardens** (1352 Pineapple Pl., 808/839-5334, www.moanaluagardens. com, 7:30am-30 minutes prior to sunset daily) is a 24-acre privately owned reserve open to the public during daylight hours. It is also the site of the home of Prince Lot Kapuaiwa, who later became King Kamehameha V. The Prince Lot Hula Festival is held at Moanalua Gardens every summer. Admission is $3 per person; children 12 and under are free. From the Moanalua Freeway H-201, take the Puuloa Road exit toward Tripler Hospital. Turn right immediately after the exit sign into the gardens. The exit is from the off-ramp.

PEARL HARBOR

TOP EXPERIENCE

★ Pearl Harbor Historic Sites

The USS *Arizona* Memorial, USS *Bowfin* Submarine Museum and Park, USS *Oklahoma* Memorial, and the Battleship *Missouri* Memorial comprise the **Pearl Harbor**

the home of King Kamehameha V at Moanalua Gardens

Pearl Harbor and Central Oahu

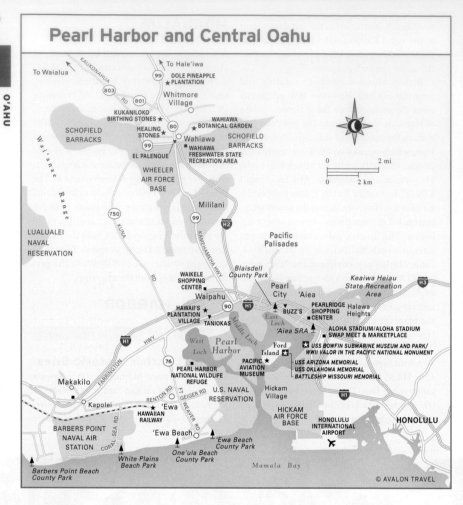

Historic Sites. Over 1.7 million people visit the USS *Arizona* Memorial and the historic sites each year, making this one of the most heavily toured areas in the state. The four sites together tell the story of Hawaii's and U.S. involvement in World War II, from the surprise attack on Pearl Harbor to the surrender of the Japanese. Pearl Harbor also serves as the central point of the **World War II Valor in the Pacific National Monument.**

Once you arrive and find free parking in one of several designated lots, enter the 17-acre park, where you'll first see the **visitors center** (808/454-1434, www.pearlharborhistoricsites.org, 7am-5pm daily) and the USS *Bowfin* Submarine Museum. If you're planning on touring any of the historic sites, especially the USS *Arizona,* arrive as early as possible and head directly to the visitors center to get in line to receive a stamped ticket for a tour time. Admission to the monument is free and the 1.25-hour program includes a 23-minute documentary and a short boat ride to the memorial. Tickets are issued on a first-come, first-served basis. On a busy day, be prepared to wait several hours for your tour.

The Military on Oʻahu

Oʻahu differs from the other main Hawaiian Islands in that there is a strong military presence here. All four branches of the military have installations on the island, and men and women in uniform are a common sight from the windward to the leeward side.

A few military strategists realized the importance of Hawaii early in the 19th century, but most didn't recognize the advantages until the Spanish-American War. It was clearly an unsinkable platform in the middle of the Pacific from which the United States could launch military operations. General John M. Schofield first surveyed Pearl Harbor in 1872, and this world-class anchorage was given to the U.S. Navy for its use in 1887 as part of the Sugar Reciprocity Treaty. In August 1898, four days after the United States annexed Hawaii, U.S. Army troops created Camp McKinley at the foot of Diamond Head, and American troops were stationed there until it became obsolete in 1907. Named in General Schofield's honor, Schofield Barracks in central Oʻahu became (and remains) the largest military installation in the state. It first housed the U.S. 5th Cavalry in 1909 and was heavily bombed by the Japanese at the outset of World War II. Pearl Harbor, first dredged in 1908, was officially opened on December 11, 1911. The first warship to enter was the cruiser *California*.

The Japanese navy attacked Pearl Harbor and other military installations on December 7, 1941. The flames of Pearl Harbor ignited World War II's Pacific theater operations, and there has been no looking back. Ever since that war, the military has been a mainstay of the island economy. Following the war, the number of men, women, and installations decreased; today there is a force of more than 55,000 active duty personnel, with all branches of the military represented.

A better option is to reserve tickets online at www.recreation.gov. You can select the date, time, tour, or tour package you'd like to take. A separate line at the visitors center awaits those who have reserved tickets.

If you do have a long wait ahead of you, check out the other historical sites, like the USS *Bowfin* Museum, or take the shuttle bus, which departs every 15 minutes, to the Battleship *Missouri* Memorial and the **Pacific Aviation Museum.** Other than the USS *Arizona* Memorial, which is free, all sites charge admission for adults

the USS *Bowfin* at the World War II Valor in the Pacific National Monument, Pearl Harbor

and children ages 4-12. There are also package tours, half-day tours, and one- or two-day passes available. Alleviate the wait time by taking advantage of the online ticket reservations to streamline your visit to Pearl Harbor.

The Pearl Harbor Historic Sites park is located off Kamehameha Highway, Route 99, just south of Aloha Stadium. There is ample signage coming from both directions. If you're on the H-1 freeway west, take exit 15A and follow the signs. You can also take TheBus, numbers 20 or 42 from Kuhio Avenue in Waikiki, or numbers 20, 42, or 52 from Ala Moana Center or downtown and be dropped off within a minute's walk of the entrance. Depending on stops and traffic, this ride could take over an hour. Also, The Arizona Memorial Bus Shuttle (808/839-0911), a private operation from Waikiki run by VIP Transportation, takes about half an hour and will pick you up at any Waikiki hotel. It charges $11 round-trip; reservations are necessary, so call a day in advance. Because the park is on an active military base, there are no bags allowed inside the area. There is a $3 bag storage fee.

Beaches

Bustling Honolulu Harbor stretches along much of Honolulu's coastline, and only a few **beaches** fall within its borders. Not to mention, the beach parks in Honolulu are more park than actual sandy beach. The beach parks draw big crowds all summer long when there's surf along the south shore, while the weekends seem to be crowded all year long. The city beaches and parks are also the stomping grounds of many members of Honolulu's pervasive homeless population.

ALA MOANA
★ **Magic Island**

Magic Island is an artificially constructed peninsula that creates the western flank of the Ala Wai Canal and Small Boat Harbor. This grassy park with shade trees, walking paths, restrooms, and outdoor showers also includes a tranquil *keiki* (child's) beach at the end of the point. It's blocked from the waves by towering rock jetties and framed in all around by beach, making it a perfect place for the kids to play

Ala Moana Beach Park

and swim safely. The jetties are constructed so that fresh ocean water can flow in and out of the lagoon without creating currents or waves. During the summer months, a wave known as Bomburas breaks beyond the jetty at the end of the point.

There is ample parking, but it does fill up during the summer and on weekends, when people turn out en masse with barbecue grills and tents to take advantage of the beautiful weather. To get to Magic Island, turn onto Ala Moana Park Drive from Ala Moana Boulevard where it intersects Atkinson Drive. After you pass the first right bend in the road, the parking lot is on the left, and it's free. The lot and park are closed 10pm-4am daily.

Ala Moana Beach Park

Connected to Magic Island, but on the west side of the peninsula, is **Ala Moana Beach Park.** Ala Moana Beach is a 4,000-foot-long, rather straight strip of sand falling into an artificial channel that runs along the entire beach. Buoys demarcate a swimming lane and one for stand-up paddling. Across the channel is a very shallow reef that stretches way out to the waves washing up on the sharp coral. There are many surf breaks along the outer reef, all the way across the beach park. A rectangular park, with busy Ala Moana Boulevard on one side and the beach on the other, has a tide-fed stream meandering through it, with a pond at each end. There are many shade trees, lots of picnic tables and barbecue areas, facilities, a snack bar, tennis courts, a community center, and lots of parking along Ala Moana Park Drive, which intersects Ala Moana Boulevard at both ends of the park. Parking can get crazy during the summer when the surf is up and on the weekends when the park is packed with families. Be sure to not use one of the designated lifeguard parking spots. Parking is free, but the park is closed 10pm-4am daily.

Water Sports

SURFING, BODYSURFING, AND STAND-UP PADDLING

The surf breaks in Honolulu come alive during the summer months, when south swells generated by storms in the southern hemisphere travel thousands of miles to Hawaiian waters. And the breaks are usually crowded with bodyboarders, shortboarders, and longboarders.

There is a channel that runs parallel and spans Ala Moana Beach entirely designated as a swimming and stand-up paddling zone. Buoys demarcate lanes. The water is flat and calm, even when it's windy because the reef protects it from the surf. It's a great place to learn how to paddle or to paddle for exercise.

There are a couple of breaks along Kewalo Basin Park as well, the most popular being a left and right peak called **Kewalo's.** The left breaks into the Kewalo Basin channel that the boats use to access the harbor. The right breaks into shallow and sharp reef. Kewalo's is often crowded since it's a favorite break for school-age kids when class is out. There are a few more breaks along the reef to the east that are usually less crowded. Access the water by carefully climbing down the seawall and paddling out over the reef. Keep in mind you'll have to come in by climbing up the seawall, which can be a challenge when the surf is big and the surges are pushing up and pulling away from it with force.

There are two small parking lots, showers, and restrooms in Kewalo Basin Park. To get to Kewalo Basin, drive east on Ala Moana Boulevard. Once you pass Ward Avenue, take the second right turn into the harbor. If you come to the signal at Ala Moana Park Road, you've missed it. Follow the road past all the boats and tour operators. It bends right at the park, and the two parking lots are just ahead on the right.

Across the Kewalo Basin Harbor channel, fronting Kaka'ako Waterfront Park and the Kewalo Marine Laboratory, is O'ahu's only strictly bodysurfing wave, **Point Panic.** It is against the law and punishable by a fine to surf the break with a board. Point Panic is a beautiful, barreling right off the rocky point. There is no beach in this area. However, there are restrooms, showers, and a small parking lot at the end of Ahui Street.

Flies is a lumpy, soft wave that breaks in front of the seawall along Kaka'ako Waterfront Park. There are several right- and left-breaking peaks that break best on a low tide, as the backwash can be a bit much on a higher tide. It is a good break for novice surfers intimidated by the crowds at other spots. Watch how the local surfers enter and exit the water. To get to the waterfront, park at the end of Ahui Street.

Outfitters

Hawaiian South Shore (320 Ward Ave., #112, 808/597-9055, www.hawaiiansouthshore.com, 10:30am-7pm Mon.-Sat., 11am-6pm Sun.) is a complete surf shop in the Ala Moana/Kaka'ako area, right by Ala Moana Beach. It sells surf-related apparel, accessories, new shortboards and longboards, and rents shortboards and longboards for $25 per day. **Blue Planet** (540 Ward Ave., 808/596-7755, www.blueplanetsurf.com, 10am-6pm daily) is just up the street and still conveniently close to Ala Moana Beach. It sells new and used longboards, shortboards, stand-up paddleboards, and accessories. It also offers long-term surfboard rentals (two or more days) starting at $40, long-term stand-up paddleboard rentals starting at $75, and 90-minute private stand-up paddle lessons for $90.

Surf Garage (2716 S. King St., 808/951-1173, www.surfgarage.com, 10am-7pm Mon.-Sat., 11am-5pm Sun.) and **Aloha Boardshop** (2600 S. King St., 808/955-6030, www.alohaboardshop.com, 10am-6pm Mon.-Sat., 11am-5pm Sun.) are right next to each other at the intersection of University Avenue and King Street. Check out Surf Garage for longboards, stand-up paddleboards, and accessories. Surf Garage rents surfboards starting at $20 and $125 weekly. Aloha Boardshop has a ton of shortboards, new and used, as well as longboards and surf accessories for sale.

Closer to Waikiki and Diamond Head in the Kapahulu area, **RV's Ocean Sport** (3348 Campbell Ave., 808/732-7137, http://rvsocean. com, 11am-5:30pm daily) is the place for used longboards and shortboards. The small shop is wall-to-wall boards, and it also specializes in ding repair. If you're looking to buy a board for your stay and then sell it back when you leave, this is the place to shop.

DIVING

Diving Honolulu waters is all about exploring shipwrecks and finger reefs. The **YO-257** and **San Pedro** wrecks are home to whitetip reef sharks, eels, and green sea turtles with deep-water reef fish on the surrounding reefs. The **Sea Tiger** wreck, rumored to be a forcibly retired smuggling vessel, rests in a protected area. Look for white-spotted eagle rays, large puffer fish, and filefish. There is also an area of finger reefs called **Turtle Canyons** that is home to a number of eel species, reef fish, and turtles. Most of the dive charters leave from Kewalo Basin.

Kaimana Divers' (1051 Ala Moana Blvd., 808/772-1795, www.waikikiscuba.com, 7am-8pm daily) two-tank boat charters start at $109, including tanks and weights. Two-tank shore dives start at $89. Gear rental is $5 per piece or $10 per full set. Kaimana also has a 10-dive package with everything included for $595. In addition to charters, it offers intro dive, private, standard, and advanced open-water courses starting at $145.

Dive Oahu (1085 Ala Moana Blvd., 808/922-3483, http://diveoahu.com, 7am-7pm Mon.-Sat., 7am-5pm Sun.) offers two-tank charters with Waikiki hotel pickup and drop-off, gear, tanks, and weights included in the rate: $139 standard, $385 five-day unlimited package. It also offers Professional

Association of Diving Instructors (PADI) online scuba courses and has a full dive shop.

Also in Kewalo Basin is **Rainbow Scuba** (1086 Ala Moana Blvd., 808/224-7857, http://rainbowscuba.com, 7am-5pm daily). Rainbow's rates include Waikiki hotel transportation, light snacks, and water on the charter, two tanks, and full gear rental. It offers two-site beginner dives for $100 for first-time divers, certified divers charter to one wreck site and one reef site for $120, and PADI certification courses starting at $420.

Breeze Hawaii Diving Adventures (3014 Kaimuki Ave., 808/735-1857, http://breezehawaiidiving.com, 7am-5pm daily) has a retail shop in the Kapahulu area and offers two-tank boat charters for $115, three-tank charters for $172, one-tank night dives $149, and two-tank sunset/night dives for $200. It also has three levels of PADI beginner dive courses and daily dives in Hanauma Bay.

While **Patrick's Diving Adventures** (85-601 Farrington Hwy., 808/589-2177, http://patricksdiving.com, 8am-2pm daily by appointment) has dive charters available only on the leeward side, it offers shore dives and scuba courses in the Honolulu area. PADI, National Association of Underwater Instructors (NAUI), Technical Diving International (TDI) and Scuba Diving International (SDI) certification starts at $379 group and $479 private.

FISHING

The bulk of the **fishing** charters are found in Kewalo Basin, where they can easily access the deeper south shore waters. If you're interested in shoreline fishing, you can cast from anywhere along the seawall at Kaka'ako Waterfront Park or from the beach at Sand Island.

Magic Sport Fishing (1125 Ala Moana Blvd., 808/596-2998, www.magicsportfishing.com) runs a 50-foot Pacifica Sportfishing Yacht out of Kewalo Basin and provides everything except lunch and beverages. The captain has over 35 years of experience in commercial fishing in Hawaiian waters, and the company will divvy up a small portion of fish per person on shared trips and larger portions for private charters. With up to six passengers, eight-hour full-day shared trips run $200 per person, private trips $975. There are also half-day private charters for $775.

Operating since 1985, **Tradewind Charters** (1125 Ala Moana Blvd., 808/973-0311, www.tradewindcharters.com) has a variety of vessels for different types of fishing expeditions, from 40-foot sailing yachts to a 65-foot sportfishing yacht, and it offers two different fishing expeditions: catch-and-release reef fishing and deep-sea sportfishing. Its private reef-fishing charter includes snorkeling and sightseeing and for 1-6 people starts at $595 for 3 hours, $795 for 4.5 hours, $995 for 6 hours, and $1,195 for 8 hours. The private deep sea charters for one to six people start at $895 for 4 hours, $1,095 for 6 hours, and $1,295 for 8 hours.

Aikane Sport Fishing (866/920-0979, www.aikanesportfishing.com) has shallow-water fishing charters for trevally and snappers or deep-sea fishing charters for big game fish like wahoo, mahimahi, blue marlin, and yellowfin tuna. It has a 42-foot Ocean Yacht and 38-foot Bertram Sportfisher. The shallow-water charters start at $500 for 4 hours and go to $625 for 8 hours; the deep-sea big game fishing charters start at $650 for 4 hours and go to $990 for 10 hours.

Established in 1950, **Maggie Joe Sport Fishing** (1025 Ala Moana Blvd., 808/591-8888, www.maggiejoe.com) has a fleet of boats designed to catch big game fish like blue marlin, yellowfin tuna, mahimahi, and skipjack tuna. It has half-day to full-day private and shared trips as well as night shark fishing for $550. The biggest boat, a 53-foot Custom Sport Fishing Yacht, starts at $890 for a three-quarter day and $933 for a private, full-day charter. Full-day shared charters are $179 per person, and half-day shared charters are $150 per person. Bananas are not permitted onboard due to superstition. If the captain deems the catch a successful haul, fishers are eligible to take home up to half of all the fish caught weighing under 100 pounds.

Hiking and Biking

HIKING

Makiki

The **Makiki-Tantalus** hike is an eight-mile loop that circles Tantalus Peak and is a great way to see a few different valleys and Ko'olau peaks up close. The trail is known for **songbirds** and some native Hawaiian flora. Look for the native white hibiscus and *'ohi'a 'ahihi*, with clusters of delicate red flowers. The hike takes advantage of the Kanealole Trail at the trailhead, which then connects in succession to the Makiki Valley Trail, the Nahuina Trail, the Kalawahine Trail, the Pauoa Flats Trail, the Manoa Cliff Trail, the Moleka Trail, and back to the Makiki Valley Trail as it rounds Tantalus. The junctions are marked well. To get to the trailhead, from Makiki Street heading north, bear left on Makiki Heights Drive. As the road switches back to the left, continue straight on an unnamed paved road into the Makiki Forest Recreation Area and past the Hawai'i Nature Center. Park on the side of the road by the gate. There is a native plant identification guide available in the nature center office for a small fee.

Manoa

In the back of rainy **Manoa Valley** are a myriad of trails all within **Lyon Arboretum** (3860 Manoa Rd., 808/988-0456, www.hawaii.edu/lyonarboretum, 8am-4pm Mon.-Fri., 9am-3pm Sat.). These trails are designed to take you through the different sections of the arboretum, so there's a wealth of interesting and colorful exotic, tropical, and native Hawaiian plants and trees everywhere you look. You could hike for a half day and not walk the same trail twice there's so much area to cover. The trails range from wide and dry to narrow, muddy, and graded. They are marked with numbers on wooden stakes that correspond to a trail map, which you can pick up in the visitors center. The main trail through

Manoa Falls

the arboretum terminates at a small waterfall. The trails offer excellent **bird-watching** opportunities. Be prepared for mud, rain, and mosquitoes. Lyon Arboretum has its own free private parking lot by the visitors center. Follow Manoa Road all the way to the back of the valley, past the houses, past Paradise Park, and turn onto the arboretum's private drive before the end of the road.

Also in the rear of Manoa Valley are several of the 18 trails that comprise the Honolulu *mauka* trail system. **Manoa Falls** is a great introduction to the area, a short 0.8-mile hike with a gradual grade under canopy and through lush foliage, up to a small waterfall and pool. Manoa is famous for its pervasive mist, so the trail can be muddy and crossed with roots in some sections. This is a popular hike, so it is well used, especially on the weekends. To get to the trailhead, either park on Manoa Road just before it narrows at the intersection with Wa'akaua Street, or continue driving on Manoa Road till you reach Paradise Park, where $5 flat-rate parking is available. If you prefer to park for free in the nearby neighborhood, tack on a 0.25-mile walk just to reach the trailhead. From the paid parking lot, continue on foot on the gravel road until it becomes the Manoa Falls Trail. The trail follows Waihi Stream to the falls and pool.

Kaimuki

At the top of Saint Louis Heights, in **Kaimuki,** you'll find a hike with views of Manoa Valley and Palolo Valley, terminating on top of Mount Olympus, a massive peak at the back of Manoa Valley. The **Wa'ahila Ridge Trail** begins in a stand of Cook pines—a misnomer since they are actually *columnar araucaria*, native to New Caledonia. The hike along the ridgeline is perfect for novices, but once you find the narrow trail that ascends to the summit, the route is more suited for intermediate hikers. At the 2,486-foot summit, in addition to breathtaking views, you'll find a thicket of native vegetation, including slow-growing *hapu'u* ferns. The hike is six miles round-trip. To get to the trailhead, park in the **Wa'ahila Ridge State Recreation Area** (www.hawaiistateparks. org, 7am-7:45pm daily Apr-early Sept., 7am-6:45pm daily early Sept.-Mar.) by following Saint Louis Drive to nearly the top of the rise and turning left on Ruth Place. There are restrooms, drinking fountains, and picnic tables by the parking lot. Parking is free, but the gate is locked when the recreation area is closed.

MOUNTAIN BIKING

While there is a plethora of trails all around O'ahu, **mountain biking** is prohibited on most of them. Fortunately for those looking to go off road on two wheels, there are a handful of mountain biking trails on the North Shore and the southeast and windward sides. Mountain biking is prohibited on all Honolulu area trails, but the big name local bicycle shops are all in town.

Outfitters

The Bike Shop (1149 S. King St., 808/596-0588, www.bikeshophawaii.com, 9am-8pm Mon.-Fri., 9am-5pm Sat., 10am-5pm Sun.) is a full-service rental, retail, and repair shop in the Kaka'ako neighborhood. It rents mountain bikes for $85 per day, road bikes starting

Verdant Lyon Arboretum is a great place to spot forest birds.

Ice in Honolulu?

A great way to cool off in the Salt Lake area is to lace up some ice skates and glide around O'ahu's only ice-skating venue, **Ice Palace** (4510 Salt Lake Blvd., 808/487-9921, www.icepalacehawaii. com). Complete with DJ and light show, it also has a closed-off section of the rink with special "walkers" that slide on the ice to help beginners get the hang of skating. Check the monthly schedule for public skating days and hours, as these do change for classes and sporting events. Generally, public skating is 9am-3pm, and admission is $8.90.

at $45 per day, and seven-speed city bikes for $25 per day. If you need a rack for your rental car, you will pay $5 per day.

The **BikeFactory** (740 Ala Moana Blvd., 808/596-8844, http://bikefactoryhawaii.com, 10am-7pm Mon.-Fri., 9am-5pm Sat., 11am-5pm Sun.), also in Kaka'ako, sells bicycles and accessories but does not rent equipment. And in Mo'ili'ili, **McCully Bicycle and Sporting Goods** (2124 S. King Street, 808/955-6329, http://mccullybike.com, 9am-8pm Mon.-Fri., 9am-6pm Sat., 10am-5pm Sun.) sells bicycles of all shapes and sizes, as well as other sporting goods, like fishing gear, tennis rackets, and athletic shoes. McCully does not rent bicycles, however.

Shopping

ALA MOANA AND KAKA'AKO
Ala Moana Center

Ala Moana Center (1450 Ala Moana Blvd., 808/955-9517, www.alamoanacenter.com, 9:30am-9pm Mon.-Sat., 10am-7pm Sun.) is the world's largest open-air shopping center, with over 290 stores and restaurants. The mall is conveniently located near Waikiki and features high-end international clothiers and jewelers, alongside popular brand-name stores. Department stores **Macy's** (808/941-2345), **Neiman Marcus** (808/951-8887), and **Nordstrom** (808/953-6100) surround the open-air central mall area. At the heart of the mall is an auditorium with seating on multiple mall levels, where daily hula performances and other shows are put on.

For technical athletic wear for yoga, running, dancing, and other aerobic pursuits, check out **Lululemon Athletica** (808/946-7220, www.lululemon.com/honolulu/alamoanacenter) on the second floor, Nordstrom wing. Also on the second level, right by Bloomingdale's, is **Na Hoku** (808/946-2100, www.nahoku.com), a local jewelry store featuring island-themed jewelry, stones, and pearls. **Shirokiya** (808/973-9111, www.shirokiya.com), next to Macy's on the second floor, is like a Japanese mall within the mall. There are food and confections, a beer garden, Japanese goods, health-care needs, as well as toys, trinkets, and other wares.

If you're in need of a bikini (or a one-piece), on the first level is **San Lorenzo Bikinis** (808/946-3200, www.sanlorenzobikinis.com), with all the best in Brazilian bikini fashion. For local surfwear, **Hawaiian Island Creations** (808/973-6780, www.hicsurf.com) is on the first floor by Bloomindale's, and **T&C Surf Designs** (808/973-5199, www.tcsurf.com) is on the third floor, Bloomindale's wing. And for authentic Hawaiian quilts and accessories, head up to the Ho'okipa Terrace and check out **Hawaiian Quilt Collection** (808/946-2233, www.hawaiian-quilts.com).

Ala Moana Center

and the Pacific. If you're in the mood for a specialty beer, wine, or liquor, the **Liquor Collection** (808/524-8808, http://liquorcollection.com) is a must.

CHINATOWN

Tin Can Mailman (1026 Nuuanu Ave., 808/524-3009, www.tincanmailman.net, 11am-5pm Mon.-Fri., 11am-4pm Sat.) is the king of Hawaiiana vintage and kitsch. It sells aloha shirts, collectibles, pin-up art, posters and hula dolls. The tiny store is packed ceiling to floor with treasures. **Hound and Quail** (920 Maunakea St., 808/779-8436, www.houndandquail.com, 1pm-6pm Mon., Wed., and Fri., 11am-4pm Sat.) sells vintage gifts, like old cameras and typewriters, furniture, home décor items and oddities like animal skulls and stuffed birds.

KAPAHULU

Kapahulu Avenue is another hub for dining and shopping in Honolulu. The mile-long stretch, running from Leahi Avenue by the fire station nearly up to the H-1 freeway, has plenty of places to grab a quick bite, sit-down restaurants, clothing stores, sporting goods stores, coffee shops, and a supermarket. There are even two tattoo parlors on the strip.

Bailey's Antiques and Aloha Shirts (517 Kapahulu Ave., 808/734-7628, http://alohashirts.com, 10am-9pm daily), next to a gas station up the street, is a score if you're looking for Hawaiiana wear and decoration. Along with over 15,000 aloha shirts in stock—new, used, and vintage—it also sells antiques like figurines, jewelry, postcards, and Hawaiian music LPs. **Island Triathlon & Bike** (569 Kapahulu Ave., 808/732-7227, http://itbhawaii.com, 10am-7pm Mon.-Fri., 10am-5pm Sat., 11am-4pm Sun.) is a one-stop shop for all things running, swimming, and biking. In addition to equipment rentals and purchases, it carries shoes, clothing, and accessories. Park in the paid lot directly across Kapahulu and the shop will reimburse the cost.

If you're looking for a great used-book store in the Kaka'ako area, check out **Jelly's** (670 Auahi St., 808/587-7001, www.jellyshawaii.com, 10am-7pm Mon.-Sat., 10am-6pm Sun.). Not only does it have a great selection of fiction, nonfiction, and children's books, but it also sells used LPs, CDs, and videos.

Ward Warehouse

Just a couple blocks west of Ala Moana Center is a small, two-story open-air mall called **Ward Warehouse** (1050 Ala Moana Blvd., 808/591-8411, www.wardcenters.com, 10am-9pm Mon.-Sat., 10am-6pm Sun.), part of a conglomerate of five open-air malls in the immediate vicinity.

For the musician on the go in Honolulu, **Island Guitars** (808/591-2910, www.island-guitars.com) is a one-stop shop for new, used, and vintage fretted instruments. **Native Books/Na Mea Hawaii** (808/596-8885, www.nativebookshawaii.com) has locally made gifts, clothing, food, and art, as well as a complete collection of books about Hawaii

KAIMUKI

If you're crafty, check out **Bead It!** (1152 Koko Head Ave., 808/734-1182, http://ibeads.com/kaimuki.htm, 10am-6pm Mon.-Sat., noon-4pm Sun.), which has a full range of beads, gemstones, books, chains, tools, and it also offers beading classes. **Gecko Books & Comics** (1151 12th Ave., 808/732-1292, 11am-7pm Sun.-Tues., 10am-9pm Wed.-Sat.) is right off Waialae Avenue and packed with books and comics. The owner is extremely knowledgeable and helpful. **SurfnHula** (3588 Waialae Ave., 808/428-5518, 11am-5pm Mon.-Fri., till 4pm Sat.) is full of surfing and Hawaiiana kitsch and memorabilia. Vintage collectibles include posters, hula dolls, toys, signs, and jewelry.

MO'ILI'ILI

J & L Trading House (2011 S. Beretania St., 808/941-8887, www.jllei.com, 10am-5pm daily) offers Hawaiiana and hula products.

Entertainment and Events

NIGHTLIFE
Chinatown

On Nuuanu Avenue, **The Dragon Upstairs** (1038 Nuuanu Ave., 808/526-1411, http://thedragonupstairs.com, 7pm-2am) is a warm and classy jazz club located above Hank's Café that also features world music. For a different beat, check out **O'Toole's Irish Pub** (902 Nuuanu Ave., 808/536-4138, http://otoolesirishpub.com, 10am-2am daily). The pub has live Irish, folk, and reggae music and is also a cigar bar, where smoking is allowed inside.

Bar 35 (35 N. Hotel St., 808/537-3535, www.bar35.com, 4pm-2am Mon.-Fri., 6pm-2am Sat.) is a warm and modern spot featuring hundreds of international beers, indoor and patio bars, daily happy hour specials, DJs, and live music. It also has table reservations and bottle service, and serves fusion-gourmet pizzas and simple tapas. **Manifest** (32 N. Hotel St., 808/523-7575, http://manifesthawaii.com, 8am-2am Mon.-Sat.) also holds valuable real estate on Hotel Street. A coffee shop by day, Manifest is a sophisticated cocktail bar after dark and a venue for artists of all mediums. Live music includes hip-hop, bluegrass, punk, and everything in between. **Downbeat Diner and Lounge** (42 N. Hotel St., 808/533-2328, http://downbeatdiner.com, 4pm-2am Tues.-Sat.) is a full-service bar and music venue hosting punk, bluegrass, reggae and indie music.

Kaka'ako

Kaka'ako has become known for its monthly outdoor street festivals. If your schedule permits, check out Eat the Street and Honolulu Night Market. **Honolulu Night Market** (449 Cooke St., 808/772-3020, www.honolulunightmarket.com, 6pm-11pm, third Sat.) is held monthly on the third Saturday and features pop-up clothing and art vendors, live entertainment and a bevy of food trucks. A full block on Cooke Street is closed to traffic and transformed into a block party atmosphere. **Eat the Street** (1011 Ala Moana Blvd., http://eatthestreethawaii.com, 4pm-9pm) is held the last Friday of the month and showcases Honolulu's eclectic food-truck culture, with over 40 food trucks every month.

Ala Moana

Rumours (410 Atkinson Dr., 808/955-4811, 8pm-midnight Tues., 5pm-2am Fri., 9pm-2am Sat.), located in the Ala Moana Hotel, has a more relaxed atmosphere focusing on the music and dancing. It plays everything from hip-hop to hits of the 1970s, 1980s, and 1990s. Tuesday is Hot Latino Tuesdays, with complimentary dancing lessons from 8:30pm-9pm.

Mo'ili'ili

Pint + Jigger (1936 S. King St., 808/744-9593, www.pintandjigger.com, 4:30pm-midnight Mon.-Wed., 4:30am-2am Thurs., 8am-2pm Fri.-Sat., 8am-midnight Sun.) is a modern public house designed to offer creative pairings of cuisine, beer, and cocktails within a relaxed atmosphere. Along with 21 beers on tap that change regularly, specialty cocktails, and a menu that also teeters to reflect the selection of libations, this bar also takes into account atmosphere, with bar seating, table seating, beer gardens, and shuffleboard.

THE ARTS

Chinatown is the home of Honolulu's art scene, and there are nearly 20 art galleries that support and promote the local artists comprising Honolulu's art community. **The ARTS at Marks Garage** (1159 Nuuanu Ave., 808/521-2903, www.artsatmarks.com, 11am-6pm Tues.-Sat.) is the heartbeat of Chinatown's art scene. With 12 major exhibits and performances, lectures, screenings, and workshops, Marks has transformed the Chinatown community through the arts. **Ong King Art Center** (184 N. King St., http://ongking.com) has carved out a niche for performance art. Whether it be through spoken word, poetry, live music, or visual art, Ong King encourages creative risk taking. **Pegge Hopper** (1164 Nuuanu Ave., 808/524-1160, http://peggehopper.com, 11am-4pm Tues.-Fri., 11am-3pm Sat.) has been a mainstay in Chinatown since the gallery opened in 1983. Famous for Pegge Hopper paintings and drawings of Hawaiian women, the gallery features Hopper's own work, as well as that of guest artists from time to time. **Art Treasures Gallery** (1136 Nuuanu Ave., 808/536-7789, http://arttreasureshawaii.com, 11am-6pm Mon.-Fri.) features world art and jewelry—think Buddha statues, Tibetan Dzi beads, jade jewelry, spiritual art, eastern antiques and artifacts.

THEATER

Downtown

On the grounds of the Honolulu Museum of Art, the **Doris Duke Theatre** (900 S. Beretania St., 808/532-8700, http://honolulumuseum.org) screens independent, documentary, and international films, performances, and concerts in a 280-seat venue. For families, the **Honolulu Theatre for Youth** (229 Queen Emma Sq., 808/839-9885, www.htyweb.org) is the perfect introduction to the dramatics for kids aged preschool through high school. The professional company presents a full season of plays every year. Another community theater in downtown Honolulu, **Kumu Kahua Theatre** (46 Merchant St., 808/536-4441, http://kumukahua.org) features Hawaiian playwrights and plays about life in Hawaii.

Chinatown

The **Hawaii Theatre** (1130 Bethel St., 808/528-0506, www.hawaiitheatre.com) is an old vaudevillian theater dating back more than 90 years and listed on the National Register of Historic Places. Today, the restored multipurpose arts center is a stage for concerts, film, musicals, and ballets. The allure and grandeur of the theater complement any performance.

Kaka'ako

The **Neil S. Blaisdell Concert Hall** (777 Ward Ave., 808/768-5400, www.blaisdellcenter.com) is the premier performing arts theater for the Honolulu Symphony and the Hawaii Opera Theatre. With 2,158 seats, a balcony, and a proscenium stage, the theater accommodates many traveling Broadway productions as well.

Manoa

Located on the University of Hawai'i at Manoa campus, **Kennedy Theatre** (1770 East-West Rd., 808/956-7655, www.hawaii.edu/kennedy) showcases productions from the university's department of theater and dance. The 620-seat mainstage theater shows Asian productions, Western productions, and contemporary works, including dance performances.

Set back in Manoa Valley, the **Manoa Valley Theatre** (2833 East Manoa Rd., 808/988-6131, www.manoavalleytheatre. com) is Honolulu's Off-Broadway playhouse. The semiprofessional theater showcases mainstream contemporary plays and musicals from Broadway, Off-Broadway, and major regional theaters.

Kaimuki

The oldest performing arts center in Hawai'i, **Diamond Head Theatre** (520 Makapuu Ave., 808/733-0277, www.diamondheadtheatre.com) opened in 1915. The historic venue shows six mainstage theatrical productions each season, including five major musicals. The theater has been dubbed the Broadway of the Pacific.

FESTIVALS AND EVENTS

The **Neal S. Blaisdell Center** (777 Ward Ave., 808/768-5400, box office 808/768-5252, www.blaisdellcenter.com) spans a city block and includes a multipurpose circular arena for concerts, shows, and sporting events; a concert hall; and an exhibition hall for expos, fairs, and events.

The **Honolulu Museum of Art** (900 S. Beretania St., 808/532-8700, http://honolulumuseum.org, 10am-4:30pm Tues.-Sat., 1pm-3pm Sun.) hosts **ART after DARK,** a monthly art party exploring different themes on rotating exhibit in the museum, like the art of tattoo or celebrating *Hina matsuri* (Girls' Day in Japan) through elaborate dolls, 6pm-9pm on the last Friday of the month, January-October. Admission is $10.

With myriad bars, nightclubs, restaurants, and art galleries, it's no wonder Chinatown is also the hub of outdoor events. Chinatown hosts annual Chinese New Year, Halloween,

St. Patrick's Day, and Cinco De Mayo Festivals, as well as the famous **First Friday.** On the first Friday of every month, people gather in the streets of Chinatown and in the galleries, museums, and art studios to celebrate the vibrant art scene. The festive event includes live music and street entertainment, and bars and restaurants cater to the crowds. Festivities begin around 6pm.

January-March

The **Honolulu Festival** (808/926-2424, http://honolulufestival.com) is a cultural event focusing on Pacific Rim cultures. The three-day festival has educational programs, activities, and performances, like cultural dances and traditional art demonstrations. The finale is a parade down Kalakaua Avenue and a spectacular fireworks display over Waikiki.

The **Hawaii Collectors Expo** (777 Ward Ave., 808/768-5400, box office 808/768-5252, http://hawaiicollectorsexpo.wix.com) in late February features all kinds of art, antiques, and collectibles. With its Hawaiiana, colored glass, handmade aloha shirts, Star Wars figurines, this three-day expo at the Neal S. Blaisdell Exhibition Hall is a favorite of local residents. There is a small entrance fee.

April-June

Memorial Day weekend is celebrated in Honolulu with the annual **Lantern Floating Hawaii** (www.lanternfloatinghawaii.com) festival on Magic Island. On the holiday itself, people from all corners of the world write remembrances and prayers on specially prepared floating lanterns to be placed in the Ala Wai Canal at dusk. The sight of over 3,000 floating lanterns is a powerful and moving experience.

On King Kamehameha Day, June 11, the **King Kamehameha Celebration Floral Parade** (www.kamehamehadaycelebration. org/floral-parade.html) is not to be missed. Beginning at 'Iolani Palace with a lei draping ceremony at the King Kamehameha Statue, the parade marches slowly to Kapi'olani

First Friday Gallery Walk

What kicked off in 2003 as a cultural community revival of the art scene in Honolulu has become one of the most attended, and most popular, monthly events on Oʻahu. In doing so, **First Friday** has transformed Chinatown into a community with a hip, vibrant art culture supporting myriad galleries, studios, cafés, and restaurants sponsoring local art and artists as a community.
First Friday, a campaign initiated by The **ARTS at Marks Garage**, is a free, self-guided gallery walk 5pm-9pm every first Friday of the month. Chinatown galleries and studios present art exhibits, and live entertainment and refreshments abound for the thousands of art enthusiasts who descend upon the area to celebrate art in all its forms. Visit www.artsatmarks.com, where you'll find a link to a Chinatown gallery map.

Park, with a beautiful display or culture, color, and flowers.

The **Islandwide Spring Crafts & Foods Expo** (777 Ward Ave., 808/768-5400, box office 808/768-5252, www.islandwidecraftexpos.com/public/public/index4.htm) is the state's largest craft fair. Over 200 artisans and food vendors come together at the Blaisdell Center to share their handmade goods and cuisine. There is also a larger Christmas show. Entrance fees apply.

July-September

In July, the **Prince Lot Hula Festival** (1352 Pineapple Pl., 808/839-5334, http://moanaluagardensfoundation.org) at Moanalua Gardens is the largest noncompetitive hula event in Hawaii. The daylong display is very popular and honors Prince Lot Kapuaiwa, who helped to revive hula by carrying on the tradition through parties at his home, which is located at the gardens.

The **Hawaii Food & Wine Festival** (www.hawaiifoodandwinefestival.com) is

a four-day epicurean delight featuring the specialties of over 50 internationally renowned master chefs and wine and spirit producers. The festival takes place across Honolulu and Koʻolina in September. Check the website for details.

October-December

Every year in early December, over 20,000 runners from around the world flock to Honolulu to participate and compete in the **Honolulu Marathon** (3435 Waialae Ave., Ste. 200, 808/734-7200, www.honolulumarathon.org). Ala Moana Boulevard between Ala Moana Beach Park and Ala Moana Center is transformed into the starting line, where runners begin their 26.2-mile trek to Hawaiʻi Kai and back to finish in Waikiki.

Downtown's historic district, at Honolulu Hale, hosts **Honolulu City Lights** (www.honolulucitylights.org) in December. The Christmas celebration of lights is punctuated by huge statues decorating the exterior of the building, most notably, Shaka Santa.

Food

CHINATOWN

Honolulu's Chinatown is chock-full of restaurants providing regional cuisine from all over the globe. Just about every other storefront is a restaurant or serves food in some fashion.

Tea

For a quaint and quiet afternoon tea, stop in at the unpretentious **Tea at 1024** (1024 Nuuanu Ave., 808/521-9596, www.teaat1024.net, 11am-2pm Tues.-Fri., 11am-3pm Sat.). Relax in the charming teahouse, don a special hat from the hat stand, and choose your china for teatime.

Asian

For a sampling of cuisine from China, Korea, Vietnam, Thailand, and the Philippines, duck inside the **Maunakea Marketplace Food Court** (1120 Maunakea St., 808/524-3409). In the center of the shopping complex that spans the small city block are vendors with stalls lined up shoulder to shoulder and family-style seating in the middle. The air is thick with the sweet smells of seafood and spices from different countries mingling together. Most vendors offer their food bento or plate-lunch style.

Chinese

In historic Chinatown, **Little Village Noodle House** (1113 Smith St., 808/545-3008, http://littlevillagehawaii.com, 10:30am-10:30pm daily, $13-50) is the quintessential Chinese restaurant for grabbing a bite. With over 100 menu items covering meat, poultry, seafood, rice, and noodle dishes, the family-friendly restaurant has every palate covered. For delicious dim sum, check out **The Mandalay** (1055 Alakea St., 808/525-8585, http://themandalayhawaii.com, 10:30am-8pmdaily, $7-13). It has plenty of entrées, but the dim sum menu is the favorite.

Pacific Rim

For exceptional Pacific Rim cuisine, check out **Lucky Belly** (50 N. Hotel St., 808/531-1888, www.luckybelly.com, 11am-2pm and 5pm-midngiht Mon.-Sat., $9-23), a very popular eatery in an arty, modern space with exposed brick walls. Seafood and pork are the main proteins in the entrées. Lucky Belly is best known for its ramen, and its slow-cooked brisket is a favorite. **The Pig & the Lady** (83 N. King St., 808/585-8255, http://thepigandthelady.com, 10:30am-2pm Tues.-Fri., 10:30-3pm Sat., 5:30pm-10pm Tues.-Sat., $14-35) combines Southeast Asian and Pacific Rim cuisine in an eclectic menu of subtle flavors and gourmet ingredients. It serves handcrafted cocktails that pair with specific entrees. For lunch, the pho French dip sandwich is a must.

Irish Pubs

J.J. Dolan's (1147 Bethel St., 808/537-4992, www.jjdolans.com, 11am-2am Mon.-Sat., $16-19) is an Irish pub serving delicious New York-style pizza. With a full bar and a selection of Irish whiskey, this small pub can get pretty rowdy when there is a packed house. **Murphy's Bar & Grill** (2 Merchant St., 808/531-0422, http://murphyshawaii.com, 11am-2:30pm Mon.-Fri., 5:30pm-9pm Sun.-Wed., 5:30pm-10pm Thurs.-Sat., $11-19) has a separate bar and dining room under one roof. The menu features a combination of bar food, burgers, and Irish food. The bar favors Irish whiskey and draught beer, with shuffleboard on offer.

American

Check out **Livestock Tavern** (49 N. Hotel St., 808/537-2577, www.livestocktavern.com, 11am-2pm and 5pm-10pm Mon.-Sat., $11-32) for seasonally inspired American plates in a rustic setting. Whether prime rib, burgers, duck, or lamb, Livestock puts a modern twist on comfort food. Reservations are suggested for supper. Across Hotel Street you'll find a diner loved by vegetarians and vegans called **Downbeat Diner & Lounge** (42 N. Hotel St., 808/533-2328, http://downbeatdiner.com, 10am-11pm Sun., 10am-midnight Mon., 10am-3am Tues.-Thurs., 10am-4am Fri.-Sat., $6-15). It serves breakfast, sandwiches, burgers, and has a variety of appetizers and a full bar. Any menu item can be prepared vegetarian or vegan style.

African
Kan Zaman (1028 Nuuanu Ave., 808/554-3847, http://kanzamanhawaii.com, 11am-9:30pm Mon.-Thurs., 11am-10:30pm Fri.-Sat., $12-24) features dishes from Morocco and Lebanon and is known for its lamb dishes and shwarma entrees. **Ethiopian Love** (1112 Smith St., 808/725-7197, www.ethiopianlovehi.com/, 5pm-10pm Mon., Wed.-Fri., 11am-2pm Thurs.-Fri., noon-10pm Sat.-Sun., $11-30) is an eat-with-your-hands restaurant, or rather with injera bread, actually. The dishes are large and meant to be shared. There is indoor and outdoor seating on the back patio.

KAKA'AKO
Quick Bites
Pa'ina Café (1050 Ala Moana Blvd., 808/356-2829, www.painacafe.com, 10am-9pm Mon.-Sat., 10am-6pm Sun., $7-12) is located in Ward Warehouse in the middle of the outdoor mall, on the bottom floor. It offers a variety of fresh and delicious poke bowls, salads, and a few tasty sandwiches. This location also serves delicious acai bowls and smoothies.

Gastropub
In the Ward Farmers Market, **REAL, a gastropub** (1200 Ala Moana Blvd., 808/591-9188, www.realgastropub.com, 2pm-2am Mon.-Sat., $3-12) is spearheading the gastropub trend in Honolulu with smart combinations of flavors in its tapas-style menu items, designed for sampling. You can combine your choice with one of over 200 bottled beers imported from all over the world and 24 rotating taps. It also has a full bar and wine.

MANOA
Hawaiian
Deep in the valley, by the Manoa Falls trailhead and Lyon Arboretum, is a restaurant set among the trees of Manoa's lush rainforest. **Treetops Restaurant** (3737 Manoa Rd., 808/988-6838, 9am-2pm daily, $7-16) serves both a weekday and a weekend buffet lunch, perfect for a post-hike meal.

Mexican
For authentic Mexican food, stop in at **Serg's Mexican Kitchen** (2740 E. Manoa Rd., 808/988-8118, 11am-9pm Mon.-Sat., 8am-8pm Sun., $4-16). With open-air, family-style seating and mariachi music, this BYOB joint is the spot for a quick taco or a sit-down meal with a big group.

KAIMUKI
Quick Bites
Rainbow Drive-In (3308 Kanaina Ave., 808/737-0177, www.rainbowdrivein.com, 7am-9pm daily, $6-8) has served choice plate lunches since 1961 and always at a reasonable price. Protein, rice, and gravy never tasted so good. **Kaimuki Superette** (3458 Waialae Ave., 808/734-7800, 7m-4pm Mon.-Sat, $7-14) serves local and seasonal dishes using locally sourced ingredients. The octopus roll is a favorite, as well the antipasti. It also has great coffee. **Sprout** (1154 Koko Head Ave., 808/737-0177, https://squareup.com/market/sproutwich, 10am-2:45pm daily, $6-8) is the stop for a fresh, handmade sandwich. Think turkey and bacon with avocado on a fresh ciabatta. Order online if you're on the go.

Steak and Seafood
On Waialae Avenue are a handful of popular restaurants. **Town** (3435 Waialae Ave., 808/735-5900, www.townkaimuki.com, 11am-2:30pm and 5:30-9:30 Mon.-Thurs.,

5:30pm-10pm Fri.-Sat., $9-28) serves breakfast, lunch, and dinner. The hip spot, with modern art decor, is a mix between Hawaii regional and Italian cuisine, all with the focus of serving organic, fresh, and locally sourced ingredients. It has a full bar, or you can BYOB for a corkage fee of $15. Limited street parking is available, but there is a small parking lot behind the restaurant as well.

12th Ave Grill (1120 12th Ave., 808/732-9469, www.12thavegrill.com, 5:30pm-10pm Sun.-Thurs., 5:30-11pm Fri.-Sat., $25-36) is just off Waialae Avenue and offers award-winning contemporary American cuisine and a commitment to locally sourced and seasonal ingredients. A well-selected wine list and scratch bar pair nicely with the flavorful fare. The small dining room is intimate, yet comfortable.

On Kapahulu is a popular and often packed **Uncle Bo's** (559 Kapahulu Ave., 808/735-8311, www.unclebosrestaurant.com, 5pm-1am daily, $12-27). Combining American bistro with Pacific Rim cuisine, Uncle Bo's is a small, modern, but casual restaurant. It has an extensive pupu menu, as well as steak, seafood, pasta, and pizza. Be prepared for a bit of a wait on the weekends, and if the bar is full, that means you'll have to stand outside.

Award-winning chef Colin Nishida creates Hawaiian-style comfort food, served as complete meals or pupu style, inside the Prudential Locations building in an offshoot of the famous Side Street Inn in Kaka'ako called **Side Street Inn on Da Strip** (614 Kapahulu Ave., 808/739-3939, http://sidestreetinn.com, 3pm-midnight daily, $12-22). The restaurant has family-style seating with a touch of fine dining, and the portions are quite large and designed to be shared.

Gastropub
Stop in for a pint and poutine at **BREW'd Craft Pub** (3441 Waialae Ave., 808/732-2337, http://brewdcraftpub.com, 4pm-11pm Mon-Thurs., 4pm-1am Fri.-Sat.,, $6-13), which has a rotating menu of craft beers on tap and bottled. The small pub is usually packed around

Town restaurant

5pm and seating can be hard to find. The menu items are served tapas style and meant to be shared. Truffle deviled eggs and jalapeño candied bacon are house favorites.

Breakfast
Koko Head Café (1145 12th Ave., 808/732-8920, http://kokoheadcafe.com, 7am-2:30pm daily, $6-16) is a very popular island-style brunch house serving Chef Lee Anne Wong's famous dumplings, egg skillets, sweet pancakes, and much more—think Pacific Rim-infused breakfast entrees. Seating is walk-in only and there is almost always a line, but it's worth it. And since it's five o'clock somewhere, you can always order a beer or craft cocktail while you wait.

Hawaiian
For authentic Hawaiian food, check out **Ono Hawaiian Food** (726 Kapahulu Ave., 808/737-2275, www.onohawaiianfoods.com, 11am-8pm Mon.-Sat., $6-22). The family-run restaurant is small and cozy, with just a few

tables. Be prepared to wait outside during peak hours.

Chinese, Thai, and Vietnamese

In Kaimuki there are three consistent picks for noodles and soup. **Hale Vietnam Restaurant** (1140 12th Ave., 808/735-7581, 11am-9:30 Thurs.-Tues., $8-14) is best known for its delicious pho. It also has barbecued pork plates and sautéed dishes with your choice of protein. **To Thai For** (3571 Waialae Ave., 808/734-3443, www.itstothaifor.com, 1am-2pm Mon. and Wed.-Sat., 5pm-9pm Sun., $9-20) has a basic Thai menu through which you can combine the dish with the protein of your liking. **Happy Days** (3553 Waialae Ave., 808/738 8666, 8am 10pm daily, $8-23) is hands down the best Chinese food in the region. It is also known for its selection of dim sum made daily. Don't forget to order the crispy gau gee appetizer.

Japanese

On Kapahulu Avenue are three noteworthy Japanese restaurants. **Irifune** (563 Kapahulu Ave., 808/737-1141, 11:30am-1:30pm and 5:30pm-9:30pm Tues.-Sat., $10-15) is a curious hole-in-the-wall with some of the best ahi on O'ahu. The entire menu consists of some combination of garlic and ahi, served with local-style sides. This restaurant is very popular, and on the weekends you can expect a wait. It does have a bench outside. Park across the street in the pay parking lot, or there is street parking in the neighborhood, behind the restaurant.

Tokkuri Tei (611 Kapahulu Ave., 808/732-6480, www.tokkuritei-hawaii.com, 11am-2pm and 5:30pm-midnight Mon.-Fri., 5:30pm-midnight Sat., 5pm-10:30pm Sun., $4-50) is a popular izakaya restaurant offering traditional Japanese food with a French influence and local uniqueness. With its sushi bar or table seating and an extensive sake and spirits selection, it will take several visits to sample the wealth of food on all 13 pages of the menu. It's located on the second floor of Hee Hing Plaza, and there is

free parking under the plaza. Reservations are necessary.

Mexican

Jose's Mexican Cafe & Cantina (1134 Koko Head Ave., 808/732-1833, www.joseshonolulu. com, 11am-10pm Mon.-Sat., 11am-9pm Sun., $14-25) serves up simple Mexican food, with seafood, beef and pork specialties, and even a few egg dishes. Jose's has a happy hour weekdays 3pm-6pm and a selection of Mexican beers and different styles of margaritas, mixed either for a glass or a pitcher.

Indian

Himalayan Kitchen (1137 11th Ave., #205, 808/735-1122, 11am-2pm and 5pm-10pm Tues.-Fri., 5pm-10pm Sat.-Mon., $11-22) serves Nepalese and Indian cuisine in a small restaurant with indoor and patio seating. This second-story BYOB is a local favorite and often packed with those seeking the eatery's variety of vegetarian and meat dishes. The entrance to the restaurant is in an alcove between a gift store, a barbecue joint, an Italian restaurant, and a salon. There is a paid parking lot with ample parking.

Sweets and Treats

You can grab a delicious pastry, dessert, or cup of coffee on Waialae Avenue at **JJ French Pastry & Bistro** (3447 Waialae Ave., 808/739-0993, www.jjfrenchbistro.com, 10am-9pm Mon.-Sat., 11:30am-9pm Sun., $5-19). It also serves pizza, pasta, sandwiches, and à la carte entrées.

On Kapahulu Avenue, residents and visitors flock to **Leonard's Bakery** (933 Kapahulu Ave., 808/737-5591, www.leonardshawaii.com, 5:30am-10pm Sun.-Thurs., 5:30pm-11pm Fri.-Sat.) in record numbers, often backing up traffic on Kapahulu while they wait for a parking stall in the small parking lot out front. Look for the neon sign and the line out the door. Leonard's is famous for its *malasadas* and doughnuts, but it also has delicious pastries, cookies, bread, pies, and wraps. For shave ice, head to **Waiola**

Shave Ice (2135 Waiola St., 808/949-2269, www.waiolashaveice.com, 10am-6pm daily Sept.-May, 9am-6:30pm daily June-Aug.). It's tucked away right off Kapahulu Avenue, across from Safeway.

MO'ILI'ILI

Health Food

Down to Earth (2525 S. King St., 808/947-7678, www.downtoearth.org, 7:30am-10pm daily) is an all-vegetarian, natural, and organic food store with a deli, salad bar, hot foods, and smoothies. Parking is on the roof behind the store. Take the alley right past the entrance and turn up the ramp.

An oasis of charm and natural food on busy and urban King Street, **Peace Café** (2239 S. King St., 808/951-7555, www.peacecafehawaii.com, 11am-9pm Mon.-Sat., 11am-3pm Sun., $9-11) serves vegan home cooking in a comfortable setting. Within its eclectic decorating scheme, Peace Café has sandwiches, salads, stews, and prepared goods like granola for the taking.

Indian

Café Maharani (2509 S. King St., 808/951-7447, http://cafemaharanihawaii.com, 5pm-10pm daily, $14-16) is an award-winning casual restaurant blending natural ingredients and a host of spices to create some of the most sought after Indian food in Honolulu.

Steak and Seafood

For modern fine dining on the best in Hawaii regional cuisine, **Chef Mavro** (1969 S. King St., 808/944-4714, www.chefmavro.com, 6pm-9pm Tues.-Sun., $75-165) offers the quintessential experience. The French-influenced cuisine is award-winning and the ingredients are locally sourced. Seasonal menus are geared toward wine pairings. Children must be 5 years of age or older, and attire is aloha casual.

Renowned chef specializing in Hawai'i regional cuisine Alan Wong pairs fine dining with fresh and local ingredients at his flagship restaurant **Alan Wong's** (1857 S. King St., 808/949-1939, www.alanwongs.com, 5pm-10pm daily, $30-50). Locally raised beef and sustainable seafood combined with O'ahu farm-fresh produce are served up with a completely local flair. In addition to entrées, it offers two set multicourse tasting menus available with wine pairings.

IWILEI

Seafood

In the Honolulu Harbor area, seafood is the main attraction. **Nico's at Pier 38** (1129 N. Nimitz Hwy., 808/540-1377, http://nicospier38.com, 6:30am-9pm daily, $13-17) is both a fish market and restaurant. It serves Hawaiian-style seafood with a French twist—gourmet food with plate-lunch delivery. The open-air restaurant also has a full bar. From Nimitz Highway, access Pier 38 from Alakawa Avenue. Open for breakfast, lunch and dinner.

On the way out to Sand Island is one of the few real tiki bars still in operation. **La Mariana** (50 Sand Island Access Rd., 808/848-2800, www.lamarianasailingclub.com, 11am-9pm daily, $14-42) is a steak and seafood restaurant located in the La Mariana Sailing Club. Nestled at the edge of Ke'ehi Lagoon, the restaurant is a veritable museum of Hawaiiana treasures and collectibles, with an unmatched ambience from the warm glow of colorful lights, wood decor, and the grin of tikis all around.

North Shore

Highlights

© AVALON TRAVEL

★ **Waimea Valley:** Part lush tropical botanical garden, part restored ancient cultural site, Waimea Valley is a bastion of beauty and education (page 96).

★ **Waimea Bay Beach Park:** This expansive sandy shore yields to turquoise water that is home to reef fish, spinner dolphins, and green sea turtles. Swim and snorkel the calm waters in summer, or watch surfers ride enormous waves in winter (page 98).

★ **Banzai Pipeline:** Watch expert surfers attempt to ride the barrel at one of the most dangerous breaks in the world (page 102).

★ **Pupukea-Waimea Marine Life Conservation District:** Comprised of Waimea Bay, Three Tables, and Sharks Cove, this

mile-long protected shoreline is where marine life abounds. It is the best area for snorkeling and shore diving on the North Shore (page 104).

★ **Skydiving:** Skydiving operators in Mokule'ia offer a once-in-a-lifetime opportunity to tandem skydive, affording you a bird's-eye view of paradise (page 109).

★ **Shopping in Historic Hale'iwa Town:** Quaint Hale'iwa is the official gateway to the North Shore. It's packed with clothing boutiques, surf shops, and art galleries (page 109).

★ **Hawaii Polo:** Enjoy the camaraderie and festive atmosphere of a polo match by the sea. Bring the family, spread out a blanket, open the cooler, and enjoy a perfect summer afternoon (page 111).

Just 30 miles from Honolulu is the famed North Shore, the big city's polar opposite. Local surfers appropriately make the distinction and have coined the regions "town" and "country."

With an average of 30 inches of rainfall annually, the North Shore is an escape to a verdant, natural haven and a simpler, almost hedonistic lifestyle. It's all about the beaches, diving, fishing, and, of course, surfing.

From the northernmost tip of the island to Ka'ena Point to the west, the North Shore's coastline looks more like a backwards *L*, or even the open jaws of a shark, and captures the powerful open-ocean swells that track across the Pacific during the northern hemisphere's winter. That's the reason for the enormous, powerful surf that pounds the reefs from October through April. Save for the town of Hale'iwa, the gateway to the North Shore, and Turtle Bay Resort, this area has remained commercially undeveloped, a mix between residential and farmland. Locals have taken great pride in their grassroots efforts to establish a marine protected area along Waimea Bay, Three Tables, and Sharks Cove, to preserve the bluff known as Pupukea-Paumalu that frames the quaint North Shore community and preserve Kawela Bay for perpetuity.

Along the extreme northern stretch of the North Shore, you'll find world-class surf spots like Laniakea, Waimea Bay, the Banzai Pipeline, and Sunset Beach. Because of the quality and sheer number of surf breaks, this part of the North Shore is known as the "Seven Mile Miracle." Hale'iwa, sitting just off the Kamehameha Highway at the bottom of the pineapple fields, is where you'll find shopping, dining, dive and surf rental outfitters, and the famous Matsumoto Shave Ice. Waialua and Mokule'ia comprise the western side of the North Shore and offer quieter, less visited beaches and the rare opportunity to watch polo during the summer months. To those who wish to jump out of a plane and skydive in paradise, head this way.

Previous: Banzai Pipeline; Turtle Bay. **Above:** Waimea Valley botanical garden.

North Shore

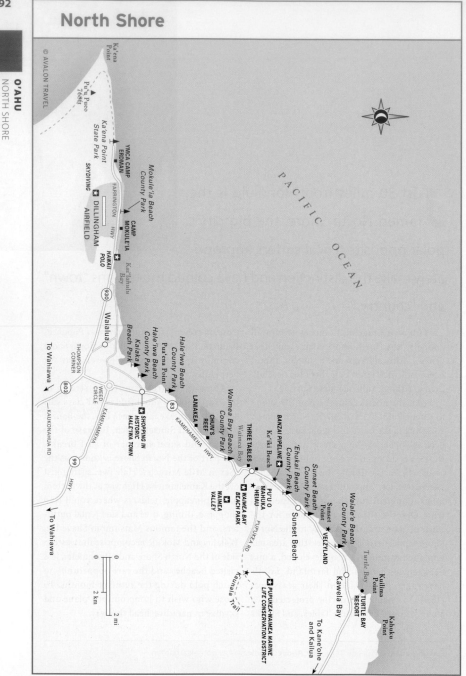

© AVALON TRAVEL

Ka'ena
Point

Pu'u Pueo
768ft

Ka'ena Point
State Park

SKYDIVING

YMCA CAMP
ERDMAN

Mokulē'ia Beach
County Park

FARRINGTON HWY

DILLINGHAM
AIRFIELD

CAMP
MOKULĒ'IA

HAWAII
POLO

Kai'ōlōhia
Bay

930

Waialua

THOMPSON
CORNER

To Wahiawa

803

KAUKONAHUA RD

KAMEHAMEHA HWY

99

To Wahiawa

WEED
CIRCLE

Hale'iwa Beach
County Park

Pua'ena Point
Hale'iwa Beach
County Park

Kaiaka
Beach Park

LANIAKEA

83

SHOPPING IN
HISTORIC
HALE'IWA TOWN

CHUN'S
REEF

Waimea Bay Beach
County Park

THREE TABLES

Waimea Bay

KAMEHAMEHA HWY

WAIMEA BAY
BEACH PARK

WAIMEA
VALLEY

PU'U O
MAHUKA
HEIAU

BANZAI PIPELINE

Ke'iki Beach

'Ehukai Beach
County Park

PUPUKEA RD

Kaunala Trail

PUPUKEA-WAIMEA MARINE
LIFE CONSERVATION DISTRICT

PACIFIC OCEAN

Sunset Beach
County Park

Sunset
Point

VELZYLAND

Sunset Beach

Kawela Bay

Waiale'e Beach
County Park

Turtle Bay

Kuilima
Point

TURTLE BAY
RESORT

Kahuku
Point

To Kāne'ohe
and Kailua

0   2 mi

0   2 km

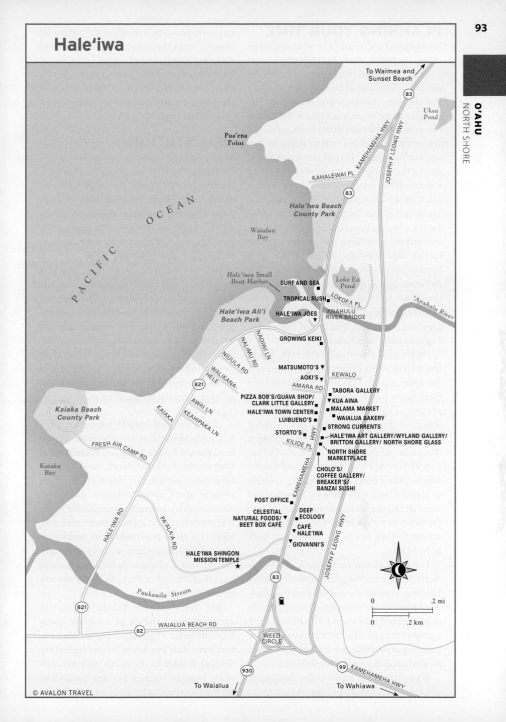

Hale'iwa

To Waimea and
Sunset Beach

83

Ukoa
Pond

Pua'ena
Point

KAHALEWAI PL

KAMEHAMEHA HWY

JOSEPH P LEONG HWY

83

Hale'iwa Beach
County Park

Waialua
Bay

OCEAN

PACIFIC

'Anahulu River

Hale'iwa Small
Boat Harbor

Loko Ea
Pond

SURF AND SEA

TROPICAL RUSH

LOKOFA PL

Hale'iwa Ali'i
Beach Park

HALE'IWA JOES

'ANAHULU
RIVER BRIDGE

NAOWI LN

GROWING KEIKI

NALIMU RD

NIUULA RD

MATSUMOTO'S

WALIKANA
HELE

AOKI'S

KEWALO

821

AMARA RD

TABORA GALLERY

PIZZA BOB'S/GUAVA SHOP/
CLARK LITTLE GALLERY

KUA AINA

AWAI LN

HALE'IWA TOWN CENTER

MALAMA MARKET

Kaiaka Beach
County Park

KAIAKA

KEAHIPAKA LN

LUIBUENO'S

WAIALUA BAKERY

STRONG CURRENTS

FRESH AIR CAMP RD

STORTO'S

HALE'IWA ART GALLERY/WYLAND GALLERY/
BRITTON GALLERY/ NORTH SHORE GLASS

KILIOE PL

KAMEHAMEHA HWY

NORTH SHORE
MARKETPLACE

Kaiaka
Bay

CHOLO'S/
COFFEE GALLERY/
BREAKER'S/
BANZAI SUSHI

POST OFFICE

DEEP
ECOLOGY

HALE'IWA RD

CELESTIAL
NATURAL FOODS/
BEET BOX CAFÉ

CAFÉ
HALE'IWA

PAALAA RD

GIOVANNI'S

JOSEPH P LEONG HWY

HALE'IWA SHINGON
MISSION TEMPLE

★

83

Paukauila Stream

821

0   .2 mi

82

WAIALUA BEACH RD

0   .2 km

WEED
CIRCLE

930

99   KAMEHAMEHA HWY

To Waialua

To Wahiawa

© AVALON TRAVEL

PLANNING YOUR TIME

No matter if it's summer or winter, rain or shine, the North Shore shouldn't be missed and can't be rushed. Take advantage of all the natural beauty and ocean activities on offer and plan for a full-day trip to the region. The 33-mile drive from Waikiki to the North Shore, taking the most direct route across the central plateau, will last an hour if all goes well and traffic is light. If your stay on O'ahu is during the summer, drive up in the morning and snorkel in the Pupukea-Waimea Marine Life Conservation District, at Waimea Bay, Three Tables, and Sharks Cove. Park at Three Tables, which is between the other two sites, and utilize the walking trail to visit all three locales without moving the car. Grab a quick lunch at Ted's Bakery at Sunset Beach or at one of the numerous establishments in Hale'iwa, then head out to Mokule'ia for Hawaii Polo, skydiving, or a glider ride. If the mountains are more your style, take a trail ride on the Pupukea bluff or in Kahuku.

During the winter the North Shore has a completely different vibe, as powerful waves push across the reefs and surfers flock to the beaches. Snorkeling and diving are out of the picture, as turbulent white water sweeps across the reefs, but watching the surf and the talented surfers taking it on can be mesmerizing. Check out the action at Waimea Bay, Pipeline, and Sunset Beach. Take a break during the day to drive to Kahuku and visit Kahuku Superette for some fresh *poke* and rice, then head back to the beach to eat while wave-watching. Enjoy dinner in Hale'iwa before setting out back to Honolulu.

For a longer, but more scenic trip to the North Shore from Waikiki, follow the Likelike Highway to Kane'ohe and drive up the windward coast in the morning. The roughly 45-mile drive will take about 1.5 hours as the sun rises over the east side. The mellow, gently meandering drive will put you in the right mood for a relaxing day on the North Shore.

If you're looking for an O'ahu destination where you can spend a portion or your entire stay surrounded by a rural coastal setting far removed from the city, then a vacation rental along the North Shore Beaches or a room at Turtle Bay Resort are great options. Just be aware that it will take a bit more time and planning for sightseeing and activities in most other island regions.

ORIENTATION

As you descend from the pineapple and coffee fields, the first town you'll come to is Historic Hale'iwa Town, the official gateway to the North Shore. On either side of town, Kamehameha Highway makes a detour through Hale'iwa. If you want to pass around Hale'iwa and continue up the coast, stay on the Joseph P. Leong Highway bypass.

Hale'iwa is full of places to eat, markets to buy food, and clothing, souvenir and surf shops, as well as art galleries. Sportfishing, shark-tour, and scuba operators are congregated in Hale'iwa Harbor, which has lovely beaches on both sides, though they are better for surfing and stand-up paddling than swimming or snorkeling. The **'Anahulu River** empties out by the harbor and beaches, offering potential for stand-up paddleboarding upriver.

Just to the west of Hale'iwa, between the Wai'anae Mountains and the coast as you head toward Ka'ena Point, are **Waialua** and **Mokule'ia.** Both are sleepy, rural agricultural communities. Farrington Highway rejoins the coast through Mokule'ia, where if it's not too windy, the beaches are nice, the water is crystal clear, and solitude surrounds you. Mokule'ia offers polo matches on Sunday afternoons in the summer, skydiving throughout the year, and a seaside hike in a natural reserve at the end of the road to the western tip of the island.

The North Shore Beaches comprise an immaculate stretch of coastline along Kamehameha Highway from **Laniakea,** just past Hale'iwa town, to the legendary **Sunset Beach** to the north. Spinner dolphins frolic in Waimea Bay, sea turtles feed off the shoreline rocks, and reef fish abound

Your Best Day on the North Shore

Surf, sun, and beaches—the rural North Shore is all about leaving behind the city and tapping into the laid-back atmosphere. Just remember, the North Shore can be very different depending if it's summer or winter.

- Drive up the H-2 freeway, through the central plateau. You'll be able to see the extent of O'ahu's agricultural base—pineapple fields as far as the eye can see. Head directly to the **Pupukea-Waimea Marine Life Conservation District,** the best snorkeling on the North Shore. Whether you post up at Waimea Bay, Three Tables, or Sharks Cove, or visit all three, you'll be amazed at the underwater beauty of the area. Snorkeling is best in the summertime.

- If it's winter during your stay, check out the waves at **Waimea Bay, Pipeline,** or **Sunset Beach.** They attract professional surfers from around the world. The action is spectacular, especially once the waves get really big.

- Stop in at **Ted's Bakery for lunch,** local style, or head out to Kahuku, just a few miles farther north, and visit **Kahuku Superette** for some of the best *poke* on the island.

- Outdoor activities are the hallmark of the North Shore. If you're daring, try **skydiving** in Mokule'ia. If staying on land suits you better, there are two outfitters that offer horseback rides in the fertile mountains above the North Shore beaches.

- During the summer, you can also spend the afternoon stand-up paddling the **'Anahulu River** in Hale'iwa Town or try a shore dive at Sharks Cove or Three Tables.

- For dinner, try **Hale'iwa Joe's** if you're in Hale'iwa town. If you're closer to the northern tip of the island, stop by Turtle Bay Resort and have a great meal at the local favorite, **Lei Lei's.**

RAINY-DAY ALTERNATIVE
What to do on the North Shore if it's raining? Simple, have a seat at **The Point at Turtle Bay.** Located right on Kuilima Point, you can enjoy the restaurant's famous **mai tai** and watch the waves roll past.

along the **Pupukea-Waimea Marine Life Conservation District,** which includes **Three Tables** and **Sharks Cove** just north of Waimea Bay, some of the best snorkeling and scuba diving on the island. In the summer, the calm water along this stretch of coast is perfect for swimming and snorkeling, but in the winter, powerful surf draws expert surfers from around the world in search of giant waves at Waimea Bay and Sunset Beach and the awe-inspiring barrels of the Banzai Pipeline. While the most popular beaches might be busy with tourists hopping off buses all year long, a short walk up or down the beach will easily remove you from the melee and most of your cares or worries. For meals you'll mostly find food trucks along the highway, and for accommodations, vacation rentals are the only way to

go, save for the only hostel in the region at Three Tables. Sunsets are remarkable from this stretch of coast.

Turtle Bay is the area along Kamehameha Highway from **Kawela Bay** to **Kahuku,** the old sugar town. This region sits at the northern tip of the island and is prone to wind and rain throughout the year. The Turtle Bay Resort on **Kuilima Point** dominates the area, with surf and golf being the main attractions, along with the bars and restaurants that many residents and visitors along the North Shore Beaches make the short drive to indulge in.

Just to the east of Turtle Bay is Kahuku, with a nine-hole golf course of its own. Kahuku is also home to a little market with great *poke* and a ranch offering trail rides.

Sights

PU'U O MAHUKA HEIAU

Located on the Pupukea bluff right above Waimea Bay and covering two acres, **Pu'u O Mahuka Heiau** is the largest *heiau* (temple) on O'ahu. Three- to six-foot stacked stone walls are what remain of the original three enclosures thought to have been built in the 17th century. The structure was integral to the social, political, and religious systems for the once-thriving Waimea Valley community. The *heiau* has views of Waimea Valley and the North Shore. There are dirt walking paths around the structure and interpretive signage, but no water or facilities. Follow the trail to the edge of the cliff for a unique view of Waimea Bay. To get there, drive up Pupukea Road and take the first right turn after the switchbacks. The paved road is rough and narrow, so drive slowly and be aware of oncoming vehicles.

★ WAIMEA VALLEY

Waimea Valley (59-864 Kamehameha Hwy., 808/638-7766, www.waimeavalley.net, 9am-5pm daily) is one of O'ahu's last partially intact *ahupua'a* (a land division stretching from the mountain to the sea), and is part botanical garden and part native Hawaiian cultural site. Once a thriving native Hawaiian community based around the river running down the valley to the sea, it offered sustenance in many forms for native Hawaiians. Today, Waimea Valley is home to many collections of tropical plants, but it is most famous for the hybrid hibiscus collection at the front of the garden and the ginger and heliconia collection at the back of the valley. Peacocks run wild through the gardens, and native **birds** are common along the stream. There are several native Hawaiian historical living sites along the 0.75-mile paved trail back to the waterfall and pool. General admission is $16 for adults and $8 for children ages 4-12 and $12 for seniors 60 and over. Golf cart transportation from the ticket booth to the waterfall is available for $4 one way and $6 round-trip. Guided hikes are led by staff on Thursday and Saturday. Reservations must be made at least three days in advance for these, and additional fees apply. Check the website for the detailed information about the guided hikes.

Hale'iwa Beach Park

Beaches

O'AHU
NORTH SHORE

The North Shore beaches are some of the finest on the island. With the natural backdrops of the Pupukea-Paumalu escarpment along the northern portion of the coast and the Wai'anae Range behind Hale'iwa stretching to Ka'ena Point, natural beauty catches your eye in every direction. Ample vegetation separates the sand from the beachfront property, and the coast is broken up by interesting rock and reef formations, sandy bays, and rugged points.

The North Shore also has two distinct personalities: benign and tranquil during the summer, from May until September; and strong and fierce in the winter, from October to April. This duality is caused by powerful storms in the North Pacific that send swell thousands of miles across open ocean, straight to the Hawaiian Islands. The North Shore reefs absorb this energy as giant waves that pound the coast, breaking up to 50 feet from crest to trough. During high surf events in the winter, the water is closed to swimming, and lifeguards monitor the spectators on the beach, as well as the surfers in the water, to make sure everyone is safe. During the biggest swell events, the beaches are closed as well.

On the other hand, summer provides perfect conditions for swimming, snorkeling, and diving. The ocean remains generally calm and flat, and the beaches are at their widest. Sunsets are also better during this time as the sun tracks farther west on the horizon.

HALE'IWA
Ali'i Beach Park

There is a small beach, framed in by rocks, at both sides of **Ali'i Beach Park,** just to the west of the Hale'iwa Small Boat Harbor, where Hale'iwa town intersects the coast. These are great places for the kids to jump around in the small shore break. Ali'i Beach Park also has a community center, restrooms, and a large,

shaded grassy park with palm trees, picnic tables, and shrubs along the vegetation line that offer shade. If there are waves breaking along the outer reef, a strong and dangerous rip current sweeps across the beach. From Kamehameha Highway, turn onto Haleiwa Road, and the beach park is past the entrance to the boat harbor. There is ample parking.

Hale'iwa Beach Park

On the other side of the harbor entrance and the 'Anahulu River, across the famous Rainbow Bridge, is **Hale'iwa Beach Park.** The water is a bit murky and the sand somewhat silty from the river mouth, but the calm waters here are a favorite for kayakers and stand-up paddlers, where you can choose to paddle in the ocean or forge up the 'Anahulu River. There is parking on the side of the road or in the designated parking area. To the north of the parking lot is a big grassy area and restrooms. The beach park is beside Kamehameha Highway. The parking lot and restrooms are closed 10pm-6am daily.

Pua'ena Point Beach Park

You'll have a different experience altogether at **Pua'ena Point Beach Park** to the immediate north of Hale'iwa Beach Park. From Kamehameha Highway, turn onto Kahalewai Place and drive to the parking lot at the end. From there walk through the ironwood trees to the small cove. The beach has lots of shade and is a great place to explore in and out of the water. Snorkel the inner waters, with their mix of sand and reef bottom, or you can walk up the beach to the rocky outcropping of Pua'ena Point.

Mokule'ia Beach Park

Situated on the western flank of the North Shore, **Mokule'ia Beach Park** is a quiet, uncrowded beach across from the Dillingham

Airfield. The sand is narrow, but stretches out in both directions, with interesting nooks and crannies along the coast. There are shrubs along the beach and some trees for shade to the east. Mokule'ia Beach Park is great for a long walk on the beach or relaxing in the sun. It's in the path of the trade winds, so it can get blustery. If you plan on swimming or snorkeling, the conditions are best with light winds. There are showers and portable toilets at the beach park along Farrington Highway, close to the end of the road. The parking lot is closed 7pm-7am daily.

NORTH SHORE
Laniakea

Famous for the turtles that rest in the sand and feed off of the rocky shelf at the water's edge, **Laniakea** is a beautiful stretch of beach once you get away from the hordes of people that jam onto the small pocket of sand where the majority of the turtles rest. Park in the dirt parking lot on the mountain side of Kamehameha Highway just north of a ranch with horses. Cross the road with extreme caution. Tour buses of all sizes stop here and direct people to the northern corner of the beach. The turtles, however, feed along the rocks that run the length of the beach, so walk to the south to escape the crowds. Where the beachfront properties begin at the southern end of the beach, the sand widens and there are beautiful views of the Wai'anae Mountains and the western side of the North Shore. If you plan on swimming or snorkeling, this is also the best place to enter and exit the water. The farther south you walk along the beach, the better the chance of finding seclusion.

Chun's Reef

A beautiful spot for a beach day, **Chun's Reef** is the next beach north of Laniakea, but without the tour buses and crowds. The wide sandy beach has tidepools in the southern corner up against the rocky point, and the water right off the beach is a bit deeper here and more suitable for swimming and snorkeling. The beach gets wider to the north end of Chun's and is lined with tall ironwood trees, providing ample shade. Little waves break over the reef quite a distance offshore almost all year long, so it's a great place for beginners to surf in the summer. It's also a favorite area for stand-up paddle surfers. Park in the dirt on the mountain side of the road across from the beach. There are lifeguards, but no facilities at Chun's.

★ Waimea Bay Beach Park

At the mouth of the Waimea River and Waimea Valley is the scenic **Waimea Bay Beach Park.** The tight bay is lined with beautiful white sand, and the water is crystal clear, perfect for swimming and snorkeling. There are rocky points on both sides of the bay, while the center is all sand, producing light-blue water. Stand-up paddle across the bay, relax on the beach, or jump off the famous Jump Rock, a 20-foot-tall rock spire right off the beach. Spinner dolphins and green sea turtles are frequent visitors. Park in the designated parking area, but if it's full, there is paid parking in Waimea Valley, which is about a 10-minute walk to the beach. Use the white pedestrian bridge to cross the river and access the beach park, which has restrooms, showers, picnic areas, and a grassy park. The beach park is closed 10pm-5am daily.

Three Tables

Once you round Waimea Bay, the first beach you come to heading north is **Three Tables,** named after three flat reef platforms that rise above the ocean surface just off the beach. This is part of the Pupukea-Waimea Marine Life Conservation District, a protected area where fishing is illegal. The resulting copious amounts of reef fish in the water mean the main draw here is snorkeling. Three Tables has a quaint beach, with shallow water stretching between rock outcroppings. Perfect for families, the beach has shade trees and picnic tables up by the bike path. There are a few parking spaces in front of the beach on the side of Kamehameha Highway, or you can park in the lot just to the north of Three Tables. Turn into the lot at the Pupukea Road traffic signal. There are restrooms here as well, although they are notoriously dingy.

Ke'iki Beach

On the north side of the prominent reef rock point that frames in Sharks Cove, **Ke'iki Beach** is the place to go if you're looking for solitude. The beach stretches out to the north, and even though the name might change every quarter mile, it's still one beautiful ribbon of sand with aquamarine water pushing up against it. The water gets deep rather quickly here, so it's also great for swimming and snorkeling. From the highway, turn onto Keiki Road and look for parking. There is also intermittent parking along Kamehameha Highway on the ocean side. Follow one of the designated public access paths to the beach. There are no facilities and no shade here.

'Ehukai Beach Park

Across from Sunset Elementary School is a small parking lot for **'Ehukai Beach Park.** Walk through the small park toward the lifeguard tower and onto the sand. To the immediate left is the world-famous **Banzai Pipeline** surf break. If it's summer, the water is beautiful and clear, but there will be no waves. To the right is 'Ehukai Beach, which stretches north up to Rocky Point. Swimming is great up and down the beach, which is lined with palms and shrubs offering midday shade. During the summer, the snorkeling is better on the Pipeline side of the park, where there is a wide shelf of reef, canyons, and caves to explore. 'Ehukai Beach Park has restrooms and showers, and there are additional public restrooms across the street in front of the school. The beach park is closed 10pm-5am daily.

Sunset Beach

To the north of Sunset Elementary School, homes line the ocean side of Kamehameha Highway, and the beach is hidden from view. But once you pass a gas station, **Sunset Beach** is all you see. A wide swath of sand from the highway to the water's edge, Sunset is also famous for its big waves during the winter, but its natural beauty is splendid, waves or not. In the summer, it's perfect for swimming and snorkeling, or you can stand-up paddle up and down the coast from here for a good look at the shore. Take a walk up the point to the north for a great view back toward Hale'iwa.

Waimea Bay Beach Park

There is parking on the ocean side of the highway, along the bike path. If you luck into one of these spots, it's pleasant enough to relax, have a snack or some coffee, and watch the ocean sparkle. During the winter, it's also a great vantage point for whale-watching. There is another parking lot on the mountain side of the highway where you'll find restrooms and showers.

TURTLE BAY
Kawela Bay

One of the most protected and secluded bays on the North Shore, **Kawela Bay** shelters a small strip of sand and a calm lagoon protected by an outer reef between Sunset Beach and Turtle Bay. It's great for snorkeling, swimming, and getting away from it all. Park on the side of the highway across from the fruit stand and walk through the trees to the beach.

Kuilima Point

Kuilima Point, today known as **Turtle Bay,** is the site of the Turtle Bay Resort, a dramatic coastline, and a sandy beach. To the west of the resort and rugged Kuilima Point is a sand and rock beach that stretches to the eastern point of Kawela Bay. Walk the beach at low tide when there is more sand or snorkel over rock and reef. On the immediate east side of the point and the main resort is a small protected cove great for families and for swimming, but you'll have to share it with the other hotel guests. Farther east of the small bay is a beach seldom visited even though it sits right next to the resort. Walk along the sand or relax under some trees. The reef is shallow right up to the shore, so this is not the best spot for swimming. Visit the beach when the winds are light, as the trade winds blow straight on shore and get quite blustery. Turtle Bay is a great stop if you're looking for a little beach time followed by lunch or dinner.

To get to Kuilima Point from the Kamehameha Highway, turn onto Kuilima Road and follow it to the main resort parking lot. There is beach access on both sides of the main resort tower.

Sunset Beach

Water Sports

SURFING

Dubbed the "Seven Mile Miracle," this area has more high-quality surf breaks packed into the scenic coastline from Hale'iwa to Turtle Bay than in any other place in the world. The powerful waves draw surfers from around the world, and for over three decades, professional surfing's elite world tour has wrapped up the title season at the infamous Banzai Pipeline.

The waves on the North Shore are also some of the most dangerous, and deadliest, in the world. With huge breaks, strong currents, and shallow reefs, even top athletes are not immune to severe injury or death. Because of these and other factors, only expert surfers should paddle out. There are lifeguards posted at most North Shore beaches; check with them for ocean conditions and safety. If you're having doubts about the waves and your ability, it's best to have a seat on the beach, enjoy the spectacle, and live to surf another day on a different wave.

Hale'iwa

HALE'IWA

Located in Hale'iwa town to the west of the harbor, **Hale'iwa** breaks off Ali'i Beach. A peak when it's small, the wave becomes exponentially more dangerous the larger it gets, breaking as a predominant right. The fast waves close out over a very shallow inside reef ledge known as the Toilet Bowl. A strong rip current is a staple at Hale'iwa. Paddle out from the west side of the beach, to the left of the Toilet Bowl section.

North Shore Beaches

LANIAKEA

Best on north swells, **Laniakea** is a right pointbreak that breaks over flat reef and sand. Depending on the direction of the swell, the wave is one of the longest on the North Shore.

Expert surfers tend to sit up at the point, while novice surfers and longboarders prefer the inside section off the south end of the beach. Paddle out from the south end of the beach. Laniakea is to the immediate north of a ranch, and there is a long dirt parking lot on the mountain side of Kamehameha Highway.

CHUN'S REEF

Just north of Laniakea, the next beach and surf spot you can see from the highway is **Chun's Reef.** Chun's is a soft-breaking right point, but also has a fast-breaking left at the top of the sandy point that most often closes out. Chun's is a favorite wave for beginners, longboarders, and kids. It's one of the most user-friendly waves on the North Shore. Keep in mind that even though the wave itself is good for learning, the shallow bottom is still dangerous, since it's covered by a sharp, flat reef. Chun's is one of the few breaks on the North Shore that also has very small waves in the summer.

WAIMEA BAY

A big wave spot that only starts to break when the waves are 15 to 20 feet on the face, **Waimea Bay** is the only chance for many to see waves of this size, a feat of nature that should not be missed if the bay is breaking. The shore break is also something to see, as huge waves barrel and detonate in spectacular fashion in inches of water. Parking at Waimea fills up quickly when the waves are big. There is limited additional parking along the highway on the west side of the bay heading west, or you can pay to park at Waimea Valley, just past the turnoff to Waimea Bay. You could also park by Three Tables and Sharks Cove and walk back along the highway. Many spectators watch and snap photos from the railing above the rocks on the east side of the bay.

★ BANZAI PIPELINE

The **Banzai Pipeline**, or simply **Pipeline**, is one of the most dangerous waves in the world. Guarded closely by a territorial crew of local surfers, Pipeline is one of those waves where visiting surfers will find it more to their advantage to sit on the beach and watch its grandeur rather than test their mettle. Breaking just 75 yards off the beach, Pipeline is a spectator's delight. Massive round and hollow lefts explode over a shallow reef, and brave surfers try to place themselves as deep as possible inside the barrel, hoping to emerge out the end on their feet. On the sand, you can feel the waves break on the beach and sense the tension and emotion in the water. Park in the 'Ehukai Beach Park lot or along the highway. Pay attention to the sporadic No Parking signs.

'EHUKAI

Also accessible from 'Ehukai Beach Park is the North Shore's only beach break, **'Ehukai.** Depending on the sand and the swells, the waves can break right or left and range from phenomenal shape to junky and lumpy surf.

SUNSET BEACH

Sunset Beach offers one of the most powerful and dangerous waves in the world, breaking from Sunset Point all the way into the bay. Strong currents and closeout sets are the hallmark of Sunset, along with a dredging inside section called **The West Bowl**, which breaks closest to the beach. A wave for experts only, when the water is gigantic, you'll find surfers attempting to ride the mountainous fluid walls. Bring binoculars to catch all the action way out to sea.

Turtle Bay
KUILIMA POINT

Kuilima Point, known locally as **Turtle Bay,** is a funky, soft wave that breaks along a sharp reef outcropping into deep water. Since the break is just off Kuilima Point, where the Turtle Bay Resort is situated, you can literally watch the surfers from Turtle Bay's pool bar. The inside has soft, rolling white water that is perfect for beginners. You can also rent longboards at the resort. The beach and water are open to the public. Paddle out from the rocky shore in front of the bungalows.

Outfitters
Hale'iwa town is full of surf shops that

The Banzai Pipeline is one of the most exciting and dangerous waves in the world.

Summer or winter, Surf 'N Sea has everything you need for the beach.

sell apparel, boards, and surf accessories. **Hawaiian Island Creations** (66-224 Kamehameha Hwy., 808/637-0991, www.hicsurf.com, 10am-8pm Mon.-Thurs., 10am-9pm Fri., 10am-5pm Sun.) and **Wave Riding Vehicles** (66-451 Kamehameha Hwy., 808/637-2020, www.waveridingvehicles.com, 9am-7pm Mon.-Sat., 10am-6pm Sun.) are two local surf brands with retail shops, and **Xcel** (66-590 Kamehameha Hwy., 808/637-3248, www.xcelwetsuits.com, 9am-5pm daily) is a local wetsuit company where you can find all manner of wetsuits to stay warm and protect yourself from the sun. **Surf 'N Sea** (62-595 Kamehameha Hwy., 808/637-9887, http://surfnsea.com, 9am-7pm daily) not only has apparel and new and used boards for sale, but it also rents shortboards and longboards by the hour, day, and week. Shortboards are $5 the first hour, $3.50 each additional hour, $24 daily, and $120 weekly; longboards are $7 the first hour, $6 each additional hour, $30 daily, and $150 weekly.

Hawaii Eco Divers (59-059 B Pupukea Rd., 888/349-3864, www.hawaiiecodivers.com, 7:30am-9pm daily) offers surf tours for experienced surfers and lessons for beginners. The surf tours include personalized surf coaching and a video of the session. Tour prices are $150 for a morning session or $250 all day for a group of up to three surfers. Surfboards are not included. Surf lessons run $100 for a three- to four-hour session focusing on catching and riding waves. The lesson rate includes boards and transportation. **Uncle Bryan's Sunset Suratt Surf Academy** (808/783-8657, http://surfnorthshore.com, 7am-5pm daily) gives beginner surfing and stand-up paddling lessons. With an arsenal of boards and vans, it drives to where the surf is best suited for learning. Book online. Standard two-hour group lessons start at $80.

Located across from Sharks Cove, **North Shore Surf Shop** (59-053 Kamehameha Hwy., 808/638-0390, 8am-8pm daily) has a huge selection of shortboards, new and used, and carries a lot of the professional surfers' used boards. It rents shortboards for $25 daily, $60 for three days, $125 weekly, and $300 for a month; longboards are $30 daily, $75 for three days, $140 weekly, and $300 for a month. It also has a retail location in the town of Hale'iwa.

At Turtle Bay Resort you can rent boards at **Hans Hedemann Surf** (57-091 Kamehameha Hwy., 808/447-6755 or 808/293-7779, www.hhsurf.com, 8am-5pm daily). Shortboards and longboards rent for $15 per hour, $40 for four hours, $50 all day, $60 overnight, $35 each additional day, and $250 per week. Two-hour private lessons go for $150, semiprivate lessons are $125, and group lessons, for up to four surfers, are $95. All equipment is included.

SNORKELING AND DIVING
North Shore Beaches
During the summer, from May to September, when the ocean is flat, the North Shore Beaches are an amazing place to snorkel. With a mix of rocks, reef, sand, calm waters,

and favorable winds, just about anywhere you jump in the water will have some interesting underwater topography, coral, and marine life.

★ PUPUKEA-WAIMEA MARINE LIFE CONSERVATION DISTRICT

The most abundant marine life is found at **Three Tables, Sharks Cove,** and **Waimea Bay,** which comprise the **Pupukea-Waimea Marine Life Conservation District.** Established in 1983 to conserve and replenish marine species at Three Tables and Sharks Cove, the reserve was expanded in 2003 to include Waimea Bay, covering 100 acres of coastline about a mile long. Fishing or the taking of any marine species is strictly prohibited in the area. Look for wrasse, surgeonfish, reef squid, puffer fish, the spotted eagle ray, palani, unicorn fish, harlequin shrimp, and frogfish, just some of the creatures that inhabit the area. Waimea Bay is also known for pods of spinner dolphins that frolic in the middle of the bay.

There are boat dives and shore dives available on the North Shore. The shore dives explore Three Tables and Sharks Cove, where there are flourishing reefs teeming with endemic fish and lava tubes, caverns, and walls to explore. The boat dives provide access to the extraordinary underwater topography and pristine offshore reefs of the North Shore Beaches: Atlantis is an area full of trenches, valleys, walls, and lava tubes, and Cathedrals has rock formations, reefs, and caverns where turtles, eels, and whitetip reef sharks are common; Grand Canyon is a drift dive along the North Shore Beaches where you'll find sponges hanging from the ledges and trevallies and rays in the deep water; two reef sites, Nanny's Reef and Nautilus Reef, are 40-foot dives with a plethora of marine life. Diving the North Shore during the winter is contingent on the size of the surf.

Outfitters

Surf 'N Sea (62-595 Kamehameha Hwy., 808/637-9887, http://surfnsea.com, 9am-7pm daily) in Hale'iwa is the North Shore's most complete surf and dive shop. It sells new gear, rents beach and ocean gear and accessories, and even leads shore and boat dives. It rents dive equipment by the piece at a daily or weekly rate. For snorkel gear, it rents by the piece or in a set, the latter runs $6.50 for four hours, $9.50 daily, and $45 weekly. Its guided

Sharks Cove is part of a marine protected area.

Snorkel vs. Surf

While Hawaii's slight seasonal changes in temperature and precipitation might not be apparent to visitors who only stay a week or two at a time, there is one natural phenomenon that differentiates strikingly between summer and winter on the North Shore—waves! During Hawaii's winter, October-April, and sometimes into spring, storms in the North Pacific create very large, open ocean swells that track toward the equator, passing by the state and expending the wave energy on the reefs and beaches. This is great news for surfers, who follow those swells closely and live to surf the powerful waves, which can break up to 60 feet on the face during the biggest surges on the outermost reefs. For snorkelers and divers, high surf is a worst-case scenario.

Once summer rolls around, the tables turn. From May to September, the North Shore becomes a tranquil swimmer's paradise. The waves usually remain flat the entire season, the sand settles, and the water becomes beautifully clear. Snorkelers and divers revel in the conditions, and the focus on the North Shore shifts from the waves above the surface to the exploration of its underwater world.

dives are operated by **Hawaii Scuba Diving,** which offers shore and boat dives as well as certification courses. The morning dives are for certified divers, while the afternoon charters to shallow reef sites are open to any level diver. One-tank shore dives are $75 for certified divers and $95 for noncertified; two-tank shore dives are $100 certified, $125 noncertified; one-tank night dives are $100; two-tank boat dives are $140. Professional Association of Diving Instructors (PADI) diving certification courses are $375 for Open Water Diver, $295 for Advanced Open Water Diver, and $650 for Divemaster.

Banzai Divers Hawaii (808/462-8290, http://banzaidivershawaii.com, 8am-6pm daily) operates diving charters from Hale'iwa Harbor seasonally May-September. Boat dives start at $180 for certified divers.

Hawaii Eco Divers (61-101 Iliohu Pl., 808/499-9177, www.hawaiiecodivers.com, 7:30am-9pm daily), operating from Hale'iwa Harbor, specializes in personalized small-group shore dives. Two-tank shore dives for certified divers, one-tank night dives and one-tank dives for noncertified divers are $109. All gear is included in the rate, along with snacks, refreshments, and photos of the dives. The company will also shoot a video of your dive for $75.

If you get to Sharks Cove and discover you

really want to snorkel but don't have any gear, you're in luck: Right across the street is **North Shore Surf Shop** (59-053 Kamehameha Hwy., 808/638-0390, 8am-8pm daily). It rents complete snorkel sets for $15 daily and $30 for three days. It also has rash guards for rent for $5, which are great for sun protection while you're snorkeling.

Hawaii Adventure Diving (66-105 Haleiwa Rd., 808/637-3474, http://hawaiiadventurediving.com) has scuba diving and pelagic diving tours and offers a private charter group, two-tank reef dive, maximum six people, for $600. The pelagic snorkel free-dive tour takes you to swim and snorkel in deep water with dolphins, whales, sharks, and pelagic fish. The two-hour tour has a three-person minimum, six-person maximum and runs $145 per person, $75 ride along.

STAND-UP PADDLING

Hale'iwa is the hub of stand-up paddling and kayaking on the North Shore, largely because of the **'Anahulu River** and the protected and calm waters off **Hale'iwa Beach Park.** You can access the shoreline in the small parking lot next to Surf N Sea or along Hale'iwa Beach Park. From there, you can paddle around the shallow river mouth, north to Pua'ena Point and beyond, or head upriver for a smooth and mellow ride.

On the North Shore, stand-up paddling is popular at **Waimea Bay, Laniakea,** and **Chun's Reef.** The conditions are best in the summer when the ocean surface is flat. Chun's and Laniakea often have very small waves in the summer, so you can even try surfing the stand-up paddleboard.

In Hale'iwa, **Surf 'N Sea** (62-595 Kamehameha Hwy., 808/637-9887, http://surfnsea.com, 9am-7pm daily) rents single kayaks for $7 the first hour, $5 for each additional hour, $20 for a half day, and $75 for a full day. The weekly rate is $300. Stand-up paddleboards rent for $10 for the first hour, $8 for each additional hour, and $40 for a full day. The weekly rate is $200. Surf N Sea also rents water bikes and pedal boats and has the distinction of being situated on the bank of the river mouth for easy ocean access.

At the Turtle Bay Resort, **Hans Hedemann Surf** (57-091 Kamehameha Hwy., 808/447-6755 or 808/293-7779, www.hhsurf.com, 8am-5pm daily) rents stand-up paddleboards for $25 per hour, $50 for three hours, $80 all day, $100 overnight, $50 each additional day, and $400 per week. Two-hour private lessons go for $150, semiprivate lessons are $125, and group lessons, up to four surfers, is $75. All equipment is included.

FISHING

During the summer, spearfishing is common along the North Shore, where reef fish and octopus are the desired take. The conditions are prime during this season with the calm, flat ocean surface. Shoreline fishing is also common from Mokule'ia out to Ka'ena Point and along the beach south of Laniakea. Remember that the area from the west side of Waimea Bay to the north side of Sharks Cove is a marine protected area and fishing or taking any marine species is strictly prohibited. Fishing gear is available in Hale'iwa at **Hale'iwa Fishing Supply** (66-519 Kamehameha Hwy., 808/637-9876, 10am-7pm Mon., Wed., Fri.-Sat.).

The North Shore is very favorable for sportfishing, with deepwater offshore and strong currents from the northwest that continually bring in bait and game fish. Several deepsea sportfishing operators are located in the Hale'iwa Small Boat Harbor if you're interested in fishing for big game fish like wahoo, mahimahi, tuna, and marlin.

Chupu Charters (66-105 Haleiwa Rd., Slip 312, 808/637-3474, www.chupu.com) operates four boats with amenities like air-conditioning, a custom Pompanette fighting chair, and top-of-the-line rods and reels. Bait, tackle, ice, and fish packaging supplies are provided.

Many people stand-up paddle the 'Anahulu River in Hale'iwa.

Chupu offers full-day exclusive charters starting at $750 for the entire boat, half-day morning private charters starting at $550, and afternoon half-day private charters starting at $550. The charters have a maximum of four to six passengers depending on the boat.

Sport Fishing Hawaii (66-105 Haleiwa Rd., 808/721-8581 or 808/450-7601, www.sport-fishing-hawaii.com) operates a 47-foot

Hatteras and charges $750 for half-day charters and $925 for the full-day, 10-hour charter, with a six-passenger limit.

Kuuloa Kai (66-195 Kaamooloa Rd., 808/637-5783, www.kuuloakai.com, 8am-10pm daily) has private charters for up to six anglers and lets you take home enough fish for a couple dinners. It offers full-day charters for $800 and half-day charters for $650.

Hiking and Biking

HIKING

You can hike to **Ka'ena Point**, the western tip of the island, from the North Shore. About five miles round-trip, the route follows an old dirt road to the point. It is a dry, windswept, but extremely beautiful hike, with views of the North Shore the entire way out. Once you reach the nature reserve at the end of the point, cross through the special predator-proof fence to see **seabird** nesting grounds, monk seals, spinner dolphins, and possibly humpback whales if you're **hiking** from November to March. Drive to the end of Farrington Highway, past Mokule'ia, park, and proceed on foot. Bring plenty of water. There are no facilities in the area.

At the very end of Pupukea Road is **Kaunala Trail** (a six-mile loop), which runs through the verdant gulches and across the ridges of the Ko'olau foothills above Pupukea. The trail is wide and well graded, with a slight elevation gain. There are great views of the North Shore on the return route. Drive to the end of Pupukea Road and park on the side of the road. Follow the dirt road past the Boy Scout camp and go around the locked gate. The trail is not far ahead to the left of the dirt road. This trail is open on weekends and holidays.

The **Kealia Trail** (seven miles round-trip) is an intermediate hike that climbs the cliff behind Mokule'ia to a summit in the Wai'anae

Range. The prize is an overlook of beautiful Makua Valley. After hiking about 4 of the 19 switchbacks you'll find amazing views of the entire North Shore, as well as native trees and shrubs along the trail. To get to the trail, take Farrington Highway through Mokule'ia. As you pass the end of the airport runway, look for an access gate in the fence and turn left. It's open 7am-6pm daily. Go past the runway and park in the lot in front of the control tower. Walk toward the mountain and go through the gate in the fence and immediately turn left.

For a walk that includes bird-watching, check out the **James Campbell National Wildlife Refuge** (66-590 Kamehameha Hwy., 808/637-6330, www.fws.gov/james-campbell). The refuge is two separate sections of wetland habitat in between Turtle Bay and Kahuku, 164 acres in total. The wetlands are dedicated to the recovery of Hawai'i's endemic waterfowl, primarily the endangered Hawaiian stilt, Hawaiian moorhen, Hawaiian coot, and the Hawaiian duck. The 126-acre Ki'i Unit is open to the public during the nonbreeding season, October-February. Also utilizing the wetlands is the bristle-thighed curlew. Guided tours are offered twice per week, on Thursday afternoons and Saturday mornings on the first two Saturdays of the month and in the afternoon on the last two Saturdays of the month. Reservations are required.

BIKING

The **North Shore Bike Path** stretches from Waimea Bay to Sunset Beach. Much of the trail is shaded, and there are ocean views along the way. Most of the trail is flat, great for a leisurely cruise or a more relaxing way to beach hop without having to worry about parking.

If you prefer going off-road, mountain bike out to Ka'ena Point on the **Ka'ena Point Trail,** an old railroad bed that is now a dirt road that hugs the coast around the point, a five-mile round-trip. The road is rough and rocky, there is no shade, and the surroundings are arid. Conversely, the scenery of the coastal dunes, the rugged shoreline, and the beautiful water is amazing. In the winter months, huge swells can wrap around the point, creating a cooling sea mist from the white water crashing against the rocks.

In Hale'iwa you can rent bikes at **Surf 'N Sea** (62-595 Kamehameha Hwy., 808/637-9887, http://surfnsea.com, 9am-7pm daily) for $10 per hour, $20 daily, and $100 weekly.

Across from Sharks Cove, the **North Shore Surf Shop** (59-053 Kamehameha Hwy., 808/638-0390, https://northshoresurf-shop.com, 8am-8pm daily) rents cruisers for $15 per day. **Hele Huli Rental** (57-091 Kamehameha Hwy., 808/293-6024, www.turtlebayresort.com) at Turtle Bay Resort rents bikes for $10 for one hour, $20 for two hours, or $25 per day. **North Shore Bike Rentals** (888/948-5666, www.northshorebikerentals.com) is a bike rental and delivery service. It delivers cruisers to any location from Mokule'ia to Velzyland. It rents cruisers for $19 a day, children's bikes for $10 a day, tandem bikes for $29 a day, pull carriers for $12 a day, and adult cruisers with a pull carrier for $28 a day. For three-day minimum rentals the $10 delivery charge is waived. Free helmets and locks are included with rental.

Adventure Sports

SHARK DIVING

There are two shark diving tour operators out of Hale'iwa Harbor. They travel 3-4 miles offshore and drop a metal shark cage in the water, where guests dive in to see Galapagos, tiger, hammerhead, and other sandbar sharks from a safe underwater vantage point. The tours are weather dependent, and no diving experience is required. If you're lucky, you'll see spinner dolphins, turtles, and even humpback whales during your time at sea. **North Shore Shark Adventures** (808/228-5900, https://hawaiisharkadventures.com) offers two-hour tours throughout the day for $120 adult, $60 children 3-13 years old. If you require transportation from Waikiki, you'll be charged an extra $55. **Hawaii Shark Encounters** (808/351-9373, http://www.hawaiisharkencounters.com) offers two-hour tours for $115.50 and $82.50 for children under 12 years old.

HORSEBACK RIDING

The North Shore is a rural enclave from Kahuku to Mokule'ia, and farms and ranches are common along the coast. Up on Pupukea, overlooking Waimea Valley and the North Shore is **Happy Trails Hawaii** (59-231 Pupukea Rd., 808/638-7433, www.happytrailshawaii.com, 8am-5pm daily). Its trails meander through forest, ranch land, and tropical orchards, offering panoramic mountain and ocean views. Two-hour tours are $99, and one-hour tours are $79. Riders must be at least six years old. **Gunstock Ranch** (56-250 Kamehameha Hwy., 808/293-2026, http://gunstockranch.com, Mon.-Sat.), just outside of Kahuku, is a family-owned and -operated working ranch at the base of the Ko'olau Mountains. It has a network of trails and tours for all riding levels, with mountain terrain and beautiful ocean views stretching all the way down the windward coast to

Kaneʻohe Bay. Its Scenic Ride is a 90-minute guided ride suitable for all skill levels for $89; the Keiki Experience is a 30-minute horse experience and ride for children ages 2-7 years old for $39; the Advanced Trail Ride is a one-hour ride with trotting and cantering during the ride for $109, and previous riding experience is required. Gunstock also offers a Moonlight Ride, a Picnic Ride, a Sweetheart Ride, a Sunset Ride, and a Dinner Sunset Ride.

★ SKYDIVING

What could be more exhilarating than seeing the entire island of Oʻahu all at once, from 20,000 feet? Jumping out of the plane that took you that high and parachuting back to earth. **Skydive Hawaii** (68-760 Farrington Hwy., 808/637-9700 or 808/945-0222, www.skydivehawaii.com) operates from Dillingham Airfield in Mokuleʻia and specializes in tandem skydiving for first-time jumpers, but its services also extend to experienced skydivers and skydiving students. It makes three jumps a day and offers a free shuttle service from several points in Honolulu. Tandem skydiving from 12,000 feet is $250 with discounted rates for online reservations. Tandem skydive from 20,000 feet is $998. Skydivers must be at least 18 years old. You can also find similar rates and services literally right next door at **Pacific Skydiving Honolulu** (68-760 Farrington Hwy., 808/637-7472, www.pacificskydivinghonolulu.com). It offers online specials for tandem skydiving starting at $139 with free Waikiki pickup.

GLIDER FLIGHTS

For those who would rather stay inside an aircraft yet still partake of those same views of the North Shore and beyond, **Hawaii Glider and Sailplane Academy** (808/222-4235, http://higlideracademy.com/) at the Dillingham Airfield offers 20-minute scenic glider flights above the Waiʻanae Mountains along the North Shore for $100. Reservations are required. Also accessing the Dillingham Airfield is **Honolulu Soaring** (808/637-0207, www.honolulusoaring.com). It has several planes in its fleet and offers scenic as well as acrobatic glider flights. The average visibility is 30 to 40 miles. One-passenger scenic flights start at $79 for 10 minutes and go to $290 for 60 minutes. Two-passenger scenic flights start at $128 for 10 minutes and go to $390 for 60 minutes. One-passenger acrobatic flights start at $165 for 15 minutes and go to $285 for 60 minutes. Combination scenic and acrobatic flights are also available.

Shopping

HALEʻIWA
★ Historic Haleʻiwa Town
Historic Haleʻiwa Town is packed full of restaurants and shops, most within a comfortable walking distance. Art galleries, surf shops, souvenir shops, and clothing and swimwear boutiques line Kamehameha Highway through this old seaside town established at the turn of the 20th century.

Directly north of the Marketplace is **Haleiwa Art Gallery** (66-252 Kamehameha Hwy., 808/637-3368, www.haleiwaartgallery.com, 10am-6pm daily), Haleʻiwa's oldest gallery. It features the work of 30 island artists in media from oil and watercolor to bronze and embroidery.

Haleiwa Store Lots (66-111 Kamehameha Hwy., 808/585-1770, www.haleiwastorelots.com, 10am-6pm daily) is a brand-new, plantation-inspired, mixed-use development in Haleʻiwa. The open-air mall has plenty of parking in back and features local retailers, dining, general stores, and lots of space to sit, relax, and enjoy the scenery. You'll find **Clark Little Gallery** (Suite #102, 808/626-5319, www.clarklittlephotography.com, 10am-6pm Mon.-Sat., 11am-5pm Sun.), featuring the underwater and wave photography of award-winning local photographer Clark Little. **Greenroom Hawaii** (Suite #201, 808/924-4404, 10am-6pm daily) features famous artists as well as popular local artist Heather Brown. Check out boutique clothing and beach shop **Guava Shop** (Suite #204, 808/637-9670, http://guavahawaii.com, 10am-6pm daily).

Waialua

If you're in Waialua, head to the old Waialua Sugar Mill, where the **North Shore Soap Factory** (67-106 Kealohanui St., 808/637-7627, www.hawaiianbathbody.com, 9am-6pm Mon.-Fri., 8:30am-6pm Sat., 10am-5pm Sun.) specializes in premier Hawaiian bath and body products, the cornerstone being its own handmade and natural soaps.

Entertainment and Events

NIGHTLIFE

Hale'iwa has two popular bars that draw the crowds at night, but also double as restaurants by day. Located in the North Shore Marketplace, **Breakers** (66-250 Kamehameha Hwy., 808/637-9898, www.restauranteur.com/breakers, 8am-2am daily, $11-24) serves breakfast, lunch, and dinner, but the surf-themed restaurant is best known for its full bar and relaxed beach vibe. Packed with surf memorabilia and one of the few places in Hale'iwa that stays open late, it often hosts big parties and has live music.

Many people on the North Shore venture to **Turtle Bay Resort** (57-091 Kamehameha Hwy., 808/293-6000 or 800/203-3650, www.turtlebayresort.com) to visit the only outdoor bar where you can grab a drink and watch the surf, the **Point** (808/293-6000, 10am-10pm daily, $8-19), better known as the Pool Bar. Stiff mai tais and other tropical drink concoctions are its specialty. Situated right on the point, this is a great place for a sunset beverage. Inside the resort there is **Surfer, The Bar** (808/293-6000, 6pm-midnight daily, $12-24), a modern mixed-media bar centered around surfing and its legacy on the North Shore. Along with a light food menu, it offers tropical drinks, wine by the glass, and a bunch of local beers. Check out

Welcome to Historic Hale'iwa Town.

The Eddie

Waimea Bay is home to the iconic **Quiksilver in Memory of Eddie Aikau,** an annual one-day event that honors the late North Shore waterman Eddie Aikau and the surfers who dedicate their lives to riding giant waves. Eddie was the first official lifeguard at Waimea Bay and a revered big-wave surfer. In 1978, Eddie was selected to help crew a Polynesian voyaging canoe, a cultural expedition bound for Tahiti. When the canoe encountered treacherous seas outside the Hawaiian Islands and capsized, Eddie struck out fearlessly on a paddleboard back to Hawai'i to save his stranded crew. He was never seen again.

Since 1985, The Eddie is staged every year to test the strongest and best big-wave surfers in the spirit of Eddie's courageous selflessness. The invitational has some impressive criteria: the waves must be at least 20-feet for the entire day of competition. Because of this minimum wave height requirement, The Eddie has only run eight times in 27 years. The waiting period is from December through February and as the saying goes on the North Shore, "The Bay calls the day."

Talk Story Wednesday, where prominent figures in the surf industry share their stories with the crowd. Video and live music also add to the experience.

FESTIVALS AND EVENTS
★ Hawaii Polo

Experience the fun and sport of seaside polo in beautiful Mokule'ia. Matches at **Hawaii Polo** matches (808/220-5153, https://hawaiipolo.org, 2pm Sun. Apr.-Sept., $10 adults, children 12 and under free) are held on Sundays April-September. Game day feels like a giant tailgate party, as people pull their vehicles right up to the field and open blankets under the ironwood trees. Bring a cooler full of food and beverages and enjoy a few chukkers (periods of play). Gates open at noon.

Haleiwa Arts Festival

The **Haleiwa Arts Festival** (62-449 Kamehameha Hwy., 808/637-2277, www.haleiwaartsfestival.org, July, free) is a weekend-long annual event that takes place at Hale'iwa Beach Park in the middle of July. The festival features the works of over 100 artists for exhibition and purchase, and has live musical and cultural entertainment, art demonstrations, and children's art activities. Food vendors accompany the open-air festival.

Vans Triple Crown of Surfing

For six weeks every winter, from early November through late December, the **Vans Triple Crown of Surfing** (www.triplecrownofsurfing.com, Nov.-Dec.) takes over the North Shore. This professional surfing event is comprised of three contests, the first at Ali'i Beach Park in Hale'iwa, the second at Sunset Beach, and the final one at the Banzai Pipeline. An international field of hundreds of competitors, as well as a cadre of hungry locals, battle it out on the biggest and best days of surf during the holding period for each event. Spectators flock to the beach to watch the action, some of the best surfing in the world. There are food vendors, restrooms, drinking water, souvenirs, and giveaways at each event. With limited parking and an influx of people on the North Shore, expect driving delays and plan to either pay for parking or park and walk quite a distance, especially during the Pipeline event.

Food

HALE'IWA

Coffee

In the North Shore Marketplace, the **Coffee Gallery** (66-250 Kamehameha Hwy., 808/637-5355, www.roastmaster.com, 6:30am-8pm daily) is a popular spot for coffee, both brewed and roasted beans. It has a great selection of bakery goods and sells local coffee by the pound. It also offers free wireless Internet for customers on the rustic covered patio or at outdoor benches.

Quick Bites

Storto's (66-215 Kamehameha Hwy., 808/637-6633, 8am-6pm daily, $5-12) is the go-to sandwich deli in Hale'iwa. The friendly staff makes big sandwiches for big appetites. For a normal serving, order a half sandwich, and don't forget the papaya seed dressing.

Café Haleiwa (66-460 Kamehameha Hwy., 808/637-5516, 7am-1:45pm daily, $4-10) is a delicious pancakes-and-eggs breakfast restaurant with Mexican specialties and a signature mahimahi plate.

Steak and Seafood

Overlooking the Hale'iwa Harbor, right by the Rainbow Bridge, is **Hale'iwa Joe's** (66-011 Kamehameha Hwy., 808/637-8005, http://haleiwajoes.com, 11:30am-9:30pm Sun.-Thurs., 11:30am-midnight Fri.-Sat., $19-40). Joe's serves up fresh and delicious seafood with Hawaiian-influenced Pacific Rim preparations. It also has meat selections and great salads. Indoor and patio seating are available or sit in the bar for a more casual experience with the full benefits of the menu. Make reservations to avoid the wait.

Pacific Rim

★ **Rajanee Thai Cuisine** (66-111 Kamehameha Hwy. Suite #1001, 808/784-0023, 12am-9pm Tues.-Sun., $12-18) has a religious local following. The flavorful Thai cuisine is consistent and delicious. Try a refreshing Thai iced tea with your meal.

For sushi, **Banzai Sushi Bar** (66-246 Kamehameha Hwy., 808/637-4404, www.banzaisushibarhawaii.com, noon-9:30pm daily, $6-48) in the North Shore Marketplace is the go-to joint. Sit at a table or try the floor seating for an authentic Japanese experience on a finely decorated outdoor covered lanai. The fish is fresh, the rolls are inventive, and It has a list of premium sake. Vegan options are on the menu, as well as large-party sushi combinations. The tempura avocado is a treat, as is the live music often on hand.

Mexican

★ **Luibueno's** (66-165 Kamehameha Hwy., 808/637-7717, http://luibueno.com, 11am-midnight daily, $6-29) serves authentic Mexican and Latin seafood, something that's hard to find on O'ahu. The restaurant decor is modern and colorful, the atmosphere is lively, and the restaurant sources its ingredients locally, including the fish that comes right off the boat at Hale'iwa Harbor.

Health Food

The **Beet Box Café** (66-437 Kamehameha Hwy. Suite #104, 808/637-3000, www.thebeetboxcafe.com, 7am-4pm daily, $6-11) offers an extensive organic vegetarian menu for breakfast and lunch. Egg dishes served all day, and acai bowls, soup, sandwiches, salads, smoothies, and raw organic vegetable juice are all possibilities.

Sweets and Treats

Established in 1951, **Matsumoto Shave Ice** (66-111 Kamehameha Hwy. Suite #605, 808/637-4827, www.matsumotoshaveice.com, 9am-6pm daily) is an integral part of the history of quaint Hale'iwa town. It has developed

Line up for shave ice.

a huge following over the years. The result is a long line that snakes around the building just to get a cup of the Hawaiian treat. Be prepared to wait quite a while, especially on the weekends and during the summer. Originally a sundries store, it still sells souvenirs, snacks, and items like sunscreen and sunglasses.

The **Waialua Bakery** (66-200 Kamehameha Hwy., 808/341-2838, 10am-5pm Mon.-Sat.) has much more than just baked goods. The locally owned bakery also has juices, a long list of smoothies, and fresh sandwiches. Much of its produce is from the family farm in Mokule'ia.

NORTH SHORE BEACHES AND TURTLE BAY
Quick Bites

Across from Sunset Beach, **Ted's Bakery**

(59-024 Kamehameha Hwy., 808/638-8207, www.tedsbakery.com, 7am-8pm daily) provides homemade bakery goods, pies, salads, burgers, sandwiches, and plate lunches. Expect a wait of 30 minutes during the lunch rush if you order hot food.

Steak and Seafood

When North Shore locals celebrate a big occasion, they go to **Lei Lei's Bar and Grill** (57-049 Kuilima Dr., 808/293-2662, www.turtlebayresort.com, 7am-10pm daily, $22-36). The open-air restaurant and bar has indoor and patio seating, just steps away from the Fazio Golf Course. It serves rich and savory fresh seafood cuisine with Hawaiian favorites like ahi *poke*. The prime rib is also a favorite, as is the escargot appetizer. Lei Lei's is open for breakfast, lunch, and dinner.

Hanauma Bay and Southeast

The southeast region is like no other on Oʻahu.

Ridges lined with mansions and green valleys with quiet communities span from Kahala to Hawaiʻi Kai, where suburban neighborhoods encircle Koko Marina, which stretches far back to the mountains. Maunalua Bay, a shallow, calm bay with a fringe reef, extends from Black Point in Kahala to the sheer cliffs of Koko Head, an impressive landmark jutting out into the bay. Windswept waves roll across shallow reefs, the turquoise water shimmers in the midday sun, and boats cruise from the marina out beyond farthest reaches of the reef.

On the east side of Koko Head is Hanauma Bay State Park, a natural area preserve known for some of the best snorkeling on Oʻahu. Past the bay, the scenery changes completely. On the dry southeastern tip of Oʻahu, the area from Koko Head to Makapuʻu, also known as the Ka Iwi Coastline, Ka Iwi State Scenic Shoreline, and Ka Iwi coast, receives 12-20 inches of rain annually, compared to the 100-inch annual average that Hoʻomaluhia Botanical Garden in Kaneʻohe receives. There are numerous lookouts to take in the rugged, dry, and wave-pummeled coastline. This stretch is also one of the best locales for whale-watching on Oʻahu during the humpback whales' annual stay from November to March.

Makapuʻu, which means bulging eye in Hawaiian, and Sandy Beach are Oʻahu's premier bodysurfing beaches. There is a short hike to the Makapuʻu lighthouse, a prime whale-watching vantage point with a great view toward Waimanalo with Manana Island, a **seabird sanctuary,** in the foreground. For beachcombers, the beaches and tidepools in between Sandy Beach and Makapuʻu are full of natural wonders and offer solace from the tour buses that stop at all the major sights in this region.

For botanical enthusiasts, Koko Crater, just inland from Sandy Beach, is home to Oʻahu's only dryland botanical garden. A short loop trail circles the inside of the crater with all variety of plants that thrive in the dry conditions. An established plumeria grove, which fragrantly blooms during the summer, graces the entrance of the garden. Hikers can also enjoy a challenge on the Koko Crater stairs, a rigorous climb up an old railway, a remnant from World War II, to the top of the crater for amazing 360-degree views. On clear days, Molokaʻi and Maui can be seen in the distance across the Ka Iwi Channel.

Previous: the rugged Ka Iwi State Scenic Shoreline; Sandy Beach Park. **Above:** Koko Crater Botanical Garden boasts a plumeria grove.

Look for ★ to find recommended
sights, activities, dining, and lodging.

Highlights

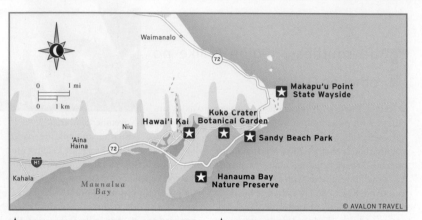

© AVALON TRAVEL

★ **Koko Crater Botanical Garden:** With its succulents, cycads, a native Hawaiian *wiliwili* tree stand, and a plumeria grove, you can't miss this garden, especially when the plumeria are in bloom (page 121).

★ **Makapu'u Point State Wayside:** Hike around the point to the lighthouse, whale-watch from November to March, swim and bodysurf at the beach, and explore the black lava tidepools (page 122).

★ **Sandy Beach Park:** The powerful break at Sandy Beach is the place for surfers to test their mettle—as it detonates right on the sand (page 124).

★ **Hanauma Bay Nature Preserve:** The first marine protected area in the state of Hawaii, this unique, circular bay lies within an extinct volcanic cone, protected from wind and waves. Live coral reef, 400 species of fish, and endangered sea turtles call it home (page 127).

★ **Hawai'i Kai:** The Hawai'i Kai Marina is the recreation hub of the southeast coast. You'll also find restaurants, shopping, and ample shoreline access along beautiful Maunalua Bay (page 130).

Hanauma Bay and Southeast

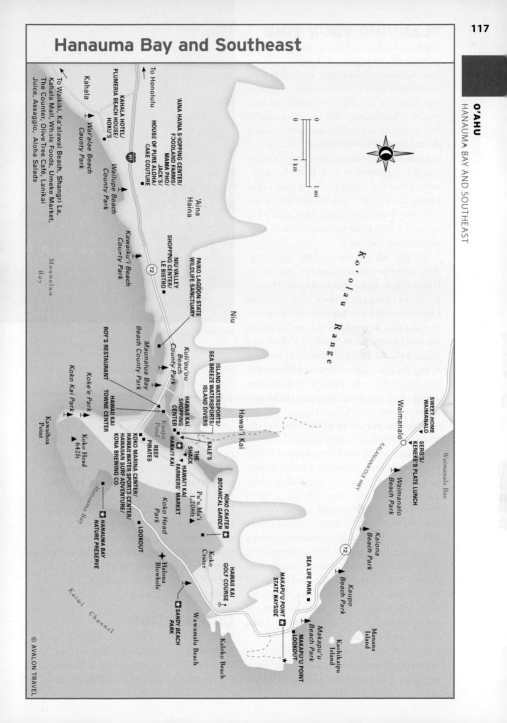

PLANNING YOUR TIME

Southeast Oʻahu is relatively small compared to other Oʻahu regions. It's about 11 miles from Kahala to Makapuʻu. With a 35 mph speed limit on the Kalanianaole Highway, that equates to about a 30-minute drive, sans traffic. While many people take advantage of this scenic-drive corridor as a way to access the windward side—Waimanalo, Kailua, and beyond—from the south shore, the southeast region is a destination all to itself. For sightseers, a half day would suffice to take in the natural beauty of the area, but for outdoor and recreation enthusiasts, plan on at least a full day to two days to see the many natural wonders without rushing.

Kahala Mall in Kahala and the three shopping centers surrounding the marina in Hawaiʻi Kai—Koko Marina Center, Hawaiʻi Kai Town Center, and Hawaiʻi Kai Shopping Center—are home to the majority of the restaurants and shopping in the region. While the neighborhoods in between Kahala and Hawaiʻi Kai all have hiking trails at the back of the valleys, Hawaiʻi Kai to Makapuʻu is where most of the recreational opportunities are centered. Snorkel, dive, and surf tour outfitters operate out of Koko Marina.

Hanauma Bay is one of the most heavily visited natural areas on the island, known for its spectacular snorkeling, but you'll have to get there early to ensure a parking spot, usually by 8am. Once the lot is full, security guards will turn cars away. The bay is closed every Tuesday. Sandy Beach, Makapuʻu, and Sea Life Park are all major tourist draws with limited parking. They are also the main beaches in the region. There's not much to do to avoid the crowds since the region is so close to Waikiki and the sights are all stops for the tour buses. The stretch of beach from the north end of Sandy Beach to the south end of Makapuʻu headland is your best chance to find a quiet patch of sand.

Since there are no major accommodations in the region, those staying in Waikiki hotels or Kailua vacation rentals will be the closest

Makapuʻu Lighthouse

to the area. While a rental car is always the easiest way to get around, the area is also accessible by taxi, ride-hailing services, and by bus. A taxi ride would run upwards of $50 (one-way); ride-hailing services like Uber and Lyft could be pricey, too. The bus, however, is an extremely affordable way to get to specific destinations along the coast without the worry of parking a rental car. The Beach Bus, route 22, runs from Waikiki to Sea Life Park, with stops at Hanauma Bay, Sandy Beach, and Makapuʻu. The bus does not run on Tuesday when Hanauma Bay is closed. Route 57 runs from Kailua to Sea Life Park, where you can transfer to route 22 to access the rest of the Ka Iwi Coastline, Hanauma Bay and on into Waikiki.

ORIENTATION

Stretching from the upscale neighborhood of **Kahala** on the east side of Diamond Head to the easternmost tip of the island at Makapuʻu, the southeast coast has two distinct zones.

Your Best Day in Southeast Oʻahu

The Southeast region offers a mix of recreational activities that include mountain, beach, and ocean settings. The region is relatively small, a 30-minute drive from Kahala to Makapuʻu, yet the activities are not to be rushed. One could easily spend a few days ticking the boxes of all the things to do along this beautiful stretch of coastline.

- Start the day by snorkeling one of the best reef habitats on Oʻahu, **Hanauma Bay Nature Preserve** in Hawaiʻi Kai. With a beautiful beach set way back in the sheltered bay, spend a couple hours viewing the immense diversity found on a healthy reef ecosystem. Keep in mind that if you arrive after 9:30am, you could be turned away if the parking lot is full. If you'd rather start your morning with a hike, walk the Makapuʻu trail to the lighthouse. From November to April, this vantage point is one of the prime locations to view Pacific humpback whales.

- After all that outdoor activity, you'll be in the mood for a delicious meal. Try **Moena Café**, a popular bistro serving breakfast and lunch, or for fresh and delicious poke bowls, check out **Paʻina Café.** They are both located in the Koko Marina Shopping Center in Hawaiʻi Kai.

- Round out the day at **Sandy Beach.** If you're a strong swimmer and enjoy bodysurfing, you'll be right at home in the barreling shore break. Otherwise, enjoy watching from the sunny beach or take a nature walk along the Ka Iwi Coast, where rocks, tidepools, and lava offer a dramatic coastline perfect for exploring on foot. For botanical enthusiasts, stroll through Oʻahu's only dryland botanical garden, Koko Crater Botanical Garden, and catch the plumeria grove in bloom during the summer.

- For dinner with live music and a relaxing atmosphere overlooking the marina, enjoy pizza, fresh fish, and great local beers on tap at **Kona Brewing Company.** Also located in the Koko Marina Shopping Center in Hawaiʻi Kai, the bar scene is lively and the food is always fresh and locally sourced.

RAINY-DAY ALTERNATIVE
Outdoor activities are the draw in this region. If you get rained out, head back into Honolulu and check out the historical district and museums.

The first area encompasses the suburban neighborhoods in the valleys and along the ridges from Kahala to **Hawaiʻi Kai. Aina Haina, Niu Valley, and Kuliʻouʻou** are the major valleys along Kalanianaole Highway, the main thoroughfare along this stretch of the island. The Portlock neighborhood lines the western flank of Koko Head and looks west over Maunalua Bay. The other part of the region, known as the Ka Iwi Coast, is dramatically different. As the highway rounds Koko Head, homes disappear and rugged volcanic landscape prevails from Hanauma Bay to Makapuʻu. Along this windy and dry stretch of coastline you'll find Koko Crater and Sandy Beach before reaching the Makapuʻu headland, the easternmost tip of the island.

Sights

KAHALA

Shangri La

A fitting estate for the upscale neighborhoods of Kahala, **Shangri La** (4055 Papu Cr., 808/734-1941 or 808/532-3853, www.shangrilahawaii.org) was the seasonal home of American heiress and philanthropist Doris Duke. Built in 1937, replete with amazing views from a small cliff above the water's edge, Shangri La was designed to hold Duke's vast collection of Islamic art, and today it serves as a center for Islamic art and culture. Portions of this home that blend Islamic architecture and Hawaiian landscaping are open to the public via guided tours led by the Honolulu Museum of Art. The 12-person group tour begins in the Arts of the Islamic World gallery at the Honolulu Museum of Art, followed by a short video about Duke and her estate, and then a minivan shuttles the group to the estate for a 1.5-hour tour featuring the public rooms of the main house and parts of the grounds. Tours are held 9am, 10:30am, and 1:30pm Wednesday-Saturday. General admission is $25, and reservations are strongly encouraged.

HAWAI'I KAI AND KA'IWI COAST

Maunalua Bay Lookout

There are several lookouts beside Kalanianaole Highway in between Hawai'i Kai and Makapu'u. The coastline is rugged, the road winds precariously close to the edge of the sea cliff, and open ocean swells constantly batter rock outcroppings. The **Maunalua Bay Lookout** is an often forgotten lookout on the mountain side of the highway, just before you arrive at the Hanauma Bay turnoff if you're heading east, with sweeping views of Koko Crater, Hawai'i Kai Marina, and Maunalua Bay, which stretches all the way to Diamond Head.

Hanauma Bay Nature Preserve Park

The first marine protected area in the state of Hawaii, **Hanauma Bay Nature Preserve Park** (7455 Kalanianaole Hwy., 808/395-2211 or 808/396-4229, www.honolulu.gov/cms-dpr-menu/site-dpr-sitearticles/1716-hanauma-bay-home.html 6am-7pm daily) is

Maunalua Bay and Hawai'i Kai Marina

the most popular snorkeling site on O'ahu. Located just to the east of Koko Head on the southeast shore, the nearly circular bay lies within a volcanic cone, with a semicircular beach and fingers of shallow reef that stretch from the edge of the bay all the way to the beach. If you're driving in, arrive as early as possible, as the parking lot usually fills to capacity by 10am and cars are turned away till others leave, usually around 2pm. There is a $1 parking fee per car and a $7.50 entry fee. Children under 13 are free. You can bring your own snorkel gear or rent snorkel sets for $12 per day. There are also food concessions at the beach. Visitors are required to view a short film and presentation about the preserve and proper etiquette while snorkeling.

Halona Blowhole

Formed by molten lava tubes meeting with the ocean, the **Halona Blowhole** funnels ocean surges through a narrow opening in the rock to create a geyser that can send a plume of spray 30 feet into the air. The blowhole isn't always active; it takes a windy day, a high tide, and high surf on the windward side to get the blast really shooting high. However, if you're there on an off day, the view toward Sandy Beach is still worth the stop.

The Halona Blowhole is located along the Kalanianaole Highway, in between Sandy Beach and Makapu'u. There is a good-sized parking lot located on the cliff side of Kalanianaole Highway, and several designated viewing areas along the cliff, right above the blowhole.

★ Koko Crater Botanical Garden

Sited inside arid Koko Crater, **Koko Crater Botanical Garden** (end of Kokonani St., 808/522-7060, www1.honolulu.gov/parks/hbg/kcbg.htm, closed Christmas and New Year's Day) takes advantage of the sheltered spot for plantings of rare and endangered dryland plant species from around the world. Koko Crater is actually two craters in one, an inner and an outer crater, of which 60 acres of the basin have been cultivated. A two-mile loop trail takes you from the fragrant and magnificent hybrid plumeria grove in the inner crater to a stand of native Hawaiian *wiliwili* trees in the back of the outer crater. In between are succulents, cycads, and over 200 species of trees. The plumeria grove is in full bloom April-June. There are no facilities on-site, except for a lone portable toilet, so it's best to use those at nearby Sandy Beach Park.

Halona Blowhole

To get here from Kalanianaole Highway, turn onto Kealahou Street, then turn left onto Kokonani Street. The paved road becomes a dirt road and ends at the garden parking lot. The gardens are open from sunrise to sunset, and there are trail maps at the entrance gate.

MAKAPU'U
★ Makapu'u Point State Wayside

Makapu'u, which translates to "bulging eye" in Hawaiian, marks the rugged and dry eastern tip of O'ahu. The rough black rock is dotted with cacti and small flowering shrubs, like the native Hawaiian *'ilima,* with its cute yellow and orange blossoms. The **Makapu'u Point State Wayside** holds several areas of interest. There are two parking lots at Makapu'u. Coming from Hawai'i Kai on Kalanianaole Highway, the first parking lot offers direct access to the trail that rounds Makapu'u Point and leads to the Makapu'u Point Lighthouse. Roughly a 3-mile roundtrip walk, the wide, paved road gains elevation gradually as it circles the point from the south to face the Pacific Ocean. On a clear day you can see the islands of Moloka'i and Maui in the far distance. The hike has an added bonus of being one of the premier whale-watching venues while the humpback whales breed and rear their young in Hawaiian waters November-March. It is also cooler during this period. The shadeless hike can get rather hot in the midday summer sun. There are informational signs along the trail about humpback whale activity and behavior.

At the end of the hike are a couple lookout platforms and the **Makapu'u Point Lighthouse,** a 46-foot-tall active lighthouse constructed in 1909. The lighthouse itself is off-limits to the public, but you can get close enough to take a nice picture with the blue Pacific as the backdrop. Feel free to scamper around the rocks and explore the summit at 647 feet, but be careful as the area is scattered with sharp rocks, boulders, and cacti.

At the second parking lot, just to the north of the first, is a magnificent lookout area with views of the Waimanalo Coast, the rugged southern end of the Ko'olau Range, and two nearby offshore islands, **Manana Island and Kaohikaipu Island State Seabird Sanctuary.** The islands are home to nesting wedge-tailed shearwaters, sooty terns, brown noodies, and several other species. It is illegal to set foot on the islands. Manana Island is commonly referred to as Rabbit Island, because a rancher actually tried to raise rabbits here prior to its designation as a seabird sanctuary.

If you consider yourself an avid hiker, from the lookout you can scramble up the backside of the point to the summit, regain the trail near the lighthouse, and follow the paved path back to the lookout for a nice loop.

Sea Life Park

Sea Life Park (41-202 Kalanianaole Hwy., 808/259-2500, www.sealifeparkhawaii.com, 9:30am-5pm daily) is an aquatic park just north of Makapu'u Point on the *mauka* side of the highway. Focused on education and interaction with exotic sea life and animals, the park is known for its adventure programs that allow guests to literally swim with the dolphins. The Dolphin Royal Swim takes you on a dorsal fin ride with two dolphins and culminates with the foot push, where the dolphins push you around the pool by your feet, $254 and park admission is included. The Dolphin Swim Adventure lets you interact with the animals and take a belly ride for $185. The Dolphin Encounter is designed for families with children to interact with dolphins in shallow water for $130. Guests can also swim with sharks, sea lions, or rays. Beyond getting in the water with the sea creatures, the park also offers a Hawaiian shark tank, dolphin shows, sea lion shows, penguins, a kids' play area, turtle feeding, and an open-air aquatic theater. Adult general admission is $40, kids age 3-12 $25.

Beaches

Because of the natural geography of Maunalua Bay, there are only a few beaches along this stretch of coast. Houses have been built to the water's edge along the highway and what little beach is accessible at low tide is soon underwater as the tide rises. Fortunately, for those looking to escape the crowds of Honolulu and Waikiki beaches, Kahala beaches offer solace from the congestion.

The beaches along the Ka Iwi Coast, from Hanauma Bay to Makapu'u, are raw, natural, and often windswept, thanks to the pervasive trade winds blowing from northwest to southeast. They are also popular destinations for visitors and locals alike. Sandy Beach and Makapu'u are the main draws with dramatic coastlines, wide beaches, and powerful shore break.

KAHALA
Ka'alawai Beach

Tucked away in the affluent Ka'alawai neighborhood, **Ka'alawai Beach** is a narrow strip of sand that runs from the end of Kulamanu Place to the Diamond Head cliffs. Framed by lavish beachfront properties beyond the vegetation line, the secluded spot draws a younger crowd and is a favorite for topless sunbathers. The shoreline is predominantly rock and reef, so getting in the water can involve finding a sandy nook to take a dip. The view to the east of Black Point is picturesque, and the clear water is often choppy from the trade winds.

To access the beach, park on Kulamanu Street and walk down Kulamanu Place to the access point. Follow the sand to the right (west) and find your own spot.

There are also some great tidepools at Ka'alawai. Once through the access point, turn left instead of right and explore. Be aware that the terrain is smooth and slippery in some spots as well as sharp and jagged in others. There are no services in the vicinity.

Waialae Beach Park

From Diamond Head Road, follow Kahala Avenue east toward the Kahala Hotel & Resort. Once you cross the Waialae Stream bridge, turn right into the **Waialae Beach Park** parking lot. Complete with free parking, showers, bathrooms, picnic benches, and a shaded arbor at the beach's edge, Waialae Beach Park is usually uncrowded and a favorite destination for kitesurfers and newlyweds taking wedding pictures. It's a fine place for a barbecue or picnic. The park is actually split in two by the stream, and a beautiful narrow beach unwinds to the west. This quiet stretch of sand, dotted with shells and bits of coral, is fringed by O'ahu's most magnificent homes and mansions. The shallow waters, with a flat sand and rock bottom, are great for snorkeling and perfect for families looking to escape the Waikiki crowds. Unfortunately, the beach is right in the path of the predominant trade winds, so be prepared to tie down umbrellas and keep your light and loose belongings secure. There are several access points along Kahala Avenue from the beach park to Hunakai Street. Park along Kahala Avenue. The beach park is closed 10pm-5am daily.

AINA HAINA
Kawaiku'i Beach Park

In Aina Haina you'll find that **Kawaiku'i Beach Park** is more of a park than a beach. At low tide there is a small strip of coarse sand fronting the park, which has mature shade trees, an expansive lawn, and bathrooms and showers. The inner waters are usually murky and not exactly inviting, but this park is still favored by anglers taking advantage of the shallow bay, and by surfers, windsurfers, kiteboarders, and stand-up paddlers for the surf spots that break along the barrier reef quite a ways out. From Kalanianaole Highway heading east, turn right at Puuikena Drive (there is a traffic signal here) to access the parking lot. Parking is free.

KULI'OU'OU
Kuli'ou'ou Beach Park

Nestled up against the Paiko Lagoon Wildlife Sanctuary in the Kuli'ou'ou neighborhood, **Kuli'ou'ou Beach Park** is one of the few areas along the Maunalua Bay coastline offering a shallow bay beside a well-maintained park. The sandy seafloor of Maunalua Bay is very shallow and dotted with bits of rock, reef, and seaweed. At low tide the water is literally ankle deep, while at high tide, it's waist deep at best. In fact, take a walk all the way out to the barrier reef, roughly 0.25 mile out to sea, keeping an eye out for sea cucumbers, crabs, and fish, all within knee-deep water. The park has facilities, picnic benches, and a free parking lot. From Kalanianaole Highway, Bay Street will take you straight there. Kuli'ou'ou Beach Park is closed 10pm-5am daily.

the west end of Waialae Beach Park

HAWAI'I KAI
★ Sandy Beach Park

A few minutes past the eastern side of Koko Head in Hawai'i Kai, along rugged and dramatic coastline, you'll find the infamous **Sandy Beach Park.** Sandy Beach is notorious for its high-impact shore break and draws bodysurfers, bodyboarders, and surfers to its challenging waves. The beach is rather wide by Hawaii standards and draws a host of locals and visitors who come to watch the aqua blue waves slam onto the shore. The ocean currents here are dangerous, the sand is studded with rocks, and the surf can get big and extremely powerful, detonating onto dry sand. The shore break has caused injuries and even fatalities, so only expert swimmers should enter the water. However, when the waves are pumping, it is quite a spectacle to watch. Parking in the dirt lot can get somewhat haphazard and choked on the weekends. And while parking is free, theft is common, so take precautions.

Sandy Beach Park is just off Kalanianaole Highway. The turnoff is visible from both directions. At the beach park, a road runs the length of the beach. Wawamalu Beach Park is at the north end. There's no sand here, just jagged lava rock running into the ocean, but it is a great place to stop and stretch or have a bite while watching waves break. There are restrooms, and a long park frequented by kite-flying enthusiasts.

Ka Iwi Coast Beaches

About 0.5 mile past Sandy Beach is a traffic signal. Pull off the road to the right just past the signal and park in the hardpack sand to access the beach, which stretches in both directions. The area is great for beachcombers and shell hunters. Walk the coastline, check out the tidepools, post up with an umbrella and enjoy the scenery. The surf tends to be rough, the currents are strong, and the coastline is rocky. Swimming is not recommended.

Makapu'u Beach Park

Makapu'u Point marks the arid southeast tip of O'ahu. Just to the north of the formidable headland, you'll find **Makapuʻu Beach Park,** a beautiful crescent of white sand set against the deep-blue ocean and dry, rugged cliffs. The scenery at Makapuʻu is breathtaking, complete with Rabbit Island and Black Rock, two seabird sanctuaries, protruding from deep water just offshore. Makapuʻu is also known for its pounding shore break, alluring to bodyboarders, bodysurfers, locals and visitors. There are strong currents here, and swimming should be done with caution. Check with the lifeguard for current ocean conditions. On days when the surf is flat and the wind is light, the water becomes very clear. Snorkeling is best at the south end of the beach, where the rocks and cliff begin. There are restrooms and showers, but parking is limited, so it's best to get there early. There is a small paved parking lot for the beach park and another dirt lot that is severely rutted and only safe for four-wheel-drive vehicles. You also can park up on the highway in the designated lookout area and walk down to the beach.

On the north side of the beach park are the **Makapuʻu Tidepools.** The coast is fringed with black lava, creating some wonderful tidepools to explore. Be aware that the surf can wash up onto the tidepools, so it's best to explore the area when the surf is small to flat. To get to the tidepools, you can walk up the coast on dirt paths from Makapuʻu Beach Park and meander across the lava as far as you'd like to go, or you can park right at the tidepools. Coming from Koko Head, turn just past Sea Life Park into the oceanside parking area.

Kaupo Beach Park

Just on the other side of the Makapuʻu Tidepools you'll come to **Kaupo Beach Park**, a great beach for snorkeling, playing on the sand, fishing, or learning to surf, with all the same great views as Makapuʻu. Here, the lava recedes to offer sandy beaches among the rocks and coastal shrubs. It has character, is safe for kids, and is a favorite for local families on the weekends. It's the perfect spot to take a break from the road and have a dip or bite to eat while enjoying the scenery. As the beach arcs north toward the Makai Research Pier, there are small, gentle waves that break just off the shore. The parking lot for Kaupo Beach Park is at the same turn as the Makapuʻu Tidepools; just stay to the left. There is also roadside parking for several vehicles right in front of where the waves break, or you can park down by the research pier. There are restroom and shower facilities in the park's lot.

Sandy Beach Park

Water Sports

SURFING, BODYSURFING, AND STAND-UP PADDLING

While there are several surf breaks in this region, none of them is both easily accessible and user friendly. Maunalua Bay sees soft and gentle waves most of the year straight out from Hawai'i Kai, but the waves are 0.5 mile out to sea and generally accessed only by boat and surf tour operator. Conversely, the waves along the Ka Iwi Coast at Sandy Beach and Makapu'u are onshore but extremely dangerous and not for beginners. As a rule of thumb, stand-up paddlers and surfers (longboarders) prefer Maunalua Bay and bodysurfers prefer Sandy Beach and Makapu'u.

The outer reefs of **Maunalua Bay** hold a wealth of surf spots for expert surfers who are comfortable with very long paddles to the breaking waves and surfing over shallow and sharp coral reefs. Because the waves break so far offshore mixed with a lack of shoreline access, it's nearly impossible for the visiting surfer to distinguish between the different breaks and know which break is surfable and which waves are breaking over dry reef.

Luckily, there are a couple surf tour operators who will take visitors out in the bay to one of the gentle, soft waves, perfect for beginner to intermediate surfers. **Hawaiian Surf Adventures** (7192 Kalanianaole Hwy., 808/396-2324, http://hawaiiansurfadventure.com, 9am-4:30pm Mon.-Sat.) accesses a secluded wave in Maunalua Bay by boat, which is a gentle surf break perfect for beginner surfers. There are no crowds to contend with, just you and the instructor. Group lessons are $89; private lessons are $149. Hawaiian Surf Adventures also offers stand-up paddle lessons and tours of Maunalua Bay starting at $99 as well as outrigger canoe tours. **Island Watersports Hawaii** (377 Keahole St., 808/224-0076,

www.islandwatersportshawaii.com, 8am-5pm daily) also taps into the uncrowded waves of Maunalua Bay with two-hour group surf lessons for $99 and 1.5-hour semiprivate lessons starting at $125. If you'd rather stand-up paddle the bay, two-hour group lessons are $99 and 1.5-hour semiprivate lessons start at $125.

To the east of Koko Head is the infamous **Sandy Beach**. As a favorite of local bodyboarders and bodysurfers, the water's edge fills with heads bobbing up and down, waiting to drop into a heaving barrel, right onto the sand. If this sounds dangerous, that's because it is. Every year people are seriously injured at Sandy Beach, everything from broken limbs to broken necks, even death. The waves can get big, especially in the summer months. If you're not a strong swimmer or comfortable in the surf zone, take solace in the fact that, from the safety of the beach, it's quite amusing to watch surfers getting slammed. Check with lifeguards for current conditions. There are also two surf breaks over a sharp and shallow coral reef, Full Point and Half Point, at the north end of the beach. Local surfers dominate them both.

Much like Sandy Beach, **Makapu'u Beach Park** is known for its powerful shore break, which can get quite big with the right swell conditions. When the surf is smaller, the shore break is a bit more playful and forgiving than Sandy Beach, but you'll still leave the beach with sand in your ears. Surfboards are prohibited in the water, but people will paddle out after the lifeguards have left for the day.

Just north of Makapu'u at **Kaupo Beach Park** there is a gentle little wave called Cockroach that breaks inside the rocky cove, perfect for beginners on big boards. During the winter months, when northeast swells sneak around Rabbit Island, the surf can get big and the currents quite strong.

SNORKELING

Snorkeling in this region is dependent on the weather. The lighter the trade winds, the better the conditions will be for snorkeling. The best bet for seeing an abundance of fish is to snorkel **Hanauma Bay** or go out with a tour operator that can take you to the best place to snorkel for the conditions. If you would like to venture out on your own, try your luck along the Kahala shoreline. You'll need to come prepared with your snorkel set, as there are no outfitters in the vicinity.

★ Hanauma Bay Nature Preserve

Hanauma Bay Nature Preserve (7455 Kalanianaole Hwy., 808/396-4229, www.hanaumabaystatepark.com, 6am-7pm Wed.-Mon., $7.50 admission, $1 parking) is the first Marine Life Conservation District in the state and the most popular snorkeling site on O'ahu. Located just to the east of Koko Head on the southeast shore, the bay lies within a volcanic cone with a semicircular beach and fingers of shallow reef that stretch from the edge of the bay all the way to the beach. After decades of preservation after rampant overuse, Hanauma Bay now boasts about 400 species of fish and an abundance of green sea turtles. Keep in mind that the water close to shore can get quite crowded with snorkelers and you'll have to swim a ways out to find some territory to yourself. If you're driving in, arrive as early as possible, as the parking lot usually fills to capacity by 10am and cars are turned away till others leave, usually around 2pm. You can bring your own snorkel gear, or snorkel sets are available to rent for $20 per day. There are also food concessions at the beach. Visitors are required to view a short film and presentation about the preserve and proper etiquette while snorkeling. Admission is free for children under 13 and Hawaii residents. There is also a 3.5-hour tour available on the state-sponsored website that includes roundtrip Waikiki transportation, snorkel set and a narrated tour to the bay for $25. There is also a tram from the parking lot to the beach ($1 down, $1.25 up).

DIVING

Island Divers (377 Keahole St., 808/423-8222, www.oahuscubadiving.com, 7am-7pm daily) is a Professional Association of Diving Instructors (PADI) Five Star Dive Center that operates out of the Hawai'i Kai Shopping Center. It caters to all levels of divers and offers PADI certification courses. It has pickup

Hanauma Bay is O'ahu's premier snorkeling area.

and drop-off services available from Waikiki hotels, or you can meet at its own private dock. Two-tank boat charter dives with full gear rental start at $124. Island Divers is a complete dive center as well, with snorkel and scuba equipment available for rent and sale. **Reef Pirates Diving** (7192 Kalanianaole Hwy., 808/348-2700, www.reefpirates.com, 6:30am-5pm daily) also operates in Hawai'i Kai, but is based in the Koko Marina Shopping Center. It is a complete dive center with sales and rentals and offers PADI certification as well as dive charters. Its two-tank charters start at $125. Ride-along passengers and snorkelers cost $45. Reef Pirates also offers multiple-day dive packages and private charters.

A complete dive shop based in the Koko Marina Center, with scuba and diving sales and rentals, **Hawaii Water Sports Center** (7192 Kalanianaole Hwy. E110, 808/395-3773, http://hawaiiwatersportscenter.com, 8:30am-5pm daily) offers 3.5-hour scuba-diving sessions from a dive boat one mile offshore in Maunalua Bay for $79. The boat leaves at 9am every day except Sunday and participants must be at least 10 years old. Call ahead to make reservations.

China Walls

Maunalua Bay, which stretches from Kahala to Koko Head along the southeastern shore, has a wealth of dive sites and several operators that specifically service this region, with charters leaving from the Hawai'i Kai Marina. Special to the area is a dive site known as **China Walls.** This vertical wall dropping off the south side of Koko Head and reaching down to depths of 75 feet is made up of

caves and ledges, and attracts sharks, turtles, jacks, rays, eels, and the endangered Hawaiian monk seal. Whale songs can be heard in the area during the winter months. China Walls is located at the southernmost tip of Koko Head, the headland that frames the eastern side of Maunalua Bay.

Maunalua Bay is home to airplane- and shipwrecks, like the WWII-era Corsair plane, a barge, and a marine landing craft known as an LST. There are also caves, reefs, and overhangs where you'll find turtles, Galapagos sharks, whitetip reef sharks, eels, countless tropical fish, and rare black coral.

Diving in the Maunalua Bay is dependent on ocean and weather conditions, and high winds or high surf can cause diving conditions to deteriorate.

FISHING

The deep waters off the southeast coast are a draw for sport anglers. The dark-blue deep is home to the bigger fish like wahoo, yellowfin tuna, and marlin. **Island Watersports Hawaii** (377 Keahole St., 808/224-0076, www.islandwatersportshawaii.com, 8am-5pm daily) is the only fishing charter operating out of the Hawai'i Kai Marina. Depending on ocean and weather conditions, it trolls for big game fish or fishes the ledges off of Maunalua Bay. The charter is $300 per hour, with a four-hour minimum and a six-passenger maximum. Fishing gear and a captain are included in the price, and you can keep some of your catch, something a lot of charters don't offer. Call the office, located in the Hawai'i Kai Shopping Center, to inquire about discounted rates.

Hiking and Biking

Kuli'ou'ou

Even though the southeast corner of O'ahu is one of the drier parts of the island, receiving less than 20 inches of rain annually, once you get off the coast and up into the southern reaches of the Ko'olau Range, the ecosystem changes dramatically. The **Kuli'ou'ou Ridge and Valley Trails** are a great example of this phenomenon. An excellent trek for any level of hiker, the mostly shaded Kuli'ou'ou Ridge trail follows Kuli'ou'ou Stream up Kuli'ou'ou Valley, traverses some switchbacks to the ridgeline, and terminates at a summit of 2,028 feet. With stunning views from Waimanalo and the windward coast all the way to Diamond Head, the five-mile round-trip hike passes through ironwood trees and Cook pines, and native *'ohi'a* and *lama* forests. At about the halfway point there are two covered picnic tables to rest at if you've gone far enough. If you prefer, at a signed junction, stay on the Kuli'ou'ou Valley trail, which passes a small pool and waterfall and terminates at a second waterfall, about two miles round-trip.

To get there from Kalanianaole Highway, turn *mauka* onto Kuli'ou'ou Road and find your way to the very back of the neighborhood, at the back of the valley. There is neighborhood street parking in the cul-de-sac. Take the one-lane paved road down to the stream and the trailhead.

Just to the west of Kuli'ou'ou Beach Park, the **Paiko Lagoon Wildlife Sanctuary** was established in 1981 to protect native Hawaiian waterbirds, migratory species, and their habitat. The sanctuary is great for a nice walk that includes **bird-watching.** Hawaiian stilts, plovers, ducks, and other fowl grace the shallow lagoon, which is naturally separated from Maunalua Bay by a small strip of earth complete with plants and trees. It is illegal to remove anything from the area. To get there from Kalanianaole Highway, turn onto Bay Street, which ends at the beach parking lot. The lagoon is directly to the west.

Hawai'i Kai

For a great cardio workout and 360-degree views of the southeast shore, the **Koko Crater**

only 1,048 stairs to the top of Koko Crater

Trail is a daunting 1,048 steps up the south side of Koko Crater. The stairs, actually railroad ties, follow the track of an old World War II military tramway that took supplies to the top of Koko Crater more than 1,000 feet to the summit. At the top you'll find several cement

military installations and amazing views all around. From Kalanianaole Highway, turn *mauka* (to the mountain side) onto Koko Head Park Road and park in the Koko Head District Park parking lot. It's about a 0.25-mile walk to the base of the stairs.

Adventure Sports

★ HAWAI'I KAI

Hawai'i Kai Marina and Maunalua Bay are home to all the aquatic thrill rides available in this region for adventure seekers. Wakeboard, water ski, and ride a Bumper Tube and Banana Boat at high speeds in the marina, or Jet Ski, parasail, and drive a sub scooter in the bay. A more recent addition to the lineup is Jetlev flight, using a controlled, water-propelled jet pack that can send you soaring 30 feet into the air.

SeaBreeze Watersports (377 Keahole St., #E-103, 808/396-0100, opens 8:30am daily), based in the Hawai'i Kai Shopping Center, has a wide range of activities. Bumper Tubes and Banana Boat rides are $52 per person, Jet Ski rentals are $55 per person for a two-seater and $80 for a single rider. Jet Ski rates are based on half-hour rides. Parasail flights are $60 per person for a 7-10-minute ride, with two people sailing at a time, and SeaBreeze is the only outfitter offering the Jetlev flight, starting at $199 for 15 minutes. It also offers snorkeling, scuba, speed sailing, and surfing lessons and has discounts for multiple-activity reservations.

Island Watersports Hawaii (377 Keahole St., 808/224-0076, www.islandwatersportshawaii.com, 8am-5pm daily), also based in the Hawai'i Kai Shopping Center, has the sub scooter, an electric submersible scooter that allows you to explore underwater without diving or scuba gear; $99 for a 20-minute ride. It has 1.5-hour whale-watching cruises November-May for $99 for adults, $79 kids 3-12 and 2-hour turtle-watching and 1.5-hour sunset cruises also for $99 per adult and

$79 per child. In addition, it offers snorkeling, scuba, and fishing adventure packages.

Based in the Koko Marina Shopping Center, behind Kona Brewing Company, **Hawaii Water Sports Center** (7192 Kalanianaole Hwy., 808/395-3773, http://hawaiiwatersportscenter.com, 8:30am-5pm daily) is another operator offering a slew of activities. Bumper tube and Banana Boat rides run $39 per person, wakeboarding and waterskiing runs $59 per person, and parasailing is $60 per person and the company flies side-by-side riders. Jet Skis are also available for $59 per person for two riders and $89 for a single-person craft. The center also offers scuba and snorkeling packages and multiple activity discounts.

HANG GLIDING

The pervasive, fresh trade winds blowing up against the Ko'olau Range, combined with the splendid beauty of clear, tropical waters and verdant cliffs, creates the perfect amphitheater for hang gliding and paragliding. Makapu'u is the premier ridge-soaring site, with five launch zones and one landing zone on the beach. Pilots also fly in the Kahana area. These are not recreational activities where you can merely rent a hang glider and jump off a cliff, but regulated endeavors for trained pilots, who must register with one of the accredited associations on O'ahu to fly from specific sites.

Visiting paragliding pilots who have their own gear should contact the **Hawaii Paragliding Association** (53-040 Pokiwai Pl., www.windlines.net). Contact any board member, whose information is listed on the website, to become a member and get in the air. Visiting hang gliding pilots with gear need to contact the **Hawaiian Hang Gliding Association** (45-015 Likeke Pl., http://files.windlines.net/hha/index.htm). Contact information is on the site about becoming a member and flying windward skies.

Food

KAHALA
Quick Bites

Puka's (4211 Waialae Ave., Ste. 2000, 808/738-0820, www.wholefoodsmarket.com/service/pukas-beerwinepupus, noon-9pm Mon.-Fri., 10am-9pm Sat.-Sun., $8-17), a small pub and restaurant inside Whole Foods Market, offers 20 craft beers on tap, wine, and a small, but delicious selection of burgers, pizza and other fresh takes on bar food. It offers beer flights, which pair nicely with the IPA-battered fish-and-chips or the fried-green-tomato BLT.

Japanese

★ Located inside Kahala Mall by the movie theater, **Goma Tei** (4211 Waialae Ave., G07, 808/732-9188, www.gomatei.com, 11am-9:30pm Mon.-Thurs., 11am-10pm Fri.-Sat., 11am-9pm Sun., $11-15) has some of the best ramen on the island. This busy, popular restaurant offers flavorful broths, fresh vegetables, soft noodles, rich cuts of meat, and crispy gyoza, which are worth any wait.

Steak and Seafood

Plumeria Beach House (5000 Kahala Ave., 808/739-8760, www.kahalaresort.com, 6:30am-10pm daily, $26-45), an open-air seaside restaurant inside the Kahala Hotel & Resort, serves breakfast, lunch, and dinner and has entrée and buffet options. The small menu selection for lunch and dinner means each dish is carefully crafted to capture the best of Hawaii regional and Pacific Rim cuisine. This comfortable island home setting takes advantage of beautiful ocean views. The Plumeria Beach House is best known for its breakfast buffet, but it also has many other à la carte choices as well.

Italian

Assaggio Bistro (4346 Waialae Ave., 808/732-1011, 11:30am-2:30pm and 5pm-9:30pm Sun.-Thurs., 5pm-10pm Fri.-Sat., $16-36) has a huge menu of classic Italian dishes. Its portions come in two sizes, small and large, with the small portion being more than enough for a complete meal. Each main dish has the choice of pasta, potatoes, rice, or vegetables for the side. Reservations are recommended. To get to Assaggio from Hawai'i Kai, take the Waialae Avenue off-ramp and turn right into the parking lot from the ramp. From Waialae Avenue eastbound, turn left onto Kilauea Avenue and then make an immediate right into the parking lot.

Mediterranean

Located on the corner of Kilauea Avenue and Pahoa Avenue is a popular BYOB called the **Olive Tree Café** (4614 Kilauea Ave., Ste. 107, 808/737-0303, 5pm-10pm daily, $11-15). Offering Mediterranean and Greek fare, the menu has plenty of vegetarian as well as meat options. The environment is warm, friendly, and casual, with both indoor and outdoor seating. The café has open seating and there is no wait service. It is a popular joint, so it's best to arrive either early or late to avoid a long wait. Luckily, there is a wine shop just next door.

AINA HAINA
Quick Bites

The small community of Aina Haina has a strip mall, the **Aina Haina Shopping**

Center (820-850 W. Hind Dr.), along Kalanianaole Highway that has a complete sampling of services and a handful of eateries. **Jack's Restaurant** (808/373-4034, 6:30am-2pm daily, $1-13) serves biscuits and gravy, eggs, omelets, and other seafood breakfast and lunch dishes. Simple and good, the eggs with corned beef hash are a local favorite.

Sweets and Treats
★ **Uncle Clay's House of Pure Aloha** (808/373-5111, www.houseofpurealoha.com, 11am-6pm Mon.-Thurs., 10:30am-8pm Fri.-Sun., $4-9) indulges in the local favorite, shave ice. Rising above the competition, with handmade syrups actually produced from locally sourced ingredients and friendly, family-style service, Uncle Clay's takes shave ice to a new culinary level. The small shop also has healthy grab-bag snacks for sale.

NIU VALLEY
Steak and Seafood
The Niu Valley Shopping Center in Niu Valley has one noteworthy tenant on the food front, **Le Bistro** (5730 Kalanianaole Hwy., 808/373-7990, 5pm-9pm Wed.-Mon., $25-40). This contemporary French restaurant, casual yet elegant, is a fixture in the Honolulu dining scene. The chef recommends his legendary short ribs, a staple on the menu since the restaurant opened over a decade ago, and the beef quartet, a sampler entrée chosen by the chef himself. Robust soups, stews, and salads round out the menu.

HAWAI'I KAI
Quick Bites
The Shack (377 Keahole St., 808/396-1919, 11am-2am daily, $7-24) is the quintessential pub and sports bar in the Hawai'i Kai area. Being dark, a bit musty, having dark wood furniture, darts, billiards, TVs all around, classic bar food, including ribs, and interesting, even curious, decorations makes this bar come alive. Not to mention, it's located right on the water in the Hawai'i Kai Shopping Center, with outside seating as well. And the

pau hana (happy hour) and daily specials will make you extra happy.

Steak and Seafood
At the water's edge in the Koko Marina Center in Hawai'i Kai is the ★ **Kona Brewing Co.** (7192 Kalanianaole Hwy., 808/396-5662, http://konabrewingco.com, 11am-10pm daily, $12-28), a local brewpub serving fresh steak and seafood, all with a twist—its signature brew is incorporated in some way into most of the recipes. It has a huge pizza menu, specialty beers on tap you can't find in the stores, and brews to go. Kona also has a great weekday happy hour 3pm-6pm: half off draft beers and select appetizer specials.

For fine dining in Hawai'i Kai, ★ **Roy's** (6600 Kalanianaole Hwy., 808/396-7697, 5pm-10pm Mon.-Fri., 5pm-10pm Sat.-Sun., $15-45) is a must. It serves signature Hawaiian fusion cuisine with exemplary service and attention to detail, and its sushi creations pair wonderfully with the entrées. It also has indoor and lanai bar seating that is first-come, first-served, accompanied by soft, live music, a much more casual option than the main, second floor dining room with beautiful views of Maunalua Bay.

Health Food and Cafés
Moena Café (7192 Kalanianaole Hwy., #D-101, 808/888-7716, www.moenacafe.com, 6:30am-3pm daily, $9-18) is a local favorite, serving breakfast and lunch. Located in the Koko Marina Center across from the theater, the small dining room is clean and bright. It offers delicious fruit bowls, Panini sandwiches, salads, pancakes, eggs Benedict, and a mean short rib loco moco. There are only a handful of tables and its very popular, so be prepared for a wait. It also uses local ingredients throughout the menu.

Pa'ina Café (7192 Kalanianaole Hwy., #E-123A, 808/356-2829, www.painacafe.com, 11am-7:30pm Sun.-Thurs., 11am-8pm Fri.-Sat., $7-12) is a small, take-out café in the Koko Marina Center. It offers a variety of fresh and delicious poke bowls, salads, and a few tasty sandwiches. If you're in the mood for poke, this is the place in Hawai'i Kai. There is plenty of outdoor seating around the marina to enjoy your meal.

Sweets and Treats

After lunch or dinner, **Bubbies** (7192 Kalanianaole Hwy., #D-103 808/396-8722, http://bubbiesicecream.com, 10am-11pm daily, $3-8) is a must. The shop is reminiscent of an old-school ice-cream parlor and has been making ice cream and desserts in Hawai'i for over 30 years. It specializes in traditional, creamy ice cream, sorbet, and mochi ice cream. If you're visiting for an event, it's a great place to pick up a homemade ice-cream cake.

MAKAPU'U
Quick Bites

Inside Sea Life Park you'll find **Pink's Hot Dogs** (41-202 Kalanianaole Hwy., 808/259-7933, 10am-3:30pm daily, $4-9). Yes, it's true. The Hollywood legend has opened a signature location on O'ahu. You'll find the same burgers and hot dogs piled high with all manner of toppings. A quirky location, you have to pay the parking attendant a small fee to park for one hour and then you'll be reimbursed when you leave with proof of receipt from Pink's.

Kailua and Windward

Known for its ample rainfall and lush, dramatic corduroy cliffs, the windward side of O'ahu, the eastern shore of the island, spans the entire length of the Ko'olau Mountain Range.

Kamehameha Highway, which winds along the shoreline, provides excellent opportunities to pull off the highway and find a nook of beach to enjoy. Windward towns, save for Kailua and Kane'ohe, are primarily residential and historically rooted in agriculture and aquaculture: *kalo lo'i* (taro), banana plantations, papaya, and fishponds. A drive up the windward coast is a trip back in time, with weathered wooden fruit stands offering family farm goods. It's a leisurely drive that should be enjoyed at every turn in the road.

The vegetation on the windward side of O'ahu is owed in large part, to the wet weather. The predominant trade winds blow out of the northeast and push air heavy with moisture up against the Ko'olau Range. As the warm, humid air rises, it cools, condenses, and forms clouds, which become saturated and dump their payload, freshwater raindrops, down on the coast and the mountains.

In addition to the stunning landscape,

Kailua and Kane'ohe have developed into major population centers and desirable destinations, each with its own draw. Kailua is full of hip shops, restaurants, and some of the best fine-white-sand beaches on O'ahu. It's also known for kitesurfing and kayaking, with several islets just offshore (two of which are only accessible via kayak). Kane'ohe town definitely caters to locals, with its dining options and shopping services, but there are more than enough reasons for a visit to the Ho'omaluhia Botanical Garden and the famous Kane'ohe Bay Sandbar, perfect for a half-day kayaking adventure.

Here, on the windward side, other than the ranch tours at Kualoa Ranch and the Polynesian Cultural Center, everything is centered around the ocean. Whether you're snorkeling, fishing, stand-up paddling, or walking along a deserted stretch of sand, the beaches and the scenery are the main attractions. If you see a nice spot along your drive and feel

Previous: Kailua Beach Park; Kane'ohe Bay. **Above:** Bird-watching on the edge of the Kawainui Marsh.

Highlights

★ **Ho'omaluhia Botanical Garden:** Backed right up to the Ko'olau Mountains, this botanical garden is known for its lake, canopy trees, and myriad species of palms from around the world. The bird-watching is phenomenal (page 140).

★ **La'ie Point State Wayside:** A dramatic offshore, wave-battered sea arch sits just off a rugged point jutting sharply out into the Pacific. It's a great place to pull up and enjoy a quiet lunch or fish from the rocks. There's a cliff-jumping spot on the south side—if you dare (page 142).

★ **Waimanalo Beach Park:** Empty white-sand beach, ironwood trees, and calm water: Waimanalo has everything you need (page 143).

★ **Kailua Beach Park:** Kailua Beach Park is the destination for ocean activities like swimming, stand-up paddling, kayaking, fishing, kiteboarding, and sailboarding (page 144).

★ **Kahana Bay Beach Park:** Where the valley opens to the ocean, you'll find this perfectly moon-shaped beach of fine, soft sand. The water is shallow and calm, and towering trees shade the deep-set bay. Remnants of an ancient Hawaiian fishpond still stand on the south side of the bay (page 147).

★ **Mokulua Islands:** Don't miss paddling out to the Mokulua Islands. When you reach an islet, turn around and look back to the mainland for an amazing view of the Ko'olaus rising up behind the beach (page 151).

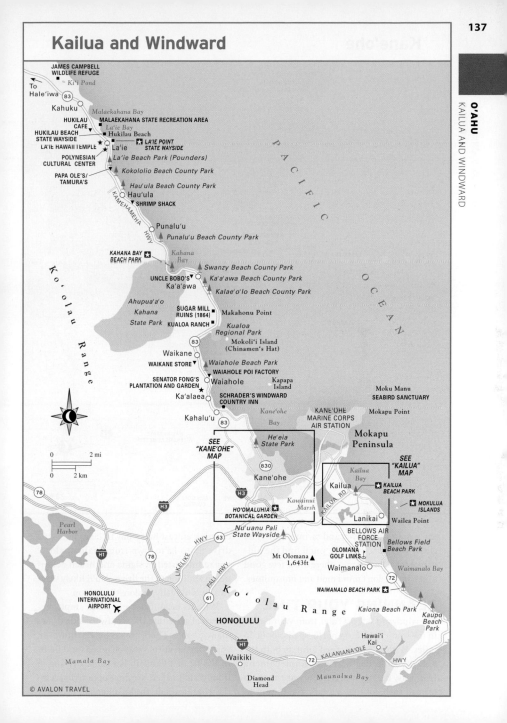

Kailua and Windward

JAMES CAMPBELL
WILDLIFE REFUGE
Ki'i Pond
To
Hale'iwa 83
Kahuku
Malaekahana Bay
HUKILAU
CAFE
MALAEKAHANA STATE RECREATION AREA
La'ie Bay
HUKILAU BEACH
STATE WAYSIDE
Hukilau Beach
LA'IE HAWAII TEMPLE
LA'IE POINT
STATE WAYSIDE
La'ie
POLYNESIAN
CULTURAL CENTER
La'ie Beach Park (Pounders)
PAPA OLE'S/
TAMURA'S
Kokololio Beach County Park
Hau'ula Beach County Park
Hau'ula
KAMEHAMEHA HWY
SHRIMP SHACK

PACIFIC

Punalu'u
Punalu'u Beach County Park

KAHANA BAY
BEACH PARK
Kahana
Bay
Swanzy Beach County Park
UNCLE BOBO'S
Ka'a'awa Beach County Park
Ka'a'awa
Kalae'o'lo Beach County Park

Ahupua'a'o
Kahana
State Park
SUGAR MILL
RUINS (1864)
KUALOA RANCH
Makahonu Point
Kualoa
Regional Park
Mokoli'i Island
(Chinamen's Hat)
83
Waikane
WAIKANE STORE
Waiahole Beach Park
WAIAHOLE POI FACTORY
SENATOR FONG'S
PLANTATION AND GARDEN
Waiahole
Kapapa
Island
Ka'alaea
SCHRADER'S WINDWARD
COUNTRY INN
Kahalu'u
83
Kane'ohe
Bay

OCEAN

Moku Manu
SEABIRD SANCTUARY
KANE'OHE
MARINE CORPS
AIR STATION
Mokapu Point
Mokapu
Peninsula

Ko'olau Range

SEE
"KANE'OHE"
MAP
He'eia
State Park

SEE
"KAILUA"
MAP
Kailua
Bay

0   2 mi
0   2 km

78
830
Kane'ohe
H3
H3
HO'OMALUHIA
BOTANICAL GARDEN
Kawainui
Marsh
Nu'uanu Pali
State Wayside
KAILUA RD
Kailua
KAILUA
BEACH PARK
MOKULUA
ISLANDS
Lanikai
Wailea Point

Pearl
Harbor
H1
78
LIKELIKE HWY
PALI HWY
63
BELLOWS AIR
FORCE
STATION
OLOMANA
GOLF LINKS
Bellows Field
Beach Park
Mt Olomana
1,643ft
Waimanalo
72
Waimanalo Bay

HONOLULU
INTERNATIONAL
AIRPORT
61
Ko'olau Range
WAIMANALO BEACH PARK
Kaiona Beach Park
Kaupo
Beach
Park

HONOLULU

Mamala Bay
H1
Waikiki
72
Hawai'i
Kai
KALANIANA'OLE
HWY
Diamond
Head
Maunalua Bay

© AVALON TRAVEL

Kane'ohe

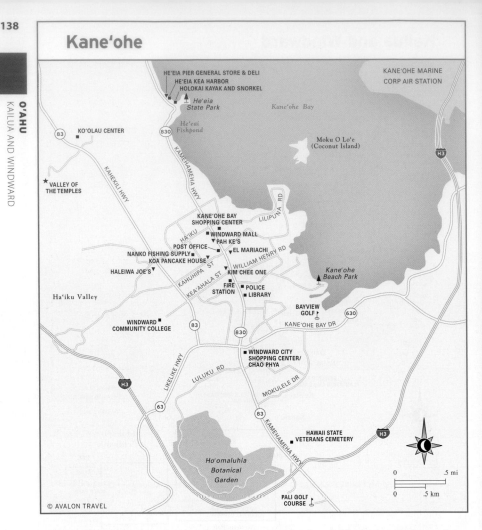

KANE'OHE MARINE
CORP AIR STATION

HE'EIA PIER GENERAL STORE & DELI
HE'EIA KEA HARBOR
HOLOKAI KAYAK AND SNORKEL

He'eia
State Park

Kane'ohe Bay

KO'OLAU CENTER

He'eai
Fishpond

Moku O Lo'e
(Coconut Island)

VALLEY OF
THE TEMPLES

KANE'OHE BAY
SHOPPING CENTER

LILIPUNA RD

WINDWARD MALL
PAH KE'S
POST OFFICE   EL MARIACHI
NANKO FISHING SUPPLY
KOA PANCAKE HOUSE
HALEIWA JOE'S   KIM CHEE ONE

Kane'ohe
Beach Park

Ha'iku Valley

FIRE
STATION   POLICE
LIBRARY

WINDWARD
COMMUNITY COLLEGE

BAYVIEW
GOLF

KANE'OHE BAY DR

WINDWARD CITY
SHOPPING CENTER/
CHAO PHYA

LULUKU RD

MOKULELE DR

KAMEHAMEHA HWY

HAWAII STATE
VETERANS CEMETERY

0   .5 mi

0   .5 km

Ho'omaluhia
Botanical
Garden

PALI GOLF
COURSE

© AVALON TRAVEL

PLANNING YOUR TIME

the need to pull over and swim, do it! The closer you look, the more you'll find the hidden gems. Don't forget, there are a few good hikes, if you don't mind mud and mosquitoes.

The windward side of O'ahu, from Waimanalo in the south to La'ie up north, spans about 35 miles. With a 35 mph speed limit on both the Kalanianaole Highway and Kamehameha Highway, it's not a drive you want to rush (or can rush, for that matter). You'll want to

earmark at least half a day to take the scenic drive up to La'ie town from Waimanalo. If you're interested in sights and beach activities in addition to the drive, you'll likely want two days to really explore this region.

With its beautiful scenery and ample recreational activities, the windward side draws many people. There are no hotels; however, you'll find plenty of vacation rentals and B&Bs in Kailua and Lanikai. For those driving in from Waikiki, there are three options to access the windward side: the Kalanianaole Highway

Your Best Day in Windward

The windward region is a mix of suburban and rural communities and covers a lot of coastline. Framed by the Pacific Ocean and the Ko'olau mountain range, the coastline is strikingly diverse and beautiful. To experience the area to its fullest, a rental car is a must to cover the distance and have the flexibility for a change of plans if the weather dictates.

- Grab breakfast and a coffee, then from Waikiki take the Likelike Highway to Kane'ohe and start your morning with a walk through **Ho'omaluhia Botanical Garden.** Or, continue on to **Kualoa Ranch** and take a tour of the ranch and the surrounding area.

- Head back south toward Kailua. For lunch, head into Waimanalo and try out **'Ai Love Nalo,** for a healthy lunch, or make your way into Kailua Town and pick up a sandwich at **Kalapawai Market.** Head to **Kailua Beach Park** or **Lanikai** for a beach day. Lanikai has beautiful views of the Mokulua Islands, and Kailua Beach is one of the most beautiful white-sand beaches on O'ahu.

- After taking in all that beauty from the beach, you'll want to get in the water and cruise around. The best way to do that is to rent a kayak. Kailua town is the hub for kayak rentals. Either stick around in Kailua and paddle to **Flat Island** and the **Mokulua Islands,** or put the kayak on the roof and go exploring. Other great areas for kayaking are **Kane'ohe Bay, Kualoa Beach Park,** and **Kahana Bay.**

- After all that outdoor activity, you'll be in the mood for a delicious meal. Try **Buzz's,** just across the street from Kailua Beach Park, for a great steak. For a more relaxed atmosphere and a local take on Pan-Latin fare, try **Cactus** in Kailua.

RAINY-DAY ALTERNATIVE

If it's raining, go shopping. The heart of **Kailua Town** is chock-full of **boutiques and shops,** all within walking distance of each other.

along the southeast shore, the Pali Highway, and the Likelike Highway. The Kalanianaole Highway will deliver you into Waimanalo, the Pali Highway directly accesses Kailua, and the Likelike Highway is a straight shot to Kane'ohe. A rental car will provide the greatest flexibility for getting around, but there are several bus routes that access the region too. Kailua town is bike friendly and there are many options for bike rentals.

Kailua is definitely the biggest draw for the area. The town offers upscale shopping and dining and the beaches are amazing: calm, clean water, white sand, and beautiful scenery. Kailua could be a day trip in itself, but plan for at least half a day here if you're driving in. It's a great locale for a nice dinner at the end of a busy day. Kailua is densely populated and gets a large amount of daily visitor traffic, so the town frequently sees heavy traffic and

the main beach parks get very crowded on the weekends and beautiful, sunny days.

Waimanalo is a great stop for a beach day and lunch, and the beaches north of Kane'ohe Bay are a getaway from the bustle of O'ahu's big towns. In these regions, you'll find small, mom-and-pop eateries, gas stations, and convenience stores. The major sights here are the Polynesian Cultural Center in La'ie and Kualoa Ranch, a few miles north of Kane'ohe. Since there are no beaches in Kane'ohe and it generally serves a local and military population, you'll most likely find yourself passing through Kane'ohe unless you'd like to hike the botanical garden or kayak out to the sandbars in the bay.

The weather changes fast on the windward side. A typical day might start out with sun in the morning, then clouds by midday, and finally heavy showers by the afternoon. Still, typical rain showers are often fleeting, localized events. Just because a shower is passing by doesn't mean you need to pack up the beach gear for the day. The best thing to do if you're planning a beach day on the windward side is to hope for the best and prepare for the worst. At least it's still warm when it rains.

ORIENTATION

The Makapu'u headland is the easternmost tip of the island. To the immediate north is Waimanalo, an agricultural town with a few food trucks, plate-lunch eateries, and white-sand beaches lined by tall wispy ironwood trees. Waimanalo is known for its local farms, ranches, and beach camping. The Kalanianaole Highway runs through Waimanalo to Kailua, where it intersects the Pali Highway.

To the north of Waimanalo is Kailua. Kailua offers boutique shopping and upscale restaurants, while the beaches are some of the prettiest on the island—fine white sand stretching for miles along the coast. The beaches are generally windy and known for kitesurfing and windsurfing. To the immediate south of Kailua is the quaint Lanikai

neighborhood, where the Mokulua Islands sit right offshore.

Complete with a mall and ample fast food, Kane'ohe is one of the larger and more congested towns on the windward coast. It's to the north of Kailua. Because of the bay there are no beaches, but the sheltered waters offer great potential for kayaking in the bay and out to the Kane'ohe Bay Sandbar. Fishing is also the draw here.

Once you travel past the northern neighborhoods of Kane'ohe, Kamehameha Highway hugs the coast from one beach town to the next. Most are quite small—maybe with just a food truck and a convenience store—and others are strictly residential. But they all have beautiful beaches in common. Kualoa Regional Park and Kualoa Ranch are points of interest in the Kualoa area. Ka'a'awa leads to Kahana Bay, with the remnants of an ancient Hawaiian fishpond and hiking in the valley. Farther north is Punalu'u, then Hau'ula, and finally La'ie, a town defined by its connection to the Church of Jesus Christ of Latter-day Saints and the home of the Polynesian Cultural Center, which is under the church's wing.

Sights

KAILUA
Ulupo Heiau State Historic Site

The massive stone platform of the **Ulupo Heiau State Historic Site** was supposedly built by the legendary *menehune* and shows remarkable skill with stone, measuring 140 feet wide by 180 feet long by 30 feet high at its tallest edge, although the stepped front wall has partially collapsed under a rockfall. The *heiau* overlooks Kawainui Marsh, and below the *heiau,* you can see traditional *kalo lo'i,* taro growing in small ponds. Ulupo Heiau was one of three *heiau* that once overlooked the former fishpond. The other two, located on the west side of the marsh, are Pahukini and Holomakani Heiau. Some restoration has

been done to Pahukini Heiau, but both remain largely untouched and inaccessible.

To get to Ulupo Heiau as you approach Kailua on the Pali Highway, turn left at the Castle Medical Center onto Uluoa Street, following it one block to Manu Aloha Street, where you turn right. Turn right again onto Manu O'o and park in the Windward YMCA parking lot. The *heiau* is directly behind the YMCA building.

KANE'OHE
★ Ho'omaluhia Botanical Garden

Ho'omaluhia Botanical Garden (45-680 Luluku Rd., 808/233-7323, www1.honolulu. gov/parks/hbg/hmbg.htm, 9am-4pm daily, closed Christmas and New Year's Day) is a botanical gem nestled at the base of the Koʻolau Range. With 400 acres of geographically organized gardens—covering the Philippines, Hawaii, Africa, Sri Lanka, India, Polynesia, Melanesia, Malaysia, and Tropical America—and a network of trails interconnecting the plantings, one could spend an entire day in the garden. The visitors center is staffed with extremely knowledgeable docents who can help identify **birds** and interesting plants in flower during your visit. You can also grab a trail map there. A paved road links all the plantings and there are separate parking lots for each, so you can pick and choose where you'd like to spend your time. Drive slowly on the road, as the path is a lovely, popular walk for residents and garden guests. Hoʻomaluhia also boasts its own lake, Lake Waimaluhia. Catch-and-release fishing is permitted on the weekends 10am-2pm. The garden is serene, quiet, lush, and often wet, so be prepared for the passing shower, mud, and mosquitoes. Rustic camping is also permitted from Friday afternoon till Monday morning. Check in at the visitors center for a pass. The garden is located in a residential area on Luluku Road, which you can access from both Kamehameha Highway and the Likelike Highway.

Coconut Island

Coconut Island (808/235-9302, http://coconutislandnews.blogspot.com), tucked away deep in Kaneʻohe Bay, literally had its 15 seconds of fame as part of the opening reel of scenic shots for the 1960s TV sitcom hit *Gilligan's Island*. But the island has a much more eclectic and interesting history than just appearing on television. Once fertile fishing grounds belonging to Kamehameha I and Bernice Pauahi Bishop, the island was purchased in the 1930s and expanded by a young heir to the Fleischmann's Yeast company. He transformed it into a zoo and aquarium, as well as a tuna-fish packing plant, the remnants of which are still visible on the island. The island changed hands several more times over the decades and today is the Hawaiʻi Institute of Marine Biology and one of the seminal locations for marine research on Oʻahu. The education outreach arm of the institute offers tours once or twice a month, depending on docent availability, for a nominal fee based on the number of people in your party. Call for a reservation or visit the blog for more information.

If you wish to simply view the island from shore, you can get a great view of the island from the elevated vantage of Lilipuna Road

Coconut Island

as it hugs the coastline. There is no public parking on Lilipuna for the institute, but you can find street parking a little way south of the dock and walk back to the point to snap some pictures. Be careful walking along the road, as there is no shoulder or designated pedestrian area. Turn onto Lilipuna Road from Kamehameha Highway at the north end of Kane'ohe town, by the Windward Mall.

KUALOA TO LA'IE

Chinaman's Hat

Just offshore from **Kualoa Regional Beach Park** (49-479 Kamehameha Hwy.) is the curious islet known as **Chinaman's Hat.** Mokoli'i Island is its Hawaiian name. The island is a quick kayak trip from the beach and has a tiny private alcove of sand on the back side. You can hike, or rather scramble, up to its 213-foot summit.

Kualoa Ranch

Kualoa Ranch (49-560 Kamehameha Hwy., 808/237-7321, www.kualoa.com, 7:30am-6pm daily) is both a 4,000-acre working cattle ranch, activity, and cultural center and the site for many of the Hollywood blockbuster movies filmed in Hawai'I (*Jurassic Park*, *Godzilla*, and *50 First Dates*, to name a few). It offers historical and cultural tours like its Movie Sites and Ranch Tour, Jungle Expeditions Tour, Ancient Fishing Grounds, and Tropical Garden Tour, or Kahiko Hula

Lessons starting at $24 adult, $15 children. For adventure tours, it provides one- and two-hour ATV or horseback packages, starting at $69. It also has venues for weddings and corporate events and even has tours that include lunch or dinner. Cultural/historic tour package tours start at $59, adventure tour packages start at $99.

★ La'ie Point State Wayside

The **La'ie Point State Wayside** is a hidden marvel, the perfect place to pull up to the edge of the rugged point, relax, have a snack, and watch waves crash against a small **seabird sanctuary** just offshore, a little island noteworthy for its sea arch. There are trashcans, but no services in the area. It is also a popular spot for cliff jumping. On the south face of the cliff is a small area where jumpers plunge roughly 30 feet to the warm water below. There is a nook in the cliff to climb out of the water and up an extremely sharp and rocky gorge to the top of the cliff. It's best to watch a few others jump and get back up before you try. There are no lifeguards, so you're on your own, quite far from a sandy beach.

Tucked away at the back of a neighborhood and out of view from the highway, turn off of Kamehameha Highway onto Anemoku Street, then hang a right onto Naupaka Street and follow it to the end of the point. Anemoku Street is across the highway from the La'ie Village Center.

Beaches

The **beaches** along O'ahu's windward coast, from Waimanalo to La'ie, are raw, natural, and often windswept, thanks to the pervasive trade winds blowing from northwest to southeast. The different ribbons of sand tend to be bastions of solitude, where you can pull off the highway and find a quiet nook under *naupaka* and palm trees. A barrier reef stretching the length of the windward coast keeps waves at most beaches to a minimum. You'll find driftwood, rocks, fine white sand, shells, and spectacular views of the lush Ko'olau Mountains from the water's edge. Beachgoers should be prepared for passing showers, as the trade winds also bring rain. Kailua beaches, especially at the two main beach parks, are usually the most crowded in the area.

Disappearing Sands

It's no secret: O'ahu's beaches are its top attractions and best commodities, for recreational, social, and cultural reasons. But in some locales where urban development has marched right up to the high-tide mark, the beaches are in serious danger of disappearing, if they're not gone already. There are natural processes in Hawaii, like large swell events, seasonal currents, and storms with heavy rainfall, that move sand up and down the beach, offshore, and then back again. This natural and transient process is called coastal erosion and has been going on for centuries and will continue to shape the beaches until the island erodes back into the Pacific altogether.

In the meantime, recent human alteration of the shoreline has played a detrimental leading role in the disappearance of sand and entire beaches altogether. On O'ahu, when the ocean shoreline encroaches within 20 feet of a structure, property owners can be granted a variance that allows them to build a seawall to protect the property. Once the natural beach dune system is stripped away and replaced with a seawall, the beach has no way to store or replenish sand for periods of natural coastal erosion, leading to a permanent state of beach erosion. You'll find this phenomenon in Kahala, Lanikai, and on other stretches of beach along the windward coast where dwellings have been built right up to sand. Where the shoreline is armored, the beaches have washed away.

WAIMANALO
Kaiona Beach Park

About a mile north of the research pier on Kalanianaole Highway in Waimanalo is a small grassy park with restrooms and showers and a narrow but beautiful beach. **Kaiona Beach Park** is a favorite area for local families, with shallow, clean, and clear water great for swimming and snorkeling. The ocean floor, a combination of white sand and reef, gives the water a magnificent azure color. Just to the south of the beach access is Pahonu Pond, an ancient Hawaiian turtle pond. Today, it's perfect for the youngest of kids to get comfortable in the water in a calm and sheltered setting. The locals also call the beach Shriners after the Shriners Beach Club at the water's edge. The free parking lot is small and fills up quickly. Use caution if you park along the road. The restroom at the beach park closes 7pm-7am daily.

★ Waimanalo Beach Park

Right in the heart of Waimanalo town, **Waimanalo Beach Park** offers the same fine white sand, great snorkeling, swimming, and azure water as all along the Waimanalo coast. The beach park has free parking, showers, restrooms, and a grassy camping area, which is predominantly used by the homeless. While lean-tos and laundry lines don't sound like paradise, the camping area is just a small portion of the three-mile beach, one of the longest on O'ahu. The beach is also lined with ironwood trees, so it's easy to duck into the shade if the sun becomes too intense. Mostly uncrowded during the week, the beach shows a different face during the weekends as families post up, fish, relax, and have a good time. It can get pretty rowdy, though. The beach park is closed 9:30pm-7am daily.

Bellows Beach Park

At the north end of Waimanalo town, Bellow Air Force Station harbors **Bellows Beach Park.** It's open to the public every Friday-Sunday. Here you'll find more of Waimanalo's signature white sand, ironwood-lined beaches. Camping complete with facilities is also available at Bellows by permit. Take the well-marked Bellows AFB turnoff from Kalanianaole Highway and follow the road to the beach, where parking is free.

KAILUA
★ Kailua Beach Park

This ocean activity hub of the windward coast offers everything—swimming, bodyboarding, kitesurfing, sailboarding, stand-up paddling, and kayaking. **Kailua Beach Park,** at the south end of Kailua, marks the start of the world-famous Kailua Beach, composed of fine grains of white sand and stretching 2.5 miles up the coast in a gentle arc. The water is shallow and often calm, perfect for families and swimming, but there can be small shore-breaking waves along parts of the beach.

Because the ocean floor is sand, ditch the snorkel mask and fins and get on top a kayak. There are outfitters within walking distance to the beach and along Ka'elepulu Stream. Popoi'a Island, better known as Flat Island, is a quick paddle offshore. There is also a boat ramp where residents launch their watercraft. Locals tend to gravitate to the small beach on the south side of the boat ramp, where they can park their trucks and anchor just off the beach.

Kailua Beach Park has restrooms, showers, and three free parking lots that fill to maximum capacity nearly every day. The park is clean, with manicured landscaping, a walking path, and beautiful canopy trees. There is also a restaurant and market right across the street. Weekends are always more crowded than weekdays, but summer weekends see the crowds swell in both the park and along the beach. Police adamantly ticket illegally parked vehicles.

To get to Kailua Beach Park from Honolulu, the Pali Highway turns into Kalanianaole Highway, which becomes Kailua Road. From Waimanalo, turn right onto Kailua Road from Kalanianaole Highway. Continue straight on Kuulei Road as Kailua Road veers right and into Kailua's shopping district. Follow Kuulei Road until it dead-ends at South Kalaheo Avenue. Turn right, then make a left at Kailua Road to access the first parking lot, or continue on Kalaheo Avenue and over the bridge as the road turns into Kawailoa Road. The next parking lot is on the left, just on the south side of the stream. At the stop sign, take a left onto Alala Road and the third parking lot is on the left side of the boat ramp. All three lots border Kailua Beach Park and are closed 10pm-5am daily. The restrooms are locked until 6am.

Lanikai Beach

Lanikai Beach fronts the affluent and quaint Lanikai neighborhood. The aesthetics

Kailua Beach is famous for its fine white sand.

Kailua

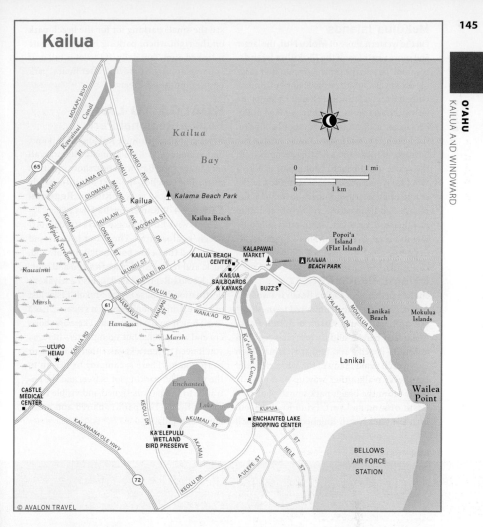

© AVALON TRAVEL

of Lanikai Beach are the same as Kailua, except Lanikai Beach gets narrower as you head south, until it disappears altogether and a seawall and multimillion-dollar homes take its place. The draw at Lanikai Beach, apart from the great swimming and calm, turquoise water, is the Mokulua Islets. A trip to "The Moks," as they are locally referred to, is the quintessential kayak destination on O'ahu. You can take a tour or paddle the 0.75 mile solo to the islands. Most people land on Moku Nui, the larger and more northerly of the two

islets. It has a small beach that offers a postcard-perfect view of the mainland and the Ko'olau Mountains, a perspective most visitors will never attain. There is also a trail to the back of the island. It is against the law to deviate from the trail, as the island is also home to nesting seabirds. Parking for Lanikai Beach is on the street through the neighborhood. There are no sidewalks, so be mindful of residents' landscaping and driveways. There are several public beach access walkways in between the homes, which are obvious and well signed.

Mokulua Islands

On the western shore of **Moku Nui**, the larger and more northern of the **Mokulua Islands,** is a small beach, the perfect respite after making the kayak crossing from Kailua or Lanikai. Once here, you'll find an amazing view of the leeward coast from a unique vantage point. The water is clear and blue, and the vibe on the beach is often festive. You can spot the burrows of the island's nesting seabirds from the white-sand beach. Moku Nui is a bird sanctuary, so public access is limited to the beach and a narrow footpath that circles the island. Paddling across via kayak, stand-up paddleboard, or other watercraft is the only way to access the beach. There are no facilities here.

Kalama Beach Park

At the north end of Kailua Beach is a wooded park that has a soft, manicured lawn, showers, and restrooms: **Kalama Beach Park.** The beach here is slightly less crowded than at Kailua Beach Park, and at Kalama Beach Park you'll avoid many of the kitesurfers and kayakers. Walk either way up or down the beach from the beach park to nab your own swath of sand and surf. From Kuulei Road, turn left onto North Kalaheo Avenue. You'll see the small parking lot for the beach park on the right where parking is free. The gate is locked 6pm-7am daily. If the lot is full or if you're planning on staying after hours, park on neighborhood streets.

KUALOA TO LA'IE

Kualoa Regional Park

After you pass through Kahalu'u, Waikane, and Waiahole on Kamehameha Highway, all set in Kane'ohe Bay, with nearshore mudflats instead of beaches, the next beautiful sandy beach you come to is at **Kualoa Regional Park** (49-479 Kamehameha Hwy., 808/237-8525, www1.honolulu.gov/parks/programs/beach/kualoa.htm). The water is clear and calm, and the ocean bottom is a mix of sand, rock, and reef, a good place to swim and snorkel. Kualoa Regional Park is also a kayaker's destination because of the Mokoli'i Islet just offshore. Chinaman's Hat, as it's known, has a small beach on the north side. There are showers and restrooms, but no outfitters here, so you'll need to rent a kayak either in Kailua or in Honolulu. There is camping by permit in the park. The parking lot is free, and the entrance to the park is signed and visible from the highway. The park is closed and gated 8pm-7am daily.

Lanikai Beach

Ka'a'awa Beaches

Just north of Kualoa you'll pass through Ka'a'awa. The Pacific Ocean pushes right up to Kamehameha Highway along much of Ka'a'awa, but there are a couple sandy nooks worth a stop. The first beach you'll come to is **Kalae'o'io Beach Park.** Simply pull off the highway under the trees. There's a grassy area, picnic tables, and a clean beach with light blue water. The beach is usually empty.

Ka'a'awa Beach Park is just a skip to the north up the highway. You'll see the restrooms and showers from the road, and notice there are only three parking spaces. If they're taken, just pull off the highway and park on the shoulder. This narrow beach is a local favorite for fishing and camping and can be packed on the weekends. The restrooms are closed 9pm-6:30am daily.

Beyond the beach park, across from the U.S. Post Office and gas station is **Swanzy Beach Park,** where camping is allowed with a permit. The beach is small and a mix of sand and rock, but it's a great zone for snorkeling when the winds are calm. The beach park has restrooms, showers, and an expansive grassy area with no shade. The views of the Ko'olaus from Swanzy are quite extraordinary. The parking lot is closed 10pm-6am daily.

★ Kahana Bay Beach Park

Kahana Bay Beach Park (52-222 Kamehameha Hwy., 808/237-7767, www.hawaiistateparks.org, 7am-7:45pm Apr.-Labor Day, 7am-6:45pm Labor Day-Mar. 31), found in dramatic Kahana Bay, offers camping by permit, a great area for a picnic, and calm, sheltered water for stand-up paddling. At the base of the bay, the Kahana Valley meets the sea and Kahana Stream spills into the Pacific, depositing fine silty sand along the beach and out into the bay. The water is often murky and a bit chilly, but remains shallow quite a ways out. The area is perfect for families with kids. Parking is right off Kamehameha Highway on the ocean side, and there are restrooms and showers. The remnants of the ancient Huilua fishpond are on the south side of the bay.

Kokololio Beach Park

Kokololio Beach Park, at the north end of Hau'ula, offers a wide beach by Hawaii standards, with a shoreline fringed with tropical almond canopy trees and *naupaka*. The ocean floor is sandy and the water is clear when the winds are light. During the winter months, when the surf is up, the shore break can get quite powerful, and a surf break appears on

Ka'a'awa has a few narrow but beautiful beaches.

the outer reef. Swimming becomes dangerous during periods of high surf due to strong currents. There are restrooms and showers in the park, as well as a generous grassy area with a large parking lot. Camping is allowed with a permit, and on the weekends, especially during the summer, the park is filled with local residents and families. The beach is also a favorite for fishing. The gated parking lot is locked 8pm-6:45am daily.

La'ie Beach Park

Just to the north, on the other side of an outcropping of limestone cliffs that marks the end of Kokololio Beach Park, is **La'ie Beach Park.** The beach park is also known as Pounders, named after the bodysurfing area near the cliffs, where the shore break can get big and powerful during the winter months. The beach is relatively small and often lined with organic debris, but the park is beautiful and dotted with picnic benches. Swimming here is better in the summer months. Stroll to the north to find another small beach on the other side of the point. There are no facilities at this beach park, but a paved parking lot is right off the highway.

Hukilau Beach

On the north end of La'ie town sits the lovely **Hukilau Beach,** a long, crescent-shaped sandy beach with dunes covered in *naupaka*. During the summer months, the water is great for swimming, but the surf and currents make for poor conditions during the winter months. Throughout the year, this area has the propensity for strong trade winds, which can also create unfavorable beach and swimming conditions. The park itself is beautiful, with

shade from ironwood trees, grass, and picnic benches—beachgoers are always welcome. There are showers, but no restrooms, and a dirt parking lot off Kamehameha Highway, which is closed on Sunday.

Malaekahana State Recreation Area

Continuing up the same crescent of sand from Hukilau Beach, you'll come to the **Malaekahana State Recreation Area** (808/537-0800, www.hawaiistateparks.org), framed in by Kalanai Point and Goat Island to the north. When the wind is not whipping onshore from the northwest and the surf is flat, the sandy bottom makes for great swimming and crystal clear water. There is more rock and reef to the north end of the beach, which is better for snorkeling if all the other weather conditions are favorable. The beach is also a favorite for fishing. Malaekahana State Recreation Area has showers, restrooms, and picnic tables, and camping is allowed with a permit on the south side of Kalanai Point. On the north side, or Kahuku side of Kalanai Point is Malaekahana Park-Kahuku section, a private 37-acre camping area. The entrance to Malaekahana State Recreation Area is off Kamehameha Highway and is well marked; the beach is not visible from the highway. Follow the road back to the parking lot, which is known as a high theft area. The entrance to the Malaekahana Park-Kahuku section is just north of the state recreation area. Look for a small faded blue sign on the side of the road. From Labor Day to March 31 the recreation area is open 7am-6:45pm daily. From April 1 to Labor Day it remains open till 7:45pm daily.

Water Sports

SURFING, STAND-UP PADDLING, AND KITESURFING

The windward side is typically just that, windy, a weather condition that can adversely affect surfing conditions unless the winds are blowing offshore. Unfortunately, the windward side usually sees onshore winds, leaving little in the way of consistent, good-quality waves for surfing. On the other hand, sports like sailboarding and kitesurfing that flourish in the windy conditions are popular in this region, centered around Kailua, where most of the outfitters are located.

Waimanalo

Just north of Makapu'u at **Kaupo Beach Park** there is a gentle little wave called Cockroach that breaks inside the rocky cove, perfect for beginners on big boards. During the winter months, when northeast swells sneak around Rabbit Island, the surf can get big and the currents quite strong.

Kailua

All along Kailua beaches, from Lanikai to Kalama Beach Park, the ocean conditions are usually just right for stand-up paddling. With a soft, sandy bottom, little to no shore break, and generally calm water, the area around **Kalama Beach Park** is perfect for distance paddling up and down the coast. If you paddle out from **Kailua Beach,** there is **Flat Island** to explore. And if you're paddling from **Lanikai Beach,** there is a bit more rock and reef off the beach, so you can explore the near-shore waters or paddle out to the **Mokulua Islands.** During the winter months, there are two surf breaks that reveal themselves on either side of Moku Nui, the larger of the two islands. Keep in mind that if the surf is big enough for waves to be breaking on the outer reefs, the ocean currents will be much stronger. Stand-up paddle surfing

should only be attempted by expert stand-up paddlers.

Stand-up paddling can become more of a chore than a pleasurable experience in extremely windy conditions. When the wind does pick up and the ocean surface becomes choppy and bumpy, sailboarders and kitesurfers take to the water in Kailua instead.

You can rent stand-up paddleboards at **Kailua Beach Adventures** (130 Kailua Rd., Ste. 101B, 808/262-2555 or 888/457-5737, www.kailuasailboards.com, 8:30am-5pm daily) for $59 half day and $69 full day, with multiday prices and free carts to walk the board to the beach. It also offers two-hour group lessons for $129, including hotel pickup and lunch, a one-hour private lessons for $199, and private group instruction for $159 per person. The retail outlet is within walking distance of Kailua Beach Park. **Windward Watersports** (33 Hoolai St., 808/261-7873, www.windwardwatersports.com, 9am-5pm daily) is a complete water-sports shop selling new and used boards and gear for many activities. It rents stand-up paddleboards starting at $49 half day and $59 full day, with two-hour lessons plus an extra two hours with the board on your own for $125. Kiteboard rentals start at $40 for one day. Actual rental of the kite is contingent upon your skill level, or beginners can take a one-hour course with a certified instructor. Located in Kailua town, the shop will help you put racks and watercraft on your vehicle for the short drive to the beach. **Hawaiian WaterSports** (167 Hamakua Dr., 808/262-5483, www.hawaiianwatersports. com, 9am-5pm daily), also located in Kailua, rents stand-up paddleboards starting at $59 for a full day with multiday rentals. It has a wide range of boards 7-14 feet and boards for all skill levels, and you can exchange your board at any time during your rental period. Group lessons start at $104 for 1.5 hours. Windsurf rentals with beginner gear starts at

$79 full day, $99 full day for advanced gear, and the shop also offers 1.5-hour lessons—groups of two start at $140, private are $199. Kiteboards are also available for rent starting at $29 per day. Different lessons are offered depending on your skill level. Private lessons start at $199 for 1.5 hours of instruction. Book online for discounted rates to all three outfitters.

Kualoa to La'ie

Just after you pass the row of oceanfront homes across from Kualoa Ranch, the road bends and Kualoa Valley opens up to your left and the beach comes into view on your right. There's immediate roadside parking for a washy surf spot called **Rainbows.** Shallow patches of flat reef amid a sandy bottom create a few different zones where mushy waves break haphazardly. Usually windblown and choppy, this break is favored by beginner surfers and longboarders. The closest outfitters for gear rentals are in Kailua.

Kahana Bay is a great spot to stand-up paddle. The bay is somewhat protected from the pervasive trade winds, and the water is usually calm and flat, with only tiny waves lapping up onshore. The sandy bottom stays shallow all around the bay, and you can paddle up to the fishponds on its southern edge or explore around the point to the north.

SNORKELING

This region has some great snorkeling locales, but it's up to you find the best spots during your stay. Because of the dips and bends in the coastline, ocean conditions can vary greatly from beach to beach, so it can be as much of an adventure to find the perfect spot to snorkel as it is to explore the water.

The windward side is heavily affected by the trade winds, which create chop on the ocean surface and wind waves can stir up sediment in the water—the stronger the trades, the choppier the ocean. Beaches with an outer reef that block the surf and shallow, protected inner waters with a mix of rock, reef, and sand are best. And unless you're heading to Kailua,

where the snorkeling is subpar, you'll need to have your own gear ready at hand because there are no shops to rent equipment along the windward coast.

Beyond Makapu'u Point, most of the windward coast is fringed by an outer reef that creates calm and shallow nearshore waters. Add an ocean floor mostly covered in rock and reef to that equation and you have the perfect conditions for snorkeling. **Waimanalo** is much like Kailua Beach with a sandy bottom. You won't see any reef fish, but you might glance a sea turtle. **Kualoa** has more potential for spotting reef fish with its reef and rock bottom. Snorkel in the area right off the beach and out toward Chinaman's Hat. **Ka'a'awa** also has some great snorkeling potential if the winds are light. Get in the water near the beach park or along the straight stretch of coast just to the south of Kahana Bay. **Hau'ula** and **La'ie** also have great beaches to explore in mask and fins, as long as weather conditions are also cooperating. You'll find a similar reef and rock bottom no matter where you jump in the water in these two towns. Just steer clear of any river mouths. Hau'ula and La'ie are also prone to high surf in the winter months, which creates dangerous ocean currents and can stir up the usually crystal clear water.

Most windward towns are small residential communities without snorkeling or diving outfitters renting or selling gear, with the exception of a few options in Kailua. **Kailua Beach Adventures** (130 Kailua Rd., Ste. 101B, 808/262-2555 or 888/457-5737, www.kailuasailboards.com, 8:30am-5pm daily) rents mask, snorkel, and fins for $12 half day, $16 full day, and $48 per week. **Twogood Kayaks** (134B Hamakua Dr., 808/262-5656, www.twogoodkayaks.com, 8am-6pm daily) has snorkel sets for $12 day, for weekly rentals pay for three days and get the next two for free. **Aaron's Dive Shop** (307 Hahani St., 808/262-2333 or 888/847-2822, www.hawaii-scuba.com, 7am-7pm Mon.-Fri., 7am-6pm Sat., 7am-5pm Sun.) also rents and sells snorkel gear.

KAYAKING
Kailua
KAILUA BEACH PARK

For all the same reasons that make **Kailua Beach Park** an attractive destination for swimming, stand-up paddling, and relaxing on the beach—white-sand beaches, shallow and calm water, and beautiful views all around—it is also the hub for kayaking on O'ahu. You can launch from Kailua Beach Park and paddle out to Flat Island, or paddle up and down the coast. Another popular place to launch from is Lanikai.

Those not comfortable with a little swell or chop on the ocean surface can also kayak in Ka'elepulu Stream, which spills into the ocean at Kailua Beach Park. The stream opens up into Ka'elepulu Pond, a wetland area that was flooded to create the Enchanted Lake neighborhood. The water in the stream will contain urban runoff, and if the mouth of the stream has not opened in some time, it can be a bit stinky. On the other side of the coin, the water will be smooth, calm, and more protected from the wind. Just try not to get wet. For first-time kayakers, a group tour is a great way to get acquainted with the kayak and the water.

★ MOKULUA ISLANDS

The **Mokulua Islands,** less than a mile offshore from Kailua Beach, are a popular draw. You can actually land on **Moku Nui,** the larger, more northern island. There's an inviting beach on the leeward side, just make sure to pull your kayak all the way up to the rocks to allow other people to land. Pack a lunch and put your camera in a dry sack because the view of mainland O'ahu from the island is breathtaking. There is a trail that circles the island. Remain on the trail because the island is a seabird nesting sanctuary.

OUTFITTERS

Windward Watersports (33 Hoolai St., 808/261-7873, www.windwardwatersports.com, 9am-5pm daily) rents single kayaks starting at $49 half day, $59 full day, and double kayaks for $55 half day and $65 full day. Triple kayaks are $79 half day and $89 full day. Kayaks can be picked up at the retail store or dropped off and ready for you at the beach. Windward offers a four-hour, self-guided tour for $49 and a four-hour, guided tour for $159 going to Flat Island, Lanikai Beach, and the Mokulua Islands.

Twogood Kayaks (134B Hamakua Dr., 808/262-5656, www.twogoodkayaks.com,

kayaking to Moku Nui, the largest of the Mokulua Islands

8am-6pm daily) rents single kayaks for $45 half day, $55 full day and tandem kayaks for $55 half day, $65 full day. Rentals come with a paddle, but there is an additional charge for a dry bag and backrest. Twogood offers free delivery of kayaks to Ka'elepulu Stream at Kailua Beach Park and basic instruction. It will deliver kayaks to other Kailua areas for $15. Twogood Kayaks offers an Adventure Package 9am-3pm for $85 per adult and $60 per child, with kayak rental, life jacket, paddle, lunch, and round-trip transportation from Waikiki included, and two guided tours, a five-hour Mokulua Islands trip for $149 adults and $104 children and a 2.5-hour Popoi'a Island Tour for $115 adults and $81 children, with extras like a guide, snorkel gear, dry bag, and backrest.

Just across the street from Kailua Beach Park you'll find **Kailua Beach Adventures** (130 Kailua Rd., Ste. 101B, 808/262-2555 or 888/457-5737, www.kailuasailboards.com, 8am-5pm daily). It rents single kayaks for $59 half day, and high-performance single kayaks and double kayaks for $69 half day. Dry bag, cooler, and backrest are an additional fee. Tour options are: a four-hour guided tour for beginners that includes snorkeling, transportation from your hotel, and lunch for $139 adults and $119 children 8-12; a five-hour guided adventure of Kailua Bay, Flat Island, and the Mokulua Islands with snorkeling, lunch, and hotel transportation for $179; and a four-hour self-guided tour for $99 adults, $89 children. Check for online discounts at all outfitters in the area.

Kane'ohe
KANE'OHE BAY
Kane'ohe Bay is a unique natural treasure in Hawaii, the largest sheltered body of water in the islands, and has several worthwhile sights that make kayaking in the bay quite an extraordinary experience. Devoid of beautiful sandy beaches, the draw in Kane'ohe Bay is what's in the bay. Coconut Island is just a stone's throw from the Kane'ohe coast, but a world all its own. The entire island is

a marine research facility, so the public cannot go onshore, but the reefs surrounding the island are protected and pristine, home to species of coral found only in Kane'ohe Bay. The water is crystal clear, and the reefs teem with fish. Farther to the north is the Kane'ohe Bay Sandbar, also known as Sunken Island. At low tide, the expansive sandbar, the size of a football field, is a favorite destination for locals and visitors. Sailboats pull right up on the sand, kayakers stop for rest, and people set up beach chairs in the sand and just relax. On the northern fringes of the bay, you'll also find the remains of several ancient fishponds.

OUTFITTERS
In Kane'ohe, **Holokai Kayak and Snorkel Adventures** (46-465 Kamehameha Hwy., 808/781-4773, www.holokaiadventures.com, 8am-4pm Mon.-Sat.) rents tandem kayaks and offers a three-hour guided tour of the bay for $120 per adult, $100 per child (4-12) kayaking from Coconut Island to the He'eia fishpond. It offers a free shuttle service to and from Waikiki and a 15 percent discount for booking online. Otherwise, you'll need to have your kayak already in tow. Many of the outfitters in Kailua or Honolulu offer free racks for your vehicle.

Kualoa to La'ie
KUALOA REGIONAL PARK
You can put your kayak in the water and paddle out to Chinaman's Hat, a small island with a distinctive profile just off the shore, from **Kualoa Regional Park.** The ocean floor off the beach is a mix of sand, reef, and rock, so there is much to see in the water. It's also very shallow, which keeps the surface rather calm. There are no outfitters in the area, so you'll need to have your kayak already on top of the car. Aside from a nice kayak adventure, the park makes a comfortable setting for a picnic lunch.

FISHING
Shoreline fishing and spearfishing are popular activities on the windward coast, whether

Fishponds

an ancient Hawaiian fishpond at Kahama Bay

Ancient Hawaiian communities were organized by *ahupua'a,* land divisions that stretched in giant swaths from the mountains all the way into the sea. Fishing was just as important as farming, and precontact Hawaiians were experts at both. Fishponds were constructed in shallow, nearshore waters by the people of the *ahupua'a* to store fish for food, because high surf and adverse ocean conditions often kept them onshore. Fishponds guaranteed a catch. Even more important, the fishponds were constructed as spawning grounds to ensure sustainability of certain species. In fact, Hawaiian fishponds were the first marine protected areas in Hawaii, and the people were not allowed to catch the fish that were spawning and considered *kapu,* off limits.

The fishponds were made by building a wall of stone on the reef that would enclose a body of water. The remnants of these fishponds are visible up and down the windward coast, and some are being restored and put into practice. There is the Moli'i fishpond at Kualoa Ranch, the Huilua fishpond in Kahana Bay, the Kahalu'u fishpond, the Pahonu Pond at Kaiona Beach Park in Waimanalo, which was also used to keep turtles, and the He'eia fishpond on the north end of Kane'ohe Bay. Friends of He'eia Fishpond is a nonprofit organization dedicated to maintaining the working fishpond for the community.

for hobby, sport, or sustenance. Between Waimanalo and La'ie, there are miles of accessible coastline where you can pull out the rod and reel, or hold your breath, and fish. You can shoreline fish from the beaches of **Waimanalo, Kailua, Ka'a'awa, Kahana, Punalu'u, Hau'ula, La'ie Point State Wayside,** and **Malaekahana State Recreation Area.** In Kane'ohe Bay, people often fish from **He'eia Pier.** In some areas, especially from Kualoa to Kahana, where the ocean pushes right up again the

highway, you can find a place to pull off on the shoulder, pop up a tent, and cast a line. Spearfishing is also popular along the shallow nearshore waters where rock and reef make up the ocean bottom. Waimanalo, Kualoa, Ka'a'awa, and Malaekahana State Recreation Area are all good spots to spearfish, and octopus, locally known as tako, is abundant in these areas—if you can find them.

If you're inclined to get out on the open water to fish, kayak fishing is the easiest way to go. Waimanalo, Kailua, and Kane'ohe Bay are more protected from the wind and better for fishing from a kayak. Ka'a'awa also has nice, long stretches of nearshore water to troll as well, but is more prone to the trade winds.

If you're coming from Honolulu and forget your fishing gear, you'll need to stop at **Nanko Fishing Supply** (46-003 Alaloa St., 808/247-0938, www.facebook.com/ NankoFishingSupply, 8am-6pm Mon., 8am-7pm Tues.-Sat., 9am-2pm Sun.), the hub of fishing gear for the windward side. Also, **Longs** (46-047 Kamehameha Hwy., 808/235-4511, 6am-10pm daily) in the Kaneohe Bay Shopping Center sells basic fishing supplies and three-prong spears.

Hiking and Biking

HIKING
Kailua

There is a popular walking trail along **Kawainui Marsh,** one of the few wetland ecosystems on O'ahu and home to several species of native waterbirds like the Hawaiian coot, Hawaiian moorhen, and the Hawaiian stilt along with a host of other feathered inhabitants. The mile-long path is a raised, paved trail that crosses the marsh from Kailua Road to Kaha Street, off Oneawa Street on the north end of the Kailua neighborhood known as Coconut Grove.

Maunawili Falls is a short hike in the shadow of Olomana that follows Maunawili Stream and terminates at the falls. From Kalanianaole Highway, turn into A'uola Road in the Maunawili neighborhood. Immediately fork left onto Maunawili Road and follow it through the subdivision and a forested area to the end at Kelewina Street. Park near the intersection and continue on foot on the one-lane private road. A sign indicates the way to the falls, which in part is on private land, so stay on the trail. Along the stream look for 'ape, a plant with huge, elephant-ear-shaped leaves. A ridgeline section offers views of Ko'olau Range, Olomana and Kane'ohe Bay. Regain the stream and follow it to a large, deep pool and Maunawili Falls. On the hike you'll cross the stream several times and the trail can be quite muddy. It is also very popular and heavily used on the weekends. There is a second smaller pool at the top of the falls and the trail continues back from there if you wish to continue exploring the forest.

Kualoa to La'ie

Just north of Ka'a'awa is the lush Kahana Valley, a state park designed to foster native Hawaiian culture. There are two trails that intermingle, loop, and wind through the valley, the **Kapa'ele'ele Trail** and the **Nakoa Trail.** The Kapa'ele'ele Trail is a one-mile loop passing cultural sites with views of Kahana Bay. And the Nakoa Trail is a 2.5-mile with *koa* and *hau* tree forests, pools along the stream, and a mountain apple grove. From Kamehameha Highway, turn *mauka* into the Ahupua'a O Kahana State Park. There is an Orientation Center, where you can find trail maps and other information, as well as restrooms. Be prepared for mud and mosquitoes on the hike.

BIKING
Kailua

Kailua is the most bike-friendly town on O'ahu. The beaches and neighborhoods are in relatively close proximity to the town center, where all the dining, shopping, and services are located. The town is flat, the weather is exceptional, and the traffic is usually so congested that it's faster to get around on two wheels. In addition to riding around town, bikes are allowed on the trail that crosses the Kawainui Marsh.

The Bike Shop (270 Kuulei Rd., 808/261-1553, www.bikeshophawaii.com, 9am-8pm Mon.-Fri., 9am-5pm Sat., 10am-5pm Sun.) is a full-service bicycle shop. It rents 21-speed cruisers for $20 per day, road bikes for $40 per day, and performance mountain bikes for $85 per day. **Kailua Beach Adventures** (130 Kailua Rd., Ste. 101B, 808/262-2555 or 888/457-5737, www.kailuasailboards.com, 8am-5pm daily) rents bikes for $20 half day, $25 full day, and $85 for seven days.

Entertainment and Events

NIGHTLIFE
Kailua

Located at the intersection of Hamakua Drive and Hahani Street, **Boardriders Bar & Grill** (201 Hamakua Dr., 808/261-4600, noon-2am daily, $9-15) is better known as a bar than a grill, but it does serve pizza, salad, steak, stir-fry, and classic bar munchies. Boardriders has a couple pool tables and is the best venue for catching live music on the windward side. The bar sees local, national, and international artists and favors reggae and jawaiian (Hawaiian reggae) music. *Pau hana* is 4pm-6pm daily.

Nestled next to the Hamakua Marsh (which has wonderful **bird-watching** opportunities) is a small but friendly blue-collar bar called the **Creekside Lounge** (153 Hamakua Dr., 808/262-6466, http://creeksidelounge.com, 10am-2am Mon-Wed., 8am-2am Thurs.-Sat., 7am-2am Sun.). Established in 1982, the Creekside is a biker bar with a cadre of friendly female bartenders. The bar shows live sporting events and is no frills, but it has a huge local following. Smoking is allowed on the patio overlooking the marsh, where most patrons regularly spill out to.

TOP EXPERIENCE

CULTURAL TOURS AND LU'AU

On the northern end of the windward side, in La'ie, the **Polynesian Cultural Center** (55-370 Kamehameha Hwy., www.polynesianculturalcenter.com, 800/367-7060, noon-9pm Mon.-Sat.) introduces visitors to the people and cultures of Hawai'i, Samoa, Maori New Zealand, Fiji, Tahiti, Marquesas, and Tonga as you walk through and visit the different villages and interact with the people demonstrating their specific arts and crafts. There is also a canoe ride that explores the villages as well. Dining is paramount to the experience, and you can choose between the Island Buffet with a mix of local Hawaiian fare, Prime Dining with prime rib, crab legs, and sushi in a secluded setting, or the famous Ali'i Lu'au, with authentic Hawaiian food, including traditional *imu* pork, a large pig cooked in an earthen oven. An evening show called "Ha: Breath of Life" is a culmination of story, dance, Polynesian music, and fire. General admission, which is for the day experience only, is $60 adult, $48 child (5-11). Admission, buffet, and evening show will run $80 adult, $64 child, and packages for admission, the lu'au, and show start at $100 adult, $80 child.

Kualoa Ranch (49-560 Kamehameha Hwy., 808/237-7321, www.kualoa.com) offers historical and cultural tours of the working ranch, bordering valleys, and coastline. Established in 1850, the ranch is steeped in tradition and has a unique perspective and story to tell about the area. There is an Ancient Fishing Grounds and Tropical Gardens Tour, Ocean Voyage Tour, Secret Island Beach Tour, and Jungle Expedition Tour, among others. The tours are $35.95 adult and $25.95 child.

FESTIVALS AND EVENTS
Kailua

The **"I Love Kailua" Town Party** (last Sunday of April) is a daytime festival in the heart of downtown Kailua. Kailua Road is closed to vehicular traffic, and people from all over the island come out to eat, shop, and celebrate Kailua. There are activities for the kids and local restaurants and retail outlets line the street with tents full of merchandise and delicious fare.

Kane'ohe

Orchids are a big deal in Hawaii and the **Windward Orchid Society** holds an annual spring show and plant sale in the King Intermediate School gym (46-155 Kamehameha Hwy., www.windwardorchidsociety.org). The two-day event showcases the best in orchid cultivars as well as other unusual plants.

Food

WAIMANALO
Quick Bites

Waimanalo has a few places to stop and grab a quick bite as you make your way along the Kalanianaole Highway. **Keneke's Plate Lunch & BBQ** (41-857 Kalanianaole Hwy., 808/259-9811, 9am-8pm daily, $2-7) serves up the typical Hawaiian plate lunch and is very popular. **Serg's** (41-865 Kalanianaole Hwy., 808/259-7374, 11am-9pm Mon.-Fri., 8am-9pm Sat.-Sun., $3-12) brings Mexican food to Waimanalo with carnitas, carne asada, carne al pastor, and its famous flauta. **'Ai Love Nalo** (41-1025 Kalanianaole Hwy., 808/259-5737, 9am-5pm Wed.-Mon., $5-10) mixes Hawaiian-style cooking with the principles of sustainability, sourcing its ingredients locally and using organic when possible. The menu is strictly fish and vegetarian and the restaurant works closely with a Waimanalo farm for all aspects of its operation. It also serves smoothies and breakfast bowls.

KAILUA
Steak and Seafood

★ **Buzz's Lanikai** (413 Kawailoa Rd., 808/261-4661, http://buzzssteakhouse.com/lanikai.htm, 11am-3pm, 4:30pm-9:30pm daily, $19-44) is famous for its kiawe charcoal-broiled burgers and steaks as well as its salads. The small, popular restaurant is quirky and fun, complete with a tree right in the middle of the lanai seating. It's right across from Kailua Beach Park, so it's usually packed, with a wait. Buzz's is also known for its signature mai tai, a mix of rum with a cherry on top.

If you'd like a juice mixer with it, order the B.F.R.D. Don't forget to ask what that stands for. No tank tops after 4:30pm.

Formaggio Grill (305 Hahani St., 808/263-2633, www.formaggio808.com, 11:30am-11pm Mon.-Thurs., 11:30am-1am Fri.-Sat., 11am-11pm Sun., $12-69) blends Italian dishes with favorites from the grill like prime rib, lamb chops, barbecued ribs, and filet mignon. Thin-crust pizzas and rich lobster bisque complement the dishes, as does the wine-by-the-glass selection, over 50 bottles. Parking is extremely limited in front of the restaurant. Try the lot across the street by Macy's.

Quick Bites

Kalapawai Market (306 S. Kalaheo Ave., 808/262-4359, www.kalapawaimarket.com, 6am-9pm daily, $4-24) is right at Kailua Beach Park, with another location in downtown Kailua (750 Kailua Rd., 808/262-3354, 5am-5pm Mon.-Thurs., 7am-5pm Sat.-Sun., $8-24). The beach park location has a small sandwich deli and a limited grocery store that also sells beer and wine. The downtown location is strictly a café and deli with a coffee and wine bar and bakery. Open for breakfast, lunch, and dinner, with indoor and outdoor seating, Kalapawai Market has made-to-order sandwiches and a selection of prepared gourmet foods.

★ **Morning Brew** (600 Kailua Rd., 808/262-7770, http://morningbrewhawaii.com, 6am-6pm daily, $1-9) is the go-to coffeehouse and bistro in Kailua. With good coffee, a great assortment of bakery goods, sandwiches, snacks, free Internet, and two stories of seating, plus outdoor seating, it's an easy all-day hangout if you have some work to do.

Mexican

Cactus (767 Kailua Rd., 808/261-1000, http://cactusbistro.com, 10am-10pm daily, $6-24) offers a blend of locally sourced ingredients and Central and South American cuisine, including influences from Cuba, Puerto Rico, and Mexico. The restaurant has a modern style, complete with regional wines and premium rums, tequilas, and liquors. It serves lunch and dinner and opens at 10am for breakfast on Saturday and Sunday.

Japanese

Noboru (201 Hamakua Dr., A-102, 808/261-3033, http://noborukailua.com, 11:30am-2:30pm, 5pm-9pm daily $4-29) is the premier sushi restaurant in Kailua. It also serves teishoku, shabu-shabu, chanko nabe, and has a modern sake bar with over 25 different kinds of sake.

Thai

Check out **Saeng's Thai Cuisine** (315 Hahani St., 808/263-9727, www.restauranteur.com/saengs, 11am-2pm, 5pm-9pm Mon.-Thurs., 5pm-11:30pm Sun., $7-11). It offers a wide range of vegetarian options alongside soups, salads, curries, seafood, meat, and noodle dishes. It is closed from 2pm-5pm to change from lunch to dinner service.

KANE'OHE

Kane'ohe is a town that has not been largely altered by tourism, the proof being that you won't find any fine-dining restaurants or chic clothing boutiques. Instead, Kane'ohe is littered with local and national fast-food chains and small and simple ethnic eateries.

Quick Bites

Once you pass through Kane'ohe, it's all about mom-and-pop places where you can grab a

quick bite. And at the top of the list is the **Waiahole Poi Factory** (49-140 Kamehameha Hwy., 808/239-2222, http://waiaholepoifactory.com, 11am-5pm daily, $5-11). Serving up real Hawaiian food like squid and beef lu'au, kalua pig, lomi salmon, lau lau, and chicken long rice, it has mini plates that come with rice and lomi salmon and combo plates for a larger appetite. It also sells hand-pounded poi, which has a firmer texture and lighter flavor than milled poi.

Just past the Poi Factory, the **Waikane Store** (48-377 Kamehameha Hwy., 808/239-8522, 9:30am-5pm Mon.-Sat.) is a historical landmark on the Hawai'i Register of Historic Places. Established in 1898, it's still serving up many of the snacks and treats it's been selling for decades: boiled peanuts, fresh cooked chicken, local fruits, and homemade peanut butter cookies.

Breakfast

For a local-style diner breakfast, stop by **Koa Pancake House** (46-126 Kahuhipa St., 808/235-5772, 6:30am-2pm daily, $2-8). It's a popular breakfast spot on the weekends and is usually packed all morning, so expect a wait. The parking lot is very small, and if it's full, park on Kawa Street.

Chinese

Pah Ke's (46-018 Kamehameha Hwy., 808/235-4505, http://pahke.com, 10:30am-9pm daily, $6-24) Chinese restaurant is just down the street from Kim Chee Restaurant and equally as popular. It's a big venue that can accommodate large parties quite easily, although it does fill up for dinner. The dishes tend to be simple combinations or a protein, vegetable, and sauce.

Thai

If you're in the mood for Thai, try **Chao Phya** (45-480 Kaneohe Bay Dr., 808/235-3555, 4pm-9pm Mon.-Thurs., 11am-10pm Fri.-Sun., $8-10) in the Windward City Shopping Center next to Starbucks. It's a good option for takeout as well.

Mexican

There is a very small Mexican restaurant in Kane'ohe called **El Mariachi** (45-1151 #B Kamehameha Hwy., 808/234-5893, 11am-9pm daily, $10-27) right behind the Aloha gas station on the *makai* side of Kamehameha Highway. With just a few tables available, it serves traditional Mexican food like burritos, enchiladas, and chilis rellenos. It also has seafood selections.

Delis

★ **He'eia Pier General Store & Deli** (46-499 Kamehameha Hwy., 808/235-2192, www. heeiapier.com, 7am-3pm Mon.-Fri., 7am-5pm Sat.-Sun., $9-13) is a breath of fresh air in terms of high-quality, fresh local food. Whether you order guava chicken, fresh fish, or burgers and fries, the deli is known for sourcing organic and local produce and meats. It also has a few old-time dishes on offer.

Steak and Seafood

For a sit-down, true steak and seafood dining experience, ★ **Haleiwa Joe's** (46-336 Haiku Rd., 808/247-6671, http://haleiwajoes. com, 4:30pm-9pm Sun.-Thurs., 4:30pm-10pm Fri.-Sat., 9am-2pm Sun., $24-35) is Kane'ohe's answer. Nestled in a lush garden setting, Joe's serves up prime rib, fresh fish, and a handful of local favorites like poke, sashimi, sizzling mushrooms, and sticky ribs. It also has a Sunday brunch.

KA'A'AWA TO LA'IE
Quick Bites

Next to the post office in Ka'a'awa is a great mom-and-pop barbeque joint called **Uncle Bobo's** (51-480 Kamehameha Hwy., 808/237-1000, www.unclebobos.com, 11am-5pm Wed.-Fri., 11am-6pm Sat.-Sun., $5-16). It offers beef and pork barbecue plates, burgers, hot dogs, chili, and daily specials like a BLT. It even has fruit smoothies for good measure.

In La'ie, stop by **Hukilau Cafe** (55-662 Wahinepee St., 808/293-8616, 6:30am-2pm Tues.-Fri., 7am-11:30am Sat., $5-13) for Hawaiian breakfast and lunch plates. Think burgers with egg and kalua pork with two scoops of white rice. The food is delicious, and the portions are ample. Cash only.

Ko Olina and Leeward

Look for ★ to find recommended
sights, activities, dining, and lodging.

Highlights

★ **Kane'aki Heiau:** This restored stone structure is a historic and spiritual window into Hawaiian culture and perseverance (page 163).

★ **Ka'ena Point State Park:** Stretching from breathtaking Yokohama Bay to the western tip of the island, Ka'ena Point State Park includes verdant valleys, a secluded beach, and a dramatic volcanic coast (page 164).

★ **Ko Olina Lagoons:** Four ocean-fed lagoons offer a safe and beautiful environment for a family day at the beach (page 165).

★ **Makaha Beach Park:** Steeped in surfing history, this dramatic point offers one of the best waves on O'ahu, which breaks nearly year-round. The wide, sandy beach forms a small bay where trees provide shade for picnicking and surf-gazing (page 166).

© AVALON TRAVEL

The leeward coast, also known as the Wai'anae Coast, is arid and rugged, with ridgelines that extend to the coast, where reef, rocks, and cliffs often take the place of sandy beaches.

Still, there is much to recommend here. The leeward coast has an unobstructed view for every day's precious sunset, where green flashes occur on a regular basis. The deep waters off the coast are prime grounds for sportfishing and a few surf spots break year-round, the most famed being Makaha, home to the first world championship professional surfing event. Spinner dolphins, humpback whales, and sea turtles frequent the waters, and the conditions are usually perfect for diving. Don't forget to look inland, where the verdant valleys of the Wai'anae Range lie in stark contrast to the parched land along the coast.

If luxury, pampering, golf, and fine dining better suit your taste, then Ko Olina, at the southwestern tip of the island, is a prime destination. A sprawling community of condos, timeshares, hotels, dining, golf, and four artificial lagoons on private land, Ko Olina is an oasis in the desert. Geared to be the next Waikiki, the area offers full-service amenities, but the price is definitely on the high side.

PLANNING YOUR TIME

If you're planning on any activity in the Ka'ena Point State Park, whether it be hiking to the natural reserve at the tip of the point, mountain biking the dirt road to the point, or kayaking in Yokohama Bay, then head there first, as early as possible, to beat the heat of the midday sun. If you have booked a fishing or diving charter departing from the Wai'anae Small Boat Harbor, then you'll need to leave Honolulu very early to account for morning traffic. After a half day in the state park, head back south and take in the sights and snap some pictures along the way. The beaches and valleys will be perfectly lit by the afternoon sun. Finish up with dinner in Ko Olina at one of its premier restaurants.

For a west side beach day, it is absolutely essential to bring an umbrella, plenty of water,

---

Previous: the arid and rugged leeward coast; Ko Olina lounging. **Above:** Ka'ena Point.

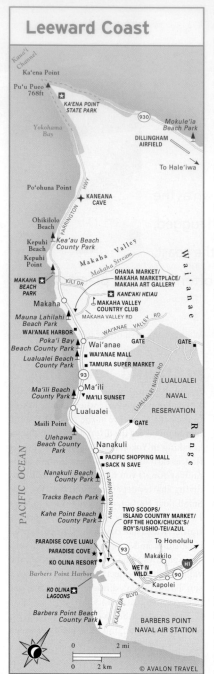

Leeward Coast

Kane'a Channel
Ka'ena Point
Pu'u Pueo
768ft
KA'ENA POINT
STATE PARK
Yokohama Bay
930
Mokule'ia Beach Park
DILLINGHAM AIRFIELD
To Hale'iwa
Po'ohuna Point
KANEANA CAVE
Ohikilolo Beach
Kepuhi Beach — Kea'au Beach County Park
Kepuhi Point
Makaha Valley
Makaha Stream
OHANA MARKET/ MAKAHA MARKETPLACE/ MAKAHA ART GALLERY
MAKAHA BEACH PARK
KILI DR
KANE'AKI HEIAU
Makaha
MAKAHA VALLEY COUNTRY CLUB
MAKAHA VALLEY RD
Mauna Lahilahi Beach Park
WAI'ANAE HARBOR
Poka'i Bay Beach County Park
WAI'ANAE VALLEY RD
Wai'anae
GATE
GATE
Lualualei Beach County Park
WAI'ANAE MALL
TAMURA SUPER MARKET
93
LUALUALEI NAVAL RD
LUALUALEI
Ma'ili Beach County Park
Ma'ili
MA'ILI SUNSET
NAVAL
RESERVATION
Lualualei
Maili Point
GATE
Ulehawa Beach County Park
Nanakuli
Range
PACIFIC SHOPPING MALL
SACK N SAVE
Nanakuli Beach County Park
Tracks Beach Park
Kahe Point Beach County Park
TWO SCOOPS/ ISLAND COUNTRY MARKET/ OFF THE HOOK/CHUCK'S/ ROY'S/USHIO-TEI/AZUL
PACIFIC OCEAN
PARADISE COVE LUAU
PARADISE COVE
KO OLINA RESORT
To Honolulu
93
Makakilo
H1
WET N WILD
90
Barbers Point Harbor
Kapolei
KO OLINA LAGOONS
KALAELOA BLVD
Barbers Point Beach County Park
BARBERS POINT NAVAL AIR STATION
FARRINGTON HWY

0   2 mi
0   2 km
© AVALON TRAVEL

and sunscreen. Shade is sparse in the region. If you're heading west just for the sunset, don't wait too late in the afternoon, as rush-hour traffic heading west could spoil your sunset plans. Lounge in one of the Ko Olina Lagoons all afternoon or post up at one of the leeward beaches, where you'll be in a prime sunset-viewing location. Keep in mind that Ko Olina is a busy resort, so there will be many people with the same sunset ideas. You'll need to keep heading west if you're in the market for your own piece of private beach real estate to watch the sun go down on another day.

If golfing is your main reason for heading to the leeward side, you can choose from two courses. The course in Wai'anae Valley is very affordable while the Ko Olina resort community offers a world-class golf experience and a shorter drive. For those staying in Ko Olina, you'll have to contend with morning rush-hour traffic heading into Honolulu as you strike out to other island locales.

ORIENTATION

Ko Olina and the windward coast are about 25 miles from downtown Honolulu. As you travel west on the H-1 to reach the locale, you'll pass Pearl Harbor and O'ahu's arid southwestern plain, home to several growing residential communities. **'Ewa**—miles and miles of apartment complexes, condominiums, and homes—is to the west of Pearl Harbor. 'Ewa Beach stretches out west to Kalaeloa and the Kalaeloa Airport, an old military operation now used for light, local air traffic. To the west of 'Ewa on the 'Ewa Plain is **Kapolei,** a brand-new planned community on the south side of the H-1 freeway. You'll also pass by Pearl City, Waipio, Waipahu, and Makakilo, all to the north of the H-1.

Ko Olina is a private resort and lifestyle community located on the coast between Barbers Point and Nanakuli, right where the highway meets the coast after crossing the 'Ewa Plain. Ko Olina has its own exit off Farrington Highway and a gated entrance manned by resort staff. This high-end community is home to three major resort hotels

Your Best Day on the Leeward Coast

The Leeward Coast is rough, rugged, and beautiful in its own right. This side of O'ahu tends to be hot and dry, so be prepared with sunscreen, hats, and plenty of water.

- If you're interested in nature, plan on hiking to **Ka'ena Point.** Mitigate the heat by arriving as early as possible, preferably as the sun is coming up. Explore the **Ka'ena Point Natural Area Reserve.** You'll most likely see Hawaiian monk seals and nesting seabirds.

- On your return to your vehicle, take a refreshing dip in the ocean at **Yokohama Bay.**

- Head south down the Leeward Coast. Grab a quick snack at **Ohana Market** in Makaha. Continue south until you get to **Ko Olina.** Have a sit-down lunch at one of the poolside restaurants at the three resort properties.

- Families should spend a playful afternoon in one of the four sheltered lagoons in Ko Olina. Couples can schedule a treatment at **Laniwai Spa.**

- For dinner, try **Roy's** for Hawaiian fusion cuisine, or **Monkeypod Kitchen** for the best in locally sourced fare.

RAINY-DAY ALTERNATIVE

While your instinct might be to get inside and stay dry, a rainy day on the west side is the perfect opportunity to swim in one of Ko Olina's **four lagoons**—solo. As visitors dash away to their hotel rooms, you'll have a lagoon all to yourself.

and four artificial lagoons for both resort guests and the public. It is also the main locale for accommodations and services in the region.

The leeward coast stretches about 20 miles from Barbers Point to Yokohama Bay in Ka'ena Point State Park and is connected by one thoroughfare, Farrington Highway. The majority of the commercial property is along the highway, as the neighborhoods snake back into the dry valleys between the massive ridges that extend to the coast. The main communities from south to north are **Nanakuli, Ma'ili, Wai'anae,** and **Makaha.** The highway dead-ends at Ka'ena Point State Park, the westernmost tip of the island.

Sights

MAKAHA
★ Kane'aki Heiau

Located deep in Makaha Valley is one of the best-preserved *heiau* on O'ahu, the **Kane'aki Heiau.** Begun in 1545, the final structure was only completed by 1812, during the reign of King Kamehameha. Two restoration phases of construction occurred to preserve the physical, spiritual, and historic aspects of the *heiau*. Originally dedicated to Lono, the Hawaiian god of harvest and fertility, it was later converted to a *luakini heiau* for human sacrifice. The thatched huts used as prayer and meditation chambers, along with a spirit tower and carved images, have all been replicated. Because the *heiau* is within a private gated community, access is limited to 10am-2pm Tuesday-Sunday. It may be closed even during those times when it's too rainy or muddy. Stop at the guardhouse and let the guard know where you're heading, at which time you will need to show your identification

Soul's Leap

Ka'ena Point is a sacred place, and not just for its natural beauty. Ancient Hawaiians thought Ka'ena Point to be a jumping-off point for the spirits of the dead to enter the afterlife. Legend has it that humankind emerged from the depths of **Kaneana Cave,** the womb of the earth goddess, and spread across the Wai'anae coast. The souls of the deceased would find their way to Ka'ena Point by following the sun past the sunset, to the eternal night. Their leap would take them to Po, the realm of ancestral spirits, a spiritual place akin to heaven and described as being a sea of eternity. Once in Po, the soul is thought to have completed the cycle of life.

and car registration or car rental agreement before you are signed in.

Kaneana Cave

Spelunkers rejoice, just off Farrington Highway on the edge of Makua Valley is the **Kaneana Cave,** a sacred ancient Hawaiian site. At 100 feet high and about 450 feet deep, this cave, *ana,* is spoken of in Hawaiian legend as the womb of the earth, where mankind emerged and spread throughout the Wai'anae coast. It is named after Kane, the god of creation. In Hawaiian lore it is also thought to be the home of Nanaue, the shark man. The cave is dark and often slippery, so bring a flashlight. It is also unmaintained, and there are several side tunnels off the main cavern that should be avoided for your own safety. Look for the painted cement road barrier that marks the entrance.

★ Ka'ena Point State Park

Ka'ena Point State Park (www.hawaiistateparks.org/parks/oahu) is the most scenic, raw, and naturally breathtaking area on the leeward side. It is also an embodiment of all things found on the leeward coast. Located at the end of Farrington Highway and stretching

all the way out to the western tip of O'ahu, Ka'ena Point State Park provides outdoor and ocean recreational activities, wildlife viewing, native plant life, green valleys, a secluded white-sand beach with turquoise water, and a dramatic volcanic coast all under the hot west-side sun. It is truly about as far removed from Honolulu and Waikiki as you can get on O'ahu.

As you round the last bend in the road with a slight elevation, the gentle arcing white sand of Yokohama Bay, also known as Keawa'ula Bay, stretches out in front of you to the west. Pristine and uncrowded, it begs for you to pull the car over and take in the serenity. Look back into the valley to catch a glimpse of the unspoiled, verdant mountains of the Wai'anae Range. As you come to the end of the paved road, a rutted, rocky dirt track completes the way to Ka'ena Point. You can walk or mountain bike out to the western tip of the island, where you'll find the **Ka'ena Point Natural Area Reserve.** This is prime territory for wildlife viewing. Look for spinner dolphins and green sea turtles in the water; on the beach you'll probably see Hawaiian monk seals basking in the sun; and the sand dunes are a protected site for nesting **seabirds.**

Beaches

If you're feeling adventurous and don't mind an hour's drive across the island, the beaches of leeward O'ahu offer wide swaths of white sand under clear, sunny skies. As the trade winds blow across the island from east to west, the leeward coast's waters remain calm and protected, offering beautiful conditions for swimming, surfing, fishing, snorkeling, diving, or just soaking up the sun. Waves are common along leeward beaches all year long, but generally get the biggest in the winter, from October to March. Make sure to exercise caution and assess the ocean conditions before entering the water. Check with a lifeguard for the safest place to swim.

KO OLINA
Paradise Cove

Just past the entrance gate to Ko Olina and next to Paradise Cove Luau is a small, yet beautiful sandy cove and lagoon called **Paradise Cove.** In the past it has been called Lanikauka'a and then Lanikuhonua Beach. Paradise Cove is one of three sacred lagoons in the immediate area where Queen Ka'ahumanu was said to have bathed and performed religious ceremonies. The shallow lagoon is protected from ocean swells by a raised reef rock shelf on its ocean side. There are trees on the beach for shade and tidepools. All in all, it's a great out-of-the-way nook to take the kids and explore. Parking is a little tricky, though. Take a right into the third driveway past the entrance gate. On the right is a small, free public parking area for about 10 cars. The sidewalk leads to a sandy pathway between two tall fences down to the beach.

★ Ko Olina Lagoons

Ko Olina has four lagoons open to the public from sunrise to sunset. The **Ko Olina Lagoons** are numbered 1-4, heading from west to east, and also have the Hawaiian names Kohola, Honu, Napa, and Ulua, respectively. They are more widely known and referred to by their number. The lagoons are artificially constructed semicircles cut from the sharp and rugged reef rock shelf that creates the shoreline. Channels were cut into the shelf to allow ocean water to flow in and out

Paradise Cove in Ko Olina

of the lagoons while blocking any surf from entering. With sandy beaches, grassy parks, a fair bit of shade from palms and trees, and a meandering pathway connecting all four lagoons, this oasis provides a sheltered, manufactured, resort-style beach experience, completely opposite to the rest of the leeward beaches. Each lagoon has its own access road from Aliinui Drive, the main road through Ko Olina. Turn right on Kamoana Place to reach Lagoon 1. The next three consecutive streets will lead to a lagoon and its parking area. There are no lifeguards on duty, but there is plenty of security, known as the Aloha Patrol, monitoring the lagoons from golf carts. Ever vigilant, they will be sure to let you know if you're breaking any rules from the long list of prohibited actions and items. Parking is free but very limited at each lagoon, with Lagoon 4 having the most available spots.

Ko Olina has four manmade lagoons.

MA'ILI
Ma'ili Beach Park
Marking the beginning of Ma'ili town and its long stretch of beach, **Ma'ili Point** is one of the more dynamic and picturesque settings along the leeward coast. There is a small park with picnic tables and grass on the southern side of the point. The shoreline rocks extend out into the water and meet up with the shallow reef here, creating a lot of whitewater and surf action to watch while relaxing or having a snack. On the north side of the point, **Ma'ili Beach Park** runs the length of Ma'ili town. Situated between two streams that run down from the mountains, the sandy beach is widest during the summer when the waves are smaller, and the gently arcing beach is great for swimming and snorkeling. During the winter, however, the sand tends to migrate elsewhere with the more frequent high surf, revealing a rock shelf along the shore. There are restrooms, picnic areas, and camping on the weekends by permit only. Ma'ili Beach Park is closed 10pm-5am daily.

WAI'ANAE
Poka'i Bay Beach Park
Between the small boat harbor and Kane'ilio Point sits a beautiful sheltered bay and wide sandy beach called **Poka'i Bay Beach Park.** There is a breakwater offshore and a reef in the middle of the bay that keep the water calm along the shoreline year-round, making this a perfect spot for swimming and families. Small waves break over the reef during the winter, which attracts novice surfers. In addition to the beautiful beach, the **Ku'ilioloa Heiau** is also out on the point and has three terraced platforms. The *heiau* is thought to have been a place for learning the arts of fishing, navigation, and ocean-related skills. The beach park is closed 10pm-5am daily.

MAKAHA
★ Makaha Beach Park
A world-class surf break with a recent history entwined with the birth of international professional surfing, **Makaha Beach Park** is the

hub of surfing on the leeward coast. The beautiful beach is framed at both ends by rocky headlands, the north end being the site of the surf break and the sharp reef that absorbs the ocean's energy. The surf here breaks all year but is biggest in the winter months, when waves can reach 40-50 feet high on the face during the biggest swell episodes. In the summer, swimming is best in the middle of the beach, or if the waves are completely flat, you can snorkel over the reef shelf. There are restrooms, showers, and a few shade trees and hau bushes along the road where everyone parks. If there is surf during your stop at Makaha, check with the lifeguards for the best place to enjoy the water.

Makua Beach

At the north end of Makua Valley, the only valley in the area fenced off and privately held by the U.S. Army, is a small parking area on the ocean side of the road under some trees with access to **Makua Beach.** This undeveloped, secluded white-sand beach is a great place to find solitude. When the waves are flat, it's also fine for swimming and snorkeling, but during high surf the ocean is dangerous at Makua Beach.

Yokohama Bay

Referred to on maps and by many as **Yokohama Bay,** Keawa'ula Bay offers by far the most picturesque beach on the leeward coast. Part of **Ka'ena Point State Park,** the white-sand beach curves to the northwest and points the way toward the western tip of the island, Ka'ena Point. The turquoise water sees waves throughout the year and is extremely dangerous for swimming during times of high surf. The surf breaks in the area are for expert surfers only. When the water is calm, the ocean is ideal for swimming. There is no shade on the beach, so be prepared with an umbrella or tent to mitigate the piercing sun. To complete the stunning views, behind the bay are several valleys that change from a dry, reddish hue to verdant green the farther back your eye takes you. There are public restrooms and lifeguards on duty.

Ma'ili Beach Park

Surfing

Much of the surf on the leeward side breaks over sharp and shallow reef, making it best suited for expert surfers. Scaling rocks and reef to enter and exit the water can be a challenge for newcomers, and the locals are quite territorial when it comes to their surf breaks. Still, with the right attitude, there's definitely a wave to be had on the leeward coast.

The leeward coast basically faces west, so it is prone to waves all year long. Southerly summer swells and the northwesterly winter swells both offer opportunities for quality surf. Winter swells can get quite big—scary big actually. When a high surf advisory is called for the coast and waves are above the 20-foot mark, it's best to leave the surfboard at home and watch the locals who are familiar with the challenging breaks.

MA'ILI
Ma'ili Point

Ma'ili Point is one of the best waves on this stretch of coastline. A predominantly left-breaking point break, the wave breaks over a shallow coral shelf, which can be a nearly dry reef at low tide. On south swells, the wave is a bit slopey and sometimes rights will break off the main peak. On northwesterly swells, Ma'ili Point is a freight-train wave, with fast breaking and barreling lefts suited for experts only. Park in the parking lot on the north side of the point. Getting in and out of the water can be tricky because of the rocky shelf along the beach, so watch or ask one of the local surfers the best way to get in without getting hurt.

WAI'ANAE
Poka'i Bay

Inside the breakwater in Poka'i Bay in Wai'anae is a rolling wave perfect for beginners. Longboarders, stand-up paddlers, and first-time surfers can get the feel of a board under their feet at this soft break. The wave breaks over a wide reef and is small and calm, even when the surf is larger elsewhere.

MAKAHA
Makaha Beach Park

Makaha is a right-hand point break steeped

Yokohama Bay

in surf history. The site of the Makaha International Surfing Championships 1954-1971, the waves at Makaha can range from fun and playful to massive and life-threatening. Makaha breaks in summer and winter, with the largest waves occurring during the wintertime high surf advisories. The wave breaks over shallow reef at the top of the point and runs into deeper water with a sandy bottom near the beach, famous for its backwash. Makaha gets crowded and has a well-established pack of locals of all ages. If you paddle out at Makaha, smile, say hello, and don't hassle anyone for a wave, or you'll be on the beach before you know it. At Makaha, you'll find people pursuing ocean sports of all kinds: surfing, bodyboarding, stand-up paddling, and bodysurfing. Parking along the road is the safest so you can keep an eye on your car.

Yokohama Bay

About eight miles past Makaha, in the Ka'ena Point State Park at the end of the road, are several challenging, barreling surf breaks. Nestled in the beautiful and secluded Keawa'ula Bay, better known as **Yokohama Bay,** swells approach out of deep water from the north and the south and detonate along the bay's shallow reefs. The waves are very dangerous as they break on extremely shallow reef shelves close to shore. This is a favorite spot for expert surfers and bodyboarders.

Outfitters

Hale Nalu (85-876 Farrington Hwy., #A2, 808/696-5897, http://halenalu.com, 10am-5pm Mon.-Fri., 10am-6pm Sat.-Sun.) has new and used boards and rents bodyboards starting at $14 per day, shortboards starting at $20 per day, longboards starting at $30 per day, and stand-up paddleboards starting at $50 per day. It also has discounts for three-day and weeklong rentals.

West Oahu SUP (84-1170 Farrington Hwy., 808/696-7873, http://westoahusup.com, 9am-5pm daily) rents bodyboards for $35 per day, $100 per five days; longboards and shortboards $35 per day, $100 per five days; and stand-up paddleboards with paddle for $15 hourly, $55 full day, and $165 per five days.

Water Sports

SNORKELING

When the surf is flat and the ocean is calm, generally during the summer, the leeward coast is a snorkeler's dream come true. Crystal clear turquoise water, ample rock outcroppings and patches of reef beside white sandy beaches, and calm nearshore waters protected from the trade winds make for excellent snorkeling all along the coast. Look for areas where a sandy beach connects to rock and reef for the best opportunities to see marine life with safe and easy passage in and out of the water. While there are many places to just pull off the road and jump in the water, it's always safer to swim or snorkel by lifeguards and first check with them about the current ocean conditions. And remember that strong currents accompany high surf, even if there are no waves breaking in your immediate locale. Green sea turtles and spinner dolphins are common sights on the leeward side.

A popular dive and snorkel spot is **Kahe Point Beach Park.** Getting in and out of the water can be tricky as small waves break on the beach, but the water becomes calm almost immediately past the shorebreak. With plenty of reef on the ocean floor, you'll see fish and turtles and plenty of corals. The visibility improves as you swim away from the beach.

Makaha also offers great snorkeling when the waves are flat. Enter the water from the beach and snorkel up the point or down the beach to the south to see live corals, fish and turtles. If there are surfers in the water, do not attempt to snorkel where the waves are breaking. If there are small waves along the point, try the south end of the beach.

Outfitters

The best bet is to bring your snorkel gear with you from your point of origin, because if you find yourself on the west side in need of snorkel gear, you'll have to drive to Wai'anae or Makaha to rent or purchase equipment. **Hale Nalu** (85-876 Farrington Hwy., #A2, 808/696-5897, http://halenalu.com, 10am-6pm Mon.-Fri., 10am-5pm Sat.-Sun.) is a sporting goods store located in Wai'anae across from Poka'i Bay renting snorkel gear for $10 per day, $20 for three days, and $35 per week. In Makaha, **West Oahu SUP** (84-1170 Farrington Hwy., 808/696-7873, http://westoahusup.com, 9pm-5am daily) rents snorkel sets for $10 full day and $38 five days.

DIVING

Nestled in the lee of the trade winds, the west side has some of the best conditions for diving on a consistent basis. The underwater world has shallow reef diving with lava tubes and arches, the Makaha caverns and rock formations—a favorite for turtles and monk seals—and several wrecks, including a plane fuselage, a landing craft unit, an airplane, and a minesweeping vessel. Look for octopus, whitemouth morays, porcupine puffer fish, whitetip reef sharks, Hawaiian stingrays, and spinner dolphins.

Outfitters

Patrick's Diving Adventures (785-371 Farrington Hwy., 808/589-2177, http://pearl-harbordivers.com), is based in Honolulu, but dives the west side in addition to the south and southern coasts. Its two-tank boat dives from the Wai'anae Small Boat Harbor are $109 per person. It also offers a special three-tank Ka'ena Point drift dive once or twice a month for $109. It has scuba courses in Honolulu, offering NAUI certification starting at $379 group and $449 private.

KAYAKING

From the water, the leeward coast is nothing less than spectacularly beautiful. Its rugged coastline, a combination of white-sand beaches, rock and reef outcroppings, and jagged cliffs, is only complemented by the deep valleys lying in succession all the way up the coast. Sea kayaking affords a perspective unmatched and unobtainable by land, far from the spiderweb of power lines over the

the rugged leeward coast

neighborhoods and the bustle of Farrington Highway. In addition, the crystal clear water runs from turquoise to deep blue, and humpback whale-watching is at its best on this side of the island during their annual stay from November to March.

As the trade winds rise over the Wai'anae Range, they create pristine conditions for ocean activities. Calm nearshore waters afford easy paddling and abundant ocean life. You can enter the water from Tracks, at the south end of the leeward coast, but be prepared to deal with small waves along the shore. From here, you can explore the jagged cliffs and find small pockets of sand only accessible from the water. Sheltered Poka'i Bay in Wai'anae is perfect for launching the kayaks. For the best views of the valleys, put in at Makaha, Makua Beach, or Yokohama Bay, but only if the surf is flat, which is more likely to occur in summer.

West Oahu SUP (84-1170 Farrington Hwy., 808/696-7873, http://westoahusup.com, 9am-5pm daily) rents two-person kayaks for $15 hourly, $55 full day, and $180 per week. The shop also rents roof racks and tie-downs for $10 each.

SAILING

If you prefer to charter a catamaran and let someone else do the navigating for you so you can focus on taking in the sights, **Wild Side Hawaii** (87-1286 Farrington Hwy., 808/306-7273, http://sailhawaii.com, reservations 8am-4pm daily) has three tours that leave from Wai'anae Small Boat Harbor: Morning Wildlife Cruise is a three-hour nearshore cruise with snorkeling, spinner dolphin swims, and seasonal whale-watching for $115; Best of the West is a 3.5-hour tour with dolphin swims, whale-watching, and tropical reef snorkeling, with a maximum of six guests for $195 per person; the Deluxe Wildlife Charter is a mid-morning three-hour cruise focusing on hands-on learning about Hawaii's marine creatures with dolphin swims, snorkeling instruction, and whale-watching for $175 adult, $145 child. It also has

a full-day cruise departing from Honolulu to the leeward coast for $335.

E O Waianae Tours (2101 Nuuanu Ave., 808/538-9091, www.eowaianaetours.com) has morning and afternoon west-side catamaran tours with snorkeling and kayaking. Adults $120, children ages 5-12 $100, children ages 4 or younger $45. It also offers transportation from Waikiki and online-booking discounts.

FISHING

While shoreline fishing is common from the cliffs and beaches in the region—papio, kumu, and moana being the sought-after take—fishing charters also run out of the area and take advantage of the frequently calm ocean conditions and the steep ledges offshore attracting pelagic fish. There is a 3,000-foot ledge just three miles from Wai'anae Harbor and another 6,000-foot ledge just seven miles out. It's also not uncommon to see people fishing from kayaks just offshore along the coast.

In the Ko Olina Marina there are several fishing charter operators. **Hawaii Charter Boat** (808/372-3868, http://hawaiicharterboat.com) offers deep-sea excursion off Ko Olina and the west coast on its luxury 43-foot fishing yacht. Its private charters are for a maximum of six passengers: the four-hour charter is $700, the six-hour goes for $850, and eight hours will run you $950. **Holopono Sportfishing Charters** (808/330-9890, http://holoponosportfishing.com) trolls for big game fish. Its four-hour charter is $700, six hours is $900, and eight hours will run you $1,100. It also offers private whale-watching tours and sunset cruises.

In the Wai'anae Small Boat Harbor you'll find **Boom Boom Sportfishing** (85-371 Farrington Hwy., Pier A, 808/306-4162, www.boomboomsportfishing.com), which offers private and shared charters for a maximum of six passengers, with two departure times daily. Four-hour private charters are $625, six hours $725, 8-10 hours $900, and 12 hours $1,300. Shared charters start at $160 for four hours and free round-trip transportation or a 10 percent discount for Ko Olina Resort guests.

Live Bait Sportfishing (808/696-1604, www.live-bait.com) also operates out of the Wai'anae Harbor, from slip B-2, and provides all equipment and tackle. You are responsible for bringing food and drinks. The company primarily fishes for marlin, wahoo, tuna, and mahimahi, and give a meal-sized portion of the catch to passengers. Half-day trips are $550 and full-day trips are $750, with a four-passenger maximum.

For fishing gear and tackle retailers, check out **Westside Tackle and Sports Shop** (87-701 Manuaihue St., 808/696-7229) in Wai'anae.

Hiking and Biking

HIKING
Leeward

The leeward side is notoriously dry, sunny, and hot, so hiking is best done early in the morning or late in the day. No matter when you go, bring plenty of water, a hat, and sunscreen.

In **Ka'ena Point State Park** (www.hawaiistateparks.org), hiking out to **Ka'ena Point** is a special experience. The rough and rocky trail, a little over five miles round-trip, follows a well-worn dirt road along the cliff out to the point. The volcanic coast is breathtaking, with tidepools, natural stone arches, and surf surging onto rock outcroppings. The road has washed away not far from the point, so follow the narrow side trail around the cliff. You'll reach a formidable fence designed to keep out invasive species; enter through the double doors. Once you are inside the **Ka'ena Point Natural Area Reserve** (www.state.hi.us/dlnr/dofaw/kaena/index.htm), an ecosystem restoration project, it is of the utmost importance to stay on the marked trails so as not to disturb the seabird nesting grounds. The dunes are covered with native Hawaiian plants and home a handful of Hawaiian and migratory seabirds. The area is also home to several species of native Hawaiian birds, including the great frigatebird, red-footed, brown, and masked boobies, sooty and white terns, and the Hawaiian short-eared owl. Other migratory birds, like the wandering tattler and the Pacific golden plover, also frequent the area. Continue down to the shoreline past some old cement installments and look for Hawaiian monk seals basking in the sun. There are no facilities along the hike and no water, so bring plenty of fluids. To get to the trail, follow Farrington Highway to Yokohama Bay. Drive along the beach till the paved road ends. Park in the dirt parking area and proceed down the dirt road on foot. The state park is open from sunup to sundown.

Explore the deep valley behind Wai'anae, in the shadow of O'ahu's tallest peak, Mount Ka'ala. The six-mile **Wai'anae Kai** loop trail is full of ups and downs, with a final climb to an overlook. It then follows an ancient Hawaiian trail back to the main route. You'll find native Hawaiian trees, shrubs, and herbs along the hike and the likes of the Japanese bush warbler. There are views of Wai'anae, Lualualei, and Makaha Valleys. The trail is unimproved and rough, so proper footwear is essential. To get there, follow Waianae Valley Road to the back of the valley. Continue on it after it turns into a one-lane dirt road. Park in the dirt lot across from the last house at the locked gate. Continue past the locked gate and follow the dirt road on foot.

BIKING

The leeward coast does have a gem of a mountain biking trail, the road to **Ka'ena Point.** Part of **Ka'ena Point State Park** (www.hawaiistateparks.org), the trail is flat, so there's no climbing or downhill involved, but the rocky, rutted, and curving cliffside dirt road is a challenging ride nonetheless. At 2.7 miles one way from the parking area to the point, the ride is extremely scenic, passing rocky coves, sea arches, and crashing waves. Once at the fence, to keep out invasive species from the natural reserve portion of the park, you can bike around the point, along the perimeter of the fence, to the Mokule'ia side and continue up the North Shore, or you can walk your bike through the double doors in the fence. However, the trails inside the reserve are narrow and sandy. The sun is intense, and there is no shade in the area, so bring plenty of water and wear sunscreen.

To get to the trail, follow Farrington Highway to Yokohama Bay. Drive along the beach until the paved road ends. Park in the dirt parking area and proceed down the dirt road on foot. The state park is open from sunup to sundown.

Hale Nalu (85-876 Farrington Hwy., #A2, 808/696-5897, http://halenalu.com, 10am-6pm Mon.-Fri., 10am-5pm Sat.-Sun.), in Wai'anae, rents mountain bikes for $30 per day, $60 for three days, or $90 for one week.

Food

MAKAHA
Markets
In the Makaha Marketplace, on the corner of Farrington Highway and Makaha Valley Road, you'll come to **Ohana Market** (84-1170 Farrington Hwy., 6am-10pm), your last chance for snacks, local sundries, and beverages if you're headed to Ka'ena Point.

KO OLINA
If you're looking for a traditional sit-down, white-tablecloth meal on the west side, then drop into Ko Olina, where top chefs have set up shop to cater to the resort guests.

Quick Bites
Island Country Markets (92-1048 Olani St., 808/671-2231, 6:30am-11pm daily) and **Two Scoops Ice Cream** (92-1048 Olani St., 808/680-9888, www.twoscoopsicp.com, 11am-9pm daily, $3-9) are both located in the Ko Olina Center & Station, near the Ko Olina entrance on the mountain side of the golf course and train tracks. The market has a full deli with hot and cold prepared foods, groceries, produce, raw foods, and alcohol. It also has tourist garb like towels, shirts, and souvenirs. Two Scoops is a locally owned ice-cream parlor with sundaes, frozen drinks, smoothies, and coffee drinks. In addition to supreme ice cream, a jumbo hot dog and Philly cheesesteak are also on the menu.

Steak and Seafood
Monkeypod Kitchen (92-1048 Olani St. Ste. 4-107, 808/380-4086, www.monkeypod-kitchen.com/ko-olina/, 11am-11pm Mon.-Fri., 9am-11pm Sat.-Sun., $14-38) is leading the charge for handcrafted and sustainable cuisine. It uses only socially conscious ingredients, like range-free Maui beef and sustainably caught fish. It serves hand-tossed, wood-fired pizza, burgers, fish, steaks, and noodle dishes like saimin, and boasts an extensive beer and wine list. Monkeypod Kitchen is can't-miss dining.

A Hawaii staple, **Roy's** (92-1220 Ali'inui Dr., 808/676-7697, www.roysrestaurant.com, 11am-2pm and 5:30pm-9:30pm Mon.-Fri., 11am-2pm and 5pm-9pm Sat.-Sun., $15-45) offers lunch and dinner in the Ko Olina Golf Club. Known for its signature Hawaiian fusion cuisine, Roy's blends fresh ingredients with European sauces and Asian spices. A prix fixe menu includes wine pairings and the exceptional desserts are made fresh to order. Indoor and outdoor seating overlooks the golf course.

Expressly Pineapple

Dole Plantation

Ananas comosus of the family Bromeliaceae is a tropical fruit that originated in southern South America. During the 1500s and 1600s, voyaging ships' captains took this unusual and intriguingly sweet fruit around the world on their journeys. **Pineapples** seem to have been brought to Hawaii from somewhere in the Caribbean in the early 1800s, but it wasn't until the mid-1880s that any agricultural experimentation was done with them. James Dole planted the first commercial pineapple plots for production on the Leilehua Plateau at Wahiawa just after the turn of the 20th century. To preserve the fruit, he built an on-site cannery in 1903 and later a second in Iwilei in Honolulu. Expanding his operation, Dole bought the island of Lana'i in 1922 and proceeded to turn the Palawai Basin into one huge pineapple plantation—some 18,000 acres at its greatest extent. The Lana'i plantation produced a million pineapples a day during peak harvest. Relying heavily on canning, Dole made the "king of fruits" a well-known and ordinary food to the American public.

Pineapple production is a lengthy process. First the ground must be tilled and harrowed to ready the soil for planting. The crowns of the pineapple fruit (which themselves look like miniature pineapple plants) or slips from the stem are planted by hand into long rows—some 30,000 plants per acre. A drip-irrigation system is then installed and the soil covered with ground cloth to help control pests and weeds. Fertilizers and pesticides are sprayed as needed, and the plants grow in the warm tropical sun. After 11-13 months these plants fruit. Generally each plant yields one fruit, which grows on a center stalk surrounded by sharp and spiky curved leaves. The plant sprouts again and, about 13 months later, a second crop is taken. Sometimes a third crop is also harvested from these same plants, before the remainders are tilled into the soil and the process begins again. Pineapples are picked by hand—a hot, dusty, and prickly job—and then placed on a boom conveyor that dumps them into trucks for transportation to the cannery. There, all are pressure-washed and sorted by size and quality before being canned or fresh-packed into boxes and shipped to market. Generally about two-thirds are sold as fresh fruit; the remainder is canned. All aspects of production are rotated to keep pineapples available for market throughout the year. There are no longer any pineapple canneries on O'ahu.

Where to Stay on Oʻahu

Waikiki

Name	Type	Price	Features	Why Stay Here?	Best Fit For
Aqua Bamboo	boutique hotel	$139-199	studios and suites with kitchens	luxury suites with outdoor lanai	couples, honeymooners
Aqua Waikiki Pearl	condo hotel	$110-425	full kitchens, private lanai	affordable suites	families
Aston at the Waikiki Banyan	condo resort	$175-269	free Wi-Fi, full kitchen, private lanai, pool, jet spa	family focus	families, large groups
Courtyard by Marriott	hotel	$229-382	high-speed Internet, business center	open spaces for business	business travelers
Diamond Head Beach Hotel	vacation rental	$95-175	studio and multiroom condos, private beach	oceanfront, near Diamond Head	couples, budget travelers
DoubleTree Alana	hotel	$249-385	pool, 24-hour fitness center	modern rooms, high-tech	business travelers, couples
★ **Halekulani**	historic hotel	$530	deep soak tubs, spa, fine dining	elegant, oceanfront	couples, honeymooners
Hilton Hawaiian Village	resort	$209-409	oceanfront, pools, saltwater lagoon	self-contained resort	couples, families, honeymooners
Holiday Inn Waikiki Beachcomber	hotel	$199-299	sundeck, swimming pool	location	families, couples
Hotel Renew	boutique hotel	$189-291	Wi-Fi	emphasis on nature	couples
Hyatt Regency Waikiki Beach	hotel	$309-379	spa, mall	location	beach lovers, couples, families
Ilikai	hotel	$249-289	full kitchens	affordable ocean views	couples, families

Waikiki (continued)

Name	Type	Price	Features	Why Stay Here?	Best Fit For
★ Moana Surfrider	historic hotel	$278-432	oceanfront pool, spa, dining	historic hotel, great location	couples, honeymooners
★ The Modern Honolulu	boutique hotel	$319-479	pool, sundeck, plush furnishings	luxury experience	couples, honeymooners
New Otani Kaimana Beach Hotel	hotel	$187-400	ocean and park views, free Wi-Fi, private lanai	oceanfront, near Diamond Head	families, couples
Outrigger Reef on the Beach	hotel	$209-309	free high-speed Internet, restaurants, shops, pool	beachfront location	groups, families, couples
★ Outrigger Waikiki on the Beach	hotel	$199-409	pool, oceanfront location	beachfront location	beach lovers, couples, families
Pacific Beach Hotel	hotel	$165-235	almost 1,000 rooms in two towers	affordable, ocean views	families, couples
★ Royal Hawaiian	historic hotel	$380-625	authentic decor, tropical gardens, spa, fine dining	historic, beachfront location	couples, honeymooners
Sheraton Princess Kaiulani	hotel	$175-257	private lanai, pool	location	families, couples
★ Sheraton Waikiki	hotel	$252-449	infinity pool, bars, restaurants	oceanfront location	couples, families, honeymooners
Waikiki Beachside Hostel	hostel	$34-273	lockers, free Wi-Fi	affordable, location	budget travelers, backpackers
Waikiki Parc	hotel	$215-440	contemporary, urban luxury	luxury and services	couples, honeymooners
Waikiki Sand Villa	hotel	$105-175	suites, kitchenettes	affordable, private	budget travelers

Honolulu

Name	Type	Price	Features	Why Stay Here?	Best Fit For
Ala Moana Hotel	hotel	$189-269	Internet access	location for business	business and budget travelers
Best Western the Plaza Hotel	budget hotel	$179-189	Wi-Fi, microwave, 24-hour airport shuttle, pool	close to airport	business and budget travelers
Pagoda Hotel	hotel	$119-149	Japanese gardens, multiroom suites	location	families, budget travelers

North Shore

Name	Type	Price	Features	Why Stay Here?	Best Fit For
Sand Island State Recreation Area	camping	$18	basic facilities	only camping in Honolulu	budget travelers, backpackers
Backpackers Hawaii	hostel	$30-150	private rooms, ocean views	accommodates large groups	backpackers, budget travelers
Kaiaka Bay Beach Park	camping	$50	beach camping	natural setting	nature lovers, budget travelers
★ Ke Iki Beach Bungalows	cottages	$160-230	bungalows, five beachfront	affordable, natural setting	nature lovers, couples, honeymooners
★ Turtle Bay Resort	resort	$320-430	suites, beach cottages, villas	only resort on the North Shore	nature lovers, couples, honeymooners, families

Southeast and Windward Coast

Name	Type	Price	Features	Why Stay Here?	Best Fit For
Ahupua'a O Kahana	camping	$18	beachfront camping	close to valley hiking	couples, nature lovers, budget travelers
Bellow Field Beach Park	camping	$30	lifeguards, gated campground	campsite on active military base	families, budget travelers, couples
Hau'ula Beach Park	camping	$50	pavilion, convenient store	location	budget travelers
Hawaii's Hidden Hideaway Bed-and-Breakfast	B&B	$175-250	private bathrooms, kitchenettes, laundry	location	couples, honeymooners
Ho'omaluhia Botanical Garden	camping	$30	basic facilities	fishing, bird-watching	groups, families, nature lovers
★ Kahala Hotel and Resort	resort	$316-796	beachfront, private lagoon, spa	luxury, beach location	luxury lovers, couples, honeymooners
Kokololio Beach Park	camping	$50	beachfront	fishing	budget travelers
Kualoa Regional Park	camping	$30-50	basic facilities	fishing and recreation	couples, families, nature lovers
★ Lanikai Bed-and-Breakfast	B&B	$175-250	suites, king-size bed, kitchenettes	beautiful setting	couples, honeymooners
Pillows in Paradise	bed-and-breakfast	$110-130	private bathrooms, pool, kitchen	location, privacy	couples, families
Sheffield House Bed-and-Breakfast	bed-and-breakfast	$139-194	private entrance, Wi-Fi, kitchenettes	beach location, privacy	couples, families
Waimanalo Bay Beach Park	camping	$50	shaded beach, basic facilities	beautiful beach	budget travelers, nature lovers, couples

Ko Olina and Leeward Coast

Name	Type	Price	Features	Why Stay Here?	Best Fit For
★ Aulani	resort	$494-699	aquatic park, spa, fine dining, suites	family-oriented Disney resort	families
Harbor Shores	apartment hotel	$120	two-bedroom units, full kitchen, private lanai	long-term stay	military families, business travelers
Hawaiian Princess	condominium	$149-209	full kitchens, laundry, private lanai, ocean views	slow pace	couples, families
Kea'au Beach Park	camping	$50	grassy campsites	affordable	budget travelers
Ko Olina Beach Villa Resort	luxury villas	$405	two- and three-bedroom villas, ocean views	private, long-term stay	luxury-loving families, couples, honeymooners
Ma'ili Beach Park	camping	$30	basic facilities	fishing	budget travelers
Marriott's Ko Olina Beach Club	villas and suites	$414-839	full kitchens, lanai, washer/dryer	family oriented	couples, families
Nanakuli Beach Park	camping	$50	shaded campsites	fishing	budget travelers

Maui
Lana'i & Moloka'i

There is a prominent Hawaiian saying about Maui: *Maui no ka oi,* "Maui is the best." Residents and visitors alike agree that there is something magical about Hawaii's second largest island. Yet it's hard to pinpoint exactly what places Maui among the most dreamed-of vacation locations in the world.

The endless stretches of golden sand are an obvious and noteworthy draw, but sand alone doesn't entice millions of visitors to flock to a 727-square-mile dot in the middle of the Pacific. Perhaps it's more than just the thought of relaxing in a lounge chair on the sand with a mai tai in hand and the soft breeze rustling the palm trees overhead. Maybe it's also the way the trade winds blow across a beach of black sand at Wai'anapanapa State Park, stirring up waves on the sparkling blue waters. Or it's the hope of a close encounter with a giant green sea turtle while snorkeling off the coast of Napili Bay. Or maybe it's the way the setting sun reflects in the waters off Makena, creating an atmosphere that's both fiery and calm in the same fleeting moment.

There's a good chance the secret to Maui's allure lies in the many moments that stick with you long after you've left the island behind. Hiking through a bamboo forest so thick it nearly obscures the sun and finding yourself at the base of a 400-foot waterfall cascading down a rocky cliff. Riding your first wave and feeling the thrill of the surf as you glide across a silky blue break. Waking at 3am to drive up a dark mountainside in the freezing cold to see the first rays of light illuminate the rich colors of Haleakala Crater.

These are the moments that make a trip to Maui truly *no ka oi.*

WHERE TO GO
Lahaina and West Maui

West Maui pulses with a unique coastal vibe. The historic town of **Lahaina** was once the capital of the Hawaiian kingdom, and it retains a port town atmosphere. Warm weather and mostly dry conditions make this region a spectacular place for outdoor adventure. Snorkel with sea turtles at **Napili Bay,** lounge on the beach in **Kapalua,** ride the zip line above **Ka'anapali,** or hike to **Nakalele Blowhole.**

Central Maui

Central Maui is the island's population center and the seat of county government. Most visitors blow through town on the way to their beachfront resort, but Central Maui has its own set of sights off the regular trail. The twisting road into **'Iao Valley** is the region's most popular attraction. **Kepaniwai Heritage Gardens** exhibits Maui's multicultural heritage, and down on the shore at **Kanaha Beach Park,** windsurfers and kitesurfers take to the waves along the stretch of Maui's north shore.

Kihei and South Maui

From the celebrity-laden resorts of **Wailea** to the condo-dwelling snowbirds of **Kihei,** South Maui is all about worshipping the sun and enjoying the procession of beaches. **Makena** remains South Maui's most adventurous venue, with snorkeling, scuba diving, hiking trails, kayaking, and some of the island's most photo-worthy beaches. Just offshore, **Molokini Crater** offers 100-foot visibility and the chance to snorkel with up to 250 species of fish.

Haleakala and Upcountry

Rural, laid-back, and refreshingly cool, Upcountry is Maui's most underrated zone. Agriculture and produce dominate **Kula,** and everything from vegetables to vineyards, coffee, and goat cheese can be found in this rural and relaxing enclave. **Polipoli** is the island's little-known adventure zone, where mountain biking, paragliding, and hiking take place in a forest shrouded in mist. Watch the dramatic sunrise from the frosty peak of towering **Haleakala,** the sacred volcano from which the demigod Maui famously snared the sun.

East Maui: the Road to Hana

The New Age town of **Pa'ia** is as trendy as it is jovial. Surfers ride waves along undeveloped beaches, patrons shop in locally owned boutiques, and the town is home to some the island's best restaurants. Along the famous, twisting **Road to Hana,** tumbling waterfalls and rugged hiking trails await. The **Pools of 'Ohe'o** spill down cliffs to the sea. The hike through a bamboo forest to the base of **Waimoku Falls** is considered the island's best trek.

Lana'i

Home to 3,500 residents and one large resort, this island is a playground of outdoor adventure. Learn about the island's history at the **Lana'i Culture and Heritage Center,** and make the journey down to **Kaunolu** to see an ancient village settlement frozen in time.

Moloka'i

Taking time to explore this island offers a chance to experience the roots of native Hawaiian culture. Take a guided tour into historic **Halawa Valley,** one of the oldest settlements in Hawaii, or ride on the back of a friendly mule as you visit the former leper colony of **Kalaupapa.** Watch the sunset from **Papohaku Beach,** one of the state's longest and most deserted stretches of sand, or climb your way high into the mists of the **Moloka'i Forest Reserve.**

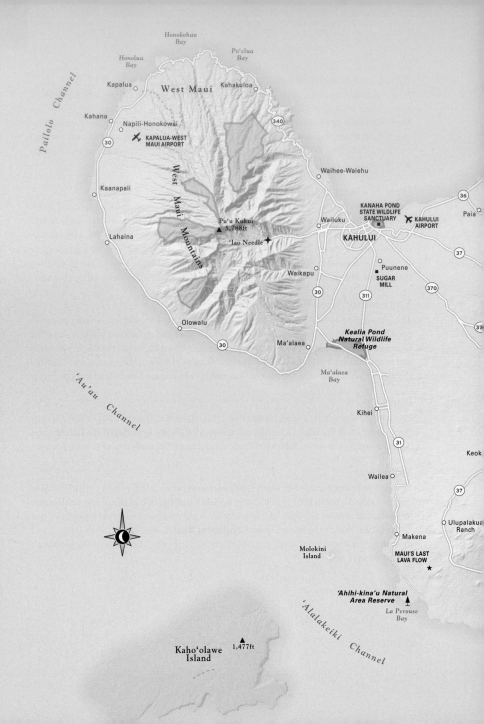

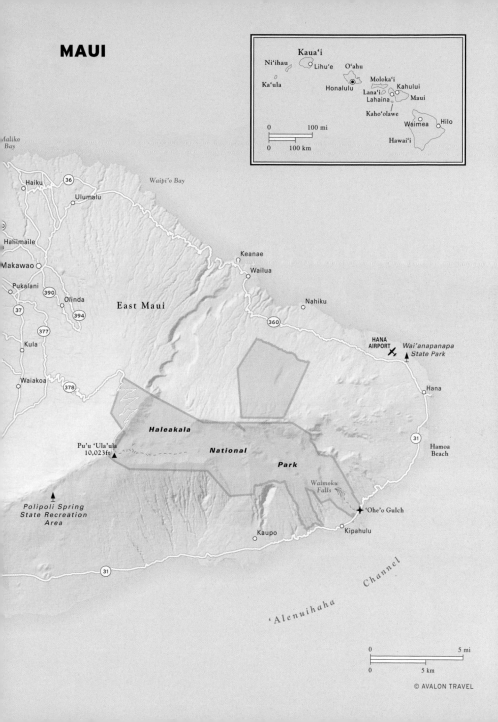

MAUI

Kaua'i

Ni'ihau
Lihu'e
O'ahu
Ka'ula
Honalulu
Moloka'i
Lana'i
Kahului
Lahaina
Maui
Kaho'olawe
Waimea
Hilo
Hawai'i

0   100 mi

0   100 km

Maliko Bay

Haiku — 36

Ulumalu

Waipi'o Bay

Haliimaile

Makawao

Keanae

Wailua

Pukalani — 390

Olinda

Nahiku

37

394

East Maui

360

Kula

HANA AIRPORT

Wai'anapanapa State Park

377

Waiakoa

378

Hana

Haleakala

Pu'u 'Ula'ula
10,023ft

National

Hamoa Beach

31

Park

Waimoku Falls

Polipoli Spring
State Recreation
Area

'Ohe'o Gulch

Kaupo

Kipahulu

31

'Alenuihaha Channel

0   5 mi

0   5 km

© AVALON TRAVEL

Lahaina and West Maui

The slopes and shores of West Maui are what many visitors picture when they close their eyes and envision paradise.

White sandy beaches, rocky coves, lush valleys, and oceanfront restaurants where the clinking glasses of mai tais and the smooth sounds of a slack-key guitar complement the setting sun—Maui is a magical place.

West Maui beaches are some of the best on the island. In winter, Honolua Bay shapes the kind of legendary right-hand point breaks that attract surfers from across the globe. In summer, this same bay offers some of the island's finest snorkeling, where bright parrotfish, shy octopi, and curious sea turtles occupy an expansive reef.

Hot, busy, and incomparably historic, Lahaina was once the whaling capital of the Pacific as well as the capital of the Hawaiian kingdom. Today, it's Maui's quintessential tourist town. The name "Lahaina" translates as "cruel, merciless sun," and, appropriately, almost every day is sunny in Lahaina. As a result, it buzzes with an energetic fervor that draws pedestrians to the streets, fishers to the harbor, and surfers to the breaks offshore.

Whether you're scouring the historic relics of Lahaina, swimming with reef fish at Napili Bay, stand-up paddleboarding along the Ka'anapali shore, or simply enjoying the sunset from an oceanfront luau, this is the Maui you were dreaming of.

ORIENTATION

West Maui, geographically, is an enormous swath of land. It technically begins once you pass through the tunnel and reach **Papalaua Beach,** and stretches all the way to **Kahakuloa** on the island's northern coast. With the exception of tiny **Olowalu village,** there's no development from the time you pass **Ma'alaea** until you reach **Lahaina.** Here you'll find Hawaii's ancient capital as well as restaurants, the harbor, and shops, whereas **Ka'anapali,** just up the road, is lined with world-class resorts. **Honokowai, Kahana,** and **Napili** meld together in a strip of oceanfront condos, and eventually give way to **Kapalua** resort about 20 minutes north of Lahaina. Past the resort, the coast gets wild and development comes to a halt,

---

Previous: Pu'u Keka'a, Ka'anapali; Honolua Bay. **Above:** inhabitant of the colorful West Maui reefs.

Look for ★ to find recommended
sights, activities, dining, and lodging.

Highlights

★ **Nakalele Blowhole:** At this thunderous blowhole, pressure transforms incoming waves into a 100-foot geyser (page 191).

★ **Lahaina Courthouse:** With an art gallery in the basement, old photos on the ground level, and a museum on the third story, this is the best way to learn the unique history of Lahaina (page 194).

★ **Honolua Bay:** In summer, snorkel with sea turtles in this legendary protected bay. In winter, watch as the island's best surfers drop into waves over 20 feet high (page 205).

★ **Surfing Lahaina:** This ancient capital is one of the island's best places for learning the Hawaiian sport of kings (page 215).

★ **Sunset Cruises off Ka'anapali Beach:** Feel the trade winds in your hair as you literally sail into the sunset off West Maui's most iconic beach (page 220).

★ **Whale-Watching:** During December through April, the waters off Maui are home to the highest concentration of humpback whales on the planet. Head out for an up-close encounter with these 50-ton creatures (page 222).

★ **Kapalua Coastal Trail:** Spend an hour scouring the coast along this luxuriant yet rugged 1.75-mile trail. Along the way you will pass some of Hawaii's most beautiful beaches (page 225).

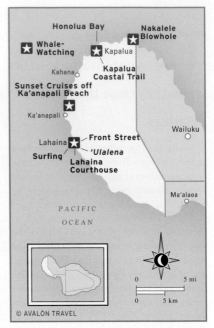

★ **Front Street:** Get your shopping, people-watching, and dining fixes by walking the length of the island's most famous thoroughfare (page 230).

★ **'Ulalena and Maui Theatre:** The history of Hawaii is told through rhythms, dance, and creative special effects inside the impressive Maui Theatre (page 233).

West Maui

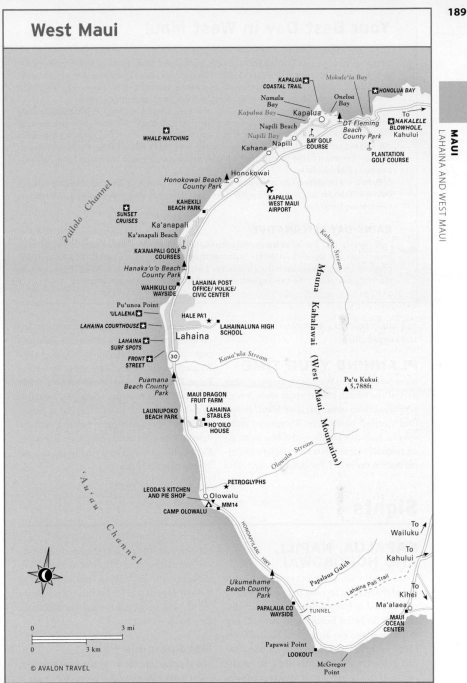

KAPALUA
COASTAL TRAIL

Mokule'ia Bay

HONOLUA BAY

Namalu
Bay

Oneloa
Bay

Kapalua Bay Kapalua

DT Fleming
Beach
County Park

To
NAKALELE
BLOWHOLE,
Kahului

WHALE-WATCHING

Napili Beach
Napili Bay

Napili

Kahana

BAY GOLF
COURSE

Kahana

PLANTATION
GOLF COURSE

Honokowai

Honokowai Beach
County Park

KAPALUA
WEST MAUI
AIRPORT

Pailolo Channel

KAHEKILI
BEACH PARK

SUNSET
CRUISES

Ka'anapali

Ka'anapali Beach

KA'ANAPALI GOLF
COURSES

Kahana Stream

Hanaka'o'o Beach
County Park

WAHIKULI CO
WAYSIDE

LAHAINA POST
OFFICE/ POLICE/
CIVIC CENTER

Pu'unoa Point

'ULALENA

HALE PA'I

LAHAINA COURTHOUSE

LAHAINALUNA HIGH
SCHOOL

LAHAINA
SURF SPOTS

Lahaina

FRONT
STREET

30

Kaua'ula Stream

Pu'u Kukui
5,788ft

Mauna Kahalawai (West Maui Mountains)

Puamana
Beach County
Park

MAUI DRAGON
FRUIT FARM

LAUNIUPOKO
BEACH PARK

LAHAINA
STABLES

HO'OILO
HOUSE

Olowalu Stream

PETROGLYPHS

LEODA'S KITCHEN
AND PIE SHOP

Olowalu

'Au'au Channel

MM14

CAMP OLOWALU

To
Wailuku

To
Kahului

HONOAPI'ILANI HWY

Papalaua Gulch

Lahaina Pali Trail

To
Kihei

Ukumehame
Beach County
Park

Ma'alaea

PAPALAUA CO
WAYSIDE

TUNNEL

MAUI
OCEAN
CENTER

0   3 mi

0   3 km

Papawai Point
LOOKOUT

McGregor
Point

© AVALON TRAVEL

Your Best Day in West Maui

Get up early and head to **The Gazebo** to be in line for the 7:30am opening. After breakfast drive up the road to **Kapalua Bay** and walk off the stack of macadamia pancakes with a stroll on the **Kapalua Coastal Trail.** Having worked up a sweat and soaked up the views, grab snacks and drinks at **Honolua Store** before embarking on the adventurous drive north.

If you feel like snorkeling and have your own gear, stop for an hour at **Mokulei'a Bay** and search for octopi and turtles, or simply take a stroll through the vines on a walk through **Honolua Valley.** Stop to photograph the world-famous bay when you reach the top of the hill, and then continue driving all the way toward **Nakalele Blowhole.** Watch your step as you clamber down to the thundering saltwater geyser, and if you're feeling up for it, continue driving to **Kahakuloa.**

By now it'll be getting late in the day, and you need to make it to **The Sea House** in Napili before 4:30pm for happy hour. Appetizers are 50 percent off, then enjoy a filling, early dinner overlooking Napili Bay.

RAINY-DAY ALTERNATIVE

Grab breakfast at **The Gazebo** and listen to the rain come down before escaping it by heading underwater on a tour with **Atlantis Submarines.** Get a burger at **Cool Cat Café,** and then brush up on your Hawaiian history inside the **Lahaina Courthouse.** Since there won't be much of a sunset, end the evening with dinner at **Sansei** and the show **'Ulalena.**

and sandy beaches give way to rocky coves and rugged cliffs.

PLANNING YOUR TIME

More people stay in West Maui than any other part of the island, and in many ways it feels separated from other parts of Maui. If you find yourself based here, it's easy to make simple, half-day jaunts to the beach, or go on tropical micro-adventures before lounging back at the resort. For other travelers who aren't based in West Maui, two full days is a good amount of time to experience the area's best sights, with one day spent in Lahaina and Ka'anapali and another exploring "up north." From Kahului Airport, it's about 40 minutes to Lahaina and an hour to Kapalua, though as the island grows, the traffic is getting particularly bad—and driving to Lahaina between 3pm and 5pm can often be bumper to bumper. Factor this in if you're trying to get to your 5pm oceanfront lu'au.

Sights

KAPALUA, NAPILI, AND HONOKOWAI

Exploring the island's northwestern coast is one of the island's best day trips—like a miniature Road to Hana without the waterfalls, but with far better beaches and views. If you continue all the way around the back of West Maui, past the town of Kahakuloa (the road isn't limited to 4WD vehicles like your rental-car map might say, but it is far narrower, curvier, and scarier than the Road to Hana), you can combine the drive with the waterfalls of Makamaka'ole Valley in Central Maui for a full-day experience. This journey is not for the timid. Most turn back toward **Kapalua** once they reach Kahakuloa.

Makalua-puna Point

For spectacular views of the northwestern coast and white-sand Oneloa Bay, take a stroll on **Makalua-puna Point**—otherwise known as "Dragon's Teeth." The jagged rocks here have been dramatically sculpted by waves crashing on the coast, and there's a large labyrinth in the middle of the point for silently reflecting on the beauty. The trailhead is located by the small parking lot at the end of Office Road. Visit without leaving a trace; this point is sacred to native Hawaiians and access can be controversial, so tread lightly when you follow the trail out onto the windswept point.

Honolua Bay

Famous for its exceptional surfing and diving, **Honolua Bay** is also one of West Maui's most beautiful sights. There is a palpable magic in this bay, from the vine-laden valley that leads to the shore and the reef that's teeming with life, to the simply legendary right-hand wave that perfectly bends around the point. When visiting Honolua Bay—particularly when the surf is breaking—either stop at the overlook on the north side of the bay after climbing the short but steep hill, or drive down the bumpy dirt road that leads to the top of the bluff. To continue the Honolua adventure on foot, walk to the where the dirt road ends, where a very thin trail connects with a network of coastal trails that lead to views of the coast.

★ Nakalele Blowhole

Eight miles past the entrance to Kapalua, by mile marker 38, is the famous **Nakalele Blowhole.** Outside of Honolua Bay this is the most popular stop along this stretch of coast. It's about a 15-minute drive past the entrance to Kapalua if you go straight through without stopping. On the right days, the Nakalele Blowhole can jettison water upward of 100 feet into the air. The best conditions for witnessing Nakalele are when the trade winds are blowing and there's northerly swell. In the full throes of its performance, Nakalele Blowhole is a natural saltwater geyser erupting on a windswept outcropping, and it's one of the most powerful forces of the sea you can witness on the island. Visitors in the past have been killed by standing too close to the blowhole, so pay attention to warning signs in the area.

Finding the blowhole can be a challenge for those who don't know where to look. At mile marker 38 there is dirt pullout on the ocean side of the highway, although the trail from here that leads down toward the water will only take you as far as the decrepit old lighthouse and a marginal view of the blowhole. A better access point is 0.5 mile farther down the road where a second dirt pullout serves as the

Nakalele Blowhole

trailhead for the path leading to the blowhole. Between the two parking areas are dozens of dirt-bike tracks that don't lead anywhere, so the best thing to do is park by mile marker 38.5 and make your way down from there. The trail to the blowhole is just over 0.5 mile long, and the last half of the trail becomes a scramble down a moderate scree slope, which is best left to those who are steady on their feet. When you reach the bottom of the rocky trail, turn around and look behind you, facing away from blowhole. If you look closely, you'll find the **heart-shaped hole in the rocks** that's a Maui Instagram darling.

The Olivine Pools

A little over four miles past the Nakalele Blowhole, by mile marker 16, the **Olivine Pools**—traditionally called Mokolea—are one of the more unique and beautiful sights on the northwestern side of the island. The coastal panoramas from here are breathtaking, and even if you don't walk down to the pools, the views alone are reason enough to stop. For most visitors, though, the goal is to swim and bathe in the shallow tide pools perfectly perched on a lava rock outcropping. On rare calm days when the wind is light and the ocean is mellow and smooth, this can be one of the most serene perches you'll find anywhere on the island. However, the ocean is treacherous here, which makes swimming in the pools risky. A good rule of thumb is to sit and watch them for a while and wait to see if any waves are crashing into them. If the ocean is calm and isn't reaching the pools, then this is the safest time for swimming or wading. Visitors *have* died trying to reach the pools, so it is especially important to be aware of your surroundings at all times. If waves are washing into the pools, keep out. Park in the dirt area on the ocean side of the road, and follow the trail leading down toward the coast to access the pools. The trail will fork at a yellow sign that warns about the dangers of continuing. Follow the trail to the edge of the bluff and then proceed down the trail leading to the pools.

KA'ANAPALI
Pu'u Keka'a

Known to most visitors as Black Rock, **Pu'u Keka'a** is the correct name for this volcanic outcropping at the northern end of Ka'anapali Beach. Today the rock is a popular spot for snorkeling, scuba diving, and cliff-jumping, although the most popular time of day is about 20 minutes prior to sunset when a torch-wielding, shirtless member of the Sheraton staff scrambles onto the rock and lights a row of carefully placed tiki torches. Once all of the torches are lit, his flaming staff is ceremoniously chucked into the water moments before he performs a swan dive off the rock. More than just a creative marketing plan, the ceremony is a reenactment of the sacred belief that this is one of the spots on the island where a person's soul leaps from this world to the next immediately following death. For a prime perch to watch the show, grab a drink at the Cliff Dive Grill inside the Sheraton Maui.

Whalers Village Museum

There's actually more to Whalers Village than high-end luxury shopping and beachfront bars. On the third story, high above the fancy stores and bustling courtyard, the **Whalers Village Museum** (2435 Ka'anapali Pkwy., 808/661-5992, www.whalersmuseum.com, 10am-6pm daily, $3 adults, $2 seniors, $1 children) is the best resource for whale education on the island's West Side. Visitors can wander through the museum to learn everything from why whales were hunted in the first place to what life was like aboard a 19th-century whaling ship. There is a large display of scrimshaw art (drawings carved on whale's teeth), and there are also movies playing throughout the day that explore the dismal yet fascinating world of 19th-century whaling. During winter, a visit to the museum is the perfect way to reinforce the knowledge gained on a whale-watching excursion.

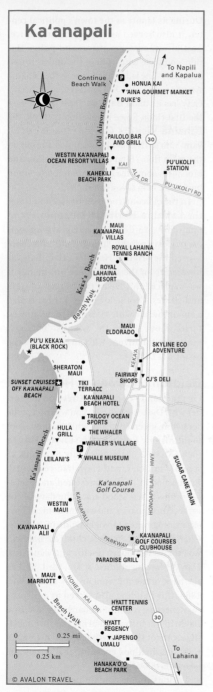

Ka'anapali

To Napili and Kapalua
Continue Beach Walk
P
HONUA KAI
'AINA GOURMET MARKET
DUKE'S
Old Airport Beach
PAILOLO BAR AND GRILL 30
WESTIN KA'ANAPALI OCEAN RESORT VILLAS
KAI
PU'UKOLI'I STATION
KAHEKILI BEACH PARK
ALA DR
PU'UKOLI'I RD
MAUI KA'ANAPALI VILLAS
ROYAL LAHAINA TENNIS RANCH
Kekaa Beach
ROYAL LAHAINA RESORT
Beach Walk
DR
MAUI ELDORADO
PU'U KEKA'A (BLACK ROCK)
SKYLINE ECO ADVENTURE
KEKAA
SHERATON MAUI
FAIRWAY SHOPS
CJ'S DELI
SUNSET CRUISES OFF KA'ANAPALI BEACH
TIKI TERRACE
KA'ANAPALI BEACH HOTEL
TRILOGY OCEAN SPORTS
HULA GRILL
THE WHALER
WHALER'S VILLAGE
Ka'anapali Beach
LEILANI'S
P
WHALE MUSEUM
HWY
SUGAR CANE TRAIN
Ka'anapali Golf Course
KA'ANAPALI
HONOAPI'ILANI
WESTIN MAUI
KA'ANAPALI ALII
ROYS
KA'ANAPALI GOLF COURSES CLUBHOUSE
PARKWAY
PARADISE GRILL
MAUI MARRIOTT
NOHEA KAI DR
Beach Walk
HYATT TENNIS CENTER
30
HYATT REGENCY
JAPENGO
UMALU
To Lahaina
0   0.25 mi
0   0.25 km
HANAKA'O'O BEACH PARK
© AVALON TRAVEL

Tour of the Stars

For a truly unique Ka'anapali experience, stand on the roof of the Hyatt and stargaze through high-powered telescopes. Held at 8pm and 9pm every night, the **Tour of the Stars** (200 Nohea Kai Dr., 808/667-4727) allows small groups of 14 people to access the roof of the resort and peer through a 14-inch reflector telescope with the resort's director of astronomy. Tours are $30 for adults and $20 for children ($25 adults, $15 children for hotel guests), and if you want to make it a romantic evening, join the nightly 10pm tour with chocolate-covered strawberries and champagne ($45 pp, $40 for hotel guests).

LAHAINA

From 1820 to 1845, the seaside town of **Lahaina**—which was originally called Lele—was the capital of the Hawaiian kingdom. At about the same time that the *ali'i* (nobility) and royalty were establishing their capital, fleets of New England whaling ships began anchoring in the Lahaina Roads. From 1820 to 1860, thousands of crusty whalers paddled ashore in wooden rowboats to reprovision their ships, soak their livers, and soothe their rusty loins. Answering the call to save these poor souls, Christian missionaries from New England began to arrive in the early 1820s, bolstered by the support of Queen Ka'ahumanu, who had embraced the values of Christianity. Lahaina became a battleground between drunken whalers and pious missionaries to win over the native Hawaiian populace, a Wild West of the Pacific. Today, scores of historic sites pertaining to this era are scattered around town.

Thanks to the tireless work of the Lahaina Restoration Foundation, many of the town's historic sites are well marked and accessible. Pick up a walking tour map from the Lahaina Visitors Center in the courthouse next to Lahaina Harbor or a *Mo'olelo O Lahaina* historical and cultural walking tour map from the offices of the Lahaina Restoration

Foundation on the grounds of the Baldwin Missionary home.

The Banyan Tree

This magnificent tree is the most recognizable landmark in West Maui. You can't miss it at the corner of Hotel and Front Streets, because it spreads its shading boughs over almost an acre. This tree is the **largest banyan in the state,** planted in April 1873 by Sheriff Bill Smith in commemoration of the Congregationalist Missions' golden anniversary. Every year in April a birthday party is held for the tree that draws hundreds of people to its shady confines. During most days you can find old-timers sitting here chatting, and artists gather on weekends to display their artwork under the tree's broad branches.

Fort at Lahaina

On the southwestern edge of the park are the restored coral remnants of the historic **Fort at Lahaina.** By 1825, the missionaries had convinced Hawaiian royalty that drunken sailors running amok in town was morally lamentable, so strict laws forbade native women from visiting the ships and whalers from coming ashore after nightfall. These rules, as you can imagine, proved a severe hindrance to lascivious pursuits, and riots frequently broke out between angry whalers and the missionaries. In 1827, whalers anchored offshore went so far as to lob cannonballs into the lawn of missionary William Richards's house, and it was decided by Hoapili—the governor of Maui—that a fort needed to be built to protect the town from the pent-up whalers. Hence, in 1832, a fort was constructed out of coral blocks with walls 20 feet high and laden with cannons, the restored remnants of which are still visible today. One of the cannons from the fort is across the street at Lahaina Harbor, facing out toward the water to serve as a reminder of the "tensions" that once gripped this town.

★ Lahaina Courthouse

The old **Lahaina Courthouse** contains the most informative museum in central Lahaina.

During its tenure as the town's political center, it also served as the governor's office, post office, customs office, and police station, complete with a jail in the underground basement. The jail is now home to the Lahaina Arts Society's **Old Jail Gallery,** and the society has its main **Banyan Tree Gallery** on the first floor. Since renovation in 1998, the **Lahaina Visitors Center** (808/667-9193, 9am-5pm daily) has also occupied a room on the main floor. Find tourist information and brochures about the town; numerous coupon books can help save a few dollars.

In the old courtroom on the second floor, the **Lahaina Heritage Museum** (9am-5pm daily, $3 donation) displays historical objects and old photographs, and there is even the original Hawaiian flag that was lowered from the courthouse on the day it was replaced in 1898 by the American stars and stripes. On the lower level there is also a small theater with informative documentaries about life in the islands. This is a must-stop for anyone with an interest in the history of Lahaina.

Baldwin Missionary House

On the inland side of Front Street, on the corner with Dickenson Street, you will notice the sprawling green lawn and whitewashed front of the historic **Baldwin Missionary House** (808/661-3262, 10am-4pm daily, $7 adults, $5 seniors, military, and Hawaiian residents). Established in 1834, this restored and peaceful property has stood since the days of the earliest missionaries and was the home of physician and reverend Dwight Baldwin, his wife, Charlotte, and their eight children. Baldwin was the first modern doctor and dentist in Hawaii, having studied at Harvard, and in the back of the museum are his tools. Until 1868, this building also served as a dispensary, meeting room, and boardinghouse, and Baldwin was instrumental not only in educating scores of Hawaiians but also in helping to fight the smallpox epidemic that struck the island in 1853.

Various rooms contain period furniture

and artifacts indicative of missionary life in Lahaina, and coin collectors will appreciate the array of historic coins that were used as legal tender in early Hawaii, including silver bullion minted in Bolivia as early as the 1500s. Entrance to the museum also covers the **Wo Hing Museum** up the street, and if you purchase a $10 Passport to the Past, admission to the A&B Sugar Museum in Kahului and the Bailey House Museum in Wailuku are also included. While visiting in the daytime is educational enough, for a true glimpse of missionary life, take part in a candlelit tour 6pm-8:30pm every Friday evening.

Plantation Museum

For a look at a period of Lahaina's history that didn't have to do with whalers, missionaries, or Hawaiian royalty, idle on over to the Wharf Cinema Center and climb the stairs to the third story for a glimpse inside the informative **Plantation Museum** (808/661-3262, 9am-6pm daily, free). Although it isn't much larger than a closet, there are dozens of old photos showing life during plantation times as well as a video detailing harvesting sugarcane. The Pioneer Mill was the social and economic engine of the West Side for the better part of 100 years, and the plantation days are just as much a part of Lahaina's heritage as harpoons, grog, and Bibles. A visit only takes a couple of minutes and is worthwhile.

Wo Hing Museum

The **Wo Hing Museum** (808/661-3262, 858 Front St., 10am-4pm daily, $7) is a small Chinese museum sandwiched between the modern commercial ventures of Front Street. Built in 1912 as a social and religious hall for Chinese workers, it's been placed on the National Register of Historic Places, showcasing Chinese immigration history on Maui, as well as Chinese cultural traditions. Downstairs are displays, and upstairs is the temple altar. In the cookhouse next door, you can see film clips of Hawaii taken by Thomas Edison in 1898 and 1906. On Chinese New Year, the Wo Hing Museum is the center of

the activities that play out on Front Street. The entrance fee also covers entrance to the Baldwin House.

Hale Pa'ahao

Where Luakini crosses Prison Street, turn left and walk a few yards to **Hale Pa'ahao** (808/661-3262, 10am-4pm daily, free), better known as Lahaina's old prison, one of the more historically informative sites. The peaceful courtyard inside the prison walls is a place of serenity and calm, where benches rest beneath the shade of a mango tree, but this compound once housed dozens of sailors and Hawaiians who broke the laws set out by the royals and their missionary advisors. To get an idea of an offense that would land you in the Lahaina slammer, read the list from the 1850s posted on the wall of one of the whitewashed wooden cells.

Hale Pa'i Printing Museum

All the way at the top of Lahainaluna Road on the grounds of Lahainaluna High School, which is the oldest high school west of the Rocky Mountains, having been founded in 1831, **Hale Pa'i Printing Museum** (808/667-7040, 10am-4pm Mon.-Wed., free) provides a phenomenally informative view into the literary past of the Hawaiian Islands. If you're involved in the education field or interested in history, this is a must-stop for a look at the history of Hawaii's printed past.

In addition to the old printing press, there are a host of native Hawaiian artifacts. This small, out-of-the-way museum in the school's parking lot provides excellent insight into the development of modern Hawaii.

SOUTH OF LAHAINA
Olowalu Petroglyphs

For every 1,000 people who snorkel at Olowalu, probably only one makes it back to the *ki'i pohaku*, the **petroglyphs** behind the Olowalu General Store. Hidden 0.5 mile back in the recesses of Olowalu valley, the 70 rock carvings on the face of Pu'u Kilea date to nearly 300 years ago, when there was

Downtown Lahaina

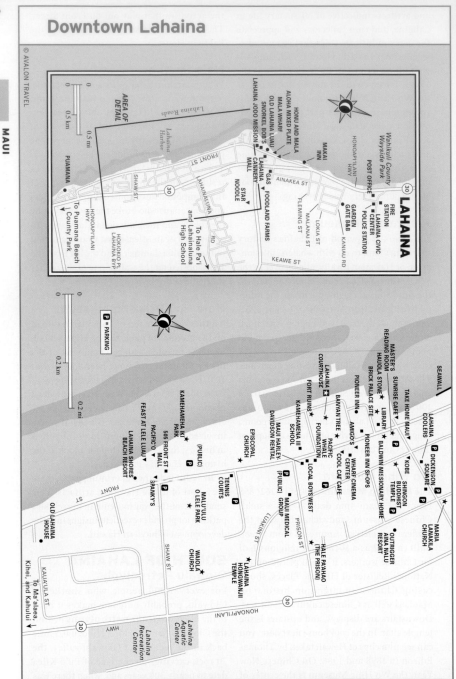

AREA OF DETAIL

0 0.5 km
0 0.5 mi

0 0.2 km
0 0.2 mi

P = PARKING

Lahaina Roads

Lahaina Harbor

LAHAINA

HONU AND MALA
ALOHA MIXED PLATE
MALA WHARF
OLD LAHAINA LUAU
LAHAINA JODO MISSION
SNORKEL BOB'S

MAKAI INN

HONOAPI'ILANI HWY

Wahikuli County Wayside Park

POST OFFICE

LAHAINA CANNERY MALL

GAS

FOODLAND FARMS

STAR NOODLE

AINAKEA ST

FLEMING ST

MALANAI ST

LOKIA ST

KANIAU RD

KEAWE ST

FIRE STATION
LAHAINA CIVIC CENTER
POLICE STATION
GARDEN GATE B&B

PUAMANA

To Puamana Beach County Park

HONOAPI'ILANI HWY

HOKIOKIO PL
LAHAINA BYP

SHAW ST

LAHAINALUNA RD

To Hale Pa'i
and Lahainaluna High School

FRONT ST

MASTER'S READING ROOM
HAUOLA STONE
BRICK PALACE SITE
PIONEER INN
LAHAINA COURTHOUSE
FORT RUINS
KAMEHAMENA III SCHOOL
MAUI HARLEY-DAVIDSON RENTAL
EPISCOPAL CHURCH
KAMEHAMEHA IKI PARK
505 FRONT ST MALL
PACIFIC'O
FEAST AT LELE LUAU
LAHAINA SHORES BEACH RESORT

SUNRISE CAFE
TAKE HOME MAUI
LIBRARY
BANYAN TREE
PACIFIC WHALE FOUNDATION
AMIGO'S
PIONEER INN SHOPS
WHARF CINEMA CENTER
COOL CAT CAFE
LOCAL BOYS WEST
MAUI MEDICAL GROUP
TENNIS COURTS
MALU'ULU O LELE PARK
3BANKY'S
WAIOLA CHURCH
LAHAINA HONGWANJI TEMPLE

BALDWIN MISSIONARY HOME

SEAWALL

LAHAINA COOLERS
DICKENSON SQUARE
KOBE
SHINGON BUDDHIST TEMPLE
OUTRIGGER AINA NALU RESORT
MARIA LANAKILA CHURCH

HALE PA'AHAO (THE PRISON)

PRISON ST

LAHAINALUNA RD

OLD LAHAINA HOUSE

FRONT ST

SHAW ST

KAUA'ULA ST

HONOAPI'ILANI HWY

To Ma'alaea,
Kihei, and Kahului

Lahaina Aquatic Center

Lahaina Recreation Center

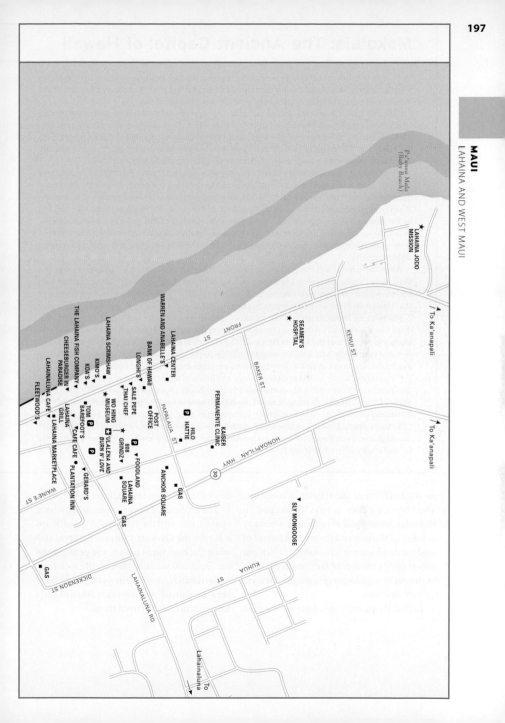

Pu'unoa Mala
(Baby Beach)

LAHAINA JODO
MISSION ★

To Ka'anapali

KENUI ST

FRONT ST

SEAMEN'S ★
HOSPITAL

BAKER ST

To Ka'anapali

PAPALAUA ST

KAISER
PERMANENTE CLINIC

HONOAPI'ILAN HWY

30

HILO
HATTIE

POST
OFFICE

808
GRINDZ ▼

'ULALENA AND
BURN N' LOVE ★

FOODLAND

LAHAINA
SQUARE

ANCHOR SQUARE

GAS

GAS

SLY MONGOOSE

KUHUA ST

DICKENSON ST

GAS

LAHAINALUNA RD

LAHAINALUNA CAFE ▼

LAHAINA MARKETPLACE

PLANTATION INN

GERARD'S ▼

CAFE CAFE

LAHAINA
GRILL

LAHAINALUNA CAFE ▼

FLEETWOOD'S ▼

WAINE'E ST

LAHAINA SCRIMSHAW ■

CHEESEBURGER IN
PARADISE ▼

THE LAHAINA FISH COMPANY ▼

KIMO'S ▼

KOA'S ▼

TOM
BAREFOOT'S

LAHAINA CENTER

WARREN AND ANABELLE'S ■

BANK OF HAWAII ■

LONGHI'S ▼

SALE PEPE ▼

THAI CHEF ▼

WO HING
MUSEUM ■

To
Lahainaluna

Moku'ula: The Ancient Capital of Hawaii

Until 1845, the town of Lahaina served as the royal capital of Hawaii. Generations of rulers from King Kamehameha on ruled the kingdom from this historic sun-drenched shore, and some of the most notable events in Hawaiian history were witnessed by this town.

If Lahaina was so important, you ask, where is the royal palace? Where is the seat of the monarchy? Where, exactly, was the capital? Unfortunately, when the capital was moved to Honolulu in 1845, the site of the former capital—Moku'ula—was abandoned and left to decay. Where once the home of ali'i and royalty existed, there is now an overgrown baseball field frequented by the island's homeless. If ever there were a fall from grace, it is the site of Moku'ula.

All hope is not lost for the former capital, however, as nonprofit group **Friends of Moku'ula** (808/661-3659, www.mokuula.com) is committed to restoring the nearly forgotten site, across from the area on Front Street where the 505 shopping center now stands. During the time when royalty called it home, there was a 25-acre *loko*, or fishpond, named Mokuhinia that was fed by the streams flowing from Mauna Kahalawai. In the middle of this pond was a small island—Moku'ula—and only the highest chiefs and Hawaiian royalty were allowed to set foot on it. Within walking distance of the ocean and framed by the mountainous backdrop, it must have been a sight to behold.

When the capital was moved, the stream was diverted to irrigate the sugar crop, and the Mokuhinia fishpond became a festering swamp of mosquitoes and bugs. Taking matters into their own hands, mill workers filled the pond with dirt in 1914. The ball field and parking structures that stand in its place were subsequently constructed on top.

Just because Moku'ula isn't visible, however, doesn't mean that it's gone. Archaeologists estimate that the site still exists about three feet below the surface, and digs have yielded artifacts that show evidence of the ancient fishpond. The Friends of Moku'ula are working to raise awareness and raise funding for a major restoration of the former royal site. The group envisions the site as a historic landmark as well as an educational resource about Hawaiian culture.

For a more in-depth look at both the history and future of Moku'ula, take one of the **Maui Nei** (505 Front St., 808/661-9494, www.mauinei.com) two-hour cultural walking tours ($50 adults, $24 ages 6-12), which not only cover many of the historic sites of Lahaina but also spend ample time discussing Moku'ula. For a truly in-depth cultural experience, book one of the 3.5-hour Discover Old Hawaii tours ($150 pp), where you'll participate in creating cultural arts at Lahaina's most sacred places. If you have an interest in Hawaiian history, there are few tours that will provide the level of insight offered on these tours.

---

no written form of the Hawaiian language. The Olowalu valley is heavily steeped in Hawaiian history, and even though a century of sugar cultivation and the encroachment of modern development has eroded traditional village sites, a number of families living back in the valley aim to perpetuate the lifestyle of their ancestors.

To find the petroglyphs, drive on the road behind the Olowalu fruit stand at mile marker 15 and proceed on the paved segment, which runs back toward the valley. After 0.5 mile are signs for the Olowalu Cultural Reserve, and when the road turns to dirt, the petroglyphs are about 200 yards farther, on the rock face. Unfortunately, some of the petroglyphs have been vandalized, so visitors are asked to keep a respectful distance from them.

Beaches

KAPALUA, NAPILI, AND HONOKOWAI

Known to locals simply as "up north," the beaches along this stretch include tropical turquoise coves sandwiched between condos and luxurious homes. **Napili** and **Kapalua** beaches are the most popular, but past the entrance to Kapalua, the shore gets wilder and the crowds start to thin. The wind can howl in the afternoons and massive surf crashes into the coast October-April. Over the winter the shore-break often grows to 10 feet or larger.

Honokowai Beach Park

The farthest point south, **Honokowai Beach Park** is a narrow stretch of sand at the northern edge of Ka'anapali. While the beach here is far from the nicest on the island, there is a large, grassy park with a playground for small children and a couple of shops across the street.

Napili Bay and Kapalua Bay

There is a lot of debate about which beach is better: **Napili Bay** or **Kapalua Bay.** There are a couple of factors that distinguish one from the other. Although a mere 0.25 mile from each other, the shore-break at Napili Bay can be larger in the winter, whereas Kapalua is more protected. The snorkeling between the two reefs is a toss-up, although Kapalua often has more fish while Napili has more sea turtles. Napili Bay is a little larger, although it can also become more crowded. If you are traveling with children, Kapalua Bay is the better bet since the water is calmer and there is easy access to beach showers and restrooms.

Your best chance for finding parking at Napili Bay is either along the side of Lower Honoapi'ilani Road between Napili Kai and the Kapalua Tennis Club, or on the south end of the beach, where there is some beach parking at the bottom of Hui Drive. The beach parking lot at Kapalua Bay fills up early. If you can't find a parking space, drop all of your beach gear by the stairs leading down to the sand and then circle back to find a spot along the road.

MAUI
LAHAINA AND WEST MAUI

Oneloa Bay or "Ironwoods"

The Best Beach in America

If a friend quizzes you on which beach in Maui was named the number-one beach in the United States, and you have to choose among Kapalua Bay, Ka'anapali Beach, D. T. Fleming Beach, Wailea Beach, and Hulopo'e Bay on Lana'i, the correct answer would be . . . all of them.

Since the rankings began in 1991, each of the five beaches listed above has held the title as the number-one beach in America, and Hamoa Beach in Hana is consistently ranked in the top five. So how, exactly, is the number-one beach determined?

The person behind the rankings is Stephen P. Leatherman, otherwise known as Dr. Beach. He has compiled a sophisticated ranking system of 50 different criteria to measure hundreds of beaches, including natural factors such as softness of the sand and width at low tide as well as human factors such as the availability of lifeguards and ease of public access. Water samples from each beach are collected to determine turbidity, suspended human material (sewage), and the amount of algae.

So why is there a different winner every year? Once a beach has won the title it is subsequently retired from future consideration. With that thought in mind, wouldn't it make sense that the best of the best would be the beach that was voted number one when the rankings first started?

If this were the case, the top beach in the United States when the rankings began in 1991 was Kapalua Bay, so the granddaddy of the best beaches in America is here on Maui.

Oneloa Bay (Ironwoods)

Hidden from view from the road through Kapalua, **Oneloa Bay** is virtually always empty. This epic expanse of shore sits right along the Kapalua Coastal Trail, although since the swimming is poor and it's out of sight, it's also out of mind. Mornings on Oneloa can be calm and still, and this is a popular spot for sunset wedding photo shoots. Oneloa is a great beach for those who just want to commune with nature and need a bit of an escape. To reach Oneloa, either park at the lot for Kapalua Bay and walk 15 minutes along the Kapalua Coastal Trail, or follow Lower Honoapi'ilani Road into Kapalua; a small beach access path and parking lot are located across from The Ridge. While there is a small beach shower for rinsing off, the nearest public restrooms are at Kapalua Bay.

D. T. Fleming Beach Park

D. T. Fleming Beach Park was the most recent of Maui's beaches to be named number-one beach in the United States, garnering the title in 2006. Fleming's is a hybrid stretch of sand where the southern half is dominated by Ritz-Carlton resort guests and the northern half is popular with locals. This is one of the best beaches on the island for bodysurfing and bodyboarding, although the surf here can get rough and dangerous in the winter. Luckily, this is one of the only beaches on the West Side with lifeguards. There are restrooms and showers at the northern end. To access D. T. Fleming Beach Park, take Honoapi'ilani Highway (Hwy. 30) past the main entrance to Kapalua 0.9 mile and turn left at the bottom of the hill. The road dead-ends in the lot.

Mokulei'a Bay (Slaughterhouse)

Mokulei'a Bay was once a secret, since you can't see it from the road, but has recently become so exceptionally popular it can be tough to find a place to park. Tucked at the base of dramatic cliffs, Mokulei'a offers some of the best snorkeling on the West Side. It's known to locals as Slaughterhouse Beach, but the name is less sinister than it sounds: a slaughterhouse was once located here but is now long gone. The bay is part of the Honolua Bay Marine Life Conservation District, so no fishing or spearfishing—or any other kind of slaughter—is allowed. This is also a popular beach for bodysurfing, although the surf can be treacherous during large winter swells.

This beach is nearly always deserted in the early morning hours, but lately is packed by 11am. To reach Mokulei'a, travel 2.5 miles past the entrance to Kapalua and park on the left side of the road, where you will notice a paved stairway leading down to the beach, as well as a sign that details the rules of the marine reserve.

Punalau Beach (Windmills)

Sandy, serene, and almost always empty, **Punalau** is little visited by tourists—but not for lack of beauty. The local name, Windmills, is derived from an old windmill that once stood here but has long since been destroyed. This is now a popular place for advanced surfers and ambitious beachcombers who scour the shore for flotsam and shells. The road down to the shore can often be rough, so unless you have a high-clearance vehicle, it's best to leave your car parked by the highway and make the five-minute trek on foot. Bring all of your valuables with you, and also pack a blanket or towel for lying in the sun and soaking up the silence. Since the reef is shallow and can be razor sharp, don't snorkel or swim here. This is also one of Maui's best spots to watch large winter surf, and the left break at the far southern end has been referred to as Maui's version of the Pipeline.

KA'ANAPALI

The beaches in Ka'anapali are long, wide, and lined by resorts. Much like Kapalua, however, the wind can often be a factor here in the afternoon, so it's best to get your water activities in early before the trade winds start blowing.

Ka'anapali Beach

Few stretches of Maui shore are more iconic than famous **Ka'anapali Beach.** This long, uninterrupted expanse of sand is lined from end to end with world-class resorts, was named the number-one beach in the United States in 2003, and is the pulsing epicenter of the West Side's see-and-be-seen crowd. It should come as no surprise that the area is a constant hotbed of activity. Pick any island beach activity—surfing, snorkeling, scuba, snuba, paddleboarding, volleyball, parasailing (summer), or whale-watching (winter)—and you'll find it on Ka'anapali Beach. A paved pathway runs the length of the beach and is popular with joggers in the morning.

The best snorkeling is found at Pu'u Keka'a (Black Rock) in front of the Sheraton at the far northern end of the beach. Most of the water sports, such as surf lessons, take place at KP Point in front of the Ka'anapali Ali'i, and the beach volleyball court is in front of the Sheraton on the north end of the beach. For bodyboarding, the best area is between Whalers Village and Pu'u Keka'a. Since the beach faces directly west, it can pick up waves any time of year. Be careful on days with big shore break, however, and use common sense.

Another favorite activity at Ka'anapali Beach is cliff-jumping off Pu'u Keka'a. While this 20-foot jump is popular with visitors and locals, the rock is one of the most sacred places on the island for native Hawaiians, who believe it's an entry point for a person's soul passing from this world into the next. To jump off Pu'u Keka'a is to mimic the soul at the moment of death, a legend still told during the evening torch-lighting ceremony that takes place before each sunset.

Since Ka'anapali Beach is exposed to the afternoon trade winds, the weather can often be wetter and windier than down the road in Lahaina. The morning hours are best for paddleboarding or snorkeling, and if the wind is blowing too hard by the Sheraton, you can find a pocket of calm at the southern end of the beach by the Hyatt. Also, if you plan on going for a morning swim, realize that there are two areas where large catamarans come ashore to pick up passengers, so be alert when you're in the water in front of Ka'anapali Beach Hotel or Whalers Village.

Unless you're staying at one of the resorts along the Ka'anapali strip, parking is going to be a challenge. Free public parking can be tough to come by, since most public spots are taken by 9am. There is one small public garage between the Sheraton and the Ka'anapali

Beach Hotel, a lot between Whalers Village and the Westin, a handful of beach parking stalls in the front lot of the Ka'anapali Beach Hotel, and a small public lot on Nohea Kai Drive just before the Hyatt. While there's always a chance that you'll luck out and snag a spot, more often than not you'll end up having to pay to park in the garage of Whalers Village. Remember, however, that if you end up shopping at a store or eating at a restaurant in Whalers Village, you can get the parking ticket validated.

Kahekili Beach Park (Airport Beach)

There was a time not too long ago when **Kahekili Beach Park,** named after the great king of Maui, was an undeveloped scrubland of *kiawe* (mesquite) trees that paled in comparison to Ka'anapali Beach. Over time, there has been so much development at Airport Beach (also known as Ka'anapali North Beach) that it's almost as busy as neighboring Ka'anapali. Yet Kahekili still has a family-friendly atmosphere where locals lounge on the grassy area in front of the beach pavilion or snorkel the offshore reef. The beach here is just as long as Ka'anapali Beach, although the steep grade of the shore makes it difficult for jogging. Most visitors use the boardwalk along the shore, and if you're up for a stroll, you can follow it as it weaves through the Royal Lahaina and Sheraton parking areas to meet up with the Ka'anapali beach path. There are public restrooms, and there is a large public parking lot at the Kai Ala entrance from the highway. If the lot is full, there's more parking on the north end of the beach, accessible from Lower Honoapi'ilani Road. The swimming here is much better than at Ka'anapali since there isn't as much catamaran traffic. If Ka'anapali Beach is too busy for you, you'll enjoy how Kahekili offers a world-class beach atmosphere at a slower pace.

LAHAINA

The beaches of Lahaina are the most underrated on the island. The swimming is poor

sunset at Makila Beach

due to the offshore reef, but they are sunnier, less crowded, and more protected from the wind than most other beaches on Maui. If it's raining in Kapalua or Napili, or windy on Ka'anapali Beach, 90 percent of the time it's going to be sunny and calm on the beaches of Lahaina.

Makila Beach

Also known as **Breakwall, 505,** or **Shark Pit, Makili Beach** is the most happening stretch of sand in Lahaina. Most visitors access the beach from Kamehameha Iki Park, and there is beach parking in a small lot or in the back of the Front Street tennis courts. This is the area where most of the surf schools set out from. There is also a beach volleyball court, which can get busy during the afternoon. Visitors are encouraged to marvel at the Polynesian voyaging canoes on display as part of the **Hui O Wa'a Kaulua Canoe Club.** Visitors rarely wander to the south end of the beach where palm trees hang over a secluded cove. Locals call this area Shark Pit for the harmless reef sharks that hang around the offshore ledge. The swimming is poor due to the offshore reef, although it provides calm water for wading with small children. There is one shower but no restroom.

Pu'unoa (Baby Beach)

On the northern end of Front Street, the beach that runs along **Pu'unoa** Point (and known to locals as **Baby Beach**) is an oasis of tranquility where you have to ask yourself if you're still in Lahaina. Shielded from visitors by its residential location—and protected from surf by the offshore reef—the sand running along this lazy promontory is the perfect spot for sitting in a beach chair and listening to the waves. Numerous trees provide shade, and the calm waters are ideal for beachgoers with young children or those who want to tan on a raft.

Finding the beach can be a challenge, and parking can be an issue. For the access point with the largest amount of parking, turn off Front Street onto Ala Moana Street by the sign for Mala Ramp. Instead of heading down to the boat launch, proceed straight on Ala Moana until the road ends by the Jodo mission. From here you will see the beach in front of you. The best section of beach is a five-minute walk to the left along the sand. Transients sometimes hang out around this parking lot; don't leave any valuables in your car. If you're walking from central Lahaina, the quickest access to the nicest part of beach is to turn off Front Street onto Kai Pali Place, where you will notice a shore access path. If you are coming from central Lahaina, this turn will be about three minutes after you pass the Hard Rock Café.

Wahikuli and Hanakao'o Beach Parks (Canoe Beach)

On the northern tip of Lahaina, these two beach parks are the strip of land between Front Street and Ka'anapali. **Wahikuli** is closer to Lahaina, and **Hanakao'o** is at the southern edge of the Hyatt. Of the two beaches, Wahikuli offers better swimming, although a secret about Hanakao'o is that on the days when the main stretch of Ka'anapali Beach is

windy, Hanakao'o sits tucked in a cove where the wind can barely reach. Hanakao'o is also known as Canoe Beach, since this is where many of the outrigger canoe regattas are held on Saturday mornings. A beach path allows you to walk or ride bicycles from the south end of Ka'anapali through Hanakao'o, Wahikuli, and down to Front Street in Lahaina.

SOUTH OF LAHAINA

On the stretch of shore between Lahaina and Ma'alaea is a grand total of zero resorts. Paddleboards and fishing poles rule this section of coast, and even though the swimming is poor, there is one spot that offers good snorkeling. Most visitors pass these beaches without giving them another thought, but if you do decide to pull over to watch the whales, visit the beach, or photograph the sunset, don't stop in the middle of the road. If you're headed in the Lahaina direction, it's easiest to pull off on the right side of the road and wait for traffic to clear before crossing.

Olowalu

Known to visitors as Mile Marker 14, the real name of this beach is **Olowalu,** after the village that stretches back into the valley. The snorkeling here is the best south of Lahaina, although plenty of beachgoers—particularly those with young children—come simply to wade in the calm waters. While the water may be calm, it's also shallow, and the swimming area is nonexistent during low tide. Parking is along the side of the highway, although it's easy to get stuck in the sand.

Launiupoko Beach Park

Located at the only stoplight between Ma'alaea and Lahaina, **Launiupoko** is the most family-friendly beach park on the West Side of Maui. It has a protected wading area for small *keiki* (children), a decent sandy beach on the south end of the park, a wide, grassy picnic area, and numerous surf breaks that cater to beginner surfers and stand-up paddle surfers. This park is so popular with the weekend barbecue crowd that local families arrive before dawn to stake their claim for a birthday party with a bouncy house. There is a large parking lot as well as restrooms and showers, and since most of the parking spots are taken by 8am, there is an overflow lot on the *mauka* (mountain side) of the highway. The water is too shallow for swimming and the snorkeling is poor, but this is a good place to put your finger on the local pulse and strike up a good conversation.

Puamana Beach Park

While there is a private gated community that goes by the same name, the public can visit the small **Puamana Beach Park** one mile north of Launiupoko. As at other beaches in the area, the swimming is poor, although the tables provide a nice setting for a picnic. For a stroll down the beach, the sandy shore fronting the condos is public property, so at low tide you can walk from the beach park to the other end of the private, gated section, although the grassy area is private. There aren't any restrooms at the beach park, but there's a refreshing shower in the parking lot with a serious nozzle.

Snorkeling

Snorkeling is the most popular activity in West Maui. Hundreds of people ply the waters of the island's western shore, flipping their fins as they chase after schools of yellow and black *manini* (convict tang). But there is always room to find your own section of reef, and the waters of West Maui teem with everything from graceful green sea turtles to the playfully named *humuhumunukunukuapua'a*—the Hawaiian state fish, whose name translates as "big lips with a nose like a pig."

Mornings are the best time of day for snorkeling. Different times of year also mean different snorkeling conditions. During the winter, places such as Honolua Bay and Napili can be dangerous due to the huge surf, so summer is the best time for exploring these reefs. Similarly, snorkeling spots on the south shore such as Olowalu can be prone to large surf

hidden lagoon at Olowalu

during summer, although with much less frequency than the northern beaches in winter. If the surf is too big or the conditions too poor, there is probably another place that is calm and beautiful just a 20-minute drive away.

KAPALUA, NAPILI, AND HONOKOWAI

★ Honolua Bay

When it comes to snorkeling along Maui's shore, **Honolua Bay** is the gold standard. This wide, scenic cleft in the coast is not only a biodiverse marine reserve, it's also protected from the afternoon trade winds. Honolua Bay is one of the most sacred and revered spots on the West Side of the island, and there has been a herculean movement over the last decade to "Save Honolua" and spare the area from development. The valley, bay, and shore exude a supernatural beauty. Somewhere between the lush green foliage of the valley and the shimmering turquoise waters is a palpable magic unlike anywhere else.

As the highway morphs into a rural county road, the first glimpse of Honolua is from the paved overlook 1.8 miles past the entrance to Kapalua. Toward the bottom of the hill, parking for the shore is in a lush and shaded valley where you might encounter some merchants selling their crafts. To reach the water, find a parking spot wherever you can (all the trails along a 0.5-mile stretch eventually lead to the shore), grab all of your snorkeling gear, and make a short five-minute trek through a dense green understory that chirps with activity and drips with vines.

The "beach" is more a collection of boulders. If you are facing the water, the right side has a much larger snorkeling area and a greater concentration of marinelife. The center of the bay has a sandy bottom and is mostly devoid of marinelife, so it's best to trace the shore and snorkel around to the right. If there aren't any charter boats tied up on the right side of the bay between 9am

and noon, it means that the conditions aren't good enough to bring paying snorkelers here. Also, if you see breaking waves out toward the point and there are more than 20 surfers in the water, it means that the visibility is going to be less than stellar and conditions will be dangerous. If it isn't raining on the shore but the stream on the left side of the bay is gushing with brown water, it means that it's raining farther up the mountain and the runoff is emptying into the bay, which also makes for subpar conditions.

If, however, the sun is shining brilliantly, here's your guide to the best snorkeling area: When you enter the water from the rocky shore, swim straight out for about 20 yards and then turn right toward the shore. You'll want to hug the shore in 5 to 10 feet of water and follow it in a ring around the right side of the bay. If you're on a mission to find Hawaiian green sea turtles, the best spot to check out is the **turtle cleaning station** on the right center of the bay. It's about 200 yards out from the boat ramp, in line with the bend in the cliff on the right side of the bay, in about 15 to 20 feet of water. If you snorkel Honolua Bay during winter, dive a few feet underwater to listen for the distant song of humpback whales. Keep a keen eye out for boat traffic, as a number of catamarans make their approach through the middle of the bay.

Mokulei'a Bay

Parking for **Mokulei'a Bay** is along the highway 1.5 miles past the entrance to Kapalua, and the best snorkeling is in the cove on the right side of the bay. Even though Mokulei'a is still a part of the Honolua Marine Life Conservation District, the reef is completely different than at Honolua Bay, so you're likely to see different species. There's still the likelihood of seeing a sea turtle, a chance for some spotted eagle rays swimming over the sand by the end of the point, and perhaps an octopus clinging to the wall at the far end of the cove. Mokulei'a is more exposed to the afternoon trade winds, so morning hours during flat, calm days are the best time for snorkeling.

Honokowai to Kapalua

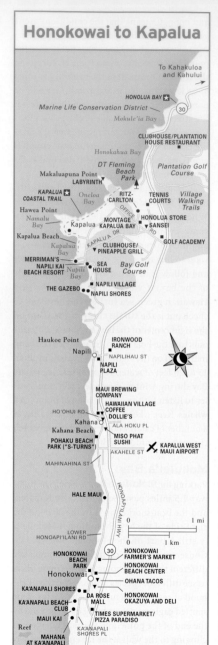

To Kahakuloa
and Kahului

HONOLUA BAY
Marine Life Conservation District   30
Mokule'ia Bay

CLUBHOUSE/PLANTATION
HOUSE RESTAURANT
Honokahua Bay

DT Fleming   Plantation Golf
Makaluapuna Point   Beach   Course
LABYRINTH   Park

KAPALUA
COASTAL TRAIL   Oneloa   RITZ-   TENNIS   Village
                 Bay   CARLTON   COURTS   Walking
Hawea Point   Trails
Namalu   HONOLUA STORE
Bay   Kapalua MONTAGE   SANSEI
                   KAPALUA BAY
Kapalua Beach   GOLF ACADEMY
          Kapalua   CLUBHOUSE/
          Bay   PINEAPPLE GRILL
MERRIMAN'S
NAPILI KAI   Napili   SEA   Bay Golf
BEACH RESORT Bay   HOUSE   Course
THE GAZEBO   NAPILI VILLAGE
              NAPILI SHORES

Haukoe Point   IRONWOOD
                      RANCH
Napili   NAPILIHAU ST
            NAPILI
            PLAZA

            MAUI BREWING
            COMPANY
            HAWAIIAN VILLAGE
HO'OHUI RD.   COFFEE
            DOLLIE'S
Kahana   ALA HOKU PL
Kahana Beach
POHAKU BEACH   MISO PHAT
PARK ("S-TURNS") SUSHI   KAPALUA WEST
            AKAHELE ST   MAUI AIRPORT
MAHINAHINA ST

HALE MAUI

                    0   1 mi
LOWER
HONOAPI'ILANI RD   0   1 km
            30   HONOKOWAI
HONOKOWAI   FARMER'S MARKET
BEACH   HONOKOWAI
PARK   BEACH CENTER
Honokowai   OHANA TACOS

KA'ANAPALI SHORES
                  DA ROSE
KA'ANAPALI BEACH   MALL
CLUB   HONOKOWAI
                  OKAZUYA AND DELI
MAUI KAI
Reef   TIMES SUPERMARKET/
        KA'ANAPALI PIZZA PARADISO
MAHANA SHORES PL
AT KA'ANAPALI
        HALAWAI DR

To   CAR
Lahaina   RENTALS   © AVALON TRAVEL

Namalu Bay

For a hidden, out-of-the-way snorkeling experience in a rocky, almost Mediterranean cove, the craggy shore of **Namalu Bay** is one of West Maui's best spots. There isn't much in the way of live coral, but you can spot green sea turtles, reef fish, and the occasional eagle or manta ray. The center of the bay is about 40 feet deep, and the areas ringing the shore are a more manageable 5 to 15 feet. As a bonus, the rocks also make for some enjoyable cliff-jumping.

Accessing the bay can be challenging, and while strong swimmers can access Namalu Bay by swimming around from Kapalua Bay, this is a long swim over deep water that's only possible when it's calm. The more practical way to reach Namalu Bay is via the dirt pathway that follows the coast. The closest public parking is at the Kapalua Bay Villas in a hidden, little-known location. To find the eight public parking spots, turn into the parking area for the Montage Hotel and make an immediate right toward the Kapalua Bay Villas. Then make a left, following the sign for beach access parking, and notice the small public parking area seemingly orphaned among the private residential lots. From here it's a short walk down to the shore and the access for the Kapalua Coastal Trail.

Now that you've found the trailhead, to find the actual snorkeling area, make your way past two brown "Trail" markers and then notice the trail goes in three different directions. The trail to the right is the Kapalua Coastal Trail; the gravel trail leading straight heads to Hawea Point, the westernmost point on the island and a great place for spotting sea turtles from shore; and the grassy trail that bends off to the left leads toward Namalu Bay. Follow the trail as it wraps to the left, past the signs that say "Proceed at your own risk." In 30 seconds you'll find yourself standing atop the cliffs overlooking hidden Namalu Bay, wondering how a place this beautiful can be so isolated and unknown.

Kapalua Bay

Kapalua Bay is a sandy cove that is a favorite for snorkeling with small children. Its relatively small size means it's easy for snorkelers to scour the entire bay. You can expect to see colorful parrotfish, lots of goatfish, and even the occasional green sea turtle. Although depths rarely exceed 20 feet, the best snorkeling is found along the right side of the bay, where the rocks extend out to the distant point. If you're a strong snorkeler and the conditions are calm, you can even snorkel around the northern point into neighboring Namalu Bay.

Napili Bay

A short walk from Kapalua Bay is neighboring **Napili Bay.** You can easily snorkel at both bays without even reparking your car. Napili Bay doesn't have quite as many fish as Kapalua Bay, but there is a higher likelihood of finding a green sea turtle. While many snorkelers hug the wall on the right side of the bay, there is another reef in the center of the bay that's almost exposed during low tide. About 20 yards farther out is a second, less visited reef, and although it's deeper, at about 15 to 20 feet, it has the highest concentration of fish. This outer reef is far from shore, so if you're uncomfortable in the water, stay on the inside reefs and enjoy the shallower areas.

Rental Shops

In Napili, **Water Works Sports** (5315 Lower Honoapi'ilani Rd., 808/298-2446, www.waterworkssportsmaui.com, 8am-5pm daily) inside Napili Shores has snorkel rentals for $7.50 per day or $25 per week. The staff can give you tips on current conditions, and also have snorkeling gear for sale.

In Kahana, **Maui Dive Shop** (4405 Honoapi'ilani Hwy., 808/669-3800, www.mauidiveshop.com, 8am-9pm daily) is within the Kahana Gateway Center and offers a full range of rentals as well as information on dive and snorkeling charters to Molokini and Olowalu.

Kahekili Beach Park

In the northern part of Ka'anapali, **Kahekili Beach Park** offers decent snorkeling off the park and at the far southern end of the beach. The reef extends from the shore out to about 25 feet of water. Expect to see a healthy amount of herbivorous reef fish. The moderate depth and easy entry make this a user-friendly snorkeling spot during the early morning hours. At the far southern end of the beach is a rock jetty that also offers good snorkeling. The rocky promontory here is the "back" of Pu'u Keka'a (Black Rock).

Pu'u Keka'a (Black Rock)

The best snorkeling in Ka'anapali is at **Pu'u Keka'a,** better known as **Black Rock.** At the far northern end of Ka'anapali Beach in front of the Sheraton, this area offers the most consistently beautiful snorkeling conditions and a relatively easy entry. The morning hours are best, and the best chance for seeing sea turtles is during high tide, when the water comes up on the side of the rock and all the *limu* (seaweed) falls into the water. Since this is a favorite delicacy of the green sea turtles, occasionally three or four of them congregate in the shallow cove in only 5-10 feet of water. Since the cliff is also a favorite place for cliff-jumping, steer clear of the immediate landing zone, and if you see the wind whipping up whitecaps out by the point, stay in the cove, protected from the wind and with gentler currents.

Ka'anapali Point

On the other end of Ka'anapali Beach is the reef at **Ka'anapali Point,** in front of the Marriott. It's not nearly as popular as the reef at Pu'u Keka'a but covers a larger area and isn't nearly as crowded. If Pu'u Keka'a is a flotilla of fins, take a 10-minute stroll to the southern end of the beach and try your luck at this less visited spot.

Rental Shops

Every major resort along the strip of Ka'anapali has a rental shack by the sand. Prices vary slightly among the operators, but expect to pay higher resort prices compared to what you'll find off the strip. The best deal in Ka'anapali on rental gear is at **The Snorkel Store** (2580 Keka'a Dr., 808/333-3705, www.thesnorkelstore.com, 8am-5pm daily), in the Fairway Shops by the highway. A full snorkel setup is around $10 per day or $27 per week, provided you book ahead online or fill out a coupon in the store. While here, ask about the guided **Snorkel Safari** ($75), where a local guide takes your party snorkeling at a spot along the shore, providing individualized attention you won't find on larger boats. It's a great option for beginner snorkelers and a nice way to find new spots.

Snorkeling Charters

A number of catamarans depart directly from Ka'anapali Beach on half-day sailing excursions along the West Maui coast. For trips to either Lana'i or Molokini Crater, you still need to go to the Lahaina or Ma'alaea harbors. For boats departing from Ka'anapali Beach, the preferred snorkeling destination is Honolua Bay. Since the surf at Honolua Bay during winter can get huge, the alternate destination is Olowalu on the south shore. Most days of the year these sleek sailing yachts are able to pull right up on the sand and load passengers directly from the beach, although on days with large surf, the shore-break can be too rough, and the trip might be moved to Lahaina Harbor. If a member of your party has restricted mobility, trips out of Lahaina Harbor are a safer option.

Of the charters departing from Ka'anapali Beach, **Trilogy** (808/874-5649, www.sailtrilogy.com) loads in front of the Ka'anapali Beach Hotel and offers 8am snorkeling trips, making it the first boat to reach Honolua Bay. The tours from Ka'anapali are usually aboard the *Trilogy IV*, a few feet smaller than other boats along the beach. The maximum capacity is about 35 people. All the food is made fresh on board. Both the Trilogy crew and the level of customer service are widely regarded as the best in the industry. Due to its slightly smaller size and its light weight, the *Trilogy IV* is the fastest of the Ka'anapali sailboats. Half-day charters are $129 for adults, $97 for teens, and $65 for children and include all food and equipment, and usually return to the beach around 1:30pm.

On the stretch of sand in front of Whalers Village, **Teralani** (808/661-7245, www.teralani.net) has two boats that regularly make excursions along the West Maui coast. The Teralani boats are larger than Trilogy's and cap their trips at 49 people. The main snorkeling tour departs at 9:30am and returns to the beach around 2:30pm. A shorter trip departs at 11am and returns to the beach at 3pm. All food, including a buffet lunch, and equipment are included in the rates. There's also an open bar once you've finished snorkeling, whereas Trilogy charges $5 per drink. With the open bar, however, the rates are also higher, at $139 for adults on the longer sail and $112 on the four-hour cruise.

Hula Girl (808/665-0344, www.sailing-maui.com), which loads on the stretch of beach in front of Leilani's restaurant, is an ornately painted boat that takes a different approach: The $98 for the five-hour tour (9:30am-2:30pm) doesn't include food, but the boat has a kitchen on board, where chefs make food to order. There is also free Wi-Fi for anyone who wants to immediately upload camera footage of an encounter with a sea turtle. Scuba diving is offered for an additional cost for both certified ($69) and introductory ($80) divers.

LAHAINA
Wahikuli Beach Park

Most of Lahaina is ringed by a barrier reef, and there are surprisingly few options for decent snorkeling. One exception is **Wahikuli Beach Park,** between Ka'anapali and Lahaina, where you can find sea turtles, corals, and large schools of goat fish at a reef just a short swim offshore. For the best results, snorkel around the north end, about 10 yards off the rocks in about 5-10 feet of water.

Mala Wharf

In Lahaina, the best snorkeling spot is **Mala Wharf,** and since it is a functioning small-boat harbor, you have to keep an eye out for boat traffic. The reward, however, is a snorkeling site where legions of sea turtles and numerous reef sharks live under the pilings littering the ocean floor. This site is most often accessed by boat, but the easiest way to reach it from shore is to park in the public parking area and cross to where the pier meets the sand. From here, it's a kick out to where the pier drops into the water. While conditions are nice year-round, the only time you don't want to snorkel here is when the river draining into the bay is a torrent of runoff.

To find the parking for Mala Wharf, turn off Front Street onto Ala Moana Street, following the signs for Mala Ramp, just on the south side of the bridge from the Lahaina Cannery Mall. Once you turn, make an immediate right down toward the boat ramp, where there are restrooms, showers, and a moderate amount of parking.

Rental Shops

Lahaina Divers (143 Dickenson St., 808/667-7496, www.lahainadivers.com, 8am-8pm daily) is a full-service dive shop but has everything you need for snorkeling. Come if you're looking to own gear for an extended period of time. Since the staff are all divers themselves, they can give you up-to-date information on the current conditions around the West Side.

If you're just looking for cheap rental gear to get through your vacation, both **Boss Frog's** (150 Lahainaluna Rd., 808/661-3333, www.bossfrog.com, 8am-5pm daily) and **Snorkel Bob's** (1217 Front St., 808/661-4421, www.snorkelbob.com, 8am-5pm daily) provide economical rentals as low as $2 per day. Remember, however, that you get what

you pay for, and you will be pitched activities and upsold on fancier equipment. If you aren't picky about a mask fitting perfectly or are on a budget, the offerings are fine and will get you through a couple of sessions at the beach.

For a similar operation in the center of Lahaina, check out **The Snorkel Store** (840 Waine'e St., 808/669-1077, www.thesnorkelstore.com, 8am-5pm daily), a small but friendly shop squirreled away in the Lahaina Square Center, a block inland from Front Street. There are often 2-for-1 specials on snorkeling gear if you book online, and prices can be as low as $10-25 per week.

Snorkeling Charters

Before sunrise, Lahaina Harbor teems with activity as fishers fuel their boats and charter captains prepare for the day. Lines form and re-form, food coolers are slung across the docks, and fresh fish is set on ice. Most **snorkeling charters** depart from behind the banyan tree on Front Street; a few set out from Mala Ramp on the northern edge of town. Snorkeling charters in Lahaina run the gamut from small inflatable rafts to massive two-tiered catamarans. It's important to find a tour company with the type of experience you want.

SAILBOATS

The company with the largest number of snorkeling charters from Lahaina Harbor is **Trilogy** (808/874-5649, www.sailtrilogy.com), which offers all-day cruises to Lana'i ($205 adults, $149 teens, $100 children) as well as a four-hour snorkel along the West Maui coast ($110 adults, $83 teens, $55 children). While a couple of other boat companies also travel to Lana'i to snorkel for the day, Trilogy is the only one with a commercial permit to have crew and facilities based on the island. The company has been running the trip to Lana'i for 45 years, and the all-day experience is far better than any other snorkel charter option.

Departing from Lahaina Harbor at 10am (during busier times of the year there can also be a 6:30am departure), the 60-foot sailing catamarans travel to Manele Harbor on Lana'i, where passengers disembark to snorkel at Hulopo'e Bay. Since Hulopo'e faces south, during summer there are a few days with large surf, so the snorkeling can be subpar. Winter is nearly guaranteed to have pristine conditions. On the beach, Trilogy has exclusive access to the left side of Hulopo'e Bay and it is the only company with lifeguards, beach mats, beach chairs, refreshments, beach volleyball, and all the snorkeling gear right on the beach. Also included in the rates is an optional guided van tour of Lana'i City.

The other sailing catamaran departing from Lahaina Harbor to Lana'i is *Sail Maui* (808/244-2087, www.sailmaui.com), a 47-foot boat that takes just 24 passengers and is the island's fastest catamaran. The seven-hour, $190-trip departs at 8:30am and docks at Manele Harbor on Lana'i. You're unsupervised while you snorkel, since the crew doesn't have permission to operate on shore, and you're given a picnic lunch to enjoy while at the beach. The trip returns to Lahaina around 3:30pm, and the crew might even hook an *ono* or a mahimahi while trolling the fishing lures under sail.

POWERBOATS

Of the larger diesel boats that operate out of Lahaina Harbor, **Pacific Whale Foundation** (612 Front St., 808/942-5311, www.pacificwhale.org) offers the most options. Its large boats can fit 149 people, and while that's a crowd, there's simply no beating the price: $83 for adults on the 9am five-hour tour to Lana'i, and each paying adult is allotted to bring one child free of charge. Unlike other boats that dock at Manele Harbor, these cruises snorkel off the boat, with the two preferred destinations being either Kaunolu (Shark Fin Cove) or the Manele reef outside of the small boat harbor. The level of customer service on a boat this size isn't the same as on the sailing vessels, but for families who are on a budget and want to go snorkeling for

the day, it's more affordable. Pacific Whale Foundation guests check in at the storefront across the street from the famous banyan tree, and loading is by the main dock at the harbor, where you wait for a crewmember to escort you to the boat.

Many of these boats go whale-watching in the winter, but during summer, **Hawaii Ocean Project** (675 Wharf St., 808/667-6165, www.hawaiiaoceanproject.com) has a fleet of aging but functional diesel boats that offer snorkeling charters ($89 adults, $57 children) to Lana'i and along the coast of West Maui. The cost is affordable, and trips are offered at 7:30am Monday, Wednesday, and Friday.

For private excursions, **Captain Woody's** (1653 A-a St., 808/667-2290, www.captainwoody.net) operates charters of only six people and leaves from Mala Ramp. Fishing, snorkeling, and seasonal whale-watching can all be included in these small group tours, which usually last six hours.

RAFTS

For those who don't like crowds, there are a number of rafts with small group sizes that place you closer to the water than any other type of vessel. Due to their bouncy nature, however, rafts aren't recommended for pregnant women or anyone with back problems. If you're prone to seasickness, the waters often become rough during the afternoon. Some companies swap their snorkeling charters for whale watching during winter, however, so check ahead.

Of all the rafts, **Ultimate Snorkel Adventure** (808/667-5678, www.ultimatewhalewatch.com) is the best option, though it only offers snorkeling trips May-November. It operates out of slip 17 of Lahaina Harbor. Group sizes are kept to 16, and this rigid inflatable is the fastest boat in Lahaina Harbor, at speeds over 35 mph. Snorkeling locations are chosen off the island of Lana'i based on the best conditions, and unlike some of the other options that go ashore on Lana'i, this excursion snorkels off the raft. Due to its small size, it can navigate close to the shore of Lanaʻi to find blowholes or follow pods of spinner dolphins hanging out by the rocks. Five-hour snorkeling trips are $139 for adults, and this is a great option for a semiprivate tour with a relaxed but professional captain and crew.

Departing from Mala Ramp at 6:30am, **Maui Ocean Riders** (808/661-3586, www.mauioceanriders.com, $139 adults, $119 children) is the only boat to circumnavigate Lanaʻi. Covering an astounding 70 miles over the course of the trip, this excursion features multiple snorkeling spots and the opportunity to witness little-seen areas of Lanaʻi, such as the waters off Shipwreck Beach, Polihua Beach, and the snorkeling area known as Three Stone. On calm days this excursion is the best of all the rafting options. On days when the trade winds are blowing early in the morning, the ride can get rough.

For a raft that docks at Manele Harbor and spends time on Lanaʻi, **Maui Adventure Cruises** (94 Kupuohi St., 808/661-5550, www.mauiadventurecruises.com) operates two trips from Lahaina Harbor, one of which allows passengers to spend three hours of beach time at Lanaʻi's Hulopoʻe Bay. This excursion ($139 adults, $109 children) operates Monday, Wednesday, and Friday, docks in Manele Harbor, and allows guests to walk Hulopoʻe Bay unsupervised. Breakfast, snacks, and a deli lunch are included. Excursions depart at 7am and 9:30am from slip 11 in Lahaina Harbor. On Tuesday, Thursday, and Saturday, an abridged 4.5-hour trip ($99 adults, $79 children) is offered, where you'll travel to Lanaʻi and snorkel off the boat rather than docking at the harbor.

SOUTH OF LAHAINA

The best snorkeling **south of Lahaina** is at **Olowalu,** otherwise known as Mile Marker 14. The reef here is a wide expanse of coral heads. The outer reef is popular with tour and dive boats, and the inside sections can teem with large parrotfish and Hawaiian green sea turtles. Directly out from the mile marker is a sand channel that leads through the shallow reef and allows access to deeper water. If you venture out from a random spot along the coast, there is a good chance you will get trapped in a maze of shallow coral heads where the water is often murky and the snorkeling is poor. If possible, get here in the morning before the winds pick up.

snorkeling in Honolua Bay

Scuba Diving

Scuba diving from the West Side of the island involves one of two options: departing from a West Side harbor for an excursion to Lana'i or diving along the West Maui shore. While certified divers should seek out a dive charter, there are also a number of shore operators that offer introductory dives. If you're a certified diver and planning on diving independently, ask at the rental shop about current conditions, and always use a dive flag. Dive spots along the northern section of the island are inaccessible during winter due to large surf. Summer is the best time for diving up north.

KAPALUA, NAPILI, AND HONOKOWAI
Dive Sites

The best shore dive in West Maui is **Honolua Bay,** although slogging all of your gear down to the water can be an exhausting undertaking. If you're diving from shore, launch from the center of the beach and hug the right side of the bay where the reef drops off into the sand channel. Maximum depth can reach about 40 feet, and you can expect to see green sea turtles and a wide variety of reef fish, and you may even have a rare encounter with spinner dolphins. Of the boats offering dive trips to Honolua Bay, *Hula Girl* (808/665-0344, www.sailingmaui.com) offers scuba diving as an add-on to the regular snorkel charter, although most dive charters head elsewhere along the West Side.

For a beginner-friendly introductory dive, **Kapalua Bay** can offer everything from a shallow dive of 25 feet to a more advanced dive of 40 feet rounding the corner toward neighboring Namalu Bay. There are showers and facilities as well as easy sandy-beach entry.

Dive Operators

Down in Honokowai, **Tiny Bubbles Scuba** (3350 Lower Honoapi'ilani Rd., 808/870-0878, www.tinybubblesscuba.com, 8am-5pm daily) operates shore dives along the West Maui coast. Under the lead of the vivacious and knowledgeable instructor Timmerz, all of the instructors for Tiny Bubbles have been diving the Maui shore for over a decade and are acquainted with the nuances of Maui diving. Introductory courses are $109, and certified divers can participate in a private guided beach dive for $89. Night dives and scooter dives are also offered. Depths on these shore dives rarely exceed 40 feet. All gear is included, and while the business is run out of the Ka'anapali Beach Club, the exact dive site is determined by the conditions.

Also operating out of Honokowai, **Scorpion Scuba** (3600 Lower Honoapi'ilani Rd., 808/669-1710, www.mauifish.net) is another trusted operator with years of experience on the shores of West Maui. The dives are an exceptional value: Introductory dives are $98, and certified beach dives are $78, with all gear included. Inquire about their certification classes, night dives, and scooter dives. The scuba operation is run out of the All About Fish store in Honokowai, where you can pick up any gear you need or ask about dive sites and conditions.

KA'ANAPALI
Dive Sites

The northernmost dive site in Ka'anapali and the one preferred by independent instructors is **Kahekili Beach Park.** The depth is shallow, rarely exceeding 35 feet, and the coral begins immediately. The reef parallels the shore, with the greatest diversity of life found at 15-25 feet. The beach is long, and the healthiest amount of coral is found right off the beach park. It is uncrowded compared to neighboring Ka'anapali Beach, and there is easier parking for lugging gear from the car. Showers and restrooms are conveniently located in the middle of the beach park.

The best dive in Ka'anapali, however, is **Pu'u Keka'a,** also known as **Black Rock.** Despite the relative ease of the dive and the fairly shallow depths, the rocky promontory draws all sorts of marinelife. Although not always guaranteed, divers frequently sight sea turtles, reef fish, eels, octopuses, and rare squid or cowries. The best way to dive Pu'u Keka'a is to do a drift dive from the southern end of Kahekili Beach Park and swim around to the front of the rock, or enter the water in front of the Sheraton, swim partway around the rock, and then double back the way you came. This is a great dive for those who have just been certified. For a real treat, consider a night dive.

To dive away from the crowds, head to the large reef at **Ka'anapali Point,** stretching from the Marriott down toward the Hyatt. The depth ranges 10-30 feet. You'll likely see a large number of turtles, corals, and technicolor parrotfish.

Dive Operators

The Ka'anapali resort diving scene is dominated by **Five Star Scuba** (www.5starscuba. com), which has operations at many of the Ka'anapali resorts. Options include pool sessions, one-tank dives, certification, and night dives. A single one-tank dive for certified divers is about $89, with the exact dive location determined by where you're staying and the conditions.

In front of Ka'anapali Beach Hotel, **the kiosk** (808/661-7789) also offers one-tank dives, pool classes, and certification courses. Introductory dives are $110, and certified dives are only $79. For a Maui dive you'll never forget, book a night dive at Pu'u Keka'a ($89).

LAHAINA
Dive Sites

Within walking distance of southern Ka'anapali, **Hanakao'o Beach Park** is the northernmost beach in Lahaina and the site of many introductory dive classes. This is a good dive if you're practicing your skills over

sand. The shallow area is also good for spotting turtles and colorful reef fish, and you can find turtles if you follow the rocks south toward Wahikuli Beach Park.

The best dive in Lahaina is **Mala Wharf,** although it's most often accessed as a boat dive. When Hurricane Iniki came storming through in 1992, the 30-foot waves it created were strong enough to destroy the outer half of Mala Ramp. Today the collapsed pilings are still lying in 25 feet of water, and the result has been decades of live coral development on what is now one of the island's best artificial reefs. The caverns of the pilings are home to numerous turtles and whitetip reef sharks, some of which can reach up to six feet. Even though the depth never exceeds 35 feet, this is a favorite of island dive charters due to its proximity to the harbors and wealth of marinelife.

The *Carthaginian* is an old whaling ship that was scuttled in 100 feet of water by Atlantis Submarines about 0.5 mile offshore from Puamana. A couple of West Side dive charters include this deep-water dive, with a maximum depth of 100 feet, in their weekly schedule. The *Carthaginian* hasn't yet developed the same amount of live coral as neighboring Mala Ramp, and it's the deepest dive in the area. Winter dives are punctuated by whale song—and you might even spot one underwater.

Dive Operators

Lahaina Divers (143 Dickenson St., 808/667-7496, www.lahainadivers.com) has the largest number of dive options available in Lahaina. Two custom-built 46-foot dive boats, departing from Lahaina Harbor, are the largest on Maui. Two-tank dives range from $149 for dives off Lana'i to $199 for a dive off Moku Ho'oniki (Moloka'i), famous for hammerhead sharks. There are also trips to the Back Wall of Molokini Crater as well as four-tank dive trips. The full-service dive shop in Lahaina has equipment sales and rentals. Since the availability of dives varies by day, inquire ahead of time.

On the north end of Lahaina at Mala Ramp, **Extended Horizons** (94 Kupuohi St., 808/667-0611, www.extendedhorizons.com) is another reputable operation that offers tours to Lana'i and the west shore of Maui. Extended Horizons takes only six passengers, and it's the only charter boat on the island to run completely on biodiesel. Morning tours check in at 6:30am at the Mala boat ramp for two-tank dives to Lana'i ($159). Other dive options include trips along the Maui shore as well as night dives, beach dives, and certification classes.

A smaller operation offering scuba tours of Lana'i, **Dive Maui** (1223 Front St., 808/661-7333, www.hawaiianrafting.com) departs from Mala Ramp aboard a rigid aluminum inflatable vessel. Group sizes are small, and a deli lunch is included with the two-tank dive. The shop is conveniently located within walking distance of Mala Ramp.

SOUTH OF LAHAINA
Dive Sites
Known to some operators as Turtle Reef or Turtle Point, **Olowalu** is an offshore, turtle-laden area popular with charter boats on the offshore reefs. Maximum depths are about 30 feet, and on nice days the visibility is close to 100 feet. This area is also popular with independent dive operators as a confined-water area for practicing dive skills. If you are shore-diving independently, the easiest way to get to deeper water is to enter around the Mile Marker 14 sign and swim in a straight line until you reach depths of 20-25 feet. When navigating your way through the coral heads, it's imperative to make sure that your gear doesn't drag across the reef, and bring a dive flag with you so that boats know you're below.

Ukumehame is a special spot accessible only by boat charter. Huge manta rays congregate here to be cleaned by reef fish who nibble algae off their wings, and the depths are a moderate 30-60 feet. It can't be done as a shore dive because the manta ray area is about a 25-minute surface swim from shore, and it takes trained dive instructors to determine if the water clarity is good enough for diving.

Surfing

Surfing is more than a hobby in West Maui—it's a way of life. Practice common etiquette, and enjoy the serenity that comes with surfing one of the most beautiful spots in the world.

KAPALUA, NAPILI, AND HONOKOWAI
Winter is the best time for surfing "up north," and the waves get larger the farther north you go. With the exception of S-Turns, however, most of the breaks on the Upper West Side are for experienced surfers. Beginners will have better luck at the breaks south of Lahaina.

Surf Spots
Pohaku Beach Park in Kahana is the epicenter of the West Side's longboard community. The break, commonly known as **S-Turns,** is perfect for beginners. Travel on Honoapi'ilani Highway until you reach the intersection with Ho'ohui Street, with the McDonald's on the corner. Turn toward the ocean, and make a left once you reach the bottom of the hill. Drive for 0.25 mile and find the parking lot for S-Turns on the right. From the parking lot, you can see two distinct breaks. To the right is Mushrooms, which can be a fun wave, but it's shallow on the inside section. To the left is S-Turns, where you'll notice a couple of A-frame peaks a long paddle offshore. Surfing at S-Turns is as much a paddle workout as a surfing workout, and you can be forgiven if you need to stop to catch your breath on the way out. Beginners stay on the inside section, while more experienced

surfers favor the outer peaks. Also, there have been some shark issues at S-Turns in the past, so be wary if the water is murky and no one else is out. S-Turns starts breaking on a moderate northwest swell, and on the largest of days can reach a few feet overhead.

The surf break at **D. T. Fleming Beach Park** is at the far northern end of the beach. The wave here is a combination of a beach break and a point break, and it can get crowded with bodyboarders during weekends. This is one of the few places on the West Side that picks up wind swell, so if it's windy and there aren't waves anywhere else, check Fleming's.

Rental Shops

Experienced surfers will get the best selection with **808 Boards** (808/283-1384, www.808boards.com, 7:30am-5pm daily, $25-35 per day), who will pick up and drop off the board at no additional charge.

Rent a board at the **Boss Frog's** locations in Napili (5095 Napilihau St., 808/669-4949, www.bossfrog.com, 8am-6pm daily) and Kahana (4310 Lower Honoapi'ilani Rd., 808/669-6700, www.bossfrog.com, 8am-5pm daily). Rates are around $20 per day for soft-top longboards or $25 per day for fiberglass boards.

For the cheapest boards you'll find on this side of the island, little-known **Annie's A&B Rentals** (3481 Lower Honoapi'ilani Rd., 808/669-0027, 9am-4pm daily) is hidden in Da Rose mall in Honokowai on the ocean side of the highway. Surfboards can be as cheap as $15 per day or $70 for the whole week.

KA'ANAPALI
Surf Spots

The only surf break in Ka'anapali is **Ka'anapali Point,** in front of the Marriott on Ka'anapali Beach. This is where the Ka'anapali surf lessons take place, although the wave here is tricky because it bends at a weird angle. Also, the inside section can be shallow and rocky, so surf school students are given booties. Ka'anapali Point can pick up both southwesterly and northeasterly swells, which means there can be surf any time of year.

Rental Shops and Schools

While the waves in Lahaina are more amenable to learning, there are still a number of operators along Ka'anapali Beach for those who would prefer to walk directly from the resort to a lesson. Since Ka'anapali gets windier than Lahaina, it's important to book the first lesson of the day for the best conditions.

Two-hour lessons ($79) can be booked at the beach shack in front of the Ka'anapali Beach Hotel. **Island Style Adventures** (808/244-6858, www.isasurfschool.com) in front of the Westin also offers two hour lessons ($75). For rentals by Ka'anapali Point, expect to pay $20-40. Booties are included in the price of all lessons and rentals.

LAHAINA

Lahaina and areas south have small waves breaking during most of the year, while summer has the most consistent surf. Most days will only have waves in the waist-high range, but the best swells of summer can reach overhead.

★ Surfing Spots

The most popular surf break in Lahaina is **Lahaina Breakwall,** located between the 505 shopping center and Lahaina Harbor. This is where most of the Lahaina surf schools operate. All of the surf schools hang out in the shallow inside section, and more experienced surfers sit farther outside. The outside section at small levels can be either a left or a right, although when it gets big on a large summer swell, it can turn into a huge left that can grow to 10 feet or more. During low tide it can get shallow enough here that you need to paddle with your fingertips and your skeg can scrape the bottom, so high tide is the optimal time for those who are concerned about falling. It shouldn't come as a surprise that this spot can get crowded, a fact of life that has earned it the moniker "Snakewall." If you're a beginner, you're better off going a few miles south to Puamana Beach Park or Guardrails.

Rental Shops and Schools

Inside the 505 shopping center, **Goofy Foot** (505 Front St., 808/244-9283, www.goofy-footsurfschool.com, 7am-9pm daily, lessons Mon.-Sat.) has helped over 100,000 students ride their first wave since opening in 1994. Two-hour lessons are $65 pp, and the owner, Tim, often enjoys time on the water as the private surf coach for Jimmy Buffett.

One block away on Prison Street are **Royal Hawaiian** (117 Prison St., 808/276-7873, www.royalhawaiiansurfacademy.com, 7am-4pm Mon.-Fri., 7am-3:30pm Sat.-Sun.) and **Maui Wave Riders** (133 Prison St., 808/875-4761, www.mauiwaveriders.com, 7am-9pm daily). Both have been operating since the mid-1990s, and all of the instructors are competent and patient professionals guaranteed to get you up and riding. Group rates run $65 pp, and for rentals, expect to pay $20 for three hours or $30 for the whole day.

To get away from the Breakwall crowds, **Maui Surfer Girls** (808/214-0606, www.mauisurfergirls.com, 8am-4:30pm daily) is the island's premier female-only surf camp operator, although it also offers coed group lessons for $85 pp. It costs a few dollars more than in town, and lessons take place a few miles south of town, along a mellow stretch of beach. At certain times of year, all-inclusive one- and two-week classes are offered to empower teenage girls through learning surfing. Lessons are offered at 8am, 10:30am, and 1pm daily.

Also south of town is **Hawaiian Paddle Sports** (808/442-6436, www.hawaiianpaddlesports.com), which offers completely private two-hour lessons ($189, $129 for 2-4

people, $109 for groups of 5 or more) and includes free photos of your time on the water. For something completely different that you'll never forget, try out **canoe surfing in an outrigger canoe** ($119-149 pp).

SOUTH OF LAHAINA

For beginning surfers and longboarders, the mile-long stretch of coast between **Puamana Beach Park** and **Launiupoko Beach Park** has numerous breaks with mellow waves for beginners. In between the two parks are peaks known as **Guardrails, Woody's,** and **Corner Pockets.** The beach parks and Guardrails have parking on the ocean side of the road, and parking for Woody's is in a dirt lot on the inland side of the highway. There can be small waves here most times of year, although summer sees the most consistent surf. If you're slightly more advanced, park in the lot for Puamana Beach Park and walk the length of shore all the way to the right along the Puamana condominium complex. At the far northern end of the beach is another break known as **Beaches or Hot Sands** that offers a fun right point welcoming to visitors.

At mile marker 12, **Ukumehame Beach Park** is another break that caters to beginners and longboarders but requires a much longer paddle than places such as Guardrails or Puamana. However, the longer effort means a longer ride. This is a favorite of island longboarders. While the beach itself is fairly long, the best waves are found directly in front of the small parking lot.

Tucked right at the base of the cliffs by mile marker 11, **Grandma's** is the name of the break on the far southern end of Papalaua Beach Park. This is a playful wave that caters to beginners and longboarders.

Stand-Up Paddling

KAPALUA, NAPILI, AND HONOKOWAI

One of the best stretches of coast for paddling is the section between Kapalua Bay and Hawea Point. The sandy entry at Kapalua Bay makes it easy to launch a board into the water. Napili Bay is another popular spot for morning paddles. Never bring a stand-up paddleboard into Honolua Bay. It's heavily frowned upon by locals and you'll likely be sent back to the beach by the surfers in the water.

Rental Shops

In Napili, rent stand-up paddleboards ($20 per hour, $40 per day) from **Water Works Sports** (5315 Lower Honoapi'ilani Rd., 808/298-2446, www.waterworkssportsmaui. com, 8am-5pm daily) inside the Napili Shores building. Be sure to get out early before the wind picks up.

If you'd prefer to have your boards delivered, **1-800-Snorkel** (800/766-7535, www.1-800-snorkel.com) offers stand-up paddleboard delivery to your hotel ($45-50 per day, depending on the type of board). Let the crew know before the morning you'd like to go, and they'll deliver it to the hotel lobby.

KA'ANAPALI

Sandy Ka'anapali is the perfect spot for stand-up paddling, but only during the morning hours before the wind picks up. On winter days, the water can be as smooth as glass, with dozens of whales breaching around you. Being out on the water during whale season can be an exciting adventure, but the same laws apply to stand-up paddlers as to boats: Stay 100 yards from humpback whales—unless, of course, they swim over to you.

Rental Shops

Almost every hotel along the main strip has activity huts offering paddleboard rentals. At **the kiosk** (808/661-7789, 8am-5pm daily) in front of the Ka'anapali Beach Hotel, boards are $25 for the first hour and $15 per additional hour. Or get them delivered to your hotel ($45 per day) from either **808 Boards** (808/283-1384, www.808boards.com)

Start the day by stand-up paddling off Ka'anapali.

Tips for Stand-Up Paddling

Stand-up paddling is very popular in Hawaii. While taking a lesson is always the best way to ensure success, here are a few tips if you'd rather rent a board and set out on your own.

- Paddle in the morning before the wind comes up.

- When first getting in the water, start on your knees to get the feel for the board.

- When you stand up, keep your feet shoulder width apart. You want to be standing in the middle of the board, about where the handle is.

- A stand-up paddleboard is like a bicycle; you need momentum for balance, so if you stop paddling, it's like trying to balance on a bicycle without pedaling. When you first stand up from kneeling, take a couple of paddles quickly to build up enough momentum so that you won't fall.

- Use the correct side of the paddle. Paddles are like an extension of your hand; you want to use the side of the paddle that would be your palm as opposed to the back of your hand.

- Instead of placing both hands on the shaft of the paddle, put one on the top and the other on the shaft. To keep a straight line you must alternate paddling on both sides of your body by taking a few strokes on your left and then a few strokes on your right, much like you would in a canoe.

- When paddling, make long, full strokes. Many first-time paddlers have a tendency to poke at the water with short, little strokes. Since this doesn't create much momentum, the board becomes wobbly and you're liable to fall. By taking long strokes, you create enough momentum for a stable platform and a much more enjoyable paddle.

- Use a leash. A leash is your lifeline if you fall off the board. If you are not sure which ankle to put the leash around, act as if you're going to do a cartwheel, and whichever foot leaves the ground second is the one you should attach the leash to.

- If you are paddling where there are waves, make sure that your board is pointing either into the waves or away from them. When waves hit the side of your board, there is a good chance you'll end up falling.

- When you fall off your board (don't worry, it happens to the best of paddlers), the best thing to do is just let it happen. Most paddleboarding injuries occur when people try to save themselves from falling and end up going down awkwardly. Accept your fate and fall gracefully into the water.

- Only competent surfers should ever try to surf on their paddleboards. Large, heavy boards can become dangerous in a surf lineup if they go crashing through a crowd, and a spate of injuries related to stand-up paddlers and their large boards have created a rift in the island surfing community. Common surf etiquette is to share the waves with surfers and stay out of the way. In the event you do fall down, make sure that your board doesn't hit someone.

or **1-800-Snorkel** (800/766-7535, www.1-800-snorkel.com).

LAHAINA

Lahaina is ringed by a barrier reef, which can make it shallow and dangerous for paddling. The trained instructors, however, know all of the *pukas* (holes) in the reef, and by allowing them to lead the way, you'll be awarded with sweeping views of the island's West Side. When you are over the Shark Pit, there's a decent chance you'll encounter an endangered Hawaiian monk seal or a harmless whitetip reef shark. While the 505 area can be a little difficult to navigate, it has the added benefit of being protected from the wind and will usually have calm, flat conditions when Ka'anapali is rough and blustery.

If you've rented your own board, the best place in the immediate area for stand-up paddling is the stretch of shore between Puamana and Launiupoko Beach Parks, where the water isn't nearly as shallow and it's still protected from the afternoon trade winds.

Rental Shops and Schools

Stand-up paddling lessons are offered in the Lahaina Breakwall area by **Royal Hawaiian** (117 Prison St., 808/276-7873, www.royalhawaiiansurfacademy.com, 7am-4pm Mon.-Fri., 7am-3:30pm Sat.-Sun.), **Goofy Foot** (505 Front St., 808/244-9283, www.goofyfootsurfschool.com, 7am-9pm daily, lessons Mon.-Sat.), and **Maui Wave Riders** (133 Prison St., 808/875-4761, www.mauiwaveriders.com, 7am-9pm daily). Rather than mingling with all the surf school students, the stand-up paddling tours go the other direction from the Lahaina Breakwall down to the section of beach known as Shark Pit. For rentals, expect to pay in the $35 range for three hours to $45 for all day.

For more personalized service in an area that isn't as crowded, **Maria Souza Stand-Up Paddle School** (808/579-9231, www.standuppaddlesurfschool.com, 8am-2pm daily) and **Hawaiian Paddle Sports** (808/442-6436, www.hawaiianpaddlesports.com) both offer lessons on beaches south of Lahaina, run by instructors who have a deep-rooted respect for the island, the environment, and Hawaiian cultural history. While they're more expensive, these tours will leave you with a deeper appreciation for the ocean. Lessons with Maria Souza's are $159 pp, and with Hawaiian Paddle Sports $189 for a private lesson, $129 pp for 2-4 people, or $109 pp for groups of five or more.

Kayaking and Canoeing

West Maui has numerous options for both **kayaking** and outrigger **canoeing**. While kayaking isn't as hard on the shoulder muscles and allows you to hug the coast, outrigger canoeing is a culturally rich experience unique to Polynesia. The morning hours are the best time to paddle, with most operators offering an early morning tour followed by another later in the morning.

KAPALUA, NAPILI, AND HONOKOWAI

The most popular kayak trip on the Upper West Side of the island is the paddle from D. T. Fleming Beach Park to Honolua Bay. Along this stretch of coast, you pass rugged rock formations inaccessible from the road, and you'll hug this dramatic coast past Mokulei'a Bay and into Honolua. Because of the high surf during winter, these tours are only offered in summer, and all trips depart D. T. Fleming Beach Park in the early morning hours before the afternoon trade winds pick up. Snorkeling in Honolua Bay is included in the excursions, and you are likely to encounter Hawaiian green sea turtles or potentially even Hawaiian spinner dolphins.

The best company offering tours up here is **Hawaiian Paddle Sports** (808/808/442-6436, www.hawaiianpaddlesports.com), with completely private excursions for kayaking ($149 pp) and outrigger canoeing ($159 pp). The educational component and respect for culture are superior to other operations.

KA'ANAPALI

Off Kahekili Beach Park in front of the Westin Villas, **Maui Paddle Sports** (808/283-9344, www.mauipaddlesports.com) offers two-hour outrigger canoe rides in a six-person outrigger

($85 pp). Trips run at 8am and 9:30am daily. This is a convenient option if you're staying in the area off Kahekili Beach.

SOUTH OF LAHAINA

The main areas for kayaking south of Lahaina are either Olowalu (mile marker 14) or Coral Gardens, off Papalaua Beach Park (mile marker 11), where you can paddle along the rugged sea cliffs that plunge down into the sea. This is a popular area for kayaking in winter since the large surf on the northern shores makes kayaking there impossible, and these are fantastic reefs for spotting Hawaiian green sea turtles. **Hawaiian Paddle Sports** (808/808/442-6436, www.hawaiianpaddlesports.com, private tours $119-199 pp) offers three-hour tours in this area. For a more budget-friendly operation, **Kayak Olowalu** (808/661-0606, www.kayakolowalu.com) offers 2.5-hour tours ($65 pp adults).

Other Water Activities

★ SUNSET CRUISES

Few Maui activities are more iconic than a sunset sail off the West Maui coast. The feeling of the trade winds in your hair as you glide along is a sensation of freedom you can't experience on land. Watch as the setting sun paints the sky every shade of orange and pink. On most days you can make out a rainbow hovering over the lush valleys of Mauna Kahalawai.

Ka'anapali

A **sunset sail off Ka'anapali Beach** can be the most magical moment of your vacation, but there are a few things to understand to make the most of the magic. Make sure to ask when you need to check in, as departure times for sunset sails are different in summer and winter. Secondly, while it's always nice to dress up a little, remember that you're going on a boat and should be outfitted accordingly. The Ka'anapali boats are all sailing catamarans, which are boarded from the sand, and since some days can have moderate shore-break, there's a good chance you'll end up wet from the shins down. Your shoes are collected prior to boarding (to prevent sand tracking onto the

view of Maui from a sunset sail

boat), so don't put too much effort into matching them with your outfit.

There's even a chance that the departure will be moved to Lahaina Harbor due to large surf on the beach. Since this isn't possible to predict until the day before the sail, it's a good idea to double-check on the morning of your sail to confirm where the boat will be loading. The northerly trade winds can often be chilly, so it's a good idea to bring a light jacket. Finally, remember that you'll be sailing. Even though the vessels are wide, stable catamarans, it may be difficult to move around, and spray may come over the sides. If your idea of a sunset sail is a stable platform that putts along at three knots, the dinner cruises from Lahaina are a better bet.

Trilogy (808/874-5649, www.sailtrilogy.com) offers sunset sails ($69) on Tuesday, Thursday, and Saturday as well as an Aloha Friday sunset sail ($79) that features live music and Pacific Rim pupus. Trilogy's sail isn't marketed as a booze cruise, but three premium alcoholic beverages are included in the rates, including mixed drink cocktails like the Moloka'i Mule. Unless the surf is high and the crew needs to load from Lahaina Harbor, the check-in for all Trilogy tours is in front of the Ka'anapali Beach Hotel.

In front of Whalers Village, **Teralani** (808/661-7245, www.teralani.net) offers two different sails departing nightly during the busier times of year. The original sunset sail ($71 adults) includes a pupu menu as well as an open bar of beer and mixed drinks. For those who would rather dine on board, the full dinner sail ($94 adults) is 30 minutes longer and includes a filling menu.

Gemini (808/669-0508, www.geminicharters.com) similarly offers sunset sails ($75 adults) that feature a pupu menu as well as Maui Brewing Company beer and mai tais.

The most yacht-like experience departing from the beach is on the *Hula Girl* (808/665-0344, www.sailingmaui.com), which not only offers the newest boat but also luxurious upgrades like throw pillows, free Wi-Fi,

panoramic viewing from the fly-bridge, and high-tech sailing. Regular sunset sails ($68) are offered Monday, Wednesday, and Friday, but you have to buy your food and drinks. For a full-service dinner cruise, *Hula Girl* also offers cruises on Tuesday, Thursday, and Saturday ($80 adults) featuring upscale Pacific Rim dining options made fresh in the onboard kitchen. In many ways, it's more like a floating restaurant with an $80 cover charge. Menu items range $5-23, and a full-service bar slings top-shelf cocktails.

Lahaina
DINNER CRUISES

A sailboat is a better venue than a powerboat for a sunset cruise, but for those who would rather be on a large, stable diesel vessel instead of a catamaran, the best **dinner cruise** from Lahaina is offered by **Pacific Whale Foundation** (612 Front St., 808/942-5311, www.pacificwhale.org). The power catamaran used for this charter is the nicest of the large diesel boats, and the menu includes locally sourced produce and sustainably harvested seafood. Regular seats are $88, but if you don't want to share a table with another party, upgrade to the premium seating ($108 adults). Three alcoholic beverages are included in the cruise, as is live music.

SAILBOATS

If you know what it means to "shake a reef," you'll be much happier watching the sunset aboard a small **sailboat** than on a large motorized platform. The fastest sailing catamaran offering sunset sails ($65 adults) from Lahaina is *Sail Maui* (808/244-2087, www.sailmaui.com), which provides sailing, pupus, beer, wine, and mai tais. Trips run Monday-Saturday, and maximum capacity of the cruise is just 24 people.

The newest catamaran in Lahaina Harbor is *Ocean Spirit,* part of the **Pacific Whale Foundation** (612 Front St., 808/942-5311, www.pacificwhale.org) fleet that sailed to Hawaii from St. Croix in only 42 days. The two-hour sunset sails ($69) include locally sourced pupus and three alcoholic beverages.

If you're a monohull sailor, **Scotch Mist II** (808/661-0386, www.scotchmistsailingcharters.com) offers evening sunset sails ($69 for Champagne Sunset Sail) aboard a Santa Cruz 50-foot racing boat, which departs from slip 2.

TOP EXPERIENCE

★ WHALE-WATCHING

Any vessel that floats is going to be offering **whale-watching** between December 15 and April 15. Even though whale season officially lasts until May 15, the whales aren't encountered with enough regularity after mid-April to guarantee sightings. The peak of the season for whale-watching is January-March, and simply being out on the water turns any trip into whale-watching.

Most snorkeling and sailing operators offer whale-watching during winter, with most boats carrying whale naturalists well-versed in the study of these gentle giants. Since most prices are about the same, the choice ultimately comes down to what sort of vessel best suits your comfort level. Small rafts from Lahaina Harbor place you the closest to the water. Sailboats also offer whale-watching

trips from both Lahaina Harbor and Ka'anapali Beach. The large 149-passenger diesel boats in Lahaina provide the most affordable rates, but you'll be sharing the vessel with over 100 other people and won't get 360-degree views.

SUBMARINE

If riding in a **submarine** is on your bucket list, **Atlantis Submarines** (Slip 18, 808/667-2224, www.atlantisadventures.com/maui, 9am-2pm daily) operates regular charters ($105 adults, $35 children) from Lahaina Harbor to the *Carthaginian,* a sunken whaling ship in 100 feet of water. Check-in is at the Atlantis shop inside the Pioneer Inn. Trips last two hours.

For those who are a little nervous about descending completely underwater and want to see fish without snorkeling, **Reef Dancer** (Slip 6, 808/667-2133, www.mauiglassbottomboat.com) is a yellow "semi-sub" that remains partially submerged for its journey along the coast. While there is an above-deck portion of the sub that never goes underwater, passengers are seated in an underwater cabin that offers 360-degree views of the underwater world. All of the boat staff double as scuba divers who can point out anything that

diving deep on Atlantis Submarines

These are the best seats in the house!

might be living along the reef such as eels, octopuses, turtles, or urchins. This is a great way for young children, elderly visitors, and non-swimmers to enjoy Maui's reef system without having to get their hair wet. Sixty-minute tours ($35 adults, $20 children) run three times each morning, with a longer 90-minute tour ($45 adults, $25 children) departing Lahaina Harbor at 2:15pm daily.

FISHING

In no place is Lahaina's port town heritage more evident than at dingy yet lovable Lahaina Harbor. The smell of fish carcasses still wafts on the breeze, and shirtless, tanned, sweat-covered sailors casually sip beer as they lay the fresh catch on ice. Some days you can buy fresh mahimahi or ono straight from the folks who caught it, or, if you'd rather take your shot at reeling one in yourself, there are a slew of sportfishing boats ready to get you on the water.

The charters that have the best chance of

catching fish are those that leave early and stay out for a full day. These are more expensive, but during a full-day charter you're able to troll around the buoys on the far side of Lana'i or Kaho'olawe. On half-day charters, you're confined to shallower water where the fish aren't biting as much, particularly during the winter. On virtually all charters you need to provide your own food and drinks. Don't bring bananas on board, since it is considered bad luck. Most boats will let you keep what you catch so you can cook it the same night.

Of all the boats in the harbor, **Start Me Up** (808/667-2774, www.sportfishingmaui.com) has the best reputation. Prices range from $129 pp for two hours to $279 pp for an eight-hour charter. Catch a 500-pound marlin, and your trip is free!

A boat with a sterling reputation is **Die Hard** (808/344-5051, www.diehardsportfishing.com), run by the legendary Captain Fuzzy. Rates for these charters vary, but expect to pay $200 pp for six-hour charters and $220 pp for full-day, eight-hour charters.

Down at the south end of the harbor, away from many of the other boats, **Luckey Strike** (808/661-4606, www.luckeystrike.com) has two different boats and operates on the premise that using live bait for smaller fish is better. Captain Tad Luckey has been fishing these waters for over 30 years, and as with most captains in the harbor, he has an enviable and well-earned amount of local knowledge to put into every trip.

PARASAILING

Parasailing isn't possible December 15-May 15. Since the waters off West Maui are part of the Hawaiian Islands Humpback Whale National Marine Sanctuary, all "thrill craft," such as high-speed parasailing boats, are outlawed during the time of year when the whales are nursing their calves. During the summer or fall, however, parasailing is a peaceful adventure option for gazing at West Maui from hundreds of feet above the turquoise waters. It's one of the best views you'll find on the island.

Ka'anapali

UFO Parasail (800/359-4836, www.ufoparasail.net) is one of the two operators departing from Ka'anapali Beach, in front of Leilani's restaurant. Only eight people are on the boat at a time, which means that your overall time on the water is only a little over an hour. Of that hour, your personal flight time lasts 10-12 minutes, depending on the length of your line (you'll end up being 400-500 feet off the water). The staff and captains who run these tours do hundreds of trips over the course of the season, and from a safety and efficiency standpoint, the crew has it down to a science. Taking off and landing on the boat is a dry entry and exit, and you will be blown away by the serenity you experience up in the air. Prices range $85-95 depending on your height; you must weigh at least 130 pounds to fly alone, and trips usually start around 9am.

In front of the Hyatt, **West Maui Parasail** (808/661-4060, www.westmauiparasail.com) offers similar tours at $75 for 800 feet or $85 for 1,200 feet. If you aren't staying in the Ka'anapali resort area, a perk of going with West Maui Parasail is that free, convenient parking can be found in the Hanakao'o Beach Park area just a three-minute walk from the Hyatt.

Lahaina

The only parasailing operation in Lahaina is **West Maui Parasail** (808/661-4060, www.westmauiparasail.com) out of slip 15. The prices are the same as at the Ka'anapali operation, but a benefit of parasailing from Lahaina is that the water is consistently calmer and glassier than in neighboring Ka'anapali.

JET SKIING

Just like parasailing, **Jet Skiing** is only possible May 16-December 14. During summer, the island's only Jet Ski operation is **Maui Watersports** (808/667-2001, www.mauiwatersports.com), in Ka'anapali, just south of the Hyatt. Even though the area is relatively protected from the wind, morning hours are still the best for the calmest conditions. Rates are $79 for a 30-minute ride and $119 for a full hour, although you can save money by booking online.

WAKEBOARDING

Captain Ryan at **Wake Maui** (808/269-5645, www.wakemaui.com) offers wakeboarding trips in the flat water between Lahaina and Ka'anapali. Wake Maui provides the only service of its kind, where a six-passenger ski boat is equipped with all the wake toys for a fun day on the water. Since Maui's winds can often be extreme, however, wakeboarding charters usually depart early to capitalize on glassy conditions. Other toys include waterskiing and wakesurfing equipment, or you can simply charter the boat ($214 for 1 hour, $428 for 2 hours, $791 for 4 hours) if you want to go whale-watching in winter.

SPEARFISHING

To take snorkeling to the next level and maybe take home dinner, **Maui Spearfishing Academy** (808/446-0352, www.maui-spearfishing.com, $169) teaches visitors how to spearfish and eradicate invasive species, and can teach you the technique behind holding your breath to spear-dive and target the right fish.

Hiking and Biking

HIKING

There aren't nearly as many hiking trails on the West Side of the island as you might expect. Much of the access in West Maui is blocked by private land or lack of proper trails. Also, since much of West Maui sits in the lee of Mauna Kahalawai, there aren't any accessible waterfalls, as there are in East Maui. Nevertheless, the hiking options in West Maui offer their own sort of beauty, from stunning coastal treks to grueling ridgeline hikes.

Kapalua, Napili, and Honokowai

★ KAPALUA COASTAL TRAIL

Even though it's only 1.75 miles long, the **Kapalua Coastal Trail** might just be the best coastal walk in Hawaii. The trail is bookended by beaches that have each been named the number-one beach in the United States: Kapalua Bay and D. T. Fleming Beach Park. While most walkers, joggers, and hikers begin the trail at Kapalua Bay, you can also access the trail from other junctions at the Kapalua Bay Villas, Oneloa Bay, the Ritz-Carlton, and D. T. Fleming Beach Park.

What makes the Kapalua Coastal Trail legendary are the various environments it passes through. If you begin at Kapalua Bay, the trail starts as a paved walkway paralleling the beach and weaves its way through ultra-luxurious residences. At the top of a short hill, the paved walkway reaches a junction by the Kapalua Bay Villas, where the path suddenly switches to dirt. Signs point to the continuation of the trail, and a spur trail leads straight out toward Hawea Point, a protected reserve that is home to the island's largest colony of 'ua'u kani (wedge-tailed shearwaters). If you follow the grass trail to the left of the three-way junction, it connects with the trail to Namalu Bay—the rocky, Mediterranean cove hidden in the craggy recesses.

Continuing along the main Kapalua Coastal Trail leads over a short rocky section before emerging at a smooth boardwalk along Oneloa Bay. The boardwalk here was constructed as a means of protecting the sensitive dunes of Kapalua, and in the morning Oneloa is one of the most gloriously empty beaches you'll find on Maui. At the end of the boardwalk, the trail leads up a flight of stairs and eventually connects with Lower Honoapi'ilani Road. From here, take a left and follow the sidewalk as it connects with the trail running in front of the Ritz-Carlton before finishing at the water's edge at D. T. Fleming Beach Park. For a side trip, hike out parallel to the golf course to **Makalua-puna Point**—otherwise known as Dragon's Teeth (page 190).

VILLAGE WALKING TRAILS

The **village walking trails** are the next most popular hikes in the Kapalua resort area. Weaving their way up the mountainside through the cool and forested uplands are the 1.25-mile Cardio Loop or the 3.6-mile Lake Loop, an uphill, butt-burning workout popular with local joggers. More than just a great morning workout, there are also sections of the trail that offer sweeping views looking out toward Moloka'i and the area around Honolua Bay. To find the access point for the trails, park in the lot for the Kapalua Village Center (between Sansei Restaurant and the Kapalua Golf Academy) and follow a paved cart path winding its way down toward an underpass, where you will find the trailhead for both loops.

MAHANA RIDGE TRAIL

The **Mahana Ridge Trail** is the longest continuous trail in the Kapalua resort area and the best option for serious hikers. Though you can access the Mahana Ridge Trail from the village trails, a less confusing and more scenic trailhead is in the parking lot of D. T. Fleming

Beach Park along the access road from the highway. The trailhead is a little hard to find, so look for the thin trail leading up the inland side of the road about 20 yards back from the parking lot. This trail climbs up the ridge for nearly six miles, all the way to the Maunalei Arboretum, and is a proper hiking trail with narrow sections, moderate uphills, and sweeping views of the coast. It is an out-and-back trip, and maps are available online at www.kapalua.com.

MAUNALEI ARBORETUM TRAIL

To climb even farther up the mountainside, follow the **Maunalei Arboretum Trail** as it winds its way through a forest planted by the great D. T. Fleming. The manager of Honolua Ranch during the 1920s, Fleming forested the mountainside with numerous plant species from across the globe in an effort to preserve the watershed. Today, over 85 years after the arboretum was established, hikers can still climb the ridges of this historic upland and be immersed in a forest of wild banyan trees as well as coffee, guava, and bo trees. Trails in the arboretum range from short 0.5-mile loops to a moderate 2.5-mile round-trip that winds down Honolua Ridge. To reach the trails, you have to hike six miles up the scenic

Mahana Ridge Trail, or book a guided hiking tour ($99) through **Ambassadors of the Environment** (808/669-6200) at the Ritz Carlton.

OHAI TRAIL

The 1.2-mile **Ohai Trail** awards hikers with panoramic vistas of the island's North Shore. This area is often windy, and the way in which the wind drowns out all other sounds makes it a peaceful respite on the northern coast. The Ohai trailhead is 10 miles past the entrance to Kapalua, by mile marker 41, between the Nakalele Blowhole and Olivine Pools. Along the moderate, winding trail are a few placards with information on the island's native coastal plants. This is also a great perch to watch for tropical **seabirds** soaring on the afternoon breeze. There isn't any readily available water on this stretch of coast, so be sure to pack a water bottle with you. There is sometimes a vendor selling drinks in front of Nakalele Blowhole, or a food truck (Mon.-Sat.) parked by Kahakuloa.

Ka'anapali
KA'ANAPALI BOARDWALK

The southern terminus of the three-mile-long **Ka'anapali Boardwalk** is in front of

Kapalua Coastal Trail

the Hyatt resort, and the easiest public beach parking is at Hanakao'o Beach Park along the highway between Ka'anapali and Lahaina. From here the boardwalk runs north all the way to the Sheraton, about 1.5 miles, although if you follow the paved walkway through the lower level of the Sheraton and through the parking lot, you will notice the trail re-forms and starts skirting the golf course. The walkway then runs through the Royal Lahaina resort and the parking lot of adjoining hotels. Following the Beach Walk signs, you eventually join another boardwalk that runs all the way down to the Honua Kai resort.

South of Lahaina
LAHAINA PALI TRAIL

Hot, dry, and with incomparable views, the **Lahaina Pali Trail** is a walk back in time to days when reaching Lahaina wasn't quite so easy. This five-mile, three-hour (one-way) hike is the most strenuous trek in West Maui, as the zigzagging trail climbs 1,600 vertical feet before reaching a crest by the Kaheawa Wind Farm. While torturous on both your legs and your thirst, the reward for the uphill slog is panoramic views over the central valley and dozens of humpback whales off the coast during winter.

Tracing its way over a part of the island that receives less than 10 inches of rainfall annually, this trail was originally constructed about 400 years ago during the reign of Pi'ilani, who envisioned a footpath wrapping around the island. When a dirt road was constructed along the coast in 1911, the trail fell into disrepair. Nevertheless, hikers still encounter evidence of ancient activity, such as stone shelters and rock walls. It's surreal to imagine that only 100 years ago this was the preferred route to reach Lahaina. To get the most out of this hike, pick up the hiking guide that the Na Ala Hele trail system has published, titled *Tales from the Trail*. It provides an interactive historical tour aligned with markers along the trail. Copies are available at the Department of Land and Natural Resources building in Wailuku (54 High St.), or, if you have a smartphone, download it as a PDF (www.mauiguidebook.com/hikes/lahaina-pali-trail).

The downside of this trail is that since it's a one-way hike, it can take some logistical planning. The Ukumehame trailhead on the Lahaina side is at mile marker 10.5, about 0.5 mile past the tunnel in a small dirt parking lot on the inland side of the highway. If you depart from the Ukumehame trailhead, the path

mountain views from the Maunalei Arboretum Trail

ascends moderately and offers pristine views of the coral reefs below. After the trail levels out at 1,600 feet, when you reach the crest by the wind farm, it descends steeply and sharply to the opposite trailhead between Maʻalaea and the junction of Honoapiʻilani Highway (Hwy. 30) and North Kihei Road. Your four options for the return route are to leave a car at the opposite trailhead, hike back the way you came, hitchhike back to the original trailhead, or turn back the way you came once you reach the wind farm (which is the shortest and most practical option).

If you plan on only hiking half the trail, setting out from the Maʻalaea trailhead offers better views of the valley and Kealia Pond, whereas departing from the Ukumehame trailhead offers better views of the coast and whale-watching opportunities. For the intrepid and those equipped with headlamps, the Ukumehame side is the best sunset perch on the West Side. Since there is absolutely no shade on this hike and it can get brutally hot, it's imperative to avoid the middle of the day and to pack more water than you would normally need.

You'll be passing over rocky, rugged terrain, so wear closed-toe shoes.

BIKING

Whether you're going for a 60-mile ride around the West Maui Mountains or a leisurely ride down Front Street on a beach cruiser, biking on the West Side of the island means cycling on roadways. For serious cyclists looking to rent a road bike, **West Maui Cycles** (1087 Limahana Place, 808/661-9005, www.westmauicycles.com, 9am-5pm Mon.-Sat., 10am-4pm Sun.), in the industrial park of Lahaina, is the best bike shop on the West Side. Mountain bikes and high-performance road bikes range $50 per day to $285 per week; basic beach cruisers are $15 per day.

Closer to the center of Lahaina, **Boss Frog's Cycles** (156 Lahainaluna Rd., 808/661-1345, www.mauiroadbikerentals.com, 8am-5pm daily) also offers beach cruisers ($15 per day, $60 per week) and high-performance road bikes ($45 per day). While this location is closer to town and more convenient, die-hard cyclists will appreciate the passion for the sport found at West Maui Cycles.

Adventure Sports

Even though water sports dominate the recreation options on the island's West Side, there are still a number of places where you can get a thrill on the land or over the water.

ATV RIDES

The best ATV ride on the West Side of the island is with **Kahoma Ranch** (808/667-1978, www.kahomaranch.com), to get dirty and rip across dirt roads on your own ATV ($222) or a shared ATV ($149). At the end, when you're all hot and sweaty, you can take a plunge down one of three different waterslides. Tour participants are awarded with views looking out at the island of Lanaʻi and back into Kahoma Valley. The tour area is closed to the public, so this is the only way you will see these views.

The waterslides look like little more than tarps stretched over a hole in the ground, but the speeds you can achieve are much faster than you'd expect. Children are $82, and those as young as age five can accompany a driver of legal age. Tours take place at 7:30am, 10am, 1pm, and 4pm daily, although the 7:30am tour doesn't include the waterslides.

ZIPLINING

The largest ziplining tour in West Maui is **Skyline Eco-Adventures** (2580 Kekaʻa Dr., 808/878-8400, www.zipline.com, 7am-6pm daily, $150), a company that was the first zipline operator on Maui. Each of the eight ziplines has a historical, environmental, or cultural connection explained by the guides, and the main draw is the view toward Lana'i and Moloka'i across the royal-blue channels.

These tours are so popular they run eight times a day, with the earliest starting from the Fairway Shops office at 7am daily. The benefit of an early tour is that temperatures are still cool and winds are calm, although there can sometimes be some lingering morning showers, and the dirt roads can be muddy from this moisture. Try to get on the 8am or 9am tour, although there is never a bad time to be up here ziplining. Children must be 10 years of age for the Ka'anapali course, closed-toe shoes are required, and the maximum weight is 260 pounds. To combine ziplining with splashing in the reservoirs, try the four-line **Zip N' Dip** tour, where you zip right into the water.

Up north, **Kapalua Ziplines** (500 Office Rd., 808/756-9147, www.kapaluaziplines. com) has a seven-line course that differs from Skyline in Ka'anapali in that all the lines are tandem. You can zip next to your loved one and watch them grimace with glee as you soar up to 2,100 feet across the Kapalua mountainside. You'll walk over one of Hawaii's longest suspension bridges and ride an ATV to the summit. Tours ($207) are offered five times per day. Since the tours can sometimes be canceled due to wind, try to go early in the morning.

Shopping

KAPALUA, NAPILI, AND HONOKOWAI

Shopping in the northwestern corner of the island is utilitarian, paling in comparison to the shops of Ka'anapali and Lahaina. Nevertheless, there are still a few stores worthy of a mention if you're staying in the area and need some emergency retail therapy.

In Kapalua, the **Honolua Store** (502 Office Rd., 808/665-9105, 6am-6:30pm daily) has a small apparel and souvenir section to accompany the food market, and if you save your receipt from any purchase, you will receive a free gift the next time you shop here.

Down the road in Kahana, **Women Who Run With Wolves** (4310 Honoapi'ilani Rd., 808/665-0786, www.womenwhorunwithwolves.com, 10am-6pm daily), downstairs in the Kahana Manor, has the best women's apparel and accessory shopping that you'll find on the northwest side.

KA'ANAPALI
Whalers Village

Without a doubt, the undisputed epicenter of the Ka'anapali shopping scene is **Whalers Village** (2435 Ka'anapali Pkwy., 808/661-4567, www.whalersvillage.com, 9:30am-10pm daily), smack in the middle of Ka'anapali Beach between the Whaler Hotel and the Westin Resort. With three levels of restaurants, clothing boutiques, jewelry galleries, and kiosks, Whalers Village is the see-and-be-seen spot for all of your island souvenir shopping. While many of the stores are name-brand outlets you're already familiar with, there are still a handful of locally run stores. Get your parking validated, since the garage rates are expensive.

If you park in the Whalers Village garage, you can't help but walk directly past **Totally Hawaiian** (808/667-4070, www.totallyhawaiian.com), a gift gallery featuring the wares of over 100 local artists. Works such as hand-painted Hawaiian gourds are on display, as is an impressive collection of Ni'ihau shell jewelry. There's also a fascinating array of ancient Hawaiian weapons handcrafted from shark's teeth and wood.

Other popular apparel favorites include **Blue Ginger** (808/667-5793, www.blueginger. com), a store specializing in women's and children's resort wear, and **Maggie Coulombe** (808/344-6672, www.maggiecoulombe.com), a world-renowned dress fashionista who has clothed top celebrities. A wide variety of pearl shops, jewelry stores, and surf outlets round out the popular mall.

LAHAINA

Frenetic and fast-paced, Lahaina is the shopping capital of Maui. The section of Front Street between the Old Lahaina Center and the 505 shopping center is where you'll find the majority of shops.

★ Front Street

Front Street is a sight in itself that centers around commerce and a voracious love of shopping. It has been listed as one of the "Great Streets in America" by the American Planning Association. Walking the length of this vivacious thoroughfare is one of the West Side's most popular activities. Along the flat oceanfront stretch, you'll find art galleries, surf shops, and more compressed in a nonstop string of merchandise. Most shops are open 9am-10pm daily.

The **Wyland Gallery** (711 Front St., 808/667-2285, www.wyland.com) offers the artist's trademark array of marinelife scenes in a perfect oceanfront location. On the opposite side of the street, acclaimed photographer **Peter Lik** (712 Front St., 808/661-6623, www.peterlik.com) has a popular showroom of his oversize art, with the ability to transport you directly into the photograph. Other galleries of note are **Sargent's Fine Art** (802 Front St., 808/667-4030, www.sargentsfineart.com), on the corner of Lahainaluna Road; the **Village Gallery** (120 Dickenson St., 808/661-4402, www.villagegalleriesmaui.com); and **Martin Lawrence** (808/661-1788, www.martinlawrence.com). Those with a passion for art should also remember that every Friday night is art night in Lahaina, when many galleries put on their finest show, featuring artist appearances or live jazz, 7pm-10pm.

Hale Zen (180 Dickenson St., 808/661-4802, www.halezen.com)—a two-minute walk up Dickenson Street—is a local favorite for everything from homewares to candles, lotions, and crafts from local artists. Just across the street, by Lahaina Divers, **Goin Left** (143 Dickenson St., 808/868-3805, www.goinleft.com, 10am-8pm Mon.-Sat., 11am-6pm Sun.) is a relatively new shop with apparel and accessories that are catered around the modern board sports lifestyle.

For jewelry, stop into **Glass Mango Designs** (858 Front St., 808/662-8500, www.glassmango.com) for a colorful selection of "wearable art." For a shop that's stuffed with work from local artists, **Maui Memories** (658 Wharf St., 808/298-0261, www.mauiislandmemories.com, 9am-8pm daily) is across from the Banyan Tree and has island-themed clothing, accessories, and gifts from dozens of Maui artists.

Classic retail outpost **Lahaina Scrimshaw** (845 Front St., 808/667-9232, www.lahainascrimshawmaui.com) showcases the seafarers' craft of carving scenes on ivory.

Banyan Tree Market

While the Friday art nights are always festive, those who prefer lesser-known artists are encouraged to visit the fair beneath the banyan tree, held 9am-5pm on various weekends throughout the year. For a full schedule on when the art fair is on, visit www.lahainaarts.com.

Lahaina Cannery Mall

Enough visitors still frequent **Lahaina Cannery Mall** (1221 Honoapiʻilani Hwy., 808/661-5304, www.lahainacannery.com, 9:30am-9pm Mon.-Sat., 9:30am-7pm Sun.) to keep a few stores open. Stores of note include **Honolua Surf Co.** (808/661-5777, www.honoluasurf.com), which has the same apparel as you would find in Whalers Village or on Front Street for slightly reduced rates, and **Maui Toy Works** (808/661-4766), for children's gifts.

Entertainment

West Maui is the island's entertainment hot spot, with the island's best lu'aus and most happening bars. You can't walk more than 10 yards in Lahaina without tripping over an evening drink special. More than just booze, West Maui is also home to family entertainment options ranging from free hula performances and whale lectures to evening magic performances.

For the most up-to-date info on the latest evening scene, pick up a free copy of *Maui Time* newspaper or check out "The Grid" section on the website at www.mauitime.com.

KAPALUA, NAPILI, AND HONOKOWAI
Evening Shows

Can't get enough of *ki ho'alu* (slack-key guitar)? The **Masters of Slack Key** (5900 Lower Honoapi'ilani Rd., 808/669-3858, www.slackkeyshow.com, 7:30pm Wed.) performance at the Aloha Pavilion of the Napili Kai Beach Resort is the best show you'll find on the island. Tickets can either be purchased online or at 6:45pm, when the doors first open. Prices for the show are normally $38, although you can also book a package dinner combo for $95, which includes a sunset dinner at the Sea House restaurant immediately before the show.

Bars, Live Music, and Nightlife

The late-night karaoke sessions at **Sansei** (600 Office Rd., 808/669-6286, www.sanseihawaii.com, 5:30pm-10pm Mon.-Thurs., 5:30pm-1am Fri.-Sat.) restaurant in the Kapalua resort are the most happening evenings on the northwestern side. This popular sushi and sake bar stays open until 1am during karaoke night, and the main draw is the award-winning late-night menu (10pm-1am) that offers dozens of sushi plates at heavily discounted rates.

In the Kahana Gateway Center, **Maui Brewing Company** (4405 Honoapi'ilani Hwy., 808/669-3474, www.mauibrewingco.

com, 11am-10pm daily) is a happening brewpub that's packed with hop-soaked locals. Sit at the bar so you can keep your beer cold on the slab of ice that's inside the bar. Over a dozen beers are available on draft, many of which are only found at the brewery.

KA'ANAPALI
Lu'aus

There is no shortage of lu'aus along the Ka'anapali strip. The best on the island, the Old Lahaina Lu'au, is in nearby Lahaina, but there are four lu'aus in Ka'anapali. If the only reason you want to go to a lu'au is for the fire dancing, choose one in Ka'anapali. All will feature buffet food mass-produced for 100 people as well as local craft artisans, and all will offer premium seating for an added price. In my opinion it isn't worth the extra cost, since it usually means you get only slightly better seats and are first in line for the food. Most shows begin at either 5pm or 5:30pm. Ka'anapali can experience higher winds and a greater likelihood of rain than nearby Lahaina, so the chances of the luau needing to be moved inside or cancelled are higher. Most nights are gorgeous, but if you want to guarantee calm conditions, you'll have better luck in Lahaina.

Of the numerous luaus in Ka'anapali, the best show is the **Wailele Polynesian Luau** (2365 Ka'anapali Pkwy., 808/667-2525, www.westinmaui.com, $115 adults, $65 children) at the Westin Maui resort. The fire dancers are the best, and the food is above average compared to the other options. Shows take place Tuesday and Thursday evenings as well as Sunday during busier times of the year, although the schedule varies. If you're driving to Ka'anapali, the one downside of this show is that parking can be challenging. Try to find free beach parking in the lot between Whalers Village and the entrance to the Westin. If you can't find a free spot, the most economical option is to park in the Whalers Village garage and then buy an ice cream or a quick beer after the show to get your parking validated for three hours.

Ka'anapali Sunset Lu'au at Black Rock (2605 Ka'anapali Pkwy., 808/877-4852, www.sheratonmauiluau.com, $108 adults, $60 children) is Monday and Wednesday evenings at the Sheraton resort. The crowds aren't quite as large as other shows, and the grassy luau grounds are more spacious. While the food is fine and the dancers are entertaining, the best part is the atmosphere, looking out at Pu'u Keka'a and experiencing the torch-lighting ceremony. While children are welcome, it mainly caters to couples and adults.

At the far end of the beach, at the southern tip of Ka'anapali, the **Drums of the Pacific** (200 Nohea Kai, 808/667-4727, www.drumsofthepacificmaui.com, Mon.-Sat., $99 adults, $69 children) takes visitors on a journey through numerous Polynesian cultures. This is Ka'anapali's largest luau, and the fire dancing and the performance are on par with other shows. If you book directly on the luau website, you can sometimes get a deal of one child admission free with each paying adult.

On the northern side of Pu'u Keka'a, facing out toward the ocean, the **Myths of Maui Lu'au** (2780 Keka'a Dr., 808/661-9119, www.mythsofmaui.com, 6pm Sun.-Fri., adults $90, children over 5 $35, children under 5 free) at Royal Lahaina is a favorite option for those traveling with children. This is the island's longest-running lu'au (but don't confuse it with Old Lahaina Lu'au, which is better), and while there's no shaking the tourist kitsch, there's a palpable charm that goes along with the old-school venue. Everything over on this side of "the rock" is more laid-back than along the main Ka'anapali strip. Although the show doesn't face the beach, it's nevertheless set along a wide stretch of sand, and guests are encouraged to watch the sun go down while sipping a drink from the lu'au grounds. The show features a fire dance finale, and the entertainers bring children on stage for an impromptu hula lesson. The food

is average, and while it isn't very Hawaiian, children enjoy the macaroni and cheese. Mai tais and Blue Hawaiians are included in the price of the ticket, but premium drinks cost extra at the bar.

Bars, Live Music, and Nightlife

Friday through Sunday, the West Side's best nightclub is the **Black Rock Lounge** (2605 Ka'anapali Pkwy., 808/662-8053), inside the Sheraton Maui, where DJs and fog machines combine to create a sexy venue for singles. The club stays open until 2am, and on Friday and Saturday the $10 cover is waived before 11pm.

During the week, the only place in Ka'anapali with anything that resembles proper nightlife is **Paradise Grill** (2291 Ka'anapali Pkwy., 808/662-3700, www.paradisegrillkb.com, until 2am), featuring live entertainment 10pm-1:30am daily. Paradise Grill and the associated Mello's Bar are on the corner of Ka'anapali Parkway and Honoapi'ilani Highway, the first building you see at the main entrance to the Ka'anapali resort. Most of the late-night entertainment takes place downstairs in Mello's, while the upstairs section of the restaurant usually has live music during dinner hours (6pm-9pm daily). Expect to find acoustic music upstairs during dinner, and rock, reggae, and karaoke later downstairs.

LAHAINA
Magic Dinner Theater

At **Warren and Annabelle's** (900 Front St., 808/667-6244, www.warrenandannabelles.com, 5pm and 7:30pm Mon.-Sat., $64-104), any skepticism you might have had about attending a magic show in Maui will immediately be erased. Much more than a simple sleight-of-hand show, this enchanting evening revolves around the legend of Annabelle, a ghost whose swanky parlor you have the pleasure of dining in for the evening. After making your way through a secret entrance, you are welcomed into a plush lounge where the sound of piano keys accompanies the clink of oversize wine glasses. It's on to the intimate

78-seat theater, and be warned, if you sit in the front row, you'll end up becoming a part of the show. Two parts magic and three parts comedy, this show will leave you laughing. Rates are $64 for the show only, but do yourself a favor and spend the extra $40 for the cocktails and appetizers package. Due to Maui County liquor laws, this show is only for ages 21 or older. The 7:30pm show is added during busier times of the year. Reservations are strongly recommended.

★ *'Ulalena* and Maui Theatre

'Ulalena (878 Front St., 808/856-7900, www.mauitheatre.com, 6:30pm Mon.-Fri., $60-80) is a captivating and sophisticated show that details the history of the Hawaiian Islands through chant, dance, and visual effects in the 680-seat Maui Theatre. Performed without words, it utilizes over 100 different instruments, played live. The most expensive tickets allow you to spend 20 minutes with the cast. If you're a fan of musicals or have an interest in Hawaiian history, this isn't an evening to be missed. A new show called *Kahiko O Lahaina* opened at the Maui Theatre, featuring the fascinating history of Lahaina.

Art Night

Friday night is **Art Night in Lahaina.** In keeping with Lahaina's status as the cultural center of Maui, three dozen galleries open their doors 7pm-10pm, throw out the welcome mat, set out food and drink, provide entertainment, and usually host a well-known artist or two for this weekly party. Take your time to stroll Front Street from one gallery to the next. Stop and chat with shopkeepers, munch the goodies, sip the wine, look at the pieces on display, corner the featured artist for a comment on his or her work, and soak in the music of the strolling musicians. People dress up, but don't be afraid to come dressed casually.

Lu'aus

Lahaina is the best place on the island to attend a lu'au. It's dry and calm and has beautiful sunsets, and the island's best lu'au is here.

Old Lahaina Lu'au (1251 Front St., 800/248-5828, www.oldlahainaluau.com, daily, $110 adults, $75 children) is hands down the best on Maui. The food is the best, the lu'au grounds are immaculate, and everything from the show to the service runs like a well-oiled machine. Despite the fact that the lu'au seats 440 people, it still manages to retain an intimate atmosphere. You are greeted with a lei made of fragrant fresh flowers. Premium bar selections are included in the rates. There is a large *imu* (underground oven) for the pig, although it gets insanely crowded, so hang by the *imu* early if you want to get a good view of the unearthing. The private oceanfront setting provides the perfect perch for watching the sun go down.

For seating, choose either traditional *lauhala* mats (closest to the stage) or at tables with chairs, which still provide a good view. The only places where it's hard to see the show are the seats in the far corners. Seating preference is given to those who book first. Remarkably, shows are offered seven days a week.

At the southern end of Front Street, the **Feast at Lele** (505 Front St., 808/667-5353, www.feastatlele.com, $125 adults, $93 children) is a lu'au on the oceanfront in the 505 shopping center. Lele is the ancient Hawaiian name for the town of Lahaina, and this show begins with dance native to Hawaiian culture. The event then migrates through various Polynesian cultures, including those of Aotearoa (New Zealand), Tahiti, and Samoa. The combination of cultures makes for a fast-paced, fiery, and heart-pumping performance capped off by everyone's favorite, Samoan fire and knife dancing. Unlike the other luaus on the island, the food features dishes from around Polynesia that reflects the show.

Bars and Live Music

Rooted in the grog-shop days of its boisterous port-town past, Lahaina is Maui's nightlife capital—unless you want to go dancing. Most places close by 11pm, but that doesn't mean you can't find live music.

For free, family-friendly live music in

a historic outdoor setting, the Lahaina Restoration Foundation hosts a **Hawaiian Music Series** (http://lahainarestoration.org, 6pm-7:30pm last Thurs. of every month) on the lawn of the Baldwin House (Dickenson St. and Front St.) in the center of town. Musical artists vary from month to month, but most sessions involve live music and *kanikapila* storytelling. Seating is limited at this popular event, and attendees are encouraged to bring a blanket or beach chair to enjoy the show.

One of the best spots for live entertainment in Lahaina is **Fleetwood's** (744 Front St., 808/669-6425, www.fleetwoodsonfrontst. com, 2pm-10pm), a two-story bar and restaurant that offers the only rooftop perch in Lahaina. This bar was opened by legendary rock musician Mick Fleetwood, and Mick himself has been known to jump in with the band for some impromptu percussion. Live music is offered most frequently on the rooftop bar, beginning around 7pm.

If you're looking to dance with a young crowd of locals, **Lulu's Lahaina Surf Club** (1221 Honoapiʻilani Hwy., 808/661-0808, www.luluslahaina.com, until 2am) is the town's only dance club, located in the Lahaina Cannery Mall. There is usually a $5 cover Saturday night. Other nights of the week sporadically feature live music. While the dance floor is large and there are a couple of pool tables in the back, the mall location detracts from the vintage Lahaina experience. Another problem here is fights.

If you're a night owl, Lahaina has a couple of watering holes that stay open until 2am. On Front Street, **Spanky's Riptide** (505 Front St., 808/667-2337, www.spankysriptide.com, 11am-1:30am Mon.-Fri., 9am-1:30am Sat., 6:55am-1:30am Sun.) in the 505 shopping center on the far southern end is a good place to grab a cheap goblet of PBR, play pool, and engage in conversation with a colorful cast of characters.

Food

The number of dining options on the West Side is overwhelming. In most places you pay a premium for the location, so prices may seem high at ocean-view tables. That said, it's still possible to get a meal for under $10 per person outside the main visitor areas. While there is an overabundance of places on the West Side to sit and casually dine, there are only a handful of decent places for an affordable lunch on the run.

KAPALUA, NAPILI, KAHANA, AND HONOKOWAI
Breakfast
One fact about Maui is that ★ **The Gazebo** (5315 Lower Honapiʻilani Rd., 808/669-5621, 7:30am-2pm daily, $9-14) restaurant has the island's best breakfast. This isn't a secret, however, and there is a line out the door by 6:45am. What makes this spot so popular

is not only the oceanfront location, gazing out toward Molokaʻi, but also the famous macadamia nut pancakes and enormously filling portions. Lunch is offered until closing at 2pm, and by then the line has shrunk. Finding parking can be challenging; try for a spot along Napili Place, or park by the Napili Bay beach access on Hui Drive and walk to the restaurant across the sand of Napili Bay. From the beach, looking toward the water, the Gazebo is on the point to the left.

Brewpub
A visit to ★ **Maui Brewing Company** (4405 Honoapiʻilani Hwy., 808/669-3474, www. mauibrewingco.com, 11am-10pm daily, $12-15) should be at the top of every beer lover's island to-do list. This is the island's original brewpub, and while you can find a number of the beers in local supermarkets, at least a dozen more can only be found on tap when

you visit. The interior is basic, but this isn't a place you come to for the decor. Even though the beer is the main draw, the Hawaiian beef burger, sliders, and coconut porter beef stew are all hearty accompaniments to a rich pint of stout. There are also filling and affordable pizzas and vegan or gluten-free options.

Coffee Shops

At the Kahana Gateway Center, **Hawaiian Village Coffee** (4405 Honoapiʻilani Hwy., 808/665-1114, www.hawaiianvillagecoffee.net, 5:30am-6pm Mon.-Sat., 5:30am-5pm Sun.) is a classic coffee shop with a strong local following and good community vibe. This is the earliest place to open on the northwest side, and the sunrise hours feature a collection of late-shift police officers refueling after a long night and sleepy-eyed locals stopping in on their way to work. Although small, the shop has a welcoming atmosphere for reading the morning paper or checking your email on the free Wi-Fi.

Hawaiian Regional

★ **Merriman's** (1 Bay Club Place, 808/669-6400, www.merrimanshawaii.com, 3pm-9pm daily, dinner from 5:30pm daily, $25-49) is one of the most scenic dining spots on the island. Arrive early to enjoy a glass of wine while watching the sunset from the oceanfront fire pit, and then enjoy a menu of farm-to-table fare, where over 90 percent of the ingredients are sourced from local farmers, fishers, and ranchers. Acclaimed chef Peter Merriman is one of the founders of the Hawaiian Regional movement, and his genius is evident in everything from the Keahole lobster and avocado salad to the Sichuan peppered day-boat mahimahi. For pairings, there are probably nations with constitutions shorter than the wine list, which features over 40 different varietals. Reservations are strongly recommended.

In Kapalua, the ★ **Banyan Tree** (1 Ritz Carlton Dr., 808/665-7096, 5:30pm-9:30pm Tues.-Sat., $25-50) restaurant inside the Ritz Carlton has phenomenally come back to life. Pair a glass from the extensive wine list with a pupu of *opakapaka* ceviche, and then treat your palate to charred ahi steak, served with bok choy and bacon. Much of the food is sourced here on island, including herbs from the garden. End the evening with a lava cake with *lilikoi* and coconut ice cream.

Another restaurant making waves in Kapalua is spectacular **Cane and Canoe** (1 Bay Dr., 808/662-6600, 7am 11am and 5pm-9pm daily), located inside the Montage Kapalua Bay looking out toward Molokaʻi, with an acoustic guitar player perched beneath the trees. Order from a menu of Hawaiian regional cuisine with a slightly Italian twist: Pacific Rim cioppino of lobster, shrimp, and mahimahi, or soba gnocchi with exotic mushrooms, served with a porcini puree. For breakfast, order the $19 local rice bowl or $28 ahi Benedict.

For one of the island's best breakfasts and happy hours, **The Sea House** (5900 Lower Honoapiʻilani Rd., 808/669-1500, www.seahousemaui.com, 7am-9pm daily, $12-45) restaurant at Napili Kai is right on the sands of Napili Bay and is a longtime island classic. Happy hour runs 2pm-5pm with half-off pupus, and if you sit down and order at 4:30pm, you can often enjoy a sunset dinner for half price. For the island's best date night, book the dinner and show package for the Wednesday-night Masters of Slack Key.

Japanese

Ask any local where to get sushi, and he or she'll tell you ★ **Sansei** (600 Office Rd., 808/669-6286, www.sanseihawaii.com, 5:15pm-10pm Sat.-Wed., 5:15pm-1am Thurs.-Fri., $8-30), a legendary outpost on the main entrance road to Kapalua resort. If you want to maximize your Sansei experience, call ahead for reservations for 5:30pm on Thursday or Friday evening. When the restaurant opens, it usually runs an early-bird special for the first 30 minutes, with selected dishes half off. If you miss the early-bird wave and would rather wait a few hours, the same specials are often offered 10pm-1am Thursday-Friday.

Local Style

From the outside, you might wonder what's so special about the hole-in-the-wall ★ **Honokowai Okazuya and Deli** (3600 Lower Honoapi'ilani Rd., 808/665-0512, 11am-2:30pm and 4:30pm-8:30pm Mon.-Sat., cash only, $9-15). Even though the front door is often closed and it's in a strip mall next to the 5A Rent-A-Space, inside you'll find huge portions, great local food, and budget-friendly prices. There are a few seats inside for dining, but most visitors order takeout to enjoy back at the condo. The food rivals any on the island, and the prices can be half as much as food served with an ocean view. Try the lemon caper mahimahi or the chicken *katsu*.

KA'ANAPALI

American

In front of the Honua Kai resort, **Duke's** (130 Kai Malina Pkwy., 808/662-2900, www.dukesmaui.com, 7:30am-9:30pm daily, $10-25) is moderately priced. Affordable breakfasts include banana and macadamia nut pancakes, while lunches tend toward sandwiches, burgers, and fish tacos. Dinner entrées are more expensive. Duke's sources ingredients from over 20 different local farms, and the Bloody Marys are always a good idea. Afternoon trade winds can make the outdoor dining frustrating, so go for breakfast before 10am or for dinner after sundown.

For the most affordable and convenient meal in Ka'anapali, **CJ's Deli** (2580 Keka'a Dr., 808/667-0968, www.cjsmaui.com, 7am-8pm daily) in the Fairway Shops has burgers, meatloaf, deli sandwiches, and comfort food ($9-15). It's also BYOB, and there's a general store a few shops down if you want to grab a drink. Up early from jet lag? You can get breakfast for under $8, beginning at 7am.

Hawaiian Regional

Even though every resort in Ka'anapali has some sort of Hawaiian Regional option, none can hold a candle to world-famous ★ **Roy's** (2290 Ka'anapali Pkwy., 808/669-6999, www.royshawaii.com, 11am-9:30pm daily, $15-45). The location, inside the golf clubhouse, would be nicer if it had an ocean view, but for what the restaurant lacks in decor, it makes up for in flavor. Chef Roy Yamaguchi was one of the founders of the Hawaiian Regional movement, and his mastery is evident in the *misoyaki* butterfish and honey mustard-braised short ribs. Even though there are over 30 Roy's locations around the country, every restaurant has a menu and a style unique to the venue. Dinner entrées are pricey; ordering sandwiches, salads, and appetizers off the lunch menu is more affordable. The chocolate soufflé will change your life. Order it halfway through your meal since it takes 20 minutes to prepare.

★ **Hula Grill** (2435 Ka'anapali Pkwy., 808/667-6636, www.hulagrillkaanapali.com, 11am-11pm daily, $13) in Whalers Village is a place that exudes the carefree nature of being on vacation in Hawaii. Sink your toes down into the sand of the outdoor barefoot bar, which has a better vibe than the pricier indoor dining room. There's live music in the afternoons, and the Kapulu Joe pork sandwich and the kalua pork and pineapple flatbread are two affordable options along an otherwise expensive shore.

Across the Whalers Village walkway, **Leilani's on the Beach** (2435 Ka'anapali Pkwy., 808/661-4495, www.leilanis.com, 11am-11pm daily, $19) serves the best fish tacos on the island. The tacos are enormous, served Cajun style, and accompanied by a special sauce that brings it all together. The restaurant has become a bit expensive, but it's heavily discounted on Tuesday afternoons. Whether you dine on the casual patio or upstairs in the dining room, save room for a world-famous Hula Pie with macadamia nut ice cream and chocolate cookie crust; it's big enough to share.

LAHAINA

American

We'll come right out and say that ★ **Lahaina Grill** (127 Lahainaluna Rd., 808/667-5117, www.lahainagrill.com, 6pm-10pm daily, $25-49) is the best restaurant in Lahaina. Opened on Valentine's Day 1990, this restaurant continues to be one of Lahaina's most romantic evenings. The ambience, service, and extensive wine list are what you would expect of a fine-dining experience. The only thing missing from the classy bistro setting is an ocean view. The food is a combination of new American cuisine infused with Pacific Rim favorites, where meat dishes include the coveted Kona coffee-roasted rack of lamb, and seafood selections include sesame-crusted ahi filets and crisp fried lobster crab cakes. Much of the produce is sourced locally from independent farmers. Reservations are recommended.

Hands down, the best burger in Lahaina is at ★ **Cool Cat Café** (658 Front St., 808/667-0908, www.coolcatcafe.com, 10:30am-10:30pm daily, $10-25). Overlooking the banyan tree, the inside portion of the restaurant is decorated in 1950s decor, while the outdoor patio is livelier. Cool Cats is consistently voted as the island's best burger. There are also fish sandwiches, blackened fish tacos, salads, and a popular bar.

Coffee Shops

For a quick coffee on the run, **Sir Wilfred's** (707 Front St., 808/661-0202, www.sirwilfreds.com, 8:30am-9pm daily) is the island's original coffee shop, having opened its doors in 1976. It's still one of the best spots in Lahaina to buy locally grown beans or inquire about fine cigars.

If you're looking for a place you can linger, grab breakfast, get free Internet access, and sip on a proper espresso, try **Café Café** (129 Lahainaluna Rd., 808/661-0006, www.cafecafelahaina.com, 7am-7pm daily).

French

If you take your fine dining seriously, then you're going to love **Gerard's** (174 Lahainaluna Rd., 808/661-8939, www.gerardsmaui.com, 6pm-10pm daily, $50) in the Plantation Inn. Chef Gerard Reversade has been serving French food with an island twist for over 30 years and was one of the pioneers of Hawaiian Regional cuisine. Classics such as foie gras and escargot punctuate the appetizer menu, and favorites include the roasted lamb and fresh fish. Gerard's has received the *Wine Spectator*'s Award of Excellence 19 times.

Hawaiian Regional

In the 505 shopping area, ★ **Pacific'O** (505 Front St., 808/667-4341, www.pacificomaui.com, 11:30am-10pm daily, $29-46) is one of the best venues in Lahaina for enjoying an oceanfront meal. Many of the ingredients are grown at the organic O'o Farm in Kula. The seaside patio is the perfect lunch spot for pairing a sesame fish salad with a crisp glass of white wine, and the fish tacos are affordable at $16.50. Reservations are necessary for dinner, when you can feast on entrées such as seafood risotto or *hapa* tempura—sashimi-grade fish wrapped in nori. Aside from the food, the wine list is one of the most comprehensive on the West Side.

On the far northern end of Lahaina, ★ **Honu** (1295 Front St., 808/667-9390, www.honumaui.com, 11am-9:30pm Mon.-Sat., 11am-9pm Sun., $18-45) offers locally sourced food in an oceanfront setting. *Honu* is the Hawaiian name for sea turtle, and there's a strong likelihood that you'll spot a turtle coming up for a breath at some point during your meal. Chef Mark Ellman, one of the original founders of the Hawaiian Regional movement, has created a menu where butternut squash coconut soup complements main courses ranging from lentil quinoa burgers to pork osso bucco. The pizzas are similarly delicious. The extensive craft beer selection features over 50 different microbrews—a rarity among island restaurants. If there's a wait, try sister restaurant **Mala** next door.

In the heart of Front Street, **Kimo's** (845 Front St., 808/661-4811, www.kimosmaui.com, 11am-10pm daily, $25-32) has a deck looking out over the waters of the Lahaina Roadstead and moderately priced lunch items ($15-18) such as coconut-crusted fish sandwiches or beach bunny turkey burgers. The dinner entrées in the dining room are pricier, including the signature Molokini Cut, a 14-ounce prime rib served with an au jus. The staff at Kimo's is as professional as they come, and the happy hour (3pm-5pm daily) has some of Lahaina's best deals.

Italian

The culinary brainchild of a chef who arrived via Brooklyn, and before that Milan, **Sale Pepe** (878 Front St., 808/667-7667, www.salepepemaui.com, 5pm-10pm Mon.-Sat., $15-30), by the Maui Theatre, is one of Lahaina's new hot spots. The authentic Italian dishes use only the freshest island ingredients, and what isn't sourced from local farmers is brought all the way from Italy.

Japanese

If there were an award for best cuisine in the most unlikely of locations, ★ **Star Noodle** (285 Kupuohi St., 808/667-5400, www.starnoodle.com, 10:30am-10pm daily, $12) would win. This popular noodle establishment on an obscure corner at the top of the Lahaina Gateway industrial area has been sculpted by Sheldon Simeon, a local chef who made it to the final three on the reality show *Top Chef.* The Asian-infused menu is spectacularly affordable, with bowls of *udon,* plates of pad thai, and dishes such as miso salmon or chicken in *ponzu* sauce. If the wait is too long (which it usually is), sit at the bar and order from the main menu.

Local Style

Believe it or not, there's a place in Lahaina where you can eat by the water and the bill won't give you a heart attack. At the northern end of Lahaina next to the Old Lahaina Luau, with which it's affiliated, ★ **Aloha Mixed Plate** (1285 Front St., 808/661-3322, www.alohamixedplate.com, 8am-10pm daily, $8-12) offers affordable plate lunches in a casual oceanfront setting. The private setting is among the most scenic in Lahaina, the food is some of the best local fare you'll find outside a luau, and it's cheap. For lunch and dinner you can sample luau items such as *lomilomi* salmon or poi. For the main course, get a kalua pig plate lunch (with two scoops of rice and macaroni salad) or spring for the Aloha Mixed Plate of *shoyu* chicken, teriyaki beef, and fresh fish served with rice and mac salad. Breakfast is just as affordable with omelets and *loco moco* dishes. There's a full bar, although alcohol isn't served at the oceanfront tables.

For breakfast where all the locals go, ★ **808 Grindz** (843 Waine'e St., 808/280-8914, www.808grindzcafe.com, 7am-2pm daily) is a hidden hole-in-the-wall by Nagasako supermarket, where an entire menu of omelets and *mocos* is only $8.08.

Natural Foods

To the delight of those who care about what they put in their bodies, ★ **Choice** (1087 Limahana Place, 808/661-7711, www.choicemaui.com, 8am-9:30pm Mon.-Sat., $8) is devoted to the benefits of a healthy, active lifestyle. When you walk in the door (where a sign informs you this is a "bummer-free zone"), you can sense the antioxidants flowing. The smoothies use all-natural superfood ingredients (spirulina, açaí, coconut meat, and almond milk), so your body will thank you. Make your smoothie "epic" by adding superfoods such as kale and blue-green algae. A large selection of freshly made kale salads are available after 11:30am each day.

SOUTH OF LAHAINA
American

The only restaurant between Lahaina and Ma'alaea is ★ **Leoda's Kitchen and Pie Shop** (820 Olowalu Village Rd., 808/662-3600, www.leodas.com, 7am-8pm daily, $8-12), in the Olowalu store building. Using many sustainable ingredients from local farms, this sandwich and pie shop has quickly become an island favorite. The deli sandwiches, potpies, and baked goods are so good, however, that you'll often find a line stretching out the front door. Try the veggie burger for a healthy lunch, or a savory chicken pot pie.

Central Maui

Central Maui is industrial, urban, and most importantly, real.

The site of Kahului International Airport, Central Maui is the first part of the island most visitors encounter. It's more built up than you'd expect of "paradise," but beyond the traffic lights, box stores, and increasing lanes of asphalt, Central Maui is the beating heart of the island's cultural past. It's also rich in natural beauty, with muddy trails leading deep into the mountains and miles of sandy shore. It's home to the island's widest array of multicultural cuisine. The sport of kitesurfing was invented here on the shores of Kanaha Beach Park. While there might not be any palm-lined resorts or tropical beach bars with mai tais, there's something that travelers might find much more interesting: a true sense of island community.

ORIENTATION

Central Maui comprises two main towns: **Kahului** and **Wailuku.** The communities of **Waihe'e, Waikapu,** and **Waiehu** are almost completely residential, and when combined with larger Kahului and Waıluku, contribute to a Central Maui population of 57,000. This is Maui's most populated region. It doesn't become rural until you pass **Waihe'e** on **Kahekili Highway.** The airport and cruise port are both in **Kahului,** and the tightest cluster of shopping and restaurants is around **Market Street** in Wailuku.

PLANNING YOUR TIME

Most visitors experience Central Maui when they drive away from the airport or take a day trip to 'Iao Valley before rushing off someplace else. Rather than devoting an hour, however, first-time visitors should spend at least half a day experiencing Central Maui's sights, whereas returning visitors looking to see new sights could easily spend two days: one day hiking, exploring the beaches, or seeing the most popular sights, and another in museums and enjoying the abundance of food.

Previous: Maui Tropical Plantation; windsurfing off the North Shore; **Above:** Kepaniwai Heritage Gardens.

Look for ★ to find recommended
sights, activities, dining, and lodging.

Highlights

★ **Maui Arts and Cultural Center:** Seeing a movie or live performance in this state-of-the-art facility is one of the best nights out on Maui (page 244).

★ **Alexander and Baldwin Sugar Museum:** Peer into the daily lives of plantation laborers and read about an era that is coming to a close on Maui after 145 years (page 245).

★ **Bailey House Museum:** See authentic Hawaiian artifacts, a surfboard ridden by Duke Kahanamoku, and the best compilation of Hawaiiana literature on the island (page 245).

★ **Kepaniwai Heritage Gardens:** This small riverside park is dedicated to Maui's immigrant communities. Sample the traditional architecture of the island's "mixed plate" community (page 246).

★ **'Iao Valley State Park:** Learn about King Kamehameha's decisive victory at the Battle of Kepaniwai and snap a photo of the iconic 'Iao Needle (page 246).

★ **Maui Tropical Plantation:** Once seemingly left for dead, this colorful agricultural land has experienced a rebirth, with ziplining, a coffee shop, a farm stand, shopping, and a phenomenal restaurant (page 247).

★ **Kanaha Beach Park:** Watch the world's best windsurfers and kitesurfers zip through the air at this unheralded beach park (page 249).

★ **Waihe'e Coastal Dunes and Wetlands Preserve:** Hike the trail of this undeveloped preserve as it passes by the ruins of Kapoho fishing village and its associated *heiau* (page 256).

★ **Waihe'e Ridge Trail:** Hike above 2,500 feet elevation to commune with the ferns and the clouds on this exceptionally scenic but muddy trail above the Waihe'e shore (page 256).

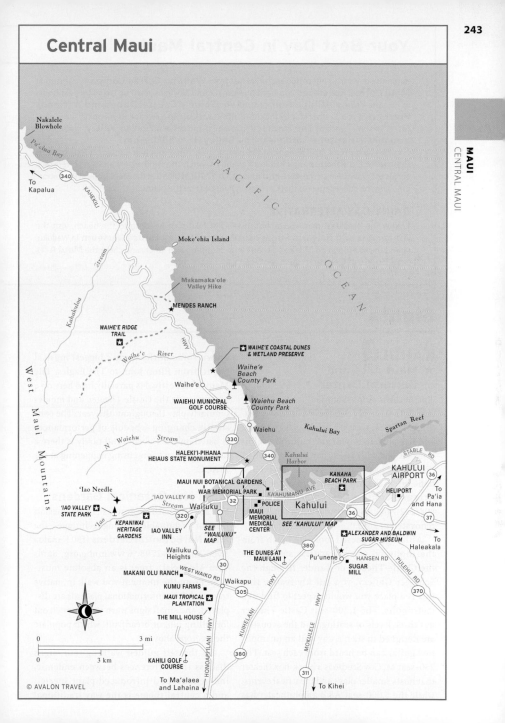

Nakalele
Blowhole

Pa'ilua Bay

PACIFIC

OCEAN

To
Kapalua

340

KAHEKILI

Kahakuloa Stream

Moke'ehia Island

Makamaka'ole
Valley Hike

MENDES RANCH

WAIHE'E RIDGE
TRAIL ★

Waihe'e River

HWY

West Maui Mountains

★ WAIHE'E COASTAL DUNES
& WETLAND PRESERVE

*Waihe'e
Beach
County Park*

Waihe'e

WAIEHU MUNICIPAL
GOLF COURSE

*Waiehu Beach
County Park*

N Waiehu Stream

Waiehu

Kahului Bay

Spartan Reef

330

HALEKI'I-PIHANA
HEIAUS STATE MONUMENT

340

*Kahului
Harbor*

STABLE RD

KAHULUI
AIRPORT 36

MAUI NUI BOTANICAL GARDENS
WAR MEMORIAL PARK

★

KANAHA
BEACH PARK
★

'Iao Needle

'IAO VALLEY RD

'Iao Valley Stream

Wailuku

32

KA'AHUMANU AVE

■ POLICE

Kahului

HELIPORT ■

To
Pa'ia
and Hana

'IAO VALLEY ★
STATE PARK

'Iao

★

MAUI
MEMORIAL
MEDICAL
CENTER

36

37

KEPANIWAI
HERITAGE ★
GARDENS

IAO VALLEY
INN

*SEE
"WAILUKU"
MAP*

SEE "KAHULUI" MAP

★ ALEXANDER AND BALDWIN
SUGAR MUSEUM

To
Haleakala

Wailuku
Heights

THE DUNES AT
MAUI LANI

380

Pu'unene

HANSEN RD

PULEHU RD

MAKANI OLU RANCH ■

WEST WAIKO RD

Waikapu

30

SUGAR
MILL

370

KUMU FARMS

305

MAUI TROPICAL
PLANTATION ★

HONOAPI'ILANI HWY

KUIHELANI HWY

MOKULELE HWY

HWY

THE MILL HOUSE ▼

0   3 mi

0   3 km

KAHILI GOLF
COURSE

380

311

To Ma'alaea
and Lahaina

↓ To Kihei

© AVALON TRAVEL

Your Best Day in Central Maui

Begin the day early with coffee and breakfast from **Wailuku Coffee Company,** or stop at **Maui Coffee Roasters** if approaching from Kahului. By 9am you'll be lacing up your boots to hike the **Waihe'e Ridge Trail,** or stroll the **Waihe'e Coastal Dunes and Wetlands Preserve** if you'd rather stay by the shore. After working up a sweat and snapping some photos, grab some lunch at **The Farmacy** in Wailuku and drive up to **'Iao Valley,** stopping at **Kepaniwai Heritage Gardens** and the **Bailey House Museum.**

Or, if you'd prefer an afternoon at the beach, grab some lunch in Kahului at **Poi by the Pound** or **Da Kitchen,** and head to Kanaha to watch the windsurfers and kitesurfers race across the waves. Finish the day with dinner at **The Mill House** at the Maui Tropical Plantation, enjoying the culinary genius that Chef Jeff Scheer puts on the plates.

RAINY-DAY ALTERNATIVE

Follow the breakfast plan above, but instead of hiking or heading to the beach, visit the **Alexander and Baldwin Sugar Museum** and **Bailey House Museum** in Wailuku, spend the afternoon on **Market Street** with shopping and lunch, and check the **Maui Arts and Cultural Center**'s schedule of events for that night.

Sights

KAHULUI
★ Maui Arts and Cultural Center

One of the reasons that Maui is *no ka oi* (the best) is that it truly does have a little of everything: tropical weather, world-class beaches, and live entertainment and cultural exhibitions on par with any urban center. Though the island has multiple venues for events, none offers the professionalism of the **Maui Arts and Cultural Center** (1 Cameron Way, 808/242-7469, www.mauiarts.org), massively renovated in 2012.

Although it doesn't look like much from the highway, when you first step inside the Castle Theater or wander through the Schaefer Gallery, you quickly realize that this is a place you would expect to find in a metropolis. The 1,200-seat Castle Theater has three levels of seating, and the acoustics are designed in such a way that an unamplified guitar can be heard from each seat. The 250-seat McCoy Studio is a black-box theater that hosts smaller plays and theatrical events, while the 5,000-seat A&B amphitheater has

drawn some of the world's biggest musical talent, from Elton John to The Eagles. The Maui Film Festival is partially held here on a screen inside the Castle Theater, and movies regularly play throughout the year. The constantly changing schedule of performances is listed on the website, and rarely is there a night there isn't something happening at the MACC.

Maui Nui Botanical Gardens

For anyone with an interest in Polynesian flora or sustainable farming techniques, the **Maui Nui Botanical Gardens** (150 Kanaloa Ave., 808/249-2798, www.mnbg.org, 8am-4pm Mon.-Sat., free) is an absolute must-stop. From the moment you walk in, native trees and their informational placards are displayed, and small signs warn you to watch out for falling *ulu,* or breadfruit, which populate the treetops above.

On the self-guided walking tour, signs discuss the differences between endemic, indigenous, and introduced plant species, and a central theme is the way traditional irrigation techniques maximize the ability to farm. Freshwater was precious to Polynesian farmers, and more than 70 species of dryland *kalo,* or taro, are successfully growing in a dry coastal dunes system. Although not as expansive as the botanical gardens in Kula, the gardens espouse the Polynesian view that humans are but stewards of the land—placed here on this earth to help protect it for future generations.

Kanaha Pond State Wildlife Sanctuary

Despite being smack in the middle of town, the **Kanaha Pond State Wildlife Sanctuary** houses as many as 90 species of native and migratory **birds.** Only five minutes from the Kahului airport, this area was once a royal fishpond that was built in the 1700s. Today this is where you'll spot the endangered Hawaiian stilt (ae'o), a slender, 16-inch bird with sticklike pink legs that, according to most recent population estimates, numbers around 2,000 statewide. The Hawaiian coot ('alae ke'oke'o), a gray-black duck-like bird that builds large floating nests, may also be seen here, and the sanctuary is open free of charge August 31-March 31. In summer, when the sanctuary is closed for nesting season, an observation pavilion is maintained on the pond's south edge, which is open year-round. To access the trails inside the sanctuary, entry is through the gates on Amala Place on the road to Kanaha Beach Park.

★ Alexander and Baldwin Sugar Museum

There's no place on the island where you can gain a better understanding of Maui's plantation heritage than at the **Alexander and Baldwin Sugar Museum** (3957 Hansen Rd., 808/871-8058, www.sugarmuseum.com, 9:30am-4:30pm daily, $7, $2 children 6-12, 5 and under free), a small, worn-down building in Pu'unene. This town, which was once the beating heart of Maui's sugar industry, has been reduced to a faint pulse: a post office, a bookstore, the museum, and the stinky sugar

mill are all that remain, and even the mill is scheduled to close at the end of 2016.

The $7 entrance fee gets you a yellow booklet called "Passport to the Past," which also includes entry to the Bailey House Museum in Wailuku, as well as Lahaina's Baldwin Home Museum and Wo Hing Museum. Here in the Sugar Museum, exhibits discuss everything from sugar's Polynesian roots to historical profiles of the island's first sugar barons. Many of the businessmen who made their fortunes in sugar—Samuel Thomas Alexander and Henry Perrine Baldwin included—were the children of New England missionary families who "came to do good and stayed to do well." Alexander and Baldwin actually met as children while growing up in Lahaina, and the 12 acres of Makawao land they purchased in 1869 would grow into a business that at one point was ranked as one of the 900 largest in the country.

In addition to educating visitors about the growth of the sugar industry, what makes the museum a must-see attraction is the window it provides into the daily lives of workers from around the globe. The cultural exhibits within the museum include everything from the hand-sewn Japanese clothing used to protect workers from centipedes to Portuguese bread ovens used by immigrants from the Azores to make their famous staple. There's even an exhibit on Filipino cockfighting.

Now, with the announcement that sugar operation will cease on Maui at the end of 2016, the museum will commemorate an era that's officially history—145 years of sugar, literally gone up in smoke.

WAILUKU
★ Bailey House Museum

Regardless of whether or not you're a museum person, every visitor to Maui should see the **Bailey House Museum** (2375-A Main St., 808/244-3326, 10am-4pm Mon.-Sat., $7 adults, $2 ages 6-12, 5 and under free) on the road to 'Iao Valley. It's listed on the National Register of Historic Places, and Duke Kahanamoku's redwood surfboard is outside on the lawn. Handcrafted in 1910 for Hawaii's "Ambassador of Aloha," the surfboard rests near a 33-foot-long canoe that's made from a single koa log, built around 1900 and one of the last of its kind.

Inside the museum, the Hawaiian Room houses artifacts of precontact Hawaii such as wooden spears, stone tools, knives made from conch shells, and daggers made from shark teeth. In the same room are stone *ki'i,* or statues, depicting the Hawaiian war god Ku; expertly crafted wooden calabashes; and an exhibit of artifacts found on the island of Kaho'olawe from both the pre- and post-bombing eras. If you need a good book or are interested in learning more about Hawaiian history and culture, the museum bookstore has the island's best selection of Hawaiian historical texts.

★ Kepaniwai Heritage Gardens

Like peanut butter to jelly—or spam to *musubi*—**Kepaniwai Heritage Gardens** (870 'Iao Valley Rd., 7am-7pm daily, free), goes hand in hand with a visit to 'Iao Valley. Tucked on the banks of 'Iao Stream, this simple but informative cultural park is far more interesting than it looks, as it details

Maui's "mixed plate" culture. In addition to pavilions that make great picnic spots (and double as great drinking spots for locals), the park features a small monument devoted to each of the island's plantation-era immigrant communities—Japanese, Chinese, Puerto Rican, and Portuguese, each monument with a small dwelling constructed in traditional style.

Along the stream are a few places where you can swim in the shallow (and cold!) waters, although use some caution when scrambling down the bank as there aren't any official trails. Unless you're a major history buff, 30 minutes here will suffice.

★ 'Iao Valley State Park

This is one of those Maui attractions you can wrongly turn into a dud—particularly if you focus on the destination, rather than enjoying the journey. Much like driving the Road to Hana and not stopping until you get there, traveling to **'Iao Valley State Park** (end of 'Iao Valley Rd., 7am-5:30pm daily, parking $5) simply to see the park is the wrong way. Rather, the journey begins the moment you leave the streets of Wailuku and make the turn down 'Iao Valley Road through a thick canopy of trees. Here you'll find chickens crossing

Bailey House Museum

Say It Right: 'Iao Needle

Given that not many English words are entirely composed of vowels, it's understandable that the name of this valley can give some visitors fits.

The most common mispronunciation of this word is "eye-ow," as in "Ow, I hurt my eye." The first step toward wrapping your tongue around the proper pronunciation is understanding that vowels are different in Hawaiian than in English. In Hawaiian they are "ah, eh, ee, oh, oo," similar to Spanish. Once you have this vowel structure in mind, it's easy to see that 'Iao Needle is properly pronounced "ee-ow."

If all else fails, remember what you would say if you sat on a 1,200-foot-tall needle: "Ee-ow!"

the road, rural houses, fields, and farms at the base of vertical cliffs.

Crane your neck and look skyward toward peaks that tickle the passing clouds, and embrace the feeling you've suddenly traveled 100 years back in time. When you reach the park at the end of the road, rather than hastily parking, walking, and rushing to see the 'Iao Needle, take a moment to read the history of all that's happened in the park, from the gruesome and bloody Battle of Kepaniwai to how soldiers would use the valley ridgelines to spot warriors approaching from sea.

When you do begin to hike the "trail," a walkway with 133 steps, admire the landscape that lines the edge of the stream. Once you conquer the stairs, you're met with a view of Kuka'emoku—better known as 'Iao Needle—rising 2,250 feet above the distant shore. While most visitors tend to photograph the needle, what's more spectacular is the rugged ridgelines and isolated interior of the mountain, which is so inaccessible and so untouched it's believed the bones of Hawaiian royalty are buried deep inside caves—so remote and shrouded in secrecy that they'll never be disturbed.

★ Maui Tropical Plantation

Talk about a place that's come back to life: There was a time when the **Maui Tropical Plantation** (1670 Honoapi'ilani Hwy., 808/244-7643, www.mauitropicalplantation. com, 9am-5pm daily, free) was a popular Maui highlight, but gradually the luster started to fade and the clientele grew old. That's changed now that new owners have set up new features such as zipline tours (page 259), a coffee shop, an ice-cream stand, an art gallery, and a fresh organic farm stand. Best of all, the palate-bending Mill House restaurant is located on the property, and much of the food served is sourced right here on the farm (page 263).

The longtime draw is the **Tropical Express Tram Tour** (800/451-6805, $20 adults, $10 children), otherwise known as "the train," a 40-minute ride that runs seven times 10am-4pm daily, making a loop through the surrounding fields as the driver discusses the crops. While children will be excited to ride on a train (it's the island's last), adults will enjoy the informative commentary. Once finished with the tram, linger for a while in plantation store and the adjoining **Rebecca Lowell Art Gallery** (808/344-1840), and visit the shed with historical photos and information about the plantation.

If it happens to be open, be sure to swing by **Kumu Farms** (808/244-4800, 10am-4pm Tues.-Sat.), to the right of the parking lot entrance. This fantastic certified-organic market is one of the island's best, where you can purchase food grown on property at a fraction of store prices. Produce is literally picked 25 feet from the farm stand, so there isn't anywhere else in Maui with produce this fresh. The farm features cilantro, peppers, chard, eggplant, carrots, and the famous sunrise papayas that are grown at the sister store on Moloka'i. You can also purchase homemade mac nut basil pesto, or cuts of grass-fed Waikapu beef for around $6 per pound. If you're staying on the West Side of the island and plan to cook in your condo, there's no better place to pick up your produce on your drive from Central Maui.

Haleki'i and Pihana Heiau

Few island visitors stop at the **Haleki'i and Pihana Heiau,** which is a shame, considering their historical importance. This site is officially classified as a Hawaii state park, but the gate to the *heiau* is no longer open for vehicular access and its condition has fallen into disrepair. Nevertheless, it's still easy to park on the street in front of the *heiau* and make the five-minute walk up the hill.

In ancient Hawaii these two *heiau* served as the religious center of the entire Wailuku *ahupua'a,* or land division. Many of Maui's ruling *ali'i* came here to either honor their deceased or commune with religious deities. It's believed that Keopuolani, the woman who would become queen, was born here at Pihana *heiau,* a site that is also believed to have been a *luakini heiau,* used for human sacrifice. Hawaiian scholars believe that one of the last human sacrifices on the island was performed here at Pihana in 1790 by King Kamehameha after his victory at the Battle of Kepaniwai. Much of Pihana *heiau* was destroyed during the 19th century when the Hawaiian monarchy converted to Christianity, but numerous walls and terraces from Haleki'i still remain.

To reach the *heiau,* travel along Waiehu Beach Road until you cross the bridge over 'Iao Stream. On the other side, make the first left onto Kuhio Place and then the first left onto Hea Place. Since the access gate to the *heiau* will likely be locked, park on the street and walk up the access road. Don't be surprised if the neighbor's dog barks—just keep walking up the hill.

Kahakuloa

Technically **Kahakuloa** is part of Wailuku, but this old fishing village is an entity unto itself. Lonely and remote, there are few places left in Hawaii that are quite like Kahakuloa. Many choose to get to Kahakuloa from the West Side of the island by following the road past Kapalua, Honolua Bay, and Nakalele Blowhole, but because this road is a loop, Kahakuloa can similarly be accessed from Wailuku. It will take you 30-45 minutes to reach Kahakuloa from Wailuku—and there aren't any gas stations—so be sure you have at least half a tank of gas before driving along the coast.

Following Kahekili Highway (Hwy. 340) past Mendes Ranch and Makamaka'ole Valley, the road becomes narrow and the foliage dense. The first stop is **Turnbull Studios** (5030 Kahekili Hwy., 808/244-0101, www.

early morning at Haleki'i and Pihana Heiau

turnbullstudios.org, 10am-5pm Mon.-Fri.), an eclectic sculpture garden with handmade crafts by local Hawaiian artists. The artist has been making sculptures at this mountainside garden for over 25 years. There are only a few parking spaces, and if it's been raining heavily, think twice before going down the short but steep driveway in a low-clearance rental car.

Farther down the road you'll reach the **Kaukini Gallery** (808/244-3371, www.kaukinigallery.com, 10am-5pm daily), inside a mountaintop home overlooking Kahakuloa Valley. The gallery features more than 120 local artists and their paintings, jewelry, and crafts, and the views from the parking lot looking up the valley make it the most scenic gallery on the island.

Finally, after a few hairpin turns on a narrow one-lane road, you reach the village of Kahakuloa, accurately called "old Hawaii" and "a place that time has forgotten." The town offers visitors a unique opportunity to glimpse Hawaiian traditions, still in practice, which managed to evade modernity. If you continue driving, you'll reach Kapalua in approximately 14 miles.

Beaches

The little-known beaches of Central Maui are defined by wind and water sports. You won't find any tiki bars or rows of beachfront cabanas, but you will find narrow stretches of sand where the world's best boarders hang out.

KAHULUI
★ Kanaha Beach Park

Kanaha Beach Park, located right next to the airport, is one of those places where you ask yourself, "How did I not know this was here?" For what it lacks in visitor friendliness (it's a frequent hangout for the homeless), the park makes up for with vibrant energy—particularly in the afternoon. You'll find windsurfers, kitesurfers, paddleboarders, and surfers out riding the waves, and on Sunday the park is bumping with barbecues and pickup games of beach volleyball.

In the early morning, before the wind picks up, this is the perfect place for a long stroll on the string of sandy beaches, where the dramatic ridgelines of Mauna Kahalawai rise from the turquoise waters. In the afternoon, the cobalt waters become flecked with whitecaps and dozens of colorful sails as windsurfers and kitesurfers race across the water—particularly in summer, when it's windier. The large, grassy beach park has showers and restrooms, and there's even a roped off area for swimming if you want to cool off or wade. It's also a convenient place to hang out if you've already checked out of your hotel and are killing time before an evening flight, since it's only minutes from the airport.

To reach Kanaha from Hana Highway, make a right at the stoplight for Hobron Avenue and then another right onto Amala Place. Drive for about 1.5 miles. The best entrances for Kanaha Beach Park are the two at the end of the road. For a shortcut, loop through the airport, past Arrivals and Departures, and make a right onto Kaʻa Street, continuing past the rental-car counters until you reach the end of the road. Turn right; the beach park is on the left.

Kite Beach

Located next to Kanaha Beach Park, **Kite Beach** is the place on the island for Maui's kitesurfing crowd. The narrow strip of sand has multiple entrances—all with sand or dirt parking lots—and you can expect kitesurfers to start launching between 11am and noon.

Stable Road

If you're looking to really get away from it all and just relax on an empty patch of sand, the string of beaches off **Stable Road** are a bit of a local secret. You'll find fishers casting rods

Kahului

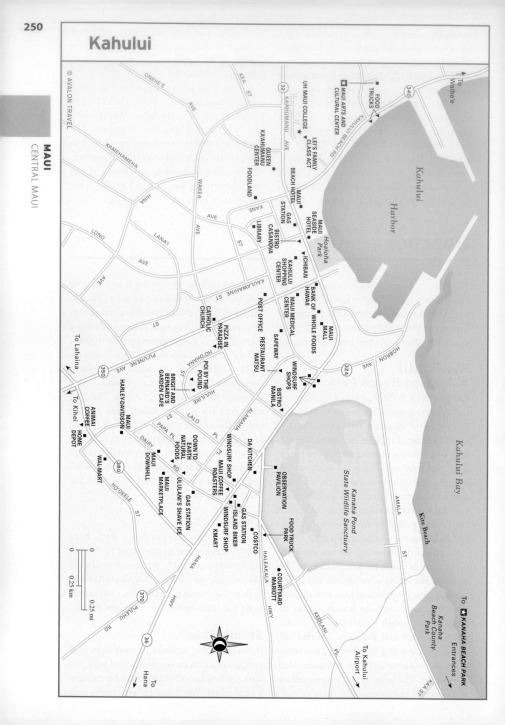

© AVALON TRAVEL

To Waihe'e

340

Kahului Harbor

Kahului Bay

Kanaha Beach County Park

ONEHE'E

KEA ST

32

KAAHUMANU AVE

KAMEHAMEHA

HINA

LONO

LANA'I

WAKEA

AVE

KANE ST

BEACH ST

KAHULUI BEACH RD

KAULAWAHINE ST

PU'UNENE AVE

HULI'ILI

LALO

PAPA PL

DAIRY RD

HO'OKELE ST

HANA HWY

HALEAKALA HWY

KEOLANI PL

AMALA ST

KAA ST

HOBRON AVE

32A

350 To Lahaina

To Kihei

380

370

PULEHU RD

36 To Hana

UH MAUI COLLEGE

MAUI ARTS AND CULTURAL CENTER

FOOD TRUCKS

LEI'S FAMILY CLASS ACT

QUEEN KA'AHUMANU CENTER

FOODLAND

MAUI SEASIDE HOTEL

GAS STATION

LIBRARY

BISTRO CASANOVA

KAHULUI SHOPPING CENTER

ICHIBAN

Ho'aloha Park

BANK OF HAWAII

MAUI MALL

MAUI MEDICAL CENTER

WHOLE FOODS

CATHOLIC CHURCH

POST OFFICE

PIZZA IN PARADISE

RESTAURANT MATSU

SAFEWAY

POI BY THE POUND

BRIGIT AND BERNARD'S GARDEN CAFE

HO'OHANA ST

WINDSURF SHOPS

BISTRO MANILA

MAUI HARLEY-DAVIDSON

ANIMAL COFFEE

HOME DEPOT

WAL-MART

MAUI DOWNHILL

MAUI MARKETPLACE

DOWN TO EARTH NATURAL FOODS

GAS STATION

'ULULANI'S SHAVE ICE

WINDSURF SHOP

MAUI COFFEE ROASTERS

DA KITCHEN

WINDSURF SHOP

ISLAND BIKER

GAS STATION

COSTCO

KMART

OBSERVATION PAVILION

FOOD TRUCK PARK

Kanaha Pond State Wildlife Sanctuary

Kite Beach

COURTYARD MARRIOTT

To Kahului Airport

KANAHA BEACH PARK Entrances

0   0
0.25 km
0.25 mi

Wailuku

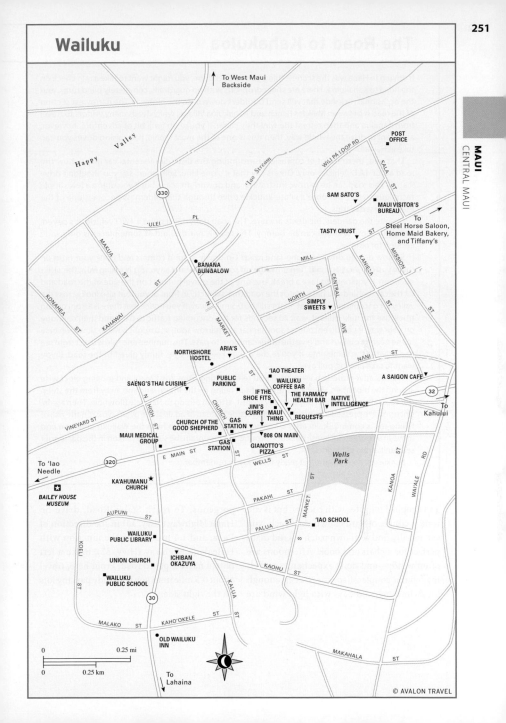

To West Maui
Backside

Happy   Valley

'Iao Stream

WILI PA LOOP RD

POST OFFICE

KALA ST

330

SAM SATO'S

MAUI VISITOR'S BUREAU

'ULEI   PL

MAKUA ST

MILL

KANIELA ST

MISSION ST

TASTY CRUST

To
Steel Horse Saloon,
Home Maid Bakery,
and Tiffany's

BANANA BUNGALOW

N MARKET ST

NORTH ST

CENTRAL AVE

KONAHEA ST

KAHAWAI ST

SIMPLY SWEETS

NANI ST

NORTHSHORE HOSTEL

ARIA'S

'IAO THEATER

A SAIGON CAFE

SAENG'S THAI CUISINE

PUBLIC PARKING

MARKET ST

WAILUKU COFFEE BAR

32

IF THE SHOE FITS

THE FARMACY HEALTH BAR

N HIGH ST

JINI'S CURRY

MAUI THING

NATIVE INTELLIGENCE

To
Kahului

VINEYARD ST

CHURCH ST

CHURCH OF THE GOOD SHEPHERD

GAS STATION

REQUESTS

MAUI MEDICAL GROUP

GAS STATION

808 ON MAIN

E MAIN ST

GIANOTTO'S PIZZA

WELLS ST

Wells Park

KANOA ST

WAIALE RD

To 'Iao Needle

320

KA'AHUMANU CHURCH

S MARKET ST

BAILEY HOUSE MUSEUM

PAKAHI ST

AUPUNI ST

PALUA ST

'IAO SCHOOL

WAILUKU PUBLIC LIBRARY

KOELI ST

UNION CHURCH

ICHIBAN OKAZUYA

KAOHU ST

WAILUKU PUBLIC SCHOOL

KALUA ST

30

MALAKO ST

KAHO'OKELE ST

OLD WAILUKU INN

0   0.25 mi

0   0.25 km

To
Lahaina

MAKAHALA ST

© AVALON TRAVEL

The Road to Kahakuloa

If driving to Hana was the scariest thing you've ever done, you might want to take a rain check on the Road to Kahakuloa. There are sheer drop-offs with no guardrails, completely blind turns, and the occasional rockslide that will send boulders down onto the highway. The narrowest section of the road is between Mendes Ranch and Kahakuloa village, which leads many visitors to travel from Kapalua and then retreat the way they came. If you're up for a bit of adventure, however, and want to drive the whole way, then this is one of the most scenic, hair-raising drives you can take in Hawaii.

That said, there's a lot of confusion surrounding the drive. Some rental car maps show the road as for 4WD vehicles only. Others say that it's one lane. Still others say you shouldn't drive it at all. This road can be narrow, frustrating, and downright scary, but if you utilize a few simple techniques, what was once a white-knuckle drive through the wilderness becomes one of the island's best day trips.

Despite the dangers, incidents are rare. The road does not require a 4WD vehicle. It's paved, although some sections can be bumpy. The road is narrow, and at some places is only wide enough for one car.

So how do you drive on a one-lane road? Go slowly around corners and honk your horn on those you can't see around. Turn the radio off so you can hear if anyone is honking from the other direction. If you need to take a break, use one of the gravel pullouts on the side of the road and let the cars behind you pass. Watch the road that's directly in front of you, but also look across the valley for oncoming traffic that might still be 0.5 mile away. If you notice that there is an oncoming truck, use the next pullout, wait 20 seconds for the oncoming traffic to pass, and then continue on your way. If you do encounter another car at a narrow spot, you might have to slowly reverse to the nearest pullout and give the other car room to pass. The number-one rule is don't sightsee and drive at the same time. If you're the driver, keep your eyes firmly glued to the road. If you want to take photos, pull over.

Try this adventurous back road. If you're departing from West Maui and moving clockwise around the mountain, you have the benefit of being on the inside lane and away from the steep cliff faces. This is the most popular way to visit, after an outing to Nakalele Blowhole. Then again, since you are pressed against the mountainside instead of against the ocean, you run the risk of falling rocks coming down after a heavy rain. If you approach from the Wailuku direction and move in a counterclockwise direction around the mountain, be sure the person in the passenger seat isn't afraid of heights.

Buckle up, hold on, and get ready for a ride to remember.

and dropped tailgates with coolers, but if you walk a couple of yards down the beach, you can usually find your own patch of sand that's perfect for a chair and book. Afternoons are often windy—and don't expect any snorkeling—but a couple of spots are deep enough for swimming, and days with light wind are gorgeous. To reach Stable Road, drive on Hana Highway (Hwy. 36) in the direction of Pa'ia, and 1.4 miles from the junction with Haleakala Highway (Hwy. 37), make a left onto a narrow paved road. From here, travel about 0.5 mile until you see sandy parking lots on the right side.

Surfing

The majority of **surfing** on this side of the island takes place from October to April. Some eastward-facing locations can pick up wind swell during the summer months, but it's choppy and sloppy. There are no surf schools that operate along this stretch of coast, and anyone opting to surf around here needs to be at least an intermediate surfer. On the biggest winter swells, teams of professional surfers have been known to tow-surf the outer reefs here, where waves can reach 70 feet. Thanks, but we'll be watching from shore.

SURF SPOTS

Kahului

For longboarding and stand-up paddle surfing, **Lowers** at Kanaha Beach Park (page 249) is a popular North Shore favorite. When standing on the sand, look for the lifeguard tower, which is where you'll paddle out. The wave at Kanaha breaks on an offshore reef and requires an arm-burning paddle, but a long paddle means a long ride, and the surf usually won't close out until the faces reach 10 feet. Mornings are best before the wind picks up, which is usually around 11am.

Wailuku

The most popular surf break in **Wailuku** is **Big Lefts** in Paukukalo. This is a long left-hand wave that can get very big on north and northeasterly swells, although it's for advanced surfers only and is heavily localized. To access the surf break, turn onto Waiehu Beach Road and then make a right on Ukali Street, following it to the end. The surf break is in front of the parking lot. Don't leave any valuables in your car, give locals the set waves, and stick to hopping the shoulder.

For a mellow longboarding wave, there's a break in front of **Waiehu Beach Park** that usually has fewer people than neighboring Paukukalo. The wave quality isn't as good, but this is still a good wave in the early morning during any north swell. To reach Waiehu Beach Park, travel along Waiehu Beach Road before taking a right turn on Lower Waiehu Beach Road, and follow it to the parking lot at the end.

dawn patrol at Paukukalo

WINDSURFING

Maui is one of world's top destinations for **windsurfing**, and at **Kanaha Beach Park,** the trade winds are so consistent during the summer months that they arrive like clockwork around 11am. In winter, the trade winds are a little less consistent, and waves can reach 15 feet or higher.

There's strictly no windsurfing before 11am, and Kanaha is split into two main launching areas conveniently named **Uppers** and **Lowers.** Many of the windsurfing schools operate by Uppers at a cove known as Kook's Beach. Lowers is located in the area by the lifeguard tower, the preferred launching point. If there are waves breaking on the reef, you'll notice a channel off the lifeguard stand where you can get past the break and out beyond the surf.

For more information on Maui windsurfing, go to www.mauiwindsurfing.net for photos, rental operators, and descriptions of the various launching sites. For a live cam of the conditions at Kanaha, check out www.mauiwindcam.com.

KITESURFING

The best place for **kitesurfing** on Maui is at the aptly named **Kite Beach** (page 249) a place of hallowed ground where the sport was born. This is the beach where all kitesurfing schools operate, and just as at neighboring Kanaha, the crowd is international. Even if you aren't a kitesurfer, this is a fantastic spot to sit and watch as dozens of colorful kites zip through the gusty trade winds. Since Kite Beach is so close to Kanaha, the unwritten rule is that kitesurfers are supposed to stay downwind (closer to Kahului Harbor) of the windsurfers to avoid high-speed entanglement. Even though this is one of the premier spots on the planet for kitesurfing, unless you're an experienced kitesurfer, lessons are imperative.

For more information about kitesurfing on Maui, check out www.kitesurfmaui.org. For a webcam of current wind and weather conditions, go to www.kitebeachcam.com.

RENTAL SHOPS

Of all the rental shops in Kahului, **Hi-Tech Surf Sports** (425 Koloa St., 808/877-2111, www.surfmaui.com, 9am-6pm daily) has the largest selection of surfboards ($25 per day) and stand-up paddleboards ($35 per day), with discounts for longer rentals.

Other reputable rental spots include the **Naish Pro Center** (111 Hana Hwy., 808/871-1503, www.naishmaui.com, 9am-5pm daily), **Second Wind** (111 Hana Hwy., 808/877-7467, www.secondwindmaui.com, 9am-6pm daily), and **Kanaha Kai** (96 Amala Pl., 808/877-7778, www.kanahakai.com, 9am-5pm daily), which is the closest shop to the beach. Expect stand-up paddleboards to cost about $35 per day, and downwind boards $35-55. Windsurfing rigs should be about $55, and kitesurf rigs about $85.

SCHOOLS AND LESSONS

When it comes to windsurfing and kitesurfing in Maui, one class isn't enough. Ideally you want to book at least a five-hour package to maximize your investment, although every school offers a single-session option if you just want to test the waters.

One of the best schools on the island is **Hawaiian Sailboard Techniques** (425 Koloa St., 808/871-5423, www.hstwindsurfing.com), located inside Hi-Tech Surf Sports. Founder Alan Cadiz has been teaching windsurfing on Maui since 1985, making this the longest-running outfit on the island's North Shore. Cadiz was one of the first instructors to teach the sport to others, and an instructor will accompany you on a stand-up paddleboard. Three-hour kitesurfing lessons are $255, and private windsurfing starts at $99. Stand-up paddle lessons begin at $89 for a two-hour class, and if you're experienced, ask about doing the Maliko Run along with a professional guide.

Stand-Up Paddling: The Maliko Run

In the sport of downwind stand-up paddling, there's no stretch of water more legendary and hallowed than the nine-mile-long Maliko Run. It's the spot where downwind racing was born, and the place where the world's best paddle surfers train for the professional tour.

In a "downwinder," paddlers position the wind at their backs and glide on the open ocean, connecting "bumps," or ocean swells, that pass beneath the board. When done properly, it's possible to feel like you're surfing on a wave that virtually has no end, and your mind and body are exceptionally aligned with the ocean movements beneath you. In the Maliko Run, paddlers begin at Maliko Gulch to the east of Ho'okipa Beach Park, and paddle downwind to either Kahului Harbor or the beach at Kanaha Beach Park. On a typical day, paddlers will be up to a mile offshore and in winds of 30 mph, riding on ocean swells that can range from knee-high to a couple of feet overhead. Average paddlers complete the nine-mile run between Maliko and the Harbor in a little under two hours, whereas the world's top paddlers can finish the course in a little over an hour—a seven-minute mile.

Maliko Runs are a favorite weekend activity of the island's water sports enthusiasts, and over 200 racers gather each year for the professional races, with one of the largest being the OluKai race at the end of April. A Maliko Run isn't an activity for anyone who isn't an avid stand-up paddler, but for stand-up paddling enthusiasts, this is the Holy Grail.

If you're a competent paddler and have lots of experience in the ocean, **Moore Water Time** (www.moorewatertime.com) has a shuttle service ($15-17 pp) with daily runs to Maliko that leave from Kanaha and Kahului Harbor. For boards, an increasing number of Kahului shops are now renting race boards, and a couple of schools will even provide lessons where an experienced instructor can accompany you.

One of the largest schools is **Action Sports Maui** (808/871-5857, www.actionsportsmaui.com), where kiting lessons range from $199 for a 2.5-hour intro class to $2,195 for a 10-day, 30-hour intensive training package. Windsurfing lessons range from $89 for 2.5 hours to a five-day course ($395 pp group, $725 private).

Kiteboarding School of Maui (808/873-0015, www.ksmaui.com) focuses specifically on kitesurfing, and offers a $199 three-hour beginner package, or $680 for eight hours (a better option for actually learning the sport).

Aqua Sports (808/242-8015, www.maui-kiteboardinglessons.com) is right on Kite Beach and offers a $195 one-day beginner special. If you just want to get the feeling for what it feels like to kitesurf without taking an entire lesson package, check out **Kiting.com** (808/852-1938, www.kiting.com) for a 30-minute tandem-kitesurfing experience ($99) riding with a professional instructor who handles the board and the steering. If you decide you're hooked on the sport, lesson packages are available.

Hiking and Biking

HIKING

'Iao Valley

From the winding drive back into the mountains, you would think that popular **'Iao Valley** would offer some good hiking. In reality, the only hike is the paved walking trail that leads to the 'Iao Needle lookout.

If you want to swim in 'Iao Stream, the best place for accessing the swimming holes is from Kepaniwai Heritage Gardens, where short trails lead down to the refreshing—and cold—water.

★ Waihe'e Coastal Dunes and Wetlands Preserve

Here's a hike that's wildly underrated (with beautiful **bird-watching** opportunities): Set on land protected by the Hawaiian Islands Land Trust, the two-mile trail in the **Waihe'e Coastal Dunes and Wetlands Preserve** runs the length of one of Maui's last undeveloped shorelines. Within the 277-acre preserve are the remains of the Kapoho fishing village as well as two different ancient *heiau* (temples) and seabirds in the low grass. Scholars estimate that the Waihe'e area was populated as early as AD 300-600, which is not surprising, as the freshwater streams, fertile valleys, and lush uplands provide all the natural resources to sustain life.

The trail parallels the shore and passes by a couple of abandoned houses before reaching the cultural relics at Kapoho. Expect the round-trip journey to take a little over an hour; add 30 minutes to explore the coast or ruins. To reach the trailhead, make a right on Halewaiu Place off Kahekili Highway (Hwy. 340) and follow the signs for Waiehu Golf Course. When the road makes a sharp turn to the right and starts heading toward the golf course, notice an unmarked dirt road going to the left. Park here, because around the corner is a stream crossing that's unsuitable for rental cars. Traveling on foot, the trailhead will be on the left, just uphill from the stream crossing. Avoid leaving valuables in your car.

★ Waihe'e Ridge Trail

The parking area for the **Waihe'e Ridge Trail** is at mile marker 7 of Kahekili Highway,

rainbow over Waihe'e Coastal Dunes and Wetlands Preserve

West Maui's Backside

across from Mendes Ranch. If the gate is open, which it usually is 7am-5pm daily, continue driving for another mile to the upper parking area. This 2.5-mile trail starts on a steep concrete incline, but fear not—if you can make it up this, you can make it the rest of the way. Eventually the trail levels out a bit and the concrete changes to dirt, which can often lead to muddy conditions, particularly if it has recently rained. But, oh, the views! This trail rises to 2,560 feet elevation, the highest hiking trail in West Maui, and offers sweeping views into Waihe'e and Makamaka'ole Valleys. In the distance, Makamaka'ole Falls tumbles dramatically through the forest; look the other direction, and the turquoise waters of the Waihe'e shore form a dramatic backdrop. The trail continues to Lanilili summit, where you can see the northern slope of the mountain on clear days. If you start hiking before 9am, you'll usually get clear conditions. This trail takes some energy, so count on three hours for the five-mile trip.

Makamaka'ole Valley

There aren't many waterfalls in Central Maui that you can access, but one exception is at **Makamaka'ole Valley,** off the side of Kahekili Highway. Approaching from Wailuku, the discreet trailhead is 0.8 mile past Mendes Ranch. At this point the road has climbed in elevation and narrowed in places to a single lane. You'll pass a sharp turn in the valley, and when the road starts pointing back toward the ocean, you'll notice a small dirt pullout that can accommodate four or five vehicles.

The trailhead is a very narrow but well-defined dirt pathway that heads downhill into the brush. There's also a false trailhead that departs from the same parking area but only goes for a few yards. If the trail suddenly ends, turn around and look for the other one. Once you are on the correct trail, it will wind its way downhill for about 10 minutes before arriving at a small swimming hole, where you'll find a rushing waterfall and a rope swing. Along the way you're rewarded with a dramatic view of

Makamakaʻole Valley as it weaves toward the ocean below.

After the first swimming hole, the trail continues deeper into the valley toward a waterfall more dramatic than the first. You have to climb over a large boulder and move branches aside to keep following the trail, which then parallels the stream over some slippery rocks. The mosquitoes can be vicious in this shaded section, so be sure you're covered. After five minutes, the trail ends at a large banyan tree whose serpentine roots snake down a near-vertical cliff face. In order to reach the pool below, climb down using the roots of the banyan as if descending a ladder. This maneuver requires athletic ability and skill, so it should only be attempted by those who are agile and accepting of the risks. The reward, however, is a small swimming hole where you can bathe beneath a waterfall in a hidden tropical setting.

HIKING TOURS

Guided hiking tours of the Waiheʻe area are available through **Mendes Ranch** (3530 Kahekili Hwy., 808/871-5222, www.mendesranch.com). The price is $110 for either the 1.5-hour Mendes Cliff morning or afternoon hike, with an additional $30 if you want the barbecue lunch. The ride offers spectacular views, and the guides have lots of local knowledge and stories. You can also book horseback riding excursions through the ranch. Rides depart at 9am and 12:30pm Monday-Saturday. Check-in is 15 minutes before departure. Show up at 11:30 for the afternoon ride if you want the barbecue lunch.

BIKING

The lone Central Maui mountain biking trail is in the **Kahakuloa Game Management Area,** where a five-mile-long 4WD road rises 1,600 vertical feet. Wear bright-colored clothing because it's also a hunting area. The turnoff from Kahekili Highway is between mile markers 40 and 41.

The **road bike ride to Kahakuloa** is one of the best on the island, where cyclists are treated to quad-burning ascents, hairpin turns through the rainforest, and sweeping views of the entire North Shore. Sharing the road with cars can be tough, considering how narrow it gets, but most cars are traveling so slowly around the tight turns that altercations are rare.

If you would prefer to be on a designated bike path that stays on level ground, the **North Shore Greenway** runs from the last parking lot at Kanaha Beach Park all the way to the town of Paʻia. To reach the Kahului terminus of the bike path, follow Amala Place all the way to the end and park in the last parking lot of Kanaha Beach Park. Parts of the bike path go directly behind the airport runway. This ride is best in the morning hours before the wind picks up.

Rental Shops

At **Crater Cycles** (400 Hana Hwy., 808/893-2020, www.cratercycleshawaii.com, 9am-6pm daily), mountain bike and road bike rentals begin at $65 per day, with discounted prices for multiple days. The staff love cycling and can offer inside info on current trail conditions and tips for enjoying your ride.

Across the street from K-Mart, **Island Biker Maui** (415 Dairy Rd., 808/877-7744, www.islandbikermaui.com, 10am-5pm Mon.-Fri., 9am-3pm Sat.) offers rentals that begin at $60 per day or $210 per week. Mountain bikes and road bikes are available.

Adventure Sports

ZIPLINE TOURS

For travelers who only go big or go home, the eight-line **Flyin Hawaiian Zipline** (1670 Honoapiʻilani Hwy., 808/463-4786, www.flyinhawaiianzipline.com, $185) covers 2.5 miles of West Maui mountainside and finishes in a different town. The most enticing reason to book this tour is the ultra-long, cheek-clenching, three-screamer zipline that runs for more than 3,600 feet—the longest on the island. The lines aren't parallel, and the height off the ground isn't as high as the fifth line at Piʻiholo, but you also get a short ATV ride at the end as they shuttle you back where you started.

In addition to views toward Haleakala, this zipline ecotour incorporates elements of habitat restoration for Hawaii's native plants and works to remove nonnative species. The company champions sustainable, educational tourism, and the ecological element of the organization isn't just something done to appear green—it's the real deal. Expect the tour to take 4-5 hours. Small snacks are included. Riders must be 10 years old and weigh 75 to 250 pounds. Guests meet at the Maui Tropical Plantation for a 4WD ride back into Waikapu Valley, where you suit up for your midair journey across the mountain. This tour often sells out well in advance, so reservations are a must.

If you'd rather ease into it, or are traveling with children, the most beginner-friendly zipline in the central valley is **Maui Zipline** (1670 Honoapiʻilani Hwy., 808/633-2464, www.mauizipline.com, $110), on the grounds of the Maui Tropical Plantation. Children as young as five and as light as 45 pounds can take part in this five-line adventure; children under age 11 must be joined by an adult. Because the course caters to young children, it isn't as extreme as some others, but the guides introduce educational elements to the program, such as the weather patterns of the area and lessons on plant species, making this a great option for families. Cable lengths range 300 to 900 feet, and there are two cables running parallel to each other, so you can go two at a time.

HELICOPTER RIDES

You heard it here first: **Helicopter** tours are the island's best splurge. They're expensive, and some people find them scary, but they are the best way to experience Maui's beauty. The majority of the island is only accessible by helicopter, and until you've seen waterfalls powerfully plunging through hidden mist-shrouded valleys, or buzzed below the world's tallest sea cliffs and seen humpback whales from the air, you'll never know the breadth of beauty that Maui really has to offer.

All pilots have logged thousands of flying hours and put an emphasis on safety, and when narrating the tours, most also provide information on geology, biology, and history. Morning tours are best because they offer the clear conditions necessary for visiting spots such as 1,100-foot Honokohau Falls or peering into Haleakala Crater. All helicopter flights depart from the **Kahului Heliport** (0.5 mile from the junction of Hana Hwy. and Haleakala Hwy.), and the two most popular tour options are those combining the West Maui Mountains with Molokaʻi, and East Maui (Hana) with Haleakala. Regardless of which operator you choose, inquire about getting the two front seats next to the pilot, since it's much easier to take photos. If you're really serious about photos, wear long sleeves and dark-colored clothing to avoid reflections in the window, and to get really pro, consider wearing gloves. Remember that you cannot have been scuba diving within 24 hours before the flight (although snuba is OK). All prices listed are for advance online reservations.

Air Maui (1 Kahului Airport Rd., Hangar 110, 808/877-7005 www.airmaui.com) has a perfect safety record and has options you won't find elsewhere, including the West Maui and Moloka'i tour ($275 pp), where you tour the mountains and marvel at thundering waterfalls. More affordable options are the 30-minute Maui Lite trip ($188 pp), occasionally offered for $100 for last-minute single seats. There are also standard West Maui-Moloka'i and Hana-Haleakala tours, including one with a cliff-side landing on the back side of Haleakala. All helicopters are the A-Star variety, which seat up to six.

The largest operator on the island, with cheaper flights, is **Blue Hawaiian Helicopters** (1 Kahului Airport Rd., Suite 105, 808/871-8844, www.bluehawaiian.com), operating both A-Star and more expensive Eco-Star helicopters, with individual bucket seats and larger viewing windows. Options include a 30-minute flight of West Maui (Eco-Star $185 pp, A-Star $153 pp) and a 1.5-hour complete island tour with a landing at Ulupalakua Ranch ($321-396 pp). For a multi-island adventure, cross the channel to the Big Island for a tour of North Kohala (sorry—no volcanoes or lava) before returning over Hana for a two-hour flight ($453-510 pp).

Also flying Eco-Star helicopters is **Sunshine Helicopters** (1 Kahului Airport Rd., Suite 107, 808/270-3999, www.sunshinehelicopters.com), which charges extra for seats in front. Tours include a 45-minute Hana-Haleakala flight ($225 pp) and a 70-minute complete island flight with deluxe seating ($480 pp). To save a little, flights are discounted $50 before 8am and after 2pm. If Mendes Ranch horseback riding or the Atlantis Submarine is also on your list of activities, you can book each as a combo package through Sunshine Helicopters and save a little on both.

After 20 years of operating flights on the Mainland, **Maverick Helicopters** (1 Kahului Airport Rd., Suite 108, 808/893-7999, www.maverickhelicopter.com) is the island's newest operator, with Eco-Star flights that include a 45-minute Hana-Haleakala tour ($299 pp) and a 70-minute complete island tour ($389 pp).

To get really extreme and have no glare in your photos, **Pacific Helicopters** (808/871-9771, www.pacifichelicoptertours.com) can fly without the doors to enjoy the dramatic scenery with no obstructions. Tours average $293-323 pp, depending on length of the tour, and since the helicopter only has room for three passengers, it's cheaper for a party of three to charter a flight ($800).

FLIGHTSEEING TOURS

If you're staying on Maui and want to see lava (which isn't guaranteed), the only way to see Kilauea volcano is with a **flightseeing tour** in an airplane. There aren't any helicopter companies from Maui that visit Kilauea volcano, although there are a couple of fixed-wing options from Kapalua and Kahului airports. **Royal Pacific Air** (808/838-7788, www.royalpacificair.com) begins its flights at Honolulu and makes stops at Kapalua Airport ($449 pp) and Kahului Airport ($425 pp) before continuing on to the Big Island. If you're staying in Ka'anapali, Napili, or Kapalua, the Kapalua airport is only a 10-minute drive, an amazingly convenient option. In addition to active Kilauea volcano, you'll experience hidden waterfalls on the Big Island as well as Hana and Haleakala Crater. It isn't cheap but compares to the most expensive helicopter tours.

The other option is **Maui Air** (808/877-5500, www.volcanoairtours.com), offering tours of the volcano. The plane can accommodate 10 passengers, and fares are about $425 from Kahului Airport and $449 from Kapalua Airport.

Shopping

KAHULUI

Kahului has the island's largest amount of shopping, though it's mainly the box-store variety. The two-story **Queen Ka'ahumanu Shopping Center** (275 W. Ka'ahumanu Ave., 808/877-4325, www.queenkaahumanucenter. com, 9:30am-9pm Mon.-Sat., 10am-5pm Sun.) is Kahului's largest mall, though many of the stores are large corporate chains. That said, there's still one shop, the **Story of Hawaii Museum** (808/283-3576, www.storyofhawaiimuseum.com, 10am-5pm daily) that sells Hawaiian prints and doubles as a Hawaiian history museum. In addition to maps and Hawaiian giclées, visitors will find exhibits on everything from Maui's involvement in World War II to the route of Hawaii's King Kalakaua—the first monarch to circumnavigate the globe.

Across town, the open-air **Maui Mall** (70 E. Ka'ahumanu Ave., 808/877-8952, www.mauimall.com, 10am-6pm Mon.-Thurs. and Sat., 10am-8pm Fri., 10am-4pm Sun.) has a couple of surf shops and clothing boutiques, and is convenient for anyone visiting on a cruise ship that's docked at Kahului Harbor.

For a classic Maui shopping experience, head to the Saturday **Maui Swap Meet** (310 W. Ka'ahumanu Ave., 808/244-3100, www.mauiexposition.com, 7am-1pm Sat., $0.50 adults, free under age 13) at UH Maui College, where over 200 local vendors gather to sell their foodstuffs and crafts. You can find everything from homemade jams to hand-turned koa wood bowls—often at prices much reduced from what you'd find in the stores.

Kahului also has the greatest concentration of water sports shops on the island, many of which are near the corner of Hana Highway and Dairy Road. Stop here for surf clothing, accessories, board shorts, or equipment sales. Favorites include **Hi-Tech Surf Sports** (425 Koloa St., 808/877-2111, www.surfmaui.com, 9am-6pm daily), **Adventure Sports Maui** (400 Hana Hwy., 808/877-7443, www.adventuresportsmaui.com, 9am-6pm daily), and **Maui Tropix** (261 Dairy Rd., 808/871-8726, 9am-8pm Mon.-Sat., 9am-6pm Sun.), which sells the ubiquitous "Maui Built" wear.

WAILUKU

Sleepy **Wailuku** is turning into a hot shopping outpost. With a tight little cluster of shops, **Market Street** rivals Lahaina, Paia, and Makawao for shopping and strolling. The difference here, however, is that many of the stores have authentic local connections—either selling products from local vendors or traditional Hawaiian crafts.

At **Native Intelligence** (1980 Main St., 808/249-2421, www.native-intel.com, 10am-5pm Mon.-Fri., 10am-4pm Sat.), visitors will find what's arguably the island's most culturally authentic store, perpetuating traditional Hawaiian culture and values, and selling everything from textbooks printed in Hawaiian to traditional lei-making supplies. You'll also find hand-carved weaponry, jewelry, and immaculate colorful feather-work, and occasional classes help introduce visitors to traditional Hawaiian culture. For anyone with an interest in traditional culture, this store is a must-visit.

Near the corner of Market and Main Streets is **Maui Thing** (7 N. Market St., 808/249-0215, www.mauithing.com, 10am-5pm Mon.-Fri., 10am-4pm Sat.), a clothing store that focuses on Maui-themed clothing and has Hawaiian books for the *keiki* (kids). This is a great store for unique Maui clothing you won't find anywhere else on the island.

For men's aloha shirts and women's clothing, **Ha Wahine** (53 Market St., 808/344-1642, 11am-3pm Mon.-Sat.) is a clothing boutique featuring clothes made on Maui, with many featuring native designs and traditional Hawaiian patterns.

Across the street is a longtime Wailuku

institution, **Request Music** (10 N. Market St., 808/244-9315, 10am-6pm Mon.-Sat.), the last holdout of true island record shops, kept alive by loyal music lovers who still want to feel the vinyl, admire the album covers, and talk with people who *really* love music. Most of the merchandise caters to the reggae and roots lifestyle, but the basement is filled with music that goes back decades.

Just a few doors down, **Sandell Artworks** (34 N. Market St., 808/249-2456, hours vary) brings creative color and flare to funky Market Street, where paintings and prints run the gamut of characters and oddities of Maui.

At the far end of Market Street are two local water sports stores, **Tri Paddle Maui** (54 N. Market St., 808/243-7235, www.tripaddlemaui. com, 10am-5pm Mon.-Fri., 10am-3pm Sat.), which specializes in accessories for outrigger paddle sports, and **Maui Sporting Goods** (92 N. Market St., 808/244-0011, 9am-6pm Mon.-Fri., 9am-5pm Sat.), the de facto fishing headquarters for most of Maui's anglers.

The string of pawn shops along Market Street always have some good deals, and at **Kama'aina Loan** (98 N. Market St., 808/242-5555, www.kamaainaloan.com, 9am-5pm Mon.-Fri., 10am-4pm Sat.-Sun.), you'll find everything from surfboards to ukuleles to ritual drums used by Nepalese shamans.

Entertainment

KAHULUI
Evening Shows
The best option for evening entertainment in Kahului is the **Maui Arts and Cultural Center** (1 Cameron Way, 808/242-7469, www.mauiarts.org), where a constantly changing schedule of live concerts, movies, exhibits, comedy shows, and family events takes place most nights of the week. Multiple events often happen on the same evening. Check the website for a list of upcoming events.

Bars
The best bar in Kahului is the **Kahului Ale House** (355 E. Ka'ahumanu Ave., 808/877-9001, www.kahuluialehouse.com, 11am-11pm Mon.-Fri., 8am-11pm Sat., 7am-11pm Sun.), which has live music every night and 24 beers on draft. There are 40 TVs for watching the game, as well as ice-cold beer, surprisingly good sushi 3pm-10pm daily, and happy hour 3pm-6pm daily.

If you would rather visit a smaller bar in a darker, more intimate setting, **Koho's Grill and Bar** (275 W. Ka'ahumanu Ave., 808/877-5588, 7am-10pm Sun.-Thurs., 7am-11:30pm Fri.-Sat.) inside the Queen Ka'ahumanu Shopping Center is a longtime local favorite, with daily drink specials and a casual crowd of margarita-sipping locals.

WAILUKU
Shows
A couple of times per year, theatrical shows take place inside historic **'Iao Theater** (68 N. Market St.), a Spanish mission-style theater that was opened in 1928. Listed on the National Register of Historic Places, the 'Iao is Hawaii's oldest theater and has hosted performers such as Bob Hope and Frank Sinatra over its lengthy history. For updated showtimes, visit **Maui OnStage** (www.mauionstage.com).

Food

KAHULUI

Coffee Shops

For local coffee beans, head to **Maui Coffee Roasters** (444 Hana Hwy., 808/877-2877, www.mauicoffeeroasters.com, 7am-6pm Mon.-Fri., 8am-5pm Sat., 8am-2:30pm Sun., $9), the best little coffee shop in town. In the same shopping complex as Marco's Grill and Deli, Maui Coffee Roasters has an assortment of brews made from Maui, Kona, Kaua'i, and Moloka'i beans. The full breakfast and lunch menu features bagels, breakfast wraps, sandwiches, and salads, and there are multiple tables and free Wi-Fi. It's five minutes from the airport.

Culinary Academy

To play a role in the next generation of Maui's most talented chefs, reserve a table at ★ **Leis Family Class Act** (310 W. Ka'ahumanu Ave., 808/984-3280, www.mauiculinary.sodexomyway.com/classact, 11am-12:30pm Wed. and Fri.), where students of the Maui Culinary Academy gain real-world experience. The students perform all roles and serve a four-course Latin, Asian, Italian, French, or Moroccan fine-dining menu that changes each week. See the website, updated each semester, for specific menus and dates. Since it's only open twice per week, advance reservations are strongly recommended. Depending on the entrée, the prix fixe menu ranges $29-41 pp, and there's no corkage fee if you bring your own wine.

German

Industrial Kahului is the last place you would expect to find a Bavarian après-ski lodge, but **Brigit and Bernard's Garden Café** (335 Ho'ohana St., 808/877-6000, 11am-2:30pm Mon., 11am-2:30pm and 5pm-9:30pm Tues.-Fri., 5pm-9:30pm Sat., www.brigitandbernards.net, $16-32) pumps out authentic stick-to-your-ribs German fare. The vaulted A-frame ceiling is hung with colorful steins, cross-country skis, and posters of alpine ski resorts. Order a massive plate of bratwurst or schnitzel served with a huge potato *rosti* and wash it down with a Bitburger brew.

Hawaiian

Usually the only time you get Hawaiian food is when you attend a luau, but here at humble ★ **Poi by the Pound** (385 Ho'ohana St., 808/283-9381, 10am-8pm Mon.-Thurs., 10am-9pm Fri.-Sat., $12-20), in industrial Kahului, the kalua pig, *lau lau, poke*, and poi are just as good—if not better—than food you'd find at a luau. To go full-on local, order the Hawaiian Plate ($19), packed with Hawaiian favorites, or get teriyaki chicken or *kalbi* ribs, made to order on the grill. Fresh poi is available for purchase, and pick up a block of sweet *kulolo*, made from taro and coconut milk.

Italian

The finest restaurant in Kahului, **Bistro Casanova** (33 Lono Ave., 808/873-3850, www.bistrocasanova.com, 11am-9:30pm Mon.-Sat., $14-38) livens up downtown with a fusion of Mediterranean and Italian cuisine. The tapas menu, served after 3pm, has crostinis, gnocchi, and grilled calamari, and a swanky bar attracts the after-work cocktail crowd.

For a quick slice of pizza, check out **Pizza in Paradise** (60 E. Wakea Ave., 808/871-8188, www.pizza-maui.com, 11am-9pm Mon.-Thurs., 11am-10pm Fri-Sat., $13-26), a family-run joint that makes its own dough and sauce. Whole pies are available, but the "by the slice" option is nice for lunch on the go. The menu also has subs and pasta, but it's the pizza that keeps locals walking through the door. The location is obscure; parking is around back.

Local Style

Let's get one thing straight: The enormous plate lunch dishes at ★ **Da Kitchen** (425 Koloa St., 808/871-7782, www.da-kitchen. com, 11am-9pm Mon.-Sat., $10-17) are the best on the entire island. Da Kitchen is the gravy-covered gold standard that all other plate lunch is measured by—it even helped serve the food at President Obama's first inauguration.

Da Kitchen is tucked in the same strip mall as Hi-Tech Surf Sports and Denny's—just look for the huge sign that says "Restaurant"— and despite the somewhat obscure location, the place is always packed. Some of the items are big enough to split (lunch for under $20), and for a tasty albeit artery-clogging meal, go all-in with fried spam *musubi* followed by Polynesian Paralysis Moco: fish tempura, kalua pork, two eggs, onion, mushrooms, and gravy over fried rice.

Mexican

For quick and authentic Mexican food, visit **Las Piñatas** (395 Dairy Rd., 808/877-8707, www.pinatasmaui.com, 8am-9pm Mon.-Sat. $7-10), next to Kinko's off Dairy Road. The Kitchen Sink burrito is so big that a growing teenager will have trouble cleaning the plate. Pair with a bottle of beer or *horchata*.

Natural Foods

Alive and Well (340 Hana Hwy., 808/877-4950, www.aliveandwellinmaui.com, 8am-7pm Mon.-Fri., 8am-6pm Sat., 10am-5pm Sun.) is a health emporium that has deli sandwiches, organic juice, and smoothies. There's also *kombucha* on tap!

WAILUKU

Old-school **Wailuku** is quietly becoming one of Maui's best places for food. Don't expect oceanfront tiki torches like you'd find at restaurants in Lahaina, since the atmosphere here is far more "authentic" in the run-down and real local sort of way. Prices are lower because rents are lower, and the wealth of affordable international cuisine is starting to garner attention.

American

Located inside the Maui Tropical Plantation, ★ **The Mill House** (1670 Honoapi'ilani Hwy., 808/270-0333, www.mauitropicalplantation.com, 11am-3pm and 5pm-9pm Mon.-Sat., 8pm-close Sun.) has gone completely next-level with the concept of farm-to-table. Nearly everything is sourced on the island, with much of it grown on the farm, and it's the island's only restaurant where the meat arrives as a whole animal and is processed on-site. Aside from the freshness, there's a creative and innovative culinary genius to all of the flavorful plates, ordered tapas-style and shared around the table. While the menu changes around what's in season, favorites include the pork *ragù* gnocchi or the beet pickled egg salad, and an extensive wine list, with 60-plus wines, accompanies the French-press coffee. Hard-core foodies can attend the **Maui Chef's Table** (6pm-9pm Sat., $150 pp), where executive chef Jeff Scheer prepares dishes that were thought up just hours before and have yet to make it on the menu. This exclusive event only has 36 seats, and reservations are strongly recommended.

Just half a block from Market Street is **808 on Main** (2051 Main St., 808/242-1111, www.808onmain.com, 10am-7pm Mon.-Fri.), where you can get filling *paninis,* sandwiches, and salads with creative culinary flare. Try the chicken mango chutney *panini* served on sourdough with pepper-jack cheese ($10), or a toasted wasabi hoagie roll with roast beef and wasabi aioli ($11). In addition to standard wine ($7 per glass) and beer, you'll also find a Beer & a Shot menu with drink combos ($8). Angry Orchard and Crown Royal, anyone? Historic black-and-white photos of Wailuku are the basic decor.

Bakeries

Wailuku is the island's epicenter for bakeries, and none is more popular than **Home**

Central Maui Food Trucks

Central Maui is the island's epicenter for quirky gourmet food trucks, and the prices compare with most of the island's budget restaurants. Expect entrées to cost $8-13, and while locations can vary, here's where you can usually find them:

FOOD TRUCK PARK ACROSS FROM COSTCO

Only five minutes from the airport, this tight little cluster of food trucks has everything from fried *poke* and ahi *katsu* at local favorite **Like Poke?** to $10 plates of chicken pad thai at the **Thai Mee Up** food truck. You'll also find local plate lunch at **Mama T's Molokai Grindz,** and three tacos for $5 at **Maui 8 Wonder Tacos.** The food truck park (10am-4pm Mon.-Tues., 10am-8pm Wed.-Fri.) is located across from the Costco gas station on Haleakala Highway.

KAHULUI HARBOR

In the dirt parking area across from the Maui Arts and Cultural Center you'll find **Geste Shrimp Truck** (Kahului Beach Rd., 808/298-7109, 10:45am-5pm Tues.-Sat., cash only), where $12 gets you 12 pieces of shrimp served with crab macaroni salad and two scoops of rice. Based on the aroma of shrimp emanating from the white truck, it's no surprise that it often runs out of food before 5pm. Next door, you'll find **Lau Hee Chicken Hekka** and their local style plate lunch of sweet salty chicken, as well as a handful of other trucks that occasionally set up shop.

MAUI FRESH STREATERY

With its rotating menu of global cuisine, **Maui Fresh Streatery** (137 Ka'ahumanu Ave., 808/344-7929, 11am-1pm Mon., Wed., and Fri.) has reached legendary status in Maui's food truck community. It's only open six hours per week and never has trouble selling out. For nearly 10 years, chef Kyle Kawakami was a professor at Maui's Culinary Academy, and he's now the overlord of a global menu that changes by the week, including chicken *katsu* curry and Furikake Fries as well as the Tres Cerditos Cubano pork sandwich. The tip jar is donated to local nonprofits, and nothing on the menu costs over $10. Since the schedule can be irregular, check ahead on social media for location and hours; you can usually find it in the parking lot of the Shell gas station.

Maid Bakery (1005 L. Main St., 808/244-7015, www.homemaidbakery.com, 5am-10pm daily), which has been serving their famous *malasadas* and *manju* since 1960. Plain *malasadas* cost $0.86, cream-filled are $1.35, and both are available 5am-10am and again 4pm-10pm.

Coffee Shops

Wailuku Coffee Company (26 N. Market St., 808/495-0259, 7am-5pm Mon.-Sat., 8am-3pm Sun., $5-8) is where "the hip come to sip." For breakfast, served until 10:30am, try a bacon, tomato, and avocado bagel served with a layer of cream cheese ($9), and for lunch try a gluten-free Life Foods burger ($11), made on Maui. You'll also find pastries, Wi-Fi, smoothies, and "pitza" served on pita bread.

Italian

Family-owned ★ **Giannotto's Pizza** (2050 Main St., 808/244-8282, www.giannottospizza.com, 11am-9pm Mon.-Sat., 11am-8pm Sun., $7) serves up homemade Italian recipes "just like Mama used to make." Located next to the Wailuku Promenade, this place is as authentic as the "Joisey" accents emanating from the kitchen. Photos of mafiosi adorn the wall, pizza by the slice is $2-4, and there's free delivery on orders over $20.

Local Style

At ★ **Sam Sato's** (1750 Wili Pa Loop, 808/244-7124, 7am-2pm Mon.-Sat., bakery until 4pm, cash only, $6), you'll probably wonder if this is really the famous restaurant, hidden deep with the Wailuku mill yard in a building you can't even see from the road. This family-run institution has been providing Wailuku plate lunch and famous *manju* pastries since the 1930s. It's the dry noodles that make Sam Sato's legendary, served with a side of homemade broth and topped with char *siu* pork and sprouts, making an affordable and addictive meal.

To order lunch like a Wailuku local, **Ichiban Okazuya** (2133 Kaohu St., 808/244-7276, 10am-8pm Mon.-Fri.) has arguably the best chicken *katsu* on Maui. You can also get tempura shrimp and veggies piled high with rice. This authentic hole-in-the-wall is take-out only. At peak times the line can be out the door, though the staff is surprisingly fast.

Natural Foods

For your daily fix of açaí and kale, head straight to ★ **The Farmacy Health Bar** (12 N. Market St., 808/866-4312, 7:30am-5:30pm Mon.-Fri., 9am-5pm Sat., 10am-4pm Sun., $6-9), where you can also score a dragon fruit smoothie or an açaí bowl with poi. Expect GMO-free organic ingredients and a strong community following.

Thai

A funky hole-in-the-wall that really has some good food in the heart of run-down Vineyard Street, ★ **Saeng's Thai Cuisine** (2119 W. Vineyard St., 808/244-1567, 11am-2:30pm and 5pm-9:30pm Mon.-Fri., $9-12) has pad thai and curries that are as tasty and authentic as they come. Pair your meal with a Singha beer or a glass of surprisingly good wine. The peaceful setting is a hidden find in the heart of industrial Wailuku.

Vietnamese

Sandwiched between a bridge and a low-income housing unit is one of Maui's most popular Vietnamese venues, ★ **A Saigon Café** (1792 Main St., 808/243-9560, 11am-10pm Thurs.-Tues., 11am-9pm Wed., $9-15). From the moment you step inside this place, you feel like you're in Vietnam, and it's a cultural as well as culinary experience that's well off the tourist radar. Opt for $12 clay pot dishes with rice, chicken, and vegetables, or try the *pho, banh hoi,* or tasty Vietnamese soup. The portions are enormous, the place is always packed, and if locals recommend eating at "Jennifer's," this is the place they mean.

Kihei and South Maui

Look for ★ to find recommended
sights, activities, dining, and lodging.

Highlights

★ **Maui Ocean Center:** Surround yourself with sharks, eagle rays, and dozens of fish, all without getting your hair wet (page 272).

★ **Hawaiian Islands Humpback Whale National Marine Sanctuary Visitors Center:** Learn about Maui's most exciting winter visitors in an oceanfront setting by Koʻieʻie Fishpond (page 273).

★ **Keawakapu Beach:** While the northern end of Keawakapu Beach teems with activity, the southern expanse is a peaceful getaway for a blanket and a book (page 276).

★ **Maluaka Beach:** The perfect place for a morning stand-up paddle is along Makena's historic coast (page 279).

★ **Makena State Park:** There are actually three beaches within the state park, known to most locals simply as "Big Beach." The sunsets are legendary (page 279).

★ **Molokini Crater:** The water inside this offshore caldera is some of the clearest in the world. The snorkeling ranks as some of the best in the state, and the scuba diving is some of the best in the world (page 281).

★ **Ulua Beach and Mokapu Beach:** These protected, sandy beaches offer friendly snorkeling conditions and an abundance of marinelife (page 285).

© AVALON TRAVEL

★ **Hoapili Trail:** This ancient footpath of kings meanders through the island's most recent lava flows. Wander deserted Hawaiian fishing villages whose stone foundations stand frozen in time (page 295).

I f one word defines South Maui, it's "beaches." South Maui is graced with dozens of sandy stretches just waiting for your footprints.

The island's longest beach is Sugar Beach; one of its smallest is Pa'ako Cove. The sound of waves lapping against the palm-lined sand is a year-round reality in South Maui. There are enough beaches that a three-week vacation isn't enough time to possibly see them all. Because much of South Maui actually faces west, the end of each day is punctuated by a sunset that somehow outdoes the last.

It's also one of the state's hottest areas, particularly in Kihei, where the smell of coconut oil wafts on the late-morning trade winds. Mornings are for stand-up paddling and snorkeling, whereas afternoons are for finding a cold drink and settling in for the sunset. At the Maui Ocean Center in Ma'alaea, you can explore the beauty of the underwater world regardless of the conditions outside, and at Molokini Crater, set just offshore, you can snorkel, dive, splash, and swim in Maui's clearest waters.

This is also Maui's fastest-growing zip code, where rows of condos and luxury resorts seem to populate every shore. Despite the hypercharged growth, however, there's still a wild side in South Maui once you venture south toward Makena, where nudist drum circles still take place on the hidden sands of Little Beach, and hiking trails follow a rocky shore that was once the pathway of kings.

ORIENTATION

South Maui runs in a long narrow column and is never far from the coast. To drive from **Ma'alaea,** the northernmost part, to the end of the road in Makena, takes approximately 30 minutes and passes through Kihei and Wailea. The high-end resorts are found in **Wailea,** whereas **Kihei** is laden with oceanfront condos and more affordable options for dining. **Makena** is where the coast gets wild and development disappears, yet it is close enough to the Wailea resorts to reach by pedaling a bike. Kihei, the commercial hub of South Maui, is sandwiched in a strip between **South Kihei Road** and **Pi'ilani Highway,** whereas Ma'alaea is the site of the harbor and the windy gateway to West Maui.

Previous: Keawakapu Beach at sunrise; a Hawaiian green sea turtle, or *honu*, off Wailea. **Above**: playing in the waves.

South Maui

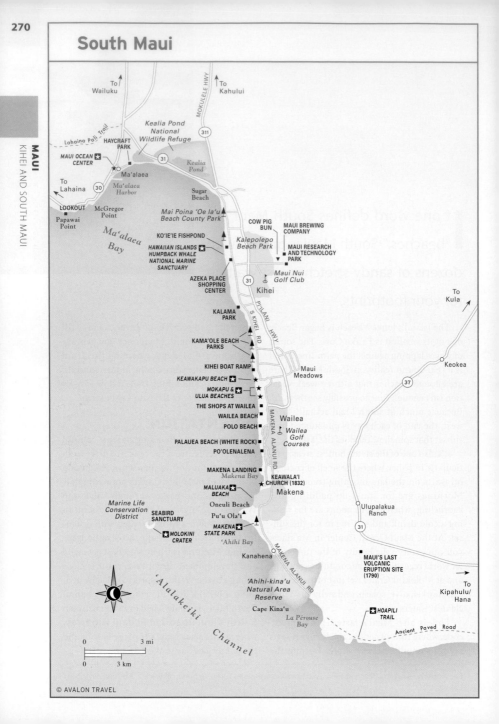

To
Wailuku

To
Kahului

MOKULELE HWY

311

Kealia Pond
National
Wildlife Refuge

Lahaina Pali Trail

HAYCRAFT
PARK

31

MAUI OCEAN
CENTER

Ma'alaea

Kealia
Pond

To
Lahaina

30

Ma'alaea
Harbor

Sugar
Beach

LOOKOUT

McGregor
Point

Mai Poina 'Oe la'u
Beach County Park

COW PIG
BUN

MAUI BREWING
COMPANY

Papawai
Point

Ma'alaea
Bay

KO'IE'IE FISHPOND

Kalepolepo
Beach Park

MAUI RESEARCH
AND TECHNOLOGY
PARK

HAWAIIAN ISLANDS
HUMPBACK WHALE
NATIONAL MARINE
SANCTUARY

AZEKA PLACE
SHOPPING
CENTER

31

Maui Nui
Golf Club

Kihei

To
Kula

KALAMA
PARK

S KIHEI RD

PIILANI HWY

KAMA'OLE BEACH
PARKS

Maui
Meadows

Keokea

KIHEI BOAT RAMP

KEAWAKAPU BEACH

MOKAPU &
ULUA BEACHES

37

THE SHOPS AT WAILEA

WAILEA BEACH

Wailea

POLO BEACH

MAKENA ALANUI RD

Wailea
Golf
Courses

PALAUEA BEACH (WHITE ROCK)

PO'OLENALENA

MAKENA LANDING

Makena Bay

KEAWALA'I
CHURCH (1832)

MALUAKA
BEACH

Makena

Ulupalakua
Ranch

Marine Life
Conservation
District

Oneuli Beach

SEABIRD
SANCTUARY

Pu'u Ola'i

31

MOLOKINI
CRATER

MAKENA
STATE PARK

'Ahihi Bay

'Alalakeiki Channel

Kanahena

MAKENA ALANUI RD

MAUI'S LAST
VOLCANIC
ERUPTION SITE
(1790)

To
Kipahulu/
Hana

'Ahihi-kina'u
Natural Area
Reserve

Cape Kina'u

La Pérouse
Bay

HOAPILI
TRAIL

Ancient Paved Road

0   3 mi

0   3 km

© AVALON TRAVEL

Your Best Day in South Maui

While there are dozens of different combinations for the perfect South Maui day, all tend to follow the same pattern of wake up early, get out on the water, and round out the day with beach time, lunch, more beach time, happy hour, and sunset.

Here's one example: wake up early and board *Kai Kanani* for the 6:30am Molokini Express tour. The tour leaves from Maluaka Beach in Makena and gets you out to **Molokini Crater** before all the other boats arrive. Spend an hour snorkeling and enjoy continental breakfast before returning to the beach at 8:30am with a full day left to explore. If you get a chance, fill up your reusable water bottle before you depart the boat.

You'll next make the drive to the "end of the road," hugging the coast and passing over the island's most recent lava flow. To stretch your legs, hike for 30 to 45 minutes on the **Hoapili Trail,** stopping to photograph the sandy beaches and watch for dolphins or whales. Back at your car, make the drive to **Makena State Park,** better known as **Big Beach,** and grab a quick lunch from whichever food truck is parked outside the First Entrance. Spend an hour strolling the beach or watching the local bodyboarders, and drive back to Maluaka Beach in Makena if you need to shower off.

At 4:30pm, park in the lot for Ulua Beach and walk to the Wailea Marriott, where dishes at **Migrant** are 50 percent off with drink specials until 6pm. Finish the day with a stroll along the **Wailea Coastal Walk,** where you can walk north past **Mokapu Beach** and watch the sunset from **Keawakapu**—leaving time to get back to your car before it's completely dark.

RAINY-DAY ALTERNATIVE

Rain in South Maui is exceptionally rare, and virtually unheard of in summer. On the drive north to Ma'alaea, stop at the **Hawaiian Islands Humpback Whale National Marine Sanctuary Visitors Center** before continuing on to the **Maui Ocean Center** to ogle sharks and rays. Get lunch downstairs at **Beach Bums Bar and Grill,** and on the drive back through Kihei, stop at **Maui Brewing Company** for a pint at the indoor tasting room.

PLANNING YOUR TIME

South Maui could be either your base for exploring the rest of the island or a sunny, sandy strip of paradise you have no plans to leave. Exploring the wild hinterlands of Makena should take about half a day, enjoying the hiking, snorkeling, beaches, and legendary sunsets. If you aren't staying in the Wailea resort, it's still nice to spend a whole day at one of the popular beaches, strolling the Wailea Coastal Walk and dining at the fancy resort restaurants. If you are staying in Wailea, do yourself a favor and spend one day where you don't leave the resort—just pool time, beach time, and maybe a massage to enjoy the luxurious surroundings. Kihei, on the other hand, deserves two days: two mornings to try out two different beaches and two afternoons to try out two different lunch spots. Ma'alaea requires only a few hours, as the only reason to go is to visit the Maui Ocean Center or catch a boat to Molokini Crater.

Sights

MA'ALAEA
★ Maui Ocean Center

There isn't a snorkeling spot on the island where you're going to see as wide a range of marinelife as at the **Maui Ocean Center** (192 Ma'alaea Rd., 808/270-7000, www.mauioceancenter.com, 9am-5pm daily Sept.-June, 9am-6pm daily July-Aug., $28 adults, $20 children). This three-acre marine park has the nation's largest collection of live tropical coral, and small children will enjoy the tidepool exhibits and the green sea turtle lagoon. Experience the 54-foot-long acrylic tunnel beneath a 750,000-gallon aquarium filled with dozens of rays and sharks, standing in a dry space and watching a tiger shark float right over you, or contemplating how spotted eagle rays look like birds as they buzz circles just a few feet from your head.

The center is deeply committed to educating visitors about the unique marine ecosystem. Did you know, for example, that nearly 25 percent of Hawaii's fish and coral species are found nowhere else on earth? The center is also a fantastic resource for learning about native Hawaiian culture, with exhibits on everything from Polynesian wayfaring to ancient Hawaiian fishponds. The center is set up to provide the animals with a realistic environment, and trained naturalists wander the grounds and give periodic talks about the various exhibits.

This is one of the island's best attractions for children as well as a rainy-day activity. Its popularity can mean crowds, however, so visit in the morning when the facility opens. There's a self-guided tour through the exhibits, and if you want to have some of them all to yourself, head directly to the last exhibit and work your way backward toward the front. Expect to spend about two hours, and if you purchase your tickets online beforehand, you can also add transportation ($5 pp). Book online for the family pass to save up to 15 percent.

KIHEI
Kealia Pond National Wildlife Refuge

The road between Ma'alaea and North Kihei

underwater magic at the Maui Ocean Center

passes through a large mudflat that parallels the shore. Most of this area is dry during summer, but on the inland side of the highway is 200-acre **Kealia Pond National Wildlife Refuge** (www.fws.gov/kealiapond). Visit to catch a glimpse of native bird species such as the *ae'o* (Hawaiian stilt) and *'alae ke'oke'o* (Hawaiian coot). Even if you aren't especially interested in **bird-watching,** the boardwalk off North Kihei Road is an informative place to stretch your legs and learn about the threats facing the island's species.

Ko'ie'ie Loko I'a Fishpond

Inside Kalepolepo Beach Park in North Kihei, the **Ko'ie'ie Loko I'a Fishpond** is the most prominent example of ancient Hawaiian life between Ma'alaea and Wailea. Estimated to be around 500 years old, it covered six acres and produced about 2,000 pounds of fish annually. It was formed by rocks passed by hand from the uplands to the sea, and thanks to the hard work of the **'Ao'ao O Na Loko I'a O Maui** (726 S. Kihei Rd., 808/359-1172, www.maui-fishpond.com)—volunteers who have been working since 1996 to restore the ancient fishpond—it can be viewed any time by visiting Kalepolepo Beach Park. For a unique experience, the organization offers guided cultural canoe trips at 8am Monday, Wednesday, and Friday for those who prearrange a visit.

★ Hawaiian Islands Humpback Whale National Marine Sanctuary Visitors Center

Right next door to Kalepolepo Beach Park is the **Hawaiian Islands Humpback Whale National Marine Sanctuary Visitors Center** (726 S. Kihei Rd., 808/879-2818, www.hawaiihumpbackwhale.noaa.gov, 10am-3pm Mon.-Sat., 10am-3pm Sat., free), a phenomenal educational resource for anyone with an interest in humpback whales. You can find plates of baleen, krill in a jar, and free binoculars out on the deck to view the whales in winter. There are also displays on turtles, dolphins, and teams that untangle whales, and while it's a bit out of the way in North Kihei, it's an easy stop when traveling from Ma'alaea back to Kihei or Wailea. Aside from the exhibits, the center also boasts some unique architecture: the 1940s-era coastal clapboard structure, seemingly better suited to Nantucket than North Kihei. The Ko'ie'ie fishpond is in front of the compound, which makes this a fun and educational side trip when visiting Kalepolepo Beach.

MAKENA

Makena has the most evidence of ancient culture and history in South Maui. This rugged, lava-strewn shore was home to a thriving population of ancient Hawaiians, and was believed to be the most populated region in South Maui during pre-contact times. When diseases and foreign plant and animal species were introduced by European explorers, however, the combination of outside forces ravaged the indigenous population, and many of the villages in Makena were abandoned. In a fitting twist to the tale, Makena is also the landing site of the first European explorer to set foot on Maui's shore—French explorer Jean-François de Galaup, compte de Lapérouse, in 1786. Despite the amount of history in Makena, many of the archaeological and cultural remnants are either on private land, in cordoned-off sanctuaries, or scattered along the shore in areas such as the Hoapili Trail. One site is open to visitors, and it parallels the plight of Makena's indigenous people.

The only horseback riding in South Maui is *way* south, at the end of the road at **Makena Stables** (8299 S. Makena Rd., 808/879-0244, www.makenastables.com), a family-run outfit that has been leading horseback riding tours since 1983. The trails meander over Ulupalakua Ranch, only accessible on a private tour. Along the way there's a good chance of spotting axis deer or wild goats that clamber across the jagged *'a'a* lava. This is one of the few horseback riding operations on the island with the possibility of riding your horse along the shore.

Beaches

When it comes to beach weather, even though South Maui is dry, other elements such as the wind and clouds can greatly affect the comfort level. The closer you are to Ma'alaea, the earlier in the day it gets windy—particularly in the summer. Since the afternoon trade winds begin their march in Ma'alaea, they progressively move from north to south through Kihei, Wailea, and ultimately Makena. During trade-wind weather patterns, the "Makena cloud" forms over Haleakala and extends out toward the island of Kaho'olawe, although this doesn't normally happen until the early afternoon. Consequently, the morning hours are the best time to hit the beach. In the afternoon, the pocket of beaches in south Kihei and Wailea have the best chance of being sunny and calm. Winter months aren't as windy, and this is also when humpback whales can be seen leaping offshore. Is it any wonder so many snowbirds choose to spend the winter here?

MA'ALAEA
Sugar Beach

If your picture-perfect vision of Hawaii is enjoying a long, lonely stroll down an isolated beach, **Sugar Beach** is going to be your favorite spot on the island. Bordered on one side by Kealia Pond National Wildlife Refuge and the waters of Ma'alaea Bay on the other, this undeveloped strip runs for five miles all the way to North Kihei.

There isn't any snorkeling here, although there can sometimes be waves for boogie boarding during summer. Rather, the main attraction here is taking a long, quiet stroll, and since most afternoons have very fierce trade winds, early morning is the best time to visit. To access Sugar Beach you can begin at the northern terminus at Haycraft Beach Park, the southern terminus in North Kihei, or at numerous entry points along North Kihei Road. If you park at Haycraft, be sure to lock your car—there are hidden homeless camps nearby.

historic Keawala'i Church in Makena

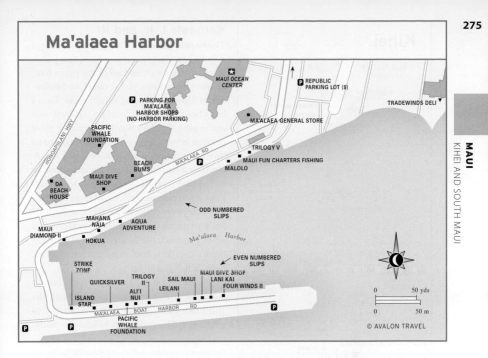

Ma'alaea Harbor

MAUI OCEAN CENTER

REPUBLIC PARKING LOT ($)

PARKING FOR MA'ALAEA HARBOR SHOPS (NO HARBOR PARKING)

TRADEWINDS DELI

PACIFIC WHALE FOUNDATION

MA'ALAEA GENERAL STORE

MA'ALAEA RD

TRILOGY V

BEACH BUMS

MAUI FUN CHARTERS FISHING

MALOLO

DA BEACH HOUSE

MAUI DIVE SHOP

ODD NUMBERED SLIPS

MAHANA NAIA

AQUA ADVENTURE

MAUI DIAMOND II

HOKUA

Ma'alaea Harbor

EVEN NUMBERED SLIPS

STRIKE ZONE

TRILOGY II

SAIL MAUI

MAUI DIVE SHOP

LANI KAI

QUICKSILVER

LEILANI

FOUR WINDS II

ALI'I NUI

ISLAND STAR

MA'ALAEA BOAT HARBOR RD

PACIFIC WHALE FOUNDATION

0   50 yds
0   50 m

© AVALON TRAVEL

MAUI
KIHEI AND SOUTH MAUI

KIHEI

Mai Poina 'Oe Ia'u Beach Park

On summer days with northerly winds, **Mai Poina 'Oe Ia'u Beach** is known as the "Kanaha of Kihei" for the windsurfing and kitesurfing crowd. In the morning hours, before the wind comes up, this beach is a nice place for taking a stroll and wandering around the dunes, and while there isn't any swimming and snorkeling is poor, there are picnic tables and pavilions for a meal by the water, and good stand-up paddling in the morning.

Kalepolepo Beach Park

Right next to the Hawaiian Islands Humpback Whale National Marine Sanctuary, **Kalepolepo Beach Park** is Kihei's most underrated beach. What makes this little-visited enclave so special is Ko'ie'ie Fishpond (page 273), which has been masterfully restored in recent years by local volunteers. Aside from its rich historical value, the fishpond is great for families with young children since it's a protected area for swimming.

Waipuilani Beach Park

Less beach and more park, the shoreline **Waipuilani Beach Park** in central Kihei is known to most locals as the dog park, since it's a popular place to run the family pet. It's a popular local gathering place—particularly for watching the sunset—and is one of North Kihei's most popular beaches, even though there's hardly any sand. To reach the parking area, turn on Waipuilani Road at the corner of South Kihei Road and the Maui Sunset condo.

The Cove

Otherwise known as "the surf lesson spot," **The Cove**, at the south end of Kalama Park, is known for its top-notch people-watching. The beach itself is just a small strip of sand, but it provides a front-row view for watching people surf. There's a volleyball court and shops across the street, and while it isn't Kihei's nicest beach, it's an action-packed hub of surfers, paddlers, and beachgoers soaking up rays.

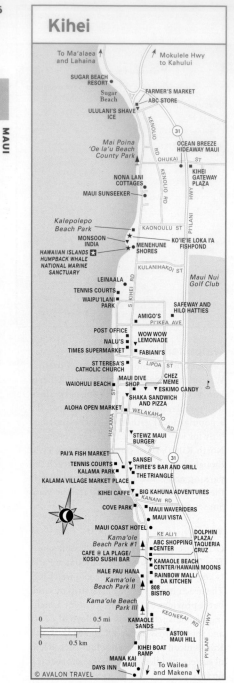

Kihei

To Ma'alaea and Lahaina

Mokulele Hwy to Kahului

SUGAR BEACH RESORT

Sugar Beach

FARMER'S MARKET
ABC STORE

ULULANI'S SHAVE ICE

KENOLIO RD

31

Mai Poina 'Oe Ia'u Beach County Park

OCEAN BREEZE HIDEAWAY MAUI

OHUKAI ST

KIHEI GATEWAY PLAZA

NONA LANI COTTAGES

KENOLIO RD

MAUI SUNSEEKER

PI'ILANI HWY

Kalepolepo Beach Park

KAONOULU ST

MONSOON INDIA

KO'IE'IE LOKA I'A FISHPOND

HAWAIIAN ISLANDS HUMPBACK WHALE NATIONAL MARINE SANCTUARY

MENEHUNE SHORES

KULANIHAKO'I ST

LEINAALA

Maui Nui Golf Club

TENNIS COURTS

WAIPU'ILANI PARK

S KIHEI RD

SAFEWAY AND HILO HATTIES

AMIGO'S

PI'IKEA AVE

POST OFFICE

WOW WOW LEMONADE

NALU'S

TIMES SUPERMARKET

FABIANI'S

E LIPOA ST

ST TERESA'S CATHOLIC CHURCH

MAUI DIVE SHOP

CHEZ MEME

WAIOHULI BEACH

ESKIMO CANDY

SHAKA SANDWICH AND PIZZA

ALOHA OPEN MARKET

HALAMA ST

WELAKAHAO RD

STEWZ MAUI BURGER

PAI'A FISH MARKET

SANSEI

31

TENNIS COURTS

THREE'S BAR AND GRILL

KALAMA PARK

THE TRIANGLE

KALAMA VILLAGE MARKET PLACE

KIHEI CAFFE

BIG KAHUNA ADVENTURES

KANANI RD

COVE PARK

MAUI WAVERIDERS

MAUI VISTA

MAUI COAST HOTEL

KE ALI'I

DOLPHIN PLAZA / TAQUERIA CRUZ

Kama'ole Beach Park #1

ABC SHOPPING CENTER

CAFE @ LA PLAGE / KOSIO SUSHI BAR

KAMAOLE BEACH CENTER / HAWAIIN MOONS

HALE PAU HANA

RAINBOW MALL / DA KITCHEN

Kama'ole Beach Park II

808 BISTRO

Kama'ole Beach Park III

KEONEKAI RD

0   0.5 mi

KAMAOLE SANDS

0   0.5 km

ASTON MAUI HILL

KIHEI BOAT RAMP

MANA KAI MAUI

PI'ILANI HWY

DAYS INN

To Wailea and Makena

© AVALON TRAVEL

Kamaole I, II, and III

The **Kamaole Beach Parks** form the core of Kihei's beach scene. Grassy areas run parallel to the roadway, and all of the parks have showers, restrooms, picnic tables, and barbecue grills for a relaxing sunset meal. Kam I has a beach volleyball court on the north side of the park. The best way to experience these beaches is to take a stroll along the coast and link all three together. The lava rock headlands can be rough on your feet and *kiawe* (mesquite) trees drop thorns, so wear footwear if you plan on walking all three beaches. The tide pools between Kam II and Kam III are a particularly nice place to explore, and when you reach the southern end of Kam III, there's a walking trail that runs for 0.75 mile to the Kihei Boat Ramp.

Mornings are the best time for stand-up paddling and snorkeling, and by noon the wind can pick up and turn the surface to whitecaps. These are great beaches for bodysurfing almost any time of year, but sometimes waves can get dangerously large on the biggest summer swells. Kam I and Kam II have street parking, whereas larger Kam III has its own parking lot exclusively for beachgoers. Kam III is also the party spot, where locals truck in horseshoes, ice chests, and bouncy houses for their three-year-olds' birthday parties. If you can't find parking, there's overflow parking between Kam III and the boat ramp.

Sometimes you will hear locals say they enjoy spending time at **Charley Young Beach;** this is just another name for the northern end of Kam I. It's protected from the wind when the southern section of the beach is choppy. Parking for Charley Young is along Kaiau Place, which is a small offshoot of South Kihei Road not far from the Cove Park.

★ Keawakapu Beach

Aside from Kam III, **Keawakapu** is Kihei's most popular beach. This long stretch of sand is more protected from the wind than the beaches farther north, and a small shop on the north end of the beach rents out stand-up paddleboards, kayaks, and snorkeling gear. In morning, before the wind picks up, this beach is a bustle of snorkelers entering the water and kids splashing in the surf, and by late afternoon, it changes into the perfect perch for the sunset. Snorkeling is best around the north and south headlands, and if you're feeling up for a really long stroll, you can connect with the Wailea Coastal Walk (page 295) at the southern end of the beach.

The north end of the beach has ample parking, and the lot is located off South Kihei Road on the north side of the Days Inn. To reach the south end of Keawakapu—which is much calmer—when South Kihei Road begins to head uphill, continue driving straight until the road dead ends in a small parking lot. There aren't many parking spaces here, although there is a small shower for hosing off. There's also a central entrance to Keawakapu that's known as Sidewalks, with public parking on the corner of Kilohana Drive and South Kihei Road.

WAILEA
Ulua Beach and Mokapu Beach
Ulua and **Mokapu** are the northernmost of Wailea's beaches, separated by a small grassy headland. Mokapu is on the north side of the hill, Ulua is on the south, and the point that separates the two is one of Wailea's best snorkeling spots. Ulua is slightly larger than Mokapu and more protected from the surf. Mokapu Beach is also the northern terminus of the Wailea Coastal Walk, although the trail technically crosses the sand dune and continues to the southern end of Keawakapu. Restrooms and showers are available. A large public parking lot is at the bottom of Ulua Beach Road, just north of the Shops at Wailea.

Wailea Beach
Home to Maui's "see and be seen" crowd, **Wailea Beach** epitomizes Wailea. Fronted by the Grand Wailea and the Four Seasons Maui, this is a beach where CEOs and professional athletes mingle with regular travelers.

The beach is constantly abuzz with activity, as there's snorkeling around Wailea Point, stand-up paddleboard rentals, outrigger canoe tours, and dozens of visitors playing in the surf who are happy to just be in Maui. Despite the private nature of the resorts, public access to the beach is quite easy, as there is a large public parking lot just before the entrance to the Four Seasons. In the parking lot are public restrooms and showers.

Polo Beach
Polo Beach is the southernmost of Wailea's resort beaches, and is the southern terminus of the Wailea Coastal Walk. The cloud-white Fairmont Kea Lani dominates the shore, its Arabian spires providing a unique backdrop

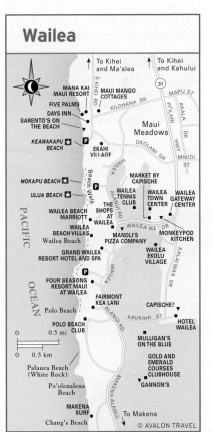

Wailea

to the shimmering blue waters. Of all of Wailea's beaches, Polo Beach is the most popular with locals due to the large public parking area being a convenient place for launching stand-up paddleboards and kayaks. There are public restrooms, showers, and one small barbecue grill. Polo Beach can also be good for boogie boarding in summer, and there is a small activity booth on the north side of the beach if you want to rent a paddleboard or kayak. To reach Polo Beach, travel south along Wailea Alanui Road before making a right on Kaukahi Street and following it to the end.

MAKENA AND BEYOND
Palauea Beach (White Rock)

If you're looking for a beach that isn't as crowded as Wailea or Polo Beach, stroll south to **Palauea Beach,** otherwise known as **White Rock.** For decades this area was about bonfires and guitars rather than gates and security cameras, but recently the mega-mansion sprawl has found its way to the shore. Parking for Palauea is along the side of Makena Road, and public access is at the southern end of the beach, next to the lonely portable toilet. Snorkeling is good around both ends of the beach, and while there aren't

any facilities, restrooms, or showers, you can find all of those at Polo Beach just a five-minute walk away.

Po'olenalena Beach

Once frequented only by locals, **Po'olenalena Beach** can now get so busy it's tough to find a space in the potholed parking lot. There are volleyball games on Sunday afternoon, and the beach is a favorite for watching the sunset. On the north end, a small trail leads from the parking lot around a rocky point, bringing you to a cove that isn't visible from the road. There are usually about 10 percent of the people on the cove beach as on Po'olenalena. It's the perfect spot to escape with a beach chair, an umbrella, and a good book.

To find Po'olenalena, travel on Wailea Alanui Road until you see Wailea Golf Club Drive on the left. Continue straight for one more minute to see the parking area for the beach on your right. For the public parking lot on the south end of the beach, look for the lot just before Makena Surf on the right side of the road. Barely visible and with only 10 spots, it's next to the yellow fire hydrant numbered 614.

Big Beach at Makena State Park

Makena

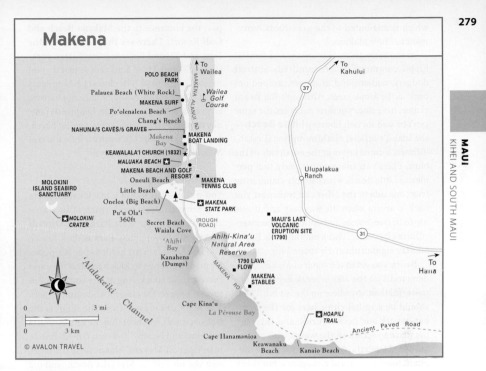

Chang's Beach

If you're looking for a pocket of sand with exceptional snorkeling and not too many people, **Chang's Beach** will be your favorite spot in Makena. Not many make it here because it's hidden from the road. Chang's Beach is about 1.5 miles past the Fairmont Kea Lani on Makena Alanui Road. Look for the small parking lot immediately past Makena Surf. If you find a spot in the parking lot *before* the Makena Surf building (the one by fire hydrant 614), walk south for 100 yards past the gated entrance, and another parking lot with six spaces is on the right, by fire hydrant 616. From here a paved walkway leads down to the shore and the fingernail of sand.

★ Maluaka Beach

Directly in front of the Makena Beach and Golf Resort, **Maluaka Beach** is everything you've ever wanted in a beach. Locals refer to it as **Prince Beach**, since the hotel used to be called the Maui Prince. There's good

snorkeling around the north end, fun waves for boogie boarding during the summer, ample parking, restrooms and showers, and a grassy area for relaxing.

Maluaka Beach has two different entrances. On the north side, coming in on Makena Alanui, make a right on Honoiki Street, then a left onto Makena Road, to the public parking lot across from Keawala'i Church. For the south entrance, continue on Makena Alanui until you pass the entrance for the Makena Beach and Golf Resort, then continue past the turnoff for the golf and tennis club. As the road bends around to the right, you'll see a sign for Makena Keone'o'io on the right. Make a right, and follow it to the parking area.

★ Makena State Park

Among the string of golden shores, none can hold a sandy candle to **Oneloa,** or **Big Beach.** As the largest beach in Makena State Park, this mile-long stretch of sand has avoided the rush of development, much of which is attributed to the grassroots movement to "Save Makena."

In the early 1970s this area was a famous hippie commune, where hundreds of draft dodgers, nudists, and dropouts camped out back in the *kiawe* trees. Although Big Beach visitors have since put their pants on, the same can't be said for neighboring **Little Beach**—the island's official clothing-optional establishment located just over the north side of the bluff. There's an anachronistic aura that permeates Little Beach, where simply clambering from one side to the other can transport you back to an era when life was easy and it was hip to be free. For an authentic Maui counterculture experience, check out the Little Beach Sunday night drum circle (page 298).

Before you get in the water at Makena, understand that the shore-break here is more powerful than anywhere on the island. There should be a spinal clinic here for the number of back and neck injuries, and this isn't the place to splash in the waves with a boogie board from the ABC Store. There are lifeguard towers in case of emergency, but think twice before entering the water on days when there's any surf.

To reach Big Beach and Makena State Park, travel on Makena Alanui road for one mile past the entrance to the Makena Beach and Golf Resort. There are three entrances; the First and Second Entrances have large parking areas, and Third Entrance is just dirt on the side of the road. The closest parking spots are at First Entrance, and be sure not to leave any valuables in your vehicle. Despite its popularity, there still are no showers at Big Beach, and the nearest place to wash off the sand is at Maluaka Beach, 0.5 mile north.

Oneuli Beach

You did it—you found a black-sand beach. The famous black-sand beach is in Hana, at Wai'anapanapa State Park, and **Oneuli Beach** in Makena State Park is dark brown and less famous. This hidden spot is a popular place for locals to kick back and fish, and there's good snorkeling at the south end of the bay only on the clearest and calmest days. The main draw, aside from the sand, is the lack of crowds, but note that the access road is potholed and bumpy. To reach Oneuli Beach, turn right off Makena Alanui Road 0.2 miles past the turnoff for Maluaka Beach, and 0.2 miles before the first entrance to Big Beach.

Pa'ako Beach (Secret Cove)

If you want to go back home and tell your

Secret Cove

friends you found the "secret beach" on Maui, take the time to visit this gem. The problem is that even though **Pa'ako Beach** is also called **Secret Cove,** the tiny inlet of sand is anything but secret. Weddings take place on a daily basis, and the chances of having it to yourself are slim. To access the beach, you have to walk through a hole in a lava rock wall just south of the Third Entrance for Big Beach. Watch carefully to find the tiny opening. As you climb up and over a little hill where Big Beach ends, you will notice a lava rock wall running along the right side of the road. Next to the speed table is a blue Beach Access sign and a shoulder-width opening in the lava rock

wall. If you're not sure if you're at the right spot, a telephone pole on the other side of the street has the code E2 3 written on it. The easiest access is to park at the Third Entrance for Big Beach and walk the rest of the way. As you might expect, sunsets here are as epic as they get.

Keawanaku Beach

If you're up for an epic hiking adventure to a beach hardly anyone knows about, put on your hiking boots and make the trek to **Keawanaku Beach.** The round-trip journey takes at least two hours on the Hoapili Trail (page 295).

Snorkeling

MA'ALAEA

Although you'll often see little red dive flags fluttering in the wind off the harbor at **Ma'alaea Bay,** these are local spearfishers who are diving for *tako* (octopus). Don't mistake this for a nice snorkeling spot. Although Ma'alaea Bay once had a teeming reef prior to the 1990s, nearly 100 percent of it has died due to invasive species of algae. It has been a case study for what will happen to all the island's reefs if environmental dangers go unmitigated.

★ Molokini Crater

When it comes to snorkeling, what Ma'alaea is known for is the harbor that serves as the starting point for boats to **Molokini Crater,** a half-submerged volcanic caldera that rises in 300 feet of water. Visibility here can be 100 feet or better nearly every day of the year. Nowhere else in Hawaii has water this consistently calm and clear. The back of Molokini Crater drops to almost 300 feet, but inside the bowl, where snorkel boats tie up, is only about 40 feet deep, and the best snorkeling is along the rim of the crater in 15 feet of water. At Molokini you have a great chance of finding colorful parrotfish,

endemic reef species, octopuses, eels, and—if you're lucky—maybe a harmless whitetip reef shark. One species notably absent from Molokini, however, are Hawaiian green sea turtles—although most tour operators combine a trip to Molokini with a second snorkeling spot along the coast of Maui so that you can check turtles off your list. Although Molokini Crater is best known for snorkeling, few people know that the 161-foot-tall islet is also a seabird sanctuary, home to a healthy population of *'ua'u kani* as well as soaring frigates. If you're an avid birder and are planning a trip to Molokini, bring binoculars to check out what's happening above water, not just down on the reef.

Because it's so massively popular, however, Molokini is a place where it can sometimes seem like there are far more humans than fish. To avoid the crowds, book your trip for as early as possible before most other boats arrive. Schedule this activity early in your trip, since you'll probably be waking up early anyway with a little bit of jet lag. If you visited Molokini 20 years ago and are returning for a second trip, you might notice there are fewer fish. Fish feeding, a popular activity during the 1980s, completely disrupted the area's natural food chain, and a handful of species took over the reef. In an effort to return the crater to its former health, Molokini is now a tightly controlled marine preserve, and you'll be required to fill out a form that outlines the rules for visiting.

Boats to Molokini fall into three categories: small, medium, and large. The cheaper the ticket to Molokini, the more people there are going to be on the boat, which also means the more people there are going to be snorkeling with you. The larger boats, which are diesel catamarans, carry 150 people during busier months. There are three sailboat companies that carry 20 to 50 people. Three raft companies carry up to 24 and get you to Molokini quickly and easily. These trips can be economical, and the small group size ensures personalized service, but the tradeoff is that the food won't be as good as on larger boats, and the restroom situation can be tight. Rafts aren't recommended for anyone who is pregnant or has back or neck problems.

morning snorkel

Nearly all boats leave for Molokini from Ma'alaea Harbor. Note that Lahaina Harbor is not a departure point for Molokini Crater. Three rafts and most scuba-diving boats leave from Kihei Boat Ramp. At Makena, the sailing catamaran *Kai Kanani* departs from Maluaka Beach; its early trip is one of the first to arrive at Molokini.

Rental Shops

The best place for renting snorkel gear in Ma'alaea is at **Maui Dive Shop** (300 Ma'alaea Harbor Rd., 808/244-5514, www.mauidiveshop.com, 6am-6pm daily) in the Ma'alaea Harbor Shops. There is a wide range of snorkeling equipment for rent or purchase, and you can pick up an optical mask if you normally wear prescription glasses.

Snorkeling Charters

Trilogy (Slip 62 and Slip 99, 808/874-5649, www.sailtrilogy.com) has been the gold standard for charter boats in Maui for 45 years. Its Molokini trip ($129 adults) is pricier than the budget options, but you get what you pay for:

Trilogy boats have only 40 to 50 passengers, snuba is available as an upgrade, and you get to enjoy a sailing catamaran to feel the breeze in your hair. The 7am trip on the *Trilogy V* departs from Slip 99, and the 8am trip is on the larger and newer *Trilogy II* from Slip 62. On Monday, Wednesday, and Friday, Trilogy also offers the adults-only Captain's Sunset Dinner Sail ($129), focusing on luxury dining and drinking.

The company with the largest presence in Ma'alaea Harbor is **Pacific Whale Foundation** (300 Ma'alaea Boat Harbor Rd., 808/249-8811, www.pacificwhale.org, 6am-9pm daily), a nonprofit organization that has its headquarters in the Ma'alaea Harbor Shops. Instead of checking in down at the harbor, check in at the shop. These cruises are more economical than some of the higher-priced excursions, although on busy days you could be sharing the boat with more than 100 people. Note that the boat cruises, Pacific Whale Foundation Eco-Adventures, are a for-profit business, and the nonprofit arm of

Molokini Snorkeling Tips

During about 80 percent of the year, the trade winds are so strong that Molokini Crater is filled with four-foot waves by noon, so boats **go there early in the morning.** A discount tour to Molokini that departs at 2pm, conditions permitting, is a scam, since conditions will rarely be permitting. You might get lucky, but chances are you'll end up snorkeling at a spot named Coral Gardens.

Most of the year, and every day in summer, **the ride back to Ma'alaea Harbor is very rough,** with 30-knot winds and sheets of spray coming over the bow. Some people love the ride, and although it's not dangerous, others are terrified. Grab a sheltered seat toward the back of the boat and brace yourself.

The water temperature in Maui fluctuates between 73°F in winter and 79°F in summer—colder than the Gulf of Mexico, but still warmer than most oceans. If you go on one of the large diesel boats, you will be asked if you want to rent a wetsuit. The crew receives a commission, so expect a sales pitch. **Don't rent a wetsuit** unless you think you will actually need one.

Molokini Crater offers dozens of species of fish, impossibly clear water, and healthy, vibrant corals, but **there are no green sea turtles.** All of the turtles are found along the southern shore, so if you want to see some turtles, book a charter that stops along the shore.

If there is large surf along the southern shore (more frequent in summer than winter), **the water color at Turtle Town will be closer to green than blue.** If the visibility along the shore isn't what you expected, it's due to increased surf.

Even if you book an early tour to beat the afternoon's trade winds, if the wind is blowing out of the north, Molokini isn't accessible. Often this wind switch can occur within minutes, so **there is a chance you'll end up snorkeling at a secondary spot,** which usually still ends up being a good trip.

Molokini Crater is a tightly controlled marine reserve. Feeding fish or stepping on coral can carry heavy penalties. **Don't feed the fish!**

the company is funded by merchandise sales and gear rentals.

The **Pride of Maui** (101 Ma'alaea Boat Harbor Rd., 808/242-0955, www.prideofmaui. com, 6am-8pm daily) offers a five-hour excursion ($101 adults) aboard a large power catamaran that features a glass-bottom viewing area and a large top deck for sunning. Trips depart at 8am next to the U.S. Coast Guard station. This popular boat can frequently load over 100 passengers. During the summer and fall months, when it isn't whale season, there's also a 3.5-hour afternoon snorkel trip ($50 adults) to a location along the West Maui shore.

The catamaran **Four Winds II** (Slip 80, 808/879-8188, www.fourwindsmaui.com) offers excursions in the morning (7am daily, $105 adults) to Molokini and in the afternoon ($49) to Coral Gardens. The catamaran has a mast, but it's often so windy in Ma'alaea Bay

that the boat isn't able to sail. Small children will love the glass-bottom part of the boat when stopped at Molokini, and unlike other boats that also make a stop along the shore, **Four Winds** makes Molokini its only stop, so you have plenty of time to relax and explore the crater at your own pace. The downside is that you won't get the chance to snorkel with turtles, although you do make a stop at a "turtle cleaning station" to view the turtles from above.

If you want to visit Molokini from Ma'alaea but don't want to spend a lot of time getting there, the **Aqua Adventure** (Slip 51, 808/573-2104, www.mauisnorkelsnuba.com) leaves at 7:15am and cruises at speeds much faster than the larger boats. The small number of passenger, capped at 40, is also a plus, and snuba gets people in the water. You can choose to snorkel, but if your main priority is getting to Molokini quickly to snuba dive, this trip

($108 adults) visits two snorkeling spots and offers an additional upgrade for snuba. Trips return by noon.

KIHEI

Mornings are the best time of day for snorkeling in **Kihei**, before the wind picks up. Winter mornings offer light winds, clear visibility, and calm water, and as an added bonus, if you dive down a few feet while snorkeling, you're guaranteed to hear whale song reverberating in the distance. Summer can have intermittent periods of high surf, which can affect visibility.

Snorkeling Spots

The northernmost beach in Kihei to **snorkel** is **Charley Young Beach,** also known as the north end of Kamaole I. There's a rocky point on the right side of the beach that offers good snorkeling, and at the southern end of the beach, the rocky points between **Kamaole I** and **Kamaole II,** and **Kamaole II** and **Kamaole III,** have colorful reef fish and turtles.

Keawakapu beach, 0.5 mile south of Kamaole III, has good snorkeling on both the north and south sides of the bay. The north end can get crowded due to the large public parking lot and bustling activity stand, and if you want to escape the crowd, either get here early, before everyone arrives, or just snorkel the outer edge of the reef in front of the Mana Kai hotel. To combine a morning snorkel with a stroll, park at the northern end of Keawakapu Beach and walk to the southern point. There are fewer crowds, it has a larger area for snorkeling, and the walk back to your car is one of the island's best beach walks.

Rental Shops

Maui Dive Shop (1455 S. Kihei Rd., 808/879-3388, 7am-9pm daily) is a reputable option for anything related to snorkeling or diving, and **Boss Frog's** (main office 1770 S. Kihei Rd., 808/874-5225, www.bossfrog.com, 8am-5pm daily) has three locations in Kihei and some of the island's cheapest rentals. The company is heavily embedded in the activities sales market, so expect a sales pitch.

Snorkel Bob's has multiple stores in Kihei, including the Kamaole Beach Center (2411 S. Kihei Rd., 808/879-7449, www.snorkelbob.com, 8am-5pm daily), and another in the Azeka II shopping area in Central Kihei (1279 S. Kihei Rd., 808/875-6188, 8am-5pm daily). Snorkel Bob's is a statewide chain that also incorporates activity sales, and you're sure to see its quirky ads if you flip through any island visitors magazines. Snorkel Bob's is known for selling gear it designs itself, and a nice feature of the operation is that you can rent gear on one island and return it on another island free of charge. Packages range from $2 per day for a basic mask and snorkel rental to $44 per week for a package that includes prescription lenses and fins.

Snorkeling Boats

The great thing about the snorkeling charters from Kihei Boat Ramp is it only takes 15 minutes to reach Molokini Crater (compared to an hour from Ma'alaea Harbor). The rafts only carry about 24 people, so if you don't like crowds, these are the trips for you, unless you're pregnant or have back or neck problems.

Blue Water Rafting (808/879-7238, www.bluewaterrafting.com) meets at the boat ramp at 6:30am. If you've already been to Molokini and are looking for an adventure snorkel, Blue Water has a trip to the Kanaio Coast, where you can snorkel along a volcanic coast most visitors will never see. This forgotten southwestern coast is pockmarked with thundering sea caves and jagged lava formations, and there are multiple places where you can see the remnants of ancient fishing villages. The captains are geologists, historians, and marine naturalists, skilled enough to hug the coast so closely you could almost reach out and touch it. The waters in this area can be rough, however, so this isn't the best trip if you're prone to motion sickness. Book the four-hour Kanaio Coastline tour ($110 adults, $89 children) or combine it with an 11am excursion to Molokini ($135 adults, $110 children). A two-hour tour to Molokini ($55 adults, $45 children) departs at 11:30am and is one of the most affordable options for visiting the crater. There is no breakfast, coffee, or restroom on board, and the minimum age for children is four.

The other primary snorkeling option from Kihei Boat Ramp is **Redline Rafting** (808/757-9211, www.redlinerafting.com), which differs from Blue Water Rafting in that this company goes to Molokini first, even taking time to snorkel the backside of the crater in 300 feet of water. From there the boat motors down toward Keoneʻoʻio (La Perouse Bay) to snorkel and search for dolphins, and then explores the northern fringes of the rugged Kanaio Coast. Because this tour visits Molokini, it doesn't go as far south as Blue Water Rafting, although it is one of the earliest boats to the crater. Tours ($135 adults, $110 children) meet at 6:30am and include breakfast, coffee, and a boat with a restroom.

WAILEA
★ Ulua Beach and Mokapu Beach

The best locations for snorkeling in Wailea are **Ulua Beach** and **Mokapu Beach,**

listed together because the rocky point that separates them is where you'll find the most marinelife. Ulua, the southernmost, is more protected and offers a gentle, sandy entry. This is the perfect spot for beginning snorkelers. Morning hours are calm and are the best time for finding turtles. Winter months have the best visibility, and if you're staying at one of the Wailea resorts, you can reach the beaches by strolling along the Wailea Coastal Walk. If you are driving, there are two small public parking lots that fill up early; arrive before 9am. To reach the parking area, turn on Ulua Beach Road off Wailea Alanui Drive just north of the Shops at Wailea, and follow the road down to the parking lots at the end.

Wailea Point

The second most popular spot for snorkeling in Wailea is **Wailea Point,** a rocky promontory rife with green sea turtles that separates the Four Seasons and Fairmont Kea Lani. The easiest point of entry is from the south side of Wailea Beach in front of the Four Seasons, but be prepared for a five-minute swim over sand.

Rental Shops

You could pay $25 per day for a set of snorkeling gear from a stand on Wailea Beach, or you

Mokapu Beach

could make the short walk over to **Maui Dive Shop** (3750 Wailea Alanui Rd., 808/875-9904, www.mauidiveshop.com, 8am-7pm daily), inside the Shops of Wailea, where snorkeling gear is $9 per day or $25 per week.

MAKENA AND BEYOND

While Makena offers some of the south side's best snorkeling, the entry and exit points can be a little more challenging than at Kihei or Wailea beaches. Makena is more exposed to southerly swell than the beaches to the north are, so visibility is affected and waves can sometimes crash into the lava rocks with such fury that it's the last place you want to be. Assess the conditions and your own abilities before venturing into the water.

Snorkeling Spots

The best place for beginner **snorkeling** in Makena is **Maluaka Beach,** in front of the Makena Beach and Golf Resort. There's a rocky point that wraps around the north end of the beach, and the entry from the sand into the water is gentle.

While Maluaka might be the easiest place to snorkel in Makena, the best snorkeling is at **Makena Landing.** The entry can be a little challenging, but once you make it out past the shallow areas, you'll be glad you made the effort. There are multiple entry and exit points for Makena Landing, the most common being the public parking area off Makena Road. To reach the parking area, drive along Makena Alanui until you reach Honoiki Street and the turn for Keawala'i Church. When you reach the bottom of Honoiki, turn right and follow the road 0.25 mile until you see a parking area on the left.

Once in the water, hug the coast toward the point on the right, and when you have rounded the tip, you'll notice there is a long finger of lava underwater that extends out toward Molokini. This is what's known as the South Finger, and there's a sea cave here that houses green sea turtles. This area is referred to as **Turtle Town** by many snorkel

boat operators, and unless you want to share the water with 200 other snorkelers, try to be out here before 10am. If you swim north from the South Finger, you will pass over lime-green coral heads. Keep an eye out for moray eels or the strange-looking flying gurnard. Eventually you'll come to the North Finger, another underwater lava formation that houses many turtles. This finger is covered in bright-red slate-pencil urchins that the ancient Hawaiians used for red dye. Eagle rays and manta rays are sometimes seen off the deeper end of the finger.

While there have been lots of complaints about the parts of Ahihi Kinau Natural Area Reserve that are closed, parts of the beautiful coast are still open, including **Waiala Cove,** a small, rocky, and mostly protected bay with crystal clear water for snorkeling. Since this area is so popular, and the road so narrow, it's common for there to be traffic jams, so rather than trying to park on the road, continue driving 0.2 miles to the parking lot for Kanahena Cove. Here you'll find a gravel trail that winds its way back toward Waiala Cove. The best entry is on the northern side, just a few feet off of the road. While Waiala has great snorkeling when the water is calm, if waves are breaking inside the bay, it's best to go someplace else. At **Kanahena Cove,** follow the trail from the large parking lot down to the rocky coast to snorkel the reef that's known to local surfers and divers as **Dumps.** This spot gets very busy, especially in winter, and in summer there is frequently large breaking surf that makes it too dangerous to snorkel.

For a map of the Makena area, staff with the Department of Land and Natural Resources have a small office in the parking lot. They've also erected signs with yellow fish that show the best places to snorkel (for the record, the fish is the *lauwiliwilinukunuku'oi'oi*—say that 10 times fast). To reach the Kanahena parking lot, travel 2.5 miles past Makena Beach and Golf Resort, or about 1 mile past Makena State Park. Because break-ins have been a problem, don't leave any valuables in the car.

a friendly critter of the reef

Finally, just when you think the road will never end, the asphalt gives way to a gravel parking lot in a spot known as **Keone'o'io,** or **La Perouse Bay.** The lava field that you drive over on the way to La Perouse is the remnants of Haleakala's last eruption. The bay is named for the French explorer Jean-François de Galaup, compte de Lapérouse, who in 1786 was the first European to set foot on Maui at this very spot. As you enter the parking area, there's a stone structure memorializing this event.

The snorkeling in La Perouse Bay can be phenomenal, although there are also times when it can be a total bust. Early mornings are best, before the trade winds fill the bay with whitecaps, and summer can bring large

surf, which turns the shore into a cauldron of white water. On calm days, however, the best snorkeling is found to the right of the parking lot, where you must scramble across a lava rock point to reach the protected inlet. The water here is an enchanting turquoise against the young black lava rock.

Snorkeling Boats

Kai Kanani (808/879-7218, www.kaikanani. com) is the snorkeling boat leaving from Makena. Only a few years old and still sparkling, it has all the added amenities you would expect from a luxury yacht, with top-notch captains. *Kai Kanani* departs directly from Maluaka Beach in front of the Makena Beach and Golf Resort, which, if you're staying in Makena, or even Wailea, makes it a far more convenient option for sailing to Molokini than driving to Ma'alaea Harbor.

If that weren't enough, it also offers free transportation to the beach from Wailea resorts. If Molokini was too crowded the last time you visited, *Kai Kanani*'s early morning Molokini Express charter ($75 adults) departs the beach at 6:30am and guarantees you're the first boat at the crater, since it only takes about 15 minutes to motor across the channel. This trip is just over two hours long, and while the second trip of the day ($150 adults) visits the crater when it's more crowded, the fact that it's four hours long as opposed to two allows for twice the amount of snorkeling time in twice the number of spots. If you're concerned about getting seasick, the journey time from Maluaka Beach to Molokini is much shorter than the journey between Molokini and Ma'alaea. On Monday, Wednesday, and Friday, it also offers a champagne and cocktail sunset cruise ($91 adults).

Scuba Diving

South Maui has some of the island's best shore diving, and with so many locations and so many different operators, planning your dives can be overwhelming. The information in this section will help you find the operations and locations that suit you best.

MA'ALAEA
Dive Sites

While **Molokini Crater** can be a great place to snorkel, to truly experience the crater's magic, you have to put on a tank. For experienced divers Molokini ranks among the best dive locations around the world, and for novices it's a window into a new aquatic universe. Only certified divers are allowed to dive at Molokini. If you aren't certified but want to experience it from below, sign up for a 20-minute snuba dive to depths of up to 10 feet.

What makes the crater such an exceptional dive spot is the combination of its pelagic location, where it's possible to see anything, and the multiple dive spots within the crater that cater to a wide range of ability levels. Novices will enjoy either Middle Reef or Reef's End, as depths don't usually exceed 70 feet. **Middle Reef** is home to pelagic species such as jacks and reef sharks, and the sand channel houses curious-looking garden eels. There's also a huge drop-off at the Middle Reef section where it can be easy to exceed your depth.

The best and most advanced dive in Molokini Crater is a drift dive of the legendary **Back Wall.** Beginning at Reef's End, divers follow the current along the back of Molokini, where a vertical wall drops 250 feet to the ocean floor. If you use nitrox or mixed gases, this is the deepest dive available anywhere in Maui County.

Even though diving at Molokini offers a chance of seeing sharks, if you want a guarantee of diving with them, the most unique dive on the island is at the **Maui Ocean Center** (192 Ma'alaea Rd., 808/270-7000, www.

mauioceancenter.com, 9am-6pm daily Jul.-Aug., 9am-5pm daily Sept.-June), where you can go diving *inside the shark tank.* As part of its **Shark Dive Maui** program, certified divers are able to spend 40 minutes surrounded by various species, including hammerhead and tiger sharks. The basic dive ($199) has a limit of four divers and is offered Monday- Friday, with a check-in at 8am. The cost includes the tank and the weight, although divers have to provide the rest of their gear. Although diving at an aquarium might seem like cheating, even some of Maui's most seasoned divers claim it's a great dive. More than just a novelty, this is your best opportunity to be completely surrounded by the ocean's most feared and misrepresented creatures. There are also deluxe ($242) and complete ($259) dive packages.

Rental Operators

The only retail operator in Ma'alaea that rents out dive gear is **Maui Dive Shop** (300 Ma'alaea Harbor Rd., 808/244-5514, www. mauidiveshop.com, 6am-6pm daily) in the Ma'alaea Harbor Shops. Although most dive operations furnish their own gear, this is a good place to pick up equipment if you're diving at the Maui Ocean Center or need accessories.

Dive Boats

Although most Molokini dive boats depart from the Kihei Boat Ramp, two that depart from Ma'alaea Harbor are the 48-foot *Maka Koa,* operated by Maui Dive Shop (808/875-1775, www.mauidiveshop.com), as well as the 40-foot *Maui Diamond II* (Slip 23, 808/879-9119, www.mauidiamond.com). Maui Dive Shop offers two-tank trips to Molokini Crater six times per week, and the second dive is either along the shore of Maui or at the *St. Anthony* wreck off Kihei. Rates for a two-tank dive are $150, and renting a buoyancy control device and a regulator is an additional $30.

exploring the contours of South Maui's shore

Keawakapu Beach. Maui Dive Shop offers dives to this part of a massive artificial reef system twice weekly as part of a two-tank excursion combined with Molokini.

Rental and Shore-Dive Operators

If you need to rent gear, get gear serviced, pick up tanks for a shore dive, or book a guided shore dive with an instructor, there are a number of different retail operators throughout Kihei. My top pick is **Maui Dreams** (1993 S. Kihei Rd., 808/874-5332, www.mauidreamsdiveco.com, 7am-6pm daily) in the shop across from the southern end of Kalama Park. These guys love to dive and offer a full range of excursions, including scooter dives ($99), night dives ($79), and regular introductory dives ($89). Guided shore dives for certified divers are $69. Maui Dreams is also the only PADI Five-Star Instructor Development Center in South Maui, so these guys literally instruct the instructors. If you want to complete your scuba certification, you can do so for as little as $299 if you've already completed the E-Learning section that's found on the PADI website.

Inside the Azeka Makai shopping center, **B&B Scuba** (1280 S. Kihei Rd., 808/875-2861, www.bbscuba.com, 8am-6pm Mon.-Fri., 8am-5pm Sat.-Sun.) offers guided shore dives ($75), night dives ($75), and scooter dives ($119) along the South Maui shore. Other operators focus on recreational diving, but B&B offers PADI certification classes and IANTD tech diving classes with trimix, nitrox, and rebreather training. B&B also provides gear rental and tank pumping.

Dive Boats

All dive boats in Kihei leave from Kihei Boat Ramp, just south of Kamaole III Beach. Parking is tight in the main lot, so head to the overflow lot on the right. The scene at the boat ramp in the morning can be hectic—especially in the dark. Most boats offer coffee aboard if you still need a wake-up, and most boats have private restrooms. Since a number

Snorkelers are allowed to accompany divers for $90. The trip is a good option for novice divers who want to explore in the 65- to 70-foot range. An added perk of booking with Maui Dive Shop is that it provides transportation from your hotel to Ma'alaea Harbor. Check-in is at 6:15am at the store in the Ma'alaea Harbor Shops.

For a few dollars less, *Maui Diamond II* offers two-tank trips to Molokini and the South Maui shore ($139), and rental of a buoyancy control device and a regulator is an additional $20. If you aren't a certified diver, you have the option of partaking in a Discover Scuba Diving introductory class, where you will snorkel at Molokini and then dive with an instructor at the second spot along the shore. The cost of the snorkel and introductory dive combo ($155) includes all your equipment.

KIHEI
Dive Sites

The only real dive site in Kihei is the *St. Anthony* **Wreck** off the south end of of boats that leave from Kihei Boat Ramp don't have offices, bring a credit card or cash so you can pay on board. If you plan on diving during your time in Maui, bring your certification card.

Of all the choices in Kihei, the top pick among locals is **Mike Severns** (808/879-6596, www.mikesevernsdiving.com), Kihei's original dive-boat operation. A number of the other operators in Kihei provide exceptional service, but it's impossible to beat Mike Severn's. An instructor will sit down with you, take out a book, and thoroughly explain the species you just saw. At Mike Severn's, the instructors wrote those books. Since Mike Severn's caters to seasoned divers, the instructors don't mandate "follow the leader," giving you the freedom to enjoy the dive at your own pace. Two-tank dives are $139, plus $15 for gear rental. Meet at 6am at the Kihei Boat Ramp aboard the 38-foot *Pilikai*.

Also among South Maui's best, **Ed Robinson's** (808/879-3584, www.mauiscuba.com) caters to advanced divers and underwater photographers. Meet at 6:30am at the Kihei Boat Ramp. Regular two-tank dives ($129) are offered Monday, Thursday, and Saturday. More advanced two-tank drift dives ($129) are offered Sunday and Friday, and a three-tank dive ($169) Tuesday. Experienced divers can join an Adventure X dive ($149) on Wednesday. Ed Robinson's has a shop in an industrial yard in central Kihei (165 Halekuai St.) that also serves as a dive museum.

WAILEA
Dive Sites

Unlike Ma'alaea or Kihei, which serve as departure points for diving elsewhere, Wailea offers shore dives with shallow depths for beginners. The entry points in Wailea are sandy and easy; the best place to enter the water is the north end of **Ulua Beach.** This is where most dive operators bring students during their certification courses, as the maximum depth is about 35 feet. Expect to see turtles, reef fish, lobsters, and perhaps a rare spotted eagle ray. There is ample parking at the

bottom of Ulua Beach Road, and the concrete walkway down to the shore is convenient for hauling tanks and gear.

The next best option is **Wailea Point,** off the south side of Wailea Beach. The nearest parking lot is between the Grand Wailea and Four Seasons resorts. Expect to see more green sea turtles than you can count, since they love the lava rock caves.

Rental Operators

The only dive shop in Wailea is **Maui Dive Shop** (3750 Wailea Alanui Rd., 808/875-9904, www.mauidiveshop.com, 8am-7pm daily), within the Shops at Wailea. You can pick up dive-related accessories and inquire about current conditions. If you're in need of gear and tank rental, you're better off visiting one of the larger outlets in Kihei.

MAKENA AND BEYOND
Dive Sites

In addition to being one of the best shore dives in Makena, **Nahuna,** also called **Makena Landing, 5 Caves,** and **5 Graves,** also has the greatest number of names. The general area is also referred to as **Turtle Town,** a name created by charter boat companies to sell snorkeling tours.

The easiest place to enter the water is the park at Makena Landing. Once in the water, turn right and follow the coast until you reach a long finger of lava. This is what's known as the South Finger, and the depth is only about 15 feet. Follow the South Finger away from the shore, and halfway to the end you will notice a large cave that you can swim through from below. There are numerous turtles that hang out here, and almost always a whitetip reef shark under a ledge. Emerging on the other side of the cave, kick your way parallel to the shore for three minutes until you reach the North Finger, which is where you're sure to find Hawaiian green sea turtles.

Another nice shore dive is **Waiala Cove,** 1.5 miles past the First Entrance for Big Beach. The depth goes to about 40 feet. Since this cove is protected from the wind, it offers pristine diving conditions as long as the surf isn't up. Expect to find green sea turtles and the rare spinner dolphin on the outer edge of the reef. Entry can be tricky since you have to navigate your way over slippery rocks, but you don't need to worry about boats in this cove, although it is often packed with snorkelers. Parking is 0.2 miles down the road at the Dumps, the Kanahena parking lot.

Surfing

If you look at a map of South Maui, you'll notice that much of it actually faces west. This means that South Maui can get waves at any time of year. The southwest swells of summer bring the best waves, but large northwest winter swells can also wrap into select areas to provide the occasional out-of-season surf. If you're a complete beginner, the only spot in South Maui you should attempt to surf is The Cove in South Kihei, but if you're an intermediate or advanced surfer, there are other spots to check out.

MA'ALAEA

Ma'alaea is one of the few spots on Maui that faces almost due south, which means that summer is the only time there will be waves.

Surf Spots

The most consistent wave in Ma'alaea is a spot known as **Off the Wall.** This is an A-frame, shifty peak that breaks directly in front of the harbor wall, and you can usually only surf here in the morning hours before the wind starts howling. To access Off the Wall, park in the dirt parking area at the end of the break wall ($0.50 per hour), and paddle to the shifty peak—which definitely beats jumping off the wall. Expect short but fun rides, and while it isn't the best break on this side of the island, it's a nice place to get wet.

Rental Shops

The only rental shop for surfboards ($30 per day) and stand-up paddleboards ($40 per day) in Ma'alaea is **Da Beach House** (300 Ma'alaea Rd., 808/986-8279, www.dabeachhousemaui.com, 10am-5:30pm daily), inside the Ma'alaea Harbor Shops. There are also boogie boards and beach chairs, and this is a good place to pick up a board if you're planning on surfing some of the breaks on the road toward Lahaina.

KIHEI

Surf Spots

The surf epicenter of Kihei is **The Cove,** at the southern end of Kalama Park, where all of the surf schools give lessons. While the waves are gentle, the downside is that it can get crowded. On some days you'll swear you could walk on water across all of the longboards crammed into the small area, but in the early morning hours, before all the surf schools show up, this is still a fun, albeit small, wave. If your goal in Hawaii is to try surfing for the first time, this is where to come.

Shortboarding in Kihei can be found at **Sidewalks** on the south-central end of Keawakapu Beach. This is a beach break that offers a fast wave, and the vibe here isn't nearly as localized as at the boat ramp or farther south. Nevertheless, it's still an intermediate wave that isn't suitable for longboards or beginners. Parking for Sidewalks is at the public lot on the corner of Kilohana Drive and South Kihei Road.

Rental Shops and Schools

In the area surrounding The Cove there are five or six operators crammed into the same city block. Even with the wide selection, it's best to make a reservation. Nearly all lessons take place in the morning between 8am and noon, before the trade winds fill in, and all operators offer standard two-hour lessons. If you've moved past the phase of learning how to pop up and ride straight, most operations also offer "surf safaris," where they act as your personal surf guide for the day.

The shop with the largest presence is **Maui Wave Riders** (2021 S. Kihei Rd., 808/875-4761, www.mauiwaveriders.com, 7am-3pm daily) who have a brand-new surf shop and building directly across from The Cove. The company also has a Lahaina location and has helped thousands of visitors ride their first wave since opening in 1997. Lesson rates are $65 pp in a group of up to six people, $85 pp for a semiprivate lesson, and $145 for one-on-one instruction.

Although it functions on a smaller scale, another operation providing lessons in Kihei as well as on the West Side is **Maui Beach Boys** (808/283-7114, www.mauibeachboys.com), a company that offers rates in the same range, $70 pp for a group lesson and $95 for a semiprivate lesson.

If you need a pro board, the best service is from **808 Boards** (808/283-1384, www.808boards.com, 7am-5:30pm daily), who will drop off and pick up the board where you're staying for no extra charge. You can get a beginner board ($25 per day, $100 per week) or a premium fiberglass board ($35 per day, $140 per week).

WAILEA
Surf Spots
On the north side of Mokapu Beach, **Stouffer's** is a local A-frame peak for intermediate shortboarders. It can pick up southwest swells in summer and large west swells in winter. Parking is at the south lot of Keawakapu Beach or in the public parking at the bottom of Ulua Beach Road.

On the southern end of Wailea is a punchy little left on the southern end of **Polo Beach** that's good for intermediate shortboarding.

MAKENA AND BEYOND
Surf Spots
There aren't any beginner surf breaks in Makena. If you're an intermediate or advanced surfer and have always wanted to surf naked, try **Little Beach,** a left that breaks on large southern swells. To reach the wave, you need to carry your board up and over the hill that separates Little Beach from Big Beach.

There is no shortage of board rentals in Kihei.

Stand-Up Paddling

KIHEI

Kihei is one of the best spots on the island for stand-up paddling, and all of the major surf schools also offer paddleboard services. Getting out on the water in the morning is imperative because once the trade winds pick up, it can become impossible to paddle upwind. For a truly meditative experience, rent a board the evening before and get up early for a sunrise paddle. You can always putt around by the Kamaole parks and stop at whichever beach is calling your name.

Rental Shops and Schools

For lessons and rentals, **Maui Stand-Up Paddleboarding** (808/568-0151, www.mauistanduppaddleboarding.com) offers private lessons and guided tours ($189 for 1 person, $139 pp for 2-4 people, $119 pp groups more than 5). The professional guide also brings along a GoPro and provides free photos of you and your group. The shop also offers rentals ($55 per day), with a minimum rental of three days, and uniquely offer inflatable Naish boards, which are convenient if you're staying upstairs or in a place without much space.

You can also try out a multisport operator such as **South Pacific Kayaks and Outfitters** (808/875-4848, www.southpacifickayaks.com), which offers two-hour lessons ($75 pp group, $99 semiprivate, $139 private). It also offers surf lessons, kayaking tours, hiking tours, and kitesurfing lessons.

If you don't feel like being packed in with the rest of the students around The Cove, you can opt for a multisport operator such as **Blue Soul** (3414 Akala Dr., 808/269-1038, www.bluesoulmaui.com) that offers private lessons ($169 for 1 person, $129 for 2-3 people, $99 pp groups of 4 or more). Blue Soul also offers surf lessons, canoe tours, hiking tours, and adventure tours to spots all over the island. Or, bundle it all together in a "Maui Adventure Day" ($950).

WAILEA

If you would prefer to take part in a guided tour, **Paddle On** (888/663-0808, www.paddleonmaui.com, $139-159) offers early-morning tours from Polo Beach in front of the Fairmont Kea Lani. There are numerous options, from Paddleboarding 101 to guided paddles down the coast, and for a morning experience you'll never forget, inquire about sunrise yoga tours that are as meditative as you can get.

Other Water Sports

KAYAKING AND CANOEING

When all factors are considered, Makena is the best area for **kayaking** and paddling. Not only is it far richer culturally, but it takes the wind about an hour longer to reach it than neighboring Kihei or Wailea.

Kihei

The best outrigger canoe tour in Kihei is with **'Ao'ao O Na Loko 'Ia O Maui** (808/359-1172, www.mauifishpond.com) at Ko'ie'ie Fishpond. This cultural tour is run by a nonprofit that's working to restore the fishpond, and along with the workout you get serious culture. Learn how this fishpond was built over 500 years ago, and be a part of the cultural awakening that's helping to bring it back to life. Affordable tours ($40) are offered at 8am Monday, Wednesday, and Friday. Meet in the parking lot of the Hawaiian Islands Humpback

Whale National Marine Sanctuary Visitors Center.

Wailea

While there are a number of options for paddling tours in **Wailea**, the one that focuses the most on Hawaiian culture is **Hawaiian Outrigger Experience** (808/633-2800, www.hoemaui.com), operating from Wailea Beach. A play on words, the acronym "HOE" translates as "paddle!" in the Hawaiian language. From the moment you begin this tour, you will realize this is as much a cultural experience as it is about the water. You'll spend time snorkeling with Hawaiian green sea turtles and gain authentic cultural insight from instructors who exude the genuine spirit of aloha. Options include a 30-minute tour ($69) and a 90-minute tour ($119) of paddling, snorkeling, and in winter, whale-watching.

Makena

The rocky shore of Makena Landing is the preferred spot of other kayak operators, most of whom also have operations elsewhere on the island. While my top pick is **Hawaiian Paddle Sports** (808/442-6436, www.hawaiianpaddlesports.com), **Aloha Kayaks Maui**

(808/270-3318, www.alohakayaksmaui.com) is another operator that employs sustainable practices, and you can also choose from **Kelii's Kayaks** (808/874-7652, www.keliiskayaks.com) as well as **South Pacific Kayaks and Outfitters** (808/875-4848, www.southpacifickayaks.com) Most tours are $65-85 for 2.5 hours and $95-110 for 4 hours. There are usually two tours offered per day. If you plan on kayaking from Makena Landing, book the early tour to beat the wind and the crowds of snorkel boats that converge on the area later in the morning.

FISHING
Ma'alaea

For four hours of recreational fishing ($159 pp), the most personalized service you'll find in Ma'alaea Harbor is **Maui Fun Charters** (Slip 97, 808/572-2345, www.mauifuncharters.com). An important difference between this boat and others is that this one focuses on bottom fishing instead of sportfishing, so instead of spending hours trolling in circles in hopes of catching the big one, you drift closer to shore and will catch a greater number of varied, albeit smaller, fish. If your goal is to take something home to fry up for dinner, this is your best bet.

exploring the Makena coast by kayak

If you want to try your luck at reeling in a trophy fish, **Strike Zone** (Slip 40, 808/879-4485, www.strikezonemaui.com) offers bottom fishing as well as sportfishing excursions. Morning charters ($168 adults) leave at 6:30am Tuesday, Thursday, and Sunday and last six hours. On Monday, Wednesday, and Friday, 2-4 hour private afternoon charters are available. This boat can accommodate up to 28 passengers and is a good option for larger groups.

Kihei

If you want to get really adventurous, **Local Fishing Knowledge** (808/385-1337, www.localfishingknowledge.com) offers kayak fishing and fly fishing excursions for the experienced and passionate angler. If you just want to rent a rod for casting in the surf, the "beach bum" setup is perfect for anglers on the sand.

Hiking and Biking

HIKING
Kihei

Hiking in Kihei is barefoot sandy strolls down the beach. For the island's longest uninterrupted beach walk, five-mile-long **Sugar Beach** runs between Kihei and Ma'alaea. You can access the beach from Haycraft Park on the Ma'alaea side, from Kenolio Park on the Kihei side, or at any of the access points along North Kihei Road.

Another popular **coastal walk** in Kihei connects the trio of Kamaole Beaches, following the trails around their headlands. Starting at Charley Young Beach on the north end of Kamaole I (parking is in a public lot on Kaiau Place), you can walk to the south end of Kamaole III along the shore and around the rocky points. Although it's always nice to feel the sand between your toes, the rocks around the headlands can be sharp, so it might be best to bring footwear.

If you want to extend the coastal walk just a little bit farther, there is a short 0.5-mile **walking path** that parallels the coast from the southern end of Kamaole III Beach to the Kihei Boat Ramp. Along the way you will pass informative signs about the coastal dune system and the *u'au kani* **seabirds** that nest in the dunes. There are a few benches sprinkled along the walking path to rest or, in winter, watch for whales.

Wailea
WAILEA COASTAL WALK

If your idea of a hike means throwing on some Lululemon, talking on your iPhone, and stopping to pick up some Starbucks, then the paved, 3.5-mile (round-trip) **Wailea Coastal Walk** is going to be your favorite hike on the island. The pathway runs from Ulua Beach to Polo Beach and is undeniably gorgeous, passing a host of native coastal plants put in to revitalize the area's natural foliage. You'll also pass the Grand Wailea, Four Seasons, Kea Lani, Marriott, and Wailea Beach Villas. To reach the "trailhead" for the walkway, park in the public lot at Ulua Beach, at the bottom of Ulua Beach Road, or in the public lot on the southern end of the trail at Polo Beach, at the bottom of Kaukahi Street. At the far northern end, the walkway becomes sand and traverses the dunes past Mokapu Beach, where it links to Keawakapu in Kihei. In front of the Marriott, you can watch whales in winter through rented binoculars ($0.50).

Makena and Beyond
★ HOAPILI TRAIL

Hot, barren, and in the middle of nowhere, the **Hoapili Trail** isn't as much about hiking as about stepping back in time. Although the 5.5-mile trail (round-trip) takes about four hours, even an hour introduces you to a side of the island most visitors never see.

The trail was once an ancient Hawaiian walking path reserved for royalty. In 1824, sections of the trail were reconstructed, and the road took on a structure that remains untouched to this day. The trailhead for Hoapili (also known as the "King's Highway") is in the parking lot of La Perouse Bay snorkeling area, 3.1 miles past the First Entrance to Big Beach. To find the trail, drive south on Makena Alanui Road until it dead-ends.

From the La Perouse Bay parking lot, you'll see the trail paralleling the shore and weaving south along the coast. Before you set out, remember that there is no shade and the trail traverses jagged ʻaʻa lava that's so sharp you'll want proper hiking boots. Since much of this hike is outside cell phone range, it's important to be prepared with food and water. Reduce the chance of overheating by starting early in the morning.

After you've followed the shoreline for 0.7 mile, passing a couple of pockets of sand and sometimes feral black goats, you'll see an abandoned lava rock structure off the right side of the trail. This is the popular surfing spot known as Laps (short for La Perouse), and on large south swells you can see death-defying surfers riding waves over jagged sharp lava. After the surf spot, the trail climbs for 10 minutes before arriving at a junction and veering off to the left. There is a sign informing you that you're entering the King's Highway and to respect the historic sites. The sign will also indicate that Kanaio Beach is two miles ahead.

On the inland section of trail where the path deviates from the coast, there's a short spur trail that leads down to the lighthouse at Cape Hanamanioa, although there isn't much to see except the old weathered light. A better side trip is the short spur trail 20 minutes later that leads down to Keawanaku Beach, where you're almost guaranteed to have the beach to yourself. To find the beach, look for a short lone palm tree springing from the black lava field surrounded by a grove of *kiawe* trees, then keep an eye out for the trail down to the shore. Although rocky, the trail is noticeable,

hiking the Hoapili Trail

and if you find yourself asking "Am I still on the trail?" then you probably aren't. After Keawanaku, the trail continues for 20 minutes to the coast at Kanaio Beach, a salt- and pepper-colored shore of black lava rock and sun-bleached coral. You'll notice the remnants of multiple structures, once part of an ancient fishing village.

Although Kanaio Beach is the turnaround point for most hikers, the King's Highway continues to Highway 31 on the "back road to Hana." To reach the highway, however, requires an overnight stay along the trail; camping is permitted along the shore from points east of Kanaio Beach. To travel just a little farther, however, a sandy road continues from Kanaio Beach and winds along the coast. Another 20 minutes of walking from Kanaio brings you to a shore that's completely bathed in bleached white coral, and on the southern end of the "white beach" is an ancient Hawaiian *heiau* set out on the point that looks much the same now as it must have when it was built.

BIKING

For a casual bike ride in South Maui, it doesn't get better than renting a beach cruiser and pedaling to beach-hop, bar-hop, and coolly cruise the strip, not worrying about traffic or finding parking. For an epic half-day road biking adventure, ride from Kihei to Makena and the lava-strewn "end of the road," where you can cycle across the island's last lava flow and relax at beaches as you go.

Kihei

If you're a hard-core cyclist, head to **South Maui Cycles** (1993 S. Kihei Rd., 808/874-0068, www.southmauibicycles.com, 10am-6pm Mon.-Sat.), across the street from Kalama Park to rent road bikes ($22-60 per day, $99-250 per week). This is a full-service bicycle shop that also offers sales and repairs.

To beach-hop for a while, beach cruisers ($15 per day, $50 per week) are available from **Boss Frog's** (1770 S. Kihei Rd., 808/661-3333, www.bossfrog.com, 8am-5pm daily). There are also mountain bikes, hybrid bikes, and proper road bikes. You can also pick up a cruiser at another Boss location in the Dolphin Plaza, across from the southern end of Kamaole II Beach Park.

Shopping

KIHEI
North End

If you turn up Pi'ikea Avenue between the Azeka Mauka Center and the Long's Shopping Center, you'll quickly come to the **Pi'ilani Village Shopping Center** (291 Pi'ikea Ave., 808/874-5151), which has the most relevant shopping options in North Kihei. A big draw is the **Hilo Hattie's** (808/875-4545, 9am-9pm daily) clothing store, with a wide range of men's and women's apparel. If you need a swimsuit, **Maui Waterwear** (808/891-8319, 9am-9pm Mon.-Sat., 9am-7pm Sun.) specializes in women's bikinis and beach accessories.

Central Kihei

The largest concentration of shopping in Kihei is in the **Kihei Kalama Village** (1941 S. Kihei Rd., 808/874-0003, 10am-7pm daily), with over 40 businesses, the most notable being **Da Beach House** (808/891-1234, www.dabeachhousemaui.com) for surf-themed apparel, **Mahina** (808/879-3453, www.mahinamaui.com) for women's apparel, and **The Love Shack Maui** (808/875-0303, www.loveshackmaui.com) for intimate moments. There are also myriad kiosks and stands where you can get henna tattoos or play with a digeridoo. This shopping area is within walking distance of the Cove Park, where most of the surf rentals take place, so if part of your group is out surfing, you can wander down here for some souvenir browsing while they are on the water.

South End

In the **Kamaole Beach Center,** the main retail outlet is **Honolua Surf Company** (2411 S. Kihei Rd., 808/874-0999, 9am-9pm daily), specializing in high-quality surf clothing. You can occasionally get the same Honolua-brand clothing cheaper than at Whalers Village in Ka'anapali or at the nearby Shops at Wailea.

Rainbow Mall is home to **Maui Fine Art & Frame** (2439 S. Kihei Rd., 808/222-3055, www.mauiartframe.com, 11am-8pm daily), one of the few art galleries in Kihei. In addition to numerous island-themed paintings and ceramics, the frames that encompass the artwork are an art form unto themselves.

WAILEA

While all of the high-end luxury resorts have a decent amount of shopping, particularly the Grand Wailea, the majority of retail on this side of the island is at the shopping centers and shops.

Shops at Wailea

Any longtime visitor to Maui will remember when the **Shops at Wailea** (3750 Wailea Alanui Dr., 808/891-6770, www.theshopsatwailea.com, 9:30am-9pm daily) were a plantation-style shopping complex with wide grassy areas and free hula shows from local *halau* (hula schools). These days, the complex has gone upscale. Inside you'll find art galleries such as **Ki'i Gallery** (808/874-1181) and **Dolphin Galleries** (808/891-8000) accompanying surf shops like **Billabong** (808/879-8330) and **Honolua Surf Company** (808/891-8229). You can often spot celebrities hanging out in luxury stalwarts such as **Tiffany and Co.** (808/891-9226), **Gucci** (808/879-1060), or **Louis Vuitton** (808/875-6980).

Aside from the high-end chain stores, you can also find a few island-themed shops offering unique and boutique souvenirs. At **Sand People** (808/891-8801, www.sandpeople.com), you can pick up coast-inspired gifts and home decor, and **Martin & MacArthur** (808/891-8844, www.martinandmacarthur.com) showcases Hawaiian-made crafts and an assortment of koa woods. If you're missing something from your cosmetics kit, **Cos Bar** (808/891-9448, www.cosbar.com) carries makeup lines, such as Bobbi Brown, that you won't find anywhere else on the island. If you're in need of a fancy gift, **Na Hoku** (808/891-8040) offers unique Hawaiian-inspired jewelry.

Entertainment

MA'ALAEA
Live Music

In the downstairs section of the Ma'alaea Harbor Shops, **Beach Bums** (300 Ma'alaea Rd., 808/243-2286, until 9pm daily) has live music 5pm-8pm daily, which coincides with the 3pm-6pm happy hour and $2.75 PBR pints. If you're staying in one of the condos at Ma'alaea, this is your best bet for a happening atmosphere and the chance to mingle with boat crews who are drinking through that morning's tips.

KIHEI
Events

For an artistic event that happens most nights, **Island Art Party** (1279 S. Kihei Rd., 808/419-6020, www.islandartparty.com, 10am-9:30pm) is a unique venue where you can join an instructor-led painting class while sipping a glass of wine. It's one of the island's best rainy-day activities and is for ages 16 and up.

Live Music and Dancing
INSIDE THE TRIANGLE

The majority of Kihei's nightlife takes place at the **Triangle**, as in, the *Barmuda* Triangle, where you could end up getting lost for days. This collection of bars within the Kihei Kalama Village can almost seem like a tropical fraternity row, with each house on the street having a different theme party.

If you're starting your night early, check out **Haui's Life's A Beach** (1913 S. Kihei Rd., 808/891-8010, www.mauibars.com, until 2am daily), aka **The Lab.** This rockin' beach bar has an outdoor patio that looks toward South Kihei Road and is a great place for people-watching. There is live music most nights, or you can shoot some pool, watch some sports, and eavesdrop on local happenings.

The best venue within the Triangle for live music is **Three's Bar and Grill** (1945 S. Kihei Rd., 808/879-3133, www.threesbarandgrill.com, until 1:30am daily), a semi-formal dining establishment that also has a VIP Surf Lounge with a built-in stage area and lighting. Weekdays often have music around dinner time, and weekend shows begin around 10pm and usually stretch until closing.

Across the parking lot, swap your draft beer for some cutting-edge mixology at

No Dancing!

The best place to go dancing in Maui is at the Kihei Kalama Village (aka the Triangle), since it's home to nearly all the places on Maui where you're legally allowed to dance. That's right—believe it or not, dancing in Maui is technically illegal at most of the island's bars.

In order for an establishment to legally permit dancing, there needs to be a designated area that is either roped off or separated in some way from the designated drinking area. There are to be no drinks on the dance floor, and randomly choosing to shake your rump while waiting in line at the bar is strictly verboten and can get you thrown out.

So why the strict rules? When it comes to the law, the dancers themselves won't get in trouble, but rather the licensed establishment can potentially lose its liquor license. The strangest part is that there is no legal definition for what constitutes dancing. Consequently, anything that involves rhythmic or purposeful movement, from a shoulder shake to a toe tap, can be construed as illicit, dangerous, and legally unacceptable. Unless, of course, you put down your drink and make your way to the designated dance floor.

Local dance advocate groups have been recommending bills to the state legislature for years in an effort to change the law (or at least define dancing), but for reasons that continue to defy logic, dancing remains an often forbidden pursuit.

Ambrosia (1913 S. Kihei Rd., 808/891-1011, www.ambrosiamaui.com, until 2am daily), a small martini bar that specializes in "upscale drinking." DJs spin on many nights of the week, and the vibe is decidedly classier and more refined than at some of the neighboring venues.

Finally, for a good old-fashioned touch of the *craic,* **Dog and Duck Irish Pub** (1913 S. Kihei Rd., 808/875-9669, until 2am daily) is a small gathering place where you can throw darts, eat bangers and mash, drink Guinness, rock out to live music, or take part in the popular quiz nights. To switch up the drinking venue, right next door is the recently opened **What Ales You** (808/214-6581, www.whatalesyoumaui.com, 11am-10pm daily), a small tap house with 16 beers on tap and about 20 wines on the wine list.

OUTSIDE THE TRIANGLE

At the other end of the parking lot of the Azeka Mauka is **Diamonds Ice Bar** (1279 S. Kihei Rd., 808/874-9299, www.diamondsicebar.com, until 2am daily), a small establishment tucked in the end unit that offers live music most nights. If you have a large group, there's a private VIP room. While it doesn't see the same amount of crowds as down at the

Triangle, it can still be a happening place if the right band is playing.

WAILEA
Shows

Surprisingly there aren't that many dinner shows on Maui, but one that will wow you is the **Willie K Dinner Show** held at **Mulligan's on the Blue** (100 Kaukahi St., 808/874-1131, www.mulligansontheblue.com, 6:30pm Wed., $65). Even if you've never heard of Uncle Willie K, once you see him play, you'll never forget him. An insanely talented local Hawaiian musician who grew up on Maui, Willie K's prowess stretches across a wide range of genres, from blues to Hawaiian to rock-and-roll and opera. The show usually happens on Wednesday, but since the schedule can vary, check the online calendar.

If you're on a budget and looking for a free public show, **Wailea Le'a** (6:30pm-8pm 3rd Wed. of the month) at the **Shops at Wailea** (3750 Wailea Alanui Dr., 808/891-6770, www.theshopsatwailea.com) usually features free performances by famous Hawaiian artists.

Lu'au

The best lu'au on the island is Old Lahaina Luau in Lahaina, but if you're staying on the south end of the island and don't want to drive that far, there are two options in South Maui. My top pick is **The Grand Luau at Honua'ula** (3850 Wailea Alanui Dr., 808/875-7710, www.honuaula-luau.com, 4pm Mon. and Thurs.-Sat., $105 adults, $57 children) because the show focuses more on Hawaiian history than the South Pacific in general. The lu'au takes place on the grounds of the Grand Wailea. Honua'ula is a name given to this section of the island by the original Polynesians who migrated here centuries ago. Call in advance to check the schedule, which can vary.

Just a few steps down the coastal walkway is **Te Au Moana** (3700 Wailea Alanui, 877/827-2740, www.teaumoana.com, 4:30pm Mon. and Thurs.-Sat., $110 adults, $63 children), at the Wailea Beach Marriott. Showtimes overlap with neighboring Grand Wailea. This show focuses more on the dance and mythology of greater Polynesia than on Hawaii, but it's still a highly entertaining performance, particularly if it's your first luau. The stage backs up to the shore in front of the hotel. The backdrop of the setting sun creates a panorama you would expect from a luau in paradise.

Live Music

For live entertainment after the sun goes down, the most popular place in Wailea is **Mulligan's on the Blue** (100 Kaukahi St., 808/874-1131, www.mulligansontheblue.com, until 1am daily). This Irish pub is owned by a real Irishman, and aside from the Willie K dinner show, the next most popular evening is at 7pm Sunday, when the Celtic Tigers Irish folk band takes to the stage. There are also periodic performances by award-winning local artists, so pick up a copy of a local entertainment catalog to see what the happenings are.

At **Monkeypod** (10 Wailea Ike Dr., 808/891-2322, www.monkeypodkitchen.com, until 11pm daily) restaurant in the Wailea Gateway Center, not only does it have Wailea's best beer selection, but it also has live music every day beginning at 1pm.

You can also find live music inside hotel lobbies, with one of the best being the **Lobby Lounge** (3900 Wailea Alanui Dr., 808/874-8000, 5pm-11:30pm daily) bar inside the Four Seasons Wailea, with hula dancers performing around sunset and live music each night. Just down the beach walk, at the Grand Wailea, the **Botero Lounge** (800/888-6100) has live music and a lively bar 5pm-10pm daily.

Food

KIHEI
American

One of the best breakfast finds on the south side is ★ **Kihei Caffé** (1945 S. Kihei Rd., 808/879-2230, www.kiheicaffe.net, 5am-2pm daily, $7-10), which gloriously opens at 5am if you're waking up early from jet lag. The portions are enormous, and breakfast is served all day. Try a generous omelet or gargantuan breakfast burrito, and since the atmosphere can be hectic, get here early to beat the crowds.

One of the best things to happen to Kihei in recent years is ★ **Nalu's South Shore Grill** (1280 S. Kihei Rd., 808/891-8650, www.nalusmaui.com, 8am-9pm daily). Many of the ingredients are local or organic, and the seared ahi club ($14) is Kihei's best sandwich. Located in the Azeka Mauka shopping center, order at the counter.

Brewery
Maui Brewing Company (605 Lipoa Pkwy., 808/213-3002, www.mauibrewingco.com, 11am-10pm daily) is slowly beginning to dominate Hawaii's beer scene. It's already the largest craft producer in the Aloha State, and with its shimmering new Kihei brewery, with 36 of its own beers on tap, this island favorite is rapidly turning into a major player. Tours of the brewery (noon-3:15pm daily,

$15 pp) are offered six times per day and include a souvenir glass and a token for a pint. Need some food to soak up the suds? There's a rotating schedule of food trucks outside 11am-10pm daily.

Coffee Shops

The most modern coffee shop in Kihei is **Java Café** (1279 S. Kihei Rd., 808/214-6095, www.javacafemaui.com, 5am-9pm daily, $7-9), in the Azeka Mauka shopping center; 75 percent of the coffee served is grown in Hawaii. You can also buy bags of beans from coffee farms on Maui, Kaua'i, Moloka'i, and the Big Island. Flatbreads and *paninis* are available for lunch; there's also a large selection of breakfast bagels.

For a coffee shop with a quirky French twist, **Café @ La Plage** (2395 S. Kihei Rd., 808/875-7668, www.cafealaplage.com, 6:30am-5pm daily) is located in Dolphin Plaza across from Kam I beach. In addition to the menu of coffee and espresso, breakfast bagels and sandwiches average $6-8.

Hawaiian Regional

Since most of Kihei's restaurants are in strip malls, there isn't an overabundance of fine dining. The exception, however, is ★ **Sarento's on the Beach** (2980 S. Kihei Rd., 808/875-7555, www.sarentsonthebeach.com, 7am-11am and 5:30pm-10pm daily, $28-49), on the water at the north end of Keawakapu Beach. You won't find a more romantic or relaxing spot in Kihei. Start off with the seared ahi or beef carpaccio before moving on to the pan-roasted island snapper or rack of lamb Placourakis. Valet parking is free, and if you show up about an hour before sunset, you'll probably get a seat with a fiery view during dessert.

Japanese

★ **Sansei** (1881 S. Kihei Rd., 808/879-0004, www.sanseihawaii.com, 5:30pm-10pm daily, $16) has been a South Maui favorite since 2002. Award-winning dishes such as the *panko*-crusted ahi rolls and signature shrimp

dynamite keep locals flocking to this nondescript spot. For a night on the town, hit up the half-priced sushi menu after 10pm Thursday-Saturday, where the *unagi* and rainbow rolls will leave sushi-lovers feeling like kids in a candy store. Late nights can be noisy, with sake and karaoke.

Local Style

The only true local-style plate lunch in Kihei is at ★ **Da Kitchen** (2439 S. Kihei Rd., 808/875-7782, www.da-kitchen.com, 9am-9pm daily, $8-15), toward the back of the Rainbow Mall in South Kihei. Although the restaurant isn't as large as its Kahului counterpart, the portions are enormous enough that you could split them and still walk away full. This hole in the wall strip-mall special is one of the best deals in town. If you're looking for a place where locals eat, this is it.

Mexican

At the very authentic **Taqueria Cruz** (2395 S. Kihei Rd., 808/875-2910, www.taqueriacruz.com, 11:30am-8:30pm Mon.-Fri.) you can hear the *norteño* music from the kitchen before it even opens. Tucked in the back of Dolphin Plaza across from Kam I beach, this is reminiscent of a roadside taqueria you might find on the back roads of Baja. The BYOB capability means you can enjoy your fish tacos with a Pacífico from your own cooler. There are taco specials ($2), burritos ($9), and live music 6:30pm-8:30pm Tuesday night.

Pizza

A favorite for south shore pizza is ★ **Fabiani's Bakery and Pizza** (95 E. Lipoa St., 808/874-0888, www.fabianis.com, 7am-9pm daily, $10-12) in central Kihei. Located in a strip mall, it's tough to find, but once you get there, you'll realize why it's a local hangout: Lunch and dinner are dominated by fresh, tasty pizzas and *paninis* crafted by a chef from Italy. There's also a decent wine selection, and the atmosphere inside is nicer than the exterior suggests. The fresh breakfast pastries are a local secret, and the 50-percent-off pizzas at the 3pm-5pm daily happy hour are one of the best deals in Kihei.

Seafood

Hidden back in the central Kihei industrial yard is ★ **Eskimo Candy** (2665 Wai Wai Place, 808/879-5686, www.eskimocandy.com, 10:30am-7pm Mon.-Fri., $10-17), Kihei's best local secret for fresh seafood. Try the seafood chowder, fish-and-chips, and *poke*, featuring four different styles of seasoned ahi tuna. There are only a few tables outside for dining, and Eskimo Candy also has wholesale rates on fish for grilling back at your condo. To find it, make the turn off South Kihei Road by Maui Dive Shop and the Avis car rental outlet, continuing toward the end of the road; the restaurant is on the right.

WAILEA

Prices in **Wailea** are much higher than in other parts of the island, and double the cost in Kihei. You're often paying for master chefs, exceptional service, and unparalleled ambience in world-class resorts.

American

The first restaurant you'll encounter in Wailea approaching from Pi'ilani Highway is ★ **Monkeypod Kitchen** (10 Wailea Ike Dr., 808/891-2322, www.monkeypodkitchen. com, 11:30am-11pm daily, $13-35), the brainchild of renowned Maui chef Peter Merriman. Ingredients are all sourced locally, supporting sustainable farming and ensuring fresh, healthy meals. Dinner options range from sesame-crusted mahimahi to *bulgogi* pork tacos in an Asian pear aioli, or an organic spinach and quinoa salad big enough to share. The craft beer list is the best in Wailea. To save a few bucks, visit during happy hour, 3pm-5:30pm and again 9pm-11pm daily, when appetizers are 50 percent off and pizzas are only $9.

Hawaiian Regional

At the beautiful Grand Wailea, **Humu-humunukunukuapua'a** (3850 Wailea Alanui Dr., 808/875-1234, www.grandwailea. com, 5:30pm-9pm daily, $30-49) is not only one of the hardest restaurants to pronounce, it's also one of the most popular. Named after the state fish, "Humu" sits in a thatched-roof Polynesian structure afloat on its own million-gallon saltwater lagoon. Large plates include the famous Hawaiian spiny lobster dish, where you can choose your lobster from the lagoon, as well as crispy mahimahi or fresh *opakapaka*. The sunset view looking over the lagoon is the classic image of paradise.

Inside the Marriott, **Migrant** (3700 Wailea Alanui Dr., 808/875-9394, www.migrant-maui.com, 4pm-10pm daily) is the brainchild of chef Sheldon Simeon of Star Noodle and *Top Chef* fame. The menu is inspired by dishes sourced from Maui's ethnic community, and chow fun noodles and *tocino* Filipino sweet pork are some popular local favorites. The food is so fresh that the menu lists the mileage to the farms where the food was sourced. Visit the "Be Happy Hour," 4pm-6pm daily, when dishes are 50 percent off. There's also a sake bar and 36 beers—8 of which are on tap.

Italian

Wailea's best pizza, ★ **Manoli's Pizza Company** (100 Wailea Ike Dr., 808/874-7499, www.manolispizzacompany.com, 11:30am-midnight daily, $16-22) is walking distance from many of the hotels, across from the Shops at Wailea. It serves 14-inch thin-crust pizzas, with organic and gluten-free options and toppings that include shrimp, pesto, kalamata olives, artichoke hearts, and feta cheese. There are salads, pasta, and a selection of 20 wines, and specials at happy hour, 3pm-6pm and again 9pm-midnight daily.

Haleakala and Upcountry

Look for ★ to find recommended
sights, activities, dining, and lodging.

Highlights

★ **Haleakala National Park:** Watch the sunrise and then spend the day hiking across the crater floor. Or visit for sunset and stay for the stars, camping overnight (page 307).

★ **Hali'imaile Distillery:** Sample vodka made from pineapples as well as flavored whiskey and rum (page 311).

★ **Kula Country Farms:** Pick up fresh produce, drink in the views, and support the island's farmers (page 313).

★ **Surfing Goat Dairy:** It's the only tour on Maui with gourmet cheese and the chance to hand-milk a goat (page 314).

★ **Maui Wine:** Sip on Maui-made wine and finish it off with an elk burger (page 315).

★ **O'o Farm:** Enjoy a romantic freshly cooked lunch in the middle of an eight-acre farm with a glass of wine, a private chef, and a vine-covered trellis (page 315).

★ **Historic Makawao Town:** Boutiques, art galleries, and ranching history—all in a two-street town (page 324).

U pcountry is Maui's little secret that's just now starting to get out. Here's a place where the smell of eucalyptus replaces the rustle of palms and truck-driving farmers with scuffed boots replace the pool boys with towels.

Upcountry is where you throw on a flannel shirt and go for a morning drive, perhaps stopping to relax on the porch of a small family-run coffeehouse. It's a place to go hiking through forests of pine trees or sip on Maui-made wine and watch the day begin or end over Haleakala Crater. It's seeing a Sunday polo game and wandering through Makawao's galleries and buying vegetables straight from the source at a stand on the side of the road. It's eating doughnuts at a family bakery that's been serving them for over a century or settling in for a colorful sunset over bicoastal views each night. Most of all, it's slowing down and taking time to breathe the mountain air and trading the glamour of beachfront resorts for the charm of a small town.

ORIENTATION

Generally speaking, Upcountry comprises Makawao, Pukalani, Kula, Keokea, and Ulupalakua. At an elevation of 1,500 to 4,000 feet, it's also home to the 10,023-foot summit of **Haleakala Crater.** From sea level, the 38-mile drive to the summit is the shortest climb to 10,000 feet of any paved road in the world. From Makawao or Kula, reaching the summit of Haleakala Crater is about an hour's drive, and from Ka'anapali or Wailea takes a little over two hours. The drive from Makawao to Ulupalakua takes 35 minutes, versus 10 minutes to the beach in Pa'ia or 15 minutes to Kahului Airport. **Makawao** has the greatest selection of restaurants, shops, and a defined center, whereas **Kula** is a patchwork of houses, farms, and restaurants that are fairly spread out. Tiny **Keokea** is the gateway between Kula and the winery in **Ulupalakua,** where the road continues all the way around to Kaupo and the "back way" to Hana.

Previous: October Kula pumpkin patch; Ulupalakua storefront. **Above:** wine tasting at Maui Wine.

Upcountry

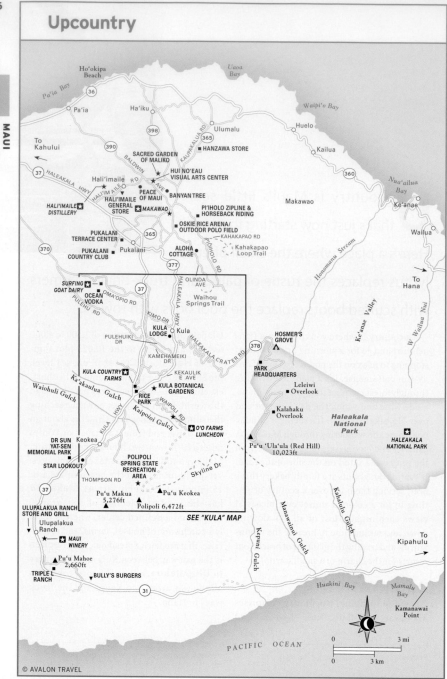

Ho'okipa
Beach

Uaoa
Bay

Pa'ia Bay

36

Waipi'o Bay

Pa'ia

Ha'iku

Huelo

398

Ulumalu

To
Kahului

390

365

■ HANZAWA STORE

Kailua

37 HALEAKALA HWY

Hali'imaile

★ HUI NO'EAU
VISUAL ARTS CENTER

360

Nua'ailua
Bay

SACRED GARDEN
OF MALIKO

Makawao

Ke'anae

HALI'IMAILE
DISTILLERY ★

PEACE
OF MAUI ★

★ BANYAN TREE

★ HALI'IMAILE
GENERAL
STORE ★ MAKAWAO

■ PI'IHOLO ZIPLINE &
HORSEBACK RIDING

Wailua

PUKALANI
TERRACE CENTER ■

370

365

Pukalani

■ OSKIE RICE ARENA/
OUTDOOR POLO FIELD

KAHAKAPAO RD

To
Hana

PUKALANI
COUNTRY CLUB

377

ALOHA
COTTAGE ■

Kahakapao
Loop Trail

SURFING ★ ■
GOAT DAIRY

OCEAN
VODKA

37

OLINDA
AVE

Waihou
Springs Trail

W Wailua Rd

PULEHU RD

KIMO DR

Ke'anae Valley

Honomanu Stream

PULEHUIKI
DR

KULA
LODGE ■ Kula

HOSMER'S
GROVE ⛺

378

KAMEHAMEIKI
DR

PARK
HEADQUARTERS

KULA COUNTRY ★
FARMS

KEKAULIK
E AVE

★ KULA BOTANICAL
GARDENS

Leleiwi
■ Overlook

Ka'akaulua Gulch

RICE
PARK

Waiohuli Gulch

Kaipoioi Gulch

WAIPOLI RD

■ Kalahaku
Overlook

Haleakala
National
Park

★ O'O FARMS
LUNCHEON

DR SUN
YAT-SEN
MEMORIAL PARK

Keokea

▲ Pu'u 'Ula'ula (Red Hill)
10,023ft

★ HALEAKALA
NATIONAL PARK

★ STAR LOOKOUT

POLIPOLI
SPRING STATE
RECREATION
AREA ★

THOMPSON RD

Skyline Dr

37

Pu'u Makua
5,276ft

▲ Pu'u Keokea

Kepuni Gulch

Manawainui Gulch

Kahulalu Gulch

To
Kipahulu

ULUPALAKUA RANCH
STORE AND GRILL

▼ Polipoli 6,472ft

SEE "KULA" MAP

Ulupalakua
▼ Ranch

★ ■ MAUI
WINERY

▲ Pu'u Mahoe
2,660ft

TRIPLE L
RANCH

▼ BULLY'S BURGERS

31

Huakini Bay

Mamalu
Bay

Kamanawai
Point

0   3 mi

0   3 km

PACIFIC OCEAN

© AVALON TRAVEL

Your Best Day in Upcountry

Begin the day in Keokea with breakfast at **Grandma's Coffee House.** Walk it off with a 30-minute stroll on neighboring **Thompson Road** before continuing on to **Ulupalakua** and a visit to **Maui Wine.** Have lunch at the **Ulupalakua Ranch Store and Grill** (try the home-made chili) before stopping for produce at **Kula Country Farms** on the drive to **Makawao** for shopping. When it's time for dinner or happy hour, head to **Polli's Mexican Restaurant** for a mango margarita, or **Casanova** at 5pm for $5 carafes of wine.

If you start your day with a **Haleakala sunrise,** spend an hour at the summit area hiking on **Sliding Sands Trail.** On the way back down, grab breakfast at **Kula Lodge** and shop at the **Kula Marketplace.** Monday through Thursday, skimp on the hiking atop the crater to squeeze in an earlier breakfast so you can make it out to **O'o Farm** for the 10:30am lunch tour. When the tour finishes at 2pm, choose to either go shopping in Makawao or drive out to **Maui Wine**—depending on how much energy you have after the early morning wake-up.

RAINY-DAY ALTERNATIVE

Start with breakfast at **Kula Lodge** and a piping cup of hot chocolate, and head downstairs to look at the artwork of Curtis Wilson Cost. Drive to Makawao for an hour of shopping and have lunch at **Polli's Mexican Restaurant,** where a lively crowd often gathers whenever the rain is coming down. Drive 10 minutes to **Hali'imaile Distillery** for an hour-long tasting and tour before treating yourself to a nice dinner at **Hali'imaile General Store.**

PLANNING YOUR TIME

While it's possible to experience Upcountry's highlights in a single day, try to spend two full days seeing the area—one day at Haleakala Crater either watching the sunrise and exploring Upcountry on the way back down, or gradually visiting Upcountry sights before heading to Haleakala for sunset. On the second day, start with horseback riding or ziplining, and then see the sights you didn't get to see the day before. While many people drive Upcountry from the beach, there are numerous lodges and bed-and-breakfasts to base yourself on the hill. It's also possible to visit Upcountry when driving the "back road" from Hana, but by the time you get here after a full day in Hana, there's really only time for the winery.

Sights

★ HALEAKALA NATIONAL PARK

"Hale-a-ka-la," House of the Sun. Few places are more aptly named than this 10,023-foot volcano. Believed to have been dormant since 1790 (the summit area has been inactive for 600 years), when measured from the seafloor, Haleakala is 30,000 feet tall—surpassed only by the peaks on the Big Island as the tallest mountain on earth.

Given its size and spellbinding nature, it's little wonder the mountain is considered sacred to indigenous Hawaiians. This is where the powerful volcano goddess, Pele, crafted her colorful cinder cones, and a *wahi pana*, or sacred place, only inhabited by the gods. It's where the demigod Maui lassoed the sun to slow its path across the sky so his people could have time to grow their crops and dry their cloth in the sun. It's also a fragile ecological treasure, with more endangered species than any other national park.

Today, the most popular activity for visitors to Maui is visiting Haleakala for sunrise—but there's far more to this national park than simply the light of dawn. Over 30 miles of hiking trails crisscross the crater, where backcountry cabins and campgrounds provide a classic wilderness experience. The sunsets and stargazing are as spectacular as viewing the crater at sunrise, and even the drive leading up to park—where the road gains 10,000 vertical feet in only 38 miles—is part of the magical, mystical experience of standing atop Haleakala.

When to Visit

The biggest question surrounding Haleakala is not if you should visit, but when. Sunrise is the most popular option, and although everyone should experience a Haleakala sunrise at least once, it's not the only time to visit. Sunrise is crowded, tough to find parking, requires waking up at 3am, and is often near or below freezing. Sunset is a display nearly as colorful but without all the crowds. You don't get the benefit of watching the sun emerge from the horizon, but there are often only 20 people instead of 400, and it isn't as cold. If you plan on hiking the crater floor, arrive at the summit in the middle of the day and time your exit for sunset.

The weather, unfortunately, can be unpredictable. Rain and even snow can fall at any time of year, but summer typically has better conditions. Statistically, on 85 percent of mornings, it's clear enough to see the sunrise. For sunset, a good rule of thumb is that if you can't see the mountain from below, you probably shouldn't bother. On the other hand, if you can see the mountain, but not the top, the sunset will seem to float on a colorful sea of clouds. To take the guesswork out of the equation, call the National Weather Service **Hotline for Haleakala Summit** (808/944-5025, ext. 4) for an up-to-date weather forecast. You can also check out the University of Hawai'i astronomy website (www.ifa.hawaii.edu/haleakalanew/weather.shtml) for up-to-the-minute weather data, including windchill, visibility, and rainfall, before heading to the summit.

Admission and Hosmer's Grove

Admission ($15 per car) to **Haleakala National Park** (www.nps.gov/hale) is good for three days and includes the Kipahulu section past Hana, home to the Pools of 'Ohe'o.

Prepare for crowds and cold at sunrise.

BRRR...

On any given morning at the top of Haleakala there is always at least one unfortunate person shivering in a tank top. People forget that Haleakala is over 10,000 feet high, which means the temperature is 30 degrees colder than it is back down on the beach. And, even though Haleakala is the "House of the Sun," the morning windchill—particularly in winter—can often be below freezing. Ice on the road is common in winter, and every few years the summit gets snow that stays for a couple of days. Naturally, whenever it snows on Haleakala, hundreds of locals rush to the summit to help their children build snowmen, and then, of course, immediately rush home to put the photos online.

Most mornings at Haleakala Crater are between 30°F and 50°F, so consider packing pants, gloves, a hat, and a jacket. No winter clothing? Use the hotel's blankets, but be sure to return them in good condition in order to avoid fees. Temperatures rise into the 60s by noon, but sunrise and sunset visitors should prepare to bundle up.

For current weather info at Haleakala summit, visit www.ifa.hawaii.edu/haleakalanew/weather.shtml or call 808/944-5025, ext. 4.

If you're driving for sunrise, head straight to the summit; if you have time to explore, take the side trip to **Hosmer's Grove,** just past the park entrance (page 316). This is one of the best **bird-watching** spots on the island.

Continuing straight past the Hosmer's Grove turnoff, you'll soon arrive at **Park Headquarters** (808/572-4400, 7am-3:45pm daily) at an elevation of 6,800 feet. Stop for information, camping permits, gifts, toilets, and a pay phone. There are some *'ahinahina* (silversword) plants outside, and sometimes *nene* (Hawaiian geese) frequent the area.

On the road toward the summit, **Leleiwi** (page 316) is an overlook that's a great alternative at sunrise. **Kalahaku,** on the other hand, is another overlook that's popular at sunrise but can only be accessed when traveling downhill.

Visitors Center and Summit Observation Building

Near the end of the road is the **Visitors Center,** at 9,740 feet. It's about 10 miles up the mountain from headquarters, about a 30-minute drive. This is where all of the bike tour companies bring you for sunrise, as it's the best view looking down into the crater. It's open sunrise-3pm daily and contains clear and concise displays on the geology of

Haleakala. Maps and books are available, and a 30-minute ranger-guided walk takes place most days at 10am and 11am.

If you want to top out above 10,000 feet and officially summit Haleakala, **Pu'u 'Ula'ula** (Red Hill) is the highest point on Maui at 10,023 feet. Here you'll find a glass-sided observation area that's open 24 hours daily. The view of the Big Island and coast of Maui is better than at the Visitors Center below. The lava rock ridge just in front of the parking area is the best place to watch the sunset. For perspective, it's 100 miles from the top of Haleakala to Mauna Loa in the distance.

Close to the summit is the **Maui Space Surveillance Complex** (www.ifa.hawaii.edu/haleakala), aka Science City. It's closed to the public and highly controversial, with protests over the construction of a telescope on culturally sacred land.

Camping and Cabins

To really appreciate Haleakala's beauty, you need to stay overnight. The most accessible campground is at **Hosmer's Grove,** where you don't even need a permit. There are a handful of tent sites, a few barbecue grills, a pit toilet, and running water. You can drive up to the campsites, which makes it an easy option. The campground is at 6,800 feet, so

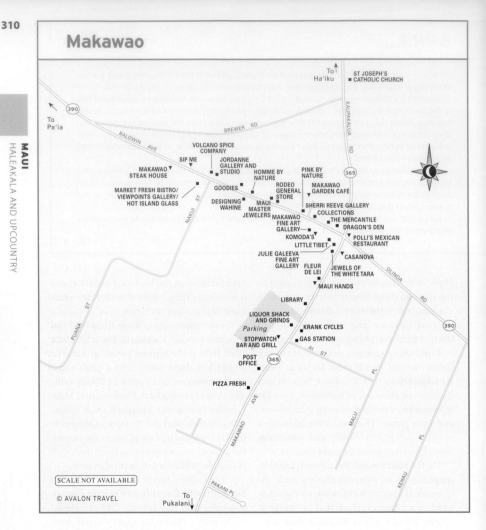

Makawao

To Ha'iku

ST JOSEPH'S
■ CATHOLIC CHURCH

390
To Pa'ia

BALDWIN AVE

BREWER RD

KAUPAKALUA RD

VOLCANO SPICE COMPANY

SIP ME ▼

MAKAWAO ▼ STEAK HOUSE

JORDANNE GALLERY AND STUDIO

HOMME BY NATURE

PINK BY NATURE

365

MARKET FRESH BISTRO/ VIEWPOINTS GALLERY/ HOT ISLAND GLASS

GOODIES

RODEO GENERAL STORE

MAKAWAO GARDEN CAFÉ

DESIGNING WAHINE

MAUI MASTER JEWELERS

SHERRI REEVE GALLERY COLLECTIONS

MAKAWAO FINE ART GALLERY—

THE MERCANTILE

DRAGON'S DEN

KOMODA'S ▼

LITTLE TIBET ■

POLLI'S MEXICAN RESTAURANT

JULIE GALEEVA FINE ART GALLERY

FLEUR DE LEI ▼

CASANOVA ▼

JEWELS OF THE WHITE TARA

MAUI HANDS ▼

OLINDA RD

LIBRARY

LIQUOR SHACK AND GRINDS

Parking

KRANK CYCLES

390

STOPWATCH ▼ BAR AND GRILL

GAS STATION

AI ST

POST OFFICE

365

PIZZA FRESH

MAKAWAO AVE

MALU

PUANA ST

NAKUI ST

PL

PL

KEHAU

SCALE NOT AVAILABLE

© AVALON TRAVEL

PAKANI PL

To Pukalani ↓

---

nights can get close to freezing. It also makes a great staging ground for driving to the summit for sunrise.

For a rugged overnight backpacking experience, there are **wilderness campsites** inside the crater at both Holua (elevation: 6,940 feet) and Paliku (6,380 feet). Camping in the crater requires a permit, which can be picked up for free from the park headquarters before it closes at 3:45pm. Both campsites have pit toilets and nonpotable water, and although the sites are first-come, first-served, they can accommodate up to 25 people and are rarely full. Maximum stay is three nights in a 30-day period, and no more than two nights in a row at the same site. Holua is accessible by a 3.7-mile hike down Halemau'u Trail and is set in a field of subalpine scrub brush looking toward the Ko'olau Gap. Paliku, on the other hand, requires hiking 9.2 miles from the Sliding Sands Trail at the summit (or a 10.3-mile hike on Halemau'u Trail), and is wet, lush, surrounded by foliage, and a good place for spotting *nene*. This is also the preferred area for hikers opting to walk out the Kaupo Gap.

In addition to campgrounds, **backcountry cabins** ($75) are available at Holua, Kapalaoa (7,250 feet), as well as Paliku. Due to their popularity, however, securing reservations can be difficult. Reservations can be made up to 180 days in advance by creating a profile on www.recreation.gov and searching for Haleakala National Park (Cabin Permits). Cabins are often booked four months in advance, so if you want to include this on your trip to Maui, plan ahead and be flexible. Cabins include 12 padded berths, a wood-burning stove, and basic kitchen utilities. Pit toilets and nonpotable water are available, and all trash must be packed out.

MAKAWAO
★ Hali'imaile Distillery

When was the last time you tried vodka made from pineapples? **Hali'imaile Distillery** (883 Hali'imaile Rd., 808/633-3609, www.halii-mailedistilling.com, tours every 30 minutes 10am-4pm Mon.-Fri., $10) is the only place in the world you'll find the sugary spirit. The team in this Quonset hut are completely redefining cocktails, from the world's only vodka aged in French oak to Kona coffee-flavored whiskey and chocolate macadamia nut vodka. Master distiller Mark Nigbur helped pioneer the process of distilling with glass, instead of copper or steel, and he's partnered with Sammy Hagar, his wild blond doppelgänger, to create Sammy's Beach Bar Rum. Tours last an hour and pass through the distillery, which is sandwiched between Hawaii's only sugar plantation and America's only pineapple plantation. Notable brands are Pau Maui Vodka and Paniolo Whiskey, and the tour is capped off by three-quarter-ounce pours for visitors over age 21.

Hui No'eau Visual Arts Center

About one mile downhill from Makawao is the **Hui No'eau Visual Arts Center** (2841 Baldwin Ave., 808/572-6560, www.huinoeau.com, 10am-4pm Mon.-Sat., $2 donation), located on a gorgeous 10-acre estate owned by the Baldwin family. The centerpiece is the neo-Spanish mansion built in 1917 and transformed in 1934 into a spectacular center for the arts. Touring the grounds is free, as is perusing the gallery, which hosts the work of local artists and has rotating exhibitions. You can pick up a self-guided tour ($6) of the property or take an hour-long guided tour ($12). History buffs should head directly to the room

Sample the spirits at Hali'imaile Distillery.

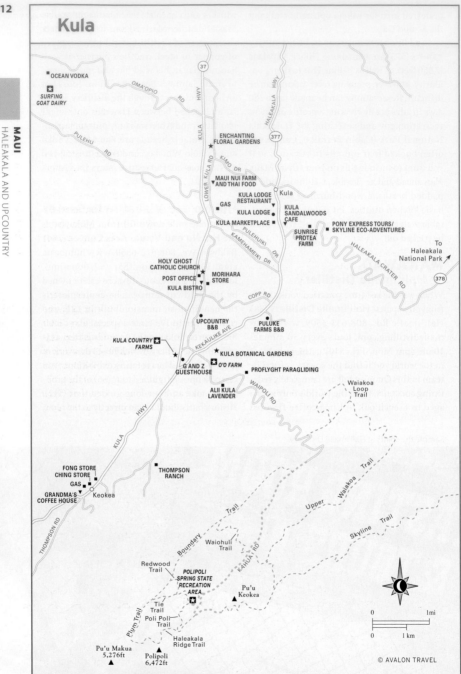

Kula

OCEAN VODKA

SURFING
GOAT DAIRY

OMA'OPIO RD

37

PULEHU RD

KULA RD

HALEAKALA HWY

ENCHANTING
FLORAL GARDENS

377

KIMO DR

LOWER KULA RD

MAUI NUI FARM
AND THAI FOOD

Kula

KULA LODGE
RESTAURANT

GAS

KULA LODGE

KULA SANDALWOODS
CAFE

KULA MARKETPLACE

PULEHUIKI DR

KAMEHAMEIKI DR

SUNRISE
PROTEA
FARM

PONY EXPRESS TOURS/
SKYLINE ECO-ADVENTURES

HALEAKALA CRATER RD

To
Haleakala
National Park

378

HOLY GHOST
CATHOLIC CHURCH

POST OFFICE

MORIHARA
STORE

KULA BISTRO

COPP RD

UPCOUNTRY
B&B

KEKAULIKE AVE

PULUKE
FARMS B&B

KULA COUNTRY
FARMS

KULA BOTANICAL GARDENS

G AND Z
GUESTHOUSE

O'O FARM

PROFLYGHT PARAGLIDING

WAIPOLI RD

Waiakoa
Loop
Trail

ALII KULA
LAVENDER

KULA HWY

FONG STORE
CHING STORE

GAS

GRANDMA'S
COFFEE HOUSE

Keokea

THOMPSON
RANCH

THOMPSON RD

Trail

Boundary

Waiohuli
Trail

Upper

Waiakoa

Trail

Skyline Trail

KAHUA RD

Pu'u
Keokea

Redwood
Trail

POLIPOLI
SPRING STATE
RECREATION
AREA

Tie
Trail

Poli Poli
Trail

Plum Trail

Haleakala
Ridge Trail

Pu'u Makua
5,276ft

Polipoli
6,472ft

0   1mi

0   1 km

© AVALON TRAVEL

full of old black-and-white photographs that show what it was like to live on the estate 100 years ago.

Makawao History Museum

If you're curious how Portugal's Azores Islands are tied to Makawao's pastures, or wonder what it was like to live on a ranch in 19th-century Maui, a short visit to the **Makawao History Museum** (3643 Baldwin Ave., 808/572-2482, 10am-5pm daily, donation) is an easy way to find out. Located in historic Makawao town amid art galleries and boutiques, the small museum has won awards for historic preservation. Look at old black-and-white photos of early Makawao ranches and read profiles of community members who helped to shape the town. The museum is completely volunteer-run and supported in part by donations. Pick up a cookbook of family recipes from Makawao's original families.

KULA

On the slopes of Haleakala between 2,000 and 4,000 feet elevation, **Kula** is the hub of Maui's rural and agricultural life. Tractors drive on two-lane roads where stands sell local produce, and flannel-clad farmers lament how deer are getting into their cabbage. For visitors, the bicoastal views are reason enough to drive here, but so are the farm tours, the winery, the shops, and the laid-back small-town vibes.

★ Kula Country Farms

Kula Country Farms (Kula Hwy., past mile marker 13, 808/878-8381, www.kulacountryfarmsmaui.com, 10am-5pm Tues.-Fri., 8am-4pm Sat.-Sun.) perfectly captures Kula's agricultural spirit. Stop in for affordable produce where colors explode off the shelves. Buy a healthy snack to enjoy with the ocean view. In October the farm gets festive and features a corn maze and an eight-acre pumpkin patch, although the main reason to visit is to support local farmers.

Ali'i Kula Lavender Farm

If you've ever wanted lavender tea . . . or lavender sunscreen, lavender body butter, or lavender scones, **Ali'i Kula Lavender Farm** (1100 Waipoli Rd., 808/878-3004, www.aliikulalavender.com, 9am-4pm daily, $3) is worth a stop. Located at the top of Waipoli Road on the way up toward Polipoli, the views at 4,000 feet elevation stretch all the way to the ocean. The air is crisp for walking around the farm,

fresh produce at Kula Country Farms

and the shrill calls of ring-necked pheasants echo above the pastures. The farm itself is 13.5 acres, and guided walking tours ($12) are given at 9:30am, 10:30am, 11:30am, 1pm, and 2:30pm daily. A small café serves scones and tea. The view, the serenity, and a warm cup of tea make this a relaxing stop.

Botanical Gardens

By Waipoli Road, the **Kula Botanical Garden** (638 Kekaulike Ave., 808/878-1715, www.kulabotanicalgarden.com, 9am-4pm daily, $10 adults, $3 children) is a 19-acre private garden with 2,500 species of plants. There are over 90 varieties of protea alone, and the self-guided walking tour takes 45 minutes. If you're on your way down from Haleakala and didn't get to see a *nene* goose, the botanical garden has two, which means you can at least get photos. You'll also find a chameleon exhibit, a Christmas tree farm, three carved wooden tiki gods, and coffee that's grown on the farm.

Meet the goats at Surfing Goat Dairy.

★ Surfing Goat Dairy

While it's a bit out of the way, eccentric **Surfing Goat Dairy** (3651 Omaopio Rd., 808/878-2870, www.surfinggoatdairy.com, 9am-5pm Mon.-Sat., 9am-2pm Sun.) is a must-see. Where else are you going to get the chance to hand-milk a goat and then feast on gourmet cheese? Three miles down Omaopio Road off Kula Highway (Hwy. 37), a line of enormous palms provides what's probably the most regal entrance to a goat dairy anywhere. There are 30-plus flavors of gourmet goat cheese and over 25 types of goat cheese truffles. The best reason to visit is the 3:15pm tour. "Casual" tours ($12) run every 30 minutes 10am-3pm daily, but the 3:15pm tour ($17) allows you to hand-milk a goat.

Ocean Vodka Organic Farm and Distillery

It isn't a vacation until you're sipping vodka at 10am. Located next door to Surfing Goat Dairy, **Ocean Organic Vodka Farm** (4051 Omaopio Rd., 808/877-0009, www.oceanvodka.com, 9:30am-5pm daily, $10) offers tours of its fully sustainable farm that produces organic vodka. The facility's energy is provided by 240 solar panels, and 30 types of Polynesian sugarcane provide the juice for vodka and rum that's distilled and bottled here. All the cane is hand-harvested, bottles are labeled by hand, and leftovers are used as organic mulch, while chickens take care of the pests.

At the outdoor thatched-roof tasting room, amid fields of waving sugarcane, sip on samples of vodka and rum sourced from different types of sugar. Some have flavors of banana and coconut despite not containing them. Even stranger, the water that's used in distilling the spirits is sourced from 3,000 feet below sea level, where heavy mineral-laden water has spent 2,000 years drifting from Greenland to the coast of the Big Island (really). Tours begin at 9:30am daily and run every 30 minutes until 4pm.

KEOKEA AND ULUPALAKUA

Once you pass Rice Park and the turnoff for Highway 377, the road begins to take on a different feel. The elevation slowly drops, the jacaranda trees provide shade over the road, and the views of South Maui begin to open up before you. Life is slow up here, in this hangout of artists, farmers, and lifelong ranchers. You'll know you've reached the community of Keokea when you see **Keokea Park** on the left, a small field that also has a playground and public restrooms.

Across from Grandma's Coffee House is the turnoff for **Thompson Road,** a one-lane pasture-lined country road that offers one of the island's best views and a leisurely spot for a stroll. By mile marker 18, on the way to Ulupalakua, is the small **Sun Yat-sen Park,** named for the revolutionary who helped found modern China.

★ Maui Wine

Yes, there is actually a winery on Maui, and yes, it's actually good. Once considered an island novelty that only served pineapple wine, **Maui Wine** (14815 Pi'ilani Hwy., 808/878-6058, www.mauiwine.com, 10am-5:30pm daily), like a fine wine, is getting better by the year. There are three varieties of pineapple wine, but there's also grenache, malbec, syrah, viognier, and chenin blanc. Aside from the wine and complimentary tastings, what makes the winery a must-see is its history and beauty.

The tasting room bar is 18 feet long and made from a single mango tree. The guest cottage where King Kalakaua stayed when he visited the ranch in 1874 is now the tasting room. There's a small historical room attached to the tasting area that details the history of the ranch (allegedly Kalakaua had too much cheer and wagered Molokini while gambling), and free tours trace the ranch's progression from potatoes to sugarcane to wine. Wondering about the cannon sitting in the yard? It was fired to greet King Kalakaua as part of his

regal arrival. Today, that heritage is carried on with the "King's Visit"—a private tasting, booked in advance, that pairs the fine estate wines with meat and produce sourced from the ranch and prepared by a private chef.

TOURS

Makawao

If you think pineapples grow underground or on trees, you should probably spend a couple of hours on the **Maui Pineapple Tour** (875 Hali'imaile Rd., 808/665-5491, www.mauipineappletours.com, 9:30am and 11:45am daily, $65). Learn why Maui's pineapples are sweet and taste like golden candy. Everyone gets a free pineapple, and you can eat Maui gold in the fields until your gums tingle. Bring a camera for the sweeping views, and don't forget the sunscreen. The minimum age is five, and the pineapple tour conveniently aligns with distillery tours next door.

For customized private tours of the island, **Open Eye Tours** (808/572-3483, www.openeyetours.com, from $825 and up for 1 or 2 adults) is based in Makawao and led by Pono, a guide who's been offering tours of Maui since 1983. The tours have an emphasis on Hawaiian culture, and through contacts built up over the years, he's able to bring visitors to properties you otherwise wouldn't get to visit. For example, a Hana tour bus won't stop at a taro field to help pull taro with the owners, but Pono will. As a former teacher, he also specializes in arranging activities for children.

Kula

★ O'O FARM

For a romantic Maui luncheon in the middle of a farm, where you can sip wine beneath a vine-covered trellis and dine on fish or chicken prepared by a chef in an outdoor kitchen, check out the **O'o Farm Gourmet Luncheon Tour** (651 Waipoli Rd., 808/667-4341, www.oofarm.com, 10:30am-2pm Mon.-Thurs., $58), where visitors take a tour around the eight-acre farm and choose from

60 different crops while picking a salad in the fields.

The air up here is misty and cool, at least when the clouds roll in, and there's nothing like a cup of French-pressed coffee. The first hour is spent touring the farm and meeting the on-site chef, who arrives at the farm at sunrise to source ingredients from the fields. Much of the produce used travels a total of 400 feet. Instead of a farm-to-table restaurant, the table has been brought to the farm. The wine is BYOB, and there's also a **"Seed to Cup"** **Coffee Tour** with coffee grown on the farm (8:30am-10:30am Tues.-Wed., $50).

For a smaller, more intimate, one-man operation of coffee, protea, and produce, the **Shim Farm Tour** (625 Middle Rd., 808/876-0055, www.shimfarmtour.com, 9am-5pm daily, reservations required, $7) runs February-June. Learn the history of the Chinese people in Kula on the affordable one-hour family-run tour.

Hiking and Biking

HIKING
Haleakala National Park
Thanks to the colorful cinder cones and trails that crunch underfoot, anyone who hikes across Haleakala Crater will swear they could be on the moon. Covering a total of 19 square miles, the crater basin is a vast wilderness with 30 miles of trails. It's a place of adventure, mythology, and silence—and home to Maui's best hiking. If you love the outdoors, no trip to Maui is complete without a spending a day on the crater floor.

Hikers need to be prepared, however, as temperatures can range from 30°F to 80°F over the course of a single day. The hiking is at high elevation, 7,000 to 10,000 feet, and hiking back up generally takes twice as long as the hike down. **Hike Maui** (808/879-5270, www.hikemaui.com, $179) is the only company that offers commercially guided hiking tours. Should you go on your own, here's a rundown of the most popular hikes, listed from shortest to longest. All mileage is round-trip.

PA KA'OAO (0.4 MILE)
If you don't feel like watching the sunrise with 200 other people, huff your way up the five-minute **Pa Ka'oao Trail** that leaves from the Visitors Center parking lot. The view from the top looks down toward the crater, and it's better than from the parking lot. Bring a flashlight for the walking the trail before sunrise.

LELEIWI OVERLOOK (0.5 MILE)
Running late for sunrise? Consider hiking to **Leleiwi Overlook** (8,840 feet). Located by mile marker 17.5, Leleiwi has smaller crowds and is usually warmer. The view looks down on the crater floor and the sheer multihued cliffs, although since the lookout faces east, it isn't as good for sunset.

HOSMER'S GROVE NATURE TRAIL (0.5 MILE)
Unlike other trails in the park, the **Hosmer's Grove Nature Trail** is at the park's lower boundary just after you enter the park. The short trail loops through a dense grove of trees, planted in 1910 as part of an unsuccessful experiment to test the viability of the lumber industry. Surrounded by sweet-smelling pine and fir, grab a fleece and go for a stroll through the 20-plus species of trees, listening for forest **birds** that flit around in the treetops. To reach the trailhead, make a left on the road pointing toward the campground immediately after entering the park. The walk, over mostly level ground, should take 30 minutes. To extend the trip, hike the **Supply Trail** for 2.3 miles to where it meets with the crater rim.

HALEMAU'U TRAIL (SWITCHBACK TRAIL) (7.5 MILES)
Beginning from an altitude of only 7,990 feet, the first 1.1 miles of the **Halemau'u Trail**

Haleakala National Park

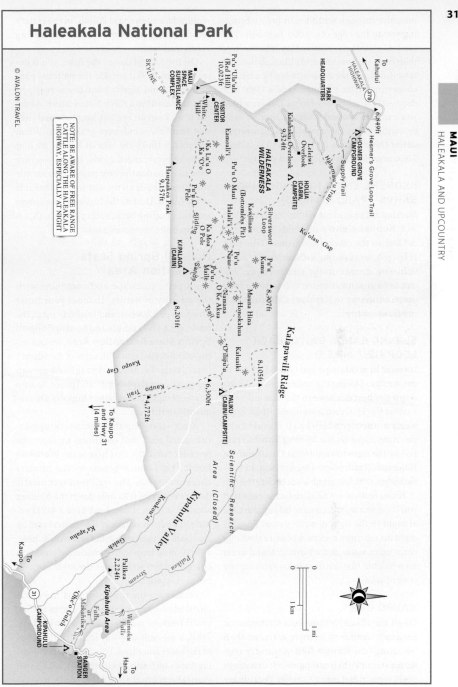

© AVALON TRAVEL

NOTE: BE AWARE OF FREE RANGE
CATTLE ALONG THE HALEAKALA
HIGHWAY, ESPECIALLY AT NIGHT

To
Kahului
(378) ▲ 6,849ft

Hosmer's Grove Loop Trail

PARK
HEADQUARTERS

▲ HOSMER GROVE
CAMPGROUND

Supply Trail

Halemau'u Trail

Kalahaku Overlook
9,324ft

Leleiwi
Overlook

HOLUA
(CABIN/
CAMPSITE)

Ko'olau Gap

Pu'u 'Ula'ula
(Red Hill)
10,023ft

SKYLINE DR.

MAUI
SPACE
SURVEILLANCE
COMPLEX

VISITOR
CENTER

White
Hill

Ka Lu'u
O
Ka 'O'o

Kaupo
and Hwy 31
(4 miles)

Eamoali'i

Pu'u O Maui

Pu'u O.
Pele

Pu'u O.
Sliding
Sands

HALEAKALA
WILDERNESS

(Bottomless Pit)

Kawilinau

Halali'i

Ka Moa
O Pele

Silversword
Loop

Pu'u
Naue

Pu'u
Maile

Pu'u'
O Ke Akua

Namana
Trail

Pu'u
Kumu

▲ 8,907ft

Maile

Mauna Hina

Honokahua

'O'ilipo'u

Kaluaiki

Kalapawili Ridge

8,105ft ▲

Haupakea Peak
9,157ft

KIPALAOA
(CABIN)

▲ 8,201ft

Kaupo Gap

Kaupo Trail

▲ 4,772ft

▲ 6,300ft

PALIKU
(CABIN/CAMPSITE)

Scientific Research Area (Closed)

To Kaupo

Koukou'ai

Ka'apahu

Kipahulu Valley

Palikea
2,224ft

Palikea Stream

Kipahulu Area

'Ohe'o Gulch

Waimoku
Falls

Falls
at
Makahiku

KIPAHULU
CAMPGROUND

RANGER
STATION

To
Hana

(31)

0   1 mi
0   1 km

meander through scrub brush before bringing you to the edge of a 1,000-foot cliff. The view down into the Ko'olau Gap is better here than from the summit, and although the trail is well-defined, the drop-offs can be a bit disconcerting. After 3.7 miles—and a 1,000 foot drop—the trail passes Holua Cabin, where you can turn around. Tack on another mile by continuing to Silversword Loop, a section of the crater known for its numerous 'ahinahina, or endangered silversword plants.

KEONEHE'EHE'E TRAIL (SLIDING SANDS TRAIL) (8 MILES)

Starting at the summit visitor center at 9,800 feet, **Keonehe'ehe'e** descends 2,500 vertical feet to the crater floor below. This trail is barren, windswept, without shade, and a stunning conduit to the cinder cones. You can turn around anytime you want to hike out. Continuing to Kapalaoa Cabin adds 3.5 miles round-trip.

SLIDING SANDS SWITCHBACK LOOP (12.2 MILES)

If you're in good shape and have a full day to devote to exploring the crater, this is hands-down the best day hike in the summit area. Park at the Halemau'u trailhead, then hitch a ride to the top, where you'll hike down to the crater floor on the **Sliding Sands** Trail. Follow the signs toward Holua Cabin and the Halemau'u Trail, where a leg-burning, switchbacking, 1,000-foot climb leads back to the car.

If you really want an island adventure that you'll never forget, consider hiking the trail at night in the light of a full moon. For this night hike, bring a backpack of extra clothing, carry extra water and a flashlight, and dress for windchill that can drop below freezing any time of year.

KAUPO GAP

Of all the hikes in Haleakala Crater, none are more legendary, or more extreme, than "shooting" the **Kaupo Gap**, a two-day trip, with a stay at Paliku campground, that drops 9,500 vertical feet over 17.5 miles. Permits are required for camping at Paliku, in the crater's remotest corner, 9.2 miles from the Sliding Sands trailhead.

On the second day of the hike, you'll descend from Paliku outside the national park boundary, and legally continue across private land until you reach Kaupo Store. Along the trail, keep an eye out for goats and deer that roam the windswept grasslands. When you finally finish the hike in Kaupo, it's best if you've prearranged a ride. If not, you may have to convince the rare passerby to shuttle your sweaty body all the way to the other side of the island. Despite the logistical challenges and the grueling backcountry terrain, this is a unique and memorable hike.

Polipoli Spring State Recreation Area

For a place to escape and commune with the serenity of nature, channel your inner Emerson or Thoreau, and meditate up in the mists, get a 4WD vehicle and head to **Polipoli Spring State Recreation Area,** an out-of-the-way forested spot with some of the island's best hiking. Trails pass through old-growth redwoods, eucalyptus, ash, and pines. Be sure to wear bright colors, since hunters are frequently in the area.

After ascending the switchbacking pasture-lined road that continues up from the lavender farm, the first hike is the **Waiakoa Loop Trail,** which begins by the hunters check-in station. The trailhead technically doesn't begin for 0.75 mile down the hunting access road, but if you don't have a 4WD vehicle, it's better to park at the hunters station and walk to the trailhead. Once you're here, a three-mile loop with a moderate elevation change of 400 feet passes through lowland brush and pines.

Farther up the road, just past the cattle guard where the road eventually turns to dirt, you'll find the trailhead for the **Boundary Trail,** a 4.4-mile one-way trail that descends to the lower fence line. This trail offers sweeping views of South Maui, and since it's 1,000 vertical feet lower than other trails, it won't

hiking in on the Waihou Spring Trail

the only person there. Even on regular days, however, Skyline is a strenuous hike providing panoramic views down the mountain's southwest rift zone. Though Haleakala has been dormant for more than 220 years, volcanologists claim that when the mountain erupts again, magma will cover the barren landscape that's visible from this trail. To reach the trailhead for Skyline Drive, turn left at the fork that leads down to the campground from the main dirt road. From here, the road continues climbing and begins to double back toward the north, along the way passing the trailhead for the 1.8-mile **Mamane Trail.** Eventually you'll reach a locked gate at an area known as the Ballpark (7,000 feet). From here it's a 3,000-vertical-foot switchbacking trail to the summit. Pack plenty of water and warm clothing, and be aware of the challenges of hiking at altitude.

Makawao

In the heart of the Makawao Forest Reserve, the **Kahakapao Loop Trail** is popular with mountain bikers and families walking their dogs. This forested 5.7-mile loop weaves through eucalyptus and pines, and the air is cool at just over 3,000 feet elevation. To reach the trailhead from Makawao, follow Makawao Avenue toward Haʻiku for 0.3 mile before turning right on Piʻiholo Road. After 1.5 miles, just past the Piʻiholo zipline tours, take a left at the fork in the road and follow it for 0.5 mile. Here you'll make a right onto Kahakapao Road and drive 1.5 miles on a narrow uphill until you reach a metal gate (open 7am-7pm daily). From the gate, a steep asphalt road continues for another 0.5 miles until it reaches a gravel parking lot. Expect to encounter some cyclists while hiking, since it's a multiuse network of trails.

If you don't feel like dealing with throngs of bikers, head to the **Waihou Spring Trail,** toward the top of Olinda Road. This two-mile trail is only open to hikers and doesn't have as steep an elevation gain as at Kahakapao. It's uniquely situated among an experimental planting of pine trees, and while the wooded

leave you as winded. It can either be done as an out-and-back hike or combined with other trails as a loop. The shortest loop is up the **Lower Waiohuli Trail,** which intersects the Boundary Trail at the 2.6-mile mark. Turning left on the Lower Waiohuli Trail, it's 1.4 miles back uphill to the main road, then a 2.5-mile trek back along the dirt road to your car.

If seven miles seems too far, most of the shorter walks in Polipoli begin and end at the campground. While some are only a mile long, the best hike in the park for first-time visitors is the 5.3-mile loop trail formed by connecting the **Haleakala Ridge Trail, Polipoli Trail, Redwood Trail,** and **Plum Trail.** Driving all the way to the campground requires a 4WD vehicle.

It's possible to hike all the way from Polipoli to the summit of Haleakala. Follow the 6.8-mile dirt road, known as **Skyline Drive,** a "back entrance" to Haleakala National Park. If it has snowed recently atop Haleakala and the rangers have closed the road, this is an alternative way to hike into the park and be trail is nice enough for walking, the treat is at the end, where a steep switchback leads to a hidden gulch. Here you'll find a 30-foot vertical rock face with tunnels bored through, and if you have a flashlight, you can climb in the tunnels and follow them for a short distance. To reach the trailhead for Waihou Springs, go to Makawao's only intersection and follow Olinda Road uphill for five very curvy miles.

Bike Down Haleakala

You've seen the brochures, you've heard the hype; here's the deal with cycling down Haleakala volcano:

It's imperative to be confident and competent on a bicycle. It is marketed as beginner-friendly, but in reality, dozens of people are seriously injured each year. In almost all cases it's because they took their eyes off the road or were riding too fast.

That said, watching the day begin from Haleakala Crater and the crisp air in your face as you weave through cow-speckled pastures is magical. Visit the shops of Makawao town and finish the ride close to the beach. A wide range of operators have different options, and the key to an enjoyable trip is choosing carefully. Decide whether you want to include sunrise at Haleakala Crater. This means waking up early, with pickups at 2am. After watching the sunrise, it's back in the van for the drive down to 6,500 feet, where all the tours begin the cycling portion, outside the national park. If you opt for a tour that doesn't include sunrise, you'll be driven to this spot, usually arriving about 10am. The next option is whether to ride with a guide. The benefit is safety, but it means you have to follow the pace of the group. For independent-minded travelers, it's probably best to choose a company that lets you ride on your own.

The third option to consider is where the tour ends: in Upper Kula with a zipline combo, or all the way to the beach. It's possible to ride from the summit to the beach with your own car and bike. **Krank Cycles** (1120 Makawao Ave., 808/572-2299, www.krank-maui.com, 9am-6pm daily) and **Haleakala Bike Company** (810 Ha'iku Rd., Suite 120, 808/575-9575, www.bikemaui.com) offer independent rentals, although **Maui Sunriders** (71 Baldwin Ave., 866/500-2453, www.mauisunriders.com) is the most convenient, as its shop is near the beach.

With those options in mind, here are some of our top picks:

Maui Easy Riders (808/344-9489, www.mauieasyriders.com, $119, online booking

Bike nearly 7,000 feet down a dormant volcano.

Tips for Biking the Volcano

- If you go with a tour, you can't ride from the summit. If you want to bike from the summit, you have to provide your own bicycle and transportation.

- Seeing the sunrise isn't guaranteed: 15 percent of the time the crater is clouded in. Variations in the weather aren't seasonal, so all you can do is hope for the best.

- If you want to spend more than 15 minutes at Haleakala after sunrise, save sunrise for a separate trip and book a midmorning bike ride. The trip will be cheaper, and you'll be able to hike and explore the crater without having to rush back to the van.

- Be prepared to wake up *really* early for a sunrise tour. Companies collect guests from the farthest hotels first, so if you're staying in Makena or Kapalua, expect to meet your driver as early as 1:45am. Try to book this excursion early in your trip, when you're still jet-lagged and waking up early.

- If you're on a budget, opt for a midmorning tour. It isn't as cold, you don't have to wake up as early, it isn't as crowded, and the trips are substantially cheaper. Companies charge more for the sunrise tours because they're popular.

- Remember that you're sharing the road with cars. There are no bike lanes, so be sure to keep your eyes on the road at all times.

- Pack closed-toe shoes, long pants, a rain jacket, and warm clothing. Early morning temperatures often dip below freezing at the summit. Although many tour companies provide rain gear, the more protection you have against the elements, the better.

- Don't expect to get any sleep in the van ride up. The road switchbacks incessantly, and drivers entertain the riders with island history and jokes.

- If you're skittish, go with a guided group. If you're an independent person, choose an independent company so you can ride without a guide.

- Don't schedule your bike ride for the day after scuba diving; decompression sickness can kill.

$99) is a small operation run by two brothers, both named Billy (really). Group size is small, only eight people, and tours begin at 9am in the parking lot of Pa'ia Bay. The ride begins at 6,600 feet, just above where other companies begin, and the 25-mile ride to the beach is longer than any other company. This guided tour makes a stop in Makawao for 30 minutes of exploring on foot, and at the end you can literally jump off your bike and into the waves.

The other top pick for guided tours is the ride with **Bike It Maui** (808/878-3364, www. bikeitmaui.com), whose sunrise tour ($140 if booked 7 days in advance, $150 within 7 days) also includes breakfast afterward. Its van is the most comfortable for the ride up

the mountain, and its bikes are exceptionally well maintained. The ride ends in Lower Kula.

Other providers who ride to the beach include **Mountain Riders** (800/706-7700, www.mountainriders.com, $67-120) and **Cruiser Phil's** (808/893-2332, www.cruiserphil.com, $89-135).

For an independent ride, **Maui Sunriders** (71 Baldwin Ave., 808/579-8970, www. mauisunriders.com) has sunrise tours ($125) that start from and end at its shop in Pa'ia, as well as an affordable "Express" tour ($76). Visitors can explore Pa'ia once the ride is over.

Other independent tours include **Haleakala Bike Company** (810 Ha'iku Rd., Suite 120, 808/575-9575, www.bikemaui.com), offering a sunrise tour ($100) and a "Haleakala Express" ride ($65) that end at Ha'iku Marketplace.

MOUNTAIN BIKING

The **mountain biking** on Maui is really good. The two main areas Upcountry are the **Makawao Forest Reserve,** about 15 minutes above Makawao, and **Polipoli,** above Kula. Thanks to the team at Krank Cycles, the Makawao Forest Reserve has recently undergone over $500,000 in trail work, which means Makawao has some of the best trails in Hawaii. With 16 miles of trail in total, there are terrain parks, single-track, two-mile climbs, and even a 30-foot banked wooden wall you'd expect to find in a place like Whistler. The "Pineapple Express" is two miles of downhill, and the west loop on the Kahakapao Trail is the most popular trail for climbing.

Polipoli, on the other hand, offers rugged downhill mountain biking, with a network of trails that switchback through redwoods, lava flows, and wide-open plains. You'll need a 4WD vehicle to reach some trailheads, and forget about visiting after a rain, since you'll get stuck in the mud. For a classic climb and single-track descent, park where the **Mamane Trail** meets the road toward the campground.

Start by riding in the direction of the campground and turn uphill at the fork, where you'll climb along the spine of the mountain before the two-mile Mamane Trail drop.

For the island's longest off-road descent, the chance to bike from 10,000 feet, have someone drive you to Haleakala for the start of **Skyline Drive.** The unpaved road begins by Science City and switchbacks its way across desolate cinder that looks like the surface of the moon. Watch for wild goats and hunters, and definitely wear bright clothing. After six miles, turn down the Mamane Trail for two fast miles of single-track. For a full 7,000-foot vertical descent, continue riding all the way down to Highway 37, then turn left for the two-mile ride on pavement to Grandma's Coffee House. Arrange to have your ride pick you up here.

For Upcountry bike rentals, **Krank Cycles** (1120 Makawao Ave., 808/572-2299, www.krankmaui.com, 9am-6pm daily) is located in Makawao and offers half-day (9am-1pm or 1:30pm-5:30pm, $35) and full-day ($75) rentals. Half day rentals are enough time for the Makawao trails, but not for Polipoli. These guys are Maui's most dedicated mountain bike shop; check out the website for current trail conditions.

Adventure Sports and Horseback Riding

PARAGLIDING

When was the last time you ran off a hill and experienced total silence? Or saw Maui from a bird's eye view without the whir of a chopper? **Proflyght Hawaii Paragliding** (1598 Waipoli Rd., 808/874-5433, www.paraglidemaui.com, 7am-7pm daily) is Hawaii's only paragliding school, and thanks to Maui's optimal conditions, flights are possible about 330 days per year. The launch and landing sites are perfect for learning, and nearly every flight takes place in the morning before the clouds

fill in. Tandem flights drop 1,000 feet ($95) or 3,000 feet ($185) over the Polipoli treetops. This unforgettable island experience is highly recommended.

ZIPLINE TOURS

Believe it or not, Upcountry is where **ziplining** was born in the United States. In 2002, **Skyline Eco-Adventures** (12 Kiopa'a Place, 808/878-8400, www.zipline.com, 7am-7pm daily) opened in Kula's misty uplands, the first in the country. Today, Skyline offers a five-line course best for beginners ($108), since the length of the lines and vertical drops aren't dramatic. There's also the option to combine a zipline with a sunrise Haleakala bike tour ($225), although the bike ride only descends 2,500 feet, so the combo is best for people who just want a sample of both activities. The course is located on the road toward Haleakala at approximately 4,000 feet elevation, and the lines run through misty, cloud-shrouded groves of eucalyptus and koa. Once you unhook from the final line, which is the longest and easily most thrilling, stroll through the neighboring lavender farm with a warm drink from the café.

In the forests above Makawao, 20 minutes away, **Pi'iholo Zipline Tours** (799 Pi'iholo Rd., 808/572-1717, www.piiholozipline.com, 7am-9pm daily, $99-219) takes the adrenaline up a notch. This is the site of the island's longest side-by-side parallel zipline, which means you can watch Mom scream in terror for 2,300 feet. At one point your feet are 600 feet above the ground, and occasionally in winter there are small waterfalls that splash through the rocky ravines. Pi'iholo can often be rainy, particularly in winter. Visitors can choose either four or five lines, but since the fifth line is the 2,300-foot screamer, it's best to get the full experience. There's also a seven- or eight-line excursion that weaves through the treetops, a great option for families with kids who aren't quite ready for the screamer.

HORSEBACK RIDING

Upcountry is horse country, and in the rolling Upcountry pasturelands, **horseback riding** is a slice of authentic Upcountry life. All of Upcountry's horseback options are on working ranches, which mean you're dealing with real *paniolo* who still ranch, wrangle, and ride.

For a small-scale intimate experience in the most beautiful pastures on Maui, **Thompson Ranch** (Middle Rd., 808/878-1910, www.thompsonranchmaui.com, $125, cash only) offers guided trail rides on its Keokea ranch. This is a family-run working cattle ranch that's far from touristy, and the ranch owners love their horses. The view here is unforgettable, with green pastures rolling down to the blue Pacific. The climb is steep, and the maximum weight for riders is 200 pounds.

In Makawao, **Pi'iholo Ranch** (808/270-8750, www.piiholo.com, 8:30am-1pm Mon.-Sat.) offers horseback tours on its 800 acre spread. Options include a two-hour ride across cattle-filled pastures ($229) and a

paragliding in Polipoli

three-hour ride with lunch at a private cabin ($349). Roping sessions are often held in the arena on Thursday afternoons. To reach Pi'iholo Ranch, go 1.5 miles up Pi'iholo Road before branching left onto Waiahiwi Road. Follow this for 0.5 mile; the sign for the ranch is on the left.

For a ranch adventure unlike any other, book the half-day Kanaio Beach ride (4.5 hours, $285) with the crew at **Triple L Ranch** (15900 Pi'ilani Hwy., 808/280-7070, www.triplelranchmaui.com, 8am-6pm daily). Located four miles past the Maui winery on the back road toward Hana, the ranch is set in windswept Kanaio, the youngest part of Maui. The cattle are all free range and roam the mountain without fences. There's no denying the magic of riding a horse to an isolated beach, even though it's rocky and lacking sand. Kanaio is laden with archaeological sites and abandoned lava-rock fishing villages. Maximum weight is 220 pounds, and minimum age is 12. Group size is limited to two or three.

Shopping

★ HISTORIC MAKAWAO TOWN

Makawao is a town of laughter, smiles, and curious moments, where a truck might pass with a goat in the back with a tailgate made out of rope, and where locals can't stroll two blocks without waving at three people they know. It's a hive of artistic, creative individuals, with strong *paniolo* ranching heritage and hitching posts lining the wood shingled storefronts that don't see much use anymore. Find a roadside parking spot and stroll around town.

Art Galleries

For Polynesian jewelry, visit **Maui Master Jewelers** (3655 Baldwin Ave., 808/573-5400, www.mauimasterjewelers.com, 10am-5pm Mon.-Fri., 10am-4pm Sat.), where works by over 30 local artists are on display. It is the island's leading source for New Zealand bone and jade carvings and also offer Tahitian pearl jewelry.

Sherri Reeve Gallery (3669 Baldwin Ave., 808/572-8931, www.sreeve.com, 9am-5pm Mon.-Fri., 10am-4pm Sat.-Sun.) showcases this ebullient Makawao artist whose distinctive floral designs have graced shirts, cards, paintings, and prints since it opened in 1997. This is a worthwhile stop among the large number of galleries in town.

In the Courtyard shopping area, **Viewpoints Gallery** (3620 Baldwin Ave., 808/572-5979, www.viewpointsgallerymaui.com, 10:30am-5pm daily) is a large, clean space that features a rotating array of artists, predominantly painters.

Back behind the gallery next to Market Fresh Bistro is **Hot Island Glass** (3620 Baldwin Ave., 808/572-4527, www.hotislandglass.com, 9am-5pm daily), the island's best-known glass studio, where you can watch artists blow glass (10:30am-4pm Mon.-Sat.). Call ahead to check the demonstration schedule.

For original oil paintings from over a dozen artists, check out the intimate **Makawao Fine Art Gallery** (3660 Baldwin Ave., 808/573-5972, www.makawaofineartgallery.com, 11am-5pm Mon.-Sat., noon-5pm Sun.), open since 1986. The gallery is a collector's haven for limited-edition pieces.

On a corner in the center of town, **Julie Galeeva Fine Art** (3682 Baldwin Ave., 808/573-4772, www.juliegaleeva.com, 10am-5pm Mon.-Sat.) showcases the highly textured paintings of this talented Russian-born artist and Maui resident.

Clothing and Gifts

The Mercantile (3673 Baldwin Ave., 808/572-1401, 10am-6pm daily) specializes in boutique women's clothing, and **Pink by Nature** (3643 Baldwin Ave., 808/572-9576, 10am-6pm Mon.-Sat., 11am-5pm Sun.) has a chic selection of the newest and trendiest styles. Its brother store, **Homme by Nature** (3643 Baldwin Ave., 808/572-3456, 9:30am-6pm Mon.-Sat., 10am-5pm Sun.) is a rustic yet modern wood-paneled enclave of vintage menswear and home decor.

The collection of clanging wind chimes announces your arrival at **Goodies** (3633 Baldwin Ave., 808/572-0288, 10am-6pm daily), an eccentric but genuinely artsy clothing boutique for women. **Designing Wahine Emporium** (3640 Baldwin Ave., 808/573-0990, 10am-6pm Mon.-Sat., 11am-5pm Sun.) offers something for everyone, including a selection of men's aloha shirts.

To pick up a rub for a sunset barbecue, the **Volcano Spice Company** (3623 Baldwin Ave., 808/575-7729, www.volcanospicecompany.com, hours vary, usually 11am-5pm Mon.-Sat., 11am-3pm Sun.) is a small shop full of spices made on the property. Try the coffee barbecue rub and the original volcano spice blend.

Fleur de Lei (1169 Makawao Ave., 808/269-8855, 10:30am-6:30pm daily) is an eco-boutique with clothing items made from organic cotton, as well as "sail bags" made from recycled windsurfing and kitesurfing sails. The store promotes fair trade and sustainable practices, and if you aren't familiar with vegan leather, stop in and ask.

For Maui-made arts and crafts such as paintings, woodwork, and jewelry, **Maui Hands** (1169 Makawao Ave., 808/572-2008, www.mauihands.com, 10am-6pm Mon.-Sat., 11am-5pm Sun.) is on Makawao Avenue right next to the Makawao library.

KULA
Art Galleries
There's only one artist on the island who really nails Upcountry. Driving past the Kula Lodge to Haleakala, make a stop at the **Curtis Wilson Cost Gallery** (15200 Haleakala Hwy., 808/874-6544, www.costgallery.com,

8:30am-5pm daily), tucked neatly beneath the restaurant. The vibe is like a fine wine cellar filled with exceptional art. Having painted the island's rural corners for over 40 years, Cost now has the longest-running one-man gallery in Hawaii. Art can be ordered with custom koa frames or individually commissioned, and the work of his daughter, Julia Cost, is also displayed.

Worcester Glassworks (4626 Lower Kula Rd., 808/878-4000, www.worcesterglassworks.com, hours vary, usually 10am-5pm Mon.-Sat., by appointment Sun.), by Kula Bistro restaurant, is a well-lit gallery inside a rustic studio mostly occupied by industrial machinery used in the glass blowing process. The resident glassblowers, Bill and Sally Worcester, operate this family-run studio and welcome guests "most days."

Gifts and Flowers
Right next to Kula Lodge is the **Proteas of Hawaii Gift Shop** (15200 Halealakala Hwy., 808/878-2533, www.proteasofhawaii.com, 8am-4pm daily), where you can pick up a bouquet of freshly cut protea ($75-140) grown only half a mile away.

Down the driveway from Kula Lodge is the exceptional **Kula Marketplace** (808/878-2135, www.kulamarketplace.com, 7am-7pm daily), an oasis of gifts from over 200 local artists, including jams, honey, coffee, music, and clothing. It's a great place to wander while digesting breakfast from neighboring Kula Lodge.

KEOKEA AND ULUPALAKUA
Art Gallery and Fine Furniture
Next to Grandma's Coffee House, tiny little **Keokea Gallery** (9230 Kula Hwy., 808/878-3555, 9am-5pm daily) has linocut collages, handmade frames, and a collection of painted surfboards. The affable artist in residence, Sheldon, is always up for a chat, and the works here are surprisingly good considering the rural location.

To return from vacation with a desk so

beautiful it will make your coworkers cry, walk to **The Kingswood Shop and Gallery** (8900 Kula Hwy., 808/878-3626, www.kingswoodshop.com, 10am-4pm Wed.-Sat.), not far from Keokea Park. The legendary woodworker Peter Naramore has exquisite pieces of koa wood furniture and exceptional heirloom antiques, and can also commission custom pieces unique to your tastes.

Clothing and Gifts

All the way out here in "deep Upcountry," the only real place for clothing and gifts is the **Ulupalakua Ranch Store** (14800 Pi'ilani Hwy., 808/878-2561, www.ulupalakuaranch.com/store, 9:30am-5:30pm daily), open for 150 years. The store features products from a dozen local vendors, and since it is on a working ranch, you'll find Wranglers and belts rather than aloha shirts and sunscreen. Consider buying a hat or shirt to help the ranch stay afloat, which helps keep the open spaces and *paniolo* heritage alive.

Visitors to Keokea should look inside **Ching Store** (9212 Kula Hwy., 808/878-1556, 7am-5:30pm daily) and **Henry Fong Store** (9226 Kula Hwy., 808/878-1525, 7:30am-5:30pm Mon.-Sat., 7:30am-3pm Sun.). These family-run businesses are fascinating time portals, where oversize cigarette boxes still serve as decor. Mrs. Fong will be quick to point out that this store is in the "new" location, since 1932; the original store opened in Keokea in 1908.

Food

MAKAWAO

American

The two best things about **Market Fresh Bistro** (3620 Baldwin Ave., 808/572-4877, www.marketfreshbistro.com, 9am-3pm Tues.-Sat., 9am-2pm Sun., dinner 6pm-8:30pm Thurs., $12) are the courtyard setting and the salmon and tomato Benedict. Emphasis is on local ingredients, and breakfast is the most popular meal, served until 11am.

A true hole-in-the-wall favorite, the **Makawao Garden Café** (3669 Baldwin Ave., 808/573-9065, www.makawaogardencafe.com, 11am-3pm Mon.-Sat., $6-9) is hidden in an alcove next to the Sherri Reeve art gallery. The café only offers outdoor seating, which means that when it rains, the restaurant closes. Laid-back and open only for lunch, options include a baby brie and bacon sandwich or quinoa salad with goat cheese. Cool down with a refreshing smoothie—flavored with mango or *lilikoi*.

If you're in the mood for a turkey or club sandwich paired with freshly squeezed juices, the deli counter inside **Rodeo General Store** (3661 Baldwin Ave., 808/572-1868, 6:30am-9pm daily, $8-10) is great for lunch on the run. The homemade chili ($4) is filling and affordable, or boost your energy with a "Green Machine"—an all-natural collection of celery, apple, parsley, cucumber, and kale thrown in the juicer.

For a juicy steak in a ranching town, **Makawao Steak House** (3612 Baldwin Ave., 808/572-8711, www.cafeoleirestaurants.com, 5pm-9pm Tues.-Sun., $25-30) has a dimly lit, dark-wood interior that makes you want to order red wine and a bowl of Maui onion soup. The steaks are expertly prepared, and this longtime local date-night venue is the most upscale restaurant downtown.

Bakery

To act like an Upcountry local, start your morning with a doughnut from ★ **Komoda Store and Bakery** (3674 Baldwin Ave., 808/572-7261, 7am-4pm Mon.-Tues. and Thurs.-Fri., 7am-2pm Sat.). Komoda's *defines* Upcountry, and the unmistakable aroma of its cream puffs wafts on the predawn air. There's a line out the door before 7am, and popular items like baked butter rolls sell out within hours. Spring for the classic Komoda "stick doughnut." Fittingly, this 100-year-old store operates without computers, so expect to pay cash.

Coffee Shops

Need to perk up after a Haleakala sunrise? **Casanova Deli** (1188 Makawao Ave., 808/572 0220, www.casanovamaui.com, 7:30am-5:30pm daily) is a Makawao classic that's been slinging cups of caffeinated cheer since 1986. Breakfast sandwiches, *paninis,* and omelets are paired with eccentric locals, and the people-watching from a front porch stool is some of the island's best.

At the edge of town, down Baldwin Avenue, **Sip Me** (3617 Baldwin Ave., 808/573-2340, www.sipmemaui.com, 6am-5pm daily) is Makawao's newest spot for espresso, Wi-Fi, and treats. It's Upcountry's earliest coffee shop to open, and 90 percent of the baked goods are gluten-free. Coffee is made from organic beans roasted on Maui, and you'll find healthy organic smoothies ($7) made from local ingredients. Best of all, there's a lovable "Pay It Forward" wall where you can buy a stranger a coffee—and maybe even receive one yourself if you meet the random criteria.

Food Tour

For a food, history, and walking tour through the heart of Makawao town, **Local Tastes of Maui** (808/446-1190, www.localtastesofmaui.com, 9:30am-11:30am daily, $45) offers tours of Makawao (Thurs.) as well as Pa'ia, Lahaina, and Kihei. Portions of proceeds are donated to local animal welfare organizations.

Hawaiian Regional

The ★ **Hali'imaile General Store** (900 Hali'imaile Rd., 808/572-2666, www.bevgannonrestaurants.com, lunch 11am-2:30pm Mon.-Fri., dinner 5:30pm-9pm daily, $22-42), which serves gourmet food in an old-school roadhouse that was once a general store, is easily the island's most unlikely location for food of this caliber. Master chef Beverly Gannon—frequently voted Maui's top chef and a founder of the Hawaiian regional cuisine movement—crafts appetizers such as sashimi Napoleon and famous crab pizza. Entrées include *paniolo* barbecue ribs and coconut seafood curry. Portions are plentiful.

Italian

On the corner at Makawao's only intersection, **Casanova** (1188 Makawao Ave., 808/572-0220, www.casanovamaui.com,

famous Komoda stick donut

lunch 11:30am-2pm Mon.-Tues. and Thurs.-Sat., dinner 5:30pm-9:30pm daily, $18-34) offers wood-fired pizzas and Italian classics like *linguine pescatore*. Easily Makawao's sexiest venue, it feels like a date-night place in a city. There's a great wine list, a $20 corkage fee if you bring your own bottle, and $5 wine carafes 5pm-6pm. On selected nights, Casanova becomes Maui's best nightclub, with Wednesday "Ladies Night" the place where singles come to party. Friday and Saturday feature Reggae or Latin from around 10pm. Cover is about $10.

Mexican

Mix some mango margaritas, a seafood burrito, and a great community atmosphere, and it's obvious why ★ **Polli's Mexican Restaurant** (1202 Makawao Ave., 808/572-7808, www.pollismexicanrestaurant.com, 11am-10pm daily, $11-22) has been a Makawao classic since 1981. Portions are enormous for the seafood enchilada, chicken burrito supreme, sizzling beef fajita, and "Makawowie" nachos appetizer. Polli's also offers Maui Cattle Company cheeseburgers, barbecue pork sandwiches, a heaping array of vegetarian options, and baby back ribs that fall off the bone. The festive interior is decorated with photographs from Mexico, surf photography from Hawaii, and authentic souvenirs from all over Latin America.

KULA
American

The **Kula Lodge** (15200 Haleakala Hwy., 808/878-1535, www.kulalodge.com, 7am-8:30pm daily, breakfast 7am-10:45am daily, $12-34) has been welcoming hungry patrons into its rustic interior for so long it's become synonymous with Kula dining. Inside a 1940s private home, this panoramic mountainside perch hasn't changed much since. At 3,200 feet elevation, it's a little bit cooler, and the dark-wood interior is a perfect fit with the low temperatures and clouds. Paintings by Curtis Wilson Cost adorn the wooden entrance (his gallery is beneath the restaurant). The Lodge

is a filling breakfast stop on the way down from Haleakala.

For an affordable, laid-back, and welcoming vibe, **Kula Sandalwoods Café** (15427 Haleakala Hwy., 808/878-3523, www.kulasandalwoods.com, 7am-3pm Mon.-Sat., 7am-noon Sun., $9-11) serves breakfast until 11am. While the outdoor lanai is nice, the cozy interior has a small fireplace with country music on the radio. For breakfast, try the Keokea omelet; at lunch, go for the kalua pig sandwich.

French

A tucked-away outdoor patio in the middle of a Kula pasture, **La Provence** (3158 Lower Kula Rd., 808/878-1313, www.laprovencekula.com, 7am-2pm Wed.-Sun., $11, cash only) is a boutique French restaurant and local Kula favorite. On Lower Kula Road just past the True Value hardware store, La Provence offers flaky croissants, café au lait, and affordable filling crepes. Order a vegetable and goat cheese crepe or a tomato and avocado Benedict, accompanied by a side of Kula greens and a cluster of roasted potatoes. Weekends can be busy, so don't come if you're in a rush. There's an ATM at the hardware store if you find yourself without cash.

Italian

For Italian food paired with local favorites, ★ **Kula Bistro** (4556 Lower Kula Rd., 808/871-2960, www.kulabistro.com, 7:30am-8pm daily, breakfast 7:30am-10:30am Tues.-Sun., $12-30) surpasses all others. Tasting the pesto chicken flatbread or jumbo lobster ravioli, it's obvious that owner Luciano Zanon has been perfecting this cuisine since his childhood in Venice. Maui-grown coffee is served at breakfast, and lunch has kalua pig *paninis* and filling hamburger steak. Most ingredients are sourced locally, the desserts are baked fresh daily, and there's no corkage fee. To pick up some booze for the BYOB, Morihara Store across the street has a decent selection.

KEOKEA AND ULUPALAKUA
American

If hunger strikes on the back road from Hana or while at the winery, head to the **Ulupalakua Ranch Store and Grill** (14800 Pi'ilani Hwy., 808/878-2561, www.ulupalakuaranch.com, 10am-5pm daily)—a carnivorous carnival of ranch-grown meats eaten on the wooden front porch. The grill features venison, lamb, elk, and beef, all raised on the 20,000 acres surrounding the store. Everything is made from scratch. Try the filling and affordable Uncle Mike's Steak Chili & Rice Bowl ($9), or an Ulupalakua Elk Burger ($12). There's also a Fresh Maui Taro Burger ($9) if you don't eat meat.

The other burger spot on the back road to Hana is **Bully's Burgers** (15900 Pi'ilani Hwy., 808/268-0123, www.triplelranchmaui.com, hours vary, usually 11am-6pm Wed.-Sun.) in Kanaio. This exceptionally simple roadside shack has grass-fed burgers ($10), raised on Triple L Ranch. Bully's is four miles past Maui Wine heading in the direction of Hana, and while there aren't any restrooms and the hours are irregular, the burgers don't disappoint.

Coffee Shop

While it doesn't look like much from the outside, there's a simple romance to ★ **Grandma's Coffee House** (9232 Kula Hwy., 808/878-2140, www.grandmascoffee.com, 7am-5pm daily, breakfast 7am-11am Mon.-Fri., 7am-noon Sat.-Sun.) that makes it Maui's best coffee shop. "Grandma" started brewing her own coffee back in 1918, and locally grown beans are roasted in the kitchen using her 100-year-old roaster. The beans are still harvested and processed by four generations of her family. For breakfast, order a Keokea crepe ($14) and enjoy it out on the porch, where slack-key musicians periodically offer live music on weekend mornings. Or grab a cup of coffee to go and enjoy a stroll on Thompson Road across the street. The only downside is that the restrooms are located at Keokea Park, a five-minute walk.

Grab brunch and coffee at Grandma's Coffee House.

East Maui: the Road to Hana

East Maui is more than a destination. It's a different mind-set.

Lush, tropical, and riddled with waterfalls, East Maui is the location of the famous Road to Hana and where Maui locals come to escape for a few days. From the windswept taro patches of the Keʻanae Peninsula to the empty pastures of Kaupo, time in East Maui ticks by at a slower place. By no means, however, does that make East Maui lazy. It's the island's adventure center, where an average day could consist of trekking to remote waterfalls, cliff-jumping in a bamboo forest, spelunking hidden caves on a black-sand beach, or body-surfing off sandy shores.

Many who drive the legendary Road to Hana ask, "This is it?" and "Where is the rest of town?" Hana is not a destination—it's famous for what it isn't more than for what it is, a sleepy little fishing hamlet. Neighbors still talk to each other and wave as they pass on the street, fishing nets hang in front yards, and the fish end up on the table. You don't come to Hana to reach something; you come out here to leave everything else behind.

East Maui is also home to Paʻia (Pa-EE-ah), a trendy, funky, and sexy town nominated by *Coastal Living* magazine as one of the "happiest seaside towns in America." Laid back and worry-free, Paʻia skanks to the beat of its own bongo. It also has the island's best shopping and food—even better than Lahaina—and the beaches are undeveloped and unheralded sanctuaries of calm.

ORIENTATION

East Maui comprises Paʻia, Haʻiku, and the famous Road to Hana. **Paʻia** is a hippie town that has become coastal beach chic, and **Haʻiku** is mostly residential, with the exception of some restaurants and B&Bs. The **Road to Hana** stretches 45 miles from Paʻia to the center of **Hana,** but continues another 37 miles around the island's back. Paʻia is only 10 minutes from Kahului Airport, although reaching Hana takes at least a couple of hours—or 20 minutes by plane. The Hana region is spread out over 22 miles from **Nahiku** to **Kipahulu,** over an hour's drive. If you're staying overnight in Hana, be sure to check exactly how far it is from the center of town.

Previous: rugged shoreline of Kipahulu; Kaupo. **Above:** Rainbow eucalyptus on the Road to Hana.

East Maui

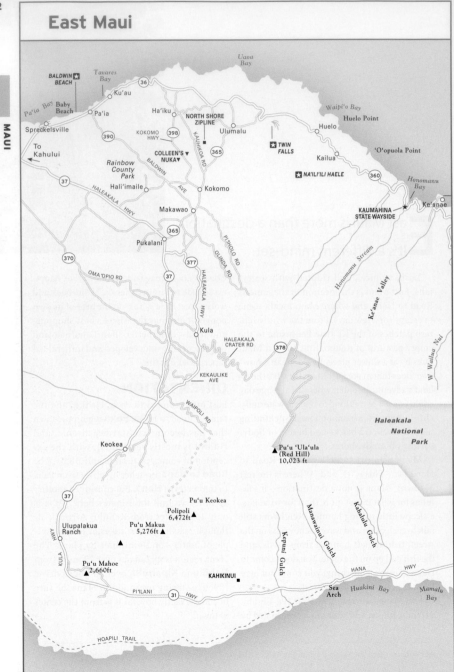

Uaoa Bay

BALDWIN BEACH

Tavares Bay

Ku'au

Pa'ia Bay

Baby Beach

Spreckelsville

To Kahului

Pa'ia

Ha'iku

NORTH SHORE ZIPLINE

KOKOMO HWY

398

Ulumalu

Waipi'o Bay

Huelo Point

Huelo

'O'opuola Point

COLLEEN'S NUKA

365

TWIN FALLS

Kailua

NA'ILI'ILI HAELE

360

Honomanu Bay

Ke'anae

Rainbow County Park

Hali'imaile

Kokomo

KAUMAHINA STATE WAYSIDE

HALEAKALA HWY

Makawao

365

Pukalani

OLINDA RD

PI'IHOLO RD

Honomanu Stream

Ke'anae Valley

377

370

OMA'OPIO RD

37

HALEAKALA HWY

W Wailua Nui

Kula

HALEAKALA CRATER RD

378

KEKAULIKE AVE

Haleakala National Park

WAIPOLI RD

Keokea

Pu'u 'Ula'ula (Red Hill) 10,023 ft

Pu'u Keokea

Polipoli 6,472ft

37

Ulupalakua Ranch

Pu'u Makua 5,276ft

Manawainui Gulch

Kahalua Gulch

Kepuni Gulch

KULA HWY

Pu'u Mahoe 2,660ft

KAHIKINUI

HANA HWY

PI'ILANI

31

HWY

Sea Arch

Huakini Bay

Mamalu Bay

HOAPILI TRAIL

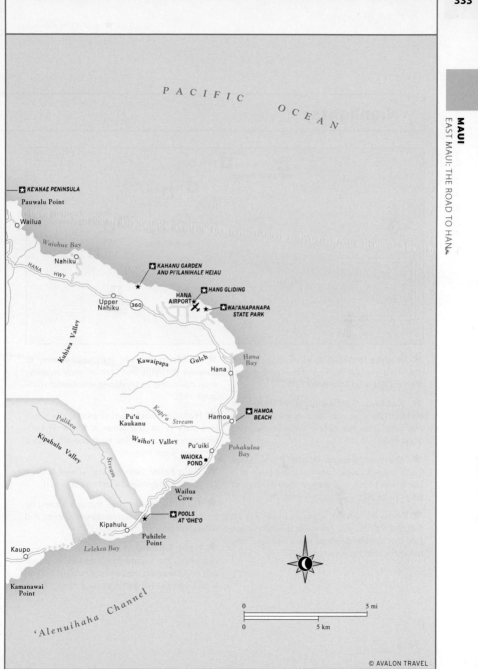

PACIFIC OCEAN

★ KE'ANAE PENINSULA
Pauwalu Point
Wailua
Waiohue Bay
Nahiku
HANA HWY
★ KAHANU GARDEN AND PI'ILANIHALE HEIAU
★ HANG GLIDING
HANA AIRPORT
★ WAI'ANAPANAPA STATE PARK
Upper Nahiku
360
Kuhiwa Valley
Kawaipapa Gulch
Hana Bay
Hana
Kapi'a Stream
Pu'u Kaukanu
Hamoa
★ HAMOA BEACH
Palikea
Waiho'i Valley
Pu'uiki
Pohakuloa Bay
Kipahulu Valley
Stream
■ WAIOKA POND
Wailua Cove
★ POOLS AT 'OHE'O
Kipahulu
Puhilele Point
Kaupo
Lelekea Bay
Kamanawai Point
'Alenuihaha Channel

0   5 mi
0   5 km

© AVALON TRAVEL

Look for ★ to find recommended sights, activities, dining, and lodging.

Highlights

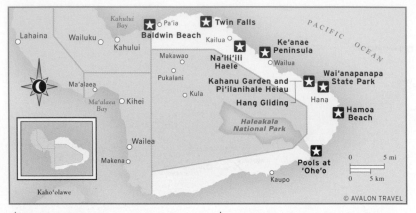

★ **Ke'anae Peninsula:** This fertile peninsula provides a glimpse into one of the last holdouts of an ancient way of life (page 338).

★ **Kahanu Garden and Pi'ilanihale Heiau:** Take a journey back to ancient Hawaii and gaze upon the largest *heiau* in the state (page 341).

★ **Wai'anapanapa State Park:** Swim inside hidden caves, bask on the shores of a black-sand beach, and walk in the footsteps of kings (page 341).

★ **Pools of 'Ohe'o:** At Maui's iconic **Seven Sacred Pools,** you can swim beneath waterfalls that tumble down to the ocean and hike through a bamboo forest (page 345).

★ **Baldwin Beach:** Start your journey to Hana on the right foot with an early morning stroll down this undeveloped white-sand shore (page 347).

★ **Hamoa Beach:** Surf or snorkel at a beach that Mark Twain and James A. Michener both recognized as one of the most beautiful they'd ever seen (page 349).

★ **Twin Falls:** Swim beneath waterfalls in an accessible, family-friendly setting (page 351).

★ **Na'ili'ili Haele:** Trek through a bamboo forest punctuated by waterfalls, guava trees, and natural swimming holes (page 352).

★ **Hang Gliding in Hana:** See the volcanic coast from the air and soar past hidden waterfalls while learning the basics of hang gliding on flights from the Hana airport (page 356).

PLANNING YOUR TIME

The biggest mistake you can make on Maui is skimping on your time in Hana. Ideally, Hana is worth three full days. Choosing to spend the night here allows more time for exploring. If you only have a day to experience the Road to Hana, devote the entire day so you can see it without feeling rushed. Pa'ia is a nice place for breakfast on the way to Hana and is worthy of at least half a day. Visit Pa'ia separately from Hana, or if you're spending the night in Hana, spend the morning at the beach in Pa'ia and then spend the afternoon enjoying the Road to Hana, when there aren't as many cars.

Driving the Road to Hana

TOP EXPERIENCE

Ah, yes, the Road to Hana—the most loved and loathed section of the island divides visitors into two camps: those who swear it's heaven on earth and those who swear never to drive it again. Most people who don't enjoy the trip didn't know what they were getting themselves into. Three words will make or break your trip: Don't rush Hana.

Devote a full day to the experience at a minimum. You're visiting one of the most beautiful places on earth; two or three days are even better. Don't expect to breeze through and see it quickly, and don't expect to be back on the other side of the island to make dinner reservations. If you're staying in Ka'anapali or Wailea, it will take you 3.5 hours just to reach the Pools of 'Ohe'o (aka the Seven Sacred Pools). That's not including stops, and the stops are what make the journey worthwhile.

No one should endure a journey to Hana without knowing exactly where the next waterfall, hiking trail, ATM, food cart, or restroom is going to be. Since sights can spring up in an instant—and making a U-turn isn't possible—be prepared. A mile-by-mile rundown of what you'll see along the side of the road follows, with specific sights and places worth stopping to linger described in greater detail.

- **Mile Marker 7:** Start in the town of Pa'ia, located around mile marker 7 on the Hana Highway (Hwy. 36). Grab breakfast from **Café des Amis** or **Paia Bay Coffee,** or go for a stroll on Baldwin Beach as the water shines turquoise in morning.

- **Mile Marker 8.8: Ho'okipa Beach Park.** In winter, stop to check out the large crashing surf and the daredevil surfers who ride it. Windsurfing picks up at 11am, but if you're trying to visit Hana in one day, you should definitely be past here by then.

- **Mile Marker 10.3: Maliko Gulch,** start of the famous Maliko Run (page 255).

- **Mile Marker 13.5:** Turnoff for **Pe'ahi,** also called **Jaws**—quite possibly the most famous surf break on the planet. If Jaws is breaking, there will be dozens of cars parked along the side of the highway. The best thing to do is park near the highway and hitch a ride to the bottom of the hill. The viewing area is from a coastal bluff at the bottom of a 4WD road, and the chances of hitching a ride increase tenfold if you barter a six-pack of beer.

- Begin Highway 360.

- **Mile Marker 0:** Note the change in mile markers at the junction of Hana Highway and Kaupakalua Road.

- **Mile Marker 0.3:** Congratulations, your first waterfall! Just joking. They get much better than this.

- **Mile Marker 2: Twin Falls** and Wailele Farm Stand.

Twin Falls

When you round the hill by mile marker 2 (remember that the mileage markers started over

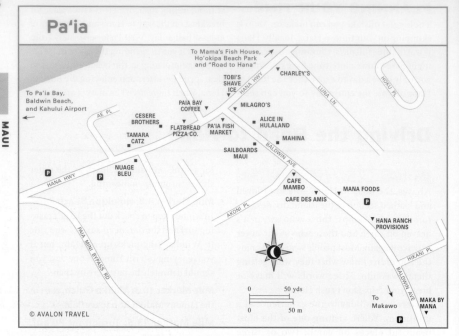

Pa'ia

To Mama's Fish House, Ho'okipa Beach Park and "Road to Hana"

CHARLEY'S

TOBI'S SHAVE ICE

To Pa'ia Bay, Baldwin Beach, and Kahului Airport

AE PL

PAIA BAY COFFEE

MILAGRO'S

CESERE BROTHERS

ALICE IN HULALAND

FLATBREAD PIZZA CO.

PA'IA FISH MARKET

TAMARA CATZ

MAHINA

SAILBOARDS MAUI

BALDWIN AVE

NUAGE BLEU

HANA HWY

HANA HWY

LUNA LN

HOKU PL

CAFE MAMBO

MANA FOODS

CAFE DES AMIS

AKONI PL

PAIA MINI BYPASS RD

HANA RANCH PROVISIONS

HIKANI PL

BALDWIN AVE

0   50 yds
0   50 m

To Makawo

MAKA BY MANA

© AVALON TRAVEL

---

at the junction of Kaupakalua Road), you'll be amazed at the large gravel parking lot on the right side of the road packed with cars. **Twin Falls** is the first set of waterfalls you encounter on the Road to Hana, and thus is the closest to many hotels. The 20-minute hike to the falls is relatively easy (page 351).

- **Mile Marker 2.8:** Your first taste of the turns that you're going to experience for the next 20 miles.

- **Mile Marker 3.4 Zipline** (page 356)

- **Mile Marker 4.5: Huelo Lookout** (7600 Hana Hwy., 808/280-4791, www.huelolookout.coconutprotectors.com, daily), the first and most official of the many fruit stands you'll find on the Road to Hana. Enjoy fresh fruit, smoothies, and coconut candy at the coastal lookout a few steps behind the stand. They also sell local arts and crafts.

- **Mile Marker 4.9:** Your first narrow bridge crossing.

- **Mile Marker 6.5: Na'ili'ili Haele** (Bamboo Forest), one of the most popular hikes in East Maui. Thundering waterfalls spill through a dense bamboo forest. Slippery rocks and flash-flood conditions have been known to cause injuries here (page 352).

- **Mile Marker 6.7:** Rainbow eucalyptus trees.

- **Mile Marker 8.1:** First scenic view of a valley looking out toward the ocean.

- **Mile Marker 8.5:** Sweeping view of dense swaths of bamboo crawling their way up the eastern flank of the mountain.

- **Mile Marker 9.5: Waikamoi Ridge Trail.** This small picnic area provides a relaxing place to stretch your legs or enjoy a roadside snack, although there are no restrooms or other facilities. There's a short loop trail that gains 200 vertical feet in the surrounding forest (page 353).

Your Best Day in East Maui

Get a good night's sleep, because this is going to be a long day. Start with a stroll on **Baldwin Beach** around 7:30am, followed by crepes and coffee at **Café des Amis.** Since you'll be spending the day driving to Hana, leave Pa'ia at 9:30am at the latest. If you want to leave earlier, get breakfast on the go from **Pa'ia Bay Coffee.**

Embark on the famous **Road to Hana,** and remember to stop often to hike, swim, and drink in the beauty of the coast. Grab a bite to eat at **Nahiku Marketplace,** and then choose a visit to either **Kahanu Garden** or **Ka'eleku Caverns.** Your next stop is **Wai'anapanapa** for a look at the black-sand beach, taking time for a short dip in the underground freshwater pools.

Continue to Hana for food and stock up on water, snacks, and gas around **Hasegawa General Store.** If you have time, make a stop at **Hamoa Beach** for a quick splash in the waves before continuing on to the **Pools of 'Ohe'o** at **Haleakala National Park.** You'll want to leave by 4:30pm for the drive around the back of the mountain, and if you've somehow made it here by 2pm, consider hiking the **Pipiwai Trail** up to 400-foot-high **Waimoku Falls.**

RAINY-DAY ALTERNATIVE
Either visit Hana in the rain (there will definitely be less traffic) or spend the day shopping in Pa'ia, escaping the rain with pizza at **Flatbread** and a drink at the happening bar.

- **Mile Marker 10: Waikamoi Falls,** the first roadside waterfall and swimming hole.

Waikamoi Falls
Simple, elegant, and easily accessible, **Waikamoi Falls** is a convenient place to take a dip. A small trail leads down to the pool, and a second waterfall is accessible above the first pool by wading across the streambed. The only inconvenience here is the lack of parking.

- **Mile Marker 10.5:** The Garden of Eden botanical garden and Coconut's Café food cart.

Garden of Eden
Up the road 0.5 mile from Waikamoi Falls is the enticing **Garden of Eden** (808/572-9899, www.mauigardenofeden.com, 8am-4pm daily, $15 adults, $5 children), an ornately manicured 26-acre rainforest utopia. In 1991, Alan Bradbury, the state's first International Society of Arboriculture (ISA)-certified arborist, began clearing the hillside and replanting native trees. It was truly a labor of love: After two decades of work, the Garden of Eden now has over 600 individually labeled plants. The entrance fee is a little steep but worth it if you're into plants. If you're traveling on a budget, you can get a similar experience at the Ke'anae Arboretum, six miles down the road. The food truck here, **Coconut's Café** (8:30am-4pm daily, $8-12), has tasty fish tacos, refreshing drinks, and even a Wi-Fi hot spot.

- **Mile Marker 11.5: Haipua'ena Falls.** Parking can be limited, and it's on the Hana side of the bridge. A short trail leads down to a pool that's nice for a refreshing dip, but you don't need to spend more than 20 minutes.

- **Mile Marker 12.2: Kaumahina State Wayside Park.** Finally—restrooms. This is the first place you'll find any official facilities.

- **Mile Marker 14: Honomanu Bay,** a gorgeous gray-sand beach in a valley that's accessible by 4WD. If you have a low-clearance vehicle, find a parking space at the top of the road and visit the beach on foot.

- **Mile Marker 16.5: Ke'anae Arboretum.** A great spot to stretch your legs and enjoy a free walk in the forest. A 30-minute paved, wheelchair-accessible trail winds back into the lush landscape. After 10 minutes of walking, the paved trail becomes dirt as you pass a fence. If you make a left once inside the boundary and head toward Pi'ina'au Stream, you'll find a small hidden swimming hole. Reaching it requires a scramble down the rocks.

- **Mile Marker 16.6:** Turnoff for Ke'anae village.

★ Ke'anae Peninsula

When you turn off the highway at mile marker 16.6, you pass through a portal to a way of life that many forgot once existed. The peninsula is a mosaic of green taro fields, vital to the livelihood of Ke'anae. Taro, also known as *kalo,* isn't just a crop, it's a representation of indigenous Hawaiian heritage. In Hawaiian mythology, a child named Haloa was stillborn and, upon being buried, turned into a taro plant. Haloa's brother became the ancestor of the Hawaiian people.

waterfalls on the Road to Hana

In addition to the taro fields, you can watch the powerful surf crash onto the rugged volcanic shore. There aren't any beaches on the Ke'anae Peninsula, and you'll often encounter locals fishing. Stop in at **Aunty Sandy's** (808/248-7448, 9am-2:30pm daily) for a warm loaf of banana bread.

- **Mile Marker 17:** Ke'anae Overlook.

- **Mile Marker 17.3:** Store and ATM. The accurately named **Halfway to Hana** (www.halfwaytohanamaui.com, 8:30am-4pm daily, $2-6, cash only) is located between the Ke'anae Overlook and the turnoff for Wailua. It's basically a hot-dog, sandwich, and shave-ice stand with an ATM around the corner, making it the closest thing to a store around Ke'anae. Ask about the freshly baked banana bread.

- **Mile Marker 18:** Turnoff for Wailua village and **Uncle Harry's** food stand.

- **Mile Marker 18.5:** Taro *lo'i* (fields) and small waterfalls coming down the road.

- **Mile Marker 18.7:** Wailua Valley State Wayside Park offers a panoramic vista looking out over the town of Wailua, a good place to stretch your legs and get a unique photo. Once in the designated parking area, look to the right for a hidden set of stairs to access the lookout. There's also a lookout in 0.1 mile on the left side of the road.

- **Mile Marker 19.6:** Upper Waikani Falls is also called Three Bears Falls. This is a great place to stop for a swim, and there is a narrow rough trail on the Hana side of the bridge.

- **Mile Marker 21:** Wailuaiki Falls.

- **Mile Marker 22.6:** Pua'a Ka'a State Wayside Park has restrooms and a small picnic pavilion on the *mauka* (mountain) side of the highway looking out over the stream. A short three-minute walk leads from the road up the stream to an underrated swimming pool and waterfall.

- **Mile Marker 24.1:** Painted Little Green Shack.

Road to Hana

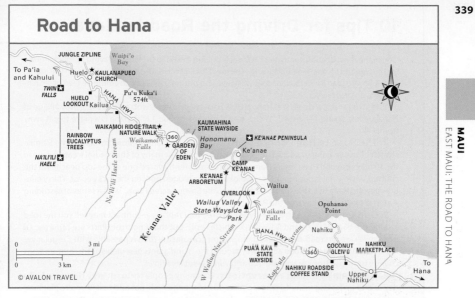

- **Mile Marker 25:** Pullout for view of Makapipi Falls. Look down from the top of the bridge!

- **Mile Marker 27.5: Coconut Glen's** (808/248-4876, www.coconutglens.com, 10:30am-5pm daily) ice-cream stand, an eccentric and uplifting outpost that serves vegan ice cream made with fresh coconut milk. Much of the building is made from recycled materials gathered around East Maui, and the ice cream is served in *lilikoi,* or coconuts, to eliminate waste.

- **Mile Marker 28.3:** Banana bread stand.

- **Mile Marker 28.7:** Nahiku Marketplace, a warm and welcoming strip mall in the forest with a surprising selection of food.

taro fields on Ke'anae Peninsula

10 Tips for Driving the Road to Hana

One of the most beautiful activities on Maui is driving the Road to Hana. Weaving 52 miles around 600 curves and 56 one-lane bridges, it's the most loved and loathed stretch of road on the island. Here's how to plan a visit to Hana that will leave you poring over a photo album instead of searching for a divorce lawyer.

1. Hana is not a destination, but a journey. Visitors who race to the sleepy village of Hana are left saying, "This is it?" With a population of around 1,800, Hana is a place to get away from it all.

2. The Road to Hana doesn't end at Hana. The famous Road to Hana is the 52-mile stretch between Kahului Airport and the town of Hana, but many of the natural treasures are in the 10 miles beyond Hana town. Hamoa Beach, consistently voted one of the top beaches in the country, is a few miles past Hana, as is Waioka Pond, a hidden pool on the rocky coast. Thirty minutes beyond Hana town are the Pools of 'Ohe'o (the Seven Sacred Pools), with a series of cascading waterfalls falling directly into the Pacific.

3. Don't drive back the way you came. Your rental-car contract may tell you the road around the back of the island is for 4WD vehicles only, but that's not true. Parts are bumpy, and a few miles are dirt road, but unless there's torrential rain, the road is passable with a regular vehicle. Following the back road all the way around the island grants new views as the surroundings change from lush tropical rainforest to arid windswept lava flows.

4. Don't make dinner reservations. Too many people try to squeeze Hana into half a day or end up feeling rushed. Hana is a place to escape the rush, not add to it. If you're planning a day trip to Hana, block off the entire day, leave early (7am), and see where the day takes you.

5. Stop early and stop often. Take a break for a morning stroll or for breakfast at a tucked-away café. Pick up some snacks and watch the waves. Stop and swim in waterfalls, hike through bamboo forests, and pull off at roadside stands for banana bread or locally grown fruit. If the car behind you is on your tail, pull over and let it pass—there isn't any rush.

6. If you're not a confident driver, take a guided tour. Local guides provide insights into Hawaiian history and culture and offer personal anecdotes that add humor to the lengthy drive. The downside is that you're on someone else's schedule.

7. Bring a bathing suit and hiking shoes. Hana is a land of adventure: Pack the necessary wardrobe and equipment for your activity of choice.

8. If you see a sign that says *kapu*, "keep out." Move along and enjoy a spot more accessible to the public.

9. Don't drive home in the dark—especially if you're going the back way. Driving on narrow one-lane roads with precipitous drop-offs is difficult enough in daylight. Leave by 4pm to ensure a well-lit journey home.

10. Stay overnight. Camp at the Pools of 'Ohe'o, or stay at a bed-and-breakfast, or at the Travaasa Hana hotel. In the morning you'll have beaches and swimming holes all to yourself before the day-trippers arrive, usually around 11am.

Nahiku Café has good coffee made with a proper espresso machine, and **Up In Smoke BBQ** has heaping bowls of kalua pig and chili ($6-9).

- **Mile Marker 29.7:** View of the Hana Airport.
- **Mile Marker 31:** Turnoff for Ka'eleku Caverns and Kahanu Garden.

Ka'eleku Caverns

As you make your way from Nahiku Marketplace, the first sights you'll encounter are a few miles before "downtown" Hana. At mile marker 31 you'll see the signs for **Ka'eleku Caverns** (808/248-7307, www.mauicave.com, 10:30am-4pm daily, $12.50 pp). Turn down 'Ula'ino Road to visit this two-mile subterranean network of lava tubes, the 18th largest in the world and the only lava tubes on Maui that are navigable and open to the public. Cave explorers are given a flashlight to examine the stalactite-encrusted surroundings. On your way out, navigate through the maze of red *ti* leaves that create the only such maze anywhere on the planet. Walking the caverns at an average pace will take about 30 minutes. There are no garbage cans or restrooms, so pack out your trash.

- **Mile Marker 31.2:** Only a few miles before the town of Hana, the legendary **Hana Farms Banana Bread Stand** (mile marker 31.2, 8am-7pm daily) features six different types of banana bread as well as a full range of fruits, coffee, sauces, and flavorings. There will be more fruit stands between Hana and Kipahulu, but none are like this. Stop for a coffee, banana bread (get a loaf with chocolate chips), and advice on your Hana adventure.

★ Kahanu Garden and Pi'ilanihale Heiau

On 'Ula'ino Road, the pavement gradually gives way to a potholed dirt road leading to **Kahanu Garden** (808/248-8912, www.ntbg. org, 9am-4pm Mon.-Fri., 9am-2pm Sat., $10, free under age 13). This 464-acre property is in Honoma'ele, an area ceded in 1848 to Chief Kahanu by King Kamehameha III. The land has remained largely unchanged since the days of ancient Hawaii. The sprawling gardens focus on species integral to Polynesian culture. You're greeted by a massive grove of *ulu* (breadfruit), and there are groves of bananas, coconuts, taro, sweet potato, sugarcane, and *'awa*. A self-guided tour details the history of the plants and the uses they had for Polynesians.

Towering **Pi'ilanihale Heiau,** a massive multitiered stone structure, is the largest remaining *heiau* in Hawaii. The walls stretch 50 feet high in some places, and the stone platforms are the size of two football fields. Multiple archaeological surveys have determined that the temple was most likely built in stages and dates as far back as the 14th century. To learn about the *heiau* and the property, you can arrange ahead of a time for an hour-long guided tour ($20 pp). To get really involved, lend a hand by volunteering (9am-noon Wed. and Fri.)—you could end up pulling taro with locals at neighboring Mahele Farm.

- **Mile Marker 31.4:** Turnoff for Hana Airport and powered hang-gliding lessons.
- **Mile Marker 32:** Turnoff for Wai'anapanapa State Park.

★ Wai'anapanapa State Park

Rugged **Wai'anapanapa State Park** is also known as "black-sand beach." At the beach overlook is one of the most iconic vistas on the drive to Hana. Take it slow on the 0.5-mile road down to the park; there are often small children playing. Once you reach the park, turn left at the parking lot and follow the road to the end, where you can access the black sand of Pa'iloa Beach and its freshwater caves.

Made of crushed black lava rock, the sand is as black as Hana's night sky. Lush green foliage clings to the surrounding coast, and dramatic sea arches and volcanic promontories jut into the frothy sea. Since it faces almost directly east, this is a popular venue for sunrise weddings, and if you spend the night in Hana, I highly recommend getting up early to come here for sunrise.

On the main paved trail by the parking lot overlook, you'll see a trail that runs in the opposite direction of the beach; this is the beginning of a popular coastal hike. One of the more popular stops along this trail is a blowhole that erupts on days with large surf. Maintain a safe distance; people have been swept into the ocean here.

The other main draw of Wai'anapanapa is the system of freshwater caves hidden in a grotto not far from the parking area. Following the cave trail from the parking lot, you'll see a sign that details the legend of the caves. Go left at the sign and travel downhill on a short loop trail. After a three-minute

Hana and Environs

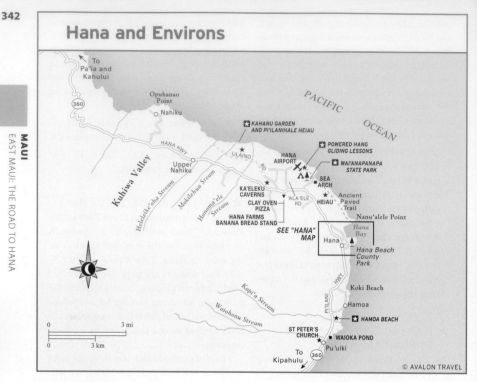

© AVALON TRAVEL

walk you'll reach the cave entrance. The clear water is crisp and cold, and if you swim back in either direction, you'll find some hidden caves. Bring a waterproof light, and don't go so far that you can't find your way back!

- **Mile Marker 32.7:** Hana school.
- **Mile Marker 34:** Fork in the road; stay left. The road rejoins the main highway in 1.5 miles via a right turn at the softball field in Hana town.

HANA TOWN

Before the arrival of Western explorers, Hana was a stronghold that was conquered and re-conquered by the kings of Maui and the Big Island. The most strategic and historically rich spot is Ka'uiki Hill, the remnant of a cinder cone that dominates Hana Bay. It's said that the demigod Maui transformed his daughter's lover into Ka'uiki Hill and turned her into the gentle rains that bathe it to this day.

Hana was already a plantation town in 1849 when sea captain George Wilfong started producing sugar here on 60 acres. After sugar production faded in the 1940s, San Francisco industrialist Paul Fagan bought 14,000 acres of what was to become the **Hana Ranch.** Today, Hana's population of 1,200 continues to be predominantly Hawaiian. There are far more sights in the Hana area than you can see in a single day.

Hana Cultural Center

While it might not look like much from the outside, the humble yet informative **Hana Cultural Center** (4974 Uakea Rd., 808/248-8622, www.hanaculturalcenter.org, 10am-4pm Mon.-Fri., $3) provides the historical backbone for the town. See ancient Hawaiian artifacts excavated from the Hana region, such as stone adzes and hand-woven fishnets, and walk around the **Hana Courthouse,**

Hana

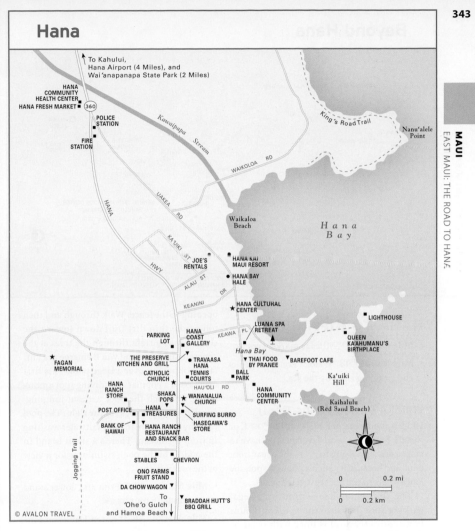

To Kahului,
Hana Airport (4 Miles), and
Wai'anapanapa State Park (2 Miles)

HANA COMMUNITY HEALTH CENTER
HANA FRESH MARKET
360
POLICE STATION
FIRE STATION

Kawaipapa Stream

King's Road Trail

Nanu'alele Point

WAIKOLOA RD

Hana Bay

Waikaloa Beach

HANA HWY

UAKEA RD

KA'UIKI ST

JOE'S RENTALS

HANA KAI MAUI RESORT

HANA BAY HALE

ALAU ST

KEANINI DR

HANA CULTURAL CENTER

LUANA SPA RETREAT

LIGHTHOUSE

PARKING LOT

HANA COAST GALLERY

KEAWA PL

QUEEN KA'AHUMANU'S BIRTHPLACE

FAGAN MEMORIAL

THE PRESERVE KITCHEN AND GRILL

TRAVAASA HANA

Hana Bay

THAI FOOD BY PRANEE

BAREFOOT CAFE

Ka'uiki Hill

CATHOLIC CHURCH

TENNIS COURTS

BALL PARK

HANA RANCH STORE

SHAKA POPS

HAU'OLI RD

WANANALUA CHURCH

HANA COMMUNITY CENTER

Kaihalulu (Red Sand Beach)

POST OFFICE

HANA TREASURES

SURFING BURRO

BANK OF HAWAII

HANA RANCH RESTAURANT AND SNACK BAR

HASEGAWA'S STORE

Jogging Trail

STABLES

CHEVRON

ONO FARMS FRUIT STAND

DA CHOW WAGON

To 'Ohe'o Gulch and Hamoa Beach

BRADDAH HUTT'S BBQ GRILL

© AVALON TRAVEL

0   0.2 mi
0   0.2 km

listed on the National Register of Historic Places. The one-room courthouse still hosts proceedings the first Tuesday of each month, and in a testament to the island's multicultural heritage, they can take place in 24 different languages.

Highway 330: Technically, Highway 360 ended at Hana Bay and Highway 330 started back at the fork in the road by the fire station. Once you drive past the center of Hana town at Hasegawa General Store and the gas station, you are on Highway 330, although the mileage markers don't start again for a couple of miles When they do, they count down instead of up. The turnoff for **Hamoa Beach** and **Koki Beach** is at the first turnoff for Haneo'o Road, about 1.5 miles past the center of Hana town, which is before the mileage markers begin again. There are two turnoffs for Haneo'o Road; take the first one, as this is the direction that local traffic naturally flows.

Beyond Hana

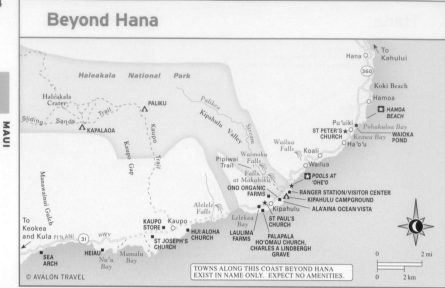

TOWNS ALONG THIS COAST BEYOND HANA
EXIST IN NAME ONLY. EXPECT NO AMENITIES.

© AVALON TRAVEL

HANA TO KIPAHULU

- **Mile Marker 51:** Mileage markers restart.
- **Mile Marker 48:** Waioka Pond, gorgeous cliff-jumping right by the sea.

Waioka Pond (Venus Pool)

Hidden at mile marker 48, **Waioka Pond,** or **Venus Pool,** is a local favorite. You have to cross a private pasture to get to the oceanfront pool, and because it's such a popular spot, the landowners haven't yet restricted access.

The first challenge is finding a legal parking spot. Because the *mauka* (mountain) side of the road is lined with residential homes, the only parking is along a fence on the *makai* (ocean) side of the road. In order for you to park legally—facing the correct direction—you have to cross the bridge past the mile marker 48 sign, pull off the road, do a U-turn, and drive back toward Hana town. Once you're facing the right way, park along the grass bordering the thin metal fence.

Once you've parked, follow the fence line toward the bridge, where you'll notice an opening in the fence. Walk through and then follow the thin dirt trail down toward the shore. Make a right through the trees at the concrete structure and you'll emerge at a cliff face looking out over a large pool. This first overlook is a popular cliff-diving spot among locals. To reach the pool without jumping, clamber down the rocks to the right. The pool is fed by both a stream and saltwater washing in from the ocean. There's a small island in the middle of the pool; swim over for a view of the rocky shore.

- **Mile Marker 47.5:** Fruit and flower stand popular with tour buses.
- **Mile Marker 46.3:** Karen Davidson Fine Art.
- **Mile Marker 45.3:** The road becomes narrow and offers dramatic views of the coast.
- **Mile Marker 45:** Laura Mango art gallery.
- **Mile Marker 44.8:** Wailua Falls, an 80-foot cascade that may be the most photographed on Maui. The best way to experience it is to take the short trail down to the base and take a dip in the swimming pools, away from the crowds.

cliff-jumping at Waioka Pond

- **Mile Marker 43.2, 42.9:** Old bridges dating to 1910.

- **Mile Marker 42.1:** 'Ohe'o Stream and bridge looking over the misnamed Seven Sacred Pools.

★ Pools of 'Ohe'o

The fabled **Pools of 'Ohe'o,** inside **Haleakala National Park** (808/248-7375, www.nps.gov/hale, $15 per vehicle), are one of the island's most popular attractions. The name **Seven Sacred Pools** is the largest misnomer on the island. There are far more than seven, and there's no record in history of them having been sacred. The name likely began as a marketing ploy by hoteliers in the 1940s. The name stuck and is used to this day. The real name is 'Ohe'o (pronounced oh-HEY-oh); locals will appreciate you using it.

This part of the island is truly stunning and a highlight of visiting Maui. The first taste you'll get of the park is crossing over 'Ohe'o Gulch on a bridge at mile marker 42.1, but try not to linger too long as you'll stop traffic. The

entrance to the park is 0.4 mile down the road, and if you have visited Haleakala National Park within the last three days, your receipt will still gain you entry.

Once inside the park you'll notice a large parking lot next to an informative visitors center. It's the best place on this side of the island to gain an understanding of the history, culture, and unique environment of the Kipahulu region. Rangers here are the best source of information on current trail and waterfall conditions in the park.

The visitors center is also where you begin the Kuloa Point Loop Trail leading down to the famous pools. Along the 10-minute walk, you'll go through groves of *hala* trees and past a number of historic sites. Eventually the trail emerges at a staircase down to the pools and one of the most iconic vistas in Hawaii.

The three main pools are open most days for exploring and swimming, although they're closed during heavy rains and flash floods. Reaching the uppermost pools requires some rock scaling; it's worth the effort, but be careful on the slippery rocks.

- **Mile Marker 41.9:** Trailhead for Pipiwai Trail and the 400-foot Waimoku Falls (parking for trailhead is inside park) (page 354).

- **Mile Marker 41.7:** Entrance to Haleakala National Park.

- **Mile Marker 41.2:** Ono Organic Farms.

- **Mile Marker 40.9:** Ho'onanea Farms fruit and coffee stand.

- **Mile Marker 40.8:** Turnoff for Palapala Ho'omau Church, the final resting place of historic aviator Charles Lindbergh.

- **Mile Marker 40.6:** Laulima Farm fruit stand and kitchen, a sprawling compound growing a wealth of organic produce and a roadside kitchen.

- **Mile Marker 39.2:** Lelekea Bay.

- **Mile Marker 39:** The road begins to deteriorate and becomes narrow, with precipitous drop-offs. This is where you should turn around if you don't want to drive around the back of the island. As a point of reference, from this point it's 50 miles to Kahului Airport via the back side, which takes about two hours without stops. If you choose to return the way you came, it's 60 miles, about 2.5 hours without stops. While bumpier, the back road is much straighter and has less traffic.

- **Mile Marker 38.8:** Trailhead for Alelele Falls, a 60-foot waterfall requiring a 10-minute hike (page 355).

- **Mile Marker 38.5:** Highway 31 begins.

- **Mile Marker 38.4:** The scariest section of road. If you make it past this without a heart attack, you'll be fine the rest of the way.

- **Mile Marker 37.8:** Road turns to dirt.

- **Mile Marker 36:** Surroundings morph from tropical and lush to windswept and arid. Welcome to Kaupo!

- **Mile Marker 34.6:** Kaupo Store.

pools of 'Ohe'o in Kipahulu

Kaupo Store

No other store on the island will amaze you quite like **Kaupo Store** (mile marker 34.6, 10am-5pm Mon.-Sat., cash only), squirreled away inside a building constructed in 1925 in surroundings that feel like the end of the earth. Inside, find cold drinks and gourmet ice-cream bars, and stock up on water and snacks for the long, winding, beautiful drive.

- **Mile Marker 33.5:** Kaupo Gap warrants a stop for the sweeping view. At the upper rim of the gap is the 6,800-foot floor of Haleakala Crater.

- **Mile Marker 31.8:** The most amazing view of Haleakala you will see. If you thought the stretch between Kipahulu and Kaupo was desolate, you're in for a treat. The southeastern flank of Haleakala opens up into the dramatic panorama—a pristine expanse of wide-open country where visitors gawk at the desolate beauty. The road

is exceptionally bumpy. After Manawainui Gulch, with its overly engineered bridge in the middle of nowhere, the road begins its gradual climb away from the coast to 3,000 feet elevation in Keokea.

- **Mile Marker 31.1:** The gate to Nu'u Bay, a rocky beach popular for fishing and scenic coastal hiking.

- **Mile Marker 30.1:** Huakini Bay.

- **Mile Marker 29:** You survived the worst part of the road—smooth pavement begins.

- **Mile Marker 28.7:** Beautiful view of a lava-rock sea arch.

- **Mile Marker 27.3:** Manawainui Bridge and Gulch.

From this point the road climbs in elevation through the rural communities of Kahikinui and Kanaio before wrapping around to Maui Wine in Ulupalakua. If it's before 5pm, toast to your success at the winery and grab a bite at the Ulupalakua Ranch Store. The closest gas is 5.2 miles down the road in Keokea.

Beaches

Beaches in East Maui are blissfully undeveloped, though due to the trade winds there isn't much snorkeling, and the water can be rough and choppy. Mornings offer the calmest conditions for a jog, a quick dip, or to commune with nature.

PA'IA
★ Baldwin Beach

The long, wide, and mostly empty **Baldwin Beach** is a popular local bodysurfing spot, although the waves can get large during winter. At the far western end, farthest from Pa'ia, is a small cove known as **Baby Beach,** where a fringing reef creates a natural pool perfect for wading with young ones. Instead of walking the length of Baldwin, you can access Baby Beach by turning on Nonohe Place off Hana Highway, followed by a right on Pa'ani Place, and a quick left onto Kealakai Place. There aren't any restrooms or showers, but you can drive to the shower a mile down the road at the main entrance. On the far eastern end of Baldwin, closest to Pa'ia, a small trail leads around the point and connects with a hidden beach next to Pa'ia Bay. This little-known stretch of sand is often occupied by sun-worshipping nudists, affable hippies, and locals passing around the *pakalolo* (marijuana). If you visit during the afternoon and the wind is howling, the cove on the far eastern end of Baldwin is sheltered and offers calm swimming most of the year.

Pa'ia Bay

The closest beach to the center of town, **Pa'ia Bay** is as active as Baldwin is calm, with a basketball court in a small park area and overflow parking for the town. The skate park at the Pa'ia Youth Center teems with area youth. Bodyboarders and surfers flock here for the waves, and a number of downhill bike companies finish tours here after descending the mountainside. There are restrooms, a beach shower, and an ever-changing cast of entertaining and colorful characters.

Kuau Cove

This beach is the scenic backdrop for **Mama's Fish House,** where many take a sunset photo. This small cove has a smattering of sand and an intriguing system of tide pools great for exploring with small children. The beach shrinks at high tide, so low tide is best for poring over the rocks to see all the slippery critters. There are a few parking spots near Mama's Fish House; the spaces with blue cones are designated as beach parking.

Ho'okipa Beach Park

The global epicenter of the windsurfing world, **Ho'okipa** also offers a thin, sandy beach that's better for tanning than swimming. A fringing reef creates a small pond nice for small children, and a wide range of people can usually be found hanging out on shore. Mornings are usually calm at Ho'okipa, and when the surf isn't too high, it's possible to snorkel in front of the rocks and find numerous *honu* (sea turtles). Every night in the hour before sunset, at least half a dozen haul out on shore in front of the pavilions. Sea turtles are protected, and it's illegal to touch them.

Rather than the pavilion area, the best place is on the stretch of sand on the left side of the beach. Parking can be tight—especially when the surf is up.

HANA TOWN
Pa'iloa Beach
(Black-Sand Beach)

The **Black-Sand Beach** at Wai'anapanapa State Park is the most popular beach in Hana. Just a few miles before the sleepy center of Hana and just past the turnoff for Hana Airport, dense foliage and black lava rock abut the crashing blue surf. The water along the shore is often rough, particularly in the afternoon. The beach is formed of crushed black lava rock, the result of the tumultuous wave erosion. The color of the sand is as black as the night sky.

To reach the shore, walk down a paved path from the parking lot of the state park. When you reach the bottom, you'll notice some sea caves you can explore at low tide. Since the sand is formed from lava rock, it isn't very comfortable; bring a blanket or a towel if you plan to hang out. Back at the parking lot, don't leave without checking out the freshwater caves. You can also walk the trail winding along the shore that leads to a thundering blowhole.

Hana Bay

Hana Bay is a laid-back crescent of gray sand in the middle of Hana town. Tucked in the lee of Ka'uiki Head, the working-class bay has a crumbling boat ramp where visitors end up when they "can't find Hana." It's nice enough for a picnic and a dip, but if you're looking for the nicest beach in Hana, keep driving out to Hamoa.

For a short, adventurous, and scenic hike, follow the trailhead at the end of the road as it snakes off into the trees. You'll reach a spot where it looks like the trail ends, but look

across the narrow ravine and you'll see it on the other side. Follow this trail to a tiny red-sand beach, and eventually all the way to the plaque that commemorates the birthplace of Queen Ka'ahaumanu. The snorkeling can be fantastic in the morning. The best way to see it is with **Hana-Maui Seasports** (808/248-7711, www.hanabaykayaks.com).

Kaihalulu Beach (Red-Sand Beach)

Before visiting **Kaihalulu**, be aware that **Red-Sand Beach** is a nude beach. It can also be dangerous to access, as there are rockslides, slippery scree slopes, and sheer drop-offs. If you're up for it, this is one of the coast's most famously scenic spots. This cavernous cove hidden in the mountainside offers decent swimming inside the rocks, and the red sand gets its color from the cinder cone.

To find the trail for Red-Sand Beach, find a legal parking area on Uakea Road by the ballpark (don't park facing the wrong direction), and walk toward an open grass field where the road dead-ends by the community center. Walk across the grass field, keeping an eye on the bushes on your right for a couple of narrow trails.

Wading for a minute through waist-high

Red-Sand Beach is beautiful.

grass, you'll eventually emerge at a small dirt trail that snakes down the roots of a tree. The footing can be slippery, so bare feet or closed-toe shoes are better than rubber slippers. The thin trail continues to the left up and over a bluff, where landslides can leave a lot of scree on the trail. Once at the top of the bluff, you'll be greeted with your first photo op of the stunning cove. From here it's a one-minute walk along a cliff until you emerge on the red shore.

HANA TO KIPAHULU
Koki Beach

To reach Hana's two famous beaches, travel 1.5 miles past the center of town (the Hana Ballpark) and then make a left on Haneo'o Road. Going downhill, first is **Koki Beach,** a favorite hangout of local surfers. On the left side of the beach, you can scramble over some rocks to reach some hidden sections of sand. Access to these smaller beaches is only possible at low tide, so most people stay on the main section of the beach. The dark-red sand is a product of a cinder cone known as **Ka Iwi O Pele** (The Bones of Pele). According to legend, this is where Pele, the volcano goddess, met her end. Her bones were stacked high on the shore before her spirit traveled southeast to the Big Island.

★ Hamoa Beach

Continuing along Haneo'o Road, paralleling the ocean, the snowcapped peak of Mauna Kea on the Big Island is occasionally visible in the distance. At low tide you can also see the remnants of the ancient Haneo'o Fishpond, although access is via private land. As the road rounds back to the right, you'll finally catch glimpses of **Hamoa Beach,** which Mark Twain considered one of the most beautiful in the world.

Parking is tight. Park only on the right side of the road so that traffic flows smoothly on the left. You might have to drive past the beach before you find a space. Access to the beach is down the stone stairway. The park area at the bottom of the stairs is property of the Travaasa Hana hotel, but the sandy beach is public property.

This is the best spot in Hana for a relaxing day at the beach. On the calmest of days it's possible to snorkel along the rocky coast, though most prefer to bodysurf the consistent playful shore break. This can also be one of the best surf breaks in the area.

windswept Koki Beach in Hana

Surfing

Surfing in East Maui is for intermediate and advanced surfers. Ho'okipa Beach Park and Hamoa Bay can see surf at any time of year, and this stretch of coast roars to life from October to April with North Pacific swells. This is some of the largest, heaviest surf on the planet. Even watching from the shore, you can feel the rush of waves large enough to shake the ground beneath you.

Pa'ia
SURF SPOTS
If you're renting a board in Pa'ia, the closest beach break is **Pa'ia Bay.** While the inside section is popular with bodyboarders, there is a second peak a little farther out that is better for surfing. Mornings are best before the wind blows the wave to pieces. Since the wave can be fast and steep, it's best for intermediate surfers.

The epicenter for surf on the island's North Shore will forever be **Ho'okipa Beach Park,** three miles past the town of Pa'ia, a legendary windswept cove. For surfers, Ho'okipa has four sections: **Pavilions (Pavils), Middles, The Point, and Lanes.** If you are standing on the beach, Pavilions is the break that's the farthest to the right and can pick up wrapping wind swell even during the summer. Since it's the most consistent, it can also be the most localized, so beginners should be wary.

SURFBOARD RENTALS
Both **Hi-Tech Maui** (58 Baldwin Ave., 808/579-9297, www.surfmaui.com, 9am-6pm daily) and **Sailboards Maui** (22 Baldwin Ave., 808/579-8432, www.sailboardsmaui.com, 9:30am-7pm Mon.-Sat., 9:30am-6pm Sun.) offer casual board rentals ($20 per day). Both shops have a full range of longboards, shortboards, and fun boards. They are an affordable option for playing in the waves of Pa'ia Bay or on a multiday safari to Hana.

SURF SCHOOLS
Given the advanced surf conditions of the island's North Shore, there aren't as many surf schools in East Maui as in Lahaina or Kihei. Professional longboarder **Zack Howard** (808/214-7766, www.zackhowardsurf.com) is one of the few instructors who offers lessons ($220 private, $260 for 2, and $100 pp for 3 or more) to surf on Maui's North Shore. While most of his lessons are conducted at locations on the south shore on the road to Lahaina, advanced surfers can paddle out on the North Shore if the conditions are right.

Hana
SURF SPOTS
The two main Hana surf breaks frequented by visitors are **Koki Beach** and **Hamoa Beach,** both on Haneo'o Road 1.5 miles past the town of Hana. Because of its easterly location, Hana

Watch for windsurfers at Ho'okipa Beach Park.

gets waves any time of the year. Since the waves are often the result of easterly wind swell, conditions can be rougher than elsewhere on the island. Koki is where many of Hana's *keiki* (children) first learn how to pop up and ride.

Around the corner at Hamoa, the protected bay offers a respite from the trade winds. Koki breaks fairly close to shore, but the wave at Hamoa breaks farther out over a combination of sand, reef, and rocks. On moderate days, this is a good place for riding a longboard or a stand-up board, since the wave isn't as steep, but the largest waves are for experts. There are no lifeguards at either beach in Hana.

WINDSURFING

The world's best flock in droves to **Ho'okipa Beach Park** to combine the trade winds with

waves that reach 20 feet in winter. Don't expect to see windsurfers on a morning drive to Hana, as windsurfing is prohibited before 11am. A better bet is to see them on the drive back in the afternoon. Parking can be difficult at Ho'okipa, so if you're coming to watch the windsurfers, park up along the highway and leave the spots closer to shore for those who need to move gear.

Windsurfing Rentals

Although most of the windsurfing rental shops are in Kahului, **Simmer Style** (137 Hana Hwy., 808/579-8484, www.simmer-hawaii.com, 10am-7pm daily) is the closest shop to Ho'okipa and the best spot on the North Shore for windsurfing rentals and supplies

Hiking and Biking

HIKING
Road to Hana
★ TWIN FALLS

At mile marker 2, which is 11.4 miles past Pa'ia, **Twin Falls** is one of the easiest and shortest waterfall hikes in East Maui. It's also the first series of waterfalls on the Road to Hana. Much of the area is private land (respect the *Kapu,* or "Keep Out" signs on driveways), and most of the "trail" is a gravel road that is wide and easy to stroll. In a few spots the footing can be tricky, but this is a good choice for a tame walk into the rainforest. Occasionally, the trails to the upper waterfalls can be closed due to hazardous conditions. If there are signs posted that say the trails are closed, respect the landowners' wishes.

An outdoor playground peppered with waterfalls, the only downside is the crowding. During the midmorning hours, as visitors make their way toward Hana, there can be 50 cars parked along the side of the road. To visit with smaller crowds, stop on your drive back from Hana; come really early, before everyone else has arrived; or make a separate

trip here in the late afternoon. Bring mosquito repellent.

Although there are myriad waterfalls at Twin Falls, two main ones are most accessible. The 1.3-mile trail begins in the gravel parking lot and leads through a small gate in a lush and forested orchard. There are portable toilets on the right side of the trail, and visitors are encouraged to leave a donation for their maintenance and upkeep. After five minutes of walking along the gravel road, you'll hear some waterfalls off to the left. These are nice for a quick photo, but the main waterfalls are still farther down the trail.

After 10 minutes of walking, you'll come to a stream crossing that can flood during heavy rain. If the trail is closed, it will be here, and if the water appears to be rushing violently, it's best to turn around. Five minutes past the stream crossing is a three-way fork in the road; go straight. After five more minutes is another fork, where the trail to the left has a wooden plank crossing a small stream. Go straight, and after two minutes of clambering around an irrigation flume, you'll find a waterfall that has a small pool for swimming. While this waterfall is nice enough, there's a second waterfall, known as Caveman, that is far more dramatic, although it can be more difficult to reach.

To get to Caveman, turn around and go back to the fork in the trail with the wooden plank. Cross the wooden plank, ascend a small hill, take the fork to the left, and then take a right 50 yards later. You'll be walking downhill, and a few minutes later you'll reach a concrete irrigation structure with steps leading up and over it. From here you'll begin to see the waterfall in the distance. To reach the base of the falls, wade across a stream that is usually about knee-deep. If the stream is manageable, a short scramble past it will bring you to a cavernous waterfall begging you to take your photo behind it. Since the water isn't clear enough to see the bottom, don't even think about jumping off the top.

★ NA'ILI'ILI HAELE

The waterfalls of **Na'ili'ili Haele** (Bamboo Forest) are one of the highlights of the Road to Hana, but this hike has steep, slippery slopes and stream crossings prone to flash floods. In the past few years firefighters have made hundreds of rescues. Access to the hike may

soon be restricted because it has become so popular. If you decide to visit, only do so if it hasn't been raining.

At mile marker 6.5, you'll know you're approaching the trailhead by the enormous hairpin turn flanked by a rock wall. The road narrows, and parking can be difficult. You can park on the right side against the bamboo. If all these spots are taken, there are more pullouts within 0.25 mile.

The correct trailhead is marked by a lone metal pole in a break in a wire fence. On the other side of the fence, the trail is narrow at first and winds downhill. After two minutes of walking is an intersection where you turn left to a steep scramble down a hill. This area can become slick, so use your hands to avoid slipping. At the bottom of the hill is a stream crossing with a wooden plank over a gap. On the other side of the stream, continue straight through a tunnel of bamboo before the path wraps around to the left and you rejoin the main trail. Make a right and follow the trail for another two minutes until you come to a major stream crossing.

It is easy to get turned around at the stream crossing because the trail ends. Across the stream is a downed tree slightly to the left. Follow the tree trunk to its base—this is the

family hiking adventures in Hana

continuation of the trail. The trail parallels the water upstream. This section has some of the densest bamboo, and even when the sun is high in the sky, the thick grove blocks out the sun. A few minutes into the bamboo is a clearing off to the left. After a few more minutes is a second clearing. When you come to a third clearing on the left, you will hear the rush of a waterfall. Turn left to cross the stream again; this leads to the first waterfall, where there's a small pool.

WAIKAMOI RIDGE TRAIL

The **Waikamoi Ridge Trail** (mile marker 9.5) provides a calming respite to stretch your legs on a 30-minute loop trail that takes you just far enough from the road that the only sounds you hear are the **birds** and the creak of swaying bamboo. The trail gains 200 vertical feet and consists of two parts: the loop trail and the spur trail to the upper picnic area. Hike in a counterclockwise direction, since this is the best-maintained section of trail. The second half of the loop, heading back downhill toward the parking lot, isn't as well maintained and is a lot muddier than the platform steps on the way up.

If you take the spur trail to the upper picnic area, there is an open clearing to explore.

The trail to the upper picnic area takes about 10 minutes and is covered in *lauhala* leaves and slippery roots. At the end of the trail is a simple picnic area where a covered pavilion provides a relaxing place for a snack and a rest. Pack mosquito repellent if you plan on stopping to eat here.

Hana Town

KING'S HIGHWAY COASTAL TRAIL

One of the few hiking options in East Maui that doesn't involve a waterfall, the three-mile **King's Highway Coastal Trail** between Wai'anapanapa State Park and the northern tip of Hana Bay is one of the few navigable remnants of the ancient King's Highway that once circled the island. Today, only scarce remnants of this ancient trail are evident, but the most prominent section is here on the coast south of Wai'anapanapa. Parking for the trailhead is in the main lot of the state park. Along the course of this three-mile trail, you'll weave around azure bays flanked by black sand, pass beneath dense groves of dry *lauhala* trees, and gaze upon lava rock arches carved from the coast by the tumultuous sea.

Wear hiking boots, as the jagged *'a'a* lava can rip rubber slippers to pieces. Carry plenty of water, as there are no facilities along the

cooling off in Wai'anapanapa Caves

trail. As you get closer to Hana Bay, the trail becomes a little more treacherous. Most people start from the Wai'anapanapa trailhead and hike about halfway before turning back. To take the road less traveled, continue north of Wai'anapanapa past a series of smaller black-sand coves before eventually emerging near the Hana Airport. Expect to devote at least three hours to this trail round-trip from the trailhead.

For a quick and easy hike that still offers a rewarding view, the trail leading from the Travaasa Hana parking lot up to **Fagan's Cross** takes about 20 minutes and has a steep enough grade to offer a good leg workout. Watch for fresh guavas in the trees, as well as fresh cow pies left by the free-range cattle.

A two-mile **walking trail** leads from the trail to Fagan's Cross south toward Hamoa Beach. The track is little more than flattened grass through the pasturelands, but you'll have the coastal views all to yourself.

Kipahulu and Beyond

TOP EXPERIENCE

PIPIWAI TRAIL
Hands down, **Pipiwai Trail** is the best in Maui. It is in the upper portion of 'Ohe'o Gulch in the area known as Seven Sacred Pools. While most visitors to 'Ohe'o only pay a cursory visit to take photos, the Pipiwai Trail, which runs on the *mauka* side of the highway, is the undisputed highlight of the Kipahulu section of Haleakala National Park.

At four miles, the trail is long enough to be adventurous and short enough to be accessible, and it maintains a moderate grade. The last 0.5 mile of the trail winds through bamboo so thick it blocks out the sun, and just when you think the scenery couldn't get any more tropical, the trail emerges at the base of 400-foot Waimoku Falls. This two-hour expedition justifies the winding drive to get here. The best way to experience the trail is to camp overnight at the Kipahulu campground and

hit the path before the throngs of day-trippers arrive.

To find the trailhead, drive 30 to 40 minutes past the town of Hana to mile marker 41.7, where you enter the Kipahulu section of Haleakala National Park. Parking for the trailhead is within the park boundaries. You'll have to pay the $15 park entry fee. Walk back to the road and 100 yards toward Hana, where you'll see signs for the trailhead on the left. The trail climbs steeply up a rocky slope to a sign outlining trail distances. Much of the Pipiwai Trail parallels 'Ohe'o Gulch, and you can hear the rush of the water as you make your way uphill toward the falls. It's not safe to access the pools or waterfalls in the river. The National Park Service advises against any attempt to access the stream.

After 10 minutes on the trail is the lookout for Makahiku Falls, a 200-foot plunge that can be anything from a trickle during drier months to a violent torrent. Past the falls, the trail begins gaining elevation for another five minutes before emerging in the shade of a beautiful banyan tree. The section between the tree and the first bridge has multiple spur trails that lead to waterfall overlooks offering views of the canyons and pools.

Ten minutes past the tree is the first of two bridges that zigzag across the stream. This is a great place to snap pictures of the waterfalls and the first bamboo forest. After crossing the second bridge, when the trail turns into stairs that climb steeply toward the bamboo, there's an opening in the railing on the left side where a path leads down to a rocky streambed. This is the Palikea Stream, and if you rock-hop up the riverbed for about 15 minutes, you'll emerge at a waterfall that is less dramatic—but also less visited—than neighboring Waimoku Falls. The waterfall here trickles down the towering canyon walls, and the pool at the bottom is occasionally used by nude bathers.

Back on the main trail, continuing up the stairs, a boardwalk leads through the densest bamboo on the island. As you emerge from the creaking cavern, five more minutes of

Alelele Falls

passing ancient lava-rock walls before emerging at the base of the pristine falls.

Hiking Tours

While many private adventure tours will take you hiking as part of the experience, one group that focuses specifically on hiking is **Hike Maui** (808/879-5270, www.hikemaui. com, $124-199), with knowledgeable guides who will take you hiking in a private area hidden behind Twin Falls. Group sizes are usually small. What makes these hikes worthwhile is not only being taken directly to the trailhead but also learning about the island's flora, fauna, history, and mythology from guides who love what they do.

BIKING

The town of Pa'ia connects two of the most popular rides on the island: the frigid ride down Haleakala and the winding journey out toward Hana. As a cycling hub, there are a few bike shops around town.

rock-hopping brings you to the pièce de résistance, 400-foot Waimoku Falls. This is one of the most beautiful corners of the island.

ALELELE FALLS

Few people make the short hike back to 60-foot **Alelele Falls,** with a refreshing pool in winter that can go dry in summer. Located on the fabled back road about three miles past the Pools of 'Ohe'o, the trailhead is at Alelele Bridge, at mile marker 38.8; park in one of the few parking spots available on the Kaupo side of the bridge.

If you have the energy left for a 10-minute hike through the jungle, the reward is a waterfall that offers just the right amount of seclusion. Although parking for the trailhead is on the Kaupo side of the bridge, the trailhead is back on the Kipahulu side, at the spot where the bridge begins. Follow this well-defined trail and cross the stream a couple of times,

Pa'ia

One of the most comprehensive cycling experiences on Maui is at **Maui Cyclery** (99 Hana Hwy., 808/579-9009, www.gocycling-maui.com, 8am-5pm Mon.-Fri., 8am-noon Sat., 8am-noon Sun.), a small but thorough shop in the heart of Pa'ia. In addition to offering rentals (from $30 per day), parts, services, and sales, the staff offer guided tours for some of the island's best rides.

Ha'iku

In the Ha'iku Cannery, **Haleakala Bike Company** (810 Ha'iku Rd., Suite 120, 808/575-9575, www.bikemaui.com, 8:30am-5pm Mon.-Sat., 9am-4pm Sun.) specializes in tour groups making the ride down Haleakala Volcano. You can rent a bike (from $40 per day), and if you arrange your own transportation to the top, you'll be able to ride from the summit of the volcano.

Adventure Sports

ZIPLINING
Ha'iku

Most adventure sports along Maui's North Shore are in the water, but **North Shore Zipline Company** (2065 Kauhikoa Rd., 808/269-0671, www.nszipline.com, 8am-4:30pm Mon.-Sat.) has seven ziplines that run through the trees of rural Ha'iku in a onetime military base. The course is family-friendly and caters mainly to first-time zippers. Children as young as five can participate as long as they're accompanied by an adult. Don't think that you won't still get a rush, however, as you can hit speeds of up to 40 mph on the last line of the course, and the viewing platforms provide a unique vantage over the rural mountainside.

RAPPELLING

If you want to get all Navy SEAL on your Maui vacation, **Rappel Maui** (808/445-6407, www.rappelmaui.com, 7am-7pm daily $200) will teach you how to strap on a harness and walk down waterfalls. The company has exclusive access to waterfalls behind the Garden of Eden. The guides are professional and completely committed to your safety. You could end up getting the best photo of your vacation. Weight limits are 70 to 250 pounds.

★ HANG GLIDING IN HANA

This is the way to see the Hana coast. On an instructional lesson with **Hang Gliding Maui** (808/572-6557, www.hangglidingmaui.com), you meet your instructor, Armin, at his man-cave hangar at the Hana Airport. All flights are private, since the hang glider only has two seats, and he teaches you the basics of steering the glider as well as lift, wind speed, and direction.

This ultralight trike has wheels and a motor, so you take off down the Hana runway as you would in a regular plane, but when you reach a cruising altitude of 2,000 to 3,000 feet, you cut the engine and hang-glide back down, listening only to the wind. The view from here is life-changing, and there aren't even windows like a helicopter—just you, Armin, and the sky. Lessons are 30-minute ($190), 45-minute ($250), and one-hour ($310) flights and are offered Monday-Tuesday and Thursday-Friday.

GLIDING AND SKYDIVING

To get even higher, another option is **Skyview Soaring** (Hana Airport, 808/244-7070, www.skyviewsoaring.com, from $165), a self-powered glider where your pilot, Hans, takes you as high as 10,000 feet before killing the engines and gliding back to the airport. This isn't for the faint of heart, although the

Walk down waterfalls with Rappel Maui.

views afforded of Haleakala Crater and the eastern flank of the mountainside surpass any from along the highway. Bring your camera, as you glide silently past towering waterfalls and above the shore of Wai'anapanapa State Park. Flights are either 30 minutes or an hour. On the longer trip you soar all the way to the rim of Haleakala Crater, reaching speeds of 50 to 100 mph on the ride down.

POWERED GLIDER FLIGHTS

If you'd rather jump out of the plane, **Skydive Hana** (400 Alalele Rd., 808/637-4121, www.skydivehana.com, 8am-3pm Sat.-Sun., from $329 pp) opened in 2015 at the Hana Airport as the island's first commercial skydive operation. The minimum age is 18, and maximum weight is 240 pounds, with a $2 per pound surcharge for those over 200 pounds.

Shopping

PA'IA

Once known for hippies, surf culture, and sugarcane, Pa'ia now features some of the island's trendiest boutiques and arguably the island's best shopping, with bikini shops, beachwear boutiques, and craft galleries populating the one-stoplight town.

Art Galleries

For amazing fine-art underwater photography from around the Hawaiian Islands, the **Cesere Brothers** (83 Hana Hwy., 808/268-4405, www.ceserebrothers.com, 10am-7:30pm daily) have a small gallery on the walk toward Pa'ia Bay where you'll find everything from colorful nudibranchs to photos of enormous tiger sharks. On the other end of Pa'ia's main strip, on the Hana side of the stoplight, **Indigo** (149 Hana Hwy., 808/579-9199, www.indigopaia.com, 10am-6pm daily) has gorgeous and inspiring photos from far-flung corners of the globe.

Surf Shops

For surf, skate, or even snowboard wear, visit **Hi-Tech Maui** (58 Baldwin Ave., 808/579-9297, www.surfmaui.com, 9am-6pm daily), **Sailboards Maui** (22 Baldwin Ave., 808/579-8432, www.sailboardsmaui.com, 9:30am-7pm Mon.-Sat., 9:30am-6pm Sun.), **Hana Highway Surf** (149 Hana Hwy., 808/579-8999, www.hanahwysurf.com, 10am-7pm daily), and **Honolua Surf Company** (115 Hana Hwy., 808/579-9593, 9am-9pm Mon.-Sat., 9am-7:30pm Sun.), all offering apparel in America's happiest surf town.

Clothing and Swimwear

The only genre that rivals surf gear in Pa'ia is women's clothing boutiques and bikini stores. Along Baldwin Avenue, **Alice in Hulaland** (19 Baldwin Ave., 808/579-9922, www.aliceinhulaland.com, 10am-8pm daily) offers a snarky range of clothing and accessories, and **Mahina** (23 Baldwin Ave., 808/579-9131, www.shopmahina.com, 9:30am-8pm Mon.-Sat., 10am-7pm Sun.) offers trendy women's clothing that can also be found in its sister stores all around the island. On the finer end of apparel are **Nuage Bleu** (76 Hana Hwy., 808/579-9792, www.nuagebleu.com, 9:30am-6pm daily) and **Tamara Catz** (83 Hana Hwy., 808/579-9184, www.tamaracatz.com, 10am-6pm Sun.-Thurs., 10am-7pm Fri.-Sat.), along Hana Highway toward the entrance to town. These are two of the more elegant and fashionable clothing boutiques.

When it comes to bikinis, sun-seekers will love bouncing between **Pakaloha** (151 Hana Hwy., 808/579-8882, www.pakalohamaui.com, 10:30am-6pm daily) and **San Lorenzo Bikinis** (115 Hana Hwy., 808/873-7972, www.sanlorenzobikinis.com, 9:30am-9pm daily), in the center of town. The bikinis are skimpy, almost Brazilian, but that's the North Shore. Even more bikinis are at **Maui**

Girl (12 Baldwin Ave., 808/579-9266, www. maui-girl.com, 9am-6pm daily) and **Letarte** (24 Baldwin Ave., 808/579-6022, www.letart-eswimwear.com, 10am-6pm daily), both with bikinis featured in *Sports Illustrated*'s swimsuit edition.

ROAD TO HANA
Gifts and Souvenirs
The best place for real shopping along the Road to Hana is at **Nahiku Ti Gallery** (mile marker 28.7, 808/248-8800, 10am-5pm daily), a small gallery within the Nahiku Marketplace. This curious strip mall in the rainforest is already strange in that it offers legitimate food options in the middle of nowhere, and the art gallery rivals those in Ka'anapali and Wailea. While nowhere near as large as the south shore shopping venues, the gallery has a varied selection of jewelry, crafts, paintings, pottery, and a surprising collection of art.

HANA TOWN
Art Galleries
By far the most comprehensive gallery in Hana, the **Hana Coast Gallery** (5031 Hana Hwy., 808/248-8636, www.hanacoast.com, 9am-5pm daily) might be the nicest art gallery on the island. A freestanding building within the Travaasa Hana hotel, the Hana Coast Gallery features fine works by Hawaiian artists. Oil paintings, ceramics, and wooden sculptures are on display in this sophisticated space, and the depth of knowledge of the staff on the intricacies of individual pieces provides an educational component to this fine-art experience.

Gifts and Souvenirs
Within the same complex as the post office and the Hana Ranch Restaurant is the small **Hana Treasures** (5031 Hana Hwy., 808/248-7372, 9am-4pm daily), selling clothing, trinkets, and "Thank God for Hana" bumper stickers.

HANA TO KIPAHULU
Art Galleries
Along the road between Hana and Kipahulu, on the ocean side of the highway, **Karen Davidson Fine Art** (mile marker 46.3, 808/248-4877, www.karendavidson.net, by appointment) focuses on the unique art of handcrafted paper. Many of the works are either oil paintings on handmade paper or an array of paper collages. There's a Hawaiian and Polynesian theme coursing through much of the artwork, unique and relevant to Hana. The studio opens to the Hana shore. If you are more interested in fine art than tumbling waterfalls, call ahead to arrange a visit.

Entertainment

LIVE MUSIC
Pa'ia
The de facto late-night watering hole for all of the North Shore continues to be **Charley's** (142 Hana Hwy., 808/579-8085, www.charleysmaui.com, 7am-10pm Sun.-Thurs., 7am-2am Fri.-Sat.), where there's live music most nights and the only place in Pa'ia where you can dance. There can also occasionally be live music in the courtyard of intimate **Café des Amis** (42 Baldwin Ave., 808/579-6323, www. cdamaui.com, 8:30am-8:30pm).

Hana
The most happening show in town is at the hotel **Travaasa Hana** (5031 Hana Hwy., 808/359-2401, www.travaasa.com) Wednesday and Thursday evening at the **Preserve Kitchen and Bar**. Local people put on their finest and come for a drink and entertainment. You never know what talent might play at the live music events held Wednesday-Friday and Sunday nights, as many famous Hawaiian artists have Hana roots.

Live music can also be found at the **Hana**

Ranch Restaurant (5031 Hana Hwy., 808/270-5280, 7:30pm-9:30pm Tues.) one night a week. A scheduled band plays the first hour, followed by an hour of open mike.

You'd be surprised how much inspiring talent a small community can foster without modern technology. Ukulele, hula, and song are ways of life in this community.

Food

HA'IKU

The town of Ha'iku is mostly residential, and aside from tropical bed-and-breakfasts has little for visitors. The exception is food, with a couple of restaurants worth the drive.

The best restaurant in Ha'iku is ★ **Nuka** (780 Haiku Rd., 808/575-2939, www.nuka-maui.com, 10am 1:30pm and 4:30pm-10pm Mon.-Sat., 4:30pm-10pm Sun., $9-19), with hand-rolled sushi that can rival the best on Maui.

PA'IA

American

Charley's (142 Hana Hwy., 808/579-8085, www.charleysmaui.com, 7am-10pm Sun.-Thurs., 7am-2am Fri.-Sat., $8-14) is as integral to Pa'ia as dawn patrol at Ho'okipa or bodysurfing at Baldwin Beach. Known as "Willie's Place" because Willie Nelson frequently dines here, Charley's has a colorful cast of characters. The saloon exterior exudes a gritty vibe, but inside it's a jovial, comfortable spot with locally sourced ingredients. Top off an early morning surf session with macadamia nut pancakes. A classic "bacon and blue" burger for lunch is filling and won't break your budget.

Italian

As the name of ★ **Flatbread Company** (89 Hana Hwy., 808/579-8989, www.flatbread-company.com, 11am-10pm daily, $16-22) implies, you won't find any Chicago-style deep dish here. All of the pizzas use organic, locally sourced ingredients and are fired in an open *kiawe* (mesquite) wood oven. Try the Mopsy (free-range kalua pork, organic mango barbecue sauce, organic red onions,

Maui pineapple, and goat cheese from Surfing Goat Dairy), or Coevolution (kalamata olives, organic and local rosemary, red onions, goat cheese from Surfing Goat Dairy, sweet red peppers, and organic herbs), both made with organic dough. A lively bar scene fills the place nightly; get there early or expect a wait. Tuesday nights, the restaurant hosts benefits for the local community, but the crowds are intense.

Mexican

On the corner of Pa'ia's only stoplight, separated by the bustling crosswalk, ★ **Milagros** (3 Baldwin Ave., 808/579-8755, www.milagrosfoodcompany.com, 11am-10pm daily, $10-19) is known for Mexican fare with a funky island twist, enormous portions, and the best happy hour in town. The black-bean nachos, ahi burrito, and blackened ahi tacos are all local favorites. Get a seat at the outdoor patio, which has some of the best people-watching in Pa'ia.

Natural Foods

Mana Foods (49 Baldwin Ave., 808/579-8078, www.manafoodsmaui.com, 8am-8:30pm daily) is the epicenter of the island's health-conscious, with a selection of organic and natural offerings. There's a hot bar as well as a deli section where you can build your own picnic lunch for the Road to Hana, or pick up filling and affordable sandwiches ($7).

Seafood

★ **Mama's Fish House** (799 Poho Place, 808/579-8488, www.mamasfishhouse.com, 11am-9pm daily, $20-55) is synonymous with Maui fine dining. Its cult-like followers claim that if you haven't been to Mama's, you've never been to Maui. The oceanfront location and romantic ambience are unbeatable, and the fish is so fresh that the menu tells you where your fish was caught that morning and who caught it. Call well in advance for reservations, timing your meal for sunset if possible. Lunch is an affordable alternative.

While your hotel concierge will recommend Mama's, local surfers will point you to ★ **Pa'ia Fish Market** (100 Baldwin Ave., 808/579-8030, www.paiafishmarket.com, 11am-9:30pm daily, $11), on the corner of the only stoplight in town. Lines stretch out the door for the popular ono and mahimahi burgers. My personal favorite is the ahi burger, paired with a Hefeweizen on draft. The fish tacos and seafood pasta are shockingly good as well.

ROAD TO HANA

There's a myth that you won't find any food while driving the Road to Hana. Stores in Pa'ia and as far away as Ka'anapali offer "Road to Hana picnic lunches" as a means of staving off starvation, even though the longest stretch without any food options is under seven miles. The best plan for food when driving the Road to Hana is to start with lunch in Pa'ia, and then make frequent stops for snacks at stands on the side of the road. As long as it's a weekday, there will be plenty of options for food when you get to Hana. For detailed info on the food stops en route, see the Road to Hana mileage guide in the beginning of this chapter.

HANA

On weekdays Hana has many lunch options. Dinner options are sparse, however, and only a handful of lunch venues are open on weekends.

Hawaiian Regional

The fanciest, freshest, and best meal in Hana is at the Travaasa Hana hotel, where ★ **Preserve Kitchen and Bar** (5031 Hana Hwy., 808/359-2401, 7:30am-9pm daily, $20-48) restaurant has fine dining rivaling the best on the island. The staff is friendly and happy to talk, and the atmosphere is welcomingly casual. Take the waiter's suggestion for the evening and order the fish of the day, which was likely caught earlier that morning in waters just off Hana. The rest of the menu features the freshest local ingredients. It's a great spot for a filling breakfast after watching the Hana sunrise.

Thai

Hana isn't a place you'd expect to find mouthwatering Thai, but ★ **Thai Food by Pranee** (5050 Uakea Rd., no phone, 8am-5pm Mon.-Sat., $10-12) is a culinary gem in the humblest of locations. Little more than a glorified food truck across from Hana Ballpark, this open-air restaurant gets packed for lunch—especially since it's open on weekends. The filling portions of pad thai and green curry are worth the wait, and if the food is too spicy you can ask them for coconut milk to bring the heat down. Parking is along Uakea Road, and be sure to park facing the correct direction, since violators are often ticketed.

KIPAHULU AND BEYOND

If you plan on driving the back road to the other side of the island, the only real food option is **Kaupo Store** (mile marker 34.6, 10am-5pm Mon.-Sat., cash only) in the dusty Kaupo hinterlands. If you're planning on venturing from Hana to 'Ohe'o (Seven Sacred Pools) and then continuing around the back side of the island, stock up on water and snacks at **Hasegawa General Store** (5165 Hana Hwy., 808/248-7079, www.hanamaui.com, 7am-7pm daily), lest you end up marooned with no water or food.

Where to Stay on Maui

West Maui

Name	Type	Price	Features	Why Stay Here?	Best For
'Aina Nalu Resort	condo	$129-400	pool, kitchen	location	couples
Camp Olowalu	camping	$20-70	restrooms, oceanfront	location, affordable	budget travelers
Ho'oilo House	B&B	$339	pool, breakfast	quiet, view	couples, honeymooners
Hyatt Regency	resort	$289-2,500	waterslides, oceanfront	location, pools	families
★ Ka'anapali Beach Hotel	hotel	$195-325	free hula show	location	families, couples
Lahaina Shores Beach Resort	condo	$199-300	pool, oceanfront	location	couples
Makai Inn	inn	$110-190	oceanfront, gardens	location, affordable	budget travelers
Maui Kai	condo	$239-400	kitchens, oceanfront	location	families, couples
★ Montage Kapalua Bay	resort	$705-2,500	kitchens, oceanfront, spa, pool	full-service resort	couples, families, honeymooners, luxury-lovers
★ Napili Kai Beach Resort	condo	$350-825	pool, oceanfront	full amenities	families, couples
Napili Village	condo	$119-139	oceanfront	location, rates	families, couples
Pioneer Inn	hotel	$159-229	garden, pool	location	couples, budget travelers
★ Plantation Inn	B&B	$187-265	pool, breakfast	location, quiet	couples, honeymooners
★ Puamana	condo	$175-600	pool, oceanfront	location, quiet	families, couples
★ Ritz-Carlton Kapalua	resort	$429-5,000	golf, spa	full-service resort	luxury-lovers, honeymooners
Royal Lahaina	hotel	$189-550	oceanfront, tennis	location	couples
Sheraton Maui	resort	$303-8,000	pool, oceanfront	full-service resort	families, honeymooners
Westin Ka'anapali Ocean Resort Villas	resort	$360-950	pool, oceanfront	full-service resort	families, couples

Central Maui

Name	Type	Price	Features	Why Stay Here?	Best For
★ Banana Bungalow	hostel	$41-126	free tours	affordable	budget travelers
Courtyard Marriott	hotel	$200-300	modern fitness room, swimming pool	location	business travelers
★ Iao Valley Inn	B&B	$100-275	quiet, breakfast	location, affordable	couples
★ Old Wailuku Inn at Ulupono	B&B	$165-195	breakfast, quiet	historic	couples

South Maui

Name	Type	Price	Features	Why Stay Here?	Best For
Aston Maui Hill	condo	$165-400	pool, kitchen	location, amenities	couples, families
Days Inn	hotel	$139-280	oceanfront, barbecue	affordable, location	budget travelers
★ Fairmont Kea Lani	resort	$459-1,775	pool, oceanfront	romantic, luxury	families, couples, honeymooners
Four Seasons Resort	resort	$600-10,000	pools, spa, oceanfront	romantic, luxury	couples, honeymooners, luxury-lovers
★ Grand Wailea	resort	$564-3,370	waterslides, spa, oceanfront	romantic, luxury, pools	families, couples, honeymooners
Hale Pau Hana	condo	$260-380	oceanfront, kitchen	location, amenities	couples, families
Hotel Wailea	hotel	$499-1400	pool, spa, amenities	boutique, romantic	couples, luxury-lovers
Maalaea Bay Rentals	condo	$100-300	pool, kitchen, laundry	location, ocean view	families, extended stay
Mana Kai Maui	condo	$240-500	kitchen, oceanfront	location, water sports	couples, families
★ Maui Coast Hotel	hotel	$169-435	pool, fitness center, shuttle	full amenities	couples, business travel

South Maui (continued)

Name	Type	Price	Features	Why Stay Here?	Best For
★ Maui Mango Cottages	cottages	$295-395	kitchen, gardens	location, amenities	couples, families
Kohea Kai	LGBT resort	$165-499	kitchenette, hot tub	quiet, location	couples
Ocean Breeze Hideaway	B&B	$109-139	gardens, breakfast	quiet, affordable	couples
Sugar Beach Resort	condo	$150-425	pool, spa, kitchen	oceanfront	couples, families
Wailea Beach Marriott	resort	$331-900	pool, spa, luau	oceanfront, watersports	families, couples
Wailea Beach Villas	condo	$850-2,500	pool, oceanfront	romantic, luxury	luxury-lovers
★ Wailea Ekolu Village	condo	$260-425	kitchen, amenities	location, affordable	couples, families

Upcountry

Name	Type	Price	Features	Why Stay Here?	Best For
★ Aloha Cottage	cottage	$239-279	hot tub, kitchen, lanai	quiet, peaceful, romantic	couples
Banyan Bed-and-Breakfast	B&B	$175-220	kitchen, breakfast	quiet, location	couples
G and Z Upcountry Bed-and-Breakfast	B&B	$149	kitchenette, breakfast	quiet, affordable	budget travelers, couples
★ Hale Ho'okipa Inn	B&B	$125-175	breakfast, garden	quiet, historic	couples
Hale Ho'omana	B&B	$119-139	breakfast, spa, wellness	location, quiet, affordable	couples, budget travelers
★ Kula Lodge	inn	$170-245	fireplace, lanai	location, romantic, quiet	couples, hikers
Kula Sandalwoods	cottage	$169-209	lanai, views	quiet, location, retreat	couples

Upcountry (continued)

Name	Type	Price	Features	Why Stay Here?	Best For
★ Lumeria	hotel	$300-459	yoga classes, garden courtyard	meditative retreat	solo travelers, couples, groups
Peace of Maui	inn	$85-175	kitchen	affordable	budget travelers
Polipoli Springs State Recreation Area	camping	$18-90	none	quiet, wilderness	budget travelers, adventure travelers
★ Star Lookout	vacation rental	$250	kitchen, views	location, quiet, romantic	couples
Upcountry Bed and Breakfast	B&B	$150	fireplace, views, breakfast	quiet, peaceful	couples

East Maui

Name	Type	Price	Features	Why Stay Here?	Best For
Ala'aina Ocean Vista	B&B	$221-231	gardens, hot tub, barbecue	quiet, peaceful	couples
★ Bamboo Inn	B&B	$195-265	ocean-view lanai, breakfast	location, romantic	couples
Haleakala National Park: Kipahulu	camping	$15	pit toilets, barbecue	location, affordable	budget travelers
★ Huelo Point Lookout	vacation rental	$250-405	hot tub, ocean view	location, quiet, peaceful	couples
★ Pa'ia Inn	inn	$199-999	oceanfront, gardens	location, boutique	couples
Sprecks Plantation House	apartment	$95-150	kitchenette	affordable, location	budget travelers, couples
★ The Inn at Mama's Fish House	inn	$250-850	kitchens, oceanfront	location, romantic	couples, honeymooners
★ Travaasa Hana	resort	$400-1,200	spa, pool, activities	location, luxury, amenities	couples, honeymooners

Lana'i

I t's hard to find an outdoor playground more stunning than Lana'i, home to a mere 3,500 residents and crisscrossed by just 30 miles of paved roads.

The late 1980s saw this island's cash crop transition from the world's largest pineapple plantation to high-end tourism. With the construction of the luxurious Four Seasons Resort, the island instantly became one of Hawaii's most exclusive getaways. In 2012, Oracle CEO Larry Ellison purchased 98 percent of the island, and while a range of projects, including a winery, a college, and a tennis center, has been discussed for the tiny island, as of yet the largest change has been the spectacular renovation of the Four Seasons Resort.

Resort life aside, visitors come to enjoy the snorkeling at Hulopo'e Beach Park, and the plantation-era charm of cozy Lana'i City—the island's only town. Choose to explore a little deeper, however, with morning hikes on pine-shrouded mountain trails, off-roading through otherworldly moonscapes, and surfing empty waves along an empty beach.

Lana'i is an island of unparalleled luxury, but it's also about 4WD trucks with deer skulls mounted to the bumper, aging Filipino plantation workers "talking story" in Dole Park, and petroglyphs scattered across rock faces that predate any of the island's modern history. It's a tight-knit community where townsfolk greet each other with first names and a smile.

ORIENTATION

The island's only town, **Lana'i City,** is in the middle of the island at about 1,700 feet elevation, 20 minutes from **Manele Harbor** and the **Four Seasons Resort Lana'i** and about 10 minutes from the **Lana'i Airport. Hulopo'e Beach** Park is a 10-minute walk from the harbor, and with the exception of the restaurants and shops at the resort, all of the island's stores and facilities are in Lana'i City. The rest of the island is a network of dirt roads perfect for off-road exploring, with many sights 45 minutes to an hour outside Lana'i City.

PLANNING YOUR TIME

Most people visit Lana'i as a day trip from Maui. If you take the 6:45am ferry from Lahaina Harbor, you have 8-10 hours to explore the island before catching the ferry

---

Previous: Keahiakawelo, or Garden of the Gods; sunset at Kaunolu. **Above:** Spinner dolphins are a common sight on the southwestern coast of Lana'i.

Look for ★ to find recommended
sights, activities, dining, and lodging.

Highlights

★ **Lana'i Culture and Heritage Center:**
Artifacts from wooden spears used in ancient
battles to old photographs of Lana'i's plantation
days adorn this cultural resource (page 369).

★ **Keahiakawelo (Garden of the Gods):**
An otherworldly landscape of tortured earth is
dotted with red boulders that appear to have
fallen from the sky (page 370).

★ **Keomoku Village:** Little more than a
collection of old homes and a haunting abandoned church, this stretch of shore shows what
life on Lana'i must have been like a century ago
(page 371).

★ **Kaunolu Village:** Explore a complex that
was once the home of King Kamehameha I, virtually untouched since the 19th century (page 372).

★ **Hulopo'e Beach Park:** This crescent of
white sand has the island's best snorkeling when
the ocean is calm and its best surf on a southern
swell (page 373).

★ **Kaiolohia (Shipwreck Beach):** The
fringing reef ringing the island's northwest coast
has been the demise of dozens of ships, including the World War II Liberty ship that provides
a dramatic backdrop for this windswept beach
(page 375).

★ **Polihua Beach:** Escape to what feels like
the end of the earth on the island's northern

coast. This is the place to make the only set of
footprints in the sand (page 376).

★ **Munro Trail:** This 12.8-mile hiking trail winds
to the island's 3,370-foot summit (page 379).

Lana'i

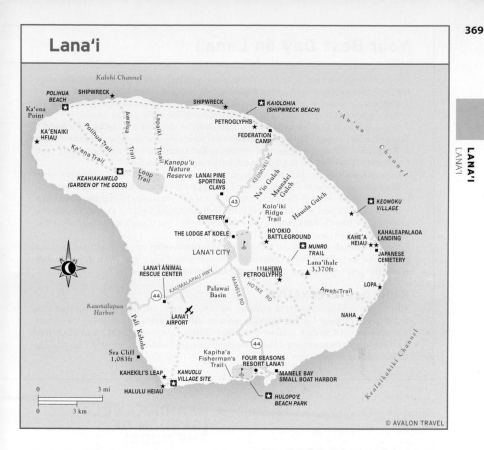

© AVALON TRAVEL

back. You'll have enough time to visit Hulopo'e Beach and do some snorkeling, hiking, and sunbathing, as well as time to rent a Jeep and explore the island's east shore. If you spend a couple of nights on Lana'i, you'll have enough time to explore the island's remote and isolated spots and still be able to relax and enjoy the island's slow pace.

Sights

★ LANA'I CULTURE AND HERITAGE CENTER

There's no better place to learn about the history of Lana'i than at the **Lana'i Culture and Heritage Center** (730 Lana'i Ave., 808/565-7177, www.lanaichc.org, 8:30am-3:30pm Mon.-Fri., 9am-1pm Sat., free). Started in 2007 in a building adjacent to the Hotel Lana'i, the exceptionally informative little museum features displays pertaining to the days of ancient Hawaii through the end of the Dole plantation. Black-and-white photos from Lana'i's ranching days are joined by stone adzes, poi pounders, and a 10-foot-long *'ihe pololu* wooden spear used as a weapon similar to a jousting lance. More than just a collection of historical photos and artifacts, the center also highlights how

Your Best Day on Lana'i

If you're visiting Lana'i as a day trip from Maui, get an early start by taking the 6:45am ferry. Make ferry reservations beforehand, and arrange for a 4WD vehicle to use on Lana'i for the day. When you arrive on Lana'i at 7:45am, take the shuttle to Lana'i City if you're renting a Jeep from **Dollar,** or if you've rented a Jeep through a local company, it might be waiting at the harbor.

Grab breakfast at **Coffee Works** by 8:30am, and pick up water and snacks at **Richard's Supermarket.** Drive to **Shipwreck Beach** and then make your way down the eastern shore to **Keomoku Village.** It's five more minutes to **Kahalepalaoa** and an empty white-sand beach, and 15 more minutes to **Lopa** beach, better protected from the wind.

Once you've left your footprints in the sand, drive for an hour back to Lana'i City for a late lunch at **Blue Ginger.** Spend 30 minutes strolling **Lana'i City** to check out the local shops, and if you rented from Dollar, return the Jeep and take the shuttle down to Manele Harbor (there's usually a shuttle around 3:30pm). Instead of going to the harbor, however, see if the shuttle can drop you at **Hulopo'e Beach Park,** where you'll swim, sunbathe, and, if you brought gear, snorkel at the nicest beach on Lana'i.

If you're feeling festive, head up to the **Four Seasons Resort** for a drink at the ocean-view pool bar, or hike to **Pu'u Pehe Overlook** as the sun sinks low in the sky. It's a 10-minute walk to Manele Harbor, where the 6:45pm ferry will take you back to Lahaina.

RAINY-DAY ALTERNATIVE

Take the rain as an opportunity to explore Lana'i City in depth. Just like a sunny day, start with breakfast and coffee at **Coffee Works,** and then walk off breakfast by exploring the **shops** that circle around Dole Park. Grab lunch at **Blue Ginger,** and then head to **Lana'i Culture and Heritage Center** for a dose of the island's history. Finish with dinner at **Lana'i City Grille** inside of **Hotel Lana'i.**

the culture of Lana'i has been influenced by historical events.

KANEPU'U PRESERVE

Six miles down Polihua Road, just before reaching Keahiakawelo (Garden of the Gods), **Kanepu'u Preserve** is the only remaining dryland forest of its kind in Hawaii. Thanks to a fence erected in 1918 by Lana'i Ranch manager George Munro, this 590-acre preserve is home to 48 species of native Hawaiian plants that covered most of the island prior to the arrival of the invasive *kiawe* tree and root-destroying goats and sheep. Managed by the Nature Conservancy, the preserve features a short, self-guided trail where visitors can see native hardwoods such as *lama* (Hawaiian ebony) and *olopua* (Hawaiian olive). The trail only takes about 15 minutes to walk, and it makes a nice stop before exploring the Garden of the Gods.

★ KEAHIAKAWELO (GARDEN OF THE GODS)

Although we've successfully put a rover on Mars, **Keahiakawelo** is the closest most of us will ever get to walking on the red planet. Despite being only seven miles from the pine-lined streets of Lana'i City, the Garden of the Gods looks like a moonscape. Erosion created ravines and rock spires in deep reds, purples, and sulfuric yellows. The best time to visit this dry, dusty, and often windswept area is at sunset, when the rich palette of color is enhanced by the afternoon light.

Keahiakawelo is almost completely devoid of vegetation, but the strangest part of the panorama is the expanse of boulders that tumble over the barren hillside. It's unclear how they got here, but the ancient Hawaiians had a number of theories. According to legend, the rocks were dropped by gods as they tended their heavenly gardens, providing the site's English name, Garden of the Gods.

Keahiakawelo remains a must-see for the consuming sense of seclusion. The road here can be rutted and rough, and a 4WD vehicle is needed if you're visiting after a heavy rain. To reach the site, take a left just after the Lodge at Koele and travel seven miles on Polihua Road, taking the right at the fork after the Koele Stables.

★ KEOMOKU VILLAGE

There isn't much to see in the abandoned village of **Keomoku,** but driving through this coastal ghost town provides a feeling of Lana'i's recent past. It also makes a great stop if you are heading out to the beach at Lopa.

Before the arrival of Europeans, it's believed there were thousands of indigenous Hawaiians living along Lana'i's eastern shore. *Heiau* were constructed as places of worship, and petroglyphs such as those found at Kaiolohia depict basic scenes from this ancient time. By the time Frederick Hayselden chose Keomoku as the site for his Maunalei Sugar Company in 1899, however, the island's population had dwindled to fewer than 200.

In one of the state's shortest-lived sugar ventures, closing in 1901 Indigenous Hawaiians attribute the company's demise to the stones from ancient *heiau* used in constructing the plantation, which angered the gods.

Keomoku remains abandoned, and there are a couple of places where you can see the remnants of its past. Driving the sandy 4WD road through the former plantation town is a tour through Lana'i's history. Simple beach-front fishing shacks dot the sandy road, their yards ringed with fishing nets.

The number-one attraction in Keomoku is **Ka Lanakila Church,** 5.5 miles from where the pavement ends on Keomoku Highway. The hauntingly beautiful wooden structure constructed in 1903 is being restored, and special sermons are still intermittently conducted in Hawaiian throughout the year.

Behind the church, a small trail leads for 10 minutes to the remains of the Maunalei Sugar Mill, and across the street, a trail passes through the coconut grove to the wooden Lahaina passenger boat. A small shrine 1.5 miles past the church honors the Japanese laborers who died on Lana'i in the few years of the plantation's existence, and 0.5 mile beyond the shrine is the abandoned pier at Kahalepalaoa, which offers good fishing and sweeping views of neighboring Maui.

looking towards Moloka'i from Keahiakawelo

★ KAUNOLU VILLAGE

The abandoned village of **Kaunolu** is difficult to reach, but its isolation has kept it underdeveloped and virtually untouched. Follow Highway 440 south from Lana'i City. Just past the airport turnoff is a large boulder inscribed with "Kaunolu." Turn left on the smooth, dusty road, accessible to any vehicle provided it hasn't rained heavily. After two miles is a historical marker and another sign pointing toward Kaunolu. Make a right down this road, which is steep, eroded, and rough. Dollar allows its Jeeps to go to the top of the road but not all the way to the bottom. To reach the bottom, drive until the road gest too rough and then get out and walk. It's three miles from here to the shore.

At the bottom of the road is a Y-junction. The road to the left leads to a set of fishing shacks used by locals who come to drink beer and fish, but turn right instead. The road abruptly ends at a wooden picnic table beneath a tree, marking the entrance to Kaunolu. This shore was home to a thriving population from the 15th century until the late 19th century. Notice that except for the wind and the waves, Kaunolu is completely silent.

The sandy ravine fronting the beach is the only successful canoe launch between here and Hulopo'e. To reach the remains of the ancient canoe *hale* (house), look for a trail that leads down the hill from where the road ends. After a rocky scramble to the dry riverbed, and follow the trail toward the water, passing some petroglyphs. An interpretive placard points out the canoe *hale*. This is the base of the Halulu *heiau*, a place of worship and of immense cultural significance to indigenous Hawaiians. It's also the best preserved *heiau* on Lana'i.

The trail bends to the right as it climbs up from the rocks, eventually crossing a footbridge toward the top of the *heiau*. Up the short hill is a Y-junction. Go left to find petroglyphs in the rocks, or go right to a viewpoint of the Kaholo Pali sea cliffs, the highest on Lana'i, with some over 1,000 feet. A notch in the cliff here is labeled Kahekili's Leap. After a warrior from the late 18th century who brought warriors here to jump into the sea to prove their valor. Medical help is far away; don't even consider jumping.

At the bottom of the road is a Y-junction. The road to the left leads to a set of fishing shacks used by locals who come to drink beer and fish, but turn right instead. The road abruptly ends at a wooden picnic table beneath a tree, marking the entrance to

Ka Lanakila Church in Keomoku Village

Lost on Lana'i

If you need a helping hand trying to plan an outing to Lana'i, the locally based **Lost On Lana'i** (808/215-0201, www.lostonlanai.com) is a one-stop shop for booking activities and ferry transportation to the island. It offers combo deals that you won't find elsewhere and can also answer questions about the island. With over 300 miles of dirt roads leading every which way, you want to make sure you don't actually end up getting lost on Lana'i.

points out the canoe *hale*. This is the base of the Halulu *heiau*, a place of worship and of immense cultural significance to indigenous Hawaiians. It's also the best preserved *heiau* on Lana'i.

The trail bends to the right as it climbs up from the rocks, eventually crossing a footbridge toward the top of the *heiau*. Up the short hill is a Y-junction. Go left to find petroglyphs in the rocks, or go right to a viewpoint of the Kaholo Pali sea cliffs, the highest on Lana'i, with some over 1,000 feet. A notch in the cliff here is labeled Kahekili's Leap. Kahekili was a fearless warrior chief from the late 18th century, with half his body tattooed black, eyelids and tongue included. He brought warriors here to jump into the sea to prove their valor. The 80-foot height of the *lele kawa* (cliff jumping) wasn't difficult, but clearing the 15-foot ledge at the base of the cliff was. Medical help is far away; don't even consider jumping.

Kaunolu. This shore was home to a thriving population from the 15th century until it was abandoned in the late 19th century. Notice that except for the wind and the waves, Kaunolu is completely silent.

follow the trail toward the water, passing some petroglyphs. An interpretive placard

Beaches

Unless you have a 4WD or high-clearance vehicle, Lana'i only has one accessible beach, which is also the only one with any facilities. If you procure a Jeep or a local's truck, there are a number of undeveloped beaches where you can run around naked with no one there to care.

★ HULOPO'E BEACH PARK

If you want to make your friends back home jealous, snap a picture of this beach. **Hulopo'e Beach Park** is the undisputed favorite hangout for islanders, named the country's best beach in 1997. Within walking distance of the Manele Small Boat Harbor, Hulopo'e is the only beach on the island with restrooms and showers. Despite being the island's most popular, it's far from crowded. The right side of the beach is used by guests of the Four Seasons Resort, who have access

to the white umbrellas and lounge chairs. Similarly, guests of Trilogy Excursions' snorkel tour from Maui inhabit the left-hand side of the beach Monday-Friday, leaving the middle section of the beach for visitors to relax in the shade or bake in the sun.

Hulopo'e Bay is a marine reserve and home to one of the few reefs in Maui County that isn't in decline. The reef extends over the left side of the bay, where colorful parrotfish the size of your forearm can easily be spotted and heard nibbling on the vibrant corals. Hulopo'e is also famous for the Hawaiian spinner dolphins that regularly enter the bay. In an effort to protect the natural sleep cycles of the dolphins, swimmers are asked not to approach them. If dolphins happen to swim toward you, consider yourself lucky.

In addition to the sugary sand and perfectly placed palm trees, there are two nature trails on each side of the beach. The **Kapiha'a**

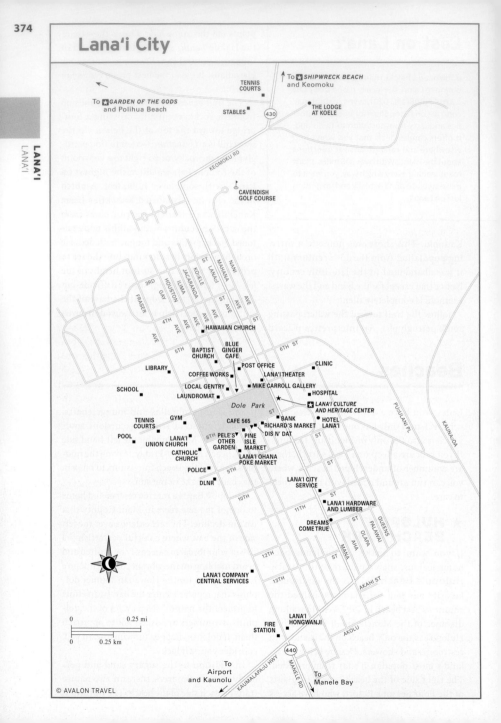

Lana'i City

TENNIS COURTS

To ☀ SHIPWRECK BEACH and Keomoku

To ☀ GARDEN OF THE GODS and Polihua Beach

STABLES

430

THE LODGE AT KOELE

KEOMOKU RD

CAVENDISH GOLF COURSE

3RD ST

FRASER AVE

GAY AVE

HOUSTON AVE

ILIMA AVE

JACARANDA AVE

KO-ELE AVE

LANA'I AVE

NANI AVE

MAHANA AVE

4TH AVE

5TH AVE

6TH ST

HAWAIIAN CHURCH

BAPTIST CHURCH

BLUE GINGER CAFE

POST OFFICE

CLINIC

LIBRARY

COFFEE WORKS

LANA'I THEATER

SCHOOL

LOCAL GENTRY

MIKE CARROLL GALLERY

LAUNDROMAT

HOSPITAL

LANA'I CULTURE AND HERITAGE CENTER

Dole Park

TENNIS COURTS

GYM

CAFE 565

ST

BANK

HOTEL LANA'I

POOL

LANA'I UNION CHURCH

8TH ST

PELE'S OTHER GARDEN

PINE ISLE MARKET

RICHARD'S MARKET

DIS N' DAT

CATHOLIC CHURCH

LANA'I OHANA POKE MARKET

ST

POLICE

9TH ST

DLNR

LANA'I CITY SERVICE

ST

10TH ST

11TH ST

LANA'I HARDWARE AND LUMBER

DREAMS COME TRUE

QUEENS ST

OLAPA ST

PALAWAI ST

AHA ST

MANA ST

12TH ST

AKAHI ST

LANA'I COMPANY CENTRAL SERVICES

13TH ST

AKOLU ST

PUUHLANI PL.

KAUNA-OA

0   0.25 mi

0   0.25 km

LANA'I HONGWANJI

FIRE STATION

440

To Airport and Kaunolu

KAUMALAPAU HWY

MANELE RD

To Manele Bay

AKOLU

© AVALON TRAVEL

Fisherman's Trail departs from the right side of the bay, and the **Trail to Pu'u Pehe Overlook** starts from the left side. There is also a fantastic system of tide pools stretching around the left point of the bay, and one is even deep enough to teach young children to snorkel. The easiest way to get to the tide pools is to use the stairway on the trail to Pu'u Pehe Overlook.

★ KAIOLOHIA (SHIPWRECK BEACH)

The most popular beach among island visitors after Hulopo'e is **Kaiolohia,** also called **Shipwreck Beach.** To get to Shipwreck, drive past the Lodge at Koele and down Lana'i's windswept "back side" by following the switchbacking, but paved, Keomoku Highway. The views as you descend this winding road stretch all the way to neighboring Maui.

Once you reach the bottom of the paved highway, a sign points left toward Shipwreck Beach. Follow the sandy road (4WD recommended) for 1.5 miles before it dead-ends in a parking area. When you pass the shacks built out of driftwood and fishing floats, you've arrived.

Traditionally this area was known as Kaiolohia. The current moniker originates with the unnamed World War II Liberty ship that was intentionally grounded on the fringing reef. Numerous vessels have met their demise on this shallow stretch of coral, but this concrete oil tanker has deteriorated more slowly than most. Stoic in its haunted appearance, the ship remains firmly lodged in the reef as a warning to passing vessels of the dangers.

Because of the persistent northeasterly trade winds, Kaiolohia is rarely suitable for snorkeling or swimming. Your time is better spent combing the beach for flotsam: Japanese glass balls used as fishing floats are the beachcomber's ultimate reward. To reach the Liberty ship is about a mile's walk along the sandy shore, although numerous rocks interrupt the thin strip of sand to give the appearance of multiple beaches.

Make a side trip to visit the **petroglyphs** on your way back to the car. About 0.25 mile after the road ends, you'll encounter the concrete base of what was once a lighthouse. If you're uncertain whether you're at the right place, check the concrete base, where names were inscribed in 1929. From the base of the lighthouse, turn directly inland and rock-hop for 300 yards until you'll see a large rock with

Splash in the tide pools of Hulopo'e Beach Park.

"Do not deface" written on it. A white arrow points to a trail behind the rock that leads to petroglyphs of dogs, humans, and a drawing known as "The Birdman."

KAHALEPALAOA

When you reach the bottom of Keomoku Highway, where the pavement ends, take a right at the fork in the road, which leads to a rugged coastal track that ranks as one of the best drives on the island. A 4WD vehicle is recommended, as the deep sand patches can drift onto the road, and depending on recent rains, the road can become rutted and rough. Nevertheless, some of Lana'i's nicest beaches are down this road, and provided there aren't enormous puddles, anyone with a Jeep or SUV should be able to navigate it.

While there are a number of small pull-outs along the side of the road leading to narrow windswept beaches, the first beach of any size is **Kahalepalaoa,** 7.5 miles from where the pavement ended. The name translates to "House of the Whale Ivory"; whale bones are believed to have washed ashore and were then used to build a dwelling. In more recent times this spot was also the site of a Club Med-style day resort named Club Lana'i. The booze-fueled excursion from Maui no longer operates, but the coconut grove that once housed the venue marks the start of a long white-sand beach that's perfect for casual strolling.

LOPA

Just over one mile past Kahalepalaoa is **Lopa,** a protected stretch of sand that is the nicest on Lana'i's back side. Although the beach isn't that different from Kahalepalaoa, Lopa faces south, so it's more protected from the north-easterly trade winds, which makes reading a book in a beach chair infinitely more enjoyable. Lopa is a popular camping spot for locals, and a couple of picnic tables have been placed beneath the thorn-riddled *kiawe* (mesquite) grove lining the beach. Although the swimming and snorkeling are poor compared to Hulopo'e Beach Park, Lopa is the perfect place for longboard surfing or paddling along the shore in a kayak (if you brought one). The chances of encountering anyone else on Lopa are higher on the weekend, when locals come to camp and fish, but as at many of Lana'i's beaches, if there happens to be anyone else, it's considered crowded.

★ POLIHUA BEACH

Polihua is so remote that even Lana'i residents consider it "out there." A vast,

the famous shipwreck of Kaiolohia

kayaking waves off Lopa

placing the only set of footprints on a deserted beach, this is the place to do it. The name Polihua derives from a Hawaiian term for "eggs in the bosom," a reference to the green sea turtles that haul out on the sand to bury eggs on the isolated shore.

The strong currents at Polihua make the water unsafe for swimming, and oftentimes the afternoon trade winds turn the entire beach into a curtain of blowing sand. The morning hours are best for a relaxing stroll through the sand dunes, and by sunset the winds have usually died down enough to watch the sun sink behind the northwest horizon. With views that stretch across the Kalohi Channel toward Moloka'i, this is one of the last beaches in Hawaii where it's still possible to feel alone.

A 4WD vehicle is imperative to reach Polihua. Travel seven miles from Lana'i City on Polihua Road to Keahiakawelo. Continue on the same road for another 25 minutes as it switchbacks down the rutted dirt track before reaching its terminus a few yards short of the beach. There are no services, so if you visit Polihua, remember to bring water and food, and to pack out everything you brought with you.

windswept, and often completely empty stretch of sand, Polihua is utterly unrivaled in its seclusion. If you've ever fantasized about

Snorkeling and Diving

SNORKELING

When it comes to snorkeling, **Hulopo'e Beach Park** easily trumps any other place on the island for the health of the reef, clarity of the water, and variety of fish. Thanks to its protected status as a marine preserve, the reef is in better shape than other places on the island, and snorkelers will revel in the large schools of *manini* (convict tang) and vibrant *uhu* (parrotfish) that flit around the shallow reef. The best snorkeling in the bay is on the left side of the beach. Since Hulopo'e faces south, it can be prone to large surf and shore break April-October. The shore break can make entry into and exit out of the water a little challenging, and

the visibility won't be as good as on days that are calmer.

Nevertheless, even a mediocre day at Hulopo'e is better than a good day at many other places. The reef never gets deeper than 25 feet. Occasionally Hawaiian spinner dolphins venture into the bay, although they usually hang out over the sand on the right, closer to the hotel.

Not far from Hulopo'e but equally as gorgeous is the vibrant reef at **Manele Bay.** Don't confuse this with snorkeling in Manele Harbor; that would be disgusting. The reef at Manele Bay is on the opposite side of the break wall between the harbor and the cliffs. Entry from shore can be tricky, since you have to come off the rocks, but if you follow the driveway of the harbor all the way to the far end, there is a little opening in the rocks where it's possible to make a graceful entry. Schools of tropical reef fish gather in abundance, and the spinner dolphins sometimes hang out in this area as well. Although Manele Bay is 0.25 mile from Hulopo'e Beach, it's still part of the marine preserve, so the same rules apply: Don't stand on the coral, and don't feed the fish. It's best not to touch anything at all.

There isn't anywhere on Lana'i to rent snorkeling equipment for the day, so your best bet is to bring your own. The snorkeling equipment at Hulopo'e Beach is only for Trilogy's day guests who come from Maui, and the gear at the Four Seasons beach kiosk is exclusively for hotel guests.

If you want to explore the island's remoter reefs, only accessible by boat, **Trilogy** (1 Manele Harbor Dr., 808/874-5649, www. sailtrilogy.com, $250 pp) provides the only snorkel charter service operating on Lana'i. The 3.5-hour snorkeling and sailing excursion usually heads around the southwestern coast to the towering sea cliffs of Kaunolu, also known as Shark Fin Cove due to the dorsal fin-shaped rock in the middle of the bay. There can occasionally be other boats from Maui here, but more often than not this trip provides the opportunity to snorkel the waters of the historic fishing village with only a handful of others. Given that Kaunolu is exposed to the deeper waters offshore, snorkelers intermittently see pelagic species such as spinner dolphins, bottlenose dolphins, eagle rays, manta rays, and whale sharks. If there's wind on the way back to Manele, the crew will hoist the sails, and since bookings are sporadic due to the low numbers on Lana'i, call the Maui office ahead of time to inquire about a charter.

SCUBA DIVING

Lana'i has some of the best diving in the state, with 14 named dive sites along the southwestern coast. The most famous are **First** and

school of *manini* at Hulopo'e Beach Park

Second Cathedrals. At First Cathedral, just offshore from Manele Harbor, the cavern entrance is at 58 feet. Inside, beams of sunlight filter down through the ceiling like light passing through a stained-glass window. There have even been a few underwater weddings here.

The best way to exit the cathedral is via a hole in the wall known locally as The Shotgun, where divers place their hands on the sides of the cathedral and allow the current to wash through a narrow opening. In addition to the main cathedral, there are a number of other swim-throughs and arches where you can catch a glimpse of spiny lobsters, frogfish, colorful parrotfish, and if you're lucky, a pod of spinner dolphins passing overhead.

Down the coast at Second Cathedral, the underwater dome is about the same size but intersected by so many openings it looks like Swiss cheese. Divers can pass in and out of the cathedral from a variety of different entry points. The highlight is a rare black coral tree that dangles from the cathedral ceiling. Large schools of *ta'ape* (blue-striped snapper) congregate on the back side of the cathedral, and you can swim through a school that numbers in the hundreds. Visibility at both of these sites regularly reaches 80 to 120 feet, and the water can be so clear that you see most of the dive site standing on the pontoon of the boat.

The most affordable way to dive off Lana'i is with a boat from Maui. The island's only dive operator, **Trilogy** (808/874-5649), only offers private charters with high prices, mainly as an amenity for the Four Seasons Resort. Check with dive operators in Lahaina about the best way to dive off Lana'i.

Hiking and Biking

HIKING
★ Munro Trail

Munro Trail doesn't look like anywhere else on Lana'i, or in Hawaii. This 12.8-mile dirt road is more like the Pacific Northwest than the tropics. Wandering around the stands of Cook pines is one of Lana'i's most iconic adventures. Get up early, throw on a light jacket, and head into the uplands, where the smell of eucalyptus wafts through an understory of ironwoods and pines. For clear skies and dry conditions, it's best to hike Munro Trail in the morning hours before enveloping clouds blow in on the trades.

To reach Munro Trail, travel past the Lodge at Koele on Keomoku Highway until you reach a sign for Cemetery Road, where you make a right just before the first mile marker. On Cemetery Road, the pavement turns to dirt and then branches off to the left, bringing you to the start of the trail. Technically Munro Trail is a single-lane dirt road navigable by anyone with a 4WD vehicle. The Dollar Jeep rental company doesn't allow its Jeeps to go on the steep and potentially muddy track, and even Hummers occasionally get stuck. The other option is to park at the trailhead and make the 5.5-mile (one-way) hike to the summit, stopping at lookouts along the way.

The first lookout, starting from Cemetery Road, is **Koloiki Ridge,** about 2.5 miles into the trail. A small red-and-white sign on the left side of the trail points the way to the ridge, and after a brief 0.25-mile jaunt, you are rewarded with grandiose views back into

Maunalei Gulch and out to the islands of Maui and Moloka'i. This lookout is also accessible as part of the **Koloiki Ridge Trail** hike, which starts behind the Lodge at Koele.

Back on the main trail, continue for a couple of miles beneath a shroud of forest until you pass some communication towers. Just past the towers is **Ho'okio Gulch,** a place that forever transformed Lana'i. In 1778, Kahekili, ruler of Lana'i and Maui, was besieged by Kalaniopu'u, a powerful chief from the Big Island whose army featured a fearless young warrior named Kamehameha. In the battle at Ho'okio, Kahekili and his warriors attempted to defend the island from the invading warriors by slinging stones down from the hilltop and hiding in crevasses carved into the cliff face. Ultimately, Kahekili and his men were defeated, and the ensuing occupation of Lana'i by Kalaniopu'u and his army drove the resource-strapped island into famine, which decimated much of the population. It's said that the spirits of those who perished in the battle still reside in the cool forests and keep watch over the eroded gulches and canyons.

Finally, after you've climbed an uphill section of trail, 5.5 miles from the end of Cemetery Road you'll find the 3,370-foot summit of Lana'ihale, or The Hale, as it's known to locals. This is the only point in Hawaii where it's possible to see five other islands on the clearest days, and during winter even the snowcapped peaks of Mauna Kea and Mauna Loa on the Big Island can be seen, over 100 miles southeast. If you continue the length of the trail, it descends for seven miles down the southern side of the ridge, past turnoffs for the Awehi and Naha trails, and eventually emerges in the remains of old pineapple fields at Highway 440 (Manele Rd.).

Pu'u Pehe Overlook

This often photographed sea stack is an iconic symbol of Lana'i and is one of the most scenic places on the island. It's not possible to climb onto Pu'u Pehe, but the **Pu'u Pehe Overlook Trail** offers hikers a sweeping panorama of the rock and the surrounding coast. To reach the overlook, take the dirt road at the south end of Hulopo'e Beach Park (the side opposite the resort) and follow it for 100 yards until it reaches a set of stairs leading down to the tide pools. From here the road becomes a trail that wraps left across the headland before reaching a hidden sandy cove popular with bodyboarders and nudist sunbathers. To get down to this sandy cove, known as Shark's Bay, requires a scramble through a chute in the rocky cliff that involves some risk.

To reach the overlook, carefully follow the edge of the cliff until it reaches a promontory about 100 feet above the shimmering reef below. Aside from the sweeping vista,

---

Lana'i on Horseback

Lana'i is steeped in its ranching heritage. The island was once a huge sheep and cattle ranch where *paniolos* roamed the terrain on horseback. Cattle no longer roam, but the island's ranching heritage lives on at the **Stables at Koele** (1 Keomoku Hwy.), where local guides who are authentic *paniolos* offer guided trail rides (1.5 hours, $190 pp) through the Lana'i City hinterlands. Keep an eye out for axis deer or mouflon sheep as you ride at your own pace on excursions geared to your skill level. The knowledgeable guides fortify the excursion with tales of the island's history. Rides are booked through the activities desk at the Four Seasons Resort (808/565-2000).

---

it's also possible to get a good view from here of the *heiau* that stands atop Pu'u Pehe, an archaeological site that is a mystery given that it's nearly impossible to access the top of the rock.

Kapiha'a Fisherman's Trail

The **Kapiha'a Fisherman's Trail** begins on the side of Hulopo'e Beach in front of the Four

Pu'u Pehe, or Sweetheart Rock, as seen from the sands of Shark's Bay

Seasons Resort and meanders past the mega-mansions on the point. Well-marked by a natural stone walkway, this 1.5-mile trail hugs the rocky coast as it weaves its way through the ancient village of Kapiha'a. Little remains of the village today, but various historical markers point out the location of *heiau* still visible in the area.

Even though this trail catches the coastal breezes off the surrounding water, there is little shade. Given the rugged nature of the path, wear closed-toe shoes. After the trail reaches a dramatic terminus atop sea cliffs on the back nine of the golf course, an easier return route is to follow the cart path back to the golf clubhouse.

Koloiki Ridge Trail

An offshoot of the Munro Trail, the **Koloiki Ridge Trail** is a five-mile out-and-back hike that begins directly behind the Four Seasons Koele Resort. On a nice day, this is the perfect way to spend two or three hours. Walking the trail is like taking a historical tour through Lana'i's past.

To reach the trailhead, go to the main entrance of the Four Seasons Koele Resort and then follow the service road toward the golf clubhouse. Once you reach the main clubhouse, another paved service road running behind the fairway ultimately leads to the trailhead. Along the initial paved section of trail, you'll encounter white-and-red signs on the trail as part of an interpretive map available at the hotel's concierge desk.

Once the dirt trail begins, you'll find yourself walking beneath a canopy of ironwood trees and Cook pines that predate the luxury hotels. Planted in 1912 by the botanist George Munro, the pines were used as a means of securing water by trapping moisture from the passing clouds, and even today they still play a major role in providing water for the island's residents.

Making a right at the red-and-white sign marked "10" places you directly on the Munro Trail. About 0.5 mile down Munro Trail at sign number 17, an arrow points the way down to the dramatic Koloiki Ridge. Once out from beneath the canopy of trees, you'll notice that the ridge is flanked on both sides by dramatic gulches. From this often windy vantage point at the end of the trail, the islands of Moloka'i and Maui appear on the horizon beyond the deep blue Pailolo Channel. When facing the islands, on the left side of the ridge is Naio Gulch, a dry rock-strewn canyon where you can occasionally catch a

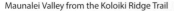
Maunalei Valley from the Koloiki Ridge Trail

glimpse of the island's elusive mouflon sheep. On the right is Maunalei Gulch, a deep cleft in the island that once had the island's only free-flowing stream. If you look closely on the valley floor, you can still see an old service road leading to a pump house. Water from Maunalei once fed the island's sugar plantation.

Food

AMERICAN

Pele's Other Garden (811 Houston St., 808/565-9628, www.pelesothergarden.com, lunch 11am-2pm Mon.-Fri., dinner 4:30pm-8pm Mon.-Sat., $7-19) is the hangout of anyone hankering for a good sandwich or a cold draft beer. The bistro also whips up healthy and affordable food options, ranging from avocado and feta wraps to pizza and chicken parmesan.

Just down the road from Richard's Supermarket, **Café 565** (408 8th St., 808/565-6622, 10am-3pm and 5pm-8pm Mon.-Sat.) is great for groups that can't agree on what they want. This hole-in-the-wall offers Italian, American, and standard local fare with calzones ($9-12), pizza ($16-22), and sub sandwiches ($6-10) as well as burgers ($7) and plate lunch options ($9). Grab a seat on the outdoor picnic tables: You can access the free Wi-Fi out here and people-watch on the street.

COFFEE SHOPS

Even sleepy Lana'i City needs help waking up in the morning, and **Coffee Works** (604 Ilima Ave., 808/565-6962, 7am-4pm Mon.-Fri., 8am-3pm Sat.) is the island's only full-time java establishment. Breakfast bagels and lunch sandwiches accompany the usual range of coffee offerings, and the outdoor porch is a great place for watching the mellow town slowly spring to life.

HAWAIIAN REGIONAL

The fanciest meal in Lana'i City is at ★ **Lana'i City Grille** (828 Lana'i Ave., 808/565-7211, www.hotellanai.com, 5pm-9pm Wed.-Sun., $15-38). The fare is more expensive than at hole-in-the-wall plate-lunch stands, but when the waiter serves a plate of miso-marinated sea bass with mushroom potato hash, cost seems less important. The Grille has the island's most comprehensive wine list. Reservations are strongly recommended, particularly on Friday evenings, when the live jazz band provides the best entertainment in town.

LOCAL STYLE

While the exterior might not look like much, at ★ **Blue Ginger** (409 7th St., 808/565-6363, www.bluegingercafelanai.com, 6am-8pm Mon., Thurs.-Fri., 6am-2pm Tues.-Wed., 6:30am-8pm Sat.-Sun., $6-11, cash only) the swinging screen door and funky plantation-style appearance are all part of the hole-in-the-wall charm. Breakfast is heaping *loco moco* plates of fried eggs, hamburger meat, rice, and gravy, and the homemade hamburger patties are the lunchtime draw that has kept patrons coming in from Dole Park since 1991. It's a true local hideout.

Neighboring **Canoes** (419 7th St., 808/565-6537, 6:30am-1pm Sun.-Thurs., 6:30am-8pm Fri.-Sat.) offers up their own special hamburger recipe, a staple of Lana'i cuisine since 1953. Canoes has the usual selection of local plate lunches and items off the grill, although a special treat is the heaping breakfast portions, available until 1pm.

When you've had your fill of plate lunches, infuse your diet with some fresh fish at the ★ **Lana'i Ohana Poke Market** (834 Gay St., 808/559-6265, 10am-3pm Mon.-Fri., $7-17, cash only), which, in classic Lana'i fashion, is either open until 3pm or until it runs out of fish. While the *poke* alone can be expensive, the best bet for a cheap and filling lunch is a *poke* bowl: one-third of a pound of fish

Where to Stay on Lana'i

Name	Type	Price	Features	Why Stay Here?	Best For
Dreams Come True	vacation rental	$141	kitchen	affordable, location	couples, budget travelers
★ Four Seasons Resort Lana'i	resort	from $960	pool, golf, oceanfront	luxury, romantic	couples, honeymooners, luxury-lovers
★ Hotel Lana'i	hotel	$174-254	lanai, breakfast	romantic, location, historic	couples
Hulopo'e Beach Park	camping	$30 + $15 pp	restrooms, water, oceanfront	location, affordable	budget travelers, groups, families

served with two scoops of white or brown rice. Simple outdoor picnic tables provide the seating for this hole-in-the-wall take-out stand.

RESTAURANTS AT FOUR SEASONS RESORT LANA'I

For dinner, ★ **Nobu Lana'i** (6pm-9:30pm daily, $35), has a selection sushi from famed chef Nobu Matsuhisa, and **One Forty** (6:30am-10:30am and 6pm-9pm daily, $40-65) has exceptional plates of Hawaiian Regional cuisine. The ahi *poke* appetizer served with dinner can compete with the best in the islands, and the hand-cut steaks and plates of fresh fish are the best that you'll find on Lana'i. For breakfast, start your day with seared ahi Benedict ($31).

Getting There and Around

GETTING THERE
Air

Flying into Lana'i requires a jump from neighboring Honolulu. **Ohana by Hawaiian** (800/367-5320, www.hawaiianairlines.com) operates turboprop planes with 25-minute flights from Honolulu (HNL) that run a couple of times per day.

Ferry

Traveling from Maui, the easiest and most practical way to get to Lana'i is the **Expeditions Ferry** (808/661-3756, www.go-lanai.com, one-way $30 adults, $20 children), which runs five times daily between Lahaina and Manele harbors. Travel time is usually about an hour, and during whale season (Dec.-Apr.), you can frequently spot humpback whales from the outdoor seating of the upper deck. Although you can buy tickets at the harbor kiosk in Lahaina the morning of your journey, make reservations ahead of time, particularly for the early morning trip. Don't be late; this is one ferry that doesn't wait around.

GETTING AROUND

If you're staying at the Four Seasons Resort, there's shuttle service to Lana'i City, the airport, and the harbor. Rates from the airport are $45 pp for a shuttle, or $195 for a luxury

SUV. From Manele Harbor, rates are $20 pp, or $85 per SUV (5 people maximum). There are complimentary shuttles to Lana'i City, and if you're staying at Hotel Lana'i, there is shuttle service to the resort. If you're staying elsewhere or visiting for the day, you'll have to rent a vehicle or take a cab.

Rentals

The longest-running and most reputable Jeep rental company on the island, **Dollar Lana'i Rent a Car** (1036 Lana'i Ave., 808/565-7227, www.visitlanai.com, 7am-7pm daily) provides 4WD Jeeps (2-door $139 per day, 4-door $169 per day). The company requests that the vehicles be returned by 5pm, so if you come from Maui on the early morning ferry, you will arrive at the harbor by 7:45am, be at the rental car counter by 8:15am, and on your way with your Jeep by no later than 8:45am, giving you more than seven hours to explore the island. Dollar provides you with a map of the island and clearly states which roads are off-limits. If you end up requiring a tow from someplace "out of bounds," it's going to cost you $500. Aside from the driver, extra passengers cost $10 pp for a shuttle from the ferry to Lana'i City.

Lanai Cheap Jeeps (800/311-6860, www.lanaicheapjeeps.com) also has rentals ($124), and **Aloha Adventure Rentals** (www.alohaadventurerentals.com) has H2 Hummers ($187) that can handle the rugged terrain.

Taxi

The island's only taxi service is **Rabaca's Limousine Service** (808/565-6670), which connects the airport, harbor, and Lana'i City for $10 pp.

Gas

There is only one station on the entire island: **Lana'i City Service** (1036 Lana'i Ave., 808/565-7227, 6am-10pm daily) supplies fuel for all 3,500 residents. Don't worry about the price; you're better off just not looking, as it's often $1 to $1.50 more per gallon than on Maui. Then again, with only 30 miles of paved roads, it isn't uncommon for a tank of gas to last a month or more.

Lahaina-Lana'i Ferry Schedule

DEPART LAHAINA HARBOR (MAUI)

- 6:45am
- 9:15am
- 12:45pm
- 3:15pm
- 5:45pm

DEPART MANELE HARBOR (LANA'I)

- 8am
- 10:30am
- 2pm
- 4:30pm
- 6:45pm

Moloka'i

Look for ★ to find recommended sights, activities, dining, and lodging.

Highlights

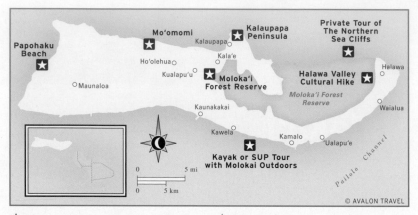

★ **Moloka'i Forest Reserve:** This is one of the few places in the state with an ecosystem identical to what the Polynesians first found over 1,500 years ago. Nearly 98 percent of the plant species are indigenous to Moloka'i (page 388).

★ **Kalaupapa Peninsula:** The Kalaupapa Peninsula fuses some of Moloka'i's darkest moments with its most dramatic surroundings. The former leper colony is now home to the most scenic mule ride on the planet (page 391).

★ **Papohaku Beach:** Nearly three miles long and virtually deserted, Papohaku Beach is the island's best spot for watching a fiery sunset (page 393).

★ **Mo'omomi:** Wild and secluded, Mo'omomi feels like Moloka'i's lost coast (page 394).

★ **Private Tour of the Northern Sea Cliffs:** Embark with an adventure guide for an unforgettable ocean tour of the tallest sea cliffs in the world (page 396).

★ **Guided Paddleboard and Kayaking Tours:** Enjoy a downwind paddle off the island's southern coast (page 397).

★ **Cultural Hike into Halawa Valley:** Travel to the roots of Hawaii on a cultural hike and swim at the base of a waterfall (page 400).

Visitors often mistake Moloka'i's lack of typical resort activities for a lack of things to do.

But the protected vibe is incomparably relaxed and epitomizes "old Hawaii," where you find yourself talking to strangers as you would with an old friend. Moloka'i is a step back to simpler times when life was slower. That doesn't mean it's boring. Imagine surfing perfect waves off an empty white-sand beach, or hiking through rainforests to thundering falls in Hawaii's original settlement. Ride mules down a steep switchbacking trail with sweeping views of the coast, or tattoo the sand with a string of footprints on a sunset stroll.

Moloka'i is Hawaii's most "Hawaiian" island in that it has the highest percentage of ethnic Hawaiians and is one of the last places you might hear Hawaiian spoken on the street. It's a place where culture and ancient tradition are preferred over modern progress.

ORIENTATION

Though the airport is located in Ho'olehua, **Kaunakakai** is the island's main town and the hub of everyday life. It's the location of the island's only gas stations and the bulk of the restaurants, and also the Hotel Moloka'i, the island's largest. The western shore is about 30 minutes away and is best for beaches and sunsets. Eastern Moloka'i has oceanfront cottages and lush **Halawa Valley.** Central Moloka'i, near **Kualapu'u,** has a handful of sights, a restaurant, and it's on the way to the misty uplands and **Kalaupapa Trail.**

PLANNING YOUR TIME

In general, 4-5 days is enough time to properly visit the island, though you can visit most of the island's highlights in a very efficient two days. Many people visit from Maui for the day, although this limits what you can do. When scheduling your trip, plan on one day for Halawa Valley and East Moloka'i, and a second day for Kalaupapa. A third day could be spent at the west end beaches or hiking Mo'omomi or the Bog, and a fourth and fifth day provide nice buffers if activities are canceled by rain.

To visit Moloka'i in two days, head to the west end to catch the sunset after a morning in Kalaupapa, and the next day go hiking in Halawa Valley before dinner at Hale Kealoha. By staying in the vicinity of Kaunakakai, most places are within a 30-minute drive, and an hour to Halawa Valley.

Previous: family sunset in West Moloka'i; Decorate coconuts at the Ho'olehua "Post a Nut."
Above: Kapuaiwa Coconut Grove.

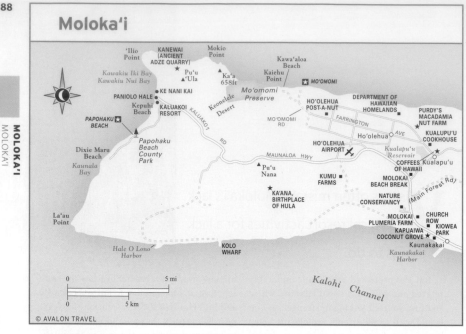

Sights

KAUNAKAKAI
Moloka'i Plumeria Farm

Have you ever wanted to make your own lei and be surrounded by the scent of plumeria? Just west of town on Highway 460, as the road starts heading uphill, is **Moloka'i Plumerias** (808-553-3391, www.molokaiplumerias.com), where you can tour the farm (10:30am daily, $25), pick your own flowers, and make a plumeria lei. Tours require advance reservations.

TOPSIDE
★ Moloka'i Forest Reserve

As you head west from Kaunakakai, slowly gaining elevation, the turnoff for the **Moloka'i Forest Reserve** is just before mile marker 4. Turn right before the bridge, and after a few hundred yards you'll pass the Homelani Cemetery, where red-dirt Maunahui Road winds way into the mountains. Your car rental agency will tell you that

this road is impassable except in a 4WD vehicle. The road is rough even when it's dry and requires at least a high-clearance truck or jeep. Follow the rutted road up into the hills into a deep forest of 'ohi'a, pine, eucalyptus, and giant ferns planted in the early 1900s. At 5.5 miles you enter the Moloka'i Forest Reserve.

After 10 miles is the **Waikolu Overlook,** a precipitous 3,700-foot drop that's frequently lined with waterfalls. Waikolu Overlook is as far as most vehicles can go. Continuing farther is the **Kamakou Preserve** and the hike to **Pepe'opae Bog** (page 398). The road is so bad that the only way forward is to park at Waikolu and walk.

Purdy's Na Hua O Ka 'Aina Farm (Macadamia Nut Farm)

A popular visitor stop is **Purdy's Na Hua O Ka 'Aina Farm** (808-567-6601, www.molo-kai.com/eatnuts, 9:30am-3:30pm Tues.-Fri.,

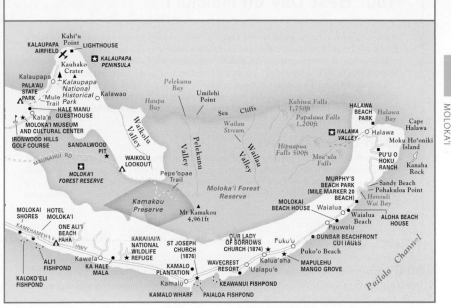

10am-2pm Sat., free) behind the public high school on Lihi Pali Avenue. This is the island's only macadamia nut farm, where you'll learn everything you wanted to know about macadamias. An informal tour led by the jovial owner teaches how to crack open the hard nut, how the nuts are grown, and how to pick out the good ones. There are no pesticides, herbicides, or other chemicals used in this 50-tree grove. While samples are included with the free tour, a small gift shop sells everything from macadamia-nut honey to mac-nut-themed clothing.

Kumu Farms

If you're into healthy, organic produce, **Kumu Farms** (Hua Ai Rd., 808/270-0301, http://mauitropicalplantation.com/kumufarms/, 9am-4pm Tues.-Fri., free) is the place for the island's best produce. Despite the recent explosion of farm-to-table cuisine, this working farm has been growing crops since 1981 and is the best place on the island to pick up fresh veggies straight from the *kumu*, or source.

Moloka'i Museum and Cultural Center

Off Highway 470, two miles north of Kualapu'u, is the **Moloka'i Museum and Cultural Center** (808/567-6436, 10am-2pm Mon-Sat., $5 adults, $1 students), a simple museum focused on the history of Kalaupapa. There's a small exhibit on Hawaiian artifacts as well as a basic gift shop, but most informative are the documentary videos and old newspaper articles about life on the Kalaupapa Peninsula. On the same grounds, behind the museum, is the **R. W. Meyer Sugar Mill,** constructed in 1878 during the island's short-lived sugar era.

Pala'au State Park

Above the residential town of Kala'e and past the mule barn, Highway 470 eventually dead-ends in the parking lot of **Pala'au State Park.** The park offers decent camping, and there are public restrooms at the parking lot, but no potable water and only basic facilities. The air is noticeably cooler than at the shore,

Your Best Day on Molokaʻi

If you only have a day to spend on the Friendly Isle, start with a hearty breakfast at **Manaʻe Goods & Grindz** before continuing on to **Halawa Valley** for the 9am cultural hike. Make the long drive past town to **Kualapuʻu Cookhouse,** where a late lunch will break up the drive to **Papohaku Beach,** where a fiery sunset and vast stretch of sand helps bring the day to a close.

If you're still hungry once back in town, or want to relax with a drink, get an oceanfront table at **Hale Kealoha** and enjoy the live local music. Feeling really ambitious? Get dessert at **Hot Bread Lane** behind Kanemitsu Bakery. This is a lot of driving for a single day, but it hits many of Molokaʻi's highlights.

RAINY-DAY ALTERNATIVE

Grab a warm drink before heading to the **Post-a-Nut** in Hoʻolehua to mail yourself a coconut. Pick up souvenirs at **Beach Break** or the strip of stores in town, and strike up conversation while listening to live music at the **Hotel Molokaʻi** bar. Sometimes if it's raining in town, it is sunny on the west end of the island for tanning or watching the sunset, so ask a local if they know what the weather is like out west.

and by midmorning the northeasterly trade winds are usually blowing.

To reach **Kalaupapa Overlook,** follow the paved path at the edge of the parking lot until it reaches a terminus at a low rock wall at the edge of a cliff. From this vantage point are unobstructed views of the town of Kalaupapa, the former leper settlement that still houses a handful of patients. Unless

you booked a mule ride or a permit to hike down, this is the closest to Kalaupapa that you can get.

Back at the parking lot, an unpaved trail leads 200 yards through a cool canopy of trees before emerging at a sacred spot named **Ka Ule O Nanahoa,** also called **Phallic Rock** for reasons that are immediately apparent. According to legend, Nanahoa, the

empty beach at Kalaupapa National Historical Park

Kaunakakai

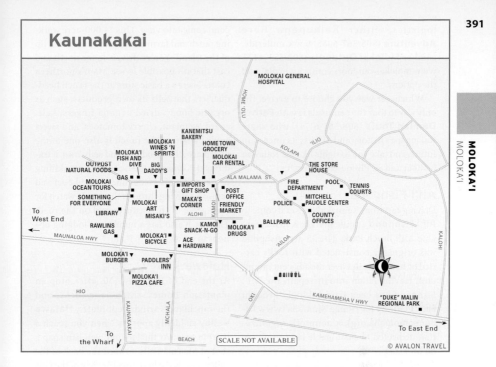

male god of fertility, once lived nearby in the forests surrounding Pala'au. One day, when Nanahoa sat to admire a beautiful young woman looking at her reflection in a pool, Kawahua, Nanahoa's wife, became so jealous that she attacked the young woman by yanking on her hair. Nanahoa was outraged in turn and struck his wife, who rolled over a nearby cliff before turning to stone. Nanahoa also turned to stone, in the shape of an erect penis, and sits here today.

★ KALAUPAPA PENINSULA

This isolated peninsula is where people with leprosy were sent to die. The story goes deeper than that, and touring the **Kalaupapa Peninsula,** now the **Kalaupapa National Historical Park,** is one of the most powerful and scenic adventures you can experience in Hawaii.

There are three ways to visit the national historical park: hiking in, riding a mule, and

flying. All are possible Monday-Saturday, and the minimum age is 16. To hike in, contact **Father Damien Tours** (808/567-6171) (page 398). To ride a mule down to Kalaupapa on the switchbacking trail, contact **Kalaupapa Rare Adventure** (808/567-6088, www.muleride.com, 8am-3:30pm daily, $199). Don't do the mule ride if you have a fear of heights, and be aware that the rides can sometimes be canceled for heavy rain. The maximum weight for riders is 250 pounds.

To fly to Kalaupapa, **Makani Kai Air** (808/834-1111, www.makanikaiair.com) has flights from the Moloka'i airport to the Kalaupapa airstrip ($75 one-way). Flight time is 15 minutes, and in order to make the 10am tour, book the 9:20am flight that arrives at 9:35am. For the return journey, there's a 2:15pm flight back. Planes only hold nine people, so advance reservations are a must. Maximum weight is 249 pounds.

For a combo tour where you hike down and fly back, or any other Kalaupapa logistics, either **Kalaupapa Rare Adventure** (808/567-6088, www.muleride.com) or **Molokai Outdoors** (808/553-4477, www.molokai-outdoors.com) can explain all the options.

Whichever way you choose to arrive, the only way to tour the peninsula is with **Father Damien Tours** (808/567-6171), who share Kalaupapa's history and discuss its uncertain future, and take you to sights like the Kalawao lookout and St. Philomena Church.

Ali'i Fishpond

Driving east from Kaunakakai, you'll come to **Ali'i Fishpond** at mile marker 3, just before One Ali'i Beach Park. The 35-acre fishpond was originally constructed with rocks carried by hand 10 miles over the adjacent mountain. Having fallen into disrepair, the Ali'i Fishpond has been painstakingly brought back to life by Ka Honua Momona (www.kahonuamomona.org), a nonprofit organization dedicated to sustainable land practices on Moloka'i.

Pu'u O Hoku Ranch

Past mile marker 20 and Waialua and Murphy's Beaches, the road narrows and runs near the sea. Honk your horn as you come around tight corners, and if you feel queasy from the drive, there's a sandy cove past mile marker 21 where you can rest. This far out on the island is very rural, and often you'll encounter groups of residents just hanging out and fishing. Be sure you have more than a quarter tank of gas if you plan to venture farther, as there are no facilities as you continue east.

Once Highway 450 starts gaining in elevation, the sweeping pasturelands of **Pu'u O Hoku Ranch** (808/558-8109, www.puuohoku.com) come into view. This 14,000-acre working ranch and farm dominates the eastern tip of the island. You've driven so far north and east that it's possible to see Maui's northern coast. There's a basic store at the ranch headquarters that sells its own products, such as organic honey, dried banana fingers, kale, chard, eggplant, cherry tomatoes, and sweet apple bananas. The ranch is also one of the only places that produces and sells 'awa, a traditional Polynesian medicinal and painkilling drink, and it also sells ranch-raised beef and venison. Driving through the ranch, watch for *nene* geese in the pastures and on the road. The ranch also has a number of lodging options to get away from it all.

Halawa Valley

At the end of Highway 450, after utopian plantation homes, single-lane turns, and the ranchland's windswept bluffs, **Halawa Valley** suddenly appears when you reach a hairpin turn. At the lookout, you can snap a shot of Moa'ula Falls, toward the back of the valley. This is the best possible view of the falls unless you take a Halawa Valley guided hike (page 400).

Halawa is believed to be Hawaii's first settlement, circa AD 650, with some evidence suggesting settlement as early as AD 300. This is the "old Hawaii," where mythology, nature, and residents commune in a way not found in modern society. The handful of residents who still inhabit this valley live a subsistence lifestyle that parallels their ancestors. Electricity is scarce, there's no cell phone reception, and taro *lo'i* (fields) weave their way up the verdant valley floor. Aside from swimming at the sandy beach or joining the guided hike, there is little to do in Halawa but snap photos and enjoy the beauty.

Beaches

If having a beach to yourself seems like your kind of afternoon, then pack a beach chair and a good book. Moloka'i's beaches are meant for sunbathing rather than snorkeling or swimming, as northwesterly swells bring large surf in winter and a reef lines the southern coast. You won't find beachside tiki bars or activity agents—in Moloka'i it's just you, the sand, the vast blue Pacific, and a fiery sunset each night.

WEST MOLOKA'I

The west end of Moloka'i has the island's best beaches, usually spared the relentless trade winds that buffet the eastern coast. Summer months are best for swimming, with the exception of Papohaku, which is always dangerous. In winter surf turns the western coast into a cauldron of white water. The empty shores are always good for sunbathing, and the sunsets are the best on the island.

★ Papohaku Beach

Over two miles long and nearly 100 yards wide, **Papohaku Beach** is easily Moloka'i's most scenic and popular. Six people is

considered a crowd, and while parts of the beach are dotted with homes, the majority of Papohaku is undeveloped with empty sand for strolling. Swimming is a terrible idea, as the rip currents and undertow are overwhelming year-round. Instead, take a morning jog or watch the sunset over the lights of Honolulu, 32 miles away.

To get here, follow Highway 460 toward the town of Maunaloa, and take a right on Kaluakoi Road. Follow Kaluakoi to sea level until it wraps around to the left. The beach park has multiple entrances on the right side of the road. For extended stays, **camping** is possible at Papohaku if you obtain a permit from the County Parks Department (808/553-3204).

Kepuhi Beach

Kepuhi Beach fronts the Kaluakoi Villas and the abandoned Sheraton resort. It's an ideal beach for swimming during the summer, and the sunset each night is the kind that ends up on your Christmas card. To reach Kepuhi Beach, follow the signs for Kaluakoi

huge Papohaku Beach

Villas off Kaluakoi Road. Public beach parking is available.

Kapukahehu (Dixie Maru)

Named after a fishing boat that sank near the bay, **Dixie's** is at the southern end of the road. From Papohaku Beach Park, follow Kaluakoi Road until it reaches Pohakuloa, turn *makai* (toward the sea), and follow it to the end of the cul-de-sac. The narrow alleyway that looks like a driveway is the beach access, and there's a small parking area about 100 yards down. For an even smaller, more hidden beach, there's a small trail through the *kiawe* (mesquite) trees that eventually leads over a fence. Follow this trail for 10 minutes, and it will bring you to sandy **Kaunala Beach,** frequented by surfers, nudists, and locals, but you'll often have it all to yourself.

Kawakiu and Pohaku Mauliuli Beach

Between Kepuhi and 'Ilio, a number of hidden, sandy coves provide splendid isolation. To reach **Kawakiu Beach,** follow the signs to the Paniolo Hale condominium complex from Kaluakoi Road by making a right on Kaka'ako and then turning left down Lio Place, following the pavement to the end. A rudimentary sign here points the way to the beach, and when the dirt road ends in a parking lot, it's a short walk to the shore. If you don't have a high-clearance or 4WD vehicle, consider parking near the end of the pavement and walking along the dirt road. While the first beach is nice, it's nothing compared to Kawakiu, so continue north by scrambling over some rocks until you arrive at **Pohaku Mauliuli.** From here, a dirt road runs along the bluff and leads to Kawakiu. If the tide is low and the surf is calm, walk along the shore. The protected cove is idyllic in summer, tumultuous in winter, and almost always empty. If you prefer to bathe in the buff, this is the place to do it. Bring lots of water as well as proper footwear for lava rocks and thorns.

The Birthplace of the Hula

Western Moloka'i history is deeply rooted in Hawaiian culture. Not far from Maunaloa, in an area known as Ka'ana, legend speaks of the goddess Laka being the first to dance the hula, having "given birth" to the dance at a hill known as Pu'u Nana. Fanning out from Ka'ana, Laka subsequently journeyed throughout Hawaii, teaching the dance to anyone who wanted to learn. To this day traditional *hula halau* (hula schools) will prepare an offering or altar to Laka, goddess of the hula, as part of their performance and ceremony. It's believed that after sharing her dance with the people of Hawaii, Laka returned to Moloka'i, where her remains are buried at Pu'u Nana overlooking the western shores. Today, the **Ka Hula Piko** (www.kahulapiko.com), an annual festival held at the end of May or beginning of June, celebrates the roots of hula and perpetuation of the craft.

Hale O Lono

Hale O Lono is incredibly remote and rarely visited. With the closing of Moloka'i Ranch, the dirt roads once used by ranch guests now are only sporadically used. **Hawela Beach,** on the east side of the old harbor entrance, is the most accessible and most protected. Rough conditions can persist at any time of the year, but on days with light winds and flat surf, the swimming and sunbathing at Hawela are on par with anywhere on the island. To find Hale O Lono, follow Highway 460 to its terminus in the town of Maunaloa. From here, Mokio Street leads to a sloping, rutted, seven-mile dirt road running to the shore. Regular vehicles with high clearance can handle this road if it hasn't been raining; a 4WD vehicle is needed if it's wet.

★ Mo'omomi

If you crave adventure, head to **Mo'omomi.** You'll need a 4WD vehicle to get to this coast, which is pristine. Its seclusion is revered and in some cases protected by local indigenous Hawaiians. Moʻomomi is currently open to visitors, but it's imperative to be respectful and keep on established trails. In the past, access has ranged from total freedom to discussion of erecting a gate. Contact **The Department of Hawaiian Home Lands** (600 Maunaloa Hwy., 808/560-6104) to inquire about current restrictions. The western portions of Moʻomomi are run by the Nature Conservancy, and visitors are asked to stay out of the dunes because of the fragile ecosystem.

To reach the Moʻomomi pavilion from Hoʻolehua, follow Farrington Avenue until the road becomes dirt, and keep right at the fork. Once parked, walking along the shore leads to a series of underwhelming beaches, but once you get back on the dirt road, the beauty of windswept **Kawaʻaloa Beach** opens up before you. Swimming is only possible in summer, as large north swells create dangerous rip currents the rest of the year. The best activity at Kawaʻaloa is strolling. For a unique way to visit, contact **The Nature Conservancy** (808/553-5236, hike_molokai@tnc.org), which hosts monthly hikes March-October.

EAST MOLOKAʻI

The eastern beaches are the most popular among residents, and morning hours offer the calmest conditions before the trade winds arrive. Like a South Pacific postcard, white-sand coves ringed by lazy palms are dotted by colorful fishing boats, and more than anywhere else on the island, there's a sense of enveloping calm. The swimming and snorkeling are best at high tide, the beachcombing and sunbathing are better at low tide, and everything is better before the afternoon wind.

Pukoʻo Beach

Just east of the Manaʻe Goods & Grindz, by mile marker 16, a small beach access sign points down a dirt driveway to hidden **Pukoʻo Beach.** You'll find water that's calm, clear, protected, and good for swimming. It's a good spot for enjoying a casual plate lunch or taking a dip to cool off.

Waialua Beach

Waialua Beach is a narrow ribbon of sand 18.5 miles east of Kaunakakai, with some of the island's best swimming. As with other beaches in the area, the wind gains in strength throughout the day, and at high tide the sand almost disappears completely.

Pukoʻo Beach

Be sure to watch for coral heads exposed at low tide.

Kumimi Beach

Also known as Twenty-Mile Beach or Murphy's Beach, **Kumimi Beach** is by mile marker 20 on Highway 450 and is the last stretch of sand before the road narrows to one lane. This is arguably East Moloka'i's most popular beach and has sweeping, spectacular views. It also has wide sand, is a nice spot for snorkeling, and in the afternoon hours you might see kitesurfers running laps down the coast.

Simple and small, **Sandy Beach** is past mile marker 21 on the winding drive toward Halawa. The beach is protected from the trade winds and, most of the time, from the surf. The beach is small, with just enough room to put down a towel. You might also share space with kids wading in the shallows or locals selling bananas out of the back of a truck.

Halawa Bay

After weaving 10 miles over the rocky coast and down through the lush eastern valleys, the two beaches that form **Halawa Bay** are like gold at the end of a rainbow. At the terminus of Highway 450, Kama'alaea Bay is the more protected beach on the far side of the stream. This is the best option for swimming and escaping the wind. Kawili Beach, at the bottom of the cliff, is more exposed to the currents and the trade winds. It's a surreal feeling to hang out on the shores of a place considered one of the oldest settlements in Hawaii. The only facilities are two portable toilets and a single trashcan by the pavilion at the end of the road.

Water Sports

Don't tell anybody, but Moloka'i has some of the best **snorkeling** and diving in Hawaii. With the exception of a few protected areas, Moloka'i's dive and snorkel spots can only be accessed by boat. **Dixie Maru Beach** on the west shore and **Kumimi Beach** on the east shore usually have calm conditions and are the only two bays to snorkel from shore. The island's southern shore is home to Hawaii's longest fringing reef, and dive outfitters have 40 named spots along its outer edge. **Moku Ho'oniki,** off the eastern tip, is known for hammerhead sharks and occasionally some larger pelagic species, from tiger sharks to whales.

CHARTERS, TOURS, AND RENTAL SHOPS

With an office right on a corner on Kaunakakai's main thoroughfare, literally inside the gas station, **Molokai Fish and Dive** (53 Ala Malama Ave., 808/553-5926, www.molokaifishanddive.com, hours vary, usually 6am-7:30pm Mon.-Sat., 6am-7pm Sun.) offers three-hour snorkeling trips ($79 pp) and scuba trips ($145) to the reef or Moku Ho'oniki ($295). This shop is the only **Professional Association of Diving Instructors (PADI)** operation on the island and can accommodate a variety of snorkel and dive excursions. Prices and open hours can vary, so call for rates and availability.

For snorkeling only, **Moloka'i Ocean Tours** (40 Ala Malama Ave., Suite 107, 808/553-3290 or 808/298-3055, www.molokaioceantours.com) can accommodate up to six passengers on the 40-foot catamaran *Manu Ele'ele* for snorkeling excursions to Kaunakakai ($75 pp). This boat visits the south shore's fringing reef, and trips usually leave around 7:30am. Rent full snorkel sets ($9 per day, $30 per week).

★ Private Tour of the Northern Sea Cliffs

Local adventure guide Walter Naki runs **Moloka'i Action Adventures**

(808/558-8184) and is one of the only people who regularly takes visitors to the tallest sea cliffs in the world. The trip is only possible when conditions allow, and since conditions are so variable, call for rates and availability. If it works out, it's guaranteed to be the most memorable day of your vacation.

SURFING, PADDLING, AND KAYAKING

The only place for beginners to surf in East Moloka'i is **Waialua Beach,** where gentle rollers provide enough push to practice getting up on two feet. While the waves can be fun, it can be shallow at low tide.

Rental Shops and Tour Operators

Airlines only allow boards up to six feet, so the best place to rent is at **Beach Break** (2130 Maunaloa Hwy., 808/567-6091, www. bigwindkites.com/beachbreak/, 10am-4pm Mon.-Sat.) at the Holomua Junction, between Kaunakakai and the airport. They have the largest selection on the island, and the owner, Zack, can provide info on where you should and shouldn't paddle out. Rent longboards ($30 per day, $150 per week), shortboards

($24 per day, $120 per week), a full range of boogie boards, beach gear, stand-up paddleboard equipment, and accessories. Check out the surf art, shot right here on Moloka'i.

In central Kaunakakai, rent Soft Top surfboards ($25 per day, $100 per week) from **Moloka'i Ocean Tours** (40 Ala Malama Ave., Suite 107, 808/553-3290 or 808/298-3055, www.molokaioceantours.com).

★ Guided Paddleboard and Kayaking Tours

Inside Hotel Moloka'i, the desk staff for **Moloka'i Outdoors** (808/553-4477, www. molokai-outdoors.com, 8am-10am and 3pm-5pm daily) can line you up with a Soft Top surfboard ($17 per day, $68 per week), fiberglass surfboard ($22 per day, $88 per week), stand-up paddleboard, paddle, or kayak. The shop offers **Guided Paddleboard and Kayaking Tours** (Mon. and Wed.-Fri.) of the island's southeastern coast that range 5-8 miles and visit the island's fringing reef—the longest of its kind in the United States. You'll paddle by fishponds, oceanfront homesteads, and colorful sections of reef, and gain fascinating insight on sustainable practices and Moloka'i's rural way of life.

tranquil coves on the eastern shore

Hiking and Biking

Even for Maui residents, Moloka'i's hiking trails are shrouded in mystery. Often the trails require a 4WD vehicle to access or permission from private landowners, although there are still a number that are accessible to the public.

HIKING
Topside

Bathed in the scent of eucalyptus and pine, the "topside" of central Moloka'i feels like the mountains. With trails ranging 1,500 to 4,000 feet in elevation, the air is cooler, and once you enter the **Kamakou Preserve,** the weather turns wetter and the surroundings more lush. Songs of native *i'iwi* birds ring from the treetops while mist hangs in the silence of deeply carved valleys. **The Nature Conservancy** (808/553-5236, hike_molokai@tnc.org) leads **bird-watching** trips into the preserve once per month March through October.

KALAUPAPA OVERLOOK

The easiest walk is the 1,500-foot paved walkway to the **Kalaupapa Overlook,** which starts at the end of the road in Pala'au State Park. Take Highway 470 past the mule barn for the Kalaupapa trail rides and continue until it dead-ends in a parking lot. There are basic restrooms here but no potable water. Be prepared for high winds that can blow your hat off, and get your camera ready for the best views of the Kalaupapa Peninsula.

KALAUPAPA TRAIL

For good reason, the **Kalaupapa Trail** (Mon.-Sat.) is the most popular hike on Moloka'i. It descends 1,700 vertical feet over the course of 3.2 miles and 26 switchbacks. There are photo-worthy views of the sea cliffs and the gorgeous, empty white-sand beach at the bottom. This trail was hand-cut into the mountain in 1886 by Portuguese immigrant Manuel Farinha to establish a land connection with the residents living topside. The trail is

still in good shape, and you need to be too: Everything that goes down must come back up. Expect the hike down to take 1.5 hours, and close to 2 hours for the return.

Since this is part of **Kalaupapa National Historical Park,** which has caps on the number of visitors, a permit is required to tour the peninsula. If you want to hike to Kalaupapa instead of riding a mule, contact **Father Damien Tours** (808/567-6171) in advance. Guides meet hikers at the bottom of the trail at 10am and provide a four-hour tour ($50 pp) of the Kalaupapa Peninsula and the national historical park. Pay them at the bottom (cash works best), and call the day before to let them know you'll be coming.

You can also book the hike through **Kalaupapa Rare Adventure** (808/567-6088, www.muleride.com, $69), optionally including a sandwich. Pick up your meal ticket and permit to the national historical park at the mule barn before hiking down. In order to be at the bottom by 10am, you should begin hiking by 8:30am at the latest. To reach the trailhead, drive 200 yards past the mule barn on Highway 470 and park on the right side of the road. Be sure to bring rain gear and a good pair of shoes, and while there's a small store in Kalaupapa where you can restock on water and snacks, it's best to pack enough food and water that you don't have to rely on the store.

PEPE'OPAE BOG

Constantly shrouded in cloud cover and dripping in every color of green imaginable, if ever there were a place to visualize Hawaii before the arrival of humans, it is **Pepe'opae Bog.** Ninety-eight percent of the plant species here are indigenous to Moloka'i, and 219 of the species are found nowhere else on earth. Following Highway 460 from Kaunakakai, make a right before the bridge at the Homelani Cemetery sign and follow the dirt road for 10 miles to the parking area at Waikolu Overlook.

Making it to Waikolu Overlook in a regular vehicle requires high clearance and the best road conditions, and you will get stuck if you go any farther. If you have a 4WD vehicle, you can drive another 2.6 miles to the trailhead, but this is precarious at best and requires advanced driving skills. The best option is to park at Waikolu and hike.

From the road, follow the signs for Pepe'opae Bog. Once the trail begins, stay on the metal boardwalk. If you step off, expect to sink shin-deep into the soggy moss and mud. The boardwalk runs for 1.5 miles through some of the most pristine rainforest left in the state. Hikers who make it to the end are rewarded with a view into **Pelekunu Valley,** plunging 4,000 feet through the uninhabited, untouched wilderness below. Hikers can attempt the climb on their own, and **The Nature Conservancy** (808/553-5236, hike_ molokai@tnc.org) leads hikes into Pepe'opae once per month March to October; advance reservations are required.

PU'U KOLEKOLE

On the same 4WD road leading to the Pepe'opae trailhead, hikers who take the fork to the right will reach the start of the **Pu'u Kolekole Trail,** a two-mile hike to the 3,951-foot summit of Pu'u Kolekole. The view overlooks the southern shore and fringing reef, the island's best view of the southern coast.

West Moloka'i

Given western Moloka'i's lack of mountains, and that the land is privately owned, all of the hikes on this side of the island follow the isolated coast.

KAWAKIU AND 'ILIO POINT

A nice walk from the condo complexes of Kaluakoi follows either the coast or a dusty dirt road to the secluded beauty of **Kawakiu Beach.** From Maunaloa Highway (Hwy. 460), take the Kaluakoi Road exit and follow it to the bottom of the hill before making a right on Kaka'ako Road. A left on Lio Place leads to the Paniolo Hale parking lot, where you can follow the signs for the beach, crossing over the fairway of the old golf course before you reach the shore. Make a right, and it's 45 minutes of walking along the coast to Kawakiu.

If the tide or surf is too high to walk along the coast, turn inland past **Pohaku Mauliuli Beach** (Make Horse Beach). After a few minutes, you'll be on a dirt road that leads north

mossy and green Pepe'opae Bog

and deposits you at Kawakiu. About 100 yards before the road drops onto the sand at Kawakiu, there's an ancient Hawaiian *heiau* out on the rocky point. To continue on to ʻIlio Point, follow the coast for another 30 minutes, where you'll eventually encounter an old Coast Guard LORAN station and refreshingly little else. Be sure to bring plenty of water, and let someone know where you're going beforehand, since this area is exceptionally remote.

MOʻOMOMI COASTAL TRAIL

Hikers with a 4WD vehicle can visit **Moʻomomi** (page 394) where a coastal trail connects a string of beaches with a windswept series of dunes. Each month March to October, **The Nature Conservancy** (808/553-5236, hike_molokai@tnc.org) leads guided hikes through the area, and while the trail is open year-round, due to the fragile ecosystem, it's imperative that hikers stay on the trail to protect the natural surroundings.

Hike to waterfalls in historic Halawa Valley.

★ Cultural Hike into Halawa Valley

You heard it here first: The **Cultural Hike into Halawa Valley** (808/542-1855 or 808/551-5538, www.halawavalleymolokai.com, $40-60 adults, $20-35 children under age 12) is the best activity in Hawaii. The caveat is that you have to be interested in Hawaiian culture, as this hike is about more than walking through a rainforest to a beautiful waterfall; it's an educational experience and a journey back in time, where you are welcomed into one of Hawaii's most sacred valleys.

You'll pass numerous *heiau,* the temples that have sat here silently for centuries, and crush *kukui* nuts straight from the trees to feel the healing oils. Depending on the season, your guide might pick *lilikoi* (passionfruit) or guava from the trees to share as a snack on the trail, and if it begins to rain back in the valley, just grab an enormous elephant ear leaf as a natural umbrella. You'll learn about taro and how it's cultivated, learn how residents hunt

pigs with knives, and hear stories of the 1946 tsunami from the last remaining resident. At the end of the hike is Moaʻula Falls, a multitiered 250-foot waterfall that spills toward a plunge pool, where the rocks are dotted with ancient petroglyphs. This is the real Hawaii, and if you schedule the hike, bring along a *hoʻokupu,* or offering—pieces of fruit or items you'd use around the house.

To book the trip, visit the tour website at halawavalleymolokai.com/hikeoverview.html, or phone and leave a message. You can also book through the **Molokaʻi Outdoors** (808/553-4477, www.molokai-outdoors.com) desk in Hotel Molokaʻi or through **Molokaʻi Fish and Dive** (53 Ala Malama Ave., 808/553-5926, www.molokaifishanddive.com). You can also just show up around 9am at the pavilion at the end of the road and hope for a last-minute spot (usually $60 pp). Be sure to pack mosquito repellent, water, snacks, and clothes and close-toed shoes that can get wet and muddy.

BIKING

The best mountain **biking** in Moloka'i is on the roads of the Moloka'i Forest Reserve, and road cyclists enjoy miles of open road with minimal traffic. The ride east from Kaunakakai to Halawa Valley is comparable to Maui's ride to Kahakuloa.

In central Kaunakakai, **Moloka'i Bicycle** (80 Mohala St., 808/553-5740 or 808/709-2453, www.mauimolokaibicycle.com, 3pm-6pm Wed., 9am-2pm Sat.) caters to every bike need: rentals (one-day $32 plus $20 per day thereafter, $120 per week), parts, and advice on good rides. They can arrange free pickups and drop-offs from a number of Moloka'i hotels, and $20-25 pickups from the airport and hotels such as Wavecrest and Kaluakoi.

Fishing

Fish are central to Moloka'i's culture, and it's the only island where **fishing** is sustainably managed around the Hawaiian lunar calendar. Fishing is a way of life on the island, and aside from the fishponds along the southern coast, many houses have traditional fishing nets hanging and drying in the yard. Offshore, the Penguin Banks between Moloka'i and O'ahu are some of Hawaii's best fishing grounds, although fishing near shore is good as well. As a general rule, the earlier you depart, the better your chances for success.

CHARTERS

The best place in Kaunakakai for buying fishing accessories is **Moloka'i Fish and Dive** (53 Ala Malama Ave., 808/553-5926, www.molokaifishanddive.com, 7:30am-6pm Mon.-Sat., 8am-2pm Sun.), which also operates four-hour trips ($695 plus $125 per additional hour) on the 38-foot Delta cruiser *The Coral Queen.*

To throw out some lines with one of Hawaii's best fishers, book a charter with captain Mike Holmes of **Fun Hogs Fishing** (808/567 6789, www.molokaifishing.com), an avid canoe racer and sailor. Aboard the 27-foot *AHI,* Holmes takes guests trolling for blue water game fish such as mahimahi, ono, ahi, and marlin on four-hour charters ($450) or very reasonably priced full-day eight-hour charters ($600). Fun Hogs can also arrange seasonal whale-watching trips ($70 adults), private snorkeling charters, or any other sort of outing for six or fewer passengers.

Also based at Kaunakakai is Captain Joe Reich of **Alyce C. Sportfishing** (808/558-8377, www.alycecsportfishing.com), who similarly offers half-day, three-quarter-day, and full-day charters aboard his 31-foot cruiser. Call for rates, and expect fresh fish for dinner.

Food

Food on Molokaʻi is mostly "local style," meaning stick-to-the-ribs plate lunches, but recent years have seen a welcome increase in culinary diversity. The options are sparse outside Kaunakakai, so be sure you have a plan for food if you venture away from town.

KAUNAKAKAI
American
The island's only restaurant to serve resort-quality food is ★ **Hale Kealoha** (1300 Kamehameha V Hwy., 808/660-3400, 7am-9pm daily, $14-24), which also has Molokaʻi's only restaurant tables with an oceanfront view. A kitchen fire closed the restaurant for four years, and it finally reopened in November 2015 in a huge leap forward for the entire Molokaʻi culinary scene. Hale Kealoha uses fresh ingredients sourced on the island, including shrimp from Keawa Nui Farms and an *ulu* (breadfruit) turkey burger. You'll also find pasta dishes, omelets, burgers, steaks, and salads, and since it's the island's only spot with a hotel liquor license, you can order a cocktail from the oceanfront bar and enjoy the nightly live music.

In the center of Kaunakakai, ★ **Paddler's Inn** (10 Mohala St., 808/553-3300, 11:30am-9pm daily, $10-16) has the best chicken *katsu* you'll find on Molokaʻi. The closest thing to a sports bar on the island, Paddler's has multiple TVs and ice-cold beer on tap, with occasional live music in the afternoon and happy hour (2pm-6pm daily) plus $3 Rolling Rocks all day. In summer, Paddler's is the place to be for the canoe races, and the fish-and-chips, burgers, plate lunches, and sandwiches are some of the best on the island. Order from the window inside, and grab a seat on the patio.

Local Style
In central Kaunakakai, ★ **Kanemitsu Bakery** (79 Ala Malama Ave., 808/553-5855, 5:30am-6:30pm Tues.-Sun., $5-9, cash only) isn't just a restaurant; it's a Molokaʻi institution that has served baked goods and bread since 1922. Breakfast and lunch are plate-lunch fare, but what catapults the bakery to legendary status is **Hot Bread Lane** (8pm-11pm Tues.-Sun.), where its famous hot bread is served from a window in a dingy, dimly lit alley out back. The experience feels illicit, trading cash for gargantuan loaves of cream cheese- and strawberry-filled bread. Other flavors include cinnamon and butter, or a blueberry with cream cheese. Loaves ($7-8) are big enough for two or three people.

Natural Foods
If you simply can't handle another plate lunch and need healthy fare, head to **The Store House** (145 Puali Place, 7am-5pm Mon.-Fri., 9am-3pm Sat., $5-10) for mango or strawberry tropical bowls ($5.75) topped with almonds, granola, coconut, banana, and honey. You'll also find kale and protein smoothies ($7.50) as well as salads, *kombucha,* and BLT sandwiches. This small spot is family run, and the fresh food is an oasis in a town of rice and mac salad.

Pizza
The de facto Molokaʻi pizza spot is **Molokaʻi Pizza Café** (15 Kaunakakai Place, 808/553-3288, 10am-10pm Mon.-Thurs., 10am-11pm Fri.-Sat., 11am-10pm Sun., $10-25, cash only), in the last building on the road toward the dock. Pizzas are served either whole or by the slice ($2.60), and there's also a decent selection of pasta dishes as well as rides and games for the kids.

TOPSIDE
Local Style
A longtime Molokaʻi classic, ★ **Kualapuʻu Cookhouse** (102 Farrington Ave., 808/567-9655, 7am-2pm Mon., 7am-8pm Tues.-Sat.,

You'll get your food when it's ready—no sooner, no later, no worries. Try the chicken *katsu* or *loco moco,* and if you're really hungry, order your plate "*kanaka*-style" for an additional $7.

WEST MOLOKA'I

Since the Moloka'i Ranch shuttered its operations, there are no restaurants on this side of the island. If you want to put together a picnic for the beach, **Maunaloa General Store** (200 Maunaloa Hwy., 808/552-2346, 9am-6pm Mon.-Sat., 9am-noon Sun.) has basic grocery items. If you're hanging out on the beach in Kaluakoi and need an overpriced snack, there's a **sundry store** (9am-5pm daily) in the otherwise abandoned resort.

EAST MOLOKA'I

The only restaurant on the east end is ★ **Mana'e Goods & Grindz** (mile marker 16, Hwy. 450, 808/558-8498, 6:30am-4pm Mon.-Fri., 7:30am-4:30pm Sat.-Sun., $6-9), where a takeout window serves everything from chicken *katsu* to freshly made fruit smoothies. If the banana pancakes happen to be on the menu, don't even hesitate—just order them.

Hotel Moloka'i under the light of a full moon

9am-2pm Sun., $8-14, cash only) is a swinging-screen-door plate-lunch institution where life moves slowly. Order inside at the counter and sit outside on the open-air lanai.

Getting There and Around

GETTING THERE
Air

The largest planes are with **Ohana** (800/367-5320, www.hawaiianairlines.com), a subsidiary of Hawaiian Airlines, with 37-seat aircraft and multiple flights per day from both Kahului and Honolulu.

Both **Makani Kai Air** (808/834-1111, www.makanikaiair.com) and **Mokulele Airlines** (808/567-6381 or 866/260-7070, www.mokuleleairlines.com) offer direct flights from Honolulu and Kahului; any other city will require a connecting flight. Be sure to check the baggage restrictions, since there isn't much space on the planes.

Moloka'i Airport

The **Moloka'i Airport** (MKK, 3980 Airport Loop, 808/567-9660) at Ho'olehua is a small open-air facility where you still walk out on the runway to board your plane. There's a single coffee shop (6am-6:30pm daily), and the only rental car operator, **Alamo** (808/567-6381, www.alamo.com, 6am-8pm daily), has offices across the street.

GETTING AROUND
Car Rental

The only rental-car agency with a booth at the airport is **Alamo** (808/567-6381, www.alamo.com, 6am-8pm daily), which has a

Where to Stay on Molokaʻi

Name	Type	Price	Features	Why Stay Here?	Best For
★ Aloha Beach House	vacation rental	$250	oceanfront, kitchen	location, romantic	couples, groups, families
Dunbar Beachfront Cottages	vacation rental	$190	oceanfront, kitchen	location, quiet	couples
Hale Malu Guesthouse	vacation rental	$55-80	kitchen	location, affordable	budget travelers, solo travelers, couples
★ Hotel Molokaʻi	hotel	$175-250	kitchenette, pool, breakfast	modern, activities desk	couples, families
Ka Hale Mala	B&B	$80-90	gardens, kitchen	quiet, affordable	budget travelers, couples, solo travelers
Ke Nani Kai	condo	$100-200	pool, kitchen	close to beach, location	couples, families
Molokai Beach House	vacation rental	$250	oceanfront, kitchen	location, full amenities	couples, groups, families
Palaʻau State Park	camping	$18	restrooms, pavilion	affordable, location	budget travelers
Paniolo Hale	condo	$110-225		oceanfront, kitchen	location, quiet
Papohaku Beach Park	camping	$10-20	toilets, water	oceanfront, quiet	budget travelers
★ Puʻu O Hoku Ranch	cottages	$200-300	kitchen, views	quiet, retreat	couples, honeymooners, families
Wavecrest Resort	condo	$100-200	pool, tennis, amenities	oceanfront, modern	couples, families

large fleet of cars and 4WD Jeeps. If you rent from Alamo, don't lose your key—they don't have extras. For an affordable cruiser, check out **Molokai Car Rental** (105 Ala Malama St., 808/336-0670, www.molokaicars.com), a casual locally owned company that can deliver the car to the airport. They don't have 4WD vehicles, but ask about their room-and-car package at Hotel Molokaʻi. The only place besides Alamo to get a 4WD vehicle, **Molokaʻi** **Outdoors** (808/553-4477, www.molokai-outdoors.com) occasionally rents SUVs for stays of three days or longer.

Gas

There are only two gas stations on the island, right next to each other in Kaunakakai. Be sure you have at least half a tank of fuel before heading out on a day trip to Halawa or Papohaku. **Rawlins Chevron** (Hwy. 450

and Kaunakakai Place, 6:30am-8:30pm Mon.-Thurs., 6:30am-9pm Fri.-Sat., 6:30am-6pm Sun.) has longer hours and more supplies, though it costs at least $0.75 more per gallon than on Maui.

Taxi

The best option for taxis on Moloka'i is **Hele Mai Taxi** (808/336-0937 or 808/646-9060, www.molokaitaxi.com), also offering private tours of the island. Expect to pay about $32 from the airport to Hotel Moloka'i. Also available is **Mid-Nite Taxi** (808/658-1410 or 808/553-5652), although service can be spotty.

Shuttle Bus

If you're on a budget, the **MEO public shuttle bus** (www.meoinc.org) operates three routes across the island—but you need to be flexible with your schedule, and there's no service on weekends. Shuttle stops include Hotel Moloka'i and in front of Misaki's Market in central Kaunakakai. The Maunaloa shuttle stops at the airport, and the shuttle runs six times Monday-Friday to Maunaloa, and eight times Monday-Friday to Puko'o in East Moloka'i. Along the routes the driver will usually let you get off wherever you want. Although it's free, donations to keep the shuttle going are accepted. For schedules visit the website.

Tours

Moloka'i Outdoors (808/553-4477, www.molokai-outdoors.com) offers an Island Tour package ($150 adults, $78 children) from Halawa Lookout all the way to Papohaku Beach. Operating three times per week, these tours cover the island in an air-conditioned van and usually carry a small group of only 4-8.

Big Island of Hawai'i

Everyone knows the Big Island of Hawai'i has beaches and sunshine. But the island is so much more than its unbelievably good weather. It's not hard to get off the beaten path here: the majority of the Big Island offers seclusion and adventure with easy access.

The Big Island of Hawai'i is the newest island, geologically speaking, in the chain of islands that make up the state of Hawai'i. While lava formed the island's physical structure, it is the sugar plantation industry, established in the mid-1800s, that is credited for creating the Big Island's culture, through bringing numerous immigrants to work the island's land. Much of the island's modern-day customs, from language (Hawaiian pidgin, or *da' kine*) to food (like the *loco moco* or Spam *musubi*) to clothing (the classic aloha shirt), reflect this merging of Chinese, Filipino, Japanese, Polynesian, Portuguese, and Mainland American cultures.

It's sometimes hard to tell locals from visitors—the only real way to confirm a true local is by checking for the Locals brand *slippahs* (flip-flops) on someone's feet. These preferred shoes embody the Hawaiian notion of *aloha,* the laid-back way of life in Hawai'i that attracts new residents and visitors every year. (Your first order of business when arriving to the island should be picking up a pair yourself.)

Many visitors are beckoned by the Big Island's warm weather and well-known spectacular landscape. Of course the island provides an array of activities for outdoor lovers, from horseback riding through paniolo (cowboy) country to surfing the popular Honoli'i Beach Park; from night snorkeling with the manta rays in Keauhou Bay to stargazing at the Mauna Kea Observatory.

The Big Island offers more than just one kind of experience: When the weather gets too hot seaside, drive upcountry to Waimea, the cool interior part of the island, where a fireside meal will be waiting for you. Or spend an early Sunday morning at one of the island's numerous farmers markets adorned with tropical fruits, *malasadas* (Portuguese doughnuts), and food carts with mouthwatering *huli huli* chicken and kalua pork.

When your visit is over, say *"a hui hou"* (until we meet again). You'll want to come back.

WHERE TO GO
Kona

Kona is dry, sunny, and brilliant. When watered, the rich soil blossoms, renowned for its diminutive **coffee plantations.** As the center of this region, **Kailua-Kona** boasts an array of art and designer shops, economical accommodations, great restaurants, and plenty of historical and cultural sites.

Kohala

North of Kailua-Kona, otherworldly black lava bleeds north into Kohala. Up the coast is **Hapuna Beach,** one of the best on the island. Peppered among resorts are **petroglyph** fields left by ancient Hawaiians. As you travel north on Highway 19 it becomes Highway 270 and you'll find yourself in the hilly peninsular thumb at the northern extremity of the island. The **Kohala Mountains** sweep down to the west to a warm and largely uninhabited coast, and to the east tumble into deep valleys cut by wind and rain. Several isolated beach parks dot the coast, and here and there are cultural sites, including a modern-day ruin at **Mahukona Beach Park.** The main town up this way is sleepy **Hawi.** At road's end is the overlook of stunning **Pololu Valley.**

Hawai'i Volcanoes National Park

The great lava fields that have spewed from **Kilauea** dominate the heart of Hawai'i Volcanoes National Park. While miles of **hiking trails** crisscross the park, most visitors see it by car (but some by bike or by foot) along the rim drive that brings you up close to sights like the impressive **Halema'uma'u Crater,** the mythical home of Madame Pele, the fire goddess. **Chain of Craters Road** spills off the *pali* through a forbidding yet vibrant wasteland of old and new lava to where this living volcano fumes and throbs. Nights in Volcano Village can be cold, but you'll be so distracted by watching the lava glow from the **Thomas A. Jaggar Museum** and then singing karaoke alongside park employees at **Kilauea Military Camp** that you'll hardly notice the drop in temperature at all.

Hilo

Hilo is the oldest port of entry and the only major city on the island's windward (east) coast. This is where it feels like old Hawaii. The city is one tremendous greenhouse where exotic flowers and tropical plants are a normal part of the landscape. The town boasts Japanese gardens, **Honoli'i Beach** (the best place to watch surfing), the **Lyman Museum and Mission House,** the **Pacific Tsunami Museum,** and a profusion of natural phenomena, including **Rainbow Falls** and **Boiling Pots** as well as black-sand beaches on the east side of town. Drive 20 minutes west of town to the mesmerizing **'Akaka Falls.** As the focus of tourism has shifted to the Kona side, Hilo has become a place where there are deals to be had.

Hamakua Coast, Waimea, and the Saddle Road

Hamakua refers to the northeast coast above Hilo, where streams, wind, and pounding surf have chiseled the lava into cliffs and precipitous valleys. The road north from one-street Honoka'a dead-ends at the lookout at **Waipi'o Valley,** the most spectacular and enchanted valley on the island. Upcountry is **Waimea,** the heart of Hawaiian cowboy country and home to the **Hawaii Regional Cuisine** movement. From Waimea one can traverse the island via the **Saddle Road** separating the mountains of Mauna Loa and Mauna Kea. Along the Saddle Road are long stretches of native forest, barren lava flow, and rangeland, plus a number of worthy spots for a stretch. From the Saddle Road, a spur road heads up to the top of **Mauna Kea,** where, at 13,796 feet, **observatories** peer into the heavens through the clearest air on earth. Heading south, another road zigzags up the slope to an atmospheric observatory, from where a hiking trail for the hale and hearty heads to the top of **Mauna Loa.**

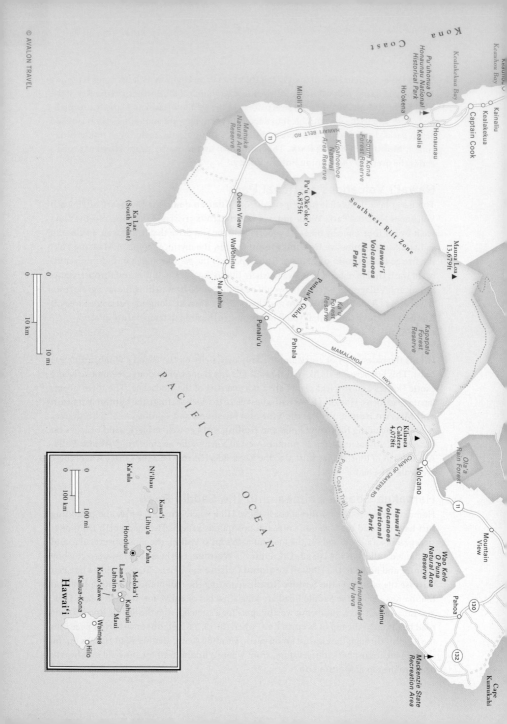

BIG ISLAND OF HAWAI'I

Kona

Kona can feel like the hottest place on the island—and not just because of its warm temperatures.

There is always something going on in Kona, from frequent festivals celebrating everything from coffee and chocolate to beer and fishing, as well as serious nightlife, which locals will tell you means anything open later than 9pm. It's no wonder that most visitors spend the majority of their time on the Kona side. Although Kona is talked about as if it were a city, it is actually a large district. From national historic sites to some of the best white-sand beaches on the island to nearly every ocean activity possible, Kona is a microcosm of what the larger island has to offer.

ORIENTATION
North of the Airport: North Kona

This is what you were imagining when you booked your trip to Hawaii: turquoise waters beside long stretches of white-sand beaches. Amazingly, there are several of these types of beaches within 20 minutes of Kona International Airport—and they are all open to the public! What might surprise you the most is that parts of this area look like a desolate moonscape. The landscape is made up of lava fields, and in recent years, the black rocks have become dotted with white stones that spell out names of favorite teams and loved ones. Don't be thrown off by the lack of infrastructure in the area: The ocean and beaches lurking behind the lava fields are some of the most magical the island has to offer for those looking for white sands and astonishing underwater life.

South of the Airport

The small area south of the international airport looks a lot like anywhere else in suburban America. When giving directions locations in this area are referred to as near or around Costco, which is a beacon of light up above Hina Lani Street, or Target in the Kona Commons shopping center. You'll likely use this area to get from one place to another and for its resource-laden shops, but don't miss out on Pine Trees, one of the best surfing spots on the island.

Ali'i Drive: Kailua and Keauhou

The heart of Kona, Ali'i Drive is the north-south thoroughfare stretching from the

Previous: public beach at the Four Seasons Resort; surf rental shop on Kona beach. **Above:** Pu'uhonua O Honaunau National Historical Park.

Look for ★ to find recommended
sights, activities, dining, and lodging.

Highlights

★ **Pu'uhonua O Honaunau National Historical Park (Place of Refuge):** Get a glimpse of ancient Hawaii at this safe haven for defeated chiefs and *kapu*-breakers. It's especially magical at sunrise (page 424).

★ **Kiholo Bay:** Get off the beaten path at Kiholo Bay, where a short 30-minute walk will take you to this pristine, rarely busy beach, a guaranteed turtle-viewing spot, with great access to swimming and snorkeling (page 425).

★ **Kikaua Point Park Beach:** Bring a picnic to this uncrowded beach—the water remains calm here, making it a perfect spot for kids (page 426).

★ **Makalawena Beach:** a favorite beach of many locals, this unspoiled beach is picture perfect with its white sand and turquoise water. There's not much shade here, so bring your sunscreen and get ready for a day cooling off in the water (page 427).

★ **Diving and Snorkeling:** Because its reef is so close to the shoreline, nearly the entire coast presents ideal snorkeling conditions. The best spots are **Kealakekua Bay** and **Pawai Bay** during the day and **Keauhou Bay** at night for the manta ray sightings (page 432).

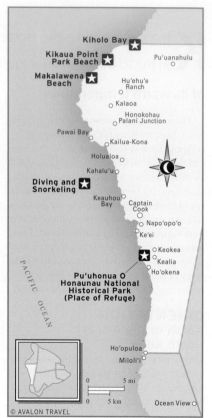

Kona

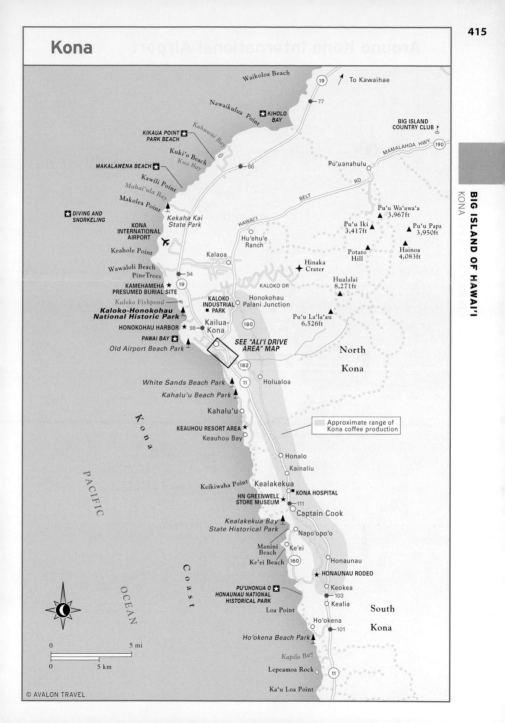

Waikoloa Beach

To Kawaihae

19

77

Nawaikulua Point

KIHOLO BAY

Kahuwai Bay

BIG ISLAND COUNTRY CLUB

KIKAUA POINT PARK BEACH

Kuki'o Beach

Kua Bay

86

Pu'uanahulu

MAMALAHOA HWY 190

KONA

BIG ISLAND OF HAWAI'I

MAKALAWENA BEACH

Kawili Point

Mahai'ula Bay

Makolea Point

RD

BELT

DIVING AND SNORKELING

Kekaha Kai State Park

HAWAI'I

Pu'u Wa'awa'a 3,967ft

KONA INTERNATIONAL AIRPORT

Hu'ehu'e Ranch

Pu'u Iki 3,417ft

Pu'u Papa 3,950ft

Keahole Point

Kalaoa

Potato Hill

Hainoa 4,083ft

Wawaloli Beach PineTrees

94

19

Hinaka Crater

KALOKO DR

Hualalai 8,271ft

KAMEHAMEHA PRESUMED BURIAL SITE

Kaloko Fishpond

KALOKO INDUSTRIAL PARK

Honokohau Palani Junction

Kaloko-Honokohau National Historic Park

180

Kailua-Kona

Pu'u La'la'au 6,526ft

HONOKOHAU HARBOR

98

PAWAI BAY

Old Airport Beach Park

SEE "ALI'I DRIVE AREA" MAP

182

North Kona

White Sands Beach Park

11

Holualoa

Kahalu'u Beach Park

K
o
n
a

Kahalu'u

Approximate range of Kona coffee production

KEAUHOU RESORT AREA

Keauhou Bay

PACIFIC

Honalo

Kainaliu

Keikiwaha Point

Kealakekua

KONA HOSPITAL

HN GREENWELL STORE MUSEUM

111

Captain Cook

Kealakekua Bay State Historical Park

Napo'opo'o

Manini Beach

Ke'ei

C
o
a
s
t

Ke'ei Beach

160

Honaunau

HONAUNAU RODEO

PU'UHONUA O HONAUNAU NATIONAL HISTORICAL PARK

Keokea

103

Kealia

OCEAN

Loa Point

South Kona

Ho'okena

101

Ho'okena Beach Park

Kapilo Bay

0   5 mi

0   5 km

Lepeamoa Rock

11

Ka'u Loa Point

Around Kona International Airport

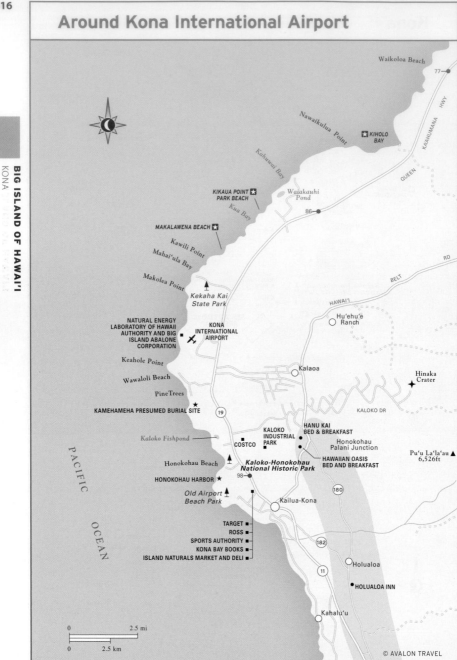

Waikoloa Beach

77

Nawaikulua Point

KAHUMANA HWY

KIHOLO BAY

Kahawai Bay

QUEEN

KIKAUA POINT PARK BEACH

Waiakauhi Pond

Kua Bay

86

RD

MAKALAWENA BEACH

Kawili Point

Mahai'ula Bay

Makolea Point

BELT

Kekaha Kai State Park

HAWAI'I

NATURAL ENERGY LABORATORY OF HAWAII AUTHORITY AND BIG ISLAND ABALONE CORPORATION

KONA INTERNATIONAL AIRPORT

Hu'ehu'e Ranch

Keahole Point

Kalaoa

Hinaka Crater

Wawaloli Beach

PineTrees

KAMEHAMEHA PRESUMED BURIAL SITE

19

KALOKO DR

KALOKO INDUSTRIAL PARK

HANU KAI BED & BREAKFAST

Pu'u La' La'au 6,526ft

Kaloko Fishpond

COSTCO

Honokohau Palani Junction

Honokohau Beach

Kaloko-Honokohau National Historic Park

HAWAIIAN OASIS BED AND BREAKFAST

HONOKOHAU HARBOR

98

Old Airport Beach Park

Kailua-Kona

180

PACIFIC OCEAN

TARGET
ROSS
SPORTS AUTHORITY
KONA BAY BOOKS
ISLAND NATURALS MARKET AND DELI

182

Holualoa

11

HOLUALOA INN

Kahalu'u

0   2.5 mi

0   2.5 km

© AVALON TRAVEL

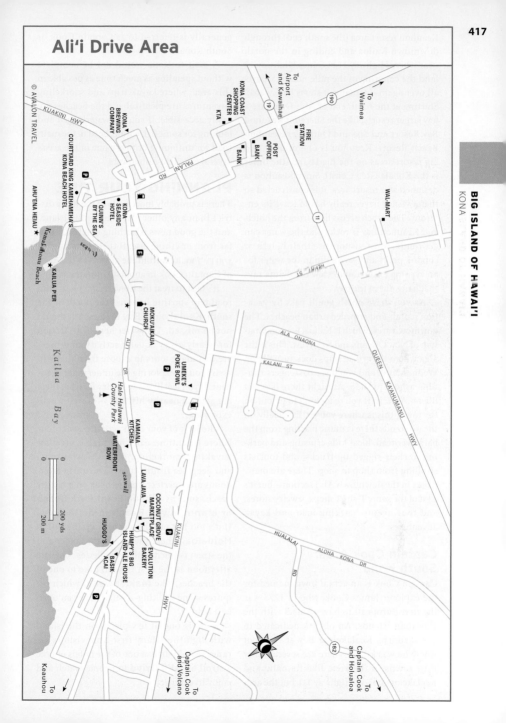

Ali'i Drive Area

© AVALON TRAVEL

To Airport and Kawaihae

To Waimea

190

19

11

KONA COAST SHOPPING CENTER

KONA BREWING COMPANY

KTA

KUAKINI HWY

FIRE STATION

POST OFFICE

BANK

BANK

PALANI RD

WAL-MART

HUALALAI ST

COURTYARD KING KAMEHAMEHA'S KONA BEACH HOTEL

P

AHU'ENA HEIAU

KONA SEASIDE HOTEL

QUINN'S BY THE SEA

Kamakahonu Beach

KAILUA PIER

Ka'iakeakua

MOKU'AIKAUA CHURCH

ALA ONAONA

KALANI ST

QUEEN KA'AHUMANU HWY

Kailua Bay

ALI'I DR

UMEKE'S POKE BOWL

P

Hale Halawai County Park

P

KAMANA KITCHEN

WATERFRONT ROW

seawall

COCONUT GROVE MARKETPLACE

LAVA JAVA

EVOLUTION BAKERY

KUAKINI HWY

HUMPY'S BIG ISLAND ALE HOUSE

HUGGO'S

BASIK ACAI

P

0   200 yds
0   200 m

HUALALAI

ALOHA KONA DR

KUAKINI RD

182

To Captain Cook and Holualoa

To Captain Cook and Volcano

To Keauhou

Keauhou resort area (the south end) through downtown Kailua and ending in the north near where Highway 11 becomes Highway 19 (and the counting of the mile markers starts all over again—actually, it starts backward). Starting at the south end of Ali'i Drive are a few larger resorts, like the Sheraton Keauhou Bay Resort and Spa and Outrigger Keauhou Beach Resort. Keauhou is one of only two big resort areas on the Big Island (the other is the Kohala Gold Coast). Since Keauhou is designed as a resort area, it is constructed so that a visitor never really has to leave its environs. The beach access here from the hotels and Keauhou Bay is rocky and the water can get rough. Most visitors use their hotel's or condo's pools and save a dip in the water for an evening excursion to view the manta rays that hang out in the bay.

As you drive north you'll pass by vacation rentals and crowded urban beaches. The downtown area, which is Kailua, is a combination of New Orleans and Key West. This is the area where the cruise ships dock (usually on Wednesdays), and you'll see passengers running ashore to shop. At night there is street life on Ali'i, so if you're looking to go out on the town, this is where you go. Especially on the weekends there is music blasting from the bars overhead, local kids cruising and parking in their rigged-up trucks, and tourists strolling from shop to shop. There are many stores in the downtown Ali'i section—but it's a lot of the same T-shirt shops, jewelry stores, and tour agents hawking luau and kayak adventures.

Captain Cook Area: South Kona

Captain Cook is an actual town, named for the explorer James Cook, who in 1778 was the first European to have contact with the Hawaiian Islands. An obelisk dedicated to Cook adorns Kealakekua Bay at the spot where he was killed. There are several other little towns in the area, like Kainaliu and Kealakekua (all off Highway 11), but the area generally is referred to as Captain Cook or South Kona.

A visit to Kona would not be complete without spending as much time as possible in this area, where kayak trips and snorkeling adventures are plentiful and the beaches are easily accessible. If you are waterlogged and looking for some drive time, head to the main road for antiquing or to try one of the area's several excellent restaurants.

PLANNING YOUR TIME

There is probably more to do in the Kona district than any other place on the Big Island, and the good news is nothing is actually that far from anything else. If there is no traffic, you can make it from the airport to the town of Captain Cook in about 40 minutes.

It's best to treat the Kona region like a mini road trip starting in either the north or the south. **Kealakekua Bay** to the south should not be missed. The water here is perfection for nearly every aquatic activity, and there are abundant tours to choose from that will assist you in exploring the underwater grandeur. If you feel like staying dry for a bit, there are several nearby historic sites well worth exploring.

The bulk of your day's activities will occur before lunchtime; early morning is great for kayaking, snorkeling, dolphin-swimming, and deep-sea fishing tours. The warm afternoons are a perfect time to relax on a nearby beach, such as **Kikaua Point Park Beach** or **Manini'owali Beach** in north Kona. If it's too hot out, head north up the hill to **Holualoa,** where the weather is cooler and the street is lined with art galleries. The late afternoon is the best time to hike to one of the beaches, like **Makalawena,** which requires some walking—usually over an open lava field.

Kona is one of few places on the island with nightlife. Many first-time visitors arrange to see a luau at one of the hotels or take a stroll on **Ali'i Drive** to people-watch and enjoy live music.

Captain Cook and South Kona

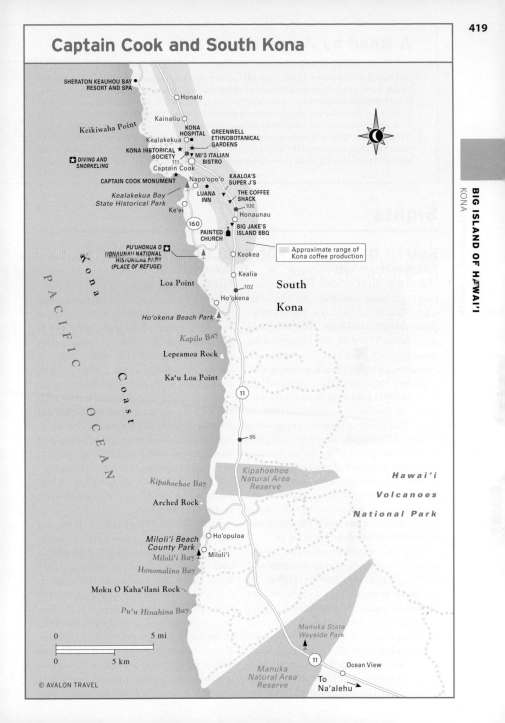

SHERATON KEAUHOU BAY
RESORT AND SPA

Honalo

Keikiwaha Point

Kainaliu

KONA
HOSPITAL

GREENWELL
ETHNOBOTANICAL
GARDENS

Kealakekua

KONA HISTORICAL
SOCIETY

MI'S ITALIAN
BISTRO

111

DIVING AND
SNORKELING

Captain Cook

CAPTAIN COOK MONUMENT

Napo'opo'o

KAALOA'S
SUPER J'S

Kealakekua Bay
State Historical Park

LUANA
INN

THE COFFEE
SHACK

106

Ke'ei

Honaunau

160

PAINTED
CHURCH

BIG JAKE'S
ISLAND BBQ

PU'UHONUA O
HONAUNAU NATIONAL
HISTORICAL PARK
(PLACE OF REFUGE)

Keokea

Approximate range of
Kona coffee production

Loa Point

Kealia

102

South

Ho'okena

Kona

Ho'okena Beach Park

Kapilo Bay

Lepeamoa Rock

Ka'u Loa Point

11

95

Kipahoehoe
Natural Area
Reserve

Hawai'i

Volcanoes

National Park

Kipahoehoe Bay

Arched Rock

Ho'opuloa

Miloli'i Beach
County Park

Miloli'i Bay

Miloli'i

Honomalino Bay

Moku O Kaha'ilani Rock

Pu'u Hinahina Bay

Manuka State
Wayside Park

0   5 mi

0   5 km

11

Ocean View

Manuka
Natural Area
Reserve

To
Na'alehu

© AVALON TRAVEL

A Road by Any Other Name

Highway 11 and Highway 19 are the main routes in the Kona region. Highway 11 has several names: Kuakini Highway, Hawai'i Belt Road, Queen Ka'ahumanu Highway, Mamalahoa Highway. These names are sometimes used in addresses, but occasionally businesses simply use Highway 11. Highway 19 on some maps and in some addresses is also called Hawai'i Belt Road, Queen Ka'ahumanu Highway, and Mamalahoa Highway where it runs through Waimea. Remember that in Kailua town, Highway 11 and Highway 19 merge, and thus it is important to note which highway you are on when looking for the mile marker (i.e., there is a mile marker 100 on Highway 11 and another on Highway 19). Using the mile markers is a great way to gauge how far you must travel.

Sights

SOUTH OF THE AIRPORT
Kaloko-Honokohau National Historical Park

Looking to learn more about the lives of ancient Hawaiians? **Kaloko-Honokohau National Historical Park** (Hwy. 19 between mile markers 97 and 98, 808/326-9057, www.nps.gov/kaho, 8:30am-4pm daily, free) houses fishponds that highlight the engineering skills of ancient Hawaiians. These fishponds are home to **birds** migrating south for the winter as well as endangered Hawaiian stilts and coots. Take a walk around the fishponds to **Honokohau Beach,** where on any given day you'll see plenty of sea turtles lounging in the sand. If you're lucky you might also see a monk seal. Continue on the sand and visit the *heiau* (temple) that sits on the south end of the beach and then follow the well-marked trail back over the lava field to the visitors center near the restrooms and parking lot.

The park is serious about locking the gate at 4pm. Another option for accessing the park is through the **Honokohau Harbor** (on Kealakehe Pkwy. off Hwy. 19 between mile markers 97 and 98), where there is a parking lot and restroom area. Although this is a national historical park, quite a few people use it solely as a beach spot. It's a nice enough beach, usually not that crowded and with calm waters, but it is at the small boat harbor and next to the airport, making the water a bit murky.

ALI'I DRIVE: KAILUA AND KEAUHOU
Historic Kailua

In reality, Kailua proper extends farther than Ali'i Drive, but commonly Kailua refers to the historic area, which is the north end of Ali'i Drive with the shops. For instance, Ali'i Drive is the location for the Hulihe'e Palace— the last royal palace in the United States of America and where King Kamehameha spent his final days. If historic Kailua is truly what you are seeking, contact the **Kona Historical Society** (808/323-3222, www.konahistorical. org, khs@konahistorical.org). The society's 90-minute tours are given only to groups of 10 or more, but if you are not part of a big group you can order online their Kailua Village Walking Map book ($10), which then must be picked up in person.

Body Glove Cruises offers historical lunch (800/551-8911, www.bodyglovehawaii. com, 1pm Wed., $98 adults, $78 children 6-17, under 5 free) and dinner cruises (4pm Sun., Tues., Thurs., Sat., $118 adults, $88 children 6-17, under 5 free) that will take you to some of the coastal historic sites; part of the proceeds from the two-hour cruise go to the Kona Historical Society. The price includes lunch or dinner, dessert, and complimentary cocktail (dinner only). It's sort of a luau on the water— combining food, entertainment, and education with the promise of seeing dolphins and/

or whales, depending on the season—and a good way to check lots of must-do activities off your list at once. Booking online through the website can save you 15 percent.

AHU'ENA HEIAU

Directly seaward of Courtyard King Kamehameha's Kona Beach Hotel (75-5660 Palani Rd.), at the north end of "downtown" Kailua, is the restored **Ahu'ena Heiau.** Built on an artificial island in Kamakahonu (Eye of the Turtle) Beach, it's in an important historical area. Kamehameha I, the great conqueror, came here to spend the last years of his life, settling down to a peaceful existence after many years of war and strife. The king, like all Hawaiians, reaffirmed his love of the *'aina* and tended his own royal taro patch on the slopes of Mount Hualalai. After he died, his bones were prepared according to ancient ritual on a stone platform within the temple and then taken to a secret burial place, which is believed to be just north of town somewhere near Wawahiwa'a Point—but no one knows for sure. It was Kamehameha who initiated the first rebuilding of Ahu'ena Heiau, a temple of peace and prosperity dedicated to Lono, god of fertility.

The tallest structure on the temple grounds is the *'anu'u* (oracle tower), where the chief priest received messages from the gods while in a deep trance. Throughout the grounds are superb *kia akua* (temple image posts) carved in the distinctive Kona style, considered some of the finest of all Polynesian art forms. The spiritual focus of the *heiau* was humanity's higher nature, and the tallest figure, crowned with an image of the golden plover, was that of Koleamoku, a god of healing. Another interesting structure is a small thatched hut of sugarcane leaves, Hale Nana Mahina, which means "house from which to watch the farmland." Kamehameha would come here to meditate while a guard kept watch from a nearby shelter. The commanding view from the doorway affords a sweeping panorama from the sea to the king's plantations on the slopes of Mount Hualalai. Though the temple grounds, reconstructed under the auspices of the Bishop Museum, are impressive, they are only one-third their original size. The *heiau* itself is closed to visitors, but you can get a good look at it from the shore.

MOKU'AIKAUA CHURCH

With a 112-foot-high steeple, the highest structure in town, the **Moku'aikaua Church**

Honokohau Beach

Your Best Day in Kona

- Visit **Pu'uhonua O Honaunau National Historical Park** in the early morning when you'll have the place to yourself.

- Join a guided **kayaking** tour of **Kealakekua Bay,** where you'll be side by side with the dolphins and experience some of the best **snorkeling** on the island.

- After a busy morning, relax at the white-sand **Manini'owali Beach/Kua Bay** in Kekaha Kai State Park (or any number of gorgeous white-sand beaches north of the Kona airport).

- In the late afternoon, cool off by heading up the mountain to gallery-filled **Holualoa,** also home of the fabulous **Holuakoa Gardens and Café,** where a dinner reservation is a must.

- Finish this long day with some bar-hopping or dancing on **Ali'i Drive.**

RAINY-DAY ALTERNATIVE

It doesn't often happen in Kona, but every once in a while you'll catch yourself in less-than-perfect weather. If so, visit the **Natural Energy Laboratory of Hawaii Authority (NELHA)** for an indoor talk on natural energy technology and the efforts to generate such energy in Hawaii. A visit here includes a tour and tasting at an abalone farm.

(75-5713 Ali'i Dr., www.mokuaikaua.org, dawn-dusk daily) has been a landmark for travelers and seafarers ever since the church was completed in January 1837. The church claims to be the oldest house of Christian worship in Hawaii: The site was given by King Liholiho to the first Congregationalist missionaries, who arrived on the brig *Thaddeus* in the spring of 1820. The walls of the church are fashioned from massive, rough-hewn lava stone, mortared with plaster made from crushed and burned coral that was bound with *kukui* nut oil. The huge cornerstones are believed to have been salvaged from a *heiau* built in the 15th century by King Umi that had occupied this spot.

Hulihe'e Palace, dating back to 1838, is full of period furniture and artifacts from the early 1900s.

Cooling Off in Holualoa

Want to get away from the beach for a few hours? The village of **Holualoa** (www.holualoahawaii.com), on the mountainside above Kailua-Kona, is quaint, and the panoramic view of Kona below is unbelievable. Plan to visit Holualoa, where the weather is cooler, for a couple of hours—or overnight in one of the choice bed-and-breakfasts here—to stroll the upscale galleries (not too upscale) and to have a meal at Holuakoa Gardens and Café. Holualoa is on Highway 180, which breaks off from Highway 11 to the south and connects to Highway 190 to the north.

Holuakoa Gardens and Café (76-5901 Mamalahoa Hwy., 808/322-2233, www.holuakoacafe.com, brunch 10am-2:30pm Mon.-Fri. 9am-2:30pm Sat.-Sun.; dinner 5:30pm-8:30pm Mon.-Sat.; café 6:30am-6pm Mon.-Fri., 8am-6pm Sat., 8am-2:30pm Sun.) is a restaurant where people actually do dress up (but you don't have to). The seating is all outdoors (but covered) in a lovely garden, and the waitstaff is attentive. The menu changes daily, the meat and greens are local when available, and the choices aren't the same old dishes seen on most menus in Hawaii. There are vegetarian and gluten-free options (including a very tasty flourless chocolate cake) and the wine list is extensive.

If you're in Holualoa during the day, be sure to check out **Holualoa Ukulele Gallery** (Hwy. 180, 808/324-4100, www.konaweb.com/ukegallery, 11am-5pm Tues.-Sat.). The building was the original town post office, and the current store owner refurbished the building's exterior with original postal boxes (not from the Holualoa post office, just from the same era). If you're thinking about buying a ukulele, but not sure what to get or how to play, Sam Rosen, the shop's owner, will patiently answer all your questions. Contact Mr. Rosen to learn more about his private workshops (from a few days to a week), where you can make your own ukulele.

Also in town is the **Donkey Mill Art Center** (78-6670 Hwy. 180, 808/322-3362, www.donkeymillartcenter.org, 10am-4pm Tues.-Sat.); check the website to see what one-day or weekend workshops the center is offering. The selections range from painting to woodcarving to silk-screening.

KONA

BIG ISLAND OF HAWAI'I

HULIHE'E PALACE

Go from the spiritual to the temporal by walking across the street from Moku'aikaua Church and entering **Hulihe'e Palace** (75-5718 Ali'i Dr., 808/329-1877, www.huliheepalace.com, 9am-4pm Mon.-Sat., except major holidays). You can look around on your own or ask the staff for a tour, which usually lasts 45 minutes. Admission is $8 adults, $6 seniors, $1 students under 18. This two-story Victorian structure commissioned by Hawaii's second royal governor, John Kuakini, dates from 1838. A favorite summer getaway for all the Hawaiian monarchs who followed, especially King Kalakaua, it was used as such until 1914. Inside, the palace is bright and airy. Most of the massive furniture is made from koa. The most magnificent pieces include a huge formal dining table, 70 inches in diameter, fashioned from one solid koa log. Upstairs is a tremendous four-poster bed that belonged

to Queen Kapi'olani, and two magnificent cabinets built by a Chinese convict serving a life sentence for smuggling opium.

The palace was opened as a museum in 1928. In 1973, Hulihe'e Palace was added to the National Register of Historic Places. Historic artifacts are displayed in a downstairs room. Delicate and priceless heirlooms on display include a tiger-claw necklace that belonged to Kapi'olani. You'll also see a portrait gallery of Hawaiian monarchs. Personal and mundane items are on exhibit as well—there's an old report card showing a grade of 68 in philosophy for King Kalakaua—and lining the stairs is a collection of spears reputedly belonging to the great Kamehameha himself.

CAPTAIN COOK AREA: SOUTH KONA

H. N. Greenwell Store Museum

It's *Little House on the Prairie* meets Hawaii.

Constructed in the 1870s to make supplies available to the Euro-American immigrant community, the **H. N. Greenwell Store Museum** (Hwy. 11 between mile markers 111 and 112, 808/323-3222, www.konahistorical. org, 10am-2pm Mon. and Thurs., $7 adults, $3 children 5-12) is the oldest surviving store in Kona and one of the oldest buildings in the area. A great experience for kids or history buffs, the volunteer-led tour of the building filled with historical pictures and relics of the area takes about a half hour and occurs on demand. Foodies will want to visit around 10am on Thursdays, when you can assist in baking Portuguese bread in the stone oven located behind the building. If you're just passing by on a Thursday, stop and pick up a loaf—but know that they are usually sold out by 2pm.

★ Pu'uhonua O Honaunau National Historical Park (Place of Refuge)

If you are going to do one historical activity while on the Big Island, do **Pu'uhonua O Honaunau National Historical Park** (off Hwy. 11 on Hwy. 160, 808/328-2326, www.nps.gov/puho). The gate is open daily 7:30am-7:15pm, while visitors center hours are 8:30am-4:30pm daily. Admission is $5 per car, $3 to walk in, free with a national park pass, or included in the $25 pass for three national parks on the Big Island. To get there from Highway 11, between mile markers 103 and 104 turn onto Highway 160 and travel down the hill a few miles to the entrance on the *makai* side.

This is where you see the true old Hawaii, circa the 1600s. A park ranger explains that there is a calming feeling here because it is a religious site dedicated to the god Lono. No killing or wars occurred at Pu'uhonua O Honaunau; it was, as it is sometimes called, a place of refuge. During times of war, women and children would seek safety on the grounds, and if defeated chiefs or those accused of sins could make it to the shore by swimming across the bay, they would be absolved of their sins and given a second chance. There were 30 such places like Pu'uhonua O Honaunau across the islands, but this site is the only one that remains.

Some of the structures at the park are original, but many are replicas. Kids tend to be particularly impressed by the imposing structures and sculptures of ancient times. The best time to visit the park is early morning—even before the gate opens. There is a wonderful sense of peace just after sunrise. Tours with

Pu'uhonua O Honaunau National Historical Park features original structures.

the knowledgeable staff are free and offered daily at 10:30am and 2:30pm, and are highly recommended. Pamphlets are also provided for self-guided tours, which would take a half hour if you just walked straight through, or you can do a self-guided audio cell phone tour by calling 808/217-9279.

The majority of tourists head straight to **Two Step** (turn *makai* off Hwy. 160 where you see the Pu'uhonua O Honaunau park sign, and instead of driving straight into the gate, turn right onto the road directly before the gate), called such because of the lava shelf that requires you to take two steps down into the water. The area offers great snorkeling and is shallow, making it popular with nonexperts and kids. There are no facilities, so it is recommended that you park in Pu'uhonua O Honaunau's lot, where there are bathrooms, and from where it's a two-minute walk to Two Step.

Beaches

Many of the best Kona **beaches** require some work to get to them. Keep in mind that often life is about the destination, not the journey. The majority of routes to the beaches can be accomplished in a good pair of sandals, but the walk, which is usually over uneven lava, can be difficult for some. There are an equal number of beaches that don't require any more walking than from the parking lot to the sand, so don't fret if you opt out of the beaches that require more effort to reach.

NORTH OF THE AIRPORT: NORTH KONA
★ Kiholo Bay

If you stop at the scenic viewpoint near mile marker 82 you get a great panorama of **Kiholo Bay** (Hwy. 19 near mile marker 81 and also between mile markers 82 and 83, gate open 7am-7pm), and chances are you'll want to get closer to it to see what looks like completely untouched paradise: a deserted beach with turquoise water and what appears to be an island off in the bay. If you start your journey at the south end of the beach, you'll find a cold freshwater lava tube bath called the **Queen's Bath** (Keanalele Waterhole). It is a sacred site, so please be respectful. A sign there asks people to refrain from using the site for bathing—but you can get in the water and peek around. This also is a good place for snorkeling when the water is clear. The beach ends and then you need to walk over the lava rock around the bend to a wonderful little shaded cove. From here you can swim out to that "island," which is actually attached to the landmass on its north side.

To drive to the south end of the bay, look for the stick with the yellow reflector on it on the *makai* side of the road between mile markers 82 and 83. If you're driving north on Highway 19 and you pass the blue Scenic Point sign, you have gone too far. The road you turn onto is gravel, but a rental car can make it to the end, where there are portable bathrooms. If you decide to walk all the way from Highway 19 to the beach, the makeshift parking lot is right before mile marker 81. Usually there are other cars parked on the side of the road. The trail, which will take you about 20 sweaty minutes to walk, starts to the left of the parking lot and veers left as you walk. The benefit in walking and not driving down is that the walk will get you much closer to the bay. If you drive, you end up on the south side of the bay and need to walk around it for about 15 minutes. I recommend wearing hiking shoes—not because the walk is challenging, but because the rocky terrain makes it a bit difficult to do in flip-flops.

Kuki'o Beach (Four Seasons Resort Beach)

The wonderful thing about Hawaii is that the entire shoreline is public—so even when the beach is at a five-star hotel, as it is in the case of **Kuki'o Beach** (Hwy. 19 between mile markers 86 and 87), the public must have access to it. Kuki'o usually offers calm water for swimming and has a pleasant, unshaded, narrow white-sand area off a paved path that extends into an excellent oceanfront jogging trail—an ideal place to get your steps in. The path is part of the historic *ala loa* (long path) route that islanders would use for a nightly procession. There is no lifeguard on duty. This bay is a fisheries management area, which means that you can fish here but a board alerts you to how many fish you can catch of each type.

To get to Kuki'o Beach, you are required to stop at the Four Seasons Resort gate and notify the guard that you are going to the public-access beach. Note: The resort itself is open to the public, so you can also say you are visiting it and go take a peek if you want. Follow the signs that read Public Access and park in the lot where the road ends.

★ Kikaua Point Park Beach

Kikaua Point Park Beach (Kuki'o Nui Dr., off Hwy. 19 between mile markers 87 and 88) is perfect in so many ways. Entry is limited (passes are handed out at the security gate), so it's never as crowded as you'd expect it to be. The water is glorious. Even when there are

waves at other places on the same shoreline it remains calm here, making it a perfect spot for kids (although there is not a lifeguard on duty). Pack a picnic and head to the grassy area shaded by coconut trees. Bathrooms, showers, and drinking water are available, and these privately maintained facilities are lovely.

To get to Kikaua Point Park Beach, turn *makai* onto Kuki'o Nui Drive and proceed to the security booth. The guards only hand out 28 passes per day, but the turnover is pretty high, so if you wait around long enough, and people do, you'll likely end up with a pass (however, the earlier you arrive the better your chances are at getting a pass quickly). Another option is to park at the Kuki'o Beach parking lot near the Four Seasons Resort and walk south to Kikaua—it's only a 10-minute walk. Don't get tricked in the parking lot with the Beach Access sign pointing to the left—this is only the tide pool area. Take the paved path straight back, about a five-minute walk, to the sandy portion. When you're done with the best beach day ever, don't forget to return your access card to the security guard so that someone else can enjoy the beach.

Manini'owali Beach (Kua Bay)

Until about 15 years ago there wasn't a road

Turtles are frequent visitors to Kiholo Bay.

to get to **Manini'owali Beach** (Hwy. 19 between mile markers 88 and 89, 9am-7pm daily) in the **Kua Bay** section of Kekaha Kai State Park. One had to really want to get there by hiking or finding a four-wheel-drive route. And even with all those barriers, people still went—so you know it has to be good. It's a smallish white-sand beach with turquoise water that is excellent for bodyboarding and snorkeling. There is not much shade, but if you're aching for sun this is a perfect place to spend the day absorbing some rays. A paved road reaches a parking lot and full facilities. It's getting so crowded that now there is sometimes a security guard at the entrance to the beach itself. To get there from Highway 19, look for the Kehaha Kai Park sign and turn *makai* across from West Hawaii Veterans Cemetery.

★ Makalawena Beach

In the state beach section of Kekaha Kai State Park, **Makalawena** (Hwy. 19 between mile markers 90 and 91, daily 9am-7pm) is a favorite beach of many locals, probably because it's an authentic Big Island experience given that it requires a little bit of hiking to get there. If you make the 30-minute trek to the beach, you'll be rewarded with isolated white sand and turquoise water. Given the walk, Makalawena is often fairly deserted (it has no facilities). The beach itself is made up of three crescent-shaped white-sand areas that are backed by trees. Bodyboarding and snorkeling are possible.

Before you get excited about coming here, you should know that while you can do it in a standard rental car, it's a slow-going 20-minute drive and then there is a 30-minute walk over a lava field. From Highway 19, look for the Kekaha Kai Park sign and turn *makai*. The initial road starts off as paved but then quickly becomes uneven lava.

To get to Makalawena, walk from the parking lot through the first beach, **Mahai'ula,** where the bathrooms are located, and then through the lava field. When you reach sand again, you're close. You might want to wear

good shoes on the walk, as the lava field can be tricky to navigate.

SOUTH OF THE AIRPORT
Pine Trees

Although famous among surfers and the site of many competitions, **Pine Trees** (Hwy. 19 between mile marker 94 and 95, access road gate open daily 7am-7pm) is not a good swimming beach, nor are there any pine trees. There are a few one-towel coves along the rocky shoreline where you can gain access to the water, but mostly it's a place from which to observe the action. To get to Pine Trees, turn *makai* where you see the sign for the Natural Energy Laboratory of Hawaii Authority (NELHA). Follow the road toward the NELHA facility a short way to **Wawaloli Beach,** a small public beach of sand and crushed coral that is used mostly by locals for relaxing and barbecuing. There are a few restrooms and some picnic tables. To continue to Pine Trees from here you'll need a four-wheel-drive vehicle. When you reach the T-intersection, turn makai on to a dirt road (the paved part continues to the right) and continue for about a mile. There is no real parking lot here—just park near the trees, where other cars likely are parked.

Old Airport Beach Park and Pawai Bay

We should thank whatever politician decided to take this old abandoned airport and turn it into **Old Airport Beach Park** (Hwy. 19 between mile markers 99 and 100). To reach it, turn makai on Makala Boulevard. Go to the end of the road, and then turn right on Kuakini to the dead end. There are nicely kept picnic areas that get busy, and the facilities are placed between the parking lot and sandy area, which doesn't make for an ideal beach. The former runway is now a jogging area, but if you're looking for some beach jogging, head north on the sand toward **Pawai Bay**. Since you are near a reef here, the little bay with sand is the best place to get in the water for some excellent snorkeling. Locals will tell you that you can camp here, but I don't recommend it.

ALIʻI DRIVE: KAILUA AND KEAUHOU
Kahaluʻu Beach Park

With a large covered picnic pavilion, barbecue pits, a guy sitting around playing ukulele on a bench, and locals drinking from the backs of their trucks in the parking lot, **Kahaluʻu Beach Park** (Aliʻi Dr. between mile markers 4.5 and 5, 6am-11pm daily) has all the makings of a quintessential urban beach park. Although there is a small, rocky beach area and a lifeguard on duty, it's not so much a place to lie out. But it is a great spot for snorkeling and ideal for kids since the water is shallow and calm. Bathroom and shower facilities are available as well as a food truck that has small storage lockers for rent; it hangs out next to the big parking area. Kahaluʻu Bay Education Center, a nonprofit organization, rents gear at fair prices and uses the profits to support the local ecosystem. The beach area is smoke free.

White Sands Beach (Laʻaloa Beach Park)

Even though **White Sands Beach** (Aliʻi Dr. between mile markers 3.5 and 4, 7am-11pm daily, gate closes at 8pm) is also right off the road, it still retains a peaceful feel to it. Officially known as Laʻaloa (Very Sacred) Beach Park and nicknamed Disappearing Sands Beach, it is popular for bodyboarding, surfing, and sunning (there is little shade here). Grab your towel and head out early because this beach gets crowded on weekends. Bathroom and shower facilities are available and there is a lifeguard on duty.

Parking can be tricky. Locals park on the *makai* side of the road or in a small lot across the street.

CAPTAIN COOK AREA: SOUTH KONA
Kealakekua Bay State Historical Park

Tourists flock to **Kealakekua Bay State Historical Park** (Beach Rd. off Hwy. 160, daylight hours) to kayak, go on ithkayak tours to the Captain Cook Monument, or to simply snorkel. The park is at the intersection of Beach Road and Napoʻopoʻo Road. There is a parking lot with a boat launch right at the intersection, and a few yards away is the historical park with bathrooms, showers, picnic areas, drinking water, and an ample parking area.

White Sands Beach

Given the proximity to the reef, the snorkeling here is excellent, and depending on the season, it's common to see dolphins swimming next to you. The kayaking here is some of the easiest ocean kayaking, so it's suitable for novices.

It is required that you obtain a permit to land at the monument across the bay. Visitors do not need to acquire their own permits when renting a kayak, but must confirm with the vessel owner that the vessel they rent possesses a valid permit for transiting the bay. There are only three companies that have valid permits (**Adventures in Paradise, Aloha Kayak,** and **Kona Boys**), so make sure you are renting kayaks from one of those companies or joining one of their tours.

You don't need a permit if you're just going to paddle around rather than land on the beach.

Manini Beach

Manini Beach (off Hwy. 160) is a prime snorkeling and kayaking area with great views of the Captain Cook Monument in the distance. Greatly affected by the tsunami in March 2011, which forced two beachfront homes into the ocean, the beach is now restored and even nicer than it was before, with a large, partly shaded grassy area and several picnic tables. There are very few places to park here so it may be hard to find a spot, but the good news is that the water never gets too crowded. From Highway 160, also called Pu'uhonua Road, turn *makai* onto Kahauloa Road and then right onto Manini Beach Road—follow it around for 0.2 mile until you see parked cars and a bay.

Ke'ei Bay Beach

A real locals' place, **Ke'ei Bay Beach** (off Hwy. 160) has a lovely strand, and it can get surprisingly busy given how you have to be in the know to get here. There is white sand and the water is calm for swimming or snorkeling. From Highway 160, also called Pu'uhonua Road, turn onto an unmarked dirt road on the *makai* side between Ke'ei transfer station and Keawaiki Road, which it is gated. Four-wheel drives are best for this road to the beach, but you can reach it in a standard car with some careful, slow driving. Drive toward the ocean (or you can walk about 15 minutes) until you can't drive anymore. Park in the semi-designated lot in front of the houses.

Ho'okena Beach Park

The road down to **Ho'okena Beach Park** (Hwy. 11 near mile marker 101) is worth the trip: It has excellent views of the coastline and the surrounding area, and if you are an advanced biker you might want to try this route for a challenge. There is an actual sandy beach here, and it makes for a nice place to bring a towel and laze the day away. There is even some shade.

The water here is not too rough, so it's a nice place to swim, snorkel, or kayak (rentals are available at the beach or by calling 808/328-8430, $20 for a single kayak for two hours or $25 for a tandem). If you get here early you might see a spinner dolphin, as this area is one of their habitats. Facilities such as showers, bathrooms, barbecues, and a large covered picnic area are available. Camping is allowed in designated areas, and permits can be obtained online (http://hookena.org/camping.html) a recommended 72 hours in advance, or at the beach from the attendant beginning at 5pm daily. It is advised that you consult the park website, as there are extensive instructions about how to obtain a permit and there is different pricing for residents and nonresidents. There is a separate area to park if you're camping here, to the left of the main parking lot. The area is popular with locals and can get crowded and rowdy at night, so it might not be the best place if you're camping with kids or looking for a peaceful evening.

From Highway 11 a two-mile paved windy road leads to the entrance. Where the road splits when you are almost at the ocean, fork to the left—don't go straight—where there is usually a sign for kayak rentals, and head on the one-lane road into the parking lot. You will see the sign for Ho'okena on the ocean side of the road.

EXCURSIONS TO KA'U

While Ka'u often serves simply as the stretch that gets visitors between Kona and Volcanoes National Park, hidden away off the main highway are magnificent secluded beaches of all colors (from green to black to white sand) and sizes. Some of these beaches require a greater sense of adventure and more than just the average rental car. An all-wheel-drive or four-wheel-drive will serve you well. Ka'u is often the hottest part of the island, thus beaches are best experienced early in the morning while the day is still cool.

Punalu'u Black Sand Beach

If you want to see some turtles lazily basking in the sun, I can almost guarantee that you will see one at **Punalu'u Black Sand Beach** (Hwy. 11 between mile markers 56 and 57). It is the most easily accessible and nicest beach in the area, so it can get pretty busy on weekends. Park on either the right side of the beach near the picnic stands and bathroom area or on the left side closer to the beach itself. Closer to the left-side parking area is a lovely, peaceful pond filled with lily pads and ducks. Camping is allowed here, and on holiday weekends local families take full advantage of it and it can get packed.

South Point

South Point is exactly what you think it is—the most southern landmass of the island and the United States of America. It lies at a latitude 500 miles farther south than Miami and 1,000 miles below Los Angeles. Known in Hawaiian as Ka Lae, it was probably the first landfall made by the Polynesian explorers on the islands. Most people drive down **South Point Road** (off Hwy. 11 between mile markers 69 and 70) so that they can say they've been there and done one of the most thrilling activities possible on the Big Island—jumping off Ka Lae and enjoying the 50-foot fall into the ocean. Luckily, there is a rope ladder available to get you back to the top. On your way down South Point Road to Ka Lae, look at the Kamoa Wind Farm—where windmills go to die—and the mostly functioning Pakini Nui Wind Farm towering overhead.

The sign to South Point Road will be obvious off Highway 11. Follow it south for 12 miles for some of the best photo opportunities on the Big Island. The drive down South Point is now paved and easy for any car, although

Ho'okena Beach Park

it is narrow, so watch for oncoming cars and pull off to the side if necessary. The road splits somewhat—stay to the right. Where the road ends you'll surely see many other cars parked, and you should also park here.

Cashing in on its proximity to South Point, the closest town, **Na'alehu,** is best known as the place that has all the "southernmost"

restaurants, bars, and bakeries. It is a mecca of southernism, and in addition to that fun fact it has some of the better culinary delights in the area. Check out the overhanging monkeypod trees forming a magnificent living tunnel in front of some of the former plantation managers' homes as you pass through on Highway 11.

Water Sports

CANOEING AND KAYAKING

Kealakekua Bay is the perfect place to **canoe** or **kayak** in the calm water, the abundance of dolphins, and the lure of boating toward the Captain Cook Monument; however, there are a lot of rules surrounding this activity. If you are a DIY kayaker and want to rent or have your own kayak to use, you are required to obtain a permit (go to www.hawaiistateparks.org/parks/hawaii and click on Kealakekua Bay State Historical Park). Please note, according to the state's website, "Transiting the bay by individuals is allowed so long as the vessel has a valid permit (both private and commercial rental vessels). Permitted vessels are prohibited from landing at Ka'awaloa flat, or launching from Napo'opo'o wharf. Visitors do *not* need to acquire their own permits when renting a kayak, but must confirm with the vessel owner that the vessel they rent possesses a valid permit for transiting the bay. There are only three kayak tour companies (listed below) that have been issued permits by the Division of State Parks.

The larger companies all offer the same tour of the bay, which includes four-hour morning or afternoon combination trips of kayaking, snorkeling, looking for dolphins, and paddling to the Captain Cook Monument. The differences between the tours are the quality of the boats and expertise of the tour guides.

The preferred company for the Kealakekua kayak tour, because of the quality of its tours

and equipment, is **Kona Boys** (79-7539 Mamalahoa Hwy./Hwy. 11, 808/328-1234, www.konaboys.com, 7:30am-5pm daily, $119-169 adults, $99-149 children), which offers both morning and afternoon tours of the bay. It also offers a trip in an old-style canoe, which leaves from the Kailua dock (1 hour, $50); someone boats you around the bay while giving you the history of the coastline.

Other choices for kayak tours include the capable **Aloha Kayak Company** (79-7248 Mamaloahoa Hwy. 11 between mile markers 113 and 114, 808/322-2868, www.alohakayak.com, 7:30am-5pm daily, $99-130 adults, $55-70 children). This company offers 3.5-hour and 5-hour tours—although both tours are not offered daily. Visit its website to receive $20 off per person on the 5-hour tour. If you are into sea spelunking (cave exploration), Aloha offers a 3.5-hour sea cave-with-snorkel tour that it touts as the best option for cruise ship passengers with limited time.

Adventures in Paradise (75-560 Kopiko Street C7-430, 808/447-0080, www.bigislandkayak.com, tours 7am and 11:30am daily, $90-$100) touts itself as the kayak company with the lowest prices for the bay trip, although its stated prices don't include taxes or the $5 state park fee or a more robust lunch like the other companies. Nonetheless, the guides are personable and knowledgeable and the small group sizes are a plus.

For a different kind of kayak adventure (and one that might be a little less crowded and a little later in the morning), try **Ocean**

Safaris (on Keauhou Bay, 808/326-4699, www.oceansafariskayaks.com, 8am-5pm daily, 3.5-hour morning tour, $85 adults, $45 children). This tour starts in Keauhou Bay and journeys to a sea cave in Kuamoo Bay. You'll snorkel on the way in an effort to view dolphins and turtles.

TOP EXPERIENCE

★ DIVING AND SNORKELING

Nearly every kayak trip or boating trip includes snorkeling, but if you're simply looking to rent gear on your own, there are several long-standing shops in the area, and good deals on snorkel sets can be had at both Costco and Target. Nearly the entire coast presents ideal snorkeling conditions given how close the reef is to the shoreline; however, some areas are harder to access due to the rocky geography. Beginners can easily start at Two Step or Pu'uhonua O Honaunau National Historical Park. The best spots are **Kealakekua Bay** and **Pawai Bay** during the day and **Keauhou Bay** at night for the manta ray sightings.

Big Island Divers (74-5467 Kaiwi St., 808/329-6068, www.bigislanddivers.com) offers competitive deals relative to other providers in the area. A two-tank guided tour ($130 per person includes snacks) is offered daily (8am-1:30pm), and most nights the company offers manta ray night dives and snorkeling trips ($120 per person diving or $100 snorkeling) with several different combinations of options, from one tank to two tanks and depending on the length of trip. This is one of the few manta ray trips with a dive and snorkel option on the same boat. The best thing about this company is that it offers discounts the more you dive—so if you think you'll go out at least twice, Big Island Divers is a good deal for you.

Captain Zodiac (Honokohau Harbor, 808/329-3199, www.captainzodiac.com, 7:30am-5pm daily) offers a four-hour snorkel and dolphin-watching tour, but does it

from a Zodiac boat and leaves from the harbor near Kailua, although the tour travels to Kealakekua Bay ($95 per adult, $79 per child with online discount). This is an extremely professional and dedicated company that truly values customer service. Also, Zodiac is a good option if you don't want to paddle around yourself but still want to be close to the dolphin and snorkeling action.

Fair Wind (78-7130 Kaleiopapa St., Keauhou Bay, 808/322-2788, www.fair-wind. com, 8am-5pm and 6:30pm-8:30pm daily, snorkel and dive tour $129 plus tax adults, $79 plus tax children, $29 plus tax toddlers under 3, manta ray diving $109 per person, discount if booked online) is your first-class deluxe option for snorkeling and diving tours. Fair Wind offers a five-hour morning snorkel and dive that includes breakfast and lunch. The boat, the *Hula Kai*, is comfortable, and staff is there to meet your every need. The manta ray night snorkel (6:30pm-8:30pm) includes all gear and a snack. Other places offer manta ray night tours, but Fair Wind's service sets it apart. A manta ray expert on board films the entire experience for purchase after the trip.

A longtime favorite of locals, **Jack's Diving Locker** (75-5813 Ali'i Dr., 808/329-7585, www.jacksdivinglocker.com, 8am-6pm Sun., 8am-8pm Mon.-Sat.) offers two-tank morning dives (8:30am, $135 per person plus gear rental for certified divers, $195 for intro divers, $65 for snorkeling; all prices include a light meal) and manta ray night trips that are really two dives, with one at sunset and a second dive to view the manta rays ($155 per person plus gear rental and $125 per person for snorkeling, not offered Tues. or Sat.). Serious divers might want to consider the Pelagic Magic dive (Tues. and Thurs., $175 for certified divers), which won the Best Night Dive category in Scuba Diving magazine's 2014 readers' choice awards. This "extreme dive" is a one-tank dive to view an underwater light display, compliments of some spectacular jellies.

Kona Honu Divers (74-5583 Luhia St., 808/324-4668, http://konahonudivers.com, 7am-5pm daily) is another outfitter with a

Watching Manta Rays

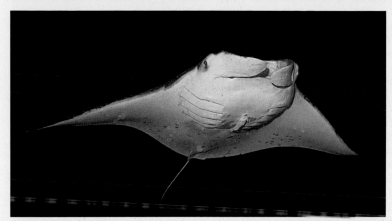

manta ray in Keauhou Bay

Many say that Kona is the number one place in the world to see manta rays, partly because they have become conditioned over time to feed at night in Keauhou Bay, eating the plankton attracted to the light at the Sheraton hotel. Snorkeling companies offer nighttime excursions into the bay so that you can snorkel with the manta rays.

Manta rays are completely harmless. Although their wingspan averages 5-8 feet, they have no teeth or stinger—but given their large size, seeing a manta ray up close can be both terrifying and exhilarating. If you are prone to seasickness, you may want to skip this trip. Even though the tour boats don't travel far, the water can be rough at night. Once one person gets sick, it seems like several more people follow.

While you won't be up close and personal with the manta rays, an alternative is simply to watch them from the Sheraton Keauhou Resort and Spa. The aptly named **Rays on the Bay** restaurant and bar (dinner served 5:30pm-9:30pm and the bar stays open until 10:30pm) has a viewing area where you can spot the mantas from dry land.

good reputation for service and luxury, and this one really specializes in diving (not just snorkeling). It offers a few different types of tours, from a manta ray night dive ($105 for one tank and $135 for two tanks) to manta ray night snorkeling ($100 per person) to two-tank daytime dives for beginning to advanced divers ($125 for divers and $65 for snorkelers). On Fridays it has a black-water night dive that takes place after the manta ray dive for those who really want to experience the ocean by night ($146). Its specialty tours are not offered daily and a minimum number of passengers is required to run charters, so availability may

dictate whether or not you decide to dive with Kona Honu. Discounts are available for multiple bookings such as a charter plus manta night dive or by adding the black-water dive to any package.

SURFING AND STAND-UP PADDLEBOARDING

Surfing is not as significant a sport on the Big Island as on the other islands. Proportionally for the size of the island, there are fewer good surfing spots here, and many of the traditional surfing sites are just not easy to access.

However, a few local sites on the Kona side do draw the faithful. Perhaps the most popular is the break along the reef at **Kahalu'u Bay** in front of the beach park. Two alternative spots are **Banyans** near White Sands Beach (aka Disappearing Sands Beach) and **Pine Trees,** north of town near the airport. Any of the shops that sell or rent boards can give you current information about surfing conditions and sites.

On the other hand, **stand-up paddleboarding** is sweeping the island. In many cases, paddleboarders can be found where the surfers are. However, you'll also see paddleboarders out with boogie boarders since smaller waves are much more practical for the stand-up paddleboard and essential for novices. If you are just beginning, try a lesson or rent a board and test it out on some flat, still water. Most places that rent surfboards also rent stand-up paddleboards.

If you need a rental, oftentimes there will be beachfront peddlers hawking boards at hourly rates (you can bargain). Many of the tour outfitters, such as the ones located near the Kailua Pier, rent boards out by the day or week. **Kona Boys** (79-7539 Mamalahoa Hwy./Hwy. 11, 808/328-1234, www.konaboys.com) is one of the few providers in Kona that offers stand-up paddleboard instruction ($99 per person for 1.5-hour group class, minimum two people, or $149 for private instruction). The company also rents stand-up paddleboards ($29 per hour or $74 per day) and offers daily 1.5-hour tours ($99 group tour, $149 private tour). If you're looking for surf instruction, contact **Ocean Eco Tours** (Honokohau Harbor off Hwy. 19, 808/324-7873, www.oceanecotours.com, 8:30am or 11:30am check-in, $95 group lessons, $150 for 2-hour private lesson), which also offers stand-up paddleboarding lessons for the same price as surfing lessons.

DOLPHIN SWIMS AND WHALE-WATCHING

Many of the kayaking and snorkeling trips offer dolphin options (both viewing and **swimming with dolphins**), since Kealakekua Bay has it all. The majority of boat trips will state that **whale-watching** is available during the winter season. Listed here are outfitters and excursions that are fully dedicated to dolphin and/or whale swims and watches. If you want to swim with the dolphins it's best to join an organized trip so that you have some instruction and assistance with this undertaking.

Dan McSweeney loves whales and wants you to love them too. At **Dan McSweeney's Whale Watching Learning Adventures** (Honokohau Harbor off Hwy. 19, 888/942-5376, http://ilovewhales.com, Dec.-Mar. only, $110 adults, $99 children), he personally conducts each tour and guarantees that you will see whales. If you're interested in learning about whales, this tour is for you. There is no open bar on the boat. Morning and afternoon departures are available and the tour lasts three hours.

Sunlight on Water (Honokohau Harbor off Hwy. 19, 808/896-2480, sunlightonwater.com) offers whale-watching tours (afternoons daily during winter, $80 adults, $60 children), a four-hour tour to swim with spinner dolphins (mornings daily, $120 adults, $80 children if booked online, includes snorkel gear) and manta ray swims (nightly, $87 adults, $75 children if booked online). The good deal here is that the company will offer you a discount if you book more than one trip with it. It is a highly recommended outfit for the dolphin swim since it is the company's real passion, but other companies might be better for whale-watching and manta ray trips.

SPORTFISHING

The **sportfishing** around the Big Island's Kona Coast ranges from excellent to outstanding. The area is legendary for its marlin fishing, but there are other fish in the sea. The best time of year for big blues is July-September; August is the optimal month. Rough seas can keep boats in for a few days during December and early January, but by February the waters have calmed. A large fleet of charter boats with skilled captains and tested crews stands ready to take you out on the water. Most of the island's 80 charter boats are berthed at Honokohau Harbor off Highway 19, about midway between downtown Kailua and Kona airport. When the big fish are brought in, they're weighed at the fuel dock, usually around 11:30am and 3:30pm.

There is some correlation between the amount you pay for your charter or tour and the experience you have. When booking a tour, check if there is a minimum number of passengers required if you are signing up for a shared boat. Not all boats have the shared option, instead requiring you to charter the entire boat. Also, for larger companies that have multiple boats and captains, you might want to check what boat/captain you'll be joining and what their success rate is out at sea. If you visit **Honokohau Harbor** (on Kealakehe Pkwy. off Hwy. 19 between mile markers 97 and 98) and walk around the dock, you'll surely find someone eager to get you onto their boat early the next morning. Here are some places to get started for booking your fishing excursion.

Several charters now offer online bookings, among them *The Silky* (808/938-0706, www.silkysportfishing.com) and *Sea Wife II*

(808/329-1806, seawifecharters.com, shared charter $109 per person for 4 hours). **Bite Me** (808/936-3442, www.bitemesportfishing.com) is a well-known corporate option, with many boats and captains, and the family-run *The Camelot* (www.camelotsportfishing.com) is excellent. The latter offers shared-boat options only if others call for the same day (it rarely happens), but charters are reasonably priced, the boat is in good shape, and the family that operates the boat is experienced and boasts a good track record.

BOAT TOURS

Boat tours are more popular during the winter season when whale-watching is at its prime; nevertheless, during off-season an evening (or day) on the water can still be a fun experience, and don't fret—the dolphins are present year-round.

Kailua Bay Charter (Kailua Harbor in front of Courtyard King Kamehameha's Kona Beach Hotel, 808/324-1749, www.konaglassbottomboat.com, 11:30am or 12:30pm daily, $40 adults, $20 children under 12) offers the unique experience of an hour-long glass-bottom boat cruise. It's sort of like snorkeling but on a boat—you get to see wonderful marine life without getting wet. It's a nice way

Boat tours are the best way to watch the sunset.

to see coral and tropical fish—and an especially easy way to show young children what lies beneath the ocean—but for the hour-long excursion your money and time might be better used elsewhere, since at times it can be difficult to actually see anything from above the glass.

What is most notable about **Body Glove Cruises** (75-5629 Kuakini Hwy., check in at Kailua Pier, 800/551-8911, www.

bodyglovehawaii.com, 7am-5pm daily) is that it can accommodate wheelchairs on the boat. Body Glove will also accommodate gluten-free and vegan dietary restrictions with 48 hours' notice. Its historical dinner cruise ($118 adults, $88 children) includes a full dinner, one complimentary cocktail, live entertainment, and a narrated tour of historical sites on the coast. A lunchtime cruise option also is available.

Hiking and Biking

HIKING

If serious **hiking** is what you're looking for, you'll want to visit other regions of the island. Instead, the Kona area offers a lot of moderate trails that are almost always the means to getting to some awesome beach.

For instance, you can hike to **Captain Cook Monument** via the inland Ka'awaloa Trail. It's not the most exciting hike ever, but the destination is the goal. The trail starts on Napo'opo'o Road just 500 feet below where it drops off Highway 11 (between mile markers 110 and 111). Look for a group of three coconut trees right near a telephone pole. The trailhead will be obvious, as it is worn there. The round-trip hike is nearly four miles. The descent will take you 60-90 minutes, with a much longer return to the top. While on the trail, if you see any side paths, remember to always keep to the left. Please note that this is a not an easy hike (look for a sign near the trailhead that explains the risks of this particular trek). Wear proper footwear and bring lots of water.

If you are looking for something more organized, try **Hawaii Forest and Trail** (74-5035B Queen Ka'ahumanu Hwy./Hwy. 19, 808/331-8505, www.hawaii-forest.com, 7am-5pm Sun., 7am-6pm Mon.-Sat.). Although their headquarters is in the heart of Kona, the tours are outside this region, mainly to Kohala and Volcano for activities such as **bird-watching.**

BIKING

Home to the famous Ironman World Championship, Kona takes **biking** seriously. Highway 19 is an ideal ride: smooth and flat and uninterrupted for many miles. On any given day you'll see many serious bikers riding along the highway, sometimes faster than the cars. Some areas have semi-designated bike lanes (the lane will be marked for part of the road, but not the entire way; many bike riders end up on the gravel road next to the paved road). Check out PATH (www.pathhawaii. org) to learn more about efforts in Hawaii to develop bike lanes.

Since Kona is a bike town, there are many shops that build custom bikes for elite athletes. If you're just looking for a rental, visit **Cycle Station** (73-5619 Kauhola St., 808/327-0087, www.cyclestationhawaii. com or www.konabikerentals.com, 10am-6pm Mon.-Fri., 10am-5pm Sat., $30-75/day). The website has an extensive list of what bikes are available, ranging from hybrid to luxury bikes; however, bikes cannot be reserved online (you need to call or email the shop). Another shop with online booking options is **Bike Works** (74-5583 Luhia St., 808/326-2453, http://bikeworkskona.com, 9am-6pm Mon.-Sat., 10am-4pm Sun., $40-60). Discounts are offered for longer rentals, making this company a good option for a multiday bike trip around the island.

Food

ALI'I DRIVE: KAILUA AND KEAUHOU

While there are many restaurants on Ali'i Drive, most of them cater to tourists and offer poor service. So beware: While a crowded restaurant usually is a sign of high quality, that's not necessarily the case on Ali'i Drive.

The only Indian restaurant on the island, **Kamana Kitchen** (75-5770 Ali'i Dr., Kailua, 808/326-7888, 11am-9:30pm daily, $12-22) is American-style Indian food. The patio area provides an ideal place to watch the sunset. The usual dishes you'd spot at your favorite Indian restaurant on the Mainland also are here: tandoori chicken, lamb curry, naan—with only a few choices of fish dishes. It serves beer and wine, with happy hour prices in effect from 3pm to 5pm.

With a great oceanfront view (the majority of seating is outside), **Island Lava Java** (75-5799 Ali'i Dr. next to the Coconut Grove shopping area, Kailua, 808/327-2161, www.islandlavajava.com, breakfast 6:30am-9:30am, lunch 9:30am-5pm, dinner 5pm-9pm daily, coffee anytime, $12-30) keeps busy. In fact, sometimes it's hard to get a table even at 7am for breakfast; luckily, it offers reservations through Open Table. The restaurant's service can be slow, but the food is consistently good and the portions are large. The non-breakfast cuisine is mostly pizzas, salads, and burgers, and the sandwiches are highly recommended.

Humpy's Big Island Alehouse (75-5815 Ali'i Dr., Kailua, 808/324-2337, www.humpyskona.com, 11am-2am Mon.-Fri., 8am-2am Sat., 9am-2am Sun., happy hour 3pm-6pm daily, $13-20) is the second location of an Anchorage mainstay. Humpy's is where to go to watch sports, to drink, and to eat breakfast. At night this place gets packed upstairs, where sometimes there is a live band. Downstairs is a bit calmer and cooler, and you can enjoy drinks on the patio facing the ocean. Lunch and dinner are good enough, with a menu featuring the usual bar food. The real winner here is weekend breakfast, perfectly paired with football watching. The blackened halibut Benedict is fantastic.

Right on the oceanfront, **Huggo's** (75-5828 Kahakai Rd., entrance off of Ali'i Dr.,

Keep an eye on the action on Ali'i Drive from Humpy's Big Island Alehouse.

Kailua, 808/329-1493, www.huggos.com, dinner 5:30pm-9pm Sun.-Thurs., 5:30pm-10pm Fri.-Sat., brunch 10am-1pm Sun., $15-37) is a great spot if you're looking for a romantic dinner or just cocktails (try getting there for the sunset). Huggo's has one of the best and most innovative mixologists on the island. The restaurant hasn't changed the menu in quite a while, offering simple dishes plated to look elegant. The fish, especially the fresh catch of the day ($36) cooked in different ways, is recommended given the restaurant's close relationship with local fishers. Huggo's has parking in a small lot right in front of the restaurant.

Essentially right in front of Huggo's, **Basik Café** (75-5831 Kahakai Rd., entrance off of Ali'i Dr., Kailua, 808/238-0184, www.basikacai.com, 7am-4pm Mon.-Fri., 8am-4pm Sat.-Sun., $6-13) has a few stools at the second-story bar overlooking the ocean. The hardest part of breakfast is picking just one antioxidant-packed bowl to try. The small (not even the large!) acai bowls and smoothies are large enough to fill two like-minded eaters.

With at least a dozen variations of fish, seasonings, sauces, and the make-your-own option, **Da Poke Shack** (76-6246 Ali'i Dr., Kailua, 808/329-7653, http://dapokeshack.com, 11am-6pm Sun.-Thurs., 11am-7pm Fri.-Sat.) is a *poke* dream come true. If you're not sure what to get, the friendly staff will let you sample as many varieties as you need to convince yourself that *poke* is for you. There isn't really anywhere to sit here, but it's not that kind of place. Grab a to-go container and bring it with you to the beach.

In the Keauhou Shopping Center, **Bianelli's Gourmet Pizza and Pasta** (808/322-0377, http://bianellis.com, 3pm-9pm Mon.-Sat., $20 for large pizza) is notable for its signature pink sauce, a white wine mushroom sauce mixed with marinara pasta sauce. If you happen to be in the area and hungry weekdays 5pm-6:30pm, try **Kenichi Pacific** (808/322-6400, www.kenichihawaii.com) for an excellent happy hour of half-price sushi and drink specials. On Saturdays stop by the **Keauhou**

Parking on Ali'i Drive

Parking is no fun on Ali'i Drive. But luckily, it's probably the only place on Hawai'i where you can't find parking. There are very few spaces on the actual street itself and only a handful of free public lots, as well as the option to pay for parking. If you are spending a night on the town, try the Coconut Grove parking lot via Kuakini Highway (it's the one with Outback Steakhouse). Usually parking is plentiful there and you can avoid the slow nighttime traffic of Ali'i Drive.

Farmers Market (8am-noon) near the movie theater and Longs Drugs.

Near Ali'i Drive

If you just landed at the Kona airport or are about to take a stroll around Kaloko-Honokohau National Historical Park, **Pine Tree Café** (70-4040 Hulikoa St., Kailua, 808/327-1234, 6am-8pm daily, $4-14) is the restaurant for you: It's quick, it's cheap, it's local food (remember that "local" on the island doesn't mean locally sourced). Breakfast includes 10 different kinds of omelets and classics like *loco moco* and Spam *musabi*. Plate lunches ($10.95) such as chicken katsu and kalbi ribs come with rice or fries and mac salad or green salad. The indoor seating area is a bit reminiscent of dorm life, but you'll be in and out of here within a half hour, so the ambience doesn't matter much.

A craft beer lover's fantasy, **Kona Brewing Company** (75-5629 Kuakini Hwy., 808/334-2739, http://konabrewingco.com, 11am-9pm Sun.-Thurs., 11am-10pm Fri.-Sat., happy hour 3pm-6pm Mon.-Fri., $5 brewery tours 10:30am and 3pm daily, $9-18) offers not only supreme beer on tap, but also good food. The "brew your own" pizza allows you to pick your toppings and sauces, and there are fish and salad options (although the salads sound much better on the menu than they appear in person). The restaurant can get crowded on the weekends, so call ahead or expect to wait for a bit. If you're going to be in town a while, pick up a growler (full growler $22, refill $13.50, 20 percent off 5pm-7pm daily) and save some money on beer.

A must-try spot for *poke* lovers, the owner of ★ **Umeke's Poke Bowls** (75-143 Hualalai Rd. #105., 808/329-3050, www.umekespoke808.com, 10am-7pm Mon.-Sat., $10-25) won the Sam Choy Poke Contest two years in a row. You could order teriyaki beef or kalua pork—but why would you? Instead, order a container (or six) filled with the various kinds of *poke* ($16.99 per pound), from spicy ahi to avocado seasoned, grab a fresh Kona-grown mamaki leaf iced tea (the ginger or cinnamon flavors), and head outside to the picnic tables to enjoy the best *poke* around. If you're interested in more of a sit-down experience, try Umeke's location in the industrial area near Target.

This is old-school Kona at its finest: A great family restaurant, **Jackie Rey's Ohana Grill** (75-5995 Kuakini Hwy., Kailua, 808/327-0209, www.jackiereys.com, lunch 11am-2pm Mon.-Fri., appetizers 2pm-5pm Mon.-Fri., happy hour 3pm-5pm Mon.-Fri., dinner 5pm-9pm daily, lunch $12-16, dinner $16-32) has a well-deserved reputation for excellence. The restaurant itself has a casual atmosphere with butcher paper lining the tables (and crayons for coloring), but the food is consistently good and the service usually attentive. Most dishes are either fish or meat served in a way that makes them local style—either by including fruit salsas or macadamia nuts or local sweet potatoes. A favorite of mine is the *mochiko*-crusted fish (*mochiko* is sweet rice flour). There is a children's menu available as well as a full wine list. If you like cocktails, try the off-menu Ling Mui martini (*li hing mui,* a salted dried plum, is a specialty flavoring in Hawaii).

Markets

Kailua has one of the larger locations of **Island Naturals Market and Deli** (74-5487 Kaiwi St., Kailua, 808/326-1122, www.islandnaturals.com, 7:30am-8pm Mon.-Sat., 9am-7pm Sun.), a local chain of natural foods stores. It has a coffee and smoothie bar as well as an excellent hot-food bar. Beer and wine (nonorganic and organic varieties) are available and on sale for 20 percent off every Friday.

CAPTAIN COOK AREA: SOUTH KONA

The best barbecue on the island, **Big Jake's Island BBQ** (Hwy. 11 near mile marker 106, *mauka* side, Honaunau, 808/328-1227, 11am-6pm Mon.-Sat., $7-12) will make you feel like you're in Memphis. The portions are huge, mouthwatering, and slow cooked on local keawe wood. The plates all come with rice, coleslaw, and beans. For Hawaiian fusion, try the barbecue bowls of pulled chicken or pork over rice. There is only outdoor picnic-style seating, so it's not the best place to be if it's raining. BYOB is encouraged and you can grab a beer from the store next door. Call ahead because hours vary.

You might not know what lau lau is, but ★ **Kaaloa's Super J's** (Hwy. 11 near mile marker 107, *makai* side, Captain Cook, 808/328-9566, 10am-6:30pm daily, $10, cash only) will teach you what it is and how it's done right. Yes, it's like you're eating lunch in your auntie's house and that might feel a bit weird for some people, but Super J's true Hawaiian home cooking offers the best lau lau on the island. The meal comes with rice, mac salad, and lomi lomi salad (tomato and salmon salad—like a salsa). Food Network's Guy Fieri has stopped by here—meaning Super J's is now on the foodie tour—but don't let that stop you from getting some of the best (and cheapest) local food you'll have on the Big Island.

★ **Mi's Italian Bistro** (81-6372 Mamalahoa Hwy. between mile markers 110 and 111, *mauka* side, Kealakekua, 808/323-3880, www.misitalianbistro.com, 11am-9pm daily, reservations a must, $18-35) is one of the better restaurants on the island. Even though the strip mall location doesn't seem ideal, the restaurant itself feels quaint and romantic. Service is attentive. The chef ensures that you order the perfect dish and pair it with the right wine. For appetizers, try the marinated beets with candied macadamia nuts. The mains come in good-size portions. Try a dish with local veal or beef, but save room for the award-winning tiramisu or flourless chocolate torte.

A good foodie choice is **Annie's Island Fresh Burgers** (79-7460 Mamalahoa Hwy./Hwy. 11 between mile markers 112 and 113, 808/324-6000, www.anniesislandfreshburgers.com, Kealakekua, 11am-8pm daily, happy hour 3pm-5pm, $15). The meat is local, the salads have local organic lettuce, and local vine-ripened tomatoes, and there are vegan options in addition to the numerous hamburgers with all kinds of toppings and savory sauces. The french fries are a must. Beer is available on draft.

The outdoor beer garden of ★ **Rebel Kitchen** (79-7399 Mamalahoa Hwy. between mile markers 113 and 114, *mauka* side, Kainaliu, 808/322-0616, www.rebelkitchen.com, 11am-8pm daily, $10-16) likely will catch your eye, as it's often packed at night and on weekends. The menu isn't huge, but it doesn't need to be because what it offers is fresh and fast. Most importantly, the prices are more reasonable when you compare them to similar offerings in the Kona and Kohala resort areas. Beer and wine are available.

An institution in town, **Teshima's Restaurant** (79-7251 Mamalahoa Hwy./Hwy. 11 between mile markers 113 and 114, *mauka* side, Kainaliu, 808/322-9140, www.teshimarestaurant.com, 6:30am-1:45pm and 5pm-9pm daily, $8-20) has been serving it up the same for years and it works well. It's a casual Japanese-style diner run for generations by the Teshima family, who opened it as a general store in 1929 and then a restaurant in 1940. Get a bento box ($9), to go or to stay. It comes with meat, egg roll, fried fish, and additional sides. Meals from fish to teriyaki beef come with a lot of extras, ensuring that you'll leave completely satisfied.

Kohala

Look for ★ to find recommended
sights, activities, dining, and lodging.

Highlights

★ **Hamakua Macadamia Nut Factory:**
Nibble on macadamia nuts of every variety imaginable while you watch the workings of the factory (page 449).

★ **Pololu Valley Lookout and Beach:**
This view of the coastline is spectacular. It's worth driving to the road's end and simply staring for a few minutes, or taking a steep hike down to the secluded beach (page 450).

★ **Puako Tide Pools:** Teeming with sealife, this watery wonderland offers some of the best snorkeling and diving on the island (page 453).

★ **Hapuna Beach State Recreation Area:** With pristine white sands and turquoise waters perfect for snorkeling, bodyboarding, and swimming, this is one of the best beaches on the island (page 453).

★ **Spencer Beach Park:** a favorite for families, this beach is a comfortable camping spot with facilities, shade, and sand (page 454).

★ **Mahukona Beach Park:** Here you'll find an underwater treasure of ruins from the plantation days—a good opportunity for beginning snorkelers (page 454).

The Kohala district, also known as the Gold Coast, is the peninsular thumb in the northwestern portion of the Big Island.

At its tip is Upolu Point, only 30 miles from Maui across the 'Alenuihaha Channel. Kohala was the first section of the Big Island to rise from beneath the sea. The long-extinct volcanoes of the Kohala Mountains running down its spine have been reduced by time and the elements from lofty, ragged peaks to rounded domes of 5,000 feet or so. Kohala is divided into North and South Kohala. North Kohala, an area of dry coastal slopes, former sugar lands, a string of sleepy towns, and lush and deeply incised valleys, forms the northernmost tip of the island. South Kohala boasts *the* most beautiful swimming beaches on the Big Island, along with world-class hotels and resorts.

South Kohala is a region of contrast. It's dry, hot, tortured by wind, and scoured by countless old lava flows. The predominant land color here is black, and this is counterpointed by scrubby bushes and scraggly trees, a seemingly semiarid wasteland. This was an area that the ancient Hawaiians seemed to have traveled through to get somewhere else, yet Hawaiians did live here—along the coast—and numerous archaeological sites dot the coastal plain. Still, South Kohala is stunning with its palm-fringed white-sand pockets of beach, luxury resorts, green-landscaped golf courses, colorful planted flowers, and inviting deep-blue water. You come here to settle into a sedate resort community, to be pampered and pleased by the finer things that await at luxury resorts that are destinations in and of themselves. Of the many scattered villages that once dotted this coast, only two remain: Puako, now a sleepy beach hideaway, and Kawaihae, one of the principal commercial deepwater ports on the island. In Kawaihae, at the base of the North Kohala peninsula, Highway 19 turns east and coastal Route 270, known as the Akoni Pule Highway, heads north along the coast.

North Kohala was the home of Kamehameha the Great. From this fiefdom he launched his conquest of all the islands. The shores of North Kohala are rife with historical significance, and with beach parks where

Previous: the view from Pololu Valley; Puako Petroglyph Archaeological Preserve. **Above:** bay at Spencer Beach Park.

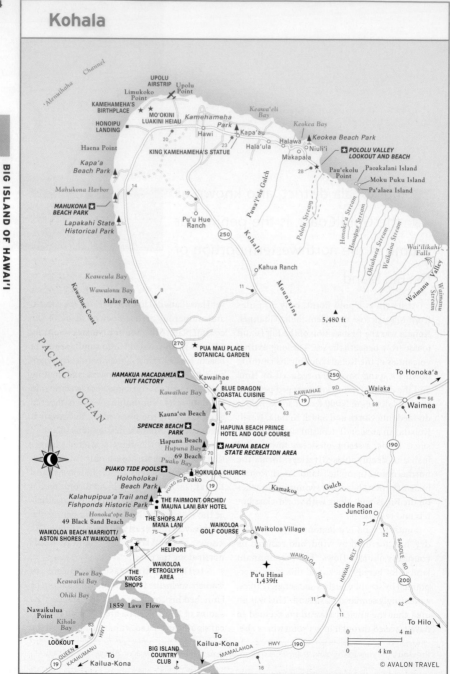

© AVALON TRAVEL

few ever go. Among North Kohala's cultural treasures is Lapakahi State Historical Park, a must-stop attraction offering a walk-through village and "touchable" exhibits that allow you to become actively involved in Hawaii's traditional past. Northward is Kamehameha's birthplace and within walking distance is Mo'okini Luakini, one of the oldest *heiau* in Hawaii and still actively ministered by the current generation of a long line of *kahuna*.

Hawi, the main town in North Kohala, was a sugar settlement whose economy turned sour when the last of the seven sugar mills in the area stopped operations in the mid-1970s. Hawi is making a big comeback, along with this entire northern shore, which has seen an influx of small boutiques and art shops. The main coastal road winds in and out of numerous small gulches, crosses some one-lane bridges, and ends at Pololu Valley lookout, where you can overlook one of the premier taro-growing valleys of old Hawaii. A walk down the steep *pali* into this valley is the Hawaii you imagined from movies and reruns of *Lost*.

ORIENTATION
South Kohala: Resort Area

Distinctive for its abundance of large resorts and rental properties, white-sand beaches lined with coconut trees, and its proximity to the airport, the Waikoloa and Mauna Lani areas are geared to meet the needs of tourists. This small area holds enough beaches and restaurants to keep you occupied for days. With three shopping centers located within the resorts, you really never have to leave the premises.

This coast's fabulous beaches are known not only for swimming and surfing, but for tide pooling and awe-inspiring sunsets as well. There are little-disturbed and rarely visited archaeological sites, expressive petroglyph fields, and the best-preserved portion of the Ala Kahakai National Historic Trail. Note: The Waikoloa Beach Resort area *(makai)* is drastically different than the Waikoloa Village area *(mauka)*. Waikoloa Village is where many

individuals who work at the resorts live. You won't find beaches there!

Kawaihae

Kawaihae is a pass-through port town with a gas station and some restaurants worthy of a stop. Some dive outfitters are based out of the harbor; they often take their clients to the waters of South Kohala or Kona, although the nearby waters are just as nice and are less crowded.

Hawi to the End of the Road

Located on the northwest tip of the island, these communities are nearly perfect small towns offering walkable main streets filled with excellent restaurants, art galleries, and coffee shops. The beaches here are rocky but offer breathtaking views of the coast and, if you're lucky, of Maui too. Unlike the southern part of the Kohala district, northern Kohala doesn't look like a lava-filled landscape from outer space. Instead, although it is quite dry in this region, there are gorgeous large trees providing shade from the sun. Spend the day strolling the streets of Hawi, explore the backroads and waters of Kohala on an ATV or kayak, watch the sunset at Pololu Valley, and then finish your day with dinner at one of the many foodie restaurants in Hawi or dancing to live music at the nearby Blue Dragon Restaurant in Kawaihae.

PLANNING YOUR TIME

The only reason to plan your time in Kohala is so that you remember to leave that perfect beach you've been lounging on for days. The afternoons in Kohala can cloud over, so plan your day accordingly. If you are spending an entire week in Kohala, as many do, take the time to explore the assorted beaches, such as the well-regarded Hapuna Beach State Recreation Area or a resort beach, which you are free to visit because all beaches must have public access points, even for nonguests. Experienced divers and snorkelers should head to the Puako tide pools for a multitude of sealife or to Mahukona Beach Park to discover

South Kohala

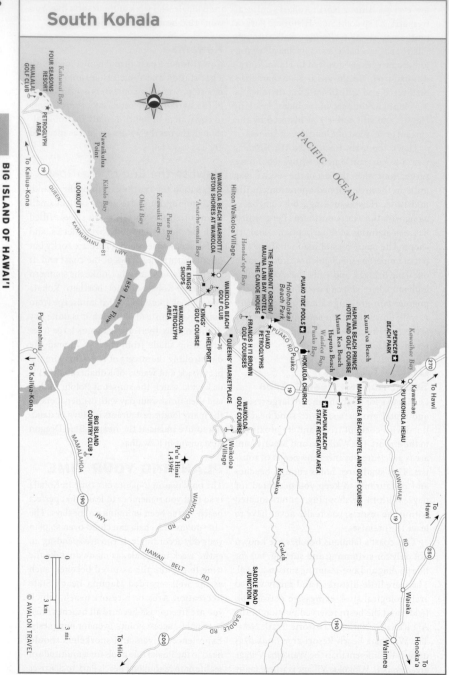

© AVALON TRAVEL

North Kohala

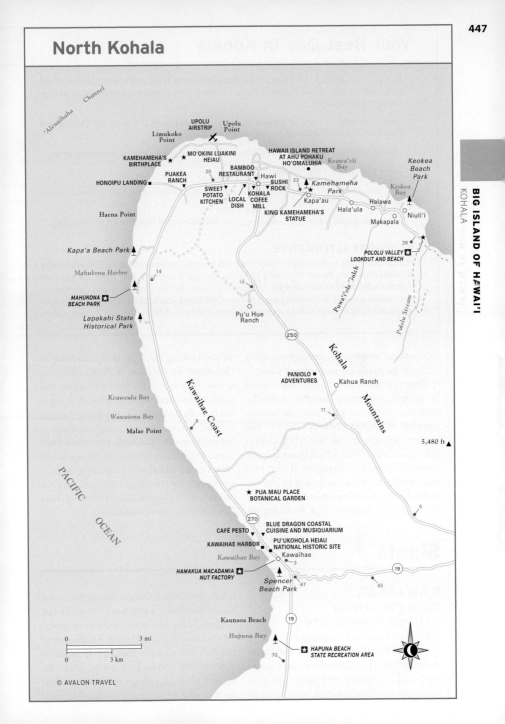

'Alenuihaha Channel

Limukoko Point

UPOLU AIRSTRIP
Upolu Point

KAMEHAMEHA'S BIRTHPLACE ★
MO'OKINI LUAKINI HEIAU

HAWAII ISLAND RETREAT AT AHU POHAKU HO'OMALUHIA

Keawa'eli Bay

Keokea Beach Park

PUAKEA RANCH
20
BAMBOO RESTAURANT
Hawi

HONOIPU LANDING ■

SWEET POTATO KITCHEN
LOCAL DISH
KOHALA COFFEE MILL

SUSHI ROCK
23
★ Kamehameha Park

Kapa'au

Keokea Bay

Halawa

Hala'ula
Niuli'i

Haena Point

KING KAMEHAMEHA'S STATUE

Makapala

Kapa'a Beach Park ▲

28 ★

POLOLU VALLEY LOOKOUT AND BEACH

Mahukona Harbor
14

13

Puwa'i'ole Gulch

Pololu Stream

MAHUKONA BEACH PARK ■

Pu'u Hue Ranch

Lapakahi State Historical Park ▲

250

Kohala

Keaweula Bay

Wawaionu Bay

Malae Point

8

Kawaihae Coast

PANIOLO ADVENTURES ■
Kahua Ranch

11

Mountains

5,480 ft ▲

PACIFIC OCEAN

★ PUA MAU PLACE BOTANICAL GARDEN

5

270

BLUE DRAGON COASTAL CUISINE AND MUSIQUARIUM

CAFÉ PESTO ▼

KAWAIHAE HARBOR ■
PU'UKOHOLA HEIAU NATIONAL HISTORIC SITE

Kawaihae Bay
Kawaihae

3

19

HAMAKUA MACADAMIA NUT FACTORY ■

Spencer Beach Park
67
63

Kaunaoa Beach

19

Hupuna Bay

★ HAPUNA BEACH STATE RECREATION AREA

70

0   3 mi

0   3 km

© AVALON TRAVEL

Your Best Day in Kohala

- Start your day on the **Ala Kahakai National Historic Trail.** Pick a point on the trail and go for a short walk, leaving plenty of time to stop at any number of beaches (especially the secret ones).

- Stop to sample all sorts of flavors of macadamia nuts and brittle at the **Hamakua Macadamia Nut Factory** on your way north to Hawi.

- Visit the galleries and shops in **Hawi** and eat lunch at one of the excellent restaurants in town.

- Try an adventure like **ziplining.**

- Drive to the lookout at **Pololu Valley** to watch the sunset and witness one of the best views on the island.

- Finish your day with dinner and dancing at the **Blue Dragon Restaurant** in Kawaihae.

RAINY-DAY ALTERNATIVE

Most people come to Kohala and never leave the beach, so there aren't many daytime indoor activities in the area. Thus, if it's raining in Kohala, take a peek to the south to Kona and then look *mauka* toward Waimea and see if you can spot any clouds in either direction—and then head to where there are none. If it's raining everywhere on the island, your best bet is to drive the 15 minutes to nearby Waimea or Kona to spend some time inside one of the museums or movie theaters.

an unofficial underwater museum of debris left from the plantation and railroad days.

There are some great trails best visited in the early morning or late afternoon—the short Kalahupipua'a Trail near the Mauna Lani Bay Hotel, the Malama Trail to view ancient petroglyphs, or the Ala Kahakai National Historic Trail, which spans most of the length of the Kohala region. If you need more breaks from the beach, hop in the car and take a scenic drive up the coast (from Highway 19 to Highway 270), watching for whales peeking out from the ocean (only in the winter) on your way to Pololu Valley for sunset. Even though the distance is short, you can take your time with this drive, stopping at the Hamakua Macadamia Nut Factory on the way and then wandering through the shops in Hawi. Or, use the afternoon for several short jaunts to the north for some of the best lunch places on the island or for ziplining the canopy or even for traveling to Waimea, which is only about 20 minutes away from the Kohala Coast and has cooler weather.

Sights

KAWAIHAE
Pu'ukohola Heiau National Historic Site

While Pu'uhonua O Honaunau is the "city of refuge," **Pu'ukohola Heiau National Historic Site** (Hwy. 270 between mile markers 2 and 3, 808/882-7218, www.nps.gov/puhe, gate hours 7:45am-4pm, park open 24 hours, free), which means "the temple on the hill of the whale," was a place of war. Today, it is one of the best-preserved and most significant temple sites in Hawaii. A walk around the park will take you about 30-45 minutes. Call 808/206-7056 for a self-guided cell phone audio tour or ask a ranger in the visitors center for a tour ($2 suggested donation) if one is available. You can also call ahead to reserve a tour. If you're bringing kids, ask the ranger for the Junior Ranger activity book, which comes with a free pin.

Visit early in the morning for the best chance of seeing blacktip reef sharks. Also keep a lookout for **birds,** as the park ranger guarantees you will see at least 10 different kinds during your visit.

★ Hamakua Macadamia Nut Factory

At the **Hamakua Macadamia Nut Factory** (Maluokalani St., off Hwy. 270 between mile markers 4 and 5, 808/882-1690, www.hawnut.com, 9am-5pm daily), imagine a room full of macadamia nuts of every variety imaginable, all available to sample for free. Candy corn, brittles, and coffee can be sampled as well. If you're planning on purchasing some nuts to take home, the prices are comparable to the local grocery stores. Or if you really love mac nuts, buy one of the four-pound bags—a good deal for about $40 depending on the variety.

Pua Mau Place Botanical Garden

This 12-acre garden doesn't get much traffic, but it's quite a sight for plant enthusiasts. The one-hour self-guided tour through **Pua Mau Place Botanical Garden** (Ala Kahua Dr., off Hwy. 270 near mile marker 6, 808/882-0888, www.puamau.org, 9am-4pm daily, adults $15, seniors $13, children 6-16 $5) takes you through the landscaped garden, an unlikely location here in arid Kohala. The focus is on flowering plants, ones that thrive and flourish in a windy and arid environment. Some of the showiest are the hibiscus, plumeria, and date palm. The garden is open for private functions such as weddings.

HAWI TO THE END OF THE ROAD
Lapakahi State Historical Park

Want to experience Hawaii as early settlers did 600 years ago? A visit to **Lapakahi State Historical Park** (Hwy. 270 between mile markers 13 and 14, 8am-4pm daily, gate closes 3:30pm, free), a reconstructed historical village, is a good place for kids and history buffs. The self-guided tour is one of the better ones on the island because the pamphlet available at the small visitors center in the parking lot is user friendly, and the trail is well marked and maintained. The trail, made up of two 0.5-mile loops, takes about 45 minutes. There are numerous home sites along the wood-chip trail. Particularly interesting to kids are exhibits of games like *konane* (Hawaiian checkers) and *'ulu maika* (a form of bowling using stones) that the children are encouraged to try.

Upolu Airport Road Scenic Drive to Kohala Historical Sites State Monument

At mile marker 20, turn off Highway 270 down a one-lane road to Upolu airstrip. You'll know you're on Upolu Airport Road when you see the wind farm on your right. You really need a Jeep to do the scenic drive. Follow the road until it reaches a dead end at the runway. Turn left onto a *very* rough dirt road, which may not be passable. This entire area is one of the most rugged and isolated on the Big Island, with wide windswept fields, steep sea cliffs, and pounding surf. Pull off at any likely spot along the road and keep your eyes peeled for signs of cavorting humpback whales, which frequent this coast November-May. After bumping down the road for about two miles (count on at least 45 minutes if you walk), turn and walk five minutes uphill to gain access to **Mo'okini Luakini Heiau.**

In 1962, Mo'okini Heiau was declared a National Historic Landmark. Legend says that the first temple at Mo'okini was built as early as AD 480. This incredible date indicates that Mo'okini must have been built immediately upon the arrival of the first Polynesian explorers, who many scholars maintain arrived in large numbers a full two centuries later.

When you visit the *heiau* (temple), pick up a brochure from a box at the entrance; if none is available, a signboard nearby gives general information. This was once a closed temple for the *ali'i* only, but the *kapu* was lifted in 1977 so that others may visit and learn. Be respectful, as this temple is still in use, and stay on the designated paths, which are cordoned off by woven rope. Along the short wall closest to the sea is a "scalloped" altar where recent offerings of flowers are often seen. Inside the *heiau* are remnants of enclosures used by the *ali'i* and space set aside for temple priests.

A few minutes' walk south of the *heiau* along this coastal dirt track is **Kamehameha's birthplace,** called **Kamehameha 'Akahi 'Aina Hanau.** Rather unpretentious for being of such huge significance, the entrance to the area is at the back side, away from the sea. Inside the low stone wall, which always seems to radiate heat, are some large boulders believed to be the actual "birthing stones" where the high chieftess Kekuiapoiwa, wife of the warrior *ali'i* Keoua Kupuapaikalananinui, gave birth to Kamehameha sometime around 1758. There is much debate about the actual year and place of Kamehameha's birth, and some place it elsewhere in 1753, but it was to the Mo'okini Heiau nearby that he was taken for his birth rituals, and it was there that he performed his religious rituals until he completed Pu'u Kohola Heiau down the coast at Kawaihae around 1791.

Together, Mo'okini Heiau, King Kamehameha's birthplace, and several other nearby historic sites make up the seven-acre **Kohala Historical Sites State Monument.** In 2005, Kamehameha Schools bought a large tract of land surrounding Kamehameha's birthplace and Mo'okini Luakini Heiau in order to protect the environs from residential and commercial development that might disturb the sacred nature of these cultural sites.

Note: You'll have to return to Highway 270 the way you came because the road is closed off on the south end (but there is a small dirt turnaround there).

★ Pololu Valley Lookout and Beach

If you are looking for the *Lost* experience on the Big Island, the **Pololu Valley Lookout and Beach** (Hwy. 270 where the road ends) is it. Park your car in the lot at the end of the highway; grab your bathing suit, tent, some food, and water; and hike the one-mile trail to the beach (about 30 minutes down and 45 minutes up for a novice hiker). If you're not

Lapakahi State Historical Park

interested in the hike, the view itself is worth driving to the road's end and simply staring for a few minutes. If you do walk down, the beach at the bottom has wonderful blackish sand, but the shoreline can be rocky and the waves hit hard depending on the day.

It's about 12 miles from Pololu Valley to Waipi'o Valley, with five deep-cut valleys in between, including the majestic Waimanu,

the largest. It's not possible to drive to Waipi'o here, but a super hiker could likely make it between the two.

Pitch your tent on top of one of the small green hills and it's likely that you will have the place to yourself, or you won't notice if anyone else is there. There are no facilities (even at the parking lot), so make sure to bring enough food and water for your visit.

Beaches

SOUTH KOHALA: RESORT AREA
Anaeho'omalu Bay (A Bay)

A long, narrow strip of inviting salt-and-pepper sand, **Anaeho'omalu Bay,** or **A Bay** (Hwy. 19 at mile marker 76, 6am-7pm daily), fronts hotels such as the Waikoloa Beach Marriott Resort and Hilton Waikoloa. Enter through the Waikoloa Beach Resort area and park behind Queens' MarketPlace. Although the beach is used by the resort hotels, it is accessible for nonguests via a huge parking lot (where the Hele-On buses wait). All the standard water sports are possible here, and rentals for equipment are available from a kiosk

in front of the Marriott. Also in front of the Marriott are lounge chairs that are open to the public. The public restrooms and showers are near the parking lot.

Holoholokai Beach Park and Malama Trail

A shaded park with a grassy area, **Holoholokai Beach Park** (Holoholokai Beach Park Rd., daily 6:30am-6:30pm daily) makes a nice place to picnic or to fish away the afternoon. There are better places to access to the ocean, but you might want to jump in after walking the Malama Trail to view the **Puako Petroglyphs,** approximately 3,000

Pololu Valley Lookout

individual rock carvings considered some of the finest and oldest in Hawaii. The trail is 1.4 miles round-trip (about a 45-minute walk), but avoid going midday when the unshaded trail can be extremely hot. A good walker can do the trail in slippahs, but others may want to wear closed-toe shoes. If you're short on time, just walk the first part of the paved trail (about 5 minutes from the parking lot) to view some of the more photogenic petroglyphs. Bathrooms and drinking fountains are available in the parking lot. To get there, from Highway 19 (between mile markers 73 and 74) turn onto Mauna Lani Drive, turn right at the first turn on the roundabout to North Kaniku Drive, and then turn right onto Holoholokai Beach Park Road.

Kalahupipua'a Trail and Fishponds Historic Park

The short, peaceful, paved **Kalahupipua'a Trail** (Mauna Lani Bay Hotel, 6:30am-6:30pm daily), which can be connected with the larger shoreline trail system, the **Ala Kahakai National Historic Trail,** passes through ancient fishponds (still stocked with fish) and the Eva Parker Woods Cottage Museum, originally constructed in the 1920s as part of a larger oceanfront estate. To get there, from Highway 19 (between mile markers 73 and 74) turn onto Mauna Lani Drive and gain access through the Mauna Lani Bay Hotel, or for public access follow Mauna Lani Drive and turn left on Pauoa Road; look for the public-access lot on the right side.

If you continue to walk south on the Kalahupipua'a Trail for a few more minutes, you'll end up at **Makaiwa Bay,** a white-sand beach that is a great spot for snorkeling, especially for beginners (the signage is so good here that there is a diagram indicating where to go snorkeling in the water based on your level of expertise). Behind the beach is the Mauna Lani Beach Club (the parking lot is not open to the public before 4:30pm, but you can walk there via the trail), housing the upscale restaurant **Napua** (1292 S. Kaniku Dr., 808/885-5022, 11am-4pm daily and 5pm-9pm Tue.-Fri., lunch $14-16, dinner $18-40). If you walk through the beach and up the stairs at the end of the beach, you'll be on **Ala Kahakai National Historic Trail,** which passes some amazing-looking homes. You can continue on this scenic path to 49 Black Sand Beach.

49 Black Sand Beach

A little-known, clean and quiet salt-and-pepper sand beach with little shade and calm

ancient fishponds located on the Kalahupipua'a Trail

water, **49 Black Sand Beach** (Honokaope Pl., Mauna Lani Resort Area, 7am-7pm daily) makes for a nice place to get away. The parking lot, including shower and bathroom facilities, is only a minute away from the sand, making this spot a good place to go if you don't want the hassle of parking and trekking to a beach.

To get there from Highway 19, between mile markers 73 and 74 turn onto Mauna Lani Drive; continue around the roundabout and turn right onto North Kaniku Drive, then left on Honokaope Place. Check in with the security guard to get a beach pass.

69 Beach (Waialea Bay)

The name of the beach is mostly what gets curious onlookers to visit it, but they are usually happy they made the trip. The **69 Beach on Waialea Bay** (Hwy. 19 between mile markers 70 and 71, 7am-7:30pm daily) is pleasant: a long, narrow stretch of white sand, lots of shade, and excellent snorkeling. Restroom and shower facilities are available and there are several picnic areas. This sometimes-crowded beach isn't the best in the area, but you won't be disappointed if you spend an afternoon here.

To get to 69 Beach from Highway 19, between mile markers 70 and 71 turn *makai* onto Puako Beach Drive and take the first right onto old Puako Road and then the first left after that; follow the road into the parking area. Note: Nonresidents must pay a $5 fee to park at the beach; however, the same parking receipt is good for both 69 Beach and Hapuna Beach.

★ Puako Tide Pools

One of the most developed fringing reefs on the island, the **Puako tide pools** (Puako Beach Dr., off Hwy. 19 between mile markers 70 and 71) are an underwater wonderland offering some of the best snorkeling and diving on the island. Once you are in the water, look for submerged lava tubes and garden eels hiding under the sandy ocean bottom. There are no facilities or rental companies located here,

so bring in what you need, including equipment and snacks.

Access is available at several different points along the shorefront, but the easiest point may be right before the road dead-ends; from Highway 19 between mile markers 70 and 71 turn *makai* onto Puako Beach Drive and follow the road through the village—even though there is a "Dead End" sign—and head toward the dead end and turn *makai* into the dirt parking area located right before the "Road Rnds in 500 Ft." sign.

★ Hapuna Beach State Recreation Area

Locals allege that the **Hapuna Beach State Recreation Area** (Hwy. 19 near mile marker 69, 7am-8pm daily) is one of the top beaches in the world, and that assertion might be true. Even on weekdays the large parking lot fills up early as locals and tourists alike rush to this white-sand beach to get a choice spot (especially since there is little shade). The turquoise waters are perfect for snorkeling, bodyboarding, and swimming. There is a lifeguard on duty, and the picnic areas, some of which are shaded, have great views of all the action on the beach. If you forgot your snorkel gear, towels, boogie boards, or chairs, you can rent from the **Three Frogs Café** (on the grassy area near the parking lot, grill 10am-4pm daily, $10, rentals 10am-4pm daily, cash only). The grill offers tacos, hot dogs, fries, shave ice, and fruit smoothies. Note: There is a $5 parking fee for nonresidents that is used for beach conservation. You can use the same parking receipt at nearby 69 Beach.

Kauna'oa Beach

All beaches in Hawaii are public; it's knowing how to access them that is the trick. The Mauna Kea Beach Hotel's beach, **Kauna'oa Beach** (Hwy. 19 near mile marker 68), is another example where you merely have to ask a security guard for a pass to park in the public lot at the hotel. Technically, there are even different bathroom and shower facilities for the public users versus the hotel guests, but since it's the same beach, there is a lot of intermingling, including public use of lounge chairs reserved for guests. Once you're in, you'll want to stay for the entire day. The water is perfect for swimming and there is a long stretch of white sand as well as a grassy area ideal for a picnic or just lounging with a book.

To get to Kauna'oa Beach, from Highway 19 turn *makai* onto Mauna Kea Beach Drive near mile marker 68 and ask the guard if you can have a parking permit for the public beach.

★ Spencer Beach Park

A top family beach and one of the best camping spots on the Big Island (you need a permit), **Spencer Beach Park** (Hwy. 270 between mile markers 2 and 3, 6am-11pm) gets crowded on weekends and holidays. It shares an entrance with Pu'ukohola Heiau National Historic Site. There are picnic pavilions with barbecues, lots of shade, a sandy beach with calm waters, restroom and shower facilities, and a general congenial atmosphere. It's more popular among locals than tourists, probably given the fact that nearby Hapuna Beach provides a more idyllic beach setting.

HAWI TO THE END OF THE ROAD

★ Mahukona Beach Park

There is no sand at this beach; instead, **Mahukona Beach Park** (Hwy. 270 between

Spencer Beach Park

mile markers 14 and 15) is a modern-day ruin. It was a shipping port during the plantation days, and you can still see the decrepit structure of the Hawaii Railroad Company (from 1930) standing in the parking lot. History or archaeology buffs or Instagrammers will want to take a quick detour just to see the modern ruins that are above ground (and snap some selfies).

Water Sports

The Waikoloa resort area and Anaeho'omalu Bay (A Bay) are not as much of an apex of ocean activities as other areas in the region. Each resort tends to offer ocean and beach equipment rental to its guests, and most also offer quick instruction for snorkeling and stand-up paddling. Fees for activities and rentals tend to be higher when purchased through hotels. You'd be better off going directly to the source to get a better price.

DIVING AND SNORKELING

Given that there is a harbor in Kawaihae, it seems like a natural location for **diving** and **snorkeling** tours; however, there isn't much activity here because most tourists prefer Kona. There really is no reason to avoid diving and snorkeling here—in fact, the benefits are that it is less crowded than the Kona Coast and the water is just as full of remarkable marine life.

Those with experience snorkeling or diving should explore the Puako tide pools, one of the most developed fringing reefs on the island. One can spend the entire day surveying sealife. There aren't rental agencies here so it is imperative to rent before you come. Alternatively, Mahukona Beach Park with its shallow water presents a good opportunity for beginners to get their feet wet and discover some nearby underwater treasure (or garbage, depending how you look at it).

If you want to join a tour, **Kohala Divers** (Hwy. 270 in Kawaihae Shopping Center, 808/882-7774, www.kohaladivers.com) has a reputation for good service and quality equipment. Kohala Divers offers a PADI open-water certification course ($530). Experienced divers can book a trip such as the popular two-tank morning charter ($139 per person), a two-tank night dive ($149), or a shorter one-tank dive ($100). Both diving and snorkeling equipment is available to rent.

The other option is **Mauna Lani Sea Adventures** (66-1400 Mauna Lani Dr., 808/885-7883, http://maunalaniseaadventures.com), although it doesn't specialize in scuba diving. For certified divers, two-tank dives with gear ($170) are offered and one-tank night dives ($125) are offered a few times a week depending on interest and must be booked over the phone. PADI-certified courses are also available ($800).

BODYBOARDING, SURFING, AND STAND-UP PADDLEBOARDING

The Kohala Coast is a good place to try out your bodyboarding and stand-up paddling skills because the waves here tend not to be too big or rough. Conversely, these conditions are not ideal for surfing. Experienced surfers head to the beach at Pololu Valley, but you have to really want to surf there since a visit requires carrying your board down (and more importantly, up) the steep trail.

Ocean Sports (Queens' MarketPlace and beach shack on Anaeho'omalu Bay, 808/886-6666, www.hawaiioceansports.com) offers rentals for all your ocean needs. Perhaps one of the best deals is on Sunday, Wednesday, and Friday from 10am to 2pm, when, for $35 per person, you receive unlimited rentals and discounts on the catamaran adventure. This isn't a bad deal considering a stand-up paddleboard rental is usually $50 for an hour. You must return at the end of each hour with your equipment and can only take it out again if no

Mahukona Beach Park

one else is waiting. If you need some help getting started, the shop offers beachboys (who are like lifeguards) to aid you in short classes. Snorkeling is $30 for 45 minutes ($10 for an extra person), and stand-up paddling is $40 for 30 minutes of instruction.

KAYAKING

After years of closure, the Kohala ditch tours are back with **Flumin' Kohala** (55-517 Hawi Rd., 808/933-4294, www.fluminkohala.com, adults $135, children $75). The Kohala Ditch is a 110-year-old system of irrigation tunnels and channels that supplied water to plantations during the heyday of the sugar industry. This three-hour adventure tour, offered four times daily (8am, 9am, 12:15pm, and 1:15pm), takes visitors on a 3-mile kayak float through the ditch system. The float is leisurely, so don't expect anything similar to white-water rafting. This slow-paced tour is led by local guides who share stories of Hawaiian history and folklore. This tour is not good idea for those who identify as claustrophobic, however.

BOAT TOURS

During winter Kawaihae Harbor is a prime location for whale-watching. Leaving from here will save you some time on the road, as this harbor is closer to the majority of the resorts and also tends to be less crowded than Honokohau. Boat trips range from snorkeling and/or diving adventures to whale- and dolphin-watching rides to sunset open-bar cruises.

Extending its monopoly on the water, **Ocean Sports** (Whale Center in Kawaihae Harbor, 61-3657 Akoni Pule Hwy./Hwy. 270, 808/886-6666, www.hawaiioceansports.com) touts a champagne sunset cruise on a sailing catamaran. It is a good deal ($129 adults, $64.50 children, *kama'aina* rates available) for those who like to combine drinking with cruising. The open bar (including a sunset champagne toast) comes with lots of appetizers, and for an extra $25 you can renew your vows on board! The Sunset Sail ($129 adults, $59.50 children) is similar to the champagne cruise, but with less food and no champagne. In summer (April-November), Ocean Sports offers a 3.5-hour morning dolphin snorkel trip ($147 adults, $73.50 children) complete with lunch and an open bar (that it assures is only available after the snorkeling is complete). In winter (December-April) one can combine drinking and whale-watching during the Whales & Cocktails cruise ($119 adults, $59.50 children). Check availability online; the schedules change with the seasons.

Mauna Lani Sea Adventures (66-1400 Mauna Lani Dr., 808/885-7883, http://maunalaniseaadventures.com) similarly has gotten in on the drinking-on-water market with its sunset sails ($99 plus tax adults, $45 plus tax children) that include whale-watching during the winter months.

Hiking and Biking

HIKING

Guided hikes aren't a big business in Kohala because there aren't too many established trails here, but the Kohala Mountains do offer some splendid scenery if you decide to explore on your own or join **Hawaii Forest and Trail** (808/331-8505, www.hawaii-forest.com, adults $179 plus tax, children $129 plus tax). This top-rated tour company offers an all-day hiking experience along the Kohala Ditch trail to Kapoloa Waterfall at the back of Pololu Valley and another hiking trek to other waterfalls in the area. It also takes guests on its six-wheel Pinzgauer vehicle into rugged former sugarcane lands for views of waterfalls and the coast. The hiking portion is pretty minimal (only 1.5 miles), making this tour accessible to anyone comfortable walking that distance over uneven terrain.

The King's Trail

A conglomeration of several trails, the **Ala Kahakai National Historic Trail** system stretching over half the island was formalized in 1847 as a way to increase access for missionaries and the transportation of goods. But even before that time, these trails were the method ancient Hawaiians used to travel the island; they linked together the kingdom of Hawaii's major districts. Thus, the trails present sites of significant events in Hawaiian history, from the arrival of the Polynesians to the islands to the arrival (and subsequent killing) of Captain James Cook in Hawaii. Historically, the trail began in the northern part of Kohala (at Upolu Point) and extended into south Puna (at Waha'ula Heiau). Much of this route is not visible anymore due to modern-day construction and/or lava covering it up.

Nowadays, the trail is most visible and walkable between Kawaihae and Pu'uhonua O Honaunau (south of Captain Cook). The National Park Service is working on improving the usability of these trails, but for now, there is about a 15-mile section that one can easily follow. If you start at Spencer Beach Park, you can follow the trail south along the coast. Another well-marked section starts at the Mauna Kea Beach Hotel, where you can travel south toward Hapuna Beach or north to a secret beach that can only be accessed via the trail. Since the trail is a combination of a historical shore trail and the *ala loa* (king's trail or long trail), you will see different signage depending on where you are (many of the signs read Ala Kahakai, though) and in some places it seems like there are two parallel trails. One of the nicest sections of the trail starts near the Mauna Lani Bay Hotel and Bungalows and takes you through ancient fishponds to some beautiful beaches, and then passes by million-dollar homes. The trail can be easily accessed in sections for a stroll of an hour or two, or you can try a larger portion of the trail from Spencer Beach Park to Hapuna Beach (about three miles one-way) if you are looking for a half-day or a whole-day activity. This route will take you through two desolate hidden beaches (Mau'umae Beach and a beach literally called "secret beach") that make for excellent stops.

BIKING

Highway 19 extending north of the airport provides a nice, flat stretch of road. It's an ideal place to ride fast, and you'll see many serious bikers doing just that. Otherwise, renting a bike simply to ride around the resort area can make for a nice afternoon. Riders wishing to follow the Kona **Ironman route** will want to continue from Highway 19 to Highway 270 north to Hawi to experience the steep climb. Beware: As you travel north on Highway 270 there is not much of a shoulder for bike riding.

For do-it-yourself rentals in the area, **Bikeworks Beach and Sport** (Queens' MarketPlace, 808/836-5000, www.bikeworkshawaii.com, 9:30am-9:30pm daily) has a nice selection of ultra-deluxe road bikes ($75 per day), deluxe bikes ($60), and cruisers ($25) and has compiled a great list of suggested rides on its website.

If you're aching for a guided or group-riding tour, consider **Velissimo Tours** (808/327-0087, http://cyclingdestinations.com/hawaii/cycling-hawaii/, $125-145 per person), which offers four different day trips. Some trips are for beginners, while others are for more experienced riders, like the ride up the Kohala Mountain Range. Both mountain and road bikes are available. Velissimo also offers week-long bicycling tours that include accommodations ($3,200) for those who want to cycle around the entire island.

Adventure Sports

ATV TOURS

ATV Outfitters (Hwy. 270 between mile markers 24 and 25, 808/288-7288, www.atvoutfittershawaii.com, 7am-6pm daily, adults $129-149, children 5-11 $80-249) offers an extreme way to experience the Kohala backcountry. There are three options of varying duration, each available twice daily: a historical tour (1.5 hours), the waterfall and rainforest tour (2 hours), and a deluxe ocean and waterfall adventure (3 hours). Prices vary depending on if you are driving the ATV or if you are merely along for the ride. Drivers with passengers must be at least 25 years old. Each tour will take you to out-of-the-way places along the coast and up into the rainforest on former Kohala sugar plantation land. You'll ride over backroads and fields, through lush gullies to waterfalls, come to the edge of ocean cliffs, or dip down to a pebble beach. These fully equipped machines let you get to places that you wouldn't be able to reach otherwise. Safe and reliable, the four-wheelers are easy to operate even for those who have had no experience on a motorcycle. Helmets, gloves, and goggles are supplied and instruction is given. Wear long pants and closed-toe shoes. Mention the website for a discount; reservations are recommended, as the tours fill up quickly.

ZIPLINING

With an excellent reputation, **Kohala Zipline** (808/331-3620, www.kohalazipline.com, $169 plus tax per adult, $129 plus tax per child) offers the only full-canopy zipline tour on the Big Island. Decide how much of your day you want to spend all strapped up: three hours or a full day. The full-day tour ($249 plus tax per person) includes lunch and waterfall swimming. Tours are offered nearly every half hour from 7:30am to 3pm; if you're on a tight schedule, book ahead of time because tours fill up.

HELICOPTER TOURS

The majority of **helicopter tours** leave from the heliport just south of the Waikoloa resort area or from a heliport next to the Hilo airport. Companies tend to focus on tours to see lava at Hawai'i Volcanoes National Park, and the longer or deluxe tours will circle the island to get a glimpse of Waipi'o Valley and waterfalls in Kohala. These tours are expensive, but if you have the funds do it. People always say that it was their favorite part of the trip—though not people who suffer from motion sickness. Tip: Wear a dark color (like black), otherwise your clothing will be reflected in the helicopter's windows and thus will show up in your photos.

Sunshine Helicopters (808/882-1233 or 800/622-3144, www.sunshinehelicopters.com), one of the larger companies with service on each island, runs a 40-minute Kohala Mountain and Hamakua Valley tour ($169 per person with online discount) and a two-hour Volcano Deluxe tour that circles the island ($520 per person with online discount or $460 for the early-bird tour).

Another large operation is **Blue Hawaiian Helicopters** (808/886-1768 in Waikoloa, 800/786-2583, www.bluehawaiian.com), which operates tours from both the Kona and Hilo sides with two helicopter options—the A-Star and the Eco-Star. The Eco-Star is touted as "the first touring helicopter of the 21st century," meaning that its seats are more comfortable, it is quieter, and it has larger windows for a less obstructed view than the A-Star. Most importantly, it costs more. From the Kona side, there are three tour options: a 90-minute Kohala Coast Adventure ($220 for A-Star, $266 for Eco-Star), the standard trip to see the waterfalls of the region; the two-hour Big Island Spectacular ($408, $510), an all-encompassing trip that circles the island to witness all its highlights; and the two-hour Big Island-Maui Trip ($453, $510), a quick jaunt over to Maui to view Haleakala Crater and then a glimpse of the Kohala waterfalls on the way back. This particular tour has a six-person minimum.

Shopping and Entertainment

SHOPPING
South Kohala: Resort Area

The two main shopping areas in Waikoloa, **Kings' Shops** and **Queens' MarketPlace,** are across the street from one another on Waikoloa Beach Drive. The Kings' Shops are high-end stores such as Coach, Tiffany, and the tiniest Macy's that you will ever see. Across the street, the Queens' MarketPlace offers typical mall selections, such as Lids, Claire's, and Quiksilver, as well as a food court (daily 7:30am-9:30pm).

Hawi to the End of the Road

Hawi and the adjoining Kapa'au are cute towns with a small main street (it's actually Hwy. 270) lined with shops, galleries, and restaurants. It's definitely worth making a short detour here, parallel parking your car and strolling from store to store. The entire walk will take you less than two hours. Yes, there is some Hawaiiana here, but this area has an artist colony feel to it, lending to goods that are higher quality than the standard kitsch you'll find in Kona or Hilo.

ENTERTAINMENT

All the resort hotels in the area have bars with live music on the weekends and sometimes also weekday evenings. The Waikoloa Beach area hosts daily events at the Queens' MarketPlace, Kings' Shops, Hilton Waikoloa Village, and Waikoloa Beach Resort. Many of the events are free and can be found on the resort's website (www.waikoloabeachresort.com). Many of the events are ideal for children—such as Hawaiian storytelling. One notable event is the weekly free concert with Big Island slack-key guitarist John Keawe. I urge you to attend that show. Keawe plays other places on the island during the week, but you usually have to pay to see him.

lu'au at The Fairmont Orchid

For something a little more local, go to **Sansei Seafood Restaurant and Sushi Bar** (201 Waikoloa Beach Dr. in Queens' MarketPlace, 808/886-6286, www.dkrestaurants.com, 5:30pm-10pm Sun.-Thurs., 9:30pm-midnight Fri.-Sat.) for weekend karaoke coupled with cheap sushi and drink deals.

North of the resort area in Kawaihae, the **Blue Dragon Restaurant** (Hwy. 270 between mile markers 3 and 4, 808/882-7771, www.bluedragonhawaii.com) has the best of both worlds: live music and dancing. It's one of the few places on the island where people get dressed up for a night out. No, it's not a club, it's more like an old-time big band dance hall—classy and romantic with excellent cocktails.

In Hawi, **Bamboo Restaurant** (Hwy. 270, Hawi, 808/889-5555, www.bamboorestaurant.info, 11:30am-2:30 and 6pm-8pm Tues.-Sat., 11:30am-2:30pm Sun.) has live music on the weekends. **Kohala Coffee Mill** (55-3412 Akoni Pule Hwy./Hwy. 270, Hawi, 808/889-5577, 6am-6pm Mon.-Fri., 7am-6pm Sat.-Sun.) also features local artists throughout the week in its small café.

The larger resorts all hold **lu'au** on alternating days during the week (see calendar online at www.waikoloabeachresort.com). They mostly feel like factory lu'au—getting people in and out and fed quickly. While it is more convenient to simply attend a luau at your hotel, you might want to venture out for a more Cirque de Soleil-style experience at **The Fairmont Orchid** (www.fairmont.com/orchid, starting at 5:30pm Sat.). This lu'au is more expensive than its counterparts, but it's a true VIP experience and the food is better than at other luau.

Food

SOUTH KOHALA: RESORT AREA

All the resorts in the area have at least one restaurant located on the premises. These restaurants, for the most part, are fine but not notable and tend to be more expensive than off-site restaurants. If you don't want to travel too far away from your hotel or condo, but still want to eat out, there are some worthwhile options nearby.

With postcard views of A-Bay and daily live music, the **Lava Lava Beach Club** (69-1081 Ku'uali'i Pl, Waikoloa, 808/ 769-5282, www.lavalavabeachclub.com, 11am-10pm Mon.-Fri., 10am-10pm Sat.-Sun., happy hour 3pm-5pm, $15-30) draws a large crowd. Dinner reservations are a must (you can make them online); however, there is open seating at the bar or at a few chairs located in the sandy area (for those who like to get their feet wet). The food is good enough here, but often you can hear guests complaining about the prices; still, the fun atmosphere and beachfront views keep the place very crowded.

If you're seeking something on the lighter side, **Juice 101** (68-1330 Mauna Lani Dr., The Shops at Mauna Lani, 808/887-2244, www.juicebar101.com, 6am-5pm daily) is just the ticket. As the name implies, it has fresh juice squeezed from fruits and greens as well as smoothies. Try the kale smoothie and acai bowl to energize you for the day. If that's not your thing, enjoy the breakfast bagels and a cup of coffee. Lunch is available, and kid friendly too, with options such as grilled cheese. It's more a takeout place than a dine-in joint, but it does have free wireless Internet.

A new addition to The Shops at Mauna Lani, ★ **The Blue Room** (68-1330 Mauna Lani Dr., The Shops at Mauna Lani, 808/887-0999, 11:30am-10pm daily, $18-32) is modeled after the Blue Room (of course) at 'Iolani Palace, the royal residence located in downtown Honolulu. The interior is decorated with beautiful historical photos of important women of Hawaiian history and the outdoor patio has a nice mixture of native plants that celebrate the land and sea. The vision of the owners was to create a Parisian café that serves high-end local drive-in food. This fusion of styles may sound confusing, but it works. The mains, such as the lau lau roasted pork, are good, but the appetizers like the Kauai shrimp, foie gras, and shrimp spring rolls are the real highlight. I recommend coming for the happy hour (3pm-5pm daily) or just ordering a dinner of several appetizers—leaving room for the flourless chocolate cake. Service is excellent.

Another new addition to The Shops at Mauna Lani is **Under the Bodhi Tree** (68-1330 Mauna Lani Dr., The Shops at Mauna Lani, 808/895-2053, www.underthebodhi.net, daily 7am-7pm, $6-15) a dream-come-true small café for the vegan/vegetarian/gluten-free/raw crowd. Its banana bread French toast breakfast ($12) is excellent; it also serves hearty egg omelets and large bowls of oatmeal. Lunch consists of locally sourced specials of the day, salads, and sandwiches. The best deal here is the happy hour (2pm-5pm daily), which includes a few different meal deals like soup, side salad, and on-tap kombucha for the bargain rate of $15.

Amid the usual humdrum of resort restaurants, **The Canoe House** (68-1400 Mauna Lani Dr., Mauna Lani Bay Hotel, 808/885-6622, www.maunalani.com/dining/canoe-house, Mon.-Sat. 5:30pm-8:30pm, $42) is a standout. The menu is thoughtful, using local ingredients (as much as possible) to create beautiful, well-executed dishes, and the wine list is extensive. I recommend any of the fresh fish or the rack of lamb. And the view! Right on the ocean, this restaurant makes for an ideal romantic evening. If you want to splurge try the "Captain's Table" blind tasting menu for $125 per person, or $175 with wine pairings.

KAWAIHAE

There is a surprisingly large number of restaurants in this small town, which attracts the overflow of resort visitors seeking food outside the bounds of their hotel. Thus prices are somewhat higher than what you'd expect. There is a harbor right in town, and many restaurants offer fresh seafood.

One of the most fun eating experiences on the Big Island, the ★ **Blue Dragon**

The Blue Room restaurant is modeled off the 'Iolani Palace.

Restaurant (Hwy. 270 between mile markers 3 and 4, 808/882-7771, www.bluedragonhawaii.com, Thurs.-Sun. 5:30pm-11pm, $18-35) is always crowded with locals and visitors alike dancing away the evening while breaking for bites of the coastal cuisine. If I could award Michelin stars (as it turns out, I can't) I'd give one to chef Noah, whom I'm sure we will be reading more about in the future. From the lillikoi julep cocktail to the "live" salad (you'll have to order it to see) to the pork chop cooked in a clove bride with guava sauce to the coconut pancetta "mash up" with flourless chocolate cake and mango sauce—chef Noah presented me with one of the best and most interactive meals of my life. And...the price point is surprisingly right. Reservations are a must, although sometimes you can get a seat at the small bar. Additionally, the restaurant offers transportation ($35 per person through Big Island Party Bus), so you should feel welcome to have that second or fourth julep cocktail as you dance the night away.

Also in the Blue Dragon parking lot (61-3616 Kawaihae Rd) is the ★ Original Big Island Shave Ice Company (808/895-6069, www.obisic.com, 11:30am-5:30pm Tues.-Sat.,). Shave ice here (small $3, regular $4) is a revelation—shaved ultra-thin and topped with real fruit flavors like mango and guava, this food truck might just win the unofficial Big Island shave ice competition. For those of you who like a little ice cream on your shave ice, not a problem: Add ice-cream flavors such as sweet potato or mac nut for just an extra $1.25. My favorite is the azuki bean toppings on a li hing mui ice.

The other choice close by is Café Pesto (Kawaihae Center, 808/882-1071, www.cafepesto.com, 11am-9pm daily, pizzas average $13 for a 9-inch wood-fired pizza, dinner mains $18-35), which feels entirely like your hometown Italian restaurant meets Hawaii. The menu is a little all over the place, from pizza and calzones to fish and Thai-style food. I'd stick with the Italian side of the menu. Reservations are recommended.

HAWI TO THE END OF THE ROAD

Hawi is the spot where ex-New Yorkers or restaurant veterans come to open restaurants, and you will reap the benefits of their decision. Nearly every restaurant in the area offers something better than the next. In fact, one of your biggest hardships in Hawi will be finding time to eat everywhere in town.

You'll think you're in Pahoa (the hippie enclave of the Big Island) when you see the menu at Sweet Potato Kitchen (55-3406 Akoni Pule Hwy./Hwy. 270, Hawi, 10:30am-3:30pm Mon.-Fri., $6-12). This (mostly) gluten-free, vegan, farm-to-table restaurant serves up breakfast and lunch delights such as maple and mac-nut granola and "forbidden" shitake congee. Don't come hungry, because this one-woman (sometimes two) show gives new meaning to the idea of "slow food." Yet if you have the time and your hunger levels can hold out, it's worth the wait, especially for the freshly made tonics and chais. Note: Seating is all outdoors and there is no restroom here.

Local Dish (55-3419 Akoni Pule Hwy./Hwy. 270, Hawi, 11am-4pm Thurs.-Mon., $15) is the Jewish deli you've been looking for in Hawaii. Classic deli sandwiches, like Reubens, are served on locally made bread. There are even a few vegetarian options.

Next door to Local Dish, one of the few authentic Mexican restaurants on the island, Mi Ranchito (55-3419 Akoni Pule Hwy./Hwy. 270, Hawi, 11am-4pm and 5pm-8pm Mon.-Sat., $9-16) is a true taquería and one of the best choices if you're looking for something a little less pricey than the majority of Hawi restaurants. The price is right and the portions are huge. Vegetarian and gluten-free options are available. You won't see the restaurant from the street; it is in the interior of the building where Local Dish is located.

If you're looking for a quick to-go treat while strolling the streets, stop in to **Kohala Coffee Mill** (55-3412 Akoni Pule Hwy./ Hwy. 270, Hawi, 808/889-5577, 6am-6pm Mon.-Fri., 7am-6pm Sat.-Sun., $7-10) for an ice-cream cone or a cookie or take a seat outdoors and listen to one of the live-music performances that tend to pop up on any given day. This is a laid-back coffee shop with beverages such as ice-cold chai as well as breakfast bagel sandwiches. Salads and hamburgers are available for lunch.

Hawai'i Volcanoes National Park

The indomitable power of Hawai'i Volcanoes National Park is apparent to all who come here.

Wherever you stop to gaze, realize that you are standing on a thin skin of cooled lava in an unstable earthquake zone atop one of the world's most active volcanoes.

Established in 1916 as the 13th U.S. national park, Hawai'i Volcanoes National Park now covers 333,000 acres. Based on its scientific and scenic value, the park was named an International Biosphere Reserve by UNESCO in 1980 and awarded World Heritage Site status in 1987 by the same organization, giving it greater national and international prestige. This is one of the top visitor attractions in the state.

With a multitude of ways to access the park—by foot, by car, by bike, and by helicopter—Hawai'i Volcanoes National Park truly does offer something for everyone. Even non-nature lovers are impressed by the environmental oddities offered here, such as the vastly different landscapes situated next to each other. Within moments one can pass through a tropical rainforest to what appears like a lunar landscape. Even if this doesn't impress, it will be hard to tear yourself away from the lava flow or glow. It's surreal.

In conjunction with a visit to the park, you'll surely pass through Volcano Village, known for the cadre of artists and scientists that live there. With wineries, farmers markets, restaurants, and galleries, it can feel like the Sonoma of Hawaii and not just somewhere to pass through on the way to somewhere else.

ORIENTATION
Hawai'i Volcanoes National Park

Practically speaking, you'll find the main entrance to the park off Highway 11 near mile marker 28; however, the park itself extends far to the north and the south of the main entrance. The upper end of the park is the summit of stupendous Mauna Loa, the most massive mountain on earth. Mauna Loa Road branches off Highway 11 and ends at a footpath for the hale and hearty who trek to the 13,679-foot summit. The park's heart is Kilauea Caldera, almost three miles across, 400 feet deep, and encircled by 11 miles of Crater Rim Drive. At the park visitors center you can give yourself a crash course in geology while picking up park maps, information,

Previous: Hawai'i Volcanoes National Park offers some of the best hiking on the island; entrance to Thurston Lava Tube. **Above:** Lava flows in Hawai'i Volcanoes National Park.

Highlights

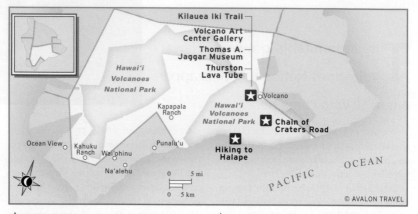

★ **Volcano Art Center Gallery:** This is one of the finest art galleries in the entire state, boasting the best the islands have to offer (page 472).

★ **Thomas A. Jaggar Museum:** This state-of-the-art museum offers a fantastic multimedia display of the amazing geology and volcanology of the area. At night you can watch the lava glow from the viewing area (page 473).

★ **Thurston Lava Tube:** Ferns and moss hang from the entrance of this remarkable natural tunnel. It's as if the very air is tinged with green (page 474).

★ **Chain of Craters Road:** Every bend of this road offers a panoramic vista. The grandeur and power of the forces that have been creating the earth from the beginning of time are right before your eyes (page 475).

★ **Kilauea Iki Trail:** This trail takes you from the top of the crater, with its lush tropical vegetation, to the crater floor, which still breathes volcanic steam (page 480).

★ **Hiking to Halape:** Your rewards for this strenuous hike are sugary sand and a sheltered lagoon—by far the most remote and pristine beach on the island (page 481).

Hawai'i Volcanoes National Park

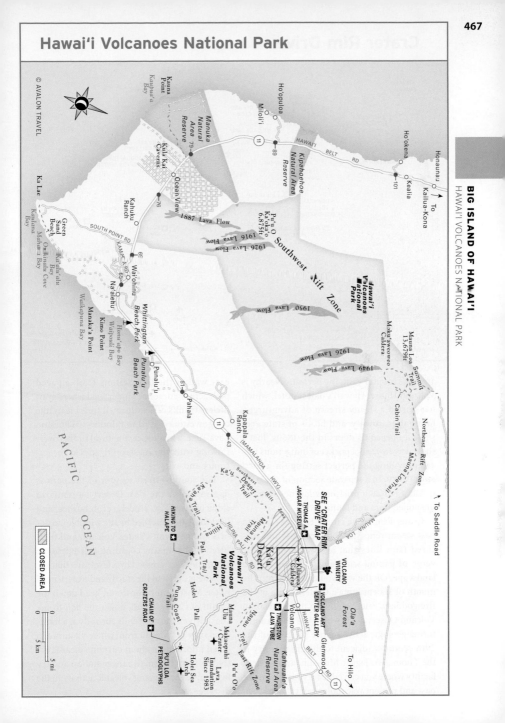

© AVALON TRAVEL

Kauna
Point

Kaupua'a
Bay

Manuka
Natural
Area
Reserve 79

Ho'opuloa

Miloli'i

HAWAI'I 11 89 BELT RD

Ho'okena

Honaunau

Kealia

101

To
Kailua-Kona

Kipahoehoe
Natural Area
Reserve

Kula Kai
Caverns

Ocean View 76

Kahuku
Ranch

SOUTH POINT RD

Ka Lae

Green
Sand
Beach

Ka'alu'alu
Bay

Kaulana
Bay

Waikapuna Bay

Manuka Cove

Manaka'a Point

Kimo Point

Waiohinu

Na'alehu

KAMA' 'AINA 65E

Waipouli Bay

Hāmu'apo Bay

Whittington
Beach Park

Punalu'u
Beach Park

Punalu'u

Pahala

11 43

Kapapala
Ranch

(MAMALAHOA HWY)

1887 Lava Flow

Pu'u O
Ka'oko'o
6,875ft

1916 Lava Flow

1926 Lava Flow

Southwest Rift Zone

1950 Lava Flow

Mauna Loa Summit
13,679ft

Moku'āweoweo
Caldera

1926 Lava Flow

1949 Lava Flow

*Hawai'i
Volcanoes
■National
Park*

Mauna Loa Trail

Cabin Trail

Northeast Rift Zone

Mauna Loa Trail

To Saddle Road

Ka'ū
Southwest Rift
Desert
Trail

Ka'ū Trail

Mauna Iki Trail

Hilina Pali Trail

Ka'ū
Desert

*Hawai'i
Volcanoes
National
Park*

**HIKING TO
HALAPE** ✚

Pali Trail

Holei
Pali

Puna Coast
Trail

**CHAIN OF
CRATERS ROAD** ✚

**PUʻU LOA
PETROGLYPHS** ✚

Kīlauea
Caldera

Mauna
Ulu

Makaopuhi
Crater

Holei Sea
Arch

Lava
Inundation
Since 1983

**SEE "CRATER RIM
DRIVE" MAP**

**THOMAS A.
JAGGAR MUSEUM** ✚

Nāpau Trail

**VOLCANO ART
CENTER GALLERY** ✚

**VOLCANO
WINERY** 🍷

**THURSTON
LAVA TUBE** ✚

Volcano

HAWAI'I

Pu'u O'o

East Rift Zone

Kahauale'a
Natural Area
Reserve

Ola'a
Forest

BELT RD 11

Glenwood,
To Hilo

PACIFIC OCEAN

▨ **CLOSED AREA**

0 ——— 5 mi

0 ——— 5 km

Crater Rim Drive

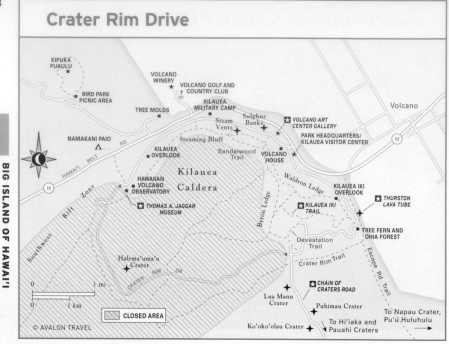

CLOSED AREA

© AVALON TRAVEL

and backcountry camping permits. Nearby is Volcano House, Hawaii's oldest hotel, which has hosted a steady stream of adventurers, luminaries, royalty, and heads of state ever since it opened its doors in the 1860s. Just a short drive away is a pocket of indigenous forest, providing the perfect setting for a **bird sanctuary.** In a separate section of the park is 'Ola'a Forest, a pristine wilderness area of unspoiled flora and fauna.

Crater Rim Drive circles Kilauea Caldera past steam vents, sulphur springs, and tortured fault lines that always seem on the verge of gaping wide and swallowing the landscape. On the way you can peer into the mouth of Halema'uma'u Crater, home of the fire goddess, Pele. You'll also pass Hawaiian Volcano Observatory, which has been monitoring geologic activity since the turn of the 20th century. Adjacent to the observatory is the Thomas A. Jaggar Museum, an excellent facility where you can educate yourself on the past and present volcanology of the park. An

easy walk is the Devastation Trail, a paved path across a desolate cinder field where gray, lifeless trunks of a suffocated forest lean like old gravestones. Within minutes is Thurston Lava Tube, a magnificent natural tunnel overflowing with vibrant fern grottoes at the entrance and exit.

The southwestern section of the park is dominated by the Ka'u Desert—a semiarid slope of lava flow, cinder, scrub bushes, and heat that's been defiled by the windblown debris and gases of Kilauea Volcano and fractured by the sinking coastline. It is a desolate region, an area crossed by a few trails that are a challenge even to the sturdy and experienced hiker. Most visitors, however, head down the Chain of Craters Road, down the *pali* to the coast, where the road ends abruptly at a hardened flow of lava and from where visitors can glean information about current volcanic activities from the small ranger station and try to glimpse the ongoing volcanic activity in the distance.

Volcano Village

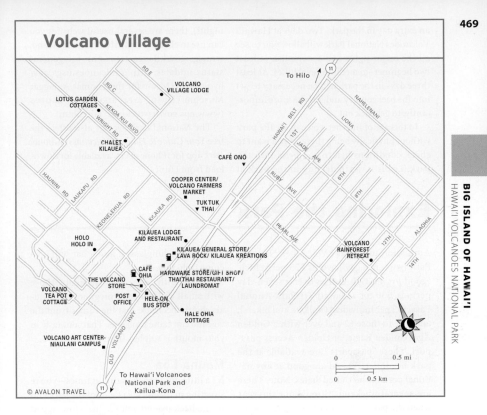

To Hilo

VOLCANO VILLAGE LODGE

LOTUS GARDEN COTTAGES

CHALET KILAUEA

CAFÉ ONO

COOPER CENTER/ VOLCANO FARMERS MARKET

TUK TUK THAI

HOLO HOLO IN

KILAUEA LODGE AND RESTAURANT

KILAUEA GENERAL STORE/ LAVA ROCK/ KILAUEA KREATIONS

VOLCANO RAINFOREST RETREAT

CAFÉ OHIA

HARDWARE STORE/GIFT SHOP/ THAI THAI RESTAURANT/ LAUNDROMAT

THE VOLCANO STORE

VOLCANO TEA POT COTTAGE

POST OFFICE

HELE-ON BUS STOP

HALE OHIA COTTAGE

VOLCANO ART CENTER– NIAULANI CAMPUS

0   0.5 mi
0   0.5 km

© AVALON TRAVEL

To Hawai'i Volcanoes National Park and Kailua-Kona

BIG ISLAND OF HAWAI'I
HAWAI'I VOLCANOES NATIONAL PARK

Volcano Village

Driving north on Highway 11, you will pass by the park's entrance before reaching the main part of Volcano town (if you are driving from Hilo, you pass the town first). Although there are residential communities on both sides of the road, the *mauka* side is the center of Volcano town. Nearly every restaurant and shop is on the short Old Volcano Road—the inner road that parallels Highway 11 through town. The golf course area, where the Volcano Winery is also housed, is on Highway 11 between mile markers 30 and 31 just south of the park.

PLANNING YOUR TIME

It's best to decide in advance how much time you want to spend at the park and whether you're visiting by car, by foot, or by bike. Regardless of your plan, your first stop should be the visitors center to check with a park ranger about any new closures in the park, new safety advisories, or a special program going on that day. Start early. The park looks entirely different in the early morning—the colors are different and it is much quieter before the busloads of tourists start to arrive. Lastly, pack a lunch. The food options in the park are minimal. Better to bring a great sandwich with you so that you don't have to return to town midday to get fed.

It is possible to see the park's "greatest hits" in one long day if you drive from sight to sight on Crater Rim and then Chain of Craters Road. You'll even have time to get out and walk around, have a leisurely dinner, and then come back to catch the glow at night. There are a handful of fairly easy hikes that only take 2-3 hours. If you're planning on doing one or more of those hikes (such as Kilauea Iki), you might want to give yourself an extra day in the park. Two days at Hawai'i Volcanoes National Park will allow you to see all the major sights and accomplish at least two beginner- to medium-level hikes. At least three days in the park will be necessary to get into the backcountry and, maybe more importantly, to get back out.

In this age of Internet, you can see the park without physically being there. If you want to check conditions before you head into the park (i.e., is it worth driving to the park at night?), there are several useful websites you can use to check **lava status** (http://volcano. wr.usgs.gov/kilaueastatus.php for general status updates, http://volcanoes.usgs.gov/ hvo/cams/HMcam for the Thomas A. Jaggar Museum viewing area) and **trail closures** (www.nps.gov/havo/closed_areas.htm).

The National Park Service also offers the free *Your Guide to Hawai'i Volcanoes National Park* app for iPhone users, available for download from iTunes.

Exploring the Park

Admission to Hawai'i Volcanoes National Park (www.nps.gov/havo) is $25 per vehicle (good for multiple entries over a seven-day period), $30 for a Hawaii Tri-Park Annual Pass, $12 per individual (walkers and bikers), and free to those 62 and over with a Golden Age, Golden Eagle, or Golden Access passport. These "passports" are available at the park headquarters and are good at any national park in the United States. Note: There are several weekends throughout the year when the park is free. Check the park's website to see if your visit coincides with one of these times.

TOP EXPERIENCE

THE VOLCANOES
Kilauea
Continuously active since 1983, Kilauea dominates the heart of Hawai'i Volcanoes National Park. Many of the park's sights are arranged one after another along **Crater Rim Drive,** which circles **Kilauea Caldera.** Most of these sights are the "drive-up" variety, but plenty of major and minor trails lead off here and there.

Expect to spend a full day atop Kilauea to take in all the sights, and never forget that you're on a rumbling volcano. It's often overcast, and there can be showers. Wear walking shoes and bring a sweater or windbreaker, maybe even a change of clothes.

Binoculars, sunglasses, and a hat will also come in handy.

People with respiratory ailments, those with small children, and pregnant individuals should be aware that the fumes from the volcano can cause problems. That sour taste in your mouth is sulphur from the fumes.

Mauna Loa
It's a little discombobulating at times—you're sweating in the hot lava fields of the park and in the background you see the snowcapped Mauna Loa. Reaching 13,680 feet in elevation, this magnificent peak is a mere 116 feet shorter than its neighbor Mauna Kea, which is the tallest peak in the Pacific (and by some accounts, the tallest in the world). Mauna Loa has had some recent volcanic activity, spilling lava in 1949, 1950, 1975, and 1980.

The summit of Mauna Loa, with its mighty **Moku'aweoweo Caldera,** is all within park boundaries. Mauna Loa's oval Moku'aweoweo Caldera is more than three miles long and 1.5 miles wide and has vertical walls towering 600 feet. At each end is a smaller, round pit crater. From November to May, if there is snow, steam rises from the caldera. This mountaintop bastion is the least-visited part of the park because this land is remote and still largely inaccessible. For now, it is possible to drive or bike the 10-mile Mauna Loa Road to the trailhead at over 6,600 feet, hike nearly

Your Best Day in the Volcano Area

- Wake up early and walk the **Crater Rim Trail.**

- Stop at the **visitors center** to chat with a park ranger (before it gets crowded).

- Visit the **Thurston Lava Tube** and hike the **Kilauea Iki Trail.**

- Get back in the car and drive the **Chain of Craters Road,** stopping at a lookout to have your packed lunch.

- In the later afternoon, after a brief rest, stop by the **Volcano Winery** for a tasting.

- Have an early dinner in **Volcano Village** or at the **Volcano House.**

- Return to the park to watch the glow from the **Thomas A. Jaggar Museum.**

- If you're not too tired, go bowling at **Kilauea Military Camp** or visit the **Lava Lounge** for some karaoke with the locals.

RAINY-DAY ALTERNATIVE

It can rain at Hawai'i Volcanoes National Park. Sometimes it's a spritz and you can continue on with only getting slightly damp, and other times it can rain hard and outdoor activity is not really possible. There are a few indoor places you can go while waiting for sunshine.

From facials to pedicures to traditional *lomilomi* massages, **Hale Ho'ola: Hawaiian Healing Arts Center and Spa** does it all and does it well, and at half the cost of spas on the Kona side. What makes this a truly great rainy-day activity is that you can call at the last minute and owner Suzanne Woolley will try to accommodate you.

Art enthusiasts will love **2400 Fahrenheit Glass Blowing,** just a few minutes north of Hawai'i Volcanoes National Park. Even if glassblowing isn't taking place, this gallery makes for a worthy stop.

If the weather still hasn't cleared up, try the **Volcano Winery** for a tasting, or drive to Hilo. Often the weather in Hilo can be drastically different from that in Volcano (you can see the clouds moving as you drive north on Highway 11).

20 miles to the summit, and stay overnight at some true backcountry cabins before you head back down.

VISITORS CENTER AREA
Kilauea Visitor Center

The park's **Kilauea Visitor Center** (808/985-6000, 9am-5pm daily) and headquarters is the first building you pass on the right after you enter through the gate. By midmorning it's jammed, so try to be an early bird. The center is well run by the National Park Service, which offers a free film about geology and volcanism, with tremendous highlights of past eruptions and plenty of detail on Hawaiian culture and natural history. It runs every hour on the hour starting at 9am. Once a day, at 11:30am, the 1959 Kilauea Iki eruption video is shown in the auditorium; it's a must-see for those planning on hiking that trail. Free ranger-led tours of the nearby area are also given on a regular basis, and their start times and meeting places are posted near the center's front doors. Also posted are After Dark in the Park educational interpretive program activities, held two or three times a month on Tuesdays at 7pm. If you are visiting with kids, ask the rangers about the free **Junior Ranger Program.** They'll give each child a park-related activity book, pin, and patch.

Many day trails leading into the caldera from the rim road are easy walks that need no special preparation. Before you head down the road, ask for a trail guide from the rangers at the visitors center, fill up your water bottle, and use the public bathroom.

Volcano House

Even if your plans don't include an overnight stop, go into **Volcano House,** across the road from the visitors center, for a look. A stop at the lounge provides refreshments and a tremendous view of the crater. Volcano House still has the feel of a country inn. This particular building dates from the 1940s, but the site has remained the same since a grass hut was perched on the rim of the crater by a sugar planter in 1846.

★ Volcano Art Center Gallery

Across the parking lot from the visitors center is the **Volcano Art Center Gallery** (808/967-7565, http://volcanoartcenter.org, 9am-5pm daily except Christmas), which occupies part of the original 1877 Volcano House. A new show featuring one of the many superlative island artists is presented monthly, and there are ongoing demonstrations and special events. The Volcano Art Center is one of the finest art galleries in the entire state, boasting works from the best the islands have to offer. Definitely make this a stop.

As a community-oriented organization, the Volcano Art Center sponsors classes and workshops in arts, crafts, and yoga, the Kilauea Volcano Wilderness Runs, and a season of performing arts, which includes musical concerts, hula, dance performances, and stage plays. Some involve local performers, while others headline visiting artists. Performances, classes, and workshops take place at the Kilauea Theater at the military camp, at the hula platform within the park, or in Volcano at the Niaulani campus building. Tickets for performances are sold individually at local outlets, or you can buy a season ticket. For current information and pricing, call the Volcano Art Center office (808/967-8222) or check its website for what's happening.

Crater Rim Trail is an easy walk that passes by many of the park's sights.

CRATER RIM DRIVE

The 11-mile road that circles the Kilauea Caldera and passes by nearly all the main sights in the park is **Crater Rim Drive.** For the past few years a part of the road has been closed due to elevated levels of sulphur dioxide gas. You can still drive on the road, but you can't usually complete the entire circle.

Along this road you will travel from a tropical zone into desert, and then through a volcanic zone before returning to lush rainforest. The change is often immediate and differences dramatic. Since you can't circle the caldera, the following sights are listed in two sections: those to the right of the visitors center and those to the left of the visitors center. The sights to the left of the visitors center can also be reached by turning left immediately after you pass through the entrance gate of the park.

To the Right of the Visitors Center

SULPHUR BANKS

You can easily walk to **Sulphur Banks** from the visitors center along a 10-minute paved trail. Your nose will tell you when you're close. Alternatively, walk the 0.6-mile trail from the Steam Vents parking lot. A boardwalk fronts a major portion of this site. As you approach these fumaroles, the earth surrounding them turns a deep reddish brown, covered over in yellowish-green sulphur. The rising steam is caused by surface water leaking into the cracks, where it becomes heated and rises as vapor.

STEAM VENTS

Within a half mile you'll come to the **Steam Vents,** which are also fumaroles, but without sulphur. In the parking lot there are some vents covered with grates, and if you walk just two minutes from the parking lot toward the caldera on the gravel trail, you'll see how the entire field steams. There are no strong fumes to contend with here, just other tourists. If you walk back toward the caldera, you'll see a gravel trail that follows the caldera around. This is the **Crater Rim Trail,** and you can walk it from here to many of the sights, including the Thomas A. Jaggar Museum—an easy 20-minute walk (one-way) through the woods from here.

KILAUEA OVERLOOK

The **Kilauea Overlook** is as good a spot as any to get a look into the caldera, and there are picnic tables near the parking lot. Unless you're stopping for lunch or making your own offering, it's perhaps better to continue on to the observatory and museum, where you not only have the view outside but get a scientific explanation of what's happening around you.

★ THOMAS A. JAGGAR MUSEUM

The **Hawaiian Volcano Observatory** (http://hvo.wr.usgs.gov) has been keeping tabs on the volcanic activity in the area since the turn of the 20th century. The actual observatory is filled with delicate seismic equipment and is closed to the public, but a lookout nearby gives you a spectacular view into the eye of **Halema'uma'u Crater** (House of Ferns), Pele's home. From here, steam rises and, even more phenomenally spectacular, a lake of molten lava forms. The lava has been rising and falling over the last few years, and when it does rise, it puts on one of the best nighttime shows you'll ever see. You can check

the glow from the Halema'uma'u Crater

Don't Take the Lava Home!

Legend has it that taking lava rock from Hawaii will bring you bad luck. **Pele,** the goddess of fire, does not like when her rocks leave Hawaii. (Although rumor has it that the legend was actually started by rangers at the national park who wanted to stop people from picking up rocks.) Every year the park receives lava rocks returned to them by mail with notes of explanation handwritten by the recipients of bad luck. I am not saying whether or not I think this legend holds true, but I can say it's best not to take the rock.

If you so happen to take something and want to send it back, you can send it to **Hawai'i Volcanoes National Park** (P.O. Box 52, Hawaii National Park, HI 96718). The park has a pile of returned rocks. If you want your rock to return with a ceremony of forgiveness, with just a $15 donation you can send your rock to Rainbow Moon (Attn: Lava Rock Return, P.O. Box 699, Volcano, HI 96785). Your rock will be returned to its source wrapped in a ti leaf. In addition, Rainbow Moon will happily send you an email to confirm that your rock was returned appropriately.

the webcam (http://volcanoes.usgs.gov/hvo/cams/hmcam) located within the crater to see what the lava is doing and decide if it's worth heading back there at night to watch its performance.

Next door to the observatory, the state-of-the-art **Thomas A. Jaggar Museum** (808/985-6049, 10am-7:30pm daily, admission free) offers a fantastic multimedia display of the amazing geology and volcanology of the area, complete with a miniseries of spectacular photos on movable walls, topographical maps, inspired paintings, and video presentations. The expert staff constantly upgrades the displays to keep the public informed on the newest eruptions. The 30-45 minutes it takes to explore the teaching museum will enhance your understanding of the volcanic area immeasurably. From the Jaggar Museum the rest of the Crater Rim Road is closed, thus it's necessary to turn around and go back the way you came.

To the Left of the Visitors Center

KILAUEA IKI OVERLOOK

The first parking lot you'll pass on the right is the gateway to **Kilauea Iki** (Little Kilauea). In 1959, lava spewed 1,900 feet into the air from a 0.5-mile crack in the crater wall (there is an amazing picture showcasing this occurrence

on a board in the parking lot). It was the highest fountain ever measured in Hawaii. Within a few weeks, 17 separate lava flow episodes occurred, creating a lake of lava. In the distance is the cinder cone, **Pu'u Pua'i** (Gushing Hill), where the lava flowed from its brownish-red base in 1959. The cone didn't exist before then. If you look down from the overlook into the crater floor you'll see something that resembles a desolate desert landscape that is still steaming in spots. Unbelievably, you can fairly easily walk across this on the Kilauea Iki trail. Surrounding the crater is a rainforest filled with native **birds** and plants.

★ THURSTON LAVA TUBE

Just up the road from the overlook is the remarkable **Thurston Lava Tube,** otherwise called Nahuku, which resembles a Salvador Dalí painting. The paved trail starts as a steep incline that quickly enters a fern forest. All about you are fern trees, vibrantly green, with native **birds** flitting here and there. As you approach the lava tube, it seems almost manmade, like a perfectly formed tunnel leading into a mine. The walk through the tube takes about 10 minutes, undulating through the narrow passage. At the other end, the fantasy world of ferns and moss reappears, and from there the trail leads back past public restrooms to the parking lot. The entire tunnel is lit and paved; however, for some extra fun take a flashlight to visit the unlit portion. As you walk up the stairway to exit the tube, you'll see on your left an open gate that looks into the darkness: This small unlit section *is* open to the public at their own risk.

★ CHAIN OF CRATERS ROAD

The 37-mile round-trip **Chain of Craters Road** that once linked the park with Kalapana village on the coast in the Puna district was severed by an enormous lava flow in 1995 and can now only be driven to where the flow crosses the road beyond the Holei Sea Arch.

When the road almost reaches the coast, look for a roadside marker that indicates the Puna Coast Trail. Just across the road is the Pu'u Loa Petroglyph Field trailhead. The lower part of the road is spectacular. Here, blacker-than-black sea cliffs, covered by a thin layer of green, abruptly stop at the sea. The surf rolls in, sending up spumes of seawater. In the distance, steam billows into the air where the lava flows into the sea. At road's end you will find a barricade and an information hut staffed by park rangers throughout the afternoon and into the evening. Read the information and heed the warnings. The drive from atop the volcano to the end of the road takes about 45 minutes and drops about 3,700 feet in elevation.

While hiking to the lava flow is not encouraged, park staff do not stop you from venturing out. They warn you of the dangers and the reality ahead. Many visitors do make the hike, but there is no trail. The way is over new and rough lava that tears at the bottom of your shoes. Many hike during the day, but if you go in the evening when the spectacle is more apparent, a flashlight with several extra batteries is absolutely necessary. To hike there and back could take three to four hours. If you decide to hike, bring plenty of water. There is no shade or water along the way, and the wind often blows along this coast. Do not hike to or near the edge of the water, as sections of lava could break off without warning. Depending on how the lava is flowing, it may or may not be worth the effort.

Craters

As you head down Chain of Craters Road, you immediately pass a number of the depressions for which the road is named. First on the right side is **Lua Manu Crater,** a deep depression

Thurston Lava Tube

now lined with green vegetation. Farther is **Puhimau Crater.** Walk the few steps to the viewing stand at the crater edge for a look. Many people come here to hear the echo of their voices as they talk or sing into this pit. Next comes **Ko'oko'olau Crater,** then **Hi'iaka Crater** and **Pauahi Crater.** Just beyond is a turnoff to the east, which follows a short section of the old road. This road ends at the lava flow, and from here a trail runs as far as **Napau Crater.**

The first mile or more of the Napau Trail takes you over lava from 1974, through forest *kipuka,* past lava tree molds, and up the treed slopes of **Pu'u Huluhulu.** (A *kipuka* is a piece of land that is surrounded by lava but has not been inundated by it, leaving the original vegetation and land contour intact.) From this cone you have a view down on Mauna Ulu, from which the 1969-1974 lava flow disgorged, and east toward **Pu'u O'o** and the active volcanic vents, some seven miles distant. Due to the current volcanic activity farther along the rift zone, you will need a permit to day-hike beyond Pu'u Huluhulu; the trail itself may be closed depending on where the volcanic activity is taking place. However, the trail does continue over the shoulder of

Makaopuhi Crater to the primitive campsite at Napau Crater, passing more cones and pit craters, lava flows, and sections of rainforest.

Roadside Sights

For several miles, Chain of Craters Road traverses lava that was laid down about 40 years ago; remnants of the old road can still be seen in spots. There are long stretches of smooth *pahoehoe* lava interspersed with flows of the rough *'a'a.* Here and there, green pokes through a crack in the rock, bringing new life to this stark landscape. Everywhere you look, you can see the wild "action" of these lava flows, stopped in all their magnificent forms. At one vantage point on the way is **Kealakomo,** a picnic overlook where you have unobstructed views of the coast. Soon the road heads over the edge of the *pali* and diagonally down to the flats, passing sections of the old road not covered by lava. Stop and look back and realize that most of the old road has been covered by dozens of feet of lava, the darkest of the dark.

The last section of road runs close to the edge of the sea, where cliffs rise up from the pounding surf. Near the end of the road is the

Ohelo berry bushes grow back quickly after a landscape has been devastated by lava.

Holei Sea Arch, a spot where the wave action has undercut the rock to leave a bridge of stone.

Pu'u Loa Petroglyphs

The walk out to **Pu'u Loa Petroglyphs** is delightful, highly educational, and takes less than one hour. As you walk along the trail (1.5 miles round-trip), note the *ahu*, traditional trail markers that are piles of stone shaped like little Christmas trees. Most of the lava field leading to the petroglyphs is undulating *pahoehoe* and looks like a frozen sea. You can climb bumps of lava, 8-10 feet high, to scout the immediate territory. As you approach the site, the lava changes dramatically and looks like long strands of braided rope.

The petroglyphs are in an area about the size of a soccer field. A wooden walkway encircles most of them and helps ensure their protection. A common motif of the petroglyphs is a circle with a hole in the middle, like a doughnut; you'll also see designs of men with triangular heads. Some rocks are entirely covered with designs, while others have only a symbolic scratch or two. If you stand on the walkway and trek off towards the two o'clock position, you'll see a small hill. Go over and down it, and you will discover even better petroglyphs, including a sailing canoe about two feet high. At the back end of the walkway a sign proclaims that Pu'u Loa meant Long Hill, which the Hawaiians turned into the metaphor "Long Life." For countless generations, fathers would come here to place pieces of their infants' umbilical cords into small holes as offerings to the gods to grant long life to their children. Concentric circles surrounded the holes that held the umbilical cords. The entire area, an obvious power spot, screams in utter silence, and the still-strong mana is easily felt.

The Big Island has the largest concentration of petroglyphs in the state, and this site holds the greatest number. One estimate puts the number at 28,000.

OTHER PARK ROADS
Hilina Pali Road

About two miles down the Chain of Craters Road, **Hilina Pali Road** shoots off to the southwest (to the left) over a narrow, roughly paved road all the way to the end at Hilina Pali Lookout—about nine miles. Soon after you leave the Chain of Craters Road, the vegetation turns drier and you enter the semi-arid Ka'u Desert. The road picks its way around and over old volcanic flows, and you can see the vegetation struggling to maintain a foothold. On the way you pass the **Mauna Iki trailhead,** Kulanaokuaiki Campground, and the former Kipuka Nene Campground—closed to help the *nene* recover their threatened population.

The road ends right on the edge of the rift, with expansive views over the benched coastline, from the area of current volcanic flow all the way to South Point. From here, one trail heads down the hill to the coast while another pushes on along the top of the cliff and farther into the dry landscape. At the *pali* lookout is a pavilion and restrooms, but no drinking water. This is not a pleasure ride, as the road is rough, but it is passable. If you drive just slightly past the turnoff for Hilina Pali Road, you'll arrive at **Devil's Throat,** a pit crater formed in 1912. It's not directly off the road, so you'll have to park your car at the small gravel area by the side of the road, cross the street, and walk back about 50 feet to catch a glimpse.

Mauna Loa Road

About 2.5 miles south of the park entrance on Highway 11, **Mauna Loa Road** turns off to the north. This road will lead you to the Tree Molds and a **bird sanctuary,** as well as to the trailhead for the Mauna Loa summit trail. As an added incentive, traveling just a minute down this road leaves 99 percent of the tourists behind.

Tree Molds is an ordinary name for an extraordinary area. Turn right off Mauna

Loa Road soon after leaving the Belt Road and follow the signs for five minutes. This road runs into the tree molds area and loops back onto itself. At the loop, a signboard explains what occurred here. In a moment, you realize that you're standing atop a lava flow, and that the scattered potholes were entombed tree trunks, most likely the remains of a once-giant koa forest. The lava stayed put while the tree trunks burned away, leaving the 15- to 18-foot-deep holes. Realizing what happened here and how it happened is an eye-opener.

Kipuka Puaulu is a sanctuary for birds and nature lovers who want to leave the crowds behind, just under three miles from Highway 11 up Mauna Loa Road. The sanctuary is an island atop an island. A *kipuka* is a piece of land that is surrounded by lava but has not been inundated by it, leaving the original vegetation and land contour intact. A few hundred yards away, small scrub vegetation struggles, but in the sanctuary, the trees form a towering canopy a hundred feet tall. The first sign takes you to an ideal picnic area called Bird Park, with cooking grills; the second, 100 yards beyond, takes you to **Kipuka**

Puaulu Loop Trail. As you enter the trail, a bulletin board describes the birds and plants, some of the last remaining indigenous fauna and flora in Hawaii. Please follow all rules. The dirt trail is self-guided, and pamphlets describing the stations along the way are available from a box near the start of the path. The loop is only one mile long, but to really appreciate the area, especially if you plan to do any **bird-watching,** expect to spend an hour minimum.

Mauna Loa Road continues westward and gains elevation for approximately 10 miles. It passes through thick forests of lichen-covered koa trees, cuts across **Kipuka Ki,** and traverses the narrow **Ke'amoku Flow.** At the end of the pavement, at 6,662 feet, you will find a parking area and lookout. If the weather is cooperating, you'll be able to see much of the mountainside; if not, your field of vision will be restricted. A trail leads from here to the summit of Mauna Loa. It takes two long and difficult days to hike. Under no circumstances should it be attempted by novice hikers or those unprepared for cold alpine conditions. At times, this road may be closed due to extreme fire conditions.

Tree Molds area off Mauna Loa Road

Hiking and Biking

HIKING

There are over 150 miles of hiking trails within the park. One long trail heads up the flank of Mauna Loa to its top; a spiderweb of trails loops around and across Kilauea Caldera and into the adjoining craters; and from a point along the Chain of Craters Road, another trail heads east toward the source of the most recent volcanic activity. But by far the greatest number of trails, and those with the greatest total distance, are those that cut through the Ka'u Desert and along the barren and isolated coast. Many have shelters, and trails that require overnight stays provide cabins or primitive campsites.

Because of the possibility of an eruption or earthquake, it is *imperative* to check in at park headquarters, where you can pick up current trail information and excellent maps. In fact, a hiking permit is required for most trails outside the Crater Rim Drive area and the coastal stretch beyond the end of Chain of Craters Drive. New fees recently have been implemented for all **backcountry and front-country campsites,** including Kulanaokuaiki Campground, and are $10 per site per night. Permits can be obtained in person from the Backcountry Office at the **Visitor Emergency Operations Center** (located on Crater Rim Dr. in the building with two rock-based columns) from 8am to 4pm daily. The earliest you may obtain a permit is the day prior to your hike. They do not accept reservations or issue permits in advance.

Much of the park is hot and dry, so carry plenty of drinking water. Wear a hat, sunscreen, and sunglasses, but don't forget rain gear because it often rains in the green areas of the park. Stay on trails and stay away from steep edges, cracks, new lava flows, and any area where lava is flowing into the sea.

If you will be hiking along the trails in the Kilauea Caldera, the free park maps are sufficient for navigation. To aid with hikes elsewhere, it's best to purchase and use larger and more detailed topographical maps. One that is readily available and of high quality is the *Hawai'i Volcanoes National Park* map by Trails Illustrated, which is available at the gift shop at the visitors center.

Self-Guided Easy Hikes

If you find yourself only having one day to venture through Hawai'i Volcanoes National Park, there are several short hikes that will offer you a glimpse of what it's like to live next to an active volcano.

VOLCANO ART CENTER'S NIAULANI CAMPUS TRAIL

Just outside the park in Volcano Village is a four-acre old-growth tropical rainforest growing in volcanic ash from the 18th century. Some of the trees at the Volcano Art Center (19-4074 Old Volcano Rd., Volcano, 808/967-8222) are at least 200 years old and more than 65 feet tall. The **Niaulani Campus Trail,** which is filled with placards explaining the area and art, is a flat 0.7-mile loop. Bird lovers will delight in this opportunity to see native **birds.** If you get there early, you can participate in an hour-long **yoga** class on Monday at 7:30am or stop by to unwind on Thursdays at 5:30pm after a day of hiking.

CRATER RIM TRAIL

Although a large part of Crater Rim Drive is currently closed due to the sulphur dioxide (vog) from Halema'uma'u, it is possible to hike along the **Crater Rim Trail.** If you park at the Thomas A. Jaggar Museum and hike along the Crater Rim Trail toward the visitors center, you will have unparalleled views of the vast Kilauea Caldera. Along the way you pass through desert-like conditions with sparse vegetation, eventually giving way to lush native tropical forests. You will also encounter the **Steam Vents,** where the water heated by the volcanic heat rises up from cracks in the earth. The hike along the Crater Rim Trail to/from the Thomas A. Jaggar Museum to the visitors center is approximately 2.5 miles and can take anywhere from 45 minutes to an hour. Parts of it are shaded; other sections cross an open field. The trailhead for this Crater Rim hike is to the left of the museum and parking lot, across the street from the visitors center (next to Volcano House). Parts of the trail have been paved and provide a good place for road or mountain biking.

SULPHUR BANKS TRAIL

From the visitors center parking lot you can get a good glimpse of some interesting volcanic geology. The **Sulphur Banks Trail** is a short and easy hike that offers intriguing sights. Bright yellow mineral deposits of sulphur line the trail as volcanic gases spew from the earth; this trail may remind some people of the volcanic vents in Yellowstone. Interpretive signs offer explanations of the volcanic activities so it's easy to understand what you're seeing. To get to this trail, walk to the left of the visitors center past the Volcano Art Center. A paved trail will lead you through a grassy field with a *heiau* (temple) and down a hill. If you see signs warning you that you may encounter volcanic gases, you're going the right way. It's 0.5 mile one-way from the visitors center to the Sulphur Banks. If you want to make it into a longer hike, you can cross the road and connect to the Crater Rim Trail by the Steam Vents and hike all the way to the Thomas A. Jaggar Museum.

EARTHQUAKE TRAIL

If you head left from the visitors center (behind the Volcano House facing the caldera) on the Crater Rim Trail, you'll walk one mile round-trip toward **Waldron Ledge** on the **Earthquake Trail,** so named due to the damage this area incurred during the 1983 6.6 magnitude earthquake. Waldron Ledge offers one of the best views in the park, and the trail, which is paved and wheelchair- and stroller-accessible as well as bike friendly, presents an easy walk.

DEVASTATION TRAIL

Farther up Crater Rim Drive, most visitors hike along the one-mile round-trip **Devastation Trail,** which could aptly be renamed Regeneration Trail. The mile it covers is fascinating; it's one of the most-photographed areas in the park. It leads across a field devastated by a tremendous eruption from **Kilauea Iki.** The area was once an *'ohi'a* forest that was denuded of limbs and leaves, then choked by black pumice and ash. The vegetation has regenerated since then, and the recuperative power of the flora is the subject of an ongoing study. Notice that many of the trees have sprouted aerial roots trailing down from the branches: This is total adaptation to the situation, as such roots don't normally appear. As you move farther along the trail, tufts of grass and bushes peek out of the pumice and then the surroundings become totally barren.

Self-Guided Moderate Hikes

If you're willing and able to complete more moderate hikes and want to experience the volcano with your own two feet, then attempt one or both of these hikes. Both hikes can easily be completed in one day.

TOP EXPERIENCE

★ KILAUEA IKI TRAIL

The **Kilauea Iki Trail** takes you from the top of the crater and lush tropical rainforest of native vegetation and native birds to the bottom of the crater floor, which is devoid of vegetation and still breathes volcanic steam. This is a moderate four-mile loop because you descend and ascend 400 feet to and from the crater floor. It takes on average three hours to complete.

The trail for this hike is clearly marked. The parking lot for Kilauea Iki is the first one on the right on the Chain of Craters Road. It's usually packed. From the parking lot go right and follow the Kilauea Iki sign, which will keep you to the left. As you hike along the rim, look to the left and down at the various railed-off lookouts. Below you is where you'll be as you descend the trail to the crater floor. Essentially you are passing along the rim and then descending across the barren landscape before returning back up through the trees.

Upon ascending the trail out of the crater floor, you will pass by the **Thurston Lava Tube** parking lot. This is a worthy addition to the hike to see a lava tube, but it is also one of the most popular stops with tour buses so it can get crowded. Note: Your car was not stolen; you are in the Thurston Lava Tube parking lot, not the lot you parked in. Keep walking through the parking lot to the next parking lot where you left your car.

The best time to do this hike is first thing in the morning, for several reasons. It's cooler in the morning, meaning a more pleasant hike in the floor of the crater. When it's cooler it's also easier to spot all the steam vents, which are an active reminder that the crater could erupt again at any time. Finally, the **birds** are also much more active in the morning. Look for them along the crater rim as they search for insects to keep their bellies filled. Pick up a trail guide for this particular trail at the visitors center or download it from the park's website for further descriptions of the sights you'll pass on your way.

PU'U HULUHULU TRAIL

Another notable hike that can be completed in just two or three hours is the 2.5-mile round-trip **Pu'u Huluhulu Trail** to Mauna Ulu. This hike is for those who like adventure, since the trail isn't marked well. Follow the signs along the Chain of Craters Road. Turn left where the road splits and there will be a sign for Mauna Ulu. Follow the road and the signs until the road ends. The trailhead will be to the left of the parking lot. This moderate hike will take you to the summit of a steaming volcanic crater that can also provide you with 360-degree panoramic views of the park; on a clear day you can even see the

ocean. The trail crosses lava flows from the 1970s, and you'll see young plants sprouting out from cracks in the lava. Follow the trail to Pu'u Huluhulu (Hairy Hill), a crater that has an island of vegetation (*kipuka*) that didn't burn during the 1970s flows. It's a short hike to the top of the *pu'u* (hill), which gives you a good view of Mauna Ulu, the big mountain right in front of you. You can't hike past Pu'u Huluhulu without a permit, but you can follow the old flows up toward the top of Mauna Ulu. There aren't official trail markers to the top but it's easy to pick your own way up the young lava and return the way you came back to the trail. From the top of Mauna Ulu you can peer into the crater, which is hundreds of feet deep, and imagine what it must have been like when lava was spewing from it up to 1,700 feet into the air. A trail guide is available at the visitors center or online on the park's website.

Self-Guided Advanced Hikes

For experienced hikers who want to do some overnight camping and hiking, the park has several options for backcountry wilderness trips.

★ HIKING TO HALAPE

A large section of the park has trails that run along the coast, providing access to several beaches that offer premier camping. By far one of the most remote and pristine beaches on the island is **Halape.** Getting here is something you have to earn, though.

The absolute closest you can get by vehicle is the **Hilina Pali Trailhead,** from where it is an eight-mile descent to the beach across hot, dry, rugged terrain. The first two miles are straight down the *pali* (cliff) with multiple switchbacks to get you safely to the bottom. Halape is the sandiest beach along the coast, but there are also other beautiful places to access the ocean that aren't quite as sandy. One stunning option: After descending the switchbacks to the bottom of Hilina Pali, take the trail to the right toward Ka'aha. This is a nice bay that offers lots of room to explore all the way to the *pali* that extends to the ocean. Some nice tide pools here offer unique snorkeling and swimming. If you keep to the left, the trail will lead you to Halape after six extremely hot miles that include some more steep ascents and descents—but your reward is a sugary beach and a sheltered lagoon that offer you sand and protection from the raw ocean that crashes just past the lagoon. This spot is popular, so you're likely see other campers, but you'll never see the crowds you would in the more accessible sections of the park. Bathroom facilities are available here. There is water available at the backcountry sites, but it must be treated before drinking because it is from a cistern of collected rainwater. Before you go, make sure to ask a ranger if there is water available; at times there is a drought.

The park requires backcountry permits to camp in these sections. They are available from the Backcountry Office at the Visitor Emergency Operation Center. There is a limit to the number of people allowed in at any given time, so plan accordingly and know to get your permits ahead of time before you begin your trek.

If you have the option for someone to pick you up, the best route with the most variety is to hike down from Hilina Pali, spend a night or two at Halape, and then enjoy a nice flat hike out by heading toward Keahou and Apua, both of which have shelter and water. This route covers a longer distance, but it is not as steep as the route you came on.

Guided Hikes

When picking a **guided hike** of the park, the most important factors to consider are: How many people will be on the tour? If the minimum isn't met, will the tour get canceled? How much hiking and walking will you actually be doing? Will the hiking be for beginners or more advanced walkers?

Ranger-led hikes are a great way to explore the park for free with certifiably experienced guides. The **Exploring the Summit hike** is offered daily at 10:30am and 1:30pm. This 45-minute walk over a paved trail meets in front of the Kilauea Visitor Center and takes

guests around the rim while the ranger lectures on Hawaiian history and geology. Check the bulletin board outside the visitors center for daily postings of additional hikes. Often, there is at least one additional hike (on some specific topic) each day.

★ **Friends of Hawaii Volcanoes National Park** (808/985-7373, http://fhvnp. org/institute/private-tours, $275-475 per group) is a nonprofit organization that uses all the proceeds from its tours to support projects and programs at the national park. The tour guides are retired park rangers and wildlife biologists.

Similarly, Warren Costa, aka ★ **Native Guide Hawaii** (808/982-7575, www.native-guidehawaii.com, $300 for one person or $150 per person for two or more) will personally pick you up (and return you safely) after guiding you through the park on a hike that includes narration on Hawaiian culture, legends, and geology of the park. Costa is concerned with not only teaching about the environment, but also raising awareness about how the environment relates to Hawaiian culture. Tours have a maximum of six guests, and children are welcome.

BIKING

Biking is permitted in the park on paved roads, paved sections of the Crater Rim Trail, and on some dirt trails. The park has created an excellent *Where to Bicycle* brochure that is available at www.nps.gov/havo/planyourvisit/bike.htm.

The suggested bike rides include a moderate 11-mile loop to circle the rim, a moderate 18-mile round-trip ride on Hilina Pali Road, a challenging 36-mile round-trip Summit to Sea ride following the path of the Mauna Ulu eruption, and a challenging 11.5-mile loop up (climbing 2,600 feet!) and down Mauna Loa Road. The guide includes several short offshoots from the Mauna Loa Road for those who want to do some mountain biking.

If you don't have a bike with you or are not an experienced rider, or you're simply looking for a different way to see the park, take a guided bike tour of the park with **Bike Volcano** (808/934-9199, www.bikevolcano.com, $110-134 per person and from $105 to ride in the van). The ride stops at all the major sights along the Crater Rim, where the tour guide, who is trained in geology and Hawaiian culture, gives informative talks about the park. Bike Volcano offers several pickup points for riders (including from Hilo), or riders may meet at the Kilauea Visitor Center.

Tours

BUS TOURS

If you have rented a car, there isn't much of a reason to take a tour bus around the park unless you really want to be able to ask questions of someone semi-knowledgeable while you're sightseeing. Otherwise, this guide as well as the brochures available at the park visitors center should provide you with enough information for your journey.

Guided tour bus trips to the park tend to be best and most utilized by day-trippers to the park—either those flying in from another island for the day or those traveling from the Kona side who don't want to worry about driving back to Kona late at night. These guided tours are also great for visitors who might need translation into languages other than English.

The Hilo-based **KapohoKine Adventures** (25 Waianuenue Ave., Hilo, 808/964-1000, www.kapohokine.com) offers a range of lengthy full-day tours to the park with possible pickup from the Kona side, a trip over the Saddle Road, and then a second (or third) pickup from Hilo before heading to the park. The entire tour, from pickup to drop-off, is 12 hours long. The tour is $299 (plus tax) with Kona pickup, $219 if you meet in Hilo or at the park. If a 12-hour tour sounds like no fun while you're on vacation, the firm also offers a shorter (10-hour) Evening Lava Expedition tour with later pickup that visits a Kona coffee farm for lunch and then heads to the park for a tour, dinner at Volcano House, and sunset at the Jaggar Museum for some lava viewing ($99 children, $119 adults plus tax).

The crème de la crème, for those leaving from the Kona side, is **Hawaii Forest and Trails** (808/331-8505, www.hawaii-forest.com, $209 adults, $169 children plus tax), with an ecofriendly ethos, extremely in-the-know tour guides, and flexibility with its small groups. This 12-hour round-trip adventure, which includes continental breakfast and lunch, is mainly a tour of the main park sights with stops along the Ka'u Coast for some sightseeing. Although you'll mostly stay on the bus during this tour, there are several less-than-a-mile walks—ideal for those who do want to do some walking in the park. A twilight trip is also available, making stops at **Mauna Kea State Park** and near Hilo to explore the **Kaumana Cave** before arriving to the park around sunset to witness the lava flow from Puna or the glow from near the Thomas A. Jaggar Museum.

HELICOPTER TOURS

A dramatic way to experience the awesome power of the volcano is to take a **helicopter tour**. The pilots will fly you over the areas offering the most activity, often dipping low over lava pools, skimming still-glowing flows, and circling the towering steam clouds rising from where lava meets the sea. When activity is really happening, tours are jammed, and prices, like lava fountains, go sky-high.

Also, these tours are not without danger, as helicopters have crashed near lava flows during commercial sightseeing flights. Nonetheless, if you are interested, contact one of the helicopter companies located in Hilo or Kona. Alternatively, fixed-wing plane tour companies also offer flights over the volcano area from both Hilo and Kona.

Sunshine Helicopters (808/882-1233

or 800/622-3144, www.sunshinehelicopters.com), leaving from Hapuna on the Kona side, offers a two-hour Volcano Deluxe tour that circles the island ($520-$595 per person with online discount or $510 for the early-bird tour).

Another large operation is **Blue Hawaiian Helicopters** (808/886-1768 in Waikoloa, 800/786-2583, www.bluehawaiian.com), which operates tours from both the Kona and Hilo sides with two helicopter options—the A-Star and the Eco-Star. The Eco-Star is touted as "the first touring helicopter of the 21st century," meaning that its seats are more comfortable, it is quieter, and it has larger windows for a less obstructed view than the A-Star. Most importantly, it costs more. From the Kona side, there is a two-hour Big Island Spectacular ($408/$510), an all-encompassing trip that circles the island to witness all its highlights, including a quick flyover of the park. From the Hilo side, the one-hour Circle of Fire Plus Waterfalls Tour ($202/$248) will take you over the waterfalls near Hilo on the way to Hawai'i Volcanoes National Park.

Food

VOLCANO VILLAGE

I wish the dining experience in Volcano—with its captive audience of tourists who are starving after a long day of touring the park—were so much better than it actually is. There are a few options, but they tend toward mediocre and overpriced, so keep your expectations low. If you're not too hungry, are in the area for a few days, or are simply in the mood for a drive, it might be worth heading to Hilo (40 minutes away) to seek better options. The choices in Volcano are listed from south to north on Old Volcano Road. They are all within minutes of one another.

The newest restaurant in the village, **'Ohelo Café** (19-4005 Haunani Rd., 808/339-7865, www.ohelocafe.com, 11:30am-2:30pm and 5:30pm-9:30pm daily, $15-35), is a good option in the Volcano Village food desert. The best bang for your buck comes from the wood-fired pizzas ($13-15), which are served at both lunch and dinner. The daily burger (offered lunch only, $14) has good flavor, but I'd skip the plate lunch because it's a bit overpriced for "local food."

In the back side of the same complex, the food at **Eagle's Lighthouse Café** (corner of Old Volcano Rd. and Haunani Rd., 808/985-8587, http://eagleslighthouse.com/, 7am-5pm Mon.-Sat., $10) (formally known as Café Ohia) is reasonably priced. There never seem to be enough people working here for as crowded as it gets. But the crowds are here for a reason: homemade breads, pastries, and lunch specials. For $9.75 you have your choice of deli sandwich with Hawaiian-style sides. The portions are large. If you're not too hungry, try the Portuguese bean soup. It's a nonvegetarian hearty stew that will warm you up during the sometimes-chilly Volcano days. There is no indoor seating, so either take your sandwiches to go into the park or enjoy them outside on picnic tables. Since the wait can get long, the staff encourages patrons to head next door to the grocery store and grab a beer to enjoy outside.

The most romantic and rustic option in town is the long-standing **Kilauea Lodge** (19-3948 Old Volcano Rd., 808/967-7366, www.kilauealodge.com, daily 7:30am-2pm and 5pm-9pm, lunch $12, dinner $32). The food is expensive, but the setting seems to match. The large fireplace sets the mood for this truly lodge-like setting, with game animals adorning the ceiling and featured on the menu. Vegetarian choices are limited here. The meat dishes are prepared well and come with satisfying sides like mashed potatoes, but overall, the meat dishes are better in the restaurants of Waimea. Foodies and those who like to drink might try their *li hing mui* (salted dried plum)-rimmed cocktails, like *liliko'i* (passion fruit) margaritas. Eating isn't a requirement for drinking here. If you solely want drinks, you can simply walk in, cozy up on the couch in front of the fireplace, and order away. Reservations are a must for dinner, and if you want to surprise your dinner guest, call ahead to ask for your name on the menu.

The food truck craze has finally made it to this side of the island. ★ **Tuk Tuk Thai** (19-4030 Wright Rd. in the Cooper Center parking lot, 808/747-3041, www.tuk-tukthaifood.com, 11am-6pm Tues.-Sat., $12) is truly the best choice around (if it's open). The standard (American-style) Thai dishes are available: fried rice, curry, pad thai noodles—all with a choice of tofu, chicken, or shrimp. It's not clear to me why the truck doesn't stick around for dinnertime (it'd make a killing!), so I recommend picking it up early for dinner and taking it back to your vacation rental to reheat later. Portions are huge. If you're in a rush or starving during your hike, you can call ahead and your order will be ready upon arrival.

Some locals say that **Thai Thai** (19-4084 Old Volcano Rd., 808/967-7969, www.lavalodge.com/thai-thai-restaurant.html, 11:30am-9pm daily, $11-26) is their favorite Thai food place on the island. The food is all spicy and authentic, with traditional dishes such as soups, rice noodles, and curries. Beer, wine, and plenty of gluten-free and vegetarian options are offered, and a children's menu is available. The restaurant is attached to a gift shop with tourist items and toiletries. Call ahead; sometimes the restaurant doesn't follow its posted hours.

Right before the road comes to a dead end, you'll find Ira Ono's place (that's what the locals call it): **Café Ono** (19-3834 Old Volcano Rd., 808/985-8979, www.cafeono.net/, gallery 10am-4pm Tues.-Sun., café 11am-3pm Tues.-Sun., $14). It's the kind of place that you either love or hate. The menu lists only four or five mains, drinks, and a few desserts each day. But the food tastes like something you could have made but you probably would have seasoned better. The service is quick enough. The setting is lovely, with a few tables in the back of the art gallery and more outdoors among the trees.

HAWAI'I VOLCANOES NATIONAL PARK

The **Volcano House** (1 Crater Rim Dr., 808/930-6910, www.hawaiivolcanohouse.com) includes two side-by-side eating options: **Uncle George's Lounge** (11am-9:30pm daily, $13) and ★ **The Rim Restaurant** (breakfast buffet 7am-10am daily, $18 per adult, $9 per child, lunch 11am-2pm, $15, dinner 5:30pm-8:30pm, $20-30), both with priceless views of the nearby crater. The lounge offers a more casual and intimate setting with pupus like kalua pork and pineapple pizza ($12) and a Big Island burger ($14) offered throughout the day. Local beers on draft are a good deal here. The restaurant is almost fancy. You'd probably want to change out of your rain-soaked pants and muddy hiking shoes to feel comfortable dining here. Reservations are a must, especially if you're booking during sunset—and that's precisely when you should dine to watch the colors change over the crater. Entrees are expensive but have the presentation one would expect for those prices—although you're likely going to be too distracted by the views to actually look at the food. I'd skip the stuffed Big Island chicken ($24) for something tastier like the Hilo coffee-rubbed lamb ($39). An extensive wine list is also available.

Hilo

Hilo is hip. It has dive bars, walkable streets, historic buildings, cheap rents, two universities, and, most important, it's an underrated foodie mecca.

It has the potential to be the new Brooklyn or the new Portland or maybe a Berkeley or Ann Arbor. But Hilo has resisted change and happily retains itself as a relic of old Hawai'i.

Hilo has the second-largest population in the state (after Honolulu). It is a classic tropical town, the kind described in books like Gabriel García Márquez's *Love in the Time of Cholera*. Many of the downtown buildings date to the early 1900s, when the plantation industry was booming and the railroad took workers and managers from the country to the big city of Hilo. You can walk the central area comfortably in an afternoon, but the town does sprawl some due to the modern-day construction of large shopping malls and residential subdivisions in the outlying areas.

In Hilo the old beat, the old music, and that feeling of a tropical place where rhythms are slow and sensual still exist. Nights are alive with sounds of the tropics, namely coqui frogs, and the heady smells of fruits and flowering trees wafting on the breeze. Days epitomize tropical weather, with predictable afternoon showers during the winter and spring months.

Hilo's weather makes it a natural greenhouse; botanical gardens and flower farms surround it like a giant lei. Black-sand beaches are close by, waiting for you to come cool off. To counterpoint this tropical explosion, Mauna Kea's winter snows backdrop the town. Hilo is one of the oldest permanently settled towns in Hawaii, and the largest on the windward coast of the island. Don't make the mistake of underestimating Hilo, or of counting it out because of its rainy reputation. 'Akaka Falls is less than 30 minutes from downtown Hilo, but there is a lot to see on the way right off the highway, including an incredible four-mile scenic drive that winds through a rainforest that smells overwhelmingly like papayas.

ORIENTATION
Downtown Hilo and the Bayfront
You'll know you are nearing downtown when

Previous: Richardson's Beach Park; Kayakers take advantage of the calm water and spectacular views of the Hilo Bay. **Above:** Rainbow Falls.

Highlights

★ **Coconut Island:** A favorite picnic spot for decades, Coconut Island offers the best panorama of the city, bay, and Mauna Kea beyond (page 495).

★ **Rainbow Falls and Boiling Pots:** The 80-foot Rainbow Falls is true to its name, its mists throwing flocks of rainbows into the air. At the potholed riverbed of Boiling Pots, river water cascades from one bubbling whirlpool tub into the next (page 497).

★ **Onomea Scenic Drive (Four-Mile Scenic Drive):** Along this four-mile route you'll see jungle that covers the road like a living green tunnel, the Hawaii Tropical Botanical Garden, and one fine view after another (page 498).

★ **'Akaka Falls State Park:** In addition to the falls, this park offers a pristine valley and an accessible foray into the island's beautiful interior (page 499).

★ **Richardson's Beach Park:** Head to this black-sand beach for terrific snorkeling, swimming, or just snoozing in the shade (page 501).

★ **Honoli'i Beach Park:** This beach is one of the finest surfing spots on this side of the island. Even if you're not a surfer, it's worth coming here to watch the local talent hit the big waves (page 501).

© AVALON TRAVEL

Hilo and Around

© AVALON TRAVEL

0 _____ 2 mi

0 _____ 2 km

To Waimea and
Mauna Kea

SADDLE RD

Wailuku River

Hawai'i Falls

Kaumana
Caves Park

Wailuku River

Wahiloa
Falls

BOILING POTS ✦

THE INN AT
KULANIAPIA
FALLS ✦

Kaiwiki
County Park

Pohākupu'a

Puhuelāohe

Stream

Waiemi
Falls

Waiēalae
Falls

To ✦ 'AKAKA FALLS STATE PARK →

Stream

Papa'ikou Park

Pauka'a

6

○ Papa'a

✦ ONOMEA SCENIC DRIVE
(FOUR-MILE SCENIC DRIVE)

Onomea Bay

RAINBOW ✦
FALLS

Kaiwiki

Waineku ○

HILO

HILO MUNICIPAL
GOLF COURSE

STAINBACK HWY

To Volcano

11

Kea'au

130

To Pahoa

MAUNA LOA
MACADAMIA NUT
FACTORY ★

HAWAII MUSEUM OF
CONTEMPORARY ART

Bayfront
Park

Hilo
Bay

Hilo

COCONUT ✦
ISLAND

HILO
INTERNATIONAL
AIRPORT ✈

SEE "GREATER
HILO" MAP

HONOLI'I ✦
BEACH PARK

Carlsmith
Beach Park

Leleiwi
Beach Park

RICHARDSON
OCEAN CENTER

Leleiwi
Point

✦ RICHARDSON'S
BEACH PARK

PACIFIC OCEAN

200

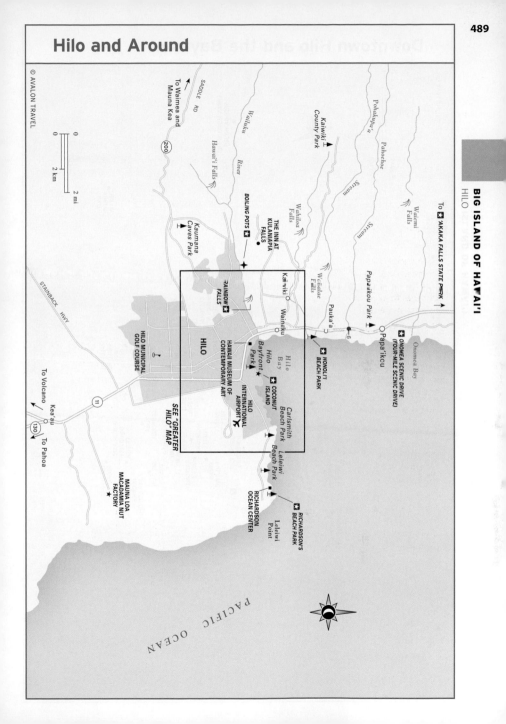

Downtown Hilo and the Bayfront

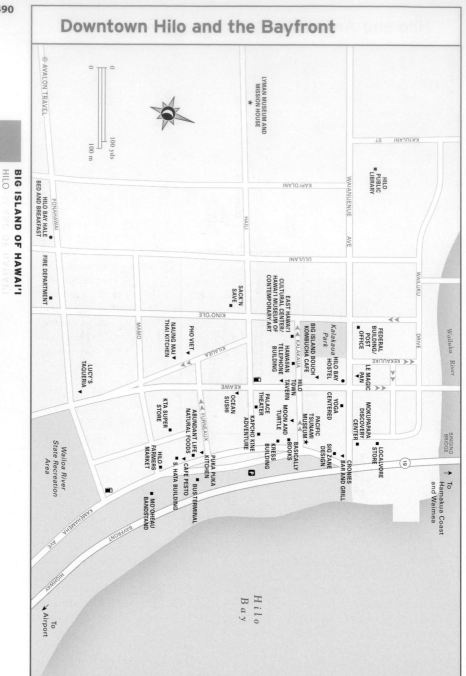

© AVALON TRAVEL

0   100 yds
0   100 m

LYMAN MUSEUM AND
MISSION HOUSE

HILO
PUBLIC
LIBRARY

KAIULANI ST

WAIANUENUE AVE

KAPI'OLANI

HAILI

ULULANI

WAILUKU DRIVE

FEDERAL
BUILDING/
POST
OFFICE

LE MAGIC
PAN

KEKAULIKE

MOKUPAPAPA
DISCOVERY
CENTER

LOCALVORE
STORE

CRONIES
BAR AND GRILL

SINGING
BRIDGE

19

To
Hamakua Coast
and Waimea

Wailuku River

PONAHAWAI

HILO BAY HALE
BED AND BREAKFAST

FIRE DEPARTMENT

SACK'N
SAVE

KINO'OLE

EAST HAWAI'I
CULTURAL CENTER/
HAWAI'I MUSEUM OF
CONTEMPORARY ART

BIG ISLAND BOUGH
KOMBUCHA CAFE

HAWAIIAN
TELEPHONE
BUILDING

Kalakaua
Park

HILO BAY
HOSTEL

HILO
TOWN
TAVERN

MOON AND
TURTLE

PALACE
THEATER

KAPCHO KINE
ADVENTURE

PACIFIC
TSUNAMI
MUSEUM

YOGA
CENTERED

BASICALLY
BOOKS

SIG ZANE
DESIGN

KRESS
BUILDING

KALAKAUA

KEAWE

KILAUEA

MAMO

PHO VIET

NAUNG MAI
THAI KITCHEN

LUCY'S
TAQUERIA

KTA SUPER
STORE

OCEAN
SUSHI

FURNEAUX

ABUNDANT LIFE
NATURAL FOODS

PUKA PUKA
KITCHEN

P

HILO
FARMERS
MARKET

CAFE PESTO

S. HATA BUILDING

BUS TERMINAL

MO'OHEAU
BANDSTAND

KAMEHAMEHA AVE

BAYFRONT

HIGHWAY

To
Airport

Wailoa River
State Recreation
Area

H i l o
B a y

you start seeing parking spaces that require parallel parking. The central downtown area is made up of Kamehameha Avenue (also called Bayfront), Kilauea Avenue (which turns into Keawe Street), and Kinoole Street—parallel streets running north to south bounded on the east by Mamo Street and on the west by Waianuenue Avenue before one has to cross over a bridge to another section of Hilo.

This area is much denser than any other part of town and easily walkable. Within this area you'll find the bus station, Hilo Farmers Market, cafés, restaurants, grocery stores, and tourist shops. While this isn't where you would come to jump in the water, this area is where you'll see cruise ship passengers walking around (with the ship in the distance towering over the town), picking up souvenirs.

Greater Hilo

Thanks to our old friend urban sprawl, Hilo begins almost right after the Kea'au Shopping Center on Highway 11. Hilo has greatly expanded from its original roots by transforming its farmlands (and the settlements of native Hawaiians) into the area on Highway 11 that now houses the Hilo International Airport, Walmart, Target, and the Prince Kuhio Mall. Where Highway 11 meets the ocean, you'll find the town's secret jewels: its beaches. Travel east on Kalaniana'ole Avenue, where beaches are situated one after another, easily recognizable from the road by their official county park signs. Although these beaches are easily accessible, you'll be entering into a coastal wonderland that couldn't feel farther from the suburban enclave just up the road.

North Hilo to 'Akaka Falls

Pass over the "Singing Bridge" leaving downtown Hilo and, soon after, you're in the North Hilo district traveling on Highway 19 toward the Hamakua Coast. This route, one of the prettiest on the island with its ocean views, passes by several old plantation towns that are still residential communities that do not offer anything of interest to tourists. Just seven miles out of Hilo, you'll pass the sign for

Four-Mile Scenic Drive. You should turn onto it immediately; it's the old route that parallels the highway. Back on the highway as you drive north, you'll arrive at the town of Honomu, the gateway to 'Akaka Falls. From here it's still necessary to climb *mauka* on Highway 220 (about 20 minutes) until you reach the entrance to this must-see sight.

PLANNING YOUR TIME

While many visitors to the Big Island stay only on the Kona side, those who know the island well and appreciate its diversity split their time between the Kona and Hilo sides. Hilo, being the largest city and main hub on the east side, is the logical place to use as a base. The city is bite-size, but you'll need a rental car to visit most of the sights around town. Hilo itself has plenty to keep a traveler busy for a number of days. First, spend time exploring the natural beauty of the city and its close-by botanical gardens, its bay and beaches, and the pretty waterfalls only a few minutes from downtown. Both Rainbow Falls and the potholed riverbed of Boiling Pots are Instagram-able and perhaps most photogenic when there's plenty of rain to make them perform at their best. Take an hour or two to walk under the giant banyan trees that canopy Banyan Drive, stroll through the relaxing Lili'uokalani Gardens, and walk the bridge to Coconut Island for a perfect view of the bay and waterfront, with snowcapped Mauna Kea as a backdrop. While you are out that way, continue on down Kalaniana'ole Avenue for a morning or afternoon in the water at one of the small beaches along the Keaukaha strip.

Hilo is an old town. Reserve a morning or afternoon for a walking tour of town, viewing its well-kept historic buildings, and then spend a few hours at both the Pacific Tsunami Museum, where you will learn about the brutal waters that destroyed much of Hilo's Bayfront, and the Lyman Museum and Mission House, where the life of early missionaries to Hawaii comes alive. A bit out of town is the Pana'ewa Rainforest Zoo, also good for a couple of hours to view tropical

Greater Hilo

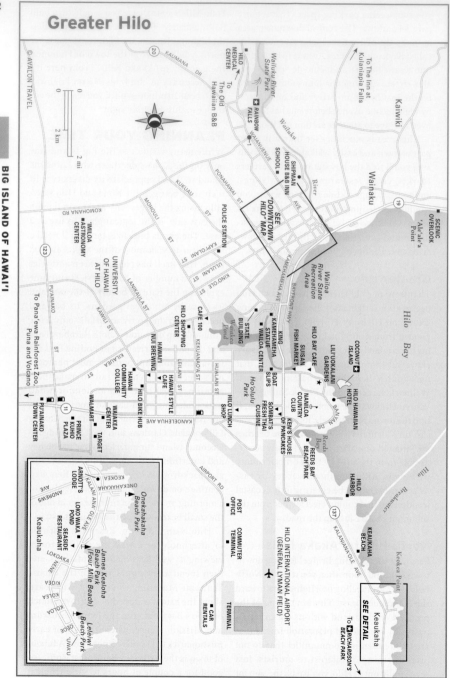

© AVALON TRAVEL

0 2 km
0 2 mi

20 KAUMANA DR

To The Inn at Kulaniapia Falls

HILO MEDICAL CENTER

To The Old Hawaiian B&B

Wailuku River State Park

RAINBOW FALLS

SHIPMAN HOUSE B&B INN

SCHOOL ST

WAIANUENUE

Wailuku River

Kaiwiki

Wainaku

19

'Ale'a Point

SCENIC OVERLOOK

SEE "DOWNTOWN HILO" MAP

PONAHAWAI ST

KUKUAU ST

POLICE STATION

KAMEHAMEHA AVE

BAYFRONT HWY

Wailoa River State Recreation Area

KOMOHANA RD

MOHOULI ST

KAPIOLANI ST

UILILANI ST

KINO'OLE ST

'IMILOA ASTRONOMY CENTER

123

PU'AINAKO ST

LANIKAULA ST

UNIVERSITY OF HAWAII AT HILO

KAWILI ST

To Pana'ewa Rainforest Zoo, Puna and Volcano

KILAUEA ST

HILO SHOPPING CENTER

CAFE 100

HAWAI'I NUI BREWING

KEKUANAOA ST

LEILANI ST

HAWAII COMMUNITY COLLEGE

HAWAI'I STYLE CAFE

HILO BIKE HUB

HUALANI ST

STATE BUILDING

KAMEHAMEHA STATUE

WAILOA CENTER

Waiakea Pond

Ho'olulu Park

KING

SUISAN FISH MARKET

HILO BAY CAFE

LILI'UOKALANI GARDENS

COCONUT ISLAND

NANILOA COUNTRY CLUB

BANYAN DR

HILO HAWAIIAN HOTEL

Hilo Bay

WALMART

WAIAKEA CENTER

TARGET

PRINCE KUHIO PLAZA

11

PU'AINAKO TOWN CENTER

KANOELEHUA AVE

HILO LUNCH SHOP

BOAT SLIPS

SOMBAT'S FRESH THAI

KEN'S HOUSE OF PANCAKES

REEDS BAY BEACH PARK

Reeds Bay

HILO HARBOR

KEAUKAHA BEACH

Breakwater

Keokea Point

Keaukaha

SEE DETAIL

To RICHARDSON'S BEACH PARK

AIRPORT RD

SILVA ST

POST OFFICE

COMMUTER TERMINAL

HILO INTERNATIONAL AIRPORT (GENERAL LYMAN FIELD)

KALANIANA'OLE AVE

137

TERMINAL

CAR RENTALS

ARNOTT'S LODGE

KALANI ANA-OLE AVE

ANDREWS AVE

KEOKEA

ONEKAHAKAHA

Onekahakaha Beach Park

LOKO WAKA POND

SEASIDE RESTAURANT

Keaukaha

James Kealoha Beach Park (Four Mile Beach)

LOKOAKA

NENE

KIOEA

KOLEA

OEOE

KOLOA

'UWA'U

Leleiwi Beach Park

Your Best Day in Hilo

- Wake up early and come to **Honoli'i Beach Park** to surf or to watch the surfers.

- If it's a Wednesday or Saturday, head to the **Hilo Farmers Market** to see the wide range of fruits that grow on the island.

- Take a **walking tour of downtown Hilo** to see the architecture of early-20th-century Hawaii.

- Stop in the **Hawaii Museum of Contemporary Art, Pacific Tsunami Museum,** or the **Lyman Museum.**

- In the afternoon, relax at one of the many black-sand beaches just 10 minutes from downtown, such as **Richardson's Beach Park.**

- Have dinner at one of Hilo's undervalued foodie joints: **Puka Puka Kitchen, Sombat's Fresh Thai Cuisine, or Hilo Bay Café.**

- For a low-key night, catch an art film or performance.

- Late at night go where the locals go to end the evening: **Ken's House of Pancakes.**

RAINY-DAY ALTERNATIVE

Hilo is a great place to spend a rainy day, given the large number of museums and movie theaters. Here are a few other ideas, and they are mostly free and kid friendly.

Right on the Bayfront, it's easy to totally miss the **Mokupapapa Discovery Center for Hawaii's Coral Reefs.** This newly renovated museum is great for spending a few minutes perusing its information about reefs and fish of the Northwestern Hawaiian Islands.

animals in a natural environment, and the opportunity to see some of the thick and luxuriant forest cover that surrounds the city. For exploration from Hilo, it's an hour's drive down to the steamy Puna Coast, about the same up to the stark lava lands of Hawai'i Volcanoes National Park or along the wet and wonderful Hamakua Coast to time-lost Waipi'o Valley, and a bit longer for a trek to the top of the Mauna Kea to see the astronomical observatories and experience a sunset from the heights.

Sights

Before the shift of tourism to the drier Kona side of the island, Hilo was the Big Island's major visitor destination. This old town and steamy tropical port still holds many attractions, from missionary homes to forest waterfalls to landscaped tropical gardens to diminutive beaches with great snorkeling options.

DOWNTOWN HILO AND THE BAYFRONT
Lyman Museum and Mission House

A few short blocks above downtown Hilo, the **Lyman Museum and Mission House** (276 Haili St., 808/935-5021, www.lyman-museum.org, 10am-4:30pm Mon.-Sat., $10 adults, $8 seniors, $3 children, $17 family, $5 students) showcases the oldest wood building on the Big Island, originally built in 1839 for David and Sarah Lyman, some of the first Christian missionaries on the island. The museum is a Smithsonian affiliate with a bit of everything, from fine art to mineral and gem collections to exhibits on habitats of Hawaii. The first-floor Earth Heritage Gallery holds a mineral and rock collection that's rated one of the best in the entire country, and by far the best in Polynesia. The museum also holds a substantial collection of archival documents and images relating to Hawaii's history.

Next door is the Lyman Mission House, which opened as a museum in 1931. The furniture is authentic "Sandwich Isles" circa 1850. Some of the most interesting exhibits are of small personal items, such as a music box that still plays and a collection of New England autumn leaves that Mrs. Lyman had sent over to show her children what that season was like. Upstairs are bedrooms that were occupied by the Lyman children. Mrs. Lyman kept a diary and faithfully recorded eruptions, earthquakes, and tsunamis. Scientists still refer to it for some of the earliest recorded data on these natural disturbances. The master bedroom has a large bed with pineapples carved into the bedposts, crafted by a ship's carpenter who lived with the family for about eight months. The bedroom mirror is an original, in which many Hawaiians received their first surprised look at themselves. Guided tours of the Lyman Mission House are included with museum admission and are given twice a day (11am and 2pm) by experienced and knowledgeable docents who relate many intriguing stories about the house and its occupants.

Pacific Tsunami Museum

Hilo suffered a devastating tsunami in 1946 and another in 1960. Both times, most of the waterfront area of the city was destroyed, but the 1930 Bishop National Bank building survived, owing to its structural integrity. Appropriately, the **Pacific Tsunami Museum** (130 Kamehameha Ave., 808/935-0926, www.tsunami.org, 10am-4pm Tues.-Sat., $8 adults, $7 seniors, $4 students) is now housed in this fine art deco structure and dedicated to those who lost their lives to the devastating waves that raked the city. The museum has numerous permanent displays, an audiovisual room, computer linkups to scientific sites, and periodic temporary exhibitions. The most moving displays of this museum are the photographs of the last two terrible tsunamis that struck the city and the stories told by the survivors of those events. Stop in for a look. It's worth the time.

Mokupapapa Discovery Center for Hawaii's Coral Reefs

This newly renovated museum right on the Bayfront, the **Mokupapapa Discovery Center for Hawaii's Coral Reefs** (76 Kamehameha Ave., Suite 109, 808/933-8180, www.papahanaumokuakea.gov, 9am-4pm Tues.-Sat., free) has a few interactive features and life-size models of wildlife, and is filled with information about the science, culture, and history of the Northwestern Hawaiian Islands and their marine life. Besides the fact that it has a great restroom (so hard to find public restrooms on Bayfront!), this center offers a perfect place to bring kids for an hour of learning masked as fun. Since the center is indoors, this visit also makes for a great pop-in on the chance that you catch yourself in a Hilo rainstorm.

Around Banyan Drive

If your Hilo hotel isn't situated along Banyan Drive, go there. This bucolic, horseshoe-shaped road skirts the edge of Waiakea Peninsula, which sticks out into Hilo Bay. Lining the drive is an almost uninterrupted series of banyan trees forming a giant canopy. Skirting its edge are the Lili'uokalani Gardens, a concentration of hotels, and Reed's Bay.

This peninsula was once a populated residential area, an offshoot of central Hilo. Like much of the city, it was destroyed during the tsunami of 1960. Park your car at one end and take a stroll through this parklike atmosphere. Or arrive early and join other Hilo residents for a morning jog around the loop.

The four dozen banyans that line this boulevard (the first planted in 1933, the last in 1972) were planted by notable Americans and foreigners, including Babe Ruth, President Franklin D. Roosevelt, King George V, Hawaiian volcanologist Dr. Thomas Jaggar, Hawaiian princess Kawananakoa, pilot Amelia Earhart, filmmaker Cecil B. DeMille, and then-senator Richard Nixon. A placard in front of most trees gives particulars. Time has taken its toll here, however, and as grand as this drive once was, it is now a bit overgrown and unkempt in spots, with much of the area needing a little sprucing up.

LILI'UOKALANI GARDENS

The **Lili'uokalani Gardens** are formal Japanese-style gardens located along the west end of Banyan Drive. Meditatively quiet, they offer a beautiful view of the bay. Along the footpaths are pagodas, torii gates, stone lanterns, and half-moon bridges spanning a series of ponds and streams. Along one side sits a formal Japanese teahouse, where women come to be instructed in the art of the tea ceremony. Few people visit this 30-acre garden,

and if it weren't for the striking fingers of black lava and the coconut trees, you could easily be in Japan.

★ COCONUT ISLAND

Coconut Island (Moku Ola) is reached by footbridge from a spit of land just outside Lili'uokalani Gardens. It was at one time a *pu'uhonua* (place of refuge) opposite a human sacrificial *heiau* on the peninsula side. Coconut Island has restrooms, a pavilion, and picnic tables shaded by tall coconut trees and ironwoods. It's been a favorite picnic spot for decades; kids often come to jump into the water from stone abutments here, and older folks come for a leisurely dip in the cool water. The only decent place to swim in Hilo Bay, it also offers the best panorama of the city, bay, and Mauna Kea beyond.

Wailoa River State Recreation Area

To the east of downtown is **Waiakea Pond,** a brackish lagoon where people often fish, although that might not be such a great idea given the rumored levels of pollution. The **Wailoa River State Recreation Area,** which encompasses the lagoon, is a 132-acre preserve set along both sides of this spring-fed

Lili'uokalani Gardens, a formal Japanese-style garden, offers idyllic views of the bay.

pond. City residents use this big, broad area for picnics, pleasure walks, informal get-togethers, fishing, and launching boats. On the eastern side are picnic pavilions and barbecue grills. Arching footbridges cross the river and connect the halves.

Stop at the **Wailoa Center** (200 Piopio St., 808/933-0416, 8:30am-4:30pm Mon.-Fri.) on the western side for tourist information and cultural displays such as exhibits by local artists. The walls in the upstairs gallery of this 10-sided building are used to display works of local artists and cultural/historical exhibits, changed on a regular basis. On the lower level hang astonishing pictures of the 1946 and 1960 tsunamis that washed through the city. The Wailoa Center sits in a broad swath of greenery, an open, idyllic, parklike area that used to be a cramped, bustling neighborhood known as Shinmachi. It, like much of the city, was almost totally destroyed during the tsunami of 1960. Nearby stands the **Tsunami Memorial** to the residents of this neighborhood who lost their lives in that natural disaster.

Also close by is the county **Vietnam War Memorial,** dedicated to those who died fighting that war, and a **statue of King Kamehameha,** a new version of which graces the town of Kapa'au at the northern tip of the island.

East of Waiakea Pond and across Manono Street you'll see **Ho'olulu Park,** with the Civic Center Auditorium and numerous athletic stadiums. This is the town's center for organized athletic events, large cultural festivals, the yearly **Merrie Monarch Festival** (www.merriemonarch.com), and the annual county fair.

GREATER HILO
Mauna Loa Macadamia Nut Factory

Mauna Loa Macadamia Nut Factory (16-701 Macadamia Road, 808/966-8618, www.maunaloa.com, 8:30am-5pm daily) is several miles south of Hilo, off Highway 11, nearly at Kea'au. Head down Macadamia Road for about three miles, through the 2,500-acre plantation, until you come to the visitors center. Inside is an informative free video explaining the development and processing of macadamia nuts in Hawaii. Walkways outside the windows of the processing center and chocolate shop let you view the process of turning these delicious nuts into tantalizing gift items; this is best viewed from August through January when most of the processing

Coconut Island is a favorite for local kids.

is done. Then return to the snack shop for macadamia nut goodies like ice cream and cookies, and to the gift shop for samples and an intriguing assortment of packaged macadamia nut items. While you're here, step out back and take a self-guided tour of the small garden, where many introduced trees and plants are identified.

Pana'ewa Rainforest Zoo

Not often can travelers visit a zoo in such a unique setting, where the animals virtually live in paradise. The 150 animals at this 12-acre zoo are endemic and introduced species that would naturally live in such an environment. While small and local, the zoo is a delight and the only natural tropical rainforest zoo in the United States. The road to the Pana'ewa Rainforest Zoo (000 Stainback Hwy., 808/959-9233, www.hilozoo.com, 9am-4pm daily, closed Christmas and New Year's Day, free) is a trip in itself, getting you back into the country. On a typical weekday, you'll have the place much to yourself. The zoo, operated by the county Department of Parks and Recreation, has a petting zoo every Saturday from 1:30pm to 2:30pm. Admission is free, although donations to the nonprofit Friends of the Pana'ewa Zoo, which runs the gift shop at the entrance, are appreciated.

Here you have the feeling that the animals are not "fenced in" so much as you are "fenced out." The collection of about 75 species includes ordinary and exotic animals from around the world. You'll see pygmy hippos from Africa, a rare white Bengal tiger named Namaste, a miniature horse and steer, Asian forest tortoises, water buffalo, monkeys, and a wide assortment of birds like pheasants and peacocks. The zoo hosts many endangered animals indigenous to Hawaii, like the *nene,* Laysan duck, Hawaiian coot, *pueo,* Hawaiian gallinule, and even a feral pig in his own stone mini-condo. There are some great iguanas and mongooses, lemurs, and an aviary section with **exotic birds** like yellow-fronted parrots and blue and gold macaws.

To get to the zoo from Hilo, take Highway 11 (Hawai'i Belt Road) south toward Volcano. About 2.5 miles past Prince Kuhio Shopping Plaza look for the Zoo sign on a lava rock wall, just after the sign reading "Kulani 19." Turn right on Mamaki.

'Imiloa Astronomy Center

Located on the upper campus of University of Hawai'i at Hilo, the **'Imiloa Astronomy Center** (600 Imiloa Pl., 808/969-9700, www.imiloahawaii.org, 9am-5pm Tues.-Sun., adults $17.50, children 5-12 $9.50, senior, military, and *kama'aina* discounts available) opened in 2006 dedicated to the integration of science and indigenous culture. The word *'imiloa* means "exploring new knowledge," and the center educates visitors by separating its exhibits into "origins" and "explorations." Although in another place, the combination of studying astronomy and voyages may not make as much sense, here in Hawaii the two matters are linked given that the ancient Polynesians used the stars to wayfind from Polynesia to Hawaii and back.

In addition to the exhibits, a planetarium hosts daily kids' programs as well as Friday night laser light shows. Special events and workshops frequently occur at the center. Check the website for more information and for the Hawaiian word of the day. Say it at the register and get a $2 discount for each individual who speaks the word.

★ Rainbow Falls and Boiling Pots

A few miles out of town as you head west on Waianuenue Avenue, two natural spectacles within Wailuku River State Park are definitely worth a look. A short way past Hilo High School a sign directs you to **Rainbow Falls,** a most spectacular yet easily visited natural wonder. You'll look down on a circular pool in the river below that's almost 100 feet in diameter; cascading into it is a lovely waterfall. The 80-foot falls deserve their name because as they hit the water below, their mists throw flocks of rainbows into the air. Underneath the falls is a huge cavern, held by legend to be the abode of Hina, mother of the god Maui. Most people are content to look from the vantage point near the parking lot, but if you walk to the left, you can take a stone stairway to a private viewing area directly over the falls (be careful; it can be slippery). Here the river, strewn with volcanic boulders, pours over the edge. Follow the path for a minute or so along the bank to a gigantic banyan tree and a different vantage point. The falls may be best seen in the morning when the sunlight streams in from the front.

Follow Waianuenue Avenue for two more miles past Hilo Medical Center to the heights above town. A sign to turn right onto Pe'epe'e Falls Street points to the **Boiling Pots.** Few people visit here. Follow the path from the parking lot past the toilets to an overlook. Indented into the riverbed below is a series of irregularly shaped depressions that look as though a peg-legged giant left his prints in the hot lava. Seven or eight resemble naturally bubbling whirlpool tubs as river water cascades from one into the next. This phenomenon is best seen after a heavy rain. Turn your head upriver to see **Pe'epe'e,** a gorgeous, five-spouted waterfall. Although signs warn you not to descend to the river—it's risky during heavy rains—locals hike down to the river rocks below to sunbathe and swim in pools that do not have rushing water. Be careful because it can get slippery; flash floods can and have occurred here.

Kaumana Cave

In 1881, Mauna Loa's tremendous eruption discharged a huge flow of lava. The river of lava crusted over, forming a tube through which molten lava continued to flow. Once the eruption ceased, the lava inside siphoned out, leaving the tube now called **Kaumana Cave** (Rte. 200). Follow a steep staircase down into a gray hole draped with green ferns and brightened by wildflowers. Smell the scent of the tropical vegetation. You can walk only a few yards into the cave before you'll need a strong flashlight and sturdy shoes. I'm not kidding: it's really dark and wet in there. A headlamp is ideal. Most people take the left

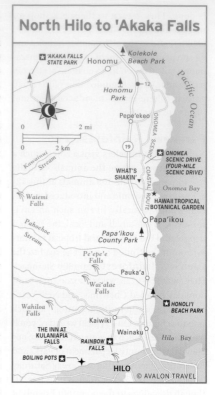

"fork" at the bottom of the stairs instead of the right one—the right one involves more crawling over uneven, tight surfaces.

To get to Kaumana Cave from downtown Hilo, turn left on Waianuenue Avenue. Just past mile marker 1 stay to the left onto Kaumana Drive (Saddle Rd.). Kaumana Cave is on the right just past mile marker 4. There are many reports of GPS leading people to the wrong location, so follow the directions here and look for the sign. Also, there have been break-ins reported in the parking area, so take proper precautions.

NORTH HILO TO 'AKAKA FALLS
★ Onomea Scenic Drive (Four-Mile Scenic Drive)

Highway 19 heading from Hilo to Honoka'a has magnificent inland and coastal views one after another. Most people find the **Onomea Scenic Drive** when coming north from Hilo. Only five minutes from the city, you'll come to Papaʻikou town. Just past mile marker 7 and across the road from the Papaʻikou School, a road posted as the scenic drive dips down toward the coast. Take it. (If you are coming from the Kona side you'll see a sign between mile markers 10 and 11). Almost immediately, signs warn you to slow your speed because of the narrow winding road and one-lane bridges, letting you know what kind of area you're entering. Start down this meandering lane past some modest homes and into the jungle that covers the road like a living green tunnel. Prepare for tiny bridges crossing tiny valleys. Stop, and you can almost hear the jungle growing. Along this four-mile route are sections of an ancient coastal trail and the site of a former fishing village. Drive defensively, but take a look as you pass one fine view after another. This road runs past the Hawaii Tropical Botanical Garden and a couple of places for quick eats before heading up to higher ground to rejoin Highway 19 at Pepeʻekeo.

If you're coming from Hilo, just a few minutes (or 1.5 miles) along the Onomea Scenic Drive is the **Hawaiʻi Tropical Botanical Garden** (27-717 Old Mamalahoa Hwy., 808/964-5233, www.hawaiigarden.com, 9am-5pm daily, last entry 4pm, adults $15, children 6-16 $5). Remember that the entrance fee not only allows you to walk through the best-tamed tropical rainforest on the Big Island but helps preserve this wonderful area in perpetuity.

The gardens were established in 1978, when Dan and Pauline Lutkenhouse purchased the 25-acre valley, and they have been open for viewing since 1984. Mr. Lutkenhouse, a retired San Francisco businessman, personally performed the work that transformed the valley into one of the most exotic spots in all of Hawaii. The locality was amazingly beautiful but inaccessible because it was so rugged. Through personal investment and six painstaking years of toil aided by only two helpers, he hand-cleared the land, built trails and bridges, developed an irrigation system, acquired more than 2,000 different species of trees and plants, and established one mile of scenic trails and a water lily lake stocked with *koi* and tropical fish. Onomea was a favorite spot with the Hawaiians, who came to fish and camp.

These inviting gardens, a "living museum" as they call it, will attract lovers of plants and flowers, and those looking to take really great photographs. The loop through the garden is about a mile long, and the self-guided tour takes about 90 minutes. As you walk, listen for the songs of the native **birds** that love this primeval spot. The walk is not difficult, but there are steps down to the gardens that are not wheelchair accessible. Golf carts ($5) are available to help those who need it down the boardwalk, and then nonmotorized wheelchairs are allowed in the garden itself.

★ ʻAkaka Falls State Park

Everybody's idea of a pristine Hawaiian valley is viewable at **ʻAkaka Falls State Park** (on Hwy. 220, gate open 8:30am-6pm daily, $5 per car or $1 per pedestrian, no charge for Hawaii residents), one of the most easily accessible forays into Hawaiʻi's beautiful interior. Take the Honomu turnoff from Highway 19 onto Highway 220 to get here. From the parking lot, walk counterclockwise along a paved "circle route" that takes you 0.4 mile in about a half hour. The footpath does require some physical exertion. Along the way, you're surrounded by heliconia, ti, ginger, orchids, azaleas, ferns, and bamboo groves as you cross bubbling streams on wooden footbridges. Many varieties of plants that would be in window pots anywhere else are giants here, almost trees. An overlook provides views of **Kahuna Falls** spilling into a lush green valley below. The trail becomes an enchanted tunnel through hanging orchids and bougainvillea. In a few moments you arrive at **ʻAkaka Falls.** The mountain cooperates with the perfect setting, forming a semicircle from which the falls tumble 442 feet in one sheer drop, the tallest single-tier waterfall in the state. After heavy rains, expect a mad torrent of power; during dry periods, marvel at liquid-silver threads forming mist and rainbows.

Beaches

If you define a beach as a long expanse of white sand covered by a thousand sunbathers and their beach umbrellas, then Hilo doesn't have any. If a beach, to you, can be a smaller, more intimate affair, where a good number of tourists and families can spend the day on pockets of sand between fingers of black lava, then Hilo has a few. Hilo's beaches are small and rocky—perfect for keeping crowds away. The best beaches all lie to the east of the city along Kalaniana'ole Avenue, an area known as the Keaukaha Strip, which runs six miles from downtown Hilo to its dead end at Leleiwi Point. Not all beaches are clearly marked, but even those that aren't are easily identified by the cars parked along the road.

DOWNTOWN HILO AND THE BAYFRONT
Hilo Bayfront Park

A thousand yards of gray-black sand that narrows considerably as it runs west from the Wailoa River toward downtown, **Hilo Bayfront Park** (along Kamehameha Ave.) at one time went all the way to the Wailuku River and was renowned throughout the islands for its beauty. Commercialism of the waterfront ruined it: By 1960, so much sewage and industrial waste had been pumped into the bay that it was considered a public menace, and then the great tsunami came. Reclamation projects created the Wailoa River State Recreation Area at the east end, and shorefront land became a buffer zone against future inundation. Few swimmers come to the beach because the water is cloudy and chilly, but the sharks don't seem to mind! The bay is a perfect spot for canoe races, and many local teams come here to train. Notice the judging towers and canoe sheds of local outrigger canoe clubs. Toward the west end, near the mouth of the Wailuku River, surfers catch long rides during winter, entertaining spectators. There is public parking along the eastern half near the canoe clubs

or at the Wailoa River mouth where the fishing boats dock.

GREATER HILO

Although these beaches are outside of the downtown area, they are really only a few minutes from downtown, and all of them are within minutes of one another. With only one exception, all the beaches are either black-sand beaches or have no sand, just a grassy area fronting the beach.

Reeds Bay Beach Park

Technically part of Hilo Bay, **Reeds Bay Beach Park** (at the end of Banyan Dr.) is a largely undeveloped area on the east side of the Waiakea Peninsula. The water here is notoriously cold because of a constantly flowing freshwater spring at its innermost end, hence the name Ice Pond. Mostly it's frequented by fishers and locals having a good time on weekends and holidays, and some sailors park their private boats here. Restrooms, water, and shower facilities are available.

Keaukaha Beach at Carlsmith Beach Park

Keaukaha Beach at Carlsmith Beach Park, located on Puhi Bay, is the first in a series of beaches as you head east on Kalaniana'ole Avenue. Look for Baker Avenue and pull off to the left into a rough parking area. This is a favorite spot with local people, who swim at Cold Water Pond, a spring-fed inlet at the head of the bay. A sewage treatment plant fronts the western side of Puhi Bay. Much nicer areas for swimming and snorkeling await you just up Kalaniana'ole Avenue, but this beach does have a restroom, shower, pavilion, and weekend lifeguard.

Onekahakaha Beach Park

Farther up the road, **Onekahakaha Beach Park** has it all: safe swimming, a small white-sand beach, lifeguards, and amenities. Turn left onto Onekahakaha Road and park in the lot of Hilo's favorite family beach. Swim in the large, sandy-bottomed pool protected by a man-made breakwater. Outside the breakwater the currents can be fierce, and drownings have been recorded; there is a lifeguard on duty during the weekends. Walk east along the shore to find an undeveloped area of the park with many small tidal pools. Beware of sea urchins.

James Kealoha Beach Park (Four Mile Beach)

James Kealoha Beach Park, also known locally as **Four Mile Beach,** is next. People swim, snorkel, and fish here, and during winter it's a favorite surfing spot. Stay to the left side of the beach since it's more protected than the right side, which can get rough with strong currents during times of high surf.

Just offshore is an island known as Scout Island because local Boy Scouts often camp there. This entire area was known for its fishponds, and inland, just across Kalaniana'ole Avenue, is the 60-acre Loko Waka Pond. This site of ancient Hawaiian aquaculture is now a commercial operation that raises mullet, trout, catfish, perch, tilapia, and other species. There is a restroom here but no other amenities.

Leleiwi Beach Park

A favorite local spot for scuba divers, thanks to its plentiful sealife, **Leleiwi Beach Park** lies along a lovely residential area carved into the rugged coastline. This park, unlike the majority of them, has a full-time lifeguard, which is good because the shore here is open to the ocean and currents may be strong.

★ Richardson's Beach Park

Adjacent to Lelewi Beach Park is Richardson Ocean Park, known locally as **Richardson's Beach Park.** A seawall skirts the shore, and a tiny cove with a black-sand beach is the first in a series. This is a terrific area for snorkeling, with plenty of marine life, including *honu*

(green sea turtles). Walk east to a natural lava breakwater. Behind it are pools filled and flushed by the surging tide. The water breaks over the top of the lava and rushes into the pools, making natural whirlpool tubs. This is one of the most picturesque swimming areas on the island and is often crowded with families since it offers a lot of shade and a full-time lifeguard on duty. Full amenities are available.

NORTH HILO TO 'AKAKA FALLS

★ Honoli'i Beach Park

Traveling north a few miles out of Hilo brings you to **Honoli'i Beach Park** (Hwy. 19 between mile markers 4 and 5). Turn right onto Nahala Street, then left onto Kahoa, and follow it around until you see cars parked along the road. The water is down a steep series of steps, and while the black-sand beach is not much appreciated for swimming, it is known as one of the finest surfing spots on this side of the island. If you're not a seasoned surfer, no worries: there is a "kiddie" area, as well as two lifeguards if any issues should arise. I highly recommend just coming for a quick viewing session to see the local talent try their hand at big waves. Restroom facilities and showers are available.

Kolekole Beach Park

Kolekole Beach Park (Hwy. 19 near mile marker 14) is popular with local people, who use its pavilions for all manner of special occasions, usually on weekends. A pebble beach fronts a treacherous ocean. The entire valley was inundated with more than 30 feet of water during the great 1946 tsunami. The stream running through Kolekole comes from 'Akaka Falls, four miles inland. Take care while wading across it—the current can be strong and push swimmers out to sea. Local kids take advantage of the ocean's pull to try their hand at bodyboarding. Amenities include portable bathrooms, grills, electricity, picnic tables, pavilions, and a camping area (county permit required); no drinking water is available.

To get to Kolekole Beach Park, look for the

tall bridge a few minutes north of Honomu, where a sign points to a small road that snakes its way down the valley to the beach park below. Slow down and keep a sharp eye out, as the turnoff is right at the south end of the bridge and easy to miss.

Water Sports

Although all water sports are possible in Hilo, it's more difficult to rent equipment on this side of the island, probably because fewer tourists come to Hilo to engage in water sports.

CANOEING AND KAYAKING

Hilo Bay is home to many outrigger canoe clubs. In fact, it's a pretty big club sport on this side of the island. If you glance out onto Hilo Bay almost any day you'll see numerous canoes and kayaks rowing by. Most canoes on the bay are owned by clubs and they do not rent out their watercraft. It may be possible to find a canoe rental if you hang out near the launch area on Bayfront and ask around. But for now, there are no businesses renting out canoes or kayaks (a business opportunity awaits!).

DIVING AND SNORKELING

Nearly all the beach parks on Kalaniana'ole Avenue offer worthy snorkeling and diving, but the best spots are at Leleiwi Beach Park and Richardson's Beach Park. Because everyone knows those are the best spots, they can become crowded. However, if you swim out just a little bit you'll leave the crowds behind and it will just be you and the turtles.

Nautilus Dive Center (382 Kamehameha Ave., 808/935-6939, www.nautilusdivehilo. com, 9am-5pm Mon.-Sat.) offers introductory diving courses ($85 per person), three- to five-day scuba certification ($360 per person), and more advanced courses. Rentals are $35 per day and discounts are available for longer rental periods. If you're looking for a guide, they do that too. For $85 you can arrange a charter tour that includes a two-tank dive.

kayaking in Hilo Bay

SURFING AND STAND-UP PADDLEBOARDING

There are some top surfing and stand-up paddleboarding destinations on this side of the island. The most popular is Honoli'i Beach Park, where surfers and boarders don't have to worry about getting in the way of swimmers. Hilo Bay also lacks swimmers, but the water is usually cold and murky. North of Hilo in Hakalau it is possible to surf near the bridge, where waves can reach up to 16 feet. At the beach parks on Kalaniana'ole Avenue, such as Richardson's, it's also possible to surf if the weather is right, but these beaches all are prime stand-up paddleboarding haunts when the water is calm.

The hardest part of your surfing/boarding attempt might not be getting up, it might be finding a board if you just want to rent one. Your best bet for renting is **Orchidland Surfboards** (262 Kamehameha Ave., 808/935-1533, www.orchidlandsurf.com, 9am-5pm Mon.-Sat., 10am-3pm Sun.).

Shopping

DOWNTOWN HILO AND THE BAYFRONT

The Bayfront area is most definitely set up to encourage shopping. Unfortunately, it doesn't always inspire shops to stay open late or to stay open at all. Don't be surprised if by 5pm downtown Hilo feels like a ghost town. Likewise, while there are a few stores that have kept their doors open for over 20 years, many more close every year. So don't be surprised if your favorite store from a past trip is nowhere to be found.

The majority of shops on the Bayfront cater to cruise ship passengers. It's difficult to distinguish one shop from another and the same Hawaiiana tchotchkes (made in China) that they offer. Nevertheless, one store that stands apart is **Basically Books** (160 Kamehameha Ave., 808/961-0144, www.basicallybooks.com, 9am-6pm Mon.-Fri., 10am-5pm Sat., 11am-3pm Sun.). This isn't where you get recently published best sellers; instead, it has a good selection of Hawaiiana, out-of-print books, and an unbeatable selection of maps and charts. You can get anywhere you want to go with these nautical charts, road maps, and topographical maps, including quadrangles for serious hikers. The store also features a good selection of travel books and national flags, as well as children's books and toys with Hawaii themes. The owners also publish books about Hawaii under the Petroglyph Press name.

Another long-standing store, **Sig Zane Design** (122 Kamehameha Ave., 808/935-7077, www.sigzane.com, 9:30am-5pm Mon.-Fri., 9am-4pm Sat.), sells distinctive island wearables in Hawaiian/tropical designs. This store is the real deal. Sig Zane designs the fabrics, and Sig's wife, Nalani, is a *kumu hula* who learned the intricate dance steps from her mother, Edith Kanakaole, a legendary dancer who has been memorialized with a local tennis stadium that bears her name. You can get shirts, dresses, and pareu, as well as affordable T-shirts, *hapi* coats, and even futon covers. The shelves also hold leather bags, greeting cards, and accessories.

GREATER HILO

The majority of shopping for everyday living happens within the same four corners off of Highway 11. More importantly, this area serves as a main wayfinding point for giving directions to all other locations around town (including the airport, which is nearby). **Prince Kuhio Plaza** (111 E. Puainako St., 808/959-3555, www.princekuhioplaza.com, 10am-8pm Mon.-Thurs., 10am-9pm Fri.-Sat., 10am-6pm Sun.) is the closest thing the

Big Island has to a mainland-looking indoor mall. You'll find a nine-screen movie theater here, too.

NORTH HILO TO 'AKAKA FALLS

The 'Akaka Falls road passes through the town of Honomu. In addition to the multitude of sarong shops dotting the main street (it's like the sarong capital of the world here), the non-sarong shops along the main street are worth a stop.

★ **Glass from the Past** (28-1672-A Old Mamalahoa Hwy., 808/963-6449, 10:30am-5pm Mon.-Sat., 7am-12pm Sun.) has been in Honomu for 25 years, and its merchandise has been in the area for nearly a hundred years. As the store's name indicates, it carries antique glass. What's so interesting about this glass is

that it is from the different area plantations—all of which had their own soda works and dairy. Each piece of glass tells a story about Hawai'i's past. Even if you're not going to make a purchase, stop in and talk with the shop owner, who scrounges the area to find his products. It's like a modern-day archaeological dig.

A few doors down, **Mr. Ed's Bakery** (28-1672 Old Mamalahoa Hwy, 808/963-5000, 6am-6pm Mon.-Sat., 930am-4pm Sun.) stocks every imaginable type of jam made from local ingredients like jaboticaba, jackfruit, starfruit, and purple sweet potato. The baked goods get bad reviews, but come in and taste one of the hundreds of jams. Low-sugar as well as no-sugar options are available; the bakery also ships jars to the mainland if you don't want to check your luggage.

Entertainment

NIGHTLIFE

People in Hilo tend not to stay out late. Maybe it's because we like to get up early and surf or maybe it's because bars open and then quickly shut down due to noise complaints from neighbors. Many of them are geared toward specific local demographics: Japanese, Korean, and Filipino clientele. If you're not with a local, you might feel a little out of place at some of these establishments.

Hilo Burger Joint (776 Kilauea, 808/935-8880, http://hiloburgerjoint.com, 11am-11pm Mon.-Sat., 11am-10pm Sun., happy hour 4pm-6pm daily, $12) is your quintessential college-town bar. In addition to 20 varieties of Big Island beef burgers, there's a full bar with lots of beers on draft. Service can be slow at times. There's live music on the weekends starting at 7pm. During the NFL season the restaurant opens early on Sundays and serves breakfast.

That sports bar you've been searching for to watch your team on the big-ish screen is **Cronies Bar and Grill** (11 Waianuenue Ave., 808/935-5158, www.cronieshawaii.

com, 11am-9pm Mon.-Thurs., 11am-10pm Fri., 11am-9pm Sat., 11am-8pm Sun., $11-20). On the weekends, it's jammed with sports lovers rooting for their favorite teams. It's right on Bayfront.

The **Hilo Town Tavern** (168 Keawe St., 808/935-2171, 11:30am-2am daily) fills a much-needed hole in downtown Hilo, where it seems like everything else closes by 5pm. You might find yourself meandering inside after hearing live music as you walk by. The bands are all local and the music styles vary. The back part of the bar has a pool table and more chairs, there is an outside patio, and the menu (which has changed several times since opening) now offers fifteen different types of sauces for chicken wings (starting at $6).

THE ARTS

Facing the peaceful Kalakaua Park, **Hawaii Museum of Contemporary Art** (141 Kalakaua St., 808/961-5711, www.ehcc.org, 10am-4pm Tues.-Sat., 5:30pm-9pm first Fri.),

Hilo Brewing

Hilo has its own microbrewery, **Hawai'i Nui Brewing** (275 E. Kawili St., 808/934-8211, www. hawaiinuibrewing.com, 12pm-5pm Mon., Tues., -Thurs., 12pm-6pm Wed., Fri., 12pm-4pm Sat.). A small operation—it produces about 1,200 barrels a year—in business since 1996, this brewery (formerly known as the Mehana Brewery) crafts five varieties of light beer with no preservatives, brewed especially for the tropical climate. Stop at the small tasting room/logo shop for a sample or gift any day except Sunday. If it's not too busy, someone may show you around.

formally the East Hawaii Cultural Center, is a nonprofit organization that supports local arts and hosts varying festivals, performances, and workshops throughout the year, here and at other locations on the island. Monthly juried and non-juried art exhibits are shown on the main-floor gallery; a venue for various performing artists is upstairs. The bulletin board is always filled with announcements of happenings in the local art scene.

Food

DOWNTOWN HILO AND THE BAYFRONT

Establishments are listed from east to west on each respective street, beginning farther from the bay and ending on Bayfront (also known as Kamehameha Avenue).

A gourmet anomaly in Hilo, **Short N Sweet Bakery and Café** (374 Kinoole St., 808/935-4446, www.shortnsweet.biz, 7am-4:30pm Mon.-Fri., 8am-3pm Sat.-Sun., $10) was proclaimed the maker of "America's most beautiful cakes" by *Brides* magazine in 2010. It was a well-deserved honor, but don't be mistaken: Short N Sweet is more than a bakery. Its lunch menu of panini and salads is a welcome break from local cuisine, and its Sunday brunch menu is gaining in popularity thanks to the homemade smoked salmon bagels and quiches. Weekdays are stocked full of deals; ask about the early-bird special (7am-10am). Vegetarian and wheat-free options are available, along with wireless Internet.

Just Cruisin' Coffee (835 Kilauea Ave., 808/934-7444, 5:30am-9pm Mon.-Fri., 5:30am-8pm Sat.-Sun., $7) has wireless Internet, drive-through windows, and outdoor seating. But where Just Cruisin' Coffee excels is with its delectable chicken macadamia nut salad with pesto sandwich, along with hot breakfast sandwiches, cold brewed coffee, smoothies, and coffee milk shakes.

Named after a famous all-Japanese fighting battalion, **Café 100** (969 Kilauea Ave., 808/935-8683, http://cafe100.com, 6:15am-8:30pm Mon.-Thurs., 6:15am-9pm Fri., 6:15am-7:30pm Sat., $7) is a Hilo institution. The Miyashiro family has been serving food at this indoor-outdoor restaurant since the late 1950s. Café 100 has turned the *loco moco* (a hamburger and egg atop rice smothered in gravy) into an art form. Offerings include the regular *loco moco,* teriyaki *loco,* Spam *loco,* hot dog *loco, oyako loco,* and, for the health conscious, the mahimahi *loco.* Breakfast choices include everything from bacon and eggs to coffee and doughnuts, while lunches feature beef stew, a salmon mixed plate, and fried chicken, or an assortment of sandwiches from teriyaki beef to good old BLT. Make your selection and sit at one of the picnic tables under the veranda to watch the people of Hilo go by.

An unassuming new restaurant located in the Pakalana Inn, the five-table ★ **Paul's**

Place Café (132 Punahoa St., 808/280-8646, http://paulsplcafe.wix.com/paulsplacecafe, 7am-3pm Tues.-Sat., $12) is delightful. Paul Cubio really cares that you, the diner, have the best experience possible at his little café. On one occasion, Chef Paul felt so badly that I had to wait for a table that he offered me a fresh smoothie while I waited and profusely apologized, even though I was the one who showed up without a reservation. A reservation isn't a must, but greatly helps given the limited seating; it's easier to get a seat later in the afternoon. There are only a few items on the menu, which has a mix of breakfast plates and fresh salads. This isn't a Spam breakfast-with-a-serving-size-for-eight kind of place. The eggs Benedict is dainty, but perfectly prepared. The Greek salad isn't large enough to split, but one can taste the flavors of each individual ingredient. The food is made with love.

If you've had enough of "local plates" then you'll be excited to find ★ Lucy's Taqueria (94 Kilauea Ave, 808/315-8246, www.lucystaqueria.com, 10:30am-9pm Sun., Mon., Wed., and Thurs.., 10:30am-10pm Fri.-Sat., $6-12). This "authentic" Mexican restaurant is quick and delicious and if it could get even better… it uses (mainly) local ingredients including Big Island beef. It's kind of a do-it-yourself place—you order at a counter, grab your own salsa (chips are free), and later bus your own table—but this DIYness keeps the prices low without compromising the quality of the food. Breakfast is served all day and you might need it after trying one of Lucy's margaritas, which are served in the separate bar area.

The competition for title of best Thai food on the Big Island continues at Naung Mai Thai Kitchen (86 Kilauea Ave., 808/934-7540, www.hilothai.com, 11am-9pm daily, $11-17), where the great lunch specials, pineapple curry, and vegan tapioca pudding give the other "best" Thai restaurants a run for their money. The space is intimate.

Front and center on Bayfront, with a black-and-white checkerboard floor, linen on the tables, an open-air kitchen, a high ceiling with whirling fans, and the calming effect of ferns and flowers, is Café Pesto (308 Kamehameha Ave., 808/969-6640, www.cafepesto.com, 11am-9pm Sun.-Thurs., 11am-10pm Fri.-Sat., reservations recommended, lunch $14, dinner $20), in the historic S. Hata Building. It offers affordable gourmet food in an open, airy, and unpretentious setting that looks out across the avenue to the bay. Pizzas from the 'ohi'a wood-fired oven can be anything from a simple cheese pie for $8.50 to a large Greek or chili-grilled shrimp pizza for $18; you can also create your own. Heartier appetites will be satisfied with the main dinner choices, mostly $15-28, which might be mango-glazed chicken, island seafood risotto, or beef tenderloin.

For well-priced food in a cute (very local) setting, it's imperative to get to ★ Puka Puka Kitchen (270 Kamehameha Ave., 808/933-2121, lunch 11am-2:30pm Mon.-Sat. and dinner 5:30pm-8:30pm Thurs.-Sat., $15). It's a must to get there early, otherwise the best dishes are gone. However, for late arrivals (after 2pm) the bento boxes are half price and quite a deal. The food is Middle Eastern-meets-Indian-meets-Hawaiian—with Japanese writing on the menu. The sautéed lamb plate is delicious. Order the house garlic rice to create the perfect plate of flavors. There are several vegetarian options on the menu and the restaurant accommodates special diets.

★ Two Ladies Kitchen (274 Kilauea Ave., 808/961-4766, 10am-5pm Tues.-Sat.) brings mochi to a whole new level, crafting it from sweet rice flour according to the secret family recipe. Each piece looks like a work of art. You can sense the sheer excitement when the sign comes up that reads, "We still have strawberry mochi today." The strawberries are real, which leads to a second sign that reads, "You can't bring them to the Mainland" (due to the agricultural inspection). You'll wish you could, though.

GREATER HILO

The menu at the ★ Hilo Bay Café (123 Lihiwai St., Hilo, 808/935-4939, www.

hilobaycafe.com, 11am-9pm Mon.-Thurs., 11am-9:30pm Fri.-Sat., lunch $15, dinner $24) seems like it was written by a food writer. It has dishes such as vegetarian flax sweet potato burger and roasted free-range chicken breast stuffed with cilantro-cumin mascarpone. The names of the dishes certainly make it hard to pick just one. The menu changes with the season and the meat, fish, and produce are from local farmers. The food here tastes good, and the café makes excellent cocktails that are classics with a Hawaii twist. A children's menu is available and reservations are a must.

You might recognize **Hawaiian Style Café** (681 Manono St., Hilo, 808/ 969-9265, 7am-2pm daily, 5pm-8:30pm Tues.-Thurs., 5pm-9pm Fri.-Sat., $12-20) from its sister brunch location in Waimea. This Hilo location serves up the same huge breakfasts with the added bonus of dinner five nights of week. Like breakfast, dinner portions are huge—but don't be embarrassed about not wanting to split a meal given the many homemade local-style choices. Try the ribs (lamb or kalbi) or one of the "family recipe" stews, and come before you're too hungry—waits can be long at times.

In same new strip mall area is **Miyo's** (564 Hinano St., Hilo, 808/935-2273, www.

miyosrestaurant.com, 11am-2pm and 5:30am-8:30pm Mon.-Sat., reservations recommended, $13-17), which touts itself as "home-style Japanese cooking." Many mourned Miyo's closing its shop in its old location (it was set up like a Japanese teahouse and overlooked a pond), but its new location suits it and modernizes not only the service, but also the cuisine. The menu is short: combination plates or bento boxes of sashimi or tempura served with chicken or beef. This is a favorite local place for power lunches, so reservations may be necessary for lunch and dinner.

It's no exaggeration to say ★ **Sombat's Fresh Thai Cuisine** (88 Kanoelehua, Hilo, 808/969-9336, www.sombats.com, 10:30am-1:30pm Mon.-Fri., 5pm-8:30pm Mon.-Sat., lunch $7, dinner $15) is probably some of the best Thai food you'll have outside of Thailand. Sombat, the owner and chef, grows the herbs in her garden in order to get her dishes flavored just right. The lunch special is an outstanding deal, with portions almost large enough to feed two people. Usually you choose between a curry and a noodle dish. Come early, as the special often sells out by 12:30pm and then only the à la carte options are available. Keep in mind that hot in

the thickest and freshest smoothie you will ever have at What's Shakin'

Hawaii is very, very hot on the mainland. So you might want to order a level down.

Pancakes make up about one-tenth of the massive menu at ★ **Ken's House of Pancakes** (1730 Kamehameha Ave., Hilo, 808/935-8711, www.kenshouseofpancakes. com, 24 hours), an institution in Hilo, so don't let the pancake part throw you off. Year after year Ken's wins awards for "Best Diner on the Island." It's one of few places in Hawaii that is open 24 hours. Sunday is all-you-can-eat spaghetti night. Breakfast is available anytime. Or, go big and order the Sumo Loco.

NORTH HILO TO 'AKAKA FALLS

The options in this area are few and far between, so plan accordingly.

Halfway through the Onomea Scenic Drive you'll come across the glorious oasis of ★ **What's Shakin'** (27-999 Old Mamaloahoa Hwy., Pepe'ekeo, 808/964-3080, 10am-5pm daily, smoothies $7, lunch $10). It might sound like a lot, $7, for a smoothie, but I can almost guarantee that it will be the best smoothie you'll ever have and it will be filling enough to split between two people. The fruit is all grown on the farm that houses this stand, and you can taste the freshness in every sip. The food, usually a daily special as well as the standard menu of nachos, salmon burgers, and burritos, is equally delicious, with huge portions and several vegetarian options. Note: If you are coming from the Kona direction, you'll pass a different smoothie stand as you turn right onto the scenic drive—What's Shakin' is just two minutes up the road from there.

Hamakua Coast, Waimea, and the Saddle Road

Look for ★ to find recommended
sights, activities, dining, and lodging.

Highlights

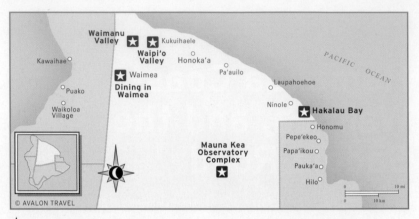

★ **Hakalau Bay:** Photographers and history buffs will be eager to visit the plantation-era ruins of Hakalau Mill, destroyed in the tsunami of 1946 (page 517).

★ **Waipi'o Valley:** Once a burial ground of Hawaiian royalty, this verdant valley is postcard perfect, with one of the best (if not the very best) views on the Big Island (page 519).

★ **Mauna Kea Observatory Complex:** View the heavens from the top of Mauna Kea, where astronomers expect an average of 325 crystal-clear nights per year (page 525).

★ **Waimanu Valley:** The hike down to Waipi'o and over the *pali* to the wild, verdant Waimanu Valley is one of the top treks in Hawaii (page 528).

★ **Dining in Waimea:** The birthplace of the Hawaii Regional Cuisine movement offers inspired dining in the heart of cowboy country (page 533).

You'll be surprised by how this northern slice of the island appears and feels so drastically different from the other regions.

The Hamakua stretch of the island, recently named the "Hilo-Hamakua Heritage Coast," draws visitors for its historical and cultural significance; there is not much beach to be had on this coast, and rough cliffs create difficult access to the ocean. Along the 50-mile stretch of Highway 19 from Hilo to Honoka'a, the Big Island grew its sugarcane for 100 years or more. Water was needed for sugar—a ton to produce a pound—and this coast has plenty. Present-day Hamakua is becoming known for its fertile growing land that is ideal for kava, mushrooms, vanilla, and macadamia nuts. Restaurants around the region source their ingredients from Hamakua, so indulge in some culinary delights on your drive around the coast.

With a population of around 2,250, Honoka'a (Rolling Bay) is the major town on the Hamakua Coast. The main street, Mamane Street, is filled with old false-front wooden buildings built in the 1920s and 1930s by Chinese and Japanese workers who left the sugar plantations to go into business for themselves. From Honoka'a, Highway 19 slips down the long Hamakua Coast to Hilo and Highway 240 heads north for nine miles to the edge of Waipi'o Valley, which you should not miss.

Waipi'o Valley (Curving Water) is the kind of place that is hard to believe unless you see it for yourself. It's vibrantly green, always watered by Waipi'o Stream and lesser streams that spout as waterfalls from the *pali* at the rear and to the side of the valley. The green is offset by a wide band of black-sand beach. From the overlook at the top of Waipi'o, you can make out the overgrown outlines of garden terraces, taro patches, and fishponds in what was Hawaii's largest cultivated valley.

Waimea, also known as Kamuela, is technically in the South Kohala district, but because of its inland topography of high mountain pasture on the broad slope of Mauna Kea, it is vastly different from the long Kohala coastal district. It also has a unique culture inspired by the range-riding *paniolo* (cowboys) of the expansive Parker Ranch. But a visit here isn't

Previous: Go riding at one of Waimea's many ranches; Waipi'o Valley overlook. **Above:** Mauna Kea summit.

one-dimensional. In town are homey accommodations, inspired country dining, and varied shopping opportunities. The town supports arts and crafts in fine galleries and has the island's premier performance venue. There's an abundance of fresh air and wide-open spaces, the latter not so easily found in the islands.

There is old lava along both sides of the road as you approach the broad tableland of the Saddle Road. Much of the lava here is from the mid-1800s, but some is from a more recent 1935 flow. Everyone with a sense of adventure loves this bold cut across the Big Island through a broad high valley separating the two great mountains, Mauna Loa and Mauna Kea. Heading up to the observatories at the top of Mauna Kea, the tallest peak in the Pacific, affords some truly stellar stargazing, while massive Mauna Loa offers one of the most extreme hikes on the island.

ORIENTATION
Hamakua Coast

Officially, the Hamakua Coast begins soon after the four-mile Onomea Scenic Drive out of Hilo and curls around to Waimea, but in reality the entire coastline should be named an official scenic drive. (This chapter is organized as if you are driving east to west on Highway 19 from Hilo along the Hamakua Coast toward Waimea. If you are coming from the Kona side, follow this chapter in reverse.) The Hamakua Coast is a good example of appreciating the journey and not necessarily the end point. The entire drive, without stopping, takes only 45 minutes.

If you are inclined to make stops along the way, there are several scenic points that allow you to soak in the magnificent ocean views down below. If you're looking for some longer excursions close to the road, stop at the Laupahoehoe Train Museum to peruse artifacts showcasing the history of the region, or visit some actual plantation artifacts (material culture for you academics out there!) at Hakalau Bay. If you really want to get out of the car and into the trees, hike one of the short trails of Kalopa Native Forest State Park, which is filled with native trees and **birds,** or try ziplining through the canopy of the World Botanical Gardens in Hakalau.

Honoka'a and Waipi'o Valley

Located on Highway 19 just 45 minutes west of Hilo and 20 minutes north of Waimea, Honoka'a is sort of a Hawaiian-style bedroom community. Follow the green sign pointing *makai* from Highway 19 to Mamane Street, the main street passing through the center of town that leads toward Highway 240 and Waipi'o Valley and the meeting points for the majority of organized Waipi'o trips. Mamane Street has a number of shops specializing in locally produced handicrafts, along with local-style restaurants, clothing and gift shops, and general merchandise stores and antiques shops. The town also holds a small health center, a post office, two banks, a movie theater, a public library, and a nine-hole golf course.

Highway 240 ends a minute outside of Kukuihaele at an overlook, and 900 feet below is Waipi'o (Curving Water), the island's largest and most southerly valley of the many that carve into the Kohala Mountains. A sacred land for ancient Hawaiians, the valley is a mile across and six miles from the ocean to its back end.

You can spend an hour in the sleepy Honoka'a town checking out the quaint handicraft boutiques and then stop back again at the end of the day after a visit to Waipi'o Valley for a happy hour cup of awa (kava) at the awa bar. And believe me, you'll be ready to relax after traveling by four-wheel-drive, horse, all-terrain vehicle, or your own two legs down the nearly vertical road to Waipi'o Valley.

Waimea

Parker Ranch, founded early in the 19th century by John Palmer Parker, dominates the heart and soul of the region. Waimea revolves around ranch life and livestock, with herds of rodeos and "Wild West shows" scheduled throughout the year.

Hamakua Coast, Waimea, and the Saddle Road

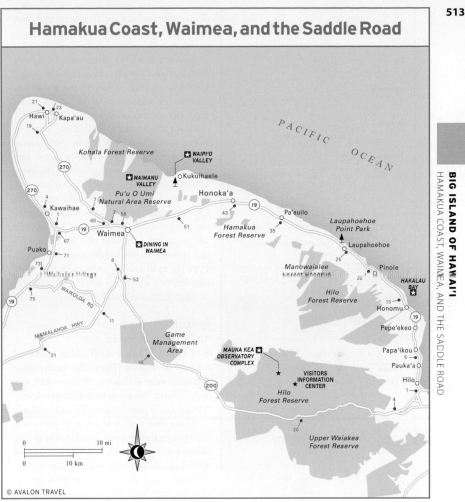

Waimea is also known as **Kamuela,** the Hawaiianized version of Samuel, after one of John Parker's grandsons. Kamuela is used as the post office address, so as not to confuse this town of Waimea with towns of the same name on the islands of O'ahu and Kaua'i.

In the last 30 years, Waimea has experienced real and substantial growth. In 1980, it had no traffic lights and was home to about 2,000 people. Now the population has grown more than threefold, there are three lights along the main highway, and there are occasional traffic jams. Waimea is modernizing and gentrifying, and its cowboy backwoods character is rapidly changing.

The town, at elevation 2,670 feet, is split almost directly down the center—the east side is the wet side, and the west is the dry side. Houses on the east side are easy to find and reasonable to rent, while houses on the dry side are expensive and usually unavailable. You can literally walk from verdant green fields and tall trees to semiarid landscape in a matter of minutes. This imaginary line also

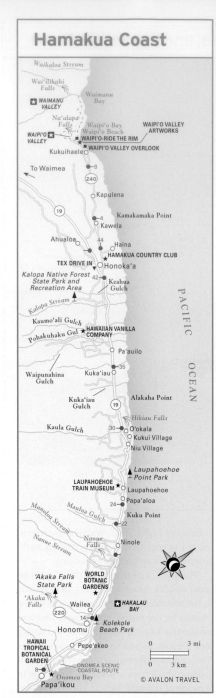

Hamakua Coast

Waikaloa Stream
Wai'ilikahi Falls
WAIMANU VALLEY
Waimanu Bay
Na'alapa Falls
Waipi'o Bay
Waipi'o Beach
WAIPI'O VALLEY
WAIPI'O VALLEY ARTWORKS
WAIPI'O-RIDE THE RIM
WAIPI'O VALLEY OVERLOOK
Kukuihaele
To Waimea — 8
240
Kapulena
19
Kamakamaka Point
Kawela
Ahualoa
44
Haina
HAMAKUA COUNTRY CLUB
TEX DRIVE IN
Honoka'a
Kalopa Native Forest State Park and Recreation Area
42
Keahua Gulch
Kalopa Stream
Kaumo'ali Gulch
Pohakuhaku Gul
HAWAIIAN VANILLA COMPANY
Pa'auilo
Waipunahina Gulch
Kuka'iau
35
Kuka'iau Gulch
Alakaha Point
19
Hikiau Falls
Kaula Gulch
30
O'okala
Kukui Village
Niu Village
Laupahoehoe Point Park
LAUPAHOEHOE TRAIN MUSEUM
Laupahoehoe
24
Papa'aloa
Manoloa Stream
Maulua Gulch
Kuku Point
22
Nanue Stream
Nanue Falls
Ninole
'Akaka Falls State Park
WORLD BOTANIC GARDENS
'Akaka Falls
220
Wailea
14
HAKALAU BAY
Honomu
Kolekole Beach Park
HAWAII TROPICAL BOTANICAL GARDEN
Pepe'ekeo
ONOMEA SCENIC COASTAL ROUTE
Onomea Bay
Papa'ikou
PACIFIC OCEAN

0   3 mi
0   3 km

© AVALON TRAVEL

demarcates the local social order: upper-class ranch managers (dry) and working-class *pani-olo* (wet).

Waimea is at the crossroads of nearly all the island's roads, the main ones being Highway 19 from Hilo (via the Hamakua Coast) and Highway 190 from Kailua-Kona. Highway 19 continues west through town, reaching the coast at Kawaihae, where it turns south and cuts along the Kohala Coast, passing by all the resorts on the way to Kailua-Kona. The upper road, Highway 190, connects Waimea to Kailua-Kona and the route looks much more like Marlboro Country than the land of *aloha,* with grazing cattle amid fields of cactus. On Highway 190 seven miles south of Waimea you'll find the turnoff to the Saddle Road (Highway 200), the road leading up to the Mauna Kea Observatory. This is the only road that travels through the middle of the island.

Mauna Kea and the Saddle Road

Slicing across the midriff of the island in a gentle arch from Hilo to the Mamalahoa Highway near Waimea is Highway 200, the Saddle Road. Access to both Mauna Loa and Mauna Kea is possible from the Saddle Road.

Along this stretch of some 55 miles you pass rolling pastureland, broad swaths of lava flows, arid fields that look a bit like Nevada, a *nene* sanctuary, trailheads for several hiking trails, mist-shrouded rainforests, an explorable cave, and spur roads leading to the tops of Mauna Kea and Mauna Loa. Here as well is the largest military training reserve in the state, with its live firing range, and the Bradshaw Army Airfield. What you won't see is much traffic or many people.

This road *is* isolated. If you do have trouble, you'll need to go a long way for assistance, but if you bypass it, you'll miss some of the best scenery on the Big Island. On the Kona side, the Saddle Road turnoff is about six miles south of Waimea along Highway 190, about halfway between Waimea and Waikoloa Road. From Hilo, follow Waianuenue Avenue

Waimea

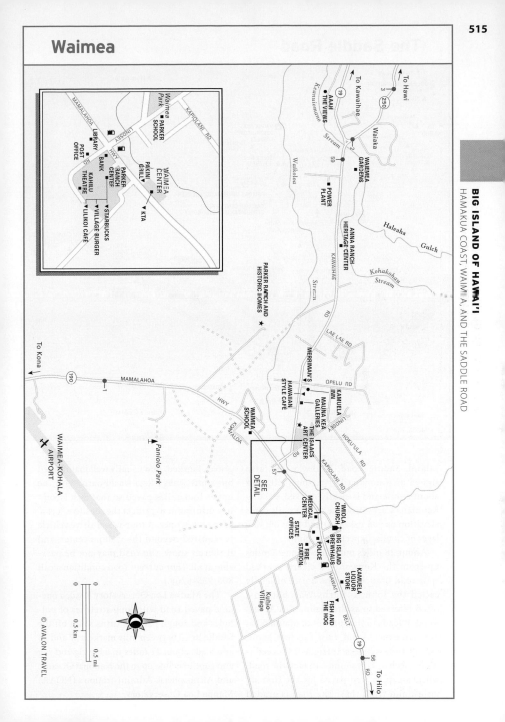

To Hawi
To Kawaihae
AAAH THE VIEWS
Waiaka
WAIMEA GARDENS
POWER PLANT
ANNA RANCH HERITAGE CENTER
Haleaha Gulch
Kohakohau Stream
PARKER RANCH AND HISTORIC HOMES
LAE LAE RD
MERRIMAN'S
OPELU RD
HAWAIIAN STYLE CAFE
KAMUELA INN
MAUNA KEA GALLERIES
THE ISAACS ART CENTER
WAIMEA SCHOOL
SEE DETAIL
MEDICAL CENTER
'IMIOLA CHURCH
BIG ISLAND BREWHAUS
STATE OFFICES
FIRE STATION
POLICE
KAMUELA LIQUOR STORE
Kubio Village
FISH AND THE HOG
To Hilo

To Kona
MAMALAHOA HWY
Paniolo Park
WAIMEA-KOHALA AIRPORT

0   0.5 km
0   0.5 mi

© AVALON TRAVEL

Waimea Park
PARKER SCHOOL
KAPIOLANI RD
LIBRARY
POST OFFICE
BANK
WAIMEA CENTER
PARKER RANCH CENTER
PAKINI GRILL
KAHILU THEATRE
STARBUCKS
VILLAGE BURGER
LILIKOI CAFE
KTA

The Saddle Road

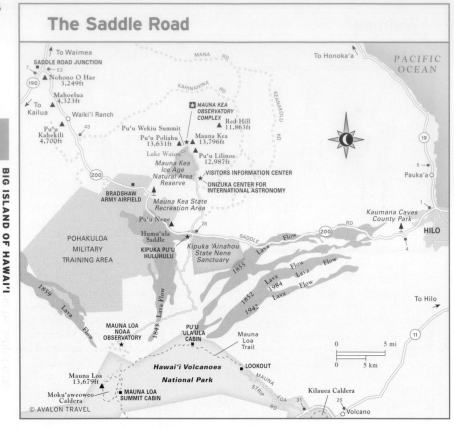

inland. Saddle Road, Highway 200, also signed as Kaumana Drive, splits left after about a mile and is clearly marked. Passing Kaumana Caves Park, the road steadily gains elevation as you pass into and then out of a layer of clouds. Expect fog or rain.

About 28 miles out of Hilo and 25 miles up from the Kona side, a clearly marked spur road branches to the north; officially called the John A. Burns Way, but most often referred to as the Mauna Kea Access Road, it leads to the summit of Mauna Kea. You can expect wind, rain, fog, hail, snow, and altitude sickness. Intrigued? Proceed—it's not as bad as it sounds. In fact, the road, while steep, is well paved for the first six miles, and from there the road is graded

gravel, banked, and usually well maintained but sometimes like a washboard, with the upper four miles paved so that dust is kept to a minimum to protect the sensitive "eyes" of the telescopes. A four-wheel-drive vehicle is required beyond the visitors center, and if there's snow, the road may not be passable at all. (For current road conditions, call 808/935-6268.)

The Mauna Loa Observatory Road, a one-lane paved road with long stretches of potholes and rough patches, turns south off the Saddle Road between mile markers 27 and 28 and leads about 17 miles in a big zig and zag and gentle incline up to the National Oceanic and Atmospheric Administration's (NOAA) Mauna Loa Observatory.

PLANNING YOUR TIME

If you came to Hawai'i not to sit on the beach, but instead to do a lot of sightseeing where it's not too hot, this region is ideal for you. Whether you're starting your trip from the east or west side of the island, you'll want to plan around being in **Waipi'o Valley** during the morning when the weather is better and when the majority of organized trips are set to leave. Unless you're going to do an overnight hiking trip through the valley, you really only need a day to see the valley and trek down it in whatever capacity.

Since the Hamakua Coast drive, without stops, is only 45 minutes, it can easily be completed in an afternoon even if you make several stops along the way. If you plan ahead, you can book reservations for a tasting at the **Hawaiian Vanilla Company** or **Hamakua Mushroom Farm Tour and Tasting** and/or soaring through the **World Botanical Gardens** with **Zip Isle**. No planning is required to stop at any of the scenic overlooks or parks along the highway.

It's unfortunate that there isn't more to see in Waimea because there is so much good food that you'll want to stay all day. I recommend visiting Waimea as a way to cool off from the hot afternoons of the Kohala Coast or to pick up provisions on your way to Mauna Kea. Stroll through the stores at **Parker Square** or tour the **Anna Ranch Heritage Center** before heading to dinner.

Regardless of how much time you want to spend at the top of **Mauna Kea,** it's important to account for how much time it will take to get there. First there is traveling on the Saddle Road to the observatory access road, which can take about an hour from Waimea, depending on weather. The drive up to the visitors center takes another 30 minutes, after which it's an additional 40 minutes to the summit after you've spent time at the visitors center to acclimate to the altitude. If you're driving in the dark, these travel times can be much longer.

The point is, a trip to Mauna Kea is hardly a quick jaunt and it's especially not quick if you're traveling on a group tour. Those planning on traveling to the summit to catch the sunset should leave a few hours ahead of time and even earlier if you might hike around the area first. After sunset, most visitors to Mauna Kea reconvene at the visitors center for an hour or two of star- and planet-gazing. Don't expect to head down before 8pm—it will be hard to walk away from the most awe-inspiring sky you might ever see.

Sights

HAMAKUA COAST
★ Hakalau Bay

There are residents of the Big Island who have never seen the abandoned plantation remnants in Hakalau Bay, a short detour off the highway. To get here from Highway 19, between mile markers 15 and 16 turn *makai* near the footbridge and follow the street around, going under the bridge and down toward the ocean and the park. Photographers and history buffs will be eager to visit the ruins of Hakalau Mill, destroyed in the tsunami of 1946. Its remnants are scattered around the parking lot.

World Botanical Gardens

Touted as the state's largest botanical garden, with over 5,000 different species, the **World Botanical Gardens** (Hwy. 19 at mile marker 16, *mauka* side, 808/963-5427, http://worldbotanicalgardens.com, 9am-5:30pm daily, self-guided tours adults $15, teens $7, children 5-12 $3, guided tours adults $57-187) is really the backdrop of the Zip Isle zipline that makes use of the botanical gardens. The entry fee to the gardens is included with the price of the zipline, and during the zip course itself you'll end up walking around a large portion of the gardens. When you are doing zipping,

Your Best Day in the Hamakua Coast, Waimea, and the Saddle Road

- Wake up early to catch the **view of Mauna Kea** from Waimea before the clouds come rolling in.

- Get breakfast at **Hawaiian Style Café** in Waimea.

- Head to **Waipi'o Valley** to join a group tour or venture down into the valley on your own.

- In the afternoon, take a drive east on Highway 19, stopping at **Hakalau Bay** to see some plantation ruins.

- Either head back the way you came or travel through Hilo and back over the **Saddle Road,** grabbing food and drinks for a picnic. Aim to arrive at the **Onizuka Center for International Astronomy** visitors information center on **Mauna Kea** just at sunset.

- Settle in for some **stargazing** that will astound you.

RAINY-DAY ALTERNATIVE

Rain or a mist is expected in Waimea—so don't let that throw you off. If it's really raining hard, you have a few options. The good news is, from Waimea you can see if it's raining down below in Kohala. If it's not, travel down the hill 20 minutes to soak up the sun.

If you want to stay in Waimea, visit the **Anna Ranch Heritage Center.** You can spend at least an hour or two touring on your own or with a guide. If you pay for the tour, for a few extra dollars you can get an "enhanced tour" that includes arts and crafts.

If you're on the Hamakua Coast, visit the **Laupahoehoe Train Museum** or the **Hawaiian Vanilla Company.**

you can walk down to the river on a short trail or drive up to catch a glimpse of a waterfall. If you are planning to just come for the botanical gardens portion, your better bet might be to visit the Hawaii Tropical Botanical Garden in Onomea Bay down the road. The guided tours occur on a Segway and can take anywhere from 30 minutes to over two hours; the longer tours visit the falls.

Laupahoehoe Train Museum

Although small in size, the **Laupahoehoe Train Museum** (36-2377 Mamalahoa Hwy./Hwy. 19 near mile marker 25, 808/962-6300, www.thetrainmuseum.com, 10am-5pm Thurs.-Sun., by appointment Mon.-Wed., adults $6, seniors $5, families $15) is big on the history of the Hamakua region. Interwoven with the history of the coastal train route, a 34-mile stretch with 21 stops that was destroyed by the 1946 tsunami, the museum offers abundant archival photos detailing what life on the Big Island looked like in the early 1900s. Next to the museum is a reconstructed train car and tracks.

Laupahoehoe Point Park

This wave-lashed peninsula is a popular place for weekend family outings. **Laupahoehoe Point Park** (Laupahoehoe Point Rd. off Hwy. 19 between mile markers 27 and 28) now occupies the low peninsula; it has nice shaded picnic tables, showers, electricity, and a county camping area. The park can get busy on the weekends with local families cooking out and playing tunes on their ukuleles. The sea is too rough to swim in, except perhaps by the boat launch ramp, but many anglers come here, along with some daring surfers. The road down to the park is narrow and winding and runs past several rebuilt homes and a restored Jodo Mission. It will take about 10 minutes to drive down to the park from the highway.

★ WAIPI'O VALLEY

Waipi'o, which means curved or arched waters, is known to Hawaiians as the Sacred Valley of the Kings. Locals know it as one of the best views on all of the Big Island—the valley really is postcard perfect, with a river running through deep green hills. The valley has been inhabited by Hawaiians for over 1,200 years and is the site of many ancient temples and burial sites. Traditionally, the valley also held importance as a fertile ground for growing taro that is made into poi, a staple of the Hawaiian diet. Today, **Waipi'o Valley** (where Hwy. 240 ends) is home to waterfalls (the two most recognizable ones are Hi'ilawe and Hakalaoa), ancient fishponds close to the front of the valley, and, closer to the shore, sand dunes intermixed with old burial grounds.

Waipi'o Beach

Stretching over a mile, **Waipi'o Beach** (access via Waipi'o Valley Rd.) is the longest black-sand beach on the island. A tall and somewhat tangled stand of trees and bushes fronts this beach, capping the dune. If you hiked the one-hour vertical road to get here you'll likely want to jump in immediately, but be careful: The surf here can be dangerous, and there are many riptides. If there is strong wave action, swimming is not advised. It is, however, a good place for surfing and fishing. There are two sections of the beach, and in order to get to the long expanse of beach across the mouth of the stream, you have to wade across. Portable bathrooms are located behind the beach near the parking area.

To get to the beach, you have to get down the Waipi'o Valley Road first. Whether you walk or drive down, when you get to the bottom turn at the first right instead of continuing straight into the valley and into private property. You'll find the next portion of your walk or drive to be muddy and filled with potholes. This road takes you directly to the beach. If you drove, park your car in the area under the trees, where there will likely be other cars. If you walked, it's often possible to hitch a ride back up with someone driving from the beach.

Getting There

You can travel down into the valley in nearly

Laupahoehoe Point Park

Culinary Delights of the Hamakua Coast

the vanilla pods of the Hawaiian Vanilla Company

Even those who are adamant in their hatred of mushrooms can't help but indulge in **Hamakua Mushrooms** (36-221 Manowaiopae Homestead Road, Laupahoehoe, 808/962-0305, http://hamakuamushrooms.com, 9am-4pm Mon.-Fri.). At one time, these exotic, buttery mushrooms were difficult to find on menus, but now one can find them at nearly every upscale restaurant on the island. If you can't get enough of these mushrooms or are just really interested in where your food comes from ("de-reifying food," as Karl Marx would say…), you might enjoy this new tour and tasting. Tours are all indoors and include a cooking demo, mushroom tasting, and lots of video watching (9:30am and 11:30am Mon.-Fri., lasts a little over an hour, adults $20 plus tax, seniors $17.50, children 5-11 $10, students $10). The price is a bit steep, so if you're short on time and low on cash I'd recommend just stopping by the gift shop and picking up some fresh or dried mushrooms to try on your own.

The rock star of foodie tours is Jim Reddekopp, owner of **Hawaiian Vanilla Company** (43-2007 Paauilo Mauka Rd., Paauilo, 808/776-1771, www.hawaiianvanilla.com, 10am-5pm Mon.-Sat.). You may have seen him on The Food Network or Travel Channel. The company's gift shop, which Jim calls "an upscale Cracker Barrel," is mainly staffed by family members and is stocked full of vanilla products both of the culinary and lotion varieties. The tour, usually led by Jim, is the kind of hour (and a half) that will make you rethink your life. You'll leave wondering, "Should I quit my job and start a farm in Hawaii?"—Jim is that excited and inspirational. Three kinds of epiphany-inducing tours are available: the **Vanilla Experience Luncheon** (12:30pm Mon.-Fri., adults $39, children under 12 $19) includes a vanilla-themed lunch (the highlight is the ice cream or sorbet depending on your lactose tolerance) and quick walk around the area; the **Farm Tour** (1pm Mon.-Fri., $25 per person) includes a "Johnny Boy," the Arnold Palmer of the vanilla experience (half vanilla ice tea, half vanilla lemonade) and dessert plus tour of the farm; and the very special **Upcountry Tea** (3pm Sat., $29 per person) includes vanilla tea (obviously), champagne toast, an appetizer, and several small courses, ending with dessert. The prices are right for this tour, Jim is hilarious, and the vanilla is sublime—you can't go wrong.

every imaginable way: by horse, by ATV, by foot, by car, and so on. Spend some time considering which method of visiting Waipiʻo meets your needs, depending on how much time you have, how much money you wish to spend, how much you want to plan ahead, and your physical prowess. For those who just want to catch a glimpse and a photo of the valley's glory from above without much effort, there is a lovely, easily accessible scenic overlook in front of the parking area (with restroom facilities).

The other important factor to consider is whether or not you want to actually go into the valley or simply travel around the rim. The majority of organized tours meet at stores in Kukuihaele, a small town just a few miles east of Waipiʻo. As you drive west on Highway 240 from Honokaʻa, when the road forks go toward the right (the sign will point to the right for Kukuihaele), follow the road and you will see the tour storefronts on the *makai* side of the road. Note: For many tours, reservations are needed. Very rarely can you just stop in and get on a tour—but if empty spaces are available due to no-shows you may be able to secure a spot at a discounted rate.

ATV

As you can probably guess, **Ride the Rim** (check in at Waipiʻo Valley Artworks, 48-5416 Kukuihaele Rd., Kukuihaele, 808/775-1450, www.ridetherim.com, morning and afternoon tours, $189 per adult ATV driver, $159 per adult buggy passenger, $99 per child buggy passenger) offers a three-hour tour around the rim (not the valley) through eucalyptus trees, stopping for a swim at a secluded waterfall. Riders must be over 16 years old and weigh between 100 and 350 pounds; however, those who can't drive can ride in an open-air buggy driven by a tour guide.

WAGON

Perhaps the most unexpected way to experience the valley is by mule-drawn wagon. This narrated cultural and historical tour organized by **Waipiʻo Valley Wagon Tours** (meet at Last Chance Store, Kukuihaele, 808/775-9518, www.waipiovalleywagontours. com, 10:30am, 12:30pm, 2:30 pm Mon.-Sat., adult $60, senior $55, child 3-11 $30) allows you to get down into the valley without exhausting yourself. The tour is only 1.5 hours and that is a bit short given the amount of time it takes to actually get down into the valley.

Waipiʻo Valley overlook

It's a good option for people short on time or families who want to travel together.

HIKING

It is possible to walk into the valley on your own. More complicated, however, is to walk the rim, as it is private property and tour companies lease rights to pass through it. Most people only take the journey into the valley as a means to the end—the end being the beach at the end of the road. To begin the vertical trek down into the valley, park your car in the lot at the end of Highway 240 or, inevitably, on the street. The road that walkers take down to the valley bottom and onward to the beach is the same paved road the cars use. Bring *plenty* of water and sunscreen for the walk—and a snack. Don't underestimate the downhill part of the journey—for many it's actually more challenging than the uphill part since it's quite hard on the knees. Give yourself about 45 minutes to get down and an hour to get back to the top. There are no public restrooms in the valley and just the portable potties at the beach, so use the nicer facilities at the Waipi'o Overlook before you head down.

HORSEBACK

If touring the valley is what you want, your best option is **Na'alapa Stables** (check in at Waipi'o Valley Artworks, 48-5416 Kukuihaele Rd., www.naalapastables.com, 9am and 12:30pm Mon.-Sat., $73-94). Known for its quality service and excellent guides who share stories of Hawaiian history and culture, this tour books up quickly, so make sure to plan ahead. Riders meet at Waipi'o Valley Artworks and then are transported down into the valley in the ranch's four-wheel vehicle. The road down to the valley is steep, so this trip might not be for the faint of heart. The entire tour is 2.5 hours, but actual horse time is not that long given the amount of time it takes to travel up and down into the valley. A printable coupon for $10 is available on the website.

Similarly, **Waipi'o on Horseback** (Hwy. 240 at mile marker 7, *mauka* side, 808/775-9888, www.waipioonhorseback.com, 9:30am and 1:30pm Mon.-Sat., $90 plus tax, discount if booked with ATV tour) is another valley trip that will get you there and near to the waterfalls. The ride through the valley is similar to those of other companies.

Waipi'o Valley

FOUR-WHEEL-DRIVE AND SHUTTLE TOUR

The road leading down to Waipi'o is outrageously steep and narrow, averaging a 25 percent gradient. If you attempt it in a regular car, it'll eat you up and spit out your bones. More than 20 fatalities have occurred since people started driving it, and it has only been paved since the early 1970s. Residents have been advocating for the last few years to cut off tourist traffic to the valley, as the cars not only create a preventable traffic mess on the road but also inflict environmental havoc on the landscape. You'll definitely need four-wheel drive to make it; vehicles headed downhill yield to those coming up.

If you want to be shuttled down to the bottom, the ★ **Waipi'o Valley Shuttle** (808/775-7121, www.waipiovalleyshuttle.com, Mon.-Sat., $59 adults, $32 children under 11, reservations recommended) makes a 90-minute descent and tour of Waipi'o Valley in air-conditioned, four-wheel-drive vans that leave from Waipi'o Valley Artworks in Kukuihaele, at 9am, 11am, 1pm, and 3pm Monday-Saturday. Along the way, you'll be regaled by beautiful legends and stories and shown the most prominent sights in the valley by drivers who live in the area. This is the easiest way into the valley, and the guides are locals who know what they're doing, as they've been at it since 1970.

WAIMEA
Parker Ranch and Historic Homes

After a bit of reorganizing, the ubiquitous **Parker Ranch** organization has finally reopened a modified version of the ranch's **historic homes** (67-1435 Mamalahoa Hwy./Hawai'i Belt Rd., 808/885-7311, www.parkerranch.com, 8:30am-3:30pm Mon.-Fri., free). Dating from the 19th century, the Puuopelu house doubles as the organization's main headquarters. Grab a self-guided tour flier in the entryway and lead yourself through the small main room filled with historical furniture and Broadway memorabilia from Richard

Smart's (the heir to the Parker Ranch) acting days. Next, visit the Mana Hale home, which was moved from its original location to this property, with relics from the early days of Parker Ranch. At least take the drive from the main road down to the site, as the views from the road and looking back at Mauna Kea are well worth the short detour.

Isaacs Art Center

One of the preeminent galleries on the island is the **Isaacs Art Center** (65-1268 Kawaihae Rd., 808/885-5884, www.isaacsartcenter.org, 10am-5pm Tues.-Sat.). This art store/museum, part of Hawai'i Preparatory Academy, is worth a stop. An expansion into two distinct spaces is under way, but for now the museum and the store are intermixed, and the pieces dating from 19th- and 20th-century Hawaii and Asia are some of the finest (and priciest) on the island.

Anna Ranch Heritage Center

Dedicated to Anna Leialoha Lindsey Perry-Fiske, the "first lady of ranching" in Hawaii, the living-history museum at **Anna Ranch Heritage Center** (65-1480 Kawaihae Rd., Hwy. 19 near mile marker 58, 808/885-4426, www.annaranch.org, 10am-3pm Tues.-Fri., guided tours 10am and 1pm by appointment (really, call ahead) $10, self-guided garden tour free) is a great entrée into what Hawaiian ranch life was like in the early 20th century. The property consists of the original house, a restored blacksmith area, and placards explaining the surrounding views of Waimea. Anna's house is nicely staged, with lots of original artifacts, including parts of Anna's extensive hat and clothing collections. If you walk around the house yourself, you might only need about 30 minutes. The guided tour, on the other hand, can run nearly two hours.

MAUNA KEA
Onizuka Center for International Astronomy

This entire mountaintop complex, plus almost all of the land area above 12,000 feet, is managed by the University of Hawai'i. Visitors are welcome to tour the observatory complex and stop by the visitors information center at the **Onizuka Center for International Astronomy** (808/961-2180, www.ifa.hawaii.edu/info/vis, 9am-10pm daily) at the 9,200-foot level. Named in honor of astronaut Ellison Onizuka, who was born and raised on the Big Island and died in the *Challenger* space shuttle tragedy in 1986. Inside are displays of astronomical and cultural subjects, informational handouts, computer links to the observatories on the hill above, and evening videos and slide shows, as well as a small bookstore and gift shop. At times, 11- and 16-inch telescopes are set up outside during the day to view the sun and sunspots; every evening they are there to view the stars and other celestial objects. The visitors center is about one hour from Hilo and Waimea and about two hours from Kailua-Kona. A stop here will allow visitors a chance to acclimate to the thin, high-mountain air—another must. A stay of one hour here is recommended before you head up to the 13,796-foot summit. The visitors center provides the last public restrooms before the summit and is a good place to stock up on water, also unavailable higher up.

Free stargazing is offered nightly 6pm-10pm, and there's a summit tour every Saturday and Sunday (weather permitting) at 1pm. These programs are free of charge. For either activity, dress warmly. Evening temperatures will be 40-50°F in summer and might be below freezing in winter, and winds of 20 miles per hour are not atypical. For the summit tour, you must provide your own four-wheel-drive transportation from the visitors center to the summit.

Going Up the Mountain

If you plan on continuing up to the summit, you must provide your own transportation and it must be a four-wheel-drive vehicle. People with cardiopulmonary or respiratory problems or with physical infirmities or weakness and women who are pregnant are discouraged from attempting the trip. In addition, those who have been scuba diving should not attempt a trip to the top until at least 24 hours have elapsed. These are serious warnings. As the observatories are used primarily at night, it is requested that visitors to the top come during daylight hours and leave within 30 minutes after sunset to minimize the use of headlights and reduce the dust from the road, both factors that might disrupt optimal

Anna Ranch Heritage Center

Mauna Kea: From Silversword to Snow

As you climb Mauna Kea (White Mountain), you pass through the clouds to a barren world devoid of vegetation. The earth is a red, rolling series of volcanic cones. You get an incredible vista of Mauna Loa peeking through the clouds and what seems like the entire island lying at your feet. In the distance the lights of Maui flicker.

Off to your right is **Pu'u Kahinahina,** a small hill whose name means Hill of the Silversword. It's one of the few places on the Big Island where you'll see this rare plant. The mountaintop was at one time federal land, and funds were made available to eradicate feral goats, one of the worst destroyers of the silversword and many other native Hawaiian plants.

Lake Waiau (Swirling Water) lies at 13,020 feet, making it the third-highest lake in the United States. For some reason, ladybugs love this area. This lake is less than two acres in size and quite shallow. Oddly, in an area that has little precipitation and very dry air, this lake never dries up or drains away, fed by a bed of melting permafrost below the surface.

Here and there around the summit are small caves, remnants of ancient quarries where Hawaiians came to dig a special kind of hard rock that is the hardest in all Hawaii. They hauled roughed-out tools down to the lowlands, where they refined them into excellent implements that became coveted trade items. These quarries, Lake Waiau, and a large triangular section of the glaciated southern slope of the mountain have been designated **Mauna Kea Ice Age Natural Area Reserve.**

A natural phenomenon is the strange thermal properties manifested by the cinder cones that dot the top of the mountain. Only 10 feet or so under their surface is permafrost that dates back 10,000 years to the Pleistocene epoch. If you drill into the cones for 10-20 feet and put a pipe in, during daylight hours air will be sucked into the pipe. At night, warm air comes out of the pipe with sufficient force to keep a hat levitating.

Mauna Kea was the only spot in the tropical Pacific thought to be glaciated until recent investigation provided evidence that suggests that Haleakala on Maui was also capped by a glacier when it was higher and much younger. The entire summit of Mauna Kea was covered in 500 feet of ice. Toward the summit, you may notice piles of rock—these are terminal moraines of these ancient glaciers—or other flat surfaces that are grooved as if scratched by huge fingernails. The snows atop Mauna Kea are unpredictable. Some years it is merely a dusting, while in other years, such as 1982, there has been enough snow to ski from late November to late July.

viewing. It's suggested that on your way down you use flashing warning lights that let you see a good distance ahead of you while keeping bright white lights unused. Some rental companies have changed their rules regarding taking cars up to the summit and it is not allowed. Others have not wavered.

Alternatively, make arrangements for a **guided tour** to the top. These tours usually last seven to eight hours and run $175-200 per person. Tour operators supply the vehicle, guide, food, snacks, and plenty of warm clothing for your trip. They also supply telescopes for your private viewing of the stars near the visitors center after seeing the sunset from the top. From the Kona side, try **Hawaii Forest and Trail** (808/331-5805 or 800/464-1993, www.hawaii-forest.com). In Hilo, contact **Arnott's Hiking Adventures** (808/969-7097, www.arnottslodge.com, discounts available for hotel guests). Take extra layers of warm clothing and your camera.

★ **MAUNA KEA
OBSERVATORY COMPLEX**

Atop the mountain is a mushroom grove of astronomical observatories, as incongruously striking as a futuristic earth colony on a remote planet of a distant galaxy. The crystal-clear air and lack of dust and light pollution make the **Mauna Kea Observatory Complex** the best in the world. At close to 14,000 feet, it is above 40 percent of the earth's atmosphere and 98 percent of its water vapor.

Temperatures hover around 40-50°F during the day, and there's only 9-11 inches of precipitation annually, mostly in the form of snow. The astronomers have come to expect an average of 325 crystal-clear nights per year, perfect for observation. Scientists from around the world book months in advance for a squint through one of these phenomenal telescopes, and institutions from several countries maintain permanent outposts there.

The second telescope on your left is the United Kingdom's **James Clerk Maxwell Telescope** (JCMT), a radio telescope with a primary reflecting surface more than 15 meters in diameter. This unit became operational in 1987. It was dedicated by Britain's Prince Philip, who rode all the way to the summit in a Rolls Royce. The 3.6-meter **Canada-France-Hawaii Telescope** (CFHT), finished in 1979 for $33 million, was the first to spot Halley's Comet in 1983.

A newer eye to the heavens atop Mauna Kea is the double **W. M. Keck Observatory.** Keck I became operational in 1992 and Keck II followed in 1996. The Keck Foundation, the Los Angeles-based philanthropic organization, funded the telescopes to the tune of over $140 million; they are among the world's most high-tech, powerful, and expensive.

In addition to these are the following: The **NASA Infrared Telescope Facility** (IRTF), online since 1979, does only infrared viewing with its three-meter mirror. Also with only infrared capabilities, the **United Kingdom Infrared Telescope** (UKIRT), in operation since 1979 as well, searches the sky with its 3.8-meter lens. Directly below it is the **University of Hawai'i 0.6-meter Telescope.** Built in 1968, it was the first on the mountaintop and has the smallest reflective mirror. Completed in 1970, the **University of Hawai'i 2.2-meter Telescope** was a huge improvement over its predecessor but is now the second-smallest telescope at the top. The **Caltech Submillimeter Observatory** (CSO) has been looking into the sky since 1987 with its 10.4-meter radio telescope. **Subaru** (Japan National Large Telescope) is a monolithic 8.3-meter mirror capable of both optical and infrared viewing. It is the most recently completed telescope on the mountain, fully operational since 2000. The **Gemini Northern 8.1-meter Telescope,** also with both optical and infrared viewing, is run by a consortium from the United States, United Kingdom, Canada, Chile, Argentina, and Brazil. Its southern twin is located on a mountaintop in Chile, and together they have been viewing the heavens since 1999. Situated to the side and below the rest is the **Submillimeter Array,** a series of eight 6-meter-wide antennae. About two miles distant from the top is the **Very Long Baseline Array,** a 25-meter-wide, centimeter wavelength radio dish that is one in a series of similar antennae that dot the 5,000-mile stretch between Hawaii and the Virgin Islands.

VISITING THE TELESCOPES

At present, only the **Subaru Telescope** (www.naoj.org) allows visitors on organized tours, and you *must* reserve at least one week ahead of time through the National Astronomical Observatory of Japan website. These free, 40-minute tours are given at 10:30am, 11:30am, and 1:30pm only on Tuesdays, Wednesdays, and Thursdays and only 15 days out of the month. Tours are run in English and Japanese, with the first and last tours of the day usually in English. The tour schedule is posted two months in advance on the telescope's website. Transportation to the telescope is the visitor's responsibility. This tour is a brief introduction to the telescope itself and the work being performed. There is no opportunity to actually view anything through the telescope. All safety precautions pertaining to visiting the summit also apply to visiting this telescope for the tour.

While the Keck telescopes do not offer tours, the visitors gallery at the telescope base is open weekdays 10am-4:30pm for a 12-minute video, information about the work being done, and a "partial view of the Keck I telescope and dome." Two public restrooms are also available to visitors. The same information and video are available in the lobby at the Keck headquarters in Waimea.

ALONG THE SADDLE ROAD
Pohakuloa

The broad, relatively flat saddle between Mauna Kea and Mauna Loa is an area known as **Pohakuloa** (Long Stone). At an elevation of roughly 6,500 feet, this plain alternates between lava flow, grassland, and semiarid desert pockmarked with cinder cones. About seven miles west of the Mauna Kea Access Road, at a sharp bend in the road, you'll find a cluster of cabins that belong to the Mauna Kea

State Recreation Area. This is a decent place to stop for a picnic and potty break. No camping is allowed, but housekeeping cabins that sleep up to six can be rented (permits are required and can be obtained through the state of Hawaii's permits website: https://camping.ehawaii.gov/camping). Nearby is a game management area, so expect hunting and shooting of wild pigs, sheep, and birds in season. A few minutes west is the Pohakuloa Training Area, where maneuvers and bomb practice can sometimes disturb the peace in this high mountain area. If the military is on maneuvers while you're passing through, be attentive to vehicles on or crossing the road.

Hiking

This region is hike central, with many different levels of hikes, from easy to difficult, with every type of scenery imaginable. Don't trespass on private land. Local residents don't want hikers wandering through their backyards on the way to find some hidden view. There are plenty of on-the-beaten-track and underutilized legal hikes in this area that will challenge you for days.

KALOPA NATIVE FOREST STATE PARK AND RECREATION AREA

This spacious natural area is five miles southeast of Honoka'a, 12 miles north of Laupahoehoe, three miles inland on a well-marked secondary road, and at 2,000 feet in elevation. Little used by tourists or residents, **Kalopa Native Forest State Park and**

Mauna Kea summit

Recreation Area (Kalopa Rd., off Hwy. 19 between mile markers 39 and 40, gate open 7am-8pm daily) is a great place to get away from the coast and up into the hills. Hiking is terrific throughout the park and adjoining forest reserve on a series of nature trails—but the trails are not marked clearly and are difficult to follow. Most of the forest here is endemic, with few alien species. Near the entrance and camping area is an **arboretum** of Hawaiian and Polynesian plants. Beyond the arboretum is a 0.75-mile nature trail loop through an *'ohi'a* forest, and a 3-mile loop trail takes you along the gulch trail and back to camp via an old road. Next to the area where you park your car there is a board with pamphlets outlining the trails. The park offers day-use picnicking, tent camping, and large furnished cabins (state permit required) that can house up to eight people. Reserve online and print your permit through the website (http://camping.ehwaii.gov).

To get to Kalopa Native Forest State Park, turn *mauka* on Kalopa Road and follow the signs up to the park—it will take about 15 minutes. There is more than one way from the highway to the park, so don't worry if you end up turning *mauka* on a different road.

★ WAIMANU VALLEY

The hike down to Waipi'o and over the *pali* to **Waimanu Valley** is considered by many one of the top three treks in Hawaii. You must be fully prepared for camping and in excellent condition to attempt this hike. Also, water from the streams and falls is not good for drinking due to irrigation and cattle grazing topside; hikers should bring purification tablets or boil or filter it to be safe. To get to Waimanu Valley, a switchback trail, locally called the Z Trail but otherwise known as the **Muliwai Trail,** leads up the 1,200-foot *pali,* starting about 100 yards inland from the west end of Waipi'o Beach. Although not long, this is by far the most difficult section of the trail. Waimanu was bought by the State of Hawaii some years ago, and the government is responsible for trail maintenance.

Kalopa Native Forest State Park and Recreation Area

The trail ahead is decent, although it can be muddy because you go in and out of more than a dozen gulches before reaching Waimanu. In the third gulch, which is quite deep, a narrow cascading waterfall tumbles into a small pool right at trailside, just right for a quick dip or to dangle your feet. Another small pool is found in the fifth gulch. After the ninth gulch is a trail shelter. Finally, below is Waimanu Valley, half the size of Waipi'o but more verdant, and even wilder because it has been uninhabited for a longer time. Cross Waimanu Stream in the shallows where it meets the sea. The trail then continues along the beach and back into the valley for about 1.5 miles, along the base of the valley's far side, to the 300-foot-high Wai'ilikahi Falls. For drinking water (remember to treat it), walk along the west side of the *pali* until you find a likely waterfall. The Muliwai Trail to the Waimanu Valley floor is about 15 miles round-trip from the trailhead at the bottom of the *pali* in Waipi'o Valley, or 18 miles round-trip from Waipi'o Lookout.

To stay overnight in Waimanu Valley, you

must have a camping permit obtained through the Division of Forestry and Wildlife (http://camping.ehawaii.gov); permits are for up to six people ($12 Hawaii residents, $18 nonresidents). Sites that are not listed on the website are temporarily unavailable for camping or hiking. Before you go, check the news release section of the Division of Forestry and Wildlife website (http://hawaii.gov/dlnr) to make sure that the trail is not closed due to hazardous conditions such as rain and/or mud.

MAUNA KEA

Hiking on **Mauna Kea** means high-altitude hiking. Although the height of the mountain (13,796 feet) is not necessarily a problem, the elevation gain in a short hour or two of getting to the top is. It takes time for the body to acclimatize, and when you drive up from the ocean you rob yourself of the chance to acclimatize easily. What you may expect to experience normally are slight dizziness, a shortness of breath due to reduced oxygen levels, and reduced ability to think clearly and react quickly. Some people are more prone to elevation problems, so if you experience more severe symptoms, get to a lower elevation immediately. These symptoms include prolonged or severe headache, loss of appetite, cramped muscles, prolonged malaise or weakness, dizziness, reduced muscle control and balance, and heart palpitations. Carry plenty of water (more than you would at a lower elevation) and food. Wear a brimmed hat, sunglasses, sunscreen, and lip balm, a long-sleeved shirt and long pants, and sturdy hiking boots or shoes. Carry a jacket, sweater, and gloves, as it can be cold and windy at and near the top. Don't alter the natural environment and stay on established trails.

There are a few good trails on the mountain. About six miles above the Onizuka Center for International Astronomy Visitors Information Center, a dirt track heads off the access road to the west and downhill to a parking lot. From the parking area, it's about one mile farther west, over the saddle between two small cones, to Lake Waiau

and its placid waters. This should take less than 30 minutes. On the way, you cross the Mauna Kea Humu'ula Trail, which starts at the third parking lot near the T intersection above and heads down the mountain to the visitors center. Taking the Humu'ula Trail to Lake Waiau should also take about 30 minutes. Continuing on down the Humu'ula Trail a couple of miles brings you past an ancient adze quarry site. Perhaps the most convenient hike is that to the true summit of the mountain. Start from the roadway across from the University of Hawai'i's 2.2-meter telescope, cross over the guardrail, and follow the rough path down into the saddle and steeply up the hill, a distance of less than half a mile.

THE SADDLE ROAD

Besides having the access road to Mauna Kea, the Saddle Road is a great place to explore by foot—especially on your way to Mauna Kea or on your way to/from the Hilo side and the Kona side.

Pu'u O'o Trail

Just after mile marker 24 on the way up from Hilo is the trailhead for the **Pu'u O'o Trail.** From the small parking lot along the road, this trail heads to the south about four miles where it meets Powerline Road, a rough four-wheel-drive track, and returns to the Saddle Road. This area is good for **bird-watching,** and you might have a chance to see the rare 'akiapola'au or 'apapane, and even wild turkeys. This area is frequently shrouded in clouds or fog, and it could rain on you. You may want to walk only partway in and return on the same trail, rather than making the circle.

Kipuka Pu'u Huluhulu

Bird-watchers or nature enthusiasts should turn into the **Kipuka Pu'u Huluhulu** parking lot, across the road from the Mauna Kea Access Road turnoff. A *kipuka* is an area that has been surrounded by a lava flow, but never inundated, that preserves an older and established ecosystem. The most recent lava around

Pu'u Huluhulu is from 1935. At the parking lot you'll find a hunters' check-in station. From there, a hiking trail leads into this fenced, 38-acre nature preserve. One loop trail runs through the trees around the summit of the hill, and there is a trail that runs down the east side of the hill to a smaller loop and the two exits on Mauna Loa Observatory Road, on its eastern edge. Pu'u Huluhulu means Shaggy Hill, and this diminutive hill is covered in a wide variety of trees and bushes, which include *mamane, naio, 'iliahi* (sandalwood), koa, and *'ohi'a*. Some of the birds most often seen are the greenish-yellow *'amakihi,* the red *'i'iwi* and *'apapane,* and the dull brown and smoky-gray *'oma'o*. In addition, you may be lucky enough to spot a rare *'io,* Hawaiian hawk, or the more numerous *pueo,* a short-eared owl. The entire loop will take you 45 minutes or less, so even if you are not particularly drawn to the birds or the trees, this is a good place to get out of the car, stretch your legs, and get acclimatized to the elevation before you head up to Mauna Kea.

MAUNA LOA

The Saddle Road is the other choice, besides near Hawai'i Volcanoes National Park, for accessing **Mauna Loa** and its trails. The **Mauna Loa Observatory Road** turns south off the Saddle Road and zigs and zags up to the **Mauna Loa NOAA Atmospheric Observatory** at 11,140 feet, which you can see high on the hillside above as you progress along this road. Use a four-wheel-drive rental vehicle that is approved for this road. Although it could be done faster, give yourself an hour to take in the surroundings, check out the distant sights, and reach the end of the road. Use your vehicle lights, particularly if there are low clouds, and straddle the reflective white line that runs down the center of this single-lane road all the way up to the observatory, pulling over only to let vehicles from the other direction get by. The atmospheric observatory is not open to the public, but you can park in a small lot below it at the end of the pavement.

About two miles in from the turnoff is a rock formation at the side of the road that, at a certain angle, looks remarkably like Charles de Gaulle, former president of France—and you don't have to use your imagination much at all. As you continue, you get a fine, distant look at the observatories on top of Mauna Kea across the saddle, Pu'u Huluhulu below at the turnoff, and the military reservation beyond to the west. About four miles in, at a turn in the road, there is a gravel road that heads over the horizon to the west, an abandoned attempt at a highway shortcut to Kailua-Kona. About eight miles up, at a point where there are a number of telephone and television transmitter towers, the road makes a big zag and heads almost in a straight-line shot, following power poles to the observatory. Notice the different colors of lava that the road crosses and the amount of vegetation on each type. The older brown lava has some grasses and small bushes growing from it, while the newer black lava is almost totally barren. There are large areas of red lava as well, and some of that has been used as road base and paving material. You will see several collapsed lava tubes near the road as you make your way up. Still farther on, areas of ropy *pahoehoe* lava stick up through newer *'a'a* lava. Around mile 15, new pavement has been laid so your ride gets smoother even as the road goes through a series of roller-coaster waves as you approach the end of the road. Beyond the end of the pavement, an extremely rough Jeep track continues—best used as a hiking trail. This track zigzags up the mountainside, eventually ending near the crater rim after about seven miles. The **Mauna Loa Observatory Trail** leaves the gravel Jeep track several hundred yards beyond the end of the pavement and heads almost straight up the mountainside, crossing the Jeep trail several times. The Observatory Trail climbs 1,975 feet over 3.8 miles up the volcano's north slope until it reaches the rim of the Moku'aweoweo Caldera summit. From this point, the Mauna Loa summit cabin is 2.1 miles. It takes about 4-6 hours altogether to hike from the observatory trailhead to the Mauna Loa summit cabin. The hike back from the Mauna Loa summit cabin to the Mauna Loa Observatory trailhead is only about three hours because you're going downhill.

A helpful resource for this hike can be found at www.kinquest.com/misc/travel/trailguide.php. This site provides a guide with a mile-by-mile description of what you'll see while you hike.

The Mauna Loa summit cabin is available to stay in for free but requires a permit from the Kilauea Visitor Center in Hawai'i Volcanoes National Park; you can only get one the day before your hike. The Mauna Loa summit cabin has 12 bunks. Visitors are allowed a three-night maximum stay. Pit toilets are available at the cabin as well as drinking water. Don't forget to treat the water. There's no water available on the trail.

Mauna Loa is at a very high altitude, so wait at least 24 hours between scuba diving and ascending Mauna Loa in order to avoid getting the bends.

Other Recreation

HORSEBACK RIDING

All the available outfitters more or less have the same restrictions for riders: usually no children under seven (the exact age might vary), and riders above 250 pounds must notify the tour operator prior to the ride of their exact weight. It is also important to be honest with the tour operator about your ability level, because some operators do not allow beginners on certain tours and others do not want advanced riders.

Views of the Kona and Kohala Coasts are abundant on **Paniolo Adventures** (Kohala Mountain Rd./Rte. 250 at mile 13.2, 808/889-5354, www.panioloadventures.com, tours range $69-175 depending on length). The company's guides have a good reputation for being professional, knowing what they are doing, and enjoying their work. With six different rides ranging from picnic adventures to sunset trots, you'll likely find a ride that suits your skill level and your schedule. A favorite tour is the 1.5-hour sunset ride ($89), suitable for all experience levels.

Dahana Ranch (47-4841 Old Mamalahoa Hwy./Hwy. 19, 808/885-0057, www.dahanaranch.com, 9am-6pm daily, $80-150) offers a menu of choices (from 1.5-hour to 2.5-hour rides) and is excellent at meeting the needs of riders. Most rides are through the ranch with lovely faraway views of Waipi'o and Mauna Kea. Whether you're looking to be the best caregiver to your child (like taking your kids or grandkids to Hawaii wasn't already enough?) or drop off your unruly children, Kids Camp at the ranch is a great place to visit. From July 1 to August 30 you can keep your kids busy from 9:30am to 3:30pm at the cost of $160 (includes lunch and riding lessons). Reservations need to be made one day in advance.

ZIPLINING

Zipline rides, also known as canopy tours, are booming on the Big Island. **Zip Isle** (Hwy. 19 at mile marker 16, *mauka* side, Hakalau, 808/963-5427, www.zipisle.com, 9am-5:30pm daily, $167 adults, $97 children, *kama'aina* discounts available) is located in the World Botanical Gardens, the state's largest botanical garden. If you have gone ziplining in Costa Rica, this course isn't for you. The thrills are minimal, but the staff is friendly and knowledgeable, making this an ideal course for first-timers and children (minimum weight requirement of 70 pounds, although they are lenient on this). Also, the course was constructed in partnership with certified engineers in order to guarantee the utmost safety for zipliners. There are three tours daily and it's a good idea to reserve a week in advance.

Entertainment

This region, luckily, attracts musicians, dancers, and performers (and some fairly big names) to its venues big and small. In Honoka'a, the **Honoka'a People's Theater** (43 Mamane St., 808/775-0000, http://honokaapeople.com) doubles as an art movie theater (tickets $6 adults, $4 seniors, $3 children) and a live music venue. Constructed in the 1930s by the Tanimoto family, who built several historic theaters on the Big Island, it was and remains the largest theater on the island, with seating capacity of 525 people. Check the schedule online for event listings. A few times a month there are live performances.

The only bar in Honoka'a, **The Landing Restaurant** (45-3490 Mamane St., 808/775-0888, 11am-10pm Sun.-Thurs., 11am-midnight Fri.-Sat.) offers live music on some Saturday nights. It also has karaoke on Thursday nights and open mic events on Wednesday nights.

In Waimea, theatergoers will be impressed by the newish (from 1981) structure built by Richard Smart, heir to the Parker Ranch, which now houses his private collection of Broadway memorabilia. The **Kahilu Theatre** (67-1186 Lindsey Rd., Parker Ranch Shopping Center, www.kahilutheatre.org, 808/885-6868) attracts first-rate local and mainland performers, like the Martha Graham Dance Company, internationally known jazz musicians, and master ukulele players. Best of all, tickets are reasonably priced and at times even free for the community events. In addition to the usual season schedule, the theater also hosts community performances, such as the Hawaii youth symphony and sometimes the **Waimea Community Theater** (65-1224 Lindsey Rd., Parker School Theater, 808/885-5818, www.waimeacommunitytheatre.org), which has been performing plays and musicals on the Big Island since 1964.

Food

HAMAKUA COAST

With the closure of the much-loved Back to the 50s Diner, there really isn't anywhere to stop for food in the area until you reach Honoka'a.

HONOKA'A AND WAIPI'O VALLEY

Don't have your heart set on eating somewhere specific in Honoka'a. Although hours are posted for restaurants, they frequently change. Waimea is only about 15 minutes away and offers many top-notch dining options, so it might be worth the extra few minutes in the car rather than eating in Honoka'a.

It's hard not to stop daily at ★ **Tex Drive In** (Hwy. 19 at the corner of Pakalana St., 808/775-0598, 6am-8pm daily, dinners $9),

a Big Island institution—and rightfully so. This long-established Hamakua restaurant is known for its fresh *malasadas:* sugared Portuguese pastries filled with passion fruit cream, chocolate, or strawberry. Best of all, you can watch the production process showcased behind plate-glass windows inside. Get there prior to 7pm before they sell out. Tex has a fast-food look, a drive-up window, a walk-up counter, and inside and outside tables, as well as a cavernous dining room in the back. Besides the *malasadas*, the restaurant serves *ono kine* local food, specializing in *kalua* pork, teriyaki chicken and beef, hamburgers, and fresh fish.

In Honoka'a town, you'll find **Café Il Mondo** (Mamane St. at the corner of Lehua St., 808/775-7711, www.cafeilmondo.com,

11am-2pm and 5pm-8pm Mon.-Sat., $12 small pizzas and calzones, cash only), an Italian pizzeria and coffee bar that's the best Honoka'a has to offer. While handmade pizzas with toppings, mostly $12-15, are the main focus, you can also get tasty calzones, pasta dishes, sandwiches, and salads for under $12, as well as ice cream and gourmet coffee. When having dinner, it's okay to bring your own bottle of wine. Cash only.

If you're looking for something a bit lighter than comfort food (not everyone's ideal breakfast includes pork chops), head to **Hina Rae's Café** (45-3610 Mamane St., 808/756-0895, http://hinaraescafe.com/#hina-raes-cafe, 8am-4pm Mon.-Fri., 8am-3pm Sat.), where acai bowls are the breakfast fare and lunch specials like spicy poke draw locals in. There is not much seating in this small coffee shop, but this café is worth a stop if you're looking for a place to get a huge almond milk coconut chai to caffeinate and rehydrate.

Another brand-new eatery on Mamane Street, **Sea Dandelion Vegetarian Cafe & Awa Bar** (45-3590 Mamane St., 802/765-0292, 11am-7pm Mon. and Thurs., 11am-4:15 am Tues., ., 4:15pm-9pm Fri., 12pm-7pm Sat.,) is the kind of place to go if you're a raw foodist and/or really want to try awa (also known as kava), sea asparagus, and vegan poke all in one place. Have some time on your hands and cash in your wallet (as the restaurant doesn't take credit cards). On Fridays, buy two cups of *awa* and get the third one free.

A much-needed addition closer to Waipi'o Valley, ★ **Waipi'o Cookhouse** (48-5370 Waipi'o Rd., 808/775-1443, 7am-7pm daily) is a barbecue joint that "broke da mouth," as we say. It's not fancy: You order at the counter and then take a seat outside in an area overlooking the ocean. All the meat is locally sourced from a nearby farm—even the lamb. The real specialties are the lamb burger ($13.50) and the kalua pork sandwich, which is slow cooked in an imu and served with papaya barbecue sauce ($14). On the first and third Saturday of the month from 3pm to 6pm there is live music as well as pork ribs and brisket served.

★ WAIMEA

It's almost guaranteed that eating in **Waimea** will lead you to exclaim, "That was the best steak of my life!" The beef doesn't get more local than this, much of it from grass-fed cattle. Waimea also is home to several long-standing upscale restaurants. Entries are listed from north to south and then east to west on Highway 19.

malasadas at Tex Drive In

You'd think there would be more barbecue in Waimea given its country feel, but **The Fish and the Hog** (64-957 Mamalaho Hwy./Hwy. 19 across from mile marker 56, 808/885-6286, 11am-8pm daily, $12-24) is the only game in town. The sampler plate is more than enough for two people and comes with brisket, ribs, pork, and homemade sausage. There are also sandwiches, quesadillas, and fish tacos on the menu, but I'd stick to the barbecue options.

There is some stiff competition in the area, yet **Lilikoi Café** (67-1185 Mamalahoa Hwy./Hwy. 19, in the back of the Parker Ranch Shopping Center, 808/887-1400, 7:30am-4pm Mon.-Sat., breakfast $7, lunch $13) still fares well. Both the atmosphere and the menu are simple: sandwiches, fresh salads that come as a combo with a choice of deli meat, and crepes for vegetarians. The breakfast choices of granola, burritos, and crepes are ideal for those looking to eat a wholesome and nourishing meal that doesn't include Spam, as many breakfast options do on the island.

Also in the Parker Ranch Shopping Center is the home of one of the best burgers you will ever have (and so agrees USA Today in its list of 50 burgers you must have before you die). **Village Burger** (67-1185 Mamalahoa Hwy./19, Parker Ranch Center Food Court, 808/885-7319, www.villageburgerwaimea.com, 10:30am-8pm Mon.-Sat., 10:30am-6pm Sun., $8-12) is a true farm-to-table establishment, with nearly every ingredient sourced from a nearby farm. The veal burger is spectacular and can be served on a beautiful bed of lettuce for those who don't want the bun. The taro burger is a well-thought-out conglomeration of garden vegetables. Try the *mamake* iced tea, a blend of a local leaf, mint, and tarragon. The restaurant is located in the food court with no ambience and little seating, so grab it go—although you'll probably finish your burger by the time you reach your car.

On weekends, be prepared to wait as visitors line up around the corner patiently anticipating the scrumptious breakfast at ★ **Hawaiian Style Café** (65-1290 Kawaihae Rd./Hwy. 19 between mile markers 57 and 58, 808/885-4295, 7am-1:30pm Mon.-Sat., 7am-noon Sun., breakfast $10, plate lunch $9-17). It's not healthy food, it's comfort food served by a friendly staff. Be prepared to make new friends because the communal counter area invokes conversation with fellow eaters. Try the *kalua* hash with eggs. It's the kind of food that's so good that you just keep eating it even though you're full. There are other local favorites on the menu, like several varieties of *loco moco*.

Waimea Coffee Company (65-1279 Kawaihae Rd./Hwy. 19, 808/885-8915, www.waimeacoffeecompany.com, 6:30am-5:30pm Mon.-Sat., 8am-2pm Sun., lunch $8) has a college-town coffee shop atmosphere. It's the kind of place where you can grab a coffee, bagels and lox, or soup or sandwich, and enjoy a book outside in the brisk Waimea air.

As one of the original homes of Hawaii Regional Cuisine, **Merriman's** (65-1227 Opelo Rd., 808/885-6822, http://merrimanshawaii.com, 11:30am-1:30pm Mon.-Fri., 5:30pm-9pm daily, and Sun. brunch 10am-1pm, reservations recommended, lunch $15, dinner $30-43) has a lot of street cred—and that's without adding the fact that its owner, Peter Merriman, is a James Beard Award finalist. The dining experience is superb, with well-trained waitstaff and white linen tablecloths. It's a good place to go if you are looking for fine dining. The menu changes, but offers the usual Hawaiian dishes of mahimahi or ahi, spicy soups, and local vegetables. Lunch is a good choice; the lunch menu is similar to the dinner menu, but less expensive.

Where to Stay
on the Big Island

Kona

Name	Type	Price	Features	Why Stay Here?	Best Fit For
Aston Kona by the Sea	condo	$180-300	sofa beds, kitchen, laundry, pool, hot tub, barbecue	location	families, couples
Casa de Emdeko	condo	$125-175	pools, barbecue, beach equipment	affordable	families, couples
Courtyard King Kamehameha's Kona Beach Hotel	hotel	$200-285	pool, luau	downtown location	families
Four Seasons Resort, Hualalai at Historic Ka'upulehu	resort	$550-1200	pools, spa, day care	truly exclusive, quality service	luxury lovers, families
Hale Kona Kai	condo	$150-250	kitchen, sofa bed, lanai, pool, barbecue, Wi-Fi	downtown location	couples, families
Hawaiian Oasis Bed-and-Breakfast	B&B	$230-320	pool, tennis courts, outdoor kitchen	downtown location	couples, large families
★ Holualoa Inn	B&B	$365-595	pool, kitchen, breakfast	views, service, quiet	honeymooners, luxury lovers
Holua Resort at Mauna Loa Village	condo	$150-250	kitchen, pool, hot tub, activities desk	uncrowded, easy parking, helpful staff	couples, families
★ Honu Kai	B&B	$230-285	laundry, kitchen, beach gear	concierge service, downtown location	first-timers, couples
Manago Hotel	hotel	$35-83	restaurant	old Hawaii feel	budget travelers
Kona Bali Kai	condo	$115-350	pool, restaurant	frequent upgrade	budget travelers, large groups
Kona Seaside Hotel	hotel	$100-140	pool	downtown location	budget travelers
Lilikoi Inn	B&B	$135-195	huge breakfast	great views of Kailua	couples, families
★ Luana Inn	B&B	$169-209	pool, delicious breakfast	views, sweet hosts	couples
Outrigger Keauhou Beach Resort	resort	$170-450	pool, tennis courts, activities desk, fitness center	one of the few true resorts in Kona, low-season deals	families

Kona (continued)

Name	Type	Price	Features	Why Stay Here?	Best Fit For
Pineapple Park	hostel	$30-100	kayak rental, free Wi-Fi	hostel scene	budget travelers
★ Sheraton Keauhou Bay Resort and Spa	resort	$125-450	pool, tennis courts, spa, business center	watching manta rays from the bar	families

Kohala

Name	Type	Price	Features	Why Stay Here?	Best Fit For
★ Aston Shores at Waikoloa	condo	$175-300	kitchen, laundry, pool, private lanai, beach gear	nice condo	families, long-term stays
★ The Fairmont Orchid	hotel	$300-500	pool, hot tub, water sports rentals, luau, fitness center, golf, tennis courts, spa	the best luau on the island	honeymooners, families, luxury lovers
Hapuna Beach Prince Hotel	resort	$250-650	golf, pool, spa, fitness center	beach location, golf	golfers, beach lovers
★ Hawaii Island Retreat at Ahu Pohaku Ho'omaluhia	boutique hotel	$195-500	lounge, ocean views, infinity pool, spa, yoga	luxury, personalized spa experience	honeymooners, weddings or reunions
Hilton Waikoloa Village	resort	$200-400	pool, penguins and dolphins, restaurants, luau	a true megaresort experience	families, luxury lovers
★ Mauna Kea Beach Hotel	hotel	$325-950	pool, hot tub, beach access, restaurant, tennis, golf	beach, trail, and golf	honeymooners, couples
Mauna Lani Bay Hotel and Bungalows	hotel	$250-800	pool, hot tub, beach, restaurant, golf	beach access	honeymooners, luxury lovers
Mauna Lani Point	condo	$250-550	pool, hot tub, kitchen, laundry	affordable access to beach and golf	golfers, couples, extended stay

Kohala (continued)

Name	Type	Price	Features	Why Stay Here?	Best Fit For
Fairway Villas Waikola by Outrigger	condo	$150-285	tennis, pool, kitchen, private lanai, beach gear	affordable, location	families, extended stay
★ Puakea Ranch	vacation rental	$235-650	pool, kitchen, horseback riding, children's play room	beautiful decor, relaxation	couples, families
Waikoloa Beach Marriott Resort and Spa	resort	$150-350	restaurants, pool, hot tub, luau	beach, location	families, Marriott members

Volcano Village

Name	Type	Price	Features	Why Stay Here?	Best Fit For
Chalet Kilauea Hotel at Volcano	hotel	$150-225	hot tub, lounge	rainforest atmosphere	couples
★ Hale Ohia	inn	$129-260	fireplaces, covered porches/lanai	cozy and warm, vintage	couples, families
Kilauea Lodge	hotel	$195-215	restaurant, breakfast included, hot tub	park access, location	couples
Volcano House	hotel	$250-380	restaurant	park access, location	park visitors
★ Volcano Rainforest Retreat	vacation rental	$190-330	kitchen, Japanese *ofuro* tubs	cozy rainforest setting	families, couples
★ Volcano Teapot Cottage	vacation rental	$195	fireplace, hot tub, kitchen	fairy-tale setting	couples
★ Volcano Village Lodge	inn	$280-375	hot tub	romance	honeymooners

Hilo

Name	Type	Price	Features	Why Stay Here?	Best Fit For
★ Hilo Bay Hale	B&B	$159	private lanai	urban experience	couples and singles, LGBTQfriendly
★ Hilo Bay Hostel	hostel	$30-79	historic building, kitchen	affordable dorm experience	budget travelers
Hilo Hawaiian Hotel	hotel	$155-300	pool, restaurant	location	conference attendees, short-term guests
★ Hilo Honu Inn	B&B	$140-250	sunporch, historic home, views	gorgeous suite that's like a Japanese tearoom	couples traveling together, honeymooners, those who like views
★ The Inn at Kulaniapia Falls	B&B	$179-289	hot tub, massage, waterfall, breakfast	a waterfall in your backyard	honeymooners
The Old Hawaiian Bed-and-Breakfast	B&B	$85-125	fridge and microwave, shared lanai, huge breakfast	best-value B&B	budget travelers
Orchid Tree Bed-and-Breakfast	B&B	$149 plus tax	pool, hot tub, shared lanai	pool near the ocean	surfers, families, couples
★ Shipman House Bed-and-Breakfast Inn	B&B	$219-249	historic, great breakfast	one of the best-known families and houses in Hawaii	couples, history buffs

the Hamakua Coast, Waimea, and the Saddle Road

Name	Type	Price	Features	Why Stay Here?	Best Fit For
Aaah the Views	B&B	$169-189	breakfast	sunset views, location	budget travelers
★ Waipi'o Rim	B&B	$220	wine and pupu hour	best views, friendly hosts	couples
★ Waipi'o Wayside	B&B	$115-200	1932 plantation house	close to town but not too far from valley	families, couples, budget travelers
★ Waimea Gardens	B&B	$160-190	farm-fresh breakfast	close to everything; the best mattress you'll ever sleep on	honeymooners, couples traveling with baby/toddler

Kaua'i

The oldest of the Hawaiian Islands, Kaua'i is a verdant retreat where natural wonders and quiet towns peacefully coexist. Its laid-back old-Hawai'i charm makes it the perfect getaway.

No one is in a hurry, and relaxing at the beach or trekking through the mountains is all the entertainment you need.

It's easy to see how the famed "Garden Isle" earned its nickname. Approximately 90 percent of the island is uninhabited, with Mount Wai'ale'ale (the wettest place on earth) and its towering ridges reaching from the center of the island out toward the sea in all directions. Sculpted by erosion, the beautiful and vast Waimea Canyon and Na Pali Coast offer majestic lookouts and hiking trails that weave from ridgelines to canyon floors. Kaua'i's waterfalls and wide rivers flow to the ocean, telling the story of the island's rain-cloaked natural history.

This gorgeous island offers civilized pleasures as well. Internationally renowned chefs showcase their one-of-a-kind Hawai'i Regional Cuisine. Kapa'a town's eclectic shops, full of locally crafted jewelry and art, draw shoppers, and couples find renewal at the luxury resorts.

But without question, the beaches are the island's main draw. Sunbathers find secluded nooks of fine white sand to soak up rays, surfers revel in the world-class waves along the north and south shores, and snorkelers rejoice in the vibrant underwater world along the island's reefs. Kaua'i is a gorgeous testament to the natural and cultural beauty of Hawai'i. It's *aloha* at its best.

WHERE TO GO
Lihu'e and the East Side
The east side, also known as the Coconut Coast, stretches from Lihu'e to Anahola. The area offers historical sites, river kayaking, waterfalls, and beautiful coastlines. **Lihu'e,** home to Kaua'i's largest airport, is the hub of commerce and government for the island. **Wailua** is home to the famous **Wailua Falls** and **Wailua River** cultural sites. The biggest draw is **Kapa'a,** a colorful town known for its whimsical cafés and eateries, as well as its eclectic shops with locally made goods. Inland behind Kapa'a are miles of great hiking trails with amazing views.

Princeville and the North Shore
The north shore is a true tropical paradise with vibrant green cliffs and streaming, ribbon-like waterfalls backing some of the island's most spectacular white-sand beaches. The area is known for surfing and snorkeling. Upscale **Princeville,** perched on a bluff high above the ocean, features luxury accommodations, vacation rentals, and a residential community. Down in **Hanalei Valley** is quaint **Hanalei** town with charming shops and great

restaurants. At the end of the road is the **Na Pali Coast,** where miles of strenuous hiking trails lead adventurers to secluded beaches, waterfalls, and valleys.

Po'ipu and the South Shore

Po'ipu is home to endless sunshine and the bulk of the island's accommodations. The region has white-sand beaches that offer snorkeling, swimming, surfing, and golfing. **Po'ipu Beach** and the **Maha'ulepu Beaches** provide an exquisite setup for the perfect beach day. On the west end of Po'ipu are some must-see sights, including **Spouting Horn** and the **National Tropical Botanical Garden.** Inland from Po'ipu is historic and local town **Koloa,** with eateries and shopping.

Waimea and the West Side

The wild and remote west side is known for its deep canyons, pristine forests, seemingly endless white-sand coastline, empty beaches, and historic towns. **Hanapepe** is home to almost 20 art galleries and popular **Art Night in Hanapepe.** Most **Na Pali Coast** tours depart from **Port Allen.** Some of the island's most spectacular viewpoints and trails are found at **Waimea Canyon** and in **Koke'e State Park.** And at the end of the road is one of the island's most beautiful and secluded beaches, **Polihale State Park.**

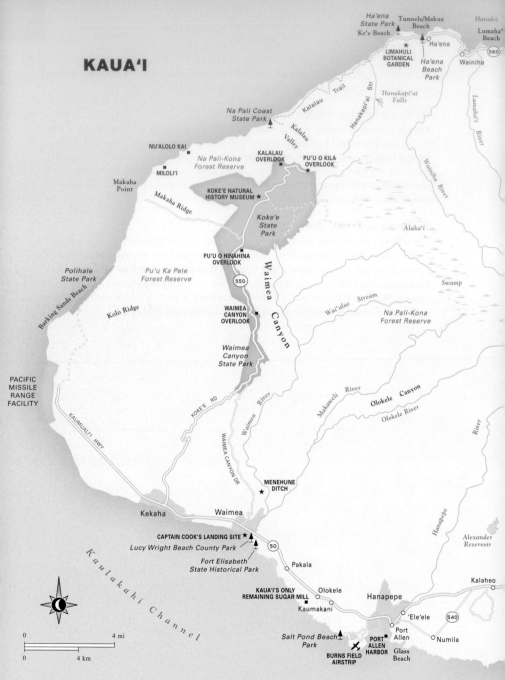

KAUA'I

Ha'ena
State Park
Ke'e Beach

Tunnels/Makua
Beach

Hanalei

Lumaha'i
Beach

LIMAHULI
BOTANICAL
GARDEN

Ha'ena

Ha'ena
Beach
Park

Wainiha

560

Na Pali Coast
State Park

Kalalau Trail

Hanakapi'ai Str

Hanakapi'ai
Falls

Lumaha'i River

NU'ALOLO KAI

Kalalau
Valley

KALALAU
OVERLOOK

PU'U O KILA
OVERLOOK

Na Pali-Kona
Forest Reserve

MILOLI'I

Wainiha River

KOKE'E NATURAL
HISTORY MUSEUM

Makaha
Point

Makaha Ridge

Alaka'i

Koke'e
State
Park

Polihale
State Park

Pu'u Ka Pele
Forest Reserve

PU'U O HINAHINA
OVERLOOK

550

Waimea Canyon

Swamp

Barking Sands Beach

Kolo Ridge

Wai'alae Stream

Na Pali-Kona
Forest Reserve

PACIFIC
MISSILE
RANGE
FACILITY

KAUMUALI'I HWY

WAIMEA
CANYON
OVERLOOK

Waimea
Canyon
State Park

KOKE'E RD

WAIMEA CANYON DR

Waimea River

Makaweli River

Olokele Canyon

Olokele River

River

MENEHUNE
DITCH

Hanapepe

Alexander
Reservoir

Kekaha

Waimea

CAPTAIN COOK'S LANDING SITE

Lucy Wright Beach County Park

Fort Elisabeth
State Historical Park

50

Pakala

KAUA'I'S ONLY
REMAINING SUGAR MILL

Olokele

Kaumakani

Hanapepe

Kalaheo

'Ele'ele

540

Salt Pond Beach
Park

BURNS FIELD
AIRSTRIP

PORT
ALLEN
HARBOR

Port
Allen

Glass
Beach

Numila

Kaulakahi Channel

0   4 mi

0   4 km

© AVALON TRAVEL

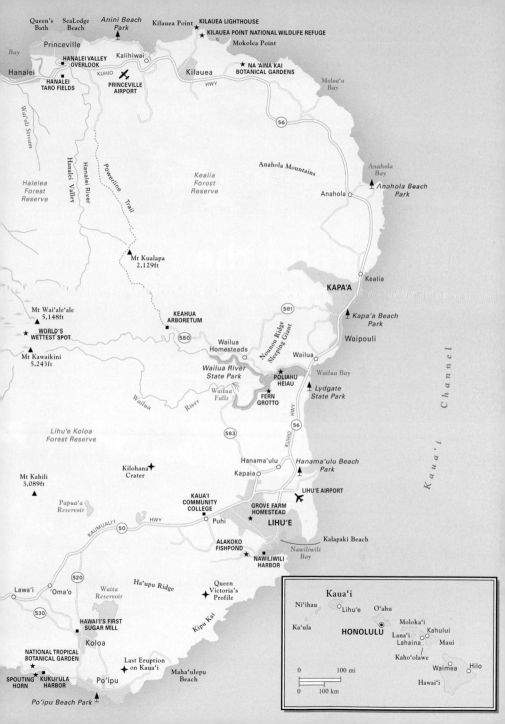

Lihu'e and the East Side

The east side of Kaua'i has many faces, from its towns to the weather.

Sometimes the sun is blazing and waves roll up on the fine, white sand at Kealia Beach, where surfers dot the lineup, or snorkelers gaze at marine life at Lydgate Beach Park. Some days can be windy and overcast, the ocean choppy and rough, a better day for cruising Kapa'a's cafés and shops. The beauty of this area is that most days are perfect to explore the rivers by kayak or stand-up paddleboard—unless it's pouring down rain, of course.

Lihu'e—a plantation town until 1996 when the sugar mill shut down—is busy, practical, and central. Its neighbor, Kapa'a, is vibrant and colorful, with a natural, laid-back vibe. Kapa'a is also known for an eclectic mix of craft shops, clothing boutiques, and galleries featuring local artists, as well as restaurants, cafés, and walk-up eateries where organic, fresh, and local food is almost always on the menu.

The stretch from Wailua Golf Course to Kapa'a's Kealia Beach is known as the Coconut Coast for the plethora of coconut trees a plantation entrepreneur planted along the highway and the coast. The Wailua River is one of the main attractions on the Coconut Coast. The name Wailua, which means "two waters,"

celebrates the beautiful ocean and bay along with the freshwater river, where *ali'i* (Hawaiian royalty) gathered for sacred ceremonies, leaving archaeological relics to tell the story. Many *heiau* (sacred rock structures) were built in the area, and their sparse remains still can be seen along the banks of the river.

Wherever you find yourself in this region, dramatic mountains and clear ocean water frame your view, and nature is in the eye everywhere you look.

ORIENTATION

Kaua'i's east side stretches from **Lihu'e,** where you'll find the airport and car rental services, a national brand shopping mall, the government center, and the Kaua'i Museum, to **Anahola,** a sleepy residential community with a few beaches and a small outdoor market. In Lihu'e, the resort area is west of the airport, near the famous **Kalapaki Beach,** which fronts **Nawiliwili Bay,** Kaua'i's port of call for cruise ships. Sister towns **Wailua** and **Kapa'a** are the main attractions for the region. The towns are funky and quaint with a natural vibe.

Everything is right along **Kuhio**

Previous: Lydgate Beach Park; kayaking the Wailua River. **Above:** Kaua'i style in Lihu'e.

Look for ★ to find recommended
sights, activities, dining, and lodging.

Highlights

★ **Kaua'i Museum:** Learn about the history and culture of Kaua'i to enhance your island experience (page 550).

★ **Kilohana Plantation:** Take a trip back in time while exploring an expansive and elegant estate. Ride the sugar train, sample locally produced craft rum, and enjoy a meal at the upscale restaurant (page 551).

★ **Wailua Falls:** Gaze at the iconic 80-foot waterfall, easily accessed by car (page 553).

★ **Lydgate Beach Park:** Bring your snorkeling gear and enjoy viewing reef fish in the calm, protected pools. Picnic tables, pavilions, and two amazing playgrounds make for an ideal day at the beach (page 557).

★ **Donkey Beach:** One of the more remote beaches in the area, this long and uncrowded stretch of white sand is perfect for sunbathing and beachcombing (page 559).

★ **Surfing at Kalapaki Beach:** The calm, crescent-moon-shaped bay is ideal for swimming, longboarding, and stand-up paddling. Watch surfers catch waves, or take a surf lesson and catch your own (page 560).

★ **Kayaking the Wailua River:** A waterfall, lush jungle, and calm waters make kayaking on the wide and smooth Wailua River a must-do adventure (page 562).

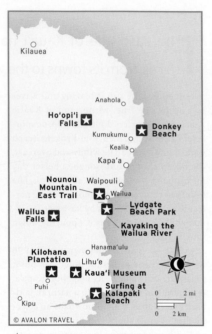

© AVALON TRAVEL

★ **Nounou Mountain East Trail:** This strenuous yet rewarding hiking trail offers solitude and spectacular coastal views from Mount Wai'ale'ale (page 564).

★ **Ho'opi'i Falls:** A gorgeous nature walk takes you through a tunnel of trees to these two waterfalls (page 565).

Lihu'e and the East Side

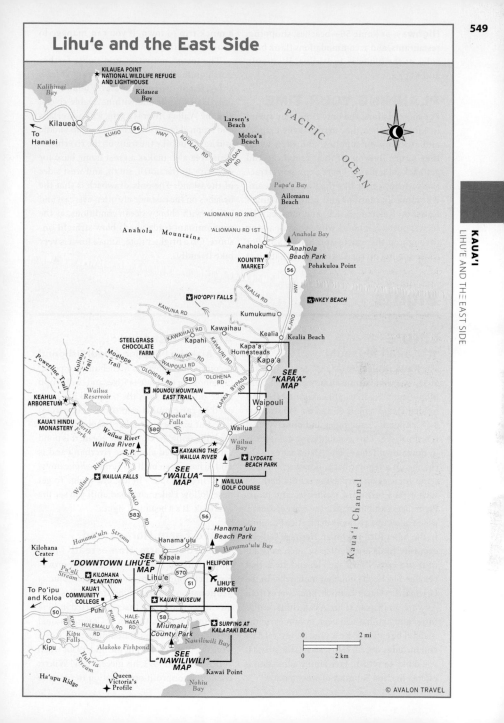

KILAUEA POINT
NATIONAL WILDLIFE REFUGE
AND LIGHTHOUSE

Kalihiwai Bay

Kilauea Bay

Kilauea

To
Hanalei

KUHIO   56   HWY

KO'OLAU RD

MOLOA'A RD

Larsen's
Beach

Moloa'a
Beach

P A C I F I C

O C E A N

Papa'a Bay

Ailomanu
Beach

'ALIOMANU RD 2ND

Anahola   Mountains

'ALIOMANU RD 1ST

Anahola Bay

Anahola

KOUNTRY
MARKET   56

*Anahola
Beach Park*

Pohakuloa Point

HO'OPI'I FALLS

KEALIA RD

KUHIO HWY

MONKEY BEACH

KAHUNA RD

Kumukumu

KAWAIHAU RD

Kawaihau

STEELGRASS
CHOCOLATE
FARM

Kapahi

Kealia

Kealia Beach

KA'APUNI RD

HAUIKI RD

Kapa'a
Homesteads

Powerline Trail

Kuilau Trail

Moalepe Trail

WAIPOULI RD

'OLOHENA RD   581

Kapa'a

'OLOHENA
RD

KAPA'A BYPASS RD

**SEE
"KAPA'A"
MAP**

KEAHUA
ARBORETUM

*Wailua
Reservoir*

NOUNOU MOUNTAIN
EAST TRAIL

Waipouli

KAUA'I HINDU
MONASTERY

North Fork

Wailua River

*Wailua River
S.P.*   580

*'Opaeka'a
Falls*

KAYAKING THE
WAILUA RIVER

Wailua

*Wailua
Bay*

LYDGATE
BEACH PARK

Wailua River

WAILUA FALLS

**SEE
"WAILUA"
MAP**

WAILUA
GOLF COURSE

MA'ALO RD

583   RD

56

*Hanama'ulu
Beach Park*

Hanama'uln Stream

Hanama'ulu

Hanama'ulu Bay

K a u a ' i   C h a n n e l

Kilohana
Crater

**SEE
"DOWNTOWN LIHU'E"
MAP**

Kapaia

HELIPORT

Pu'ali Stream

KILOHANA
PLANTATION

Lihu'e   570

51   LIHU'E
AIRPORT

To Po'ipu
and Koloa

KAUA'I
COMMUNITY
COLLEGE

50   Puhi

PUHI RD

HALE-
HAKA RD

58

KAUA'I MUSEUM

SURFING AT
KALAPAKI BEACH

KIPU RD

HULEMALU RD

*Miumalu
County Park*

Nawiliwili Bay

Kipu
Falls

Kipu

Alakoko Fishpond

**SEE
"NAWILIWILI"
MAP**

Kawai Point

Hule'ia Stream

Ha'upu Ridge

Queen
Victoria's
Profile

*Nohili
Bay*

0   2 mi

0   2 km

Highway, or Route 56—beaches, shopping, restaurants, and accommodations flank both sides of the highway in Wailua, Waipouli, and Kapa'a.

PLANNING YOUR TIME

For most visitors, the only time they spend in Lihu'e is when they arrive at the airport and stock up on supplies, and then when they return to drop off their rental car and get back on a plane. There are a few attractions worth seeing, like the Kaua'i Museum, Kilohana Plantation, and lunch at Duke's Kauai on Kalapaki Beach, and most can be seen in just a few hours while you're passing through on the way to another region. For those staying on the Coconut Coast, it's just a quick trip to town, if you can manage to avoid the traffic.

The towns, activities, and sights farther north on the Coconut Coast warrant at least a day, if not two, of your stay. Kaua'i is the only Hawaiian Island with navigable rivers, and the Wailua River is a gem, with waterfalls and tropical forests. You can stand-up paddle and kayak or hike the trails on the riverbank. This area also makes a great home base for day trips to the north, south, and west sides of the island. The only drawback is that the beaches on the east side are often overcast and windy with choppy ocean conditions, as the predominant trade winds blow straight onshore. On a brighter note, Kapa'a town is very bike friendly.

Sights

LIHU'E

★ Kaua'i Museum

The **Kaua'i Museum** (4428 Rice St., 808/245-6931, www.kauaimuseum.org, 10am-5pm Mon.-Sat., $15 adults, $10 *kama'aina* (Hawaii residents), $12 seniors 65 and up, $10 students 8-17, children 7 and under and military free) is a must-see. This two-building complex is in downtown Lihu'e. The island art exhibits change on a regular basis; however, the museum focuses on displaying ethnic heritage such as koa furniture, feather lei, and more. Permanent exhibits include the *Story of Kaua'i*, which takes up two floors in the Rice Building. In the Juliet Rice Wichman Heritage Gallery, exquisite finds are on display, such as beautiful and rare N'ihau shell lei and items that belonged to Kaua'i *ali'i* and monarchs. In the Oriental Art Gallery exhibit, housewares from Asia are on display as are Asian china, sculptures, and art that had been in homes on the island. The entrance fee is valid for several days and includes docent tours, so ask for a pass if you'd like to return. Free family admission is offered the first Saturday of every month.

Alakoko Fishpond

The **Alakoko (Rippling Blood) Fishpond** is commonly known as Menehune Fishpond. Overlooking the Hule'ia River and the Ha'upu ridge on the far side, the fishpond has been used to raise mullet and other commercial fish. But unlike most other fishponds, which are built along the edge of the ocean, this pond was constructed along the riverbank and is said to have been built by the *menehune* (mystical "little people") in just one night. To get here, follow Hulemalu Road until you see the overlook. It's a beautiful sight.

Grove Farm Homestead

The **Grove Farm Homestead** (4050 Nawiliwili Rd., 808/245-3202, www.grove-farm.net, tours 10am and 1pm Mon.-Thurs., $20 donation adults, $10 children 5-12) is a former sugar plantation that was started in 1864 by George Wilcox, the son of Congregational missionary teachers. The homestead was a working plantation until the mid-1930s when Wilcox died. In 1971, his niece, Mabel Wilcox created a nonprofit organization to preserve

The Best Day on the East Side

To experience the best of the best on the east side, begin early and be ready for a busy day. Because Kaua'i's most spectacular beaches are found on other parts of the island, a day on the east side should be spent with activities rather than lounging on the sand. Begin in Kapa'a and work your way toward Lihu'e because some of the Kapa'a and Wailua sights are best in the morning. If you begin your day early with breakfast around 8am, you should be finished and ready for dinner around 7:30pm.

- Welcome the day with breakfast at **Kountry Kitchen** or **Art Café Hemingway** in Kapa'a.

- Next, kayak the **Wailua River** or walk along the river to **Ho'opi'i Falls.** If you choose the hike, just head up the road, but if you'd rather paddle up the Wailua River, make sure to book a reservation in advance. Check with your outfitter to see if it provides lunch; you can grab lunch in Kapa'a afterward if it doesn't. If you're looking to skip strenuous activity for a day, take the drive up to **Wailua Falls** for a quick-stop photo op.

- After your morning nature experience, head back to Kapa'a for lunch at **Mermaids Café** or **Olympic Café.**

- After lunch, head south to **Lydgate Beach Park.** Cool off and snorkel in the calm pools. Spend some time viewing the underwater world and relaxing in the sun. Don't forget your snorkel equipment.

- Head over to Lihu'e for a visit to the **Kilohana Plantation.** Browse the shops and plantation grounds, or take a ride on the historical train.

- For dinner there are two great options in Lihu'e. For a spectacular dinner featuring local cuisine, try **Gaylord's.** To enjoy a classic Hawaiian restaurant in a semi-formal atmosphere, have a meal on the water at **Duke's.**

RAINY-DAY ALTERNATIVE

If rain and wind have you running for cover, spend some time exploring the **Kaua'i Museum,** which offers a rich history of the island through permanent and rotating exhibits. Then, head down to **Kalapaki Beach Park** and post up in the bar at **Duke's.** With oceanfront seating, once the rain clears you'll be in the right spot to get back in the water.

KAUA'I
LIHU'E AND THE EAST SIDE

Grove Farm Homestead as a historical living farm. Reservations for tours are preferred, but the staff will most likely accommodate unexpected visitors. They ask that visitors call at least 24 hours in advance to book a tour. Reservations are also accepted up to three months in advance by emailing tours@grove.org. Exact directions will be given over the phone. Wear comfortable shoes that can be slipped off because, as in most homes in Hawaii, shoes are not worn indoors here. Tours are sometimes canceled on rainy days.

★ Kilohana Plantation

For an elegant trip back in time, visit the

Kilohana Plantation (3-2087 Kaumuali'i Hwy., 808/245-5608, www.kilohanakauai.com, shops open 9:30am-9:30pm Mon.-Sat., 9:30am-5pm Sun., free), a sprawling estate with manicured lawns, fruit, flowers, a train, and the former mansion of Gaylord Wilcox. At the time that Gaylord Wilcox moved the business offices of Grove Farm from the homestead site, he had the 16,000-square-foot Kilohana plantation house built in 1936. After decades of family use, the building was renovated in 1986 and turned into shops that sell arts and crafts. Exploring the antique mansion's rooms, still decorated with original furnishings, jewelry, and other elegant

Downtown Lihu'e

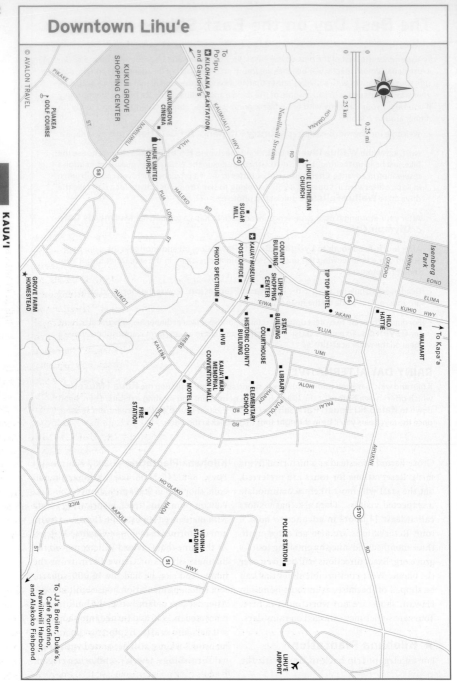

© AVALON TRAVEL

PIKAKE

KUKUI GROVE SHOPPING CENTER

PUAKEA GOLF COURSE

KUKUIGROVE CINEMA

ST

NAWILIWILI

RD

58

KAUMUALI'I HWY

50

To Po'ipu,
KILOHANA PLANTATION,
and Gaylord's

LIHUE UNITED CHURCH

HALA

PUA LOKE ST

HALEKO RD

SUGAR MILL

Nawiliwili Stream

RD

HO'OMANA

LIHUE LUTHERAN CHURCH

KAUA'I MUSEUM

POST OFFICE

PHOTO SPECTRUM

COUNTY BUILDING

LIHU'E SHOPPING CENTER

'EIWA

'EHIKU

OXFORD

Isenberg Park

EONO

ELIMA

KUHIO HWY

WALMART

To Kapa'a

56

TIP TOP MOTEL

'AKAHI

HILO HATTIE

STATE BUILDING

'ELUA

'UMI

GROVE FARM HOMESTEAD

AUKOI

HISTORIC COUNTY BUILDING

COURTHOUSE

HVB

LIBRARY

KALENA

KRESS ST

KAUA'I WAR MEMORIAL CONVENTION HALL

MOTEL LANI

ELEMENTARY SCHOOL

HARDY RD

PUAKOLE RD

'ALOHI

IHOTI

PALAI

FIRE STATION

RICE ST

HO'OLAKO

HAVA

AHUKINI

KAPULE

RICE

ST

51 HWY

VIDINHA STADIUM

POLICE STATION

570 RD

To J's Broiler, Duke's,
Cafe Portofino,
Nawiliwili Harbor,
and Alakoko Fishpond

LIHU'E AIRPORT

0.25 mi
0.25 km

To Kapa'a

Wailua Falls

Fern Grotto

The Wailua River's **Fern Grotto**, a natural rock amphitheater where a dense forest of ferns hangs from the grotto, is a popular place to visit. An upriver tour run by **Smith's Kauai** (3-5971 Kuamoʻo Rd., 808/821-6895, www.smithskauai.com, boats depart 9:30am, 11am, 2pm, and 3:30pm daily, $20 adults, $10 children 3-12) is the way to access it. A two-mile, 90-minute round-trip river journey takes you to the grotto. On the trip you'll also be treated to a hula dance and Hawaiian music.

Kamokila Hawaiian Village

For a cultural experience, explore **Kamokila Hawaiian Village** (5443 Kuamoʻo Rd. along the Wailua River, 808/823-0559, www.villagekauai.com, 9am-5pm daily, $5 adults, $3 children 5-12). Kamokila means stronghold, and is Kauaʻi's only re-created Hawaiian village. It was built on the site of an ancient royal village, the first of seven ancient villages in this valley. Village sites include the canoe house, the *Outbreak* movie set, a birth house, taro patches, a wood-carving house, the village lagoon, petroglyphs, medicinal plants, and a lot more. The village also offers outrigger canoe rides, hiking and swimming, access to Secret Falls, weddings, and a luʻau.

★ Wailua Falls

One of Kauaʻi's most beautiful and easy-to-view waterfalls is the 80-foot **Wailua Falls**, which was featured on the opening credits of the television show *Fantasy Island*. Legend says the Hawaiian *aliʻi* would dive off the falls to prove their physical prowess, and commoners were not allowed to participate. Surrounded by wide-open pasture, it's a beautiful drive up Maʻalo Road to get to the falls. It's about four miles to the end of the road, so you can't miss it. The falls can be viewed from a lookout spot where there is a parking lot, which is a perfect place for a photo op. The lookout spot is the only place to view the falls unless you take one of the two trails

artifacts, serves as a tangible experience of history.

Kilohana Plantation has several restaurants, as well as Luʻau Kilohana every Tuesday and Thursday evening. A horse-drawn carriage operates 11am-6pm daily. Just show up and stand in line near the front entrance to take a ride. The 20-minute carriage ride is $12 for adults and $6 for children; call 808/246-9529 for reservations.

The **Kauai Plantation Railway** (www.kauaiplantationrailway.com) is a popular attraction on the plantation. Complete with a whistle, the 1939 Whitcomb diesel engine, named Ike, pulls mahogany coaches modeled after King Kamehameha's personal car. The Signature Train Tour is 40 minutes and tours 105 acres. It costs $19 adults, $14 children 3-12, infants are free. The tours run daily at 10am, 11am, noon, 1pm, and 2pm. Check in 30 minutes before departure. There also are packages that include the train tour and nature walk and lunch, as well as a train tour and luʻau.

Wailua

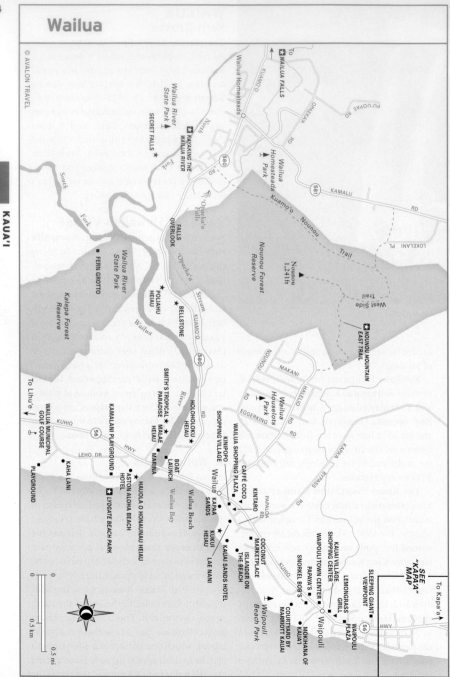

© AVALON TRAVEL

To
WAILUA FALLS

Wailua Homesteads Rd

KUAMO'O RD

ORAKA RD

PU-UOPAE RD

Wailua River State Park

SECRET FALLS

North Fork

South Fork

KAYAKING THE WAILUA RIVER

Wailua Homesteads Park

'Opaeka'a Falls

580 RD

581 KAMALU RD

Kuamo'o - Nounou Trail

LOKELANI PL

FALLS OVERLOOK

'Opaeka'a Stream

Nounou Forest Reserve

Nounou 1,241ft

West Side Trail

FERN GROTTO

Kalepa Forest Reserve

Wailua River State Park

POLIAHU HEIAU

BELLSTONE

KUAMO'O

Wailua River

580

NOUNOU MOUNTAIN EAST TRAIL

MAKANI RD

HALELIO RD

Wailua Houselots Park

EGGERKING RD

NOUNOU RD

To Lihu'e

KUHIO

56

LEHO DR

KUHIO HWY

WAILUA MUNICIPAL GOLF COURSE

KAMALANI PLAYGROUND

SMITH'S TROPICAL PARADISE

MALAE HEIAU

HOLOHOLOKU HEIAU

BOAT LAUNCH

Wailua River

Wailua Bay

PLAYGROUND

KAHA LANI

ASTON ALOHA BEACH HOTEL

HAUOLA O HONAUNAU HEIAU

LYDGATE BEACH PARK

Wailua Beach

KINIPOPO SHOPPING VILLAGE

WAILUA SHOPPING PLAZA

CAFFE COCO

Wailua

KAPAA SANDS

KINTARO

KUKUI HEIAU

KAUAI SANDS HOTEL

LAE NANI

PAPALOA RD

COCONUT MARKETPLACE

ISLANDER ON THE BEACH

Waipouli Beach Park

KUHIO HWY

KAPA'A BYPASS RD

KAUAI VILLAGE SHOPPING CENTER

WAIPOULI TOWN CENTER

PAPAYA'S

SNORKEL BOB'S

COURTYARD BY MARRIOTT KAUAI

SLEEPING GIANT VIEWPOINT

LEMONGRASS GRILL

MOKIHANA OF KAUA'I

WAIPOULI PLAZA

Waipouli

56

HWY

To Kapa'a

SEE "KAPA'A" MAP

0 0.5 km

0 0.5 mi

down to the falls, but both are slippery and can be dangerous.

Smith's Tropical Paradise

Smith's Tropical Paradise (3-5971 Kuhio Hwy., 808/821-6895, www.smithskauai.com, 8:30am-4pm daily, $6 adults, $3 children 3-12) is a 30-acre botanical and cultural garden along the Wailua River. There are two main buildings here; one is home to a lu'au and the other is a lagoon theater used for music shows. A path over one mile long leads you around the property. There is also a Japanese garden.

Opaeka'a Falls

Two miles up Kuamo'o Road are the 150-foot majestic **Opaeka'a Falls.** The scenic lookout is on the right after the first mile marker and has a large parking lot and restrooms. The beautiful falls are easy to see and make for a good photo opportunity. Along Kuamo'o Road on the way to the falls, look out for sacred *heiau,* such as the Poliahu Heiau.

KAPA'A
Kaua'i Hindu Monastery

A very intriguing place to visit is the **Kaua'i's Hindu Monastery** (107 Kaholalele Rd., 888/735-1619, www.himalayanacademy.com, 10:45am-noon daily, 9am-noon daily for worshippers). Located up the Wailua River, the monastery is built completely from hand-carved stones from India. Each stone takes seven years to carve and there are 4,000 of them. Free, guided tours are offered once a week, but it is open for visitation daily. The holidays vary with the Hindu calendar. Wear long pants and shirts that cover the shoulders; no miniskirts for women or going shirtless for men. On-site are the Kadaval Hindu Temple, Ganesha Shrine, and Bangalore Gallery. Call for specific guided tour dates and to reserve a parking space.

Nounou, the Sleeping Giant

Legend says that a long time ago, a giant lived in Kawaihau behind Kapa'a town. He was very friendly and helped the people of the area. He had a hard time staying awake

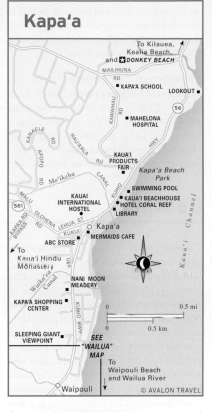

for more than a hundred years at a time, and when he would sleep, he would use a small hill as a pillow. The people called him Kanaka Nunui Moe, the sleeping giant. After a chief requested that the people bring rocks and trees from Koke'e and Waimea to build a *heiau* for him, the giant helped, bringing all the material down. To show appreciation, the people provided the giant with a wonderful meal of poi, pig, and fish. He filled his belly and was so full he lay down to rest for the last time.

At Kipuni Place is the **Sleeping Giant Viewpoint** pull-off. From this angle you can see the mountain, and with some imagination you can see why they call it Sleeping Giant. Trails go up both the front and the back of this hill, bringing you up to a picnic spot on the chest; from there a narrow trail leads over the throat to the chin and forehead. Note that these hikes are composed of narrow trails along a ridgeline with vertical cliffs on both sides. They are very dangerous.

Steelgrass Chocolate Farm

Steelgrass Chocolate Farm (5730 Olohena Rd., 808/821-1857, www.steelgrass.org, 9am-noon Mon., Wed., and Fri., $75 adults, children 12 and under free) offers a tour called Chocolate from Branch to Bar. The eight-acre farm specializes in vanilla, bamboo, and cacao, the chocolate tree. The tour reveals everything about growing and harvesting cacao fruit and turning it into chocolate. Smelling and tasting is part of the three-hour tour, where you explore the gardens and the orchard and enjoy an 11-course chocolate tasting. Exploring a chocolate farm in Hawaii is an experience unique from what the rest of the United States has to offer, as Hawai'i is the only state with an environment hospitable to cacao.

Beaches

The shoreline on the east side is dotted with numerous white-sand beaches, and every nook has a different look and feel. Sunbathe or surf in Lihu'e, snorkel and barbecue in Wailua, or bodysurf or enjoy a beachside bike ride in Kapa'a. They're all tropical gems; however, a few are some of the more popular and crowded beaches in Kaua'i. If you're staying in Lihu'e and don't want to go far, they will more than satisfy, but the pervasive trade winds can whip up choppy ocean conditions, blowing sand and thick cloud cover at a moment's notice. Conversely, if you happen to be on the east side when the trade winds are light or blowing from a northerly direction, the east-side beaches change face into some of the most dynamic, inviting, and easily accessible beaches on the island.

LIHU'E
Kalapaki Beach

Although **Kalapaki Beach** fronts the Kaua'i Marriott Resort, the beach is open to the public. The sand is white, but down by the stream it's a little darker from dirt and sediment. The nearshore waters are great for swimming, and occasionally snorkeling. Farther out on a shallow reef in the bay, stand-up paddlers, longboarders, and bodyboarders take advantage of the gentle, yet perfectly shaped waves. The popular eatery Duke's fronts the beach here, and is another reason why it's a well-known spot.

Kalapaki Beach fronts **Nawiliwili Bay.** To get here, take Rice Street down toward the ocean and stick to your right as it becomes Route 51. Access is via the hotel on your left if you park in the visitors' area. Or, if you keep going, on the north end of Nawiliwili Park before the Anchor Cove Shopping Center there's a small parking lot. Look for the narrow footbridge going over Nawiliwili Stream to the hotel property and the beach.

Ninini Beach

Located to the harbor side of Ninini Point and the lighthouse, **Ninini Beach** is a narrow, sandy beach fronting the low cliff. It's calm most of the year, but during large surf or windy days the beach can be a little rougher. This is a small and less-visited beach that is very good for sunbathing and a secluded beach day. Snorkeling can be good on the left side by the rocks, but it's dangerous. To get here, take Pali Kai Road past the Marriott, walk along the edge of the Kaua'i Lagoons Golf Club, and keep to your right until you see the steep trail to the beach below. If you take the fork on your left you'll find its sister beach, also known as Ninini, which is another less-visited area for sunbathing and swimming.

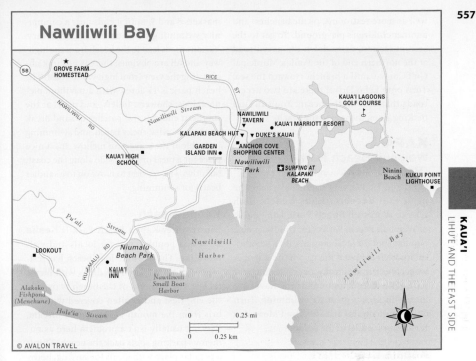

Nawiliwili Bay

© AVALON TRAVEL

WAILUA
Wailua Beach

Wailua Beach stretches from the mouth of the Wailua River to the first rocky point heading north. Surfers sometimes catch waves breaking along a shallow reef offshore, but the blustery trade winds, choppy ocean conditions, and strong currents tend to keep beachgoers away. However, when the ocean and wind are calm, it is a local favorite for a beach stroll and sunbathing. The river mouth adds an element of action, but when the river is flowing heavily it's an extremely unsafe place to hang out in the water. Petroglyphs can be seen carved into rocks at the mouth of the river when the tide is very low. You can pull up roadside off Route 56.

★ Lydgate Beach Park

On the south side of the Wailua River and behind the Aston Hotel lies **Lydgate Beach Park**, where two protected pools are the highlight of the beach. The pools are protected by lava rock barriers that create perfect places to swim and snorkel, regardless of surf conditions. It's safe for young children and anyone else who prefers to relax in the water worry-free. There is a lifeguard here, as well as sheltered picnic tables, grills, and restrooms and showers, but camping is not allowed.

The **Kamalani Playground** is located on the mountain side of the beach parking lot. The castle-like, wooden playground has towers, bridges, slides, swings, balancing beams, climbing features, and interactive areas such as a huge xylophone, which means it's easy to entertain children for a long time. A large pavilion on-site is perfect for lunch or a birthday party. To get to the beach park and playground, turn off Route 56 onto Leho Drive and then onto Nalu Road. You will find several parking lots along the beach. The pools and playground are located at the northern end of the beach.

A newly created section of the beach park has a number of bike paths and walkways as well as more restrooms, picnic benches, and another children's playground. To get to the second section, drive down the paved road at the northern end of the Wailua Municipal Golf Course until it branches toward the sea. Turn onto Leho Drive; there are two access roads that head to the ocean. You can find parking along the way to the beach.

KAPA'A
Waipouli Beach Park (Baby Beach)

While on Kaua'i, you'll probably hear the name **Fuji Beach** or **Baby Beach**. Both refer to **Waipouli Beach Park**, lying north of Waipouli Beach. Perfect for children and a popular spot for local families, it's a wonderful location to spend the day in the water. A long, natural stone breakwater protects a large part of the ocean, and unless the waves are huge, this spot is great for swimming. Turn onto Pahihi or Makana Street and Moanakai Road runs parallel to the ocean.

Kapa'a Beach Park

A little north of Baby Beach is another local favorite, **Kapa'a Beach Park**. The white-sand beach scattered with rocks runs north from Waikaea for almost a mile between mile markers 8 and 9, until it ends near a community swimming pool and the Kapa'a library. Various roads lead to the beach from the highway and all are obvious; there is nothing obstructing the view from highway to coast. The beach park is 15 acres, with a pavilion, picnic tables, showers, toilets, and grills at the southern end. Several patches of sand break up the somewhat rocky beach, and swimming is doable if the waves are mellow. It's a nice place for a meal or a bike ride along the coast, but otherwise it's best to move on to a sandier beach for swimming.

Kealia Beach

Shortly after Kapa'a Beach Park is **Kealia Beach**, a popular spot for locals and visitors alike. The 0.5-mile-long beach has restrooms, lifeguards, and pavilions with picnic tables. The east end of the beach is usually the emptiest and is often covered with debris from the mouth of the Kapa'a Stream. Parking usually isn't a problem here as numerous parking spots back the beach. This is a popular place with locals for surfing, bodysurfing, and bodyboarding, and it's good for swimming when the waves are small. This is definitely one of the more crowded beaches on Kaua'i, but it makes for an easy swim while in

Kealia Beach

the area. The shore break often pounds the shore, so it's best to stay on the beach if you're not a strong swimmer and the waves are up. The beach begins about 0.5 mile before mile marker 10.

★ Donkey Beach

A short distance down the road from Kealia Beach is **Donkey Beach**. This is a beautiful, remote white-sand beach where the swimming is less than ideal but the atmosphere is wonderful. It is a hidden treasure thanks to the 10-minute walk down to the beach. Swimming can be rough, but it's a peaceful zone to relax and sunbathe thanks to the ample space and the good chance you'll be alone. The ocean here is choppy with strong currents on a regular basis and has no lifeguards. The occasional monk seal is spotted here; if you see one, stay a good distance away. This is a beach known to be a favorite for those who like nude sunbathing, but most likely you'll find the beach empty or see a few people enjoying it with their suits on.

To get here, turn right about 0.5 mile past mile marker 11 at the brown sign with hikers on it. Parking is up top near the restrooms, and the easily noticeable trailhead is on the east end of the parking lot.

ANAHOLA TO KILAUEA
Anahola Beach Park

Like many of Kaua'i's beach parks, **Anahola Beach Park** has an open area for picnic tables, grills, showers, restrooms, and various camping spots if you have a county permit. This is a popular camping spot for locals, who like to set up elaborate camps for the weekend, so it's generally not a secluded spot, but visitors are welcome to enjoy it. The swimming is safe in the protected cove on the eastern end of the beach as well as in the river. Toward the north end the currents are usually stronger and the waves are bigger. If you plan to camp, don't leave your possessions unattended for too long; the area is known for occasional incidents of theft. The ironwood trees provide natural shade and a break from the sun. To get here, take either Aliomanu Road or Anahola Road from Route 56.

On the north side of the stream is **Aliomanu Beach.** Homes and vacation rentals border this less-visited beach. It's long with white sand, and there are some rocky spots in the water, but it can be a nice place to stroll and, most likely, be alone. The northern end of the beach is nicer. To get here, turn right onto the second Aliomanu Road, just a bit after mile marker 15, and keep to your right to access the eastern beach, or take the first left and then right to access the northern beach.

Water Sports

SNORKELING AND DIVING

The east side of Kaua'i has one spectacular **snorkeling** spot—Lydgate Beach Park—and several other reefs worth exploring. More often than not, however, the trade winds and choppy ocean conditions will have you traveling elsewhere to snorkel. Remember, if you're a water lover, it's a great idea to keep a complete snorkel set in the car no matter where you go on Kaua'i. That way you're always prepared to jump in the water if the conditions are right. On the east side it's easy to make a quick stop and pick up any last-minute beach gear because the shops and beaches are in very close proximity.

Wailua
LYDGATE BEACH PARK

Lydgate Beach Park is your best bet for snorkeling on the east side, with two protected ocean pools that offer an easy and relaxing place to snorkel and swim. There are plenty of fish to see. The ponds are almost always swimmable and calm, unless the surf is abnormally huge. Don't forget your underwater camera. Keep in mind that there are normally quite a few other snorkelers and general beachgoers sharing the sights.

OUTFITTERS AND RENTALS

At **Boss Frog's Dive & Surf** (4-746 Kuhio Hwy., 808/822-4334, www.bossfrog.com, 8am-5pm daily), divers and snorkelers can find everything they need to explore Kaua'i's underwater world. Snorkel rentals include basic to full professional snorkel sets. The average snorkel set that will get you through an enjoyable session rents for $9 per day or $27 per week. You can also purchase your own snorkel set. The shop offers all other beach needs, such as board rentals and other beach gear. The service is friendly and the workers are happy to guide you to the best spots.

Another tried-and-true place for snorkel rentals is **Snorkel Bob's** (4-734 Kuhio Hwy., 808/823-9433, www.snorkelbob.com, 8am-5pm daily). It offers complete sets, including a mask, snorkel, and net gear bag with grade-A surgical-quality silicone for ultimate comfort and water seal. The adult package goes for $35 per week or $22 per week for children. The budget crunch package offers a basic mask, snorkel and fins, and dive bag for $9 per week. A unique rental package is what the shop calls the 4 Eyes RX Ensemble, to compensate for nearsightedness while snorkeling. This includes a mask with a prescription lens for $44 per week for adults and $32 for kids. It also offers rentals for single snorkels ($7-12/week), various fins ($8-12/week), wetsuits ($20/week), snorkel vests, life jackets, and flotation belts ($20/week), and boogie boards ($26/week). A fish identity card is a fun thing to pick up so you can tell friends later on what you saw.

Seasport Divers (4-976 Kuhio Hwy., 808/823-9222, www.seasportdivers.com, 9am-5pm daily) has been in business since 1987 and is locally owned and operated. The Kapa'a location only rents gear and takes reservations for tours. The shop offers complete snorkel gear sets for *kama'aina* rates of $6 per day or $19 per week and visitor rates of $8 per day or $25 per week. Seasport Divers offers

the Ni'ihau, or Forbidden Island, dive, where you explore the waters around Ni'ihau and Lehua Island. Thanks to the lack of visitors and fishing on the island, Ni'ihau's waters are alive and thriving. There are wall dives, lava formations, and caves to explore. Dives off a boat are offered from $200 for just snorkeling or $335 for 2-3-tank dives for certified divers.

SURFING AND STAND-UP PADDLING

Surfing on the east side is usually at two main surf breaks: Kalapaki Beach and Kealia Beach. If you want to try surfing on the Coconut Coast and are a beginner, it's a good idea to get a surf lesson at Kalapaki Beach rather than renting a board and going for it alone. Experienced surfers will have fun at these breaks but should be comfortable in crowded waves with some currents. If you're not traveling with your own board, there are several surf shops that offer rentals; rentals are also available on the sand at Kalapaki Beach. Stand-up paddling is best done at Kalapaki Beach, where you can surf the wave or paddle the sheltered bay.

Lihu'e

TOP EXPERIENCE

★ **KALAPAKI BEACH**

A great place for beginner surfers, stand-up paddling, and bodyboarding, **Kalapaki Beach** is a local favorite. Right out in front of Duke's restaurant is a small and mellow right-and left-breaking wave over a shallow reef. The rights are longer and gentler. The lefts tend to be steeper and shorter, and end on a very shallow reef. Mornings usually provide the best conditions. From Rice Street, turn into the small dirt parking lot by the river. You'll see signs for Duke's Kauai parking.

OUTFITTERS

For surfing lessons at popular Kalapaki Beach, try **Kauai Beach Boys** (3610 Rice St., 808/246-6333, http://kauaibeachboys. com), which offers 90-minute classes at the beach with no more than four people in a class. Classes begin with about 30 minutes on land, and the rest of the class is in the water. Classes include boards, rash guards, and booties for foot protection. Lessons are daily at 10am, noon, and 2pm and also are $82 per person. Stand-up paddle lessons are also 90-minute lessons for $82 per person, but they are offered daily at 9am, 1pm, and 3pm. Kauai Beach Boys also offers 45-minute canoe rides for $51 per person.

To explore a river on a surfboard, try the stand-up paddle tour offered by **Outfitters Kauai** (2827A Poʻipu Rd., 808/742-9667, www.outfitterskauai.com, 7am-5pm). The tour starts with a paddle up the calm Huleʻia River and includes a hike to waterfalls, a picnic lunch, and even some water zipline action. The two-mile paddle lasts about a half day. The tour is $128 for adults and $90 for children 3-14. It is offered Monday, Wednesday, Friday, and Saturday and departs at 7:45am.

Kapaʻa
KEALIA BEACH
Kealia Beach is very popular, and is generally crowded with locals hanging out on the beach, surfing, bodyboarding, and bodysurfing. The waves break outside and then re-form and break on shore, offering a pounding shore

break. The conditions are usually choppy and windy with strong ocean currents, but when the trade winds are light, it can be a great wave. Best suited for intermediate to experienced surfers, the crowds can make catching a wave a bit tough. You can't miss Kealia. It's in full view from Route 56, near mile marker 10 at the northern end of Kapaʻa. The parking lot stretches the length of the beach, and you can even pull up in the sand, right to the shore, on the north end of the beach. Just make sure to drive on the hard-packed path.

OUTFITTERS
Tamba Surf Company (4-1543 Kuhio Hwy., 808/823-6942, www.tambasurfcompany.com, 9am-5pm Mon.-Sat., 10am-3pm Sun.) is the premier east-side surf shop for surfboards, gear, and rentals. It's the locals' choice for good reason. It offers all different kinds of shortboards, even a few fun shapes and mini-tankers, as well as soft-top longboards and stand-up paddleboards. Surfboard rentals are $25 for 24 hours, $40 for two days, $55 for three days, and every day after that is an additional $10 per day. Stand-up paddleboards rent for $40 for 24 hours and $20 per day for each day thereafter. Racks for your vehicle are provided if you need them.

Calm conditions make Kalapaki a favorite spot for stand-up paddling.

Kapaa Beach Shop (4-1592 Kuhio Hwy., 808/212-8615, www.kapaabeachshop.com, 8am-6pm Sun.-Fri.) rents all kinds of beach gear. It has beach chairs and umbrellas for $5 per day, bodyboards for $7 per day, and eight-foot soft-top surfboards for $20 per day.

KAYAKING

Kayaking is an extremely popular activity on east-side rivers, especially the wide and gentle Wailua River. Kayakers will find exciting river adventures, beautiful scenery, and calm water. While you can launch into the ocean, the pervasive trade winds and choppy ocean conditions make river kayaking the obvious choice.

Lihu'e

OUTFITTERS

Outfitters Kauai (2827A Po'ipu Rd., 808/742-9667, www.outfitterskauai.com, 7am-5pm) offers a half-day adventure on the gentle Hule'ia River. Kayak two miles downwind taking in the sights of the surrounding national wildlife refuge, hike through lush jungle to a secluded waterfall, and relax on the way back aboard a motorized canoe. The tour is $112 for adults and $92 for children 3-14. The tour departs at 8:45am. The firm also rents kayaks at its Hule'ia and Wailua River locations.

Kapa'a

★ WAILUA RIVER

The Wailua River is Kaua'i's most popular spot for kayaking. Up the river you'll find Fern Grotto, a natural amphitheater where ferns hang in abundance; Secret Falls with its swimmable pool; and gorgeous views inland and along the banks. Uluwehi Falls, also known as Secret Falls, lies on the north side and is reachable after a paddle and a hike. It's about five miles round-trip and roughly three hours without stopping to explore the river. The most common way to navigate the river is with a guided kayak tour. Only a few companies rent kayaks for independent paddling up the river.

OUTFITTERS

Ali'i Kayaks (174 Wailua Rd., 808/241-7700, www.aliikayaks.com, 7:30am-7:30pm Mon.-Sat., $55 includes tax) offers a Wailua River kayak tour. A local guide shares Hawaiian history and legends during the adventure. The tour heads up the river's north fork and takes a short hike through the rainforest, ending at Secret Falls. Offered every day except Sunday, tour check-in times are 8:30am, 9am, 10am or 10:30am, and reservations are required. Ali'i provides kayak equipment, a dry bag, and walking sticks. The tour lasts approximately 4.5 hours and includes four miles of kayaking and 1.5 miles of moderate hiking.

Another reliable option is Kayak Kaua'i (3-5971 Kuhio Hwy., 808/826-9844, www.kayakkauai.com, 7am-8pm daily, $85 plus tax adults, $60 children under 12). It offers a five-hour guided paddle up the Wailua River and hike to Secret Falls. The tour is great for families and allows you to swim in the freshwater stream or pool of the falls. Offered daily except Sunday, this tour has a 12-person capacity. Check in is at 7:45am, 9am, and 12:15pm. The company provides kayaks with foot pedals and rudders, dry bags, life vests, juices and water, and a deli-sandwich lunch with snacks and a vegetarian option.

Kayak Kaua'i is one of the few selected by the state to be an exclusive outfitter for lone kayaking up the Wailua River. The Wailua River rental package includes double kayaks with a permit, life preservers, car racks, paddles, back rests, a map, and bow line. Dry bags, coolers, and walking sticks can also be rented separately. Kayakers need to bring lunch and other necessary supplies on this trip. The kayaks are dispatched 8:30am-11:30am and can be returned after sunset or before 8am the next day to the Kapa'a shop. No singles are available, and the price is $85 per day.

A favorite with many is Outfitters Kauai (2827A Po'ipu Rd., 808/742-9667, www.outfitterskauai.com, 7am-5pm daily), which offers a guided Wailua River tour to Secret Falls. A lunch is included, and cold drinks are available throughout the day. Prices are $112 per adult and $92 for children 5-14. The company asks that participants are comfortable kayaking for 60-90 minutes and walking two miles of rugged trail.

One of the original kayak companies on the Wailua River, **Wailua Kayak and Canoe** (169 Wailua Rd., 808/821-1188, www.wailuakayakandcanoe.net) offers both 4.5-hour guided kayak tours as well as five-hour kayak rentals (single $50, double $85, $125 triple). The 4.5-hour waterfall guided tour includes a class I easy paddle and a short hike to Secret Falls for $90 per person with lunch (8am tour) and $70 without (12:30 tour). The company provides a deli-sandwich lunch with the tour.

WATERSKIING, WAKEBOARDING, AND OTHER POWER SPORTS
Wailua

The only company to offer these kinds of boarding opportunities is **Kaua'i Water Ski and Surf Co.** (4-356 Kuhio Hwy., Kinipopo Shopping Village, 808/822-3574, www.kauaiwaterskiandsurf.com, 9am-5pm Mon.-Fri. and 9am-noon Sat.). For a unique experience on the gorgeous Wailua River, hop on some water skis for an experience you'll never forget. The company also offers wakeboarding on the river, kneeboarding, and hydrofoil, where your board rises above the water while supported by a hydrofoil wing that remains under the water. The company offers the experience for beginners as well as experienced boarders who want to work on their technique while in Kaua'i. The boat fits five extra passengers, who can come along for free and watch while you board around the river. Rates are $90 for a half hour or $175 per hour, and reservations are required.

FISHING
Lihu'e

Departing from Lihu'e's Nawiliwili Harbor, **Kai Bear Sportfishing Charters** (808/652-4556, www.kaibear..com, reservations required, 6am-10pm Mon.-Sat., 6am-9pm Sun.) offers a variety of shared and exclusive private charters for a range of interests and budgets. Charters go out on one of two boats, the 38-foot *Kai Bear* or the 42-foot *Grander*. The boats offer at least one custom-made Blue Water Rod and Penn International Gold two-speed reel. Four-hour charters are $159 shared

waterskiing the Wailua River

and $800 private. Six-hour charters are $212 shared and $1,050 private. Eight-hour charters are $300 shared and $1,350 private, and for a to-be-determined price you keep all the fish. Bottled water and soft drinks are provided, and guests are allowed to bring their own food and alcoholic beverages, but no glass containers.

Lahela Sportfishing (Slip 109, Nawiliwili Small Boat Harbor, 808/635-4020, www.la-hela-adventures.com, reservations required) leaves out of Nawiliwili Harbor and takes guests out on the 34-foot *Lahela*. The boat is the only fishing boat certified by the Kauai Coast Guard in operation on the island and takes up to 14 passengers. Private fishing charters range from $400 for two hours to $1,200 for eight hours. Deluxe, shared charters are priced at $200 with spectators at half price. Economy shared charters require a minimum of six anglers at $150. Guests must be at least seven years old.

Kapa'a

C-Lure Charters (Nawiliwili Harbor, 808/822-5963, www.clurekauai.com) takes anglers out on the *Mele Kai*, a custom-built 41-foot Noosa cat equipped with Shimano tackle, depth sounders, and a GPS. It seats six people in the shade and has a fighting chair. Guests must bring their own food and alcoholic beverages, but C-Lure provides fishing tackle, bait, soft drinks, and water. The company cannot take more than six people but can arrange for additional boats to caravan if you want to bring more people. Charters range from half-day to whole-day trips and custom multiday charters. Prices range from $100 for non-fishing spectators to $1,250 for a full day with up to six anglers.

Going out with **Hawaiian Style Fishing** (1651 Hoomaha Pl., 808/635-7335, www.hawaiianstylefishing.com) means cruising on a 25-foot Radon. The company offers sport and bottom fishing and say they're prepared for any fish. You're invited to bring along your lucky lure or pole. Four-hour shared charters run from $140 per person, while private charters are $600. Eight-hour private charters are $1,050.

Hiking and Biking

HIKING

Miles of trails weave through the east side's interior behind Wailua and Kapa'a. You can hike trails that wind through lush green forest, along rivers, to waterfalls, or out in the open sun. The air is thick with moisture and the smell of wild tropical fruit like guava and passion fruit, the views are abundant, and the scenery—both along the trail and up and down the coast—is breathtaking.

Wailua

Three trails comprise the Nounou Mountain Trails. They are all in the mountains above **Wailua** and zigzag over Nounou Ridge, the Sleeping Giant.

★ NOUNOU MOUNTAIN EAST TRAIL

Many feel the nearly two-mile-long (each way) east trail is the prettiest of the three, and it can easily take up most of the day if you take your time enjoying views and lunch. The trail, which climbs to 1,000 feet in elevation, is strenuous. The east side of the trail begins off Haleilio Road. The trailhead leads to a series of well-defined switchbacks. It continues with an incline through lush forest providing some shade. At the 0.5-mile mark there is a fork; *be sure not to go to the left here.* It's dangerous, as are most side trails on this hike. At the 1.5-mile marker the west trail intersects, but stick to the east trail. Farther along at the main fork in the trail, take the left path, which leads to a picnic table, shelter, and bench. Take in the views because they're spectacular. At the table, you'll see a trail that goes south up to the giant's head and face. If you're a novice hiker, your hike should end here, at the table.

The remainder of the trail is for expert hikers only. The trail is narrow, steep, and dangerous. If you proceed, you'll walk along the spine of the mountain with sheer cliffs on each side. To get to the trailhead, drive 1.2 miles up Haleilio Road. Parking is by the 38th pole on the right, which has a sign indicating it is pole 38.

KUAMO'O-NOUNOU TRAIL

The **Kuamo'o-Nounou Trail** is about two miles one way and is tough, but suitable for a fit family. The trail begins with a wooden bridge over the Opaeka'a Stream. From here you veer left gradually at an incline. It takes about one hour each way and sees about an 800-foot elevation gain or loss depending on which way you're going. This trail is steeper than the east trail. The end of the trail intersects the west-side trail. About 0.75 mile from the trailhead is a shelter on a perch with great views of Kaua'i's highest point, Kawaikini, Wailua Homesteads, and views to the northwest. At the 1.8-mile point, it begins the decline to the west trail. You can usually see waterfalls if it's been raining. To get to the trailhead, head up Kuamo'o Road, after Opaeka'a Falls. There is a pasture on the near corner of Maile Street on the right side and a home on the far corner. You'll see the Nounou Trail sign.

NOUNOU MOUNTAIN WEST TRAIL

The **Nounou Mountain West Trail** is 1.5 miles long and one hour each way. A little shorter and less steep than the east trail, the west trail has more shade and meets up with the Kuamo'o-Nounou Trail after about 0.5 mile in. The trail ascends faster than the others, making it quite a workout. Keep going and you'll meet up with the east trail and then have access to the incredibly dangerous trail to the summit and giant's head.

Kapa'a

★ HO'OPI'I FALLS

This low-impact hike is a forest walk along Kapa'a Stream that leads to two waterfalls. The 2.2-mile hike stays under the forest canopy. Along the trail are thimbleberry bushes that have bright-red berries similar to raspberries. When you come down to the river, hang a right slightly up from the river and continue on the well-worn, narrow trail. You'll see multiple offshoot trails going down to the river. They're a bit steep, and the red dirt can be slippery. When you can hear the falls, take a side trail down to the top of the falls. Here you can sit and spend some time, eat, or just hang out near the falls and along the river. To get to the bottom of the falls, you'd have to continue downstream then head back up in the water. When you're done here, backtrack up the side trail and continue on.

Eventually you'll have to go down to the river and walk along the edge. Stay near the water's edge to keep off private land. Right before the second waterfall the trail goes over the river and to the top of the falls; this is the end of the trail. If you want to really enjoy this hike, bring mosquito repellent.

To get to the trailhead, turn onto Kawaihau Road from Kuhio Highway. Head inland for about 12 minutes and then take a right onto Kapahi Road. Look for the yellow metal post on your left at the trailhead. Right past here is a dirt pull-off spot that fits about three cars. Please go very slowly on this neighborhood road to show respect to the residents.

POWERLINE TRAIL

The 13-mile, strenuous **Powerline Trail** hike will take you from the east side to the north shore over the course of the day. The trail is actually a rough road built for the installment of power transmission lines between Lihu'e and Hanalei, although some believe the trail was originally a connection between the two areas for early Hawaiians. If you choose to complete the whole thing, you'll need a pickup on the north shore, or you can take the bus back to the east side. For a shorter hike, just go as far as you like and turn around when you're ready.

Starting at the Kapa'a trailhead, you'll encounter a rather steep incline for a little while, and from there it's pretty level traveling with an eventual descent into Hanalei. Not too far from the beginning you'll see **Kapakaiki Falls** on your right, and soon after is **Kapakanui Falls.** While the scenery may be dense, lush, and green, the road itself is bare, dry, and hot, with no shade. Remember to bring plenty of water for this trail. After completing the incline from the trailhead, you'll be treated to great views of **Mount Wai'ale'ale.**

On this trail you might encounter mountain bikers, dirt bikers, and hunters and their dogs in season. To get to the trailhead, head up Kuamo'o Road and pass the Wailua Reservoir till the pavement ends, then go about a mile to the Keahua Arboretum, where you should park. At the arboretum, cross the stream and walk up the steep road; you'll see a four-wheel-drive track heading uphill to your right. This is the start of the trail.

KUILAU AND MOALEPE TRAILS

The 4.5-mile **Kuilau Trail** begins about 200 yards before the entrance to the Keahua Arboretum and takes about 2-3 hours round-trip. There are a few parking spots at the trailhead marker on the right side of Kuamo'o Road. This somewhat mellow trail leads to a picnic area with tables and shelter after about a mile. Not long after this, you'll come upon the prize of this trail— views to Mount Wai'ale'ale and the crater and down to Kilohana and Ha'upu Ridge. From here, keep following the trail, circling around the hill until you come to a small wooden footbridge. Here, about two miles from where you began this nature stroll, the Kuilau Trail meets the **Moalepe Trail**. After crossing the bridge, the Kuilau Trail weaves through a tunnel of trees to an open flat spot and then turns east. The Moalepe Trail begins at the end of Olohena Road. This trail is popular with local

horseback riders and offers awesome views before joining back with the Kuilau Trail almost three miles from Olohena Road.

SWIMMING POOL TRAIL

For a cool pool and Mount Wai'ale'ale views, take this hike, which is about five miles round-trip. This trail heads into the center of the island and leads to a stream-gauging station and dammed section of the river. The locked gate at the beginning of the trail is where scenes of the entrance gate were filmed for *Jurassic Park*. Walk around the gate and head up the inclined road for roughly 45 minutes till you make it to the gauging station and the dammed part of the river. From here you can see the crater, and if it's been rainy, as the center of Kaua'i usually is, you may see many waterfalls cascading down the green cliffs.

From here it's about 1.5 hours via either a walk through a tunnel in the hill that requires most people to hunch over or a trek over the hill to the falls and the refreshing pool at the bottom. A flashlight is a good idea for the tunnel. Soon after, you'll see the chilly and refreshing pool, and if you swim through it and stick to the right for just a few minutes you'll come to the falls, with another small and refreshing bubbling pool. Only go in if the water flow is calm—it's a highly enjoyable experience.

To get to the trailhead, head to the Keahua Arboretum off Kuamo'o Road and follow the gravel road running across the stream at the arboretum. Stick to the main road for about four miles. The road is marked as being for four-wheel drives, but it is usually fine for two-wheel drives unless it is very muddy. At the fork in the road, keep to the left. Then there's another fork with a gate. If the gate is open, keep driving, and if it's closed, park here and you'll just have to walk longer. The second gate is the *Jurassic Park* gate. Go around the gate and begin your adventure.

HIKING TOURS AND GEAR

For all the hiking gear you could need, stop by **Da Life** (3500 Rice St., on Kalapaki Beach,

808/246-6333, www.livedalife.com, 8am-6pm Mon.-Sat., 9am-5pm Sun.). The shop offers a thorough array of outdoor gear. Name brands fill the store, providing all the hiking gear you could need. Stop by for anything you might have forgotten, especially before any serious hikes.

For a private guided tour, contact **Kaua'i Hiking Adventures** (808/822-4453, www.kauaihikingadventures.com, full-day tours $285, half-day tours $185). The tours are suitable for all fitness and ability levels. Each tour is customized to the hiker's personal preference, ability, and weather conditions. The guide shares knowledge of Hawaii's plants, history, and culture while hiking. Prices include you and up to three of your friends. The guide is a National Outdoor Leadership School Certified Outdoor Skills and Ethics Trainer and has explored Kaua'i extensively.

BIKING

Much of Kaua'i's narrow, winding roads can be unsafe for biking, but if you really enjoy cruising on two wheels, you're in luck because the east side is home to the 6.6-mile **Ke Ala Hele Makalae bike path.** The name translates to "the path that goes by the coast," and true to its name, the bike path stretches along part of the east coast while staying almost entirely level. Multiple beaches, swimming, and picnic spots are located along the path. The path begins at the Lihi Boat Landing to the south and winds north to Kealia Beach.

Lihu'e

Longtime bike doctor **Bicycle John** (2955 Aukele St., 808/245-7579, 10am-6pm Mon.-Fri., 10am-3pm Sat.) offers a thorough selection of road and mountain bikes to rent and own. Also available is a selection of other biking gear, including bikes, helmets, lights, repair services, and more. Bicycle John himself is known to be a straight-to-the-point kind of guy, no bells (except for bikes) or whistles, but he knows what he's doing.

Kapa'a

At **Coconut Coasters Beach Bike Rentals** (4-1586 Kuhio Hwy., 808/822-7368, www.coconutcoasters.com, 9am-6pm Tues.-Sat., 9am-4pm Sun.-Mon.), you will find a variety of bikes: classic and three-speed cruisers ($22 half day, $25 full day, $95 weekly) for adults and children, tandem bikes ($36 half day, $45 full day, $190 weekly), mountain bikes ($25 half day, $30 full day, $120 weekly), trainers that attach to adult bikes

the Ke Ala Hele Makalae bike path

for 6-9-year-olds, and covered trailers for toddlers that connect to the back of the bike. The classic beach cruiser is slightly less expensive. Rates for kids' mountain bikes and cruisers vary. Reservations are required for rentals.

Kauai Cycle (934 Kuhio Hwy., 808/821-2115, www.kauaicycle.com, 9am-6pm Mon.-Fri., 9am-4pm Sat.) offers cruisers, road bikes, and mountain bikes for rent. It also provides maps, trail information, clothing, accessories, and guidebooks. Rentals include a helmet and a lock and start at $20 per day. Multiday rates are also available, as well as car racks. It also has a certified repair shop in case your own bike needs help.

Adventure Sports and Tours

LIHU'E
Zipline and Tubing
Kaua'i Backcountry Adventures (3-4131 Kuhio Hwy., 808/245-2506, www.kauaibackcountry.com, 7am-6pm daily) offers ziplining and tubing on 17,000 acres of old sugar plantation land. You have the choice of seven different courses for your zipline experience. Zipline sessions begin at 9am and 1pm daily for $125.

Tubing begins at 8am, 9am, 10am, noon, 1pm, and 2pm daily for $106. The ride takes you down the plantation's old irrigation system. Float through open canals and several tunnels dug in the late 1800s.

Outfitters Kauai (2827A Po'ipu Rd., 808/742-9667, www.outfitterskauai.com, 7am-5pm daily) offers ziplining in the Kipu area on the southern border of Lihu'e. The Zipline Trek Nui Loa offers a 1,800-foot tandem zipline over the Ha'upu Mountains, valleys, waterfalls, and huge trees. Zip for about 0.25 mile, enjoying over 90 seconds of airtime. This tour includes a picnic lunch and cold water. It costs $158 for adults and $138 for children 7-14. Another zipline trek is the Kipu Zipline Safari, which includes kayaking two miles up a river, exploring swimming holes and waterfalls, enjoying views of features that appeared in the films *Jurassic Park* and *Raiders of the Lost Ark,* and ziplining through jungle terrain. This tour includes snacks, a picnic lunch, and cold drinks. It costs $195.83 for adults and $154.17 for children 7-14.

ATV
Drive an all-terrain vehicle (**ATV**) with **Kipu Ranch Adventures** (Kipu Rd., 808/246-9288, www.kiputours.com, 6:30am-6pm daily). Guided ATV tours take adventurous drivers into 3,000 acres of Kaua'i's uninhabited interior. Driving yourself into otherwise inaccessible parts of the island offers awesome views, mud puddles to plow through, and exciting terrain in Kipu Ranch just outside of Lihu'e and up to Kilohana Crater. Drivers must be 16 or older, but there are other vehicles available for younger guests. Long pants and shoes are a must. Three different tours are offered and range $45-168 depending on guests' ages and the tour chosen.

Aloha Kaua'i Tours (1702 Haleukana St., 800/452-1113, www.alohakauaitours.com, 7am-7pm daily) offers a range of tours into the interior of the island. The rainforest hike is actually a combo of four-wheel-driving and hiking. The tour goes inland from Wailua into the heart of the island. The tour walks from the gate where scenes from *Jurassic Park* were shot. Guests walk for about three miles to freshwater pools while learning about Hawaiian culture and history. The guides provide umbrellas, ponchos, and walking sticks as well as backpacks, snacks, and beverages. Groups are required to be a minimum of 4 and maximum of 12. Adults cost $77 and children 5-12 are $60. For the same prices, Aloha also offers the half-day SeaFun Ocean Adventures tour that includes snorkeling. Both tours depart at 8am and 1pm. Guests should arrive 15 minutes early for check-in..

Helicopter Tours

Blue Hawaiian Helicopters (3651 Ahukini Rd., 808/245-5800 or 800/745-2583, www.bluehawaiian.com, 7am-5pm daily) offers a tour it calls the Kaua'i ECO adventure. The company's new American Eurocopter ECO-Star offers more interior room to take you over the Hanapepe Valley, then on to Manawaiopuna, otherwise known as Jurassic Falls. Then it's on to the Olokele and Waimea Canyons, then over the Na Pali Coast, Bali Hai Cliffs, and Hanalei Bay. If weather permits, you get to explore the crater of Mount Wai'ale'ale by air for a finale. Regular price is $246.56, with special online prices.

Near the airport is **Jack Harter Helicopters** (4231 Ahukini Rd., 808/245-3774, www.helicopters-kauai.com, 8am-6pm daily), which offers two tours. The 60-65-minute tour hits all of Kaua'i's major scenic areas in AStar and Hughes 500 helicopters. Price totals $289, including fuel surcharge. A longer tour of 90-95 minutes flies at slower speeds and explores deeper into Kaua'i's valleys and canyons. In this tour the helicopter takes more turns than in the other, providing more photo opportunities. The only tour on the island of this length, it takes flight only on the Astars. Regular price is $434 including fuel surcharge.

With **Safari Helicopters** (3225 Akahi St., 808/246-0136, www.safarihelicopters.com, 7:30am-5:30pm daily) you have the opportunity to tour a waterfall owned by the owner of Ni'ihau. The Deluxe Waterfall Safari is a 60-minute trip to Wai'ale'ale Crater, Waimea Canyon, and the Na Pali Coast. Regular price is $239 per person, with special web fares. For the Kaua'i Refuge Eco Tour Safari offers a 90-minute trip over the same sites as the other tour as well as a stopover at the Kaua'i Botanical Refuge overlooking Olokele Canyon. The price is $304 per person, with special web fares.

Shopping

Lihu'e town serves the daily functional needs of island residents. Auto dealerships, a shopping mall, national brand stores, and industrial supplies are found here.

KILOHANA PLANTATION

The historic **Kilohana Plantation** estate (3-2087 Kaumuali'i Hwy., 808/245-5608, www.kilohanakauai.com, 9:30am-9:30pm Mon.-Sat., 10:30am-3pm Sun.) has a selection of shops with art, knickknacks, handmade items, clothing, and other island-style products. The shops can be found on both levels of the house. At **Sea Reflections** you can find unique objects from the sea as well as Hawaiian shells. The **Artisan's Room** on the lower level of the house is decorated with work from local artists. A popular shop is **Clayworks at Kilohana,** a working ceramics gallery. Browse work by local artists or take a workshop and clay-making class yourself. **The Hawaiian Collection Room** has an array of intriguing island finds, like Ni'ihau shell lei, Hawaiian collectibles, and local jewelry and gifts.

KAPA'A AND WAILUA
Galleries

Aloha Images (4504 Kukui St., 808/639-2756, www.alohaimages.com, 10am-6pm daily) prides itself on being a "candy store for art lovers" for 20 years. It's a good slogan as the shop is loaded with affordable local art. Hundreds of original works line the walls, along with giclées, prints, and other things for the home. Featured artists paint in the gallery daily.

Inside **Kela's Glass Gallery** (4-1354

Kuhio Hwy., 808/822-4527 or 888/255-3527, www.glass-art.com, 10am-7pm Mon.-Sat., 11:30am-4:30pm Sun.) is a dreamy, glistening underwater world of sculpted glass. With over 150 glass artists' work on display, Kela's displays Kaua'i's natural beauty in jewelry to wear and decorative pieces. The staff is friendly and happy to help you find that perfect gift.

Clothing and Accessories

At **Island Hemp and Cotton** (4-1373 Kuhio Hwy., 808/821-0225, www.islandhemp.com, 9:30am-6:30pm Mon.-Sat., 10am-5pm Sun.) you will find a wide selection of clothing made from, you guessed it, hemp. The airy shop is in the center of downtown Kapa'a, and here you can find dresses, boxers, surf shorts, shoelaces, smoking pants, and even some really nice aloha shirts.

Women love the clothing at **The Root** (4-1435 Kuhio Hwy., Ste. 101, 808/823-1277, 10am-6pm daily), where quality clothing is available in a combination of relaxed and classy. The skirts, dresses, and shirts are comfortable yet stylish and perfect for island wear or anywhere else.

Sweet Bikinis (4-871 Kuhio Hwy. #B, 808/821-0780, sweetbikinikauai.com, 10am-6pm daily) offers a selection of swimwear in a seemingly infinite array of colors and styles. Separates, tankinis, Brazilian-cut bottoms, and accessories like beach wraps and jewelry can also be found. The shop also has activewear swim attire. The staff is knowledgeable about which fabric holds up well for surfing and about sizing.

With all the hikes and beaches on the island, a stop at **Work It Out, Kaua'i's Active Clothing Store** (4-1312 Kuhio Hwy., 808/822-2292, 10am-6pm Mon.-Sat.) is necessary. The store is loaded with stylish apparel for hiking, biking, jogging, yoga, martial arts, and paddling. A running and walking group meets at the shop on Wednesdays at 6pm and runs the Ke Ala Hele Makalae bike path, a 3-7-mile jaunt, before returning to the shop for refreshments. The staff is always happy to share input on Kaua'i activities.

Shopping Centers

Located on the ocean side of the highway, **Coconut Marketplace** (4-484 Kuhio Hwy., 808/822-3641www.coconutmarketplace.com, 9am-7pm Mon.-Sat., 10am-6pm Sun.) is home to many shops and eateries. From high-end and locally made souvenirs to classy resort wear and amazing jewelry, you'll find it all

Island Hemp and Cotton in Kapa'a

here. Apparel can be found at **Crazy Shirts** (808/822-0100), which has an abundance of souvenir clothing; **By the Sea** (808/821-1979), which offers jewelry and resort clothing; and **Nakoa Surf Co** (808/822-6955), which has loads of surf-related stuff. Other highlights include **Style World** (808/821-8181), featuring designer clothes made with natural fibers, and **Elephant Walk Gift Gallery & Boutique** (808/822-2651), where you will find unique art, home decor, jewelry, accessories, and clothing. The **Coconut Marketplace Farmers Market** takes place 8am-noon every Tuesday and Thursday and is worth a look, with locally made gifts and locally grown food.

Surf Shops

Deja Vu Surf outlet (4-1419 Kuhio Hwy., 808/822-4401, www.dejavusurf.com, 9:30am-6pm daily) in Kapa'a has an extensive selection of surf gear: clothing, swimwear, boards for rent and sale, and everything else for catching waves or relaxing on the beach.

The locally owned and operated **Tamba Surf** (4-1543 Kuhio Hwy., 808/823-6942, www.tambasurfcompany.com, 9am-5pm Mon.-Sat., 10am-3pm Sun.) is a popular shop and brand with locals. It carries its own brand of clothing, as well as name-brand clothing, accessories, gear, and boards. Boards for rent and sale are also offered.

Gifts and Souvenirs

Densely stocked with souvenirs and beach gear, the **ABC Stores** (4-831 Kuhio Hwy., 808/822-2115, www.abcstores.com, 8am-9pm daily) chain is a bit of a tourist trap, but it does have some last-minute necessities like sunscreen and bottled water. The stores are loaded with all kinds of not-one-of-a-kind souvenirs, shirts, snacks, and general-store basics. Drinks and alcoholic beverages are also for sale, along with underwater cameras, limited snorkel and beach accessories, and beach supplies.

Shell lovers must make a stop at the **Shell Factory** (4-901 Kuhio Hwy., 808/822-2354, www.shellskauai.com, 9am-5pm daily). The shop is adorned with beautiful tropical shells, although most are not from Hawaii. Still, they are perfect, fully intact, and exhibit some of nature's most intricate work.

Jewelry

Imperial Jewelers (4-831 Kuhio Hwy., 808/822-0094, 10am-6pm Mon.-Sat.) sells Hawaiian handcrafted heirloom jewelry. Pendants, bracelets, rings, and earrings are available in the local style of carved 14-karat gold with a name in black if you like. The carvings come in an array of Hawaiian designs, like whales, sea turtles, flowers, and more. A highlight is the plumeria lei flowers collection, where elegant small plumerias are connected in a permanent lei.

Jim Saylor Jewelers (4-1318 Kuhio Hwy., 808/822-3591, 9:30am-5:30pm Mon.-Sat.) sells unique pieces. The designer uses precious stones, black pearls, and diamonds in his unique settings and styles. Saylor's been designing on Kaua'i for over two decades.

A very fun stop is **Kauai Crafters** (4-1176 Kuhio Hwy., 808/346-7700, www.kauaicrafters.com, 9am-6pm Mon.-Sat., 9am-5pm Sun.). The small shop is jam-packed full of local crafts with a strong shell theme. it sells *kahelelani* jewelry, koa and mammoth ivory fishhook necklaces, coconut faces, and a lot more.

Outdoor Markets

A "no import" market, **Kealia Kountry Market** (4100-4199 Kealia Rd., 808/635-5091, 11am-4pm Sun.) brings local vendors together offering locally grown and made products. There is usually live music, and local crafts, produce, and ready-to-eat food are available. Locals come to shop and socialize.

On the way north out of Kapa'a is the **Anahola Marketplace** (4523 Ioane Rd., 9am-5pm Wed.-Sun.), another place for residents to sell fruit and veggies, locally made crafts, and other things. It's worth a stop to or from the north shore.

Health-Food Stores

In Kapaʻa, **Hoku Natural Foods** (4585 Lehua St., 808/821-1500, www.hokufoods.com, 10am-6pm daily) has natural products and food. Natural and organic baby and body products, household cleaners, and food fill the spacious store. It also sells BPA-free water containers and other products.

Papaya's (4-831 Kuhio Hwy., 808/823-0190, www.papayasnaturalfoods.com, 8am-8pm Mon.-Sat., 10am-5pm Sun.) has long been the east side's staple health-food store (and where the hippies gather). It has a full selection of vitamins, body products, cleaning supplies, books, food, and more. If you're going to be around for a while, ask for the deli and frequent shopper card.

Entertainment

LIHUʻE
Polynesian Dance, Luʻau, and Theater

Luʻau Kalamaku takes place at Kilohana Plantation (3-2087 Kaumualiʻi Hwy., 877/622-1780, www.kilohanakauai.com, $50-146) and entertains with hula, poi, food, music, and a full-scale theater experience. Luʻau Kalamaku is Kauaʻi's only theatrical luʻau. Hula dancers, fire poi ball twirlers, traditional Polynesian fire knife dancers, and a vivid story line all combine for an exciting evening and view of Hawaiian culture. Your main course is cooked in the plantation's *imu,* an underground oven, and is unearthed while you are there. Then it's time for live Tahitian music, Hawaiian games, and hula dancing. The evening begins outside in the estate's garden for fun and games before entering the theater. A storyteller tells of the settling of the island by voyagers from Tahiti.

WAILUA
Luʻau and Theater

A riverside luʻau takes place at **Smith's Tropical Paradise** (5971 Kuhio Hwy., 808/821-6895, www.smithskauai.com, 5pm Mon.-Fri. Jun.-Aug., 5pm Mon. and Wed.-Fri. Feb.-May and Sept.-Oct., 4:45pm Mon., Wed., and Fri. Nov.-Jan., $88 adults, $30 children 7-13, $19 children 3-6). The garden luʻau dinner includes *kalua* pig cooked in an *imu,* teriyaki beef, mahimahi, chicken adobo, poi, and more. Hula is presented later on, and guests may go on stage to try out some moves. Tahitian drum dances and a Samoan fire knife dance are also treats. Guests are welcomed with an *imu* ceremony, cocktails, and music, followed by the luʻau feast and ending with the rhythm of an aloha show. Those who choose to eat dinner elsewhere can purchase show-only tickets.

Food

Kauaʻi's east side is home to many great restaurants and eateries. This is where you'll find the majority of the island's high-end and elegant restaurants, but there's also a great selection of hole-in-the-wall local eateries.

LIHUʻE
American

A Lihuʻe staple is ★ **JJ's Broiler** (3416 Rice St., 808/246-4422, www.jjsbroiler.com, 11am-11pm daily, $11-39) on Kalapaki Bay. It has a Chart House feel, with sailboats hanging from the ceiling, and is a classic Lihuʻe stop. Meats and local fish are offered on the extensive menu. The bi-level restaurant overlooks Kalapaki Bay, which enhances the experience. The bottom level is more casual, offering a full bar and a veranda. Upstairs is more formal and romantic. JJ's claim to fame is the Slavonic Steak, a thin, broiled tenderloin dipped in butter, wine, and garlic sauce. The portions are large, the food is good, and it rarely disappoints.

The tried-and-true **Kalapaki Beach Hut** (3474 Rice St., 808/246-6330, www.kalapaki-beachhut.com, 7am-8pm daily, $6-10) serves up breakfast and lunch with burgers that have proved to be a local favorite and never a letdown. The restaurant offers views of the harbor, and for breakfast has the standard fare plus local dishes like *loco moco*. Lunch includes fish and chips and sandwiches along with buffalo, turkey, fish, veggie, and beef burgers. Also on the premises is **Kalapaki Shave Ice** (11am-6pm daily) serving shave ice, smoothies, and ice cream; and **Kalapaki Coconuts** (7am-8pm daily), serving fresh coconut water straight from the shell.

Hawai'i Regional

★ **Gaylord's** (3-2087 Kaumual'i Hwy., 808/245-9593, www.gaylordskauai.com, 11am-2:30pm and 5:30pm-9:30pm Mon.-Sat., 9am-2:30pm Sun. for brunch, $27-36) is a farm-to-table restaurant at the Kilohana Plantation. Using local ingredients, the classy restaurant features American comfort food and Asian-fusion cuisine options. Gaylord's uses produce grown in the fields at Kilohana, and its meat and fish come from Kaua'i ranchers and fishers. Some of the main dishes include potato-crusted mahimahi, sesame seed-seared ahi tuna, chipotle barbecued pork chop, and grilled rib eye steak. Lunch mains include salads, sandwiches, fish-and-chips, steak frites, and vegetarian quiches ranging $9-19, and it has a Sunday brunch buffet for $30 per person and $15 for children 5-12, including a Bloody Mary bar starting at 9am.

A classic eatery on Kaua'i, ★ **Duke's Kauai** (3610 Rice St., 808/246-9599, www.dukeskauai.com, 11am-10:30pm, $19-36) is a must-stop on the to-eat-at list in Hawai'i. Named after the legendary Hawaiian surfer Duke Kahanamoku, the restaurant is split into two levels, where railing-side seats with unobstructed ocean views are the best. The downstairs Barefoot Bar is steps from the sand and serves up sandwiches, burgers, fish tacos, Hawaiian plates, and more for $11-20. The dining room serves dinner daily and offers fresh fish and seafood, steaks and prime rib, and a salad bar. It has live music several nights a week.

Duke's Kauai at Kalapaki Beach

The Mighty Coconut

While on the Coconut Coast, make sure to try a fresh coconut. Available at several fruit stands in Kapa'a, the coconut water is a refreshing and very healthy drink. Although the name calls it a nut, it is a seed and fruit. Packed with electrolytes, coconut water is also full of fiber, protein, antioxidants, vitamins, and minerals. It's become a hot packaged commodity in recent years and now is stocked on supermarket shelves, but for many islanders there is nothing more satisfying and refreshing than a coconut straight from the tree. When you sample coconut water, make sure to ask the supplier if you can try the coconut meat. Lining the inside of the coconut, the fleshy white meat is also a tasty treat with a nutty flavor. The coconut meat in a young, green coconut is generally softer and more gelatinous than in an older one, which has thicker and firmer meat. Don't miss out on this Coconut Coast treat.

Italian

The open air and views over Kalapaki Bay from ★ **Café Portofino** (3481 Ho'olaule'a Way, 808/245-2121, www.cafeportofino.com, 5pm-9:30pm daily, $19-45) offer one of the most ideal backdrops, especially to enjoy excellent Italian food. The food is authentic and the wine selection is robust for Kaua'i standards. The owner is Italian, which reflects in the quality of the food. Seafood, pasta, veal, filet mignon, and other meat dishes are available, along with enough meat-free options for vegetarians. Homemade gelato and fruit sorbets are also served. This is romantic fine dining.

A local favorite, **Kaua'i Pasta** (4-939B Kuhio Hwy., 808/822-7447, www.kauaipasta.com, 11am-9pm daily, $12-33) is a family-owned, chef-driven Italian restaurant focusing on comfort food and upscale specials. Tasty appetizers, unique salads, panini, and an array of main dishes are combined with a few Pacific-inspired appetizers on the lounge menu. It also offers a gluten-free menu. There are locations in Lihu'e (called KP Lihue there) and Kapa'a. The atmosphere is modern, yet warm. The lounge is open till midnight Monday-Saturday and till 10pm on Sunday.

WAILUA AND KAPA'A
American

The quaint and simple ★ **Kountry Kitchen** (1485 Kuhio Hwy., 808/822-3511, 6am-1:30pm daily, $6-14) is a perfect place to grab a classic breakfast of eggs, omelets, pancakes, French toast, coffee, and more. The place is a favorite with locals and visitors, and you may have to wait a few minutes on a weekend morning. True to its name, a country theme sets a homey feeling for the decor. Portions are large and service is friendly.

At **Olympic Café** (1354 Kuhio Hwy., 808/822-5825, 6am-9pm daily, $6-14), the open-air side of the café overlooks the sidewalk in downtown Kapa'a. Usual breakfast fare like eggs and pancakes are offered for breakfast. Lunch is wraps, burgers, salads, and sandwiches. Dinner offerings include pasta, fish, burgers, Mexican dishes, steaks, and more. The restaurant is known for its large portions. You won't leave here hungry.

Coffee and Bakeries

Situated next to the Moikeha canal in a historic two-story building, **Art Café Hemingway** (4-1495 Kuhio Hwy., 808/822-2250, www.artcafehemingway.com, 8am-2pm and 6pm-9pm Wed.-Sun., $6-22) is a sophisticated and artsy café owned by a friendly German couple. Find your own nook upstairs, downstairs, or on the porch. Table and couch seating is available. The café serves gourmet coffee with a true European feel, and is a testament to the eclectic nature of Kapa'a town.

Sweet describes **Sweet Marie's Hawaii Bakery** (4-788 Kuhio Hwy., 808/823-0227, www.sweetmarieskauai.com, 7am-2pm Tues.-Sat., $1-6), a quaint and cute bakery. The small bakery is in with today's health trends of serving up gluten-free baked goods, desserts, and wedding cakes, as well as gluten-free catering. Freshly baked pastries, muffins, and cookies are a delightful treat. Try the amazing *liliko'i* (passion fruit) burst. You can even take home some gluten-free muffin mixes and pizza dough. Great for breakfast or dessert.

Hawai'i Regional

Escape reality at ★ **Oasis** (4-820 Kuhio Hwy., in Waipouli Beach Resort, 808/822-9332, www.oasiskauai.com, 11:30am-3pm and 4pm-9pm daily, $16-35), which offers oceanfront dining in an environment that is truly an oasis from the outside world. Service is always on point, and the eatery focuses on local cuisine, using 90 percent ingredients from Kaua'i, from veggies to fish. It's the perfect location for a romantic dinner or a celebratory meal. The eatery opens to a white-sand beach. Its main dishes are available in half and full portions. It is open for lunch and dinner with happy hour 4pm-6pm daily. Sunday brunch is 10am-2pm.

★ **Caffe Coco** (4-369 Kuhio Hwy., 808/822-7990, www.caffecocokauai.com, 5pm-9pm daily, $15-30) is a garden bistro emanating a relaxed island ambience and offering made-to-order gourmet food with a Pacific theme. It specializes in vegan, vegetarian, and gluten-free fare. Enjoy outdoor seating in the courtyard surrounded by numerous fruit trees, tiki torches, delicate lighting, and umbrellas. Indoor seating is offered, and there is also an indoor art gallery. Order at the counter, and don't forget to use the house's "jungle juice" if the mosquitos get bothersome. A full espresso bar and desserts are also available.

Health Food

Rainbow Living Foods (4-1384 Kuhio Hwy., 808/821-9759, www.rainbowlivingfoods.com, 10am-5pm Mon.-Fri., 10am-3pm Sat., $6-14) is an organic, raw, and vegan café offering healthy and gourmet meals like Russian caviar, kale oahu, and delicious juices and desserts. Check the daily specials and enjoy the healthy meals.

A true hole in the wall, ★ **Mermaids Café** (1384 Kuhio Hwy., 808/821-2026, www.mermaidskauai.com, 9am-9pm daily, $9-12) is nestled between shops in downtown Kapa'a. The food is delicious, and definitely on the healthy side, although not all vegetarian. The order-at-the-window café serves wraps, burritos, sandwiches, and stir-fry, all with unique

Olympic Café

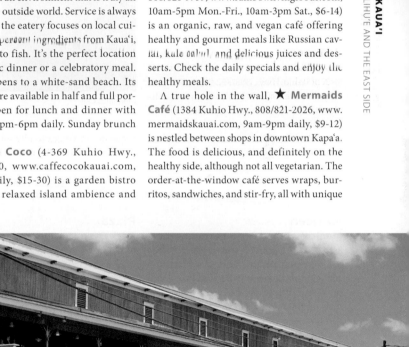

twists and most with tofu, chicken, and fresh-fish options. Mermaids serves breakfast, lunch, and dinner. Check for daily specials. Try the ahi nori wrap and the spearmint and lemongrass iced tea and hibiscus lemonade. There's limited sidewalk seating and a small bar tucked around the side.

Papaya's (4-831 Kuhio Hwy., 808/823-0190, www.papayasnaturalfoods.com, 8am-8pm Mon.-Sat., 10am-5pm Sun.) has an all-day hot bar and salad bar for $7.99 a pound; a deli that makes sandwiches, smoothies, and juices to order; and pre-made foods in the refrigerator. The food is good, organic, and vegetarian, but can feel repetitive if you eat there a lot. The food is served as takeout, but there are seats outside to eat at.

Japanese

For spectacular food, stop by ★ **Kintaro** (4-370 Kuhio Hwy., 808/822-3341, 5:30pm-9:30pm Mon.-Sat., $11-21), which has delicious sushi, a full bar, and teppanyaki seating. The fish is local and always fresh, the service is outstanding, and the atmosphere is sophisticated enough to get dressed for an evening. Make reservations for the teppanyaki. Lobster, filet mignon, and other seafood are available for those not in the mood for Japanese food.

Mexican

Monico's Taqueria (4-356 Kuhio Hwy., 808/822-4300, monicostaqueria.com, 11am-3pm and 5pm-9pm Tues.-Sun., $8-17) serves up authentic Mexican food with a local twist. The restaurant is clean and the food is consistent. It also serves meals to go. Try the fish tacos.

Verde (4-1105 Kuhio Hwy., 808/821-1400, www.verdehawaii.com, 11am-9pm daily, $10-17) is located in the Kapa'a Shopping Center. The restaurant is modern and fresh with an

Mermaids Café

urban decor. Verde proudly sources produce, meat, and fish locally and has a bold menu with authentic dishes as well as vegetarian and gluten-free options. For handcrafted cocktails, check out the margarita bar.

Pizza

Brick Oven (4-4361 Kuhio Hwy., 808/823-8561, http://brickovenpizzahi.com, 11am-9pm daily, $8-33) in Wailua has been a local favorite since 1977. It's very child friendly and offers kiddos a free ball of dough to play with. Wheat or white crust is offered, as well as the option to have garlic butter brushed on the dough. Thursday night is Brick Oven's signature all-you-can-eat buffet. It's a good place for a group or family dinner or a very casual date.

Princeville and the North Shore

Highlights

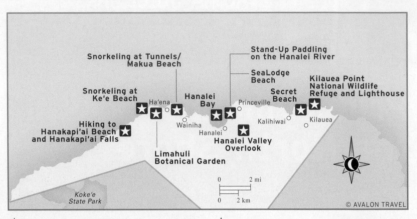

★ **Kilauea Point National Wildlife Refuge and Lighthouse:** Enjoy great views of the coastline; then walk through the lighthouse and learn about the seabird sanctuary (page 581).

★ **Hanalei Valley Overlook:** This overlook provides views of a wildlife preserve and acres of the Hawaiian staple taro and other farmlands (page 583).

★ **Limahuli Botanical Garden:** Take a botanical stroll through history along terraced taro fields used by ancient Hawaiians (page 585).

★ **Secret Beach:** Located at the end of a short downhill hike, Secret Beach offers a refreshing waterfall and fine white sand. Just beyond are crystal-clear tide pools and a lovely oceanside waterfall (page 587).

★ **SeaLodge Beach:** This beautiful and secluded white-sand beach is perfect for sunbathing, swimming, and snorkeling. Picturesque views abound from the trail (page 589).

★ **Hanalei Bay:** Nearly two miles of fine white sand make up this heavenly crescent-moon-shaped beach. Enjoy several surf breaks, swimming, and full amenities (page 591).

★ **Snorkeling at Tunnels/Makua Beach:** One of the best snorkeling sites on the island features unique reef formations just off the beach (page 595).

★ **Snorkeling at Ke'e Beach:** Marking the beginning of the Na Pali Coast, Ke'e's protected cove creates a natural swimming pool and spectacular snorkeling (page 595).

★ **Stand-Up Paddling on the Hanalei River:** Rent a board in Hanalei and paddle the calm, long, and winding river that empties into Hanalei Bay (page 598).

★ **Hiking to Hanakapi'ai Beach and Hanakapi'ai Falls:** Enjoy splendid views along the famous Kalalau Trail on the Na Pali Coast. The finale is a majestic waterfall and its icy-cold pool. This is the ideal hike for a daylong nature experience (page 604).

The north shore of Kaua'i is one of the most beautiful, intriguing, and naturally preserved locales across the island—even the entire state.

The coast unfolds to the east with undulating bays, white-sand beaches, rocky headlands, and picturesque river mouths until it slams up against the dramatic Na Pali Coast—with cliffs that rise thousands of feet from the crashing waves.

The north shore is a place of both opulence and simplicity. World-class golf courses, a luxury resort, and high-end condominiums give way to a taro fields; a quaint, historic town; and a slow, easy way of life centered around the ocean. Farms abound, **seabirds** nest on cliffs, and whales breech offshore as winter waves pound the reefs along the coast. All the while, Mount Wai'ale'ale, the wettest place on earth, stands watch over the region, and white ribbons of waterfalls slice through the lush green mountains.

The north shore is raw and unadulterated. It's also soft and inviting as the colors of the sky change from sunrise to sunset, the dichotomy a reflection of its native Hawaiian past, when this region was a place for both *ali'i* (royalty) and commoners.

Today, the north shore is for everyone, though visitors with an eye for nature will no doubt have a hard time leaving. Recreation is the cornerstone of life here.

In the winter, surfers flock to Hanalei Bay to catch long waves. In the summer, snorkelers and divers explore the reefs along the entire stretch of coast. Kayakers and stand-up paddlers take to the river for its calm water.

Hikers relish the challenge of walking the infamous Kalalau Trail, an 11-mile, one-way journey that offers beautiful, timeless views and tests the mind and body. Wherever you trek on the north shore, the verdant mountains frame the view.

ORIENTATION

There is no hard line dividing the east side of the island from the north, as rolling hills, pasture land, and agricultural estates provide the scenery. Heading northwest from Anahola, **Kilauea** is the first town you'll encounter on the north shore. It's home to the **Kilauea Point National Wildlife Refuge**

Previous: fresh eats in Hanalei town; Limahuli Botanical Garden. **Above:** a sunny day at the beach.

Princeville and the North Shore

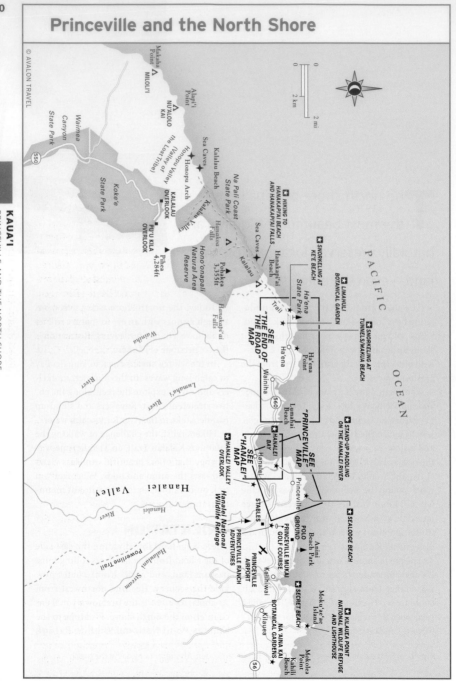

© AVALON TRAVEL

PACIFIC

OCEAN

Makahu Point

MILOLI'I

Alapi'i Point

NUALOLO KAI

Honopu Arch

Sea Caves

Sea Caves

Na Pali Coast State Park

Kalalau Beach

Kalalau Valley

Hanakoa Falls

Pihea 4,284ft

Pohakea 3,335ft

Hono'onapali Natural Area Reserve

Hanakapi'ai Falls

Hanakapi'ai Beach

Kalalau Trail

Ha'ena State Park

Ha'ena Point

Ha'ena

Wainiha

Lumahai Beach

Wainiha

Waimea Canyon State Park

Koke'e State Park

KALALAU OVERLOOK

PU'U KILA OVERLOOK

550

☒ HIKING TO HANAKAPI'AI BEACH AND HANAKAPI'AI FALLS

☒ SNORKELING AT KE'E BEACH

☒ LIMAHULI BOTANICAL GARDEN

☒ SNORKELING AT TUNNELS/MAKUA BEACH

"THE END OF THE ROAD" MAP
SEE

560

Lumahai River

Wainiha River

River

Hanalei Valley

Hanalei River

River

Hanalei

Halulani Stream

Powerline Trail

Powerline Trail

Hanalei Valley

SEE "PRINCEVILLE" MAP

SEE "HANALEI" MAP

☒ HANALEI BAY

☒ HANALEI VALLEY OVERLOOK

☒ STAND-UP PADDLING ON THE HANALEI RIVER

Hanalei

Princeville

Hanalei National Wildlife Refuge

STABLES

PRINCEVILLE RANCH ADVENTURES

PRINCEVILLE RANCH

PRINCEVILLE AIRPORT

PRINCEVILLE GOLF COURSE

PRINCEVILLE MAKAI GOLF COURSE

Kaithiwai

POLO GROUND

Anini Beach Park

Moko'ae'ae Island

☒ SEALODGE BEACH

☒ SECRET BEACH

☒ KILAUEA POINT NATIONAL WILDLIFE REFUGE AND LIGHTHOUSE

NA 'AINA KAI BOTANICAL GARDENS

Kilauea

Mokolea Point

Kahili Beach

56

0   2 mi

0   2 km

and **Lighthouse** as well as marvelous white-sand beaches, secret tide pools, and waterfalls. Nearby, **Kalihiwai** is the access point to beaches like Kalihiwai Beach and Anini Beach. A few miles north is **Princeville** on a high bluff. It's composed of 9,000 acres of planned luxury homes, condos, and a luxury hotel with a view of Hanalei Bay that can't be beat. Descending into Hanalei Valley is historic **Hanalei town,** backed by prominent green cliffs of Mount Wai'ale'ale, lined with waterfalls. From Hanalei to the start of the **Na Pali Coast** at the end of the road, the coast is made up of some of the state's most spectacular beaches. Beginning at **Ke'e Beach,** the **Kalalau Trail,** leading for miles along the wild and gorgeous Na Pali Coast, leads to waterfalls, secluded beaches, and camping far off the beaten path.

The **Kuhio Highway** (Route 56) is the only highway in this region, so getting around is easy.

PLANNING YOUR TIME

The north shore should not be rushed, and there's no way a day trip from another side of the island will do it justice. The best way to explore this area entails finding accommodations that fit your budget and planning on at least an overnight stay. Three days is sufficient to see the sights, visit a few beaches, get in the water, and even take a hike, but the more time you can muster here, the better.

You'll find the lion's share of the region's accommodations in **Princeville;** however, the locale requires driving out of the resort area to access most of the area's attractions. Luckily, it's not a far drive in either direction to Kilauea or Hanalei. **Hanalei** is a great home base for food, shopping, and supplies. No matter if you're planning a beach day or a day hike, you'll most likely be eating at least one meal in Hanalei. It offers the user-friendliest beaches, and the business district is centrally located in the middle of town. You can literally park and walk to almost all of the restaurants and shops Hanalei has to offer. There is phenomenal snorkeling on the north shore when ocean conditions permit, and you can stand-up paddle up the rivers almost any time of year. **Kalalau Trail** along the Na Pali Coast is the ultimate for avid hikers.

Sights

KILAUEA
★ Kilauea Point National Wildlife Refuge and Lighthouse

A picture-perfect view of a beautiful inlet speckled with white seabirds nesting in the cliffs and gliding overhead, monk seals on the rocks below, and even humpback whales in the winter months, makes the **Kilauea Point National Wildlife Refuge and Lighthouse** (end of Kilauea Rd., 808/828-1413, www.fws.gov/refuge/kilauea_point, 10am-4pm daily) a must-see stop. Upon arrival, the initial view from the cliff-top parking lot is photo-worthy. After this, take a stroll on the narrow peninsula to the Kilauea Lighthouse, a designated National Historical Landmark and visitors center. This is also a great place for dedicated **bird-watchers,** and people who just enjoy watching wildlife. Permanent and migrating seabirds spend their time here, including the frigate bird, boasting its eight-foot wingspan; and the red-footed booby with white feathers, black-tipped wings, and, of course, red feet; as well as the wedgetail shearwater and red- and white-tailed tropic birds.

Sea turtles, dolphins, and Hawaiian monk seals can all be seen from the cliffs occasionally. The waters here are also part of the Hawaiian Islands Humpback Whale National Marine Sanctuary, and whales can be seen here during winter and spring. The visitors center holds a wealth of information worth checking out about bird and plant life, the history

The Best Day on the North Shore

The best day on the north shore is all about good food, beach-hopping, colorful sunsets, snorkeling, and catching a few waves. It can all be experienced in one day if you begin early (around 9am).

- Begin your day on the north side with views of the **Kilauea Point National Wildlife Refuge.** Gaze down into the clear blue water of the cove, where birds nest and whales make wintertime visits. It's a classic photo opportunity with the lighthouse standing proudly above the cove.

- Head back up to **Kilauea Bakery & Pau Hana Pizza** for a quick but quality breakfast of sweet and savory pastries, coffee, and other treats. If you'd like, you can drop into some other shops here.

- Next, it's off to **Anini Beach** for a beautiful beach walk. The east side of the beach has long strips of white sand that hug the shallow and clear nearshore water. Past the beach park to the west you'll find the white sand dotted with rocks and tide pools, depending on the tide.

- After working up an appetite strolling in the sand, stop at the **Hanalei Valley Overlook** for a photo and then head down to Hanalei for a healthy local lunch at the **Hanalei Taro and Juice Co.** This is a great place to try some healthy Hawaiian dishes.

- Now, to experience what the north shore is all about—go for a surf. There are two easy options: rent a surfboard at **Hanalei Surf Company** or **Backdoor Surf** for a self-guided surf lesson, or if you're more comfortable with a surf school, visit the **Titus Kinimaka Hawaiian School of Surfing** in Hanalei and book a lesson. Another option is renting a stand-up paddleboard and hitting the **Hanalei River** or **Hanalei Bay** if the waves are flat.

- If it's summer and the waves are small, **Tunnels Beach** is the next stop for excellent snorkeling, so don't forget your snorkel gear.

- Next, it's time to go spelunking, Kaua'i style. If you parked at Ha'ena Beach Park and walked down to Tunnels Beach, you won't need to drive anywhere. Back at the beach park, cross the highway to the **Maniniholo Dry Cave** and take a quick peek. It's fun to take photos here. After that, stop for photos and dipping your feet in the cold water at **Waikapala'e Wet Cave.** Some people like to swim here, but the cave is rather dark and eerie.

- To end the day, head down to **Ke'e Beach** for more snorkeling in the natural pool, or just relax and enjoy the sunset.

- On the way back, stop in Hanalei at **Postcards Café, The Dolphin Restaurant,** or **Bar Acuda Tapas and Wine** for dinner. If you're looking for entertainment, hit up **Bouchons Hanalei** or **Tahiti Nui** for live music.

RAINY-DAY ALTERNATIVE

To best enjoy the north shore, don't let the rain get you down. Since the majority of activities in the region are outdoors, just embrace it and revel in its beauty—more rain means more waterfalls. If you really can't get into it, then duck into a restaurant for a meal or go for a shopping spree, because passing showers are just a part of life here.

of the lighthouse, and Hawaiian history. To get here, turn into Kilauea at the Shell gas station near mile marker 23, then down Kilauea Road. Drive straight to the end to the lighthouse, where entrance is free for people 16 and under, and all others cost $5 per person.

Na 'Aina Kai Botanical Gardens

Just past the Quarry Beach access road is **Na 'Aina Kai Botanical Gardens** (808/828-0525, www.naainakai.org, 8am-noon Mon. and Fri., 8am-5pm Tues.-Thurs.), encompassing a whopping 240 acres of tropical hardwoods, fruit trees, ornamental plantings, and statues. Over 100 acres of the property is a tropical hardwood plantation with about two dozen types of trees, including teak, mahogany, zebra wood, rosewood, and cocobolo, along with a lot of tropical fruit trees. The gardens take a creative twist in the central areas, where theme gardens feature various types of plants and 60 lifelike bronze sculptures add life to the experience. Admission may feel a bit pricey, from $25 for a 90-minute walk to $70 for a five-hour walk and tram ride through all areas, but the view from the parking lot is enticing, and it's truly an enjoyable treat. The visitors center and gift shop are a fun stop to explore the gifts, books, and plants. To get here, turn down Wailapa Road after mile marker 21 and go to the end.

PRINCEVILLE
Sunset on the Lawn

In front of the **St. Regis Princeville Resort** (5520 Ka Haku Rd., 808/826-9644, www. stregisprinceville.com), where the last remnants of a *heiau*'s rock walls can be seen, is a perfect place to end a beautiful north shore day. On any clear day, drop by the lawn to take in the array of colors as the sun sets over

Hanalei Bay and the green mountains backing the coast. During winter months, surfers may be seen dropping in on mountainous waves at the same time.

HANALEI
★ Hanalei Valley Overlook

The sights over Hanalei Valley inspire a dreamy feeling that harken back to the days of old Hawai'i. Different photo opportunities present themselves as the soft morning light changes to bright afternoon sun and then to demure sunset hues, all bringing out different colors in the taro patches below. Right after the Princeville turnoff on the left is the Hanalei Valley scenic overlook. The Hanalei River cuts through the valley until it meets the ocean, and along its banks myriad shades of green radiate from the valley, which reaches back into the 3,500-foot *pali* (cliffs) for almost nine miles. There's a saying on Kaua'i's north shore: "When you can count 17 waterfalls, it's time to get out of Hanalei."

Wai'oli Hui'ia Church and Wai'oli Mission House Museum

The **Wai'oli Hui'ia Church** (5-5363 A Kuhio Hwy., 808/826-6253) lies near the west end of town and stands tall with its colorful

Kilauea Lighthouse

Princeville

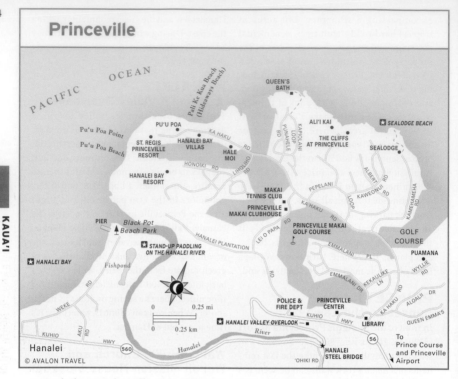

stained-glass windows illuminated by sunlight. Wai'oli means "joyful water," and it pays to go inside to look at the windows and take in the open-beam ceiling of the quaint church. Built in 1912, the church was part of a mission station that also included a home for the preacher, a school for Hawaiian boys, and accommodations for the teacher.

Behind and slightly to the right of the church is the **Wai'oli Mission House Museum** (808/245-3202, www.grovefarm.org/waiolimissionhouse, 9am-3pm Tues., Thurs., and Sat., free), which was originally the teacher's house. The lush green parking lot welcomes visitors to the home, which boasts a New England-style interior that was built in 1836 by Reverend William P. Alexander. Inside you enter the parlor, where Lucy Wilcox taught Hawaiian girls how to sew and paintings of the families are on the walls. Around the house are artifacts, including dishes, knickknacks, and a butter churn

from the 1800s. Tours are given on a first-come, first-served basis.

Ho'opulapula Haraguchi Rice Mill

The **Ho'opulapula Haraguchi Rice Mill** (5-5070 A Kuhio Hwy., 808/651-3399, www.haraguchiricemill.org, kiosk hours 11am-3pm Mon.-Fri.) is an agrarian museum nestled in the taro fields of the Hanalei Valley within a national wildlife refuge usually not accessible to the public. Dating back to the 1800s, it's listed on the National Register of Historic Places. This mill is the last remaining rice mill in all of Hawai'i, although it stopped operating in 1960 when the rice industry ceased to thrive. A nonprofit organization was formed to preserve and share the mill. Guided tours and private tours are available by reservation on Wednesdays only, so you need to call first. Tours ($87 adults) share Hawaii's agricultural and cultural history, and visitors can view

Hanalei

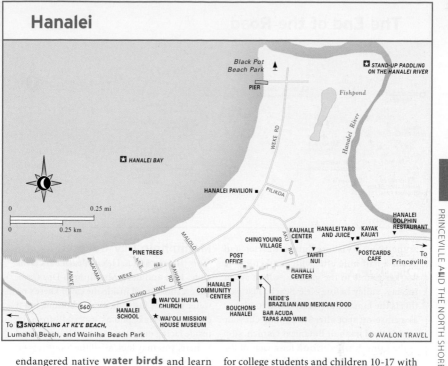

endangered native **water birds** and learn about taro cultivation and the uses of taro. A complimentary picnic lunch, including taro grown at the farm, is offered. When making a reservation, you must choose between a sandwich or Hawaiian plate lunch. The entrance kiosk is one mile after the Hanalei one-lane bridge, on the north side of the road.

TO THE END OF THE ROAD
★ Limahuli Botanical Garden
At the **Limahuli Botanical Garden** (5-8291 Kuhio Hwy., 808/826-1053, http://ntbg.org/tours/limahuli, 9:30am-4pm Tues.-Sat.), you'll take a trip back in time to see the native plants that decorated Hawaii before invasive species moved into the islands. Visitors have a choice of self-guided or guided walking tours. Self-guided tours are $20 for adults, $10 for college students with identification, and free for children under 18. Guided tours are $40 for adults and $20

for college students and children 10-17 with paying adult. Kids under 10 are not recommended. Guided tours are 2.5 hours, and self-guided ones last 1.5 hours. Reservations are required for the guided tour only.

Part of the National Tropical Botanical Garden, the gardens lie in front of Mount Makana (*makana* means "gift") on 1,016 acres that help both ancient and modern plants flourish. The original 14 acres were donated by Juliet Rice Wichman in 1976, then expanded to 17 acres, and the final 985-acre parcel in the above valley was donated by Wichman's grandson, Chipper Wichman, in 1994. It's a good idea to wear proper shoes, and umbrellas are provided. The visitors center is where the tours begin, and this is where books, crafts, gifts, and other items are on sale. The taro *lo'i* (patches) here are believed to be around 900 years old. The brochure and the tour guide share legends of the valley.

To get to the gardens, take a left inland

The End of the Road

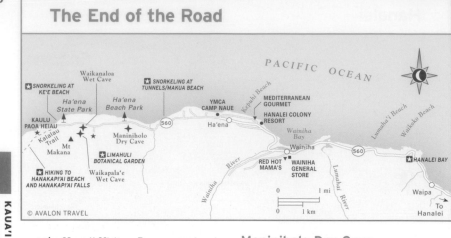

PACIFIC OCEAN

★ SNORKELING AT KE'E BEACH

Waikanaloa Wet Cave

★ SNORKELING AT TUNNELS/MAKUA BEACH

Ha'ena State Park

Ha'ena Beach Park

YMCA CAMP NAUE

Kepuhi Beach

MEDITERRANEAN GOURMET

HANALEI COLONY RESORT

KAULU PAOA HEIAU

Ha'ena

560

Wainiha Bay

Lumaha'i Beach

Waikoko Beach

Kalalau Trail

Mt Makana

Maniniholo Dry Cave

★ LIMAHULI BOTANICAL GARDEN

Wainiha

560

★ HANALEI BAY

★ HIKING TO HANAKAPI'AI BEACH AND HANAKAPI'AI FALLS

Waikapala'e Wet Cave

Wainiha River

RED HOT MAMA'S

WAINIHA GENERAL STORE

Lumaha'i River

Waipa

© AVALON TRAVEL

0   1 mi
0   1 km

To Hanalei

at the Hawaii Visitors Bureau warrior sign about a half mile after mile marker 9. The marker points to the gardens, which are in the last valley before Ke'e Beach. Just past this is the Limahuli Stream, which locals use as a rinse-off spot after swimming. On your way to the Limahuli Botanical Garden, stop at the **Lumahai Overlook** for a view of the Lumahai Beach and a great photo op. After the fifth mile marker you'll notice a small pull-off area where an HVB sign points to the ocean.

Maniniholo Dry Cave

Directly across from Ha'ena Beach Park is the wide, low, and deep Maniniholo Dry Cave. Take a short stroll inside the cave. There's no water in here, just a dusty dirt bottom, but it can be fun to take photos, especially from the inside facing out. Sometimes walking around in here, you may look at all the footprints on the ground and wonder how long they go undisturbed. Although the cave seems to stay dry, there is no archaeological evidence that it was used for permanent habitation.

Limahuli Botanical Garden

Waikapala'e Wet Cave

The earth opens up here to crystal-clear water after you've walked up a short hill to look down into the **Waikapala'e Wet Cave**. Also known as the "Blue Room" because of another hidden cave here that's accessible only through an underwater tunnel that turns a vibrant blue, the cave is a contradiction. It's beautiful and spacious, but since the trees have grown up and block the light, it exudes a slightly eerie feeling. Visitors will find a tranquil place to spend time, and many people swim in the cold water. To get here, drive about three minutes past Ha'ena Beach. It's on the left just past the big overflow parking lot on your right, and is only identifiable by the obviously worn path up the rocky hill and the pull-off spot across the street. It's about a 1.5-minute walk up, where you can peer into the cave from above or take a short but steep and slippery trek down into it.

Waikanaloa Wet Cave

The **Waikanaloa Wet Cave** is clearly seen from the road a little before Ke'e Beach. The cave is a nice sight and another good photo opportunity. There is no swimming allowed, as the sign indicates. Look at the floor of the pond itself to see some interesting patterns.

Kaulu Paoa Heiau and Kaulu O Laka Heiau

To the right of **Ke'e** are **Kaulu Paoa Heiau** and **Kaulu O Laka Heiau**, where it's said that the art of hula was born. Legend says the goddess Laka bestowed hula to the Hawaiians here. At these *heiau* as well as at any others, please respect everything in the area, meaning do not disturb or touch. The views up here are wonderful, especially during sunrise or sunset when the sky changes to all shades of color. At Ke'e Beach look for the trail weaving inland through the jungle up to the *heiau*.

Beaches

No matter what kind of beach lover you are, Kaua'i's north shore has a beach that will make your day: surfers revel in the world-class waves during the winter months, snorkelers enjoy pristine reefs during the summer, beachcombers can easily find shells and driftwood, and sunbathers will love the white sand and myriad nooks and crannies along the coast to find their own slice of paradise. You can post up next to a lifeguard or spend the day without seeing another soul at Secret Beach. Some beaches, like Hideaways, requires a hike and a thirst for adventure, while others, like Pine Trees, provide the convenience of beachfront parking under the ironwood trees for the perfect beach picnic. North shore beaches are dynamic, raw, and some of the most beautiful beaches in the Hawaiian Islands.

KILAUEA
Larsen's Beach

Named after the former manager of Kilauea Plantation, L. David Larsen, **Larsen's Beach** offers seclusion and enough space to stroll and see what you can find on the beach. Larsen's is another place where the crowds are usually nonexistent, and many times you will be alone or a good distance from other visitors. The very dangerous Pakala Channel is right before the point on the north end and features an extremely strong current that beachgoers absolutely must stay out of. For the rest of the beach, if the waves are flat and conditions are very calm, snorkeling can be marvelous here. To get to Larsen's Beach, turn down the second Ko'olau Road headed north, right before mile marker 20, and a little over one mile down take the left Beach Access road to the end. After the cattle gate is a trail; it's about a 10-minute walk to the bottom.

★ Secret Beach

Secret Beach is a wonderful treasure at the end of a dirt road and short trail. The beach is very, very long, and when the waves are really small, generally in the summer months, swimming is possible. Conversely, during the winter months the waves pound the shore and the current is extremely strong. Steep, tall cliffs back the beach, and about halfway down the beach you'll find a small waterfall—perfect for rinsing off.

Secret Beach is full of surprises, and depending on the season, wave size, rain, currents, and tides, you may find swimming ponds in the sand or exposed rock and tide pools. The walk down takes about 10 minutes and is a steep trail on roots and dirt. Secret Beach is also the unofficial nude beach on the north shore.

Secret Beach is also known as **Kauapea Beach**, and the Kilauea Lighthouse is visible on the point at the east end. There are awesome, even more secret tide pools and another waterfall farther west past the beach. To get here, turn onto the first Kalihiwai Road heading north and take the first right onto a dirt road. Head to the end of the road; parking is behind large homes.

Kahili/Quarry Beach

A long, fine white-sand beach backed by an ironwood forest, **Kahili Beach** is also known as **Quarry Beach**. A popular spot with locals for surfing and bodyboarding, Kahili Beach is gorgeous, but not a good choice for swimming. The ironwood forest growing out of the red dirt backing the beach makes for a fun place to experiment with photography. There are two sides to the beach, with a ridge of rock dividing them. The east side serves as an unofficial campsite. It's not a wide section of rock, and crossing over is simple when the waves are small. A river meets the ocean on the west end of the beach, and along the river can be a good, calm zone for swimming. During weekdays, there's a good chance Quarry Beach will be empty, but it's popular with locals on weekends. To get to Kahili Beach, head north and turn right onto Wailapa Road between mile markers 21 and 22. Turn left at the yellow post and cement blocks marking the top of the road and go about a half mile down to the beach.

KALIHIWAI
Kalihiwai Beach

Kalihiwai Beach is another beautiful bay nestled between two rocky points with a river at the west end that usually offers a perfect place for a refreshing and calm swim. The sand is white and very fine, and the right-hand breaking wave along the cliff at the east end of the bay is a draw for expert surfers. There are no amenities here, but there is sufficient parking under the ironwood trees. Swimming in the river is great for children, but make sure to stick by them. The edge of the water varies from a gradual slope to a steep drop. If you rented stand-up paddleboards or kayaks and have them strapped to your rental car, launch them into the river for a solitary paddle. Kalihiwai is a favorite spot for locals and families because the vibe is low key and the ocean activities are endless.

Coming from the east side, turn down the first Kalihiwai Road to get here. The road ends at the river, where the other side is visible. The road used to connect, but was destroyed in a 1946 tsunami. To reach the other side, take the second Kalihiwai Road and take a right at the first fork. It leads to the other side of the beach, where locals sometimes come to fish or paddle across the river to the beach.

Anini Beach

The seemingly endless white sand of **Anini Beach** stretches for approximately two miles. Much to the delight of beachgoers who like to laze about in the water, a barrier reef stretches the entire length of Anini and creates a shallow lagoon and great swimming for children and others who appreciate calm waters. The swimmable water here is a highlight. There's really no safer swimming on the north side than at Anini, and the water is surprisingly shallow, even very far out. Along the drive down, various pull-offs on the shoulder dot the road. They are all near small patches of beach where it's likely you'll be alone.

Anini Beach Park, about halfway down the road, is a popular beach with a camping area, restrooms, showers, picnic tables, and barbecue pits. The beach park is almost always crowded. If you're looking for less of a crowd, try any of the beach areas before or after the beach park. Past the beach park, beach access continues until the end of the road, where a stream meets the ocean. Feel free to pull over anywhere and take a dip or enjoy the beach. Near the end of the road is a swing hanging from a false kamani tree, a perfect opportunity for an ocean-side swing. To get here, take the second Kalihiwai Road headed north. Keep to the left at the fork in the road (going right leads to the north side of Kalihiwai Beach) and keep driving until you find your patch of beach.

Wyllie Beach

After the stream at the end of Anini Beach is **Wyllie Beach**, named after the road that accesses it from Princeville. If you want to check it out, park at the end of Anini and walk across the stream. It's the narrow strip of sand before the point and is lined with false kamani trees. The water is very calm here.

PRINCEVILLE
★ SeaLodge Beach

Seclusion, white sand, shade, and a pristine cove of crystal-clear water—everything a beach lover could want—are what you'll find at **SeaLodge Beach**. Accessed by a shaded hike through the trees and then a short walk along the rocky coast, the beach provides good snorkeling when the ocean is calm. There's no lifeguard or amenities. Located near the SeaLodge condos at the end of Kamehameha Road in Princeville, parking is in the unmarked stalls toward the top of the parking lot. The trailhead is in front of building A and marked with a sign. On the way down you'll find amazing panoramic views worth taking a minute to indulge in and snap a few photos.

Take the dirt trail down past the small stream on the way to the ocean. Once you reach the ocean keep to your left, where you can walk along the black rocks or on the narrow trail a little up on the dirt. After a minute you'll see SeaLodge Beach, nestled in its own cove and backed by a vertical cliff. The back of the beach is lined with trees that provide enough shade that you can spend a few hours at the beach. It's quite an amazing beach and worth the effort.

KAUA'I
PRINCEVILLE AND THE NORTH SHORE

Kalihiwai Beach

Queen's Bath

Queen's Bath is a tide pool at the bottom of a cliff looming above the ocean. Erosion has created an extremely unique and picturesque natural rock pool that is at its best when the waves are small, but big enough to wash into the pool. This spot is extremely dangerous. There's a plaque at the base of the trail with a safety warning stating that as of 2011, 28 people have died here, which speaks for itself. On very calm days, normally during the summer, the pool is crystal clear and swimmable. When the ocean is rough at any time of the year, it's risky. During the winter, when large waves pound the cliff, it's suicidal. A five-minute walk from the bottom of the trail to the pool puts visitors at the edge of the cliff and the pool. The hike down is intriguing in itself and offers several sights along the way, including a river, a couple of waterfalls, and a pool that usually has a few fish resting in it.

To get here, turn right onto Punahele Road and take the second right onto Kapiolani Loop. The parking lot is on the left-hand corner, bordered by a green cement wall. The trailhead is easy to find, marked with a warning sign and another sign giving notice of the shearwater breeding grounds. About 10 to 15 minutes down the dirt trail, it veers to the left at a waterfall pouring right into the ocean. Go left past the warning signs, and almost right on the edge of the cliff is the pond. Remember that during the winter months, from about September through April, the pool is unusable due to the large surf.

Hideaways Beach/Pali Ke Kua

Hideaways is a great beach for snorkeling, as is its sibling beach on the far side of the rocky point on the right. When the surf is small, snorkelers will usually see a gorgeous variety of fish and some green sea turtles. As at many other north shore beaches, false kamani trees provide shade. The trail down the cliff is very steep, slippery, muddy, and strenuous. Ropes stretch along the trail for assistance. Although it's a very short hike, it takes agility and balance and is not suitable for young children.

Check ocean conditions before going to this beach. When the waves are big in Hanalei Bay, the surf will be washing far up the beach at Hideaways. The beach is at its best when the winds are light. To get here, take the trail that starts shortly before the St. Regis Princeville Resort gatehouse, next to the Pu'u Poa tennis courts. To reach the other side of the beach, either swim to the right from Hideaways (when

Anini Beach

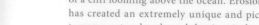

conditions allow, of course) or walk the paved trail from the **Pali Ke Kua** condominiums.

Pu'u Poa Beach

Directly below the St. Regis Princeville Resort is the easily accessible and popular **Pu'u Poa Beach**. Swimming and snorkeling are both good here when ocean conditions allow. The white-sand beach reaches toward the mouth of the Hanalei River to the left. The ocean right off the beach is a mix of shallow sand and reef. It's the perfect area for beginning snorkelers and children. When the surf is up, the break on the outer reef is where experienced and elite surfers catch some of the biggest waves the north side musters up in the winter. For hotel guests, access is by the hotel pool area. For those not staying at the hotel, there is a small parking area by the guardhouse at the hotel entrance, and a cement path behind the hotel leads to the beach.

HANALEI
★ Hanalei Bay

Hanalei Bay is a crescent-moon-shaped, two-mile stretch of unbroken white-sand beach with several different named beaches along the heavenly stretch. The bay was used as one of Kaua'i's three main ports until recently and is still visited by large yachts. Constructed in 1912 for rice transportation, the pier on the right side of the beach is now utilized mostly by children, who love to jump off it, and by fishers, who enjoy lazing on it with a pole.

To the left of the pier is **Queen Reef,** and to the right is **King Reef.** Surfing for both experts and beginners takes place here, along with bodyboarding, sailing, swimming, and stand-up paddling. At the end of Weke Road between the pier and river is **Black Pot Beach Park.** The name refers to the days when a large black pot was always cooking over a fire on the beach here with a big meal for everyone to share. Nearby and *mauka* (on the mountain side) of Weke Road is the headquarters of the Hanalei Canoe Club. You will see the sign when driving in, along with the sign for a shave ice wagon.

West of that is **Hanalei Pavilion** by the pier, recognizable, of course, by the large pavilion on the side of the road. Farther west and roughly in the center of the bay is **Pine Trees,** a popular surf spot for local children and families. Access to Pine Trees is at the end of He'e, Ama'ama, and Ana'e Roads. It's a good place to watch locals surf or take surfing lessons yourself. More access is available near the west end of the bay before the bridge. Hanalei

Pu'u Poa Beach fronts the St. Regis Princeville Resort.

Pavilion and Pine Trees both have lifeguards, and all of these spots are county-maintained and have showers, restrooms, picnic tables, and grills. When in Hanalei, turn off Route 560 onto Aku Road right before Ching Young Village. Turn right onto Weke Street, and near the end you'll see the beach where the pier is. Turn left onto Weke and then right onto He'e, Ama'ama, or Ana'e Roads to reach Pine Trees.

Waikoko Beach

Located at the west end of Hanalei Bay is **Waikoko Beach** and surf break. Another white-sand beach with black rocks dotting the area in the water and on the beach, it can be a less-crowded place to hang out, perhaps because the number of visitors here is limited by the roadside parking. To get here, look for the small parking area on the side of the road after the bridge and mile marker 4. If a spot is available, look for the short trail through the trees.

TO THE END OF THE ROAD

Lumahai Beach

After Waikoko Beach is the first access to **Lumahai Beach**. Lumahai is slightly over a mile long, running between mile markers 5 and 6, and has two accesses. The locals call the north end by the river "local" Lumahai and the east end "tourist" Lumahai. Don't be put off by nicknames, as tourist Lumahai has a nice trail down, and this end of the beach is prettier. Heading north, about a mile after the last bridge at the end of Hanalei Bay is a curve in the road with several parking spots alongside. This is before mile marker 5. Look for the trailhead, located where the trees open up to the ocean the most.

To access the north end of the beach, head about a mile past the first access. If you pass mile marker 6 and the bridge, you've gone too far. The best thing about this end of Lumahai is the river. The river is a great place for children to swim and play in the sand, but only upriver from the mouth. It's best to stay out of the open ocean here. Lumahai is one of the most dangerous beaches to swim on the north side. There is no lifeguard.

Tunnels/Makua Beach

Named after the surf break on the outer reef, **Tunnels/Makua Beach** offers some of the best snorkeling on the island, when the waves are flat. Reef fish can usually be found enjoying the waters not far from shore, and the sea caves to the left entertain bigger fish. There is

Hanalei Bay

a drop-off farther out that is intriguing, but this area is for experienced snorkelers and divers only, and should only be explored when the waves are small. This part of the beach is generally less crowded than Ha'ena Beach Park on the north end of Tunnels thanks to the limited parking. The beach is beautiful and long and makes a perfect place for a walk or run. Access borders homes located on two narrow side roads past mile marker 8. The first is just short of a half mile past the marker, and the second is slightly farther and most recognizable by the bent metal post with red paint. It is across from the 149th telephone pole, although at press time the 9 was missing so it looks like pole 14.

Ha'ena Beach Park

A picturesque beach with a backdrop of lush green mountains highlighted by perfect surfing waves and a river, **Ha'ena Beach Park** is a must-visit. Before the sand is a grassy lawn for tent camping, along with restrooms, showers, and picnic tables. A river bordering the east end of the park area runs over the road as you drive in. Swimming is good here only when the waves are small. The reef has great snorkeling, again, only when the waves are small in the summer. If the main parking lot

is filled up, which it often is, there is a bit more parking at the west end right past the showers. For those intending on camping on the north side, Ha'ena is one of the most ideal places because of its location, scenery, and surrounding sights. Past the rocks on the west end the beach keeps going, and it's a great, long, solitary stroll if you're up for it, passing two *heiau* and eventually the area formerly known as Taylor Camp. Ha'ena Beach Park is located off Kuhio Highway after mile marker 8 and just before mile marker 9, across from the Maniniholo Dry Cave.

Ke'e Beach

The pot of gold at the end of the road is **Ke'e Beach** and its large natural swimming pool. The snorkeling here is truly wonderful. Unfortunately because it's also the start of the Kalalau Trail, the parking lot is almost always full, day or night. You may have to wait in the car for a few minutes for a spot to open up, or drive back up the road to an upper parking lot or even on the side of the road past that. Either way, Ke'e Beach is breathtakingly beautiful, provides amazing photo opportunities, and has full amenities and a lifeguard. Venturing east down the beach will lead you to several *heiau* and the spot where Taylor Camp stood,

the north end of Lumahai Beach

which makes for a nice beach stroll. To get here, drive to the very end of Route 560; the road turns into a parking area at the beginning of the Na Pali Coast.

NA PALI COAST
Kalalau Trail Beaches

For those who continue on foot and are dedicated to a serious hike, about a two-mile hike from Ke'e Beach is **Hanakapi'ai Beach.** There's a freshwater stream, and it's a favorite campsite for hikers.

After Hanakapi'ai Beach and four more strenuous miles is **Hanakoa Beach,** another good place to camp. The biggest thrill here are the falls that are another 0.5 mile inland. In this area you'll also see wide terraces and wild coffee trees.

Five miles down the coast from Hanakoa is **Kalalau Beach.** It's important to note that this is a serious hike, requiring proper prepping and serious dedication. Kalalau Beach is about a half mile long with a small waterfall, often used by campers for a shower, and portable toilets. Many people who camp here like to pitch tents in the caves for protection from the wind and rain.

Past Kalalau is **Honopu Beach,** and the only legal way to get there is to swim from Kalalau. No surfboards, boats, or other crafts are allowed on shore, but you could paddle in a ways, anchor in the water, and swim up to the beach. Honopu Beach is actually composed of two picturesque, undisturbed beaches separated by an impressive arch. These are perhaps the most magical beaches on the island. You'll find a wonderful waterfall here and a stream to rinse off the saltwater. Vertical cliff walls that are more than 1,000 feet high back these beaches.

Water Sports

SNORKELING AND DIVING

During the summer months—from May through September—or when the ocean conditions in the winter are very calm, the north shore offers great opportunities for **snorkeling**. When snorkeling, always remember to only go out when the waves are very small or the ocean is completely calm, and it's safest with a partner. In addition to a mask and snorkel, dive fins are always a must, as strong currents are prevalent even on the calmest days.

A water camera or GoPro is always a good idea. Snorkel gear rentals are available at the **Hanalei Surf Company** (808/826-9000, www.hanaleisurf.com, 8am-9pm daily). It offers complete sets for $5 for 24 hours, $12 for three days, $18 for five days, and $20 for seven days. **Pedal-N-Paddle** (in Ching Young Village, 808/826-9069, www.pedalnpaddle. com, 9am-6pm daily) has complete adults'

sets for $5 per day and $20 per week, and kids' sets for $4 per day and $15 per week. It also has flotation devices and fins or mask- and snorkel-only rentals. The last chance for snorkel rentals would be the **Wainiha General Store** (5-6607 Kuhio Hwy., 808/826-6251, 11am-6pm daily). It offers complete sets for $9 per day.

Kilauea
ANINI BEACH

The calm water and the long, fringing reef make for great snorkeling at **Anini Beach**. The water stays shallow shockingly far out and maintains a depth of around four feet. Some of the safest snorkeling on the north side can be experienced at Anini Beach. Snorkelers who head far enough out will see the ledge dropping into the deep sea. To get here, take the second Kalihiwai Road headed north. Keep to the left at the fork in the road (going right leads to the north side of Kalihiwai Beach).

Princeville
HIDEAWAYS BEACH

Hideaways Beach is the best snorkeling in Princeville, as long as the waves are small. Snorkelers will usually be treated to a colorful array of tropical fish. Green sea turtles are known to cruise through the water at a leisurely pace. To get here, take the trail shortly before the St. Regis Princeville Resort gatehouse and next to the Pu'u Poa tennis courts. To reach the other side of the beach, either swim to the right from Hideaways (when conditions allow, of course) or walk the paved trail from the Pali Ke Kua condominiums.

SEALODGE BEACH

For more Princeville snorkeling, hike down to **SeaLodge Beach** for seclusion and a pretty lively underwater world. There's a reef right off the beach here in a cove, which means some pretty fish will be lingering around. There's no lifeguard here, so don't go out too far. If you haven't rented gear yet, you can buy some at the Princeville Foodland.

To get here, drive to the SeaLodge condos at the end of Kamehameha Road in Princeville; parking is in the unmarked stalls toward the top of the parking lot. The trailhead is in front of building A and marked with a sign. Take the dirt trail down past the small stream on the way to the ocean. Once you reach the ocean, keep to your left, where you can walk along the black rocks or on the narrow trail a little up on the dirt. After a minute or so you will see SeaLodge Beach.

Hanalei
WAIKOKO BEACH

If you're going to check out **Waikoko Beach** anyway, you can hop in with a snorkel and mask since you're there. The reef draws in fish and it's worth a glance, but it's not the best snorkeling on the north side. This area is rocky, and waves break here quite often. It's at the north end of Hanalei Bay; to get here, look for the small parking area on the side of the road after the bridge and mile marker 4.

If a spot is available, look for the short trail through the trees.

To the End of the Road
★ TUNNELS/MAKUA BEACH

To see a rainbow of brightly colored reef fish, hop in the water at **Tunnels**. With the outer reef, it's no surprise that fish like to wander in here. Reef fish spend their time not far from shore, and the sea caves to the left are a favorite hangout for bigger fish, along with the outside drop-off. The outer area is for experienced snorkelers and divers only, and should only be accessed when the waves are very small or the ocean is flat. Sea turtles, the occasional reef shark, caves, and fish can be seen. Access borders homes located on two narrow side roads past mile marker 8. The first is just short of 0.5 mile past the marker, and the second is slightly farther and most recognizable by the bent metal post with red paint. It is across from the 149th telephone pole, although at press time the 9 was missing so it looks like pole 14.

★ KE'E BEACH

Another location known for spectacular snorkeling, **Ke'e** offers great underwater views inside the natural pond, where there is usually a crowd of snorkelers. Outside in the open ocean the views get even better, but snorkeling here should only be attempted when the waves are flat in the summer months. Advanced snorkelers find that heading a bit to the left and snorkeling along the reef offers the best views. To get here, drive to the very end of Route 560; the end of the road turns into a parking area at the beginning of the Na Pali Coast.

Na Pali Coast

The best and safest way to snorkel along the **Na Pali Coast** is definitely with a boat tour company. Tours leave from the east side and head down the coast, but many also leave from the west side. The underwater world along the coast is nothing short of amazing: sea turtles, a spectrum of fish, the occasional reef shark, underwater caves, and marine mammals.

Na Pali Catamaran (5-5190 Kuhio Hwy., 808/826-6853, www.napalicatamaran.com) has been launching out of Hanalei Bay for almost 40 years. Guests ride an outrigger canoe to a 34-foot catamaran that takes 16 passengers maximum. The company offers snorkeling cruises and provide all the gear. A deli-style meal is provided; visitors have the option of a meat or veggie sandwich. Snack, drinks, and water are also provided. All tours depend on ocean conditions. Adults pay $179, children 5-11 are $130 plus tax and harbor fees. The office is right next to the Hanalei Post Office.

Also leaving from Hanalei Bay is **Captain Sundown** (P.O. Box 697, Hanalei, HI, 96714, 808/826-5585, www.captainsundown.com). A six-hour Na Pali snorkel sail ($195 including tax and fees) takes you down the coast and stops at a sea-turtle cleaning station where triggerfish clean the turtles. Trampoline nets allow great views below to dolphins and other sea life. Captain Sundown also offers a three-hour Na Pali sunset sail ($144) down the coast. Snacks, soft drinks, and bottled water are provided.

Na Pali snorkeling tours leaving from the west side are much higher in number, and include **Holo Holo Charters** (4353 Waialo Rd., Ste. 5A, Eleele, 808/335-0815 or 800/848-6130, www.holoholokauaiboattours.com), which offers a Na Pali snorkel sail ($109-149). The well-established company's cats, one motorized and one sailing, run out of Port Allen Harbor. The company has a reputation for treating guests well.

Catamaran Kahanu (4353 Waialo Rd., Eleele, 808/645-6176 or 888/213-7711, www.catamarankahanu.com) is a Hawaiian-owned tour company offering Na Pali Coast snorkeling combined with a glimpse into Hawaiian culture. Aboard the boat, passengers are treated to craft demonstrations such as basket, hat, and rose weavings, which guests take home as mementos. Rates are $80-122 with special children's rates. Boats also leave from the west side.

SURFING AND STAND-UP PADDLING

The coast from Kilauea to the Na Pali Coast is peppered with A-plus surf breaks, best suited for expert surfers. The area has also produced

No matter how big the waves are, Ke'e Beach is a great place to snorkel.

a number of professional surfers, including Bruce Irons and his late brother Andy, Bethany Hamilton, and others. If you haven't brought a board, you can rent a surfboard and head out yourself, or take surf lessons. Surf lessons are a good idea if you're a novice to the sport. Besides the goal to eventually surf down the line, there are some basic tips to learn, like how to paddle for a wave and stand up.

If you'd like to learn to stand-up paddle (SUP) or are already a fan of the sport, there are several beaches and rivers ideal for paddling. Rental SUPs are easily found on beaches all around Kaua'i.

If you're spending time on the north shore, board rentals are available from **Hanalei Surf Company** (in Hanalei Center, 808/826-9000, www.hanaleisurf.com, 8am-9pm daily). It rents beginner surfboards for $20 per day, $50 for three days, $75 for five days, and $90 per week. It also rents high-performance surfboards for $25 per day, $60 for three days, $90 for five days, and $110 per week. **Backdoor Surf** (Ching Young Village, 808/826-1900, www.hanaleisurf.com, 8:30am-9:30pm daily) rents stand-up paddleboards with paddles and car racks for $40 per day, $100 for three days, $150 for five days, and $200 for a full week. For lessons, **Hawaiian**

Surfing Adventures (5134 Kuhio Hwy., 808/482-0749, www.hawaiiansurfingadventures.com, 8am-5pm daily) and the **Titus Kinimaka Hawaiian School of Surfing** (in the Quiksilver shop, 5-5088 Kuhio Hwy., 808/652-1116, www.hawaiianschoolofsurfing.com) will take you out and most likely get you on a wave. It offers 1.5-hour lessons—group lessons are $65 per person, private lessons are $100 for children under 13 years old and $150 for others, and for families it offers semiprivate lessons with two students per instructor for $200 and three students per instructor for $225. **Hanalei Activity Center** (Ching Young Village, 808/826-1898) also arranges surf lessons.

Kilauea
KALIHIWAI BEACH AND QUARRY BEACH

When the conditions and swell direction are right, **Kalihiwai Beach** has a heavy, right-hand-breaking wave off the rocky point on the east side of the bay. Locals surf and stand-up paddle here, and when the surf spot is breaking, the shore break across the beach is usually intense too. The river is an ideal place for stand-up paddling, and paddlers can head up and down the river as well as across from

Surfing at Kalihiwai Beach is for experts only.

the beach to the end of the second Kalihiwai Road. **Quarry Beach** offers another good wave for experienced surfers, and is mostly utilized by locals. There are no lifeguards at either beach.

To get to Kalihiwai when coming from the east side, turn down the first Kalihiwai Road. The road ends at the river, where the other side is visible. To reach the other side, take the second Kalihiwai Road and go right at the fork. It leads to the other side of the beach, where locals sometimes come to fish or paddle across the river to the beach. To get to Quarry Beach when headed north, turn right onto Wailapa Road between mile markers 21 and 22. Turn left at the yellow post and cement blocks marking the top of the road and head about a half mile down to the beach.

Hanalei

HANALEI BAY

All of **Hanalei Bay** is ideal for stand-up paddling, either on waves for experienced paddlers or around the bay when the waves are small. Most of the sea floor across the bay is covered in sand, save for the points on either side, which is a flat and sharp reef. **The Bay,** the outside break stretching from the St. Regis hotel to the pier, is one of the most famous waves on Kaua'i. Located on the east side of the bay, it generally breaks during the winter months when swells arrive from the west and north. This break is for experienced surfers only. The bay is a fast and hollow right-hand point break. Shortboarders prefer to sit farther up the reef and try for the barrels, while longboarders and stand-up paddle surfers prefer the end bowl, which is slopier and breaks right into the channel. Spectators at the pier or Black Pot Beach Park will have a great view of the end bowl, but the wave actually stretches way up the reef. Paddle out in the channel straight out from Black Pot Beach Park. When in Hanalei, turn off Route 560 onto Aku Road right before Ching Young Village. Turn right onto Weke Street, and near the end you'll see the beach.

PINE TREES

Roughly in the center of Hanalei Bay is **Pine Trees**, a perfect break for all levels of surfers. The waves break right and left over a shallow, sandy bottom. Beginners and kids generally catch waves near the shore where the whitewater is smaller, while more experienced surfers will sit farthest out for the longest rides. When the waves get bigger, Pine Trees becomes very powerful with strong ocean currents. On most days the lineup will probably be packed with kids, so it can be a good idea to paddle out before the nearby elementary school is out for the day (around 2pm). Surfboard rentals are located nearby in Hanalei. When in Hanalei, turn off Route 560 onto Aku Road right before Ching Young Village. Turn left onto Weke and then right onto He'e, Ama'ama, or Ana'e Roads to reach Pine Trees.

★ HANALEI RIVER

The Hanalei River is a favorite for stand-up paddlers. While crossing the Hanalei Bridge into town, you'll probably see paddlers enjoying a leisurely paddle on the river. Morning is a nice time to paddle before it gets too hot, and it's a great way to start the day. You'll first notice the river as you come into Hanalei and drive over the one-lane bridge. **Kayak Kaua'i** (5-5070 Kuhio Hwy., 808/826-9844, www.kayakkauai.com) offers SUP lessons and rentals from its dock up the Hanalei River. It's about a 20- to 30-minute paddle down the river to the ocean. Lessons cost $85, and rentals are $45 per day or $225 per week. Both include leash and, if requested, a car rack.

WAIKOKO BEACH

At the north end of Hanalei Bay is **Waikoko Beach**. It's a left-breaking rocky reef break. Although it's not one of the *most* dangerous spots, it's a good idea to leave it alone unless you're an experienced surfer. The break requires walking out on a very shallow and sharp reef, and hopping off at the end of the wave into a shallow reef. To get here, look for the small parking area on the side of the road after the bridge and mile marker 4. If a spot is available, look for the short trail through the trees.

To the End of the Road
TUNNELS/MAKUA BEACH

Right before Ha'ena Beach Park, Tunnels Beach has an epic, right-breaking wave. **Tunnels** is for expert surfers only. This is where local surfer Bethany Hamilton lost her arm to a shark at the age of 13. If the big waves don't keep you on the beach, that might. The movie *Soul Surfer* was released in 2011, documenting the Kaua'i native's loss and her comeback. The beach at Tunnels is beautiful, and if the waves are good it can be fun just to watch the surfers in the water.

A little west down the beach from Tunnels is the surf break known as **Cannons.** Again, this is another wave reserved for expert surfers due to the intensity of the barreling, left-hand breaking wave as well as the shallow reef in front of it. This can be another fun spot to watch the surfers from the beach when the waves are good.

Access borders homes located on two narrow side roads past mile marker 8. The first is just short of a half mile past the marker, and the second is slightly farther and most recognizable by the bent metal post with red paint.

It is across from the 149th telephone pole, although at press time the 9 was missing so it looks like pole 14.

KAYAKING
Hanalei

Kayak Kaua'i (5-5070 Kuhio Hwy., 808/826-9844, www.kayakkauai.com) offers a leisurely adventure on the Hanalei River with kayak rentals and guided tours where kayakers have the option of a single kayak for $29 or a double for $54.

A tour of the Hanalei River and Hanalei Bay is also offered by **Kayak Hanalei** (5-5190 Kuhio Hwy., in Ching Young Village, 808/826-1881, www.kayakhanalei.com) from March through October. Suitable for all ages, the tour explores the bay and river and takes paddlers snorkeling. A complete sandwich lunch is provided, with vegetarian as an option, and is enjoyed on the beach. The price for children is $95.38, adults $106.10.

Na Pali Coast

Kayaks can be rented for a trip down the Na Pali Coast ending at Polihale, but only in summer months when seas are calm. **Outfitters Kauai** (2827A Po'ipu Rd., Po'ipu, 808/742-9667 or 999/742-9887, www.outfitterskauai.

stand-up paddling the Hanalei River

com, $238) runs a 16-mile sea kayak adventure along the coast. The trip features an exploration of sea caves, opportunities to see waterfalls, dolphins, and sea turtles, and respites on deserted beaches that feel far from civilization. The tour offers tandem, open-cockpit, or sit-on-top self-bailing kayaks with foot pedal controls, and the tour is only available from mid-May until mid-September on Tuesdays and Thursdays.

Kayak Kaua'i (5-5070 Kuhio Hwy., 808/826-9844, www.kayakkauai.com) also offers sea kayaking along the Na Pali Coast. It's a serious adventure only for the very fit and hardy and can only be done in the summer. The kayaking adventure requires 5-6 hours of paddling and runs about $240.

Na Pali Kayak (5-5070 Kuhio Hwy., 808/826-6900, www.napalikayak.com) takes adventurous day-trippers, honeymooners, and campers on various trips along the Na Pali Coast. Adventures include guided day kayaking trips, camping along the coast, a honeymoon private charter for two, and private guided tours. Fees vary $200-3,000 for a group charter, so please call for the most up-to-date rates and details.

FISHING
Na Pali Coast
Na Pali Sportfishing (808/635-9424, www. napalisportfishing.com) will take you down the coast, but it leaves out of Kikiaola Harbor on the west side. The boat generally leaves at 6am because, according to the company, that's when serious anglers fish; that time can be hard to make if you're on the north shore, but Na Pali does schedule later trips as well. The company takes people out on a 35-foot Baja cruiser with a fly bridge and outriggers for a maximum of six people. Boaters must bring their own food and snacks, but the company provides soft drinks, fishing tackle, and zipper-lock bags so guests can take fish home. Half days shared run $135 an angler, full days are $220, and a full-day fishing charter runs $1,050. Check for other rates and tours. Restrictions include no pregnant women, no recent back surgeries or injuries, and no children under four years old.

WHALE-WATCHING
During the months of December through March or April, humpback whales *(kohola)* spend time in the islands singing and giving birth. After bulking up on weight in Alaska through the summer, the whales don't eat while they're here and may lose up to about one-third of their weight. During these months, keep an eye out for whales any time you look at the ocean. They breech, they spout, and it's one of the best sights to be seen.

From November through March **Bali Hai Tours** (808/634-2317, www.balihaitours.com) heads north from Kapa'a, taking people out to see the whales. Although the boat can handle 12 people, Bali Hai takes no more than 6 people out on its 20-foot Zodiac, with a two-stroke 100 hp Mercury motor. The company provides snorkel gear, floater noodles and bodyboards, dry bags, and snacks. Prices are $175 for adults and $110 for children.

Hiking and Biking

HIKING

The north shore is home to some of the most outstanding hikes on the island. From short walks and secluded beaches, to hidden waterfalls and the 19-mile trek along the Na Pali Coast, the north shore is a hiker's dream scene. Pair ample **hiking** with pristine beaches and mountain views, and the value of a mile-long beach walk shouldn't go underestimated; it can be one of the most peaceful and memorable experiences to be had on Kaua'i.

Kilauea
SECRET BEACH TIDE POOLS AND WATERFALL

Tide pools and an ocean-side waterfall are the beautiful rewards at the end of this half-hour, one-mile hike. It's important to note that this hike should only be done during the summer months, when the ocean is completely flat. At the northern end of the beach at the bottom of the access trail, head over the rocks. After the small, sandy area is a pretty spot where the water juts into the cliffs, and you'll need to pass behind this. There's a roughly 10-foot-tall vertical cliff to climb that presents two options: climb up over the cliff and stick to the rocks, or climb up on the end that's over the water.

After passing this, stick to the trail high on the wall that backs the small cove. You'll eventually reach some **tide pools.** Then, right before another finger of water juts into the cliffs, you'll see the wonderful deep and smooth boulder-bottomed pools. Once you're here it looks like this could be the end, but it's not. There are several five- to six-foot-deep pools. They are beautiful pools that are generally clean and clear, and the rock bottom is smooth. The pool closest to the edge of the cliff needs to be avoided when the waves are anything but flat.

Where the cliff meets the finger, there is another small vertical cliff, about six to eight feet high. For an even better reward, climb it and head a very short distance inland to see the waterfall coming out of a small, lush green crevice, pouring into more tide pools. This is far from Kaua'i's tallest waterfall, but the combination of an oceanside waterfall with salt tide pools is a unique sight to see and enjoy. The falls pour down onto a fairly flat rock area, and there is a small cave in back of the water perfect for sitting in as long as the falls aren't pouring too heavily. The rock leading to the falls is extremely slippery, so taking your time is important, although walking above the falls and coming back down and around works too. In front of this are several salt tide pools that the freshwater runs into. There's another, easier way to get here. Take the first Kalihiwai Road and pass the road to Secret Beach, then stop at the yellow fire hydrant. Take the trail here about 10 minutes down to the top of the waterfall. This isn't nearly as exciting as the hike from **Secret Beach,** but it's shorter and safer.

To get here, turn onto the first Kalihiwai Road heading north and take the first right onto a dirt road. Head to the end of the road, where parking is behind large homes.

Princeville
POWERLINE TRAIL

It takes a powered-up person to attack the entire daylong journey along the roughly 13-mile **Powerline Trail.** Completing it is only recommended for those who have a ride waiting on the other side, where the trail ends at the Keahua Arboretum in Wailua. The sights range from a few views into Hanalei Valley to an abundance of mountain views, the north and south shores, the center of the island, and the Hanalei region. The trail is hot and dry and lacking in shade. It's best for hikers to go as far as they like but then return to the Princeville trailhead. Around two hours from the start of the trail, the pass is a good place to turn around and head back. To get to the northern trailhead, turn at the Princeville Ranch Stables about a half mile east of Princeville. Head uphill for about two miles until the pavement ends. Go a little farther to the parking area near the green water tank. This is a serious trail for mountain bikers, but it's strenuous. Don't attempt to go four-wheeling here.

Hanalei

'OKOLEHAO TRAIL

This intense 1.5-hour, 2.3-mile hike is a good hike to prep for the Kalalau Trail. 'Okolehao refers to the Hawaiian version of moonshine, made from the ti root planted up here. It's said the literal translation is "iron bottom" for the iron pots used to ferment it. The hike provides a serious workout that will most likely be experienced in solitude. The trail gains about 1,200 feet and will have hikers huffing and puffing in no time. The effort is well worth it, though. The **'Okolehao Trail** offers amazing views of the island that begin about 0.5 mile up. From the end of the trail the Kilauea Lighthouse, Hanalei River, Wai'ale'ale, Hanalei Bay, and the area by Ke'e and as far as Anahola can be seen. When hiking after a rain, be very careful, as the trail gets slippery. To get to the trailhead, turn left immediately after the one-lane bridge into Hanalei onto Ohiki Road. A little over a half mile down the road, there's a parking lot on the left. A small bridge marks the trailhead on the opposite side of the road.

HANALEI NATIONAL WILDLIFE REFUGE

At the 917-acre **Hanalei National Wildlife Refuge** in Hanalei Valley, endangered native **water birds** such as the Hawaiian coot, black-necked stilt, koloa duck, and gallinule can be spotted, as well as several migrant species that have reclaimed their ancient nesting grounds. The area is decorated with taro lo'i, the square patches where taro is grown. Although visitors are allowed in Hanalei Valley, no one is permitted in the designated wildlife area other than for fishing or hiking along the river. After crossing the first one-lane bridge into Hanalei, turn left onto Ohiki Road.

Na Pali Coast

The heavenly and harsh **Na Pali Coast** is where all of nature's wonder joins together, a world that will both amaze and test those who choose to explore it. Other than the ocean, this is the only access to the rugged coastline with sea cliffs, five lush valleys, waterfalls, and camping along the 15-mile stretch from Ke'e to Polihale. The cliffs rise up to 4,000 feet in certain areas, and sea level is found only at the four main beaches along the way. The largest and most magnificent valley here is the Kalalau Valley, where ancient Hawaiians lived and archaeological evidence still remains. Other valleys also hold evidence of inhabited sites, as Hawaiians lived in various locations along the way. Rain falls here in excess, creating an abundance of waterfalls and streams.

The Na Pali Coast State Park comprises 6,175 acres of raw, pristine nature. The remaining cliffs, coastline, and valleys are either state forests or natural area reserves. There is a ranger stationed at Kalalau Valley who oversees the park and who will ask campers for permits. There is a trailhead by Ke'e Beach that you can't miss, and at Kalalau Valley there's a sign-in box. Day-use permits are required to go beyond Hanakapi'ai (where there are composting toilets), about two miles in, and a camping permit is necessary to stay overnight at Hanakapi'ai, Hanakoa, or Kalalau. Camping is permitted for up to five nights total, but two consecutive nights are not allowed at Hanakapi'ai or Hanakoa. Permits are $20 per day per person. Hawaii residents receive a $5 discount. Permits issued are limited to protect the natural area, and during busy times can sell out a year in advance. The Department of Land and Natural Resources offers an online reservation system (camping.ehawaii.gov) where you can check for availability and purchase permits.

THE KALALAU TRAIL

What may be the best way to experience the coast is the 11-mile **Kalalau Trail**, which begins right at Keʻe Beach. Mother Nature dictates what condition the trail is in, so hikers may find a somewhat dry and firm trail or a narrow trail so steep and wet they must scoot along on a cliff's edge while digging their hands deep into the dirt to hang on. Upon reaching Kalalau Beach, hikers may be welcomed to the beach by nude campers, as some people take advantage of the remote location and leave swimwear in their packs.

The path was originally created by Hawaiians as a land route between Kalalau Valley and Heʻena. The Kalalau Trail was built in the late 1800s and rebuilt in 1930 for horses and cows to pass over. To experience the trail is to experience what old Hawaii must have been like, when people lived off the land and close to nature. It usually takes a full day to get to Kalalau Beach, and it's hands down the best hike in the state. The trail is well worn from decades of use, so you're not likely to get off track and lost.

The currents along the coast are dangerous too, so stay out of the water from around September through April, when winter swells pound the cliffs and beaches. In summer, the sand usually returns to Hanakapiʻai Beach, the most commonly visited part of the hike, after being swept away by the winter's large surf. Hanakapiʻai, like Queen's Bath, has a list of the names and ages of people who have died at this beach due to the pounding surf often washing over bare rock.

To access the Kalalau Trail, park at the end of the road at Keʻe Beach. The lot is often full, but there is an overflow lot a short walk up the road. You can park overnight, but never leave anything visible in the car to avoid a break-in. Some hikers who have a permit to stay multiple nights choose to hitchhike to and from the trailhead to avoid leaving their car overnight. However, hitchhiking presents its own challenges, like not knowing how long you'll be waiting for a ride. After hiking 22 miles, are you prepared to walk back to your room?

the Kalalau Trail

More than the basics are needed to camp out here. You'll need a waterproof tent, mosquito repellent, first-aid kit, biodegradable soap, food, sleeping bag, and whatever else you think you may need and don't mind carrying on your back mile after mile. Water bladders as opposed to water bottles are a good idea, because they're lighter and run a constant line of water to the mouth. Tree cutting is not allowed, and there isn't much natural firewood, so bring a stove if you want to cook. Drinking out of the streams is not advised; doing so can cause serious stomach illness, so boil the water or bring a water filter or purification tablets. Please remember not to litter and to take out what you carried in. Reachable only by boat or kayak, the Nuʻalolo Kai can be visited for the day only, and Miloliʻi offers camping for a maximum of three nights with very basic campsites. The most accurate idea of what to expect is from hikers who have recently made the journey, because the trail changes with the weather.

★ **HANAKAPI'AI BEACH AND HANAKAPI'AI FALLS**

It's about two miles and a two-hour hike from Keʻe to **Hanakapiʻai Beach**. The first mile goes uphill to about 800 feet, with the last mile going down and ending at the beach. Depending on the season, you may get lucky and see some brave and slightly crazy surfers out here. During low tide and only during the summer, people will camp in caves on the beach, but on the far side of the stream up from the beach is the best place to camp.

From the west side of the stream at Hanakapiʻai Beach the Hanakapiʻai Trail starts, leading two miles inland up into the valley to the wonderful **Hanakapiʻai Falls**, passing old taro fields and crumbling rock walls. The trail crosses the stream several times on the way up, so if the stream looks full and rushing, just turn around and head back. It can be dangerous during high water. If the stream is low, keep going. The hike to the 300-foot-high falls is rewarding and worth it. There is a wonderful ice-cold swimmable pool at the bottom, but don't swim directly under the falls. From Hanakapiʻai Camp near the beach, the hike should take around 2-3 hours, and it's about 5-6 hours from Keʻe Beach.

HANAKAPI'AI BEACH TO HANAKOA

It's a strenuous 4.5-mile, three-hour trek from **Hanakapiʻai Beach to Hanakoa**. The trail climbs steadily and doesn't go back down to sea level until Kalalau Beach, nine miles later. Switchbacks lead you out of Hanakapiʻai Valley. The trail passes through the hanging valleys of Hoʻolulu and Waiahuakua, both parts of the Honoʻonapali Nature Area Preserve and loaded with native flora, before arriving at Hanakoa. In the past, Hanakoa was a major food-growing area for Hawaiians, and many of its terraces are still intact. Wild coffee plants can be seen here. Hanakoa is a bit rainy, but it's intermittent and the sun usually dominates throughout the day. To get to Hanakoa Falls from here, which are even more amazing than Hanakapiʻai Falls, you'll need to take a worthwhile half-mile detour inland. Cross the Hanakoa Stream and hang a left at the trail near the shelter. Walk for about 150 feet or so, take a left at the fork, and continue for 15 to 20 minutes.

HANAKOA TO KALALAU BEACH

From **Hanakoa to Kalalau Beach** the trek is less than five miles, but it's a tough one and takes around three hours. It's important to start this one early in the morning to get as much time in as possible before the heat sinks in. The trail gets drier and more open as you approach Kalalau, but the views along the way make it all worth it. Around mile marker 7 is land that until the late 1970s was part of the Makaweli cattle ranch. After Pohakuao Valley is Kalalau Valley, spanning two miles wide and three miles deep. Freshwater pools dot the area and look inviting after the long, hot hike. Camping is only allowed in the trees along the beach or in the caves west of the waterfall—not along the stream, its mouth, or in the valley. The falls have a wonderful, refreshing pool. On the far side of the stream is a *heiau* on top of a little hill. If you follow the trail here inland for around two miles you'll find Big Pool, which is really two pools connected by a natural waterslide.

HONOPU, NU'ALOLO KAI, AND MILOLI'I

If you somehow have it in you to keep going, other destinations include **Honopu**, **Nuʻalolo Kai**, and **Miloliʻi**. Honopu is less than 0.5 mile west of Kalalau Valley, and is known as "Valley of the Lost Tribe" by legend of the small Mu people said to once inhabit the area. The beach is separated by a big rock arch that has been used in at least two movies. You can get to Nuʻalolo Kai by staying on the Kalalau Trail; it is right after Awaʻawapuhi Valley, about nine miles down the coast. It has a lovely beach and dunes right up against a tall cliff. There's a pair of reefs here that provide good snorkeling opportunities when the water is calm. A community of Hawaiians lived out here until 1919, and their archaeological remnants still exist as stone walls and *heiau* platforms. They cultivated taro in the adjoining Nu'alolo 'Aina Valley, and they reaped the bounty of the ocean as well. Another mile west is Miloli'i, another site inhabited by native Hawaiians. At Miloli'i you'll find a very basic camping area with restrooms and a simple shelter. Down the beach is another *heiau*. Miloli'i only gets about 20 inches of rain a year, a big contrast from the rest of the wet Na Pali Coast.

BIKING

Hanalei and Princeville are the best areas on the north shore for **biking**. After Hanalei there are numerous one-lane bridges and a narrow winding road to Ke'e that could push bikers into the traffic. Princeville is the safest and most convenient place for a leisurely ride, although the steady incline heading up can be rough. To rent a beach cruiser to explore Hanalei, stop at **Pedal-N-Paddle** (Ching Young Village, 808/826-9069, www.pedalnpaddle.com, 9am-6pm daily) for hybrid road bike and cruiser rentals for $12 daily or $50 for the week. Biking accessories are also available, along with water-sport supplies.

Adventure Sports and Tours

ZIPLINING
Princeville
For the thrill of flying through the air over verdant landscapes on a private ranch, **Princeville Ranch Adventures** (5-4280 Kuhio Hwy., 808/826-7669 or 888/955-7669, princevilleranch.com, by appt.) has three different **zipline** tours and one zipline and horseback ride tour, which start at $159 per person. The lines travel through valleys with mountain and ocean views and will get your adrenaline pumping. You can't miss the ranch entrance on the north side of Kuhio Highway

before Princeville. Tour fees also include a picnic lunch and an experienced guide.

HELICOPTER TOURS
Princeville
Departing out of the small Princeville airport is **Sunshine Helicopters** (Princeville Airport, 866/501-7738, www.sunshinehelicopters.com). A 40- to 50-minute flight will take you over the Na Pali Coast, Waimea Canyon, and many places utilized in Hollywood films. Open seating is priced at $289, and first class is $364. Check for discounts on the website.

Shopping

KILAUEA
Kilauea Plantation Center
The **Kilauea Plantation Center** on Kilauea Road is home to the **Healthy Hut** (4480 Ho'okui Rd., 808/828-6626, www.healthyhutkauai.com, 8:30am-9pm daily), where you'll find organic produce, fruit, and other natural foods. There are natural home wares and gifts, along with a health and beauty section, vitamins, and natural baby products.

A very small wine and beer selection is also available.

Kong Lung Historic Market Square
Also on Kilauea Road is the **Kong Lung Historic Market Square** (2484 Keneke St., 808/828-1822, konglungkauai.com). The building is now listed on the National Register of Historic Places for its role in the town's

development. The market square is home to an array of shops and eateries, including the **Lotus Gallery** (808/828-9898, www.jewelofthelotus.com, 10am-5pm daily), selling a spectrum of antique and modern Asian art and elegant jewelry made from pearls, opals, black diamonds, jade, and other stones, as well as Hawaiian *kahelelani* and sunrise-shell jewelry. The shop is also stocked with carvings, garden art, and various artifacts.

Island Soap and Candle Works outlets (808/828-1955, www.islandsoap.com, 9am-8pm daily) can be found around the island. The Kilauea location is not only a retail shop, but also a working factory where visitors can watch the soap being made by hand. The shop offers a full line of all-natural products.

PRINCEVILLE
Princeville Center

A variety of shops to fit most needs can be found in the **Princeville Center** (5-4280 Kuhio Hwy., 808/826-9497, www.princevillecenter.com). Visit the **Hawaiian Music Store** (808/826-4223, www.hawaiianmusicstore.com, 9am-9pm daily) to find a soundtrack for your trip. It's actually a kiosk near the Foodland entrance. Listening to the music back at home will always take you back to Kaua'i. The kiosk usually has local music playing on speakers, adding an element of island style to the shopping center.

For a select bottle of wine, the **Princeville Wine Market** (808/826-0040, 10am-7pm Mon.-Sat., 1pm-7pm Sun.) holds an array of wines, something for every connoisseur's palate. Pick up a bottle for a romantic night at your accommodation or to enjoy a sunset beverage on the beach.

At the **Magic Dragon Toy & Art Supply** (808/826-9144, 9am-6pm daily), a compilation of unique and educational toys, games, activities, and kites can be found. Great art supplies are also available.

HANALEI
Kauhale Center

In the **Kauhale Center** (4489 Aku Rd.), on the oceanside of the road, **The Bikini Room** (808/826-9711, www.thebikiniroom.com, 10am-6pm Mon.-Sat., 11am-5pm Sun.) is where unique and quality Brazilian bathing suits can be found. A sale rack can often be found in front of the shop, and the staff is especially helpful with insight on what suits are best for swimming or sunning.

The Root (808/826-2575, 9:30am-7pm Mon.-Sat., noon-6pm Sun.) has an array of fun, funky, simple, sweet, and trendy women's clothing. From dressy to relaxed, it's of high quality and pretty.

Hanalei Center

The historic **Hanalei Center** (5-5121 Kuhio Hwy.), on the *mauka* side of the highway, has an array of shops and eateries. **Harvest Market Natural Foods and Cafe** (5-5161 Kuhio Hwy. #F, 808/826-0089, http://harvestmarkethanalei.com, 9am-7pm Mon.-Sat., 9am-6pm Sun.) brings healthy food to Hanalei. The shelves are stocked with organic and natural food, produce, body products, and vitamins.

At the west and back side of the center is **Havaiki Oceanic and Tribal Art** (5-5161 Kuhio Hwy. #G, 808/826-7606, www.havaiki-art.com, 10:30am-6:30pm daily), where a visit feels like an exploration through the Pacific. The collection resembles what you may find while visiting a museum, with all the most prized gifts the area has to offer. Interesting and amazing artifacts, statues, carvings, jewelry, and much more pack this store full, ranging from affordable to outrageous. Every piece tells a story.

The **Yellowfish Trading Company** (808/826-1227, 10am-8pm daily) is an interesting store that feels like a journey through Hawaiian history and memorabilia. The store is loaded with Hawaiiana, collectibles, hula girl lamps, aloha shirts, carvings, swords, candles, jewelry, and so much more.

At the far east end of the old Hanalei school building is the **Hanalei Surf Company** (808/826-9000, www.hanaleisurf.com, 8am-9pm daily), which sells and rents boards and water gear, along with a good stock of clothing and swimwear for the whole family.

Ching Young Village

The bustling **Ching Young Village** (5-5190 Kuhio Hwy., 808/826-7222, www.chingyoungvillage.com) has many shops, including **Divine Planet** (808/826-8970, www.divineplanet.com, 10am-6pm daily) and **Aloha From Hanalei** (same phone and hours), which are two connected shops, but with different themes. The former features bamboo women's clothing, beads, Asian-themed collectibles, and pretty and fun paper star lanterns. The latter shop has a unique array of local gems, handmade creamy soaps and lotions made by a local goat dairy, and Hawaiiana.

Robin Savage Gifts & Gourmet (808/826-7500, 8:30am-7pm daily) may be the most fun gift shop in Hanalei. Local cards, children's clothing, books, lotions, home and kitchen wares, and gourmet foods fill the shop. The shop is stocked with an abundance of products, and it's almost hard to move, but there are a lot of good finds.

On the east end of the shopping center is **Backdoor Surf** (808/826-1900, www.hanaleisurf.com, 8:30am-9:30pm daily). It rents and sells surfboards, and offers a large array of men's, women's and children's swimwear, surf gear, and clothing.

Colorful and cute describes the clothing in **Kokonut Kids** (808/826-0353, www.kokonutkidskauai.com, 10am-6pm Mon.-Sat., 10am-5:30pm Sun.), which offers all things local for children. From play clothes to dress clothes, Kokonut Kids can deck out the children for the whole trip. The **Hanalei Toy and Candy Store** (808/826-4400, 10am-6pm daily) has a unique selection of quality toys and candy.

Hanalei Colony Resort

Na Pali Art Gallery & Coffee Shop (5-7132 Kuhio Hwy., 808/826-1844, www.napaligallery.com, 7am-5pm daily) is a wonderful art gallery filled with local art, jewelry, house decorations, tribal carvings, and more. The collection of Ni'ihau and sunrise shell jewelry at the back of the small shop should not be missed. Paintings, scratchboard art, and local shell puzzles decorate the place. Coffee, smoothies, and bagels are offered too.

Entertainment

The very best entertainment on the north shore may very well be the waves, snorkeling, or the sunset. But for those looking for a little more action, there are a few places in town with live music.

PRINCEVILLE

At the **St. Regis Lobby Bar** (inside the St. Regis Princeville Resort), those looking for a mellow social evening or date night will find a 180-degree view of Hanalei Bay accented by local music. Live jazz or Hawaiian music highlights the evening. The bar is open 3:30pm-10:30pm daily.

HANALEI

At **Tahiti Nui** (5-5134 Kuhio Hwy., 808/826-6277, www.thenui.com, dinner and music 6pm-8:30pm, late music 9:30pm-1am) dinner is offered nightly, but more importantly, it's the only place that could be considered a real nighttime entertainment venue in Hanalei, featuring karaoke and Hawaiian music. Check the website for monthly schedules.

Bouchons Hanalei (5-5190 Kuhio Hwy., 808/826-9701, www.bouchonshanalei.com) in Ching Young Village has live music Thursday-Sunday nights. Call for hours and music selection.

TO THE END OF THE ROAD

The oceanfront lu'au at **Mediterranean Gourmet** (5-7132 Kuhio Hwy., 808/826-9875, www.kauaimedgourmet.com, 6pm-8:15pm Thurs.) offers the opportunity to fill your belly with a buffet dinner of traditional Hawaiian food while taking in hula dancing, fire knife dancing, and local music. Some of the mouthwatering buffet highlights include *lomilomi* salmon, traditional *kalua* pork, *haupia*, coconut cake, and, of course, Hanalei poi. Because it's limited to 80 guests, reservations are required, so call to get your spot. The adult charge is $83, which includes a drink, those ages 12-20 pay $60, and for children 11 and under it's $35.

Food

KILAUEA

Quick Bites

★ **Banana Joe's** fruit stand (5-2719 Kuhio Hwy., 808/828-1092, www.bananajoekauai.com, 9am-6pm Mon.-Sat., 9am-5pm Sun.) is a family-run, small yellow shop that sells smoothies, fresh fruit, baked goods, and local honey. The variety of fruit here makes Carmen Miranda's hat look boring. It's a perfect place for a pre-beach snack stop, a gift run, or an after-scenic-route stop.

Seafood

"There's a whole lot more than fish in store" is the self-described motto of the **Kilauea Fish Market** (Kilauea Plantation Center, 4270 Kilauea Rd. #F, 808/828-6244, 11am-8pm Mon.-Sat., $10-30), and it's true. Free-range beef, salads, and plate lunches are also available, along with vegetarian specials. Enjoy the outdoor seating area or take it to go for a room or beach meal.

Health Food

Kauai Juice Company (Kilauea Plantation Center, 4270 Kilauea Rd., http://kauaijuiceco.com, 8am-5pm Mon.-Sat.) offers cold-pressed, organic juices made from locally sourced ingredients. Start your day or rehydrate with one of its delicious and fresh concoctions. Kauai Juice also has elixirs and kombuchas.

Hawaiian

The Bistro (Kong Lung Historic Market Square, 2484 Keneke St., 808/828-0480, www.lighthousebistro.com, noon-2:30pm and 5:30pm-9pm daily, happy hour 5:30pm-6pm daily, $8-26) is near the lighthouse, not right by it. This is the closest to fine dining in Kilauea, but it isn't entirely formal; you can dress up for fun or go low-key. Lunch includes garden and fish tacos, garden and beef burgers, fish sandwiches, soups, and salads and runs $7.50-10 or $15 for all-you-can-eat pasta. Dinner includes ginger-crusted fresh catch, shrimp parmesan, coconut-crusted pork, ribs, and a lot more, along with salads and another all-you-can-eat pasta bar. Vegetarians will have plenty of options here. Wine, beer, and cocktails are available.

Deli, Pizza, and Bakery

★ **Kilauea Bakery & Pau Hana Pizza** (2484 Keneke St., 808/828-2020, www.kilaueabakery.wordpress.com, 6am-9pm daily, $15-33) in the Kong Lung Historic Market Square serves up satisfying breakfasts and coffee along with tasty pizzas. Mornings usually bring a line of loyal locals coming in for the sweet and savory breakfast pastries. Pizzas go in the oven at 10:30am and come with a heap of toppings.

PRINCEVILLE

American

The **Kaua'i Grill** (808/826-9644, www.kauaigrill.com, 5:30pm-9:30pm Tues.-Thurs., 5:30pm-10pm Fri.-Sat., $32-72) inside the

St. Regis Princeville Resort offers sweeping views of beautiful Hanalei Bay. The eatery stays true to its surroundings with a nautilus shell-spiraling ceiling. Chef Colin Hazama, who was recently recognized by the James Beard Foundation as a finalist in the Rising Star Chef of the Year category, cooks up a tasting menu, unique salads, a vegetarian menu, and lamb, meats, and fish, all with a unique island twist. A kids' menu helps keep the prices down.

Mexican

★ **Federico's Freshmex Cuisine** (Princeville Center, 5-4280 Kuhio Hwy., 808/826-7177, 9am-8:30pm Mon.-Sat., $6-15) offers big portions of authentic Mexican fare. Carnitas, carne asada, and *al pastor* are favorites at this busy little family-run restaurant. From tortas to tacos, the fresh food is accompanied by a fresh salsa bar. Be prepared to wait a few more minutes than usual for your food because each meal is prepared to order. Federico's also has a great kids' menu. For a few extra cents you can request biodegradable wares.

HANALEI
Cafés and Breakfast

The scent alone in **Java Kai** (5-5161 Kuhio Hwy., Ste. 210, 808/823-6887, www.javakai. com, 6am-7pm daily, $8-13) in the Hanalei Center will make anyone who enters want to try the local coffee. The coffee is great, and the food is limited but includes a really good Belgian waffle, papaya and bagels, and a small selection of breakfast dishes including a breakfast burrito. Eat and run or drink your cup of joe on the porch.

Japanese and Seafood

★ **Bouchons Hanalei** (5-5190 Kuhio Hwy., 808/826-9701, www.bouchonshanalei.com, 11:30am-8:30pm daily, lunch $9-15, dinner $11-30) delivers Pacific-American cuisine. The lunch menu, served 11:30am-3:30pm, features a range of foods from burgers and ribs to taco salads and chicken dishes. Dinner is served 5pm-8:30pm and includes exquisite sushi, a Pacific-themed menu, ribs, burgers, and other Asian dishes. An array of drinks and live music on certain nights are also offered. The restaurant is the best of two previous ones fused together by the owner.

Just after entering Hanalei you'll see ★ **The Dolphin Hanalei** (5-5016 Kuhio Hwy., 808/826-6699, www.hanaleidolphin. com), consisting of the restaurant, a fish market, and sushi lounge. The restaurant (lunch 11:30am-3pm daily, $10-16, dinner 5:30pm-9pm daily, $20-35) serves an array of Pacific Rim salads, burgers, and seafood in all of its glory. Enjoy your meal at the riverside tables or in the open-air restaurant. You can go casual here, but it's also nice enough to dress up. The sushi lounge (5:30pm-9pm daily) has a wonderful array of sushi and a good sake selection. The Hanalei Fish Market (10am-7pm daily) offers a wide selection of fresh fish and pre-made sushi rolls. You'll find a good variety of seafood, specialty cheeses, organic produce, beef, and desserts.

Hawaiian

The family-run ★ **Hanalei Taro and Juice Co.** (5-5070A Kuhio Hwy., 808/826-1059, www.hanaleitaro.com, 11am-3pm daily, $4-10.50) serves up a modern take on traditional Hawaiian food. Established in 2000, the company is part of the Haraguchi family farm (of the rice mill) and creates the meals with local foods and taro. The restaurant puts a new twist on Hawaiian food, as with the taro smoothie and taro veggie burgers, while staying traditional with *kalua* pig, *laulau*, poi, *lomilomi* salmon, and a whole lot more.

★ **Postcards Café** (5 Kuhio Hwy., 808/826-1191, http://postcardscafe.com, 6pm-9pm daily, $18-38) is a vegetarian's (or seafood lover's) dream, with a spectacular menu of gourmet vegetarian and seafood cuisine. No meat, poultry, or refined sugar is used here, which makes the abundance of organic ingredients and local produce stand out. Many dishes are vegan or can be made vegan. If you like lobster, try the fennel-crusted lobster tail.

Health Food

Harvest Market Natural Foods and Cafe (Hanalei Center, 5-5161 Kuhio Hwy. #F, 808/826-0089, http://harvestmarkethanalei. com, 9am-7pm Mon.-Sat., 9am-6pm Sun., hot bar $7.99/pound) brings healthy food to Hanalei. The shelves are stocked with organic and natural food, produce, and body products. Pre-made meals are in the refrigerator at the back of the store, and a salad bar offers an array of food. Coffee and pastries are available in the morning, and the deli takes orders off its menu. Slightly on the pricey side, but it's healthy.

American

Hanalei Gourmet Cafe, Bar, and Delicatessen in the Hanalei Center (5-5161 Kuhio Hwy., 808/826-2524, www.hanaleigourmet.com, 8am-10:30pm daily, lunch $7.50-13, dinner $10-27) offers a variety of restaurants in one. It's in the old school building, which adds a historical element to the laid-back atmosphere. Happy hour is 3:30pm-5:30pm daily. Dinner is 5:30pm-9:30pm. Early-bird specials are offered 5:30pm-6:30pm, and selected sports are available on cable TV. A really unique thing about this place is that it offers picnic

services. The crew will help you pack your food and wine into insulated backpacks or coolers so you can hike the Na Pali Coast or paddle up a river. The meal selection is varied, from appetizers of seafood, nachos, and the tasty artichoke dip to dinners of pork loin, poultry, steak, and pastas, many with a Pacific twist. Salads are available in abundance, as well as sandwiches and burgers. This place has plenty of vegetarian options. There are two sides to the café, a sit-down restaurant and a take-out kitchen. Check the chalkboard out front for the daily specials.

Brazilian and Mexican

★ **Neide's Salsa and Samba** (Hanalei Center, 808/826-1851, 11:30am-2:30pm and 5pm-9pm daily, $10-20) serves up some really good margaritas, as well as unique dishes. The head chef from Brazil has a unique take on South American food, like adding cabbage and carrots to the dishes. The service is very laid-back, and there is outdoor and indoor seating. It can be a good place to bring kids because the porch seating lies on a yard-like area with a picnic table and garden, so children can roll around while you enjoy a really tasty, strong, and slightly

fresh juice served from a street-side stand

pricey margarita. Vegetarians will not leave here with an empty belly.

Tropical Taco (5-5088 Kuhio Hwy., 808/827-8226, www.tropicaltaco.com, 8am-8pm Mon.-Fri., 11am-5pm Sat.-Sun., $5-14) is in the green Halele'a Building on the ocean side of the highway, the green being similar to the green lunch wagon the owner ran the business out of for 20 years. The tacos, burritos, and tostadas are tasty, simple, and can be grabbed on the run or enjoyed sitting at the location. Vegetarians will find a sufficient meal here. It's very popular, so expect a bit of a wait. The Baja-style fish tacos are the bomb.

Tapas

★ **Bar Acuda Tapas and Wine** (808/826-7081, www.restaurantbaracuda.com, bar 5:30pm-10pm daily, dinner 5.30pm 9.30pm daily, $6-16) in the Hanalei Center may be home to the most modern decor in Hanalei. It serves tapas, which are defined on the menu as a variety of small, savory dishes typically shared communally among friends. To never have a boring month, the menu here changes by the week and the season; offerings include local honeycomb with goat cheese, short ribs, local fish, salads, desserts, and a great wine menu.

TO THE END OF THE ROAD
Mediterranean

★ **Mediterranean Gourmet** (5-7132 Kuhio Hwy., 808/826-9875, www.kauaimedgourmet.com, noon-3pm and 5pm-8:30pm Tues.-Sun., 6pm-8:15pm (lu'au only) Thurs., happy hour 3pm-6pm Tues.-Sun., $17-65) was voted by *Honolulu* magazine as the best new restaurant on Kaua'i in 2007, best restaurant on Kaua'i in 2008, 2009, 2010, and 2011, and best Greek restaurant in 2012 and 2013. If that doesn't speak for itself, then the oceanfront location paired with the menu will amaze you. Lebanon native and chef Imad Beydoun and his wife, Yarrow, feature Greek, French, Spanish, Italian, and Lebanese-influenced dishes for lunch or dinner. Dinner reservations are recommended, and music is provided each night. Tuesday has Hawaiian music and hula dancers, Wednesday has jazz and half-price wine night, Thursday has a lu'au, Friday has singer and guitarist Anjela Rose and half-price wine, and Saturday has singer and guitarist Sara Thompson during dinner. Try the homemade sangria or a mojito. Lunch includes wraps, vegetarian dishes, fish, and more. For dinner, there are vegetarian, lamb, beef, fish, chicken, and vegetarian dishes, along with the famous rack of lamb for two.

Po'ipu and the South Shore

There's a not-so-secret phenomenon that is known by locals and returning visitors alike: For an almost guaranteed sunny beach day, just head to Po'ipu and the south shore.

Even if it's raining on the north shore or windy and overcast on the east side, it's always sunny here. In fact, if it's pouring in the mountains, rain stretches down to historic Koloa town, where the showers abruptly turn off, as if there is a line in the sand.

This region tends to be dry and hot, and the cactus and succulents that line the road and open spaces confirm that. There's even a beautiful succulent botanical garden at the Outrigger Kiahanu Plantation planted back in the 1930s that still thrives today.

The south shore holds claim to an important part of state history: It was home to the first successful sugar mill in Hawaii. Located in Koloa, the mill brought together seven different ethnic groups, the main source of labor on the plantations, shaping the state's diverse cultural demographic. The sugar mill was the central feature of society and life on the south shore. From 1835 to 1880, Koloa was Kaua'i's most densely populated area. Koloa Landing, down in Po'ipu, was among the top three most active whaling ports in the entire state, and

sugar was a booming business for well over a century. The newest mill, the McBryde Sugar Co. Koloa Mill, shut its doors in 1996, ending the sugar dynasty on Kaua'i. Its remains can still be seen off Maha'ulepu Road.

Today, resorts, golf, ocean recreation, and dining are what you'll find in the region, with Po'ipu holding the lion's share of the amenities. While Koloa has evolved into a quaint and quiet residential town, Po'ipu has expanded with massive development over the last couple decades. Visitors who stayed on the south shore 10 years ago might not recognize the coastal locale, as luxury developments and high-end resorts now line the beach and spread inland to Koloa. There might not be as much open space as there once was, but the beaches remain beautiful and the water invitingly clear.

ORIENTATION

The south shore includes **Kalaheo, Koloa, Lawa'i,** and **Po'ipu,** stretching from the dry and sunny shoreline surrounding Po'ipu to

---

Previous: Lawa'i Bay, National Tropical Botanical Garden; monk seal on Po'ipu Beach.
Above: Spouting Horn.

Look for ★ to find recommended
sights, activities, dining, and lodging.

Highlights

★ **Tunnel of Trees:** Eucalyptus trees form a natural tunnel over Maluhia Road, creating a beautiful sight and great photo opportunity (page 616).

★ **Spouting Horn:** Saltwater erupts through a hole in the lava sea cliffs at the south shore's claim to fame (page 616).

★ **Sunset in Po'ipu:** End a lovely south shore day by watching the spectacular sunset in Po'ipu. Several locations offer great views from the beach or sand-free lawns (page 619).

★ **National Tropical Botanical Garden:** The only tropical plant research facility in the United States boasts two gardens with a vast array of plants. Informative tours speak to the history of the region (page 619).

★ **Kukui O Lono Park:** This lovely park is perfect for a stroll through Japanese gardens. It's also a quiet place to picnic with an ocean view (page 620).

★ **Maha'ulepu Beaches:** Visiting these sunny beaches is the closest you'll get to venturing into the wild on the south shore. The long dirt road keeps many people out, and the expansive beaches offer space for everyone (page 621).

★ **Po'ipu Beach Park:** A joy for all beach-goers, this beach offers protected swimming and a manicured park perfect for picnicking and relaxing. It's a wonderful place for children (page 622).

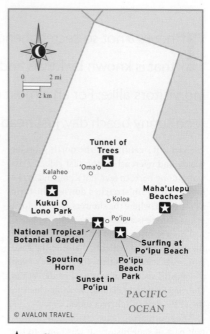

© AVALON TRAVEL

★ **Surfing at Po'ipu Beach:** This is the only beach in the region where the surf is very accessible for novices. Lessons are available, and you'll find expert surfers and surf schools pushing kids into waves in close proximity (page 626).

Po'ipu and the South Shore

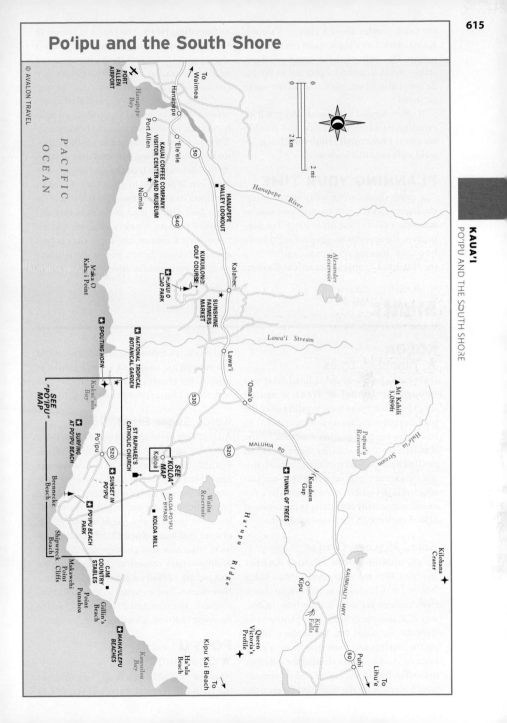

© AVALON TRAVEL

PORT ALLEN AIRPORT

To Waimea

Hanapepe

Hanapepe Bay

PACIFIC OCEAN

Port Allen

'Ele'ele

KAUAI COFFEE COMPANY VISITOR CENTER AND MUSEUM

Numila

HANAPEPE VALLEY LOOKOUT

Hanapepe River

Alexander Reservoir

50

540

Kalaheo

KUKUIOLONO GOLF COURSE

'ILIKUI O PARK

SUNSHINE FARMERS MARKET

Lawa'i Stream

Lawa'i

SPOUTING HORN

NATIONAL TROPICAL BOTANICAL GARDEN

Kukui'ula Bay

Kukui'ula Bay

Ma a O Kalae i Point

SEE "PO'IPU" MAP

SURFING AT PO'IPU BEACH

Po'ipu

520

SUNSET IN PO'IPU

ST RAPHAEL'S CATHOLIC CHURCH

Koloa

SEE "KOLOA" MAP

'Oma'o

530

KOLOA-PO'IPU BYPASS

KOLOA MILL

MALUHIA RD

520

TUNNEL OF TREES

'Knudsen Gap

Papa'a Reservoir

▲ Mt Kahili 3,089ft

Wahiawa Reservoir

Ha u p u Ridge

Kipu

Kilohana Crater

KAUMUALI'I HWY

Queen Victoria's Profile

Kipu Falls

Puhi

50

To Lihu'e

PO'IPU BEACH PARK

Brennecke Beach

Shipwreck Beach

CJM COUNTRY STABLES

Makawehi Point Cliffs

Point Punahoa

Gillin's Beach

MAHA'ULEPU BEACHES

Kawailoa Bay

Ha'ula Beach

To Kipu Kai Beach

0

0

2 km

2 mi

the thick jungles above Kalaheo. Kalaheo, Koloa, and Lawaʻi are quiet, residential towns. The bulk of the accommodations, shops, restaurants, and sights are in Poʻipu. Poʻipu is also where you'll find all the ocean activities.

If you're headed to the west side, you'll inevitably pass through and Lawaʻi and Kalaheo because the **Kaumualiʻi Highway** (Route 50) is the only road that leads west.

PLANNING YOUR TIME

The south shore can be a day trip if you're staying up on the north shore or east side, or it can be a destination all to itself. For daytrippers, the appeal is hanging out at **Poʻipu's beaches,** soaking up the sun, and visiting the **National Tropical Botanical Garden**

or **Spouting Horn.** The region is known to be dry and hot, so botanical garden explorers should plan their tours in the morning and head to the beach in the afternoon where they can cool off in the water.

Visitors staying in Poʻipu will find ample accommodations, including condos, bed-and-breakfasts, vacation rentals, and hotel rooms. The variety of condos and vacation rentals makes it easy for long-stay travelers to stock up the kitchen with food to avoid eating every meal out. While you might be able to see all the sights in a day or two, this is also a great home base for day trips to the west side and Waimea Canyon. Visitors who want to arrive at their accommodation, put the car keys away, and play at the beach every day will love what this region has to offer.

Sights

KOLOA
★ Tunnel of Trees

Entering Koloa via Maluhia Road takes you through the **Tunnel of Trees**, a natural tunnel of eucalyptus trees bending over the road, branches and leaves laced together. The trees were brought in from Australia by the Knudsen family to stabilize the road. If you can find a safe pull-off spot along the road, this is a wonderful photo opportunity if you can get a traffic-free shot. On very sunny days, the tunnel is especially intriguing as diamonds of light shine through the leaves overhead.

Koloa History Center

At the quaint **Koloa History Center** (Building 10 in the Waikomo Shops on Koloa Rd., www.oldkoloa.com, 9am-9pm daily, free), you can get some insight into the history of Koloa via artifacts and photographs from the plantation era. The center is small, yet the displays and photographs are a good place to start a south side visit for a deeper understanding of the region and its agricultural history. Near the Waikomo Stream, the

center is at the former site of an old hotel and provides picnic tables and a small garden to enjoy in the courtyard, which is shaded by a very old and impressive monkeypod tree.

Koloa Sugar Plantation

All that's left of the foundation of Koloa town is the remnants of the old sugar mill, the first successful mill in Hawaii. The mill, which was established in 1835, is located across from the shops at the end of Maluhia Road. A plaque gives a brief history and explains the significance of the mill and sugar industry. You can see and touch about 12 different varieties of sugarcane that grow on-site. A bronze sculpture pays respect to the seven ethnic groups that worked on Hawaii's plantations: Hawaiians, Chinese, Japanese, Puerto Ricans, Filipinos, Koreans, and Portuguese. If you're shopping in Koloa, it's worth a quick stop.

POʻIPU
★ Spouting Horn

Near the end of Lawaʻi Road, shortly after the National Tropical Botanical Garden, is

The Best Day on the South Shore

Spouting Horn

You can easily experience the best of the south shore in one day without missing out on anything. While the best days on other parts of the island require visitors to move quickly through many activities, you can see the best of the south shore in a more relaxed manner. If you start with breakfast around 8am, you should be able to get it all done by sundown.

- Begin your day with breakfast at **Kalaheo Café.** Sit down or order takeout; either way you'll have plenty of time for the day. If you prefer takeout, head over to **Kukui O Lono Park** and enjoy breakfast amid a Japanese garden overlooking the ocean.

- Enjoy a walk through the **National Tropical Botanical Garden.** With two gardens and tours to choose from, you could easily spend anywhere from an hour to half a day exploring the exquisite gardens.

- While you're in the immediate vicinity, stop at **Spouting Horn.** Wait for a couple of big bursts from the blowhole, snap a few photos, and then it's on to the next stop.

- Head down the road to **Po'ipu Beach** for a surf. If you're an experienced surfer, renting a board is easy, or beginners can take a lesson. Make sure to book the lessons in advance. Afterward, grab lunch at **Living Foods Market and Café** in **The Shops at Kukui'ula.**

- For a relaxing time with full amenities, bask in the sun and salt at **Po'ipu Beach Park.** This is an especially good option if you have children. For a much more secluded beach time, make the drive to the **Maha'ulepu Beaches.**

- To end the day, enjoy the sunset in Po'ipu. Watch the sunset over the boats and Spouting Horn from **Kukui'ula Small Boat Harbor** or from the **Beach House Restaurant.**

- For dinner, stay at the **Beach House Restaurant,** or head back to The Shops at Kukui'ula in Po'ipu and take your pick between five excellent, high-quality restaurants.

RAINY-DAY ALTERNATIVE

Grab a black trash bag or pull out that poncho that's wedged at the bottom of your bag and explore the **Allerton Garden** and **McBryde Garden.** Part of the McBryde Garden is seen by tram and the Allerton Garden tour takes place mostly under the canopy of shade trees. Bring an umbrella.

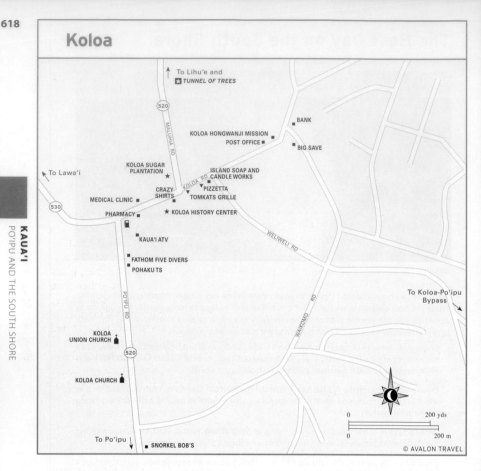

Koloa

To Lihu'e and
➕ TUNNEL OF TREES

520
MALUHIA RD

BANK

KOLOA HONGWANJI MISSION
POST OFFICE ■
■ BIG SAVE

To Lawa'i

KOLOA SUGAR
PLANTATION ★
KOLOA RD
ISLAND SOAP AND
CANDLE WORKS ■

CRAZY
SHIRTS ■
■ PIZZETTA
TOMKATS GRILLE

MEDICAL CLINIC ■

530

PHARMACY ■

★ KOLOA HISTORY CENTER

WELIWELI RD

■ KAUA'I ATV

■ FATHOM FIVE DIVERS
POHAKU TS

POIPU RD

To Koloa-Po'ipu
Bypass

WAIKOMO RD

KOLOA
UNION CHURCH ✝

520

KOLOA CHURCH ▟

0   200 yds
0   200 m

To Po'ipu ↓
■ SNORKEL BOB'S

© AVALON TRAVEL

the south side's claim to fame, the explosive **Spouting Horn**. Saltwater erupts through a hole in the lava sea cliffs, bursting high into the air (the bigger the waves, the bigger the spray). Listen for a low moaning sound following each eruption from another hole that blows only air. Hawaiian legend says that a huge lizard called Mo'o (*mo'o* is Hawaiian for lizard) lived in this area. The lizard would eat anyone who tried to fish here. A man named Liko made that mistake, and Mo'o attacked him, only to get speared in the mouth and stuck where the blowhole is. According to the legend, the noise is the sound of the lizard's pain.

There is ample parking, a grassy lawn, and a picnic table along with souvenir and jewelry booths. The main viewpoint is from the gated area just in front of the spout, where everyone huddles together to get the best shot. Don't forget your camera for this one, and do not go down to the blowhole.

Koloa Heritage Trail

To learn about five million years of the south side's natural and cultural history, follow the 10-mile-long **Koloa Heritage Trail**. Don't be fooled by the name, as the trail is actually along the coast in Po'ipu. Weaving along the trail by car, foot, or bicycle, you will visit 14 cultural, historical, and geological sites of significance to the area. Each site has a numbered marker, and it's a good idea to pick up the *Koloa Heritage Trail* guide, which offers descriptions of each site as you follow the trail. Call 888/744-0888 to pick up the trail guide or visit www.poipubeach.org/local-resources/visitor-info/koloa-heritage-trail to download a copy. The self-guided tour stretches from Spouting Horn to Makawehi and Pa'a Dunes to the east, and then to Koloa town.

★ Sunset in Po'ipu

Po'ipu has a clear view west, and there are many places to watch the vibrant and colorful sunset. An ideal spot is at the **Beach House Restaurant** (5022 Lawa'i Rd., 808/742-1424, www.the-beach-house.com, 5pm-10pm daily, $26-48) on Lawa'i Beach. The open-air restaurant serves dinner, pupu, and drinks overlooking the ocean. For sunset worshippers, a waterfront lawn offers tiki-torch-lit outdoor lounging while watching the sunset and surfers at PK's. Although many locals and visitors like to spend the evening on the lawn here without eating at the restaurant, the lawn is technically part of the restaurant grounds.

At the very end of Lawa'i Road is **Kukui'ula Small Boat Harbor.** Here you will find a pavilion, a lawn backing a small strip of sand, picnic tables, and a small pier to watch the sunset over Spouting Horn. Swimming here isn't recommended, but it is a great place to end the day watching boats bob in the harbor as the sun sets on the horizon.

Prince Kuhio Park and Ho'ai Heiau

Across from the ocean on Lawa'i Road and across from Ho'ona Road is the birthplace of beloved Prince Kuhio. The well-maintained monument and park has a large lawn, a pond, a pavilion, Ho'ai Heiau, and foliage. The beautiful area is a great place for culture and history buffs. The *heiau* (sacred rock structure) is in great condition.

★ National Tropical Botanical Garden

Composed of McBryde and Allerton Gardens, the **National Tropical Botanical Garden** (visitors center, 4425 Lawa'i Rd., 808/742-2623, www.ntbg.org, 8:30am-5pm daily, combined tour $60 adults, $30 children 12 6-12, 5 and under free) in Po'ipu is the only tropical plant research facility in the United States. With three gardens on Kaua'i, one on Maui, and one in Florida, the garden's mission is to enrich life through discovery, scientific research, conservation, and education by perpetuating the survival of plants, ecosystems, and cultural knowledge of tropical regions.

Over 6,000 tropical plant species flourish at the 259-acre **McBryde Garden.** Here you can explore a seemingly infinite array of plants and flowers ranging from bamboo to orchids. The gardens are divided into sections dedicated to medicinal and nutritional plants, herbs and spices, endangered species, fruits, and much more. Trams take visitors into McBryde Garden every hour 9:30am-2:30pm daily; self-guided tours cost $30 for those 13 years old and up, $15 for children 6-12, and children 5 and under are free.

The 80-acre **Allerton Garden** is named after the garden's creator, John Allerton, a member of a mainland cattle-raising family that founded the First National Bank of Chicago. The garden dates back to the 1870s, when Queen Emma first planted here at one of her summer vacation homes. In 1938, Robert Allerton bought the property, and for the next two decades he and his son John cleared the land. John traveled the Pacific extensively, bringing back exotic plants to Kaua'i. Cutting through the property is the Lawa'i River, and small garden rooms and pools make it quite an enchanting experience. The garden is complete with statuary and fountains. Guided tours start at 9am, 10am, 1pm, and 2pm Monday-Saturday. Reservations are necessary, and you'll want to make them about a week in advance as the tours are often booked up, especially during holiday seasons. The fee is $50 for those 13 years old and up and $25 for children 8-12. Children under eight are not allowed on the tour. Even for those who aren't generally interested in botany, this is an informative tour that covers the history of the area, Hawaiian culture, art, and design.

Drop by the visitors center across from Spouting Horn to check out the gift shop and displays in the restored plantation manager's house. It has Hawaiian crafts, Ni'ihau shell lei, and books about Hawaii. Around this center, which was constructed in 1997 after the last center was destroyed in Hurricane 'Iniki, are the demonstration gardens, which are worth exploring even if you aren't going on a tour. Tours leave from the visitors center. Be prepared with water, comfortable walking shoes, and your camera.

KALAHEO
★ Kukui O Lono Park

Oftentimes public parks aren't exceptional places to visit, but **Kukui O Lono Park** (Pu'u Rd., 7am-6pm daily) is quite an enjoyable experience. A unique combination of Japanese gardens, rocks used by Hawaiians for various purposes, abundant plumeria trees, and a public golf course, the park is beautiful and has a great ocean view. It was given to the people of Kaua'i in 1919 by plantation owner Walter D. McBryde. After entering through the large stone and metal gate, go straight to find the gardens and memorial, or take the

right at the fork in the road to find the golf clubhouse about a half mile up. The views in every direction are amazing. Pink plumeria flourish here, and the collection of rocks used by Hawaiians for various functions is quite interesting. If you're a runner, this is a great place to get some exercise. There is even designated parking for joggers.

To get here, turn onto Papalina Road in Kalaheo. About two miles in, turn right at the large gate on the second Pu'u Road.

LAWA'I

Along the hillside at **Lawa'i International Center** (3381 Wawae Rd., 808/639-4300, www.lawaicenter.org, free, donations accepted), 88 Buddhist shrines replicate the 88 temples along the thousand-mile trail and pilgrimage route in Shikoku, Japan. The center opened in 1904 in a small, lush valley that had been used by Hawaiians as a place of worship and then by Japanese Taoists and Shintoists. The area had become rundown and ignored until the 1960s, when a local woman organized the repair and eventual acquisition of the property. The area is lush with tropical foliage and dotted with orchids. During the tour you'll learn the history of the property and enjoy tea and local pastries. The tour begins

Kukui O Lono Park

through a small cave and leads to the miniature shrines, where previous visitors have left jewelry, shells, coins, and other offerings. The shrines can be viewed on the second and last Sunday of each month with tours taking place at 10am, noon, and 2pm.

Beaches

Some of Kaua'i's best **beaches** are found on the south side. They're blanketed in fine white sand and range from popular and crowded to secluded and rarely visited. All of the beaches are in the Po'ipu area, as Koloa, Kalaheo, and Lawa'i are all inland areas. The beaches are great for all kinds of ocean activities, such as snorkeling, surfing, swimming, and sunbathing.

PO'IPU
★ Maha'ulepu Beaches
Adventure into the outskirts of the south side and drive out to the **Maha'ulepu Beaches** at the east end of Po'ipu. You'll travel down a long and bumpy dirt road through undeveloped land with great views of the green mountains inland. The road is fit for two-wheel-drive cars but is usually pocked with ruts and potholes. Fortune favors the brave, though. Drive slowly and eventually you'll get to the long strip of beaches. Gillin's Beach is the first you come to, Kawailoa Bay is the second, and the third and most secluded is Ha'ula Beach. To get here, drive past the Grand Hyatt Kauai until the road turns to dirt. You'll see the CMJ Stables sign as the road turns to dirt and a gate. The access is privately owned, and the gates are locked at 6pm. Respect the area and pack out everything you brought in.

Gillin's Beach is accessed via a short trail through some dense shoreline brush. Parking is out of sight from the beach, so bring your valuables to the beach or leave them at home. The beach is very, very long, with fine white sand. It's a nice beach for swimming, but be careful and use good judgment as the conditions are often windy and strong currents prevail. Although the beach is very long, it's not the widest from dunes to ocean. As the tide gets higher the sand gets narrower, and you will most likely see sunbathers bordering the dunes. To the right of the beach after Elbert Gillin's house is the Makauwahi Sinkhole, which is fun to explore. The open sandstone sinkhole has some fun elements to check out including unearthed archaeological finds.

Swimming is best east of Gillin's at **Kawailoa Bay,** where the water is most protected. To get here, drive past Gillin's and you'll see Kawailoa Bay from the roadside, or walk from Gillin's east around the bend, but it's a bit of a walk. The cove is calmer here than anywhere else on the beach, but the beach isn't quite as nice as the rest. Since the beach is in a semi-protected cove, the whipping winds can be less offensive here.

To get to **Ha'ula Beach,** walk for a while along the lithified cliffs. The cliffs look wild and prehistoric; they're rough, and you'll want shoes for this beach walk. After about 15 minutes of walking, you'll reach Ha'ula Beach. Swimming out here is always dangerous, but secluded beachcombing and sunbathing is ample. Serenity and isolation is the main appeal of making the trip.

Shipwreck Beach
Shipwreck Beach fronts the Grand Hyatt Kaua'i Resort and Spa. Named after an old shipwreck that used to rest on the eastern end, the beach is generally crowded because of its location. It offers plenty of space with about 0.5 mile of sand, but the ocean here is usually too rough for swimming except for those who are experts in the water. Local surfers and bodyboarders congregate on the east end of the beach and surf the waves along the outer reef. Also on the eastern end is Makawehi Point, the high cliff that locals like to jump

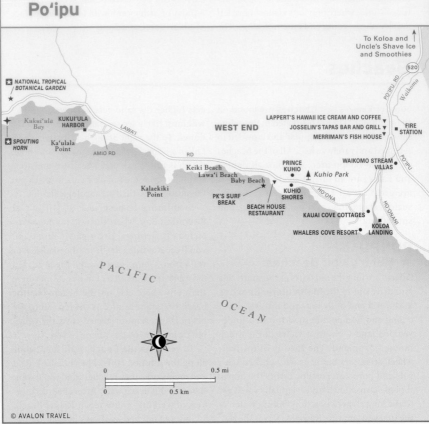

Po'ipu

NATIONAL TROPICAL
BOTANICAL GARDEN

Kukui'ula
Bay

KUKUI'ULA
HARBOR

SPOUTING
HORN

Ka'ulala
Point

AMIO RD

LAWA'I

RD

WEST END

LAPPERT'S HAWAII ICE CREAM AND COFFEE
JOSSELIN'S TAPAS BAR AND GRILL
MERRIMAN'S FISH HOUSE

FIRE
STATION

Keiki Beach
Lawa'i Beach
Baby Beach

Kalaekiki
Point

PK'S SURF
BREAK

BEACH HOUSE
RESTAURANT

PRINCE
KUHIO

Kuhio Park

KUHIO
SHORES

WAIKOMO STREAM
VILLAS

HO'ONA

KAUAI COVE COTTAGES

WHALERS COVE RESORT

KOLOA
LANDING

HO'ONANI

PO'IPU RD

Waikomo

To Koloa and
Uncle's Shave Ice
and Smoothies

520

PO'IPU RD

PACIFIC

OCEAN

0   0.5 mi
0   0.5 km

© AVALON TRAVEL

off for fun. To get here, drive toward the Hyatt on Weliweli Road and turn right onto Ainako Road. Park in the small parking lot at the end.

★ Po'ipu Beach Park

Po'ipu Beach Park (at the end of Kuai Road) is hands down the most ideal beach for families and children on the south side. A protected swimming area, playground, full amenities, and grassy lawn come together to create everything necessary for a full day at the beach. It's often crowded with visitors and local families, a testament to its popularity. The shallow ocean pool is semi-enclosed by a short rock wall, providing calm water within the rock barrier. It's a great swimming pool for children to float and play. The water isn't as protected on the west side of the beach, but if the waves are small it's safe and a great zone for swimming and snorkeling. Monk seals frequent the beach too, so if you see a seal, please respect all signs and safety zones and give the seal plenty of space to snooze in the sun.

An elaborate playground for children is located at the east side of the park alongside a shade-offering tree. Picnic tables dot the grassy lawn, showers and bathrooms are on-site, and there are lifeguards on duty. There is parking available across the street from the beach, but on most days the spots are full. Get there early to grab a spot or be prepared to wait for someone to leave.

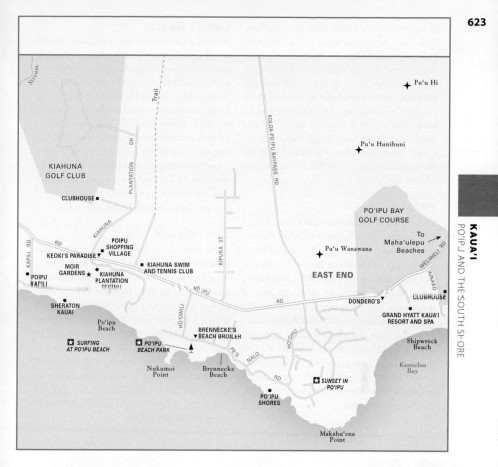

Just east of Po'ipu Beach Park is **Brennecke Beach.** The waves are great for bodyboarding and bodysurfing. Surfboards are not allowed. Beginners can rent a bodyboard from **Nukumoi Beach & Surf Shop** (2080 Ho'one Rd., 808/742-8019, www.nukumoisurf.com, 8am-sunset daily) across the street and charge the little waves. To get here, turn down Ho'owili Road off Po'ipu Road. The beach is right at the bottom along Ho'one Road.

Po'ipu Beach

Also known as **Sheraton Beach** (because it fronts the Sheraton Kaua'i) and **Kiahuna Beach, Po'ipu Beach** is a popular, and therefore a generally crowded, beautiful beach. The swimming just offshore is usually pretty mellow thanks to the outer reef where the surfers find great waves. Surf lessons are also given here. It's also a good spot for snorkeling if the ocean is calm, so bring your gear. There are restrooms at the grassy lawn above the sand. Parking here and along the street can be tight, so keep a lookout for several parking areas along the road. The beach is at the end of coastal Ho'onani Road.

Baby Beach

True to its name, **Baby Beach** is perfect for small children and babies. The small beach is nearly always calm, still, and shallow. The water here feels more like a saltwater swimming pool than the open ocean. There is a narrow strip of white sand descending into the water, leading to a rocky bottom. Hawaiian rocks can always be a bit tough on the feet, so bringing water shoes is a good idea. Kids will love jumping around in the water with floats here. To get here, turn off Lawaʻi Road onto Hoʻona Road and look for the beach access sign. The beach is behind the oceanfront homes.

PK's

Located right across from the Prince Kuhio monument, hence the name **PK's**, the narrow strip of sand is most notable by the surf break to the right of the Beach House Restaurant. The wave here is also called PK's. Snorkelers will find a lot of fish here since the bottom is so rocky, but the ocean surface is usually rough. It's best to snorkel when the waves are very small and the wind is calm. The beach is narrow and just off the road, so it's less than ideal for a day at the beach. Drive down Lawaʻi Road and you'll see the small beach below the roadside rock wall directly across from the monument.

Lawaʻi Beach

A small white-sand beach in an almost always sunny area, **Lawaʻi Beach** offers swimming and decent snorkeling along a narrow strip of white sand. The grounds of the Beach House Restaurant jut out on the left side of the beach, while condominiums act as a backdrop across the road. Across the street is a small parking lot with restrooms and a small shop. This is a popular hangout for local surfers, who enjoy a few beers at day's end while watching the waves at PK's. Head down Lawaʻi Road and you can see the beach from the street right past the Beach House Restaurant.

Keiki Beach

A few yards down from Lawaʻi Beach is **Keiki Beach**. A secluded and very small strip of sand just below the road, the small beach is accessible by hopping over the rock wall and stepping down past a few boulders. There's a little tide pool here that's good for a very shallow dip or for kids, only at low tide. The nice thing about this spot is that it's nearly always uninhabited. During high tide you'll find yourself sitting up against the rock wall, so it's best at low tide. Although small, Keiki Beach is a change from Lawaʻi Beach just because it's usually empty.

Brennecke Beach

Lawa'i Bay

Bordering the National Tropical Botanical Garden is **Lawa'i Bay**. The bay is usually only reached by those with a passion for serious ocean adventuring. If you kayak about a mile west from **Kukui'ula Small Boat Harbor** you will reach it. Those who make it there are asked to be respectful and not enter the gardens. Needless to say, you'll most likely be alone here if you make the trip. Park your vehicle at Kukui'ula Small Boat Harbor at the end of Lawa'i Road. Hop in the water with your kayak and paddle about a mile west down the coast.

Water Sports

SNORKELING AND DIVING

The south side has great **snorkeling** at several popular beaches. One of the highlights underwater is the large number of green sea turtles that feast on the seaweed that covers the shoreline rocks. They move slowly and are gentle creatures. Green sea turtles are a federally protected species, and it is against the law to touch them.

Po'ipu

BEACHES

Hop in the water at **Lawa'i Beach** and you'll see colorful reef fish. The water is clear and the bottom is rocky, which means fish are attracted to the area because they eat the seaweed and algae growing on the rocks. Just east of Lawa'i Beach and across from the Prince Kuhio monument is **PK's**. The snorkeling conditions are very similar to Lawa'i Beach, but the beach is rarely visited because it's right off the road. Down the road, **Po'ipu Beach Park** is a good option for snorkeling. There's usually something to see at either end of the beach, and the water is often calm here. The beach park is heavily used, so be prepared to rub shoulders with other snorkelers.

SNORKELING AND DIVING GEAR RENTALS

You can rent or buy snorkel gear at **Nukumoi Beach & Surf Shop** (2080 Ho'one Rd., 808/742-8019, www.nukumoisurf.com,

Po'ipu Beach

8am-6:30pm daily). It rents all kinds of beach gear, including complete snorkel sets for about $6 per day and $20 per week. At **Snorkel Bob's** (3236 Po'ipu Rd., 808/742-2206, www.snorkelbob.com, 8am-5pm daily) you'll find a wide variety of gear for rent. It offers complete sets including a mask, snorkel, and net gear bag with grade A surgical-quality silicone for ultimate comfort and water seal. The adult package goes for $35 per week or $22 per week for children 12 and under. The budget crunch package offers a basic mask, snorkel, fins, and dive bag for $9 per week. A unique rental package is what is called The 4 Eyes RX Ensemble, to compensate for nearsightedness while snorkeling. This includes a mask with a prescription lens for $44 per week for adults and $32 for kids.

Fathom Five (3450 Po'ipu Rd., 808/742-6991, www.fathomfive.com, 7am-6pm daily) offers everything you could need for casual snorkeling to professional diving. It rents complete snorkel sets for $6 daily. For diving, the company has over 26 boat dive locations and a few shore dives. A complete list of its dives is featured on its website, with exceptional detail about each dive. If you need to rent dive equipment, shore dives start at $102, and two-tank boat dives start at $150. The boats leave from Kukui'ula Small Boat Harbor. **Boss Frog's** (5022 Lawa'i Rd., 808/742-9111, www.bossfrog.com, 8am-5pm daily) has rental snorkel gear for $8 per day or $30 per week. It's at Lawa'i Beach in the same building as the Beach House Restaurant.

SURFING AND STAND-UP PADDLING
★ Po'ipu
BEACHES

The break at **Po'ipu Beach,** also known as Waiohai, is a great wave for beginners and intermediate surfers. It breaks best when it's head high or smaller and breaks right and left. The lefts break into a very shallow section of the reef on the inside that is a favorite for bodyboarders. It can get crowded with locals and visitors staying in the surrounding hotels. For a local spot with both left- and right-hand breaking waves, paddle out to **PK's** in front of Lawa'i Beach. The waves here mostly break left, but the section directly in front of the restaurant breaks as a right sometimes. Paddle out from the beach, but keep an eye out for sections of shallow reef. The wave is a local favorite, so be mellow and respectful. During the right swell, a powerful and intense right-hand breaking

checking the surf at PK's

Top Kid-Friendly Activities on the South Shore

Although just about every site and activity on the south shore is fit for kids, there are a few high-lights for them, especially outdoor activities.

- The south shore is filled with beaches galore, but take the kids to **Po'ipu Beach Park.** There isn't a more perfect beach for kids than this, with its protected, shallow area for swimming, a playground, showers, and a grassy park.

- At **Spouting Horn** kids love watching the ocean water blast through a hole in the lava rock. There are also picnic tables on a well-manicured lawn and plenty of chickens to chase.

- **Surf lessons at Po'ipu Beach** will make any Kaua'i trip complete. Kids will love a chance to try to catch some waves.

- There is a really nice **playground** on Omao Road. Swings, slides, a small rock-climbing wall, a large field, a picnic table, and more make for a nice break from the car. Heading up from the bottom of the road, the playground is around three-quarters of the way up on your right.

- Kids love pizza, and **Brick Oven Pizza** in Kalaheo is a great place for lunch or dinner. Stop by on Monday and Thursday nights for an all-you-can-eat buffet.

wave called **Acid Drops** is to the west of PK's. This wave is heavy, but a coveted wave for experienced surfers.

SURF LESSONS AND GEAR

Po'ipu is a hot spot for surfing, and a Hawaiian vacation wouldn't be complete without at least trying to catch a few waves. If you haven't surfed before, a lesson is the way to go. The instructor will teach you the basics of the sport and current ocean conditions. Several surf schools offer lessons at Po'ipu Beach. Experienced surfers can simply rent a board and hit the surf.

The **Garden Island Surf School** (808/652-4841, www.gardenislandsurfschool.com) offers group lessons at Po'ipu Beach for $75 and private lessons for $150, or $120 for two students. All lessons are two hours in duration at 8am, 10am, noon, and 2pm and require reservations. For something different try outrigger canoe surfing, where you'll catch waves in a canoe. It also gives stand-up paddle lessons; 90-minute classes are $70. You'll find the Garden Island kiosk at the Ko'a Kea Hotel & Resort poolside kiosk. The entrance to the resort is off Po'ipu Road.

To rent a board, contact **Poipu Surf** (2829

Ala Kalanikaumaka Rd., Ste. H-151, 808/742-8797, 9am-9pm daily). Located in The Shops at Kukui'ula, it rents high-performance surf-boards for $25 per day or $110 per week and bodyboards for $8 per day with fins or $25 per week. **Nukumoi Beach & Surf Shop** (2080 Ho'one Rd., 808/742-8019, www.nuku-moisurf.com, 8am-6:30pm daily) rents soft longboards for $25 per day and $75 per week, epoxy shortboards for $30 per day and $90 per week, and stand-up paddleboards starting at $60 per day and $250 per week. It charges $6 for soft surfboard racks for the duration of your rental.

KAYAKING
Po'ipu

You can kayak the south shore's coastline with **Outfitters Kauai** (2827A Po'ipu Rd., 808/724-9667, www.outfitterskauai.com) on its kayaking and whale-watching secluded beach adventure, which is available Tuesday-Saturday from mid-September through May. Outfitters uses tandem, open cockpit, or sit-on-top-type self-bailing kayaks with foot-pedal-controlled rudders to explore the coast. You'll paddle to secret beaches and snorkel and bodysurf at beaches that are only accessible by water. Because the tours are done in the wintertime, whale sightings are common, as well as dolphin and sea turtle sightings. Price for adults is $165 and children 12-14 are $133.

Adventure Sports and Tours

ATVS
Koloa
Ride ATVs with **Kaua'i ATV** (3477-A Weliweli Rd., 866/482-9775, www.kauaiatv.com, 7:30am-5pm daily, $113-170). It has a large collection of vehicles and can take family groups or individuals. It offers two tours: the Waterfall Tour, a four-hour, 23-mile adventure that includes a stop at a waterfall with a pool and lunch, and the Koloa Tour, a three-hour tour on 22,000 acres of private land with mountain and ocean views. It hase clothing to loan, so you don't have to get yours dirty. It also offers 'ohana (family) buggies to ride with your group. Reservations are required.

ZIPLINING
Lawa'i
Adrenaline junkies can fly through the air with **Just Live** (3416 Rice St., 808/482-1295, ziplinetourskauai.com, 7am-5pm daily). The adventure sports company offers three different zipline ecotours as well as a ropes course. The Zipline Treetop Tour covers seven different zipline courses and lets you walk over four canopy bridges for $120. The ziplines run up to 800 feet long and are suspended 60-80 feet in the air. The Wikiwiki Zip Tour utilizes three different ziplines, two of which are over 700 feet long, and three bridge crossings for $79. The Zipline Eco Adventure combines three ziplines, three bridges, rappelling, a monster swing, and rock-wall climbing for $125. Tours include a snack and water.

BOAT TOURS
Po'ipu
Several boat tour companies cruise Po'ipu waters. They also offer **whale-watching** from December through April. **Captain Andy's**

Sailing Adventures (4353 Waialo Rd., 808/335-6833, www.napali.com) offers various boat cruises, and each one includes whale-watching in season. During the winter months, combine whale-watching with the two-hour Po'ipu Sunset Sail, which takes you down to the secluded Maha'ulepu Beaches and Kipu Kai. Adults cost $69, children $49, and kids under two are free. The sail includes live Hawaiian music, appetizers, beer, and wine. In season, whales and dolphins are a common sight.

Blue Dolphin Charters (4354 Waialo Rd., 808/335-5553, www.kauaiboats.com) offers a two-hour South Side Sunset Sail in the Po'ipu area. Food, cocktails, and romantic sunsets are enjoyed on this tour, along with whales in season. This company prefers December through March as whale season, and rates run $75 for adults 18 and up, $75 for youth 12-17, and $55 for children 2-11 (check the website for discounts).

GUIDED HIKING TOURS
Koloa
Kaua'i Nature Tours (808/742-8305, 888/233-8365, www.kauainaturetours.com) offers guided hikes in the Maha'ulepu area on the east end of the south side. It also offers hikes in other parts of the island. The guides, authors of *Kaua'i's Geologic History,* share insight into the island's geological formation and history. On this hike you'll see wildlife and enter a sinkhole where fossil-filled sediment speaks to the island's history. The 2.5-mile coastal walk begins after a 9am pickup at Po'ipu Beach Park. The company provides lunch after a four-hour walk to a private beach cove, and snorkeling and swimming in Kawailoa Bay. The rate is $135 for adults and $100 for children 5-12.

Shopping

Shopping on the south side is contained to several areas where shops are clustered together. The area is filled with many boutiques, galleries, souvenir shops, and clothing stores. Most daily shopping needs are found in nearby Lihu'e.

KOLOA

Clothing

For a unique array of clothing, check out **Jungle Girl** (5424 Koloa Rd., 808/742-9649, 9am-9pm daily). It also has a collection of accessories and housewares. There are some locally made items as well as creations from around the world. If you're looking for aloha wear, drop into **Pohaku Ts** (3430 Po'ipu Rd., 808/742-7500, www.pohaku.com, 10am-6pm Mon.-Sat., 10am-5pm Sun.). It offers cotton aloha shirts that are designed, cut, and sewn on Kaua'i for men, women, and children. Bikinis galore decorate the inside of **South Shore Bikinis** (3450 Po'ipu Rd., 808/742-5200, 9am-7pm daily), which specializes in the tiny-backed Brazilian bikini. It also carries a variety of other suits along with beachwear for all ages, hats, sandals, and other accessories. A huge spectrum of Kaua'i and Hawaii souvenir shirts can be found in **Crazy Shirts** (5356 Koloa Rd., 808/742-7161, www.crazyshirts.com, 10am-9pm). A chain found throughout the islands, it sells shirts and a few other items for men, women, and children with a heavy Kaua'i and Hawai'i theme.

Gifts, Crafts, and Souvenirs

Island-style souvenirs and gifts can be found at **Hula Moon Gifts** (5426 Koloa Rd., 808/742-9298, 9am-9pm Mon.-Sat., 10am-9pm Sun.). It sells unique locally made crafts, gifts, and jewelry. At the **Emperor's Emporium** (5330 Koloa Rd. #3, 808/742-8377, 9am-9pm daily) you will find a resort-style store offering jewelry, gifts, and clothing. The fragrant scents emanating from **Island Soap and Candle Works** (Koloa Rd., 808/742-1945, www.kauaisoap.com, 9am-9pm daily) will draw you in. The locally run store has shops island-wide where it manufactures natural Hawaiian botanical products, beeswax candles, and other gifts. While shopping you'll get a behind-the-scenes look into how it's all made.

Wine

The lovely **Wine Shop** (5470 Koloa Rd., 808/742-7305, www.thewineshopkauai.com, 10am-7pm Mon.-Sat.) in Koloa offers a great selection of wine along with other spirits. Fun and cute wine accessories, gift baskets, and gourmet foods are also available.

PO'IPU

Most of Po'ipu's recommended shops are located within **The Shops at Kukui'ula** (2829 Ala Kalanikaumaka St., 808/742-9545, www.theshopsatkukuiula.com, 10am-9pm daily), the south shore's premier high-end outdoor mall, home to award-winning restaurants, boutiques, and contemporary art galleries.

Galleries

Admire the work of local crafters and artists at **Halele'a Gallery** (The Shops at Kukui'ula, Ste. K, 808/742-9525, www.haleleagallery.com, 10am-9pm daily), a chic boutique gallery. Island artisans and designers showcase their creations, like wall art, jewelry, photography, koa furniture, and apparel. A wonderful source for locally made products is **Palm Palm** (The Shops at Kukui'ula, Ste. H157, 808/742-1131, www.palmpalmkauai.com, 10am-9pm daily). It's well stocked with fashionable clothing, bath products, high-end jewelry, and quality accessories. The owner has been in the jewelry industry for a decade and brings style to the shop.

Clothing, Accessories, and Swimwear

Also found at The Shops at Kukui'ula are a handful of clothing boutiques ranging from surfwear and resortwear to unique island-style apparel. For high-quality aloha wear, stop at **Tommy Bahama** (The Shops at Kukui'ula, Ste. A107, 808/742-8808, www.tommybahama.com, 10am-9pm daily). The store offers high-end casual island wear for men and women.

Hopefully you brought sunglasses to Kaua'i, because you'll need them. If not, there's the **Sunglass Hut** (The Shops at Kukui'ula, Ste. E129, 808/742-9065, www.sunglasshut.com, 10am-9pm daily), which offers a huge selection of sunglasses for men and women. **Quiksilver** (The Shops at Kukui'ula, Ste. F131, 808/742-8088, 10am-9pm daily) has a great selection of men's, women's, and children's surf-themed clothing for in and out of the water. Accessories like sunglasses, hats, and sandals also are available.

Arts, Crafts, and Jewelry

At the intriguing **Red Koi Collection** (The Shops at Kukui'ula, Ste. G143, 808/742-2778, www.redkoicollection.com, 10am-9pm daily) you'll find fine arts, from hand-painted silks to original paintings, to koa furniture and jewelry. The high-end products make it feel like a hip and modern island museum combined with the home decor of a wealthy world traveler. Expect high prices. Amazing Kaua'i outdoor photography decorates **Scott Hanft Photography** (The Shops at Kukui'ula, Ste. H155, 808/742-9515, www.scotthanftoutdoorphotogallery.com, 10am-9pm daily), showcasing wonderful air, underwater, nature, and landmark shots from around the island. Originals and prints are available, along with magnets, cards, jewelry, and more.

Local island jewelry can be found at **Ocean Opulent Jewelry** (The Shops at Kukui'ula, Ste. G141, 808/742-9992, www.oceanpoipu.com, 10am-9pm daily). Look for freshwater pearls and island-themed jewelry among the gold, silver, and platinum.

Bath and Beauty

Malie Organics (The Shops at Kukui'ula, Ste. F133, 808/332-6220, www.malie.com, 10am-9pm daily) is a locally owned line of organic and all-natural Hawaiian luxury spa products. The company captures the glorious, decadent scents from the islands with its skin care line, hand soaps, and other pampering products, made from organically grown ingredients.

LAWA'I

General Store

The small **Lawai General Store** (3586 Koloa Rd., 808/332-7501, 6am-11pm daily) sells snacks, beer, ice, and some general store needs. The shop is tiny and local, and much of the stock is covered in dust. Lawai is known for its Spam *musubi*.

KALAHEO

Music

In Kalaheo, **Scotty's Music** (2-2436 Kaumuali'i Hwy. #A3, 808/332-0090, 11am-4pm Mon.-Sat.) offers an array of instruments, guitars, and ukuleles. Ukuleles are a great take-home souvenir for music lovers.

Entertainment

PO'IPU

Lu'au

If you're in the mood for dinner and a show, Hawaiian style, check out the **Grand Hyatt Kaua'i Lu'au** (1571 Po'ipu Rd., 808/240-6456, www.grandhyattkauailuau.com, 5:15pm-8pm Thurs. and Sun.). Guests are treated to cocktails, music, and a lu'au dinner with traditional foods from Hawaii and the Pacific, along with arts and crafts and bar drinks. This includes a Polynesian dancing show, hula, and fire knife dancing.

Bars and Live Music

The **Grand Hyatt Kaua'i** (1571 Po'ipu Rd., 808/742-1234, www.grandhyattkauailuau, com) is also home to several lounges and bars, including **Stevenson's Sushi & Spirits** (808/240-6456, 5:30pm-midnight daily), which features sushi and live jazz nightly 8:30pm-11pm. Minors are permitted 6pm-9pm. There is also live music at the **Seaview Terrace** (808/240-6456, 4:30pm-10pm daily). The evening begins with a torch-lighting

ceremony, and performances may include a Hawaiian soloist, Hawaiian duet, or a children's hula show.

Surrounded by flaming tiki torches and the Moir Gardens of the Outrigger Kiahuna Plantation Resort, the **Plantation Gardens Bar and Restaurant** (2253 Po'ipu Rd., 808/742-2121, www.pgrestaurant.com, 5:30pm-9:30pm daily) mixes classic elegance with tropical nights. The restaurant and full bar feature a unique and delicious Pacific Rim menu with a Hawaiian flair. You can sit outside on the lanai and enjoy specialty cocktails, tropical drinks, wine, and beer.

KALAHEO

Live Music

Kalaheo is quiet at night, but **Kalaheo Steak and Ribs** (4444 Papalina Rd., 808/332-4444, www.kalaheosteakandribs.com, 5pm-9:30pm Tues.-Sun.) has live music every Thursday and Sunday at 7pm and karaoke on Friday and Saturday nights at 7pm. Happy hour is 4pm-7pm.

Food

KOLOA

Italian

If you're in the mood for really good pizza, head over to ★ **Pizzetta** (5408 Koloa Rd., 808/742-8881, www.pizzettarestaurant.com, 11am-9pm Mon.-Fri., 11am-10pm Sat.-Sun., $12-25) for great pizza and other wonderful Italian dishes, such as calzones and chicken parmigiana. Nestled in a historic clapboard Koloa building, the restaurant is central in Koloa town and the atmosphere is laid-back. In honor of Kaua'i's wild chickens, Pizzetta offers Rooster Brew, a custom beer brewed specifically for the eatery. Pizzetta uses homemade sauces. Try the spinach artichoke dip.

Seafood and Local Cuisine

Koloa Fish Market (5482 Koloa Rd., 808/742-6199, 10am-6pm Mon.-Fri., 10am-5pm Sat., $8-11) offers fish, of course, along with plate lunches and other local dishes like *laulau, poke,* cucumber salad, and sashimi. The selection is limited, but it's really popular with locals. The market is takeout only, great for a snack on the beach.

Local-style **Sueoka's Snack Shop** (5392 Koloa Rd., 808/742-1112, 9am-8pm Tues.-Sat., 9am-4pm Sun., $5-10) is a quick stop to pick up local food. It serves teriyaki burgers, curries, chili, and plate lunches. It also has sliced-up fruit available in the same style as small

New York City delis. Drinks, chips, and the usual convenience store snacks are also available. This is another affordable option for a beach lunch.

Ice Cream and Shave Ice

For a treat, try **Koloa Shave Ice** (Poʻipu Rd., 808/651-7104, 10am-6pm daily). Located in the Old Koloa Town shops, it serves up a very finely shaved cone, which is the make-or-break aspect with shave ice.

Koloa Mill Ice Cream and Coffee (5424 Koloa Rd., 808/742-6544, www.koloamill.com, 7am-9pm daily, $4 for a single scoop) serves up items to satisfy the sweet tooth and provide a caffeine fix. It prides itself on serving only Hawaiian-made foods, such as Kauaʻi coffee, ice cream made on Maui, and locally made baked goods and snacks. The ice-cream shop atmosphere is classic and offers free wireless Internet.

POʻIPU
Steak and Seafood

A beautiful, tropical atmosphere and great food are found at ★ **Keoki's Paradise** (2360 Kiahuna Plantation Dr., 808/742-7534, www.keokisparadise.com, 11am-10:30pm daily, $22-35), where ponds, a small waterfall,

greenery, and a large beautiful tree create a very relaxing vibe. You'll find a mix of visitors and locals enjoying a drink at the bar. Service is friendly, and the Pacific cuisine menu features several dishes with locally sourced ingredients. Steak and seafood are the specialties. Keoki's is in the Poipu Shopping Village with covered, open-air seating.

Overlooking the ocean is the ★ **Beach House Restaurant** (5022 Lawaʻi Rd., 808/742-1424, www.the-beach-house.com, 5pm-10pm daily, $26-48). The open-air restaurant has a prime oceanfront location on Lawaʻi Beach with a front lawn dotted with tiki torches—the perfect spot for watching the sunset. Open for dinner, the Beach House serves seafood, steaks, and even a roasted duck dish. It can get pretty crowded, so reservations are a very good idea. It also has a great wine list.

The Dolphin Poipu (The Shops at Kukuiʻula, Ste. A100, 808/742-1414, www.hanaleidolphin.com, 11:30am-3:30pm and 5:30pm-9:30pm daily, $20-35) serves exotic sushi, local fish, and steak entrées. The fish market sells fresh fish, choice-cut steaks, and premade sushi rolls and is open 10am-7pm daily—perfect for a meal back at the condo.

the view from Beach House Restaurant

Hawaii Regional

Two farm-to-table sister restaurants by Chef Peter Merriman are **Merriman's Gourmet Pizza & Burgers** (The Shops at Kukui'ula, Ste. G147/149, 808/742-8385, www.merrimanshawaii.com, 11am-10pm daily, $13-18), which is downstairs, and ★ **Merriman's Fish House** (808/742-8385, 5:30pm-9pm daily, $15-59), located upstairs. Delicious fare and sustainability are combined to produce high-quality, Hawaii regional cuisine. Both eateries utilize locally grown or caught ingredients, constituting 90 percent of the food they use. The downstairs café offers casual dining, while the upstairs fish house offers mountain and ocean views with a full bar.

Consistency is key at ★ **Eating House 1849** (The Shops at Kukui'ula, Ste. A201, 808/742-5000, www.eatinghouse1849.com, 5pm-9:30pm daily, $13-38), where Chef Roy Yamaguchi offers his dynamic and modern version of plantation cuisine inspired by the region's past. The menu changes nightly, depending on the fresh local fish, produce, meats, and game that are available that day. The menu is small and the service is excellent. Reservations can be made by phone or online.

Italian

At the elegant ★ **Dondero's** (1571 Po'ipu Rd., 808/240-6456, 6pm-10pm Mon.-Sat., $15-44) in the Grand Hyatt Kauai, you will be treated to a wonderful meal with a romantic and high-end atmosphere. You can sit outdoors under the stars, overlooking the ocean, or enjoy your meal inside with Italian decor of murals and tiles. A robust wine list complements Dondero's fresh local fish, veal, pastas, and decadent desserts. Resort casual wear is required.

Shave Ice

For a local treat, head to ★ **Uncle's Shave Ice and Smoothies** (The Shops at Kukui'ula, Ste. K158B, 808/742-2364, www.uncleskauai.com, 11am-9pm daily, $4-8). It offers 25 shave ice flavors with extras like cream caps, fruit, and ice cream. It also sells other snacks like caramel-apple bites and popcorn. Sugar-free syrups sweetened naturally with stevia are a progressive option here.

Quick Bites

The south shore's **Savage Shrimp** (The Shops at Kukui'ula, Ste. K158A, 808/742-9611, 11am-9pm daily, $12) serves up shrimp plates, fish tacos, shrimp tacos, fish and chips, and

Merriman's sister restaurants at The Shops at Kukui'ula

fried shrimp. A favorite with beach-going locals, it used to be in a lunch wagon and now has a permanent home.

The popular Kaua'i eatery **Bubba Burgers** (The Shops at Kukui'ula, Ste. L163, 808/742-6900, www.bubbaburger.com, 10:30am-9pm daily, $4-8) is family owned and operated and serves Kaua'i grass-fed beef, chicken, fish, and vegan burgers. The burgers are priced by weight. It also has the usual burger joint sides like shakes, fries, and soda.

Living Foods Market and Café (The Shops at Kukui'ula, Ste. D124, 808/742-2323, www.livingfoodskauai.com, 7am-9pm daily) offers local and organic prepared foods, salads, smoothies, produce, and groceries. It also has homemade breads and dips, made-to-order pizzas, sandwiches, and more. The shop is spacious and elegant, but it's rather expensive. It has a good array of wines and liquors. Outside tables are provided, or you can take away for a picnic at the beach or dinner back at the condo. The café closes at 8pm.

KALAHEO
American
The always-good ★ **Kalaheo Café** (2-2560 Kaumuali'i Hwy., 808/332-5858, www.kalaheo.com, 6:30am-2:30pm Mon.-Sat., 6:30am-2pm Sun., dinner at 5pm Tues.-Sat., $2-13) is the south side's answer to the cute, local, friendly café where you can relax reading the paper or have Sunday brunch with 10 friends. Order at the counter and then choose a table,

but there's no rush to get out of the spacious hardwood-floored café, which is adorned with local art and music. Coffee is served with eggs, breakfast burritos, waffles, pastries, and sides. Salads and off-the-grill specialty sandwiches are available for lunch, along with bottled beer. Vegetarians can find a decent array of meat-free options.

The name says it all at **Kalaheo Steaks and Ribs** (4444 Papalina Rd., 808/332-4444, www.kalaheosteakandribs.com, Tues.-Sun. 4pm-10pm, dinner 5pm-9:30pm, $16-33). For three decades the restaurant has been serving ribs, steaks, fresh fish, pastas, appetizers, and salads. A full bar, the Saloon, adds to the fun. The atmosphere also fits the name with a knotty pine interior with the usual steakhouse theme. At the Saloon, happy hour is held 4pm-7pm daily with a selection of appetizers.

Italian
A local favorite is ★ **Brick Oven Pizza** (2-2555 Kaumuali'i Hwy., 808/332-8561, http://brickovenpizzahi.com, 11am-9pm daily, $10-33). It's great for family night or a casual date. Also very kid-friendly, it gives kids free dough to play with during dinner. It offers a selection of pizza, beer, and wine, and you can get your crust in white or wheat dough as well as basted with garlic butter. The decor has a country feel, and the walls are covered in license plates from around the country that almost all say something Hawaii-related on them. All-you-can-eat buffet nights are 5pm-9pm Monday and Thursday.

Waimea and the West Side

Look for ★ to find recommended
sights, activities, dining, and lodging.

Highlights

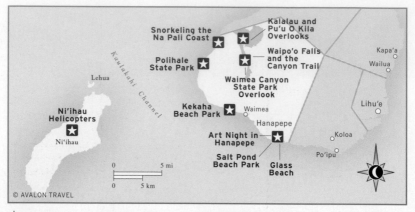

★ **Waimea Canyon State Park Overlook:** The views from this overlook into the vast and deep-red Waimea Canyon are not to be missed. Make sure to take Waimea Canyon Drive inland, because the sights from there are just as valuable (page 643).

★ **Kalalau and Pu'u O Kila Overlooks:** Feast your eyes on dramatic and pristine vertical mountain cliffs reaching down to the sea from two overlooks in Koke'e State Park. They are regarded as the best views in the Pacific (page 643).

★ **Glass Beach:** This unique beach has a colorful, sparkling layer of beach glass atop dark sand (page 645).

★ **Salt Pond Beach Park:** The family-friendly beach is an ideal place for children to swim and frolic in the protected swimming area, an oversized sand-bottom tide pool. A large lawn, lifeguards, and restrooms make it perfect for a picnic (page 645).

★ **Kekaha Beach Park:** Marking the beginning of 15 miles of white sand, Kekaha Beach Park offers all the amenities for a full day at the beach:

pavilions, picnic tables, a barbecue pit, and a lifeguard (page 646).

★ **Polihale State Park:** This is the epitome of tropical Hawaii paradise, with endless fine white sand and bright-blue water framed by sacred cliffs. The western-most end of the main Hawaiian Island chain, Polihale State Park has the best sunset-viewing in the entire state (page 647).

★ **Snorkeling the Na Pali Coast:** Hop on a boat with Captain Andy's Sailing Adventures or any of the other outfitters in Port Allen for an unforgettable snorkeling trip (page 648).

★ **Waipo'o Falls and the Canyon Trail:** Hikers who endure the trek to Waipo'o Falls are rewarded with an 800-foot double waterfall (page 651).

★ **Ni'ihau Helicopter:** Virtually the only way to explore Ni'ihau's beaches is on a tour with Ni'ihau Helicopters. The company offers beach-combing and snorkeling tours (page 655).

★ **Art Night in Hanapepe:** Check out the local art scene as a plethora of galleries open their doors 6pm-9pm every Friday (page 658).

Locally known as the west side, Kaua'i's leeward coast is a world unto itself.

Miles of white-sand beaches wrap the island to the north where the vertical cliffs of the Na Pali Coast strike down to meet the ocean, and dramatic canyons cut deep into the island's interior. Small towns seem frozen in the plantation era, and red dirt covers everything. The west side is as local as it gets. From the artists in Hanapepe who relocated to the area to paint Kaua'i's beauty to the west-side born-and-raised Hawaiians in Waimea, the people are warm and friendly.

Hanapepe town and Port Allen welcome visitors to the west side. Hanapepe, which means "crushed bay," originally thrived as a hub for taro cultivation and later evolved into a rice-farming community, then became a bustling town from the early 1900s until just after World War II. At one point the town was an economic center and, shockingly, one of the biggest towns on the island. In the 1940s, thousands of GIs were trained here before being sent away for duty. Today, the riverside town offers country charm and artisan creations that can be experienced via a stroll or walking tour of the historic buildings, over 40 of which are listed in the National Register of Historic Places. In historic Old Hanapepe, art galleries have a monopoly on the main strip.

Waimea town, to the west of Hanapepe, has a story all its own—a moment in time that changed the course of Hawaii's history. Captain James Cook first set foot in Hawaii on the beach in Waimea on January 20, 1778, and is remembered by two monuments in the small town. Once home to the last great king of Kaua'i, Kaumuali'i, Waimea was for many years a bustling town and port until the Nawiliwili and Port Allen harbors were created and the sugar mill closed in 1969.

Waimea is also the portal to Waimea Canyon, which has been called the "Grand Canyon of the Pacific," and Koke'e State Park. Koke'e State Park is known for its amazing trails, a high-elevation swamp ecosystem found nowhere else in Hawai'i, and majestic lookouts over the Na Pali Coast. Back down on the coast, Kekaha marks the 15-mile stretch to the end of the road and the Na Pali Coast's sacred cliffs at Polihale State Park. Out here, the silence is broken only by the picturesque and dangerous waves that crash on the beach and lull campers to sleep.

Previous: Kalalau Overlook; Waimea town. **Above:** Waimea Canyon.

Waimea and the West Side

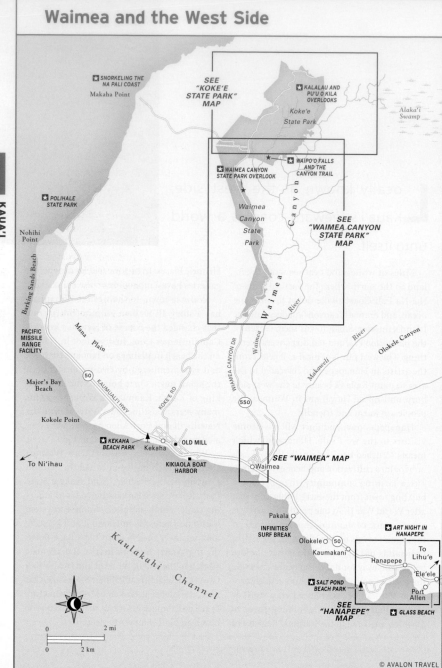

SNORKELING THE
NA PALI COAST

Makaha Point

SEE
"KOKE'E
STATE PARK"
MAP

KALALAU AND
PU'U O KILA
OVERLOOKS

Koke'e
State Park

Alaka'i
Swamp

WAIPO'O FALLS
AND THE
CANYON TRAIL

WAIMEA CANYON
STATE PARK OVERLOOK

POLIHALE
STATE PARK

Nohihi
Point

Waimea
Canyon
State
Park

SEE
"WAIMEA CANYON
STATE PARK"
MAP

Canyon

Waimea

River

Olokele Canyon

Makaweli

River

PACIFIC
MISSILE
RANGE
FACILITY

Mana Plain

Major's Bay
Beach

50

KAUMUALI'I HWY

KOKE'E RD

WAIMEA CANYON DR

Waimea

550

Kokole Point

To Ni'ihau

KEKAHA
BEACH PARK

Kekaha

OLD MILL

KIKIAOLA BOAT
HARBOR

SEE "WAIMEA" MAP

Waimea

Barking Sands Beach

Pakala

INFINITIES
SURF BREAK

Olokele

Kaumakani

50

Hanapepe

ART NIGHT IN
HANAPEPE

To
Lihu'e

'Ele'ele

SALT POND
BEACH PARK

Port
Allen

SEE
"HANAPEPE"
MAP

GLASS BEACH

Kaulakahi Channel

0   2 mi

0   2 km

© AVALON TRAVEL

ORIENTATION

The west side stretches from 'Ele'ele all the way to the Na Pali cliffs at the end of the road in Polihale State Park. It includes **Port Allen,** from where many of the sightseeing tours to the Na Pali Coast depart, **Hanapepe,** which carries the moniker "Kaua'i's Biggest Little Town," historic **Waimea** town, **Waimea Canyon** and **Koke'e State Parks, Kekaha Beach Park,** and **Polihale State Park.**

The **Kaumuali'i Highway** (Route 50) is the main thoroughfare along the coast all the way to the end of the road. Waimea Canyon is accessed by **Waimea Canyon Drive** (also known as Route 550) in Waimea town, and **Koke'e Road** in Kekaha.

PLANNING YOUR TIME

There are a few options for accommodations on the west side, but most travelers make day trips to this region. From Po'ipu it takes approximately 20 minutes to get to Waimea town and another 20-30 minutes to get to the Waimea Canyon State Park Overlook. From the north shore, it takes about 1-1.5 hours to get to Waimea town, depending on traffic in Kapa'a and Lihu'e.

Some visitors camp on the beach at Polihale State Park or in the cool forests in Waimea Canyon and Koke'e State Parks. It is a long and slow drive to both of these remote locations. Once you've arrived at your destination, whether it's a secluded beach or a canyon lookout, you'll probably be ready to have a snack and stretch your legs before getting back in the car. Be prepared with food and water at these remote locations. Serious hikers could spend their entire vacation just hiking the state park trails in this region.

If you'd like to explore the towns as well, stop in historic Waimea town or artsy Hanapepe after your day at the beach or in the mountains. Have a meal, then explore without rushing since you've already accomplished your big sightseeing goals. For those not interested in the great outdoors, a day trip of sightseeing at Waimea's historic sites and Hanapepe's art galleries, paired with a trip to the plantation at Kaua'i Coffee, will hold your attention for a full day. Those who wish to stay out of the sun, have a hard time walking in sand, or dislike eroded, washboard dirt roads should avoid Polihale altogether. The sunset may be "the best" from Polihale, but it's still amazing from anywhere along the west side's long and drawn-out coastline.

If you've booked a tour along the Na Pali Coast, most of which are at least half-day adventures, you'll need to make your way to either Port Allen or Waimea, where the tours depart from. Upon your return, check out nearby Hanapepe and make it a full day.

Sights

Sights from Hanapepe to the end of the road share two common themes: history and natural wonders. They're generally all easily accessible and very camera worthy.

HANAPEPE

Hanapepe Valley and Lookout

As you come around the bend from Kalaheo and first lay eyes on the Port Allen area, a Hawai'i Visitors Bureau sign points out an overlook pull-off for Hanapepe Valley. It offers a peek down into the valley and is easily accessible.

Hanapepe Swinging Bridge

Extended over the Hanapepe River, this wooden plank footbridge runs between the historic town and the inland side of the river. With enough bounce and shake to inspire a little excitement as well as a lovely view down the river, the **Hanapepe Swinging Bridge** is fun to take a walk on. It's easily accessible

The Best Day on the West Side

Waimea Canyon State Park Overlook

The best of the west can be experienced in one day if you start early, but be prepared to spend much of the day driving.

- Your one-day Kaua'i western adventure begins with a quick stop at **Glass Beach,** where you can take a morning dip in the tide pool before heading up to **Old Hanapepe** to browse local art, walk on the swinging bridge, and have breakfast at **Grinds Café.**

- Head farther west and inland to the **Waimea Canyon State Park Overlook.** It's a good idea to pack snacks and drinks before heading up Waimea Canyon Road (the views are much better along this route compared to Koke'e Road). Remember to keep an eye out for the waterfall at the 1,500-foot elevation sign.

- After taking in the sweeping views up the red-earth canyon, head back down to the coast or visit the **Kalalau and Pu'u O Kila Overlooks.** If it's cloudy and misty at the Waimea Canyon Overlook, chances are the weather will be the same or worse at the other overlooks. Either way, take Koke'e Road back down to the coast and turn left to Waimea town for lunch at **Island Taco,** then take a break from the heat with a **JoJo's Shave Ice.** If you're out of snacks and drinks, you'll want to restock before heading out to **Polihale State Park** for the rest of the afternoon.

- Once on the road into Polihale, you'll come to a fork in the road at the big tree about three miles in. From here you can go right to the parking area with showers and restrooms, or you can go left about a tenth of a mile to **Queen's Pond.** At Queen's Pond, swimming is generally safe and suitable for kids. Since you most likely will need a break from the car, spend the remainder of the day at the beach and watch the sun set over Ni'ihau. Maybe you'll see the elusive green flash just as the sun drops below the horizon.

RAINY-DAY ALTERNATIVE

A rainy day on the west side is the perfect opportunity to explore **Hanapepe.** Stroll along the **boardwalk,** visit the **art galleries,** and enjoy **local coffee.** No need to rush.

Hanapepe

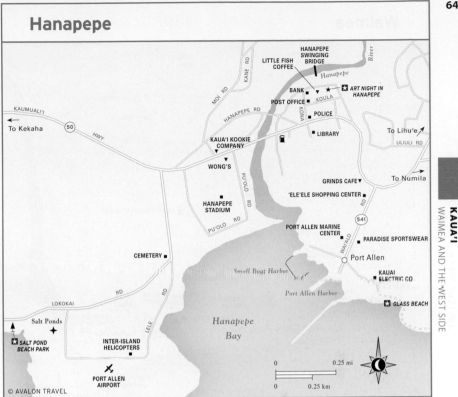

from the town and free. Once off the bridge take a left to walk the levee back to the old vehicular bridge and come back into town along Hanapepe Road. A stroll across the bridge fits in easily with any stroll through town.

Kauai Coffee Company Visitor Center and Museum

In 2011, Italian coffee giant Massimo Zanetti Beverage bought **Kaua'i Coffee Company**, which grows Hawaiian arabica coffee bean plants on its 3,400-acre drip-irrigated property and produces roughly four million pounds of coffee a year. Harvest is done mechanically and takes place September through November, which is the busiest time of year on the estate. The largest single coffee estate in Hawaii, Kaua'i Coffee has a hold on about 60 percent of the Hawaiian coffee market. If

you use Route 540, and especially if you love coffee, stop at the **Kaua'i Coffee Company Visitor Center and Museum** (1 Numila Rd., 808/335-0813 or 800/545-8605, 9am-5pm daily, free). A refurbished plantation building houses the gift shop and museum. Historical artifacts are available for viewing, and information explains how coffee is handled and processed at each stage. Gifts, clothing, food items, and, of course, coffee can be purchased and tasted.

WAIMEA
Fort Elisabeth State Historical Park

Just before the Waimea River and right past mile marker 22 is **Fort Elisabeth State Historical Park**. The shape of this Russian fort somewhat resembles an eight-pointed

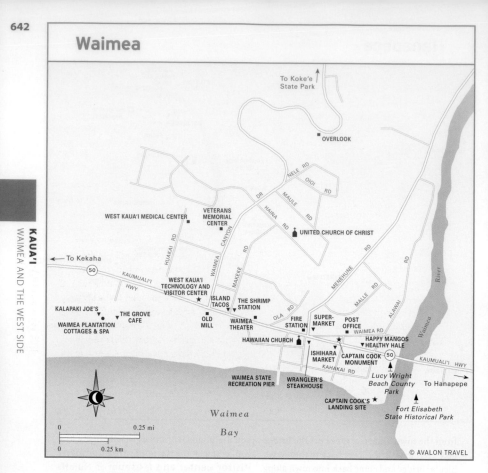

Waimea

star. It dates back to 1817, when, according to traditional history, a German doctor named Georg Anton Schaeffer constructed it in the name of Czar Nicholas of Russia and named it after the czar's daughter. University of Hawai'i at Hilo anthropologist Peter R. Mills studied the fort and drew the conclusion that the fort was originally built and used by Hawaiians as a *heiau,* a Hawaiian sacred site. He shows that after the Russians' departure, Hawaiians continued to use the fort, but in ways that reflected an ongoing transformation of cultural values as a result of contact with outsiders and the development of multiethnic communities in Waimea and other port settlements throughout the Hawaiian chain. For more information, read Mills's book *Hawai'i's Russian Adventure.*

Captain Cook Monuments

The **Captain Cook monuments** pay tribute to James Cook, the explorer who is credited with "discovering" the Hawaiian Islands (for the Western world). A life-size statue of Cook is located on the strip of grass that is Hagaard Park, between Waimea Road and Route 150. Benches are nearby if you'd like to have a seat and enjoy a snack. The other monument is a plaque attached to a boulder at Lucy Wright Beach Park.

West Kaua'i Technology and Visitor Center

At the bottom of Waimea Canyon Drive, audiovisual displays, books, and wall displays at the **West Kaua'i Technology and Visitor Center** (9565 Kaumuali'i Hwy., 808/338-1332, www.westkauaivisitorcenter.org, 10am-4pm Mon.-Fri.) offer visitors a glimpse into the history of the town and surrounding areas. There is some Ni'ihau shell jewelry on display, and other artifacts tell the story of the area's sugar past and technological present. Brochures for Waimea businesses and restaurants, books, Internet access, and printing services are also available.

★ Waimea Canyon State Park Overlook

Waimea Canyon State Park Overlook and the drive up offer a series of majestic sights of the canyon. The canyon's colors change throughout the day as the sun moves across the sky, so if you gaze into the 10-mile-long, 3,000-foot-deep canyon for any length of time, different photo opportunities usually present themselves. Make sure to take Waimea Canyon Drive rather than Koke'e Road (which the street sign in Waimea recommends). This road provides clear views of Ni'ihau, multiple valley lookouts, and a small waterfall flowing over bright red dirt at the 1,500-foot elevation sign. Each lookout holds different views of the canyon, and you will probably be able to spend some time at one by yourself. To get there, take Waimea Canyon Drive and stick to the right at the fork in the road at the Koke'e State Park sign. At the top there is a lookout with wheelchair accessibility, bathrooms, and often a snack and gift tent. On the way back down, take Koke'e Road just to see the other views. At the bottom are several gift shops and a general store.

Koke'e Natural History Museum

The **Koke'e Natural History Museum** (3600 Waimea Canyon Dr., after mile marker 15, 808/335-9975, www.kokee.org, 10am-4pm daily, suggested donation of $1) offers several displays. The museum calls the outdoors the real plant displays, but inside is an exhibit called Treasury of Trees, Resources of a Traditional Lifestyle. The exhibit is on forest trees and their traditional Hawaiian uses. It's interesting to visualize how the Hawaiians utilized their natural resources. Game animals that were introduced to the island are also on display, including a wild boar, a stag, goats, game birds, and trout. A weather exhibit focuses on devastating Hurricane 'Iniki. Perhaps the most interesting display is a collection of land and sea shells from Ni'ihau and Kaua'i. A large whale vertebrae and a sea turtle shell are quite intriguing. The museum staff can help you choose which of the 19 trails and hikes in the park are right for you, which is very helpful. Detailed hiking maps are also available.

★ Kalalau and Pu'u O Kila Overlooks

Many regard these two overlooks as the best views on Kaua'i, and even the best in the Pacific. At mile marker 18 the **Kalalau Overlook** opens to an expansive view over Kalalau Valley, the biggest valley on the Na Pali Coast. The valley was inhabited until the beginning of the 1900s.

About a mile down the road is the even better **Pu'u O Kila**, which offers a window into Kalalau Valley, from the Alaka'i Swamp to Mount Wai'ale'ale. If you get there on a cloudy day, there's a chance the views won't be visible at all. Earlier in the day is better, or if scheduling allows, check the weather and go when it looks best. To get here, go past the Koke'e Lodge and onto a road that turns into potholes and broken-up pavement.

Waimea Canyon State Park

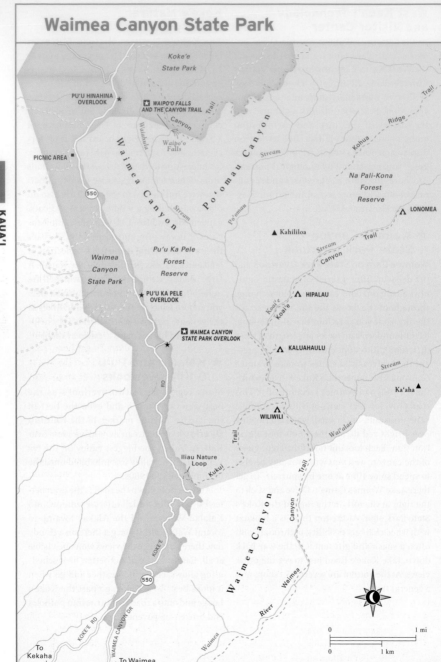

Koke'e
State Park

PU'U HINAHINA
OVERLOOK ★

⊞ WAIPO'O FALLS
AND THE CANYON TRAIL

Waipo'o
Falls

PICNIC AREA ■

Waialae

Waimea Canyon

Canyon

Po'omau Canyon

Kohua Ridge Trail

Trail

Po'omau Stream

Na Pali-Kona
Forest
Reserve

550

Stream

▲ LONOMEA

▲ Kahililoa

Stream

Trail

Canyon

Waimea
Canyon
State Park

Pu'u Ka Pele
Forest
Reserve

★ PU'U KA PELE
OVERLOOK

Koai'e

Koai'e

▲ HIPALAU

⊞ WAIMEA CANYON
STATE PARK OVERLOOK

▲ KALUAHAULU

Stream

Ka'aha ▲

RD

▲
WILIWILI

Trail

Wai'alae

Iliau Nature
Loop

Kukui

Canyon Trail

Waimea Canyon

Waimea River

KOKE'E

550

KOKE'E RD

WAIMEA CANYON DR

Waimea

0   1 mi

0   1 km

To
Kekaha

To Waimea

© AVALON TRAVEL

Beaches

Kaua'i's west coast is the driest side of the island, which makes its bountiful **beaches** all the more inviting. They range from sufficient to spectacular, narrow to wide, black to white, remote to popular, and, depending on Mother Nature's mood, swimmable to unsafe. The Pacific is easily accessible from many areas along the coastline. Peruse all the beaches on offer and find your own nook to enjoy this often overlooked side of the island. Just like at any beach, do not leave valuables in your car. You'll be on your own most of the time, so stay out of the water if the waves are big or if you're unsure about the ocean conditions. If in doubt, don't go out.

HANAPEPE
★ Glass Beach

The saying "one person's trash is another's treasure" describes **Glass Beach** to a T. On this small, black- and gray-sand beach, colored beach glass blankets the sand, making a colorful landscape that sparkles in the right light. The amount of glass varies with the tide and ocean conditions, but there's usually a good amount. Located near a former dumpsite and right in front of large gas tanks in an industrial area, the small beach is easily accessible. The water is not necessarily inviting; it's darker than at other beaches because of the underlying reef, but you can still enjoy a dip in the natural tide pool almost directly in front of the beach access. At high tide, small waves rush into the pool, but at low tide it provides safer swimming than the rest of the beach. It's not uncommon for monk seals to frequent the beach. To get here, head west on Route 50 from Po'ipu and turn left onto Waialo Road toward Port Allen. Turn left onto Aka Ulu then right at the fork in the dirt road and you will see the beach.

★ Salt Pond Beach Park

Salt Pond Beach Park offers the best of Hawaii's beaches: white sand, black rocks, tide pools, a protected swimming area, and a large lawn. This beach is popular with visitors and locals, so it can be crowded. It has restrooms, showers, and lifeguards. A lunch wagon even stops by on a regular basis. It's easily accessible and convenient if you don't have time to venture out farther west. It's also great for children and swimmers who prefer calm and safe ocean conditions.

Its name comes from the nearby salt ponds, where locals harvest salt (*pa'akai*, in Hawaiian, translating to "firm sea from evaporative basins scraped out of the earth"). Utilized for generations, the basins are lined with black clay, and after drying they're filled with seawater. When the seawater evaporates, salt is left behind and harvested. The salt is spoken for, so please don't take any if you see it. The rock salt with a reddish tint from the red dirt is called *alae*. To get here from Route 50, turn onto Route 543 at the street sign pointing toward the ocean, then go right on Lele Road.

Pakala's

A three-minute walk through brush and trees takes you to **Pakala's**. The river-mouth beach is roughly 500 yards long and is composed of compact dark sand. It's remote and quiet, although not as picturesque as other west-side beaches. Its length makes it a great place for a morning stroll, and the compact sand is perfect for a jog or a few yoga poses. The beach is a favorite for surfers who surf the long left-hand point break along the reef. The small rock pier to the left is a good place to enjoy the morning sun and watch surfers catch waves. The water here is murky because of the sand flowing in from the river. To get here, park on the side of the road just after mile marker 21. There is a trail by the guardrail and fence.

WAIMEA

The **Waimea** district lies along a black-sand beach. It is long, narrow, and made of fine black sand mixed with river sediment and green olivine. Rivers are common in this area and during heavy rain cause the surrounding ocean to become murky with the red dirt, resulting in less-than-perfect swimming conditions. The beaches are still worth checking out, and are great for a picnic or walk.

Lucy Wright Beach County Park

Named after the first native Hawaiian schoolteacher, who passed away in 1931, **Lucy Wright Beach Park** is located at the mouth of the Waimea River on the western bank and is home to Captain Cook's landing site. Consisting of a small ball field, restrooms, and a couple of picnic tables, the black-sand beach is usually covered in driftwood. It's a popular hangout for locals; a canoe club launches here. Swimming isn't recommended along this entire beach. To get here, turn left after the bridge just as you enter Waimea town. Looking west down the beach, the Waimea State Recreation Pier juts off the beach into the ocean. It's a good place for picnicking and a popular spot for pole fishing. To access the

pier, walk along the beach or down a back street behind the Waimea Library.

THE WILD WEST

This is where dreamy, seemingly endless beaches begin and stretch all the way to the Na Pali Coast. You'll encounter miles of soft sand and a multitude of opportunities for oceanside four-wheel-driving, camping, surfing, and sunbathing.

★ Kekaha Beach Park

Kekaha Beach Park marks the beginning of about 15 miles of white sand that stretches to the Na Pali Coast. Pavilions, picnic tables, portable toilets, and a barbecue pit set the stage for a complete day at the beach. Riptides are frequent and dangerous when the surf is up, but when the ocean conditions are calm, it's great for swimming. Locals hang out, fish, and surf here, and it's a good place to spend the day if you don't want to drive another 30 or 40 minutes to Polihale. This is the last beach with a lifeguard on duty, something to keep in mind when deciding where to post up for a beach day. Ni'ihau is in full view from here. Kekaha Beach Park stretches west for a few miles, but this is the last area with facilities until Polihale. The beach is at mile marker 27.

Salt Pond Beach Park

★ Polihale State Park

Imagine sitting on a long white-sand beach, a distant island in view, clear blue sky overhead, looming cliffs behind you, and waves rolling in as your soundtrack. This is **Polihale State Park**. At the very end of the beach, where the cliffs meet the ocean, are **End of the Road** and **Echoes,** popular surf breaks for only the most experienced surfers. The sand gives way to cliffs that fall into the ocean, which marks the beginning of the Na Pali Coast. The area is also home to the Polihale Heiau. This sacred spot is said to be where the souls of the dead leap off the cliffs to the land of the dead, a mythical underwater mountain a few miles off the coast. Polihale is also popular for four-wheel-driving and camping. For the adventurous who make the trek and plan to stay till dark, the reward is the most amazing sunset over the "forbidden" island of Ni'ihau.

To get to Polihale, drive until the pavement ends on Route 50 and turn left onto the dirt road at mile marker 33. It's about a 3.5-mile, or 20- to 30-minute drive to the big tree at the fork in the road. The left fork leads to **Queen's Pond,** where a fringe reef creates a protected swimming area. Look for a dirt parking lot and walk down to the beach. The right fork leads to another section of beach and facilities. Drive another 0.1 mile and near the north end of the beach you'll see a dirt parking area with covered picnic tables, restrooms, and showers. Park where the ground is firm. You can walk as far up or down the beach as you'd like. Lifesaving devices are attached to a post near the back of the beach in this area.

For those setting out for the end of the road, the final three miles of dirt road become very treacherous due to erosion and soft sand. A Four-Wheel-Drive Only sign is posted at the beginning of the road for good reason. It is not recommended to drive a two-wheel-drive vehicle past this area. For rental vehicles, driving on the dirt road will void any insurance you've signed for. Two-wheel-drive vehicles get stuck all the time. In this situation, you'll either have to wait for a local with a vehicle that can assist you or call for a tow truck, which is extremely expensive. Also, most cell phones do not get reception here. For those who are willing to take a chance and drive a two-wheel-drive vehicle on the dirt road, do not drive any faster than 5 miles per hour. If you're in doubt about the surface of the road, exit the vehicle and check for soft sand before proceeding on. For better or worse, you'll most likely be on your own at the end of the road.

Kekaha Beach Park

Water Sports

SNORKELING AND DIVING

Beach **snorkeling** on the west side isn't the best on Kaua'i, but remember that almost anywhere the sea is calm it is worth it to hop in the water with your snorkel gear. In Hawaii's lively waters there's always the chance of seeing a green sea turtle or some tropical fish. Numerous boat tour companies that leave from the west side offer guided trips along the Na Pali Coast for spectacular snorkeling. Fish, sea turtles, and reef life can be seen while snorkeling, and dolphins and whales in the winter and early spring months can be seen from the boat. Port Allen and Kikiaola Boat Harbor are the main mooring and departure points for Na Pali cruises.

Hanapepe
SALT POND BEACH PARK

West-side snorkeling is best at **Salt Pond Beach Park**. The water is almost always calm and the area is protected from open ocean waves, making it a great place for children and beginners to check out the underwater life. Snorkeling is best out by the rock wall, but it's worth it to swim all over and see what's below.

★ Na Pali Coast
BOAT TOURS FROM PORT ALLEN

Holo Holo Charters (Port Allen Marina Center, 4353 Waialo Rd., Ste. 5A, 808/335-0815 or 800/848-6130, www.holoholokauai-boattours.com) offers the only tour available to the island of Ni'ihau ($190 adults, $124 children 6-12). (This tour lets visitors explore the Ni'ihau reefs. To visit Ni'ihau itself, book a tour with Ni'ihau Helicopters.) It also offers a 3.5-hour Na Pali sunset tour ($104 adults, $84 children 5-12) as well as a five-hour Na Pali snorkel sail ($134 adults, $94 children 6-12). The company has two catamarans, one 50 feet long and another with a shaded cabin and large bar area, to get oceangoers to their destination from the Port Allen Harbor. It provides a deli-style buffet for lunch along with soft drinks, beer, and wine. The company has a reputation of treating guests well.

Catamaran Kahanu (Port Allen Marina Center, 4353 Waialo Rd., 808/645-6176 or 888/213-7711, www.catamarankahanu.com) is a Hawaiian-owned, 22-year-old tour company offering a year-round, five-hour Na Pali Coast swimming and snorkeling tour ($145 adults), a whale-watching/snorkel tour ($79), and a sunset dinner tour ($89) available December through April. On the boat guides give visitors a glimpse into Hawaiian culture with craft demonstrations such as basket, hat, and rose weavings, which guests take home as mementos. The company also offers private charters, and online rate specials are available at its website.

Kaua'i Sea Tours (Port Allen Marina Center, 4353 Waialo Rd. #2B, 808/826-1854 or 800/733-7997, www.kauaiseatours.com), operating for over 29 years, offers dinner or snorkeling power sailing catamaran tours aboard the 60-foot *Lucky Lady* and ocean raft snorkeling tours aboard rigid-hulled inflatables. The catamaran has a maximum of 49 passengers. Half-day morning snorkeling tours are $156 adults, $146 children 13-17, and $116 children 3-12; the afternoon snorkeling and dinner cruise is offered May through September for the same rate as the morning tour; and the four-hour sightseeing sunset dinner cruise is $120 adults, $110 children 13-17, and $95 children 3-12. There are four raft tours: a 5.5-hour morning or afternoon snorkel picnic tour, a four-hour sightseeing tour that will take you up to the cliffs and sea caves, and a 6.5-hour tour with a beach landing that's available April through October. The raft tours start at $115 adults, $105 children 13-17, and $75 children 7-12. Rate specials are available at the website.

To explore the outskirts of Niʻihau, try **Bubbles Below Scuba Charters** (Port Allen Marina Center, 4353 Waialo Rd., 808/332-7333 or 866/524-6268, www.bubbles-belowkauai.com) for unique three-tank diving experiences in the waters of Niʻihau and Lehua Island ($345), and two-tank dives along the Na Pali Coast and Mana Crack ($245), including a night crustacean dive and a twilight dive. Mana Crack is an 11-mile-long sunken barrier reef of finger coral and is home to the largest eel in the world. The company offer private boats and instruction as well.

BOAT TOURS FROM WAIMEA

Na Pali Explorer (9643 Kaumualiʻi Hwy., 808/338-9999 or 877/335-9909, www.napal-iexplorer.com, $105-149 with children's rates) is in Waimea right next to Island Taco and offers various tours on its rigid-hulled inflatable boats, called RHIB. These under-30-foot boats are maneuverable and get up close to the natural geography and wildlife on the Na Pali Coast. The expeditions include dolphin and whale-watching (Nov.-Mar., $69), shore landings to an ancient fishing village and sea cave explorations (Apr.-Sept., $149 adults, $129 children 8-12), and a 4.5-hour snorkeling tour (year-round, $139 adults, $119 children 5-12).

Kauaʻi native Liko Hoʻokano is the captain at **Liko Kauaʻi Cruises** (4516 Alawai Rd., 888/732-5456, www.liko-kauai.com, $140 adults, $95 children 4-12), where a five-hour Na Pali snorkeling and sights tour is available year-round. Dolphin-watching is included, and whale-watching is part of the tour during the season. A deli lunch and soft drinks are included aboard the 49-foot powered catamaran. Morning and afternoon tours depart daily.

SURFING AND STAND-UP PADDLING

Some of the most intense and powerful barreling waves can be found on the west side, especially during the winter months. West-side waves in general are suited for expert surfers due to their size, strong currents, and the lack of lifeguards. Chances are, if you are planning on surfing on the west side, you have your own board, you know where to go, and you have a few local friends to paddle out with. For the beginner or intermediate traveling surfer, your best option is to stick to the more user-friendly waves on the south shore. A good slogan to live by, whether you're surfing or swimming, is if in doubt, don't go out. If you have your heart set on getting on a board, your best bet is to stand-up paddle along the **Waimea River** where it is calm and flat. You'll need to come equipped with your own board and paddle though.

Hanapepe

Salt Pond Beach Park is a calm place for stand-up paddling. There are no rentals on the beach, so you'll need to come ready with your own board and paddle. To get here from Route 50, turn onto Route 543 at the street sign pointing toward the ocean, then go right on Lele Road.

Waimea

Infinities (between mile markers 21 and 22) is a long, left-hand-breaking wave located at Pakala's Beach. The popular surf break is almost directly in front of the small rock pier at the east end of the beach, just past the river mouth. The wave's name refers to the seemingly endless ride surfers get out here. Although Infinities isn't the most dangerous wave, only experienced surfers should venture out. It's a very localized break, and only those with thorough knowledge of surf etiquette and respect should paddle out.

FISHING

From trout to sport fishing, visitors have the option to reel in some fish in either freshwater or saltwater.

The Wild West

Na Pali Sportfishing (7923 Bulili Rd., Kekaha, 808/635-9424, www.napalisport-fishing.com, 8am-7pm daily) leaves out of the Kikiaola Boat Harbor and offers the captain's lifetime of Hawai'i fishing experience catching mahimahi, ahi, wahoo, blue marlin, and more. The fish caught on the trip become property of the captain, but he will send you home with fillets. You must bring your own lunch on this boat. Make sure to inquire about departure times because the first cruise leaves at 6am. The half-day shared rate is $135 per angler and the full-day shared rate is $220 per angler. Half-day charters are $650 and full-day charters are $1,050. The company also offers a five-hour Na Pali sightseeing cruise ($150/person).

Koke'e State Park

Rainbow trout can be found in the **Pu'u Lua Reservoir** on the west side of Koke'e. Koke'e trout season is from the first Saturday in August for 16 consecutive days, then weekends and holidays until the end of September. Call the **Division of Aquatic Resources, Department of Land and Natural Resources** (3060 Eiwa St., Lihu'e, 808/274-3344) for any questions. **Cast and Catch** (located in Koloa, 808/332-9707) provides guided freshwater fishing trips. Fishing licenses can be obtained from **Lihu'e Fishing Supply** (2985 Kalena St., Lihu'e, 808/245-4930).

Hiking and Biking

HIKING
Waimea Canyon State Park

Waimea Canyon State Park is home to vast, breathtaking canyons and decorated with numerous trails weaving through the forest from ridgeline to the canyon floor, ranging from serious hikes to short walks. Once you've gazed at the views on the drive up, take a walk or a long hike to immerse yourself in the natural splendor of the canyon.

ILIAU NATURE LOOP

A perfect family walk, the **Iliau Nature Loop** begins off Koke'e Road and also marks the beginning of the Kukui Trail. Pull all the way off the road between mile markers 8 and 9 to access the easy, 0.25-mile-long trail, which takes about 15 minutes to complete. Views of Waimea Canyon and Wai'alae Falls open up about midway along the loop. The trail is at an elevation of about 3,000 feet and is home to its namesake, the *iliau* plant. The *iliau* is a relative of the silversword, which grows high on Haleakala on Maui, and the greensword, which grows on the Big Island. This rare plant grows only on the dry mountain slopes of western Kaua'i. White-tailed tropic **birds** and the brown-and-white *pueo* (Hawaiian owl) are known to fly through the area.

KUKUI TRAIL

The **Kukui Trail** leads down into Waimea Canyon and is the trailhead for the Iliau Nature Loop as well, so begin at the same location between mile markers 8 and 9. This 2.5-mile trail takes about 60-90 minutes to complete the walk in. It is strenuous as it descends over 2,000 feet very quickly, which of course you have to climb up on the way out. Don't forget to bring plenty of water if you're planning on hiking all the way down and up. There are gorgeous views of the canyon along the way. The Wiliwili Campground marks the end of the Kukui Trail. You can set up camp for the night (permit required) and continue on other trails or head back out the same day.

KOAI'E CANYON TRAIL

From the end of the Kukui Trail, serious hikers can head up the Waimea River for about 0.5 mile and then cross the river to find the trailhead for the three-mile-long **Koai'e Canyon Trail**. This trail has about a 720-foot change in elevation. If the river water is high and rushing, do not cross it. Flash flooding is always a concern. The trailhead is near the Kaluahaulu Campground on the east side of the river. The trail leads you to the south side of Koai'e Canyon, where there are many

Waimea Canyon Trail

the hikes begin along Koke'e Drive or the dirt roads that veer off it. The trails generally fall into five categories: Na Pali Coast overlook trails, Alaka'i Swamp trails, forest trails, canyon overlook trails, and even a few **birdwatching** trails. Remember to bring good hiking shoes, lots of water, sunblock, food, and even swimwear, depending on which trail you take.

Koke'e Natural History Museum (3600 Waimea Canyon Dr., after mile marker 15, 808/335-9975, www.kokee.org, 9am-4pm daily) offers trail maps and information. A basic trail map called *Trails of Koke'e* can be picked up at **Na Pali Explorer** (9643 Kaumuali'i Hwy., 808/338-9999 or 877/335-9909, www.napaliexplorer.com) in Waimea, but much more thorough trail maps are Hawaii Nature Guide's *Koke'e Trails* map and *Northwestern Kaua'i Recreational Map* by Earthwalk Press.

freshwater pools, which have higher water levels in the winter. The canyon was once used for farming. There are two more campsites at the end of this trail. It is strongly advised to avoid this trail during rainy weather.

WAIMEA CANYON TRAIL

If you head south from the Kukui Trail, you can connect with the 11.5-mile, strenuous, and usually hot and dry **Waimea Canyon Trail**. This is a lengthy trail that parallels the Waimea River through the canyon. It can also be reached by hiking eight miles inland from Waimea town. This trail is popular with serious hikers who enjoy a challenge, but many regard the trail as lacking in sights and views. The hike is well worn and passes back and forth over the river, which usually has plenty of water. Note that river water needs to be boiled or treated before drinking.

Koke'e State Park

There are about 45 miles of trails in **Koke'e State Park** that vary in difficulty. Most of

THE CLIFF TRAIL

For an easy family trail, take a 10-minute walk on the **Cliff Trail**. Located off Halemanu Road, it's a leisurely stroll and leads to a wonderful viewpoint overlooking Waimea Canyon. From the lookout you may see some wild goats hanging out on the canyon walls. This trail also accesses the Canyon Trail.

TOP EXPERIENCE

★ WAIPO'O FALLS AND THE CANYON TRAIL

The semi-strenuous 1.8-mile Canyon Trail branches off the Cliff Trail and leads to the upper section of the 800-foot **Waipo'o Falls** before going up and along the edge of the canyon. It takes about three hours and could be done by a family, if the family is up for a bit of a challenge. Wonderful views of the canyon are offered on this popular trail, and the reward of swimming in freshwater pools makes it a choice hike. The trail goes down into a gulch and then weaves along the cliff to the Koke'e Stream and the falls. It follows the eastern rim of the canyon. Parking

Koke'e State Park

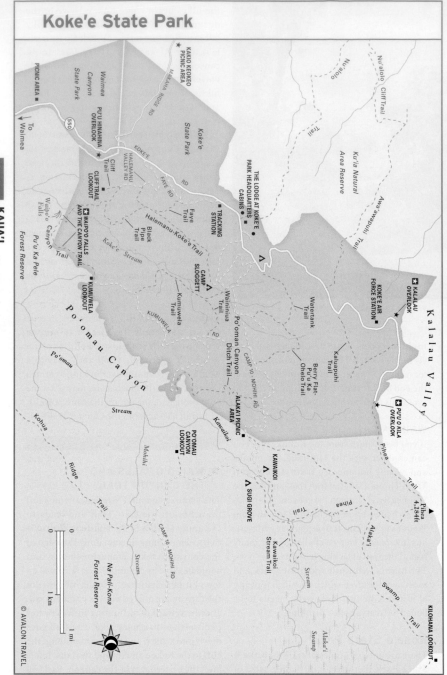

© AVALON TRAVEL

is at the Puʻu Hinahina Lookout between mile markers 13 and 14. The trailhead is at the back of the parking lot. The trail ends at the Kumuwela Lookout, where you can head back on the **Canyon Trail** or walk back on Kumuwela Road.

NATURE TRAIL

A good trail for children is the 0.1-mile **Nature Trail**. Starting behind the Kokeʻe Natural History Museum, it parallels the meadow. It's an easy and enjoyable walk through forest and offers good examples of native vegetation. Before beginning the trail, pick up a free copy of a plant guide at the museum. This trail takes about 15 minutes to complete.

KUMUWELA TRAIL

Off Mohihi Road is the Kumuwela Trail (1.6 miles round-trip). It takes about one hour on the way in and offers lush native vegetation and fragrant flowers. It's a good **birdwatching** trail, and you can connect to the Canyon Trail at Kumuwela Road at the end of the trail.

PUʻU KA OHELO/ BERRY FLAT TRAIL LOOP

Near park headquarters is pole #320, which marks the beginning of Camp 10-Mohihi Road. This is generally a four-wheel-drive road, but occasionally two-wheel-drive cars can make it if the weather has been really dry. Numerous trails start here and head into the forest along ridges with canyon views, crossing a couple of minor streams. The roughly 1.6-mile loop called the **Puʻu Ka Ohelo/Berry Flat Trail** is a semi-strenuous trail that has a beautiful forest of sugi pine, California redwoods, Australian eucalyptus, and the valuable native koa as well as the ʻohiʻa tree. Small, red strawberry guava with a thick flesh and edible seeds grows here, and this is a popular spot for locals to harvest the fruit. Picking season is midsummer, so it's important to check with park headquarters

before snacking on the fruit while hiking. To access this trail, begin at the Puʻu Ka Ohelo trailhead near some cabins about a quarter mile up a road off Camp 10-Mohihi Road, and hike clockwise, which will take you downhill.

POʻOMAU CANYON DITCH TRAIL

The beautiful **Poʻomau Canyon Ditch Trail** is less than 0.5 mile past the Berry Flat Trail. Developed to maintain the Kokeʻe irrigation ditch, this trail is less than four miles long round-trip. It's fairly strenuous and deserves plenty of time to be completed. This trail leads to wonderful views of the Poʻomau Stream, lush green forests, and a great view of two waterfalls from a peninsula of land that extends out into the canyon. If you bring a picnic lunch you'll find a grassy overlook to rest and enjoy the views. Take Waineke Road across from the Kokeʻe Museum to Mohihi Road. You will need to park well before the trailhead on Mohihi Road, a little over 1.5 miles from Route 550. Walk about 0.75 mile to an unmarked trailhead on your right.

PIHEA TRAIL AND ALAKAʻI SWAMP TRAIL

Beginning at the end of Waimea Canyon Drive at the Puʻu O Kila Overlook is the **Pihea Trail**, about 3.8 miles in length. It leads to the **Alakaʻi Swamp Trail**, about 3.5 miles long. The Pihea Peak, accessed by a very steep trail, is about 1.3 miles after the lookout. This trail runs along the back edge of the Kalalau Valley, and you will be treated to wonderful views into the valley and out to the ocean. About 1.6 miles in, a wooden boardwalk has been constructed to help keep hikers from getting submerged in mud. When you hit the Alakaʻi Trail take a left, and it's about two miles to the end. A majestic, gorgeous, and unique trail, the Alakaʻi Swamp Trail heads down toward the Kawaikoi Stream and then up a ridge across boggy forestland to the Kilohana Overlook, the trail's ultimate destination. When you can catch a very clear day, which can be tough, the views of the Wainiha and Hanalei Valleys are awesome.

The approximately five-million-year-old swamp is about 4,500 feet above sea level, and is one of the most distinctive experiences on the island. The environment is otherwordly. Mossy trees, birds, and fog create an ecosystem different from anywhere else in the state. It's a great **bird-watching** trail, but the views are iffy with the lingering mist and clouds of the area. The entire trail totals about eight miles.

KALUAPUHI TRAIL

The **Kaluapuhi Trail** is 4 miles round-trip and one of the flattest trails on Kaua'i. The easy hike is a forest trail from start to finish, passing through moist forest where native **birds** can be seen. Walk in as far as you'd like to go and then return on the same trail to avoid walking back on the highway. To get to the trailhead from the Koke'e Museum, drive 1.9 miles north on Route 550. There is a small pull-off on the right side of the road at the trailhead. The trail ends 0.25 mile past the Kalalau Lookout.

HALEMANU-KOKE'E TRAIL

Take a stroll on the **Halemanu-Koke'e Trail** for **bird-watching** in native koa forest. The round-trip hike to Halemanu Valley and back is 2.4 miles. The trail climbs 300 feet through koa forest, follows the ridge, and then drops into the valley. To get to the trailhead, turn right onto the dirt road that leads to YMCA Camp Sloggett and park near the Camp Sloggett sign. Walk toward the cabins. The trailhead is by the first cabin on the right.

BIKING

Sunrise and sunset group bike tours are offered for an 11-mile downhill ride, but of course you can always take the ride on your own. Starting in the cool mountain air along the rim of Waimea Canyon at around 3,600 feet, the ride skirts the rim and then heads down the roller coaster foothills to the coast at Kekaha. All of the tours are groups, and participants are given a helmet and jacket to wear. Cruiser bikes with comfortable seats are available for the half-day tour. Refreshments and information on Hawaiian culture are offered. Sunglasses, sunscreen, and sometimes pants are a necessity. A sag wagon follows for bikers who need a rest and to alert traffic from behind. If you'd like to spend about five hours on a bike tour, contact **Outfitters Kauai** (2827 Po'ipu Rd., Po'ipu, 808/742-9667 or 999/742-9887, www.outfitterskauai.com). The rate is $113 for adults, $92 for children 12-14, and van riders are $56.25.

For the serious mountain biker, the **Waimea Canyon Trail** is an adventure. This eight-mile trail leads back down to Waimea town via an old dirt track and crosses through a game management area. Because of this, a special permit is required to walk though the area and is available at the trailhead. You can connect to the Waimea Canyon Trail by going south from the Kukui Trail. This trail is for dedicated mountain bikers only.

Adventure Sports and Tours

West-side tours explore Kaua'i's coffee industry, history, and nature. Get a glimpse of history through town walking tours, gain insight into the tropical flora and fauna in Koke'e, explore the beaches of Ni'ihau, and see Kaua'i from a bird's-eye view. Unique to the west side is the opportunity for skydiving, offered nowhere else on the island. The adventure sports add some real action to an otherwise mellow locale.

SKYDIVING

Skydive Kauai (Port Allen Airport, Kuiloko Rd., 808/335-5859, www.skydivekauai.com, $239) will help you free fall out of a plane to 4,500 feet, where the chute opens and you glide back to the airfield. The ride only takes people 18 and older and under 200 pounds. The company offers video or photo packages of your experience starting at an additional $70.

HELICOPTER TOURS
★ Ni'ihau Helicopters

Virtually the only way to visit the beaches of Ni'ihau unless invited by an islander is via a **Ni'ihau Helicopters tour** (877/441-3500, www.niihau.us, 8am-2pm Mon.-Sat., $385 including lunch and refreshments), which will take you there for a half day on the beach to snorkel and sunbathe. A safari/hunting excursion is also offered ($500-1,750). Owned and operated by the owners of Ni'ihau, the company offers free-chase hunting for boars, sheep, and oryx. Five people are required for both tours, and you reach the island in a twin-engine Agusta 109A helicopter that was originally set up to provide medical services for Ni'ihau residents.

Island Helicopters

Movie and waterfall buffs will enjoy a trip to **Manawaiopuna Falls,** which was used in Steven Spielberg's 1993 blockbuster *Jurassic*

Park and is located on land that is said to belong to the Robinsons, the same family that owns Ni'ihau. The nearly 400-foot-tall falls are hidden in a valley near Hanapepe and have been restricted to the public for years. Around five years ago the owner and pilot at **Island Helicopters** (Ahukini Rd., Lihu'e, 808/245-8588 or 800/829-5999, www.islandhelicopters.com) began pursuing permits from the state and county to land at the falls. He was successful and now flies people to the remote location five days a week for a 25-minute landing at the falls as part of an 85-minute circle island tour for a regular rate of $371 with online discounted fares.

WALKING TOURS
Hanapepe

A self-guided walking tour through Hanapepe town can be done with or without the *Historic Hanapepe Walking Tour Map* that is available without charge in many of the shops in town. The map provides background information on the historical buildings and churches. For map-free walkers, plaques with information can be found on the front of most of the buildings.

The **Kaua'i Coffee Company** (800/545-8605, www.kauaicoffee.com, 9am-5pm daily), the largest single coffee estate in Hawaii, offers a free walking tour where visitors can learn about Kaua'i coffee. The tour includes interpretive signs that identify the five different varieties of coffee as well as the entire coffee bean growing process, from initial blossoming through harvesting and processing, to the final roasting and into your cup.

Waimea

A local volunteer offers two tours in Waimea free of charge. A walking tour of Waimea town is offered on Monday and begins at the **West Kaua'i Technology Center** (9565 Kaumuali'i Hwy., 808/338-1332) at 8:30am.

She also guides a tour on Saturday of a plantation neighborhood dating back to the 1900s; it meets at the lobby of the **Waimea Plantation Cottages** (9400 Kaumuali'i Hwy., 808/338-1625). Reservations are required and can be made by calling 808/337-1005.

Shopping

High-end fashion and big-box stores are absent on the west side. Small boutiques, local crafts, jewelry, and art are abundant. The west side offers some unique souvenirs, from Ni'ihau jewelry to local art.

HANAPEPE

Art galleries featuring photography, paintings, drawings, sculptures, glass, and more line the streets of **Hanapepe**. The town is always worth a stroll through, whether window shopping or purchasing a masterpiece.

Art Galleries

Giorgio's Gallery (3871 Hanapepe Rd., 808/335-3949, www.giorgiosart.com, 11am-5pm daily) is an extravaganza of color reflecting the beauty of the islands in landscape, floral, and abstract paintings. Using a method called plein air, Giorgio creates palette knife oil paintings, often on location around Kaua'i. You will usually find a friendly staff member overseeing the spacious gallery during business hours, who's happy to chat about the island and art. The walls are covered in bursts of color that seem to leap off the canvas.

If you look to your left as you enter **Banana Patch Studios** (3865 Hanapepe Rd., 808/335-5944, www.bananapatchstudio.com, 10am-4:30pm Mon.-Thurs., 10am-9pm Fri., 10am-4pm Sat.) you will see art being made through a large window looking right into the studio. This is a great place for souvenirs such as ceramic tiles saying "please remove shoes," and "aloha." Owner Joanna Carolan creates the tiles, an array of jewelry, and nature-inspired paintings. Island-style trinkets and home decor from other crafters are also in stock.

Traditional watercolors and incredible island photography capturing nature's spectacular moments can be found in the **Arius Hopman Gallery** (3840C Hanapepe Rd., 808/335-0227, www.hopmanart.com, 10:30am-2pm Mon.-Thurs., 10:30am-2pm and 6pm-9pm Fri.), where the artwork can be printed up to 12 feet long. Both the paintings and photos reflect Kaua'i's beauty, life, and energy. Hopman's artistic ability is in his blood; his mother was a world-renowned artist who was commissioned to sculpt Mahatma Gandhi twice. The native of India moved to Hawai'i in 1985 and lives in Hanapepe.

Crafts and Books

There's something warm and cozy about independently owned bookstores, and **Talk Story Bookstore** (3785 Hanapepe Rd., 808/335-6469, www.talkstorybookstore. com, 10am-5pm Sun.-Fri., 10am-9:30pm Fri.) doesn't disappoint. The family-run business is Kaua'i's only new and used bookstore and is located in the historic Old Yoshiura Store. Over 40,000 used, rare, and collectible books are available, along with Hawaiian gifts, crafts, records, and Hawaiian slack-key and ukulele lesson courses. Any books you want to unload can be traded in for in-store credit. The shop stays open late on Art Night, offering live entertainment.

Crafts and jewelry decorate **J J Ohana** (3805-B Hanapepe Rd., 808/335-0366, www. jjohana.com, 8am-6pm Mon.-Thurs., 8am-9pm Fri., 8am-5pm Sat.). The highlight here is the Ni'ihau shell jewelry made by the owner, whom you may find overseeing the shop. She makes beautiful earrings, necklaces, and bracelets that are some of the most valuable Kaua'i souvenirs.

PORT ALLEN
Clothing

At the **Red Dirt Factory Outlet** (4350 Waialo Rd., 800/717-3478, www.dirtshirt. com, 9am-5pm daily) in Port Allen, a natural resource has been used to create one of the most famous Kaua'i souvenirs. The shirts are dyed with real Kaua'i red dirt, and there's an interesting story behind the making of the shirts. Self-guided tours are available at the factory store 9am-noon and 1pm-4pm daily to watch the silk-screening process. There is also a smaller red dirt store in Waimea.

WAIMEA
Gourmet Treats and Beauty Products

Known as one of the tastiest tropical flavors and used across the culinary board from desserts to entrées, the *liliko'i,* or passion fruit, is used in all of its glory at **Aunty Liliko'i** (9875 Waimea Rd., 808/338-1296, www.auntylilikoi. com, 10am-6pm daily). The sweet and sour fruit is the highlight in jams, jellies, mustards, dressings, syrups, and even skin-care products. Drop by the quaint shop in Waimea to pick up a snack.

Antiques

Antiques from around the islands can be found at **Collectibles and Fine Junque** (9821 Kaumuali'i Hwy., 808/338-9855). An array of Hawaiiana, books, trinkets, jewelry, and so much more fills the small shop to the brim. The staff is usually happy to talk story with shoppers, and even just browsing here can be fun. The small building that houses the shop is an antique itself. Those looking for it may question if the rundown building is being utilized, but the historic look adds to the shop's spirit.

Giorgio's Gallery

Entertainment

If you're looking for nightlife, the west side isn't where you'll find it. Art Night in Hanapepe is really the only action at night other than a dinner out or stargazing on the beach (which is quite enjoyable).

★ ART NIGHT IN HANAPEPE

Around 16 art galleries open their doors for a night of art celebration 6pm-9pm each Friday on Hanapepe Road. **Art Night** is an opportunity to socialize with locals and other visitors, explore the town, and meet artists. The night can be enjoyed casually if you're coming straight from the beach, but it can also be an opportunity to dress up for a night out on the small, historical town. You'll find live music on the boardwalk, artists working away at their latest masterpieces, and plenty of food and refreshments. If you're considering purchasing a piece of local art, meeting the artist can often provide context and a deeper story to the work that is fun to share with family and friends back home and creates a connection to your time in the islands.

CLASSES
Waimea

Create your own souvenir at **Kaua'i Art Classes** (808/631-9173, www.kauaiartclasses. com). All materials are provided for creating silk paintings, acrylics, and pastels at Waimea Plantation Cottages. Classes are offered at multiple locations on the west side, so check the website for directions and addresses.

To get the most out of your photo opportunities on Kaua'i, take a **digital photography class** from Hanapepe painter and photographer Arius Hopman (808/335-5616, www. hopmanart.com).

Food

Good food isn't hard to find out west. There are a number of *ono* (delicious) places to eat, from snacks and desserts to local brews and dinner. For such small towns there's a wide array of cuisines and a decent number of vegetarian dishes scattered through the eateries.

HANAPEPE
Cafés

The roadside **Grinds Café** (4469 Waialo Rd., 808/335-6027, www.grindscafe.net, 5:30am-9pm Mon. and Fri.-Sun., 6am-3pm Tues.-Thurs., $5-22) serves its entire menu all day long. It offers pizzas, sandwiches, pasta, salads, and more. Breakfast options start at $5, while dinner entrée options range $13-20. Indoor and patio seating is available, where you will find a mix of locals picking up a cup of coffee and visitors passing through.

Grab a smoothie, coffee, bagel, acai bowl, salad, or a fresh sandwich at **Little Fish Coffee** (3900 Hanapepe Rd., 808/335-5000, 6:30am-5pm Mon.-Sat., $3-11). The artsy café has indoor seating and patio seating in the backyard. The coffee is fair trade, organic, and roasted by Kauai Roastery. The kitchen closes at 3pm, and it's open till 9pm during Hanapepe Art Night. Check the Little Fish Coffee Facebook page for more information.

Local Food

Located on Kaumuali'i Highway, you can't miss **MCS Grill** (1-3529 Kaumuali'i Hwy., 808/431-4645, www.mcsgrill.com, 10:30am-8:30pm Mon.-Fri., 5pm-9pm Sat., $10-21) with the red flame logo on the front of the restaurant. It serves breakfast, lunch, and dinner and offers a few vegetarian items. MCS Grill is

Little Fish Coffee

best known for its saimin as well as its plates, served with rice as well as potato, macaroni, or tossed salad.

Treats and Desserts

The tropical- and traditional-flavored ice creams and sorbets at ★ **Lappert's Ice Cream** (1-3555 Kaumuali'i Hwy., 808/335-6121 or 800/356-4045, www.lappertshawaii.com, 10am-6pm daily, $4 for a single scoop) are the perfect cool accent to a warm Hawaiian day. Originating on Kaua'i, the shop now has outlets statewide. The ice cream has about 16 percent butterfat in its regular flavors and around 8 percent in its fruit flavors, making for some pretty creamy ice cream.

WAIMEA
American

The decor is true to the name at ★ **Wrangler's Steakhouse** (9852 Kaumuali'i Hwy., 808/338-1218, www.wranglersrestaurant.com, lunch 11am-4pm Mon.-Fri., dinner 4pm-9pm Mon.-Sat., $18-33),

where the restaurant is decorated with cowboy trinkets and gear. Indoor and outdoor seating are offered. Wrangler's is known for its great steaks, and it offers a salad and soup bar with each meal. A full bar is stocked with a variety of liquors, wines, and beers to please any palate. The menu offers a hefty assortment of red meats, poultry, and seafood. Service is friendly, and there is also a small *paniolo* (Hawaiian cowboy) museum as well as shell jewelry for sale.

To peel, or not to peel, that is the question at ★ **The Shrimp Station** (9652 Kaumuali'i Hwy., 808/338-1242, 11am-5pm daily, $11-12), where shrimp is served up in a number of ways. At this very laid-back eatery, seating is at picnic tables under a tent right on the side of the main road. The menu includes shrimp entrées, drinks, desserts, and ice cream. It's located across from Island Taco.

Local Treats

Finely shaved ice and 60 flavors can be found at ★ **JoJo's** (9734 Kaumuali'i Hwy., across from mile marker 23, www.jojosshaveice.com, 11am-5:30pm daily, $3-6). The line can be long, but it's a testimony to JoJo's great shave ice. Try some local flavor combos like lychee and coconut or *liliko'i* and *melona*.

Mexican

★ **Island Taco** (9643 Kaumuali'i Hwy., 808/338-9895, www.islandfishtaco.com, 11am-5pm daily, $3-12) in Waimea is a simple order-at-the-counter taco stand with seating, reminiscent of roadside taco stands in Mexico. The large menu offers local fish, pork, chicken, and even a wide variety of satisfying vegetarian and vegan options. Portions are large, with unique toppings like a wasabi-spiked aioli sauce and the option of fat-free dishes. Perfect for a quick stop on a drive through Waimea or to satisfy a craving after camping at Polihale, this place is really good. Island even serves fresh homemade tortillas.

Health Food

Organic, vegetarian, vegan, and natural

breakfasts, lunches, smoothies, and desserts can be found at the family-run ★ **Happy Mangos Healthy Hale** (Alawai Rd., 808/338-0055, www.happymangos.com, store 6:30am-5pm Mon.-Fri., 7am-3pm Sat., café 6:30am-4pm Mon.-Fri., 7am-2pm Sat., $3-9). The owners serve freshly made food along with natural and organic groceries and produce. Located in a small plantation-style building across from Lucy Wright Beach Park, the health-food store is the only natural and organic choice in Waimea. It serves non-vegetarian sandwiches too.

KOKE'E STATE PARK
Local Food

Breakfast and lunch are served daily at the restaurant of the **Koke'e Lodge** (808/335-6061, www.kokeelodge.com/, 9am-2:30pm daily, $6-8). The soups accent the cool weather, and Koke'e's banana bread and its corn bread make a great treat. Meat entrées are common, but there are a few vegetarian options too, along with local dishes like *kalua* pork and *loco moco*. Wine, beer, and cocktails are also on the menu. The next eatery is about 15 miles away unless you bring a picnic lunch.

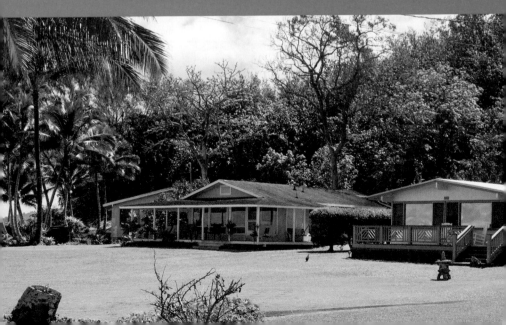

Where to Stay on Kaua'i

The East Side

Name	Type	Price	Features	Why Stay Here	Best Fit For
Aloha Hale Orchid	studio	$55	mini fridge	on orchid farm, affordable	budget travelers
★ Aston Aloha Beach Hotel	hotel	$113-195	pool	affordable, good location	families, couples
Fern Grotto Inn	cottages	$150-190	kitchens	privacy	families, couples
Garden Island Inn	small inn	$134-143	kitchenettes, beach gear	affordable, central location	couples
Honu'ea International Hostel Kaua'i	hostel	$25-70	common kitchen area	affordable	budget travelers, young people
Hotel Coral Reef	hotel	$125-245	pool	oceanfront	couples
Kaha Lani	condos	$188-268	tennis court, pool	oceanfront	families, couples
Kapa'a Sands	condos	$135-225	pool, barbecue	oceanfront, affordable	families, couples
Kaua'i Beach House Hostel	hostel	$33-75	kitchen area	near the water	budget travelers
Kauai Beach Villas	condos	$145-185	pool, jet spa, tennis	beachfront	families on a budget
Kauai Country Inn	B&B	$179-219	breakfast	Beatles museum	couples
★ Kaua'i Marriott Resort	large resort	$309-459	full resort amenities, childcare	full-service resort	families, couples
Kaua'i Palms Hotel	budget hotel	$79	free muffins and coffee	affordable	budget travelers
★ Kaua'i Sands Hotel	budget hotel	$80-152	pool	oceanfront, affordable	budget travelers
★ Lae Nani Resort Kauai	condos	$189-359	pool, tennis court	oceanfront	families, couples
★ Motel Lani	hotel	$64	showers	affordable	budget travelers
Rosewood Kaua'i Bunk House	rooms	$75-85	kitchenettes	affordable	budget travelers
Wailua Bay View	condos	$155	pool, ocean views	affordable	couples

The North Shore

Name	Type	Price	Features	Why Stay Here	Best Fit For
★ Ali'i Kai	condos	starting at $110	pool, tennis	location	couples, families
Bamboo at Kalihiwai	apartment	$200	spa tub, kitchen	privacy	couples
Bed, Breakfast and Beach at Hanalei	B&B	$120-170	breakfast	location	couples
The Cliffs at Princeville	condos	$324-414	pool, tennis	views, location	couples, families
Emmalani Court	condos	starting at $125	pool, barbecue	affordable	couples
Green Acres Cottages	B&B	$75-90	studios	location, affordable	budget travelers
★ Hanalei Bay Resort	condos	starting at $109	pool, tennis courts	location, decent price	families, couples
Hanalei Bay Villas	stand-alone homes	starting at $165	mountain views	location	families, couples
★ Hanalei Colony Resort	condos	$279-479	pool	oceanfront location	honeymooners, couples
Hanalei Inn	motel	$149-159	barbecue, TV, hammock	simple, location	couples
Kaua'i Coco Cabana	private home	$175-190	outdoor shower, beach gear	location	couples
North Country Farms	cottages	$160	orchard	location, kid-friendly	nature lovers
Plumeria Moon Cottage and Hideaway Bay	cottage and main home	$335-795	hot tub, beach gear	privacy	couples
Plumeria at Anini Beach	private home	$375	near beach	privacy	couples, families
Puamana	condos	starting at $100	pool	affordable	families, couples
The River Estate	private homes	$275-295	hot tub	location	couples, families
★ SeaLodge	condos	$110-175	pool, barbecue	location, price	couples, families

The North Shore (continued)

Name	Type	Price	Features	Why Stay Here	Best Fit For
★ St. Regis Princeville Resort	luxury resort	$552-747	pools, beach, restaurants, spa	luxurious stay	lovers of luxury
Westin Princeville Ocean Resort Villas	villas	$369-686	pools	resort amenities	luxury-seeking families and couples
YMCA Camp Naue	cabins, tents	$15	oceanfront	affordable, simple	budget travelers

The South Shore

Name	Type	Price	Features	Why Stay Here	Best Fit For
Boulay Inn	apartment	$85	beach gear, private room	affordable	budget travelers
Classic Vacation Cottages	vacation rentals	$70-150	beach gear, hot tub	lots of options	families, couples, groups
Grand Hyatt Kaua'i Resort and Spa	resort and spa	$448-1,136	two pools, golf course, restaurants, spa	location, luxury	families, couples
Hale Kua	B&B	$120-175	kitchenettes, beach gear	private units	families, couples
Hideaway Cove Villas	high-end villas	$185-725	Jacuzzi tubs, kitchens, beach gear	high end, amenities	luxury lovers
★ Kalaheo Inn	inn	$82-156	kitchenettes	affordable, location	families, couples
Kaua'i Banyan Inn	private suites	$155-230	kitchenettes	location	families with children 10 and older
Kaua'i Cove Cottages	cottages	$129-239	kitchens	honeymoon cottages	couples
Kaua'i Garden Cottages	private-home suites	$145-165	lanai	privacy	couples

The South Shore (continued)

Name	Type	Price	Features	Why Stay Here	Best Fit For
★ Kiahuna Plantation Resort	cottages	$269-415	gardens, restaurant	lovely grounds	couples
Marjorie's Kaua'i Inn	B&B	$170-225	pool, hot tub	affordable	couples
Nihi Kai Villas	condos	$145-625	heated pool, oceanfront, hot tub, tennis	full amenities	families, couples
★ Prince Kuhio	condos	$85-155	pool, barbecue	affordable, location	families, budget travelers
Seaview Suite	rooms in home	$75-95	kitchenette	location, affordable	groups, nature lovers
Sheraton Kaua'i	resort	$339-746	two pools, spa shopping	full-service resort	families, couples
Turtle Cove Cottage	private home	$275-285	lanai, full home	close to beach	families, couples
Waikomo Stream Villas	condos	$130-270	pool, hot tub, kiddie pool, tennis	amenities	families, couples
★ Whalers Cove Resort	condos	$366-975	pool, hot tub, oceanfront	location	couples

The West Side

Name	Type	Price	Features	Why Stay Here	Best Fit For
Coco's Kaua'i Bed-and-Breakfast	B&B	$120-140	breakfast, off grid	unique	green travelers
★ Koke'e Lodge	cabins	$93	wood-burning stoves, cooking utensils	affordable, in nature	outdoorsy types or budget travelers
Monolithic Dome	private home	$95	lanai, kitchenette	private and relaxing	solitude-seekers

The West Side (continued)

Name	Type	Price	Features	Why Stay Here	Best Fit For
★ Waimea Plantation Cottages	hotel	starting at $149	pool, oceanfront	historic, unique	families, couples
West Inn Kaua'i	small hotel	$199-349	kitchens in some rooms	location	families, couples
YMCA Camp Sloggett	tents, cabins	$15-225	fireplace, kitchen	time in nature	outdoors types

Background and Essentials

The Landscape

Ancient Hawaiians worshipped Madame Pele, the fire goddess whose name translates equally well as Volcano, Fire Pit, or Eruption of Lava. When she was angry, she complained by spitting fire, which cooled and formed land. And so the Hawaiian Islands were born.

The islands' volcanic origins have a basis in science as well as myth. From a stationary hotspot in the earth's mantle, the islands of Hawaii are created as molten lava rises through weak points in the earth's crust. On the Big Island, Mauna Kea, the world's tallest mountain, reaches to 13,796 feet above sea level, or 31,000 feet tall when measured from the ocean floor, almost 3,000 feet taller than Mount Everest. And it's still growing. Once islands move past the hot spot on the Pacific Plate, volcanic activity ceases, and they begin a slow process of erosion, moving northwest across the vast Pacific Ocean. Over thousands of years, the mountains erode to shoals and atolls (barrier reefs just below the ocean surface), returning to their underwater origins. The Lo'ihi Seamount, located southeast of the Big Island, is likely to be the next Hawaiian island. Emerging from the flank of Mauna Loa, its summits are about 50 miles apart. Lo'ihi is roughly 3,000 feet below sea level and isn't expected to become a full-fledged island for at least 10,000 years or longer, depending on volcanic activity.

Lava comes in two distinct types, for which the Hawaiian names have become universal geological terms: 'a'a and pahoehoe. They're easily distinguished by appearance, but chemically they're the same. 'A'a is extremely sharp, rough, and spiny. Conversely, pahoehoe is billowy, ropelike lava that can mold into fantastic shapes. Examples of both are visible across the islands.

GEOGRAPHY

About 2,400 miles from the nearest continental shore, Hawaii is the most isolated group of islands on the planet. There are eight main Hawaiian Islands: Ni'ihau (the Forbidden Island), Kaua'i (the Garden Isle), O'ahu (the Gathering Place), Moloka'i (the Friendly Isle), Lana'i (the Pineapple Isle), Kaho'olawe (the Target Isle), Maui (the Valley Isle), and Hawai'i (better known as the Big Island). The Hawaiian archipelago consists of 132 islands, islets, and atolls, stretching roughly 1,500 miles from northernmost Kure Atoll to the still-growing Big Island of Hawai'i at the southeastern end of the chain. The eight main islands have a total area of 10,931 square miles. The Big Island is the largest island, accounting for about 63 percent of the state's total landmass; the other islands could fit within it two times over. Next largest is Maui, followed by O'ahu, Kaua'i, Moloka'i, and Lana'i. There are approximately 750 miles of coastline in the state. The main Hawaiian Islands are located in the Tropic of Cancer.

Hawaii's landscape is extremely diverse, offering everything from arid desert to snowcapped mountains. There are rivers, streams and waterfalls, vertical cliffs, extinct tuff cone volcanoes, tranquil bays and high-elevation plateaus. Because of their dramatic rise out of ocean depths, the islands include examples of 11 of the world's 13 climate zones.

CLIMATE
Temperature

Hawaii has comfortable weather year-round. Near the coast, the average daytime high temperature in winter is about 82°F, with the average daytime high in summer raising the thermometer only a few degrees to 87.5°F. Nighttime temperatures drop about 10 degrees. Elevation, however, does reduce temperatures: about three degrees for every 1,000 feet you climb.

Temperatures are both constant and moderate because of the trade winds, prevailing northeast breezes that blow at about 10-20 miles per hour. You can count on the trades to be blowing on an average of 300 days per year, hardly missing a day during summer and occurring half the time in winter. Although usually calm in the morning, they pick up during the heat of the afternoon, then weaken at night.

The Tropic of Cancer runs through the center of Hawaii, yet the latitude's usually oppressively hot and muggy weather is most often absent in the islands. Honolulu, on the same latitude as sweaty Hong Kong and Havana, has an acceptable 60-75 percent daily humidity factor.

Winds blowing from the south and southwest are known as kona winds. *Kona* means leeward in Hawaiian. Kona winds bring hot, humid air and unstable weather. If they persist for more than a couple of days, they also bring vog, a thick haze caused by the Kilauea Volcano on the Big Island. Kona winds are most common October-April.

Rainfall

Precipitation is the biggest differentiating factor in Hawaii's climate. Rainfall is most often localized and comes in waves of passing showers. Precipitation also occurs mostly at and below the 3,000-foot level, with the mountains acting as rain magnets. As the trade winds push warm, moist air up against the mountains, the air rises, cools, and drops a payload of rain to the ground. The heaviest rainfall occurs on the windward side of the islands and over mountain ranges, and dry conditions prevail on the leeward sides and south shores. For example, the Honolulu International Airport and Waikiki average only 20-25 inches of rain per year, while the Nu'uanu Reservoir in the mountains above Honolulu gets a whopping 120-130 inches yearly.

Localized weather means that weather patterns are very specific. If it's raining where you are, simply relocate to another part of the island or just wait a few minutes for the precipitation to pass. You can usually depend on south shore beaches and the leeward side to be sunny and bright. Ocean temperatures run 75-80°F year-round.

Severe Weather

Tsunami is the Japanese word for tidal wave. Hawaii's location in the middle of the Pacific Ocean puts it in the path of tsunamis as they travel from their point of origin and spread across the Pacific. A Hawaiian tsunami is actually a seismic sea wave that has been generated by an earthquake or landslide that could easily have originated thousands of miles away in Japan, South America, or Alaska. Not actual waves that break like the ones seen along the reefs, tsunamis show up as a series of three to five tidal surges that affect coastal waters and shorelines over several hours, with about 30 minutes between each surge. Tsunamis can range from simply a larger than usual fluctuation in sea level over the duration of the event to a devastating tidal surge that can floor and damage shoreline property, especially the harbors, and cause loss of life. For visitors staying in shoreline hotels with six or more stories, the safest place to be during a tsunami event is on the third floor or higher. Otherwise, shoreline areas should be evacuated.

Hurricanes are also a threat in Hawaii. They are rare, but destructive. Most hurricanes originate far to the southeast off the Pacific coast of Mexico and Latin America; some, particularly later in the season, start in the midst of the Pacific Ocean near the equator south of Hawaii. Hurricane season is considered June through November. Most hurricanes pass harmlessly south of Hawaii, but some, swept along by kona winds, do strike the islands. The most recent and destructive was Hurricane 'Iniki, which battered the islands in 1992, killing eight people and causing an estimated $2 billion in damage. It had its greatest effect on Ni'ihau, the Po'ipu Beach area of Kaua'i, and the leeward coast of O'ahu.

Plants and Animals

The Hawaiian Islands, about 2,500 miles from any continental landfall, were originally devoid of plant or animal life. Over time, as plants, animals, and insects found their way to the islands, they slowly evolved into highly specialized organisms occupying the gamut of each island's microclimates. In Hawaii, it is not uncommon for a particular plant species only to be found in a single valley across the entire island chain.

The unique plants and animals found only in Hawaii are known as endemic, those species naturally occurring in Hawaii but found elsewhere in the world are known as native, and those brought to the islands by people are called introduced species. Introduced species that are fast growing, rapidly increase in number and easily spread over a region are referred to as invasive species. Invasive species and loss of habitat have been detrimental to the survival of Hawaii's highly specialized native and endemic flora and fauna. Hawaii is also known as the endangered species capital of the world, with most of its endemic plants and animals listed as rare and endangered, with many species having already gone extinct. The majority of the remaining pockets of native Hawaiian flora in Hawaii have been relegated to inaccessible valleys and steep mountain cliffs.

INTRODUCED PLANTS

Before settlement, Hawaii had no fruits, vegetables, coconut palms, edible land animals, conifers, mangroves, or banyans. The early Polynesians brought in 27 varieties of plants that they needed for food and other purposes, like banana, sweet potato, breadfruit, sugarcane, and taro. They also carried along gourds to use as containers, 'awa to make a basic intoxicant, and the *ti* plant to use for offerings or to string into hula skirts. About 90 percent of plants on the Hawaiian Islands today were introduced after Captain James Cook first set foot here. Non-Hawaiian settlers over the years have brought mangoes, papayas, passion fruit, pineapples, and the other tropical fruits and vegetables associated with the islands. Also, most of the flowers, including protea, plumeria, anthuriums, orchids, heliconia, ginger, and most hibiscus, have come from every continent on earth. Tropical America, Asia, Java, India, and China have contributed their most beautiful and delicate blooms.

TREES

Koa and *'ohi'a* are two endemic Hawaiian trees still seen quite often in the state. Both have been greatly reduced by the foraging of introduced cattle and goats, and through logging and forest fires. The *koa* (*Acacia koa*) is Hawaii's finest native tree. It can grow to more than 70 feet high and has a strong, straight trunk, which can measure more than 10 feet in circumference. The Hawaiians used *koa* as the main log for their dugout canoes, and elaborate ceremonies were performed when a log was cut and dragged to a canoe shed. *Koa* wood was also preferred for paddles, spears, and even surfboards. Today it is still considered an excellent furniture wood. To protect fine specimens found in reserves, *koa* is now being grown on plantations for future harvesting for commercial purposes.

The *'ohi'a* (*Metrosideros polymorpha*) is a survivor and a pioneer plant, one of the first types of plants to colonize lava flows. It is the most abundant of all the native Hawaiian trees. Coming in a variety of shapes and sizes, it grows as miniature trees in wet bogs or as 100-foot giants on cool slopes at higher elevations. The *'ohi'a* produces a tuft-like flower—usually red, but occasionally orange, yellow, or white, the latter being very rare and elusive—that resembles a bottlebrush. The flower was considered sacred to Pele; it was said that she would cause a rainstorm if *'ohi'a* blossoms were picked without the proper prayers. The flowers were fashioned into lei that resembled feather boas. The strong, hard wood was used to make canoes, poi bowls, and especially for temple images. 'Ohi'a logs were also used as railroad ties and shipped to the mainland from the Big Island. It's believed that the "golden spike" linking rail lines between the U.S. East and West Coasts was driven into an 'ohi'a log from the Big Island when the two railroads came together in Ogden, Utah, in 1869.

MARINE LIFE

Although decades of overfishing have taken their toll on the marine life along island reefs, entire populations of reef dwellers are bouncing back in specific locations thanks to managed Marine Protected Areas. These managed zones are designed to promote reef health and bolster populations of reef dwelling species. In turn, these healthy areas allow populations of fish to grow rapidly and reproduce in exponentially larger numbers, spilling over into unprotected waters and benefiting species higher up the food chain. Hawaii has over 200 species of native fish.

Whales and **dolphins** are also common in Hawaiian waters. The most famous whale, and commonly seen, is the **North Pacific humpback,** but others include the sperm, killer, false killer, pilot, Cuvier's, Blainsville, and pygmy killer. There are technically no porpoises, but dolphins include the common, bottlenose, white-sided, broad- and slender-beaked, and rough-toothed. Small and sleek spinner dolphins are the ones you'll often see near the shore. The **mahimahi,** a favorite food fish found on many menus, is commonly referred to as dolphin fish but is unrelated and is a true fish, not a cetacean.

The **Hawaiian monk seal** is one of only two mammals native to Hawaii (the Hawaiian hoary bat is the other). These curious seals are critically endangered and protected by law. Monk seals frequently relax on the beach and have a nap in the sun. If you see a monk seal, give it ample space and do not disturb or touch the seal in any way. **Green sea turtles**

at rest are also common along island shorelines. They share the endangered designation and should be given the same respect.

BIRDS

Due to the lack of native mammals and reptiles in precontact Hawaii, native birds flourished, becoming widespread and highly specialized. Not to mention, they were able to feast on over 10,000 species of native insects. However, one of the great tragedies of natural history is the continuing demise of Hawaiian birdlife. Since the arrival of Captain Cook in 1778, 23 species have become extinct, with 31 more in danger. And what's not known is how many species were wiped out before white explorers arrived. Experts believe that the Hawaiians annihilated about 40 species, including seven species of geese, a rare one-legged owl, ibis, lovebirds, sea eagles, and honeycreepers—all gone before Captain Cook showed up. Hawaii's endangered birds account for 40 percent of the birds officially listed as endangered or threatened by the U.S. Fish and Wildlife Service. Most of the remaining indigenous Hawaiian birds can be found on any island below the 3,000-foot level.

Hawaii's shoreline cliffs, dunes and islets are home to thriving colonies of marine birds. Look for several birds from the tern family, including the **white, gray,** and **sooty tern.** Along with the terns are **shearwaters** and the enormous **Laysan albatross,** with its seven-foot wingspan. **Tropicbirds,** with their lovely streamer-like tails, are often seen along the windward coasts.

If you're lucky, you can also catch a glimpse of the *pueo* (Hawaiian owl) in mountainous areas. Deep in the forests you can sometimes see elusive birds like the 'elepaio, 'amakihi, and the fiery red '*i'iwi.* The 'amakihi and '*i'iwi* are endemic birds not endangered at the moment. The '*amakihi* is one of the most common native birds; yellowish-green, it frequents the high branches of the 'ohi'a, koa, and sandalwood trees looking for insects, nectar, or fruit. It is less specialized than most other Hawaiian birds, the main reason for its continued existence. The *'i'iwi,* a bright red bird with a salmon-colored, hooked bill, is found in the forests above 2,000 feet. The most common native bird, the *'apapane* is abundant and easiest to see. It's a chubby, red-bodied bird about five inches long with a black bill, legs, wingtips, and tail feathers.

Exotic, introduced birds are the most common in the beach parks and in urban areas. **Black myna birds,** with their sassy yellow eyes, are common mimics around town. **Sparrows,** introduced to Hawaii through Oʻahu in the 1870s, are everywhere. **Munia,** first introduced as caged birds from Southeast Asia, have escaped and can be found almost anywhere around the island of Oʻahu.

INTRODUCED ANIMALS

Almost all of the mammals in Hawaii are introduced, and many have had severe and detrimental consequences for Hawaii's natural environment and native species. **Rats, mice,** and **mongooses** thrive and are responsible for disease and the decline of ground nesting bird populations. Feral ungulates like **pigs** and **goats** destroy native forests as they root up and eat vegetation, creating fetid pools of water where mosquitoes thrive, contributing to the decline of forest bird populations through disease. In years past, grazing **cattle** were responsible for the deforestation of watersheds that led to landslides. **Geckos, anoles,** and **chameleons** are a few of the introduced reptiles that are common.

History

HAWAII'S SETTLERS

The great "deliberate migrations" from the southern Pacific islands seem to have taken place AD 500-800, though the exact date is highly contested by experts. The first planned migrations were from the violent cannibalistic islands called the Marquesas, 11 islands in extreme eastern Polynesia. The islands themselves are harsh and inhospitable, breeding toughness into the people that enabled them to withstand the hardships of long, unsure ocean voyages and years of resettlement. They were masters at building great double-hulled canoes, with the two hulls fastened together to form a catamaran, and a hut in the center provided shelter in bad weather. The average voyaging canoe was 60-80 feet long and could comfortably hold an extended family of about 30 people. These small family bands carried all the staples they would need in the new lands.

For five centuries, the Marquesans settled here and lived peacefully on the new land. The tribes coexisted in relative harmony, especially because there was no competition for land. Cannibalism died out. There was

much coming and going between Hawaii and Polynesia as new people came to the settlement over the course of hundreds of years. Then, it appears that in the 12th century a deliberate exodus of warlike Tahitians arrived and subjugated the islanders. This incursion had a terrific significance on the Hawaiian religious and social system. The warlike god Ku and the rigid *kapu* system were introduced, through which the new rulers became dominant. Voyages between Tahiti and Hawaii continued for about 100 years, and Tahitian customs, legends, and language became the Hawaiian way of life. Then suddenly, for no recorded or apparent reason, the voyages discontinued and Hawaii returned to total isolation.

CAPTAIN COOK

The islands remained forgotten for almost 500 years until the indomitable English seafarer, Captain James Cook, sighted Oʻahu on January 18, 1778, and stepped ashore at Waimea on Kauaʻi two days later. At that time Hawaii's isolation was so complete that even the Polynesians had forgotten about it. The

Englishmen had arrived aboard the 100-foot flagship HMS *Resolution* and its 90-foot companion HMS *Discovery*. The first trade was some brass medals for a mackerel. Cook provisioned his ships by exchanging chisels for hogs, while common sailors gleefully traded nails for sex. Landing parties were sent inland to fill casks with freshwater. After a brief stop on Ni'ihau, the ships sailed away, but both groups were indelibly impressed with the memory of each other.

Almost a year later, when winter weather forced Cook to return from the coast of Alaska, the *Discovery* and *Resolution* found safe anchorage at Kealakekua Bay on the Kona Coast of the Big Island on January 16, 1779. By the coincidence of his second arrival with religious festivities, the Hawaiians mistook Cook to be the return of the god Lono. After an uproarious welcome and generous hospitality for over a month, it became obvious that the newcomers were beginning to overstay their welcome. During the interim a sailor named William Watman died, convincing the Hawaiians that the *haole* were indeed mortals, not gods. Inadvertently, many *kapu* were broken by the English, and once-friendly relations became strained. Finally, the ships sailed away on February 4, 1779.

After plying terrible seas for only a week, *Resolution*'s foremast was badly damaged. Cook sailed back into Kealakekua Bay, dragging the mast ashore on February 13. The natives, now totally hostile, hurled rocks at the sailors. Confrontations increased when some Hawaiians stole a small boat and Cook's men set after them, capturing the fleeing canoe, which held an *ali'i* named Palea. The Englishmen treated him roughly, so the Hawaiians furiously attacked the mariners, who abandoned the small boat.

Next, Cook made a fatal error in judgment. He decided to take nine armed mariners ashore in an attempt to convince the venerable King Kalani'opu'u to accompany him back aboard ship, where he would hold him for ransom in exchange for the cutter. The old king agreed, but his wife prevailed

upon him not to trust the *haole*. Kalani'opu'u sat down on the beach to think while the tension steadily grew.

Meanwhile, a group of mariners fired on a canoe trying to leave the bay, and a lesser chief, No'okemai, was killed. The crowd around Cook and his men reached an estimated 20,000, and warriors outraged by the killing of the chief armed themselves with clubs and protective straw-mat armor. One bold warrior advanced on Cook and struck him with his *pahoa* (dagger). In retaliation Cook drew a tiny pistol and fired at the warrior. His bullets spent themselves on the straw armor and fell harmlessly to the ground. The Hawaiians went wild. Lieutenant Molesworth Phillips, in charge of the nine mariners, began a withering fire; Cook killed two natives.

Overpowered by sheer numbers, the sailors headed for boats standing offshore, while Lieutenant Phillips lay wounded. It is believed that Captain Cook stood helplessly in knee-deep water instead of making for the boats because he could not swim. Hopelessly surrounded, he was knocked on the head, then countless warriors passed a knife around and hacked and mutilated his lifeless body. A sad Lieutenant King lamented in his diary, "Thus fell our great and excellent commander."

UNIFICATION OF THE HAWAIIAN ISLANDS

In the 1780s, the islands were roughly divided into three kingdoms: Kalani'opu'u ruled Hawaii and the Hana district of Maui; wily and ruthless warrior-king Kahekili ruled Maui, Kaho'olawe, Lana'i, and later O'ahu; and Kaeo, Kahekili's brother, ruled Kaua'i. War ravaged the land until a remarkable chief, Kamehameha, rose and subjugated all the islands under one rule. Kamehameha initiated a dynasty that would last for about 100 years, until the independent monarchy of Hawaii forever ceased to be.

Hawaii under Kamehameha was ready to enter its "golden age." The social order was medieval, with the *ali'i* as knights, owing their military allegiance to the king, and the serf-like *maka'ainana* paying tribute and working the lands. The priesthood of *kahuna* filled the posts of advisers, sorcerers, navigators, doctors, and historians. This was Polynesian Hawaii at its apex. But like the uniquely Hawaiian silversword plant, the old culture blossomed, and as soon as it did, it began to wither. Ever since, all that was purely Hawaiian has been supplanted by the relentless foreign influences that began bearing down upon it.

MISSIONARIES AND WHALERS

Kamehameha was as gentle in victory as he was ferocious in battle. Under his rule, which lasted until his death on May 8, 1819, Hawaii enjoyed a peace unlike any the warring islands had ever known. However, the year 1819 was of the utmost significance in Hawaiian history. With the death of Kamehameha, came the overthrow of the ancient *kapu* system, the arrival of the first whalers in Lahaina, and the departure of Calvinist missionaries from New England determined to convert the heathen islanders. Great changes began to rattle the old order to its foundations. With the *kapu* system and all of the ancient gods abandoned (except for the fire goddess Pele of Kilauea), a great void opened the souls of the Hawaiians. In the coming decades Hawaii, also coveted by Russia, France, and England, was finally consumed by America. The islands had the first American school, printing press, and newspaper west of the Mississippi. Lahaina, in its heyday, became the world's greatest whaling port, accommodating more than 500 ships of all types during its peak years.

In 1823, the first mission was established in Lahaina, Maui, under the pastorate of the Reverend William Richards and his wife. Within a few years, many of the notable *ali'i* had been, at least in appearance, converted to Christianity. By 1828, the cornerstones for Waine'e Church, the first stone church on the island, were laid just behind the palace of Kamehameha III.

THE GREAT MAHELE

In 1840, after moving the royal court to Honolulu, the new center of commerce in the islands, Kamehameha III ended his autocratic rule and instituted a constitutional monarchy. This brought about the Hawaiian Bill of Rights, but the most far-reaching change was the transition to private ownership of land, known as The Great Mahele. Formerly, all land belonged to the ruling chief, who gave wedge-shaped parcels called *ahupua'a* to lesser chiefs to be worked for him. The commoners did all the real labor, their produce heavily taxed by the *ali'i*. The fortunes of war, the death of a chief, or the mere whim of a superior could force a commoner off the land.

The Hawaiians, however, could not think in terms of owning land. No one could *possess* land, one could only *use* land, and its ownership was a foreign concept. As a result, naive Hawaiians gave up their lands for a song to unscrupulous traders, and land-ownership issues remain a basic and unrectified problem to this day. In 1847, Kamehameha III and his advisers separated the lands of Hawaii into three groupings: crown land (belonging to the king), government land (belonging to the chiefs), and the people's land (the largest parcels). In 1848, 245 *ali'i* entered their land claims in the *Mahele Book,* assuring them ownership. In 1850, the commoners were given title in fee simple to the lands they cultivated and lived on as tenants, not including house lots in towns. Commoners without land could buy small *kuleana* (farms) from the government at $0.50 per acre. In 1850, foreigners were also allowed to purchase land in fee simple, and the ownership of Hawaii from that day forward slipped steadily from the hands of its indigenous people.

THE END OF A KINGDOM

Like the Hawaiian people themselves, the Kamehameha dynasty in the mid-1800s was dying from within. King Kamehameha IV (Alexander Liholiho) ruled 1854-1863; his only child died in 1862. He was succeeded by his older brother Kamehameha V (Lot

Kamehameha), who ruled until 1872. With his passing the Kamehameha line ended. William Lunalilo, elected king in 1873 by popular vote, was of royal lineage, but not of the Kamehameha bloodline. He died after only a year in office, and being a bachelor, he left no heirs. He was succeeded by David Kalakaua, known far and wide as the "Merrie Monarch," who made a world tour and was well received wherever he went. He built 'Iolani Palace in Honolulu and was personally in favor of closer ties with the United States, helping to push through the Reciprocity Act. Kalakaua died in 1891 and was replaced by his sister, Lydia Lili'uokalani, last of the Hawaiian monarchs.

REVOLUTION
AND ANNEXATION

When Lili'uokalani took office in 1891, the native population was at a low of 40,000, and she felt that the United States had too much influence over her homeland. She was known to personally favor the English over the Americans. She attempted to replace the liberal constitution of 1887 (adopted by her pro-American brother) with an autocratic mandate in which she would have had much more political and economic control of the islands.

When the McKinley Tariff of 1890 brought a decline in sugar profits, she made no attempt to improve the situation. Thus, the planters saw her as a political obstacle to their economic growth; most of Hawaii's American planters and merchants were in favor of a rebellion. A central spokesperson and firebrand was Lorrin Thurston, a Honolulu publisher, who, with a core of about 30 men, challenged the Hawaiian monarchy. Although Lili'uokalani rallied some support and had a small military potential in her personal guard, the coup was relatively bloodless—it took only one casualty. Naturally, the conspirators could not have succeeded without some solid assurances from a secret contingent in the U.S. Congress as well as outgoing president Benjamin Harrison, who favored Hawaii's annexation. Marines from the *Boston*

went ashore to "protect American lives," and on January 17, 1893, the Hawaiian monarchy came to an end.

Sanford B. Dole, who became president of the Hawaiian Republic, headed the provisional government. Lili'uokalani surrendered not to the conspirators, but to U.S. ambassador John Stevens. She believed that the U.S. government, which had assured her of Hawaiian independence, would be outraged by the overthrow and would come to her aid. Incoming president Grover Cleveland *was* outraged, and Hawaii wasn't immediately annexed as expected.

In January 1895, a small, ill-fated counterrevolution headed by Lili'uokalani failed, and she was placed under house arrest in 'Iolani Palace. Officials of the Republic insisted that she use her married name (Mrs. John Dominis) to sign the documents forcing her to abdicate her throne. She was also forced to swear allegiance to the new Republic. Lili'uokalani went on to write *Hawaii's Story* and the lyric ballad "Aloha O'e." She never forgave the conspirators and remained queen in the minds of Hawaiians until her death in 1917.

On July 7, 1898, President William McKinley signed the annexation agreement, arguing that the U.S. military must have Hawaii in order to be a viable force in the Pacific.

PEARL HARBOR ATTACK

On the morning of December 7, 1941, the Japanese carrier *Akagi*, flying the battle flag of Admiral Togo of Russo-Japanese War fame, received and broadcast over its public-address system island music from Honolulu station KGMB. Deep in the bowels of the ship, a radio operator listened for a much different message coming thousands of miles from the Japanese mainland. When the ironically poetic message "east wind rain" was received, the attack was launched. At the end of the day, 2,325 U.S. soldiers and 57 civilians were dead; 188 planes were destroyed; 18 major warships were sunk or heavily damaged; and the United States was engaged in World War

II. Japanese casualties were ludicrously light. The ignited conflict would rage for four years until Japan, through the atomic bombing of Nagasaki and Hiroshima, was brought into total submission. By the end of hostilities, Hawaii would never again be considered separate from America.

STATEHOOD

Several economic and political motivations explain why the ruling elite of Hawaii desired statehood, but put simply, the vast majority of people who lived there, especially after World War II, considered themselves Americans. The first serious mention of making the Hawaiian Islands a state was in the 1850s under President Franklin Pierce, but the idea wasn't taken seriously until the monarchy was overthrown in the 1890s. For the next 50 years, statehood proposals were made repeatedly to Congress, but there was stiff opposition, especially from the southern states. With Hawaii a territory, an import quota system beneficial to mainland producers could be enacted on produce, especially sugar. Also, there was prejudice against creating a state in a place where the majority of the populace was not white.

During World War II, Hawaii was placed under martial law, but no serious attempt to confine the Japanese population was made, as it was in California. There were simply too many Japanese, and many went on to gain the respect of the American people through their outstanding fighting record during the war. Hawaii's own 100th Battalion became the famous 442nd Regimental Combat Team, which gained notoriety by saving the Lost Texas Battalion during the Battle of the Bulge and went on to be *the* most decorated battalion in all of World War II. When these GIs returned home, *no one* was going to tell them that they were not loyal Americans. Many of these Americans of Japanese Ancestry (AJAs) took advantage of the GI Bill and received higher education. They were from the common people, not the elite, and they rallied grassroots support for statehood. When the vote finally occurred, approximately 132,900 voted in favor of statehood with only 7,800 votes against. Congress passed the Hawaii State Bill on March 12, 1959, and on August 21, 1959, President Dwight Eisenhower announced that Hawaii was officially the 50th state.

People and Culture

POPULATION

Of the nearly 1.4 million people that reside in Hawaii, 963,607 live on O'ahu, with slightly less than half of these living in the Honolulu metropolitan area. Statewide, city dwellers outnumber those living in the country by nine to one. O'ahu's population accounts for 70 percent of the state's population, yet the island comprises only 9 percent of the state's land total. Sections of Waikiki can have a combined population of permanent residents and visitors as high as 90,000 per square mile, making cities like Tokyo, Hong Kong, and New York seem roomy by comparison. The next most populous islands are the Big Island, at more than 185,000 residents, and Maui with

nearly 150,000 residents. Kaua'i has just over 68,000 people. Molokai has just over 7,000, while Lana'i is home to just over 3,000.

PEOPLE

Nowhere else on earth can you find such a kaleidoscopic mixture of people as in Hawaii. More than 50 ethnic groups are represented throughout the islands, making Hawaii the most racially integrated state in the country. Ethnic breakdowns for the state include 25.3 percent Hawaiian/part Hawaiian, 20.5 percent Caucasian, 18.4 percent Japanese, 10 percent Filipino, 8.9 percent Hispanic/Latino, and 4.2 percent Chinese.

Ni'ihau, a privately owned island, is home

to about 160 pure-blooded Hawaiians, representing the largest concentration of Hawaiians per capita in the islands. The Robinson family, which owns the island, restricts visitors to invited guests only. The second-largest concentration is on Moloka'i, where 2,700 Hawaiians, living mostly on a 40-acre *kuleana* of Hawaiian Home Lands, make up 40 percent of that island's population. The majority of mixed-blood Hawaiians, 240,000 or so, live on O'ahu, where they are particularly strong in the hotel and entertainment fields.

Native Hawaiians

When Captain Cook first sighted Hawaii in 1778, there were an estimated 300,000 natives living in relative harmony with their ecological surroundings; within 100 years a scant 50,000 Hawaiians remained. Today, although more than 240,000 people claim varying degrees of Hawaiian blood, experts say that fewer than 1,000 are pure Hawaiian.

Ancient Hawaiian society was divided into rankings by a strict caste system determined by birth, and from which there was no chance of escaping. The highest rank was the *ali'i,* the chiefs and royalty. A *kahuna* was a highly skilled person whose advice was sought before any major project was undertaken, such as building a house, hollowing a canoe log, or even offering a prayer. The *mo'o kahuna* were the priests of Ku and Lono, and they were in charge of praying and following rituals. They were very powerful *ali'i* and kept strict secrets and laws concerning their various functions.

Besides this priesthood of *kahuna,* there were other *kahuna* who were not *ali'i,* but commoners. The two most important were the healers (*kahuna lapa'au*) and the sorcerers (*kahuna 'ana'ana*) who could pray a person to death. The *kahuna lapa'au* had a marvelous pharmacopoeia of herbs and spices that could cure over 250 diseases common to the Hawaiians.

The common people were called the *maka'ainana,* "the people of land"—the farmers, craftspeople, and fishers. The land they lived on was controlled by the *ali'i,* but they were not bound to it. If the local *ali'i* was cruel or unfair, the *maka'ainana* had the right to leave and reside on another's lands. *Maka'ainana* who lived close to the *ali'i* and could be counted on as warriors in times of trouble were called *kanaka no lua kaua* (a man for the heat of battle). They were treated with greater favor than those who lived in the backcountry, *kanaka no hi'i kua,* whose lesser standing opened them up to discrimination and cruelty. All *maka'ainana* formed extended families, called *'ohana,* who usually lived on the same section of land, called *ahupua'a.* Those farmers who lived inland would barter their produce with the fishers who lived on the shore, and thus all shared equally in the bounty of land and sea.

A special group called *kauwa* was an untouchable caste confined to living on reservations. Their origins were obviously Polynesian, but they appeared to be descendants of castaways who had survived and became perhaps the aboriginals of Hawaii before the main migrations. It was *kapu* for anyone to go onto *kauwa* lands; doing so meant instant death. If a human sacrifice was needed, the *kahuna* would simply summon a *kauwa,* who had no recourse but to mutely comply. To this day, to call someone *kauwa,* which now supposedly only means servant, is still considered a fight-provoking insult.

A strict division of labor existed among men and women. Men were the only ones permitted to have anything to do with taro. This crop was so sacred that there were a greater number of *kapu* concerning taro than concerning a man himself. Men pounded poi and served it to the women. Men were also the fishers and the builders of houses, canoes, irrigation ditches, and walls. Women tended to other gardens and shoreline fishing and were responsible for making tapa cloth. The entire family lived in the common house called the *hale noa.*

Ali'i could also declare a *kapu* and often did so. Certain lands or fishing areas were temporarily made *kapu* so that they could be revitalized. Even today, it is *kapu* for anyone to remove all the *'opihi* (a type of limpet) from a rock. The greatest *kapu, kapu moe*, was afforded to the highest-ranking *ali'i*: anyone coming into their presence had to prostrate themselves. Lesser-ranking *ali'i* were afforded the *kapu noho*: lessers had to sit or kneel in their presence. Commoners could not let their shadows fall on an *ali'i*, nor enter the house of an *ali'i* except through a special door. Breaking a *kapu* meant immediate death.

RELIGION

The Polynesian Hawaiians worshipped nature. They saw its forces manifested in a multiplicity of forms to which they ascribed godlike powers, and they based daily life on this animistic philosophy.

Any object, animate or inanimate, could be a god. Anything or anyone could be infused with *mana,* especially a dead body or a respected ancestor. *'Ohana* had personal family gods called *'aumakua* on whom they called in times of danger or strife. There were children of gods called *kupua*, who were thought to live among humans and were distinguished either for their beauty and strength or for their ugliness and terror.

Ancient Hawaiians performed religious ceremonies at *heiau*, temples. The basic *heiau* was a masterfully built and fitted rectangular stone wall that varied in size, from about as big as a basketball court to as big as a football field. Once the restraining outer walls were built, the interior was backfilled with smaller stones, and the top dressing was expertly laid and then rolled, perhaps with a log, to form a pavement-like surface. All that remains of Hawaii's many *heiau* are the stone platforms or walls. The buildings on them, constructed in perishable wood, leaves, and grass, have long since disappeared.

The Hawaiian people worshipped gods who took the form of idols fashioned from wood, feathers, or stone. The eyes were made from shells, and until these were inlaid, the idol was dormant. The hair used was often human hair, and the arms and legs were usually flexed. The mouth was either gaping or formed a wide figure eight lying on its side, and more likely than not was lined with glistening dog teeth. Small figures made of woven basketry were expertly covered with feathers taken from specific birds.

In the 1820s, missionaries brought Congregational Christianity and the "true path" to heaven to Hawaii, setting out to convert the pagan Hawaiians and "civilize" them. Catholics, Mormons, Adventists, Episcopalians, Unitarians, Christian Scientists, Lutherans, Baptists, Jehovah's Witnesses, the Salvation Army, and every other major and minor denomination of Christianity that followed in their wake brought its own brand of enlightenment. Chinese and Japanese immigrants established major sects of Buddhism, Confucianism, Taoism, and Shintoism. Today, Allah is praised, the Torah is chanted in Jewish synagogues, and nirvana is available at a variety of Hindu temples, even the Church of Scientology is selling books and salvation.

LANGUAGE

In Hawaii, English is the primary language spoken, yet the beat and melody of the local dialect is noticeably different. Hawaii has its own unmistakable linguistic regionalism. The many ethnic people who make up Hawaii have enriched the English spoken with words, expressions, and subtle shades of meaning that are commonly used and understood throughout the islands. The greatest influence on the English spoken here comes from the Hawaiian language, and words such as *aloha, hula, lu'au,* and *lei* are familiarly used and understood by all.

Pidgin

Other migrant peoples, especially the Chinese, Japanese, and Portuguese, influenced the local dialect to such an extent that the simplified plantation lingo they spoke has become known as "pidgin." English is the official language of the state, business, and education, but pidgin is the language of the people. Hawaiian words make up most of pidgin's non-English vocabulary, but it includes a good smattering of Chinese, Japanese, and Samoan as well. The distinctive rising inflection is provided by the melodious Mediterranean lilt of the Portuguese. Pidgin is not a stagnant language. It's kept alive by new slang words introduced by younger generations of speakers. *Maka'ainana* of all socio-ethnic backgrounds can at least understand pidgin. Most islanders are proud of it, but some consider it a low-class jargon.

Hawaiian

The Hawaiian language sways like a palm tree in a gentle wind. Its words are as melodious as a love song. With its many Polynesian root words easily traced to Indonesian and Malay, Hawaiian is obviously from this same stock. The Hawaiian spoken today is very different from old Hawaiian. Its greatest metamorphosis occurred when the missionaries began to write it down in the 1820s. Still, it nearly vanished. There has been a movement to reestablish the Hawaiian language over the last couple of decades. Not only are courses offered at the University of Hawai'i, but there is also a successful elementary school immersion program in the state, some books are being printed in it, and more and more musicians are performing in Hawaiian.

Hawaiian is, by and large, no longer spoken as a language except on Ni'ihau and in Hawaiian-language immersion classes and family settings; the closest tourists will come to it is in place-names, street names, and words that have become part of common usage, such as *aloha* and *mahalo*. There are sermons in Hawaiian at some local churches. Kawaiaha'o Church in downtown Honolulu is the most famous of these, but each island has its own.

Thanks to the missionaries, the Hawaiian language is rendered phonetically using only 12 letters. They are the five vowels, *a-e-i-o-u*, sounded as they are in Spanish, and seven consonants, *h-k-l-m-n-p-w*, sounded exactly as they are in English. Sometimes *w*

is pronounced as *v*, but this only occurs in the middle of a word and always follows a vowel. A consonant is always followed by a vowel, forming two-letter syllables, but vowels are often found in pairs or even triplets. A slight oddity about Hawaiian is the glottal stop called *'okina*. This is an abrupt break in sound in the middle of a word, such as "oh-oh" in English, and is denoted with a reverse apostrophe ('). A good example is the one in *ali'i* or, even better, the O'ahu town of Ha'iku, which actually means Abrupt Break.

Pronunciation Key

For those unfamiliar with the sounds of Spanish or other Romance languages, the vowels are sounded as follows:

A—pronounced as in "ah" (that feels good!). For example, *tapa* is "tah-pah."

E—short *e* is "eh," as in "pen" or "dent" (thus *hale* is "hah-leh"). Long *e* sounds like "ay" as in "sway" or "day." For example, the Hawaiian goose (*nene*) is a "nay-nay," not a "nee-nee."

I—pronounced "ee" as in "see" or "we" (thus *pali* is pronounced "pah-lee").

O—pronounced as in "no" or "oh," such as "oh-noh" (*ono*).

U—pronounced "oo" as in "do" or "stew." For example, "kah-poo" (*kapu*).

Diphthongs and Stresses

Eight vowel pairs are known as "diphthongs" (ae-ai-ao-au-ei-eu-oi-ou). These are the sounds made by gliding from one vowel to another within a syllable. The stress is placed on the first vowel. In English, examples would be **soil** and **bail.** Common examples in Hawaiian are *lei* and *heiau*.

Many Hawaiian words are commonly used in English, appear in English dictionaries, and therefore would ordinarily be subject to the rules of English grammar. The Hawaiian language, however, does not pluralize nouns by adding an *s*; the singular and plural are differentiated in context. The following are some examples of plural Hawaiian nouns treated this way in this book: *haole* (not *haoles*), *kahuna,* lei, and lu'au.

FOOD

Thanks to Hawaii's plantation past, immigrants from around the world also brought their cuisine to the islands, and many of the dishes remain local favorites to this day. You'll find Chinese dim sum and bao, char siu stuffed steamed buns called manapua, Korean kimchi, Vietnamese pho, Puerto Rican pasteles, Portuguese malasadas, tonkatsu from Japan, and SPAM, biscuits, and gravy from World War II Americans in ethnic eateries and on menus across the state.

While local Hawaiian food is rooted in Polynesian techniques and flavors, it is also an amalgam of the cuisine from the immigrants who became an integral part of Hawaiian culture. Plate lunches, found mainly at drive-in restaurants (island-style fast food), are served with two scoops of rice, macaroni salad, and a protein, including chicken katsu, kalbi, or kalua pork. This affordable and filling meal incorporates Japanese, Korean, American, and Hawaiian cooking. Loco moco is another favorite plate for lunch as well as breakfast: two fried eggs, a hamburger patty over rice smothered in gravy—talk about East meets West.

The food served at luʻau is very similar to what you'll find at a Hawaiian food restaurant, and there are several staple dishes no matter where you go. Kalua pig is a favorite, a smoky-flavored pulled pork tossed with cabbage. Traditionally, it is cooked in an *imu*, an underground earthen oven. Chicken long rice has bits of thigh meat cooked with ginger, green onions, and long rice noodles in a chicken broth. Lau lau is fish, pork, or chicken wrapped in taro leaves and steamed in *ti* leaves, lomi salmon is raw cubed salmon tossed with tomatoes, onion, and chile peppers, and squid luʻau is young taro leaves and squid cooked in coconut milk, the end product a tasty dish resembling creamed spinach. *Poke* (pronounced like okay with a p), is a raw fish salad made with ahi tuna, soy sauce (called shoyu in Hawaii), and sesame oil. There are all different kinds of *poke*, some have onions and seaweed, some are spicy, some are mayonnaise based, and sometimes the fish is replaced with *tako* (octopus). No Hawaiian luʻau is complete without poi, a staple starch made from pounded taro root, and haupia, a coconut milk-based dessert usually served as a congealed pudding.

THE ARTS
Music

Ancient Hawaiians passed along stories through chants, in which the emphasis was placed on historical accuracy, not melody. The missionaries were the first to introduce the Hawaiians to melody through Christian hymns, and soon singing became both an individual and group pastime. Early in the 1800s, Spanish vaqueros from California were imported to teach the Hawaiians how to be cowboys. With them came guitars and moody ballads. Immigrants who came along a little later in the 19th century, especially from Portugal, helped create Hawaiian-style music. Their biggest influence was a small, four-stringed instrument called a *braga* or *cavaquinho*, the prototype of the homegrown Hawaiian instrument that became known as the ukulele. "Jumping flea," the translation of ukulele, is an appropriate name devised by the Hawaiians when they saw how nimble the fingers were as they jumped over the strings. Over many decades, Hawaiian music has evolved through techniques like slack key tuning, the twang and easy slide of the steel guitar, and the smooth falsetto singing that accompanies the relaxed melodies. Today, popular Hawaiian music has fused with the beat of reggae, creating a style of music locally known as jawaiian.

Hula

The hula is more than an ethnic dance; it is the soul of Hawaii expressed in motion. It began as a form of worship during religious ceremonies and was danced only by highly trained men. It gradually evolved into a form of entertainment, but in no regard was it sexual. It was history portrayed in the performing arts. In the beginning an androgynous deity named

The Lu'au

The lu'au is an island institution. Local families have big lu'au for a baby's first birthday, anniversaries, graduations, and family reunions. Commercial operators have packaged the lu'au as nightly dinner and entertainment so visitors can get a glimpse of the tradition and traditional Hawaiian fare—kalua pig, lau lau, chicken long rice, lomi salmon, white rice, and poi. For a fixed price, you can gorge yourself on a tremendous variety of island foods, sample a few island drinks, and have an evening of entertainment as well. Lu'au run from about 5pm to 8:30pm. On your lu'au day, eat a light breakfast and skip lunch.

All commercial lu'au have pretty much the same format, though the types of food and entertainment differ somewhat. The tourist variety of lu'au is a lot of food, a lot of fun, but definitely a show. To have fun at a lu'au you have to get into the swing of things, like the Polynesian Revue. Local performers dance and lead the tourist hula—the fast version with swaying hips and dramatic lighting—a few wandering troubadours sing Hawaiian standards, and a muscular, sweaty man will swing flaming torches. Some offer an *imu* ceremony where the pig is taken from the covered oven, as well as traditional games, arts, and crafts. Food is usually served buffet style, although a few do it family style. Most tourist lu'au have American and Asian dishes for those less adventurous souls.

Laka descended to earth and taught men how to dance the hula. In time the male aspect of Laka departed for the heavens, but the female aspect remained. The female Laka set up her own special hula *heiau* at Ha'ena on the Na Pali coast of Kaua'i, where it still exists. As time went on women were allowed to learn the hula. Scholars surmise that men became too busy wresting a living from the land to maintain the art form.

Men did retain one type of hula for themselves called *lua*. This was a form of martial art employed in hand-to-hand combat that evolved into a ritualized warfare dance called *hula ku'i*. During the 19th century, the hula almost vanished because the missionaries considered it vile and heathen. King Kalakaua saved it during the late 1800s, when he formed his own troupe and encouraged the dancers to learn the old hula. Many of the original dances had been forgotten, but some were retained and are performed to this day.

Today, hula *halau* (schools) are active on every island, teaching hula and keeping the old ways and culture alive. Hula combines the chanting of the *mele* (story) and is accompanied by traditional instruments like the *ipu* (gourd). Performers spend years perfecting their techniques telling stories through dance.

They show off their accomplishments during the fierce competition of the Merrie Monarch Festival in Hilo every April. The winning *halau* is praised and recognized throughout the islands.

Almost every major resort offering entertainment or a lu'au also offers a hula revue. Most times, young island beauties accompanied by proficient local musicians put on a floor show for the tourists. It's entertaining, but it's not traditional hula.

Weaving and Carving

Hawaiians became the best basket makers and mat weavers in all of Polynesia. *Ulana* (woven mats) were made from *lau hala* (pandanus) leaves. Once split, the spine was removed and the leaves stored in large rolls. When needed they were soaked, pounded, and then fashioned into various floor coverings and sleeping mats. Intricate geometrical patterns were woven in, and the edges were rolled and well fashioned. A wide variety of basketry was made from the aerial root *'ie'ie*, and the shapes varied according to use. Some baskets were tall and narrow, some were cones, others were flat like trays, and many were woven around gourds and calabashes.

Wood was a primary material used by

Hawaiian artisans. They almost exclusively used *koa* because of its density, strength, and natural luster. It was turned into canoes, woodware, calabashes, and furniture for the *ali'i*. Temple idols were another major product of woodcarving. A variety of stone artifacts were also turned out, including poi pounders, fish sinkers, and small idols.

The most respected artisans in old Hawaii were the canoe makers. With little more than a stone adze and a pump drill, they built canoes that could carry 200 people and last for generations—sleek, well-proportioned, and infinitely seaworthy. The main hull was usually a gigantic *koa* log, and the gunwale planks were minutely drilled and sewn to the sides with sennit rope. Apprenticeships lasted for years, and a young man knew that he had graduated when one day he was nonchalantly asked to sit down and eat with the master builders. Small family-sized canoes with outriggers were used for fishing and perhaps carried a spear rack; large ocean-going double-hulled canoes were used for migration and warfare. On these, the giant logs had been adzed to about two inches thick. A mainsail woven from pandanus was mounted on a central platform, and the boat was steered by two long paddles. The hull was dyed with plant juices and charcoal, and the entire village helped launch the canoe in a ceremony called "drinking the sea."

Lei Making and Featherwork

Any flower or blossom can be strung into lei, but the most common are orchids or the lovely smelling plumeria. Lei are all beautiful, but special lei are highly prized by those who know what to look for. Of the different stringing styles, the most common is *kui*—stringing the flower through the middle or side. Most "airport-quality" lei are of this type. The *humuhumu* style, reserved for making flat lei, is made by sewing flowers and ferns to a *ti,* banana, or sometimes *hala* leaf. A *humuhumu* lei makes an excellent hatband. *Wili* is the winding together of greenery, ferns, and flowers into short, bouquet-type lengths. The most traditional form is *hili,* which requires no stringing at all but involves braiding fragrant ferns and leaves such as *maile.* If flowers are interwoven, the *hili* becomes the *haku* style, the most difficult and most beautiful type of lei.

The highly refined art of featherwork was practiced only on the islands of Tahiti, New Zealand, and Hawaii, but the fashioning of feather helmets and idols was unique to Hawaii. Favorite colors were red and yellow, which came only in a very limited supply from a small number of birds such as the *'o'o, 'i'iwi, mamo,* and *'apapane.* Professional bird hunters in old Hawaii paid their taxes to *ali'i* in prized feathers. The feathers were fastened to a woven net of *olona* cord and made into helmets, idols, and beautiful flowing capes and cloaks. These resplendent garments were made and worn only by men, especially during battle, when a fine cloak became a great trophy of war. Featherwork was also employed in the making of *kahili* and lei, which were highly prized by the noble *ali'i* women.

Tapa Cloth

Tapa, cloth made from tree bark, was common throughout Polynesia and was a woman's art. A few trees such as the *wauke* and *mamaki* produced the best cloth, but a variety of other types of bark could be utilized. First the raw bark was pounded into a felt-like pulp and beaten together to form strips (the beaters had distinctive patterns that helped make the cloth supple). The cloth was then decorated by stamping (a form of block printing) and dyed with natural colors from plants and sea animals in shades of gray, purple, pink, and red. They were even painted with natural brushes made from pandanus fruit, with an overall gray color made from charcoal. The tapa cloth was sewn together to make bed coverings, and fragrant flowers and herbs were either sewn or pounded in to produce a permanent fragrance. Tapa cloth is still available today, but the Hawaiian methods have been lost, and most tapa comes from other areas of Polynesia.

Getting There and Around

AIR

With its isolated location in the middle of the Pacific Ocean, the only way to get to Hawaii is via airplane. Most commercial flights to Hawaii are routed to the **Honolulu International Airport** (code: HNL, 300 Rodgers Blvd., 808/836-6411, http://hawaii.gov/hnl); however, some carriers provide direct service to neighbor islands. The Honolulu airport has three terminals: the **Overseas Terminal** accommodates international and mainland flights, the **Interisland Terminal** handles Hawaiian Airlines flights, and the **Commuter Terminal** handles the small interisland carriers. There is a free intra-airport shuttle service for getting around the airport. Ground transportation is available just outside the baggage claim areas on the lower level, along the center median. The airport is 10 miles from Waikiki and six miles from downtown Honolulu.

The Big Island has two major airports. The **Kona International Airport** (code: KOA, 73-200 Kupipi St., 808/327-9520, hawaii.gov/koa) serves international, overseas and interisland flights. It is the island's primary airport, located on the west side of the island, seven miles from Kailua. The **Hilo International Airport** (code: ITO, Kekuanaoa St., 808/961-9300, hawaii.gov/ito), on the east side of the island just two miles east of Hilo, serves interisland carriers.

In Maui County, the **Kahului Airport** (code: OGG, 1 Kahului Airport Rd., 808/872-3830, hawaii.gov/ogg) is the primary airport on Maui, a hub for overseas and interisland flights. Two smaller airports are serviced by only commuter airlines: **Hana Airport** (code: HNM, 808/248-4861, hawaii.gov/hnm) on the northeast coast and the **Kapalua Airport** (code: JHM, 808/665-6108, hawaii.gov/jhm) on the west side, a quick drive from Ka'anapali and Lahaina.

The **Moloka'i Airport** (code: MKK, 808/567-9660, hawaii.gov/mkk), located about seven miles northwest of Kaunakakai, is serviced by interisland and commuter planes, while the tiny **Kalaupapa** Airport (code: LUP, 808/838-8701, hawaii.gov/lup) is serviced by commuter planes for residents and visitors touring the Kalaupapa National Historic Park. A permit from the **Hawaii Department of Health** (808/567-6924, health.hawaii.gov) is necessary prior to making air reservations. **Lana'i Airport** (code: LNY, 808/565-7942, hawaii.gov/lny), located three miles southwest of Lanai City, is serviced by interisland and commuter planes.

On Kaua'i, the **Lihue Airport** (code: LIH, 3901 Mokulele Loop, 808/274-3800, hawaii.gov/lih) is the primary airport on the island, handling domestic, overseas, and interisland commercial flights, including commuter and air taxis. It's located on the southeast coast, about 1.5 miles east of Lihue town.

Air is the only commercial way to island hop, except for ferries between Maui and Moloka'i and Lana'i. **Hawaiian Airlines** (800/367-5320, hawaiianairlines.com) is Hawaii's leading commercial carrier, with the largest selection of flights between the main Islands. **Mokulele Airlines** (866/260-7070, mokuleleairlines.com) utilizes a prop caravan service to ferry passengers to and from Moloka'i and Lana'i. Their small prop planes also service the smaller airports in Hana and Kapalua, Maui. **Island Air** (800/652-6541, islandair.com) has a fleet of turboprop planes that service routes from Kaua'i, Maui, Moloka'i, and Lana'i to O'ahu.

Everyone visiting Hawaii must fill out a Plants and Animals Declaration Form and present it upon arrival in the state. Anyone carrying any of the prohibited items, including fruits, vegetables, plants, seeds, and soil, as well as live insects, seafood, snakes, and amphibians, must go through an inspection at the airport. For additional information

BACKGROUND AND ESSENTIALS
GETTING THERE AND AROUND

on just what is prohibited, contact any U.S. Customs Office or check with an embassy or consulate.

Before you leave Hawaii for the mainland, all of your bags are subject to **agricultural inspection** before you enter the ticketing line to check luggage and get your boarding pass. There are no restrictions on beach sand from below the high-water line, coconuts, cooked foods, dried flower arrangements, fresh flower lei, pineapples, certified pest-free plants and cuttings, and seashells. However, papaya must be treated before departure. Other restricted items are berries, fresh gardenias, jade vines, live insects and snails, cotton, plants in soil, soil itself, and sugarcane. Raw sugarcane is acceptable if it is cut between the nodes, has the outer covering peeled off, is split into fourths, and is commercially prepackaged. For any questions about plants that you want to take to the mainland, call the **Agricultural Quarantine Inspection office** (808/861-8490) in Honolulu.

Shuttle Service

Several shuttle services offer transportation to most hotels and resorts, including **Roberts Hawaii Express Shuttle** (808/539-9400 or 800/831-5541, www.robertshawaii. com) **SpeediShuttle** (877/242-5777, www. speedishuttle.com), and **Executive Airport Shuttle** (800/833-2303, hawaiiexecutive-transportation.com).

CAR

The easiest way to get around each island is by car. If you haven't booked a **rental car** online prior to your arrival, the registration counters are located in the baggage claim area or just outside. All car rental shuttles stop in the designated area of the airports just outside the baggage claim areas.

In Hawaii, there are several local courtesies to follow on the road. Drivers don't honk their horns except to say hello or in an emergency. It's considered rude to honk to hurry someone along. Hawaiian drivers reflect the climate: They're relaxed and polite. Often on small roads, they'll brake to let you turn left when they're coming at you. They may assume you'll do the same, so be ready, after a perfunctory turn signal from another driver, for him or her to turn across your lane. The more rural the area, the more likely this is to happen. On all roadways, it is customary to let a signaling motorist change lanes in front of you. If you need to change lanes and someone lets you in, always give a thank-you wave. When merging, people allow every other car into the lane.

Hawaii has a **seat-belt law** as well as a **ban on cell phones** while driving. Speed limits change periodically along the highways, particularly when they pass through small towns. Police routinely check the speed of traffic with radar equipment, often hiding in a blind spot to radar and ticket speeding motorists.

BUS

On Oʻahu, **TheBus** (808/848-4500, www. thebus.org) provides island-wide transportation, including from the airport. If you're planning on riding the bus from the airport to your hotel, keep in mind that your bags have to be able to fit under the seat or on your lap without protruding into the aisle. There are several bus stops on the second level of the airport on the center median. Route Nos. 19, 20, and 31 access the airport, and Route No. 19 eastbound will take you to Waikiki. Fares are $2.50 for adults, $1.25 children ages 6-17, children 5 and under are free if they sit on an adult's lap. The Visitors Pass, a four consecutive day pass, is $25 with unlimited use. Call 808/848-5555 for route information.

The **Maui Bus** (808/270-7511, www. co.maui.hi.us/bus) system has eight routes for an inexpensive way to get around to the major towns. Fares are $2 per boarding or $4 for a day pass, and monthly passes are also available. Although the bus does run to the airport, riders are not allowed to board with luggage that can't fit under their seat. For a full listing of island bus schedules refer to the timetables on the website.

The **Kaua'i Bus** (808/241-6410, www.kauai.gov/Transportation, 5:27am-10:40pm Mon.-Fri. and 6:21am-5:50pm Sat., Sun., and holidays) runs island-wide, with stops from Hanalei to the west side. The bus is a green, convenient, and affordable way to get around. The last stop in Hanalei is the old Hanalei courthouse, so the bus doesn't go out to the end of the road, and on the west side it runs to Kekaha, not out to Polihale. Fares are $2 for adults, $1 for children and seniors. Monthly passes are also available.

On the Big Island, the **Hele-On Bus** (www.heleonbus.org) operates daily routes all around the island. The main bus terminal is in downtown Hilo at Mo'oheau Park, just at the corner of Kamehameha Avenue and Mamo Street. There are a number of intra-Hilo routes, with additional intercity routes to points around the periphery of the island, but these all operate on a very limited schedule, sometimes only once a day.

TAXI

On **O'ahu,** taxi service is available at the Honolulu International Airport. From the terminal to Waikiki costs about $35-40 during non-rush-hour periods with a maximum of four passengers. The fare is by meter only, and there is a charge of $0.35 per bag. To get around the island by taxi, it's best to call and make arrangements directly from a company, as it is technically illegal for taxi drivers to cruise around looking for a fare. Call **Charley's Taxi** (808/233-3333 or 877/531-1333, http://charleystaxi.com), **City Taxi** (808/524-2121, www.citytaxihonolulu.com), and **The Cab** (808/422-2222, www.thecabhawaii.com). For earth-conscious travelers, try **Eco Cab** (808/979-1010, www.ecocabhawaii.com). If you need some special attention like a limousine service, try **Cloud 9 Limousines** (808/524-7999, www.cloudninelimos.com). It is one of about 50 limo services on the island.

More than two-dozen taxi companies operate island-wide service on **Maui.** From Kahului Airport, the fare to Lahaina should be roughly $65, $80 to Ka'anapali, $100 to Kapalua, and $55 to Wailea. Expect $5-10 in and around Kahului, and about $14 to the hostels in Wailuku. Those in need of a taxi can call **Surf Taxi** (807/870-9974, www.surftaximaui.com), **West Maui Taxi** (808/661-1122, www.westmauitaxi.com), **Kihei Taxi** (808/298-1877, www.kiheitaxi.com), or **Aloha Maui Taxi** (808/661-5432, www.alohamauitaxi.com).

On the **Big Island,** both the Hilo and Kona airports always have taxis waiting for fares, which are regulated. From Hilo's airport to downtown costs about $15, to the Banyan Drive hotels about $10. From the Kona airport to hotels and condos along Ali'i Drive in Kailua fares run $25-40, north to Waikoloa Beach Resort they run about $50, and fares are approximately $70 as far north as the Mauna Kea Beach Hotel.

On **Kaua'i,** most taxi services run island-wide. Taxi rates are $3 per mile and $0.40 a minute. Prices are per minivan not per person. **Pono Express** (808/635-3478, www.ponoexpress.com) offers taxi, airport shuttle, and tour services. **North Shore Cab Co.** (808/639-7829, www.northshorecab.com) provides island-wide rides and sightseeing tours. For a more upscale ride, try **Kaua'i North Shore Limousine** (808/828-6189, www.kauainorthshorelimo.com). **Ace Kaua'i Taxi Services** (808/639-4310) will take you wherever you need to go.

Visas and Officialdom

Entering Hawaii is like entering anywhere else in the United States. Foreign nationals must have a current passport and most must have a proper visa, an ongoing or return air ticket, and sufficient funds for the proposed stay in Hawaii. A visa application can be made at any U.S. embassy or consular office outside the United States and must include a properly filled out application form, two photos, and a nonrefundable fee. Canadians do not need a visa but must have a passport. Visitors from many countries do not need a visa to enter the United States for 90 days or less. This list is amended periodically, so be sure to check in your country of origin to determine whether you need a visa for U.S. entry.

Everyone visiting Hawaii must fill out a Plants and Animals Declaration Form and present it to an airline flight attendant or the appropriate official upon arrival in the state. Anyone carrying any of the listed items must have those items inspected by an agricultural inspection agent at the airport. These items include but are not limited to fruits, vegetables, plants, seeds, and soil, as well as live insects, seafood, snakes, and amphibians. For additional information on just what is prohibited, contact any U.S. Customs Office or check with an embassy or consulate in foreign countries.

Hawaii has a very rigid pet quarantine policy designed to keep rabies and other diseases from reaching the state. All domestic pets are subject to 120 days' quarantine (a 30-day quarantine or a newer five-day-or-less quarantine is allowed by meeting certain pre-arrival and post-arrival requirements), and this includes substantial fees for boarding. Basically, it is not feasible to take your pet with you on your Hawaiian vacation. For complete information, contact the **Department of Agriculture, Animal Quarantine Division** (99-951 Halawa Valley St., Aiea, HI 96701, 808/483-7151, http://hdoa.hawaii,gov) in Honolulu.

Travel Tips

TRAVELING WITH CHILDREN

If you're traveling with young children, consider leaving all the gear at home to make your luggage lighter and less cumbersome. Car rental companies rent car seats for a small fee, and you can rent all kinds of other products for your stay on O'ahu, like a crib, pack-n-play, stroller, and high chair, even beach gear. **Paradise Baby** (808/561-1061, www.paradisebabyco.com) rents luxury baby equipment with free island-wide delivery and pickup. **Baby Aboard** (808/393-7612, www.babyaboard.com) serves the entire island, and **Baby's Away** (808/640-6734 or 800/496-6386, https://babysaway.com) rents equipment for Honolulu and Waikiki area visitors as well as those staying on Maui and the Big Island. On Kaua'i, contact **Ready Rentals** (800/599-8008, www.readyrentals.com) to rent various baby supplies. Cribs, tents, strollers, high chairs, and more are available to rent during your stay. One of the best sites on Maui for kids (other than the beach) is the **Maui Ocean Center,** which is full of hands-on activities and educational experiences. On the other hand, if you want to bring the little ones on vacation, but want to sneak away for a romantic dinner, the best service on the island for a short-term sitter is **The Nanny Connection** (808/875-4777, www.thenanny-connection.com), where professional sitting staff will meet you at your hotel and take care of your loved one in your absence.

Pet Quarantine

Hawaii has a very rigid pet quarantine policy designed to keep rabies and other mainland diseases from reaching the state. All domestic pets are subject to a **120-day quarantine** (a 30-day quarantine and five-day-or-less quarantine are allowed by meeting certain pre-arrival and post-arrival requirements). The process is expensive and time-consuming, and there are additional airline fees as well. Unless you are contemplating a move to Hawaii, it is not feasible to bring pets. Exceptions to the quarantine are made for animals originating in other rabies-free locales like Guam, Australia, New Zealand, and the British Isles. For complete information, contact the **Department of Agriculture, Animal Quarantine Division** (99-951 Halawa Valley St., 'Aiea, HI 96701, 808/483-7151, http://hdoa.hawaii.gov/) in Honolulu.

TRAVELERS WITH DISABILITIES

For a smooth trip, travelers with disabilities should make as many arrangements ahead of time as possible. Tell the transportation companies and hotels you'll be dealing with the nature of your restrictions in advance so they can make arrangements to accommodate you. Bring your medical records and notify medical establishments of your arrival if you'll need their services. Travel with a friend or make arrangements for an aide on arrival. Bring your own wheelchair if possible and let airlines know if it is battery-powered. Boarding interisland carriers sometimes requires steps. They'll board wheelchairs early on special lifts, but they must know you're coming. Most hotels and restaurants accommodate persons with disabilities, but always call ahead just to make sure.

The state Commission on Persons with Disabilities was designed with the express purpose of aiding disabled people. It is a source of invaluable information and distributes self-help booklets, which are published jointly by the Disability and Communication Access Board and the Hawaii Centers for Independent Living. Any person with disabilities heading to Hawaii should write first or visit the office of the **Hawaii Centers for Independent Living** (414 Kuwili St., #102, Honolulu, HI 96817, 808/522-5400, www.hcil.org). Additional information is available on the **Disability and Communication Access Board** (www.hawaii.gov/health/dcab/home) **Access Aloha Travel** (414 Kuwili St., #101, Honolulu, 808/545-1143 or 800/480-1143, www.accessalohatravel.com) rents wheelchair lift-equipped vans on Oʻahu for $200 per day or $723 per week; monthly rentals are also possible. This is a full-service travel agency and a good source of information on traveling with disabilities. Valid out-of-state **wheelchair-accessible parking placards** may be used throughout the state of Hawaii.

LGBT TRAVELERS

The overall mindset in Hawaii has long been acceptance of the LGBT community. In 2011, the state legalized civil unions for same-sex couples. Oʻahu has gay and lesbian bars, nightclubs, accommodations, and beaches. **Hula's Bar & Lei Stand** in Waikiki is a well-known hangout, as is **Queen's Beach** and the surrounding area of Kapiʻolani Park on Oʻahu, just a short walk from Hula's.

The **Travel Alternative Group** (www.tagapproved.com), a resource for accommodations and attractions, has approved **Aqua Hotels & Resorts** (www.aquaresorts.com/special-offers/lgbt-travel/), which offers discounts on reservations for LGBT travelers, and **Aston Hotels & Resorts** (www.AstonHotels.com). Another resource for finding accommodations and tours is the **International Gay and Lesbian Travel Association** (954/630-1637, www.iglta.org). They have tapped **Hotel Renew** (www.hotelrenew.com), **Discover Hawaii Tours** (808/690-9050, www.discoverhawaiitours.com) as gay and lesbian friendly. A few bed-and-breakfast establishments particularly cater to these groups; look for them on **Purple Roofs** (www.purpleroofs.com), a website dedicated to LGBT travel.

Health and Safety

In Hawaii, the most common health risks come from heatstroke, sunburn, intoxication, dehydration, and drowning.

SUN

The warming yet harmful rays of the sun come through more easily in Hawaii because of the sun's angle, and you don't feel them as much because there's always a cool breeze. The worst part of the day to be in direct sun is 11am-3pm. Oʻahu lies about 21.5 degrees north latitude, not even close to the equator, but it's still more than 1,000 miles south of sunny Southern California beaches. Use sunscreen on your face and exposed skin every day, even if you're not at the beach. Hats, sunglasses, beach umbrellas, plenty of water, and a dose of common sense will keep you active outdoors without a sunburn souvenir. And just because it's cloudy doesn't mean you can skip the sunscreen.

Whether out on the beach, hiking in the mountains, or just strolling around town, be very aware of dehydration. The sun and wind tend to sap your energy and your store of liquid. Carry bottled water with you at all times. Make sure to drink even more water than normal to account for the stress on your body under the strong Hawaiian sun.

MOSQUITOES AND COCKROACHES

Mosquitoes were unknown in the Hawaiian Islands until their larvae stowed away in the water barrels of the *Wellington* in 1826 and were introduced at Lahaina. They bred in the tropical climate and rapidly spread to all the islands. They are a particular nuisance in the rainforests, watersheds, and periodically damp areas like the windward coast and mountains. Be prepared, and bring a natural repellent like citronella oil, available in most health stores on the islands, or a commercial product available in grocery and drugstores.

Cockroaches are common in Hawaii. One comforting thought is that they aren't a sign of filth or dirty housekeeping. They love the climate like everyone else, and it's a real problem keeping them under control. Just do your best to handle it, they won't hurt you.

LEPTOSPIROSIS

Present in streams, ponds, and muddy soil, leptospirosis is a freshwater-borne bacteria deposited by the urine of infected animals. From 2 to 20 days after the bacteria enter the body, there will be a sudden onset of fever accompanied by chills, sweats, headache, and sometimes vomiting and diarrhea. Preventive measures include staying out of freshwater sources and mud where cattle and other animals wade and drink, not swimming in freshwater if you have an open cut, and not drinking stream water. Although not always the case, leptospirosis may be fatal if left untreated.

OCEAN SAFETY

More people drown in Hawaii than anywhere else in the world. In addition, powerful shore breaks are also the cause of severe injuries like broken backs and necks. But don't let these statistics deter you from enjoying the ocean. Instead, educate yourself on the day and area's ocean conditions and enjoy the water responsibly. Ask lifeguards or beach attendants about conditions and follow their advice. Common sense, good judgment, and respect for the ocean go a long way. And never turn your back on the ocean while enjoying the shoreline. Rogue waves can wash over reef, rock, and beach and pull you out into the water. Obey all warning signs posted on the beach, and if you're swimming, surfing, or snorkeling, return to shore before you get tired. If you engage in an ocean activity by yourself, make sure you tell others in your party your planned whereabouts in the event of an emergency. If you find yourself on the beach psyching yourself up to get in the water, it's probably better to heed the warning, "If in doubt, stay out."

Sharks, Urchins, and Coral

Sharks live in all the oceans of the world. Most mind their own business and stay away from shore. Hawaiian sharks are well fed—on fish—and don't usually bother with unsavory humans. If you encounter a shark, don't panic! Never thrash around because this will trigger their attack instinct.

Portuguese man-of-wars and other jellyfish put out long, floating tentacles that sting if they touch you. Jellyfish are blown into shore by winds on the 8th, 9th, and 10th days after the full moon. Don't wash the sting off with freshwater because this will only aggravate it. Locals will use hot saltwater to take away the sting, as well as alcohol (the drinking or rubbing kind), aftershave lotion, or meat tenderizer (MSG), but lifeguards use common household vinegar. After rinsing, soak with a wet towel. An antihistamine may also bring relief. Expect to start to feel better in about a half hour.

Coral can give you a nasty cut, and it's known for causing infections because it's a living organism. Wash the cut immediately and apply an antiseptic. Keep it clean and covered, and watch for infection. With coral cuts, it's best to have a professional look at it to clean it out. Most infection comes from tiny bits of coral that are left deep in the cut. Never stand on or grab coral. It damages the fragile life form and can send you to the hospital.

Poisonous sea urchins, like the lacquer-black *wana,* are found in shallow tidepools and reefs and will hurt you if you step on them. Their spines will break off, enter your foot, and severely burn. There are cures. Soaking a couple of times in vinegar for half an hour or so should stop the burning. If vinegar is not available, the local cure-all is urine.

EMERGENCIES AND MEDICAL SERVICES

For **police, fire, or ambulance,** dial **911.** For **nonemergency police** assistance and information, call 808/529-3111. In case of a natural disaster such as hurricanes or tsunamis on O'ahu, call the **Civil Defense** at 808/523-4121 or 808/733-4300. The **Coast Guard Search and Rescue** can be reached at 800/535-3230. The **Sex Abuse Treatment Center Hotline** is available at 808/524-7273 for cases involving sexual assault or rape crisis.

On O'ahu, full service hospitals include **The Queen's Medical Center** (1301 Punchbowl St., Honolulu, 808/538-9011, www.queensmedicalcenter.org), **St. Francis Medical Center** (2230 Liliha St., Honolulu, 808/547-6011, www.stfrancishawaii.org), and **Straub Clinic and Hospital** (888 S. King St., Honolulu, 808/522-4000, www.hawaiipacifichealth.org/straub) in Honolulu; **Castle Medical Center** (640 Ulukahiki St., 808/263-5500, http://adventisthealth.org/castle/) in Kailua; **Wahiawa General Hospital** (128 Lehua St., 808/621-8411, www.wahiawageneral.org) in Wahiawa; and **Kahuku Medical Center** (56-117 Pualalea St., 808/293-9221, www.kmc-hi.org) in Kahuku on the North Shore.

On Maui, between downtown Kahului and downtown Wailuku, **Maui Memorial Medical Center** (221 Mahalani St., 808/244-9056, www.mauimemorial.org/) is the only full-service hospital on the island. Several clinics are dotted around the island, including the following in Kihei: **Urgent Care Maui/Kihei Physicians** (1325 S. Kihei Rd., Ste. 103, 808/879-7781, www.medicalclinicinmauilcom), **Kihei-Wailea Medical Center** (808/874-8100, www.kiheiwaileamedicalcenter.com) in the Pi'ilani Village Shopping Center, and **Kihei Clinic** (2349 S. Kihei Rd., 808/879-1440). **Kaiser Permanente** has clinics in Lahaina (910 Waine'e, 808/662-6800, http://www.kpinhawaii.org/), Wailuku (80 Mahalani St., 808/243-6800), and Kihei (1279 S. Kihei Rd., 808/891-6800). In West Maui, the **Urgent Care West Maui** (808/667-9721, www.westmauidoctors.com/) maintains an office at the Whalers Village shopping mall, and in Hana, the **Hana Community Health Center** (808/248-8294, http://hanahealth.org/) is along the highway just as you enter town.

In Lihu'e, on Kaua'i, stands the island's main medical center, **Wilcox Memorial Hospital** (3-3420 Kuhio Hwy., Ste. B, 808/245-1100 or 808/245-1010 for emergencies, www.hawaiipacifichealth.org/wilcox/). The smaller **West Kaua'i Medical Center** (4643 Waimea Canyon Dr., 808/338-9431, www.kvmh.hhsc.org/) is open for emergency care and surgical needs. Both facilities are open 24 hours. Associated with Wilcox Memorial Hospital and located at the same address is the **Kaua'i Medical Clinic** (3-3420

Kuhio Hwy., Ste. B, 808/245-1500, www.hawaiipacifichealth.org/wilcox/). It has an urgent-care walk-in clinic (8am-5pm Mon.-Fri. and 8am-noon Sat.). There are other branches in 'Ele 'Ele (808/335-0499), Kapa'a (808/822-3431), and Koloa (808/742-1621).

On the Big Island, hospitals include the **Kona Community Hospital** (79-1019 Haukapila St., 808/322-9311, https://kch.hhsc.org/), **North Hawaii Community Hospital** (77-311 Sunset Dr., 808/329-7314, http://www.nhch.com/cms/view.aspx/Show/Home), and **Straub Clinic & Hospital** (75-Nani Kailua Dr. #6B, 808/329-9744, www.hawaiipacifichealth.org/straub). The largest facility on the Hilo side is the **Hilo Medical Center** (1190 Waianuenue Ave., 808/932-3000, www.hilomedicalcenter.org/).

Information and Services

TOURIST INFORMATION

The **Hawaii Visitors and Convention Bureau** (HVCB, 2270 Kalakaua Ave., Ste. 801, 808/524-0722 or 800/464-2924, www.gohawaii.com) is the state of Hawaii's official tourism agency and website. The great thing about the HVCB is that everything it offers is free. The staff is extremely knowledgeable, and the office is packed with excellent brochures on virtually every facet of living in, visiting, or simply enjoying Hawaii. The website features travel tips, quick facts, regional information, and service providers to help inform your vacation.

Maps

Aside from the simple maps in the ubiquitous free tourist literature, the Hawaii Visitors and Conventions Bureau and other organizations put out folding pocket maps of the island that are available free at the airport and tourist brochure racks around the island. Various street maps can be found at bookstores around the islands. Other useful and detailed maps of the

islands are the Rand McNally *O'ahu, Honolulu* map and the AAA *Honolulu Hawaii* map.

The **Waikiki Business Improvement District** (www.waikikibid.org) publishes a free detailed map of Waikiki with an entertainment calendar, important phone numbers, and a TheBus quick reference guide to major attractions. You can pick up a map at the police substation at Kuhio Beach Park or from one of the friendly aloha ambassadors that walk Waikiki's main drags solely to help visitors. They wear fluorescent yellow shirts, blue hats, and blue shorts.

Weather, Marine Report, and Time of Day

For recorded information on O'ahu island weather, call 808/973-4381; for marine conditions phone 808/973-4382; and for the surf report, call 808/973-4383. For surf information on the Internet, check www.surfnewsnetwork.com or call 808/596-SURF. For time of day, call 808/643-8463. On the Big Island, for recorded information on **local island** weather, call 808/961-5582; for the **marine report,** call 808/935-9883; and for **volcano activity,** call 808/985-6000. For a recorded weather report on Kaua'i call 808/245-6001. For the surf conditions call 808/245-3564.

MONEY

Hawaii uses U.S. currency. Full-service bank hours are Monday-Thursday 8:30am-4pm and Friday 8:30am-6pm. A few banks offer limited Saturday service, and weekday hours will be a bit longer at counters in grocery stores and other outlets. Traveler's checks are accepted throughout Hawaii at hotels, restaurants, rental car agencies, and in most stores and shops. However, to be readily acceptable they should be in U.S. currency.

Taxes

Hawaii does not have a state sales tax, but it does have a general excise tax of 4.712 percent, which will be added to sales transactions and services. In addition, there is an accommodations tax of 9.25 percent, so approximately 14 percent will be added to your hotel bill when you check out.

Index

INDEX

M

N

INDEX

List of Maps

Photo Credits

Title page photo: © Kyle Ellison
page 4 © Kristin Belew; page 5 © Heather Ellison; page 6 (top left) © Dreamstime.com, (top right) © Kevin Whitton, (bottom) © Kristin Belew; page 7 (top) © RightFramePhotoVideo | Dreamstime.com, (bottom left) © Kevin Whitton, (bottom right) © spectruminfo/123rf.com; page 8 © Photoquest | Dreamstime. com; page 10 (top) © Featurecars | Dreamstime.com, (bottom) © Mark Wasser; page 11 © Mark Driessen; page 12 (top) © Ritu Jethani/123rf.com, (middle) © Berneunion | Dreamstime.com, (bottom) © gigra/123RF. com; page 13 (top) © Desertsolitaire/Dreamstime.com, (middle) © chrishowey/123RF (bottom) © 123RF; page 14 © Eddy Galeotti/123RF; page 15 © Kevin Whitton; page 16 © Engel Ching | Dreamstime.com; page 17 © Gilles Gaonach | Dreamstime.com; page 18 © Daleksan | Dreamstime.com; page 19 © Izanbar | Dreamstime.com; page 20 © Kristin Belew; page 21 © Kevin Whitton; pages 26-175 © Kevin Whitton; page 181 © Alexandra Baackes; page 186 (top) © Heather Ellison, (bottom) © Kyle Ellison; page 187 © Kristin Belew; page 191 © Mark Driessen; page 199 © Kyle Ellison; page 202 © Kyle Ellison; page 204 © Jenna Strubhar; page 211 © Kyle Ellison; page 217 © Kyle Ellison; page 220 © Kyle Ellison; page 222 © Alexandra Baackes; page 223 © Kyle Ellison; page 226 © Kyle Ellison; page 227 © Kyle Ellison; page 240 (top) © Kyle Ellison, (bottom) © Kyle Ellison; page 241 © Kyle Ellison; page 246 © Kyle Ellison; page 248 © Kyle Ellison; page 253 © Kyle Ellison; page 256 © Kyle Ellison; page 267 (top) © Kyle Ellison, (bottom) © Jenna Strubhar; page 269 © Jenna Strubhar; page 272 © Jenna Strubhar; page 274 © Kyle Ellison; page 278 © Kyle Ellison; page 280 © Jenna Strubhar; page 282 © Kyle Ellison; page 285 © Kyle Ellison; page 287 © Kyle Ellison; page 289 © Kyle Ellison; page 292 © Kyle Ellison; page 294 © Kyle Ellison; page 296 © Kyle Ellison; page 302 (top) © Jenna Strubhar, (bottom) © Kyle Ellison; page 303 © Heather Ellison; page 308 © Kyle Ellison; page 311 © Kyle Ellison; page 313 © Kyle Ellison; page 314 © Alexandra Baackes; page 319 © Jenna Strubhar; page 320 © Alexandra Baackes; page 323 © Alexandra Baackes; page 327 © Kyle Ellison; page 329 © Kyle Ellison; page 330 (top) © Kyle Ellison, (bottom) © Heather Ellison; page 331 © Jenna Strubhar; page 338 © Jenna Strubhar; page 339 © Kyle Ellison; page 345 © Mark Driessen; page 346 © Jenna Strubhar; page 348 © Heather Ellison; page 349 © Heather Ellison; page 350 © Kyle Ellison; page 352 © Jenna Strubhar; page 353 © Heather Ellison; page 355 © Kyle Ellison; page 356 © Kyle Ellison; page 361 (top) © Jenna Strubhar, (bottom) © Alexandra Baackes; page 366 (top) © Kyle Ellison, (bottom) © Heather Ellison; page 367 © Kristin Belew; page 371 © Kyle Ellison; page 372 © Kyle Ellison; page 375 © Heather Ellison; page 376 © Kyle Ellison; page 377 © Kyle Ellison; page 378 © Kristin Belew; page 380 © Kyle Ellison; page 381 © Kyle Ellison; page 385 (top) © Heather Ellison, (bottom) © Kyle Ellison; page 387 © Kyle Ellison; page 390 © Heather Ellison; page 393 © Mark Driessen; page 395 © Heather Ellison; page 397 © Heather Ellison; page 397 © Heather Ellison; page 399 © Kyle Ellison; page 400 © Mark Driessen; page 403 © Kyle Ellison; page 407 © Birdiegal717 | Dreamstime.com; pages 412-535 © Bree Kessler, except page 412 (bottom) © Vacclav | Dreamstime.com; page 433 © Marty Wakat | Dreamstime.com; page 437 © Leia Grossman; page 441 (bottom) © Dreamstime.com; page 443 © Dreamstime.com; page 459 © Leia Grossman; page 461 © Leia Grossman; page 464 (bottom) © George Burba | Dreamstime.com; page 465 © Dreamstime.com; page 486 © Photoeuphoria | Dreamstime.com; page 487 © Dreamstime.com; page 509 (top) © Mark Wasser, (bottom) © Dreamstime.com; page 511 © Dreamstime.com; page 527 © Mark Wasser, page 541 © Dreamstime.com; pages 546-661 © Kevin Whittion except page 635 (top) © Dreamstime.com; page 667 © MNStudio | Dreamstime.com

Also Available

BIG ISLAND OF HAWAI'I

Including Hawai'i Volcanoes National Park

BREE KESSLER

HONOLULU & O'AHU

KEVIN WHITTON

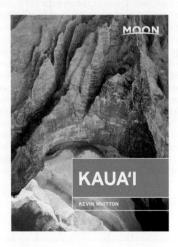

KAUA'I

KEVIN WHITTON

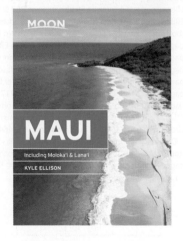

MAUI

Including Moloka'i & Lana'i

KYLE ELLISON